Economics
for South African students

FOURTH EDITION

Philip Mohr, Louis Fourie
and associates

Van Schaik
PUBLISHERS

Published by Van Schaik Publishers
1064 Arcadia Street, Hatfield, Pretoria

First edition 1995
Second impression 1996
Third impression 1997
Fourth impression 1998
Fifth impression 1998
Sixth impression 1999
Seventh impression 1999
Eighth impression 2000
Ninth impression 2000
Second edition 2000
Second impression 2001
Third impression 2002
Fourth impression 2003
Third edition 2004
Second impression 2004
Third impression 2004
Fourth impression 2005
Fifth impression 2005
Sixth impression 2006
Seventh impression 2007
Fourth edition 2008
Second impression 2008

ISBN 978 0 627 02712 3

Commissioning editor Lydia Reid
Production manager Werner von Gruenewaldt
Editorial manager Daleen Venter
Copy editor & proofreader Yvonne Kemp
Cover design by Gisela van Garderen
Cover image Digital Source Image Library
Illustrations by Jon Inggs
Typeset in 9.3 on 11 pt Century Old Style by Pace-Setting & Graphics
Printed and bound by Paarl Print, 22 Oosterland Street, Dal Josafat, Paarl, South Africa

NOTE TO LECTURERS

Contact the marketing department at marketing@vanschaiknet.com or on (012) 342 2765 for a CD-ROM with a test bank and a Microsoft PowerPoint slide show that accompanies this book.

The title *South African workbook for economics* is also available as a guide to assist students to master the material. The book is in a question-and-answer format.

Specifications

Authors: Corné van Walbeek, Waldo Krugell, Nicholas Samouilhan
ISBN: 978 0 627 02720 8

For any further information on this book contact the marketing department at marketing@vanschaiknet.com or on (012) 342 2765.

NOTE TO STUDENTS

Visit our supplementary website to *Economics (for South African students)* at *learnactive.co.za*

With the help of Trydian Interactive (Pty) Ltd, an e-learning development company, a supporting website has been developed for this textbook. The aim of the website is to give students further guidance as they work through the concepts and content covered by the textbook.

The website is supplementary to the textbook and is not a compulsory element for the completion of your studies, but it is a powerful resource.

Where can I find the website?

The supporting website is part of Trydian Interactive's *learnactive.co.za* e-learning solution and can be accessed at the following web address:

www.learnactive.co.za/vanschaik

Can anyone use the website?

Yes, the website is open for general use and any student can get access to it. But before you can use the site, you need to register – there's no charge, and it takes a few seconds. Just follow these easy steps:

1. Go to the website: www.learnactive.co.za/vanschaik.
2. Click on "Create your own profile".
3. You will be taken to a screen where you must submit information such as your name, your email address, the course you are studying, the institution you are studying at, as well as some other geographical information.
4. You will also be asked to choose a username and a password.
5. After you have keyed in all the information needed, you will submit the information online and a unique profile will be generated for you.
6. At this stage you will be asked to enter a course code. Enter the following code: **VS-Econ001**
7. You now have full access to the website!

Once you have registered, you don't need to repeat this process. The next time you enter the website, you just key in your username and password, and you're ready to go.

Navigation on *learnactive.co.za*

Navigation is very simple and straightforward. Just follow the instructions on screen!

After you log on to the website, you are presented with a simple menu structure that can be used to jump between the various functionalities.

Features of the website

learnactive.co.za gives you a series of value-adding functionalities. These include:

- **E-workbook:** The e-workbook is an interactive compilation of case studies, questions and answers that you can work through, as part of your exam preparation, in order to make sure that you understand the content.
- **E-forum:** A forum will be available for you to voice your opinions on the content and to discuss or debate certain economic topics and questions with your fellow students.
- **Events calendar:** You will also get access to your own calendar where you can schedule events, appointments and important dates. Each time you log on to the website, you will receive a reminder about these scheduled events.

We believe that *learnactive.co.za* will truly add value to your learning experience and that it will assist in giving you a better understanding of the subject matter. We invite all economics students to try the website!

If you need any further information on the *learnactive.co.za* website, please email us at learnactive@trydian.com.

SUGGESTED COURSE OUTLINES

1. COMPREHENSIVE FIRST-YEAR COURSE IN ECONOMICS

Whole book – up to the lecturer(s) to decide which sections or subsections to leave out.

2. COMPREHENSIVE ONE-SEMESTER MODULE IN MICROECONOMICS

- *Introduction to economics.* Chapter 1
- *The economic problem.* Chapter 2, Sections 2.1 to 2.4
- *The circular flow of income and spending.* Chapter 3, Sections 3.1 and 3.2
- *Basic tools of analysis.* Chapter 6 (as background)
- *Demand, supply and prices.* Chapter 7
- *Demand and supply in action.* Chapter 8
- *Elasticity.* Chapter 9
- *Consumer choice.* Chapter 10, Sections 10.1 to 10.5 (rest optional)
- *Production and cost.* Chapter 11
- *Perfect competition.* Chapter 12
- *Monopoly and imperfect competition.* Chapter 13, Sections 13.1 to 13.5 (certain subsections optional)
- *Labour market.* Chapter 14, Sections 14.1 to 14.3 (rest, including the Appendix, optional)
- *Market failure and government failure.* Chapter 16, Sections 16.2 to 16.5

3. COMPREHENSIVE ONE-SEMESTER MODULE IN MACROECONOMICS

- *Introduction to economics.* Chapter 1 (if not covered yet)
- *The circular flow of income and spending.* Chapter 3
- *Measuring the performance of the economy.* Chapter 4
- *The South African economy.* Chapter 5 (as general background)
- *Basic tools of analysis.* Chapter 6 (if not covered yet)
- *The monetary sector.* Chapter 15
- *The public sector.* Chapter 16, Sections 16.7 to 16.11 (16.12 optional)
- *The foreign sector.* Chapter 17 (certain subsections optional)
- *Basic macroeconomic model.* Chapter 18
- *Extensions of the basic model.* Chapter 19
- *The AD-AS model.* Chapter 20, Section 20.1
- *More on macroeconomic theory and policy.* Chapter 20, Section 20.3 (20.2 and 20.4 optional)
- *Inflation.* Chapter 21 (certain subsections optional)
- *Unemployment and the Phillips curve.* Chapter 22, Section 22.1 (Section 22.2 optional)
- *Economic growth and business cycles.* Chapter 23, Sections 23.1 to 23.4

4. BASIC FIRST-YEAR COURSE IN ECONOMICS

- *Introduction to economics.* Chapter 1
- *The economic problem.* Chapter 2, Sections 2.1 to 2.4
- *The circular flow of income and spending.* Chapter 3, whole chapter
- *Measuring the performance of the economy* (may be studied in conjunction with chapters 18 to 23). Chapter 4, Sections 4.1 to 4.5
- *The South African economy.* Chapter 5 (for general background) – has to be studied in conjunction with (or after) Chapter 4
- *Basic tools of analysis.* Chapter 6 (again a background chapter)
- *Demand, supply and prices.* Chapter 7, Sections 7.1 to 7.4
- *Demand and supply in action.* Chapter 8, Sections 8.1 to 8.4
- *Elasticity.* Chapter 9, certain subsections can be omitted
- *Consumer choice.* Chapter 10, Sections 10.1 to 10.3
- *Production and cost.* Chapter 11, Sections 11.1 to 11.4
- *Perfect competition.* Chapter 12, Sections 12.1 to 12.4
- *Monopoly and imperfect competition.* Chapter 13, Sections 13.1 (selected parts), 13.2 (selected parts), 13.5 (selected parts)

- *Labour market.* Chapter 14, Section 14.2
- *Monetary sector.* Chapter 15, Sections 15.1 to 15.8
- *Public sector.* Chapter 16, Sections 16.1, 16.4, 16.7, 16.8, 16.10, 16.11
- *Foreign sector.* Chapter 17, Sections 17.1, 17.3, 17.4
- *Basic macroeconomic model.* Chapter 18
- *Extensions of the basic model.* Chapter 19 (selected parts)
- *Aggregate demand and supply.* Chapter 20, Section 20.1 (optional)
- *Inflation.* Chapter 21, Sections 21.1, 21.2 (optional), 21.3, 21.4 (selected parts)
- *Unemployment.* Chapter 22, Section 22.1
- *Economic growth and development.* Chapter 23, Sections 23.1 to 23.3

5. BASIC ONE-SEMESTER MODULE IN MICROECONOMICS

- *Introduction to economics.* Chapter 1
- *The economic problem.* Chapter 2, Sections 2.1 to 2.4
- *The circular flow of income and spending.* Chapter 3, Sections 3.1 and 3.2
- *Basic tools of analysis.* Chapter 6 (as background)
- *Demand, supply and prices.* Chapter 7, Sections 7.1 to 7.4
- *Demand and supply in action.* Chapter 8, Sections 8.1 to 8.4
- *Elasticity.* Chapter 9 (selected parts only)
- *Consumer choice.* Chapter 10, Sections 10.1 to 10.3 (optional)
- *Production and cost.* Chapter 11, Sections 11.1 to 11.4
- *Perfect competition.* Chapter 12, Sections 12.1 to 12.4
- *Monopoly and imperfect competition.* Chapter 13, Sections 13.1 and 13.2 (selected parts)
- *Labour market.* Chapter 14, Section 14.2 (optional)

6. BASIC ONE-SEMESTER MODULE IN MACROECONOMICS

- *Introduction to economics.* Chapter 1 (if not covered yet)
- *The circular flow of income and spending.* Chapter 3, whole chapter
- *Measuring the performance of the economy.* Chapter 4, Sections 4.1 to 4.5
- *The South African economy.* Chapter 5 (for general background) – optional
- *Basic tools of analysis.* Chapter 6 (if not covered yet)
- *The monetary sector.* Chapter 15, Sections 15.1 to 15.8
- *The public sector.* Chapter 16, Sections 16.4, 16.7, 16.10 and 16.11
- *The foreign sector.* Chapter 17, Sections 17.1, 17.3 and 17.4
- *Basic macroeconomic model.* Chapter 18
- *Extensions of the basic model.* Chapter 19 (selected parts)
- *Aggregate demand and supply.* Chapter 20, Section 20.1 (optional)
- *Inflation.* Chapter 21, Sections 21.1, 21.2 (optional), 21.3 and 21.4 (selected parts)
- *Unemployment.* Chapter 22, Section 22.1
- *Economic growth and development.* Chapter 23, Sections 23.1 to 23.3

7. COURSE/MODULE IN ECONOMICS FOR BUSINESS SCHOOLS (MBA, MBL, MDP, AEP, etc)

- *Introduction to economics.* Chapter 1
- *Some basic concepts.* Chapter 2
- *The circular flow of income and spending.* Chapter 3, whole chapter
- *Demand, supply and elasticity.* Chapter 7, 8 and 9 (selected topics)
- *The theory of the firm.* Chapter 11-13 (selected topics)
- *The labour market.* Chapter 14 (selected topics)
- *The monetary sector.* Chapter 15 (selected topics)
- *The public sector.* Chapter 16 (selected topics)
- *The foreign sector.* Chapter 17 (balance of payments and exchange rates)
- *Measuring the performance of the economy.* Chapter 4 (selected topics)
- *The South African economy.* Chapter 5
- *Aggregate demand and supply.* Chapter 20, Section 20.1
- *Inflation.* Chapter 21 (selected topics)
- *Unemployment.* Chapter 22 (selected topics)
- *Economic growth and business cycles.* Chapter 23 (selected topics)

CONTENTS

PART IV MACROECONOMICS

PREFACE

This fourth edition of *Economics (for South African students)* is an updated version of the popular third edition.

As its predecessors, this edition covers the full spectrum of economic issues, while emphasising the institutional features of the South African economy. The latter are presented together with standard economic theory to give students an introduction to economics that they can relate to the world around them. The emphasis is on relevance, but rigour is not sacrificed.

Like most texts, the book contains more material than can be covered comfortably in a year course or two semester modules at universities, universities of technology, business schools or other institutions of higher learning. It is thus up to the lecturers who use the book to decide which parts to emphasise and which to leave out or perhaps cover in second-year courses or modules. To assist with this choice, some suggested course and module outlines are provided. See page iv for more information.

An important feature of the book is the liberal use of practical examples and additional explanations of important concepts and issues, which are presented as boxed text. These increase the topicality and relevance of the text without interrupting the main thread. Review questions have also been added to stimulate discussion and students' interest in the subject.

Plan of the book

The book is divided into four main parts. Part I is a comprehensive introduction to economics, the South African economy and the economic way of thinking. This part of the book is quite long, since it is essential to a sound understanding of the subject and of the economic environment around us. Too often, students start studying economic theory without really knowing what the subject is all about or what the main issues are. Part II focuses on basic microeconomic concepts, topics and issues such as supply, demand, consumer choice, firms' decisions and the labour market. The material is mostly standard, neoclassical theory but it is supplemented by South African data and examples. This part lays the foundation for the discussion in Part III of three major sectors of the economy – the monetary sector, the public sector and the foreign sector. In each case the basic tools of microeconomic analysis developed in Part II are used to explain and analyse certain important issues. At the same time, the student is introduced to the major concepts and variables of macroeconomic analysis. In Part IV those concepts and variables are joined together in a series of macroeconomic models. The advantage is that students are already thoroughly acquainted with all the individual elements by the time they start working with these models. The emphasis in this part is on Keynesian macroeconomics, but the reader is also introduced to a variety of other approaches and to various views on macroeconomic issues such as unemployment, inflation and economic growth.

Each part of the book starts with an introductory page outlining the purpose and content of the chapters in that part, and listing some learning outcomes. Likewise, each chapter starts with an introductory page linking it to the rest of the book and indicating what it is all about. Again we provide some learning outcomes to focus the reader's attention on the essential elements. The most important concepts are listed at the end of each chapter in more or less the order in which they appear in the text and each chapter concludes with some review questions.

The sections, tables, boxes and figures are numbered according to the chapters. For example, Box 2-6 is the sixth box in Chapter 2 and Section 14.2 is the second section of Chapter 14. This numbering system is used to facilitate cross-referencing.

To the student

Courses and modules in economics are typically regarded as being among the most challenging of all those presented at universities, universities of technology, business schools or other tertiary institutions. But studying economics can be fun, provided that you approach it correctly. Economics is not a subject that you can study by simply reading the material or trying to memorise it. Such an approach is bound to fail. You have to try to understand it.

Because students who study economics come from widely varying backgrounds, we have not assumed any prior knowledge of economics in this book. We start from scratch and provide fairly detailed explanations, particularly as far as the most fundamental concepts and theories are concerned. As a result, some of the chapters are quite long. We believe that clear and detailed explanations are better than more concise explanations that are possibly more difficult to follow. Since it is so important to understand what you are learning, longer may prove to be quicker and easier.

Gary Player, the famous South African golfer, once remarked that "the more I practise, the luckier I get". The same applies in economics. You have to practise, that is, study actively. Always study with a pen or pencil, working through the arguments, drawing the graphs and summarising the main points. This book requires no mathematics beyond simple high school algebra. In fact, the only requirements are a basic knowledge of arithmetic and the ability to solve a simple equation and understand a graph. Those of you who do not have any formal training in mathematics should thus not be alarmed by the symbols, equations and graphs. They are simply shorthand ways of expressing economic variables, relationships and theories. When you use the symbols, equations and graphs, you must always remember what *economic* variables and relationships they represent – this is a book about economics, not about algebra or geometry.

Follow the economics news in the newspapers and on television, and try to relate it to what you are learning. You will be surprised how much you can understand by combining the basic tools of economic analysis with some common sense. Many renowned economists have commented that of all the courses in economics, the introductory course is the most useful.

A textbook is written, first and foremost, for students, not for lecturers. We trust that you will find the book useful and that you will derive some pleasure from using it.

Acknowledgements

We wish to thank Marcel Kohler for his contribution to the revision of Chapter 17, Johan Lötter for assisting with some of the data, Cilliers Swart for perusing the manuscript and Willie le Roux and Thea Uys for comments on various aspects of the book. As usual, Elna van Rensburg did the word-processing, while Yvonne Kemp served as copy editor and proofreader. Thanks are also due to Leanne Martini, Lydia Reid, Daleen Venter, Werner von Gruenewaldt and all their co-workers at Van Schaik Publishers.

PHILIP MOHR
LOUIS FOURIE
September 2007

PART I

Introduction

The purpose of this part of the book is to introduce you to the main issues, concepts and tools of economics. Part I consists of six chapters. Chapter 1 is an introductory chapter which deals with the definition of economics and the way economists think. Chapter 2 takes a closer look at the economic problem by focusing on the three key questions: What? How? and For whom? We outline the potential solutions to these questions and describe the major types of economic system. We also introduce you to three famous economists who are linked to these systems. Interdependence is the subject of Chapter 3. We illustrate and explain the various relationships between households, firms, the government and the rest of the world. Chapter 4 explains how the performance of the economy is measured. The issues dealt with include the measurement of the level of economic activity, unemployment, inflation and the distribution of income. This paves the way for the discussion in Chapter 5 of the major features and problems of the South African economy. We conclude Part I in Chapter 6 with an explanation of some essential concepts and tools which are used in the rest of the book.

Once you have studied Part I you should be able to

- explain what economics is all about
- describe the main elements of the economic problem
- distinguish between different economic systems
- sketch how the various sectors of the mixed economy fit together
- describe how the performance of the economy is measured
- summarise the major features of the South African economy
- explain why we use models in economic analysis
- read and interpret graphs

The most important concepts that you have to master are listed at the end of each chapter.

1 What economics is all about

Learning outcomes

Once you have studied this chapter you should be able to

- explain what economics is all about
- define economics
- explain what the economic problem is
- define the important concept of opportunity cost
- describe a production possibilities curve or frontier
- distinguish between microeconomics and macroeconomics
- distinguish between positive and normative economics
- explain why economics is a social science
- comment on why economists disagree on certain issues
- identify some common mistakes in reasoning about economics

Economics is a study of mankind in the ordinary business of life.
ALFRED MARSHALL

Economics is the art of making the most out of life.
GEORGE BERNARD SHAW

Economics is the only profession in which one can gain great eminence without ever being right.
GEORGE MEANY

In this chapter we introduce you to economics. We first use a number of examples to indicate what economics is all about and we then introduce the important concepts of **scarcity**, **choice** and **opportunity cost**. We explain these concepts with the aid of a **production possibilities curve**. Next we give some important definitions, including various definitions of economics. We explain the difference between **microeconomics** and **macroeconomics**, as well as the difference between **positive** and **normative** economics. This is followed by a brief discussion of the major reasons for the apparent tendency for economists to disagree. The chapter concludes with an explanation of some common mistakes in reasoning about economics.

Fifty years ago economics was not as familiar a term in South Africa as it is today. The political debate was dominated by racial issues. There was no television, and economic journalism was in its infancy. There were few periodicals that dealt with economic issues, and economic matters received little coverage in the newspapers. Students who went to university to study subjects like accounting, statistics and management found that they also had to study economics, but they usually had no idea what the study of economics would entail.

All this has changed. Nowadays everyone has heard about economics and everyone knows that it is important. Economic affairs play an important role in the political debate, and economic issues are reported and analysed every day on television. There are a number of weekly and monthly periodicals, many websites and even some television channels that deal almost exclusively with economic issues. Every newspaper has a large and expanding section which focuses on economic and financial matters. Economics is taught in our schools and many students go to university specifically to study economics.

There is thus a much greater awareness of economic issues today than at any time in the past. But this does not mean that people know what economics is all about. Many people are convinced that economics is only concerned with making money. Some believe that economics is concerned mainly with buying and selling shares on the JSE Securities Exchange. Others think that economics is the study of balance sheets and profit statements. As we shall point out in this book, all these views are extremely narrow and do not capture the essence of what economics is all about.

What then is economics? What is it concerned with? The two definitions of economics quoted on the previous page indicate that it is a wide-ranging discipline. These definitions point to the fact that the subject is concerned with virtually every aspect of human existence.

The following example gives some indication of the wide-ranging nature of economics, and of the types of question and issue that it is concerned with.

Let us take a fictitious character – we shall call him Simon Mokgatle – who lives in Diepkloof. And let us think about some of the decisions that he has to make once he has finished his secondary education. Should he continue with his studies at a residential technical college, university of technology or university, or should he try to find a full-time job? Or should he try to find a job while at the same time continuing his studies through Unisa? If he is going to further his studies, which field of study should he choose? If he decides to try and find a job, what type of job should he apply for? What type of transport should he use to travel to work or lectures: a taxi, a bus or a train? What should he wear when he goes to work or when he attends lectures? If he opts for and finds a job, how should he spend his first pay cheque? If he cannot find a job and cannot afford to study further or obtain a bursary, what should he do? Should he remain in Diepkloof and continue looking for work or should he move to another area or town in pursuit of employment? If he does find a job and also enrols as a student at Unisa, what should he do on a Saturday night – study, watch television or go to the movies?

The list is virtually endless. Simon has to make choices every day of his life. And this is what economics is essentially about. It deals with the **choices** that people have to make – what to eat, what to wear, what career to pursue. The word **economics** is derived from the Greek words *oikos*, meaning house and *némein*, meaning manage. Economics is thus the science of household management and as such is indeed concerned with the ordinary business of life.

But economics is not only concerned with the choices that individuals like Simon Mokgatle have to make. It also studies the decisions of businesses, government and other decision makers in society. Should Toyota expand its production of motorcars? Should Benson & Hedges increase the price of its cigarettes? Or should it rather reduce the price in an attempt to increase sales? Should government spend more on education or on housing? Or should health be a greater priority? And what about safety and security? Should taxes be raised or lowered? Should the government raise more taxes through the value-added tax (VAT) and less through personal income tax? Should more basic necessities carry a zero VAT rate to help the many poor people in South Africa? Or should the government rather subsidise the prices of necessities such as bread and maize, or perhaps even hand out food parcels to the needy?

Like Simon, businesses and government also have to make choices every day. But why are these choices necessary? This brings us to the basic fact of economic life – **scarcity**. Without scarcity it would not be necessary to make choices. Individuals, businesses and government all want to do many things, but the means with which these wants can be met are limited. **Wants** are plentiful – we all want a lot of things – but the **means** are scarce. We therefore have to make **choices** all the time.

The relationship between unlimited wants and scarce resources is so central to economics that most definitions of economics focus almost exclusively on this relationship. A few definitions are listed in Box 1-1.

The definitions in the box are all by authors of well-known introductory economics textbooks. Apart from these definitions and that of Marshall given at the beginning of the chapter, two of the most widely-quoted ones are those of Jacob Viner and Lionel Robbins. Viner (1892–1970), a well-known 20th century American economist, simply stated that "economics is

BOX 1-1 SOME DEFINITIONS OF ECONOMICS

Economics is the study of how our scarce productive resources are used to satisfy human wants.

George Leland Bach

Economics is the study of how individuals and societies choose to use the scarce resources that nature and previous generations have provided.

Karl Case and Ray Fair

Economics is the study of how scarce resources are allocated among various uses.

Richard Eckhaus

Economics is the study of how people allocate their limited resources to provide for their wants.

Jack Harvey

Economics is the study of how individuals and groups of individuals respond to and deal with scarcity.

James Kearl

Economics is the study of the use of scarce resources to satisfy unlimited human wants.

Richard Lipsey

Economics is the study of how society manages its scarce resources.

N Gregory Mankiw

Economics is concerned with the efficient use or management of limited productive resources to achieve maximum satisfaction of human material wants.

Campbell McConnell

Economics is the study of how people use their limited resources to try to satisfy unlimited wants.

Michael Parkin

Economics is the study of how societies use scarce resources to produce valuable commodities and distribute them among different people.

Paul Samuelson

Economics is the study of how individuals, firms, governments and other organizations within our society make choices and how those choices determine how the resources of society are used.

Joseph Stiglitz

what economists do." This is quite a catchy definition, but it is not a particularly useful one.

Lionel Robbins (1898–1984), a prominent 20th century British economist, set the tone for most modern definitions in the 1930s by defining economics as "the science which studies human behaviour as a relationship between ends and scarce means which have alternative uses".

We shall not try to provide yet another definition of economics. It should be obvious that economics has to do with the use of scarce resources to satisfy unlimited wants. The central elements of economics are therefore **scarcity** and **choice**.

Although scarcity and choice lie at its heart, economics is not merely concerned with the types of choice indicated earlier. Economics also seeks to describe, explain, analyse and predict a variety of phenomena such as economic growth, unemployment, inflation, trade between individuals and countries, the prices of different goods and services, poverty, wealth, money, interest rates, exchange rates and business cycles.

Consider the following questions:

- What determines the price of petrol? Why does the petrol price increase from time to time? What are the effects of such increases on individuals, households, businesses, government and society at large?
- What is money? How is it created? How do changes in the amount of money in the country affect the various participants in the economy (households, businesses, etc)?
- What are interest rates? Why are they important? Why are interest rates raised or lowered from time to time? How do such changes affect households, businesses and government?
- What is unemployment? What causes unemployment? What can the government do to reduce unemployment?
- What is inflation? Does inflation have anything to do with unemployment?
- Why has the rand often depreciated sharply against the major international currencies such as the US

dollar and the euro? Why did it appreciate so sharply in 2002?

- What is the difference between capitalism and socialism? And between socialism and communism? Why did communism collapse in Eastern Europe towards the end of the 1980s?
- What is nationalisation? How does it differ from privatisation? Why are some goods and services such as electricity provided by government-owned institutions while other goods and services are provided by privately-owned firms?
- Why did certain East Asian economies expand so rapidly in the 1980s and early 1990s? Why did African economies generally fare badly? Why is South Africa richer than most other African countries?
- Why are certain provinces in South Africa so much richer than others? Why are some South Africans richer than others?
- What are South Africa's economic prospects? Will the country prosper and be able to provide a better life for all? Or will the economy stagnate or decline?

These are just some of the issues that economics is concerned with, and we shall deal with many of these questions in this book.

1.1 Scarcity, choice and opportunity cost

Economics is concerned with scarcity. The basic fact of economic life is that there are simply not enough goods and services to satisfy everyone's wants. Wants are unlimited but the means with which the wants can be satisfied are limited.

Note that **wants** are not the same as **needs** and **demand**:

- **Wants** are human desires for goods and services. Our wants are unlimited – we all want everything. For example, we would all want to own a fully-equipped, fully-serviced luxury villa in each of the ten most beautiful places in the world. As individuals and as a society we always want or desire more or better goods and services. Individuals have biological, spiritual, material, cultural and social wants while people as a group have **collective wants** for things such as law and order, justice and social security.
- **Needs** are necessities, the things that are essential for survival, such as food, water, shelter and clothing. Needs, unlike wants, are not absolutely unlimited. For example, it is possible to calculate the basic needs which have to be met if a person or household is to survive. The Bureau for Market Research at the University of South Africa has worked out what goods and services a household needs in its "shopping basket" every month in order to sustain a minimum living level. What such a "basket" contains gives a good idea of the basic needs of a household.
- **Demand** differs from wants, desires or needs. There is only a demand for a good or service if those who want to purchase it have the necessary means to do so. In other words, demand has to be backed by purchasing power. Demand will be studied in detail in Part II.

Now that we have examined wants, let us see why we say that **resources** are limited. There are three types of resource: natural resources (such as agricultural land, minerals and fishing resources), human resources (such as labour) and man-made resources (such as machines). These resources are the means with which goods and services can be produced. In economics we call these resources **factors of production**. Since the resources are limited, it follows that the goods and services with which we can satisfy our wants are also limited.

All individuals and societies are confronted by the problem of unlimited wants and limited means. They therefore have to make choices.

- Hendrik Mathibela goes to the shop with R5 in his pocket. He wants an ice cream, a cool drink, a chocolate and a packet of chips. But his resources are limited. He cannot buy all the things he wants with the R5. He therefore has to choose what to buy and what to sacrifice.
- It is Saturday night. Anne van der Merwe has to study for an examination on Wednesday. She also wants to watch television, go to the movies and visit her friends. But she cannot do all these things at the same time. She has to choose what to do and what not to do.
- The South African government has, say, R10 billion to spend on new development programmes during a given financial year. It wants to provide houses, jobs, free health services and free education for all needy South Africans. But the resources are limited. The government has to decide what it will do immediately and what will have to be postponed until later years.

In all these cases difficult choices have to be made. Some wants will be satisfied but many will be left unsatisfied. In each case it has to be decided which of the available alternatives will have to be sacrificed.

Economic decisions are all difficult. The fact that we live in a world of scarcity forces us to make difficult choices. When resources are used to produce a certain good, they are not available to produce other goods. A decision to produce more of one good therefore also means that less of another good can be produced. Similarly, a student who decides to study through Unisa while holding down a job has to sacrifice a lot of other things if he or she is to succeed in obtaining a degree. As the proverb says: "You cannot have your cake and eat it."

Because resources are scarce, the use of resources can never be costless. There are always **costs** involved even if these costs are not always apparent to the consumer of the goods or services in question. To emphasise this point, economists made up a principle, which they call the TANSTAAFL principle. TANSTAAFL is an acronym for "There ain't no such thing as a free lunch." Someone always has to pay. Other opportunities always have to be sacrificed. The main point of this principle is that there are always costs involved in any use of scarce resources.

Because economics deals with scarcity it is not a popular science. More than a century ago Thomas Carlyle called it the "dismal science". "This science," he said, is "not a gay science ... no, a dreary, desolate and indeed quite abject and distressing one; what we might call, by way of eminence, the dismal science." The 1950s Russian leader, Nikita Khrushchev, was also fond of reminding us that "economics is a subject that does not greatly respect one's wishes." Because economists frequently have to emphasise scarcity and the need for hard, unpopular decisions, they are generally not a popular group of people. They are frequently the ones who have to bring the bad news. For example, economists often have to remind politicians that many of their well-meant spending programmes are simply not affordable.

Scarcity must not be confused with poverty. Scarcity affects everyone. The rich are also subject to scarcity. Even the richest person on earth will have unsatisfied wants and will have to make economic decisions. For example, no matter how rich you are in terms of money or material wealth, you only have 24 hours a day in which to sleep, eat, work and relax. Everyone has to deal with the fact that time is a limited resource.

Although scarcity is an essential element of the economic problem, the need for decision making only really arises when the scarce resources have to be allocated between competing alternatives. If you have only one goal in life but you do not have sufficient resources to completely achieve that goal, your resources are scarce. However, with only one goal you will not have an economic problem to solve, since you do not have to decide how to allocate your limited resources. This is not a realistic example since no one has only one goal in life, but it does illustrate the importance of choosing between different alternatives in making economic decisions. In our earlier examples, Hendrik Mathibela, Anne van der Merwe and the South African government were all faced with difficult choices between different alternatives. This is what the economic problem is all about.

When we are faced with such a choice we can measure the cost of the alternative we have chosen in terms of the alternatives that we have to sacrifice. This is called **opportunity cost**. When there are only two alternatives, the opportunity cost is quite straightforward. For example, if Anne only has to choose between studying and going to the movies, the opportunity cost of studying would be the visit to the movies that she has to forgo. Likewise, if Hendrik only has to choose between a cool drink and a chocolate, the opportunity cost of the cool drink would be the chocolate which he has to sacrifice (assuming that he cannot afford both). When there are more than two alternatives, the opportunity cost is somewhat more complicated. We then measure the opportunity cost of a particular alternative in terms of the **best** alternative that has to be sacrificed.

The opportunity cost of a choice is the value to the decision maker of the best alternative that could have been chosen but was not chosen. In other words, the opportunity cost of a choice is the value of the best forgone opportunity.

Every time a choice is made, opportunity costs are incurred and economists always measure costs in terms of opportunity costs. For the economist the cost of something is what you have to give up to to get it.

Opportunity cost is one of the most important concepts in economics since it captures the essence of the problems of scarcity and choice. It is also an essential element of the economic way of thinking. Economists do not only consider explicit monetary costs (often called accounting costs). They also consider implicit costs, always asking how the scarce resources could have been used alternatively.

The production possibilities curve

Scarcity, choice and opportunity cost can be illustrated with the aid of a **production possibilities curve**, also called a production possibilities frontier.

Consider an isolated rural community along the Wild Coast whose main foods are potatoes and fish. The people have found that by devoting **all** their available time and other resources to fishing, they can produce 5 baskets of fish per working day. On the other hand, if they spend **all** their production time gardening, they can produce 100 kilograms of potatoes per working day. It is possible for them to produce either 5 baskets of fish or 100 kilograms of potatoes, but in each case the entire production of the other good must be sacrificed.

The only way that the inhabitants can enjoy a diet which includes both fish and potatoes is by using some of their resources for fish production, and some for potato production. Resources must be shifted from one production possibility to produce the other. By experimentation, they find that it is possible for them to produce any of the combinations shown in Table 1-1. These combinations represent the maximum amounts which can be produced with all the available resources. If the people decide to produce combination E, they will be able to produce 4 baskets of fish and 40 kilograms of potatoes per day. But in producing this combination they have had to decide not to produce more fish or more potatoes. In producing 4 baskets of fish, they have had to forgo the additional 60 kilograms of potatoes which they could have produced if they had used all their resources to grow potatoes. Likewise, in producing 40 kilograms of potatoes they have decided to forgo the extra (5th) basket of fish which they might have produced.

TABLE 1-1 Production possibilities for the Wild Coast community

Possibility	*Fish (baskets per day)*	*Potatoes (kg per day)*
A	0	100
B	1	95
C	2	85
D	3	70
E	4	40
F	5	0

The opportunity cost of producing the 40 kilograms of potatoes is the basket of fish; and the opportunity cost of producing the 4 baskets of fish is 60 kilograms of potatoes that have to be forgone. The community therefore has to choose between more potatoes and less fish or more fish and less potatoes. Given the available resources, it is impossible to produce more of one good without decreasing the production of the other good.

The different alternatives can be illustrated graphically in a **production possibilities curve** as in Figure 1-1. The curve shows the possible levels of output in an economy with limited resources and fixed production techniques. If you find it difficult to understand or "read" Figure 1-1, turn to Chapter 6, where we explain graphs in more detail.

Fish production is measured along the horizontal axis and potato production on the vertical axis. The combinations in the table are represented by points A, B, C, D, E and F in the diagram. Note that we have joined the different points to form a curve. This actually implies that there are also other possible combinations apart from the six that are given in Table 1-1. However, we only focus on these six points.

The production possibilities curve indicates the combinations of any two goods or services that are attainable when the community's resources are fully and efficiently employed.

FIGURE 1-1 A production possibilities curve for the Wild Coast community

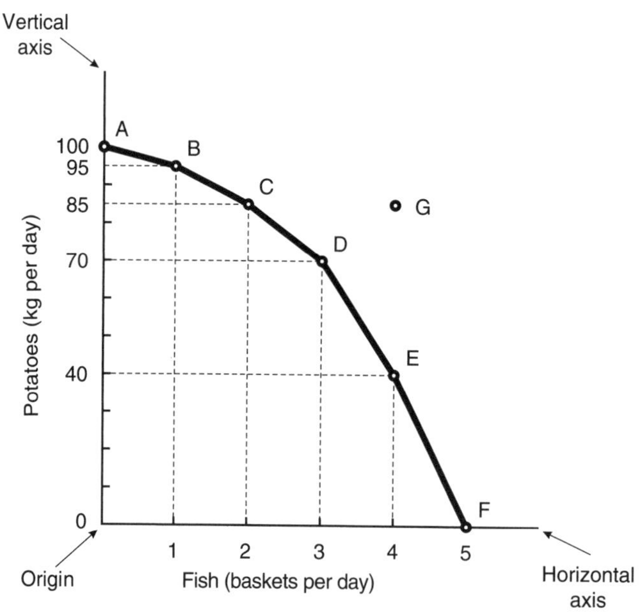

The various points on the curve show the combinations of fish and potatoes that can be produced daily with the available resources.

As we move along the production possibilities curve from point A to point B through to point F, the production of fish increases while the production of potatoes decreases. To produce the first basket of fish the community has to sacrifice 5 kilograms of potatoes (from 100 to 95). To produce the second basket of fish the sacrifice is an additional 10 kilograms of potatoes (the difference between 95 and 85). To produce the third basket of fish an additional 15 kilograms of potatoes have to be forgone (the difference between 85 and 70). The **opportunity cost** of each additional basket of fish therefore **increases** as we move along the production possibilities curve. This is why the curve bulges outwards from the origin. In technical terms we say that the curve is **concave** to the origin.

The production possibilities curve is a very useful way of illustrating scarcity, choice and opportunity cost. We go into it in more detail in Chapter 2, but for the time being note the following. **Scarcity** is illustrated by the fact that all points to the right of the curve (such as G) are unattainable. The curve thus forms a frontier or boundary between what is possible and what is not possible. **Choice** is illustrated by the need to choose among the available combinations along the curve. **Opportunity cost** is illustrated by what we refer to as the negative slope of the curve, which means that more of one good can only be obtained by sacrificing the other good. Opportunity cost therefore involves what we call a **trade-off** between the two goods.

The production possibilities curve is the first analytical tool which you encounter in this book. Like all other tools of analysis, it is not necessarily based on a practical situation in a particular economy. However, as we shall explain later, particularly in Chapter 6, such analytical tools (or theories or models) are essential devices for understanding, explaining and predicting what is going on in the world around us. We shall return to the production possibilities curve in Section 2.1.

1.2 Economics as a science

Economics is a social science

Economics is a **science**. Like any other science, economics involves a systematic attempt to discover regular patterns of behaviour. These patterns are used to **explain** what is happening, to **predict** what might happen and to assist policymakers to devise or choose appropriate economic **policies**. Take the petrol price as an example. Economics assists us in **explaining** the level of the petrol price or why it has changed. It helps us to **predict** what the price will be in future or what will happen in the rest of the economy if the petrol price changes. Economics also provides useful information to the authorities who have to decide on a **policy** in respect of the petrol price. The emphasis on **explanation**, **prediction** and **policy** will be a recurrent theme of this book.

Economics is a **social science**. It studies the behaviour of human beings, both individually and as groups. Other social sciences include sociology, social psychology, anthropology and political science. The social sciences are distinguished from the natural sciences like physics, chemistry, botany, astronomy and zoology, which study the natural universe.

So the natural sciences differ from the social sciences in respect of **what** is studied. But there are also differences in respect of **how** it is studied. In many natural sciences it is possible to conduct controlled laboratory experiments. However, this method is generally not available to social scientists. Economists cannot discover regular patterns of behaviour by conducting laboratory experiments, nor can they test their theories in this way. Economists study the behaviour of people in a constantly changing environment. They cannot place people in test-tubes to determine how they will react to any particular change. They cannot hold other things constant while the impact of one particular change is investigated. Economists therefore have to resort to other methods.

Another important difference between economics and a natural science like physics is found in the **nature of their generalisations**. In the natural sciences certain natural laws can be identified. For example, the law of gravity states that when an apple falls from a tree, it will always fall to the ground. But when the price of apples falls, the best an economist can say is that more apples will probably be purchased. This outcome is a very likely outcome and economists are so confident about it that they generally also talk about a law, the Law of Demand, which will be discussed in Chapter 7. But this law is not as absolute or exact as the laws of the natural sciences. It is a **conditional** law which says that the quantity demanded will increase when price falls, **provided all other things remain the same**. This condition, that all other factors remain constant, is called the *ceteris paribus* condition or assumption. *Ceteris paribus* (which is the Latin term for "all things being equal") is the economist's substitute for the natural scientist's controlled laboratory experiments. It is not a perfect substitute but it is the best we can do in our attempt to explain the complex and often unpredictable behaviour of human beings. The *ceteris paribus* condition is an essential part of economic reasoning. You will encounter it at various places in this book.

Economics is an **empirical science**. This means that actual experiences are studied and measured. But measurement is generally also far less precise in economics than in the natural sciences. Particularly in the case of macroeconomics, which involves amounts like total spending, income and production, measurement can only be approximate. Nevertheless, we have to measure things in economics. The measurement of the performance of the economy will be explained in Chapter 4.

Microeconomics and macroeconomics

The study of economics is usually divided into two parts: microeconomics and macroeconomics. In **microeconomics** the focus is on individual parts of the economy. The prefix "micro" comes from the Greek *mikros* meaning small. In microeconomics the decisions or functioning of decision makers such as individual consumers, households, firms or other organisations are considered in isolation from the rest of the economy. The individual elements of the economy are, figuratively speaking, each put under the microscope and examined in detail. Examples include the study of the decisions of individual households (what to do, what to buy, etc) and of individual firms (what goods to produce, how to produce them, what prices to charge etc). It also includes the study of the demand, supply and prices of individual goods and services like petrol, maize, haircuts and medical services. You will study microeconomics in Part II of this book.

Macroeconomics is concerned with the economy as a whole. The prefix "macro" comes from the Greek word *makros* meaning large. In macroeconomics we focus on the "big picture." We develop an overall view of the economic system and we study total or aggregate economic behaviour. The emphasis is on topics such as total production, income and expenditure, economic growth, aggregate unemployment, the general price level, inflation and the balance of payments. Macroeconomics is therefore the world of totals. You will study macroeconomics in Part IV of this book.

Further examples of the distinction between microeconomics and macroeconomics are provided in Box 1-2.

Thus, while microeconomics studies the operation of the economy at the level where the basic decisions are taken, macroeconomics focuses on aggregate economic behaviour and the aggregate performance of the economy.

The distinction between microeconomics and macroeconomics is not watertight. There are many overlaps. What happens at the individual (micro) level affects the overall (macro) performance of the economy and vice versa. The difficulties that are sometimes experienced in distinguishing between micro-

BOX 1-2 MICROECONOMICS VERSUS MACROECONOMICS: SOME EXAMPLES

In microeconomics we study	In macroeconomics we study
The price of a single product	The consumer price index
Changes in the price of a product, like tomatoes	Inflation (ie the increase in the general level of prices in the country)
The production of maize	The total output of all goods and services in the economy
The decisions of individual consumers, like Simon Mokgatle or Anne van der Merwe	The combined outcome of the decisions of all consumers in the country
The decisions of individual firms or businesses, like a shop or factory	The combined decisions of all firms in South Africa
The market for individual goods, like bananas	The market for all goods and services in the economy
The demand for a product, like maize	The total demand for all goods and services in the economy
An individual's decision whether or not to work	The total supply of labour in the economy
A firm's decision whether or not to expand its production of, say, motorcars	Changes in the total supply of goods and services in the economy
A firm's decision to export its product	The total exports of goods and services to other countries
A firm's decision to import a product from abroad	The total imports of goods and services from other countries

economics and macroeconomics have given rise to the creation of an "in-between" level called **mesoeconomics**.

The term mesoeconomics is not used very often. We shall stick to the conventional distinction between microeconomics (which is the subject of Part II) and macroeconomics (which is dealt with in Part IV). As we progress, you will realise, however, that the dividing line is often somewhat vague or artificial. This will be particularly evident in Part III which examines three important sectors of the economy at the micro and macro levels. Nevertheless, the distinction between microeconomics and macroeconomics is very useful in our attempt to understand, explain and predict economic events and to examine economic policy.

Positive and normative economics

Another important distinction is between positive and normative economics. A **positive statement** is an objective statement of fact. A **normative statement** involves an opinion or value judgement. Consider the following examples:

- Kaizer Chiefs won the Supa 8 in 2006.
- Jacob Zuma was the South African Newsmaker of the Year in 2006.
- Tiger Woods won the US Open in 2006.
- In 2006 the average South African inflation rate, based on the consumer price index, was 6,0 per cent.
- The rand appreciated against the euro in 2006.
- Bafana Bafana can play much better than they did against Swaziland on 13 March 2007.
- Economic policy in South Africa should be primarily aimed at reducing unemployment.
- Ernie Els is a better golfer than Retief Goosen.
- *One flew over the cuckoo's nest* is one of the best movies ever made.
- The South African inflation rate is too high.

The first five are positive statements. The last five are normative statements which involve opinions or value judgements. Positive statements can be proved or disproved by comparing them with the facts. Normative issues can be debated but they can never be settled by science or by an appeal to facts.

Statements which include words like "should", "ought", "desirable" and "must" are all normative statements. But not all normative statements contain these words. Consider the following two examples:

- Capitalism exploits workers.
- Poverty is the direct result of the apartheid system.

Both these statements might sound like positive statements but they are in fact normative statements. Both contain value judgements and neither of them can be proved or disproved objectively. This can be very frustrating. We always want definite answers to questions, but we simply have to accept that economics can never be a value-free science. Economics deals with people, their hopes, fears and ambitions. Human behaviour can never be analysed totally objectively and policy always involves judgement. Values, faith, belief, conviction, prejudice and ideology are therefore frequently decisive in economic matters. This helps to explain why economists often disagree on certain important issues.

Why economists disagree

Economists are notorious for their tendency to differ on important issues. This prompted George Bernard Shaw to state that if all the economists in the world were laid end to end, they would reach no conclusion. Likewise, Arthur Motley claimed that if the nation's economists were laid end to end, they would point in all directions! Roberto Alazar also once said that economics is the only field in which two people can share a Nobel prize for saying opposing things! Winston Churchill is reported to have stated, when he was the British Chancellor of the Exchequer, that whenever he asked England's six leading economists a question, he got seven answers – two from Mr Keynes! The fact that Keynes reputedly submitted two answers is also not surprising. Economists are often unwilling to commit themselves to a single answer. Ask an economist a question and you will usually receive more than one answer: "On the one hand ... but on the other hand ...". That is why it is often jokingly said that one-handed economists are in great demand!

Why do economists tend to disagree on certain important issues?

- **They might make different value judgements.** As explained above, many economic issues involve value judgements. Thus even when economists agree on the facts, they may differ because they have different views about what **ought** to be. For example, two economists who agree that a government subsidy on bread will lower the cost to the consumer, might disagree about whether there ought to be such a subsidy.
- **They might not agree on the facts.** As will be explained in Chapter 4, measurement in economics is often only approximate. Moreover, it takes time to compile data on the performance of the economy. There is therefore always some uncertainty about the actual performance of the economy at any particular time.
- **They might be biased.** Economists are human beings and like all other human beings they might find it difficult to be completely objective. They might be forced to reach conclusions that serve the

interests of their employers. For example, an economist who is employed by government will find it difficult to be critical of government policy. Likewise, economists who are employed by private companies could face dismissal or could sacrifice promotion if they make public statements about economic issues that are not in their employers' interests.

- **They might hold different views about how the economy operates.** Many economic issues are complex, particularly at the macroeconomic level. Even if economists are in a position to be as objective as possible, they might still hold different views about how the various parts of the economy fit together or about the speed with which certain parts react to changing circumstances.
- **They might have different time perspectives.** Some economists may be more concerned with short-term prospects while others might tend to focus on the long run. This might lead to different conclusions.

There is a well-known story about a person who visited her economics professor thirty years after she had left university. Seeing an examination paper on the professor's desk, she commented that the questions were still the same as thirty years before. "Quite true," came the reply, "but the answers are different!" Although this might be somewhat far-fetched, it is not completely ridiculous. As circumstances change, new explanations are often needed. Economists are therefore often forced to change their minds about important issues. Those who do will then differ from those who stick to their previously held views. We have already referred to John Maynard Keynes, a famous 20th century British economist. He often changed his mind on important policy issues when circumstances or the nature of problems changed. This made him unpopular in certain circles. He reacted as follows: "I seem to see the elder parrots sitting around and saying 'You can rely upon us. Every day for 30 years, regardless of the weather, we have said "What a lovely morning!". But this [Keynes] is a bad bird. He says one thing one day and something else the next'."[1] In a similar vein he once told a critic: "If the facts change, I change my mind. What do you do, sir?"

Nevertheless, economists agree on many issues. This agreement is particularly obvious when economists talk to non-economists. Any experienced economist will be able to provide many examples of how economists of different persuasions will tend to agree with one another when discussing economic issues with politicians, business people, lawyers, accountants, engineers, mathematicians and other non-economists. The reason is that the economists have all been trained in the economic way of thinking, while the other people have not. Let us now take a look at this "economic way of thinking".

1.3 Some common mistakes in reasoning about economic issues

The economic way of thinking

Many people think that economics is a difficult subject. The main reason for this opinion is that economics has a language of its own. People who do not understand the terms that economists use tend to believe that economics is difficult.

Other people maintain that economics is easy, since much of it is simply common sense. As indicated in the introduction to this chapter, economics deals with a number of very ordinary issues. Much of it is indeed common sense. But it is **structured** common sense. It is a **way of thinking** about everyday issues. As John Maynard Keynes once put it:

> The theory of economics does not furnish a body of settled conclusions immediately applicable to policy. It is a method rather than a doctrine, an apparatus of the mind, a technique of thinking which helps its possessor to draw correct conclusions.[2]

Likewise, Milton Friedman, an American economist who won the Nobel Prize in 1976 (and who belongs to a totally different school of thought than Keynes), has also emphasised that economics is a way of reasoning, of thinking about problems.

Unfortunately the economic way of thinking does not come easily to people who have not been trained in or exposed to economics. In the remainder of this section we indicate some of the common mistakes non-economists make when reasoning about economic issues. Even economists fall into one or more of these traps from time to time.

The blinkered approach (or biased thinking)

Any particular individual looks at the world from his or her own vantage point. In other words, we all look at reality through different eyes. Those who are not trained to recognise the various interrelationships in the economy tend to make highly simplified and biased diagnoses of economic issues. They also often propose very simple solutions to the country's economic problems.

In the late 1970s a lecturer in engineering at the University of Stellenbosch wrote a letter to *Die Burger* in which he diagnosed South Africa's economic prob-

1. Quoted by Lord Kaldor in Thirlwall, AP (Ed). 1982. *Keynes as a policy adviser.* London: Macmillan, 17.
2. Keynes, JM. 1923. Introduction. In Robertson, DH, *The control of industry.* New York: Macmillan, vii.

lems and offered easy solutions. According to him there were only two major causes of the problems: engineers were being paid too little compared with other workers and personal income tax rates were too high. The solutions were therefore simple – pay engineers more and reduce personal income tax. This is a typical example of blinkered reasoning. Here we had a tax-paying engineer looking at the economy from his particular vantage point and proposing a solution that suited him personally.

This tendency to produce oversimplified and biased diagnoses and policy prescriptions is not restricted to the engineering fraternity – although they are notorious among economists for their lack of economic understanding (along with accountants and medical practitioners). Most non-economists tend to come up with simple explanations and proposals based on their own particular experience or interests. In other words, there is a tendency to provide the One Big Explanation. Some politicians, for example, argue that most of South Africa's economic problems can be traced to the policy of apartheid. Others again argue that South Africa's economic problems started when the apartheid system came under pressure, pointing out that there was rapid growth and economic stability during the heyday of apartheid. Workers tend to blame big business for our economic woes, while some businessmen regard trade union pressure for higher wages as the major cause of South Africa's poor economic performance. The list is almost endless.

Ask anyone to explain an economic problem like inflation or unemployment and you will usually get a simple explanation and a simple solution which can be traced to that person's personal circumstances. Few people are trained to step outside their own circumstances when looking at economic problems and even fewer are honest enough to admit that they might be part of the problem. In fact, even economists find it difficult (if not impossible) to be completely objective in their analyses of real-world economic problems.

Fallacy of composition[3]

A second, related mistake often made in reasoning about economic issues is to assume that the whole is always equal to the sum of the parts. This is called the **fallacy of composition**. Something that is true for the single case (or a part of the object being studied) is not necessarily true for the whole.

Have you ever seen a spectator seated in the stands at a soccer match suddenly stand up to get a better view of the action? If one person does it, he or she might see better. But if all the spectators stand up at the same time, nobody will see any better than they would have if everybody had remained seated in the first place. In fact, the short ones will probably have a worse view.

Likewise, if a farmer – let us call him Walter Pitso – increases his production of tomatoes while the production of the other farmers remains the same, he can be fairly sure of an increased income. But if all farmers follow Walter's example, their total income as well as their individual incomes may decline as a result of an oversupply of tomatoes and a fall in the price of tomatoes. This will be explained in Part II.

One person can withdraw money from a bank without causing any problems. But if most of the bank's clients withdraw their deposits, the bank could collapse. Similarly, one worker or group of workers could benefit by obtaining a wage increase. But if the wages of all workers in the economy are increased, the result could simply be inflation. This would leave no one better off than before. In fact, they could perhaps even be worse off.

Another example is the paradox of thrift. One household could benefit by saving more, but if all households save more, everyone may end up in a worse position than before. If saving increases, spending decreases. With lower levels of spending there will be lower levels of production and income. Ultimately, all households may therefore end up with less income to save than before. This paradox will be explained in Part IV.

The fallacy of composition often occurs in reasoning about macroeconomic issues because people tend to generalise from their own experience as individuals when trying to explain the operation of the economy as a whole.

Post hoc ergo propter hoc

Post hoc ergo propter hoc is a Latin phrase meaning "after this, therefore because of this". When two events follow each other closely in time, people often assume that the second event is the consequence of the first. In other words, the first event is regarded as the cause of the second event. This is called the *post hoc ergo propter hoc* fallacy or *post hoc* fallacy for short.

For example, in a South American village there is a witchdoctor who puts on a green costume each year just before the rainy season and then dances through the village. A few weeks later the trees and the grass turn green. Was this because of the witchdoctor's dance? Obviously not. Likewise, the fact that the rooster crows before dawn does not mean that the rooster is responsible for the sunrise.

A certain group of economists – the monetarists – attribute inflation to earlier increases in the money supply. They justify their position by pointing to observations about increases in the money supply and subsequent increases in prices. Two British researchers, Llewellyn and Witcomb, have found, however, that there was a stronger correlation

3. Note that when an argument is branded as a fallacy or error of logic, it does not imply that the argument is necessarily incorrect – it merely means that it is not necessarily correct.

between the incidence of dysentery (a stomach infection) in Scotland and the inflation rate in the United Kingdom one year later than between increases in the money supply and the subsequent price increases. Using the monetarists' line of argument it could therefore be concluded that Scottish dysentery (and not increases in the money supply) was the real cause of inflation in the United Kingdom!

We are often tempted to say: "Look what happened after that event occurred last time!" But the trouble is that there are so many things at work all the time. Therefore, unless you know more about a situation apart from the fact that one thing **followed** the other, you really cannot conclude anything. Always be extremely careful not to fall into the *post hoc ergo propter hoc* trap.

Correlation and causation

The *post hoc* fallacy is a specific example of the more general confusion between correlation and causation. If two events occur together or tend to follow one another, it does not necessarily follow that the one is the cause of the other. In other words, correlation does not imply causation.

It is sometimes stated, for example, that bowls is the most dangerous sport in the world since more people die on bowling greens than on any other sports fields. This is of course a nonsensical argument. Bowls is a very safe sport. It is quite true that many people die on bowling greens. But this is simply because so many elderly people play bowls.

Likewise, it can be claimed that Tab, Coca-Cola Light or any other diet cool drink makes one put on weight. Why? Because most people who drink these beverages are overweight. This is again a fallacy. Many people drink sugar-free or diet drinks in an attempt to lose weight.

The following is a famous example. It has been established that there is a positive correlation between the number of babies born in various cities in northwestern Europe and the number of storks' nests in those cities. Does this mean that storks really do bring babies? No, cities with larger populations (and more babies) tend to have more houses, which offer storks more chimneys on which to build their nests.

There is also a positive correlation between shoe sizes and the mathematical ability of school children. What does this mean? It only means that older children, with bigger feet, can do more mathematics than younger, smaller children with smaller feet. This example shows how one can go wrong by focusing on one thing (shoe size) while ignoring other more important things (like age).

A statistical correlation between two variables does not prove that one has caused the other or that the variables have anything to do with each other. For causation to be established there must be a logical theory explaining the effect of one variable on the other.

Levels and rates of change

Many people mistakenly believe that economics is only about numbers. Economics is an empirical science and economists often use numbers. But they use them only to illustrate principles or to quantify or analyse those things that can be expressed in numbers.

When dealing with numbers you must be very careful. One of the most common mistakes is to confuse **levels** with **rates of change**. The following examples illustrate the importance of distinguishing between levels and rates of change.

- We often read or hear that "the latest consumer price index is 10 per cent." As we shall explain in Chapters 4 and 21, the consumer price index measures the **level** of prices in the country. We then calculate the **rate of change** of that level to determine the inflation rate. The statement should therefore read: "the latest **rate of increase** in consumer prices is 10 per cent" or "the latest inflation **rate** is 10 per cent." This example illustrates the fact that people often confuse the level of prices with the rate of increase in prices. In other words, people tend to confuse high prices with rapidly increasing prices. Moreover, when they hear that the inflation rate has declined, they often mistakenly think that it means that prices have fallen when, in fact, prices are still increasing, but at a slower rate than before.
- The average level of wages of black workers in South Africa is still significantly lower than the average wages of white workers. But during the past three decades wages of black workers have on average increased much faster than white workers' wages. It is thus possible for a variable (such as the wages of black workers) to be at a relatively low level even after increasing at a high rate. The base from which a rate is calculated should always be taken into account. See Box 1-3.
- Industrialised countries, such as the United States, Japan, Switzerland and Germany, have higher levels of income per person than developing countries such as Malaysia, Korea, Chile and Brazil. But incomes in the latter countries grew much faster than in the former in recent decades. In fact, Botswana had the highest growth rate in the world during the 1970s and 1980s. But Botswana is still not a rich country. Why? Because the growth in Botswana started from a very low base. In the 1960s Botswana was one of the poorest countries in the world. Since then the economy has grown rapidly but the actual level of production and income in Botswana is still low compared to the richer countries of the world.

BOX 1-3 LEVELS AND RATES OF INCREASE: SOME NUMERICAL EXAMPLES

Rates of increase are usually expressed as percentages. For example, if the consumer price index increases from 200 to 220, the rate of increase is 10 per cent. This is calculated by expressing the difference of 20 (ie 220 minus 200) as a fraction of the original level (200) and multiplying the result by 100.

In other words, the percentage increase from 200 to 220

$$= \frac{220 - 200}{200} \times \frac{100}{1}$$
$$= \frac{20}{200} \times \frac{100}{1}$$
$$= \frac{2\,000}{200}$$
$$= 10$$

A large percentage of a low number is still a low number. On the other hand, a small percentage of a large number can be quite large. For example, 50 per cent of 300 is equal to 1 per cent of 15 000:

$$50\% \text{ of } 300 = \frac{50}{100} \times \frac{300}{1} = \frac{15\,000}{100} = 150$$
$$1\% \text{ of } 15\,000 = \frac{1}{100} \times \frac{15\,000}{1} = \frac{15\,000}{100} = 150$$

Thus if John earns R300 per month while Harry earns R15 000 per month, a 50 per cent increase in John's monthly earnings will be required to match a 1 per cent increase in Harry's monthly earnings.

Likewise, 20 per cent of 100 is less than 5 per cent of 500. It is therefore extremely important to distinguish carefully between levels and percentages or rates.

As we proceed we shall provide more examples of the need to distinguish carefully between levels and rates of change.

There are many other examples of mistaken reasoning. Most of them are not confined to economics. They are mistakes that people often make in reasoning about a wide variety of issues. But they are mistakes and we always have to be careful of falling into one or more of these traps. Economics, like any other science, calls for disciplined, structured and logically correct reasoning.

IMPORTANT CONCEPTS

Wants and needs
Means or resources
Scarcity (unlimited wants and limited resources)
Choice
Opportunity cost (or trade-off)
Production possibilities curve
Social science (versus natural science)
Ceteris paribus
Microeconomics
Macroeconomics
Positive economics
Normative economics
Biased thinking
Fallacy of composition
Post hoc ergo propter hoc
Correlation and causation
Levels versus rates of change

REVIEW QUESTIONS

1. Use everyday examples to illustrate the relationship between scarcity, choice and opportunity cost.
2. Construct your own version of a production possibilities curve (or frontier) and use it to explain scarcity, choice and opportunity cost.
3. Give two examples of microeconomic problems in South Africa today as well as two examples of pressing macroeconomic problems.
4. Give three examples of positive statements about the economy, and three examples of normative ones.
5. Use the principle of opportunity cost to explain:
   (a) why students watch more TV the week after the examinations than the week before the examinations.
   (b) why a self-employed person plays more rounds of golf per week while on holiday than during the rest of the year.
   (c) why Ernie Els does not tend to his own garden (at Herolds Bay, Wentworth or in Florida), even if he can perhaps do it better and faster than anyone else.
6. "The fact that economists often disagree proves that economics is not a science." Do you agree with this statement? Explain your viewpoint.
7. "The fact that the South Korean economy has grown rapidly since the Korean War (in the early 1950s) implies that South Korea is one of the richest countries in the world today." Do you agree? Explain your view.

2 A closer look at the economic problem

Learning outcomes

Once you have studied this chapter you should be able to

- describe the three central economic questions
- distinguish between the four main factors of production
- explain what the distribution issue is all about
- describe the major differences between traditional, command, market and mixed economies
- briefly describe the contributions of Adam Smith, Karl Marx and John Maynard Keynes to economic science

Under capitalism, man exploits man, under socialism it is just the opposite.

ANONYMOUS

Question: "What is socialism?" Answer: "The longest way to capitalism."

POLISH JOKE

It is not from the benevolence of the butcher, the brewer, or the baker that we expect our dinner but from their regard to their own interest. We address ourselves not to their humanity but to their self-love.

ADAM SMITH

In Chapter 1 you were introduced to the central concepts of scarcity, choice and opportunity cost. We now introduce you to three central economic questions that have to be solved in any economic system.

- **What** goods and services will be produced and in **what** quantities? These are **output** questions.
- **How** will each of the goods and services be produced? How much of the scarce resources will be used in the production of each good? These are **input** questions.
- **For whom** will the various goods and services be produced? Who will receive the goods and services? How much of them will they receive? And **where** will the production occur? These are **distribution** questions.

In this chapter we use these three questions (What? How? and For whom?) as a framework to introduce a number of further important concepts and issues. We shall also revisit some concepts and issues that we have already introduced. We point out, for example, what different **types of goods and services** are produced. We also explain the major **resources** that are used to produce these goods and services. We then turn to some aspects of the **distribution issue**, and we examine different possible solutions to the three central questions. We ask how different societies go about solving the questions. In the process we describe the major types of **economic system**. We also introduce you to three important economists whose ideas have helped to shape these systems.

In the first three sections we use the three central questions (What? How? For whom?) to introduce a number of important concepts and distinctions. The different solutions to these three questions are then discussed in Section 2.4. The chapter is concluded by a brief overview of the ideas of three important economists whose views helped to shape the various answers to the three central questions.

2.1 What should be produced?

The purpose of economic activity is to satisfy human wants. Humans have different types of wants, including material wants and spiritual wants. Most wants are satisfied by **goods and services**. **Goods** are tangible objects like food, clothing, houses, books and motorcars. **Services** are intangible things like medical services, legal services, financial services, the services of an economics lecturer and the services provided by public servants. Because much of economics is concerned with the production and distribution of goods and services, the term "goods and services" is used frequently. For the sake of convenience, however, we often refer to "goods" only when we really mean "goods and services".

The words "goods" and "services" both have positive connotations. They satisfy wants and are therefore "good" and "serve" a purpose. We do not call them "bads" and "disservices". We assume (for the time being at least) that all goods and services serve a useful purpose and that maximum production is therefore desirable.

There are different types of good. In the paragraphs that follow we distinguish between consumer goods and capital goods, different categories of consumer goods, final goods and intermediate goods, private goods and public goods, free goods and economic goods, homogeneous goods and heterogeneous goods.

Consumer goods and capital goods

Consumer goods are goods that are used or consumed by individuals or households (ie consumers) to satisfy wants. Examples include food, wine, clothing, shoes, furniture, household appliances and motorcars. **Capital goods** are goods that are not consumed in this way but are used in the production of other goods. Examples include all types of machinery, plant and equipment used in manufacturing and construction, school buildings, university residences, roads, dams and bridges. Capital goods do not themselves yield direct consumer satisfaction, but they permit more production and satisfaction in future. Choosing between producing consumer goods and producing capital goods therefore means choosing between present and future consumption. However, like all other goods, capital goods also have a limited lifetime. They are subject to wear and tear and may also become obsolete. Their value therefore **depreciates** over time.

Capital goods are an important factor of production. We discuss them in greater detail when we introduce the different factors of production.

Different categories of consumer goods

Consumer goods can be classified into three groups: non-durable goods, semi-durable goods and durable goods.

- **Non-durable goods** are goods that are used once only. Examples include food, wine, tobacco, petrol and medicine.
- **Semi-durable goods** are goods that can be used more than once and which usually last for a limited period. Examples include clothing, shoes, sheets and blankets and motorcar tyres.
- **Durable goods** are goods which normally last for a number of years. Examples include furniture, refrigerators, washing machines, dishwashers and motorcars.

Apart from purchasing goods, individuals and households can also satisfy some of their wants by purchasing **services** such as those listed earlier.

Final goods and intermediate goods

Final goods are the goods that are used or consumed by individuals, households and firms. A loaf of bread, for example, is a final good. **Intermediate goods**, on the other hand, are goods that are purchased to be used as inputs in producing other goods. Intermediate goods are thus processed further before they are sold to end users. Flour used by a baker is an intermediate good. The baker does not consume it. The flour is processed into bread, cake or something else. However, when a household purchases flour it is a final good since the purpose is to consume it in some form or another. The distinction between final goods and intermediate goods becomes very important when economic activity is measured. If we do not distinguish between these two types of good, we can easily count goods twice (double counting) and so overestimate total production. This is explained in Chapter 4.

Private goods and public goods

A **private good** is a good that is consumed by individuals or households. All typical consumer goods (like food, clothes, furniture and motorcars) are private goods. The distinguishing feature of private goods is that consumption by others can be excluded. A **public good**, on the other hand, is a good that is used by the community or society at large. Consumption by individuals cannot be excluded. A traffic light, for example, is a public good. Other examples are defence and weather forecasts. We discuss the distinction between private goods and public goods in more detail in Chapter 16.

Economic goods and free goods

An **economic good** is a good that is produced at a cost from scarce resources. Economic goods are therefore also called scarce goods. Naturally, most goods are economic goods. A **free good** is a good that is not scarce and therefore has no price. Air, sunshine and sea water at the coast are usually regarded as free goods. Nowadays, however, air and sea water are often polluted, with the result that clean air and sea water are not always freely available. Anyone living in a town like Witbank, Vanderbijlpark or Alexandra in winter will appreciate that clean air can be a scarce commodity. Even sunshine can become scarce in large cities with high-rise buildings. People who live at street level (or even beneath it) in one of these cities may not enjoy light or heat from the sun. If they want maximum access to sunshine, they have to move to the higher floor levels for which they have to pay higher rentals. In these cases clean air and sunshine are economic goods rather than free goods.

All the gifts of nature are sometimes regarded as free goods, since they are not produced by humans. But in many instances it requires effort and cost to make them useful to humans. Minerals have to be mined and even water has to be stored and piped, often at great expense.

Note also that some goods or services which are labelled "free" are not really free. The term free education is used to indicate that the pupils concerned do not have to pay for their education. But the education is not free in the economic sense since someone, for example the taxpayer, still has to pay for it. Remember the TANSTAAFL principle – "there ain't no such thing as a free lunch."

Homogeneous and heterogeneous goods

Homogeneous goods are goods that are all exactly alike. There are few examples of such goods in the real world. A fine ounce of gold is one example – one fine ounce is exactly the same as another. **Heterogeneous** or differentiated goods are goods that have different varieties, qualities or brands. Most goods are heterogeneous goods – even something like bread, which comes in different shapes, sizes and qualities. Think of virtually any good (eg shirts, shoes, video recorders, radios, cassette tapes, meat, eggs) and you can immediately list different varieties or brands of that good.

The production possibilities curve once again

The fact that a variety of goods and services are produced and consumed does not answer the question **what** should be produced. A simple answer to the question would be that enough of all goods and services should be produced to satisfy all human wants. But as we have emphasised repeatedly, this is not possible. Resources are limited and choices have to be made. In Chapter 1 we illustrated the problems of scarcity, choice and opportunity cost by using a **production possibilities curve**. This curve, which is sometimes also called the production opportunity curve, summarises the first central economic question. Let us take another look at this curve.

The production possibilities curve given in Figure 1-1 in Chapter 1 was based on a hypothetical example of an isolated Wild Coast community that produces fish and potatoes. Figure 2-1 is a reproduction of Figure 1-1.

The production possibilities curve shows the different combinations of fish and potatoes that can be produced with the available resources and the available production techniques. For example, C indicates that the community can produce 85 kilograms of potatoes **and** 2 baskets of fish per day. The curve also indicates

FIGURE 2-1 The production possibilities curve once again

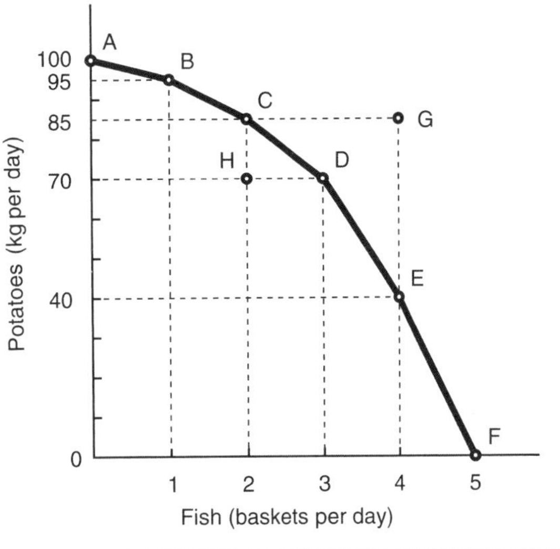

ABCDEF is a reproduction of the production possibilities curve in Figure 1-1. It indicates the maximum attainable combinations of potatoes and fish that can be produced by the Wild Coast community. Point G is unattainable since it lies beyond the curve. Point H is an attainable combination, since it lies inside the curve, but it represents an inefficient use of resources.

that more fish can only be produced by sacrificing part of the potato production. For example, at D more fish (3 baskets) can be produced per day than at C but this means that fewer potatoes (70 kilograms) will be produced. In other words, 15 kilograms of potatoes have to be sacrificed to produce an extra basket of fish. By moving from C to D the community actually **transforms** part of the production of potatoes into fish. That is why the curve is sometimes also called the **transformation curve**.

With a given level of resources and a given state of technology, the community can produce different combinations of potatoes and fish. But it cannot move beyond ABCDEF (or AF for short). That is why the curve is sometimes also called the production possibility **boundary** or **frontier**. It indicates the maximum attainable combinations of the two goods, also called the **potential output**. You will recall that a production possibilities curve such as the one in Figure 2-1, that is **concave** to the origin, illustrates increasing opportunity costs.[1]

There are, of course, also other attainable combinations. Point H, which indicates a combination of 70 kilograms of potatoes and 2 baskets of fish, is one such combination. In fact, any combination within the frontier (ie below the curve) is attainable. But such combinations are **inefficient** – either the available resources are used inefficiently or some of them are idle (ie unemployed). Instead of producing combination H the community can produce C or D. At C the production of fish is the same as at H, but 15 kilograms more potatoes are produced. Likewise, at D the production of potatoes is the same as at H, but one extra basket of fish is produced. In any economic system the first challenge therefore is to produce one of the maximum attainable combinations of goods and services. In other words, the scarce resources should be used fully and as **efficiently** as possible. This occurs when it is impossible to produce more of the one good without sacrificing some production of the other good. On the production possibilities curve **actual** output is equal to **potential** output.

The community would, of course, have preferred a combination beyond the production possibilities curve or frontier, such as G in Figure 2-1. Point G indicates a combination of 85 kilograms of potatoes and four baskets of fish. But any point beyond AF is unattainable. Given the **available resources** and the **current production techniques**, a combination such as that indicated by G is impossible.

However, the quantity of available resources can increase and/or production techniques can improve over time. If this happens, it can be illustrated by a production possibilities curve that shifts outwards. Such an outward movement illustrates **economic growth**. To explain this, we use a production possibilities curve which illustrates the production of consumer goods and capital goods, the two broad types of good produced in the economy. The potential production of consumer goods and capital goods can be increased in a number of possible ways.

- If an improved technique for producing capital goods is developed, it will be possible to produce more capital goods with the available factors of production. The original production possibilities curve is illustrated in Figure 2-2 as AB. If we assume that the available factors of production and the technique for producing consumer goods remain the same, the maximum potential production of consumer goods remains at A. But the maximum potential output of capital goods (if all available resources are used to produce capital goods) increases from B to C. The new production possibilities curve is thus indicated by AC. Except at point A, it is now possible to produce more capital goods **and** more consumer goods than before. For example, at point Y more of both types of good are produced than at point X.

FIGURE 2-2 Improved technique for producing capital goods

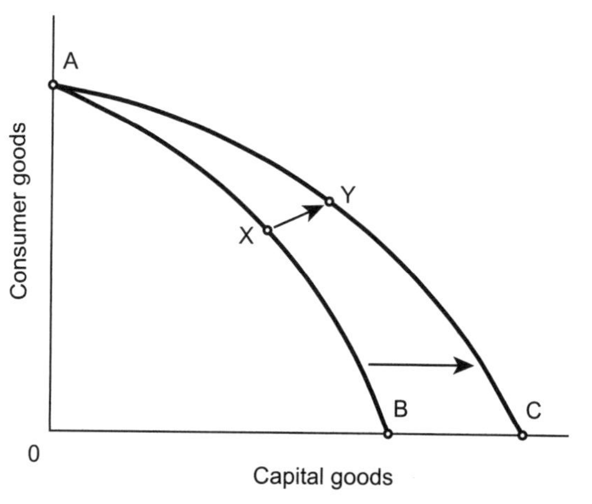

An improved technique for producing capital goods makes it possible to produce more capital goods with the available resources. The production possibilities curve swivels outwards from AB to AC.

- Similarly, if a new technique for producing consumer goods is developed, while the available resources and the technique for producing capital goods remain the same, the maximum potential output of consumer goods will increase. This is illustrated in Figure 2-3. The original production possibilities curve is again indicated as AB. But this time the maximum potential output of con-

1. Opportunity cost may also be constant, in which case the production possibilities curve will be a straight line, rather than bulged as in Figure 2-1.

FIGURE 2-3 Improved technique for producing consumer goods

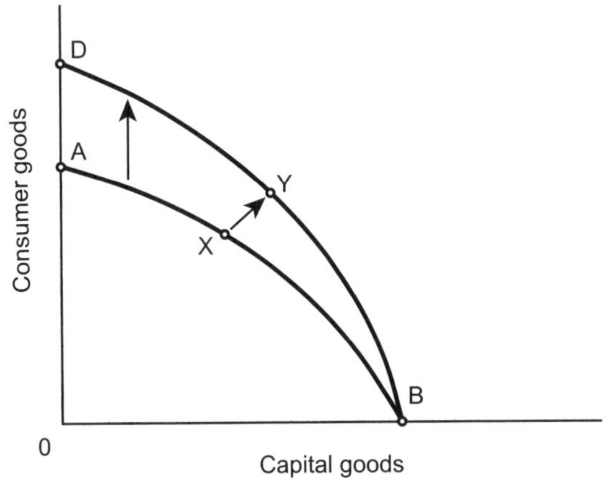

An improved technique for producing consumer goods makes it possible to produce more consumer goods with the available resources. The production possibilities curve swivels outwards from BA to BD.

FIGURE 2-4 Increase in the quantity or productivity of the available resources

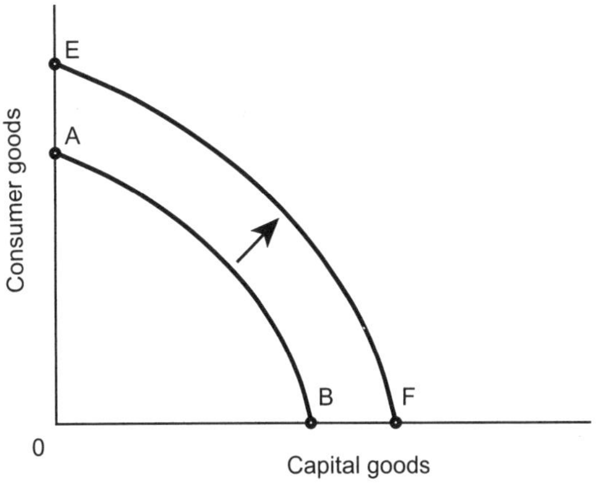

An increase in the quantity or productivity of resources makes it possible to produce more consumer goods and capital goods. The production possibilities curve shifts outwards from AB to EF.

sumer goods increases (from A to D), while the maximum potential output of capital goods remains unchanged (at B). Again, the production possibilities curve swivels, but this time on point B rather than on point A. Except at point B, it is now possible to produce more consumer goods **and** capital goods than before, as illustrated, for example, by the movement from point X to point Y.

- If the amount of available resources (eg the number of workers) and/or the productivity of the available resources increase, it will be possible to produce more consumer goods **and** more capital goods than before. This can be illustrated by a shift of the original production possibilities curve (AB) to the right (to EF) as in Figure 2-4. Figures 2-2, 2-3 and 2-4 all illustrate economic growth. We discuss economic growth at various points in this book, particularly in Chapter 23.

The amount of resources or their productivity (or efficiency) can, of course, also decrease, resulting in a decline in potential output. This can be illustrated by inward shifts of the production possibilities curve (ie a reversal of the shifts illustrated in Figures 2-2, 2-3 and 2-4).

The production possibilities curve also illustrates how important it is to use scarce resources fully and efficiently. If the economy is operating at less than the potential output (ie if **actual** output is less than **potential** output), illustrated by a point inside or below the production possibilities curve, some of the available resources are unemployed or not employed efficiently – see point H in Figure 2-1. In such a case it is possible to expand production simply by using the existing resources fully and more efficiently (given the state of technology). With a fuller or more efficient use of the available resources actual output can be increased from H to C or D in Figure 2-1. See also Table 2-1.

The production possibilities curve illustrates potential output but it does not indicate which of the possible combinations should be produced. The final choice will depend on the preferences of society. For example, from an efficiency point of view it is possible to produce various combinations of military goods and civilian goods but the actual combination chosen will depend on the preferences of consumers, or of political office-bearers as their representatives.

The example of the choice between the production of consumer goods and capital goods can be used to indicate a further important aspect of economic growth. By this time you are aware that an increased

TABLE 2-1 The production possibilities curve (PPC): a summary

Description	*Illustrated by*
Attainable combinations	All points on or inside the PPC
Unattainable combinations	All points beyond the PPC
Efficient combinations	All points on the PPC
Inefficient combinations (or unemployment)	All points inside the PPC
Increase in potential	Outward shift of the PPC

availability of resources (factors of production) will raise the potential output of the economy. But you also know that capital goods are man-made factors of production (see Section 2.2 as well). Thus, the greater the amount of capital goods produced, the greater the potential output will be. The choice between the production of consumer goods and capital goods is therefore not a neutral one as far as the potential growth rate of the economy is concerned. The greater the amount of resources that are devoted to the production of capital goods (machinery, equipment etc), the fewer the amount of resources available to produce consumer goods that can be enjoyed by the population. But, and this is important, the greater the current production of capital goods, the greater the potential output of the economy and therefore also the greater the potential future production of consumer goods. If, on the other hand, most resources are currently used to produce consumer goods, the capital stock of the economy will not expand rapidly and the potential output of the economy and the potential future production (and enjoyment) of consumer goods will suffer.

Finally, note that while economic growth can help to reduce the gap between wants and means in the economy, it will not eliminate the problem of relative scarcity. In other words, economic growth will never succeed in solving the economic problem.

The decision about **what** to produce incorporates the decision **how much** of each good and service to produce, as well as the decision what **not** to produce. The decision about what to produce is therefore really a decision about how to allocate the scarce resources among different possible uses. That is why the decision about **what** to produce is called the problem of **resource allocation**. The different types of resource are discussed in the next section. Different possible answers to the question of **what** should be produced are discussed in Section 2.4.

2.2 How should it be produced?

Once a decision has been taken about what goods and services should be produced, the next question is **how** these goods and services should be produced. Because the resources are scarce, they have to be used efficiently. But what are these resources? In this section we focus on the different types of resource that are used to produce goods and services. They are called **factors of production**.

Factors of production

There are four main factors of production: natural resources (or land), labour, capital and entrepreneurship. Natural resources and labour are sometimes called **primary** factors of production, while capital and entrepreneurship are called **secondary** factors. Another possible distinction is between **human resources** (labour and entrepreneurship) and **non-human resources** (natural resources and capital). We now discuss each of the four factors of production separately.

■ NATURAL RESOURCES (LAND)

Natural resources (sometimes called land) consists of all the gifts of nature. They include mineral deposits, water, arable land, vegetation, natural forests, marine resources, other animal life, the atmosphere and even sunshine. Natural resources are fixed in supply. Their availability cannot be increased if we want more of them. It is, however, often possible to exploit more of the available resources. For example, new mineral deposits are still being discovered and exploited every year. But once they are used, they cannot be replaced. We therefore refer to minerals as **non-renewable** or **exhaustible assets**.

As with all other factors of production, both the **quality** and the **quantity** of natural resources are important. Some countries cover a vast area but the land is of limited value. A desert, for example, has little or no agricultural value. But it may contain valuable mineral deposits. Some countries have a relatively small geographical area but a plentiful supply of arable land and minerals.

The situation can also vary within a country. For example, in South Africa there are large areas with little or no agricultural or mineral value. But there are also areas that are rich in minerals or arable land.

Because natural resources are in fixed supply, the rate at which they are exploited is often a cause of concern. Nowadays environmentalists are extremely concerned about pollution and the destruction of natural resources such as the rain forests. These concerns, and the idea of environmentally sustainable development, were put firmly on the global agenda by the Earth Summits held in Rio de Janeiro in 1992 and in Johannesburg in 2002.

■ LABOUR

Goods and services cannot be produced without human effort. **Labour** can be defined as the exercise of human mental and physical effort in the production of goods and services. It includes all human effort exerted with a view to obtaining reward in the form of income. The efforts of goldminers, rubbish collectors, professional boxers, civil servants, engineers and university lecturers are all classified as labour. In modern societies there is a high degree of specialisation of labour – see Box 2-1.

The **quantity** of labour depends on the size of the population and the proportion of the population that is able and willing to work. The latter, in turn, depends on factors such as the age and gender distribution of the population. The proportion of children, women

BOX 2-1 SPECIALISATION AND THE DIVISION OF LABOUR

The three main economic activities in each modern society are **production**, **consumption** and **exchange**. The ultimate aim of economic activity is to satisfy human wants. Different people produce different goods and services which are then exchanged (or traded) and eventually consumed. But this was not always the case. In primitive societies each household provided for the wants of the members of the household. Production and consumption occurred within the same household and there was little or no exchange or trade of goods and services between different households.

But even in these primitive households there was some **specialisation**. For example, women performed tasks in and around the home while men would go hunting. But there was no division of labour. **Division of labour** occurs when a production process is broken up into different steps or parts, each of which is performed by an individual worker or group of workers. Each worker can then focus on a particular task. For example, a person who is competent in all the manual trades can construct a house without any assistance from anyone else. But it will take a lot of effort and time. Houses are usually constructed by teams which each specialise in a different part of the task, eg bricklayers, plasterers, plumbers, electricians, tilers and carpenters. This division of labour creates opportunities for specialisation and enables a group of people to build more houses than they would have been able to do if each one tried to build a whole house alone.

The importance of the division of labour was recognised in the 18th century by Adam Smith, who is often regarded as the father of modern economics. His example of producing pins has become famous in economics and is quoted in virtually every introductory textbook. On the first page of his famous book, *The wealth of nations* (see Section 2.5), he wrote:

> To take an example … from a very trifling manufacture … the trade of the pinmaker; a workman not educated to this business … nor acquainted with the use of the machinery employed in it … could scarce, perhaps … make one pin in a day and certainly could not make twenty. But in the way in which this business is now carried on, not only the whole work is a peculiar trade, but it is divided into a number of branches … One man draws out the wire, another straightens it, a third cuts it, a fourth points it, a fifth grinds it at the top for receiving the head … ten persons … could make among them upwards of forty-eight thousand pins a day. Each person, therefore, … might be considered as making four thousand eight hundred pins in a day.

The division of labour has a number of advantages, including the following:

- It **saves time**. One person handling different tools and moving from one work position to another entails a considerable waste of time. With the division of labour each worker performs a single task, which saves a lot of time.
- It enables workers to be **allocated to tasks that they are best suited for**. People have different abilities – for example, some are physically strong while others are more skilled at performing intricate tasks which do not require physical strength.
- It enables workers to **develop specific skills**. If the production process is divided into specific tasks, each worker becomes skilled at his or her task. It is also easier to train workers in specific tasks.
- It makes **mechanisation** possible. The division of labour breaks a single task up into a number of simpler tasks that can often be performed by machines, which can work for 24 hours a day. Workers then only need to supervise the process. Some processes can be refined further so that even the supervision can be performed by machines. This is referred to as **automation**.
- It **leads to better quality**. The division of labour allows greater uniformity in quality and makes it possible to exercise quality control at various stages in the production process.

However, the division of labour also has some disadvantages. The most important disadvantage is that work can become monotonous and boring. Workers often feel bored, less responsible and less fulfilled if they are performing simple, repetitive tasks which require little thought. They also cannot appreciate their individual contributions to the end product, and they may therefore lose interest in the quality of their work – this is known as **worker alienation**. Another important disadvantage is that people (and processes) become more and more interdependent. If a breakdown occurs at one point, then everyone is affected. In fact, modern societies are highly interdependent. One person's well-being depends on the activities of other people; one production process depends on the smooth running of other production processes; one firm depends on other firms, and so on. In the modern economy this interdependence even reaches across national boundaries, with production processes in one country being dependent on inputs received from other countries. As we emphasise in Chapter 3, **interdependence** is one of the major features of any modern economy. This means that individuals, sectors and countries are all vulnerable to changes in the domestic and international economy.

Note that the specialisation of labour is a broader concept than the division of labour. **Specialisation** refers to the tendency of people, businesses and countries to concentrate on different activities to which they are best suited: some people specialise in law, others in medicine; some firms produce clothes while others produce food; some countries specialise in producing minerals, while others produce machines, and so on. The **division of labour** refers to the act of assigning individual workers to different tasks which form part of a production process.

As emphasised by Adam Smith (see Section 2.5), specialisation creates wealth. But the gains from specialisation can only be achieved if there is **exchange** or **trade** between the different participants. Individuals, businesses and countries trade the goods and services in which they specialise for goods and services produced by others. Without exchange, specialised producers cannot satisfy their consumption wants from their own production.

As stated at the beginning of this box, the three major economic activities in modern societies are production, consumption and exchange. Along with specialisation and the division of labour, these activities form the basis of the interdependent economic system.

and elderly people all affect the available quantity of labour, which is called the **labour force**.

The **quality** of labour is even more important than the **quantity** of labour. The quality of labour is usually described by the term **human capital**, which refers to the skill, knowledge and health of the workers. Education, training and experience are all important determinants of human capital.

■ CAPITAL

Capital comprises all manufactured resources, such as machines, tools and buildings, which are used in the production of other goods and services. Capital goods, which were also defined in the previous section, are not produced for their own sake but to produce other goods. Capital can be a confusing concept, particularly because it is often used in a financial or monetary sense. Business people, bankers and accountants all have their own definition of capital. Even in economics the term sometimes has a financial connotation. It is important to remember, however, that when we talk about capital as a **factor of production**, we are referring to all those tangible things that are used to produce other things.

To produce capital goods, current (ie present) consumption has to be sacrificed in favour of future consumption. As explained earlier, the more capital goods that are produced in a particular period, the fewer the number of consumer goods that will be produced in that period, but the greater the production capacity will be in future. On the other hand, if all current resources are used for producing consumer goods, the future means of production will be fewer.

Like all other goods, capital goods do not have an unlimited life. Machinery, plant, equipment, buildings, dams, bridges and roads are all subject to wear and tear. Equipment can also become outdated or obsolete because of technological progress. For example, huge mainframe computers installed a decade or two ago have been replaced by much smaller, cheaper and more efficient personal computers. Provision therefore has to be made for the replacement of existing capital goods. This is called the provision for **depreciation** (or depreciation allowance). In the national accounts (see Chapter 4) it is referred to as **consumption of fixed capital**.

■ ENTREPRENEURSHIP

The availability of natural resources, labour and capital is not sufficient to ensure economic success. These factors of production have to be combined and organised by people who see opportunities and are willing to take risks by producing goods in the expectation that they will be sold. These people are called entrepreneurs. The word entrepreneur comes from the French word *entreprendre* which means "to undertake". The term was coined at the beginning of the 19th century by the French economist Jean-Baptiste Say (see Box 2-7).

The entrepreneur is the driving force behind production. Entrepreneurs are the initiators, the people who take the initiative. They are also the innovators, the people who introduce new products and new techniques on a commercial basis. And they are the riskbearers, the people who take chances. They do this because they anticipate that they will make profits. But they may also suffer losses and perhaps bankruptcy.

The entrepreneur is more than a manager. The entrepreneur is dynamic, a restless spirit, an ideas person, a person of action who has the ability to inspire others. Because entrepreneurship is such an important factor of production, a lot of research has been done to identify the characteristics of successful entrepreneurs. What drives an entrepreneur? What differentiates entrepreneurs from other human beings? Unfortunately there are no simple answers. There is, for example, still a lively debate on the question of whether entrepreneurial talent comes naturally or whether it can be acquired (eg through appropriate training).

All that can be stated with certainty is that entrepreneurship is an important economic force. In countries where entrepreneurship is lacking, the government is sometimes forced to act as entrepreneur in an attempt to stimulate economic development.

■ TECHNOLOGY

Technology is sometimes identified as a fifth factor of production. At any given time, a society has a certain amount of knowledge about the ways in which goods can be produced. When new knowledge is discovered and put into practice, more goods and services can be produced with a given amount of natural resources, labour, capital and entrepreneurship. If this happens we say that technology has improved. The discovery of new knowledge is called **invention**, while the incorporation of this knowledge into actual production techniques and products is called **innovation**. The wheel, the steam engine and the modern computer are all examples of important inventions. For these inventions to be used in actual production, new machines (ie capital goods) have to be developed. In other words, the inventions have to be embodied in capital. The application of inventions also requires entrepreneurs to identify the opportunities and exploit them. Thus, while technology is important, it can be argued that it forms part of capital and entrepreneurship. In this book, we therefore do not deal with it as a separate factor of production.

Money is not a factor of production

Money is often regarded as the key to everything else. People frequently say "money can buy anything" or "money is power". Money is important, but it is not a factor of production. Goods and services cannot be produced with money. As we explain in Chapter 15, money is a medium of exchange. Money can be exchanged for goods and services. Money is therefore something which facilitates the exchange of goods and services. But money cannot be used to produce goods and services. To produce goods and services we need factors of production such as natural resources, labour and capital.

The choice of technique

The question of how the goods and services should be produced essentially involves choosing the best methods of production to produce the various goods and services. Frequently, various techniques are available to produce a particular good. For example, a dam or a road may be built with large machines and relatively little labour, or it may be built with less sophisticated equipment and more labour. When the production process is dominated by machines we talk about **capital-intensive** production. On the other hand, if the emphasis is on labour, the technique is **labour intensive**. The appropriate choice of technique will depend on the availability and quality of the various factors of production as well as their relative cost. In a rural community which does not have access to capital goods such as tractors there may be no option but to use unsophisticated equipment and a lot of physical effort to produce food or other goods. However, in the modern economy, where different options are available, the choice of technique will depend, *inter alia*, on the relative prices of the factors of production (eg wages and interest rates).

2.3 For whom should it be produced?

The third central question of economics is how the production is distributed among the different individuals and groups in the economy. In other words, who will receive the goods and services that are produced in the economy? Since goods and services are consumed to satisfy human wants, this question is the same as asking whose wants will be satisfied.

The distribution of the production among the various participants in the economy is a normative issue, and often a very emotional one, particularly in societies where the distribution is highly unequal. As we show in the rest of this book, South Africa has a highly unequal distribution of income and wealth. It therefore comes as no surprise that the **distribution question** is high on the agendas of many South African interest groups.

But the distribution question is not only about what each individual gets. It is also concerned with the relative shares of different sectors and of the different factors of production. In the previous section we introduced the four major factors of production: natural resources, labour, capital and entrepreneurship. These factors earn incomes, called **rent** (natural resources), **wages** and **salaries** (labour), **interest** (capital) and **profit** (entrepreneurship). The distribution among these forms of income is called the **functional distribution** of income. The distribution among the various individuals or households in the economy (irrespective of the source of the income received) is called the **personal distribution** of income. The distribution of **income** must also be distinguished from the distribution of **wealth**.

As we explain in Chapter 3, income is a flow which is earned during a period (day, week, month, year). Wealth, on the other hand, is a stock – the stock of physical and financial assets that have been accumulated over time. Physical assets include things such as houses, cars, furniture, paintings and land, while financial assets include savings deposits, shares in companies and investments in unit trusts. Although income and wealth are different concepts, they are linked, and the distribution of income is related to the distribution of wealth. The reason is that many of the assets owned by the owners of wealth yield an income, for example in the form of rent, interest or dividends.

The distribution of income will also affect **what** goods and services will be produced. Income is the source of spending, and consumers "vote" for what they want by spending their income on goods and services. In this way production is determined by the "money votes" of the consumers. The types of goods and services that are produced will thus also depend on the distribution of income. For example, in societies where income is distributed very unequally, the production of goods will tend to be concentrated on the wants of the wealthy people. In addition, many people will be employed by the wealthy as domestic servants, drivers and gardeners.

Income is also distributed very unequally among different countries. More than half of the world's population live in poor countries and receive only about 5 per cent of the total world income. In contrast, about one-sixth of the world's population live in the rich, industrialised countries and receive about 80 per cent of the total world income.

Other aspects of the distribution issue include the distribution of economic activity between the government sector (which we call the **public sector**) and the rest of the economy (which we call the **private sector**); the geographic distribution of economic activity between different **regions** in one country; and the distribution between the **primary sector**, the **secondary sector** and the **tertiary sector** – see Box 2-2.

In the rest of this chapter we show how the distribution question is approached in different economic systems. We also touch on various aspects of the distribution question in the rest of the book.

2.4 Solutions to the central questions: an introduction to economic systems

In this section we look at some of the mechanisms that are used to solve the central economic questions. There are essentially three such coordinating mechanisms: **tradition**, **command** and the **market**. These three mechanisms form the basis of the most important economic systems, along with property rights – see Box 2-3. We discuss four systems: the traditional system, the command system, the market system and the mixed system. Our emphasis is on the market system and the mixed system, since most economies today are mixed systems in which the market plays a central role.

A **system** is a network of parts which interlock to form an overall pattern. Examples include the nervous system of the human body, the solar system, the transport system of a country and its political system. An **economic system** is a pattern of organisation which is aimed at solving the three central questions discussed in the previous sections. Economic systems do not always work well, but they are often so vast and complicated that it is quite marvellous that they work at all.

The traditional system

The oldest solution to the three central questions is **tradition**. By this we mean that the same goods are produced and distributed in the same way by each successive generation. In a traditional system each participant's task and methods of production are prescribed by custom. Men do what their fathers did. Women do what their mothers did. People use the same techniques of production as their parents did and production is distributed according to long-established traditions.

A **traditional economic system** provides clear and easy answers to the three central questions. It is, however, a rigid system, which is slow to adapt to changing conditions and stubbornly resists innovation. Tradi-

BOX 2-2 THE PRIMARY, SECONDARY AND TERTIARY SECTORS

The production of goods and services in a country occurs in three broad sectors: the primary, secondary and tertiary sectors.

- The **primary sector** is the sector in which raw materials such as agricultural, fishing, forestry and mining products are produced.
- The **secondary sector** is the manufacturing part of the economy in which raw materials and other inputs are used to produce other goods. This includes the beneficiation of primary products (eg canning fruit and vegetables and processing minerals into mineral products such as steel), and the manufacturing of consumer goods (like clothing, footwear and furniture) and capital goods (such as machinery, buildings, roads and railways).
- The **tertiary sector** comprises the services and trade sections of the economy. It is often referred to as the services sector. Activities in the tertiary sector include trade, transport, communication and education, as well as financial, personal and government services.

During the early phases of economic development, agriculture and other primary activities usually account for a large share of total production. As development proceeds, first the secondary sector and then the tertiary sector become more important. In developed economies the tertiary sector usually accounts for the bulk of the total economic activity. As indicated in Chapter 5, this process has also occurred in South Africa.

tional systems tend to be subsistence economies. They therefore tend to be characterised by economic stagnation, that is, an absence of economic progress. But this is usually not considered a drawback by the participants themselves. In traditional systems economic activity is not the first priority. Economic activity is usually secondary to religious and cultural values and the desire to perpetuate the status quo.

A good example of a traditional system was the manorial system in medieval Europe. Nowadays, purely traditional systems are not as common as they used to be. They tend to be limited to isolated and largely self-sufficient communities, for example in the Canadian Arctic, certain remote parts of Latin America, island communities in the Pacific, and various parts of Africa. This does not mean, however, that tradition is no longer an important mechanism for solving the central questions, even in more advanced societies. Important aspects of economic behaviour are still governed by tradition. Some children still follow in their parents' footsteps. In wealthy families status and tradition are still important. Nicky Oppenheimer had little choice but to become a leading figure in the Anglo American Group, while Johann Rupert was groomed to succeed his father at the head of the Rembrandt empire. But people like Nicky Oppenheimer and Johann Rupert are not bound by tradition when they have to make important decisions about what to produce and how to produce it.

The command system

The second solution to the central questions is **command**. In a **command system** the participants are instructed what to produce and how to produce it by a central authority which also determines how the output is distributed. Because the economy is governed and coordinated by a central authority, command systems are also called **centrally planned systems**.

Central planning is obviously a tremendous task. Decisions have to be taken on how, where and for what purpose every natural resource, every labourer and every capital good are to be applied. The planners have to determine what consumer goods should be produced, how to produce them and how they are to be divided among consumers; how many resources should be allocated to the production of capital goods and how many to consumer goods; and what types of capital good should be produced. These are but a few of the problems that the planners have to solve. This is an extremely difficult task, particularly in a changing environment. Mistakes are inevitable. Nevertheless, in the 1970s and early 1980s more than a third of the world's population lived in countries that relied heavily on central planning. These countries included Russia, China, Poland, Romania, North Korea and East Germany. Since then, however, central planning has become almost obsolete. At the time of writing, North Korea was generally regarded as the best

BOX 2-3 CLASSIFYING ECONOMIC SYSTEMS

No two economies have identical solutions to the questions **What**? **How**? and **For whom**? Each country has different institutions and there are almost as many kinds of economic systems as there are national economies. Certain common features can be used, however, to classify economic systems.

The two basic criteria are property rights and the coordinating mechanism.

- **Property rights**. The oldest known classification of economic systems distinguishes between economies according to the predominant form of ownership of the factories, farms and other productive assets (ie according to property rights). Property rights refer to the right to possess, use or dispose of tangible assets (eg houses) and intangible assets (eg patents) as well as the right to all or part of the income generated by those assets. Property can be owned **publicly** or **socially** by different levels of government (central, provincial or local government), the personnel of a firm (workers' management) or public boards (as in **socialism**), or it can be owned **privately** by individuals, partnerships, cooperatives and companies (as in **capitalism**).

- **Coordinating mechanisms**. Every economy has to: determine what is to be produced, where, how and how much; allocate the aggregate amount of goods and services produced between private consumption, collective consumption and investment in capital goods; distribute the material benefits among the members of society; and maintain economic relations with the outside world. A **coordinating mechanism** is a means of providing and transmitting information so as to coordinate the economic activities of the great number of participants in an economy. Economic systems are often classified according to their predominant coordinating mechanism. In a **market economy** coordination is achieved through the market mechanism or price system, ie through the free and spontaneous movement of market prices, as determined by the operation of the forces of supply and demand. In a **centrally planned economy** coordination of decisions is achieved by means of a central plan, drawn up by a central planning authority.

On the basis of these two criteria, economic systems may be classified broadly as:

- market capitalism, planned socialism or market socialism

A **capitalist market economy** is characterised by the private ownership of the factors of production. Decision making is decentralised and rests with the owners of the factors of production. Their decisions are coordinated by the market mechanism. Examples of capitalist market economies include the USA and Canada. When people refer to a **capitalist** economy, **market** economy or **free enterprise** economy, they actually have in mind a capitalist market economy. When people refer to a **mixed capitalist** economy, they are drawing attention to the fact that not all the productive assets are in the hands of private people, but that some are government owned. In a **mixed market economy** (or market-oriented system) economic decisions are made partly through the market and partly by government. The degree of the mix varies from country to country. In a **free-market economy** all decisions are made by individual households and firms with no government intervention. A free-market economy is a theoretical construct and does not exist in real life.

Planned socialism (or **centrally planned socialism** or **command socialism**) is an economic system characterised by public ownership of the factors of production. Decision making is centralised and is coordinated by a central plan, which contains binding directives (commands) to the system's participants. Examples of socialist planned economies are North Korea and the former Soviet Union. A **mixed command economy** is a planned economy that makes some use of markets, as in the People's Republic of China in recent decades.

Market socialism is an economic system characterised by the public ownership of the factors of production. Decision making is decentralised and is coordinated by the market mechanism. Examples are the former Yugoslavia and the post-war economic system in Hungary prior to the late 1980s.

Note that communism is not defined as an economic system. **Communism** is a political system rather than an economic system. Communist countries function under a single, dominant communist party.

remaining example of a country in which the economy is still largely based on central planning.

Command economies are often described as **socialist** or **communist systems**. Although central planning has been used mostly in socialist or communist systems, central planning is not necessarily synonymous with socialism or communism. Central planning refers to the way in which economic activity is coordinated, while socialism and communism refer to the ownership of the factors of production – see Box 2-3. In a pure socialist system, all the factors of production except labour are owned by the state. In a pure communist system all resources are in principle owned by everybody – everything is common property. In practice, however, command systems are characterised not only by central planning but also by state ownership of all goods, services and factors of production (except labour). Command systems therefore tend to be socialist systems.

As mentioned, there are few centrally planned or command systems in force today. Even in the few remaining countries where central planning is still proclaimed to be the basis of the economic system, increasing reliance is being placed on the market as a mechanism for coordinating economic activity. Nevertheless, some elements of the command mechanism are used in all economies. The government plays an important role in every country. All government activity has to be planned and coordinated by some central body or bodies. In other words, even in market or capitalist systems the command mechanism is still alive and well. We shall return to this point in our discussion of the mixed economic system.

The market system

Whereas traditional and command systems are relatively easy to comprehend, the market system requires more detailed explanation. In a market system the method of coordination is so subtle and intricate that it could not have been invented. It simply happened. To explain this, we first have to explain what a market is.

Most people think of markets as specific places (or locations) where certain goods are bought and sold. Most of you have seen a meat market, fish market, vegetable market, fruit market or flea market in action. These markets all have particular venues. But a market does not require a specific location. A **market is any contact or communication between potential buyers and potential sellers of a good or service**. This contact can be personal, or it can take place by means of a telephone, a fax machine, a computer, newspaper advertisements or any other means.

Any institution or mechanism which brings potential buyers ("demanders") and prospective sellers ("suppliers") of particular goods and services into contact with each other is regarded as a market. Markets can be local, regional, national or international. The corner café and a spaza shop are examples of local markets. The JSE Securities Exchange is a national market where shares are traded. The London gold market is an example of an international or world market. When we explain how markets work, in the rest of this book, we shall often use concrete examples of markets with a specific location, such as fruit and vegetable markets. But you will also encounter more abstract national markets such as the labour market, the money market, the capital market and the foreign exchange market, which have no specific location. In the foreign exchange market, for example, dealers in foreign exchange buy and sell currencies like dollars, pounds sterling, euros, yen and rands through national and international telephone, facsimile and computer networks.

For a market to exist, the following conditions have to be met:

- There must be at least one potential buyer and one potential seller of the good or service.
- The seller must have something to sell.
- The buyer must have the means with which to purchase it.
- An exchange ratio – the market price – must be determined.
- The agreement must be guaranteed by law or by tradition.

In practice, sellers usually fix their prices, and prospective buyers shop around to find the best bargain. For example, if you want to buy a refrigerator you will go to a number of shops that sell refrigerators before you decide from which seller you are going to buy.

A market system is one in which individual decisions and preferences are communicated and coordinated through the market mechanism (ie the mechanism which meets the conditions listed above). The most important elements of this mechanism are market prices. **Market prices** are signals or indices of scarcity which indicate to consumers what they have to sacrifice to obtain the goods or services concerned. At the same time market prices also indicate to the owners of the various factors of production how these factors can best be employed. In Section 2.3 it was pointed out, however, that the types of goods and services produced also depend on the distribution of income – the consumers with the most "money votes" have the largest impact on demand, market prices and the structure of production. They therefore dominate the outcome of the market processes.

Market systems are often called capitalist systems. Like socialism, capitalism refers to a particular type of ownership of the factors of production. Whereas most factors of production in a socialist system are owned by the state (or by society at large), a capitalist system is characterised by **private ownership**. Market systems are, however, not necessarily capitalist systems. The market mechanism can also be used in socialist systems. It is thus possible to have market socialism. But just as the command mechanism tends to be used primarily in socialist systems, the use of the market mechanism tends to coincide with the capitalist system of ownership. In the rest of this book we shall concentrate on market systems in which most of the factors of production are privately owned. In other words, the focus will be on **market capitalism**.

Such an economic system is characterised by individualism, private freedom, private property, property rights, decentralised decision making and limited government intervention. Most of the means of production are owned by individuals who take decisions based on their self-interest. While the government does own property, such as government offices and embassies in other countries, most property is owned privately. Moreover, individuals' property rights are protected by law and they are usually free to sell their property as they choose (subject only to certain laws and regulations governing such transactions). The most basic condition is that they may not infringe on the legal property rights of others.

In market capitalism, economic activity is driven by **self-interest**. Consumers want to maximise their satisfaction. Business people wish to maximise their profits. Workers want the highest possible income for a given amount of work. How does a system in which self-interest plays a crucial role succeed in solving the central questions? Two centuries ago, Adam Smith, the Scottish professor who is generally regarded as the father of the capitalist market system, dealt with the same issue as follows:

> [E]very individual ... generally, indeed, neither intends to promote the public interest, nor knows how much he is promoting it ... he intends only his own gain, and he is in this, as in many other cases, led by an invisible hand to promote an end which was no part of his intention. Nor is it always the worse for the society that it was no part of it. By pursuing his own interest he frequently promotes that of the society more effectually than when he really intends to promote it.
>
> (Adam Smith. 1776. *The wealth of nations*, 423)

In other words, Smith claimed that the **market mechanism** works like an **invisible hand** which coordinates the selfish actions of individuals to ensure that everyone is better off. Let us take a closer look at how this is achieved.

What will be produced in a market system? The answer is those goods and services that consumers are willing to spend their income on and which can be supplied profitably. Goods that consumers do not want will not be produced. If some uninformed business person happens to produce unwanted goods, he or she will incur losses and cease to produce the goods in question. Only those goods which can be produced and sold profitably will continue to be produced.

How will it be produced? In a market system producers are forced to combine resources in the cheapest possible way (for a particular standard or quality). Their decisions on the combination of factors of production are governed by the prices of the various factors and their productivity.

For whom will the goods and services be produced? In a market system the goods and services go to those who have the means to purchase them. This, in turn, is linked to the production process. Production generates income and freemarketeers argue that in a pure market system the income earned will reflect the value placed on each person's resources. In other words, they argue that there is a direct link between what you put into the system and what you get out of it. Exceptions only arise if a society, through its government, chooses to assist certain individuals and groups, for example the handicapped and the elderly.

In a capitalist market economy the different economic agents pursue their self-interest by responding to pecuniary (ie monetary) **incentives**. Workers work harder, smarter or longer if they have the prospect of increasing their money income, and therefore their ability to purchase goods and services. Firms invest time, money and effort and take risks if they have the prospect of earning profits or increasing their profits. All agents respond to price signals. For example, if one of the leading supermarkets advertises "specials", consumers react by purchasing more of the goods concerned. When high profits are earned in a particular industry, more firms will be attracted towards that industry. Likewise, occupations or professions in which remuneration is high will tend to attract most new entrants. In recent decades, for example, the increasing professionalisation of sport and the astronomical amounts that successful sportsmen and women earn have persuaded an increasing number of young people to enter the world of professional sport. For some it can be lucrative, but success is by no means guaranteed. Sports people compete against each other and only the successful ones are rewarded – see Box 2-4.

Competition is an important feature of market capitalism. It occurs on each side of the market, that is, among suppliers (sellers) or among buyers (consumers). Competition should not be confused with **negotiation** which occurs between buyers and sellers, that is, across the different sides of the market. Competition among sellers protects consumers against exploitation and promotes efficiency and growth. Such competition creates order among suppliers. The successful ones are rewarded in the form of profit while the unsuccessful ones make losses and are eliminated.

Unfortunately competition is not always free and fair. As you will see in Part II, most markets in the real world are characterised by imperfect competition. Even the protagonist of the market system, Adam Smith, wrote:

> People of the same trade seldom meet together, even for merriment and diversion, but the conversation ends up in a conspiracy against the public, or in some contrivance to raise prices.
>
> (Adam Smith. 1776. *The wealth of nations*, 130)

The existence of imperfect competition does not imply that the market system does not work. But it does mean that the results are not always as favourable as the proponents of the free market system would have us believe. The pure market system has a number of serious defects, including a tendency to inequality and instability. These defects are discussed in some detail in Chapter 16. A number of adjustments have to be made to compensate for these defects and the government has to take responsibility for these adjustments.

After all is said and done, however, the market system is still a wonderful thing – see Box 2-5. It is almost inconceivable that a complicated economic system can function quite smoothly without some agency to coordinate the millions of decisions taken by the various participants every day. In a market system, decisions are reflected in **market prices** which constitute a vast **signalling system** that directs and controls economic activity. The role of money in this system is explained in Box 2-6.

BOX 2-4 THE WINNER TAKES ALL

In 2003, Ernie Els started his golfing year on an extremely high note. After winning the Nedbank Challenge in December 2002 (earning prize money of $2 million), he won four of the first seven tournaments he played in 2003, finishing a close second in two more. In the space of a few months he earned almost R40 million in prize money alone. Many aspiring young golfers turn professional, dreaming of emulating Ernie's performance. Some are quite successful, but the majority struggle to earn a decent living. In the 2002/2003 season, for example, 15 events were played on the Sunshine Tour. Trevor Immelman played in the richest four of these tournaments, won two and earned more than R2 million in prize money. Seven golfers earned more than R500 000 and twenty-eight earned more than R200 000. Professional golf can undoubtedly be rewarding. However, of the 462 professional golfers who qualified to play in at least one of these tournaments (and many did not qualify to play in any), 256 won no prize money at all. One golfer, who shall remain nameless, succeeded in qualifying for 14 tournaments but did not make the cut after the first two rounds in any of these tournaments and therefore earned absolutely nothing. Of those who did succeed in earning money, most were hardly able to cover their costs. In fact, the bottom 35 who earned prize money received a combined total of R95 253,10. The top 15 players earned half the total prize money, while the bottom 78 per cent won only five per cent of the total prize money.

This example from the world of professional sport applies to the rest of the economy as well. In a capitalist market system the successful participants are often richly rewarded, but for every winner there are many who cannot compete successfully. As a result, the distribution of income tends to be highly unequal in such a system.

BOX 2-5 THE MIRACLE OF THE MARKET ECONOMY

The market economy is a wonderful thing. In most countries there are millions of consumers whose needs and wants have to be satisfied. Their wants also change from time to time as their income or tastes change. On the other hand there are thousands of firms that produce or supply the goods and services that are required to satisfy the consumers' wants. They use various production techniques which are also subject to change. Goods or inputs that are not available domestically have to be imported. How are all these activities coordinated in a market economy? This question was asked as long ago as 1845 by the Frenchman Frédéric Bastiat in his *Sophismes économiques*.

> On coming to Paris for a visit, I said to myself: Here are a million human beings who would all die in a few days if supplies of all sorts did not flow into this great metropolis. It staggers the imagination to try to comprehend the vast multiplicity of objects that must pass through its gates tomorrow, if its inhabitants are to be preserved from the horrors of famine, insurrection, and pillage. And yet all are sleeping peacefully at this moment, without being disturbed for a single instant by the idea of so frightful a prospect. On the other hand, eighty departments (a French term for districts) have worked today, without cooperative planning or mutual arrangements, to keep Paris supplied. How does each succeeding day manage to bring to this gigantic market just what is necessary – neither too much nor too little? What, then, is the resourceful and secret power that governs the amazing regularity of such complicated movements, a regularity in which everyone has such implicit faith, although his prosperity and his very life depend upon it? That power is an *absolute principle*, the principle of free exchange. (Emphasis in original.)

More than a century later Paul Samuelson, the American economist who was awarded the Nobel Prize for Economics in 1970, returned to the same issue (and the same quotation) in his well-known textbook, *Economics*:

> To paraphrase a famous economic example, let us consider the city of New York. Without a constant flow of goods in and out of the city, it would be on the verge of starvation within a week. A variety of right kinds and amounts of food is involved. From the surrounding counties, from 50 states, and from the far corners of the world, goods have been travelling for days and months with New York as their destination.
>
> How is it that 10 million people are able to sleep easily at night, without living in mortal terror of a breakdown in the elaborate economic processes on which the city's existence depends? For all this is undertaken without coercion or centralised direction by any conscious body!
>
> Everyone notices how much the government does to control economic activity ... What goes unnoted is how much of economic life proceeds without direct government intervention. Hundreds of thousands of commodities are produced by millions of people more or less of their own volition and without central direction or master plan.

The market economy, with all its imperfections, is indeed a wonderful thing. In a market economy no one is consciously concerned with production or distribution. The three central questions – What? How? and For whom? – are solved by an invisible force which Adam Smith called the **invisible hand** – see quote in text.

The mixed economy

In the real world no economic system is based purely on tradition, command or the market. All economic systems are a mixture of traditional behaviour, central control and market determination. They are therefore often described as mixed systems, although one of these three mechanisms usually dominates.

During most of the 20th century there was a great debate about the relative merits of command and the

BOX 2-6 THE ROLE OF MONEY IN A MARKET SYSTEM

People often associate markets (and, for that matter, economics) with money and activities aimed at making money. As we have mentioned, the capitalist market system is based on the pursuit of self-interest and maximum gain. But economic activity is aimed at the maximum satisfaction of human wants, not at making money. Money is only a **means** towards an end and, as explained in Section 2.2, money is **not a factor of production**. Money is also not to be confused with income – see Chapter 15.

In a market system money is primarily used as a medium of exchange. Money is a standard good that everyone knows and that everyone will accept in exchange for other goods and services. Money is a very convenient way of exchanging goods and services. It also makes specialisation possible. In a moneyless society people have to resort to barter. A **barter system** is a system in which goods and services are directly exchanged for other goods and services. This requires what is called a **double coincidence of wants**. For example, if Dolly makes shoes and wants a spade, she must find someone who makes spades and wants shoes. If she finds John who makes spades and finds out that he wants a shirt rather than shoes, then Dolly must first find someone who makes shirts and wants shoes. Once her shoes have been traded for a shirt, she can then trade the shirt for the spade she really wants.

Barter is clearly a very complicated, cumbersome and time-consuming activity. Money eliminates the need for bartering and a coincidence of wants. It is therefore a very important invention. Money allows people to specialise. Every person can specialise in a particular type of economic activity. Some can work in factories, while others can work in mines. Some can be teachers, others can be nurses. Some can be doctors and others can be university professors. In the end they all earn money incomes which can then be used to purchase whatever they require and can afford. Without money this would not be possible.

The monetary sector is discussed in detail in Chapter 15.

market as mechanisms for coordinating economic behaviour. There was also great competition between the capitalist and communist countries – the so-called Cold War between the largely capitalist West and the communist bloc. This debate or competition was, for all practical purposes, settled internationally by the collapse of central planning in the 1980s and early 1990s. Nevertheless, the correct mixture between the market mechanism and government intervention, or between the private sector and the public sector, will always be an important issue. In other words, the appropriate "mix" of the mixed economy will always be debated. The mix also depends on the perceived problems of the society concerned and is thus likely to change over time.

The South African economy is a mixed economy in which private property, private initiative, self-interest and the market mechanism all play an important role. The South African economy is, however, also characterised by a substantial degree of government intervention. In this sub-section we take a brief look at South Africa's mixed economy. Most of the features of the South African economy are examined in greater detail in the rest of the book.

In pure market capitalism all factors of production are privately owned. In South Africa, as in all other countries, some enterprises, or significant shares of them, are owned directly or indirectly by the state. At the time of writing, examples included Transnet, the Post Office, Eskom, Armscor, the South African Broadcasting Corporation and Rand Water. State ownership of enterprises is a contentious issue. Some economists and politicians are in favour of selling these assets to the private sector. This is called **privatisation**. During the 1980s a number of state-owned enterprises were privatised, the largest of which was Iscor, which was privatised in 1989. During the early 1990s, however, there was strong support for **nationalisation**, that is, for the acquisition of privately owned assets by the state. Nationalisation, which is the opposite of privatisation, was originally one of the cornerstones of the economic policy of the African National Congress (ANC). The ANC repeatedly called for greater state ownership and government intervention to redress past inequities. However, by the time of the 1994 elections nationalisation was a relatively minor element of the ANC's *Reconstruction and Development Programme* and in due course the privatisation drive, which had been abandoned in 1990, was resumed. Nowadays privatisation is often referred to as the restructuring of state assets. In 1997 Telkom was partly privatised, when the government sold shares in Telkom to Malaysian and American firms. The process was taken a step further in 2003 when shares in Telkom were sold to the public.

A second element of pure market capitalism is an absence of direct state interference in the economic decisions of consumers and producers. Consumers are free to decide what to consume while production is left to privately-owned firms. In practice, however, government participates in the economy in various ways, as buyer and seller of goods and services, as employer and as regulator. Some of these actions restrict the freedom of private consumers and producers. As we show in later chapters, government's share in the South African economy grew quite rapidly during recent decades. Again this is a major source of contention and debate. Freemarketeers call for less government interference in private decision making while others call for more intervention, particularly to combat poverty and to improve the material conditions of those who suffered under the apartheid system.

One particular area of government intervention is price control. In a pure market system all prices are established through the market mechanism. South Africa, however, has a long history of price control and other forms of price-fixing by the government. Most of these controls and practices were abolished during the 1980s but certain prices, particularly the price of petrol, are still fixed or controlled by government.

In pure market capitalism there is usually assumed to be **perfect competition** among sellers and among buyers of goods and services. Perfect competition is examined in Part II. The distinguishing feature of perfect competition is that no buyer or seller can influence the price of the good or service in question. In practice, however, there are many instances where individual buyers or sellers (or groups of buyers and sellers) do have the power to influence prices. When this happens we have **imperfect competition**, which we discuss in Chapter 13. The existence of imperfect competition is one of the arguments that is used in support of government intervention in the economy.

From this brief discussion it should be clear that South Africa does not have a pure market system. The system is a mixed one in which both the market mechanism and command or central direction (in the form of government intervention) play a significant part. Moreover, the mix between the market and central organisation, or between the private sector and the public sector, changes all the time. In the rest of this book both the market mechanism and the role of government are examined in some detail. Tradition also plays a role in directing economic activity in the mixed economy, but this role is relatively unimportant and we do not examine it any further.

2.5 The men behind the systems: Smith, Marx and Keynes

Economic systems do not just happen. They evolve over time. And they are shaped by a variety of social, political, economic, historical, cultural and other influences. The ideas of economists also help to lay the foundations for economic systems. In this section we introduce you to three famous economists, Adam Smith, Karl Marx and John Maynard Keynes, whose ideas have helped to shape various economic systems.

Adam Smith (1723–1790)

Adam Smith was born in 1723 in Kirkcaldy, a small fishing town near Edinburgh in Scotland. He studied at Oxford and at the age of 28 he was appointed as Professor of Logic at the University of Glasgow. Eight years later, in 1759, he published his first book, *The theory of moral sentiments.* This book on philosophy immediately made him famous and in 1764 he was appointed as the tutor of a young Scottish duke. He accompanied the wealthy duke on a two-year educational tour of Europe for which he was paid £300 a year plus expenses and a pension of £300 a year for life. This was almost twice as much as Smith ever earned as a professor. On his return from the tour, Smith settled at Kirkcaldy where he spent most of the next ten years working on what was to become probably the most influential book on economics ever written. The book, published in 1776, was titled *An inquiry into the nature and causes of the wealth of nations* (see Box 2-7). This book, which is usually referred to simply as *The wealth of nations*, laid the foundation of economic science as we know it today. Much had been written on economics prior to 1776, but it was Smith who transformed the subject into a science and who first provided a detailed intellectual justification for free markets, both domestically and internationally. He is therefore universally regarded as the intellectual father of the market system and of capitalism.

As the title of his book indicates, Smith's primary aim was to find the sources of the wealth of nations. At that stage wealth was believed to be money, and more specifically gold and silver. Smith, however, said that the purpose of economic activity is to satisfy human wants. To him, therefore, the wealth of a nation consisted of the annual production of goods which can be used to satisfy human wants. In other words, he emphasised the importance of total output or national product.

As far as the sources of wealth (or the national product) are concerned, Smith emphasised the importance of three interrelated things: the **division of labour**, **free trade** and a **limited role for government**.

BOX 2-7 SOME IMPORTANT AUTHORS AND BOOKS IN THE HISTORY OF ECONOMIC THOUGHT

The following books are among the most important written during the past few centuries. We refer to all these authors in this book.

YEAR	AUTHOR	TITLE
1776	Adam Smith (1723–1790)	*An inquiry into the nature and causes of the wealth of nations*
1798	Thomas Malthus (1766–1834)	*An essay on the principles of population*
1803	Jean-Baptiste Say (1767–1832)	*Traité d'economie politique* (A treatise on political economy)
1817	David Ricardo (1772–1823)	*Principles of political economy*
1848	Karl Marx (1818–1883) Friedrich Engels (1820–1895)	*The communist manifesto*
1867	Karl Marx (1818–1883)	*Das Kapital* (Capital)
1890	Alfred Marshall (1842–1924)	*Principles of economics*
1936	John Maynard Keynes (1883–1946)	*The general theory of employment, interest and money*
1953	Milton Friedman (1912–2006)	*Essays in positive economics*

Adam Smith, Karl Marx, Friedrich Engels and John Maynard Keynes are all discussed in the text. Smith is usually regarded as the father of the classical school. This school included economists like Malthus, Say and Ricardo. Thomas Malthus was a parson who was worried about the rapid population growth of his time. He predicted that food production would not grow fast enough to provide food for the rapidly growing population. His main ideas are summarised in Chapter 14.

Jean-Baptiste Say was a French economist who is credited with coining the word "entrepreneur" (see Section 2.2) and formulating the theory that supply creates its own demand. This theory, which became known as Say's law, is discussed in Part IV.

David Ricardo was a famous British economist who made many lasting contributions to economic science during his relatively short life, including the law of diminishing returns (discussed in Part II) and the principle of comparative advantage (discussed in Chapter 17).

Alfred Marshall is generally regarded as the person who refined neo-classical economics as we know it today. Much of the economic theory in Part II of this book can be traced to Marshall's work.

Milton Friedman was the leader of the monetarist school of thought which became very influential in the 1970s. The main ideas of the monetarists are presented in Chapter 20.

The first chapter of *The wealth of nations* deals with the division of labour – see also Box 2-1. The very first sentence reads as follows: "The greatest improvement in the productive powers of labour and the greater part of the skill, dexterity, and judgement with which it is anywhere directed, or applied, seem to have been the effects of the division of labour." Smith was not the first to emphasise the importance of the division of labour but his contribution in this regard was unique in two respects. First, he used a very apt example to illustrate the point and, second, he realised that the division of labour is limited by the size of the market. Smith's example of a pin factory is one of the classic examples in economics and was also quoted in Box 2-1.

The division of labour (and the specialisation it entailed) was unquestionably an important determinant of economic growth. Smith realised, however, that the scope for the division of labour (and therefore economic growth) was limited by the size of the market, both domestically and internationally. Markets had to be expanded. Larger markets would lead to greater division of labour and increased economic growth. The necessary increase in the size of markets could only be achieved, however, if there were no impediments to free trade, both domestically and internationally.

Smith believed in the effectiveness of decentralised decision making. According to him, individuals should be allowed to pursue their own self-interest and the market would then act as an **invisible hand** to ensure that their decisions would promote the national interest. He did not argue that private individuals are philanthropic or in any way devoted to promoting the public interest. The benefits only occur when individuals seek their own self-interest through the market mechanism. Why should this happen? The answer is that individuals who seek their own advantage will be more efficient than any set of politicians or bureaucrats. In trying to produce the most value for themselves, individuals will in effect be producing the greatest possible value. By contrast, governments tend to be inefficient and wasteful.

Smith's belief in the efficiency of the market system extended to the trade between nations. The generally accepted view at the time was that nations should export as much as possible and import as little as possible. In this way a country could add to its stock of gold and silver, which was regarded as the wealth of the nation. Smith favoured free trade between nations and showed that this would be to everyone's benefit as it would expand markets and the production of goods and services. He therefore argued strongly against restrictions on international trade as well as against all other forms of government intervention in economic affairs.

However, he did not argue that government should adopt a completely "hands-off" approach. He simply believed that the role of government had to be limited to an absolute minimum. He identified three things which governments ought to do: the provision of national defence, the administration of justice and the provision of certain socially desirable services (such as education) that private interests might neglect.

Adam Smith is a truly remarkable figure in the history of economics. He is important not only because of his writings but also because of the influence of his work on others. *The wealth of nations* laid the foundation for a whole school of economics, the **classical school**, which, in turn, provided the basis for the **neo-classical school** which is still very active today. In fact, much of the economic theory contained in this book can be traced to his original contribution and the impact it had on his followers.

Karl Marx (1818–1883)

Karl Marx was born in Germany in 1818. He was a versatile scholar and a passionate revolutionary. He studied in Germany and in 1848 published *The communist manifesto* with his close friend and collaborator, Friedrich Engels. He practised journalism from time to time but his radical ideas cost him the chance of an academic appointment at a German university. In 1849 he settled in England where he did most of his scholarly writing in the British Museum in London. Marx's ideas were never popular in establishment circles and his life was often hard – see Box 2-8. Had it not been for the financial support of his friend, Engels, he would probably not have survived and written what he did. In 1867 Marx published the first volume of his major work, *Das Kapital* (Capital). A further two volumes were issued by Engels after Marx died.

Marx was a political scientist, historian, sociologist and economist. The central theme of his work was the historical evolution of institutions. In particular he regarded capitalism as a specific and temporary form

BOX 2-8 MARX IN LONDON

The Prussian police spied on Marx while he was living in London. The following is an extract from a report submitted by a police spy who had infiltrated Marx's rooms:

> Marx lives in one of the worst, therefore one of the cheapest, quarters of London. He occupies two rooms. The one looking out on the street is the salon, the bedroom is at the back. In the whole apartment there is not one clean and solid piece of furniture. Everything is broken, tattered and torn, with a half inch of dust over everything and the greatest disorder everywhere. In the middle of the salon there is a large old-fashioned table covered with an oilcloth, and on it there lie manuscripts, books and newspapers, as well as the children's toys, the rags and tatters of his wife's sewing basket, several cups with broken rims, knives, forks, lamps, an inkpot, tumblers, Dutch clay pipes, tobacco ash – in a word, everything topsy-turvy and all on the same table. A seller of second-hand goods would be ashamed to give away such a remarkable collection of odds and ends.

Quoted in Galbraith, JK. 1977. *The age of uncertainty*. London: BBC and Andre Deutsch, 98.

of social organisation. He argued that capitalism was self-destructive and that it would be replaced by a classless system in which there would be no private property. His argument went roughly as follows:

Labour is the source of all value. The value of every commodity ultimately depends on the labour embodied in it. Workers, however, are only paid enough to survive (ie a subsistence wage). Capitalists extract a surplus value from the workers, since the value of the workers' contribution exceeds the amount they receive in wages. The primary aim of capitalists is to increase this surplus value. They attempt to achieve this by employing more machinery and equipment. This increases total production but causes technological unemployment, which Marx called the industrial reserve army of the unemployed.

Unemployment succeeds in keeping wages down but cannot create surplus value. Surplus value can only be created by the employment of labour.

Marx thus saw internal contradictions in the working of the capitalist system. Capitalists want to increase surplus value (ie profit) but in the process they displace the real source of surplus value (labour) by machines. The poor, exploited working class is united into a powerful political force that is capable of seizing power through revolutionary action. Marx regarded such a revolution as inevitable, but he never provided any details about the new, classless socialist system that was to succeed capitalism. This is perhaps understandable, given his belief in the inevitable historical evolution of institutions such as economic systems. What is strange, however, is that he saw communism, which would succeed socialism, as a final system which would not be succeeded by anything else. This part of his argument is inconsistent with his basic idea of the historical evolution of institutions.

Although there were undoubtedly flaws in Marx's line of reasoning, his analysis of capitalism contained many important insights which had either escaped the attention of, or were ignored by, Adam Smith and his followers. These included the importance of mechanised, large-scale production and the worker alienation it produces (see Box 2-1), the problem of the business cycle, that is, the recurring expansion and contraction of industrial production (see Chapter 22), and the growing importance of purely financial activity. He also emphasised the importance of power and conflict in economic affairs.

What he failed to anticipate, however, was the possibility that the capitalist system would adapt in order to deal with these problems. Among the most important changes that occurred were the rise of the trade union movement, which strengthened the bargaining power of workers, and the increasing degree of state intervention in the mixed economy, which helped to smooth the business cycle and improve the living conditions of the working class.

Marx's most powerful impact, however, was in the political sphere. His ideas were popular among revolutionaries and the working classes and there were many socialist and communist revolutions in the 20th century as a result of his influence. But whereas Marx had predicted that the ultimate socialist revolution would occur in the rich capitalist countries, the actual revolutions were mostly limited to poor, non-industrial countries. The new rulers therefore had to devise their own ways and means of dealing with the central economic questions once the revolution had occurred. The results were often disappointing and by the end of the 20th century the wheel had almost turned full circle. Nowadays economic systems are largely based on private ownership, private initiative and the advantages of the market system.

Karl Marx's influence, however, is still felt all over the world. Marxist principles are still taught and Marxist scholars, schools of thought and political parties are still to be found in virtually every country in the world, including South Africa.

John Maynard Keynes (1883–1946)

John Maynard Keynes (pronounced "canes", as in cane furniture, sugar or spirits) was born in England in the year in which Karl Marx died. Whereas Marx had predicted the demise of capitalism, Keynes helped to lay the foundation for the mixed economy as we know it today. It can therefore be argued that Keynes helped to transform the capitalist system in such a way that Marx's predictions of a popular revolution were never realised in the highly developed industrial countries.

John Maynard Keynes was the son of an eminent Cambridge logician and political economist, John Neville Keynes. (It was his father who introduced the distinction between positive and normative economics explained in Chapter 1.)

John Maynard Keynes was very versatile. At various times in his career he was a senior government official, an editor, publisher, businessman, teacher, college administrator and the foremost economist of his age. He was a prolific writer who wrote on a wide range of topics. His *Collected writings*, compiled by the Royal Economic Society, comprises 30 volumes. His most important book, *The general theory of employment, interest and money* (usually simply called the *The general theory*) was published in 1936. This is generally regarded as the first systematic macroeconomic text.

During the first few decades of the 20th century most economists believed in the efficiency and effectiveness of the market system. Like Adam Smith, they believed that private markets should be allowed to function freely without government intervention. If there were problems, these problems were ascribed to factors which interfered with the functioning of the market mechanism. The solution, therefore, was to eliminate these interferences. At the macroeconomic level, economists believed that there could not be a sustained period of unemployment. Unemployment was regarded as a temporary phenomenon which would be solved automatically if government, trade unions or other institutions did not interfere with the functioning of the market mechanism.

This belief that there would always be a natural tendency towards full employment was put to a severe test by the Great Depression, which started in 1929 and which affected most Western countries. From 1929 to 1933 the major industrial countries experienced falling production and high and increasing unemployment. For example, in the United States the value of total output was 46 per cent lower in 1933 than in 1929. During the same period the unemployment rate increased from 3,2 per cent to 24,9 per cent. Even in South Africa the value of total output fell by 21 per cent between 1929 and 1932, before recovering in 1933. This experience was clearly not an example of temporary problems regarding the functioning of the market mechanism. The intensity and international extent of the problem forced economists to reconsider their earlier positions.

Keynes, who had been brought up in the classical tradition, realised that the foundations of classical thinking about the functioning of the economy had to be re-examined. He had no quarrel with the theory about how the market mechanism works at the microeconomic level. But he had serious doubts about the validity of transferring these principles to the macroeconomic level. In *The general theory* he deals primarily with large economic aggregates such as the total output of the economy, total employment and the general price level.

His main message was that the aggregate level of economic activity is determined by the **aggregate demand** for goods and services. This was directly in contrast to the idea of the classical economists that total production (or aggregate supply) would create its own demand. This was called Say's law, after the French economist Jean-Baptiste Say – see Box 2-7. While the classical economists believed that there could never be a sustained deficiency of demand at the macroeconomic level, Keynes explained why aggregate demand could be insufficient to sustain the levels of production and employment. When this happened, the government had to stimulate the total demand for goods and services by applying the appropriate policy measures. These measures included raising government spending or decreasing taxes. Keynes therefore provided intellectual justification for government intervention to stimulate economic activity and reduce unemployment.

Unlike Smith and Marx, Keynes did not propagate a new type of economic system, nor did he foresee major political changes. He was merely an economist who realised that the economic theory of his time was flawed in a number of respects. In particular, he realised that the analysis of individual markets was not appropriate to an analysis of the economy at the aggregate level. He did not invent **macroeconomics** – classical economists had also examined macroeconomic issues – but by focusing on aggregates he laid the foundation for modern macroeconomics, which is usually called Keynesian economics. Such was the impact of Keynes and his followers that it is often referred to as the Keynesian revolution in economics. Most of the macroeconomic analysis in this book also has its origin in *The general theory* and we shall refer to Keynes frequently in later chapters.

Because he justified government intervention in the economy, Keynes is often blamed for the rapid growth in government's share in the economy. Nevertheless, he was undoubtedly the most influential economist of the 20th century. He had a lasting impact on economic theory and policy and probably helped to save market capitalism from the collapse that Marx had predicted.

IMPORTANT CONCEPTS

Consumer and capital goods
Final and intermediate goods
Private and public goods
Economic and free goods
Homogeneous and heterogeneous goods
Economic growth
Factors of production
Natural resources
Labour
Capital
Entrepreneurship
Distribution of income and wealth
Primary, secondary and tertiary sectors
Tradition
Command
Market
Traditional system
Command system
Market system
Capitalism
Socialism
Mixed economy
Division of labour

REVIEW QUESTIONS

1. Which of the following can be classified as capital (as a factor of production)? Explain your answer in each case.
   (a) the amount of money in Mrs Zwelithini's savings account
   (b) a truck owned by a transport company
   (c) an amount of money invested by foreigners on the JSE Securities Exchange
   (d) the building that houses the headquarters of Rand Merchant Bank in Sandton
2. Use an example to explain how one can use a production possibilities curve to illustrate scarcity, choice and opportunity cost.
3. Use production possibilities curves to illustrate the following (putting goods on the vertical axis and services on the horizontal axis):
   (a) an increase in productivity in the goods sector
   (b) an increase in the potential output of the economy due to a greater availability of factors of production
   (c) a shift in production from goods towards services
4. Give an example of an economic problem involving opportunity cost that the South African government is currently facing.
5. Explain the difference between labour and entrepreneurship as factors of production.
6. What do you regard as the main advantages of a free market economy compared to a command economy?

Some useful websites in economics

General websites (containing resources for economists and links to other useful websites) .... www.rfe.org
http://econwpa.wustl.edu
http://netec.wustl.edu/WebEc

International economic organisations

International Labour Organisation .... www.ilo.org
International Monetary Fund .... www.imf.org
Organisation for Economic Cooperation and Development .... www.oecd.org
United Nations .... www.un.org
United Nations Development Programme .... www.undp.org
World Bank .... www.worldbank.org

Other international websites

American Economic Association .... www.vanderbilt.edu/AEA/
Centre for Economic Policy Research .... www.cepr.org

South African websites

Business Unity South Africa .... www.busa.org.za
Chamber of Mines of South Africa .... www.bullion.org.za
Cosatu (trade union federation) .... www.cosatu.org.za
Department of Labour .... www.labour.gov.za
Economic Society of South Africa .... www.essa.org.za
Human Sciences Research Council .... www.hsrc.ac.za
National Treasury .... www.finance.gov.za
South African Government .... www.gov.za
South African Reserve Bank .... www.resbank.co.za
Statistics South Africa .... www.statssa.gov.za

3 The interdependence between the major sectors, markets and flows in the mixed economy

Learning outcomes

Once you have studied this chapter you should be able to

- describe how total production, total income and total spending in the economy are related
- distinguish between stocks and flows
- distinguish between households and firms and show how their decisions and activities are interrelated
- describe the government sector and show how it interacts with households and firms
- show how the foreign sector interacts with the domestic economy
- show where the financial sector fits into the overall picture

In economics everything is related to everything else, often in more than one way.

ANONYMOUS

Consumption is the sole end and purpose of all production.

ADAM SMITH

The whole of science is nothing more than the refinement of everyday thinking.

ALBERT EINSTEIN

In this chapter we introduce the major participants in the economy. They are **households**, **firms**, the **government** and the **foreign sector**. We also introduce the major markets and flows and show how all these elements are interrelated in a mixed economy. The major markets are the **markets for goods and services**, the **factor markets** and the **financial markets**. The major flows are **production**, **income** and **spending**. Total spending in the economy consists of spending by households, firms, the government and the foreign sector.

The various circular flows illustrated and explained in this chapter might seem very simple, but they are essential guides towards understanding how the different sectors and markets are interrelated.

Experienced economists often stress that you need a good imagination to understand the functioning of the economy as a whole. When you are studying **microeconomics**, that is, when you are examining individual parts of the economy by putting them under a "**micro**scope", you can often fall back on your own experience. For example, everyone is a consumer and can therefore rely on his or her own experience when analysing individual or household decisions on what goods to buy, how time is spent, etc. In other words, you can place yourself in the position of the decision maker to try to understand how he or she behaves. You have probably also seen a vegetable market or a flea market and can therefore envisage what an individual market looks like and how it operates.

However, at the **macroeconomic** level, that is, when you are dealing with the economy as a whole, things are different. No one has ever seen the South African economy and no one ever will. Moreover, the concepts we deal with at the macroeconomic level (like the market for all goods and services produced in a country) do not refer to things that really exist. There is no physical market where all goods and services are bought and sold. Likewise, the general price level is an abstract concept which does not exist in a physical sense.

When dealing with the economy as a whole we therefore have to imagine things. We have to have mental pictures about how the economy fits together. A useful way of obtaining such pictures is to use simplified diagrams which set out the most important interrelationships between the major components of the economic system. In this chapter we introduce you to some of these diagrams. In addition we emphasise an important fact of economic life which non-economists often ignore or neglect when presenting their diagnoses and remedies for a country's economic problems. This feature is the high degree of **interdependence** in an economic system. In an economic system everything does indeed depend on everything else.

The chapter focuses on how things fit together in a mixed economy. We start by emphasising the three major flows in the economy as a whole: total **production**, total **income** and total **spending**. As you will see later, particularly in Part IV, these three flows and their interdependence form the cornerstone of the study of macroeconomics. In Sections 3.2 to 3.5 we construct a variety of pictures which show the major sectors and interrelationships in the economy. This is done on a step-by-step basis.

We start off by considering an economy that consists only of **households** and **firms**. After describing what is meant by households and firms, we construct a simple picture of how they are linked. In the following section we introduce and describe the **government**, and then add it to the picture presented in the previous section. The next step is to introduce the rest of the world, which we call the **foreign sector**. At that stage we have various pictures of how households, firms, the government and the foreign sector interact. The overall picture is completed by also pointing out where the **financial sector** fits into the picture.

As mentioned earlier, the purpose of these pictures is to obtain some mental image of how the economy fits together. We show the major parts and how they are interrelated. These pictures are gross simplifications, since we ignore many details. But they are essential to our understanding of how the economy works. Without such pictures it is virtually impossible to make sense of the complicated workings of the economic system.

3.1 Production, income and spending

As we saw in Chapter 2, economics is essentially concerned with what to produce, how to produce it and how to distribute the products between the various participants. Note that the focus is on **production**. It stands to reason, therefore, that the total production of goods and services is of major concern to economists. But production is not pursued for its own sake. The ultimate aim is to use or consume the products to satisfy human wants. The logical sequence is therefore as follows: production creates income (earned in the production process by the various factors of production) and this income is then spent to purchase the products. The sequence contains three major elements: **production**, **income** and **spending**. In practice, of course, everything is happening at the same time: production occurs, income is earned, and all or part of the income is spent to buy the goods and services that are available. In other words, there is a continuous circular flow of production, income and spending in the economy – see Figure 3-1.

One aspect of the economic problem that is not included in this simple diagram is how the income is **distributed** among the various participants in the economy. This important issue was introduced in Chapter 2 and you will encounter it again at various places in the rest of the book. At this stage, however, we are primarily interested in how the major components of the mixed economy are linked. We therefore ignore the details of the distribution problem for the time being. These details are not essential to a basic understanding of how things fit together, and might divert your attention from the essential elements. We assume that the income earned by the various factors of production are the "correct" amounts and focus on total income rather than its distribution.

Production, income and spending are all **flows**. To understand what this means, we have to distinguish between **stocks** (which are measured at a particular point in time) and **flows** (which are measured over a period). To illustrate this, consider the level of the water in a dam. The level of the water in a dam can

FIGURE 3-1 The three major flows in the economy

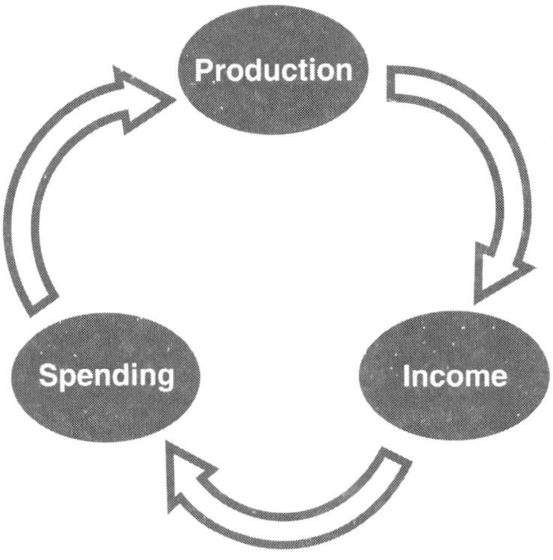

Production generates income (for the various factors of production) and part or all of this income is then spent to buy the available goods and services. All these things are happening at the same time.

only be measured exactly at a particular point in time. For example, at 00:00 on 1 May 2007 the level of the Gariep dam was at 72,64 per cent of its capacity. This kind of variable, which can only be measured at a particular point in time, is called a **stock variable**, or simply a **stock**. The flow of water into the dam, on the other hand, can only be measured over a period, that is as a rate, irrespective of how short such a period might be. Thus, the flow into the Gariep dam can be expressed as so many cubic metres of water per second, per minute, per hour or per day. For example, on 1 May 2007 the inflow into the Gariep dam was measured at 250 cubic metres per second. This kind of variable, which can only be measured over a period, is called a **flow variable** or simply a **flow**. Production, income and spending all fall into this category – they are all flows which can only be measured over a period. In practice the total production, income and spending in the economy are measured quarterly but the main interest is in the annual levels of production, income and spending.

Further examples of stocks and flows are provided in Box 3-1. In the rest of this book we shall frequently remind you of the difference between stocks and flows.

In a mixed economy the households, firms, the government and the foreign sector all participate in the production process. They all contribute towards total production, they all earn an income and they all spend their incomes. Apart from production, income and spending, the other important economic activity that links the various sectors in an economy is **exchange**. In a mixed economy exchange usually occurs in markets. Goods, services and factors of production are all exchanged in markets. The two fundamental sets of markets in the economy are the markets for goods and services, usually simply called the **goods markets**, and the markets for the various factors of production, usually simply called the **factor markets**.

We now show how these sectors, activities and markets are interrelated. We start by considering the interrelationships between households and firms.

3.2 The interdependence between households and firms

Households

A **household** can be defined as all the people who live together and who make joint economic decisions or who are subjected to others who make such decisions for them. A household can consist of an individual, a family or any group of people who have a joint income and take decisions together. Every person in the economy belongs to a household.

The household is the basic decision-making unit in the economy. In primitive societies households were the only decision-making units. The others (firms, the government and the foreign sector) only came later. Recall, from Chapter 1, that the word "economics" is derived from a Greek word meaning the management of the household. This underlines the central role of households in the economy.

Members of households consume goods and services to satisfy their wants. They are therefore called **consumers**. The act of using or consuming goods and services is called **consumption**. The total spending of all households on consumer goods and services is called total or aggregate consumption expenditure, or simply total consumption. We use the symbol C to indicate total consumption or consumer spending in the economy. (Note that **a symbol is merely an abbreviation or shorthand for a concept or a variable**.)

Because households are the basic units in the economy, we often use the term households when we refer to individuals or consumers. In other words, the terms households, individuals and consumers are used interchangeably. In a market economy it is households or consumers who largely determine **what** should be produced.

In a mixed economy most of the factors of production are owned by households. Labour is obviously owned by the members of households. Many of the other means of production, such as capital goods, are also owned by individuals. For example, even large business concerns like Anglo American, Sanlam and Pick 'n Pay are owned by their shareholders. The factors of production of these companies are therefore ultimately owned by individuals or households.

BOX 3-1 STOCKS AND FLOWS

When considering any economic variable it is important to determine whether it is a stock variable (or stock) or a flow variable (or flow).

A **stock** has no time dimension and can only be measured at a specific **moment**. When a shopkeeper takes stock, she counts all the goods in the shop at that particular time. A **flow** has a time dimension and can only be measured over a **period**. When a shopkeeper calculates her sales, profit or loss, the calculation is done for a period. Whenever we use a flow variable, the period concerned has to be specified. Stock statistics are "still pictures" of the economy, while flow statistics provide "moving pictures" of the economy. The classic distinction between stocks and flows, referred to in the text, is between the level of water in a dam and the rate at which water is flowing in or out of the dam. The following are some additional examples:

Stock	**Flow**
Wealth	Income
Assets	Profit
Liabilities	Loss
Capital	Investment
Population	Number of births and deaths
Balance in savings account	Saving (ie the difference between income and spending during a period)
Unemployment	Demand for labour
Gold reserves held by the South African Reserve Bank	Gold sales, gold production

Stocks and flows are related. Stocks can only change as a result of flows. The level of water in a dam can only increase if water flows into the dam; the capital stock can only increase if investment occurs; the population (stock) will change if the number of births (flow) or the number of deaths (flow) change.

There are other types of variable apart from stocks and flows. Prices, for example, are **ratios** between different flows. Ratios between two stocks or between two flows have no time dimension, but a ratio between a stock and a flow or between a flow and a stock has a time dimension. The most important distinction, however, is between stocks and flows. Failure to distinguish between stocks and flows can easily lead to faulty reasoning and analysis. This will become apparent once we start analysing the economy. Whenever you encounter a variable in economics, you must therefore always first ascertain whether you are dealing with a stock or a flow.

Although households own the factors of production, these factors cannot satisfy human wants directly. Households therefore sell their factors of production (labour, capital, etc) to firms that combine these factors and convert them into goods and services. In return for the factors of production that they supply, the households receive income in the form of salaries and wages, rent, interest and profit. This income is then used to purchase consumer goods and services which satisfy their wants.

In economic analysis we assume that consumers are rational. By this we mean that households always attempt to maximise their satisfaction, given the means at their disposal. The decisions of households are examined in Part II, particularly in Chapter 10.

To summarise: Every individual is a member of a household. Households are the basic units in an economic system. They own the factors of production and sell these factors on the factor markets to firms. In exchange for the services of their factors of production, households receive an income which they use to purchase consumer goods and services in the goods markets. These goods and services are then consumed to satisfy human wants.

Firms

The next component of the mixed economy is the firm. A firm can be defined as the unit that employs factors of production to produce goods and services that are sold in the goods markets. Firms are the basic productive units in the economy. A firm is actually an artificial unit. It is ultimately owned by or operated for the benefit of one or more individuals or households. As mentioned above, even large firms are ultimately owned by their shareholders. Firms can take different forms – see Box 3-2.

BOX 3-2 DIFFERENT TYPES OF FIRM

Firms can take various forms. The following are the most common types of firm in South Africa.

- **Individual (or sole) proprietorships**. Many firms are owned by a single person who makes all the decisions, receives the entire profits and is legally responsible for the debts of the firm. Examples include shops, cafés, farms, hairdressers and plumbing services. This type of firm is particularly suited to activities which require personal supervision but where the scale of operations and the financing requirements are not large. It is relatively easy to form or to dissolve. All the decision-making power is vested in the owner and there is a strong incentive to manage the business efficiently. A sole proprietorship has no separate existence from the owner – the assets of the firm are the assets of the owner. Its main weakness is its unlimited liability: the owner is responsible for all the debts and losses incurred by the firm. All the owner's assets may therefore have to be used to settle the debts of the firm. Another weakness is the limited ability to raise funds for expansion.
- **Partnerships**. This form of business does not differ much from individually owned businesses. Partnerships are suited to activities which do not require large amounts of financing but which need specialised ability. Partnerships are therefore often set up in the case of professional services. Doctors, dentists, attorneys, engineers and accountants frequently form partnerships. Although this type of firm can realise the benefits of specialisation and also potentially has greater access to finance, it is also characterised by unlimited liability. Moreover, the partners are the joint owners of the firm, and the actions of any one partner are therefore binding on the others.
- **Companies**. A company is a business whose identity in the eyes of the law is separate from the identity of its owners. It is the least risky form of business, since the liability (and thus the risk) of the owners (or shareholders) is usually limited to the value of the shares they own. Companies can generally also attract more financing than other types of firm, through the sale of shares (equity) or bonds or via bank credit. Another benefit is the fact that specialists can be appointed to manage the business, although the separation of ownership and management (control) can create problems – see the discussion of the principal-agent problem in Box 11-1. This type of firm, which requires a significant amount of red tape to establish, is also sometimes abused by unscrupulous business people. There are two types of companies: private companies and public companies.

  A **private company** is limited to a maximum of 50 members and the right to transfer its shares is restricted. Private companies need have only one shareholder. In South Africa a private company can be identified by the abbreviation (Pty) Ltd which appears after its name. This is an abbreviation for "proprietary limited." Examples include Alusaf (Pty) Ltd, Clicks Stores (Pty) Ltd, Johnson Tiles (Pty) Ltd and Sapekoe (Pty) Ltd.

  In contrast, a **public company** may not have fewer than seven shareholders. There is, however, no maximum number of shareholders in the case of public companies. A public company is a company that wishes to raise capital (in the financial sense) from the public and its shares are therefore easily transferable. Many public companies are listed on the JSE Securities Exchange where their shares are traded every weekday. They are called **listed companies**. Examples include Anglo American, Remgro, Richemont, Old Mutual, Sappi, Sanlam, Pick 'n Pay and Sasol.

Many foreign-owned or **multinational companies** also operate in South Africa. They include Shell, Microsoft, Siemens, Colgate-Palmolive, IBM, Philips and BMW.

- **Close corporations.** In 1985 a new form of business enterprise was introduced in South Africa. This is called the close corporation and it has to display the letters cc after its name. Close corporations are easier to establish than private or public companies. A close corporation can have a maximum of ten members. Each member holds a specified interest, expressed as a percentage of the total. This interest can only be disposed of with the consent of all the other members. The close corporation is a type of business that lies somewhere between a sole proprietorship or partnership and a company. It was created to afford members some of the advantages of a company without having to register as a fully-fledged company under the Companies Act. By the early 1990s there were already more close corporations than companies in South Africa.
- **Other forms.** Other forms of business enterprise include cooperatives (often used in agriculture), trusts and public enterprises such as public corporations – see Box 3-3. There are also numerous informal sector businesses, that is, businesses which are not formally registered. They include hawkers, street vendors, spaza shops, subsistence farmers, smugglers, prostitutes and shebeens.

Whereas households are engaged in consumption, firms are engaged primarily in **production**. Firms are the units that convert factors of production into the goods and services that households desire. Firms are therefore the buyers in the factor markets and the sellers in the goods markets. In a market economy it is firms which largely decide **how** goods and services will be produced.

In economic analysis we assume that firms, like households, are also rational. By this we mean that firms always aim to achieve maximum profit. **Profit** is the difference between revenue and cost. When analysing the decisions of firms, we ignore the differences between different types of firm. This enables us to treat the firm as the basic decision-making unit on the production or supply side of goods markets. The behaviour of firms comes under the spotlight in Part II, particularly in Chapters 11 to 13.

All individuals who own or work for a firm are also members of a household. They are therefore engaged in two sets of decisions. They make consumer decisions like any other individual or household but when they are at work they make business decisions relating to the objectives of the firms that they own or work for.

One of the factors of production purchased by firms is **capital**. As explained in Chapter 2, capital goods are man-made factors of production, such as machinery and equipment, which are used to produce goods and services. The act of purchasing capital goods is called **investment** or **capital formation**, which is denoted by the symbol I. Whereas households are responsible for spending on consumer goods (C), firms are responsible for spending on capital goods (I).

To summarise: Firms purchase factors of production in the factor markets. They transform the factors into goods and services which are then sold in the goods markets.

Goods market

Recall from Section 2.4 that a market is any contact or communication between potential buyers and potential sellers of a good or service. There are thousands of markets for consumer goods and services in the economy. To understand how the different elements of the economy are related, we lump all these different markets together under the heading "the **goods market**". In economics we call this "aggregation".

In **macroeconomics** we treat the goods market as if there were only one market for all goods and services in the economy. In **microeconomics** we analyse each of the markets individually.

Factor market

Factors of production are purchased and sold in many different markets. They are called factor markets. The factor markets include the labour market and the markets for capital goods. The incomes earned by the factors of production (ie their prices) can be grouped into four categories: wages and salaries, rent, interest and profit.

In **macroeconomics** we tend to aggregate the factor markets and treat them as if there were only one market for factors of production in the economy – "the **factor market**". In **microeconomics** we examine the individual markets in detail.

The circular flow of goods and services

The interaction between households and firms can be illustrated with the aid of a simple diagram. This diagram, which is called the **circular flow of goods and services**, is an example of the type of picture that is required to understand how the different parts of the economy fit together. It is the most basic description of the production process in the economy.

We show the households, the firms, the goods market and the factor market in Figure 3-2. The households offer their factors of production for sale on the factor market where these factors are purchased by the firms. The firms combine the factors of production and produce consumer goods and services. These goods and services are offered for sale on the goods market where they are purchased by the households.

FIGURE 3-2 The circular flow of goods and services

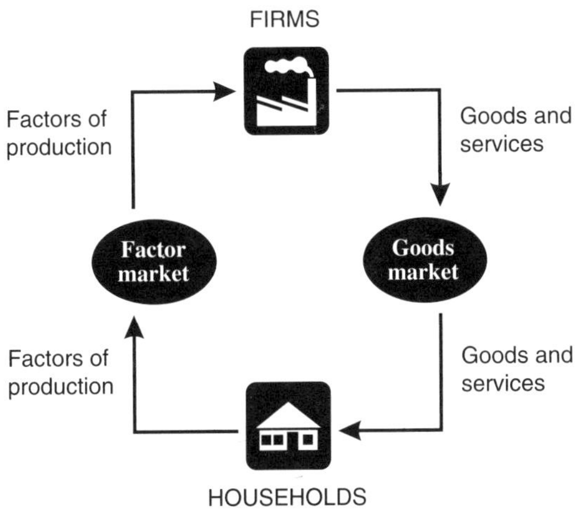

Households sell their factors of production to firms in the factor market. The firms transform these factors into goods and services which are then sold to households in the goods market.

The circular flow of income and spending

In Figure 3-2 we show how goods and services flow between households and firms. The interaction between households and firms can also be illustrated by showing the flow of income and spending. This is done in Figure 3-3. The flow of income and spending is usually a **monetary flow** (ie a flow of money). Its direction is **opposite** to the flow of goods and services. Firms purchase factors of production in the factor market. This spending by firms represents the income (wages, salaries, rent, interest and profit) of the households. The households, in turn, spend their income by purchasing goods and services in the goods market. The spending by the households represents the income of the firms.

FIGURE 3-3 The circular flow of income and spending

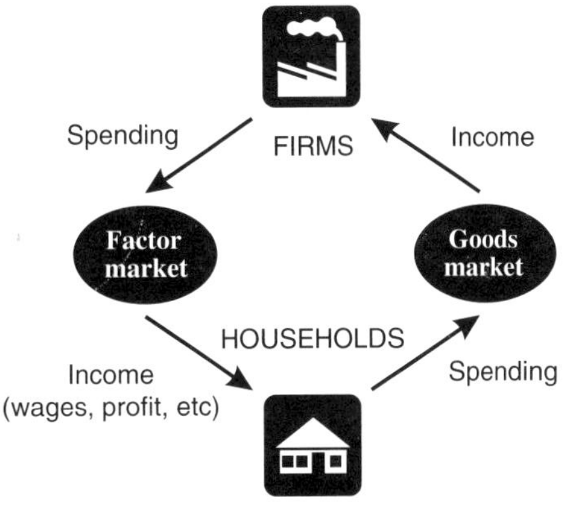

Firms purchase factors of production in the factor market. Their spending represents the income of the households (ie the sellers of the factors of production). Households then spend their income in the goods market to purchase goods and services. Their spending represents the income of the firms.

The links between households and firms that are illustrated in Figures 3-2 and 3-3 are quite simple. But they are also very important. As emphasised earlier, it is absolutely essential to have some mental images of how the different parts of the economy fit together.

3.3 Introducing the government

Government is a broad term that includes all aspects of **local**, **regional** (or **provincial**) and **national** government. In economics we often refer to the **public sector**, which includes everything that is owned by government as the representative of the people. The composition of the public sector in South Africa is described in Box 3-3. The public sector is more closely examined in Chapter 16.

Government includes all politicians, civil servants, government agencies and other bodies belonging to or under the control of government. It therefore includes the President, cabinet ministers, provincial premiers, mayors, everyone working for central government, provincial governments and municipalities, and public corporations such as Eskom, Transnet and the South African Reserve Bank.

In their official capacities, the President, the Minister of Finance, all other politicians and all civil servants are part of the government sector, but in their private capacities they are all members of households as well. When they decide which goods to consume, they are driven by the same motives as any

BOX 3-3 THE PUBLIC SECTOR IN SOUTH AFRICA

The composition of the public sector in South Africa is outlined in the diagram below. The core of the public sector is **central government**. Central government includes all the different government departments, extra-budgetary agencies such as the Council for Scientific and Industrial Research and the South African Bureau of Standards, and universities.

The next level is **general government**. This is obtained by adding provincial government and local government to central government. **Provincial government** includes the administrations of the nine provinces. **Local government** includes metropolitan councils, municipalities and district councils.

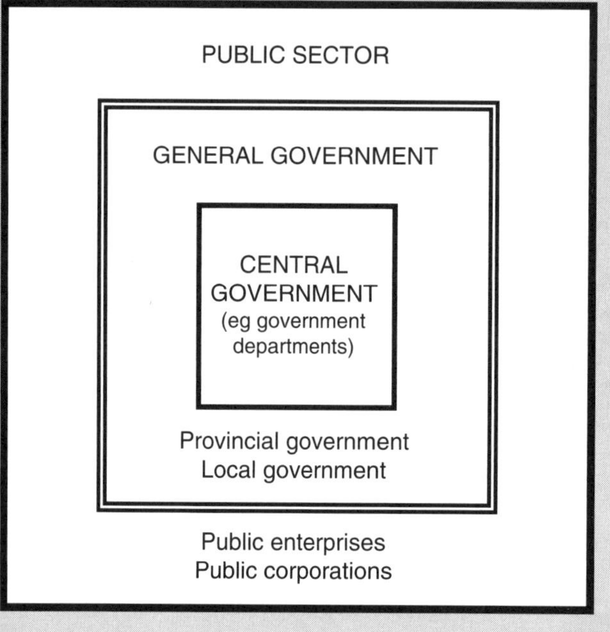

The final level is the **public sector**. The public sector includes the general government and the public corporations and other state enterprises. Public corporations are firms that are controlled by the government, either by the number of shares the government owns in them or through the appointment of members of the board of directors. Examples include Eskom, Armscor, the Atomic Energy Corporation, the Industrial Development Corporation, Rand Water, the SABC, the Post Office and Transnet. Although public corporations form part of the public sector, their decisions are often based on the same principles as those of other business concerns. In terms of our circular flow diagrams they can therefore be regarded as firms rather than as part of the government sector.

other individual or household, but in their official capacities they are supposed to serve the community at large.

In contrast to households and firms, who are assumed to act rationally and consistently, we do not assume that government always acts in a consistent fashion. Government is supposed to attain national goals which may vary from time to time. For example, the objectives of the ANC government elected in South Africa in June 1999 differed radically in many respects from the objectives that were pursued by the National Party government during the heyday of apartheid. Another reason why government does not necessarily act consistently is to be found in the objectives of politicians and public officials (or bureaucrats). Every politician or public official has personal objectives (such as re-election, promotion, power, prestige) as well as public service objectives. For example, in a democratic system the main objective of politicians is to achieve success at the next elections. This often results in a bias towards policies which will yield immediate or short-term benefits.

The role of government in the economy has already been touched on in Chapter 2 and is discussed further in Chapter 16. For the present it is sufficient to note a few important aspects of government activity. The primary function of government is to establish the framework within which the economy operates. Government also participates in the circular flow of production, income and spending. It purchases factors of production (primarily labour) from households in the factor market and also purchases goods and services from firms in the goods market. In return, government provides households and firms with public goods and services such as defence, law and order, education, health services, roads and dams. These services are financed mainly by levying taxes on the income and expenditure of households and firms. Government also transfers some of its tax revenue directly to needy people such as old-age pensioners.

Government's economic activity thus involves three important flows:

- government **expenditure** on goods and services (including factor services) – this is usually denoted by the symbol *G*
- **taxes** levied on (and paid by) households and firms – taxes are usually represented by the symbol *T*
- **transfer payments**, that is, the transfer of income and expenditure from certain individuals and groups (eg the wealthy) to other individuals and groups (eg the poor)

Unlike government spending and taxation, transfer payments do not directly affect the overall size of the production, income and expenditure flows. We therefore focus only on government spending *G* and taxes *T*. **Government spending** constitutes an **injection** into the flow of spending and income while **taxes** constitute a **leakage** or **withdrawal** from the circular flow of income between households and firms.

The various links between government, on the one hand, and households and firms, on the other, are illustrated in Figure 3-4. Part of the circular flow diagram, which illustrates the interaction between households and firms, is exactly the same as in Fig-

FIGURE 3-4 The government in the circular flow of production, income and spending

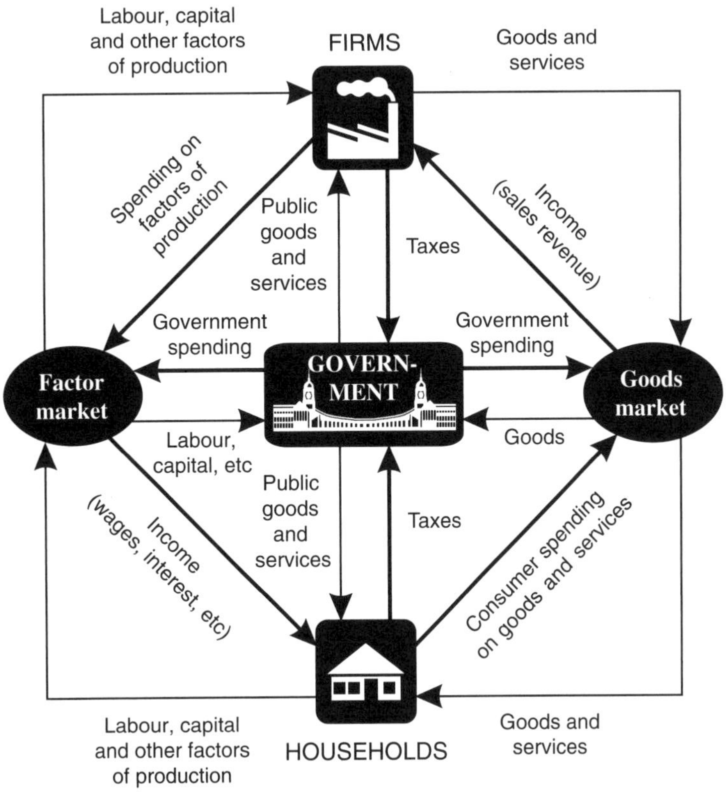

The government purchases factors of production (mainly labour) from households in the factor market, and goods from firms in the goods market. Government provides public goods and services to households and firms. Government spending is financed by taxes paid by households and firms.

ures 3-2 and 3-3. The only new parts are those relating to the government, which has been placed in the centre of the diagram.

3.4 Introducing the foreign sector

The fourth major sector to consider is the rest of the world, which we call the **foreign sector**. The South African economy has always had strong links with the rest of the world. The South African economy is thus an **open economy**. Many of the goods produced in South Africa are sold to other countries while many of the consumer and capital goods consumed and used in South Africa are produced in the rest of the world. In addition, many foreign companies operate in South Africa while some South African firms also operate elsewhere. The various flows between South Africa and the rest of the world are summarised in the **balance of payments**, which is introduced in Chapter 4.

In recent years the economic links between different countries have become stronger and more complex. This is usually described as globalisation. Advances in transport and communication have opened up international markets. Many firms therefore tend to look at the whole world as a potential market for their goods or services. Nowadays people often say that the world has become a global village in which firms from different countries have to compete with each other. It has also become very easy to shift funds between countries. Economic or political developments in a country can thus easily result in massive flows of funds into or out of that country.

As you learn more about economics, you will come to realise that a country's economic links with the rest of the world are often crucial determinants of the level and pace of economic activity in the domestic economy. This point is emphasised at various points in the rest of the book.

The foreign sector consists of all countries and institutions outside the country's borders – see Box 3-4. South Africa's foreign sector is discussed in more detail in Chapter 17.

The flows of goods and services between the domestic economy and the foreign sector are **exports**, which we denote with the symbol X, and **imports**, which we denote with the symbol Z.

Exports (X) are goods that are produced within the country but sold to the rest of the world. Imports (Z) are goods that are produced in the rest of the world but purchased for use in the domestic economy. South Africa's exports consist mainly of gold and other minerals while the country's imports are mainly

BOX 3-4 THE FOREIGN SECTOR

The foreign sector consists of all the countries in the rest of the world as well as international institutions which govern the flow of goods and services and the flow of funds between different countries.

The countries of the world can be divided into two broad categories: **industrial countries** and **developing countries**. The World Bank classifies its members into four groups: **low-income economies**, **lower-middle-income economies**, **upper-middle-income economies** and **high-income economies**.

- The high-income economies are the **industrial countries**. They include countries such as the United States, Japan, Germany, the United Kingdom, France, Canada, Australia and Italy. Most of the industrial countries are in Europe.
- The other three categories identified by the World Bank are all **developing countries** (which are sometimes called less developed countries or LDCs). The developing countries are heavily concentrated in Africa, Asia and South America. For example, most of the low-income countries are situated in Africa, with Ethiopia, Burundi and Sierra Leone among the poorest. Most South American countries are middle-income developing countries, as is South Africa.

Most of South Africa's trade and other economic links are with the industrial countries. For example, in 2005 about 60 per cent of South Africa's exports went to the industrial countries while more than half of the country's imports also came from these countries. By contrast, only about 9 per cent of our exports went to the rest of Africa, while Africa only provided about 4 per cent of South Africa's imports.

The most important international economic organisations are the International Monetary Fund, the World Bank and the World Trade Organisation. We provide more detail about these institutions and our links with other countries in Chapters 5 and 17.

capital and intermediate goods that are used in the production process.

In the case of South Africa's exports the spending originates in the rest of the world. This spending represents the income of our exporters. Exports are a component of the total income earned in South Africa. **Exports** thus constitute an **addition** or **injection** into the circular flow of income and spending in the domestic economy.

In the case of imports the spending originates in the domestic economy. This spending by importers represents the income of the other countries' exporters. **Imports** thus constitute a **leakage** or **withdrawal** from the circular flow of income and spending in the domestic economy.

As in the other cases, the flow of income and spending is in the opposite direction to the flow of goods and services. We concentrate on the flow of income and spending between the domestic economy and the foreign sector rather than on the flow of goods and services. This flow of income and spending is shown in Figure 3-5.

FIGURE 3-5 The foreign sector in the circular flow of income and spending

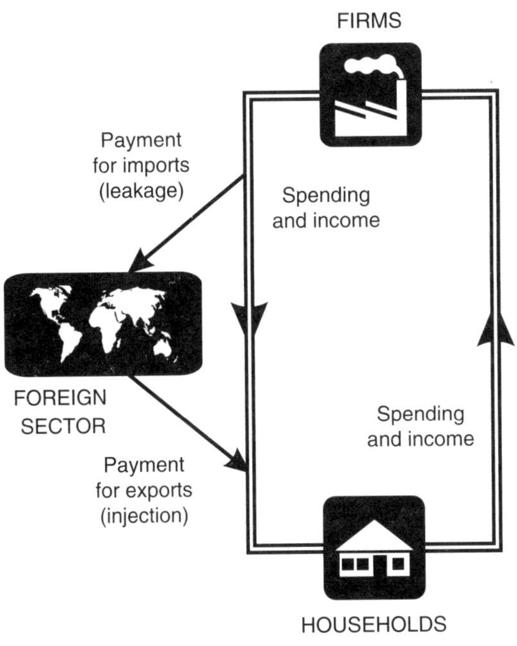

Domestic firms and households import goods and services from the rest of the world. Payment for imports constitutes a leakage of income and spending to the rest of the world. Goods and services are exported to other countries. Payment for exports constitutes an injection into the circular flow of domestic income and spending.

3.5 Financial institutions in the circular flow of income and spending

In this section we show where financial institutions fit into the overall picture. **Financial institutions** include banks such as Standard Bank and Nedbank, insurance companies such as Old Mutual and Sanlam, pension funds such as the Mine Employees Pension Fund, and the JSE Securities Exchange. These institutions are not directly involved in the production of goods. They act as links between households or firms with surplus funds and other participants that require funds, for example firms that wish to expand their activities. In this regard one can distinguish between **surplus units** (ie those who are in a position to save because they spend less than they earn) and **deficit units** (ie those who require funds because their spending exceeds their income).

To indicate the position of financial institutions or the **financial sector** in the economy, we use a simple circular flow which excludes government and the foreign sector. Households and firms who do not spend all their income during any particular period (ie surplus units) **save** some of their income. We use the symbol S to indicate saving. As far as households are concerned, the decision to save is a decision not to consume. In other words, saving can be defined as the act of not consuming. Likewise, firms can also save by not spending all their income. When saving occurs, there is a **leakage** or **withdrawal** from the circular flow of income and spending. Saving is channelled to financial institutions, for example in the form of saving deposits with banks. These funds are then available to firms that wish to borrow to expand their productive capacity (ie deficit units). Firms expand their productive capacity by purchasing capital goods such as machinery and equipment. Recall that this is called **investment** (I). When firms purchase capital goods, that is, when they invest, there is an **addition** or **injection** into the circular flow of income and spending.

The main function of the financial sector is therefore to act as a funnel through which saving can be channelled back into the circular flow in the form of investment spending.

In Figure 3-6 we show the circular flow of income and spending between households and firms. To keep things as simple as possible, the factor market, goods market, government and foreign sector have all been omitted. The financial sector acts as an intermediary between those who save and those who wish to invest. Households and firms channel their savings to the financial sector which then lends the funds to those firms that wish to borrow to invest. **Saving** is a **withdrawal** or **leakage** from the circular flow, whereas **investment** is an addition or **injection**. This also points to a connection between the expansion of the production capacity (through investment) and the

FIGURE 3-6 Financial institutions in the circular flow of income and spending

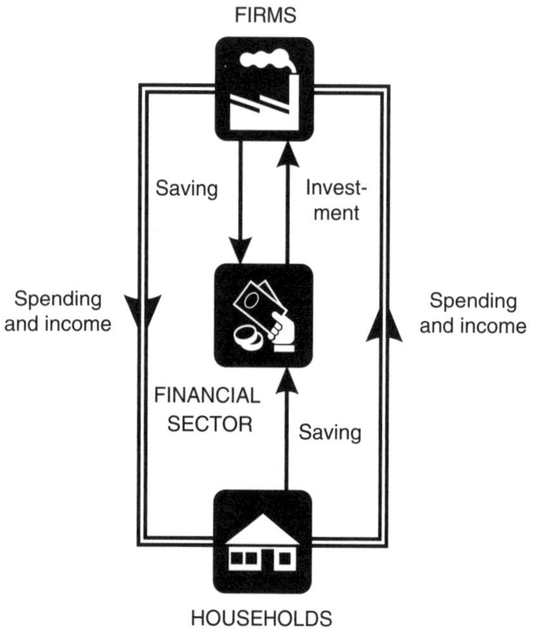

Households and firms do not spend all their income. Part of their income is saved. The saving flows to the financial sector which then lends funds to firms to finance investment spending.

decision to refrain from spending on consumer goods (saving). The importance of saving and investment is emphasised at various places in the rest of the book, particularly in Part IV. We deal more fully with the financial sector in Chapter 15.

3.6 Total production, income and spending revisited

In this chapter we introduced three important flows in the economy: production, income and spending. Total (or aggregate) production is simply the production of all goods and services in the economy. This production generates an income, the value of which is equal to the total production. Total income in the economy is the income that is earned by the various factors of production, that is, wages and salaries, rent, interest and profit. The equality between the value of production and the value of income is explained further in the next chapter.

We also introduced total spending (or expenditure) in the economy. Note that "total" and "aggregate" are synonyms and that spending and expenditure also have the same meaning. These terms are used interchangeably in the rest of the book. In other words, when we talk about total spending and aggregate expenditure we are referring to the same flow. Aggregate spending on South African goods and services consists of spending by the four sectors:

- spending by households on consumer goods and services (C)
- spending by firms on capital goods (I)
- spending by government on goods and services (G)
- spending by foreigners on South African goods and services (X) *minus* spending by South Africans on imported goods and services (Z)

Total expenditure can therefore be written as $C + I + G + X - Z$. You will encounter these components of total expenditure frequently in the rest of the book, particularly in Part IV.

Apart from these elements of total spending, we have introduced two other important flows. They are taxes (T), which are paid to government and saving (S), which refers to income that is not spent. T and S represent **leakages** or **withdrawals** from the circular flow of income and spending in the economy. The other important leakage is imports (Z), which have to be subtracted from exports (X), as we have done above.

These flows and the four sectors have been combined to construct a number of pictures of how the main elements of the economy fit together. All the details were not included in every picture. Many other possible pictures can therefore also be constructed. Figure 3-7 represents one such picture. It is a combination of Figures 3-4, 3-5 and 3-6, and summarises most of the important concepts introduced in this chapter.

As an exercise you can try to construct your own detailed picture of how the flows, markets and sectors are interrelated. This will help to give you that all-important "feel" for the basic fact of economic interdependence which is so essential in understanding how the economy works.

FIGURE 3-7 The major elements of the circular flow of income and spending

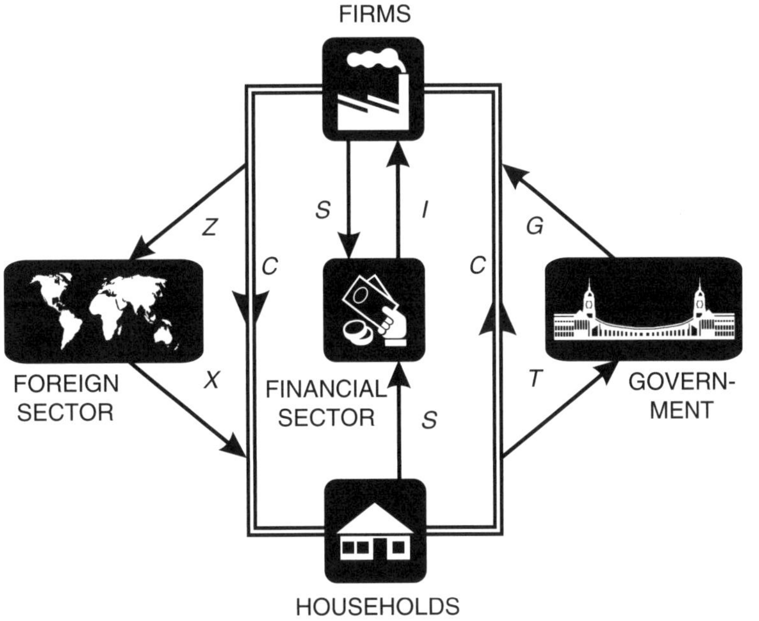

This figure summarises the essence of the previous circular flow diagrams. The basic flow is between households and firms. This represents consumption expenditure (C). Saving (S), taxes (T) and imports (Z) are all leakages from the circular flow. Investment spending (I), government spending (G) and exports (X) are all injections into the circular flow.

IMPORTANT CONCEPTS

Production (or output)	Government	Investment spending *(I)*
Income	Foreign sector	Government spending *(G)*
Spending (or expenditure)	Goods market	Exports *(X)*
Stocks and flows	Factor market	Saving *(S)*
Households	Circular flow	Taxes *(T)*
Firms	Consumption expenditure *(C)*	Imports *(Z)*

REVIEW QUESTIONS

1. Use examples to explain the difference between stock variables (stocks) and flow variables (flows) in economics.
2. Explain how (a) the government sector, (b) the foreign sector and (c) financial institutions fit into the circular flow of income and spending in the economy.
3. Describe the circular flow of income and spending in the economy.
4. List the main injections into the circular flow of income and spending, and the main leakages from this flow.
5. Discuss the main categories of spending in the economy.

Some words of wisdom

Many are the occasions on which I have participated in discussions about policies involving economic issues in which those participating have included economists of all shades of political opinion together with non-economists of all shades of political opinion. Almost whatever the subject of discussion, the outcome after a brief interval is predictable. The economists will be found aligned on one side of the subject – the free enterprisers along with the central planners, the Republicans along with the Democrats, libertarians and generally even socialists; the bulk of the group – academics, businessmen, lawyers, you name it, generally on the other.

MILTON FRIEDMAN
(Foreword to Allen, WR. 1981. *The midnight economist.* Chicago: The Playboy Press, xiii-xiv)

To a well-trained economist [his way of looking at things] seems so natural and obvious that he is likely to dismiss it as trivial. One of the important things I have learned in twenty years of intimate contact with non-economists of all kinds – civil servants, engineers, scientists and politicians – is that it is not an obvious procedure to other people, and is therefore far from trivial.

CHARLES HITCH
(Brookings Institution. 1961. *Research for public policy*. Washington, DC: Brookings Institution, 92-93)

The more I studied economic science, the smaller appeared the knowledge which I had of it, in proportion to the knowledge that I needed.

ALFRED MARSHALL
(Quoted in James, S. 1984. *A dictionary of economic quotations* (2nd edition). London: Croom Helm, 56)

You don't need to have a PhD in economics to realise that the government has made a mess of South Africa's economy.

TREVOR MANUEL
(*Sunday Times*, 15 September 1991)

4 Measuring the performance of the economy

Learning outcomes

Once you have studied this chapter you should be able to

- explain the five main macroeconomic objectives
- explain what the national accounts represent
- define the most important national accounting concepts
- show how the basic national accounting concepts are linked
- define the unemployment rate
- define and interpret the consumer price index (CPI)
- explain the balance of payments
- explain a Lorenz curve and the Gini coefficient

When you cannot measure what you are speaking about, when you cannot express it in numbers, your knowledge is of a meagre and unsatisfactory kind.

LORD KELVIN

When you can measure what you are speaking about, when you can express it in numbers, your knowledge is still of a meagre and unsatisfactory kind.

FRANK KNIGHT

Statistical figures referring to economic events are historical data. They tell us what happened in a non-repeatable historical case.

LUDWIG VON MISES

Economists are frequently confronted with questions such as: How is the economy performing? What are our economic prospects? Are things going to improve and, if so, when? Why are certain economies doing so well while others are struggling?

The people who ask these questions are usually only interested in their own wellbeing. They want to know what is going to happen to their own living standards. But the economist must take a broader view and must be able to judge the overall or macroeconomic performance of the economy. This raises two important questions:

- What criteria should be used?
- How can these criteria be quantified or measured?

In this chapter we explain how the performance of the economy is measured. We first outline the major **macroeconomic goals** or **objectives** and then explain how the performance in respect of each objective is measured. We devote a large part of the chapter to a discussion of the **national accounts**, which contain information about total production, income and spending in the economy. We also explain the **consumer price index**, the **balance of payments** and the measurement of **unemployment** and **income distribution**.

The performance of a company such as Sasol, Impala Platinum or Pick 'n Pay is usually judged in terms of its profitability, and standard accounting techniques are used to measure profit. But how do we assess the performance of the economy as a whole? This is what this chapter is all about. In the first section we identify five basic criteria for judging the performance of the economy and in the subsequent sections we take a closer look at the measurement of the performance of the economy in respect of each of these criteria. Since we are dealing with the economy as a whole, the focus is on macroeconomic objectives, rather than on the position of individual participants or groups of participants in the economic process.

4.1 Macroeconomic objectives

Economists usually distinguish five macroeconomic objectives which can be used to judge the performance of the economy:

- economic growth
- full employment
- price stability
- balance of payments stability (or external stability)
- equitable distribution of income

The first and arguably the most important criterion is **economic growth**. In a growing economy, the total production of goods and services will increase from one period to the next. If the population is growing and there is no economic growth, average living standards cannot increase, and it will also not be possible to create enough jobs for the growing population. The measurement of economic growth requires a yardstick for measuring the total production of goods and services. This is no simple matter and much of this chapter is concerned with this question. We return to the measurement of economic growth in Chapter 23.

A second, related objective is **full employment**. Ideally all the country's factors of production, particularly labour, should be fully employed. In practice, however, every country experiences unemployment. Unemployment has serious costs, both to the people who are unemployed and for society at large. At a personal level the people who are unemployed suffer materially as well as psychologically. At the macro level unemployment poses a serious threat to social and political stability. Unemployment should therefore be kept as low as possible, but this is a daunting challenge. In fact, as we mention in Section 4.4, even the measurement of unemployment is no easy task.

As mentioned above, one of the purposes of economic growth is to create additional employment opportunities for a growing population. But economic growth does not guarantee full employment. A group of workers can, for example, use more or better machines to produce an increased amount of goods and services. In other words, production can be raised without employing more people. Nevertheless, economic growth is a **necessary** condition for the expansion of employment opportunities. It is highly unlikely that the number of jobs in a country will increase if the total production of goods and services is not increasing. Unemployment is discussed in more detail in Chapter 22.

The third objective is **price stability**. Price stability does not mean that all prices should always stay constant. In a market-based mixed economy individual prices should respond to changes in supply and demand, as we explain in detail in Chapters 7 and 8. But anyone living in South Africa during the period since the Second World War, and particularly since 1973, knows that most (if not all) prices have tended to increase from one year to the next. The process of increases in the general level of prices is called **inflation**. Inflation has various harmful effects. When economists talk of **price stability** as an objective, they refer to the objective of keeping inflation as low as possible. When we judge the performance of the economy we therefore have to look at what is happening to prices. In order to do this we must have a measure or yardstick of the movements in *all* the prices in the economy. The most important yardstick is the consumer price index, which we explain in Section 4.5. Other measures of inflation are discussed in Chapter 21.

The fourth objective is **balance of payments or external stability**. In the previous chapter we emphasised the interdependence between the various sectors which comprise the economy. We also showed how the domestic economy interacts with the rest of the world. Nowadays there is a high degree of interdependence between different countries. South Africa is no exception. Many of the goods produced in South Africa, particularly metals and minerals, are exported to other countries. South Africa also has to import machinery, equipment and other goods from abroad. To pay for these imports the country has to earn the necessary foreign currency (dollars, pounds, euros, yen, etc) by exporting goods and services. Some balance between exports and imports is therefore required. In technical terms we say that the balance of payments and exchange rates should be fairly stable. This is what the objective of balance of payments stability (or external stability) is all about. The balance of payments is introduced in Section 4.6. Other aspects relating to the foreign sector, including the exchange rate, are dealt with in more detail in Chapter 17.

The fifth objective is an **equitable** (or **socially acceptable**) **distribution of income**. Like the other economic objectives, the distribution objective is partly a subjective or normative issue. Value judgements are always important when priorities have to be assigned to the different objectives. But, as we mentioned in Chapter 2, the distribution issue is often a particularly emotional issue. While most people will agree that economic growth, full employment, price stability and external stability are all desirable objectives that ought to be pursued, not everyone will agree that the distribution of income should be meddled with. Some, for example, regard an unequal distribution of income as a means of stimulating saving and investment which will eventually also benefit the poor. However, apart from possible unfairness or injustice, a highly unequal distribution of income tends to generate social and political conflict. It can also have important effects on the structure and development of the economy. We explain the measurement of the distribution of income in Section 4.7 and the distribution issue is touched upon at various other places in this book.

4.2 Measuring the level of economic activity: gross domestic product

The first step in measuring economic growth is to determine a country's total production of goods and services in a specific period. In other words, the production of all the different goods and services must be combined into one measure of total production or output. This complicated task is performed in South Africa by the national accounting sections of Statistics South Africa (Stats SA) and the South African Reserve Bank (SARB). The officials who are responsible for this task may be regarded as the accountants or bookkeepers of the economy as a whole. Just like an ordinary accountant has to keep record of the activities of an individual firm, the national accountants have to draw up a set of accounts which reflect the level and composition of the total activity in an economy during a particular period. Obviously, this is a daunting task.

The central concept in the national accounts is the gross domestic product (GDP). **The gross domestic product is the total value of all final goods and services produced within the boundaries of a country in a particular period (usually one year).** GDP is one of the most important barometers of the performance of the economy. At first glance it seems to be a clear and simple concept. But how do the national accountants succeed in adding up all the different types of economic activity in the country during a particular period? To explain this, we have to examine the various elements of the definition of GDP.

The first important element is **value**. How is it possible to add together various goods and services such as apples, pears, skirts, shoes, medical services, education and computers to arrive at one meaningful figure of the total production of goods and services? The solution is to use the **prices** of the various goods and services to obtain the **value** of production. Once the production of each good or service is expressed in rands and cents, the total value of production can be determined by adding the different values together. Twenty apples cannot be added to thirty pears, but the market value of twenty apples can be added to the market value of thirty pears to obtain a combined measure of the two. For example, if apples cost 80 cents each and pears R1,00 each, then the value of 20 apples will be R16 (ie 20 × R0,80) and the value of 30 pears will be R30 (ie 30 × R1,00). The combined value of the two will thus be R46 (ie R16 + R30).

The second important element is the word **final**. In Section 2.1 we distinguished between final goods and intermediate goods and we mentioned that this distinction is very important as far as the measurement of economic activity is concerned. One of the major problems that national accountants have to deal with is the problem of **double counting**. If they are not careful they can easily overestimate or inflate the value of GDP by counting certain items more than once. Consider the following simple example:

- A farmer produces 1 000 bags of wheat which he sells to a miller at R10 per bag, yielding a total of R10 000.
- The miller processes the wheat into flour, which he then sells to a baker for R12 500.
- After baking bread with the flour, the baker sells it to a shop for R18 000.
- The shop subsequently sells the bread to final consumers for R21 000.

What is the total value of these four transactions? A spontaneous reaction to this question will probably be to add the value of all the sales together. This gives an answer of R61 500 (ie R10 000 + R12 500 + R18 000 + R21 000); see the first column of Table 4-1. But this is clearly wrong. The total value of the farmer's production cannot be added to the total value of the miller's sales to the baker, since the value of the production of the wheat is included in the value of the flour sold by the miller. The same applies to the value of the bread.

To avoid the problem of double counting, the national accountants use a concept which became familiar to most South Africans with the introduction

TABLE 4-1 Calculating value added: a simple example of the production and distribution of bread

Participant	*Value of sales*	*Value added*
Farmer	R10 000	R10 000
Miller	12 500	2 500
Baker	18 000	5 500
Shopkeeper	21 000	3 000
	R61 500	**R21 000**

of value-added tax (VAT) on 30 September 1991. Starting with the full value of the farmer's production they subsequently add only the **value added** by each of the other participants in the production process. This is summarised in the last column of Table 4-1. Nowadays GDP is often also called **gross value added** (GVA).

One way of avoiding double counting is therefore to count, in each transaction, only the value added (ie the addition to the value of the output). In our example this yields an answer of R21 000.

But what has all this got to do with the adjective **final** in the definition of GDP? In our example the value of the shop's sales to the final consumers also amounts to R21 000. The fact that this is exactly equal to the total value added is no accident.

Double counting can also be avoided by only counting the value of those sales where a good or service reaches its final destination. Such sales involve **final** goods and services which have to be distinguished from **intermediate** goods and services. As explained in Section 2.1, any good or service that is purchased for reselling or processing is regarded as an intermediate good or service. Intermediate goods and services do not form part of GDP. Thus, in our example the national accountants will ignore the sales of the farmer to the miller as well as those of the miller to the baker and of the baker to the shopkeeper.

Note, however, that it is the **ultimate use** of a product which determines whether it is a final or an intermediate product. If the flour in the above example is bought by consumers, it would be classified as a final good. Moreover, if the flour is not sold during the period in question it becomes part of the miller's **inventories**, which (as we explain later) form part of investment in the national accounts.

There is another way in which double counting can be avoided. That is by considering only the **incomes** earned during the various stages of the production process by the owners of the factors of production. In our example R10 000 is earned during the farming stage, R2 500 (ie R12 500 minus R10 000) during the milling stage, R5 500 (ie R18 000 minus R12 500) during the baking stage, and R3 000 (ie R21 000 minus R18 000) during the final selling stage. This again yields a total of R21 000 (R10 000 + R2 500 + R5 500 + R3 000). Note, in addition, that the **income** earned during each stage of the production process is **equal to the value added** during that stage. This is also no accident. **Income is earned by producing, that is, by adding value to goods and services.** For the economy as a whole, income can only be increased if production increases (ie if more value is added). The fact that value added, spending on final goods and income all yield the same answer means that there are three different ways of calculating GDP. These three methods measure the same phenomenon and must necessarily all yield the same answer.

Three methods of calculating GDP

The three methods of calculating GDP illustrated in the example are

- the **production method** (value added)
- the **expenditure method** (final goods and services)
- the **income method** (incomes of the factors of production)

Why do they yield the same answer? The value of final goods and services must necessarily be made up of the successive values added in the different stages of production. In addition, production and income can be viewed as two sides of the same coin. Production is the source of income – the only way in which income can be generated in an economy is by producing (and selling) goods and services.

As explained in Chapter 2, the income earned by the various factors of production (labour, capital, natural resources and entrepreneurship) consists of wages and salaries, interest, rent and profit. The total value of production in the economy will therefore be equal to the total value of wages and salaries, interest, rent and profit.

The equality between production, income and expenditure can also be explained in terms of the circular flows discussed in Chapter 3, where we saw that production requires factors of production (purchased in the factor markets). The reward of the factors of production constitutes the income that is used to purchase the production on the goods markets. In other words, **the three methods essentially measure the same thing, albeit at different points in the circular flow**.

The actual measurement of GDP is, of course, infinitely more complex than our simple example. If you think how difficult it is to construct a set of accounts for an individual undertaking, you can imagine how complicated it must be to estimate the value of the total production of goods and services in a country in a particular year. Fortunately, the fact that there are three ways of calculating GDP serves to improve the accuracy with which it is measured. The national accountants use all three methods or approaches and have to arrive at the same answer. In other words, the national accounts have to balance, just as any other set of accounts has to balance.

In our example we have already shown that production (or value added) equals spending on final goods and services. We shall now expand on this simple example to illustrate that the production, expenditure and income approaches all yield the same answer.

The value the baker adds to the final product (bread) amounts to R5500 (R18000 – R12500 = R5500). To be able to produce this added value, the baker has to employ certain factors of production (primary inputs). Suppose the values of these inputs are as follows:

Wages and salaries	R2 500
Rentals (buildings)	1 000
Interest on loans	500
Total	**R4 000**

This means that the baker's entrepreneurial profit, that is, the difference between his revenue and his payments to the other factors of production, has to be R1 500. Profit includes the compensation for the entrepreneur's own labour. The selling price of the baker (R18 000) is therefore apportioned as follows:

Primary inputs	
Wages and salaries	R2 500
Rentals	1 000
Interest	500
Profit	1 500
Secondary inputs	
Intermediate goods and services (flour)	R12 500
Total	**R18 000**

Note that the value of the baker's intermediate goods and services is the same as the value of the miller's sales. This amount of R12 500 can therefore, as in the case of the R18 000 above, be apportioned between primary and secondary inputs. In this way all sales (R61 500) in the chain can be apportioned to the payment for factors of production (primary inputs) on the one hand and intermediate goods and services (secondary inputs) on the other. In the statement set out below it is assumed, somewhat unrealistically, that the farmer has bought no intermediate goods or services. Note also that the entrepreneurial profit is treated as a balancing amount (residual item) throughout.

	Value of sales	Payment for factors of production (primary inputs)	Value of intermediate goods and services
Farmer	R10 000	R10 000	–
Miller	12 500	2 500	R10 000
Baker	18 000	5 500	12 500
Shopkeeper	21 000	3 000	18 000
Total	**R61 500**	**R21 000**	**R40 500**

In view of the above, the following equality may be derived for the economy as a whole:

Value of total sales	=	**total primary income (wages and salaries, rent, interest and profit)**	+	**value of intermediate goods and services**
(R61 500)	=	(R21 000)	+	(R40 500)

The following will also apply:

Value of total sales	–	**value of intermediate goods and services**	=	**total primary income**

Since the left-hand side of this equation is also equal to the value of all final goods and services, and the value of total primary income is synonymous with the total income in the economy, the following will also be true:

The value of final goods and services = total income

It should therefore be clear that **output expressed in monetary terms** must be equal to the **total monetary income** derived from it. As mentioned earlier, production (or output) and income are simply two sides of the same coin.

Further aspects of the definition of GDP

Recall that GDP was defined as the total **value** of all **final** goods and services produced **within the boundaries of a country** during **a particular period** (usually one year). Two elements of this definition have now been explained: the meaning of value and the meaning of final goods and services. Two further aspects need to be highlighted.

The first is the term "within the boundaries of a country". In some definitions this term is replaced by "in the economy". The important point is that GDP is a **geographic** concept that includes all the production within the geographic area of a country. This is what is signified by the term **domestic** in gross domestic product. We shall return to this aspect when other measures of economic activity are discussed.

The last important aspect to note is that only goods and services produced **during a particular period** are included in GDP. GDP therefore concerns the production of **new** goods and services (also called **current** production) during a specific period. Goods produced during earlier periods and sold during the period under consideration are not included in GDP for the latter period. Moreover, the resale of existing goods such as houses or motorcars is also not part of GDP. GDP only reflects production which occurred during the period in question. Also note that GDP is a **flow** which can only be measured over a period of time (usually one year).

In our discussion of the measurement of GDP we emphasised that production and income are two sides of the same coin. This means that "income" can be substituted for the "product" in GDP. Gross domestic product is therefore the same as gross domestic income. In practice, however, we usually refer only to GDP, even when we want to indicate the total income generated in an economy in a particular period.

One element of GDP that has not yet been explained is the word **gross**. The description of total output as gross product means that no provision has been made for that part of a country's capital equipment (buildings, roads, machinery, tools, etc) which is "used up" in the production process.

During the period for which GDP is calculated, obsolescence and wear and tear cause capital equipment to **depreciate**. Provision should therefore be made for such depreciation and this provision should be subtracted from the value of output. Subtracting the provision for depreciation (also called **consumption of fixed capital**) from the **gross** total, changes it to a **net** total. The net amount is a more correct measure of economic performance since it adjusts gross production for the decrease in the value of capital goods. In practice, however, the gross measure is used more often than the net measure. One of the reasons for using the gross measure is the fact that depreciation is difficult to estimate. For example, it is difficult to determine by how much diverse assets such as buildings, tractors, machines and computers depreciated during a particular period.

The fact that depreciation is often ignored when measuring economic growth does not mean that it is an unimportant element of the national accounts. It is important because it shows what proportion of the total output should actually be saved in order to maintain the economy's production capacity at the same level. In 2006 consumption of fixed capital constituted more than 12 per cent of South African GDP. Depreciation is therefore clearly significant.

Measurement at market prices, basic prices and factor cost (or income)

The three methods of calculating GDP will only yield the same result if the same set of prices is used in all the calculations. There are, however, three sets of prices that can be used to calculate GDP, namely **market prices**, **basic prices** and **factor cost** (or **factor income**).

In practice, market prices are used when calculating GDP according to the expenditure method, while basic prices are used when the production (or value added) method is applied. Factor cost (or factor income) is used when the income method is followed. Different valuations of GDP will thus yield different results and you should therefore always check at which prices GDP is expressed.

The differences between market prices, basic prices and factor cost (or factor income) are due to various taxes and subsidies on goods and services. When there are **indirect taxes** (ie taxes on production and products) or **subsidies** (on production or products) the amount paid for a good or service differs from both the cost of production and the income earned by the relevant factors of production. For example, the amount paid by a consumer for a packet of cigarettes is much higher than the combined income earned by the merchant, the manufacturer, the workers, the tobacco farmer and everyone else involved in the process of producing and selling the packet of cigarettes. The difference is the result of excise duty and value-added tax (VAT), which together constitute almost 50 per cent of the market price of a packet of cigarettes in South Africa. Indirect taxes (ie taxes on production and products) thus have the effect of making the market prices of goods and services higher than their basic prices or factor cost.

Subsidies have just the opposite effect. They result in market prices being lower than basic prices or factor cost. For example, for many years there was a subsidy on bread in South Africa, which kept the market price of a loaf of bread below the cost of producing it. Certain suburban transport services and certain exports are still subsidised.

The national accountants distinguish between two types of tax and subsidy on production and products. They distinguish between taxes on products and other taxes on production. Likewise, they distinguish between subsidies on products and other subsidies on production. **Taxes on products** refer to taxes which are payable per unit of some good or service (eg value-added tax, taxes and duties on imports and taxes on exports). **Other taxes on production** refer to taxes on production that are not linked to specific goods or services (eg payroll taxes, recurring taxes on land, buildings or other structures and business and professional licences). **Subsidies on products** include direct subsidies payable per unit exported to encourage exports, and product-linked subsidies on products used domestically. **Other subsidies on production** refer to subsidies that are not linked to specific goods or services (eg subsidies on employment or the payroll).

The following identities apply:

- GDP at market prices – taxes on products + subsidies on products ≡ GDP at basic prices
- GDP at basic prices – other taxes on production + other subsidies on production ≡ GDP at factor cost (or factor income)

Likewise:

- GDP at factor cost + other taxes on production – other subsidies on production ≡ GDP at basic prices
- GDP at basic prices + taxes on products – subsidies on products ≡ GDP at market prices

Measurement at current prices and at constant prices

Another important distinction that needs to be made is that between **GDP at current prices** (or **nominal GDP**) and **GDP at constant prices** (or **real GDP**). When GDP is measured for a particular period, the prices ruling during that period have to be used. For example, when they calculated the GDP for 2007 the national accountants had to use the prices paid for the various goods and services in 2007. We call this **measurement at current prices** or in **nominal** terms (see Box 4-1). However, we are not only interested in the size of GDP during a particular period. We also want to know what happened to GDP from one period to the next. We want to know, for example, how the 2007 GDP compared with the GDP for 2006. Recall, from Section 4.1, that the **growth** in economic activity is one of the major macroeconomic objectives. This can be measured by calculating the percentage change in GDP from one year to the next.

But in a world in which prices tend to increase from one period to the next (ie a world of **inflation**), it makes little sense to simply compare monetary values between different years. We have to allow for the fact that prices may have increased. For example, in 2006 the South African GDP at current market prices was 12,2 per cent higher than in 2005. But this did not mean that the actual production of goods and services was 12,2 per cent greater in 2006 than in 2005. The largest part of this increase simply reflected the fact that most prices were higher in 2006 than in 2005.

BOX 4-1 NOMINAL VALUES, REAL VALUES AND PURCHASING POWER

In a world in which prices are changing it is essential to distinguish between **nominal** values and **real** values. You will encounter this crucial distinction at numerous places in the rest of the book, and you will therefore make things far easier for yourself if you make sure, now, that you understand the difference between the two terms.

The distinction between nominal and real is quite easy to understand. Consider the following questions:

- John Smith earned a salary of R5 000 per month in 1992; Sipho Mashego earned a salary of R5 000 per month in 2007. Are these two salaries the same?
- Koos van der Merwe paid R1 500 for a new 66 cm colour television set in 1976; Krish Naidoo paid R1 500 for a new 66 cm colour television set in 2007. Did they pay the same amount?

In both cases the answer is yes and no. **Nominally** (ie in monetary or rand terms) John and Sipho earned the same salary and Koos and Krish paid the same amount for the TV set. In **real** terms, however, (ie bearing in mind the inflation during this period) John earned more than Sipho and Koos paid more than Krish. In other words, although the amounts concerned are the same in rand or monetary terms, they actually differ because the **value** (or **purchasing power**) of money changes over time.

Nominal means "in terms of the name". The nominal value of something is therefore its face value. In our examples the nominal values of the salaries and prices of TV sets are expressed in rands. Nominal values are therefore also called monetary values.

Real means "actual" or "essential". The real value of a salary therefore refers to its actual or essential value in terms of what it can buy. We call this the **purchasing power** of the salary. In the same way, the real value of the price of a TV set refers to the actual purchasing power required to buy the TV set.

Take a fifty-rand note. What is the nominal value of the note? Can it change? The nominal value of the note is fifty rands and it cannot change. The face value of the note cannot change. *What is the real value of the note? Can the real value change?* The real value of the note depends on the prices of goods and services, that is on how much it can purchase. As prices increase, the real value or purchasing power of the note decreases. The real value of the note can therefore change.

The difference between nominal and real values will be explained further once the consumer price index has been explained – see Box 4-5.

To solve this problem, the national accountants at Stats SA and the SARB convert GDP at current prices to GDP at **constant prices** (or **real** GDP – see Box 4-2). This is done by valuing all the goods and services produced each year in terms of the prices ruling in a certain year, called the **base year**. At the time of writing, 2000 was the base year used by Stats SA and the SARB. In other words, each year's GDP was also expressed at 2000 prices. This is what we mean when we talk about GDP at constant prices or real GDP.

Once this adjustment had been made, the national accountants found that the South African GDP was 5,0 per cent greater in 2006 than in 2005. The growth in GDP at constant prices (or real GDP) was therefore only 5,0 per cent. The difference between this rate and the 12,2 per cent growth in GDP at current prices (or nominal GDP) was the result of price increases (ie inflation).

Table 4-2 shows South African GDP at current prices and at constant (2000) prices for the period 1997 to 2006. Note that the GDP at current prices is lower than the GDP at constant prices in the years prior to the base year. In the base year the two values are equal, since the same prices are used in both instances. After the base year, the current price values exceed the constant price values.

As you might imagine, the transformation of GDP at current prices (nominal GDP) to GDP at constant prices (real GDP) is a complicated process. It is not necessary for us to go into any details of the process. What is important, however, is to understand the difference between the two concepts. You will come across the difference between nominal and real variables on a number of occasions throughout this book. In a world of inflation all values (not only GDP) have to be expressed in nominal and real terms. Otherwise you can easily reach wrong conclusions when comparisons are made. Some additional problems relating to the measurement and interpretation of GDP are discussed in Chapter 23.

TABLE 4-2 GDP at current prices and constant prices, 1997–2006

Year	*GDP at current prices (R millions)*	*GDP at constant (2000) prices (R millions)*
1997	685 730	860 516
1998	742 424	864 968
1999	813 683	885 365
2000	**922 148**	**922 148**
2001	1 020 007	947 373
2002	1 168 699	982 121
2003	1 260 693	1 012 763
2004	1 398 157	1 061 768
2005	1 539 253	1 115 875
2006	1 726 688	1 171 508

Source: South African Reserve Bank, *Quarterly Bulletin*, March 2005, December 2006, March 2007

4.3 Other measures of production, income and expenditure

In this section we introduce some other measures of aggregate economic activity. While GDP is undoubtedly the most widely used barometer of total production in an economy in a particular year, the other measures also have specific uses. Our explanation of these other measures will help to further clarify some aspects of GDP.

Gross national income or gross national product

As mentioned earlier, GDP is a geographic concept – the adjective **domestic** indicates that we are dealing with what occurred within the boundaries of the country. It does not matter who produces the goods or who owns the factors of production. It could be a German, Taiwanese or any other firm. Nor does it matter to whom the goods are sold. They could be sold locally or exported to another country. As long as the production takes place on South African soil it forms part of South African GDP.

But economists also want to know what happens to the income earned and standard of living of all South African citizens or permanent residents in the country. To answer this question, all income earned by foreign-owned factors of production in South Africa has to be subtracted from GDP. In this way the South African element of GDP can be ascertained. In addition, all income earned by South African factors of production in the rest of the world also has to be taken into account. Once these adjustments have been made, we have an indication of the **national** income, that is, the income of all permanent residents of the country. This is called the **gross national income (GNI)**, which equals the gross national product (GNP).

To derive GNI from GDP the following must therefore be done:

Subtract from GDP:

- all profits, interest and other income from domestic investment which accrue to residents of other countries (eg the profits earned in South Africa by foreign owners of companies such as Lever Brothers, Colgate-Palmolive or BMW and the interest paid by South Africans to foreign lenders)
- all wages and salaries of foreign workers engaged in domestic production (eg the wages earned by residents of Lesotho, Mozambique and Malawi on the South African gold mines)

BOX 4-2 NOMINAL AND REAL GDP: A SIMPLE EXAMPLE

We can use a simple example to illustrate the difference between nominal GDP (ie GDP at current prices) and real GDP (ie GDP at constant prices).

Suppose that only three goods are produced in a particular economy: apples, bananas and oranges. In 2000, 100 apples were produced and sold at 50 cents each, 200 bananas were produced and sold at 25 cents each, and 150 oranges were produced and sold at 30 cents each.

The total value of production in 2000 was thus (100 × R0,50) + (200 × R0,25) + (150 × R0,30) = R50 + R50 + R45 = R145.

In 2006, 150 apples were produced and sold at R1,00 each, 200 bananas were produced and sold at 40 cents each and 100 oranges were produced and sold at 50 cents each. The total value of production in 2006 was thus (150 × R1,00) + (200 × R0,40) + (100 × R0,50) = R150 + R80 + R50 = R280.

This was significantly higher than the R145 recorded for 2000. In percentage terms the increase was 93,1 per cent. But the R145 and R280 are both **nominal** values. **Current prices** were used to value the production in each year.

Did the production actually increase? What happened to the **real** production? To answer this question we must measure the production in both years at the same prices. In this way we eliminate the effect of price increases.

We can do this by using 2000 as the base year and using 2000 prices to obtain the value of production in 2006 at constant (2000) prices. By doing this we find that the total value of production in 2006 was (150 × R0,50) + (200 × R0,25) + (100 × R0,30) = R75 + R50 + R30 = R155. In other words, we use the prices of 2000 along with the quantities of 2006 to determine **real** GDP (or GDP at **constant prices**) in 2006. We now see that the actual increase in the value of production was the difference between R145 (2000) and R155 (2006). This represents an increase of 6,9 per cent. This was the **real** increase in production between 2000 and 2006.

The calculations above can be summarised as follows:

Nominal GDP in 2000		Nominal GDP in 2006		Real GDP in 2006 (at 2000 prices)	
100 apples at 50c	= R50	150 apples at R1	= R150	150 apples at 50c	= R75
200 bananas at 25c	= R50	200 bananas at 40c	= R80	200 bananas at 25c	= R50
150 oranges at 30c	= R45	100 oranges at 50c	= R50	100 oranges at 30c	= R30
	R145		R280		R155

Increase in nominal GDP between 2000 and 2006

$$= \frac{280 - 145}{145} \times \frac{100}{1} = \frac{135}{145} \times \frac{100}{1} = 93{,}1 \text{ per cent}$$

Increase in real GDP between 2000 and 2006

$$= \frac{155 - 145}{145} \times \frac{100}{1} = \frac{10}{145} \times \frac{100}{1} = 6{,}9 \text{ per cent}$$

Add to GDP:

- all profits, interest and other income from investments abroad which accrue to permanent residents (eg the profits earned by a South African construction company that builds roads in the rest of Africa and the dividends earned by South African owners of shares in foreign companies such as Microsoft and Wal-Mart)
- all wages and salaries earned by permanent residents outside South Africa (eg the income earned by South Africans working in Britain)

In the case of South Africa, foreign involvement in the domestic economy has always been larger than the involvement by South African factors of production in the rest of the world. In technical terms we say that the country's **primary income payments** to the rest of the world (ie the remuneration of foreign-owned factors of production in our economy) exceed our **primary income receipts** (ie the remuneration earned by South African factors of production in the rest of the world). South Africa's GNI has therefore always been smaller than its GDP. For example, in 2006 South Africa's GNI was R1 690,9 billion while the GDP was R1 726,7 billion. Net primary income payments to the rest of the world amounted to R35,8 billion.

Formally:

GNI = GDP + primary income receipts
− primary income payments

or (since payments are larger)

GNI = GDP − net primary income payments to the rest of the world

where net primary income payments
= primary income payments − primary income receipts

In some countries GNI is larger than GDP. Take Lesotho, for example. Lesotho is a small, landlocked, mountainous country. Production in Lesotho is limited. Most citizens of Lesotho work in South Africa, particularly on the mines. Lesotho's GNI is thus greater than its GDP. In certain industrial countries which invest heavily abroad, like the United States, the United Kingdom and Germany, GNI is also usually larger than GDP.

Economists use both GDP and GNI (or GNP) when measuring or analysing the state of the economy. GDP is the best measure of the **level of economic activity** in the country and of the potential for creating jobs for the country's residents. Economic growth is therefore usually measured by calculating the percentage change in real GDP from one year to the next. GNI, on the other hand, is a better measure of the **income** or **standard of living** of the citizens of a country. If we want to know how South Africans as a group are faring, we therefore examine the level and rate of change in real GNI (or GNP). More details about the calculation and significance of real GDP and real GNI (or GNP) are provided in Chapter 23.

Expenditure on GDP

In Section 4.2 we explained that there are three approaches to calculating GDP: the **production approach** (which measures the value added by all the participants in the economy), the **income approach** (which measures the income received by the different factors of production) and the **expenditure approach** (which measures the spending on final goods and services by the different participants).

With the expenditure approach, the national accountants add together the spending of the four major sectors of the economy: households, firms, government and foreign sector. You learnt about the elements of total spending in Chapter 3. Recall that they are:

- consumption expenditure by households (*C*)
- investment spending (or capital formation) by firms (*I*)
- government spending (*G*)
- expenditure on exports (*X*) minus expenditure on imports (*Z*)

In symbols we can therefore write:

$$\text{GDP} = \text{expenditure on GDP} = C + I + G + X - Z$$

The composition of expenditure on GDP in South Africa in 2006 is shown in Table 4-3. Expenditure on GDP is always valued at market prices. Note that the published figures do not conform precisely with the equation above. For example, investment spending (called capital formation in the national accounts) includes spending by both firms and the government, while government spending pertains to final consumption expenditure only. However, to link up with the macroeconomic theory explained in Part IV, we use the above equation throughout this book.

From the table it is clear that **final consumption expenditure by households** is the largest single element of total expenditure in the economy. In the national accounts this is subdivided into spending on durable goods, semi-durable goods, non-durable goods and services – see also Section 2.1. In 2006 spending on services represented about 40,9 per cent of private consumption expenditure in South Africa. The shares of the other components were as follows: non-durable goods 38,6 per cent, durable goods 10,3 per cent and semi-durable goods 10,2 per cent.

TABLE 4-3 Composition of expenditure on GDP in South Africa, 2006

	R millions
Final consumption expenditure by households (*C*)	1 080 074
Gross capital formation (*I*)	350 669
Final consumption expenditure by general government (*G*)	336 073
Residual item	18 012
Exports of goods and services (*X*)	515 355
minus Imports of goods and services (*Z*)	–573 495
Total	**1 726 688**

Source: South African Reserve Bank, *Quarterly Bulletin*, March 2007

Gross capital formation requires some clarification. By now you know that **capital formation** or **investment** refers to additions to the country's capital stock, that is, the purchase of capital goods. You also know that **gross capital formation** means that no provision has been made for the consumption of fixed capital. In the national accounts, gross capital formation is subdivided into two components: gross **fixed** capital formation and **changes in inventories**. Fixed capital formation refers to the purchase of capital goods like buildings, machinery and equipment, while changes in inventories reflect goods produced during the period that have not been sold, or goods produced in an earlier period but only sold during the current period. Changes in inventories can therefore be positive or negative. They are usually very small in relation to the size of fixed investment. In 2006, for example, gross fixed capital formation amounted to R320 642 million while the change in inventories was R30 027 million. This yielded the gross capital formation of R350 669 million shown in Table 4-3. As can be seen from the table, gross capital formation is much smaller than final consumption expenditure by households. However, as we show in Chapter 18, investment spending is a very important component of total spending in the economy and also the most volatile.

The next element of expenditure on GDP is **final consumption expenditure by general government**. As the name indicates, this does not include capital expenditure (ie investment) by the government. The government's capital formation is included in gross capital formation.

In the national accounts you will also find a relatively small **residual item**. This item merely serves to balance the national accounts when the three methods discussed in Section 4.2 do not yield exactly the same answer.

A substantial portion of the expenditure on South African GDP occurs in the rest of the world. This spending on South African **exports** has to be **added** to the other components of spending on GDP. On the other hand, C, I, G and X all contain spending on goods and services not produced in South Africa. Such **imports** of goods and services therefore have to be **subtracted** to obtain the total expenditure on South African produced goods and services. **Spending on GDP does not include imports**, since **imports are produced in the rest of the world. Expenditure on GDP includes spending on South African produced goods and services only**.

As we explain in Part IV, the components of expenditure on GDP play an important role in macroeconomic analysis.

Gross domestic expenditure (GDE)

Expenditure on GDP is always equal to GDP at market prices. It indicates the total value of spending on goods and services produced in the country. However, it does not indicate the total value of spending **within the borders** of the country. As indicated above, part of the expenditure on South African GDP occurs in the rest of the world while part of the spending in the country is on goods and services produced in the rest of the world.

The three central domestic expenditure items (C, I and G) do not distinguish between goods and services manufactured locally and those manufactured in the rest of the world (such as French wine, Italian shoes, Japanese CD players and German machinery). These three items constitute **gross domestic expenditure** (GDE). Economists are particularly interested in GDE, which indicates the total value of spending within the borders of the country. It **includes imports** but **excludes exports**, since spending on exports occurs in the rest of the world.

The relationship between GDP (or expenditure on GDP) and GDE is very important and needs to be emphasised. In symbols we have

$$\text{GDE} = C + I + G$$
$$\text{GDP} = C + I + G + (X - Z)$$

GDE includes imports (Z) and excludes exports (X), while GDP includes exports (X) and excludes imports (Z).

The difference between GDE and GDP is therefore the difference between exports and imports ($X - Z$). This can be seen clearly by examining the equations for GDE and GDP given above. Incidentally, ($X - Z$) is often called **net exports** (NX).

The difference between domestic production and domestic expenditure is therefore reflected in the difference between exports and imports. If GDP is greater than GDE for a particlar period, it follows that exports were greater than imports during that period. This is quite logical. If the value of production in the domestic economy exceeded the value of spending within the country, it follows that the value of exports was greater than the value of imports. Thus if GDP > GDE, it follows that $X > Z$.

Similarly, if the value of spending within the country exceeded the value of production within the country, it follows that the value of imports was greater than the value of exports. Thus if GDE > GDP, it follows that $Z > X$.

The importance of these relationships is emphasised in later chapters.

A summary of the basic national accounting totals

In this subsection we summarise the basic national accounting totals discussed above and show how they are interrelated.

We start from the expenditure side. **Gross domestic expenditure** (GDE) consists of expenditure on final goods and services by households (*C*), firms (*I*) and government (*G*) during a particular period. GDE includes spending on imported goods and services (*Z*) and excludes exports (*X*). GDE is expressed at market prices. In symbols we have

$$GDE = C + I + G$$

where *C*, *I* and *G* include imported goods and services.

To move from GDE to **gross domestic product** (GDP) at market prices, that is, the total market value of all the final goods and services produced in the period concerned, imports have to be subtracted from GDE and exports added. In symbols the relationship can be expressed as follows:

$$\text{GDP at market prices} = \text{GDE} + X - Z$$
$$= C + I + G + X - Z$$

To move from GDP at market prices to **gross national income** (GNI) at market prices, net primary income payments to the rest of the world have to be subtracted from GDP:

$$\text{GNI at market prices} = \text{GDP at market prices} - \text{net primary income payments}$$

The relationships between these national accounting concepts are summarised in Table 4-4 which contains the South African figures for 2006.

TABLE 4-4 National accounting totals in South Africa in 2006

	R millions
Final consumption expenditure by households	1 080 074
Gross capital formation	350 669
Final consumption expenditure by general government	336 073
Residual item	18 012
equals	
Gross domestic expenditure	**1 784 828**
plus Exports of goods and services	515 355
minus Imports of goods and services	−573 495
equals	
Gross domestic product at market prices	**1 726 688**
minus Net primary income payments to the rest of the world	−35 756
equals	
Gross national income at market prices	**1 690 932**

Source: South African Reserve Bank, *Quarterly Bulletin*, March 2007

4.4 Measuring employment and unemployment

We now turn to the second macroeconomic objective, namely full employment. In **principle** it is quite easy to measure employment and unemployment. To measure employment you simply have to find out how many people have jobs at the time the measurement is done. To measure the number of unemployed persons you simply have to ascertain how many people are willing and able to work but do not have jobs at that time. The number of unemployed persons can then be expressed as a percentage of the total number of people who are willing and able to work. This percentage is called the **unemployment rate**.

In **practice**, however, total employment and unemployment in the economy are quite difficult to measure. When exactly is a person employed? What about part-time or seasonal workers? Are housewives employed or unemployed? When is a person unemployed? What about someone who does not have a job but is also not actively seeking work? What about people who are making a living by selling things on the pavement or from illegal activities like prostitution and dealing in drugs? These are but some of the problems that government agencies or private researchers are faced with when trying to estimate total employment and unemployment in the economy.

We shall not deal with these issues in any further detail at this stage. The measurement of employment and unemployment in South Africa is discussed in Chapters 5 and 22.

4.5 Measuring prices: the consumer price index

Prices and purchasing power

The third macroeconomic objective is price stability. As we have mentioned in Section 4.1, economists are interested in what is happening to the prices of goods and services. They want to know what is happening to **inflation**. They also need information about price movements to be able to distinguish between **nominal** and **real** values – recall the discussion of nominal and real GDP.

Since World War II most prices in South Africa have increased from year to year. The prices of all goods increased considerably but the prices of different goods increased at different rates.

When the prices of goods and services increase, the purchasing power of our income decreases. A South African consumer can purchase much less with R100 today than in 1980, when prices were much lower. In other words the **real** value (or purchasing power) of R100 is much less today than it was in 1980.

Economists want to know what is happening to the purchasing power of the consumer's rand. But to estimate changes in purchasing power, they have to know what is happening to prices **in general**. Instead of investigating what is happening to individual prices, we therefore use one of the general or composite price indices compiled and published by Stats SA – see Box 4-3. The best-known of these is the consumer price index (CPI). In the remainder of this section we explain the CPI. Other price indices, such as the production price index (PPI), and the different ways of measuring inflation are explained in Chapter 21.

The consumer price index (CPI)

The consumer price index (CPI) is an index of the prices of a representative "basket" of consumer goods and services. The CPI thus represents the cost of the "shopping basket" of goods and services of a typical or average South African household. In constructing the CPI, Stats SA

- selects the goods and services to be included in the **basket**
- assigns a **weight** to each good or service to indicate its relative importance in the basket
- decides on a **base year** for calculating the CPI
- decides on a **formula** for calculating the CPI
- **collects prices** each month to calculate the value of the CPI for that month

To select the goods and services to be included in the **basket** and to determine their relative **weights**, Stats SA conducts a comprehensive, in-depth survey of household income and expenditure in South Africa. The weight allocated to each good or service is based on the relative importance of the item in the average consumer's budget or "shopping basket". This requires a lot of time and effort and is therefore only done every five years or so. The fact that such surveys are not undertaken more regularly is not really a problem, since the pattern of household spending does not change significantly from one year to the next. In other words, the relative weights of the differ-

BOX 4-3 INDEX NUMBERS

An **index number** expresses the value of some series in any given period as a percentage of its value in the base period. Economists often use index numbers to express relative changes or to combine different series in an average. To express relative changes they use **specific** indices and to combine different series they use **general** or **composite** indices.

To explain a **specific index**, we use the following table, which contains the average annual price of gold (per fine ounce) from 2004 to 2006 in US dollars (USD) and in rand (ZAR):

Year	USD	ZAR
2004	409	2 637
2005	445	2 825
2006	604	4 085

The relative fluctuations in both series can be expressed and compared better by setting the values in 2004 equal to 100 and expressing the other values as percentages of these values. In the USD column, 409 is set equal to 100 and all the other figures therefore also have to be divided by 409 and multiplied by 100. To convert the rand values, 2637 is set equal to 100 and all the other figures are also divided by 2637 and multiplied by 100. The results are as follows:

Year	USD	ZAR
2004	$(409/409) \times 100 = 100{,}0$	$(2\,637/2\,637) \times 100 = 100{,}0$
2005	$(445/409) \times 100 = 108{,}8$	$(2\,825/2\,637) \times 100 = 107{,}1$
2006	$(604/409) \times 100 = 147{,}7$	$(4\,085/2\,637) \times 100 = 154{,}9$

We can now immediately see, for example, that the average dollar price of gold was 47,7 per cent higher in 2006 than in 2004, while the rand price increased by 54,9 per cent over the same period.

In the case of a **general** or **composite index** several different series are combined into an average. Each series has to be weighted according to its relative importance. The best-known composite index in South Africa is the consumer price index (CPI), which is explained in this chapter.

ent goods and services usually do not change much in the short run.

The **base year** is the year in which the survey of household expenditure is done. Once the items in the basket and their relative weights have been determined, this information is inserted into a standard price index formula. All that is then required to calculate the CPI, are the prices of the goods and services concerned. In Box 4-4 we provide a simple example of how the prices of two goods can be combined into a price index. This example shows, for instance, that the effect of the price of a particular good or service on the price index depends on the weight of the good or service concerned. The CPI is based on the same principle.

At the time of writing, the South African CPI was based on a household income and expenditure survey conducted in October 2000. The total CPI basket consists of about 1 500 different consumer goods and services. These goods and services are classified into more than 40 groups and sub-groups for which separate indices are constructed. In addition, different CPIs are published each month for, *inter alia*, five expenditure groups, for pensioners, for the nine provinces and for twelve metropolitan areas in South Africa. Separate CPIs are also published for the metropolitan and other urban areas and (since 2003) for the rural areas. Stats SA collects the price information each month mainly by sending out questionnaires (6 700 per month). On average 110 000 price quotations are obtained every month. Some prices are collected directly by officials of Stats SA and the information supplied by the retailers is checked for consistency and possible errors.

You will appreciate that the compilation of the CPI for each month takes some time. The CPI for a particular month (which is based on the prices during the first seven days of the month) is therefore usually published during the second half of the following month.

The weights of the different groups of goods and services included in the CPI basket in South Africa in 2007, based on the 2000 survey, are shown in Table 4-5. Also included are the values of the CPI for each

BOX 4-4 CONSTRUCTING A PRICE INDEX: A SIMPLE EXAMPLE

Suppose that only two goods, meat and bread, are consumed. Suppose further that it has been established that the typical or average consumer purchases 4 kg of meat and 10 loaves of bread per week, in other words, the typical consumer basket consists of 4 kg of meat and 10 loaves of bread. In 2005 meat cost R30 per kilogram and bread cost R4 per loaf. In 2006 meat cost R40 per kilogram and bread R4,80 per loaf. By how much did the cost of the basket (ie the weekly cost of living) increase between 2005 and 2006?

We first calculate the cost of the basket in 2005. The total cost of the basket in 2005 is $(4 \times R30) + (10 \times R4) = R120 + R40 = R160$.

The total cost of the same basket in 2006 is $(4 \times R40) + (10 \times R4{,}80) = R160 + R48 = R208$. If we were to set the cost of the basket in 2005 (or the consumer price index) equal to 100, then the relative cost in 2006 would be

$$\frac{208}{160} \times 100 = 130{,}0$$

In this example the increase in the consumer price index between 2005 and 2006 thus amounted to 30,0 per cent. The price of meat increased by 33,3 per cent while the cost of bread increased by 20 per cent. But because the value of meat has a much greater weight in the consumer basket than the value of bread, the overall increase in the cost of living was much closer to the increase in the price of meat than to the increase in the price of bread.

This example also illustrates one of the problems of the consumer price index. It represents the cost of a typical basket of goods and services and therefore does not apply to every consumer. In our example a consumer who purchased bread only would have experienced a cost of living increase of just 20 per cent (not 30 per cent). However, since the consumer price index contains a large basket of goods and services – more than 1 500 items in South Africa – it nevertheless provides a reasonable indication of the cost of living of most consumers. Changes in the CPI reflect changes in the average cost of living fairly accurately.

TABLE 4-5 The South African consumer price index (metropolitan areas), 2005 and 2006 (2000 = 100)

Group	*Weight*	*Index for 2005*	*Index for 2006*	*Percentage change between 2005 and 2006*
Goods				
Food	*22,1*	138,1	147,9	7,1
Furniture and equipment	*2,5*	116,6	115,3	–1,1
Clothing and footwear	*3,2*	92,3	84,6	–8,3
Vehicles	*6,0*	116,5	115,6	–0,8
Transport: running costs	*5,5*	152,7	174,0	13,9
Beverages and tobacco	*2,5*	157,2	169,6	7,9
Other goods	*15,3*	124,1	128,1	3,2
Services				
Housing	*24,3*	115,4	119,2	3,3
Transport	*3,4*	123,6	127,5	3,2
Other services	*15,2*	139,0	145,3	4,5
Total	***100,0***	**128,0**	**133,9**	**4,6**

Note: These figures sometimes differ slightly from those published by Statistics South Africa.
Source: South African Reserve Bank, *Quarterly Bulletin*, March 2007

group as well as for the total basket in 2005 and 2006. These values are average values for the year. The last column shows the percentage increases for each group and for the total between 2005 and 2006.

Note that more than a fifth of the basket consisted of food while housing represented almost a quarter. It follows therefore that changes in the prices of food, housing rentals and mortgage rates had a major impact on movements in the CPI. Also note that the highest group indices for 2006 were those for transport: running costs (including petrol), beverages and tobacco, food and other services. This means that the prices of these groups of goods rose most quickly between 2000 (the base year) and 2006.

The figure at the bottom of the last column (4,6 per cent) is the figure that is usually taken to be the average South African inflation rate in 2006. We examine the measurement of inflation in more detail in Chapter 21, where we also discuss core inflation and the CPIX, which serves as the basis for calculating the inflation targets pursued by the South African Reserve Bank. In Box 4-5 we explain how the CPI can be used to calculate changes in purchasing power.

4.6 Measuring the links with the rest of the world: the balance of payments

The fourth macroeconomic objective concerns a country's economic links with other countries. Each country keeps a record of its transactions with the rest of the world. This accounting record is called the **balance of payments**. The South African balance of payments summarises the transactions between South African households, firms and government and foreign households, firms and governments during a particular period (usually a year) – see Box 4-6.

The balance of payments consists of two major accounts, the **current account** and the **financial account**.

- Just as each business keeps a record of its purchases and sales of goods and services, so does a country. All the sales of goods and services to the rest of the world (ie **exports**), all the purchases of goods and services from the rest of the world (ie **imports**) as well as all the primary income receipts and payments are recorded in the **current account** of the balance of payments.
- Just as everyone with a bank account has an accounting statement showing all the funds going into the account and all the funds going out of the account, so does a country. All the **purely financial flows** in and out of the country, like purchases and sales of assets such as bonds and shares, are recorded in the **financial account** of the balance of payments.

If there is a **surplus** on the **current account**, it indicates that the value of the country's exports exceeded the value of its imports during the period under review. If there is a **deficit**, then imports were greater than exports.

BOX 4-5 CHANGES IN PURCHASING POWER

The difference between nominal values and real values was explained in Box 4-1. In that box we also indicated that real values refer to purchasing power. Now that you know something about the CPI, we can explain the meaning of changes in purchasing power with the aid of numerical examples.

At the time of writing, the base period of the South African CPI was 2000. In other words, the CPI for 2000 was 100,0. In 2006 the CPI was 133,9. This meant that the basket of goods and services purchased by the average consumer cost 33,9 per cent more in 2006 than in 2000. Another way of stating this is that the purchasing power of a given amount of money declined between 2000 and 2006.

If a particular basket of goods and services cost R100,00 in 2000, it would have cost R133,90 in 2006. Thus, whereas R100,00 was enough to buy one basket in 2000, it could only buy a fraction of a basket in 2006. This fraction is given by the ratio between the price levels in 2000 and 2006 respectively, that is,

$$\frac{100,0}{133,9} = 0,75$$

Between 2000 and 2006 the purchasing power of the consumer's rand thus fell from R1,00 to R0,75 (ie 75 cents).

Suppose Sandra Johnson earned R1 000,00 per month in 2000. According to our example she could (at R100,00 per basket) have purchased 10 baskets per month in 2000. If her **nominal** income remained unchanged between 2000 and 2006, the **real** value or **purchasing power** of her income would have fallen. In 2006 she would only have been able to afford 7,5 baskets (ie R1 000,00 divided by R133,90). Price increases (ie inflation) therefore erode the **real** value or **purchasing power** of a fixed **nominal** amount. The real value is obtained by dividing the nominal amount by the price level. As the price level increases, the real value of the nominal amount falls.

The relationship between nominal values, prices and real values (or purchasing power) can be used to calculate various things. For example, we can calculate that something which cost R1,00 in 2006 would have cost about 1,6 cents in 1950. Put differently, compared to 1950 a rand was worth only 1,6 cents in 2006. Note that we can only make such comparisons if the base year is clearly specified. A statement such as "the rand is only worth 10 cents today" is meaningless unless the base year is specified. We therefore have to say, for example, that in 2006 the rand was worth only 10 cents (or 10 per cent) compared to what it was worth in 1981.

During a period of inflation, the purchasing power of a given nominal amount falls. Prices can, however, also decrease. For example, between 1920 and 1930 prices actually fell in South Africa. As a result the purchasing power (or **real** value) of R1,00 increased by 40 per cent between 1920 and 1930.

BOX 4-6 ALL TRANSACTIONS WITH THE REST OF THE WORLD ARE RECORDED IN THE BALANCE OF PAYMENTS

The balance of payments is always compiled by an official agency. In South Africa it is compiled by the South African Reserve Bank, with the South African Revenue Service being one of its most important sources of information.

The fact that the balance of payments is an official document often creates the illusion that it only records transactions between the government and foreign governments, or that the government somehow controls (or is responsible for) all the transactions with the rest of the world. This is not the case. The South African balance of payments is simply a summary record of the transactions of **all** South African households, firms and levels of government with households, firms or governments in the rest of the world.

Likewise, if there is a **surplus** on the **financial account**, it indicates that more funds flowed into the country than flowed out during the period concerned. In this case we say that there was a **net inflow of foreign capital** into the country. If there is a **deficit**, it indicates that the outflows exceeded the inflows. We then say that there was a **net outflow of foreign capital**.

Both the current account and the financial account can be in surplus or in deficit. If we add the two balances (ie the balance on current account and the balance on financial account), we obtain the **change in the country's gold and foreign exchange reserves**. This change serves as the balancing item on the balance of payments.

All these concepts are explained more fully in Chapters 5 and 17. For the time being, the most important thing to note is that all transactions with the rest of the world are recorded in the balance of payments and that this account is one of the major indicators of the current and prospective state of the economy.

4.7 Measuring inequality: the distribution of income

The fifth macroeconomic objective concerns the **distribution of income** among individuals or households.[1] As we have indicated, the measurement of the performance of the economy in respect of the macroeconomic objectives is no easy task. The most difficult of all to measure is the distribution of income. To obtain an accurate picture of the distribution of income we must have reliable information about the income of each individual or household in the economy during a particular period. This information is difficult to obtain. Nevertheless, researchers use data from population censuses, tax returns and other sources to estimate the distribution of income. Once this information has been obtained, certain measures or criteria then have to be applied to estimate the degree of equality or inequality. This whole process is difficult and time-consuming. Estimates of the distribution of income are therefore only undertaken sporadically.

In this section we explain three of the measures that are often used to measure the equality or inequality of the distribution of income, once the necessary basic information has been obtained.

Lorenz curve

The first measure is the **Lorenz curve** (named after the American statistician Lorenz who developed it in 1905). The Lorenz curve is a simple graphic device which illustrates the degree of inequality in the distribution of income (or any other variable). We first explain the Lorenz curve and then use a simple example to show how it is constructed.

To construct the Lorenz curve illustrating the distribution of income, the different individuals or households in the economy first have to be ranked from poorest to richest. This is done on a cumulative percentage basis. In other words, we start with the poorest per cent of the population, the second poorest per cent and so on until we come to the richest per cent of the population. The cumulative percentages of the population are plotted along the horizontal axis. The vertical axis shows the **cumulative** percentage of total income. In other words, if the poorest per cent of the population earns 0,1 per cent of the total income in the economy, that number will be plotted vertically above the first per cent of the population. If the second poorest per cent of the population earns 0,2 per cent of the total income in the economy, it means that the first two per cent earned a cumulative share of 0,3 per cent (ie 0,1 plus 0,2 per cent) of the income. This number (0,3) will then be plotted vertically above the 2 on the horizontal axis.

The construction of the Lorenz curve can be explained with the aid of a simple example. Table 4-6 shows a hypothetical distribution of income. To keep things simple, we only show the income of each successive 20 per cent of the population.

The first two columns in Table 4-6 contain the basic data. The last two columns are simply the cumulative totals. For example, these two columns show that the first 60 per cent of the population (the poorest 60 per cent) earn 25 per cent of the total income.

The last two columns are then plotted as in Figure 4-1. Point **a** shows that the poorest 20 per cent of the population earns 3 per cent of the income, point **c** shows that the poorest 60 per cent of the population earns 25 per cent of the income, and so on.

Note two other features of the diagram. The first is that the axes have been joined to form a square. The second feature is the diagonal running from the origin 0 (bottom left) to the opposite point B (top right) of the rectangle. The **diagonal** serves as a reference point. It indicates a **perfectly equal distribution** of income. Along the diagonal the first 20 per cent of the

TABLE 4-6 A hypothetical income distribution

Percentage		*Cumulative percentage*	
Population	*Income*	*Population*	*Income*
Poorest 20%	3	20	3
Next 20%	7	40	10
Next 20%	15	60	25
Next 20%	25	80	50
Richest 20%	50	100	100

1. Recall that the personal distribution of income (discussed here) differs from the functional distribution of income, which refers to the distribution of income between the different factors of production.

FIGURE 4-1 A Lorenz curve

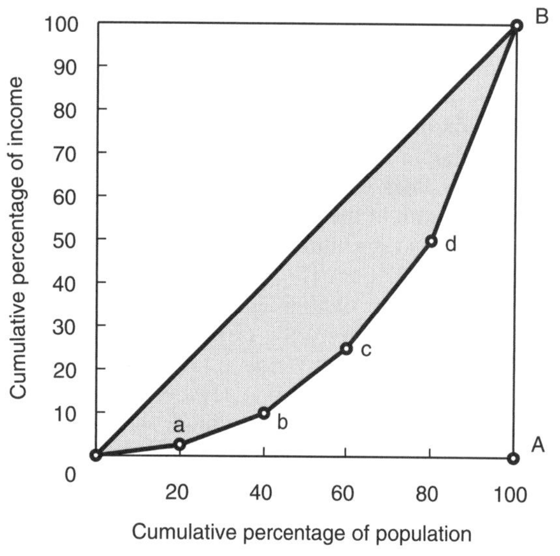

The cumulative percentage of the population (from poor to rich) is shown on the horizontal axis. The cumulative percentage of income is shown on the vertical axis. The line that goes through a, b, c and d is the Lorenz curve. The diagonal 0B is the line of perfect equality. The shaded area is the area of inequality.

population receives 20 per cent of the total income, the first 40 per cent receives 40 per cent, and so on. Like the diagonal, any Lorenz curve must start at the origin 0 (since 0 per cent of the population will earn 0 per cent of the income) and end at B (since 100 per cent of the population will earn 100 per cent of the income).

The degree of inequality is shown by the deviation from the diagonal. The greater the distance between the diagonal and the Lorenz curve, the greater the degree of inequality. In Figure 4-1 the area between the diagonal and the Lorenz curve has been shaded. This **shaded area** is called the **area of inequality**. The greatest possible inequality will be where one person earns the total income. If that is the case, the Lorenz curve will run along the axes from 0 to A to B.

Gini coefficient

Another measure of inequality is the **Gini coefficient** (or Gini ratio), named after the Italian demographer, Corrodo Gini, who invented it in 1912. This is obtained by dividing the area of inequality shown by a Lorenz curve by the area of the right-triangle formed by the axes and the diagonal (the line of equality). In Figure 4-1 the latter area is shown by the triangle formed by points 0, A and B. The Gini coefficient can vary between 0 and 1. The Gini coefficient is sometimes also multiplied by 100 to obtain the **Gini index**, which varies between 0 and 100.

If incomes are distributed perfectly equally, the Gini coefficient is zero. In this case the Lorenz curve coincides with the line of perfect equality (the diagonal) and the area of inequality is therefore zero. At the other extreme, if the total income goes to one individual or household (ie if the incomes are distributed with perfect **inequality**) the Gini coefficient is one. In this case the area of inequality will be the same as the triangle 0AB. In practice the Gini coefficient usually ranges between about 0,30 (highly equal) and about 0,70 (highly unequal).

Quantile ratio

A third possible way of expressing the equality or inequality of the distribution of income is to use a **quantile ratio**. A quantile ratio is the ratio between the percentage of income received by the highest x per cent of the population and the percentage of income received by the lowest y per cent of the population. For example, we can compare the income received by the top 20 per cent with that earned by the bottom 20 per cent of the population. Using the figures in Table 4-6, the answer will be 50 ÷ 3 = 16,7. The higher the ratio, the greater the degree of inequality. The ratio between the top 20 per cent and the lowest 40 per cent (50 ÷ 10 = 5 in our example) is also often used to compare income distributions between countries.

The distribution of income is discussed further in Chapters 5 and 14.

IMPORTANT CONCEPTS

Economic growth
Full employment/unemployment
Price stability/inflation
Balance of payments (or external) stability
Distribution of income
Gross domestic product (GDP)
Final and intermediate goods
Value added
Production method
Expenditure method
Income method
Market prices
Basic prices
Factor cost
Current prices
Constant prices
Nominal GDP
Real GDP
Gross national income (GNI)
Net primary income payments
Consumption of fixed capital
Gross domestic expenditure (GDE)
Purchasing power
Specific index
General (composite) index
Consumer price index
Balance of payments
Current account
Financial account
Lorenz curve
Gini coefficient
Gini index

REVIEW QUESTIONS

1. Explain why GDP can be measured in three different ways.
2. Explain why nominal GDP data have to be adjusted before economic growth can be calculated.
3. List South Africa's main macroeconomic goals (or objectives) and rank them in order of priority. Substantiate your ranking. Would you classify your ranking as an example of positive or normative economics? Explain.
4. If you are told that the South African GDP at current prices increased by seven per cent last year, what conclusions can you draw from this fact? Explain your answer.
5. Explain why only final goods and services are included when GDP is estimated (according to the expenditure method).
6. Explain why the total value of the sales of each industry or sector in the economy cannot be added together to obtain an estimate of GDP (according to the production method).
7. Which of the following should be taken into account when South African GDP is estimated (according to the expenditure method) for a particular year? Indicate, in each case selected, whether the item should be classified as private consumption spending (*C*), investment spending (*I*), government spending (*G*), exports (*X*) or imports (*Z*).
   (a) a new motorcar produced by Daimler Chrysler in East London that remained unsold at the end of the year
   (b) the expenses incurred by Ms VA Nity, a private patient, who underwent plastic surgery at the Carstenhof Clinic in Midrand
   (c) chickens bought by Kentucky Fried Chicken outlets to sell to their customers
   (d) Ms IN Vestor's purchase of 2 000 Sasol shares
   (e) Mr G Ambler's purchase of 100 Lotto tickets
   (f) Maans Wiese's purchase of an existing house in Moorreesburg from Pietie Rossouw
   (g) the estate agent's commission from the sale of Pietie's house

(h) the purchase of new tractors, imported from the United States, by a group of farmers in Mpumalanga
(i) Thabo from Tshwane mowing his own lawn
(j) Indira from Durban depositing money in a savings account

8. Explain the difference between GDP and GNP.

9. Why are economists primarily interested in real GDP, not nominal GDP?

10. Explain the difference between gross domestic expenditure (GDE) and expenditure on gross domestic product (GDP).

5 The South African economy

Learning outcomes

Once you have studied this chapter you should be able to describe each of the following in respect of South Africa:

- recent growth, employment and inflation record
- position on the balance of payments
- international economic position
- factor endowment
- economic links with the rest of the world

> *South Africa has advanced politically by disasters and economically by windfalls.*
>
> CW DE KIEWIET
>
> *South Africa, renowned far and wide for politics and little else beside.*
>
> ROY CAMPBELL

This chapter deals with the South African economy. Before we proceed to an analysis of the various elements of the economy, we first give you some background about the development, recent performance and important features of the South African economy. We start with a brief overview of the **development of the economy**. This is followed by a closer look at the **performance** of the South African economy in recent years, using the various measures explained in Chapter 4. This performance is placed in a **historical** and **international context** by comparing it with past trends and with the performance of other countries.

The next section indicates South Africa's **international economic position**. There is also a brief discussion of South Africa's **factor endowment**, that is, the availability of the various factors of production, which will give you some indication of the major strengths and weaknesses of the South African economy. The chapter concludes with a discussion of South Africa's **economic links** with the rest of the world.

Studying this chapter will give you a good grasp of the most important features, strengths and weaknesses of the South African economy, which will serve as a useful background to the remainder of the book.

5.1 The development of the South African economy: a brief overview

The earliest inhabitants of Southern Africa were originally hunter-gatherers and later crop and stock farmers. When Jan van Riebeeck settled at the Cape in 1652, vegetables, grain and meat were produced for the crews of the ships of the Dutch East India Company. Towards the end of the 17th century, surpluses of wheat and wine were produced. Efforts to export these products failed, however, largely because of the great distances to the markets of Europe and Indonesia.

Besides the long-established trade in gold, copper, ivory and other hunting products with Arabs along the east coast (via Mozambique), the only noteworthy export market during the 18th century was the sale of foodstuffs to the crews of war ships passing the Cape. Following the occupation of the Cape by the British at the beginning of the 19th century, the Cape was declared a free port in the hope that it would become a clearing house for the rich wares of the East. This also failed, but British efforts to stimulate private enterprise gradually paid dividends. For example, in 1836 the first private commercial bank was established at the Cape. Meanwhile, some 4 000 British immigrants had settled in the eastern parts of the Cape Colony in the 1820s. After their initial crop-farming efforts had failed, they switched to animal husbandry and by 1842 wool had surpassed wine as the most important export product of the Cape.

Until the 1860s the Southern African economy was dominated by agriculture. The only significant mineral production was the mining of copper in Namaqualand. The turning point was the discovery of alluvial diamonds in 1867 and, in particular, the discovery of the diamond "pipes" of Kimberley in 1870 and 1871. This heralded the start of a boom in mining activity. Immigrants with a variety of skills were attracted to South Africa and the activities in and around Kimberley created new markets for farm produce. As a result many farmers switched from subsistence farming to market-oriented production. Diamond mining also led to the extension of railways and other forms of communication as well as to the inflow of foreign capital.

The greatest single event in the history of the South African economy was the discovery of gold on the Witwatersrand in 1886, which had the same kind of effects as the discovery of diamonds, but on a much larger scale. The effects were also more sustained. Today, more than a century later, gold is still one of the most important products in the South African economy.

When the Union of South Africa was formed in 1910, the South African economy was still largely based on the exploitation of natural resources. Agriculture and mining accounted for almost half of GDP, while the contribution of manufacturing was about 4 per cent – see Table 5-1. World War I provided a great stimulus to South African manufacturing. The country was cut off from its traditional sources of manufactured goods, providing an incentive to local industries to fill the gap. By 1920 the share of manufacturing in GDP had risen to 7,4 per cent.

During the 1920s manufacturing was promoted by a deliberate policy of industrialisation through import replacement. Important milestones included the establishment of the Board of Trade and Industries in 1921, the Electricity Supply Commission (now Eskom) in 1922 and the South African Iron and Steel Corporation (Iscor) in 1928.

Along with the rest of the Western world the South African economy suffered a severe setback during the Great Depression which commenced towards the end of 1929. During this period, much of the country also experienced severe drought conditions, which exacerbated the problem. GDP declined in 1930, 1931 and 1932. The 1928 level of GDP was only reached again in 1934, after the price of gold had increased and the drought had been broken.

The devaluation of the South African pound at the end of 1932 triggered significant industrial growth from 1933 onwards. World War II provided a further boost to economic activity in South Africa. Manufacturing was stimulated by the demands of the war effort and by the need to meet domestic demand in the absence of imported goods. During the war years manufacturing surpassed both agriculture and mining to become the most important sector of the South African economy. Another significant development during the war period was the establishment of the Industrial Development Corporation (IDC) in 1940. The IDC played a major role in the establishment of capital-intensive industries such as Sasol. From 1949 onwards the development of the Orange Free State goldfields gave a further stimulus to the growth of the South African economy. Gold production, which had reached a peak in 1941 and subsequently fell, started increasing again from 1953 onwards. As we explain in the rest of the chapter, the South African economy is still heavily dependent on the exploitation of its mineral resources.

Another important point to note is the growth of the service sector. The early phases of economic development in any country are usually dominated by the **primary sector** (agriculture and mining), followed by a phase in which the **secondary sector** (manufacturing, gas, water, electricity, etc) becomes the most important. The next stage of the process is characterised by strong growth in the **tertiary sector**, particularly in financial and government services. As indicated in Table 5-1, South Africa's economic development also followed this general pattern. The first part of the table provides information on the shares of certain kinds of economic activity in GDP and the second part indicates the percentage contributions of the

TABLE 5-1 Contributions of different kinds of economic activity to South African GDP, selected years

	Percentage contribution to GDP						
	1911	1920	1930	1940	1960	1990	2006
A. Kind of economic activity							
Agriculture	21,5	22,7	14,3	12,6	12,4	5,2	2,7
Mining	27,3	17,5	15,2	19,4	12,7	10,6	7,9
Manufacturing	4,2	7,4	9,7	12,8	21,0	25,4	18,2
Trade	12,8	15,6	14,9	13,9	14,2	13,4	13,9
Financial services	2,8	2,6	2,6	2,8	10,8	14,5	22,0
General government	5,5	7,1	8,4	10,5	8,6	14,0	14,8
Other	25,9	27,1	34,9	28,0	20,3	16,9	20,5
B. Sector							
Primary sector	48,8	40,2	29,5	32,0	25,1	15,8	10,6
Secondary sector	5,9	10,0	13,6	17,1	26,6	33,0	23,0
Tertiary sector	45,3	49,8	56,9	50,9	48,3	51,2	66,4

Sources: Statistics South Africa, *South African Statistics 2002*; South African Reserve Bank, *Quarterly Bulletin*, March 2007

primary, secondary and tertiary sectors. See also Box 2-2.

Having outlined some elements of the historical development of the South African economy, we now turn to a description of more recent developments.

5.2 The performance of the South African economy in recent years

In this section the various measures developed in Chapter 4 are used to assess the performance of the South African economy in recent years, and to compare it with the performance of earlier years and with the performance of some other countries.

Economic growth

Table 5-2 shows what happened to economic growth in South Africa from 1990 to 2006. The first column shows the annual percentage change in real gross **domestic** product (real GDP). As indicated in Chapter 4, the measurement of economic growth only makes sense if we use **real** data, that is, if the figures have been adjusted for the effect of inflation. The second column shows the annual percentage change in real gross **national** income (real GNI). The average real GDP per head of the population (ie the **per capita** real GDP) is shown in the third column. This falls when real GDP growth is lower than population growth.

The figures in the table show clearly that the South African economy performed badly between 1990 and 1993. Growth was actually negative during the first three years of the 1990s. A negative growth rate means that the real value or volume of production in that particular year was lower than in the previous year. If population growth is taken into account, the picture is even worse. In a number of the years the growth in real GDP was lower than the population growth and when real GDP per capita increased, the rate of increase was usually low. From 1994 onwards, however, the growth performance improved significantly, albeit not spectacularly.

Table 5-3 compares the growth of the South African economy between 1960 and 2005 with that of some other countries. The other countries selected are:

- **three highly developed industrial countries**: Japan, the United Kingdom and the United States
- **three East Asian countries** that have developed rapidly in recent decades: Korea, Malaysia and Thailand
- **three South American countries** which share certain important features with South Africa: Argentina, Brazil and Chile
- **three sub-Saharan African countries** that, like South Africa, were also British colonies: Kenya, Zambia and Zimbabwe

These countries are used in most of the international comparisons we present in this chapter.

Table 5-3 clearly shows how the growth performance of the South African economy deteriorated from the 1960s onwards. Whereas growth had been fairly high during the 1960s, it fell during the 1970s, 1980s and 1990s. Also note that even the relatively high growth of the 1960s was not particularly rapid by international standards. Note, in particular, the high

TABLE 5-2 Economic growth in South Africa, 1990–2006

	Annual percentage change in		
Year	*Real gross domestic product GDP*	*Real gross national income GNI*	*Real GDP per capita*
1990	–0,3	–1,2	–2,4
1991	–1,0	–0,8	–3,1
1992	–2,1	–2,1	–4,2
1993	1,2	1,6	–0,9
1994	3,2	5,1	1,1
1995	3,1	2,2	1,0
1996	4,3	4,6	2,1
1997	2,6	2,1	0,5
1998	0,5	–0,3	–1,6
1999	2,4	1,2	–0,2
2000	4,2	3,7	2,1
2001	2,7	2,5	0,8
2002	3,7	5,1	1,9
2003	3,1	3,5	1,5
2004	4,8	5,8	3,4
2005	5,1	5,3	3,7
2006	5,0	6,3	3,6

Source: South African Reserve Bank, *Quarterly Bulletin*, March 2007

growth achieved by Japan in the 1960s, Korea, Malaysia and Thailand throughout the period under review and Brazil in the 1960s and 1970s.

However, as we emphasised at the end of Chapter 1, growth rates can sometimes be misleading. They depend on the **level** from which the growth occurred. For example, in 1960 Korea, Malaysia and Thailand were all still very poor countries. Since then they have all grown rapidly, but average living standards in these countries are still well below the average living standards in the major industrialised countries. Similarly, the relatively low growth in the industrialised countries in recent years occurred off very high levels. The wealthier a country becomes, the more difficult it is to continue growing rapidly. If you do not follow this argument, you should review Box 1-3 at the end of Chapter 1.

Unemployment and employment

The decline in economic growth in South Africa contributed to an increase in unemployment. As mentioned in Section 4.4, unemployment is particularly difficult to measure. In South Africa this problem was aggravated by an almost deliberate tendency to underestimate unemployment among black workers during the apartheid era. As a result most economists regarded official estimates of total unemployment in South Africa as unreliable. In the 1990s, the official measurement of unemployment became more reli-

TABLE 5-3 Economic growth in various countries, 1960–2005

	Average annual percentage growth in real GDP				
Country	*1960–1969*	*1970–1979*	*1980–1989*	*1990–1999*	*2000–2005*
Japan	10,0	5,1	5,2	1,7	1,9
United Kingdom	3,1	2,4	2,4	2,1	2,7
United States	4,4	3,2	2,7	3,0	2,7
Korea	7,7	9,3	8,0	6,1	5,2
Malaysia	n/a	7,9	5,7	7,1	5,2
Thailand	8,3	7,3	7,2	5,1	5,0
Argentina	3,1	3,1	–1,0	4,0	1,5
Brazil	9,1	7,9	3,0	2,3	2,5
Chile	4,5	1,6	3,5	6,4	4,4
Kenya	5,7	6,4	4,6	2,2	4,2
Zambia	5,5	1,2	1,4	1,0*	n/a
Zimbabwe	n/a	2,5	4,7	1,6	–5,9
South Africa	**5,9**	**3,3**	**2,2**	**1,4**	**3,8**

Notes: n/a = not available; figure marked with an asterisk is for 1990–1997; Zimbabwe's last figure is for 2000–2004.
Source of basic data: International Monetary Fund, *International Financial Statistics Yearbook*, various issues

able. There is, however, no consensus on whether the strict or expanded definition should be used (see Chapter 22). In September 2006 the strict definition, which is currently regarded as the official definition, yielded an unemployment rate of 25,6 per cent, compared to the 37,3 per cent yielded by the expanded definition.

Unemployment is arguably the most important and vexing problem facing the South African economy. The unemployed suffer mental and physical hardship and unemployment poses a serious threat to social and political stability. For example, when unemployment increases, crime and social unrest also tend to increase. We examine unemployment in South Africa in more detail in Chapter 22.

It should be noted, however, that the increase in unemployment is not unique to South Africa. Unemployment has increased in many countries in recent years. Even in the industrial countries people have increasingly been replaced by machines in the manufacturing sector. The result has been an increase in production without an accompanying increase in employment. This phenomenon is often referred to as **jobless growth**.

Although employment, like unemployment, is difficult to measure, we have estimates of the number of people who are employed in a full-time capacity in the so-called formal sector of the South African economy. Table 5-4 indicates the employment in the major sectors of the economy in 2005. Note the large employment in the services (tertiary) sector.

Inflation

Table 5-5 shows what happened to inflation in South Africa from 1990 to 2006. The inflation rate is measured by the annual percentage change in the consumer price index (CPI). As indicated in the table, inflation in South Africa tended to decline during this period. After having been in double digits – but remarkably stable – between 1973 and 1992, the rate fell to below 10 per cent for the first time since 1973 in 1993 and subsequently the trend was downwards until the end of the decade. It then remained fairly steady until increasing sharply in 2002 in the wake of a sharp depreciation of the rand against the major international currencies. Subsequently the rate declined significantly again.

TABLE 5-4 Employment in the main non-agricultural sectors of the South African economy, 2005

	Employment	
Sector	*Number*	*Percentage of total*
General government	1 505 000	21,2
Public business enterprises	99 000	1,4
Mining	444 000	6,2
Manufacturing	1 186 000	16,7
Construction	424 000	6,0
Trade	1 383 000	19,4
Financial institutions	1 503 000	21,1
Private sector (total)	5 507 000	77,4

Note: Only selected sectors are shown; private sector figures therefore do not add up to total of private sector.

Source: South African Reserve Bank, *Quarterly Bulletin*, March 2007

TABLE 5-5 Inflation in South Africa, 1990–2006

Year	*Annual percentage increase in CPI*
1990	14,3
1991	15,6
1992	13,7
1993	9,9
1994	8,8
1995	8,7
1996	7,3
1997	8,6
1998	6,9
1999	5,2
2000	5,4
2001	5,7
2002	9,2
2003	5,8
2004	1,4
2005	3,4
2006	4,7

Source: Statistics South Africa

Table 5-6 compares South Africa's inflation rate since 1960 with the inflation rates of our selected group of countries. As shown in the table, South Africa had a very low inflation rate during the 1960s. In the 1970s and 1980s inflation in South Africa escalated. Note, in particular, the difference between the figures for South Africa and for the industrial countries in the 1980s. Whereas South Africa's inflation rate had compared favourably with the inflation rates of all other countries in the 1960s, a large gap developed in the 1980s between inflation in South Africa and in countries like Japan and the United States.

Another significant feature of the table is the high inflation recorded in the three South American countries. These average figures do not tell the full story. In fact, annual inflation reached a mammoth 3 080 per cent in Argentina in 1989, 2 938 per cent in Brazil in 1990 and 505 per cent in Chile in 1974. Even higher annual figures were recorded in the 1980s in Bolivia

TABLE 5-6 Inflation in various countries, 1960–2005

	Average annual percentage increase in consumer prices				
Country	*1960–1969*	*1970–1979*	*1980–1989*	*1990–1999*	*2000–2005*
Japan	5,3	9,0	2,5	1,2	–0,5
United Kingdom	3,5	12,5	7,4	3,7	2,5
United States	2,3	7,1	5,5	3,0	2,7
Korea	15,7	15,1	8,1	5,7	3,1
Malaysia	0,7	5,4	3,6	3,7	1,7
Thailand	2,2	7,8	5,7	5,0	2,1
Argentina	22,7	106,5	319,2	58,6	8,2
Brazil	44,3	30,0	230,0	332,4	8,4
Chile	25,1	129,9	21,2	11,5	2,8
Kenya	1,8	10,8	11,6	16,5	8,2
Zambia	4,5	10,1	36,5	68,1	21,2
Zimbabwe	1,9*	7,2	12,7	28,1	87,7**
South Africa	**2,4**	**9,7**	**14,6**	**9,8**	**5,1**

Notes: *Figure pertains to 1965–1969; no earlier data available.
**Figure pertains to 2000–2002. Subsequently exploded.

Source of basic data: International Monetary Fund, *International Financial Statistics Yearbook*, various issues

(11 750 per cent in 1985), Nicaragua (10 205 per cent in 1988), Peru (3 399 per cent in 1989) and in Zimbabwe (over 4 000 per cent in mid-2007). When inflation reaches these levels, we call it **hyperinflation**. On the other hand, when inflation becomes negative (as in Japan and Argentina) it is called **deflation**.

Inflation is examined in greater detail in Chapter 21.

Balance of payments

The main elements of South Africa's annual balance of payments between 1990 and 2006 are summarised in Table 5-7. The first column shows the **balance on the current account**, that is, the difference between the exports and imports of goods, services and income. The second column shows the **balance on the financial account**, that is, the net inflow (denoted by a plus) or net outflow (denoted by a minus) of capital. The third column shows the **change in the country's net gold and other foreign reserves** after unrecorded transactions have been taken into account. This reflects the overall balance of payments position. The balance of payments is explained in more detail in Chapter 17.

One of the most important features of the South African economy between 1985 and 1993 was a significant and sustained net **outflow of capital**. The problem started in 1985 when South Africa could not meet its foreign debt commitments and had to reach agreement with its foreign creditors on the repayment of its foreign debt. During the following years these debt commitments, the weak economic performance, political unrest and uncertainty caused massive net outflows of capital. At the same time financial sanctions prevented significant inflows of capital. The average annual outflow between 1985 and 1993 was R5 334 million or 2,2 per cent of GDP. This was in stark contrast with the experience between 1946 and 1974 when South Africa experienced a net average annual **inflow** of foreign capital of 2,5 per cent of GDP.

When a country has to repay foreign debt and cannot borrow funds on the international financial markets, it has to maintain a surplus of exports over imports to offset the outflow of capital. This is exactly what South Africa had to do between 1985 and 1993. As shown in the first column of Table 5-7, the country had a surplus on the current account of its balance of payments during each of the years from 1990 to 1993. These surpluses largely offset the financial account deficits. As a result, the country's net gold and other foreign reserves, shown in the third column, did not always decline. In 1994, however, there was a dramatic change. A small current account surplus was recorded but there was again a net inflow of foreign capital. As a result, the country's net foreign reserves increased. The financial account surpluses in most of

TABLE 5-7 South Africa's balance of payments, 1990–2006

Year	Current account balance (R millions)	Financial account balance (R millions)	Change in net reserves (R millions)
1990	5 471	–1 501	3 552
1991	6 241	–2 543	4 137
1992	5 552	–1 491	564
1993	4 867	–5 669	8 913
1994	336	4 359	2 887
1995	–7 989	19 781	8 586
1996	–7 963	13 394	–5 103
1997	–10 231	27 049	10 827
1998	–13 100	17 300	–4 377
1999	–4 156	19 379	11 816
2000	–1 192	1 909	5 366
2001	2 869	–23 247	–12 237
2002	9 679	3 853	16 080
2003	–13 660	–14 503	–4 858
2004	–44 631	45 781	37 528
2005	–58 384	68 395	34 263
2006	–111 082	101 203	29 792

Note: The sum of the current account balance and the financial account balance does not add up to the change in net reserves. The difference is the result of unrecorded transactions and (to a lesser extent) the capital transfer account.

Source: South African Reserve Bank, *Quarterly Bulletin*, various issues

the subsequent years can be ascribed to the abolition of financial sanctions and South Africa's subsequent re-entry into the international capital market.

As we explain at the end of this chapter, balance of payments developments have always had a significant impact on South Africa's economic fortunes.

Personal income distribution

South Africa has a highly skewed distribution of personal or household income. As mentioned in Chapter 4, income distributions are difficult to measure and are therefore not estimated regularly. Moreover, the estimates are subject to a significant margin of error. In some countries the distribution of income among individuals or households has never been estimated, while in other countries such estimates are made only infrequently. Nevertheless, it is widely accepted that South Africa has one of the most unequal distributions of personal income in the world. In South Africa the Gini coefficient (which was explained in Section 4.7) has been estimated to be as high as 0,68. This is one of the highest Gini coefficients ever estimated in the world. Estimates for the industrial countries tend to vary between about 0,30 and 0,45, and for developing countries the estimates generally vary between about 0,40 and 0,60. Clearly, South Africa's figure is very high. Gini coefficients for the countries included in the earlier tables are given in Table 5-8.

South Africa's personal income distribution has traditionally followed racial lines, with whites earning the most, followed by Asians, coloureds and blacks. In recent years, however, the gaps between the different races have tended to become smaller. At the same time the distribution within the black group has become much more unequal. This can be ascribed to the increasing unemployment, the relatively fast rate of increase in the wages of blacks employed in the formal sector of the economy and increased poverty in the rural areas as a result of the impact of severe droughts, floods and other natural disasters. Gini coefficients for the different population groups in 2000 have been estimated as 0,57 (blacks), 0,51 (coloureds), 0,50 (Asians) and 0,45 (whites).[1]

TABLE 5-8 Gini coefficients for various countries

Country	Year	Estimate of Gini coefficient
Japan	1993	0,25
United Kingdom	1999	0,36
United States	2000	0,41
Korea	1998	0,32
Malaysia	1997	0,49
Thailand	2002	0,42
Argentina	2003	0,53
Brazil	2003	0,58
Chile	2000	0,57
Kenya	1997	0,43
Zambia	2002	0,42
Zimbabwe	1995	0,50
South Africa	**2000**	**0,58**

Source: World Bank, *World Development Report 2006*

Functional distribution of income

As explained in Chapter 2, the functional distribution of income refers to the income received by the various factors of production, that is, rent (natural resources), wages and salaries (labour), interest (capital) and profit (entrepreneurship). Unfortunately no aggregate data for the various types of income are available in South Africa. The only available data pertain to the distribution between the compensation of employees (ie wages, salaries and other employment benefits) and the so-called gross operating surplus (which includes rent, interest and profit). Together these two comprise gross value added (or GDP) at factor cost.

1. Du Toit, J. 2002. *The structure of the South African economy.* Rivonia: Absa Group, 17.

Their relative shares tend to vary with the growth of the economy. When GDP grows relatively rapidly, the share of compensation of employees tends to fall as the gross operating surplus increases (because of increased profits). The opposite occurs when GDP is stagnating or declining. Between 1994 and 2006 the share of compensation of employees varied between 49,4 per cent (2006) and 56,3 per cent (1998).

Geographical distribution of economic activity

As in other countries, there is an unequal distribution of economic activity (and income and wealth) between the various provinces, regions and cities in South Africa. On a provincial basis, Gauteng, KwaZulu-Natal and the Western Cape contribute by far the largest share of South African GDP. As far as metropolitan areas are concerned, Johannesburg, Cape Town, Durban, Pretoria and the East Rand together contribute more than 50 per cent of GDP. In recent years, however, certain other regions and some of the poorest provinces have grown relatively rapidly (even if sometimes off a very low base). Two regions that have grown fast in recent years are Nelspruit (in Mpumalanga) and Rustenburg (in Northwest Province). One of the main determinants of growth in the Nelspruit area was the increased spending by Mozambicans, while Rustenburg's growth was a spin-off of the boom in platinum prices and production.

As in the case of the distribution of income, the geographical distribution of economic activity in South Africa also has strong racial and political overtones, having been linked to successive apartheid policies of bantustans, homelands and self-governing states. Not surprisingly, therefore, the highest poverty rates are in areas which were self-governing or "independent" homelands (eg in the Eastern Cape, Limpopo and KwaZulu-Natal). A similar phenomenon occurs in the urban areas where, for example, the average income in Randburg and Sandton is much greater than that in Soweto. The disparities between rural and urban areas and even more between the metropolitan areas and the rest of the country have given rise to large-scale movements of people to the more developed and dynamic urban areas. This process is, of course, not unique to South Africa, but it was suppressed and significantly delayed during the apartheid era.

Summary

The South African economy performed badly from 1990 to 1993. During this period the country experienced negative economic growth, falling average living standards, high and rising unemployment, serious balance of payments problems and high inflation. After the political reform in 1994, the country's economic performance improved significantly.

5.3 South Africa's international economic position

In the previous section we compared South Africa's economic growth and inflation **rates** with those of some other countries. In this section we look at the **levels** of certain economic and social indicators in relation to the levels in other countries. The general conclusions are that South Africa is neither a particularly rich nor a particularly poor country and that while the level of economic development is fairly high, the level of social development still leaves much to be desired. The low level of social development can be linked to the high degree of inequality and widespread poverty in the country.

International organisations such as the World Bank and the United Nations regularly rank the different countries in the world on the basis of certain criteria. For example, each year the World Bank ranks its member countries according to their real GNI per capita in US dollars and in so-called international dollars, both adjusted for differences in purchasing power. These countries are then classified into four groups: low-income countries, lower-middle-income countries, upper-middle-income countries and high-income countries. South Africa tends to be either at the top of the lower-middle-income group or at the bottom of the upper-middle-income category. On the basis of the World Bank's classification South Africa can therefore perhaps appropriately be described as a middle-middle-income country!

Further perspective on South Africa's position can be gained from Table 5-9 which shows the rankings of some other countries with which you may be familiar.

Although these rankings are subject to a significant margin of error, they do give some indication of the relative levels of economic development in different countries.

In the African context South Africa is an economic giant. Table 5-10 shows how the South African economy compares with other Southern African countries. Note the huge difference between the South African GDP and the GDP of the other countries in the table. Also note that Botswana had a relatively high per capita income in 2004. Botswana has a small population and the economy is largely based on its rich diamond mining industry. The result is that the average income per head of the population is quite high.

It is disconcerting that South Africa's **social indicators**, such as births, deaths and life expectancy, compare quite badly with those of other middle-income countries. This is shown in Table 5-11, which includes some of the middle-income countries that are comparable with South Africa. With a few exceptions, South Africa's indicators are generally worse than those of the other countries in the table. Life expectancy is the lowest (due mainly to the prevalence of HIV/Aids), while the fertility, birth and infant mortality rates rank

TABLE 5-9 World Bank classification according to 2004 GNI per capita in adjusted US dollars

Low-income countries		*Lower-middle-income countries*	
Country	*GNI per capita ($)*	*Country*	*GNI per capita ($)*
Sierra Leone	550	Bolivia	2 600
Malawi	630	Egypt	4 200
Burundi	660	Morocco	4 250
Tanzania	670	Philippines	4 950
Congo, Dem Rep	680	China	5 890
Guinea-Bissau	690	Colombia	6 940
Congo, Republic	740	Namibia	7 520
Ethiopia	750	Thailand	7 930
Niger	780	Brazil	7 940
Upper-middle-income countries		*High-income countries*	
Country	*GNI per capita ($)*	*Country*	*GNI per capita ($)*
Botswana	9 580	New Zealand	22 260
Mexico	9 640	Germany	28 170
Russian Federation	9 680	Australia	29 340
Malaysia	9 720	France	29 460
Chile	10 610	Japan	29 810
South Africa	**10 960**	Netherlands	31 360
Mauritius	11 950	United Kingdom	31 430
Argentina	12 530	Switzerland	35 660
Poland	12 730	United States	39 820

Note: Adjustments based on World Bank Atlas method.
Source: World Bank, *World Development Indicators 2006*

among the highest for the group, indicating a poor level of social development. The government is making a determined effort to rectify this situation by, for example, trying to improve housing, health and education facilities and conditions in South Africa.

5.4 South Africa's factor endowment

South Africa, like other countries, is well endowed with certain factors of production and poorly endowed with others. This section provides a brief overview of South Africa's position in respect of the different factors of production: natural resources (or land), labour, capital and entrepreneurship.

Natural resources

One of the first features to consider when examining a country's resources is its **geographical location**. Situated at the southern end of the African continent, South Africa forms part of sub-Saharan Africa, the worst-performing economic region in the world. It is also isolated from the industrial countries and from the important international growth centres. The physical location of the country is therefore definitely a disadvantage.

The natural resources for **agriculture** are generally poor by world standards. Only about 13 per cent of South Africa's land surface is suitable for cultivation. Another major problem is the climate. Most of the country is arid or semi-arid with a low and variable rainfall. Other problems include severe winter frosts and hail damage in the summer rainfall areas and severe and prolonged droughts which often end in floods. As a result of the general lack of rainfall only a small percentage of the country is suitable for dryland crop production. In the rest of the country crops have to be grown under irrigation. On the positive side, the variety of climatic conditions allow farmers to grow almost every type of crop and to rear all types

TABLE 5-10 The economies of Southern Africa, 2004

Country	GDP in millions of US dollars	GNI per capita in PPP dollars*
Botswana	7 700	9 580
Lesotho	1 300	3 250
Malawi	2 000	630
Mozambique	5 300	1 170
Namibia	4 800	7 520
Tanzania	11 600	670
Zimbabwe	8 000	2 040
South Africa	**165 300**	**10 960**

Note: * PPP dollars calculated according to purchasing power parity (PPP).
Source: World Bank, *World Development Report 2006*

of livestock. South Africa can therefore produce a wide variety of agricultural products.

As far as **forestry** is concerned, South Africa has some beautiful natural forests that enhance the country's tourist potential. They are, however, of little commercial value, having been overexploited prior to World War II. For the rest there are a large number of commercial plantations which mainly produce pulp for making paper and board and timber for the mining industry.

South Africa has an extensive coastline with some of the finest beaches in the world. The sunny climate and the beaches are among the country's most important tourist attractions. It is also fairly well endowed with marine resources. The **fishing** industry is relatively small, however.

South Africa's primary natural asset is its exceptional **mineral wealth**. The country is blessed with a large variety of minerals. South Africa is the world's largest producer of a number of minerals and also has the largest known reserves of some minerals – see Table 5-12. Production and exports of minerals are, however, dominated by **gold**, **coal**, **diamonds** and **platinum group metals** (PGMs) – see Box 5-1. The contribution of the other minerals is also important but relatively small in comparison to the four most important ones. Minerals are non-renewable or exhaustible resources. South Africa cannot, therefore, base its economy on its mineral wealth forever. Other sectors of the economy must also be developed.

As mentioned earlier, South Africa is a beautiful country with a variety of attractions and a wonderful sunny climate for tourists. Its **natural tourist potential** is a resource which has not been exploited fully as yet.

On the negative side, South Africa does not have **navigable rivers** (which would have reduced transport costs significantly). It also has no significant **crude oil** reserves. **Natural gas** was found off the southern Cape coast in the 1980s and exploited by Mossgas, but this venture was based on strategic rather than economic considerations. Nevertheless, South Africa is fortunate to have massive coal resources which are used for the generation of **electricity** (by Eskom) and the production of **synthetic fuel** at the various Sasol plants. Its energy resources are supplemented by some hydroelectric power and a nuclear power plant at Koeberg near Cape Town.

Labour

The most important resource of any country is its people. Witness, for example, the economic success of Japan, South Korea and other East Asian countries which do not have abundant natural resources. In

TABLE 5-11 Social indicators in some middle-income developing countries, 2004

Country	Life expectancy at birth (years)	Total fertility rate	Crude birth rate (per 1 000 population)	Infant mortality rate (per 1 000 live births)
Argentina	75	2,3	18	16
Brazil	71	2,3	20	32
Chile	78	2,0	16	8
Korea	77	1,2	9	5
Malaysia	73	2,8	22	10
Poland	74	1,2	9	7
Thailand	71	1,9	16	18
Turkey	70	2,2	19	28
South Africa	**45**	**2,7**	**24**	**54**

Note: The total fertility rate represents the number of children that would be born to a woman if she were to live to the end of her childbearing years and bear children at each age in accordance with prevailing age-specific fertility rates.
Source: World Bank, *World Development Indicators 2006*

TABLE 5-12 Selected mineral resources of South Africa, 2003

Mineral	*Reserves*		*Production*	
	% of world reserves	*World ranking*	*% of world production*	*World ranking*
Platinum group metals	87,7	1	59,3	1
Manganese	80,0	1	14,8	1
Chrome	72,4	1	49,0	1
Vanadium	44,0	1	41,0	1
Gold	40,7	1	14,4	1
Vermiculite	40,0	2	41,3	1
Alumino-silicates	37,4	1	29,8	2
Titanium	29,8	2	n/a	n/a
Zirconium	19,4	2	n/a	n/a
Fluorspar	16,7	2	n/a	n/a
Uranium	9,6	4	2,1	10
Coal	3,7	7	4,7	5
Iron ore	0,9	11	3,5	7

Note: n/a = not available
Source: Department of Minerals and Energy

contrast, a number of African countries that are well endowed with natural resources have suffered economic stagnation or decline.

Recall from Chapter 2 that labour includes the **number** of people engaged in or available for the production of goods and services and their physical and intellectual **skills** and **effort**. Both the **quantity** and the **quality** of labour are thus important. South Africa has a fairly large population which is growing rapidly. The natural growth is supplemented by large inflows of migrant workers from neighbouring countries. The number of workers or potential workers is therefore not a problem. The main problem is a lack of skills.

South Africa's labour supply problems have been exacerbated in recent years by the prevalence and spread of HIV/Aids. It has been estimated that more than 3,5 million South Africans were HIV positive in 2000 and that this number would increase to 7,5 million in 2010. Apart from all its other effects, HIV/Aids is set to have a significant unfavourable impact on the supply of skilled and experienced workers and therefore also on the productive capacity of the South African economy.

One of the greatest challenges facing the South African economy is to try to increase the supply of skilled labour. How can this be achieved? The answer lies in areas such as education, training and human development in general. In this regard it should be noted that South Africa's labour position has been adversely affected by racial discrimination in the provision of education and training and by job reservation during the apartheid era. Things have changed, but unfortunately it takes time to improve the situation through education and training. In the meantime South Africa is still faced with a surplus of unskilled labour and a shortage of skilled labour, particularly when the economy grows. In the short run the lack of skills can be alleviated through immigration but in the long run the quality of the South African labour force must be improved.

Capital

Recall from Chapter 2 that capital as a factor of production refers to all man-made assets that are used in the production of goods and services. This includes things such as machines, plant, buildings, roads, bridges and dams – all things that are not wanted for their own sake but which are required to produce other goods and services.

South Africa is a capital-poor country. Many capital goods, such as heavy or specialised machinery and equipment, cannot be manufactured locally on a profitable basis and therefore have to be imported. About 40 per cent of South African imports consist of capital goods. To pay for these goods, South Africa requires foreign exchange (eg dollars, pounds, yen and euro), which has often been in short supply. The large import component of capital has important implications for economic policy. When domestic demand expands, capital spending and imports increase, placing pressure on the exchange rate of the rand against other currencies (such as the US dollar and the Japanese yen). These relationships are explained in more

BOX 5-1 PLATINUM GROUP METALS: SOUTH AFRICA'S NEW GOLD

South African gold production reached a peak of 1002 tons in 1970 and subsequently declined to a level of 275 tons in 2006. During the 1980s the price of gold (in US dollars) declined from an annual average of $613,07 in 1980 to $381,54 in 1989. During the 1990s the gold price was initially fairly steady but by 1999 the average annual price had declined further, to $278,92. It stayed around that level in 2000 and 2001 before increasing to $310,16 in 2002. By 2006 it reached $604,46. Fortunately for South Africa, the fall in gold output and the volatility of the gold price were neutralised to a significant extent by a rise in the production and international prices of the platinum group metals (PGMs), namely platinum, palladium and rhodium. The following table contains data on the estimated international demand and supply of PGMs in 2006. Note South Africa's dominant position and the various uses of the metals.

Estimated demand and supply of platinum group metals, 2006

		Platinum ('000 oz)	Palladium ('000 oz)	Rhodium ('000 oz)
SUPPLY (by country)				
South Africa		5 290	2 905	690
Russia		880	3 900	95
North America		345	985	20
Other		270	270	19
Total supply		**6 785**	**8 060**	**824**
DEMAND (by application)				
Auto catalyst:	gross	4 195	4 015	868
	recovery	–855	–800	–170
Chemical		360	420	48
Dental		–	800	–
Electrical		425	1 065	9
Glass		390	–	60
Investment		–40	–	–
Jewellery		1 605	995	–
Petroleum		205	–	–
Other		490	140	22
Total demand		**6 775**	**6 635**	**837**
Movement in stocks (supply minus demand)		10	1 425	–13

Source: Johnson Matthey

detail at the end of this chapter, in Chapter 17 and in Part IV.

In the 1970s and 1980s the scarcity of capital in South Africa was exacerbated by an increase in the capital intensity of production. The **capital intensity of production** refers to the amount of capital required to produce each unit of output. The ratio between the country's capital stock and its annual output is called the average **capital-output ratio**. An increased capital intensity of production is thus reflected in an increase in the capital-output ratio. Another indication of capital intensity is the average **capital-labour ratio**, which is the stock of capital per worker. As shown in Table 5-13 both the capital-output ratio and the capital-labour ratio were significantly higher in 2006 than in 1970. However, both the capital-output ratio and the capital-labour ratio fell during the 1990s. The reason for this fall was the low rate of investment spending during this period. Additions to the capital stock were often lower than the increases in production and in the number of workers, with the result that the ratios tended to fall.

An increase in the capital intensity of production is a worrying trend. In a country where labour is plentiful and capital is scarce the appropriate trend would have been towards labour-intensive rather than capital-intensive production. An increase in capital intensity is, however, a complicated matter. For example, there are certain industries, like the chemical and engineering industries, which are capital intensive by nature. Even mining requires large capital outlays. South Africa also has to keep up with international technological developments in many industries to remain internationally competitive.

Table 5-14 indicates the composition of South Africa's stock of capital at the end of certain years between 1950 and 2006. Note that it reflects some of the structural changes in the South African economy discussed in Section 5.1 and shown in Table 5-1. For example, the share of agriculture, forestry and fishing decreased considerably while the share of the secondary sector (manufacturing and electricity, gas and water) increased significantly. In the tertiary sector the increase in the share of community, social and personal services until 1990 was quite significant. The increase in the share of mining and quarrying between 1980 and 1990 reflected a move towards more capital-intensive methods of mining.

TABLE 5-13 Indicators of capital intensity, 1970–2006

Year	*Average capital-output ratio*	*Average capital-labour ratio (R)*
1970	1,8	97 590
1975	2,1	127 875
1980	2,3	146 885
1985	2,6	147 163
1990	2,6	139 098
1995	2,6	129 288
2000	2,4	124 236
2006	2,1	124 593

Notes: Average capital-output ratio obtained by dividing real capital stock by real GDP at basic prices (both at constant 2000 prices); average capital-labour ratio obtained by dividing the real capital stock (at constant 2000 prices) by number of workers (mid-year estimates).

Source: South African Reserve Bank, *Quarterly Bulletin*, March 2007

A positive aspect of South Africa's capital stock is its infrastructure, particularly if we compare it with the standards of other developing countries. South Africa has a relatively sound physical infrastructure, with wide-reaching road, rail and air links and a sophisticated communications network. In addition it also has a highly developed financial infrastructure.

Entrepreneurship

As explained in Section 2.2, the entrepreneur is vital to economic growth and development. The entrepreneur is the person who identifies opportunities and

TABLE 5-14 Composition of fixed capital stock by kind of economic activity, selected years

Economic activity	*Percentage composition*					
	1950	*1970*	*1980*	*1990*	*2000*	*2006*
Agriculture, forestry and fishing	14,3	8,7	6,4	4,3	3,4	3,4
Mining and quarrying	5,2	6,3	6,7	8,9	8,1	7,3
Manufacturing	8,2	10,5	12,9	12,4	14,8	13,2
Electricity, gas and water	6,0	7,2	8,7	9,7	6,7	5,9
Construction (contractors)	0,4	0,6	0,8	0,6	0,5	0,8
Wholesale and retail trade, catering and accommodation	5,4	5,7	5,1	4,8	5,1	5,3
Transport, storage and communication	17,0	14,8	15,0	13,1	17,6	17,4
Finance, insurance, real estate and business services	25,4	22,8	20,1	21,3	22,8	23,7
Community, social and personal services	18,1	23,4	24,3	24,9	21,0	23,0
Total	**100,0**	**100,0**	**100,0**	**100,0**	**100,0**	**100,0**

Source: South African Reserve Bank, *Quarterly Bulletin*, various issues combines the other factors of production. The entrepreneur is the one who develops new ideas (or puts them into practice), who develops new markets, who takes risks in the pursuit of profit and who creates employment and income.

In the *South African Executive Report* of the *Global Entrepreneurship Monitor 2006*, published by the Graduate School of Business at the University of Cape Town, South Africa was placed 30th in a group of 42 participating countries as regards the level of overall entrepreneurial activity. Significantly, only 5,29 per cent of adult South Africans engaged in entrepreneurial activity, the second lowest rate of all the developing countries that participated in the study. Studies such as this one yield a wide array of data, but also demonstrate how difficult it is to define or measure entrepreneurship. The overall impression, nonetheless, is that South Africa is not particularly well endowed with entrepreneurship as defined in the previous paragraph. This is often regarded as one of the fundamental problems of the South African economy.

5.5 South Africa's links with the rest of the world

South Africa has an **open economy**, which means that the economy has strong links with other economies. Openness is usually measured either by the proportion of GDP that is exported, or the proportion of domestic spending (GDE) that is spent on imports, or both. Table 5-15 gives some indication of the openness of the South African economy in comparison to the other countries that have been used in most of the comparisons in this chapter.

Apart from their overall levels, the **composition** of South Africa's imports and exports is also important. South Africa's **exports** are dominated by mining products. Although the general economic importance of gold declined significantly from the early 1980s, gold exports still constituted 8,2 per cent of all merchandise exports in 2006. In 1980, an extraordinary year, the figure was as high as 51 per cent. The composition of merchandise exports and imports is summarised in Table 5-16.

The fact that South Africa still exports mainly mineral and other primary commodities and related manufactured goods means that the economy is very vulnerable to changes in demand and prices in the international commodity markets. For example, when the price of gold, platinum or diamonds falls, it has a strong impact on the value of South African exports and therefore also on the welfare of South Africans. Likewise, a fall in the demand for coal, iron ore, steel or manganese also has a significant impact on the domestic economy. As a mineral-exporting country, South Africa is faced with different problems and challenges than countries such as Japan, Korea and Taiwan whose economies are largely based on capital, labour and entrepreneurship.

South Africa's **imports** consist mainly of capital and intermediate goods. On average, capital goods and intermediate goods each constitute about 40 per cent of total merchandise imports. The rest consists of consumer goods. The importance of capital goods can also be seen in Table 5-16 which shows the high share of machinery and transport equipment in total mer-

TABLE 5-15 Measures of openness, South Africa and selected other countries, 2005

Country	*1* *Exports as % of GDP*	*2* *Imports as % of GDE*	*3* *Average of **1** and **2***
Japan	14,3	13,1	13,7
United Kingdom	26,4	29,0	27,7
United States	10,5	15,3	12,9
Korea	42,5	41,0	41,8
Malaysia	123,4	130,6	127,0
Thailand	73,7	74,1	73,9
Argentina	24,6	20,2	22,4
Brazil	16,8	13,0	14,9
Chile	41,8	36,6	39,2
Botswana	49,8	41,1	45,5
Kenya	26,7	33,8	30,3
Zimbabwe	24,7	29,4	27,1
South Africa	**27,5**	**28,1**	**27,8**

Source: International Monetary Fund, *International Financial Statistics*

TABLE 5-16 Composition of South Africa's merchandise exports and imports, 2006

Category	Exports (% of total)	Imports (% of total)
Agriculture	3,5	2,1
Mineral products (including oil)	14,6	19,3
Precious metals (including gold)	27,7	1,6
Base metals	17,5	4,9
Chemicals, plastics and rubber	7,4	11,2
Machinery and electrical equipment	10,0	26,3
Transport equipment	9,4	19,4
Textiles, clothing, leather and paper	3,4	6,1
Food, beverages and tobacco	3,3	2,4
Other	3,2	6,7
Total	**100,0**	**100,0**

Source: South African Revenue Service

chandise imports. The South African manufacturing sector is heavily dependent on imports. When the manufacturing sector grows, there is therefore a strong surge in imports. This often creates serious problems for policymakers. We shall return to this point shortly.

The direction of international trade

Most of South Africa's international trade is conducted with the major industrial countries. This is shown in Table 5-17 which indicates the most important destinations of South Africa's exports as well as the origin of the country's imports in 2005. The countries in the table have been ranked on the basis of the combined value of exports to and imports from each country.

From the table it is quite obvious that South Africa's strongest trade links are still with the major industrial countries. The rankings vary from year to year but Germany, the United States, the United Kingdom and Japan have generally been South Africa's most important **trading partners**. This means that South Africa's economic fortunes are closely linked to economic conditions in those countries.

The balance of payments constraint

The balance of payments was introduced in Section 4.6 and discussed again in Section 5.2. Recall that the balance of payments consists, *inter alia*, of a **current account** and a **financial account**. The current account reflects the imports and exports of goods, services and income, while the purely financial transactions between South Africa and the rest of the world are recorded in the financial account. Also recall that the overall balance of payments position is reflected in the **change in the country's gold and other foreign reserves**.

The balance of payments is often a crucial determinant of the level of economic activity and the direction of economic policy in South Africa. In order for the South African economy to grow, capital goods have to be imported. But these imports have to be paid for in the currencies of the exporting countries. To obtain these currencies, which we call **foreign exchange**, goods and services have to be exported. If the value of exports (X) is less than the value of imports (Z), the current account is in deficit. In principle, however, this deficit can be financed by a surplus on the financial account of the balance of payments. Such a surplus is achieved if there is a net inflow of capital into the country. This net inflow can be the result of a spontaneous inflow of foreign capital or of overseas borrowing by South African companies, banks or the government.

During the first thirty years after World War II, South Africa could generally afford to run deficits on the current account of the balance of payments. In other words, the country could afford to import more goods and services than it exported. This was made possible by a net inflow of capital to South Africa, that is, by a surplus on the financial account of the balance of payments.

TABLE 5-17 South Africa: major destinations of exports and origins of imports, 2005

Country	Exports to the country (R millions)	Imports from the country (R millions)
Germany	21 229	49 123
United States	31 155	37 306
Japan	32 783	23 656
United Kingdom	32 023	19 365
China	8 714	31 485
France	6 505	15 393
Saudi Arabia	1 916	19 397
Netherlands	14 907	5 420
Italy	7 391	10 342
Australia	9 008	7 325

Notes: Data are for merchandise exports and imports only.
The countries are ranked according to the total value of South Africa's trade (exports plus imports) with each country.

Source: South African Revenue Service

From 1976 onwards, however, increased political and economic instability meant that South Africa could no longer rely on net inflows of capital, and from 1985 to 1993 the country experienced large net outflows of capital. South Africa was also denied access to international capital markets. When there is a net outflow of capital (ie a deficit on the financial account of the balance of payments), this usually has to be balanced by a surplus on the current account. The latter implies that exports have to be greater than imports.

But how can this be achieved in a country like South Africa? Given the nature of the country's exports, there is relatively little that can be done to increase exports in the short run – the value of our exports depends largely on the demand for and prices of our mineral exports. These, in turn, depend on the state of the international commodity markets. To generate the required surplus of exports over imports, the authorities therefore have to take steps aimed at reducing imports. Since imports are linked to the level of domestic economic activity, the latter has to be reduced by applying restrictive policies. When this happens, we say that the authorities (and the economy) are subject to a balance of payments constraint. Although the authorities would like to stimulate economic activity, they are virtually forced to put a brake on economic expansion because of balance of payments considerations.

In 1994, however, South Africa regained access to the international capital markets. The country could again afford to run deficits on the current account of the balance of payments. The balance of payments constraint on economic activity and policy thus became less acute. This was one of the main reasons for the positive economic growth recorded from 1994 onwards.

We realise that you may not yet be able to understand the logic of this argument fully. It is so important, however, that we have included it in this early chapter. We shall return to the importance of the balance of payments in Parts III and IV.

IMPORTANT CONCEPTS

Primary sector	Unemployment	Social indicators	Foreign exchange
Secondary sector	Inflation	Capital-output ratio	Balance of payments constraint
Tertiary sector	Balance of payments	Capital-labour ratio	
Economic growth	Income distribution	Open economy	

REVIEW QUESTIONS

1. List the main strengths and weaknesses of the South African economy.
2. Discuss South Africa's economic links with the rest of the world.

6 The economist's analytical toolkit

Learning outcomes

Once you have studied this chapter you should be able to

- explain what a theory is
- describe the different ways in which a theory can be presented
- identify the main elements of a theory
- explain what equilibrium, comparative statics and *ceteris paribus* mean
- describe the main elements of a graph

Knowing how to simplify one's description of reality without neglecting anything essential is the most important part of the economist's art.

JAMES S DUESENBERRY

Economic science is but the working of common sense aided by appliances of organised analysis and general reasoning.

ALFRED MARSHALL

Say it in words, demonstrate it in graphs and tables, and if technical details are needed, place them in appendices or provide references.

IRVING FISHER

By now you should have gained some idea of the types of issue an economist is concerned with. We have introduced you to the central economic questions and the different economic systems that have been devised to solve these questions. We have also shown you how the main elements of the mixed economy are interrelated and how the performance of the economy can be measured, and we have outlined the major features of the South African economy.

Most of what you have encountered up to now can be regarded as **descriptive economics** – we have described many important features of economics and the economy. The time has now arrived to start **analysing** things. Much of the rest of this book will be concerned with **economic theory**.

Economic theory is not particularly difficult. On the contrary, much of the economic theory in this book is simply common sense. But it is **structured** common sense. To arrive at the correct conclusions you must "think straight", that is, you must argue in a logical, disciplined fashion. The problem with economics is that many of the issues are familiar to everyone. Economics is so mixed up with everyday life that people often think they know the answers to important questions without analysing them carefully or systematically. Without realising it, people often accumulate opinions, ideas, hearsay and half-truths which make "straight" thinking difficult.

In this chapter we introduce a number of concepts and tools required for straight thinking in economics. You will encounter them regularly in the rest of the book. We use some examples to explain and illustrate the essential ingredients of disciplined, clear thinking.

6.1 Theory and reality

Theory is not a popular word. Most people are not interested in theory. They want to deal with the real world, not with some theory about how the world is supposed to function. Students often complain that economics is too abstract or unrealistic. People often say: "That is all very well in theory, but it does not work that way in practice."

Everyone wants to deal with reality. But economic reality is very complex. Economists study human behaviour in a world in which virtually everything is related to everything else, and often in more than one way. To deal with this complex reality we have to simplify. We have to scale things down to manageable proportions by focusing on the essential elements only. This is what theory is all about.

Theory is not something that is reserved for economic textbooks. Theory is also not monopolised by economists. All scientists use theory all the time. Although they probably do not realise it, every citizen uses theory every day. Suppose an economist explains how prices are determined by the market forces of supply and demand and someone responds by saying it is fine in theory but that it does not work that way in practice. When asked how things actually work in practice, the person responds by saying that the shops charge whatever prices they want to charge. What the person is actually doing is offering an alternative theory about how prices are determined. Any explanation of how things work in practice is a theory.

Theory involves **simplification** or **abstraction**. No theory (in any science) captures every detail of the phenomenon being studied. A theory only captures details which are regarded as essential or crucial for analysing a particular problem. All theories are thus simplifications of, or abstractions from, reality. The aim is to make sense of an extremely complicated world by focusing on the most important factors, while allowing all the unimportant details to fade into the background.

Theorising is a **systematic** attempt to understand the world around us. It is thus a way of **organising** our thinking. Logical, structured, organised or clear thinking always involves simplification. Reality is just too complicated to allow us to think clearly about everything at once.

A theory is like a map – see Box 6-1. A map is a simplified version of reality – it is an abstraction which focuses on the essential information that the user needs in order to locate a certain place or address. The degree of abstraction depends on the purpose for which the map is to be used. For example, there are maps which show you how to get from Cape Town to Pretoria, but they will not show you how to get to the

BOX 6-1 THEORIES AND MAPS

In his inaugural lecture as Professor of Economics at the University of South Africa, Christopher Torr used the following analogy to explain the features of a good theory:

> A theory should be likened to a map. Like a theory, a map provides an unrealistic account of the world, if by unrealistic we mean that there is not a one-to-one correspondence between what appears on the map and what appears in that part of the world under consideration. The more realistic a map is, the less likely it will be of assistance. Imagine trying to find one's way around Pretoria with the aid of a map the size of several rugby fields. In the first place, the map would not fit into your car. In the second place, the profusion of detail would confuse you. A map the size of Pretoria would be of no assistance at all. Since theory is by definition unrealistic, a good theorist must know what to leave out of his analysis. Such a decision is at least as important as knowing what to leave in.
>
> Last year we received visitors from the Cape. My wife drew a map and I faxed it. I have kept a copy of this map for posterity. It is not only an account of what to do after passing Johannesburg. It is also a work of art, lovingly produced, and captures in vivid detail, most of the natural and synthetic objects that could conceivably be encountered between Johannesburg and Pretoria. By the time nightfall had arrived, our guests hadn't. As we drank our sundowners alone, I felt obliged to point out that (1) maps are by definition unrealistic, (2) a good map is a simple map and (3) the usefulness of a map is dictated as much by what it omits as by what it includes. By the time I had extended the analogy to theory, my wife had fallen asleep and our guests had arrived, having decided to turn back once they passed Cullinan.

University of South Africa (Unisa). You will need another map to show you how to get from Unisa to Mamelodi and yet another one to locate a specific street or house in Mamelodi. Each map will contain the features that are essential for the purpose of that particular map.

When different economic theories are examined in the rest of this book, you will see how the appropriate degree of abstraction depends on the purpose of the analysis. For example, we simplify much more when explaining the total demand for all goods and services in the economy than when we examine an individual household's demand for a particular product (say tomatoes). In explaining the total demand for goods and services we focus on the total income of all households in the economy. On the other hand, when examining an individual household's demand for tomatoes we focus on variables such as the price of tomatoes, the prices of related products and that particular household's income. **The main requirement (or secret) of good analysis or theorising is to identify the most important elements and relationships in the complex world that we need to explain, and to ignore the rest.** This way we will not be confused by irrelevant detail.

Theories are sometimes also called **models, laws, principles, explanations** or **hypotheses**. An **economic model** is a formal statement of a theory. It can be likened to a model aircraft or model car. It is much simpler and contains far less detail than the real thing. Just like engineers at Boeing or Toyota build and use models (nowadays usually computer models) to examine or predict how actual aircraft or cars will work, economists also build models of the economy. Theories, models, laws and hypotheses all refer to ideas or stories about how the world works. Economic theory has three main purposes:

- to **explain** (or understand) how different things are related in the complex real economic world
- to **predict** what will happen if something changes
- to serve as a basis for the formulation and analysis of decisions on economic **policy**

These three purposes are interrelated. We first have to explain before we can predict and we have to do both before we can start analysing or proposing economic policy measures. Prediction is not necessarily the same as forecasting. Forecasting refers to future outcomes in the real world. Prediction, however, refers primarily to "what if" questions. Economists want to determine **what** will happen **if** something changes. Forecasts and predictions that are based on economic theories are never completely accurate, but they are usually much better than those which are not based on economic theories or models.

One of the purposes of science is to increase our ability to control our environment. In economics this means that economic policy is important, but we can only formulate appropriate policy if we understand our environment. We thus need good economic theory which links explanation, prediction and policy. The emphasis on explanation, prediction and policy is a recurrent theme of the rest of this book.

6.2 Different ways of expressing a theory

Economic theory is an attempt to explain and analyse economic behaviour by isolating certain important relationships, patterns or regularities. It can be expressed in words, numbers, symbols and equations, or graphs. We use two simple examples to illustrate this point.

Any theory or relationship can be expressed in **words** (ie **verbally**). For example, we can say that there is a relationship between the size of the maize harvest and rainfall – as rainfall increases, the volume of maize production also increases. Similarly, we can say that there is a relationship between the total spending by households on consumer goods and services and their income – as households' income increases, their spending also increases.

The same relationships can also be expressed in numbers by using numerical **tables**, which are called **schedules**. For example, Table 6-1 contains hypothetical figures about a relationship between the size of the maize harvest and the annual rainfall. The higher the rainfall, the greater the number of tons of maize that are harvested. This is called a **positive** relationship since both variables move in the same direction.

TABLE 6-1 Annual rainfall and maize production

Annual rainfall in maize producing areas (mm)	*Annual maize production (millions of tons)*
200	5
300	7
400	9
500	11
600	13

Similarly, Table 6-2 contains hypothetical figures about a **positive** relationship between total household income and total spending on consumer goods and services by households.

A third, very useful way of expressing a theory or relationship is to use **symbols** and **equations**. This has three major advantages. Using symbols is an economical or **shorthand** way of expressing a relationship. By using the symbols m for maize production and r for rainfall we can simply write that $m = f(r)$.

TABLE 6-2 Total household income and total household spending on consumer goods and services

Total household income (R millions)	*Total household spending on consumer goods and services (R millions)*
90 000	82 500
110 000	97 500
132 000	114 000
158 000	133 500
185 000	153 750
216 000	177 000
251 000	203 250

This simply means that m (ie maize production) is a function of (or depends on) r (ie rainfall). This notation is explained and discussed more fully in the next section. Similarly, we can use the symbols C for household spending on consumer goods and services and Y for total household income and write that $C = f(Y)$.

The second important advantage of expressing theories or relationships as equations is that we can then **use the rules of algebra** (ie mathematics) to analyse the relationship. Those of you who have a mathematical background will immediately realise the advantage of expressing the relationships such as those in our examples as

$$m = 1 + \frac{1}{50}r$$

$$C = 15\,000 + \frac{3}{4}Y$$

In these equations, each symbol has a specific meaning. By expressing the relationships in this way it should be obvious that there is a positive relationship between m and r, as well as between C and Y.

The third major advantage of using equations is that a **large number of variables can be analysed** using the algebraic method. When there are only two variables involved (eg maize production and rainfall) it is still relatively easy to express the relationship in words and to derive certain conclusions from the basic relationship. But as soon as we allow for more variables and for the interaction between different sets of variables, matters become complicated and it is often very difficult (in fact almost impossible) to keep track of everything using words only. However, provided the basic elements of the theory are expressed correctly in algebraic terms, we can use the rules of mathematics to derive all the possible relationships between different variables or sets of variables.

The major drawback, however, is that many students do not have a basic background in mathematics. For that reason, we use very little mathematics in this book. We do use symbols as a form of shorthand but as far as the manipulation of equations is concerned, we never go beyond simple addition, subtraction, multiplication and division. Wherever possible, we also always present the alternative formulations of the theory concerned (ie in words, numbers or graphs).

The fourth possible way of presenting relationships or theories is by making use of **graphs**. This method is used extensively in economic analysis. It is an extremely useful method since it gives a visual indication of the major elements or relationships in any theory. As the Chinese proverb states, **one picture is worth a thousand words**. To be successful in the study of economics, you must be able to read or interpret graphs and to draw them. The basic rules are very simple but because they are so important we devote a special section of this chapter (Section 6.5) to the meaning, interpretation and use of graphs.

Although the graphical method is extremely useful, it has one potential drawback in that ordinary graphs have **only two dimensions**. This means that we can only use graphs to express the relationship between two variables. Two-dimensional pictures are nevertheless still very useful. As we have emphasised, the whole idea of theory is to simplify, that is, to identify and analyse the most important factors. This means that we usually focus on the relationship between two variables. Moreover, there are ways and means of incorporating the effects of all the other possible influences on a particular variable into our analysis. We shall see, for example, that certain things that we cannot see directly on a graph can be incorporated **indirectly** by means of the **intercept** or **position** of a particular graphed line or curve. This will become clearer when we use graphs to analyse particular economic issues.

6.3 Elements and types of functional relationship

The study of economics is essentially a search for relationships between different economic variables. In this section we take a closer look at different types of variable and functional relationship.

A **variable** is anything that can be measured and that can change. Examples include temperature, height, mass, distance, speed, rainfall and time. Economic examples include prices, wages, profit, interest rates, exchange rates, quantities bought and sold, production, income and employment. A variable is thus a quantity, magnitude or amount that can assume any of a set of values.

Economic theory involves the search for relationships between different economic variables. The purpose is to explain one variable in terms of other variables. When different variables are linked in a cause-effect relationship we call it a **functional rela-**

tionship. Functional relationships are often simply referred to as functions. A **function** is a statement of how one variable depends on one or more other variables. As indicated in Section 6.2, we express functional relationships by using the notation f( ). This notation is simply a shorthand for "depends on the things in brackets". For example, we write that

maize production = f(rainfall, soil quality, fertiliser, ...)

By this we mean that maize production depends on rainfall, soil quality and fertiliser. The three dots indicate that there may also be other variables which affect maize production. Cause-effect relationships rarely involve only two variables. Often there are a number of possible factors or variables which can affect the variable that we want to explain. We therefore always have to allow for this possibility. However, as we have emphasised, the secret of good theory is to focus on the most important variables and thus avoid being confused by relatively unimportant things.

The variable being explained is called the **dependent** variable and the variables on which it depends are called the **independent** or **explanatory** variables or **determinants**. Thus, if we wish to explain maize production, then maize production becomes the dependent variable, while rainfall, soil quality, fertiliser, etc are the independent or explanatory variables or determinants. Which variable is selected as the dependent variable is determined by the purpose of the theory. Any particular variable can be a dependent variable in one context and an independent variable in another context. For example, if we wish to explain the income of farmers in South Africa, then the volume of maize production will be one of the independent or explanatory variables or determinants.

In economic theory we also often refer to **autonomous** or **exogenous variables**. They are similar to independent or explanatory variables. The feature that they have in common is that they are used in a theory to explain other things but they are not themselves explained by the theory. For example, our theory uses rainfall to explain maize production but it does not explain rainfall. Meteorologists, on the other hand, will have theories to explain rainfall. In their theories rainfall thus becomes a **dependent** (also sometimes called an **endogenous**) variable, whereas it is an independent (or exogenous) variable in our example.

Broadly speaking, there are two types of functional relationship: direct (or positive) relationships and inverse (or negative) relationships. A **direct** or **positive relationship** means that the changes in the dependent and independent variables are in the **same direction**. If maize production increases when rainfall increases, there is a positive relationship between maize production and rainfall. An **inverse** or **negative** relationship means that the change in the dependent variable is in the **opposite direction** to the change in the independent variable. The statement that the quantity of apples demanded will fall if the price of apples increases is an example of an inverse or negative relationship between the quantity of apples demanded (dependent variable) and the price of apples (independent variable) – when the independent variable goes up, the dependent variable goes down, and when the independent variable goes down, the dependent variable goes up.

Functional relationships are often expressed as **equations**. An equation is a form of **equality** (which is quite simply a statement that something is equal to something else). There are two types of equality: **conditional equalities** or **equations** and **identical equalities** or **identities**. Pointing out the difference between the two may seem to be splitting hairs, but it is actually quite important. Confusion between equations and identities often results in faulty reasoning and incorrect conclusions.

An **identity** is an equality which is a definition and is therefore always true, while an equation is an equality which is only true for specific values of the variables concerned. Consider the following equality: $a^2 = a \times a$. This is simply the definition of a^2, and it is always true (ie for any value of a). It is thus an identity. Similarly, a statement that the money value of a number of apples is equal to the number of apples times the price of an apple is also an identity. But $a^2 = 16$ is not an identity. It is true only if $a = 4$ or -4, and it is therefore a conditional equality or **equation**.

All the national accounting definitions that were introduced in Chapter 4 are identities. The following are a few examples:

- GNI = GDP *minus* net primary income to the rest of the world
- Market prices = basic prices *plus* taxes on products *minus* subsidies on products
- GDE = $C + I + G$
- GDP = $C + I + G + X - Z$

All these national accounting relationships are **true by definition** and are therefore **identities**. Identities are often indicated by using a ≡ sign, instead of the usual = sign. For example, $a^2 \equiv a \times a$. We shall sometimes use this notation to emphasise that an equality is an identity.

Whereas identities are simply definitions, **equations** are the equalities which represent functional relationships, that is, theories about how the variables are related. As mentioned earlier, equations are conditional equalities which only hold for certain values of the variables concerned. There are two important types of equation in economics: **behavioural equations** and **equilibrium equations** (or equilibrium conditions). **Behavioural equations** reflect functional relationships or theories about the behaviour of individuals, groups or institutions in the economy. For example, if we express the relationship between consumption spending by households (*C*) and their total income (*Y*) as an equation (eg $C = 100 + \frac{3}{4}Y$), we have an example of a behavioural equation. It is an equation which expresses a view or theory about the behaviour of households. Most of the equations that you will encounter in the rest of the book are behavioural equations.

The other main type of equation is an **equilibrium condition** or **equation**, which indicates the equilibrium state of the variables concerned (ie it pinpoints the equilibrium position). Equilibrium equations are important equations which are used frequently in economic theories or models.

6.4 Equilibrium, comparative statics and *ceteris paribus*

In their attempts to identify and analyse the important relationships between variables in the economy, economists have to use a certain **method** or **approach**. Here they are at a disadvantage compared to most natural scientists (eg physicists or chemists) who can use controlled experiments and other laboratory methods to establish and analyse cause-effect relationships. For example, if a chemist wants to discover the reaction of chemical A with chemical B, he or she can take two identical and sterile test tubes with the same amount of B in both and then add a certain amount of A to one of the test tubes. The result in this tube is then compared to the unchanged tube and the difference can be ascribed to the reaction between A and B. If this experiment is repeated under the same conditions, the same result will be obtained. The chemist can also use the same method to determine the effects of varying the proportions of A and B.

This experimental method is generally not available to economists (or other social scientists) – see Box 6-2. The economist deals with the complex real world in which many things are changing all the time and in which outcomes depend on human decisions and reactions. For example, an economist who wishes to study the impact of changes in tax rates cannot get everyone in the economy to pause while income tax rates are raised by five percentage points to see what the effects of such a change will be. Nor can the economist obtain an answer by locking a number of people in a room and raising their income tax rates by five percentage points.

The economist has to employ other methods to understand, explain and predict economic phenomena. Two essential elements of the economist's toolkit are the concept of **equilibrium** and the *ceteris paribus* assumption. They are essential ingredients of **comparative statics** which is the most common method of economic analysis. The concepts equilibrium, comparative statics and *ceteris paribus* may all sound quite daunting but they are actually not so complicated.

Equilibrium

The concept of equilibrium plays a central role in economic theory. It represents a situation in which none of the participants has any incentive to change his or her behaviour – everyone is content to continue with things as they are. Equilibrium can also be described as a state of balance, that is, a state in which all opposing forces are balanced. A system is in equilibrium when the different forces offset each other so that

BOX 6-2 EXPERIMENTAL ECONOMICS

Some economists believe that controlled experiments are possible in economics. In fact, in 2002, Vernon Smith, a professor at George Mason University in Virginia in the United States and a leader in the development of **experimental economics**, was awarded the Nobel Prize for Economics for his work in this field. Although subject to criticism (eg that the experiments are not as clean and the inferences not as clear cut as in the physical sciences), Smith's work has yielded interesting results, for example, that market participants are not nearly as rational as conventional economic theory would have us believe. Smith shared the Nobel Prize with Daniel Kahneman, a psychologist from Princeton University, who has demonstrated how individuals systematically behave less rationally (or more illogically) than orthodox economists believe they do. The contributions by Smith and Kahneman prompted Joseph Stiglitz, himself a former Nobel Laureate, to emphasise how important it is to study people as they behave, not as we want them to behave. Only by understanding actual human behaviour can policymakers and their advisers hope to design policies that will help to improve the functioning of the economy.

Interestingly enough, Smith's experiments appear to suggest that people are more altruistic and less selfish than economists have assumed – except for one group: the economists themselves!

there is no net tendency for the system to change.

The meaning of equilibrium can be illustrated with the aid of the following analogy. A shopkeeper has two assistants. The shopkeeper wants to keep the shop open for six days a week. He also wants at least one assistant to help him on a Saturday. But the assistants want to work only five days a week and each wants at least two free weekends every month. The solution is fairly simple. Each assistant works every second Saturday but gets a day off during the week when he or she works on the Saturday. Here we have three participants who each have their own plans. These plans can, however, all be satisfied in the manner indicated, and the solution can be regarded as a state of equilibrium. This is essentially what equilibrium is all about. It is a situation in which all the plans under consideration are realised. No plans are frustrated and all opposing forces (eg the shopkeeper's need for assistance on weekends and the assistants' need for free weekends) are balanced.

If the assistant who is due to work on a given Saturday falls ill on the Friday, the equilibrium will be disturbed. The other assistant will have to change his or her plans. Once the first assistant has recovered, he or she will then have to work an additional Saturday to restore the balance. However, if one of the assistants resigns, or if a third assistant is hired, or if the shopkeeper wants to do business seven days a week, new solutions will have to be found. The new equilibrium position can then be compared to the original one to determine the impact of the change.

Equilibrium can also be explained with a physical example. Suppose you sit motionless on a swing. All the forces are balanced and there is no tendency for things to change. Then someone gives you a push. You start swinging to and fro. If you are not pushed again, your movements will become progressively smaller until you are motionless again. Equilibrium is thus restored and things will remain that way until the equilibrium is disturbed again.

In economic theory we examine all the forces at work in the particular situation that we are investigating and then formulate the conditions under which there will be equilibrium (ie a condition of balance in which all plans are realised or all opposing forces offset each other).

Statics and comparative statics

Equilibrium is a fundamental concept in economic analysis. The description of an equilibrium state is called **static analysis** (or simply **statics**). It is called "static" since it does not involve time or motion.

One of the underlying forces is then changed and a new equilibrium is described. We compare the new equilibrium with the original one and ascribe the difference to the change in the underlying force. This method of **comparing** two **static** equilibrium states to determine the effects of a change is called **comparative statics**.

Comparative statics does not involve time. An equilibrium state is a state of rest or balance that does not involve any time, action or change. It can be likened to a photograph. We then change one element of the static picture and describe the new equilibrium state. In other words, we take another photograph. The two equilibria (photographs) are then compared. This is what the method of comparative statics is all about. It is the method that is used most often by practising economists and also the method that is used in the economic theory or analysis in the rest of this book. As we proceed, you will get plenty of exercise in this method of analysis.

Ceteris paribus

It is all very well to construct a picture in which all forces are balanced or at rest and then change one element only and determine the results of such a change. **But how can we be sure that none of the other elements or forces will change**? Economists deal with this problem **by assuming that all the other factors or forces remain constant or unchanged**. This is the *ceteris paribus* assumption. *Ceteris paribus* is a Latin term which means "other things being equal." You will encounter this assumption from time to time in the rest of this book and in your future studies in economics. The *ceteris paribus* assumption may seem very implausible but it is in fact an absolutely essential (and probably the most useful) assumption in economic analysis.

To determine cause-effect relationships, or to predict the results of a change, we can only allow one thing to change at a time. This applies to all sciences, including the natural sciences. If a chemist adds two substances (say Y and Z) to another substance (say X), he or she cannot ascribe the result either to Y or to Z. To find out how each of Y and Z reacts with X, separate experiments have to be conducted to test the reaction between Y and X and between Z and X. Similarly, we can only allow for **one change at a time** in economic theory. We have to isolate the impact of each change that we want to investigate.

In the real world, of course, most things are changing all the time. In other words, the real world is never in equilibrium – see Box 6-3. But, as we have stressed in Section 6.1, theory is not a description of actual events. It is an attempt to understand how the real world works, and to reach such an understanding we have to use "unrealistic" concepts and methods such as equilibrium, *ceteris paribus* and comparative statics. These concepts and methods will become clearer once we start using them in the next chapter.

Once you have studied Chapters 7 and 8, you should study this chapter again to ensure that you understand the logic of economic theory. You should

BOX 6-3 EQUILIBRIUM AND THE REAL WORLD

Water, as you know, seeks its own level. In its equilibrium state the sea must therefore be flat and smooth. You therefore decide to go to the beach, where the waves are rolling in, to wait for equilibrium (ie for the surf to become absolutely smooth). While waiting, you grow old and die. That is also about how long you would have to wait for long-run equilibrium in the economy or in a particular market. Like the surf, the economy never reaches a stable equilibrium.

Equilibrium is not a description of something which exists in the real economic world. Nevertheless, the **concept** of equilibrium is an essential element of the economist's toolkit. Without it we cannot come to an understanding of how things work, or of what will happen if certain things change. Without the equilibrium concept we also cannot analyse the effects of economic policy.

repeat this exercise while studying Chapters 18 and 19. If you understand the meaning and basic methods of economic theory, then at least half the battle is won.

6.5 Reading and working with graphs

If you page through this book, or through any other economics textbook, you will come across a large number of graphs (or diagrams or figures). The aim of these graphs is to help you understand and visualise the operation of an economy and its parts.

We have already referred to the Chinese proverb which states that one picture is worth a thousand words. This saying is, however, only true if you are able to "read" (ie understand or interpret) the picture (or diagram). As a student of economics, you must also be able to draw a diagram or graph as you will often be asked to explain concepts or theories "with the aid of a diagram." The purpose of this section is to help you "read" and construct diagrams or graphs.

Graphs are used to

- illustrate economic facts and figures
- present an economic theory (or model) visually

In this book the emphasis is on the use of graphs in the visual representation of economic theory. To understand these graphs, you have to know how graphs are constructed. If you do not have a mathematical background, do not despair. The graphs in this book are all simple and easy to understand. By now you have already encountered some graphs, and you have probably interpreted them correctly. All you need in order to understand graphs and work with them, is some discipline, common sense and plenty of practice.

The axes

A graph is drawn in a two-dimensional space, called a coordinate space. The basic elements are two lines, one horizontal and the other vertical, labelled x and y respectively in Figure 6-1. The horizontal line is called the **horizontal axis** (or x **axis**) and the vertical line is called the **vertical axis** (or y **axis**). The y axis is drawn perpendicular (ie at a right angle) to the x axis, forming a **set of axes**. The two axes cross (or intersect) at zero (which is called the **origin**).

The horizontal axis (x axis) starts on the left-hand side at minus infinity and the values measured on the axis then increase (the negative values become smaller) up to zero. To the right of the origin the values become positive and increase as we move to the right. The vertical axis (y axis) is measured from the bottom to the top, the numbers increasing from minus (or negative) infinity at the bottom to plus (or positive) infinity at the top. Infinity is denoted by the symbol ∞.

The axes in Figure 6-1 divide the figure into four squares known as **quadrants**. Combinations of x and y, where the values of both are positive are shown in the first quadrant. Combinations of x and y, where the values of both are negative, are shown in the third quadrant. In the second quadrant the values for y are positive, those for x negative and in the fourth quadrant the values for y are negative and those for x positive. Because most economic data and variables are positive, **economists usually only work with the first quadrant**. This was the case, for example, with the production possibilities curves in Chapters 1 and 2. There are a few cases when economic data are negative. In those cases the fourth quadrant will also be employed. The second and third quadrants are rarely used in economics.

A graph like the one in Figure 6-1 can be drawn on graph paper where equal distances on the horizontal and vertical axes represent the same magnitudes, that is, each little square on the graph paper is equal to one unit (or any multiple or fraction of one) on both the horizontal and vertical axes. The scale of a graph, however, does not have to be drawn like this. The horizontal and vertical axes often represent different things and therefore have different scales, for example, as in Figure 1-1 in Chapter 1, which showed various production possibilities. The important point to

FIGURE 6-1 The basic elements of a graph

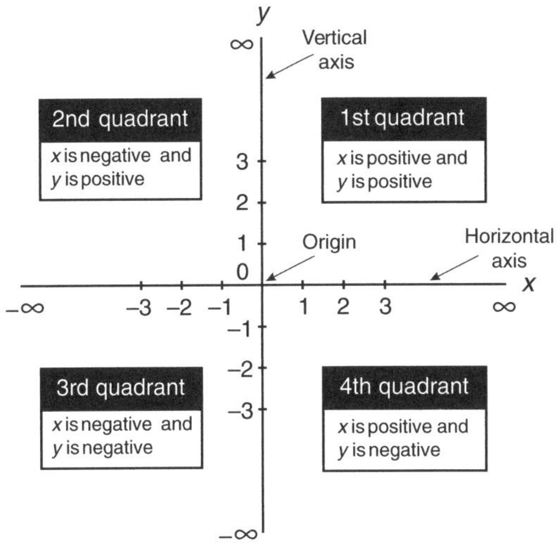

The horizontal (x) axis and the vertical (y) axis cross (or intersect) at zero (the origin). On the horizontal axis negative numbers are to the left of zero, positive numbers are to the right. On the vertical axis positive numbers are above zero, negative numbers are below. The two axes divide the area, which is called a coordinate space, into four quadrants.

note is that **once a scale has been decided on, that scale must be applied to the whole axis**. For example, in Figure 1-1 each segment on the vertical axis represents 20 kilograms of potatoes, and on the horizontal axis each segment represents one basket of fish. See also Figure 6-2, where the distance between every 100 millimetres of rainfall on the horizontal axis is the same, and the distance between every 1 million tons on the vertical axis is the same, but the two axes do not have the same scale.

Drawing a graph from a table

Now that we have explained the axes, we can proceed to the actual drawing of a graph that illustrates a functional relationship between two variables. We again use the example of the relationship between maize production (the dependent variable) and rainfall (the independent variable). In Table 6-1 we showed the following possible combinations of rainfall and maize production:

Rainfall (millimetres per year)	*Maize production (millions of tons per year)*
200	5
300	7
400	9
500	11
600	13

Maize production (m) depends on rainfall (r). In symbols this function can be expressed as $m = f(r)$ *ceteris paribus*, where m = annual maize production (in millions of tons) and r = annual rainfall (in millimetres). (As will be explained later, this specific functional relationship can be represented by the equation $m = 1 + \frac{1}{50} r$, where 1 is the intercept on the vertical axis and $\frac{1}{50}$ is the slope of the curve.)

From the information provided it is clear that there is a **direct** (or **positive**) **relationship** between rainfall and maize production. As rainfall (the independent variable) increases, maize production (the dependent variable) also increases, and as rainfall decreases, maize production also decreases. To plot this information, we use only the first (or positive) quadrant, where the values of both variables are positive – neither rainfall nor maize production can be negative. As mentioned earlier, most graphs in economics are confined to the first quadrant – the other quadrants are used in exceptional cases only. We plot maize production on the vertical axis and rainfall on the horizontal axis. This is in accordance with the general mathematical principle of plotting the dependent variable on

FIGURE 6-2 Plotting points on a graph

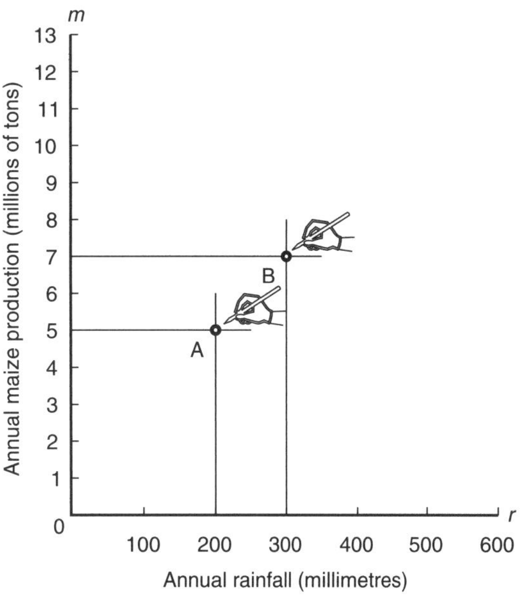

Maize production (m) is plotted on the vertical axis and rainfall (r) on the horizontal axis. On each axis there is a different, but consistent scale. Each point plotted represents a specific combination of rainfall and maize production. Point A indicates a combination of 200 millimetres of rainfall and 5 million tons of maize, while point B indicates a combination of 300 millimetres of rainfall and 7 million tons of maize.

the vertical axis and the independent variable on the horizontal axis. In economics, however, this convention is not always followed – see Box 6-4.

In Figure 6-2 we do not use the same scale on both axes, that is, the divisions on the two axes are not the same. We do this because the numbers of the two variables differ quite considerably – on the horizontal axis the numbers go up to 600 (millimetres), while the numbers on the vertical axis go up to 13 (million tons) only. Note, however, that **equal distances or segments on each axis must reflect equal quantities**. On the horizontal axis, the distance between 300 and 400 must be the same as the distance between 400 and 500. Similarly, on the vertical axis the distance between 7 and 9 must be the same as the distance between 9 and 11.

The next step is to plot the data. We illustrate this by using two of the combinations in the table. The first, which we call combination A, is the combination of 200 millimetres of rainfall and 5 million tons of maize. To plot this combination, we first go to 200 millimetres on the horizontal axis and draw a vertical line at that point. At each point along that line, rainfall r is equal to 200 millimetres. Similarly, we draw a horizontal line at a level of maize production of 5 million tons. At each point along this line, maize production m is equal to 5 million tons. At the point where these two lines intersect (and at that point only), rainfall is 200 millimetres *and* maize production is 5 million tons. This point, indicated by A in Figure 6-2, thus represents a combination of 200 millimetres of rainfall and 5 million tons of maize. We repeat this procedure for a combination of 300 millimetres of rainfall and 7 million tons of maize and label this point B. We have now used two of the combinations given, and we have found two points, A and B, in the first quadrant.

Having explained how different points are plotted, we can now proceed to the actual drawing of a line or curve. In Figure 6-3 we use all the information provided in the table to plot five combinations of rainfall and maize production. We then join these points to form a line or curve. In this particular example the points were specifically selected to represent a straight line.

FIGURE 6-3 A graphical presentation of the relationship between maize production and rainfall

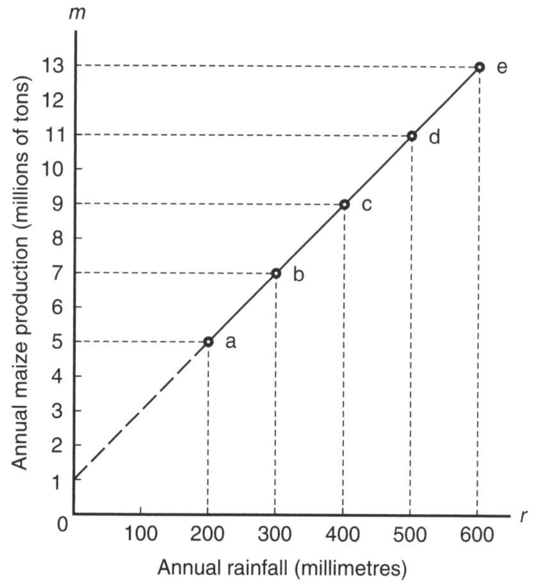

Points a to e represent the information in Table 6-1. These points are then joined to form a straight line which indicates the relationship between maize production and rainfall. If the line is extended, it intersects the vertical axis at a level of maize production of 1 million tons.

In practice, functional relationships between two variables can seldom be plotted as continuous, precisely straight lines. In economics, however, it is often quite plausible to represent functional relationships

BOX 6-4 PLOTTING DEPENDENT AND INDEPENDENT VARIABLES

In mathematics it is customary to indicate an independent variable by the symbol x and to indicate it on the horizontal axis. A dependent variable is indicated by the symbol y and is indicated on the vertical axis. In economics, however, this custom is not followed consistently. The main reason is that many economic variables are interdependent, as was indicated in Chapter 3. In microeconomics, for example, we want to explain how the price of a product is determined by the demand for and supply of the product. But the quantity demanded and the quantity supplied are both dependent on the price of the product. Since the ultimate aim is to determine the price, we always put it on the vertical axis, but when we examine the demand and supply curves individually this means that the independent variable (price) is on the vertical axis. In economics you always have to check which is the dependent and which is the independent variable – you cannot simply assume that the variable on the vertical axis is the dependent variable.

by straight lines. Such straight lines are called **linear** relationships. Most of the functional relationships in the rest of this book are assumed to be linear, but we sometimes also use **non-linear** (or **curvilinear**) relationships. Note that the line between the different points has been extended to intersect the vertical axis at a level of maize production of 1 million tons. This point where the line meets or intersects the vertical axis is called the **intercept** and will be referred to again later.

In any figure **the origin, the axes and the lines, curves or functions must be labelled clearly, otherwise no one will be able to read or interpret the picture**.

Relationships between economic variables

Figure 6-3 illustrates a **direct** (or **positive**) linear **relationship** between two variables. There are many such relationships in economics. There are, however, also many **inverse** (or **negative**) **relationships** between economic variables. An inverse relationship means that the value of the dependent variable increases when the value of the independent variable decreases, or that the value of the dependent variable decreases when the value of the independent variable increases.

Some of the possible relationships between economic variables are summarised in Figure 6-4.

Figure 6-4(a) shows a direct (positive) linear relationship (AA) between y and x. An example of such a relationship in microeconomics is the relationship between the quantity of a product supplied and the price of the product. This is called a supply curve and it is examined in Part II of this book. A macroeconomic example is the relationship between total spending and total income in the economy, which is examined in Chapters 18 and 19.

Figure 6-4(b) shows a direct (positive) non-linear relationship (BB) between y and x. An economic example is the increasing part of a firm's marginal cost curve, which is examined in Chapter 11.

Figure 6-4(c) shows an inverse (negative) linear relationship (CC) between y and x. A microeconomic example of such a curve is the relationship between the quantity demanded of a good or service and the price of that good or service. This is called a demand curve and it is examined in Part II of this book. A macroeconomic example is the relationship between investment spending and the interest rate, which is explained in Chapter 18 and used in Chapter 20.

Figure 6-4(d) shows an inverse (negative) non-linear relationship (DD) between y and x. An economic example is the decreasing part of the marginal product of a factor of production, which is examined in Chapter 11.

In Chapters 18 and 19 we frequently want to draw a line which indicates all the possible points where the value of the variable on the vertical axis (y) is equal to the value of the variable on the horizontal axis (x). In mathematical terms this means that we want to plot the function or equation $y = x$. If the same scale is used on both axes, this function is represented graphically by a line which goes through the origin and is equidistant from both axes, as in Figure 6-5. Since this line is at an angle of 45 degrees to both the axes, it is usually referred to as "the 45-degree line". Note, however, that this result only holds when the line starts at the origin and both axes are drawn to exactly the same scale.

FIGURE 6-4 Some possible relationships in economics

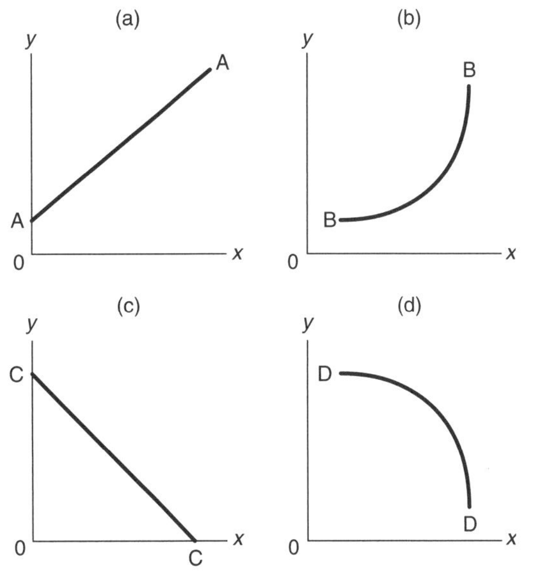

AA in (a) shows a direct (positive) linear relationship between y and x, while BB in (b) shows a direct, non-linear (or curvilinear) relationship between the two variables. CC in (c) shows an inverse (negative) linear relationship between y and x and DD in (d) shows an inverse, non-linear (or curvilinear) relationship between the two variables.

Plotting a graph from an equation

In Figure 6-3 we drew (or plotted) a graph from information provided in a table. In Section 6.2 we said that information about a functional relationship contained in a table can also be represented by an equation. Instead of using a table, we can plot a graph directly from the corresponding equation. Any straight line can be represented by the general equation $y = a + bx$, where y is the dependent variable, x the independent variable, a the y intercept (usually the vertical intercept) and b the slope of the line. The equation representing the relationship between maize production and rainfall in Table 6-1 is given by $m = 1 + \frac{1}{50} r$,

FIGURE 6-5 The 45-degree line

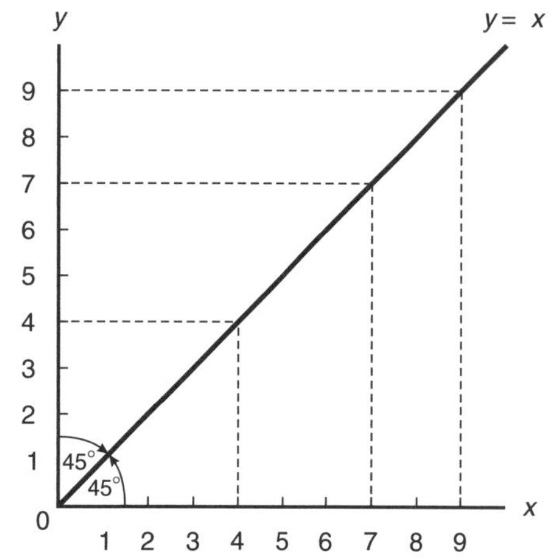

The figure illustrates a function of the type y = x. Both axes are drawn to the same scale. At each point on the curve the value of y is equal to the value of x. This curve forms a 45-degree angle with each of the axes.

where m = annual maize production (in millions of tons) and r = annual rainfall (in millimetres). The intercept is 1 (million tons) and the slope is $\frac{1}{50}$. To confirm that the equation is correct, we can substitute rainfall levels from the table into the equation and calculate the corresponding levels of maize production. For example, when $r = 200$, then $m = 1 + \frac{1}{50}(200) = 1 + 4 = 5$; when $r = 300$, then $m = 1 + \frac{1}{50}(300) = 1 + 6 = 7$, and so on. Using the equation we thus obtain the same curve as in Figure 6-3.

One of the advantages of using the equation of a linear relationship between two variables is that the equation contains information about the **intercept** and the **slope** of the function.

■ THE INTERCEPT

The intercept of a graph or curve is the point at which it crosses (or intersects) one of the axes. The y intercept is obtained by setting the value of x equal to zero (because $x = 0$ along the y axis). Similarly, the x intercept is obtained by setting the value of y equal to zero (because $y = 0$ along the x axis). For example, with $m = 1 + \frac{1}{50}r$ we obtain the intercept on the m-axis by setting $r = 0$. With $r = 0$ the last term falls away (since $\frac{1}{50}(0) = 0$) and we are left with $m = 1$. In Figure 6-3 we see that this is the point where the curve intersects the m axis. What does this tell us? The fact that the m intercept is equal to one means that one million tons of maize will be produced even if there is no rainfall. Some maize may, for example, be grown under irrigation, while the natural moisture in the soil may also yield some maize.

■ THE SLOPE

The second important element of an equation of a linear relationship between two variables is the slope. The **slope** of a function, curve or graph indicates the response of one variable to changes in the other variable. In everyday language the slope of a curve reflects the **relative steepness** or **flatness** of the curve.

The slope of a linear function is defined as the ratio between the change in the variable on the vertical (y) axis and the corresponding change in the value of the variable on the horizontal (x) axis. Thus:

$$\text{Slope} = \frac{\text{change in } y \text{ values (ie on vertical axis)}}{\text{change in corresponding } x \text{ values (ie on horizontal axis)}}$$

Alternatively it can also be expressed as:

$$\frac{\text{vertical difference}}{\text{horizontal difference}}$$

In our example of maize production and rainfall we can use the difference between any two points to obtain the slope of the curve. Consider points a and b in Figure 6-3. As we move from a to b, annual rainfall increases from 200 to 300 millimetres and annual maize production increases from 5 to 7 million tons. Applying the definition of a slope we obtain the following:

$$\begin{aligned}\text{slope} &= \frac{\text{difference in values on vertical axis}}{\text{difference in values on horizontal axis}}\\ &= \frac{\text{change in maize production}}{\text{change in rainfall}}\\ &= \frac{7-5}{300-200}\\ &= \frac{2}{100}\\ &= \frac{1}{50}\end{aligned}$$

The same result could have been obtained by using points A and B in Figure 6-2. In Figure 6-2 the difference in m (which we indicate by Δm) is 2 and the difference in r (which we indicate by Δr) is 100. (The symbol Δ is the Greek capital letter delta which is often used to indicate a change in a variable or a difference between two values.) Thus

$$\begin{aligned}\text{slope} &= \frac{\Delta m}{\Delta r}\\ &= \frac{2}{100}\\ &= \frac{1}{50} \quad \text{(as before)}\end{aligned}$$

Note also that $\frac{1}{50}$ occurs in the equation of the function. This is no accident. The linear function $m = 1 + \frac{1}{50} r$ indicates both the intercept (1) and the slope ($\frac{1}{50}$) of the curve.

Linear functions are represented by the general equation

y = a + bx
where a = intercept on the y axis (ie when $x = 0$)
and b = slope (ie the number of units by which y will change if x changes by one unit)

All that is required to plot a linear function is information about the intercept and the slope of the function, and both these pieces of information are contained in the equation of the function. We now use two further examples to illustrate the intercept and the slope of linear functions.

■ EXAMPLES

In Figure 6-6 we show both a direct (positive) linear relationship (in [a]) and an inverse (negative) linear relationship (in [b]). They are similar to the relationships illustrated in Figure 6-4(a) and Figure 6-4(c) respectively.

Figure 6-6(a) shows a direct (positive) relationship, which is similar to the supply curve which we introduce in Chapter 7. Figure 6-6(b) shows an inverse (negative) relationship which is similar to the demand curve, which we also introduce in Chapter 7.

The equations of the two curves are $y = 4 + \frac{1}{2}x$ and $y = 10 - 2x$ respectively. The first term on the right-hand side of each equation indicates the y intercept of each curve, that is, 4 and 10 respectively. These are the values of y when $x = 0$. The coefficients of x indicate the slopes of the two curves, namely $\frac{1}{2}$ and -2 respectively. The two slopes can be illustrated by considering what happens to y when x changes from 2 to 4. This is indicated by the movement from A to B in the two graphs. In (a) we see that y increases by 1 (from 5 to 6) and in (b) it decreases by 4 (from 6 to 2). The slope is given by the change in y (ie Δy) divided by the change in x (ie Δx).

The slope is often simplified as the **rise** (ie the change on the vertical axis) over the **run** (ie the change on the horizontal axis). In Figure 6-6(a) this yields a result of $\frac{1}{2}$ and in Figure 6-6(b) the result is $-\frac{4}{2} = -2$. This minus sign indicates that the change in y (the rise) is in the opposite direction to the change in x (the run). A straight line has a constant slope that can be calculated between any two points on the line. You can check this by considering the difference in the y and x values between any two other points along the curves.

In economic theory we are interested in the direction of functional relationships, in other words we want to know whether the dependent variable changes in the same direction as changes in the independent vari-

FIGURE 6-6 Examples of intercepts and slopes

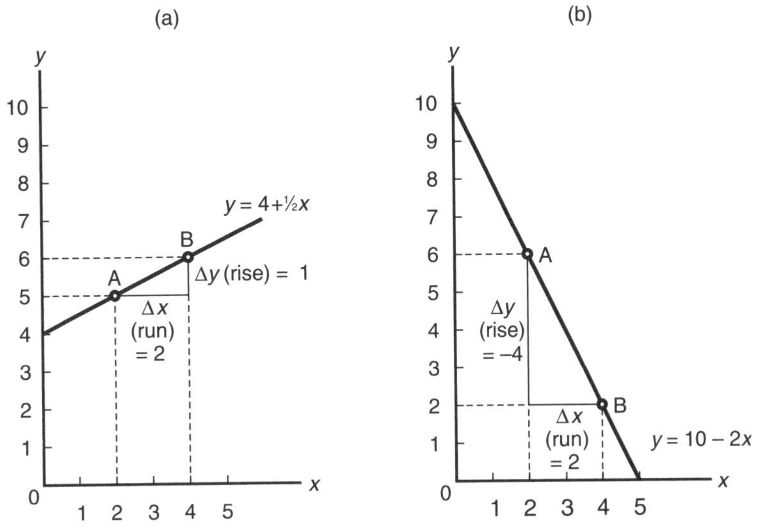

The functional relationship in (a) is a direct or positive one, represented by the equation y = 4 + ½x. Its y intercept is 4 and its slope is ½. The functional relationship in (b) is an inverse or negative one, represented by the equation y = 10 – 2x. Its y intercept is 10 and its slope is –2. The two functions are similar respectively to the supply curve and the demand curve introduced in the next chapter.

able, or whether it changes in the opposite direction to changes in the independent variable. When the function is illustrated graphically, we can immediately see whether there is a direct or an inverse relationship between the variables. In economic theory we also want to determine or show by how much the dependent variable changes when the independent variable changes. This is illustrated by the **slope** (ie the relative steepness or flatness) of the curve. Note, however, that the steepness or flatness of a curve can be changed by changing the scale (or measuring units) on one of the axes (or both). The apparent steepness or flatness of a curve may therefore be misleading. That is why we refer to the **relative** steepness or flatness – the only true comparisons are the differences between two curves drawn to exactly the same scale and using the same measuring units.

Concluding remarks

In this chapter we introduced various essential items in the economist's toolkit. In the next chapter we start using these tools to analyse the economy. In the process of doing this, the meaning and significance of the concepts introduced in this chapter should become even clearer. If you experience problems while studying Chapter 7, you should refer back to this chapter. Economic theory and its application require a proper understanding of the basic tools of economic analysis.

IMPORTANT CONCEPTS

Abstraction
Economic model
Schedules
Equations
Graphs
Variables
Functional relationships (or functions)
Dependent and independent variables
Direct (positive) relationships
Inverse (negative) relationships
Equations and identities
Behavioural equations
Equilibrium equations
Equilibrium
Statics and comparative statics
Ceteris paribus
Horizontal and vertical axes
Quadrant
Linear relationships
Non-linear (curvilinear) relationships
45-degree line
Intercept
Slope

REVIEW QUESTIONS

1. "Theories should contain as much detail about actual events as possible." Do you agree? Explain.
2. In reality many things change at the same time. Why then do economists often assume that "all other things are constant"?
3. What type of relationship (positive or negative) would you expect between the following?
   (a) the price of music videos and the sales of music videos
   (b) the sales of toothbrushes and the sales of toothpaste
   (c) the price of maize and the production of maize
4. What is the special feature of a 45-degree line?
5. Explain the three main purposes of economic theory.
6. Explain the difference between:
   (a) dependent and independent variables
   (b) endogenous and exogenous variables
   (c) equations and identities
   (d) behavioural equations and equilibrium equations

(e) statics and comparative statics
(f) a direct relationship and an inverse relationship between two variables

7. How would you explain to a friend or family member the Latin phrase *ceteris paribus* and its use in economic theory?

8. What does the term "equilibrium" mean in economic analysis?

9. Use an example to illustrate the intercept and the slope of a linear function and relate these concepts to the general equation that represents a linear function.

PART II

Microeconomics

In this part of the book we analyse the goods market and the labour market by examining the decisions of households and firms. In Chapter 7 we look at households' demand for consumer goods and services, and we then analyse firms' supply of these goods and services. We also examine equilibrium in goods markets.

Chapter 8 focuses on changes in equilibrium, while Chapter 9 deals with the responsiveness of the quantity demanded to price changes, which is called the price elasticity of demand. Other elasticity concepts are also introduced. This is followed, in Chapter 10, by an examination of consumer behaviour.

The next three chapters in this part of the book focus on the behaviour of firms. We introduce various production and cost concepts in Chapter 11, followed by an examination of the behaviour of profit-maximising firms under different competitive conditions. In Chapter 12 we deal with perfect competition, and in Chapter 13 we look at the behaviour of firms under conditions of monopoly and imperfect competition. Chapter 14 focuses on the labour market, which is the most important factor market in the economy.

Once you have studied this part of the book you should be able to

- show how prices and quantities exchanged are determined by demand and supply
- analyse changes in demand and supply
- explain the meaning and significance of the price elasticity of demand
- explain the utility approach to consumer equilibrium
- use indifference curves to derive a demand curve
- explain the various production and cost concepts
- derive the equilibrium of the firm under conditions of perfect competition
- analyse the position of the firm under conditions of monopoly and imperfect competition
- explain the supply of and demand for labour

7 Demand, supply and prices

Learning outcomes

Once you have studied this chapter you should be able to

- identify the most important determinants of the quantity demanded
- show how demand can be expressed in words, numbers, graphs and equations
- explain the difference between demand and quantity demanded
- differentiate between a movement along a demand curve and a shift of a demand curve
- explain the determinants of the quantity supplied
- distinguish between a movement along a supply curve and a shift of a supply curve
- explain how the equilibrium price and quantity are determined
- distinguish between the consumer surplus and the producer surplus

You can make even a parrot into a learned economist – all it has to learn are the words "supply" and "demand".

ANONYMOUS

A very poor man may be said in some sense to have a demand for a coach [a horse-drawn carriage] ... he might like to have it; but his demand is not an effectual demand.

ADAM SMITH

Economics and economists are often associated with demand and supply. In 1872 Thomas Carlyle described economics as the science "which finds the secret of this Universe in 'supply and demand'." Although something of an exaggeration, demand and supply are indeed among the most important (and useful) tools in the economist's toolkit.

In Chapter 3 we introduced the circular flow of income and spending in the economy and showed where the goods market and the factor market fit into the overall picture. In this chapter, and in the rest of Part II, we focus on the **goods market**, by analysing individual markets for goods and services. Figuratively speaking, we put the goods market under the microscope and examine the behaviour of households (as purchasers of consumer goods and services) and firms (as suppliers of these goods and services). The households are the driving force behind the demand for consumer goods and services, whereas the firms are the driving force behind the supply of goods and services.

We start with a brief overview of supply and demand. We then explain an **individual household's demand** for goods and services. This is followed by an examination of **market demand**. We also explain the important distinction between a **movement along a curve** and a **shift of a curve**. This is followed by a similar analysis of an **individual firm's supply** and **market supply**. Market demand and market supply are combined to obtain the **equilibrium price** and **quantity** of a product, and the concepts of **consumer surplus** and **producer surplus** are introduced.

The analysis of demand and supply is probably your first encounter with economic theory. We therefore proceed systematically and fairly slowly in this chapter. The study of demand and supply yields important results. It also illustrates the basic elements of systematic, clear thinking in economic theory. It is important to follow the method and the logic of each argument, since they establish the pattern for most of the reasoning in the rest of this book. If you master the way of thinking set out in this chapter, most of the other economic theories in this book should be fairly easy to follow. In fact, in many cases the same tools are used to analyse a variety of issues. We start with a brief overview of demand and supply.

7.1 Demand and supply: an introductory overview

In Chapter 3 we explained how households and firms interact. Households own factors of production (natural resources, labour, capital and entrepreneurship). They sell these factors to firms in the factor markets and receive rent (natural resources), wages and salaries (labour), interest (capital) and profit (entrepreneurship). Firms combine these factors of production to produce goods and services that are sold in the goods markets to households who use the income (derived from selling their factors of production) to purchase the goods and services.

In this and the next six chapters (ie up to Chapter 13) we focus on the goods markets. In these markets, firms are the suppliers and households the consumers who demand the goods and services concerned. In a market economy, the prices and quantities traded in the goods markets are determined by the interaction of demand and supply.

The links between households and firms are illustrated in Figure 7-1, which is an adaptation of the basic circular flow illustrated in Figure 3-3.

Demand and supply are often likened to the two blades of a pair of scissors that interact to determine the equilibrium price and equilibrium quantity in the market. In the next two sections we take a closer look at demand (Section 7.2) and supply (Section 7.3). In other words, we examine each blade separately before putting them together again.

FIGURE 7-1 The interaction between households and firms

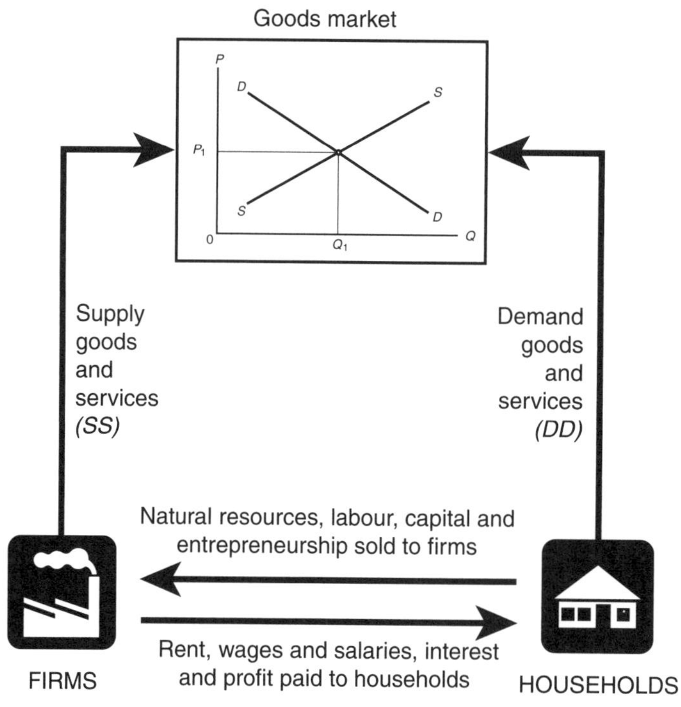

Households sell their factors of production to firms. Firms use these factors to produce goods and services that are sold in the goods markets to households who use their income to buy the goods and services. In the goods markets firms thus determine the supply (SS), while households determine the demand (DD). The interaction of supply and demand determines the price (P_1) and quantity (Q_1) of each good or service.

7.2 Demand

Demand is the outcome of decisions about which wants to satisfy, given the available means. If you demand something (in the economic sense), it means that you **intend** to buy it **and** that you **have the means** (ie the purchasing power) to do so. In other words, when we talk about demand we are referring to the **quantities of a good or service that the potential buyers are willing and able to buy**.

As mentioned in Section 1.1, demand should not be confused with **wants**. Wants are the unlimited desires or wishes that people have for goods and services. How many times have you seen something you wanted, and thought, "if only I could afford it"? The basic fact of economic life is that only some of our wants can be satisfied. There are simply not enough means to satisfy them all. Demand is only **effective** if the consumer is able and willing to pay for the good or service concerned.

You should also not confuse demand with **needs** or **claims**. We often hear or read that workers in a particular firm or industry **"demand"** or **claim** a certain increase in their wages. Such "demands" are requests (often supported by the threat of action) for certain wants or needs to be satisfied.

Demand is a **flow** concept which is measured over a period (recall the distinction we made between stocks and flows in Section 3.1). We should always specify the period concerned (eg day, week, month or year). For example, if you demand three litres of milk at the usual price, your demand might be regarded as large, average or small, depending on whether it refers to a day, a week or a month. We should therefore always specify the time dimension, but it can be quite cumbersome to do so all the time. In the analysis which follows we do not always indicate the time dimension explicitly. We frequently refer simply to quantities rather than (more correctly) to quantities per period (day, week, month, quarter, year). We do this to keep the analysis as simple and uncluttered as possible. You should always remember, however, that concepts such as demand, supply, production, output, income and expenditure are all **flow variables** that are measured over a period rather than at a particular time.

Demand refers to the quantities of a good or service that prospective buyers are willing and able to purchase during a certain period. It relates to the **plans** of households, firms and other participants in the economy, not to events that have already occurred.[1] The fact that demand is concerned with plans means that the quantity demanded may differ from the quantity actually bought. The quantity bought or exchanged will depend on the availability of the good or service in question. The quantity demanded may be less than, equal to or greater than the quantity actually bought.

1. Economists often use the Latin terms *ex ante* to refer to plans and *ex post* to refer to events that have already occurred.

Like many economic concepts, demand can be expressed in **words**, **schedules** (or numbers), **curves** (or graphs) and **equations** (or symbols). In this chapter we use all four of these ways to examine the demand for goods and services. We deal only with the market for consumer goods and services, which we refer to simply as the **goods market**.

Because we are dealing with **microeconomics**, we focus on the demand for particular goods and services. We first examine the demand of an individual consumer or household for a particular good or service, and then we look at the market demand. The total (or aggregate) demand for all goods and services in the economy is examined in Part IV, which focuses on macroeconomics.

Individual demand

To illustrate the determinants and properties of individual demand, we consider the demand for tomatoes of an imaginary consumer, Anne Smith. Anne is a single parent with two school-going children.

What determines the quantity of tomatoes that Anne plans to purchase in a particular period, say one week?

- **The price of the product**. The lower the price of tomatoes, the larger the number of tomatoes Anne will be willing and able to buy, *ceteris paribus*.
- **The prices of related products**. Anne's decision about how many tomatoes to purchase will also depend on the prices of related products. Here we have to distinguish between complements and substitutes. **Complements** are goods that are used jointly. In the case of tomatoes, complements include bread (for tomato sandwiches), onions (for tomato salad or tomato and onion stew) and lettuce (for a salad). **Substitutes** are goods which can be used instead of the good in question. Tomatoes can be replaced by, for example, beans (in a stew) or avocados or other ingredients (in a salad). The relationship between the demand for a particular good and the prices of its complements and substitutes is examined more fully later. For the time being it is sufficient to note that the prices of related goods also affect Anne's decision about how many tomatoes she plans to buy.
- **The income of the consumer**. Anne's plans will also be affected by her income, in this case her weekly income. Anne's income determines her purchasing power, that is, her ability to purchase tomatoes. The higher her income, the more tomatoes she can afford (and plan) to buy.
- **The taste (or preference) of the consumer**. Anne's decision will also be influenced by her taste (as well as her children's tastes). The more she

likes tomatoes or dishes which require tomatoes as an ingredient, the more tomatoes she will plan to buy. On the other hand, she might not like them or she may be under doctor's orders not to eat them (because of their high acidity). All these non-measurable influences on consumers' decisions are usually lumped together under "taste" (or "preference"). Taste can have a positive or a negative impact on the quantity demanded.

- **The size of the household.** In our example Anne has two children. She will therefore tend to buy more tomatoes than a household consisting of one person, but fewer than a larger household.

One of the things that does **not** determine Anne's demand is **the availability** or **supply** of tomatoes. When asked to identify the factors which determine the quantities of goods demanded (ie the **determinants** of demand), many people instinctively put availability or supply at (or near) the top of their lists. The confusion probably arises because most people realise that tomatoes will be expensive when they are in short supply. Anne's demand decision is, however, **independent of the supply situation**. She bases her plans on the information she has available. In particular, she considers the price of tomatoes without knowing or worrying about how the price is determined. If tomatoes are in short supply, the price will be high and Anne will take the higher price into consideration.

Tomatoes may not be available in the market. When this happens, she will not be able to satisfy her demand for tomatoes, that is, she will not be able to purchase the quantity that she plans to buy. The availability of tomatoes can therefore affect the **actual outcome** in the market. Anne's plans (ie her demand), however, are unaffected. This is a very important point. As we emphasised in Chapter 6, much of economic theory is simply common sense, but it is **structured**, **disciplined** or **logical** common sense. To arrive at the correct conclusions, you must always consider very carefully what you are dealing with. You must always be careful not to confuse different issues (eg demand and supply decisions).

We have now identified the most important determinants of Anne's demand for tomatoes. We can state that the quantity of tomatoes demanded weekly by Anne Smith (ie the quantity that she plans to purchase every week) is determined by the price of tomatoes, the prices of related goods, her weekly income, her taste (including her children's tastes) and the size of her household.

More generally:

The quantity of a good demanded by an individual (or household) in a particular period depends on (or is a function of) the price of the good, the prices of related goods, the income of the individual (or household), taste, the number of people in the household and any other possible influence.

This is a verbal statement of the determinants of individual demand. As mentioned in Chapter 6, all economic theory can be stated in **words**. But words are sometimes quite cumbersome. They can also become very confusing. We therefore often use **symbols** as a shortcut or shorthand method of expressing economic theories.

Let Q_d = quantity of tomatoes demanded in a particular period
P_x = price of tomatoes
P_g = prices of related goods
Y = household's income during the period
T = taste of the consumer(s) concerned
N = number of people in household concerned
... = allowance for other possible influences

Given these symbols, we can express the individual's demand for tomatoes as follows:

$$Q_d = f(P_x, P_g, Y, T, N, \ldots) \quad \text{(7-1)}$$

Equation 7-1 is simply a shorthand way of stating what we said earlier. Although much simpler than the long sentence used earlier, Equation 7-1 might seem quite complicated. It contains no fewer than six variables. One **dependent variable** (Q_d) is expressed as a function of five **independent variables** (P_x, P_g, Y, T, N). Although this is a useful starting point, we need to make things simpler. Recall, from the previous chapter, that the whole purpose of theory is to understand things by reducing the details to the barest minimum. We must concentrate on the most important determinants. We do not ignore or abandon the other determinants – we simply focus on the ones that have the largest impact or which are crucial to the rest of our analysis, and we keep the remaining ones constant.

The most important determinant of the quantity demanded of a particular good is probably its **price**. In terms of Equation 7-1, the focus is on the relationship between Q_d and P_x. This relationship is so important that it has been accorded the status of a "law". The **law of demand** states:

Other things being equal (ie *ceteris paribus*), the higher the price of a good, the lower is the quantity demanded.

The relationship between quantity demanded and price can be illustrated in various ways. One possibility is to use a demand schedule. A **demand schedule** is a table which lists the quantities demanded at different prices when **all other influences on planned purchases are held constant**. Table 7-1 is an example of a demand schedule. In the table we show the various quantities of tomatoes that Anne Smith plans to purchase weekly at different prices, on the assumption that all the other determinants (P_g, Y, T, N) remain constant. For example, if the price is R1,00 per kilogram, she plans to purchase six kilograms per week. This is labelled possibility *a*. If the price is R4,00, she plans to purchase three kilograms per week (possibility *d*), and so on.

TABLE 7-1 Anne Smith's demand schedule for tomatoes

Possibility	*Price of tomatoes (R/kg)*	*Quantity demanded (kg per week)*
a	1	6
b	2	5
c	3	4
d	4	3
e	5	2

The information in the demand schedule can also be illustrated graphically by drawing a **demand curve**. Figure 7-2 contains the demand curve that corresponds to the information in Table 7-1. The points on the demand curve correspond to the different possibilities indicated in the demand schedule. (The fact that we join these points to form a continuous curve implies that other, intermediate prices and quantities, such as a price of R1,50 and a quantity of 5,5 kilograms, are also possible.)

Since this is the first graph in this part of the book, we examine it in detail to check whether you have mastered the art of drawing and reading graphs, as explained in Section 6.5. From now on we shall use graphs frequently. It is important, therefore, to ensure that you read the graphs correctly and that you can draw them. If you have any problems with Figure 7-2, first study Section 6.5 again. Graphs or diagrams are particularly useful for expressing the essentials of economic theories. They are also quite simple to understand, provided you follow the basic rules for drawing and interpreting them.

The basis of any diagram is the axes. In Figure 7-2 the price of tomatoes (in rand per kilogram) is shown on the vertical axis, while the quantity of tomatoes demanded (in kilograms per week) is shown on the horizontal axis.[2] Each point in the diagram represents a particular combination of the price of tomatoes and the quantity demanded. For example, point *a* shows that six kilograms of tomatoes will be demanded if the price is R1 per kilogram.

Similarly, point *b* shows that five kilograms are demanded at a price of R2 per kilogram, and so on. By

2. Note that the independent variable is on the vertical axis and the dependent variable on the horizontal axis.

FIGURE 7-2 Anne Smith's weekly demand for tomatoes

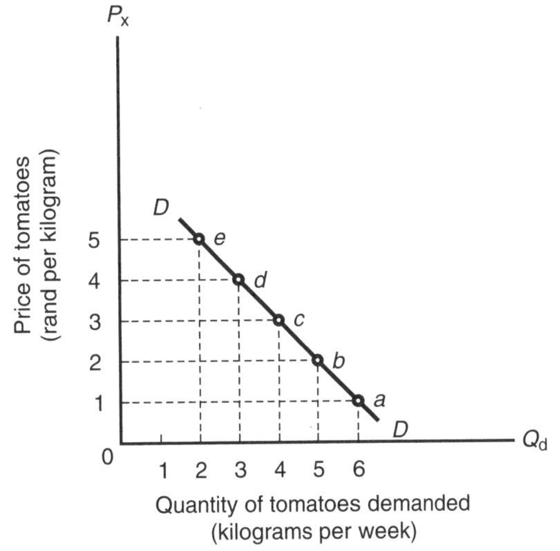

Each point indicates the quantity of tomatoes demanded at that price. By joining the points we obtain the demand curve DD. The demand curve indicates the relationship between the quantity of tomatoes demanded weekly and the price of tomatoes, on the assumption that all other things remain equal.

plotting all these points from the demand schedule and joining them we obtain a **demand curve**, *DD*, which slopes down from top left to bottom right. This indicates a **negative** or **inverse relationship** between the price and the quantity demanded. The higher the price, the smaller the quantity of tomatoes demanded. As we have already mentioned, this inverse (or negative) relationship between price and quantity demanded is called **the law of demand**.

The demand curve is a simple and useful way of indicating the relationship between the quantity demanded and the price of a good or service, on the assumption that **all other determinants are constant** (ie *ceteris paribus*).

Let us now return to Equation 7-1 which states that

$$Q_d = f(P_x, P_g, Y, T, N, \ldots)$$

When we focus on the relationship between Q_d and P_x, as in the demand schedule of Table 7-1 and the demand curve of Figure 7-2, we are assuming that P_g, Y, T and N do not change. We do not ignore or abandon these (or any other) determinants of the quantity demanded. We simply **assume that they do not change**. To indicate this, we rewrite Equation 7-1 as

$$Q_d = f(P_x, \bar{P}_g, \bar{Y}, \bar{T}, \bar{N} \ldots) \quad \text{(7-2)}$$

where the bars above P_g, Y, T and N indicate that these variables or determinants are held constant.

Equation 7-2 is usually abbreviated to

$$Q_d = f(P_x) \textit{ ceteris paribus} \quad \text{(7-3)}$$

which also indicates that all the other determinants are held constant (or assumed to be constant). (Remember that *ceteris paribus* is the Latin term for "all other things being equal". It can be abbreviated as *cet par.*)

No variable in economics can be explained by only one other variable. All economic relationships are similar to Equation 7-1. But since we always want to focus on the relationship between a dependent variable (which we want to explain) and a particular independent variable (or determinant), all relationships are expressed (and used) in the form indicated by Equations 7-2 and 7-3. In other words, we **always** use the ***ceteris paribus*** condition. To keep things simple, we do not always state this condition or assumption explicitly. In other words, we often simply write $Q_d = f(P_x)$. You must remember, however, that such expressions are based on the **assumption that all other things remain constant**. As we proceed, we shall slip in a *ceteris paribus* now and then to remind you of this fact.

Later in this chapter, we examine what happens if any of the other determinants do change. In the meantime, we recap on the various ways in which individual demand and the law of demand can be expressed:

- **Using words. Demand** refers to the **entire relationship** between the quantity demanded and the price of a good or service, on the assumption that all other influences are held constant. The law of demand states that this is an inverse or negative relationship. The higher the price of the good, the lower the quantity demanded, *ceteris paribus.*
- **Using numbers: the demand schedule**. The demand schedule is a table which shows the quantities of a good demanded at each possible price, *ceteris paribus*. Table 7-1 is an example of a demand schedule. The figures in the table indicate that the quantity demanded decreases as the price increases. The **entire demand schedule** in Table 7-1 represents Anne Smith's **demand** for tomatoes.
- **Using graphs: the demand curve**. The demand curve is a line which indicates the quantity demanded of a good at each price, *ceteris paribus*. Figure 7-2 contains an example of a demand curve. The negative slope of the curve clearly indicates that the quantity demanded increases as the price decreases. This is a visual representation of demand. The **entire demand curve** in Figure 7-2 represents Anne Smith's **demand** for tomatoes.
- **Using symbols: the demand equation**. The demand equation is a shorthand way of expressing the relationship between the quantity of a good demanded and its price, *ceteris paribus*. Equations 7-2 and 7-3 are both demand equations:

$$Q_d = f(P_x, \bar{P}_g, \bar{Y}, \bar{T}, \bar{N}, \ldots) \quad \text{(7-2)}$$

$$Q_d = f(P_x) \textit{ ceteris paribus} \quad \text{(7-3)}$$

These equations (which are actually two ways of expressing the same thing) are often reduced to $Q_d = f(P_x)$, since the *ceteris paribus* assumption is usually taken for granted in economics. The equations above both represent Anne Smith's **demand** for tomatoes. They do not explicitly indicate the fact that there is an inverse relationship between quantity demanded and price. To do this, we have to formulate a more precise equation. This is done in Appendix 7-1, where demand and supply are analysed algebraically.

Market demand

The individual demand curve is one of the most important building blocks of microeconomic theory. But firms are interested in the total (or market) demand for the goods and services that they supply, rather than in the demand of a particular individual or household. In a market system the plans of **all** the consumers and producers of a good or service have to be taken into account.

To move from individual demand to market demand is quite straightforward. Market demand is simply the sum of all the individual demands. Suppose there are only three prospective buyers of tomatoes in a particular market: Anne Smith, Helen Rantho and Purvi Bhana. To obtain the **market demand schedule**, the three individual demand schedules are simply added together. This is shown in Table 7-2, where the market demand is obtained by adding the individual quantities demanded horizontally at each price.[3]

Similarly, the **market demand curve** can be obtained by adding the individual demand curves horizontally (ie at each price). This is shown in Figure 7-3 which shows the individual demand curves of Anne (A), Helen (H) and Purvi (P) and the market demand curve (*DD*). The market demand curve can, of course, also be obtained by plotting the market demand schedule (ie by plotting the quantities in the last column of Table 7-2 against the relevant prices in the first column).

The market demand curve shows the relationship between the price of tomatoes and the quantity demanded in the market (by all the consumers) during a particular period (in this case a week), again on the assumption that all other factors remain unchanged. Like the individual demand curve, the market demand curve also slopes downwards from

3. Note that we assume here that the three demand schedules are independent of each other. This is not always the case. A consumer's decisions are sometimes affected by what other consumers do.

TABLE 7-2 Deriving the market demand schedule from individual demand schedules

Price of tomatoes (R/kg)	*Kilograms of tomatoes demanded weekly by*			*Total quantity demanded per week (kg)*
	Anne	*Helen*	*Purvi*	
1	6	4	5	15
2	5	3	4	12
3	4	2	3	9
4	3	1	2	6
5	2	0	1	3

left to right. In other words, it also shows an inverse or negative relationship between the price of tomatoes and the quantity demanded, *ceteris paribus*.

What determines the quantity of tomatoes demanded in the market at each price? Since market demand is derived from individual demand, it follows that the same factors which determine the individual quantities demanded also determine the total quantities demanded in the market. In symbols we can therefore write

$$Q_d = f(P_x, \bar{P}_g, \bar{Y}, \bar{T}, \bar{N}, \ldots) \quad (7\text{-}4)$$

where Q_d = quantity of tomatoes demanded in the market

P_x = price of tomatoes

P_g = prices of related goods

Y = total income of all prospective purchasers of tomatoes

T = tastes of all prospective purchasers of tomatoes

N = total number of potential consumers of tomatoes (ie the total population in the market area concerned)

… = allowance for any other possible influences on the quantity of tomatoes demanded in the market

The market demand curve has the same characteristics as the individual demand curve. The only difference, of course, is that we are now dealing with all the prospective buyers of tomatoes in a particular market, not just one. The total income of all the prospective buyers, the tastes of all of them and the total number of people served by the market therefore have to be taken into account. We also explicitly provide for other factors which may influence the demand for tomatoes. These include things like expected future prices and the quality of the tomatoes. The algebraic formula for market demand is given in Appendix 7-1.

Having derived the market demand curve, we now turn to the important distinction between **move-**

FIGURE 7-3 The market demand curve

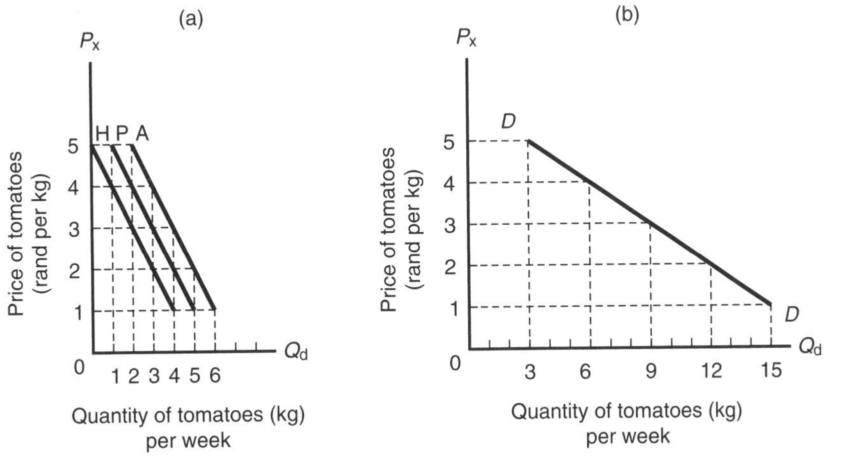

The market demand curve is obtained by adding the individual demand curves horizontally. In (a) Anne's demand curve is labelled A, Helen's H and Purvi's P. In (b) these three demand curves have been added to obtain a market demand curve DD.

ments along the demand curve and **shifts** of the curve.

Movements along the demand curve and shifts of the curve

From now on we often use diagrams to explain things. These diagrams all contain curves which represent important economic relationships, like the demand curve in Figure 7-3. To understand and interpret the diagrams you have to understand the difference between a **movement along** a curve and the **shift of** a curve. This is crucial for understanding economic theory. Because this is so important, we explain it in detail in this section. You will notice that the movement along a curve relates to the **slope** of the curve, while the shift of a curve relates to its **position** or **intercept**. Make sure that you are able to distinguish between the meaning of a movement along a curve and the meaning of a shift of a curve. If you understand this, you will find much of economic theory fairly easy.

A movement along a demand curve (a change in the quantity demanded)

Consider the market demand curve *DD* in Figure 7-4. What does it show? The market demand curve simply shows the quantities demanded at different prices of the good or service. For example, the demand curve *DD* in Figure 7-4 (which is the same as *DD* in Figure 7-3(b)) shows that 15 kg of tomatoes will be demanded weekly at a price of R1,00; 12 kg at a price of R2,00; and so on.

What will happen to the quantity demanded if the price of tomatoes falls from R4,00 to R3,00 per kg? To find the answer, we first determine how many kilograms are demanded at a price of R4,00. From Figure 7-4 we see that the answer is 6 (point *d*). Then we determine how many kilograms of tomatoes are demanded at a price of R3,00. This is indicated by point *c*. The answer to the question can thus be obtained by comparing points *d* and *c*. This shows that the weekly quantity of tomatoes demanded will increase from 6 kg to 9 kg, if the price of tomatoes falls from R4,00 per kg to R3,00 per kg. Correct? Not quite. To be fully accurate we have to add the *ceteris paribus* condition. In other words, the result will hold only if all other factors remain the same.

If the **price of the product changes**, we obtain the change in the **quantity demanded** by comparing the relevant points on the fixed, given or unchanged demand curve, that is, by **moving along the curve**. This is how we determine a **change in the quantity demanded**.

The market demand curve shows the relationship between the price of the product (P_x) and the quantity demanded (Q_d), *ceteris paribus*. To find out what happens to Q_d if P_x changes, we simply compare the relevant points **on the given demand curve**, since the demand curve shows the relationship between price and quantity demanded, on the assumption that all other influences on demand are constant. This relationship can also be expressed in symbols as in Equation 7-5.

FIGURE 7-4 A movement along a demand curve

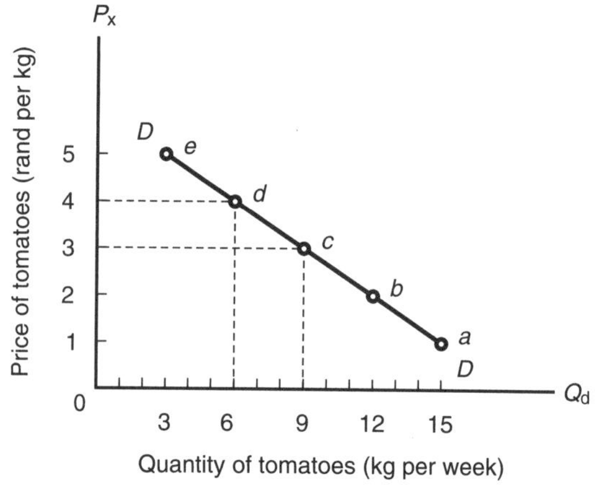

Demand curve DD is the same as the demand curve in Figure 7-3(b). Points a to e correspond to the figures in the first and last columns of Table 7-2. A fall in the price of tomatoes from R4,00 per kg to R3,00 per kg increases the quantity demanded from 6 kg to 9 kg. This is represented by a movement along the demand curve (as the price changes).

$$Q_d = f(P_x, \bar{P}_g, \bar{Y}, \bar{T}, \bar{N}, \ldots) \quad (7\text{-}5)$$

where the symbols have the same meanings as before and the bars indicate which determinants are assumed to be constant.

But what happens to the relationship between Q_d and P_x if P_g, Y, T, N or any other influence on demand should change? Graphically this is indicated by a **shift** of the demand curve.

A shift of the demand curve (a change in demand)

What are the factors that can cause a **change in demand**, that is, a **shift of the demand curve**? A change in any of the determinants of demand **other than the price** of the product will **shift** the demand curve. Because we have elevated the price of the product to centre stage by measuring it on the vertical axis, changes in the other determinants of demand are reflected only as shifts of the curve itself. When this happens, we describe it as a **change in demand**. The difference between a change in the quantity demanded (illustrated by a movement along a given demand curve) and a change in demand (illustrated by a shift of the whole demand curve) is summarised again later (in Figure 7-7). We now examine changes in the other determinants of demand, which cause the **demand curve to shift**.

▪ A CHANGE IN THE PRICE OF A RELATED GOOD

The quantity of tomatoes that consumers or households plan to buy does not depend only on the price of tomatoes. It also depends on the prices of related goods. As mentioned earlier, these related goods fall into two categories: **substitutes** and **complements**.

Substitutes

A **substitute** is a good that can be used in place of another good to satisfy a certain want. Examples include butter and margarine, beef and mutton, tea and coffee, apples and pears, bus trips and train trips, hamburgers and hot dogs, compact discs and audio cassette tapes. An increase in the price of a substitute will cause an increase in the demand for the product in question, *ceteris paribus*. To illustrate the point, we examine an example of two goods that are generally accepted as being substitutes, namely butter and margarine.

An increase in the price of butter will increase the **demand** for margarine, *ceteris paribus*. **If the price of butter increases, a greater quantity of margarine will be demanded at each price of margarine than before.** If the price of butter increases, the demand curve for margarine will therefore **shift** to the right. This is called an **increase in demand**.

This is shown in Figure 7-5. In (a) we show the demand for butter (D_BD_B). At a price of R12,00 per kg, 200 kg of butter are demanded. This is indicated by point *a*. Suppose the price of butter increases to R15,00 per kg (eg because butter is in short supply). According to the demand curve, the quantity of butter demanded falls to 150 kg, as indicated by point *b*. On the market for butter we therefore have a **movement along the demand curve**, from *a* to *b*. The difference between *a* and *b* shows what happens to the **quantity demanded** as the price of butter changes.

But what happens in the market for margarine? This is shown in (b). The original demand curve for margarine is indicated by D_MD_M. This curve was derived on the assumption that the price of butter is R12,00 per kg. It shows, for example, that 300 kg of margarine are demanded at a price (for margarine) of R9,00 per kg, as long as the price of butter is R12,00 per kg. This is indicated by point *c*. However, if the price of butter increases to R15,00 per kg, then 350 kg of margarine are demanded at a margarine price of R9,00 per kg, as indicated by *d*. At any other price of margarine, more margarine will be demanded after the rise in the price of butter than before the price rise.

FIGURE 7-5 Two substitutes: butter and margarine

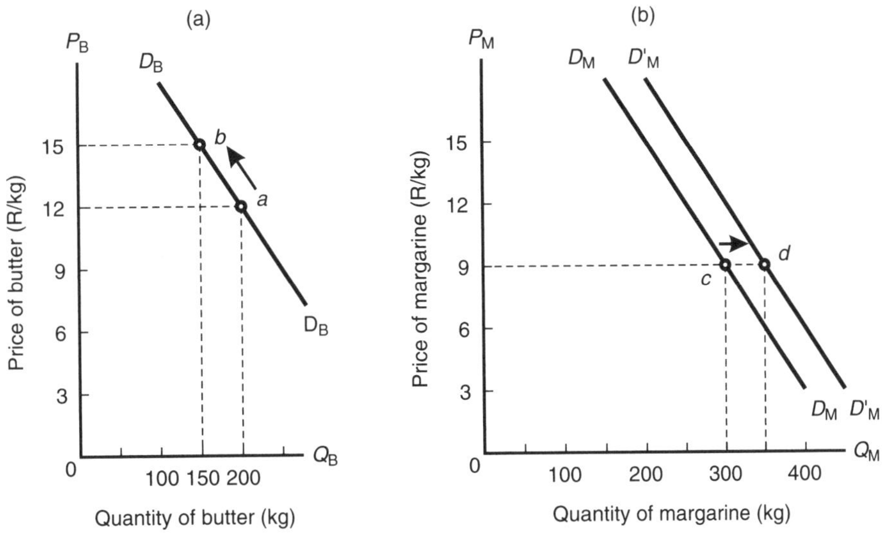

The demand for butter is shown in (a) and the demand for margarine in (b). The original demand curves are D_BD_B and D_MD_M respectively. If the price of butter increases from R12 to R15 per kg, the quantity of butter demanded falls from 200 kg to 150 kg. The increase in the price of butter leads to an increase in the demand for margarine. At each price of margarine more margarine is demanded when the price of butter is R15 per kg than when the price of butter is R12 per kg. The demand curve in (b) thus shifts to the right, to $D'_MD'_M$.

At each price of margarine a greater quantity of margarine will be demanded when the price of the substitute (butter) is R15,00 per kg than when it is R12,00 per kg. **An increase in the price of a substitute** (butter) **will thus lead to a rightward shift of the demand curve of the product concerned** (margarine). The new demand is indicated by $D'_M D'_M$ in Figure 7-5(b).

Similarly, **a decrease in the price of a substitute will lead to a decrease in the demand** for the good concerned (ie a **leftward shift** of the demand curve). If the price of butter should fall to R9,00 per kg, fewer kilograms of margarine will be demanded than before **at each price** of margarine, ***ceteris paribus***. The demand for margarine will therefore decrease.

Complements

Complements are goods that tend to be used jointly to satisfy a want. Examples include fish and chips, "pap en vleis", motorcars and petrol, coffee and milk, tea and sugar, spaghetti and meat balls, golf clubs and golf balls, compact discs and CD players, video cassettes and video cassette recorders, tomatoes and onions, tomatoes and lettuce.

If the price of the complement of a good changes, the demand for the good will also change. For example, the fact that video cassettes can only be used with video cassette recorders (VCRs) means that a change in the price of VCRs will affect the demand for video cassettes. This is illustrated in Figure 7-6. Figure 7-6(a) shows the demand for VCRs. At a price of R2 000 the quantity demanded is 10 000 per time period (point *a*). If the price of VCRs falls to R1 500, the quantity demanded increases to 14 000 (point *b*). The fall in the price of VCRs increases the **quantity** of VCRs **demanded** and this is illustrated by a **movement along the demand curve** for VCRs from *a* to *b*.

What happens in the market for video cassettes? Since cassettes and VCRs are complements, the fall in the price of VCRs and the consequent increase in the quantity of VCRs demanded will cause the quantity of cassettes demanded to rise at each price of cassettes, *ceteris paribus* (ie the **demand** for video cassettes will increase). If VCRs cost R1 500 each, more video cassettes will be demanded at each price of cassettes than when the price of VCRs is R2 000. The fall in the price of VCRs therefore increases the demand for video cassettes. This is shown in Figure 7-6(b) as a rightward **shift of the demand curve**. The original demand curve $D_C D_C$ was derived for a price of VCRs of R2 000. It shows, for example, that 50 000 video cassettes are demanded per period at a price of R30 per cassette (point *d*). If the price of VCRs falls to R1 500, then 70 000 video cassettes will be demanded per period at a price of R30 per cassette (point *e*). The same will occur at any other price of video cassettes and the

FIGURE 7-6 Two complements: video cassette recorders (VCRs) and video cassettes

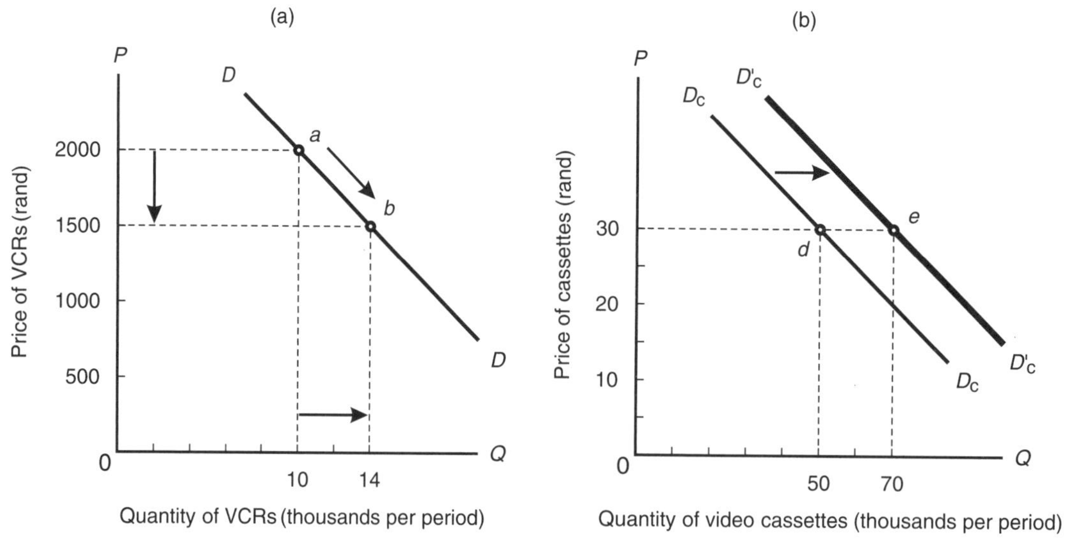

The demand for VCRs is shown in (a) and the demand for video cassettes in (b). The original demand curves are DD and $D_C D_C$ respectively. If the price of VCRs falls from R2 000 to R1 500, the quantity of VCRs demanded per period increases from 10 000 to 14 000. The increased quantity of VCRs demanded (as a result of the lower price) leads to an increase in the demand for video cassettes. At each price of cassettes more cassettes are demanded per period when the price of VCRs is R1 500 than when it is R2 000. The demand curve in (b) thus shifts to the right to $D'_C D'_C$.

demand curve shifts to $D'_C D'_C$, as in Figure 7-6(b). **A fall in the price of a complementary product** (VCRs) **increases the demand for the product** (video cassettes) and this is illustrated by a rightward **shift of the demand curve**.

Similarly, **an increase in the price of the complement** (VCRs) **will lead to a decrease in the demand for the product** (video cassettes). In this case the demand curve for video cassettes will shift to the left.

■ A CHANGE IN THE INCOME OF CONSUMERS

A change in consumer income will lead to a change in **demand**. Graphically this is illustrated by a **shift** of the demand curve. An increase in income will normally lead to an increase in demand, while a fall in income will result in a decrease in demand. **The demand curve will thus shift to the right when income increases and to the left when income decreases.** When this happens, the good is called a **normal good**.

In some exceptional cases, demand decreases when income increases. When this happens, the goods in question are called **inferior goods**. Poor consumers may, for example, reduce their consumption of bread when their income increases. This will happen when the increase in income enables them to switch to other, more expensive, foodstuffs such as meat. Note that the adjective "inferior" does not refer to any physical attribute of the good concerned. It merely indicates that demand increases as income decreases, or decreases as income increases.

■ A CHANGE IN CONSUMERS' TASTES OR PREFERENCES

When consumers' tastes or preferences change, **demand** changes. For example, if doctors discovered that the acidity of tomatoes can cause serious health problems, the demand for tomatoes would fall. In other words, the demand curve would shift to the left, *ceteris paribus*. Similarly, if doctors discovered that tomatoes contain substances that are good for one's health, demand would increase, that is, the demand curve would shift to the right, *ceteris paribus*. **Advertising** and **fashion** can also change consumers' tastes or preferences. Any change in taste or preference will be illustrated by a **shift** of the demand curve.

■ A CHANGE IN POPULATION

Demand also depends on the size of the population served by the market in question. Other things being equal, the larger the population, the greater will be the demand for the product, and the smaller the population, the smaller will be the demand for the product. An increase in the population will thus **shift** the demand curve to the right, *ceteris paribus*.

■ OTHER INFLUENCES ON DEMAND

A change in expected future prices

One important influence on economic decisions which we have not yet introduced is **expectations**. A change in consumers' expectations in respect of any of the determinants of the quantity demanded can cause a change in demand. For example, expected price changes can cause a change in current demand. If the price of a good is expected to fall, *ceteris paribus*, consumers will tend to reduce their current demand, preferring to wait and buy more later at a lower price. Similarly, expected price increases can cause an increase in demand, *ceteris paribus*. Sometimes price increases are announced in advance, for example the monthly adjustment in petrol prices. If a price increase is announced, the demand for petrol rises sharply before the actual price increase. Likewise, if a price decrease is announced, consumers will tend to delay their purchase until after the price decrease comes into effect.

The *ceteris paribus* condition is extremely important in this case. During inflation all prices tend to increase. What we are dealing with here, however, is an expected increase in the price of one good only. Put differently, we are dealing with a situation in which the **relative price** of the good is expected to change (see Box 7-1).

The distribution of income

Demand may also change if a constant total income is redistributed among the different households in the economy. For example, if income is redistributed from high-income households to low-income households, the demand for goods bought mostly by low-income households will increase, while the demand for goods purchased mostly by high-income families will decrease, *ceteris paribus*. The distribution of income is an important determinant of the composition or structure of demand in a market economy, since in such an economy only money votes count.

Demand: a summary

The impact of the most important influences on demand and the quantity demanded is summarised in Table 7-3 and Figure 7-7. The impact of a change in the price of a good on the quantity demanded of that good can also be separated into a substitution effect and an income effect – see Box 7-2. Some possible exceptions to the law of demand are discussed in Chapter 10, where the background to demand is discussed in greater detail.

We have taken quite some time to explain demand. In the process we emphasised certain important principles and aspects of economic analysis which you will encounter time and again in the rest of this book. Now that we have emphasised these principles and

BOX 7-1 THE IMPORTANCE OF RELATIVE PRICES

The law of demand states that the quantity demanded of a good decreases when its price rises and increases when its price falls, *ceteris paribus*. The effects of price changes are illustrated by movements along the demand curve. All these conclusions depend on the *ceteris paribus* condition, that is, they only apply if all other influences on the quantity demanded are held constant.

The *ceteris paribus* condition has an important implication regarding the meaning of the **price** of the good (shown on the vertical axis when we construct a demand curve). If all other factors are kept constant, a fall in the price of the good does not only mean that the **absolute price** (in rands and cents) falls – it also means that the **relative price** (ie the ratio between the price and the prices of other goods) falls. The good therefore becomes absolutely and relatively cheaper than before. In other words, all other goods become **relatively** more expensive in comparison with that good.

In the market system, relative prices are very important. The relative prices are the signals which govern the allocation of resources. If all prices change in the same proportion (eg if all prices and incomes increase by 10 per cent during inflation), the plans of households and firms will be unaffected and the allocation of resources will remain unchanged. But if a good becomes **relatively** cheaper or **relatively** more expensive, the plans of the various participants in the economy will be affected.

To summarise: for a given demand curve the price on the vertical axis indicates both the absolute and the relative price of the good in question. A movement along the demand curve indicates that both the absolute price and the relative price have changed. Changes in **relative** prices are the driving force in the market mechanism.

TABLE 7-3 The market demand curve: a summary

Determinant	*Change*	*Effect on market demand curve*	*Correct description of effect*
Price of the good	Increase	Upward movement along the demand curve	A fall in the quantity demanded
	Decrease	Downward movement along the demand curve	An increase in the quantity demanded
Prices of related goods			
– Substitutes	Increase	Rightward shift of the demand curve	An increase in demand
	Decrease	Leftward shift of the demand curve	A fall in demand
– Complements	Increase	Leftward shift of the demand curve	A fall in demand
	Decrease	Rightward shift of the demand curve	An increase in demand
Income (normal good)	Increase	Rightward shift of the demand curve	An increase in demand
	Decrease	Leftward shift of the demand curve	A fall in demand
Taste/preferences	An increased desire to buy	Rightward shift of the demand curve	An increase in demand
	A reduced desire to buy	Leftward shift of the demand curve	A fall in demand
Population	Increase	Rightward shift of the demand curve	An increase in demand
	Decrease	Leftward shift of the demand curve	A fall in demand
Expected future price of the good	Price is expected to increase	Rightward shift of the demand curve	An increase in demand
	Price is expected to fall	Leftward shift of the demand curve	A fall in demand

FIGURE 7-7 A change in the quantity demanded versus a change in demand

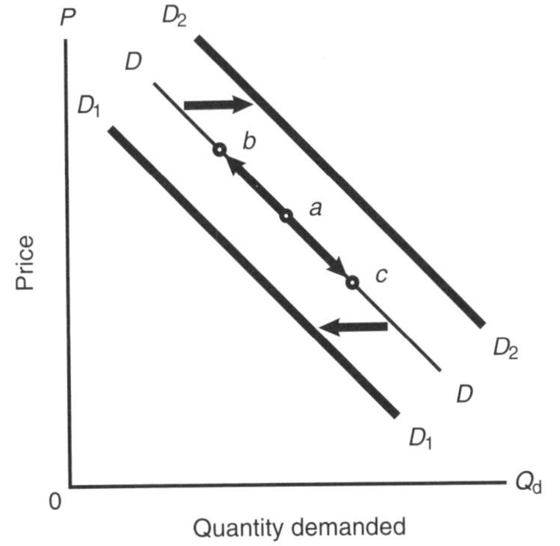

*When the **price of a good changes, there is a movement along the demand curve and a change in the quantity demanded**. Along demand curve DD a movement from a to b indicates a decrease in the quantity demanded, while a movement from a to c shows an increase in the quantity demanded. If one of the **other influences on demand changes, there is a change in demand which is represented by a shift of the demand curve**. An increase in demand is represented by a rightward shift of the demand curve, such as the shift from DD to D_2D_2. A decrease in demand is represented by a leftward shift of the demand curve, such as the shift from DD to D_1D_1.*

aspects, we can proceed a little faster with the analysis of supply.

7.3 Supply

Supply can be defined as **the quantities of a good or service that producers plan to sell at each possible price during a certain period.** As in the case of demand, supply refers to **planned** quantities – the quantities that producers or sellers plan to sell at each price. Just as consumers must be able to carry out their plans, producers must be willing and able to supply the quantities concerned. There is also no guarantee that the quantity supplied will actually be sold. The quantity actually sold or exchanged will depend, amongst other things, on the demand for the good or service in question. The quantity supplied during a specific period may therefore be greater than, equal to or smaller than the quantity actually sold or exchanged.

Like demand, supply is a **flow** concept which is measured over a period of time (hour, day, week, month, etc). It can also be expressed in **words**, schedules (**numbers**), curves (**graphs**) or equations (**symbols**). As we have mentioned, we deal only with the goods market in this chapter. We do not investigate the supply of factors of production such as labour.

As in the case of demand, we first examine the supply of an individual producer, seller or firm before we look at the market supply. We again focus on the supply of a particular good. The **total** (or aggregate) **supply** of all goods and services in the economy is a **macroeconomic** issue which will be discussed in Part IV.

BOX 7-2 THE SUBSTITUTION EFFECT AND THE INCOME EFFECT OF A PRICE CHANGE

As mentioned in Box 7-1, relative prices are the key to understanding the inverse relationship between price and quantity demanded (ie the law of demand). We can distinguish two fundamental reasons for the law of demand: the **substitution effect** and the **income effect**.

If the price of tomatoes falls while the prices of all other goods and services remain constant, tomatoes become **relatively** cheaper (and all the other things relatively more expensive). This will result in a shift in spending away from the goods which have become relatively more expensive towards the goods which are now relatively cheaper. This shift is called the **substitution effect**. Consumers will plan to substitute the cheaper tomatoes for the more expensive beans, sprouts, etc. **The substitution effect is always towards the goods which have become relatively cheaper** (or away from the goods which become relatively more expensive).

The substitution effect is not the only effect that is at work. If the price of a good changes, while a household's income and the prices of all other goods remain the same, the actual value or effective purchasing power of the household's income changes. The purchasing power of income is called **real**

income. When prices change, real income changes, even if money income remains the same. If the price of tomatoes increases, real income decreases, *ceteris paribus*. Similarly, if the price of tomatoes decreases while all other things remain the same, the household's real income increases. If a consumer's real income increases, he or she will plan to buy more tomatoes, *ceteris paribus*. Likewise, if a consumer's real income falls, he or she will plan to buy fewer tomatoes. We call this the **income effect**. In the case of a normal good the income effect works in the same direction as the substitution effect.

We can summarise the two effects as follows:

Change in the price of the good (*ceteris paribus*)	Type of effect	How it works	Impact on quantity demanded
Price increases	Substitution effect	Good becomes relatively more expensive as a result of higher price	Quantity demanded decreases
	Income effect	Real income falls as a result of higher price	Quantity demanded decreases
Price decreases	Substitution effect	Good becomes relatively cheaper as a result of lower price	Quantity demanded increases
	Income effect	Real income increases as a result of lower price	Quantity demanded increases

The income effect of a change in the price of a single product is usually quite small. Such a change will normally have an almost imperceptible impact on the purchasing power of a consumer or group of consumers and on the demand for the product. The substitution effect is therefore usually more important. There may be exceptions (see Chapter 10) but they are comparatively rare and tend to apply to individual demand rather than market demand.

Individual supply

As stated above, supply refers to the quantities of a good or service that prospective sellers plan to sell at various prices. To illustrate the determinants and properties of individual supply, we consider the supply of tomatoes of an imaginary farmer, Johnny Ramos. Johnny is a vegetable farmer in Gauteng who sells his produce on the Pretoria fresh produce market.

What determines Johnny's supply of tomatoes in a particular year?

- **The price of tomatoes**. The higher the price of tomatoes, the greater the quantity that Johnny will plan to grow and sell, *ceteris paribus*.
- **The prices of alternative products**. Johnny's decision about how many tomatoes to produce will also depend on the prices of alternative products (outputs). As a vegetable farmer, he must decide which vegetables to grow, and how much of each. If the price of cauliflower increases, relative to the price of tomatoes, he might plan to produce more cauliflower and fewer tomatoes. Likewise, if the price of cabbages falls, relative to the price of tomatoes, he might plan to produce fewer cabbages and more tomatoes. Producers will always consider the prices of alternative outputs that they can produce with the same resources. These outputs are sometimes referred to as substitutes in production.
- **Prices of factors of production and other inputs**. The quantities of tomatoes that Johnny plans to sell at different prices will also depend on the cost of production. To make a profit, he has to cover his costs of production. If the prices of one or more of his inputs (eg labour, fertiliser, machinery) increase, a smaller quantity of tomatoes will be supplied by Johnny at each price than before, *ceteris paribus*. The reason, of course, is that it will cost more to produce each quantity.
- **Expected future prices**. Whereas consumers can make decisions fairly quickly, producers often have to plan long in advance. Johnny will therefore not only be influenced by what is happening at present, but also by what he expects to happen in future

when his tomatoes reach the market. For example, the higher he expects the future price of tomatoes to be, *ceteris paribus*, the more tomatoes he will plan to produce. In the case of non-perishable crops, like wheat or maize, farmers may even withhold some of their produce from the market in anticipation of a price increase. In other words, they may postpone their supply to a future period.

- **The state of technology**. New technologies (or production techniques) that enable producers to produce at lower costs will increase the quantity supplied at each price. For example, the introduction of new fertilisers or a new tomato which is less susceptible to plant disease will tend to increase the supply of tomatoes, *ceteris paribus*.

Supply decisions must not be confused with demand decisions or with actual outcomes in the market. As mentioned earlier, much of economic theory is simply structured common sense. But you must argue in a disciplined fashion by always considering carefully the question you are dealing with and taking care to avoid confusing supply decisions with demand decisions.

So, in deciding what quantities of tomatoes to supply, Johnny considers the price of tomatoes. This price is affected by the demand for tomatoes, but he does not worry about how the price is determined. He wants to make a profit by selling tomatoes at prices that more than cover the costs of his inputs. He has no guarantee, however, that he will be able to sell all the tomatoes he plans to produce at each price. For example, when the market price is lower than the price he expected, he may have to sell some tomatoes at a loss, or even destroy them.

We have now identified the most important determinants of Johnny's supply of tomatoes. We can state that the quantity of tomatoes supplied annually by Johnny (ie the quantity that he plans to produce each year) is determined by the price of tomatoes, the prices of related commodities, the prices of his inputs, the expected future prices of tomatoes and the state of technology.

More generally:

The quantity of a good supplied by an individual producer (seller, firm) in a particular period is a function of the price of the good, the prices of alternative outputs, the prices of the factors of production, the expected future prices of the good and the state of technology.

This is a **verbal** statement of the determinants of individual supply. Supply can also be expressed in a shorthand way by using **symbols**.

Let Q_s = quantity of tomatoes supplied
P_x = price of tomatoes
P_g = prices of alternative outputs
P_f = prices of factors of production and other inputs
P_e = expected future prices of tomatoes
T_y = technology

The individual supply of tomatoes can then be expressed as

$$Q_s = f(P_x, P_g, P_f, P_e, T_y) \quad \text{(7-6)}$$

As in the case of demand, we focus primarily on the relationship between the quantity supplied and the price of the good.

We therefore state that:

$$Q_s = f(P_x, \bar{P}_g, \bar{P}_f, \bar{P}_e, \bar{T}_y) \quad \text{(7-7)}$$

or

$$Q_s = f(P_x)\ \textit{ceteris paribus} \quad \text{(7-8)}$$

where the bars indicate that the relevant variables are kept constant.

We can also construct a **supply schedule**. Table 7-4 is an example of such a schedule. It shows the various quantities of tomatoes which Johnny will supply at various prices during a particular year. In contrast to the quantity demanded, the quantity supplied increases as the price of the product increases.

The information in the supply schedule can be illustrated graphically by drawing a **supply curve**. Once again we accord priority status to price above all other determinants of the quantity supplied by indicating it on the vertical axis. Figure 7-8 contains the supply curve that corresponds with the information in Table 7-4. It has a positive slope, indicating that the quantity supplied increases as the price increases. The points on the supply curve correspond to the different possibilities indicated in the table. The fact that we join the points to draw a supply curve implies that there are also other, intermediate possibilities (eg a price of R1,50 per kg and a quantity supplied of 750 kg). Supply curves are not necessarily linear (as in Figure 7-8) but to keep things simple we assume (for the moment) that all supply curves can be represented by straight lines.

Make sure that you understand what the supply curve indicates. If you have problems in interpreting it, revise the more detailed explanation of the demand

TABLE 7-4 Johnny's supply schedule of tomatoes

Possibility	*Price of tomatoes (R/kg)*	*Quantity supplied (kg per year)*
a	1	500
b	2	1 000
c	3	1 500
d	4	2 000
e	5	2 500

FIGURE 7-8 Johnny's annual supply of tomatoes

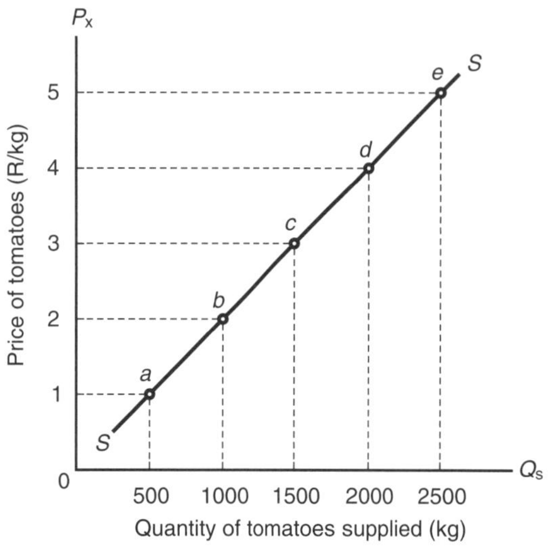

Each point indicates the quantity of tomatoes supplied at that price. By joining the points we obtain a supply curve SS. The supply curve indicates the relationship between the quantity of tomatoes supplied annually and the price of tomatoes, on the assumption that all other things remain unchanged.

curve in Section 7.2 and the explanation of graphs in Section 6.5.

Supply can be expressed in four ways:

- **Using words. Supply** refers to the **entire relationship** between the quantity supplied of a commodity and the price of that commodity, other things being equal. The law of supply states that this is usually a **positive** (or **direct**) relationship. The higher the price of the good, the greater the quantity supplied; and the lower the price of the good, the lower the quantity supplied, *ceteris paribus*.
- **Using numbers: the supply schedule**. The supply schedule is a table which shows the quantity of a good supplied at each price, *ceteris paribus*. Table 7-4 is an example of a supply schedule. The figures in Table 7-4 indicate that the quantity supplied increases as the price increases. The **entire supply schedule** in Table 7-4 represents Johnny's **supply** of tomatoes.
- **Using graphs: the supply curve**. The supply curve is a line or graph which indicates the quantity supplied of a good at each price, *ceteris paribus*. Figure 7-8 contains an example of a supply curve. The slope of the curve shows that the quantity supplied increases as the price increases. This is a visual representation of supply. The **entire curve** in Figure 7-8 represents Johnny's **supply** of tomatoes.
- **Using symbols: the supply equation**. The supply equation is a shorthand way of expressing the relationship between the quantity supplied of a good and its price, *ceteris paribus*. Equations 7-7 and 7-8 are both supply equations:

$$Q_s = f(P_x, \overline{P}_g, \overline{P}_f, \overline{P}_e, \overline{T}_y) \quad (7\text{-}7)$$

$$Q_s = f(P_x) \textit{ ceteris paribus} \quad (7\text{-}8)$$

These two equations are often reduced to $Q_s = f(P_x)$, since the *ceteris paribus* assumption is usually taken for granted in economics. Note that an **entire equation** represents the **supply** of the product. A more precise equation of the supply curve is formulated in Appendix 7-1, in which demand and supply are analysed algebraically.

Market supply

To move from individual supply to market supply, the individual supplies are added together horizontally. The market supply curve is obtained in the same way as the market demand (see Table 7-2 and Figure 7-3) – except that we now add the individual supply curves.

The market supply curve shows the relationship between the price of the product and the quantities supplied (by all the firms) during a particular period. Like the individual supply curve, the market supply curve also slopes upwards from left to right. In other words, there is a direct or positive relationship between price and quantity supplied.

What determines the quantity of a good supplied in the market at each price? The same factors that determine the individual quantities supplied also determine the total quantities supplied in the market. In symbols we can write

$$Q_s = f(P_x, P_g, P_f, P_e, T_y, N, \ldots) \quad (7\text{-}9)$$

where Q_s = quantity supplied in the market
P_x = price of the product
P_g = prices of alternative outputs
P_f = prices of factors of production and other inputs
P_e = expected future prices of the product
T_y = technology
N = number of firms supplying the product
... = allowance for other possible influences on the quantity supplied

In principle the market supply curve is the same as the individual supply curve. The only real difference is that the market supply pertains to all the prospective sellers of the product in a particular market. The total number of firms (N) supplying the product therefore has to be taken into account. In addition we allow explicitly for all the other factors which may influence the supply of the product. These other possible determinants include:

- **Government policy**. Subsidies on particular goods or services tend to raise their supply, while taxes tend to reduce supply.
- **Natural disasters**. Floods, earthquakes and droughts have an impact on supply. In 1995, for example, a major earthquake in Kobe in Japan destroyed many factories and reduced the supply of a number of goods (including golf balls). In South Africa we are familiar with the devastating impact of severe droughts or flooding.
- **Joint products and by-products**. Some products are produced jointly (eg sugar and molasses, wheat and bran, lead and zinc, beef and leather) with the result that a change in the supply of the major product results in a similar change in the supply of the by-product. Joint products are sometimes called complements in production.
- **Productivity**. This is related to, amongst other things, technology. A change in the productivity of the factors of production (eg as a result of improved technology) will lead to a change in supply. If productivity falls, production costs increase, *ceteris paribus*, and supply decreases. The relationship between productivity and supply is examined in Chapter 11.

FIGURE 7-9 A movement along a supply curve: a change in the quantity supplied

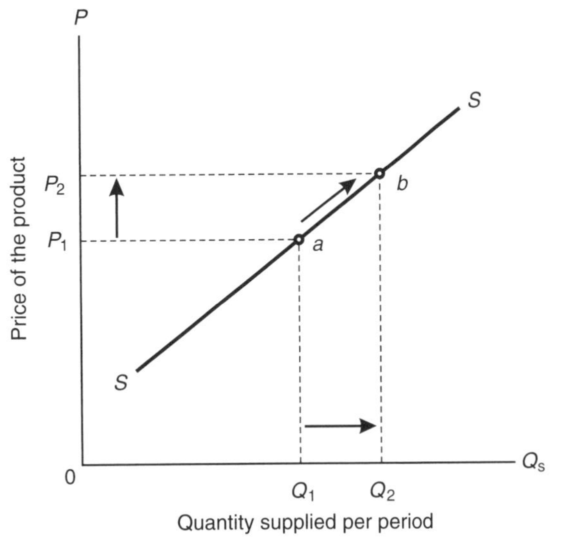

A change in the price of the product leads to a movement along the supply curve SS. For example, when the price of the product increases from P_1 to P_2 the quantity supplied increases from Q_1 to Q_2. In other words, there is a movement along SS from a to b.

Some of the determinants of supply are interdependent. For example, if the relative price of a product is expected to increase, the number of firms supplying the market will tend to increase.

Now that we have introduced the market supply curve, we turn to the important distinction between **movements along** the supply curve and **shifts** of the curve. In dealing with the demand curve, we discussed this distinction quite extensively. Since the principles are the same, we shall be fairly brief.

Movements along the supply curve and shifts of the curve

The supply curve in Figure 7-9 shows the relationship between the price of the product and the quantity supplied, *ceteris paribus*. At a price of P_1 the quantity supplied is Q_1, as indicated by combination *a* in the figure. If the price increases to P_2, the quantity supplied will increase to Q_2, as indicated by combination *b* in the figure. The supply curve shows that the quantity supplied will increase if the price increases, *ceteris paribus*. If we want to know what will happen if **the price of the product** changes, we simply **move along the curve**. Such a movement represents a **change in the quantity supplied**.

However, if one of the **other determinants** of the quantity supplied changes, then the whole supply relationship changes. Graphically this is indicated by a **shift** of the supply curve. Whereas **a movement along a supply curve** (as a result of a change in the price of the product, which we measure on the vertical axis) is referred to as **a change in the quantity supplied**, **a shift of the supply curve** (as a result of a change in any factor other than the price of the product) is called **a change in supply**. The two possible changes in supply are indicated in Figure 7-10. Any factor which leads to an increase in supply (ie an increase in the quantity supplied **at each price** of the product) will **shift** a supply curve such as *SS* in Figure 7-10, to S_2S_2. On the other hand, any factor which results in a decrease in supply (ie a fall in the quantity supplied at each price of the product) will **shift** a supply curve such as *SS* in Figure 7-10 upwards, to the left, to S_1S_1.

A change in any determinant of the quantity supplied except the price of the product will be illustrated by a shift of the supply curve. The impacts of the most important determinants of supply are summarised in Table 7-5.

The derivation of a supply curve is explained in Chapter 11. The supply curve mainly reflects the cost of producing the product concerned. In Chapter 11 we show how costs of production are related to the prices of the inputs used in the production process and their productivity.

TABLE 7-5 The market supply curve: a summary

Determinant	*Change*	*Effect on market supply curve*	*Correct description of effect*
Price of the good	Increase	Upward movement along the supply curve	An increase in the quantity supplied
	Decrease	Downward movement along the supply curve	A decrease in the quantity supplied
Prices of alternative products (substitutes in production)	Increase	Leftward shift of the supply curve	A decrease in supply
	Decrease	Rightward shift of the supply curve	An increase in supply
Prices of joint products (complements in production)	Increase	Rightward shift of the supply curve	An increase in supply
	Decrease	Leftward shift of the supply curve	A decrease in supply
Prices of inputs	Increase	Leftward (upward) shift of the supply curve	A decrease in supply
	Decrease	Rightward (downward) shift of the supply curve	An increase in supply
Expected future prices[4]	Price is expected to increase	Rightward shift of the supply curve	An increase in supply
	Price is expected to fall	Leftward shift of the supply curve	A decrease in supply
Technology	Cost-reducing improvement in technology	Rightward shift of the supply curve	An increase in supply
	Cost-increasing changes in technology	Leftward shift of the supply curve	A decrease in supply
Number of firms (sellers)	More firms enter market	Rightward shift of the supply curve	An increase in supply
	Firms leave market	Leftward shift of supply curve	A decrease in supply

7.4 Market equilibrium

Equilibrium, excess demand and excess supply

Having explained demand and supply, we can now combine them to explain equilibrium in the market for a particular good or service. The market is in equilibrium when the quantity demanded is equal to the quantity supplied, that is, when the plans of the households (buyers, demanders) coincide with the plans of the firms (sellers, suppliers). The price at which this occurs is called the equilibrium price. At any other price there will be disequilibrium, in the form of excess supply or excess demand. When there is disequilibrium, forces are set in motion to move the market towards equilibrium.

We now use demand and supply schedules and curves to explain equilibrium and disequilibrium in the market for a consumer good (tomatoes). The algebraic derivation of equilibrium is explained in Appendix 7-1.

Table 7-6 shows the market demand and supply schedules for tomatoes in a market on a particular day. The first column shows various prices of tomatoes (in rands per kilogram); the second column

4. Note that the reasoning here excludes speculative behaviour – see Box 8-1.

FIGURE 7-10 Shifts of the supply curve: changes in supply

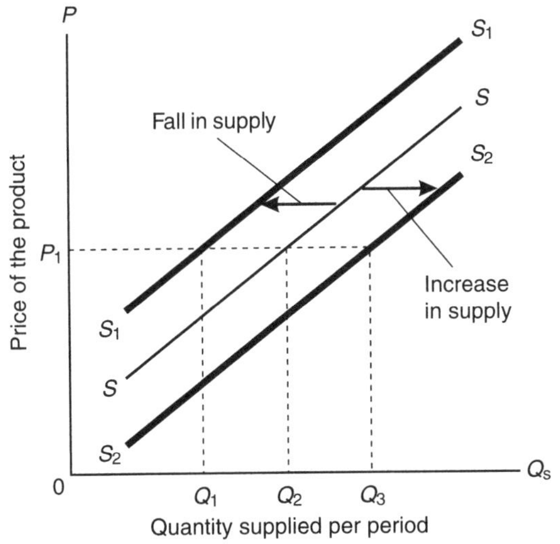

The original supply curve is SS. A change in any of the determinants of the quantity supplied other than the price of the product will lead to a change in supply, illustrated by a shift of the supply curve. Any factor which reduces supply will shift the supply curve to the left, to S_1S_1. Any factor which increases supply will shift the supply curve to the right, to S_2S_2. Note, for example, the differences in the quantities supplied at price P_1.

shows the quantity of tomatoes demanded at each price; the third column shows the quantity supplied at each price; the fourth column shows the difference between the quantity demanded and the quantity supplied; and the last column shows the direction of any pressure on the price of the product. When the quantity demanded is greater than the quantity supplied, there is **excess demand** (or a **market shortage**) at that particular price. When the quantity supplied is greater than the quantity demanded, there is **excess supply** (or a **market surplus**) at that particular price. When the quantity demanded is equal to the quantity supplied, there is **equilibrium** in the market. Recall, from Section 6.4, that equilibrium is a state of rest in which opposing forces are balanced and in which there is no tendency for things to change (as long as the underlying forces remain unchanged).

The data in Table 7-6 are illustrated graphically in Figure 7-11. In the table and in the figure we see that the quantity demanded is greater than the quantity supplied (ie that there is excess demand) at all prices lower than R5 per kg. For example, at a price of R2 per kg 320 kg are demanded, while only 50 kg are supplied. The excess demand (or market shortage) of 270 kg is indicated by *bc* in Figure 7-11. At all prices higher than R5 per kg the quantity supplied is greater than the quantity demanded (ie there is an excess supply or surplus). For example, at a price of R7 per kg only 120 kg are demanded, while 300 kg are supplied. The excess supply (or market surplus) of 180 kg is indicated by *df* in Figure 7-11.

When there is excess demand (ie a market shortage), firms sell their total production but households do not obtain the quantity of the product which they would like to buy at that particular price. In an effort to obtain a greater quantity of the product, households bid up the price of the product (ie they offer to pay more for the product), while the firms realise that they can charge a higher price. As the price rises, the quantity supplied increases along the supply curve – existing firms produce more – while the quantity demanded falls along the demand curve. This process continues until equilibrium is reached where the quantity demanded is equal to the quantity supplied.

When there is excess supply (ie a market surplus), firms find that they cannot sell all their products – they are left with unsold stocks (also called inventories) of the product. They cut their production and compete with each other to find buyers for their products by reducing the price. This results in a fall in the quantity supplied along the supply curve. Some existing firms produce less. At the same time the falling price raises the quantity demanded along the demand curve. This process continues until equilibrium is reached where the quantity demanded is equal to the quantity supplied. See Box 7-3.

Market equilibrium occurs at the intersection of the demand and supply curves. This is the point at which both buyers and sellers agree upon the quantity of goods to be exchanged and the price at which they will be exchanged.[5] Once equilibrium is reached, no further change will occur (as long as the underlying forces remain the same). In Chapter 8 we examine what happens when an underlying force (ie any of the non-price determinants of demand and supply) changes. The purpose is to predict how equilibrium prices and quantities will respond to changes in market forces.

The functions of prices in a market economy

As explained above, prices cause adjustments in the quantities demanded and supplied of each good. Prices serve two important functions in a market economy: a rationing function and an allocative function.

As emphasised in Chapter 1, scarcity is the universal feature of economic life. Prices serve to ration the

5. Note that equilibrium occurs when the **quantity** demanded is equal to the **quantity** supplied, not when demand equals supply. Strictly speaking, demand is only equal to supply when the demand and supply curves are identical.

TABLE 7-6 The demand and supply of tomatoes in a market on a particular day

Price of tomatoes (R/kg)	*Quantity demanded (kg)*	*Quantity supplied (kg)*	*Excess supply or demand (kg)*	*Pressure on price*
1	360	0	360 (excess demand)	Upward
2	320	50	270 (excess demand)	Upward
3	280	100	180 (excess demand)	Upward
4	240	150	90 (excess demand)	Upward
5	200	200	0 (equilibrium)	None
6	160	250	90 (excess supply)	Downward
7	120	300	180 (excess supply)	Downward
8	80	350	270 (excess supply)	Downward

scarce supplies of goods and services to those who place the highest value on them (and can afford to pay for them). This is the **rationing function** of prices.

Prices also serve as signals which direct the factors of production among different uses in the economy. In markets where there is excess demand, prices increase. Higher prices mean increased profit opportunities, *ceteris paribus*. The possibility of increased profits attracts additional factors of production (labour, capital, etc) towards the activities concerned. On the other hand, excess supply results in falling prices and losses, which drives factors of production away from the activities concerned. This is the **allocative function** of prices, which may be

FIGURE 7-11 Demand, supply and market equilibrium

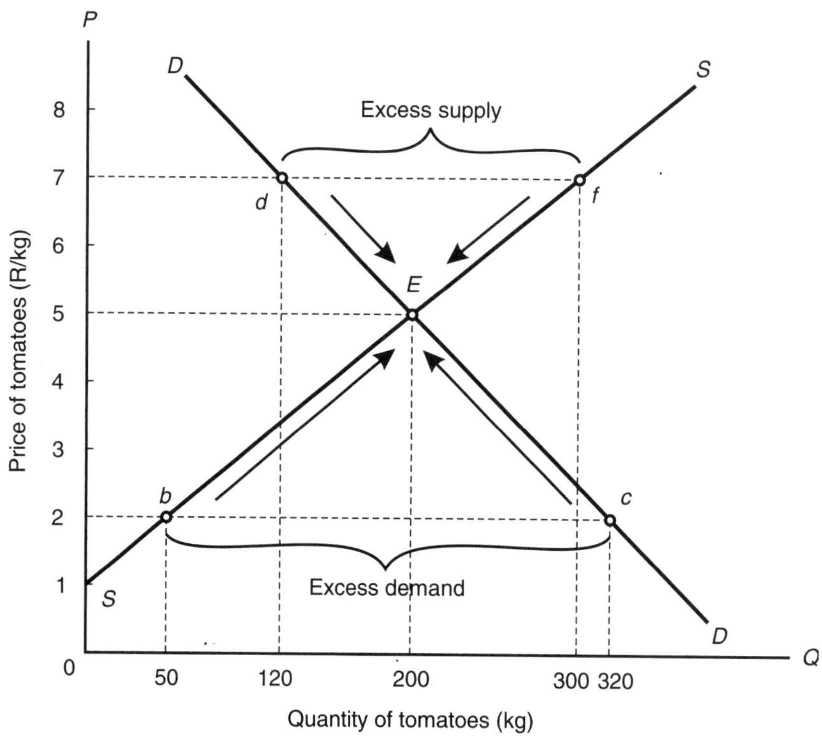

The demand curve DD intersects the supply curve SS at a price of R5 per kg – this is the equilibrium price. The equilibrium quantity is 200 kg. At a price of R2 the quantity demanded is 320 kg and the quantity supplied 50 kg. The excess demand of 270 kg is indicated by bc. At a price of R7 per kg the quantity demanded is 120 kg and 300 kg are supplied. The excess supply of 180 kg is indicated by df.

BOX 7-3 MARKET EQUILIBRIUM

In Chapter 6 we explained that equilibrium is an analytical concept that we use in our attempt to explain how markets behave in the real world. We also emphasised that markets are seldom, if ever, in equilibrium.

The model illustrated in Figure 7-11 implies that consumers and producers only trade once the equilibrium price and quantity have been established. In other words, we assume that markets work like auctions where auctioneers call out different prices and only allow trade to take place once they are satisfied that an equilibrium price has been agreed upon. At that price both the seller and buyer are satisfied that they are getting the best possible deal.

Markets do not behave in this fashion. There is no guarantee that buyers are buying the best goods at the lowest possible prices or that sellers are getting the highest possible prices for their goods. Markets operate under conditions of uncertainty and equilibrium is never actually reached. Nevertheless, and this is the important point, markets generally tend to move towards equilibrium. If there is excess demand, prices tend to rise and if there is excess supply, prices tend to fall. Although unrealistic, in the strict sense of the word, the notion of equilibrium is a useful and indispensable element of the economist's toolkit.

regarded as the driving force behind Adam Smith's "invisible hand", which we referred to in Chapter 2.

In Chapter 8 we show how price controls and other forms of interference with the market mechanism prevent prices from fulfilling their rationing and allocative functions.

Always bear in mind, however, that markets only reflect the plans of those who are able to participate as consumers or suppliers. Those who lack purchasing power or command over factors of production are not able to signal their wants or plans via the market. **In markets only money votes count**. Advocates of free markets claim that markets produce the most efficient allocation of resources and that the problem of income distribution is not an economic issue. Market outcomes, however, depend on the distribution of income. For each income distribution there is a different "efficient" allocation of resources. Economists therefore cannot simply dismiss the distribution of income as a non-economic issue.

7.5 Consumer surplus and producer surplus

As indicated in the previous section, the equilibrium or market-clearing price is determined by the interaction between demand and supply. With a normal, downward-sloping demand curve and a normal, upward-sloping supply curve the uniform market price implies that some consumers are paying less than the maximum they are willing to pay, while certain suppliers are receiving more than the minimum they were willing to accept. To understand this, we have to examine two important concepts, the **consumer surplus** and the **producer surplus**.

Consumer surplus

A downward-sloping demand curve and a uniform market price imply that consumers actually receive more than their money's worth. The reason is that the market price is usually lower than the highest prices consumers are willing to pay for all but the last (or marginal) unit of the product concerned. The difference between what consumers pay and the value that they receive, indicated by the maximum amount they are willing to pay, is called the **consumer surplus**.

In Figure 7-12 *DD* is the demand curve and P_1 the market price. The demand curve indicates the highest prices that consumers are willing and able to pay for different quantities of the good. If the market price is P_1 the consumers pay that price for **each** of the units purchased. This is less than the highest prices they are prepared to pay for all of the units purchased except the last one. For every quantity between zero and Q_1 consumers therefore pay less than they are prepared to pay. The total amount gained in this way by the consumers is indicated by the shaded triangle in Figure 7-12. This is called the **consumer surplus**.

Producer surplus

Parallel to the concept of consumer surplus, is that of producer surplus. Whereas the consumer surplus involves the idea of consumers being willing to pay more than the market price for units of a product, the producer surplus involves the idea of producers being willing to supply units of the product at less than the market price.

In Figure 7-13 the supply curve *SS* indicates the different quantities that producers are willing to supply at

FIGURE 7-12 The consumer surplus

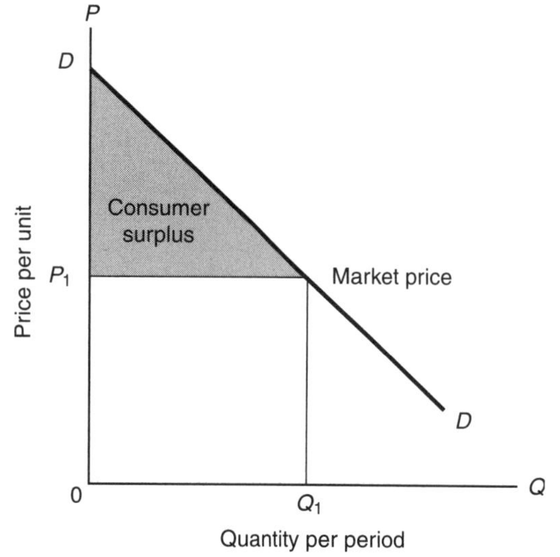

DD is the demand curve, P_1 the market price and Q_1 the quantity demanded at the market price. For each quantity between 0 and Q_1 (ie except Q_1), consumers are willing to pay more than the price P_1 they are actually paying. The shaded area thus represents a gain to consumers, called the consumer surplus.

FIGURE 7-13 The producer surplus

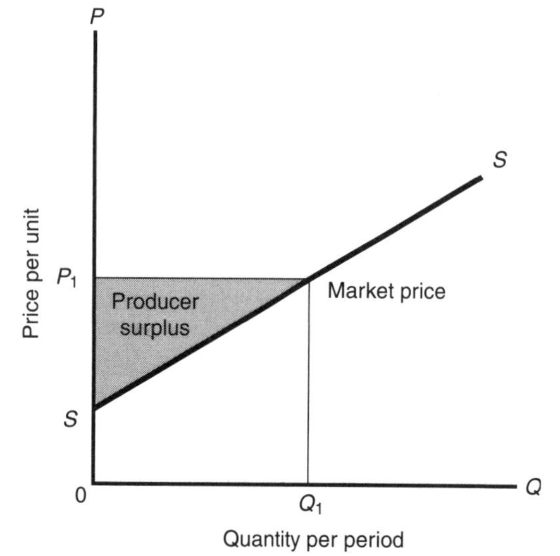

SS is the supply curve, P_1 the market price and Q_1 the quantity supplied at the market price. For each quantity between 0 and Q_1 (ie except Q_1), producers are willing to supply at a lower price than the price P_1 that they are actually receiving. The shaded area thus represents a gain to producers, called the producer surplus.

different prices. With a uniform market price P_1 and an equilibrium quantity Q_1, it implies that up to Q_1 there is a positive difference between the lowest prices at which producers are willing to supply the different quantities and the price they actually receive. This is indicated by the shaded area in Figure 7-13. This total gain to producers is called the **producer surplus.**

Consumer surplus and producer surplus at market equilibrium

In Figure 7-14 we combine Figures 7-12 and 7-13 to illustrate consumer surplus and producer surplus at market equilibrium. The consumer surplus is indicated by the darker shaded triangle DP_1E and the producer surplus by the lighter shaded triangle SP_1E.

Consumer surplus and producer surplus have many important applications in economic analysis, some of which will be illustrated in the remainder of this part of the book.

FIGURE 7-14 Consumer surplus and producer surplus at market equilibrium

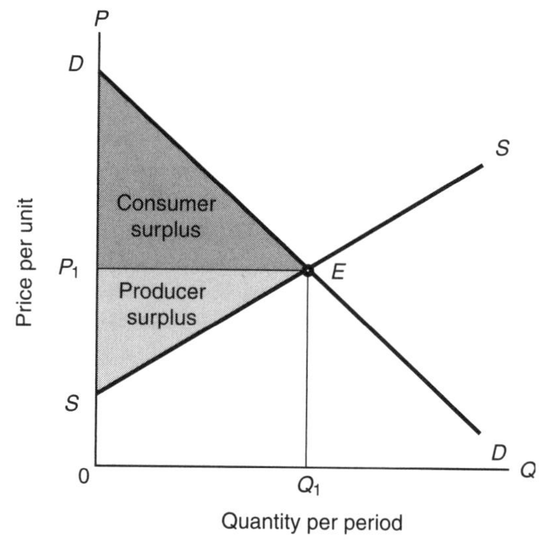

DD is the demand curve, SS the supply curve, P_1 the equilibrium price and Q_1 the equilibrium quantity. At all quantities less than Q_1 consumers pay a lower price (P_1) for the product than the highest prices they are willing to pay (as indicated by the demand curve). There is thus a consumer surplus, indicated by the darker shaded triangle DP_1E. Likewise, at all quantities less than Q_1 producers receive a higher price (P_1) than the lowest prices they are prepared to supply the product for (as indicated by the supply curve). There is thus also a producer surplus, indicated by the lighter shaded triangle SP_1E.

IMPORTANT CONCEPTS

Demand
Individual demand
Market demand
Complements
Substitutes
Law of demand
Demand schedule
Demand curve
Change in quantity demanded
Movement along demand curve
Change in demand
Shift of demand curve
Normal and inferior goods
Relative prices
Substitution effect
Income effect
Supply
Individual supply
Market supply
Supply schedule
Supply curve
Change in quantity supplied
Movement along supply curve
Change in supply
Shift of supply curve
Equilibrium
Excess demand (shortage)
Excess supply (surplus)
Rationing function of prices
Allocative function of prices
Consumer surplus
Producer surplus

REVIEW QUESTIONS

1. This question provides some examples of changes in tastes or preferences, identified as among the possible causes of changes in demand. Explain, with the aid of a diagram, the impact of:
   (a) the spread of HIV/Aids on the demand for condoms
   (b) the dissemination of information about the hazards of smoking on the demand for cigarettes
   (c) a change in fashion from bell-bottomed trousers to narrowly-cut trousers on the demand for bell-bottomed trousers
   (d) increased crime on the demand for private security services
2. Explain what is meant by excess demand and excess supply in a goods market and explain how excess demand and excess supply are eliminated by market forces.
3. What do economists mean by demand?
4. List the main determinants of the demand for (a) economics textbooks and (b) cellular phones in South Africa.
5. Is the following statement true or false? "As the price of bananas increases, the demand for bananas falls." Explain your answer.
6. "The average price of bananas increased from R3,00 per kilogram in May to R3,50 per kilogram in June. This implies that the demand for bananas increased between May and June." Do you agree? Discuss.
7. "The price of golf balls increases from year to year but every year golfers purchase more golf balls. This implies that the demand curve in respect of golf balls slopes upward." Explain the error in this argument.
8. Use an example to distinguish between a change in supply and a change in the quantity supplied.
9. Use an example to distinguish between a movement along a demand curve and a shift of a demand curve. What terms do we use to distinguish between these two types of change?

10. Use a diagram to illustrate and explain consumer surplus and producer surplus.
11. Explain, with the aid of a diagram, the meaning of equilibrium in the market for a particular good.
12. What are the functions of prices in a market economy?
13. Use an example to explain the difference between an increase in demand and an increase in the quantity demanded.

APPENDIX 7-1
ALGEBRAIC ANALYSIS OF DEMAND AND SUPPLY

In this appendix we show how linear demand and supply curves can be expressed algebraically in the form of equations and how these equations can be used to determine equilibrium prices and quantities. Demand and supply curves are not necessarily linear, but we stick to linear functions to keep the algebra as simple as possible. The general form of the equation of a straight line (ie a linear function) is:

$y = a + bx$

where y = dependent variable
x = independent variable
a = y intercept of the function (ie where $x = 0$)
b = slope of the function (which indicates how y will change if x changes)

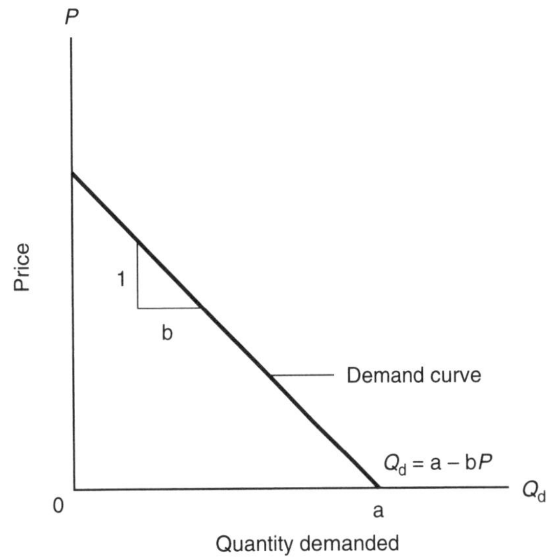

A linear demand curve is represented by the following equation:

$Q_d = a - bP$ .... (1)

where Q_d = quantity demanded (dependent variable)
P = price of the product (independent variable)
a = quantity demanded when $P = 0$ (intercept on quantity axis)
–b = inverse of the slope of the demand curve

Note that the slope is negative, since a change in price leads to a change in quantity demanded in the **opposite direction** to the change in price. Also note that –b represents the inverse of the slope (as it is usually measured), since the independent variable is depicted on the vertical axis instead of the horizontal axis. This demand curve is shown graphically in the figure on this page.

A linear supply curve is represented by the following equation:

$Q_s = c + dP$ .... (2)

where Q_s = quantity supplied (dependent variable)
P = price of the product (independent variable)
c = presumed quantity supplied when $P = 0$ (intercept on the quantity axis)[1]
d = inverse of the slope of the supply curve

Note that the slope is positive, since a change in price leads to a change in the quantity supplied in the **same direction** as the change in price. Again note that d represents the inverse of the slope, since the independent variable is depicted on the vertical axis. This supply curve is shown graphically in the following figure.

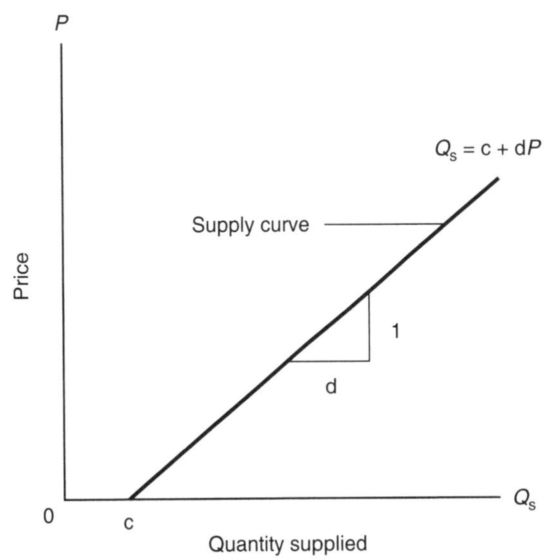

Equilibrium occurs when the quantity supplied in the market is equal to the quantity demanded in the market, that is, $Q_s = Q_d$. To obtain the **equilibrium price**,

1. Note that this is a presumed quantity (obtained by extending the supply curve), since it is unrealistic to assume that a positive quantity will be supplied when the price of the product is zero.

we use the right-hand sides of Equations 1 and 2. Since $Q_s = Q_d$, it follows that:

$$c + dP = a - bP$$
$$\therefore \quad dP + bP = a - c$$
$$\therefore \quad P(d + b) = a - c$$
$$\therefore \quad P = \frac{a - c}{d + b} \quad \text{.................... (3)}$$

The equilibrium quantity can be obtained by substituting the right-hand side of Equation 3 for P in the demand equation (Equation 1) or the supply equation (Equation 2). Substituting it into Equation 1 yields the following **equilibrium quantity** Q:

$$Q = a - b\left(\frac{a - c}{d + b}\right) \quad \text{....................... (4)}$$

Equations 3 and 4 may look quite intimidating. However, they simply show how the intercepts and slopes of the demand and supply curves may be used to obtain the equilibrium price and quantity.

We now work through a numerical example to show how it is done. We first use Equations 1 and 2 and then use Equations 3 and 4 to check whether they yield the same answers.

Suppose that the market demand and supply curves are given by $Q_d = 200 - 2P$ and $Q_s = 50 + P$. At equilibrium $Q_d = Q_s$, therefore:

$$200 - 2P = 50 + P$$
$$\therefore \quad -2P - P = 50 - 200$$
$$\therefore \quad -3P = -150$$
$$\therefore \quad P = \frac{-150}{-3}$$
$$= 50$$

Substituting $P = 50$ into the equation for the demand curve, yields $Q_d = 200 - 2(50) = 200 - 100 = 100$. Since $Q_d = Q_s$ at equilibrium, Q_s will also be equal to 100. In this example, therefore, the equilibrium price is 50 and the equilibrium quantity is 100. The same answer can be obtained by substituting the equilibrium price of 50 into the equation of the supply curve, ie $Q_s = 50 + P$.

We now use Equations 3 and 4 to see whether or not they yield the same results. In Equation 3 we had $P = (a - c)/(d + b)$. Substituting the values by the specific ones in our example yields:

$$P = \frac{200 - 50}{1 + 2}$$
$$= \frac{150}{3}$$
$$= 50 \quad \text{(as before)}$$

In Equation 4 we had $Q = a - b\left(\frac{a - c}{d + b}\right)$.

Again substituting the values in our examples for the symbols, we obtain:

$$Q = 200 - 2\left(\frac{200 - 50}{1 + 2}\right)$$
$$= 200 - 2\left(\frac{150}{3}\right)$$
$$= 200 - 2(50)$$
$$= 200 - 100$$
$$= 100 \quad \text{(as before)}$$

8

Demand and supply in action

Learning outcomes

Once you have studied this chapter you should be able to

- explain how a change in demand affects the equilibrium price and quantity in the market
- explain how a change in supply affects the equilibrium price and quantity in the market
- predict the effects of simultaneous changes in demand and supply
- analyse the interaction between related markets
- show what happens if the government interferes in the price mechanism by setting minimum or maximum prices

Other Things Being Equal – One of the old-time greats in economics; you can generally tell whether a man is an economist by the number of times he uses this particular phrase.

WILLIAM DAVIS

When there is a real scarcity, it is in the interest of the great body of consumers that the price of corn should be raised sufficiently high, to cause such a degree of economy in consumption as may enable the supply to last throughout the year.

ROBERT TORRENS

As we have already pointed out, demand and supply are among the most useful analytical devices available to the economist. In Chapter 7 we introduced demand and supply and showed how they combine to determine the equilibrium price and quantity exchanged in a goods market. In this chapter we show how demand and supply can be used to analyse certain situations in the economy. The emphasis is on predicting what will happen if something changes.

We start by examining how equilibrium prices and quantities react to **changes in demand**. This is followed by a discussion of **changes in supply**. We then look at **simultaneous changes in demand and supply**, followed by an analysis of the **interaction between related markets**. The next section deals with **government intervention** in the form of price fixing. Finally we give brief attention to the problems of **agriculture**.

In Chapter 7 we mentioned a number of factors which can cause a change in market demand as well as the factors which can cause a change in market supply. Remember that a change in any determinant of demand or supply *except* the price of the product will cause a change in demand or supply, illustrated by a shift of the demand curve or the supply curve. We now examine the impact of changes in demand or supply on the equilibrium price and quantity of the product concerned. We first look at changes in demand.

8.1 Changes in demand

An **increase in demand** (represented by a rightward shift of the demand curve) will result in an increase in the price of the product and an increase in the quantity exchanged, *ceteris paribus*. This is illustrated in Figure 8-1(a) where the demand curve shifts from *DD* to D_1D_1. The increase in demand can be the result of a change in any of the determinants of demand *except the price of the product* – a change in the price of the product will result in a change in the quantity demanded, illustrated by a movement along the demand curve. As explained in Chapter 7, the sources of an increase in demand include:

- an increase in the price of a substitute product
- a decrease in the price of a complementary product
- an increase in consumers' income
- a greater consumer preference for the product
- an expected increase in the price of the product

What happens to supply when demand increases? Supply (represented by the supply curve) remains unchanged, but the quantity supplied increases as the price of the product increases. In other words, there is an upward movement along the supply curve, such as the movement from *E* to E_1 in Figure 8-1(a). When demand increases, there is an excess demand at the original price P_0. As explained in Chapter 7, an excess demand (or market shortage) results in an increase in the price of the product. The price of the product is bid up as purchasers compete to obtain the available quantity supplied. As the price rises, suppliers increase the quantity supplied, while the quantity demanded falls. This process continues until equilibrium is re-established at E_1, that is, at a higher price (P_1) and a higher quantity (Q_1) than before.

A **decrease in demand** will result in a decrease in the price of the product and a decrease in the quantity exchanged, *ceteris paribus*. This is illustrated in Figure 8-1(b) by a leftward *shift* of the demand curve from *DD* to D_2D_2. The decrease in demand could be the result of a change in any of the determinants of demand *except the price of the product*. As explained in Chapter 7, the possibilities include:

FIGURE 8-1 Changes in demand

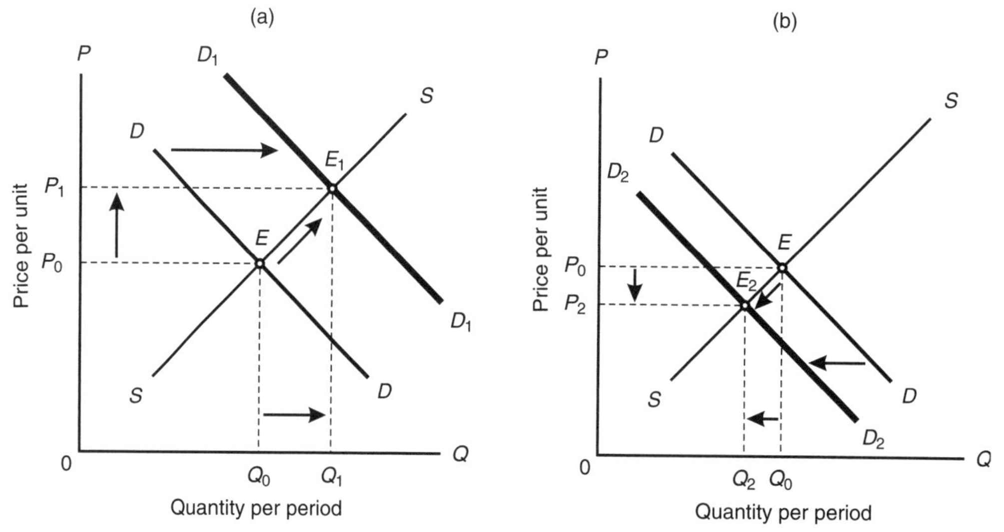

An increase in demand is illustrated in (a). The demand curve shifts from DD to D_1D_1 and as a result the equilibrium price increases from P_0 to P_1, while the equilibrium quantity increases from Q_0 to Q_1. There is an upward movement along the supply curve from E to E_1. In (b) we show a decrease in demand, illustrated by a shift of the demand curve from DD to D_2D_2. Both the equilibrium price and the equilibrium quantity fall, to P_2 and Q_2 respectively. There is a downward movement along the supply curve from E to E_2.

- a fall in the price of a substitute product
- an increase in the price of a complementary product
- a fall in consumers' income
- a reduced preference for the product
- an expected fall in the price of the product

Supply (represented by the supply curve) again remains unchanged. When demand decreases, the price of the product falls and this leads to a reduction in the quantity supplied. The supply curve remains unchanged, but there is a downward movement along the supply curve, such as the movement from E to E_2 in Figure 8-1(b). When demand decreases, there is an excess supply at the original price P_0. As explained in Chapter 7, an excess supply (or market surplus) results in a reduction in price as sellers compete to sell their excess stocks. As the price falls, the quantity supplied also falls, while the quantity demanded increases, until equilibrium is re-established at E_2, that is, at a lower price (P_2) and a lower quantity (Q_2) than before.

A range of possible changes in the demand for a product X is illustrated in Figure 8-2.

8.2 Changes in supply

An **increase in supply** will result in a fall in the price of the product and an increase in the quantity exchanged, *ceteris paribus*. This is illustrated in Figure 8-3(a) where the supply curve shifts to the right (or downwards) from SS to S_1S_1. Such an increase in supply means that more goods are supplied at each price than before or, alternatively, that each quantity is supplied at a lower price than before. The shift of the supply curve could be the result of a change in any of the determinants of supply *other than the price of the product*. As explained in Chapter 7, the possibilities include:

- a fall in the price of an alternative product or a rise in the price of a joint product
- a reduction in the price of any of the factors of production or other inputs (ie a decrease in the cost of production)
- an improvement in the productivity of the factors of production (eg as a result of technological progress) – this also lowers the cost of production

What happens to demand when supply increases? Demand (represented by the demand curve) remains unchanged but the **quantity demanded** increases as the price of the product falls. There is a downward movement along the demand curve, such as the movement from E to E_1 in Figure 8-3(a). When supply increases, there is an excess supply at the original price P_0. As explained in Chapter 7, an excess supply (or market surplus) results in a decrease in the price of the product. Firms compete with each other by lowering the price of the product. As the price falls, the quantity demanded increases, while the quantity supplied falls. This process continues until equilibrium is re-established at E_1, that is, at a lower price (P_1) and a higher quantity (Q_1) than before.

A **decrease in supply** will result in an increase in the price of the product and a decrease in the quantity exchanged, *ceteris paribus*. This is illustrated in Figure 8-3(b) by a leftward (upward) shift of the supply curve from SS to S_2S_2. Such a decrease in supply means that fewer goods are supplied at each price than before or, alternatively, that each quantity is supplied at a higher price than before. The shift of the supply curve could be the result of a change in any of the determinants of supply *other than the price of the product*. As explained in Chapter 7, the possibilities include:

- an increase in the price of an alternative product or a fall in the price of a joint product
- an increase in the price of any of the factors of production or other inputs (ie an increase in the cost of production)
- a deterioration in the productivity of the factors of production (which also raises the cost of production)

What happens to demand when supply decreases? Demand remains unchanged but there is an upward movement along the demand curve, such as the movement from E to E_2 in Figure 8-3(b). When supply decreases, there is excess demand at the original price P_0. As explained in Chapter 7, excess demand (or a market shortage) results in an increase in the price of the product. Consumers bid up the price of the product in their attempt to obtain the available quantity supplied. As the price increases, the quantity demanded decreases, while the quantity supplied increases. This process continues until equilibrium is re-established at E_2, that is, at a higher price (P_2) and lower quantity (Q_2) than before.

A few possible changes in the supply of a product X are illustrated in Figure 8-4.

8.3 Simultaneous changes in demand and supply

When only demand or only supply changes, it is possible to predict what will happen to equilibrium prices and quantities in the market. However, if demand and supply change simultaneously, the precise outcome cannot be predicted. This is a special case of a more general problem in economic theory (as well as in most other theories). When one factor is allowed to change, it is usually possible to determine or predict the effects of such a change. But when more than one

FIGURE 8-2 Examples of changes in demand

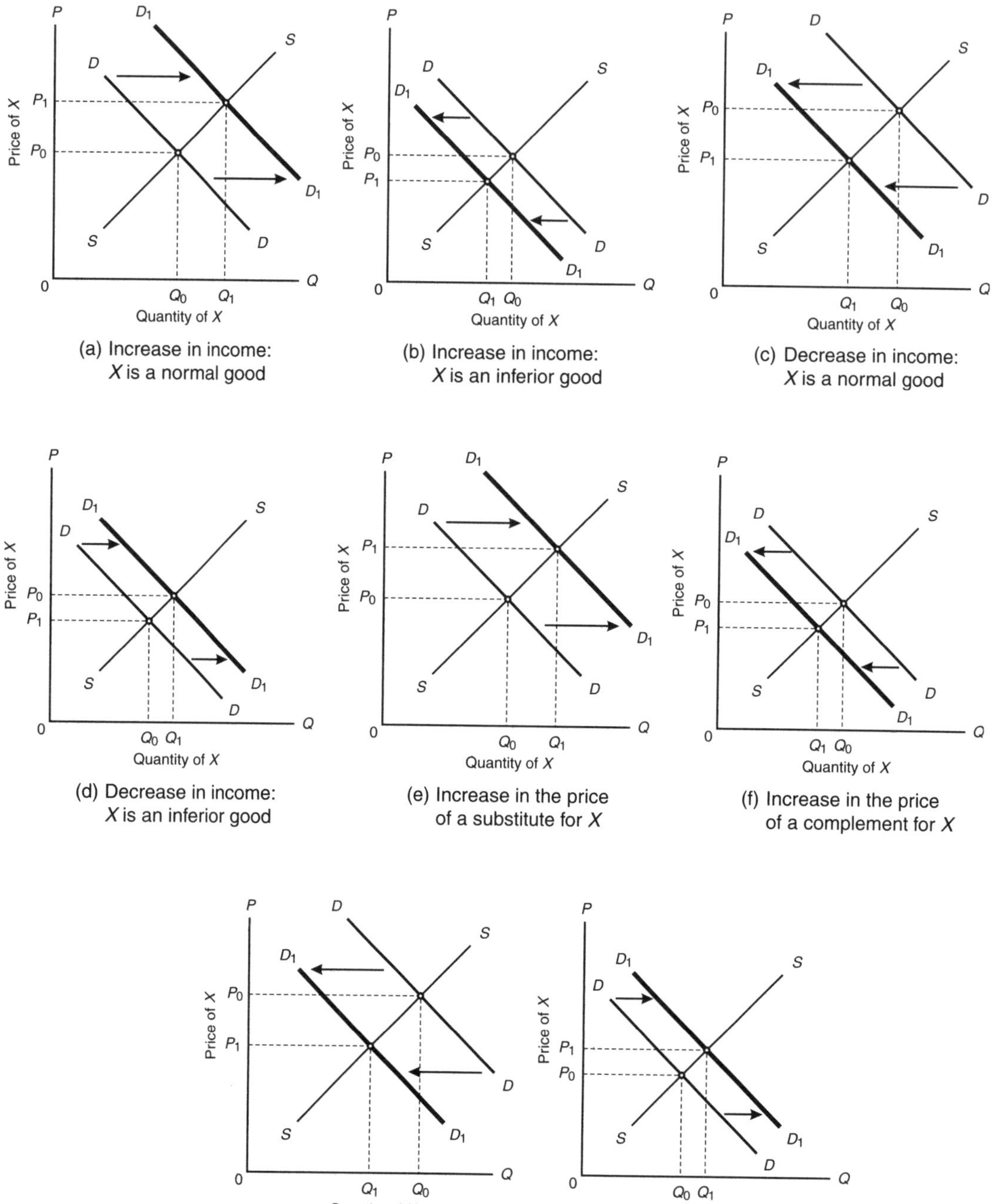

(a) Increase in income: X is a normal good

(b) Increase in income: X is an inferior good

(c) Decrease in income: X is a normal good

(d) Decrease in income: X is an inferior good

(e) Increase in the price of a substitute for X

(f) Increase in the price of a complement for X

(g) Decrease in the price of a substitute for X

(h) Decrease in the price of a complement for X

change is involved, it is seldom possible to predict the outcome, since the changes may work in opposite directions. The method of **comparative statics**, which we use here and which was explained in Chapter 6, requires that only one variable or force is allowed to change at a time.

We have seen that an increase in demand leads to an increase in the equilibrium price and that a decrease in supply also leads to an increase in the equilibrium price. It follows, therefore, that an increase in demand accompanied by a decrease in supply will raise the equilibrium price of the product

FIGURE 8-3 Changes in supply

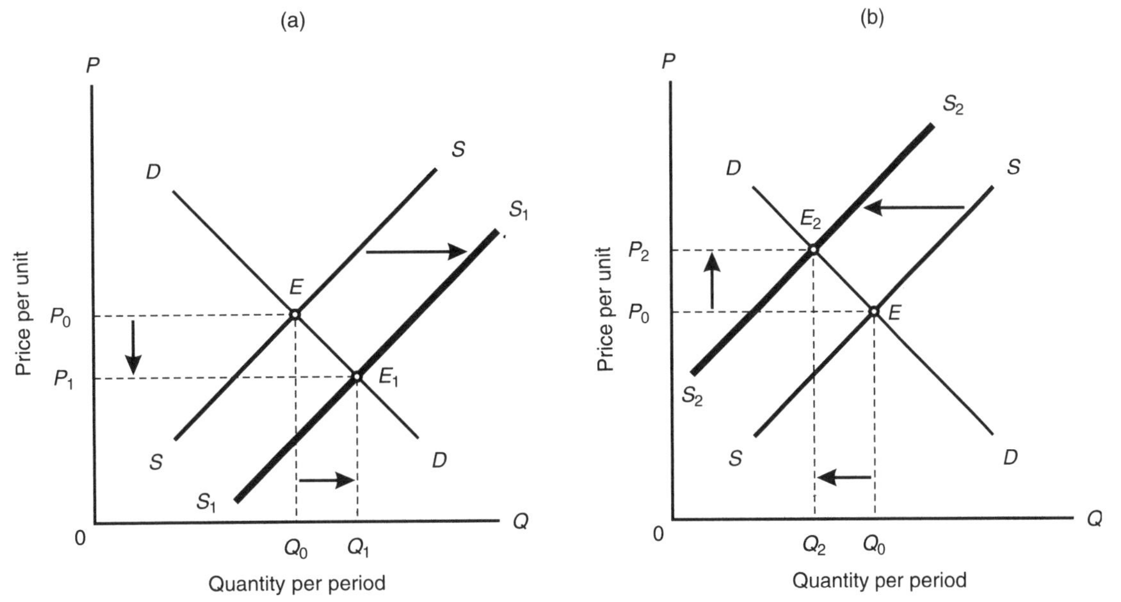

In (a) we show an increase in supply, illustrated by the shift of the supply curve from SS to S_1S_1. The equilibrium price falls to P_1 and the equilibrium quantity increases to Q_1. There is a downward movement along the demand curve from E to E_1. A decrease in supply is illustrated in (b) by a shift of the supply curve from SS to S_2S_2. The equilibrium price increases to P_2 while the equilibrium quantity falls to Q_2. In this case there is an upward movement along the demand curve from E to E_2.

concerned. What we cannot predict, however, is what will happen to the equilibrium quantity exchanged in the market. An increase in demand raises the equilibrium quantity, *ceteris paribus*, while a decrease in supply lowers the equilibrium quantity, *ceteris paribus*. The two forces work in opposite directions as far as the equilibrium quantity is concerned and the outcome will depend on the relative magnitudes of the changes in demand and supply.

Similar problems occur in other cases. For example, when demand and supply both decrease it is possible to predict what will happen to the quantity exchanged, since both forces have the same impact on the equilibrium quantity. Their combined impact on the equilibrium price is, however, uncertain, since a decrease in demand reduces the price, *ceteris paribus*, while a decrease in supply raises the price, *ceteris paribus*. The equilibrium price could rise, remain unchanged, or fall, depending on the relative magnitudes of the changes in demand and supply.

The results of the various combinations of simultaneous changes in demand and supply are summarised in Table 8-1. Figure 8-5 illustrates the problem by showing the possible outcomes of a simultaneous increase in demand and decrease in supply. In Figure 8-5(a) the relative changes in demand and supply are equal; in (b) the relative change in supply is greater than the relative change in demand; and in (c) the relative change in demand is greater than the relative change in supply. The changes in demand and supply both raise the equilibrium price of the product but the change in the equilibrium quantity is uncertain. In Figure 8-5(a) the equilibrium quantity remains unchanged; in (b) it falls; and in (c) it rises. The figure clearly shows how the outcome depends on the relative changes in demand and supply.

TABLE 8-1 Simultaneous changes in demand and supply

Change in demand	*Change in supply*	*Change in price*	*Change in quantity*
Increase	Increase	Uncertain	Increase
Increase	Decrease	Increase	Uncertain
Decrease	Increase	Decrease	Uncertain
Decrease	Decrease	Uncertain	Decrease

A special case of changes in demand and supply in speculative markets is explained further on, in Box 8-1.

FIGURE 8-4 Examples of changes in supply

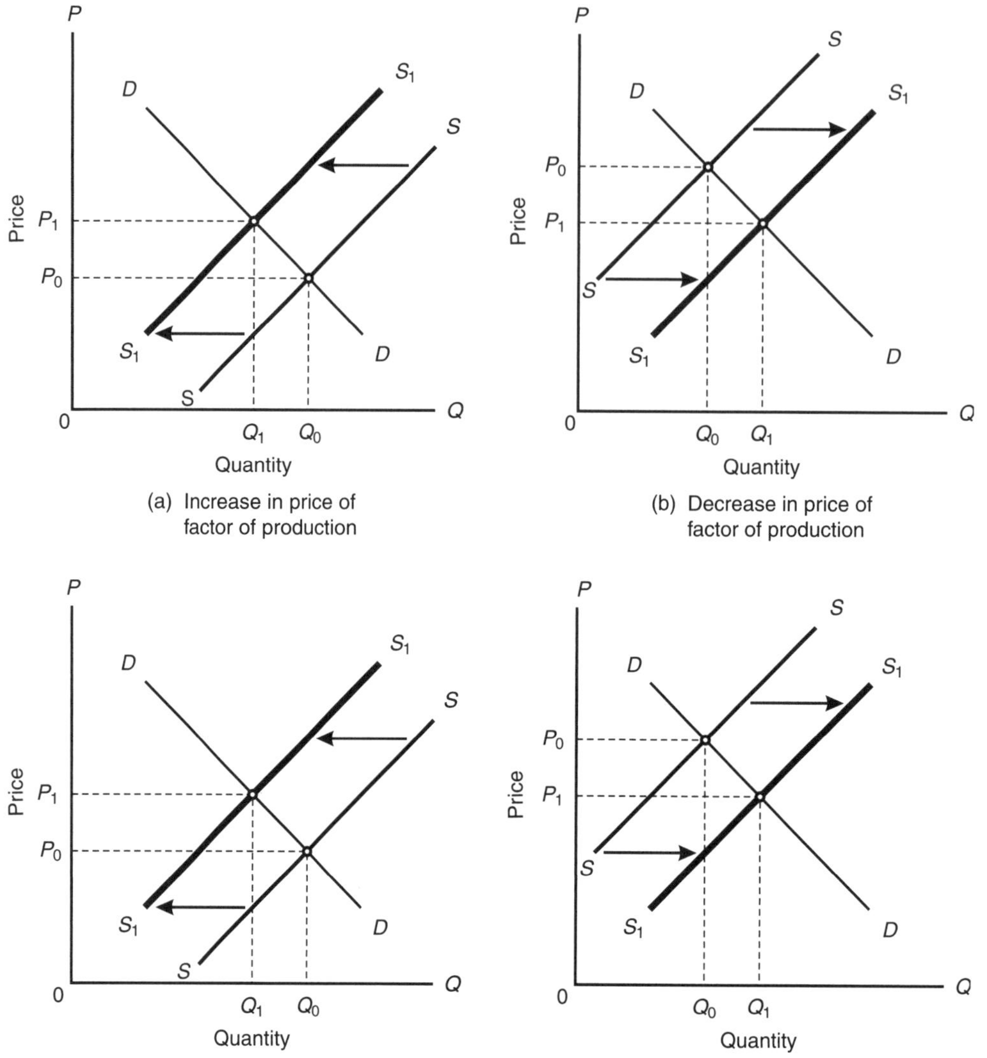

(c) Decrease in productivity

(d) Increase in productivity

8.4 Interaction between related markets

As we saw in Chapter 7, many products are related to each other in some way or another. For example, some are substitutes (in consumption), some are complements (in consumption), some are substitutes in production, some are joint products, and so on. In this section we extend the analysis in the previous section and provide some examples of interrelationships between different markets.

Fish and meat

Until 1966 Roman Catholics were not allowed to eat meat on Fridays and tended to eat fish instead. In 1966 the Pope lifted the ban and announced that Catholics could eat meat on Fridays. What was the probable impact of this decision on the prices and average weekly sales of fish and meat respectively?

Economic theory tells us that in predominantly Catholic areas the demand for fish would have declined, illustrated by a leftward *shift* of the demand curve, as in Figure 8-6(a), while the demand for meat would have increased, illustrated by a rightward *shift* of the demand curve, as in Figure 8-6(b). As a result the price and weekly sales of fish would have declined, while the price and weekly sales of meat would have increased, as illustrated in the two diagrams. Research by an American economist, Frederick Bell, showed that fish prices and sales did indeed decline. This is an example of the impact of a change in tastes (broadly defined) on demand, and therefore on the equilibrium prices and quantities, in the case of substitute products.

FIGURE 8-5 A simultaneous increase in demand and decrease in supply

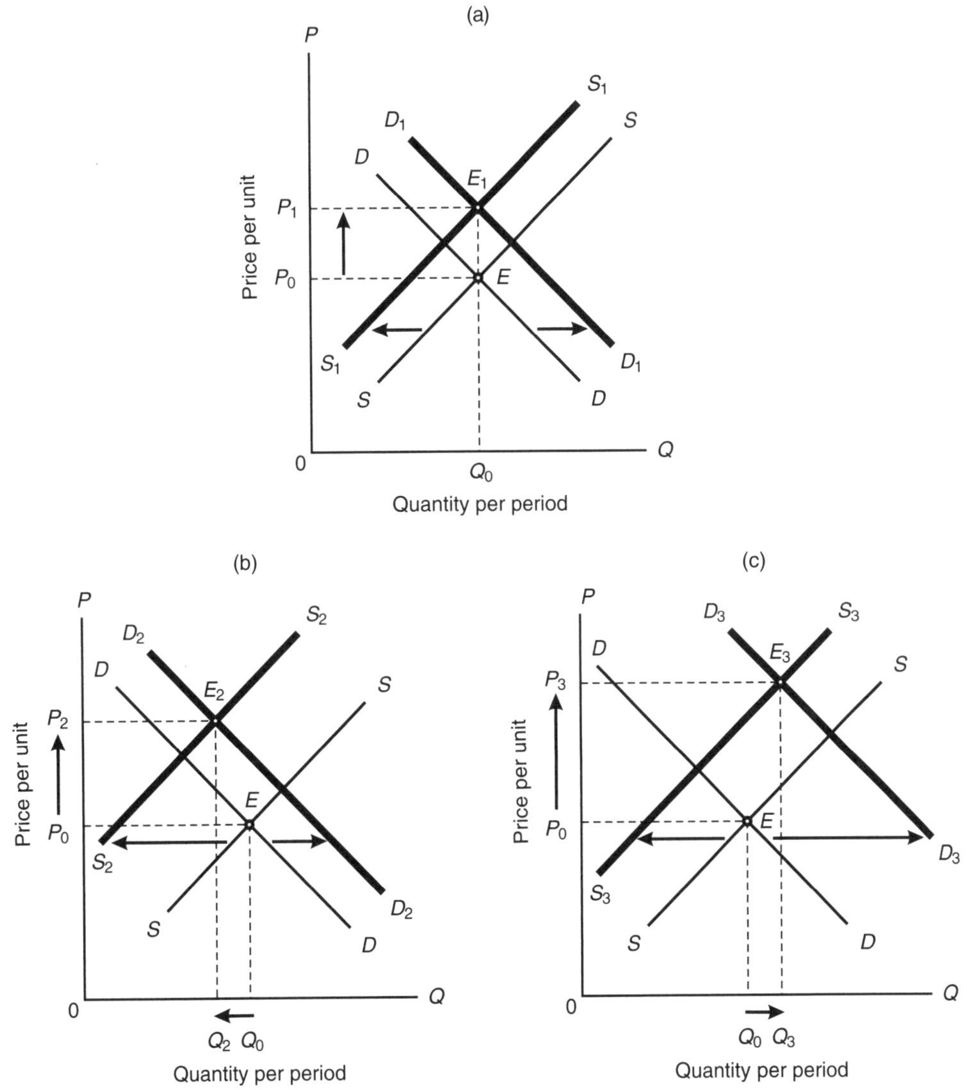

In all three diagrams the original demand, supply, equilibrium price and equilibrium quantity are represented by DD, SS, P_0 and Q_0. A simultaneous increase in demand (illustrated by a rightward shift of the demand curve) and decrease in supply (illustrated by a leftward shift of the supply curve) raises the price of the product. The impact on the equilibrium quantity depends on the relative magnitude of the changes. In (a) the quantity remains unchanged at Q_0. In (b) it falls to Q_2 and in (c) it increases to Q_3.

Conclusive medical evidence that fish is much healthier than meat could have exactly the opposite effect to that shown in Figure 8-6. This can be illustrated by simply exchanging the diagrams for fish and meat.

Motorcars and tyres

What will happen, *ceteris paribus*, in the market for new tyres if the cost of producing motorcars increases (eg as a result of successful wage claims by trade unions in the motorcar industry)? The increase in costs in the motorcar industry can be illustrated by a leftward (upward) *shift* of the supply curve, as in Figure 8-7(a). As a result, the equilibrium price of motorcars will increase from P_0 to P_1 and the equilibrium quantity will fall from Q_0 to Q_1. With fewer motorcars being produced, the demand for new tyres (a complementary good) will decrease, illustrated by a leftward (downward) *shift* of the demand curve in Figure

FIGURE 8-6 Interaction between the markets for fish and meat

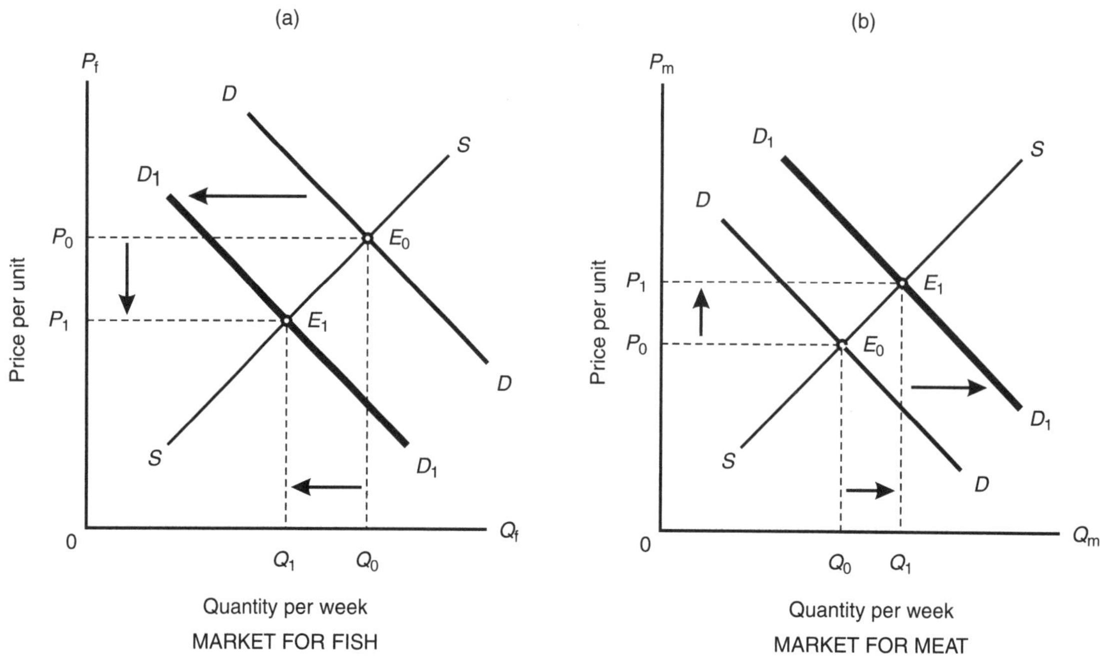

The markets for fish and meat are illustrated in (a) and (b) respectively. The original demand and supply curves are DD and SS and the equilibrium prices and quantities are P_0 and Q_0 respectively. In (a) the decrease in the demand for fish is illustrated by the leftward (downward) shift of the demand curve from DD to D_1D_1. The equilibrium price of fish declines from P_0 to P_1 and the weekly quantity traded falls from Q_0 to Q_1. In (b) the increase in the demand for meat is illustrated by the rightward (upward) shift of the demand curve from DD to D_1D_1. The equilibrium price of meat increases from P_0 to P_1 and the weekly quantity traded rises from Q_0 to Q_1.

8-7(b). As a result, the equilibrium price of tyres will fall from P_0 to P_1 and the equilibrium quantity will also decrease, from Q_0 to Q_1.

A cost-saving technological improvement in the production of motorcars or an increase in the productivity of the workers in the industry (without a concomitant increase in wages) will have exactly the opposite impact to that illustrated in Figure 8-7.

The interaction between the foreign exchange market and the domestic market for hake

In 2001 the price of the rand fell sharply in terms of the major international currencies. This depreciation of the rand, from about R8,00 per US dollar in September to more than R13,00 to the US dollar in December, can also be illustrated with the aid of demand and supply curves, as we shall explain in Chapter 17. When the rand depreciates, the domestic prices of imported goods inevitably increase. At the same time, however, it becomes more profitable for South African firms to export, and sometimes the increase in exports occurs at the expense of domestic consumers. For example, towards the end of 2001 South African fishing companies were getting such good prices for hake (in rand terms) on the export market, that it became almost unobtainable in the domestic market. This resulted in a sharp increase in the domestic price of hake. In the end, limited quantities of hake were available in the South African market but only at prices about equal to those that fishing firms could obtain by exporting it. This is illustrated in Figure 8-8. Prior to the depreciation of the rand, the demand curve was *DD*, the supply curve *SS*, the equilibrium price P_0 and the equilibrium quantity Q_0. After the depreciation of the rand, the domestic supply fell to S_1S_1, causing an increase in the price of hake to P_1, and a fall in the quantity to Q_1.

The subsequent appreciation of the rand against the major international currencies in 2002 had the opposite type of effect on the market for hake in South Africa, *ceteris paribus*.

FIGURE 8-7 Interaction between markets for motorcars and tyres

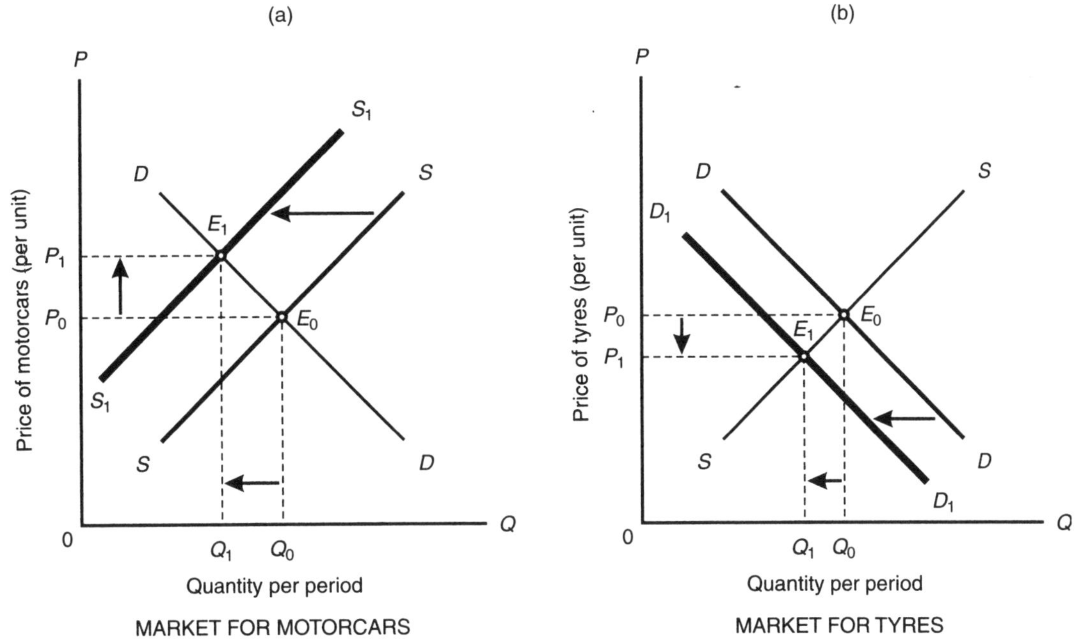

The markets for motorcars and tyres are illustrated in (a) and (b) respectively. The original demand and supply curves are DD and SS and the equilibrium prices and quantities P_0 and Q_0 respectively. In (a) the impact of an increase in the costs of producing motorcars is illustrated by the leftward (upward) shift of the supply curve from SS to S_1S_1. The equilibrium price of motorcars increases from P_0 to P_1 and the equilibrium quantity falls from Q_0 to Q_1. In (b) the consequent decrease in the demand for tyres is illustrated by a leftward (downward) shift of the demand curve from DD to D_1D_1. The equilibrium price of tyres falls from P_0 to P_1 and the equilibrium quantity also decreases from Q_0 to Q_1.

8.5 Government intervention

The changes explained in the previous sections will occur only if the market forces of supply and demand are free to establish the equilibrium prices and quantities of goods and services. Quite frequently, however, consumers, trade unions, farmers, business people and politicians are not satisfied with the prices and quantities determined by market demand and supply. Their dissatisfaction leads them to put pressure on government to intervene to influence prices and quantities in the market. This intervention can take different forms, including:

- setting maximum prices (price ceilings)
- setting minimum prices (price floors)
- subsidising certain products or activities
- taxing certain products or activities

In this section we examine the impact of maximum prices. Minimum prices are dealt with in the next section and more examples of government intervention are provided in Chapter 14 (minimum wages), Chapter 16 (excise taxes) and Chapter 17 (import tariffs and quotas).

Maximum prices (price ceilings, price control)

Governments often set maximum prices for certain goods and services. In the 1970s the prices of many goods and services in South Africa were controlled by government (eg the prices of bricks, sand, cement, sugar, firearms, television receivers, glass and metal containers, glass, yellow margarine, bread, electrical appliances, radios, tyres, sanitary ware, windows and pharmaceutical products). During the 1980s, however, almost all the price controls were abolished, and nowadays most prices are determined by market forces. It is nonetheless important to analyse the impact of maximum price fixing. Many consumers call for price control and there is always the possibility that the government may reintroduce it.

FIGURE 8-8 The impact of the depreciation of the rand on the market for hake in South Africa

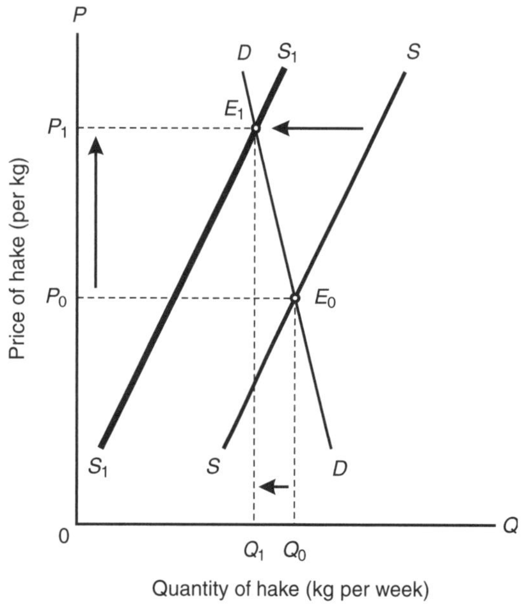

The initial demand and supply are indicated by DD and SS. The initial equilibrium price is P_0 and the equilibrium quantity Q_0. After the depreciation, the supply curve shifted to S_1S_1 causing an increase in price from P_0 to P_1 and a decrease in the quantity traded from Q_0 to Q_1.

Governments set maximum prices

- to keep the prices of basic foodstuffs low, as part of a policy to assist the poor
- to avoid the exploitation of consumers by producers, that is, to avoid "unfair" prices
- to combat inflation
- to limit the production of certain goods and services in wartime

If a maximum price is set **above** the equilibrium (or market-clearing) price, it will have no effect on the market price or the quantity exchanged. Prices and quantities will still be determined by demand and supply. However, when a maximum price is set **below** the equilibrium price (as is usually the case), it will have significant effects.

In Figure 8-9 we show a demand curve (*DD*), a supply curve (*SS*), the equilibrium price (P_0) and the equilibrium quantity exchanged (Q_0). Suppose the government then sets a maximum price (P_m) **below** the equilibrium price (P_0). At the lower price (P_m) consumers will demand a quantity (Q_2) which is higher than the equilibrium quantity (Q_0). Suppliers, however, will only be willing to supply Q_1, which is lower than Q_0. There is thus a **market shortage** (or **excess demand**) equal to the difference between Q_2 and Q_1 (or *ab*).

In the absence of price control this excess demand will raise the price until equilibrium is re-established at P_0 and Q_0. But when price control is introduced, different ways have to be found to solve the problem of excess demand. When market prices are not allowed to fulfil their rationing function, someone or something else must do the job. The basic problem is how to allocate the available quantity supplied (Q_1) between consumers who demand a total of Q_2 of the good concerned.[1] This can be done in various ways:

- Consumers may be served on a "first come first served" basis, resulting in queues or waiting lists.
- Suppliers may set up informal rationing systems (eg by limiting the quantity sold to each consumer or by selling to regular customers only).
- Government may introduce an official rationing system by issuing ration tickets or coupons which have to be submitted when purchasing the product.

Queues and informal rationing systems all entail additional private costs (to the consumers and/or the sup-

FIGURE 8-9 Maximum prices

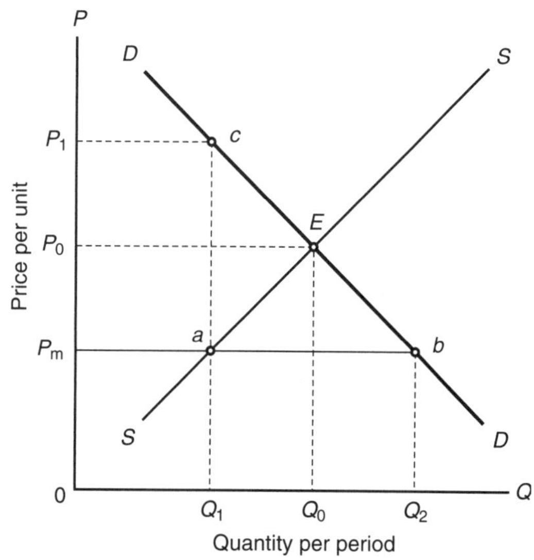

If the government sets a maximum price of P_m below the equilibrium price of P_0, this results in an excess demand of $Q_2 - Q_1$ (or ab).

1. One possibility is to import the difference between Q_2 and Q_1, provided such imports are available at a price of P_m or less. This will eliminate the shortage, but if such imports are available, price control is unnecessary to start with.

BOX 8-1 SELF-FULFILLING EXPECTATIONS

When all the participants in a market expect that the price of the product will move in a certain direction and they all incorporate this expectation in their decisions, the expected movement will be realised almost immediately (provided the product is of such a nature that purchases or supplies can be brought forward or postponed easily). This is an example of self-fulfilling expectations.

To explain this phenomenon, let us look at the international gold market. If all participants in the gold market expect the price of gold to increase significantly, everyone will try to purchase as much gold as possible before the price goes up. At the same time the suppliers of gold will hold back their supplies as long as possible. In the accompanying figure, *DD* and *SS* represent the original demand and supply of gold. The equilibrium price is P_1 and the quantity exchanged is Q_1. A general expectation of a price increase which is incorporated into participants' decisions will increase demand to *D'D'* and reduce supply to *S'S'*. The result is an increase in the price to P_2. The only reason for this increase is the expectation that the price will increase. In this case, therefore, the participants' expectations are fulfilled.

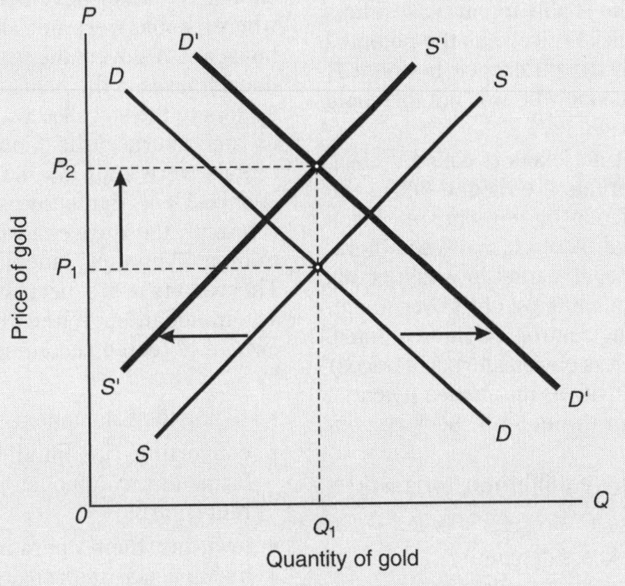

The same type of effect can occur when everyone expects the price of gold to fall and they incorporate this expectation into their decisions. Other markets in which self-fulfilling expectations can occur include other international commodity markets (eg the markets for platinum, silver and maize), the stock market (eg the JSE Securities Exchange), the capital market (in which long-term securities are traded) and the foreign exchange market (in which currencies are traded). These markets are all speculative markets in which expectations play an important role. Self-fulfilling expectations cannot occur in all markets – in many markets supply cannot adjust instantaneously and inventories of the product cannot be hoarded. Even in the markets where self-fulfilling expectations may occur, the various participants usually have different expectations, with the result that changes in demand, supply and price are unpredictable. Nevertheless, this example serves to emphasise the importance of expectations and explains why certain prices sometimes move in a particular direction for no apparent reason.

pliers). For example, consumers have to spend time queueing, while suppliers have to use scarce resources to administer the rationing system. Official rationing systems amount to additional government intervention and stimulate corruption (eg bribery of rationing officials). Another consequence of maximum price fixing is the development of black markets.

Black markets occur in any situation where the market forces of supply and demand cannot (or are not allowed to) eliminate excess demand. For example, when there is a major sporting event (such as the Wimbledon tennis finals, the World Cup soccer final or a rugby test between South Africa and New Zealand), or a rock concert featuring, say, the Rolling Stones, Iron Maiden or Pearl Jam, tickets are in limited supply. The tickets are issued at fixed prices and the quantity of tickets is limited by how many people the venue can accommodate. Although the prices may be high, there are still more people who want to attend the event than there are tickets available. This situation is similar to the one illustrated in Figure 8-9. Anyone who succeeds in getting a ticket (eg by queueing through the night) can sell this ticket to someone else at a much higher price. In Figure 8-9 we see that consumers are willing to pay a price of P_1 for a quantity of Q_1. Anyone who is able to purchase a ticket at a price of P_m (the official price) has the potential to make a profit equal to the difference between P_1 and P_m by selling it to someone who was not fortunate enough to get hold of a ticket.

This alternative market in tickets is called a black market. Not all black markets are illegal, but in the case of maximum price fixing by government, black market activity is outlawed. A black market is therefore often defined as an illegal market in which goods are sold above the maximum price set by government. All price controls (including controls on interest rates, exchange rates and other less obvious forms of prices) stimulate black market activity as unsatisfied potential purchasers seek to obtain the good or service concerned.

Fixing prices below the equilibrium (or market-clearing) price thus

- creates shortages (or excess demand)
- prevents the market mechanism from allocating the available quantity among consumers
- stimulates black market activity by providing an incentive for people to obtain the good and resell it at a higher price to those consumers who are willing to pay higher prices to obtain it

Price controls are invariably implemented in the sincere belief that they are in the best interests of society – in many cases they are motivated by an honest concern for the well-being of poor consumers or low-income citizens. Price controls, however, create many problems of their own. They are nowhere near as attractive as those who propose them would like us to believe, and the controls usually have to be abolished sooner or later. Nevertheless, price control is introduced every now and then. Many politicians are apparently under the impression that the basic forces of demand and supply (ie Adam Smith's proverbial invisible hand) can be eliminated simply by passing a law.

Rent control

Rent control provides one of the best examples of the problems created by imposing a maximum price below the equilibrium (or market-clearing) price. It has been said that one of the surest ways of destroying a city (short of dropping a nuclear bomb on it) is to implement rent control. Like all other controls, the motives of rent control are praiseworthy. In South Africa, for example, rent control was introduced in the late 1940s to protect tenants from being exploited by the owners of rented accommodation during the post-war housing shortage. This shortage arose because, during the war, production had been geared to the war effort and the construction of dwelling units had been curtailed. The problem was exacerbated by the return of ex-servicemen who did not have accommodation and could not afford to purchase houses. A similar situation developed later in the townships, where people were not allowed to purchase land or houses and government stopped constructing additional houses in the belief that blacks were temporary visitors to the so-called white areas and would sooner or later return to the "homelands". At the same time rentals were kept low, so as to assist the generally poor residents in the townships.

In both these cases market forces were prevented from fulfilling their rationing and allocative functions. The results were permanent shortages of rented accommodation. When rent controls are imposed, owners of rented accommodation (eg flats) can react by

- selling the flats under sectional title
- converting the buildings into offices or other forms of accommodation which are not subject to rent control
- lowering their operating costs by skimping on maintenance and repairs (ie by reducing the quality of their service) – in some cases the buildings deteriorate to such an extent that they are eventually simply abandoned
- ceasing to erect new rented accommodation – the supply of new rented accommodation falls (while the population and demand increase) and the shortage becomes worse

All these actions aggravate the shortage of rented accommodation.

When rent control is in force, the market cannot fulfil its rationing function and alternatives have to be found. Prospective tenants are at the mercy of agents and landlords, and often resort to bribery to get their names moved up on the long waiting lists (queues). Corruption and favouritism are rife. Those who are fortunate enough to obtain accommodation (ie the existing tenants) benefit – at least for as long as the condition of the units does not deteriorate too much. Prospective tenants often have to pay "black market prices", for example in the form of exorbitant "finder's fees" or "key deposits".

The longer the controls are maintained, the greater the difference between controlled rentals and market-clearing rentals will become, and the more difficult it becomes to lift the controls, since rentals will soar when the controls are abolished. In the end no one gains – those fortunate enough to obtain accommodation find that the condition of the buildings deteriorates over time (possibly even to the point where they become uninhabitable); the owners cannot make a profit and leave the market; and many people cannot find accommodation at all. The irony is that those who were supposed to benefit from the controls probably suffer the most.

The welfare costs of maximum price fixing

The concepts of consumer surplus and producer surplus, introduced in Chapter 7, can be used to illustrate the welfare loss associated with maximum price fixing. In Figure 8-10 a maximum price P_m is set **below** the market-clearing price P_1. As a result the quantity exchanged falls from the equilibrium level Q_1 to Q_m.

FIGURE 8-10 The welfare costs of maximum price fixing

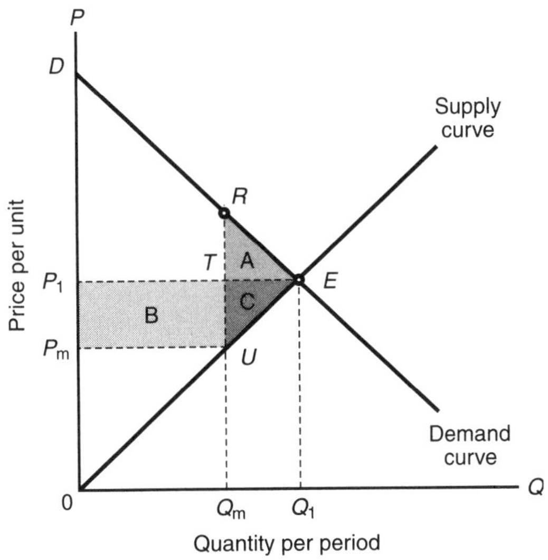

*Prior to price fixing the equilibrium price is P_1 and the equilibrium quantity Q_1. Government then fixes a maximum price P_m **below** the equilibrium price. The quantity exchanged falls to Q_m. Rectangle B is transferred from the producer surplus to the consumer surplus. Triangle A, which used to be part of the consumer surplus, and triangle C, which used to be part of the producer surplus, both disappear. The total deadweight loss to society is equal to A plus C.*

At the market-clearing price P_1, the consumer surplus was P_1DE (see Figure 7-12). At the new fixed price, P_m, the consumer surplus is P_mDRU. Consumers have lost the shaded triangle indicated by A, since only Q_m is exchanged, but they have gained rectangle B, since those who can obtain the product now pay less for it than before. Area B used to be part of the producer surplus but now becomes part of the consumer surplus. In the absence of the maximum price, the producer surplus is indicated by the triangle $0P_1E$ (see Figure 7-13). All that remains of this surplus after the maximum price is set, is the small triangle $0P_mU$. As mentioned above, rectangle B is transferred to the consumer surplus. Triangle C simply disappears, since only Q_m is produced and exchanged. The total welfare loss to society is triangle A plus triangle C. This is usually referred to as **deadweight loss**. Too little is being produced and in the end society (which consists of consumers and producers) is worse off as a result of the interference in the market system.

Administered prices

Although price control, in the sense of government control of the prices of goods and services produced by private firms, has for all practical purposes been abolished in South Africa, government departments or other public sector agencies still determine the prices of a range of goods and services in South Africa. These prices are usually called **administered prices**, to indicate that they are the result of administrative processes rather than of market forces of supply and demand. Administered prices often feature strongly in the debate on the causes of inflation in South Africa and appropriate anti-inflation policy.

According to the South African Reserve Bank, the prices of more than 20 per cent of the goods and services in the CPI basket can be classified as administered prices. The most important of these are the prices of medical services, petrol and diesel, communication services, electricity and education (in that order). Other prices administered by the public sector include those of public transport services, water and licences.

The term "administered prices" was first coined in the United States in the 1930s to indicate private sector prices that were determined discretionally by the suppliers of goods and services instead of by market forces. In South Africa, however, the term is used exclusively to indicate government involvement in price determination. The different prices are administered according to different conventions, rules and formulae. For example, a specific formula is used to determine the monthly adjustments in fuel prices, while other administered prices are determined in other ways, often on a cost-plus basis. Price determination is discussed further in the rest of this book, particularly in Chapter 13. For the moment the important point to bear in mind is that many prices in the economy are not determined by the impersonal market forces of supply and demand. Discretion often plays an important role.

8.6 Agricultural prices

Fluctuations in agricultural prices

The prices of agricultural products generally fluctuate much more than the prices of manufactured goods. Why is this the case? The answer lies in the supply conditions. The supply of agricultural products varies from season to season and is affected by the weather, disease, and by the fact that many products are perishable and therefore cannot be stored for long periods. As supply varies (illustrated by shifts of the supply curve), prices vary, even if demand conditions (illustrated by the demand curve) remain unchanged.

These fluctuations may be intensified by the reaction of farmers, particularly in the case of annual crops. Suppose, for example, that the price of potatoes increases sharply in Year 1 as a result of a bad harvest. The high price of potatoes induces existing potato farmers to plant more potatoes in Year 2 and also induces other farmers to plant potatoes instead of alternative crops. If the weather and other market conditions in Year 2 are normal, the result will be a significant increase in the supply of potatoes in Year 2 and a fall in the price of potatoes, *ceteris paribus*. The extent of the price decline may actually leave potato farmers worse off than they would have been if the supply of potatoes had not increased.

This example illustrates the **fallacy of composition**, which was explained in Chapter 1. An individual potato farmer may improve his position by producing more potatoes, but if all farmers do the same, potato farmers (as a group) may end up being worse off than before. This is illustrated in Figure 8-11.

In the figure the demand and supply in Year 1 are represented by DD and S_1S_1. The equilibrium price is P_1, the equilibrium quantity is Q_1 and farmers' total income from potatoes is represented by the area $0P_1E_1Q_1$ (ie the price (P_1) times the quantity sold (Q_1)). Expecting high prices for potatoes, farmers increase their supply of potatoes to S_2S_2 in Year 2. With demand unchanged, the quantity sold increases to Q_2 but the price falls to P_2. Farmers' total income from potatoes in Year 2, represented by the area $0P_2E_2Q_2$, is lower than in Year 1 (ie $0P_1E_1Q_1 > 0P_2E_2Q_2$). As a group they are thus worse off in Year 2 than in Year 1, despite having produced and sold more potatoes.

FIGURE 8-11 An increase in supply as a result of an expected high price of potatoes

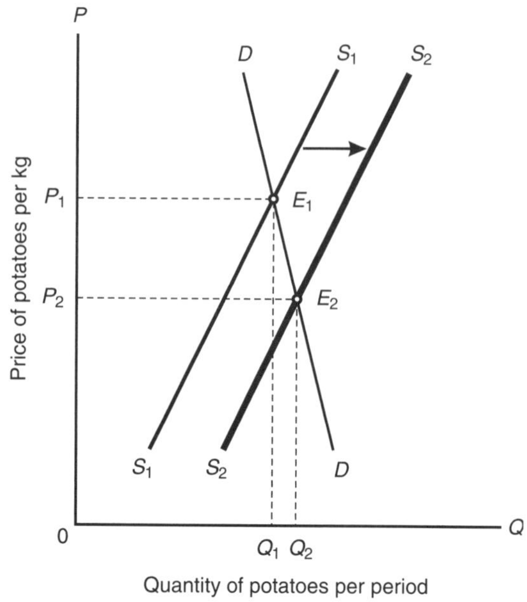

DD represents the demand for potatoes and S_1S_1 the supply of potatoes in Year 1 (when the harvest was bad). The equilibrium price and quantity are P_1 and Q_1 respectively. Farmers expect prices to be high in Year 2 as well and plant more potatoes. S_2S_2 represents the supply of potatoes in Year 2. The equilibrium quantity increases to Q_2 but the price falls to P_2. Farmers' total income from potatoes in Year 2 ($0P_2E_2Q_2$) is lower than in Year 1 ($0P_1E_1Q_1$).

Minimum prices (price supports, price floors)

Markets for agricultural products are usually characterised by a relatively stable demand, but also by a supply which is subject to large fluctuations (as illustrated in Figure 8-11). Prices therefore tend to fluctuate and farmers' income is unstable and uncertain. To stabilise farmers' income, governments often introduce minimum prices (or price floors) which serve as guaranteed prices to producers. If the minimum price is **below** the ruling equilibrium price, the operation of market forces is not disturbed, but if the minimum price is **above** the ruling equilibrium price (as is often the case) there is a surplus (or excess supply). This is illustrated in Figure 8-12.

In Figure 8-12 we show a hypothetical market for beef. DD is the demand curve and SS the supply curve. The equilibrium price is R15 per kilogram (kg) and the equilibrium quantity 7 million kg. Suppose the government sets a minimum price of R20 per kg. At that price the quantity demanded is 4 million kg and the quantity supplied is 9 million kg. There is thus an excess supply, or surplus, of 5 million kg (represented by the difference between a and b in the figure).

FIGURE 8-12 A minimum price

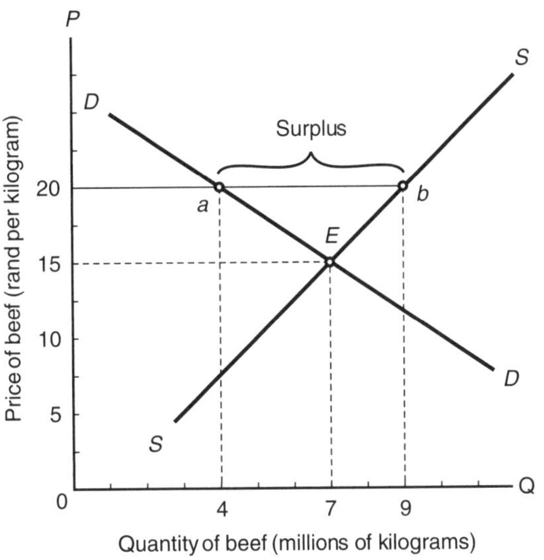

DD and SS represent the demand and supply of beef. The equilibrium price is R15 per kg and the equilibrium quantity is 7 million kg. The introduction of a minimum price of R20 per kg results in a market surplus of 5 million kg (represented by ab).

When government fixes a minimum price above the equilibrium price, it creates a market surplus. This usually requires further government intervention. The options are essentially the following:

- Government purchases the surplus and exports it.
- Government purchases the surplus and stores it (provided the product is non-perishable).
- Government introduces production quotas to limit the quantity supplied to the quantity demanded at the minimum price – in Figure 8-12 the aim would be to limit production to 4 million tons, thus eliminating the surplus.
- Government purchases and destroys the surplus.
- Producers destroy the surplus.

The artificially high price is usually justified by arguments that it is in consumers' interests that farmers receive a stable income (and keep producing the products) or that the surplus can be exported to earn foreign exchange. However, when the surplus is exported, it is often exported at a loss, and always at the expense of domestic consumers who have to pay an artificially high price for the product. If the surplus cannot be exported, further government intervention is required to dispose of the surplus. This often results in additional cost to taxpayers, and always entails a welfare loss to society.

Instead of merely fixing a minimum price, government can also fix a producer price and a lower consumer price, and subsidise producers by the difference. Suppose, for example, a producers' price of maize is set at R1 000 per ton and a consumer price at R900 per ton. The difference between the two prices (ie R100 per ton) is paid by government to producers as a subsidy. This reduces or eliminates the surplus but still involves a cost to taxpayers. It represents a redistribution of income from taxpayers to users of maize.

What government cannot do, is sell the surplus to domestic consumers at a lower price – this will defeat the whole purpose of setting a price floor. If government does not purchase the surplus, it has to prevent producers from selling the surplus illegally to consumers at lower prices. This requires administrative and other forms of control and therefore involves additional costs to taxpayers and further welfare losses.

Another alternative is to give the surplus to the poor. Surpluses of perishable products are often offered to charitable institutions, but the collection and distribution of the products entail significant costs and the products are seldom collected. There is also a danger that the distributors may consume some of the products themselves or sell some of it at low prices to consumers who would otherwise have bought the products at the floor price. This will reduce the quantity demanded in the market and increase the market surplus.

Setting minimum prices above equilibrium prices is a highly inefficient way of assisting small or poorer farmers, since

- all consumers, including poor households, have to pay artificially high prices
- the bulk of the benefit accrues to large farmers or farming concerns owned by big companies
- inefficient producers are protected and manage to survive
- the disposal of the market surpluses usually entails further cost to taxpayers and welfare losses to society

If government wishes to assist certain farmers, then direct cash subsidies paid only to those farmers is a better alternative. With direct subsidies there is no interference in the price mechanism. Only those who are supposed to benefit receive the subsidy and the cost of the subsidy is explicit, instead of being hidden (as in the case of minimum prices).

The welfare costs of minimum price fixing

The concepts of consumer surplus and producer surplus can also be used to illustrate the welfare loss of minimum price fixing. In Figure 8-13 the equilibrium price and quantity are P_1 and Q_1 respectively. The government now fixes a minimum price P_m above the equilibrium price. If we assume that **producers respond to actual demand**, then the quantity supplied (and exchanged) will fall to Q_m. In the absence of price fixing, the consumer surplus is P_1DE and the producer surplus $0P_1E$. After minimum price fixing the consumer surplus is P_mDR. Consumers thus lose

FIGURE 8-13 The welfare costs of minimum price fixing

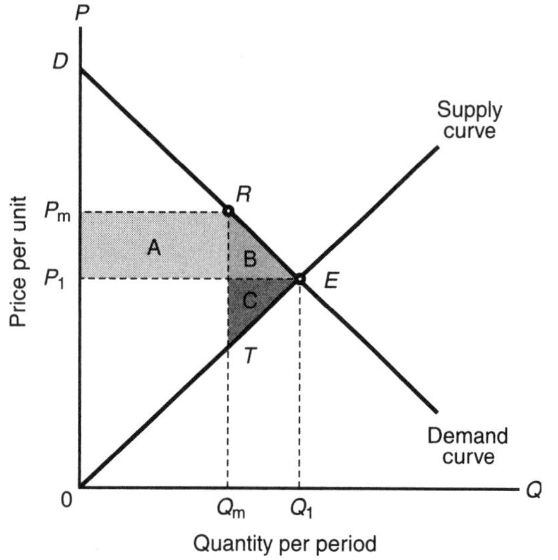

*Prior to price fixing the equilibrium price is P_1 and the equilibrium quantity Q_1. Government then fixes a minimum price P_m **above** the equilibrium price. **If producers respond to actual demand**, the quantity supplied (and exchanged) falls to Q_m. Rectangle A is transferred from the consumer surplus to the producer surplus. Triangle B, which used to be part of the consumer surplus, and triangle C, which used to be part of the producer surplus, both disappear. The total deadweight loss to society is equal to B plus C.*

rectangle A (to the producers) and triangle B (which disappears). The producer surplus becomes $0P_mRT$. Producers gain rectangle A at the expense of consumers but triangle C disappears. The total **deadweight loss** to society is thus triangle B plus triangle C. As in the case of maximum price fixing, too little is produced and society is worse off as a result of the interference in the market system.

If producers ignore and do not respond to actual demand, the situation is slightly more complicated, since a surplus will be produced, as explained earlier. The welfare costs of such a situation are not examined here.

Concluding remarks

In this chapter we showed how the tools of demand and supply can be used to analyse real world situations. We focused on the **direction** of change. By now you have probably realised that the impact of a given change in demand or supply on the equilibrium price and quantity (ie the **magnitude** of the change) will depend on the shape of the supply and demand curves. The information we require is contained in the price elasticity of supply or demand, which is examined in the next chapter.

IMPORTANT CONCEPTS

Change in demand
Change in supply
Market shortage (excess demand)
Market surplus (excess supply)
Maximum prices (price ceilings)
Minimum prices (price floors)
Rationing
Black market
Deadweight loss
Administered prices

REVIEW QUESTIONS

1. Explain what is wrong with the following line of reasoning: "If the supply of a good increases, the price will fall, but if the price falls then more will be demanded. This rise in demand will then push up the price. The increased price will cause less to be demanded and so on. Therefore it is impossible to say what the effect of the original increase in supply will be."

2. Illustrate the impact of the following on the demand curve and the equilibrium price and quantity for product *X:*
   (a) An increase in consumers' taste for *X*
   (b) An expected increase in the price of *X*
   (c) An official health warning against the consumption of *X*

3. Use demand and supply curves to illustrate and explain why a rare item such as a painting by Rembrandt, Rubens or Van Gogh is sold at such a high price.

4. Use demand and supply curves to show how the shift from video cassette recorders (VCRs) to digital video disc (DVD) players affected the markets for (a) VCRs and DVD players and (b) video tapes and DVDs.

5. Use a diagram to illustrate and explain the following:
   In 1995 a 45 kg bag of potatoes sold for $8 in the United States. As a result of this relatively high price, potato farmers earned high profits. Due to these high profits more farmers planted potatoes in 1996. As it happened, weather conditions were also particularly favourable for the growth and harvesting of potatoes. In 1996 a 45 kg bag of potatoes sold for about $2, one dollar less than the cost of producing a bag.

6. Suppose all the oil wells in Iran, Iraq and Kuwait are set alight, resulting in a dramatic and prolonged decline in the world output of oil. Use demand and supply curves to illustrate how this will affect: (a) the price of oil, (b) the price of coal, (c) the price of motorcars and (d) taxi fares.

7. Analyse the following statement critically: "An increase in supply will cause a reduction in price. This decrease in price will then cause a decrease in supply, which will continue until supply is back at its original level."

8. Use a diagram to explain why rent control resulted in a shortage of rented accommodation in South Africa in the 1960s.

9. Explain, with the aid of a diagram, how each of the following will affect the market for coffee:
   (a) A severe frost destroys much of the Brazilian crop.
   (b) Coffee is shown to cause cancer in laboratory experiments on mice.
   (c) The price of tea declines sharply.
   (d) Coffee prices are expected to rise rapidly in the next few months.
   (e) Workers in the coffee industry form a trade union and succeed with claims for higher wages.

10. Explain, with the aid of a diagram, why the price of DVD players fell when the sales of DVD players increased.

More words of wisdom

The study of economics does not seem to require any specialised gifts of an unusually high order. Is it not, intellectually regarded, a very easy subject compared with the higher branches of philosophy and pure science? Yet good, or even competent, economists are the rarest of birds. An easy subject at which very few excel! The paradox finds its explanation perhaps, in that the master-economist must possess a rare combination of gifts. He must reach a high standard in several different directions and must combine talents not often found together. He must be mathematician, historian, statesman, philosopher - in some degree. He must understand symbols and speak in words. He must contemplate the particular in terms of the general, and touch abstract and concrete in the same flight of thought. He must study the present in the light of the past for the purposes of the future. No part of man's nature or his institutions must lie entirely outside his regard. He must be purposeful and disinterested in a simultaneous mood; as aloof and incorruptible as an artist, yet sometimes as near the earth as a politician.

JOHN MAYNARD KEYNES
(Quoted in Heilbroner, R. 1967. *The worldly philosophers*. London: Allen Lane, 261)

Almost the only firms that today employ economists are banks and securities houses. These people are not really valued for their advice: they are entertainers who perform before clients and advertise their employers' services on breakfast television.

JOHN KAY
(*Financial Times*, June 5 2003)

9 Elasticity

Learning outcomes

Once you have studied this chapter you should be able to

- define elasticity
- explain the meaning and significance of price elasticity of demand
- distinguish between five categories of price elasticity of demand
- explain the determinants of price elasticity of demand
- define income elasticity and cross elasticity of demand
- explain the meaning and significance of price elasticity of supply

The elasticity (or responsiveness) of demand in a market is great or small according as the amount demanded increases much or little for a given fall in price, and diminishes much or little for a given rise in price.

ALFRED MARSHALL

All demand curves are inelastic.
All supply curves are inelastic too.

GEORGE STIGLER

In this chapter we focus on the responsiveness of the quantity demanded and the quantity supplied to changes in price and other determinants of the quantity demanded and the quantity supplied. By now we know how the equilibrium price and quantity in the market will respond to changes in demand and supply. But what will the absolute or relative sizes of the changes in price and quantity be? By how much, for example, will the equilibrium price increase if supply decreases? And by how much will the equilibrium quantity change? What will happen to the total revenue of the suppliers, which is equal to the average price per unit multiplied by the quantity sold? Will it fall or will it increase? Will suppliers benefit from higher prices or from lower prices, bearing in mind that the quantity demanded will probably react to a price change? What determines the responsiveness of the quantity demanded to changes in price? By how much does the quantity demanded respond to changes in income or changes in the prices of substitutes or complements? And what about supply – how responsive is the quantity supplied to changes in price and what determines this responsiveness?

These are the questions that are examined in this chapter. We start with a general definition of **elasticity**. This is followed by an analysis of the **price elasticity of demand**, which constitutes the main part of the chapter. In the subsequent sections we examine the **income elasticity of demand**, the **cross elasticity of demand** and the **price elasticity of supply**.

We have said repeatedly that demand and supply curves are among the most useful analytical tools in economics. The reasons for this are that we can use demand and supply to:

- **explain** a number of economic phenomena (eg how the price of a product is determined)
- **predict** what will happen if an economic variable changes (eg what will happen to the price of a product if the price of a substitute for that product changes)
- analyse the effects of **policy** decisions (eg what will happen to the price of cigarettes, the quantity exchanged and tax revenue if the tax on cigarettes is raised)

We have dealt with some of these issues in Chapter 8, and in the rest of this book we use demand and supply curves to examine a variety of issues. It is therefore important to have a good grasp of the basic principles of demand and supply.

Up to now we have concentrated on analysing the **direction** of change when supply or demand changes. But economists, business people and the government are also interested in the **magnitude** of the change. By **how much** will price and quantity change if demand or supply changes? How will a change in the price of a good or service affect the total amount that consumers plan to spend on that particular good or service? Will the change in the quantity demanded be proportionally larger or smaller than the change in the price? Will it be profitable for the suppliers of a product to raise the price of the product, or should they rather lower it? What will the relative impact on price and quantity be if price control were to be imposed on a particular product? These are some of the many questions that economists are interested in, but which we can only answer if we know how **responsive** the quantity demanded and the quantity supplied are to price changes. In other words, we want to know by how much the quantity demanded and the quantity supplied will change in response to changes in price. In technical terms we say that information is required about the price **elasticity** of demand and supply. But what does elasticity mean?

A general definition of elasticity

Elasticity is a **measure of responsiveness or sensitivity**. When two variables are related, one often wants to know **how sensitive or responsive the dependent variable is to changes in the independent variable**. We know, for example, that the size of the maize crop is dependent on rainfall. But how sensitive or responsive is the size of the maize crop to (say) a one per cent change in rainfall? In economics there are many cause-effect relationships which raise similar questions. How responsive is investment spending to changes in the interest rate? How responsive is government's tax revenue to changes in taxpayers' income? How responsive is the quantity of labour supplied to changes in the wage rate? How responsive is the demand for imports to changes in domestic income? The list is almost endless. In each case we are interested in the responsiveness or sensitivity of a dependent variable to changes in an independent variable. The **measure of such responsiveness or sensitivity is called elasticity.** Elasticity can be defined as the **percentage change in a dependent variable if the relevant independent variable changes by one per cent.** This is obtained by dividing the percentage change in the dependent variable by the percentage change in the independent variable:

$$\text{elasticity} = \frac{\text{percentage change in dependent variable}}{\text{percentage change in independent variable}}$$

In the rest of this chapter we introduce four types of elasticity:

- the price elasticity of demand
- the income elasticity of demand
- the cross elasticity of demand
- the price elasticity of supply

The most important of these is the price elasticity of demand, to which we now turn. Once we have explained the price elasticity of demand in some detail, we deal briefly with the other three.

9.1 The price elasticity of demand

In the case of a demand curve the dependent variable is the quantity demanded and the independent variable is the price of the product. The **price elasticity of demand** is the **percentage change in the quantity demanded if the price of the product changes by one per cent**, *ceteris paribus*. This is obtained by dividing the percentage change in the quantity demanded by the percentage change in the price of the good or service concerned. Using the symbol e_p for the price elasticity of demand, we therefore write:

$$e_p = \frac{\text{percentage change in the quantity demanded of a product}}{\text{percentage change in the price of the product}}$$

For example, if the price of the product changes by 5 per cent and this results in a 10 per cent change in the quantity demanded, *ceteris paribus*, then e_p = 10 per cent ÷ 5 per cent = 2. This implies that a one per cent change in the price of the product will lead to a two per cent change in the quantity demanded.

Some important aspects and implications of this definition must be emphasised:

- Elasticity is calculated by using **percentage changes**, which are **relative changes, not absolute changes**. We cannot use absolute changes in prices and quantities because prices are expressed in monetary units, while quantities are expressed in physical units. But if we use percentage changes, the **units in which prices and quantities are measured do not affect the result**. Prices may be measured in rands, cents, dollars, euros, yen or any other currency unit, and quantities may be measured in bags, boxes, cartons, bottles, kilograms, pounds, litres, gallons, metres, yards or any other unit of measurement.
- The price elasticity of demand is the ratio of the percentage change in the quantity demanded to the percentage change in price. This ratio is called the **elasticity coefficient**, which is simply a number and is not measured in units, percentages or anything else.
- Elasticity coefficients enable us to **compare** how consumers react to changes in the prices of **different goods and services**, such as matches, motorcars, meat, petrol and university tuition. We cannot compare a change in the absolute quantity of matches demanded with a change in the number of motorcars demanded. We also cannot compare the impact of, say, a R1 change in the price of matches with the impact of a R1 change in the price of a motorcar. A R1 change in the price of a box of matches is a massive change, while a R1 change in the price of a motorcar is negligible. But we can compare the elasticity coefficient for matches with the elasticity coefficient for motorcars, which gives us a comparison between the sensitivity of each to changes in price.
- Strictly speaking, the measured price elasticity of demand has a **negative sign**, since the change in the price of a product and the change in the quantity demanded move in opposite directions. When the price increases, the quantity demanded falls and when the price falls, the quantity demanded increases. This problem is sometimes overcome by including a minus sign in the definition of price elasticity of demand, but this is a cumbersome approach. In this book we ignore the negative sign and simply concentrate on the **absolute value** of the price elasticity of demand. When we say that the price elasticity of the demand for tomatoes is 0,5, we mean that a one per cent **increase** in the price of tomatoes will lead to a 0,5 per cent **decrease** in the quantity demanded (or that a one per cent **decrease** in the price of tomatoes will lead to a 0,5 per cent **increase** in the quantity demanded).

Calculating price elasticity of demand

To calculate the price elasticity of demand we have to calculate the percentage change in the quantity demanded and divide it by the percentage change in the price of the product. If we denote the quantity demanded by Q, and the change in quantity demanded by ΔQ, then

$$\text{percentage change in quantity demanded} = \frac{\Delta Q}{Q} \times 100$$

Similarly, if we use the symbols P and ΔP for the price of the product and the change in price, then

$$\text{percentage change in price of the product} = \frac{\Delta P}{P} \times 100$$

Thus, price elasticity of demand (e_p)

$$= \frac{\text{percentage change in quantity demanded}}{\text{percentage change in price of product}}$$

$$= \frac{\frac{\Delta Q}{Q} \times 100}{\frac{\Delta P}{P} \times 100} = \frac{\frac{\Delta Q}{Q}}{\frac{\Delta P}{P}} \quad \text{(since the 100s cancel out)}$$

$$= \frac{\Delta Q}{Q} \times \frac{P}{\Delta P}$$

$$\therefore e_p = \frac{\Delta Q}{\Delta P} \times \frac{P}{Q} \quad \ldots\ldots\ldots\ldots \quad (9\text{-}1)$$

The slope of a linear demand curve is given by the change in price (ΔP) divided by the change in quantity (ΔQ). The first part of the right-hand side of Equation 9-1 (ie $\Delta Q/\Delta P$) thus represents the **inverse of the slope of a linear demand curve**. Since the slope of a straight line is constant, the inverse of the slope is also constant. The second part of the right-hand side of Equation 9-1 (ie P/Q) represents the ratio between the price (P) and the quantity (Q) at a point on the demand curve. Since this ratio varies along the demand curve, it follows that the price elasticity of demand will be different at each point on the demand curve.[1] This can be explained by using a numerical example.

Figure 9-1(a) represents a linear demand curve with a constant slope of ½ (ignoring the minus sign). The inverse of the slope is 2 and is also constant. We now apply the formula in Equation 9-1 to calculate the price elasticity of demand at points A, B, C, D and E. In each case we simply have to multiply 2 (ie the inverse of the absolute value of the slope) by the ratio of P to Q.

At A the price P is 10 and the quantity Q is zero. The ratio of P to Q is thus $^{10}/_{0}$ which is infinitely large,

1. The elasticity coefficient calculated at a point on a demand curve is usually called point elasticity (in contrast to arc elasticity, which is explained later).

FIGURE 9-1 Price elasticity of demand at different points along a linear demand curve

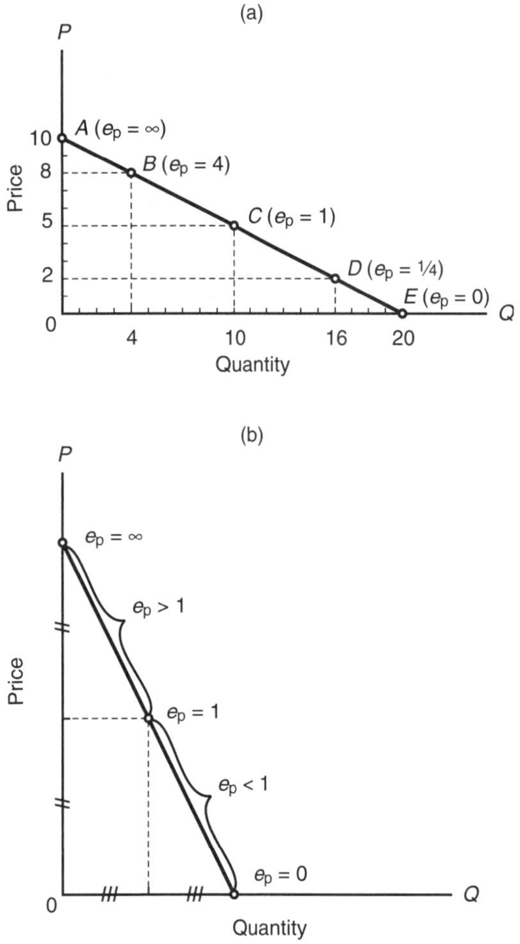

The line through points A, B, C, D and E in (a) represents a linear demand curve. The price elasticity of demand is different at each point along the curve, varying from infinity (∞) where it meets the price axis to zero where it meets the quantity axis. The results are summarised in (b).

or infinity (indicated by the symbol ∞).[2] Multiplying infinity by 2 is still infinity; thus e_p at $A = \infty$. At *B* the price *P* is 8 and the quantity *Q* is 4; thus $P/Q = 2$ and $e_p = 2 \times 2 = 4$. At *C* the price *P* is 5 and the quantity *Q* is 10; thus the ratio of *P* to *Q* is ½ and $e_p = 2 \times (\frac{1}{2}) = 1$. At *D* the price *P* is 2 and the quantity *Q* is 16; thus $P/Q = \frac{2}{16} = \frac{1}{8}$ and $e_p = 2 \times (\frac{1}{8}) = \frac{2}{8} = \frac{1}{4}$. At *E* the price *P* is zero and the quantity *Q* is 20; thus $P/Q = \frac{0}{20} = 0$ and $e_p = 2 \times 0 = 0$.

2. Strictly speaking, a ratio with zero as the denominator is undefined and one should really say that e_p tends towards infinity as *Q* approaches zero.

In the case of a linear demand curve, the price elasticity of demand (e_p) varies from infinity (∞) where the demand curve meets the price axis to zero (0) where the demand curve meets the quantity axis. As we move downwards to the right along the demand curve, the elasticity coefficient e_p falls from ∞ to 0. Between *A* and *C* the elasticity coefficient is larger than one, at *C* it is equal to one, and between *C* and *E* it is smaller than one. This is no accident. Along any linear demand curve which is extended to meet or intersect both the price and quantity axes, the price elasticity is infinity where it meets the price axis, zero where it meets the quantity axis, and equal to one at the point which is precisely in the middle of the curve (the midpoint or centre).

At any point above the midpoint the elasticity is greater than one and at any point below the midpoint the elasticity is less than one. These results are summarised in Figure 9-1(b). Although the figure shows a linear demand curve with a steeper slope, the results are still the same. Note that horizontal and vertical lines drawn from the midpoint of the demand curve towards the axes divide the price and quantity axes between the origin and the intercepts into two distances of equal length.

Figure 9-1 is technically correct, but it is unrealistic, since prices seldom (if ever) fall to zero or rise so high that the quantity demanded becomes zero. In practice only a portion of "complete" demand curves such as those in Figure 9-1(a) and (b) are encountered. This is illustrated in Figure 9-2 which shows a hypothetical "complete" market demand curve for beef and the portion of the curve which is relevant in a particular period. When the price is zero, ten thousand kilograms of beef are "demanded", but when the price is R60 per kg, no beef is "demanded". At a price of R30 per kg (ie in the middle of the price range) the price elasticity of demand (e_p) is equal to one. At prices above R30 per kg, e_p is greater than one and at prices below R30 per kg, e_p is less than one. In the market, however, the price of beef does not fall to zero or rise to R60 per kg. Suppose the price is expected to vary only between R36 and R48 per kg during the period under consideration. This implies that the only relevant part of the demand curve is the section between *A* and *B*, which is amplified in the figure. At any point between *A* and *B* the price elasticity of the demand for beef is greater than one.

We now examine this relevant range of the demand curve and determine the price elasticity of demand in the price range between R36 and R48 per kilogram. What is the price elasticity of demand (e_p) in this range (ie between *A* and *B* in Figure 9-2)?

From our definition we know that

$$e_p = \frac{\text{percentage change in quantity demanded}}{\text{percentage change in price}}$$

FIGURE 9-2 The relevant part of a "complete" demand curve

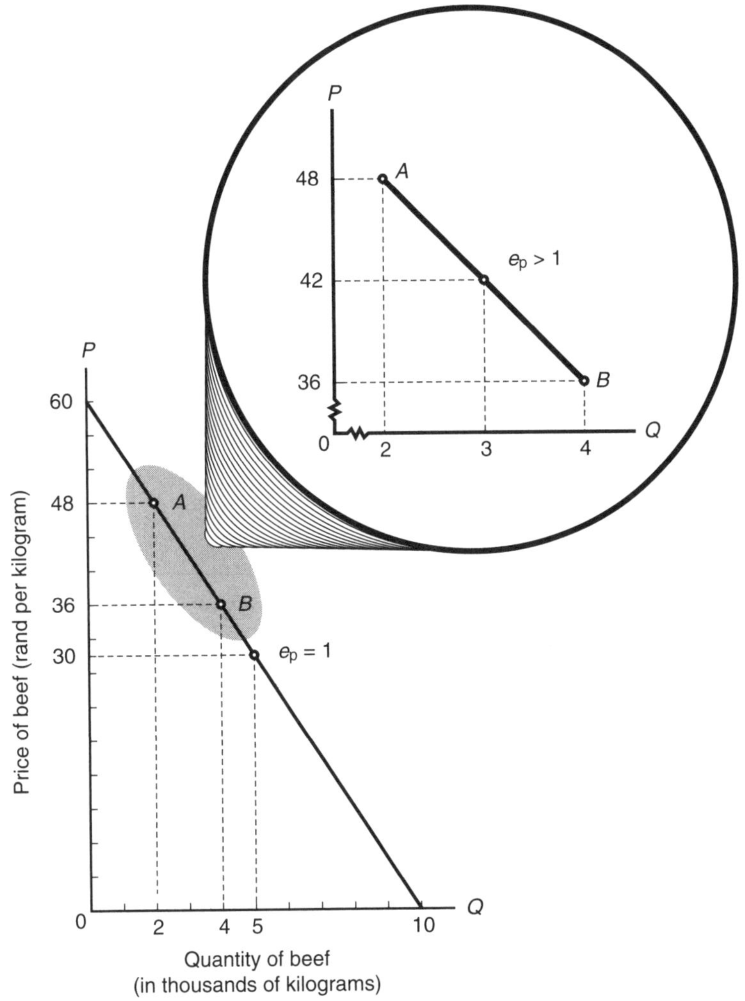

The basic diagram shows a "complete" demand curve for beef which extends from axis to axis. Suppose, however, that only the part between A and B is relevant. This part is amplified in the figure. Note that the axes in the amplified part have been "cut off" – the irrelevant prices and quantities are omitted.

In principle the answer is straightforward. We simply need to calculate the two percentage changes and divide the percentage change in quantity demanded by the percentage change in price. There is, however, a technical problem. When we want to calculate the percentage change between two different points on a demand curve the answer will depend on which point we use as the basis for our calculation (ie on the direction of the change). For example, if we take *A* as the basis, then the percentage change in price is calculated by dividing the difference between *A* and *B* (ie R12) by R48 and multiplying the answer by 100. This yields a percentage change of $(^{12}/_{48}) \times 100 = {}^{1}/_{4} \times 100 = 25\%$. But if we use R36 (point *B*) as the basis, the percentage change is calculated by dividing the change (again R12) by R36 and multiplying the result by 100. This yields a percentage change of $(^{12}/_{36}) \times 100 = {}^{1}/_{3} \times 100 = 33\,^{1}/_{3}\%$. With the same basic information we can thus obtain two different answers. The same problem occurs when calculating the percentage change in quantity. But we want an answer which is independent of the starting point or direction of change. The solution is to **use the average of the two points as the basis**. In this way we always obtain the same answer, irrespective of the basis or direction of change.

In our example we therefore use $(36 + 48) \div 2 = 42$ as the basis for calculating the percentage change in the price of beef. The result is a percentage change of $(^{12}/_{42}) \times 100 = (^{1200}/_{42}) = (^{200}/_{7})\%$. Similarly, the percentage change in the quantity of beef is the change between A and B (2 000) divided by the average of the quantities indicated by A and B (ie [2 000 + 4 000] ÷ 2 = 3 000) multiplied by 100. This yields a percentage change of (2000⁄3000) × 100 = (200⁄3) %. The price elasticity of demand is then obtained by dividing the percentage change in the quantity demanded (ie 200⁄3) by the percentage change in the price (ie 200⁄7).

$$\therefore \; e_p = \frac{\frac{200}{3}}{\frac{200}{7}} = \frac{200}{3} \times \frac{7}{200} = \frac{7}{3}$$

Note that the answer is greater than one. This should come as no surprise, since we are dealing with the part of the demand curve where the elasticity at each point is greater than one. The elasticity coefficient calculated by comparing two points on a demand curve is called **arc elasticity**. To calculate arc elasticity, we use the average of the two quantities and the average of the two prices as a basis for calculating the percentage change.

The formula for calculating **arc elasticity** is

$$e_p = \frac{(Q_2 - Q_1)/[(Q_1 + Q_2)/2]}{(P_2 - P_1)/[(P_1 + P_2)/2]} \quad \text{............ (9-2)}$$

Since we have percentages above and below the line we do not have to multiply the expressions above and below the line by 100. The 100s cancel out. The 2s also cancel out and can therefore be dropped from Equation 9-2, as in Equation 9-3 below:

$$e_p = \frac{(Q_2 - Q_1)/(Q_1 + Q_2)}{(P_2 - P_1)/(P_1 + P_2)} \quad \text{................ (9-3)}$$

We ignore the negative sign again by taking the absolute differences between Q_2 and Q_1 and between P_2 and P_1. Now work through the example in Box 9-1 to make sure that you know how to calculate arc elasticity.

Price elasticity of demand and total revenue (or total expenditure)

The price elasticity of demand can be used to **determine by how much the total expenditure by consumers on a product (which is also the total revenue of the firms producing that product) changes when the price of the product changes**. This is probably the most important reason why economists, business people and policymakers are so interested in information concerning the price elasticity of demand.

The total revenue (*TR*) accruing to the suppliers of a good or service (or the total expenditure by the consumers) is equal to the price (*P*) of the good or service multiplied by the quantity (*Q*) sold. We know that there is an inverse relationship between the quantity demanded (*Q*) and the price of a product (*P*). Any change in price leads to a change in the quantity demanded **in the opposite direction** to the change in price. The effect of a price change on total revenue will thus depend on the relative sizes of the price change and the change in the quantity demanded.

- If the change in price *P* leads to a proportionately greater change in quantity demanded *Q* (ie if the price elasticity of demand is greater than one), total revenue *TR* (= *PQ*) will change in the opposite direction to the price change.
- If the change in price leads to an equi-proportional change in the quantity demanded (ie if the price elasticity of demand is equal to one), total revenue will remain unchanged.
- If the change in price leads to a proportionally smaller change in the quantity demanded (ie if the price elasticity of demand is smaller than one), total revenue will change in the same direction as the price change.

Much of the rest of our discussion of the price elasticity of demand is concerned with these important relationships.

■ A NUMERICAL EXAMPLE

We now use a numerical example to show how changes in total revenue are related to the price elasticity of demand. Suppose the first two columns of Table 9-1 represent the demand schedule for hamburgers in a particular town in a certain period. The first column shows the price of hamburgers *P*, the second column the quantity demanded (and sold) *Q* at each price and the third column the total revenue ($TR = P \times Q$) at each price. The last column shows the price elasticity of demand e_p at each point (which we have calculated using Equation 9-1).

The demand curve corresponding to the demand schedule of Table 9-1 is shown in Figure 9-3(a). As explained earlier, the price elasticity of demand will be equal to one at the point on the demand curve which is exactly midway between the intersections with the price and quantity axes. In this example the midpoint is at a price of R10 and a quantity of 10 000. At any point on the demand curve above the midpoint the price elasticity of demand will be greater than one, and at any point below the midpoint it will be smaller than one. (You can verify these statements by calculating the point elasticity of demand at various points along the demand curve, using Equation 9-1 and the information in Table 9-1.)

In Figure 9-3(b) we show the total revenue (*TR*) at each quantity of hamburgers sold. As the price of hamburgers falls, and the quantity of hamburgers demanded (and sold) increases, so the total revenue (*TR*) rises at first, reaches a maximum and then declines. Figure 9-3 illustrates three important results:

BOX 9-1 CALCULATING ARC ELASTICITY: AN EXAMPLE

Suppose the following combinations represent two points on a demand curve:

Point 1: $P_1 = 10;\ Q_1 = 17$

Point 2: $P_2 = 8;\ Q_2 = 19$

These points are shown in the following diagram:

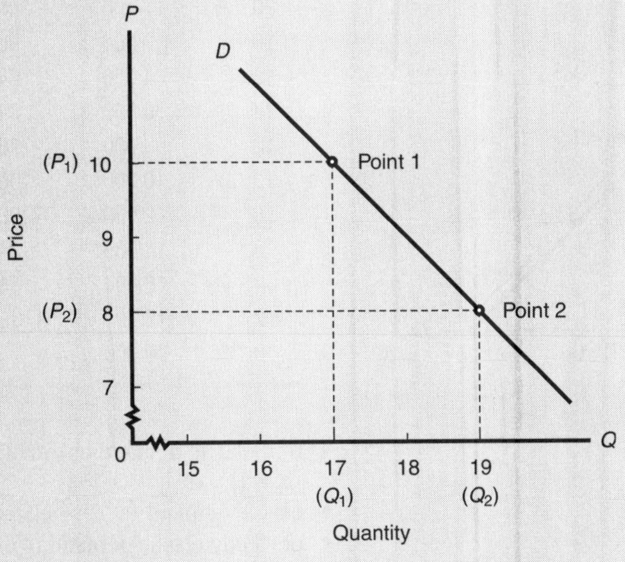

To calculate the arc elasticity between these two points we use the formula in Equation 9-3:

$$e_p = \frac{(Q_2 - Q_1)/(Q_1 + Q_2)}{(P_2 - P_1)/(P_1 + P_2)}$$

Above the line we have the difference between the two quantities divided by their sum and below the line we have the difference between the two prices divided by their sum. Thus

$$e_p = \frac{(19 - 17)/(17 + 19)}{(8 - 10)/(10 + 8)} = \frac{2/36}{2/18} \text{ (remember, we ignore the negative sign)}$$

$$= \frac{2}{36} \div \frac{2}{18} = \frac{2}{36} \times \frac{18}{2} = \frac{1}{2}$$

- As long as the price elasticity of demand is greater than one, total revenue *TR* (or the total expenditure by consumers) increases as the quantity sold *Q* increases.
- *TR* reaches a maximum when the price elasticity of demand is equal to one.
- When the price elasticity of demand is less than one, *TR* falls as the quantity sold *Q* increases.

Figure 9-3 is an important diagram to which we refer again in Chapter 13. The relationship between the price elasticity of demand and total revenue can be explained further by distinguishing five different categories of price elasticity of demand. See also Box 9-2.

Different categories of price elasticity of demand

Five categories of price elasticity of demand can be distinguished:

- perfectly inelastic demand ($e_p = 0$)
- inelastic demand (e_p lies between 0 and 1)

FIGURE 9-3 The relationship between price elasticity of demand and total revenue

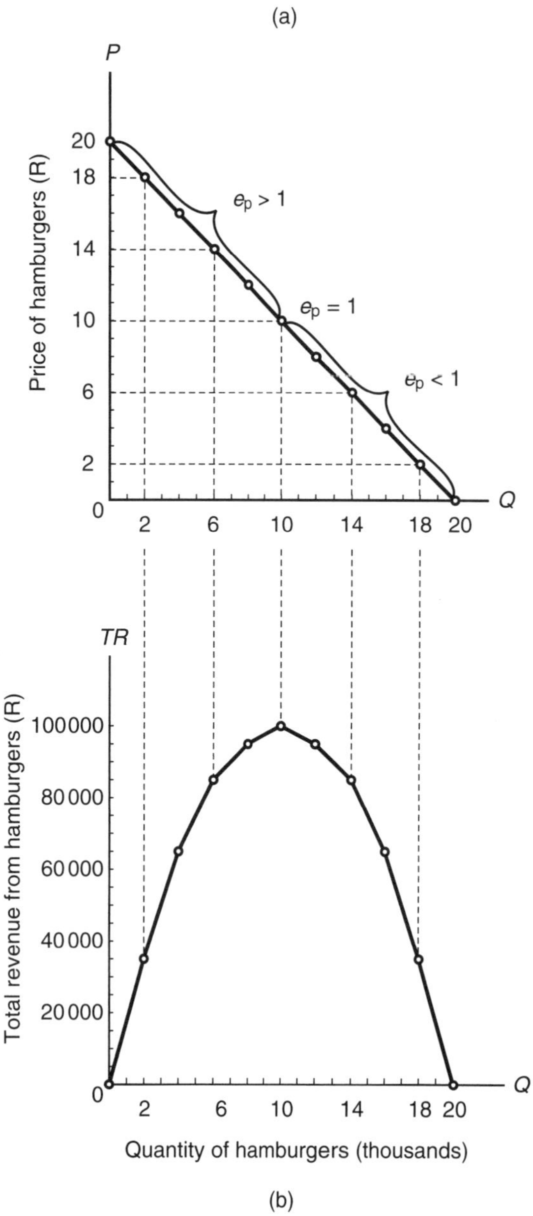

Panel (a) depicts the demand for hamburgers and the price elasticity of demand (e_p) along the curve, based on the data in Table 9-1. Panel (b) shows the corresponding total revenue (TR) from the sale of hamburgers. When e_p is greater than one, TR increases as the quantity of hamburgers increases. When e_p is equal to one, TR is at a maximum. When e_p is less than one, TR falls as the quantity of hamburgers increases. This relationship holds for all downward-sloping linear demand curves.

TABLE 9-1 The demand for hamburgers and total revenue from hamburger sales

Price per hamburger (R) P	Quantity demanded Q	Total revenue from hamburger sales (R) TR = PQ	Price elasticity of demand e_p
20	0	0	∞
18	2 000	36 000	9,0
16	4 000	64 000	4,0
14	6 000	84 000	2,3
12	8 000	96 000	1,5
10	10 000	100 000	1,0
8	12 000	96 000	0,7
6	14 000	84 000	0,4
4	16 000	64 000	0,3
2	18 000	36 000	0,1
0	20 000	0	0

- unit elastic demand or unitary elasticity of demand ($e_p = 1$)
- elastic demand (e_p lies between 1 and ∞)
- perfectly elastic demand ($e_p = \infty$)

These five categories are illustrated in Figure 9-4.

■ PERFECTLY INELASTIC DEMAND

Perfectly inelastic demand (which is unlikely to occur in the real world) refers to a situation where the price elasticity of demand is **zero**. A perfectly inelastic demand curve is represented by a vertical line parallel to the price axis, such as *DD* in Figure 9-4(a). This shows that consumers plan to purchase a fixed amount of the product, irrespective of its price.

If the demand for a product is perfectly inelastic, the producers can raise their revenue by raising the price of the product. As explained earlier, the producers' total revenue *TR* is equal to the price of the product *P* times the quantity sold *Q* (ie $TR = P \times Q$). When *P* increases and *Q* remains constant, *TR* increases.

■ INELASTIC DEMAND

Demand is said to be **inelastic** when the quantity demanded changes in response to a change in price, but the percentage change in the quantity is less than the percentage change in the price of the product. The value of the price elasticity of demand, or the **elasticity coefficient**, is thus **greater than zero but smaller than one**. In contrast to the case of perfect inelasticity, we cannot draw a linear demand curve (ie a straight line) which represents inelastic demand all along the curve. As explained earlier, the elasticity

FIGURE 9-4 The different categories of price elasticity of demand

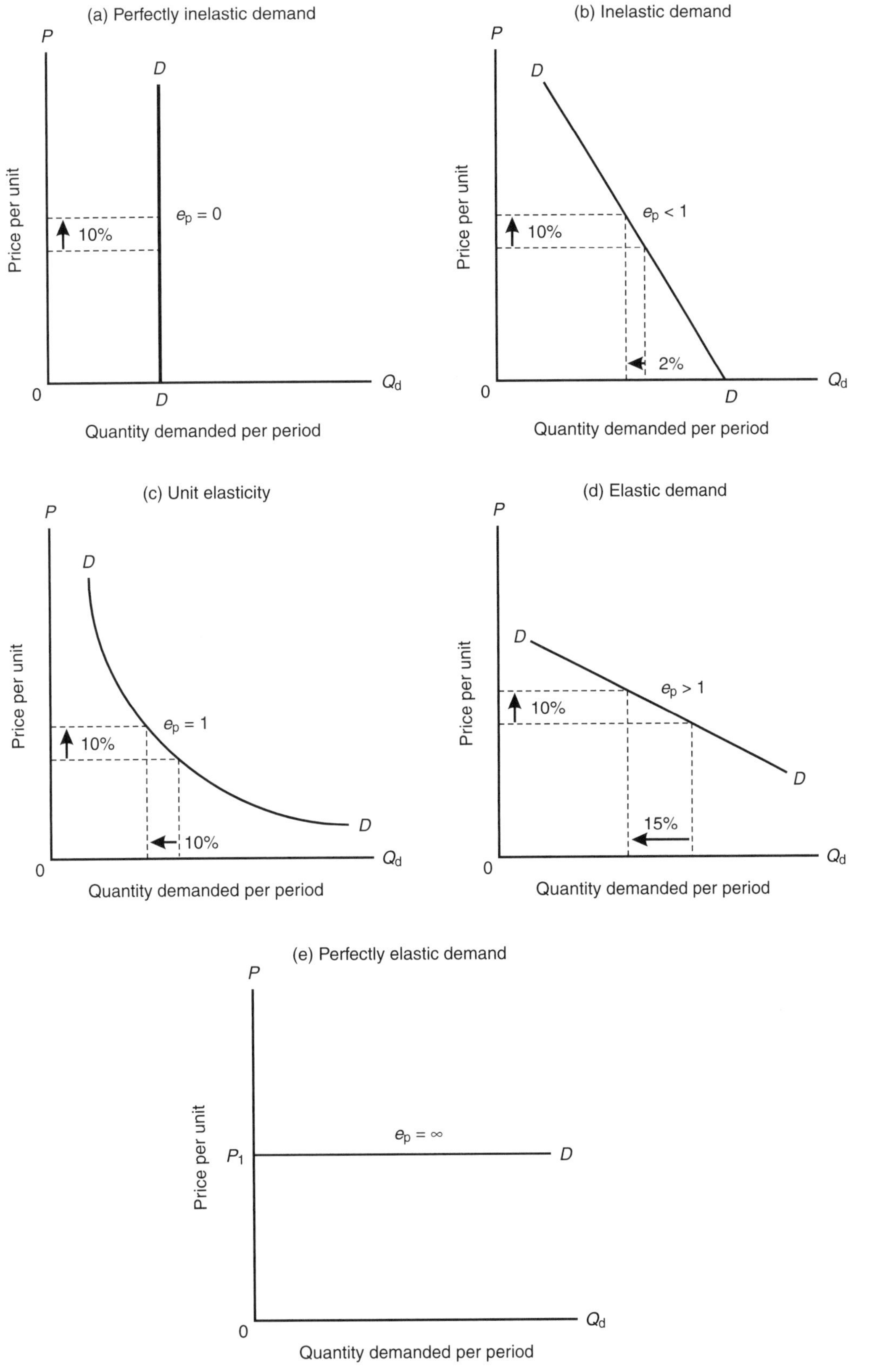

BOX 9-2 PRICE ELASTICITY OF DEMAND, PRICE CHANGES AND CHANGES IN TOTAL REVENUE

In any market the total revenue (*TR*) of the sellers is equal to the total spending (*PQ*) by the buyers. The relationship between price elasticity of demand (e_p), changes in price (*P*) and changes in total revenue ($TR = PQ$) in the three non-extreme cases of price elasticity of demand (ie inelastic, unitary elastic and elastic demand) can be illustrated as follows:

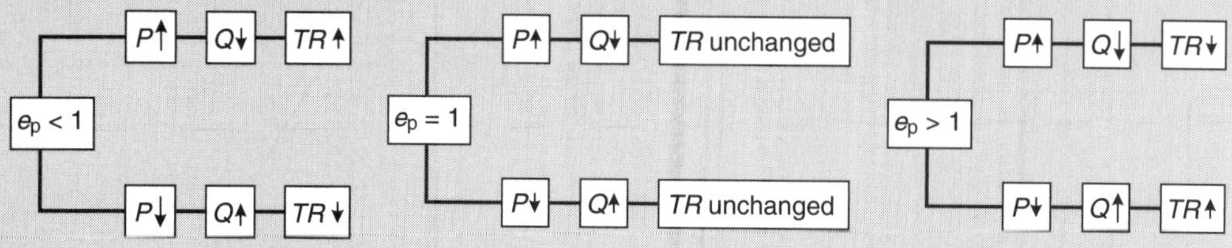

coefficient varies from point to point along any downward-sloping linear demand curve. Nevertheless, we use a steep curve, such as the one in Figure 9-4(b), to approximate an inelastic demand curve (bearing in mind that it is not fully accurate, as we explain in Box 9-3).

If producers are faced with an inelastic demand for their product, they will have an incentive to raise the price of the product, since the percentage fall in the quantity demanded *Q* will be smaller than the percentage increase in the price *P* of the product. In other words, if the price of the product increases, the producers' total revenue *TR* (= $P \times Q$) will increase. By the same token there will be no incentive for the producers to drop the price of the product, since the increase in the quantity demanded will be proportionally smaller than the percentage decrease in the price, that is, their total revenue *TR* (= $P \times Q$) will decrease.

■ UNIT ELASTIC DEMAND (UNITARY ELASTICITY)

Unitary elasticity occurs when the percentage change in the quantity demanded is exactly equal to the percentage change in price. The elasticity coefficient is thus **equal to one**. Unitary elasticity is the dividing line between inelastic and elastic demand. It cannot be represented by a straight line demand curve, but those of you with a mathematical background will realise that a unit elastic demand curve can be represented by a rectangular hyperbola, as in Figure 9-4(c).

If producers are faced with a unit elastic demand curve, they cannot raise their total revenue by decreasing or increasing the price of the product. In both cases the percentage change in the price will be exactly offset by a corresponding percentage change in the quantity demanded (in the opposite direction to the change in price). *TR* (= $P \times Q$) will therefore remain unchanged.

■ ELASTIC DEMAND

Demand is said to be **elastic** when a price change leads to a proportionally greater change in the quantity demanded, that is, when the elasticity coefficient is **greater than one**. An elastic demand curve cannot be represented by a unique downward-sloping linear demand curve, since the elasticity coefficient varies along such a curve. Nevertheless we use a relatively flat demand curve, such as the one in Figure 9-4(d), to represent an elastic demand curve (bearing in mind that it is not fully accurate).

If producers are faced with an elastic demand for their product, they can increase their total revenue by lowering the price of the product. When the price of the product *P* decreases there will be a proportionally greater increase in the quantity demanded *Q*. Total revenue *TR* (= $P \times Q$) will thus increase. An increase in total revenue should not, however, be confused with an increase in total profit. The impact on profit will also depend on the change in total cost.

When faced with an elastic demand, producers will have no incentive to raise their prices, since the resulting decrease in the quantity demanded will be proportionally greater than the increase in the price of the product, so total revenue will fall.

■ PERFECTLY ELASTIC DEMAND

A perfectly elastic demand curve has an elasticity coefficient of **infinity** and is depicted by a horizontal line, as in Figure 9-4(e). This curve shows that consumers are willing to purchase any quantity at a certain price (P_1), but if the price is raised only fractionally, the quantity demanded falls to zero. An example of a perfectly elastic demand curve is provided in Chapter 12, where we discuss the position of an individual firm in a perfectly competitive market.

The most important features of the five categories of price elasticity are summarised in Table 9-2.

TABLE 9-2 Price elasticity of demand: a summary

Category	*Meaning*	*Effect on total revenue (TR = PQ) when price (P) changes*
Perfectly inelastic demand ($e_p = 0$)	*Q* does not change when *P* changes	*TR* changes with *P* in the same direction as *P;* there is thus an incentive for suppliers to raise prices
Inelastic demand ($0 < e_p < 1$)	Percentage change in *Q* is smaller than percentage change in *P*	*TR* changes in the same direction as change in *P;* there is thus an incentive for suppliers to raise prices
Unit elastic demand ($e_p = 1$)	Percentage change in *Q* is equal to percentage change in *P*	*TR* remains unchanged
Elastic demand ($1 < e_p < \infty$)	Percentage change in *Q* is greater than percentage change in *P*	*TR* changes in the opposite direction to change in *P;* there is thus an incentive for suppliers to lower prices
Perfectly elastic demand ($e_p = \infty$)	Indeterminate quantity *(Q)* demanded at given price *(P)*; nothing demanded at a fractionally higher price	When *P* increases, *Q* falls to zero; *TR* therefore also falls to zero

Price elasticity of demand and the impact of a change in supply

We now examine the impact of a change in supply when demand curves have different price elasticities. In Figure 9-5 we show two demand curves, D_1 and D_2, and a supply curve S_1 which all intersect at point A_0. The equilibrium price is P_0 and the equilibrium quantity is Q_0. Total expenditure on the product (and total revenue) equals $0P_0A_0Q_0$. Suppose supply increases to S_2 (eg because of an increase in the number of firms). The intersection of D_1 and S_2 is at A_1 (with an equilibrium price P_1 and an equilibrium quantity Q_1) and the intersection of D_2 and S_2 is at A_2 (with an equilibrium price of P_2 and an equilibrium quantity of Q_2). Total revenue in the case of D_1 is $0P_1A_1Q_1$ and in the case of D_2 it is $0P_2A_2Q_2$. This figure illustrates the important points made earlier with respect to changes in total revenue (*TR*):

- In the case of D_1, the relatively elastic demand curve, the increase in quantity is greater than in the case of D_2, the relatively inelastic demand curve.
- In the case of D_1, the relatively elastic demand curve, the fall in price is less than in the case of D_2, the relatively inelastic demand curve.
- In the case of D_1, the relatively elastic demand curve, total revenue *TR* after the increase in supply (represented by the area $0P_1A_1Q_1$) is greater than in the case of D_2, the relatively inelastic demand curve. In the latter case the total revenue *TR* after the increase in supply is represented by $0P_2A_2Q_2$.

If supply decreases, the opposite will happen, as you can verify using similar initial curves and shifting the supply curve upwards to the left. Note that such comparisons are valid only if we proceed from an initial point where all the curves intersect, such as at point A_0 in Figure 9-5.

Figure 9-5 can be used to add to the explanation of fluctuations in agricultural prices in Section 8.6. The demand for most agricultural products (which are generally regarded as necessities) tends to be inelastic, such as D_2 in Figure 9-5. When supply fluctuates (eg as a result of changes in climatic conditions), the fluctuations result in large changes in the prices of the products concerned, while the quantities do not change much. In other words, the problems of agriculture are exacerbated by the inelastic nature of the demand for agricultural products. The technique applied in Figure 9-5 can be used to analyse a variety of other real-world phenomena, some of which we touch on in later chapters.

Determinants of the price elasticity of demand

We have now defined the price elasticity of demand, shown how it is related to total revenue, identified five different categories of price elasticity of demand, and shown how it influences the impact of a change in supply. But what are the determinants of the price elasticity of demand? Why are certain goods characterised by an inelastic demand while other goods have an elastic demand? What types of goods and services tend to have elastic demands and which tend to have inelastic demands? We now discuss some of the determinants of price elasticity and give some practical examples. In discussing each determinant we have to assume once more that all other things remain unchanged (ie we have to make the *ceteris*

FIGURE 9-5 The impact of an increase in supply

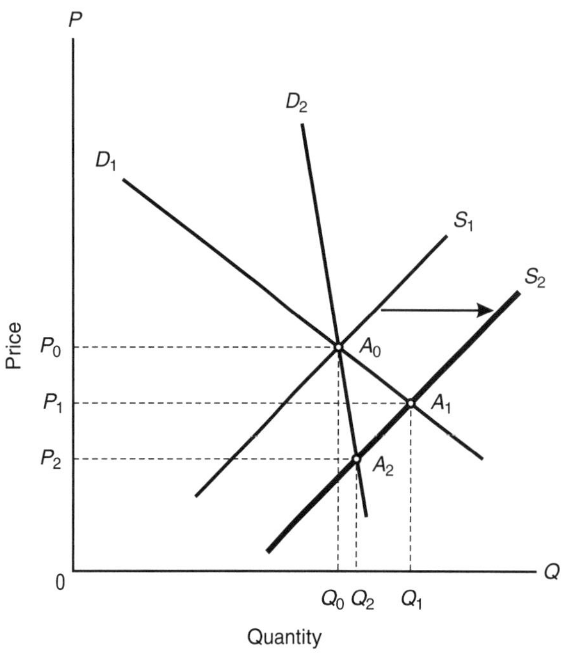

D_1 and D_2 represent two demand curves which intersect each other and a supply curve S_1 at point A_0. If supply increases to S_2, the price impact is larger in the case of the relatively inelastic demand curve D_2 and the quantity impact is greater in the case of the relatively elastic demand curve D_1. After the increase in supply the total revenue in the case of D_1 ($0P_1A_1Q_1$) is greater than in the case of D_2 ($0P_2A_2Q_2$).

paribus assumption). In practice, however, all things can change. This means that the impact of one determinant can be neutralised by another determinant which works in the opposite direction. Moreover, different consumers or groups of consumers (eg poor and rich consumers) may respond differently to price changes. Therefore, in deciding whether the demand for a particular good or service will tend to be elastic or inelastic, all the relevant information must be considered (ie all the possible determinants have to be taken into account).

■ SUBSTITUTION POSSIBILITIES

The availability of substitutes is undoubtedly the most important determinant of consumers' reactions to a price change. The larger the number of substitutes and the closer (or better) the substitutes are, the greater is the price elasticity of demand, *ceteris paribus*. Goods and services with good substitutes (shown here in brackets) include beef (mutton), butter (margarine), taxi services (bus services, train services), hamburgers (hot dogs) and apples (pears). These goods and services will therefore tend to have an elastic demand. For example, if the price of a good with close substitutes increases, consumers will tend to switch to the substitutes, which become relatively cheaper. On the other hand, if a good has no close substitutes, like salt, petrol, electricity or certain medicines, demand will tend to be inelastic.

■ THE DEGREE OF COMPLEMENTARITY OF THE PRODUCT

In the case of highly complementary goods (ie goods which tend to be used jointly with other goods rather than on their own) the price elasticity of demand tends to be low. Examples of goods with complements (shown here in brackets) include sugar (tea, coffee and many foodstuffs), motorcar tyres (motorcars), petrol (motorcars), salt (food), golf balls (golf clubs) and audio cassettes (cassette players). In many cases it may be argued that it is the absence of good substitutes, rather than the degree of complementarity, which is responsible for the inelastic demand of highly complementary goods. This is not always the case, however. Whereas a fall in the price of a product without close substitutes will tend to increase the quantity demanded, the quantity demanded of goods with a high degree of complementarity will not necessarily increase if their prices fall. Salt is a good example. People will not start buying more salt simply because the price of salt has fallen (relative to the prices of other goods).

■ THE TYPE OF WANT SATISFIED BY THE PRODUCT

The price elasticity of the demand for **necessities**, like basic foodstuffs, electricity, petrol, medical care and postage stamps, tends to be lower than the price elasticity of **luxury goods and services** such as recreation, entertainment, swimming pools and luxury motor vehicles. There are no hard and fast rules to determine whether a particular good or service is a necessity or a luxury. All we can really say is that the demand for a product that is considered a necessity tends to be relatively inelastic, whereas the demand for a product that is considered a luxury tends to be relatively elastic. (See also the discussion on the income elasticity of demand in Section 9.2.)

■ THE TIME PERIOD UNDER CONSIDERATION

Demand tends to be more price elastic in the long run than in the short run. When the price of a product changes, *ceteris paribus*, consumers usually need time to adjust to the change in relative prices. In the 1970s, for example, the price of crude oil increased more than twenty-fold. In the short run consumers could do

BOX 9-3 ELASTICITY AND SLOPE

Elasticity is often confused with slope. From the discussion in the text it should be clear, however, that elasticity and slope are not the same thing. Although the slope of a linear demand curve (or, rather, the inverse of the slope) forms part of the formula for the point elasticity of demand, we have seen that the price elasticity of demand varies from point to point along a linear demand curve. Except for the two extreme cases of perfectly elastic and perfectly inelastic demand, a demand curve with a constant slope represents a collection of price elasticities, varying from zero to infinity.

Another reason why slope cannot be used to compare elasticities is that one can obtain demand curves with different slopes by varying the scales on the axes. Where different products are involved (eg beef and milk), different units of measurement are used. Therefore it is impossible to compare the elasticity of the demand curves of different products (eg beef and milk) using a diagram.

The only valid graphical comparison of the price elasticity of demand is to compare two demand curves for the same product at the point where they intersect. This is shown in the accompanying figure.

In the figure we show two demand curves, D_1 and D_2, which intersect at point A. At that particular point the price elasticity of demand curve D_1 is greater than that of D_2. Recall, from Equation 9-1, that $e_p = (\Delta Q/\Delta P) \times (P/Q)$. Where the demand curves intersect, the price P and quantity Q are the same for both curves, ie P/Q is the same for both curves. But $\Delta Q/\Delta P$, the inverse of the slope, differs. It is greater for D_1 than for D_2 (since D_2 has a greater slope than D_1). The price elasticity of D_1 at A is thus greater than the price elasticity of D_2 at A. This is the only valid graphical comparison of the price elasticity of two downward-sloping linear demand curves.

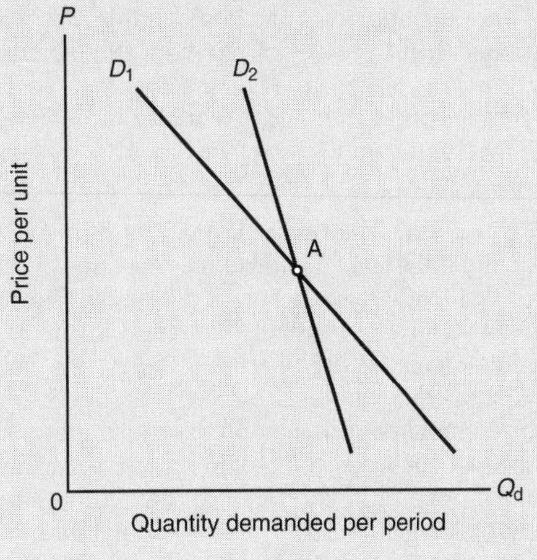

little about it and sales did not fall significantly. In due course, however, consumers switched to smaller, more fuel-efficient cars.

Another example is the price elasticity of demand for airline tickets. Someone who has to fly somewhere at short notice does not have the opportunity to shop around for the best deal. In many cases he or she purchases the first available ticket without paying too much attention to the price. However, if someone in Gauteng plans to go on holiday to Cape Town in a few months' time, he or she has plenty of time to compare the prices offered by different airline companies, as well as to compare the cost of flying with the cost of alternative modes of transport (train, bus, motorcar). The long-run demand for airline tickets will therefore be more price elastic than the short-run demand. The airline companies realise this and base their fare structure on the differences in price elasticity. The practice of charging different prices to different sets of customers according to differences in price elasticity is called **price discrimination**, which we discuss in Chapter 13. Empirical studies conducted in other countries have confirmed that demand curves tend to be relatively inelastic in the short run and significantly more elastic in the long run.

■ THE PROPORTION OF INCOME SPENT ON THE PRODUCT

It is often argued that the greater the proportion of income spent on a product, the greater the price elasticity of demand will be (or that the smaller the proportion, the lower the price elasticity of demand will be). The expenditure on products such as matches, salt and paper clips constitutes a small share of a consumer's budget, so it is argued that a price change will have a negligible effect on the quantity demanded. In many cases, however, the low price elasticity of demand can probably also be explained by the lack of substitutes, the degree of complementarity or the type of want that is satisfied.

■ OTHER POSSIBLE DETERMINANTS OF PRICE ELASTICITY OF DEMAND

The following factors can also affect the price elasticity of demand:

- **The definition of the product**. The broader the definition of the product, the smaller the measured price elasticity of demand will tend to be. This is again related to the substitution possibilities. Broader definitions reduce the number of possible substitutes. The price elasticity of the demand for food, for example, will be less than the price elasticity of demand for any particular type of food. Meat and beef is another example – the price elasticity of demand for beef is greater than the price elasticity of demand for meat. Similarly, the price elasticity of the demand for a particular motorcar will be greater than the price elasticity of the demand for motorcars. In the United States, for example, it was estimated that the price elasticity of demand for Chevrolet motorcars was four times as great as the price elasticity of demand for motorcars in general.
- **Advertising**. The price elasticity of demand for a particular brand of a product (eg Omo washing powder) will be greater than the price elasticity of demand for the product (washing powder). The reason again is that one brand (eg Omo) may be substituted by another (eg Surf). Producers spend large amounts of money on advertising and other forms of non-price competition, such as packaging, distribution and service, to develop a loyalty among consumers to their particular brands. In other words, they try to convince consumers that their particular products have no real substitutes. To the extent that they are successful, they reduce the price elasticity of demand for their brands.
- **Durability**. The more durable the good, the more elastic the demand will tend to be, *ceteris paribus*. For example, if the price of washing machines or refrigerators increases, consumers may decide to keep their existing machines for a longer period than they had originally intended. Non-durable goods, like household cleaning materials, cannot be used more than once and therefore tend to have a more inelastic demand.
- **Number of uses of the product**. It is sometimes argued that the greater the number of uses of a particular product, the greater the price elasticity of demand will tend to be. The argument is that substitutes may be available for certain of the uses. Electricity, for example, has a variety of uses. A rise in the price of electricity may cause consumers to switch to other means of cooking. Less important uses of electricity (such as heating) may be eliminated altogether.
- **Addiction**. Products that are habit forming (eg cigarettes, alcohol, drugs) will tend to have a relatively low price elasticity of demand. For consumers who are totally addicted, the demand may even be perfectly price inelastic.

■ THE COMBINED EFFECT OF THE DETERMINANTS

As we mentioned earlier, there are no hard and fast rules as far as the determinants of the price elasticity of demand are concerned. Each of the determinants will probably have the effects that we have indicated, but only if viewed in isolation. Sometimes they all work in the same direction. Salt is the classic example: it has no real substitutes; it is a complement to many foodstuffs; it is essential; it is non-durable; and spending on salt comprises a small proportion of the average consumer's income. It is therefore not surprising that the price elasticity of the demand for salt was estimated at about 0,1 in empirical studies in the United States.

In many cases, however, the various determinants counteract each other and the final result is therefore uncertain. For example, a television set is almost regarded as an essential product today. It has no close substitutes and has no alternative uses. On the other hand it is a durable good on which the consumer spends a significant portion of his or her income.

In deciding whether the demand for a particular product is price elastic or inelastic, all the determinants, and the relative importance of each, must be considered. Usually, however, the **substitutability of the product is the crucial factor**. As we have indicated, many of the other determinants are related to the existence of substitution possibilities.

No wide-ranging empirical investigation of price elasticity of demand has been conducted in South Africa, but in empirical studies undertaken in the United States the following goods and services have been generally found to have inelastic and elastic demands:

- **Inelastic demand** ($e_p < 1$): salt, matches, toothpicks, cigarettes, bread, milk, petrol, electricity, water, eggs, potatoes, meat, postage stamps, medical care, legal services, motorcar tyres
- **Elastic demand** ($e_p > 1$): motor vehicles, mutton, furniture, entertainment, restaurant meals, overseas holidays, butter, chicken, veal, apples, peaches

Can you use the determinants that we have identified to explain each of these empirical results?

Applications

Price elasticity of demand has many applications in economic analysis. Firms and policymakers require information about price elasticity when making pricing or policy decisions. For example, the distribution of the burden of excise taxes or import tariffs, or of the benefit of subsidies, depends on the price elasticity of demand. Firms also require information about how the quantity demanded will respond when the price of their good or service changes. Box 9-4 provides one example of the importance of price elasticity of demand. Many further examples are provided in the review questions at the end of this chapter and in the rest of this book. Whenever demand and supply can be used to analyse a particular situation, price elasticity becomes important.

9.2 Other demand elasticities

Elasticity is a measure of responsiveness which can be applied to any causal relationship between two variables. Since the quantity demanded of a product does not only depend on the price of a product, it is possible to calculate other demand elasticities as well. In this section we briefly examine two such demand elasticities: the **income elasticity of demand** and the **cross elasticity of demand**.

Income elasticity of demand

The quantity demanded of a product depends on the income of the consumers. As consumers' incomes rise, the quantity demanded usually increases, *ceteris paribus*. The question is, by how much will the quantity demanded change, relative to the change in income? The **income elasticity of demand** (e_y) measures the responsiveness of the quantity demanded to changes in income. Applying our general definition of elasticity, it is defined as the ratio between the percentage change in the quantity demanded (the

BOX 9-4 DRUG ADDICTION, LAW ENFORCEMENT AND DRUG-RELATED CRIME

The use of illegal drugs, such as heroin, cocaine and crack, is a major problem in modern society. Drug addiction can ruin the lives of addicts and their families. Moreover, addicts often resort to crime (eg prostitution, shoplifting, burglary, mugging, armed robbery) to obtain the money they need to buy drugs. Many communities in South Africa are severely affected by drug-related activities.

To discourage the use of illegal drugs, governments across the world (including the South African government) take steps to reduce the flow of such drugs into their countries. To the extent that they are successful, they reduce the supply of drugs in the domestic market, but since the demand for illegal drugs is highly price inelastic the result tends to be a sharp increase in price. As we have seen, a reduction in supply (illustrated by a leftward shift of the supply curve) when demand is price inelastic results in an increase in total spending (*PQ*) and therefore in the total revenue (*TR*) of the suppliers (in this case the drug producers and dealers). Faced with higher prices, drug addicts increase their criminal activity in an attempt to finance their greater expenditure on drugs. Paradoxically, therefore, success in the fight against drugs may increase the prevalence of drug-related crime. The ideal solution, of course, would be to combat drug addiction and drug-related crime by reducing the demand for drugs. It is sometimes argued, however, that such a reduction in demand (illustrated by a leftward shift of the demand curve) cannot be achieved and that the only sensible solution is to legalise the drugs. Proponents of this view call for drugs to be legalised for adults and to be regulated for purity and potency (as in the case of alcohol). Legalisation would reduce drug trafficking by reducing prices and profits in the industry and because the demand is price inelastic, the increase in the quantity consumed would be relatively small. Total expenditure on drugs would decrease and as a result drug-related crime would also diminish.

Opponents of such legislation argue that there is a segment of the drug market in which the price elasticity of demand is high. The consumers in this market segment are the occasional users of drugs. When drug prices are low, more people (particularly the youth) will tend to experiment with drugs and be exposed to the risk of becoming drug addicts. Conversely, if the price is very high, fewer people will experiment with drugs, and in time the number of addicts (and the prevalence of drug-related crime) will decline.

There are no easy solutions to drug addiction and drug-related crime. For our purposes, however, it is important to note how demand and supply analysis and elasticities can be used to assess different approaches to dealing with the problem. As an exercise you should draw diagrams to illustrate the various arguments outlined in this box.

dependent variable) and the percentage change in consumers' income (the independent variable), that is,

$$e_y = \frac{\text{percentage change in the quantity demanded of the product}}{\text{percentage change in consumers' income}}$$

Income elasticity of demand may be positive or negative. A positive income elasticity of demand means that an increase in income is accompanied by an increase in the quantity demanded of the product concerned (or that a decrease in income is accompanied by a decrease in the quantity demanded). Goods with a **positive income elasticity** of demand are called **normal goods**. A negative income elasticity of demand means that an increase in income leads to a decrease in the quantity demanded of the good concerned (or that a decrease in income leads to an increase in the quantity demanded). Goods with a **negative income elasticity** of demand are called **inferior goods**.

Normal goods are further classified as luxury goods or essential goods. When the income elasticity of demand is **greater than one**, that is, when the percentage change in the quantity demanded is greater than the percentage change in income, the good is called a **luxury good**. When the income elasticity of demand is **positive but less than one**, that is, when the percentage change in the quantity demanded is smaller than the percentage change in income, the good is called an **essential good**.

Information about the income elasticity of demand is important to the suppliers of goods and services. They want to know what will happen to the quantities demanded of the goods and services they supply as the incomes of consumers increase. In the 1960s, Japanese entrepreneurs assumed, quite correctly, that incomes in the industrial countries would increase rapidly. They therefore identified a number of goods with relatively high income elasticities of demand and were ready to supply them (eg electronic equipment and motorcars) when the quantities demanded of these goods subsequently increased faster than the incomes of consumers in the industrial countries.

On the other hand, the low income elasticity of demand of basic foodstuffs is one of the reasons why developing countries which export agricultural products fared relatively badly during the post-war economic boom. Consumers' income increased, but the quantities of basic foodstuffs demanded did not increase to the same extent. In other words, the demand for these commodities did not keep pace with the growth in income and the demand for manufactured goods.

Table 9-3 contains some examples of income elasticities of demand that have been calculated for South Africa. Although the table is somewhat dated, it contains some interesting results. Note how the income elasticities of demand tend to differ between high-income and low-income households. Can you explain the differences (eg why certain goods are luxuries to low-income households but necessities to high-income households)? Can you also explain why paraffin, candles and ordinary radios are inferior goods to low-income households? See also Box 9-5.

TABLE 9-3 Some estimated income elasticities of demand in South Africa, 1985

Item	*Income elasticity of demand*	
	High-income households	*Low-income households*
Brown/wholewheat bread	0,25	0,23
Maize meal	0,31	0,00
Rice	0,02	0,60
Cakes and biscuits	0,78	2,27
Meat	0,32	0,90
Biltong	1,36	1,11
Fresh fish	0,51	1,61
Fresh milk	0,21	0,66
Cheese	0,46	2,01
Pure fruit juice	0,83	2,03
Tea	0,21	0,25
Women's clothing	0,98	1,14
Men's clothing	0,99	1,26
Paraffin	0,55	−0,51
Candles	0,82	−0,20
Transport	1,26	1,25
Medical care	0,65	0,98
Furniture	1,40	1,30
Electrical equipment	1,06	2,18
Ordinary radio	0,88	−0,56
Television set	0,37	1,65

Source: Loubser, M. 1990. *Income elasticities of the demand for consumer goods and services*. Research report No. 175. Pretoria: Bureau of Market Research (University of South Africa)

Cross elasticity of demand

The quantity demanded of a particular good also depends on the **prices of related goods**. The **cross elasticity of demand** measures the responsiveness of the quantity demanded of a particular good to changes in the price of a related good. Applying our general definition of elasticity, we can define the cross elasticity of demand (e_c) as the ratio between the percentage change in the quantity demanded of a product (the dependent variable) and the percentage change in the price of a related product (the independent variable), that is,

BOX 9-5 ENGEL'S LAW

If the income elasticity of demand for a product is greater than one, the quantity purchased rises more rapidly than income and an increased share of income is spent on the product. If the income elasticity is less than one, the proportion of income spent on the product declines as income increases.

In the 19th century a German statistician, Ernst Engel, studied family budgets in different countries and found that as family income increased, the share of the budget spent on food declined. Subsequent statistical studies confirmed this finding. In South Africa, for example, Statistics South Africa conducts a five-yearly *Survey of Household Income and Expenditure* to determine the weights to be used in compiling the consumer price index (see Chapter 5). In 2000, the very low expenditure group spent an estimated 51 per cent on food, compared to a figure of 16 per cent for the very high expenditure group.

This statistical regularity, which simply means that the income elasticity of the demand for food is less than one, has come to be called **Engel's law**. This law explains why the share of agriculture in economic activity (referred to in Section 5.1) tends to decline during the course of economic development. It also helps to explain why some food-exporting developing countries (particularly those that rely heavily on exports of one or a few basic foodstuffs) tend to experience lower rates of economic growth than the industrialised countries and other growing economies to which they export their agricultural products.

$$e_c = \frac{\text{percentage change in the quantity demanded of product A}}{\text{percentage change in the price of product B}}$$

When two goods are unrelated (eg motorcar tyres and margarine) the cross elasticity of demand will be zero.

In the case of **substitutes** (eg butter and margarine) the cross elasticity of demand is **positive**. A change in the price of the one product (eg butter) will lead to a change in the same direction in the quantity demanded of the substitute product. For example, when the price of butter increases, more margarine will be demanded, *ceteris paribus*, as consumers switch to the relatively cheaper margarine.

In the case of **complements** the cross elasticity of demand is **negative**. A change in the price of the one product (eg motorcars) will lead to a change in the opposite direction in the quantity demanded of the complementary product (eg motorcar tyres). For example, if the price of motorcars falls, the quantity of motorcars demanded will increase and as a result more motorcar tyres will be demanded.

9.3 The price elasticity of supply

We conclude this chapter by examining the price elasticity of supply.

The price elasticity of supply measures the responsiveness of the quantity supplied of a product to changes in the price of the product. More formally, the **price elasticity of supply** (e_s) is the ratio between the percentage change in the quantity supplied of a product (the dependent variable) and the percentage change in the price of the product (the independent variable), that is,

$$e_s = \frac{\text{percentage change in the quantity supplied of a product}}{\text{percentage change in the price of the product}}$$

Different categories of supply elasticity

Since the quantity supplied usually increases as the price of the product increases (ie since there is a direct relationship between the variables), the price elasticity of supply is easier to interpret than the price elasticity of demand. As in the case of price elasticity of demand, five different categories of supply elasticity can be distinguished:

- perfectly inelastic supply ($e_s = 0$)
- inelastic supply (e_s greater than 0 but smaller than 1)
- unit elastic supply ($e_s = 1$) (unitary elasticity)
- elastic supply (e_s greater than 1)
- perfectly elastic supply ($e_s = \infty$)

These five categories are illustrated in Figure 9-6. The supply curve in Figure 9-6(a) is perfectly inelastic. It has the same shape as a perfectly inelastic demand curve, indicating that the quantity supplied is unresponsive to (or independent of) changes in the price of the product. The supply curve in Figure 9-6(b) is an inelastic supply curve. Any upward-sloping linear supply curve which intersects the horizontal (quantity) axis has a positive elasticity of less than one (but greater than zero). This indicates that the percentage change in the quantity supplied is less than the percentage change in the price of the product. The supply curve in Figure 9-6(c) has unitary elasticity. Any upward-sloping linear supply curve which passes through the origin has an elasticity of one, indicating that the percentage change in the quantity supplied is equal to the percentage change in the price of the product. The supply curve in Figure 9-6(d) is an elastic supply curve. Any upward-sloping linear supply curve which intersects the vertical (price) axis has an elasticity greater than one but less than infinity. This indicates that the percentage change in the quantity supplied is greater than the percentage change in the

FIGURE 9-6 Different categories of price elasticity of supply

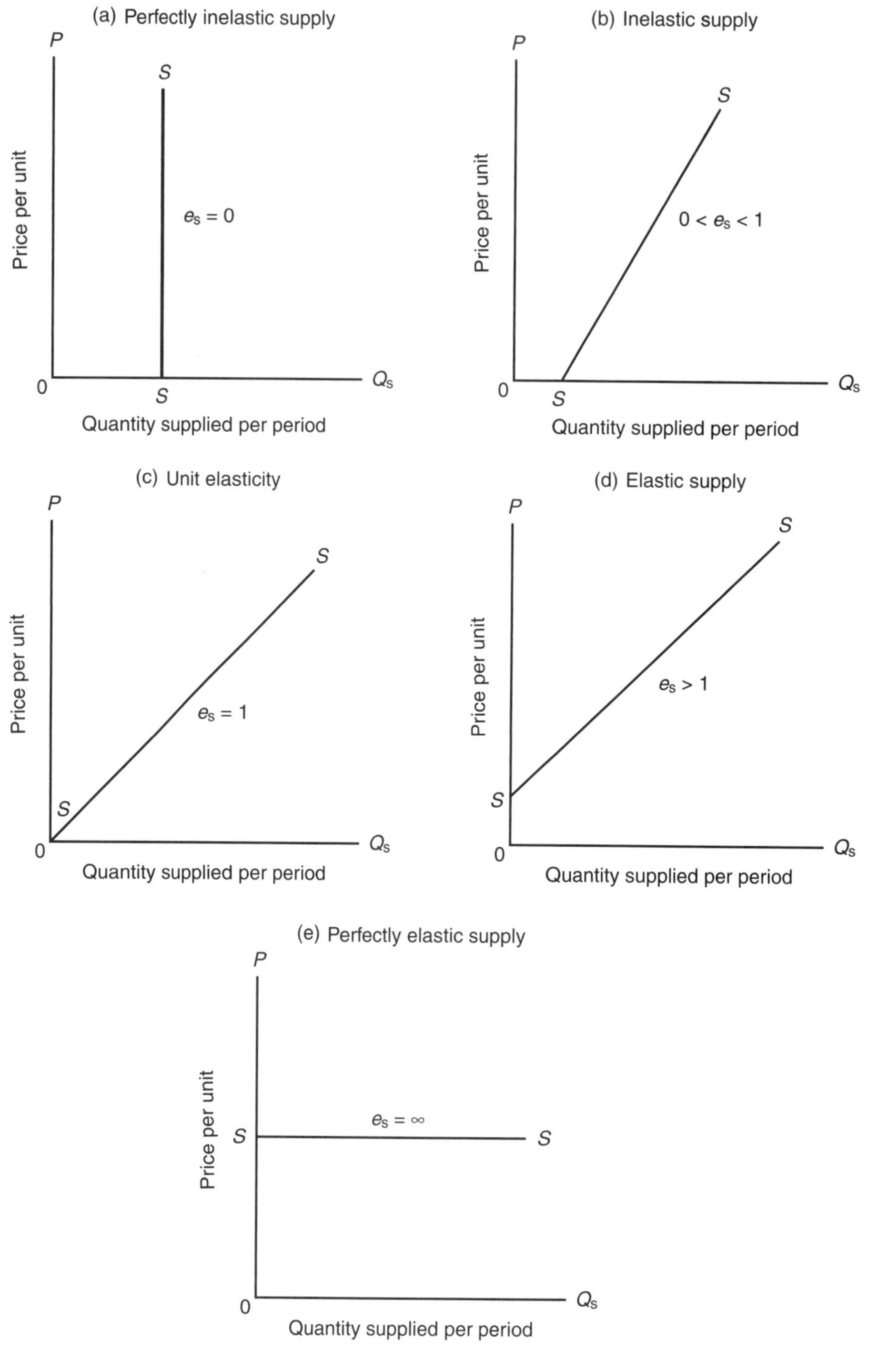

price of the product. The supply curve in Figure 9-6(e) is perfectly elastic, indicating that any quantity can be supplied at a given price. It, too, has the same shape as a perfectly elastic demand curve.

The determinants of the price elasticity of supply

Like the price elasticity of demand, the price elasticity of supply depends on the length of **time** that has elapsed since the change in price. In the short run, most supply curves are inelastic, as suppliers do not have sufficient time to respond to a price change. In the long run, however, they can adjust their levels of production in response to changes in price. An obvious example relates to the planting cycle of crops – if the maize price increases, farmers need a full growing season to adjust their production to the price increase. Inelastic short-run supply curves (such as the one illustrated in Figure 9-6(b)) may thus become elastic (like the one in Figure 9-6(d)) in the long run. In the United States it has been estimated, for example, that the short-run and long-run price elasticities of supply of fresh cabbage are 0,36 and 1,2 respectively. Similar results were obtained for all other fresh vegetables. Even factories and other production units cannot adjust immediately to price changes. For example, if the price of aluminium, steel, copper, platinum or gold increases, it may take months, if not longer, to increase production in response to the price increase.

Supply may also be inelastic with regard to a *decrease* in price in the short run. A fall in the price of apples, for example, will not necessarily result in a rapid reduction in the quantity supplied. Farmers with apple orchards will probably still be forced to harvest and sell the apples at the lower price, rather than lose all their income. They will also not switch to other types of fruit since the price of apples will probably recover in subsequent years.

The previous example suggests that price **expectations** are also an important determinant of supply elasticity. Expectations of higher prices will result in increased supply. By the same token, reductions in price which are regarded as temporary by producers will tend to lead to an inelastic response. However, if a price reduction is perceived by producers to be a long-term phenomenon, they will reduce their production capacity. In such conditions supply will tend to be more elastic.

Other determinants of supply elasticity include the possibility of **stockpiling** the product and the existence of **excess capacity**. Products that can be stockpiled have a more elastic supply than perishable goods which cannot be stockpiled. Firms with excess production capacity will be able to respond more quickly to a price increase than firms that are operating at full capacity. Finally, the **availability of inputs** can also affect the ability of producers to respond to price increases. If essential inputs are not available, firms cannot increase their output in reaction to an increase in the price of their product.

Elasticity: a summary

Table 9-4 summarises the different elasticities explained in this chapter.

TABLE 9-4 Different elasticities: a summary

Type	*Definition*	*Possibilities*	*Description*
Price elasticity of demand	$\frac{\text{Percentage change in quantity demanded}}{\text{Percentage change in price}}$	$e_p > 1$ $e_p < 1$ $e_p = 1$ $e_p = \infty$ $e_p = 0$	Elastic Inelastic Unit elastic Perfectly elastic Perfectly inelastic
Cross elasticity of demand	$\frac{\text{Percentage change in quantity demanded of one good}}{\text{Percentage change in price of another good}}$	$e_c < 0$ $e_c > 0$ $e_c = 0$	Complements Substitutes Independent goods
Income elasticity of demand	$\frac{\text{Percentage change in quantity demanded}}{\text{Percentage change in income}}$	$e_y > 0$ $e_y < 0$ $e_y > 1$ $e_y < 1$	Normal good Inferior good Income elastic Income inelastic
Price elasticity of supply	$\frac{\text{Percentage change in quantity supplied}}{\text{Percentage change in price}}$	$e_s > 1$ $e_s < 1$ $e_s = 1$ $e_s = \infty$ $e_s = 0$	Elastic Inelastic Unit elastic Perfectly elastic Perfectly inelastic

IMPORTANT CONCEPTS

Elasticity	Inelastic demand	Income elasticity of demand
Price elasticity of demand	Unit elastic demand	Normal and inferior goods
Elasticity coefficient	Elastic demand	Essential and luxury goods
Arc elasticity	Perfectly elastic demand	Cross elasticity of demand
Total revenue (or expenditure)	Slope and inverse of slope	Price elasticity of supply
Perfectly inelastic demand	Determinants of price elasticity	Elastic and inelastic supply

REVIEW QUESTIONS

1. Define the price elasticity of the demand for potatoes and discuss its determinants.
2. For each of the following pairs of goods, which good would you expect to have a greater price elasticity of demand and why?
   (a) Elvis Presley recordings or rock-and-roll recordings in general
   (b) prescribed textbooks or science fiction novels
   (c) airline tickets purchased by business travellers or airline tickets purchased by tourists
3. Suppose that you are the owner of an ice-cream shop and that you have established that the price elasticity of the demand for ice-cream in your particular market is 1,8. Would you sell ice-cream at R5,00 per litre or R4,50 per litre? Explain.
4. Suppose that you are the managing director of a firm that produces three goods: X, Y and Z. The price elasticity of the demand for X is 2,5; for Y it is 1,00; and for Z it is 0,50. The firm is experiencing serious cash flow problems and you have to increase total revenue as soon as possible. If you are in a position to set the prices for these goods, what would be your pricing strategy for each product? Explain.
5. Suppose that you are the manager of a soccer stadium where all the tickets always have to be sold at the same price. Two matches are scheduled to be played during the next fortnight: the first between Sundowns and Pirates and the second between two First Division sides.
   (a) Market research indicates that you can sell 40 000 tickets for the Sundowns-Pirates clash at R10 each, or 30 000 tickets at R20 each. Which option would you choose? What is the price elasticity of the demand for this particular game?
   (b) Likewise, market research indicates that you can sell 15 000 tickets for the First Division fixture at R10 each, or 5 000 tickets at R20 each. Which option would you choose? What is the price elasticity of the demand for this game?
6. Suppose you are the owner of a supermarket. Each week you offer some goods at "special prices". Would it make more sense to offer specials on goods with a low price elasticity of demand or on those with a high price elasticity of demand? Explain your choice.
7. In 1973/74 the Organisation of Petroleum Exporting Countries (OPEC) engineered a relatively small restriction in the international supply of crude oil, resulting in vast revenue gains for OPEC members. Use your knowledge of demand, supply and elasticity to explain these gains.

8. Suppose that you are appointed as the chief executive officer of Spoornet at a time when it is making a loss on passenger transport. You are informed that the price elasticity of passenger rail services is 1,4. What pricing strategy would you follow in your attempt to restore profitability at Spoornet?

9. You are still the CEO of Spoornet. Analysts have determined that the price elasticity of 1,4 is a weighted average figure. During peak hours in the morning and evening the price elasticity of demand is 0,8 and during the rest of the day it is 2,6. How would this information affect your pricing strategy?

10. In 1977 a frost in Brazil, the world's largest supplier of coffee, caused a sharp reduction in the supply of coffee. This led to an increase in the international spending on coffee. Far from hurting coffee producers, the frost actually made them better off. Use your knowledge of demand, supply and elasticity to explain this somewhat paradoxical result.

11. If you were the Minister of Finance and you wanted to raise revenue by taxing a specific good, would you tax a good of which the price elasticity of demand is high or one of which the price elasticity of demand is low? Explain.

12. Use your knowledge of supply and demand curves and elasticity to explain why *farmers as a group* may prefer bad weather to good weather, even though an *individual farmer* prefers good weather to bad weather.

13. Explain the difference between a normal good and an inferior good.

14. Use the concept of the income elasticity of demand to explain the difference between necessities, luxuries and inferior goods.

15. Developing countries that export agricultural products to industrialised countries frequently argue that unless they expand their manufacturing sectors, they will always remain relatively poor. Use the elasticity concept to explain such an argument.

16. What does it mean when we say that supply is perfectly inelastic?

Nobel Laureates in economics

The Alfred Nobel Memorial Prize for Economic Science was established in 1968 by the Swedish central bank (the Riksbank). Candidates for the Nobel Prize are elected by the Swedish Royal Academy of Sciences. The final choice, from proposals received from various individuals and organisations, is announced in mid-October of each year.

The following people were awarded the Nobel Prize for Economics from 1969 to 1987 (with their country of residence in brackets):

1969 Ragnar Frisch (Norway), Jan Tinbergen (Netherlands)
1970 Paul Samuelson (United States)
1971 Simon Kuznets* (United States)
1972 Kenneth Arrow (United States), John Hicks (Britain)
1973 Wassily Leontief* (United States)
1974 Friedrich von Hayek (Britain), Gunnar Myrdal (Sweden)
1975 Leonid Kantorovich (Soviet Union), Tjalling Koopmans* (United States)
1976 Milton Friedman (United States)
1977 James Meade (Britain), Bertil Ohlin (Sweden)
1978 Herbert Simon (United States)
1979 W Arthur Lewis* (Britain), Theodore W Schultz (United States)
1980 Lawrence R Klein (United States)
1981 James Tobin (United States)
1982 George J Stigler (United States)
1983 Gerard Debreu* (United States)
1984 Richard Stone (Britain)
1985 Franco Modigliani* (United States)
1986 James M Buchanan Jr (United States)
1987 Robert M Solow (United States)

* Kuznets and Leontief were born in Russia, Koopmans in the Netherlands, Lewis in the West Indies, Debreu in France and Modigliani in Italy.

The Nobel Laureates from 1988 to 2006 are listed on page 222.

10

Background to demand: the theory of consumer choice

Learning outcomes

Once you have studied this chapter you should be able to

- define utility, marginal utility and weighted marginal utility
- explain the relationship between total, average and marginal values
- state the conditions for consumer equilibrium
- use weighted marginal utility to derive a demand curve
- explain what indifference curves are and list their important properties
- define the budget line and explain consumer equilibrium
- examine the effects of changes in income or prices

By the principle of utility is meant that principle which approves or disapproves of every action whatsoever, according to the tendency which it appears to have to augment or diminish the happiness of the party whose interest is in question.

JEREMY BENTHAM

A person distributes his income in such a way as to equalise the utility of the final increments of all commodities consumed.

WILLIAM STANLEY JEVONS

My first rule is never to buy anything you can't make your children carry.

BILL BRYSON

In the discussion of demand and supply in the previous three chapters, we assumed that demand curves usually slope downward from left to right. This is in accordance with the law of demand, which states that the quantity demanded of a good will increase if the price of the good falls, and will decrease if the price rises, *ceteris paribus*. In this chapter we examine consumer behaviour in greater detail. In the process we provide an explanation for why demand curves slope downward from left to right. We focus on two approaches to the study of consumer choice: the **utility approach** and the **indifference approach**. The utility approach is based on the notion of **cardinal utility** while the indifference approach is based on the notion of **ordinal utility**.

Among the most important concepts introduced in this chapter are **utility, marginal utility** and **weighted marginal utility**. The concept of marginal utility, which provides a justification for the law of demand, is the first marginal concept you encounter in this book. Marginal concepts play an important role in neoclassical economic analysis and we therefore explain the **difference between total, marginal and average values** in some detail. We also explain what **indifference curves** are and we indicate their important properties. We then introduce the **budget line** and combine it with indifference curves to explain **consumer equilibrium**. This is followed by an investigation of the effects of changes in income and prices and the derivation of the demand curve.

In this chapter we introduce the theory of consumer behaviour. This theory should be relatively easy to understand. We are all consumers and can therefore rely on our own experience when analysing consumer behaviour. It is important to remember, however, that theory is always a simplification of reality and therefore always abstract. In analysing consumer behaviour we have to make certain simplifying assumptions. This can be a source of frustration to anyone who confuses theory with description. As we emphasised in Chapter 6, the purpose of theory is not to describe behaviour but to **explain** and **predict** it and to analyse **policy** decisions. To achieve these aims, we need general theories which we can then apply to specific cases. To formulate such theories we have to make certain simplifying assumptions.

10.1 Utility

Consumption is not an end in itself. Households and individual consumers do not simply engage in consumption in order to consume goods and services. The purpose of consumption is to satisfy wants. In the analysis of consumer behaviour it is assumed that households or consumers attempt to **maximise their satisfaction of wants**, given the available means and the alternatives at their disposal.

Utility is simply a term for consumer satisfaction. This term was devised by economists in the 19th century to express **the degree of satisfaction that a household or consumer derives or expects to derive from the consumption of a good or service**. The purpose of consumer behaviour can thus be restated as the **maximisation of utility**, given the available means and alternative consumption possibilities.

The utility of a particular good or service is the degree to which it satisfies human wants. It is, however, an **abstract** and **subjective** concept. A particular product does not have a unique, measurable utility which applies to all consumers. Tastes and wants differ from one consumer to the next. A product will also provide different amounts of satisfaction to a particular consumer at different times and at different places. An umbrella, for example, will yield greater consumer satisfaction when it rains than when it does not rain. Similarly, a refrigerator will have a greater utility in the tropics than at the South Pole. There is also no instrument or yardstick with which utility can be measured objectively. We therefore cannot compare one consumer's level of utility (or satisfaction) with that of another consumer.

Cardinal and ordinal utility

Economists use two notions of utility: cardinal utility and ordinal utility. **Cardinal utility** involves the idea that utility can be measured in some way, while **ordinal utility** involves the ranking of different bundles of consumer goods or services in order of preference ("ordinal" is derived from "order(ing)"). The **utility approach** to the analysis of consumer behaviour is based on the assumption that a consumer can assign values to the amount of satisfaction (utility) that he or she obtains from the consumption of each successive unit of a consumer good or service. It is also assumed that it is possible to compare the utility of different consumer goods and services quantitatively. In other words, the utility approach is based on the notion of **cardinal utility**. The **indifference approach**, on the other hand, employs the notion of **ordinal utility**, which only requires consumers to rank different bundles of goods or services in order of preference.

We can explain the difference between cardinal and ordinal magnitudes by considering the measurement of length. The metric scale is an example of a cardinal scale. It enables us to measure distances and allows us to compare different distances with each other; for example, if distance A is 100 metres and distance B is 200 metres, then we know that B is exactly twice as long as A. An ordinal scale, on the other hand, simply indicates that some distances are shorter than, longer than or the same as other distances. Such a scale enables us to rank the distances, say, from shortest to longest but it does not enable us to determine precisely how the distances compare. In contrast to cardinal numbers, the size relationship of ordinal numbers cannot be established.

The cardinal utility approach is based on the assumption that satisfaction (utility) is somehow measurable on a cardinal scale and that differences in utility can be precisely quantified. Ordinal utility, on the other hand, simply means that the satisfaction which a consumer obtains from consuming different products or bundles of products can be **ranked** or **ordered**. The consumer can rank different products or combinations of products in order of preference but can say nothing about the absolute level of satisfaction that each product or combination of products yields. **The size of the utility differences cannot be established**. The consumer can only rank things from highest to lowest, best to worst, most satisfying to least satisfying, and so on.

We first examine the utility approach, based on cardinal utility.

10.2 The utility approach: marginal utility and total utility

The utility approach to the analysis of consumer behaviour is based on the assumption that an individual consumer can and does **subjectively** assign units of value to the utility derived from the consumption of successive units of a product. To distinguish these units from other units of measurement (such as metres, litres and rands) we call them **utils**.

Let us consider John Smith's consumption of bananas during a particular period. Suppose that the first banana he consumes gives him a utility of, say, 50 utils. After he has consumed a banana, the intensity of his want for bananas decreases, and the second banana's utility is only 35 utils, and so on. The extra or additional utility that a consumer derives from the consumption of one additional unit of a good is called **marginal utility**. In our example, the marginal utility of the first banana is 50 utils and the marginal utility of the second banana is 35 utils. Table 10-1 contains hypothetical values for the marginal utility of bananas consumed by John Smith during a particular period. His **total utility** is the sum of all the marginal utilities. The total utility of one banana is 50 utils, the total utility of two bananas is 85 utils (ie 50 + 35), and so on. This relationship between **total** values and **marginal** values is very important in economic analysis. In Box 10-1 the relationships between total, average and marginal values are explained in greater detail.

Table 10-1 illustrates that if identical (or homogeneous) units of a good are consumed one after the other, the **marginal utility** will decline until it reaches zero. Thereafter it becomes negative. Negative utility is usually called **disutility**. **Total utility** increases as long as marginal utility is positive. It reaches a maximum when marginal utility is zero (ie when the consumer is satiated) and then decreases when marginal utility becomes negative (ie when disutility sets in). In the table, satiation is reached after the consumption of the seventh banana.

You can conduct your own experiment to test this theory. Take a box of chocolates, a packet of sweets, a packet of cigarettes or a case of beer and consume the contents one after the other. Assign a value to the satisfaction derived from each additional unit consumed. The result will probably be similar to the trend illustrated in Table 10-1. This trend is called the **law of diminishing marginal utility**. The law of diminishing marginal utility states that **the marginal utility of a good or service eventually declines as more of it is consumed during any given period**. This law is sometimes called Gossen's first law, after the German economist, Hermann Heinrich Gossen (1810–1858), who formulated it in 1854.

The law of decreasing marginal utility can also be expressed in terms of total utility. When a consumer consumes more units of a particular good, the consumer's total utility in respect of that good will increase at a decreasing rate, *ceteris paribus*. In other words, the addition to total utility from consuming each additional unit of the good will decrease. This addition to total utility is, of course, the marginal utility of the product.

The distinction between total utility and marginal utility also offers a possible solution to a problem with which Adam Smith struggled in the 18th century. This problem is usually called the paradox of value – see Box 10-2.

TABLE 10-1 John Smith's marginal utility and total utility from the consumption of bananas during a specific period

Number of bananas consumed	*Marginal utility (utils)*	*Total utility (utils)*
1	50	50
2	35	85
3	29	114
4	18	132
5	12	144
6	6	150
7	2	152
8	0	152
9	–4	148

We now use total utility, marginal utility and the law of diminishing marginal utility to examine consumer choice.

10.3 Consumer equilibrium in the utility approach

In the analysis of consumer behaviour it is assumed that every consumer attempts to maximise his or her satisfaction of wants by consuming goods and services. The aim is thus to obtain the **highest attainable level of total utility**. The adjective "attainable" is important, since a consumer's income and the prices of the various goods and services limit or constrain his or her capacity to satisfy wants. For a given income and a given set of prices of goods and services, a consumer will be in equilibrium if he or she obtains the maximum possible total utility. Recall that equilibrium is a situation in which there is no incentive for the participants (in this case the consumers) to change their plans. When a consumer obtains the maximum possible total utility from his or her income, given the prices of the various goods and services, there is no incentive for the consumer to change his or her plans.

In marginal utility theory it is assumed that consumers are aware of their wants and of the utility they will derive from satisfying these wants. It is therefore assumed that each consumer is in a position to arrange his or her wants in order of importance and to draw up a list of the things that he or she would prefer to purchase. This list, which reflects the tastes of the consumer, is called a **scale of preferences**. The assumption that there is a scale of preferences does not suggest that consumers actually go so far as to write down their scales of preferences and assign numbers to the satisfaction derived from the consumption of each unit. It simply suggests that consumers can only take ration-

BOX 10-1 TOTAL, AVERAGE AND MARGINAL MAGNITUDES

Total, average and marginal magnitudes and their interrelationships play a key role in economic analysis. In this chapter we explain total and marginal utility. In Chapters 11 and 12 we introduce various total, average and marginal magnitudes: total, average and marginal product; total, average and marginal cost; and total, average and marginal revenue. The marginal concept also plays an important role in macroeconomics. In Part IV, for example, we introduce concepts such as the marginal propensity to consume, the marginal propensity to save and the marginal propensity to import. **To understand economic theory, it is essential to understand what a marginal magnitude represents, and how it relates to total and average magnitudes.**

We now use two non-economic examples to explain what total, average and marginal magnitudes mean and how they are interrelated. We then summarise the main points.

Example 1: Sam Sibanda, an economics student, has to submit ten assignments during the year. Each assignment carries 100 marks. For his first assignment he obtains 70 marks. At this stage his total, marginal and average marks are all equal to 70. For the second assignment he obtains 50 marks. This **addition** to his total marks now becomes his **marginal** mark, which is 50. His **total** marks at this stage are 70 plus 50, that is, 120. His **average** mark is now 120 divided by 2, that is, 60. Why has his average mark fallen? Because his marginal mark (50) is lower than his previous average (70). **When the marginal value is lower than the previous average value, the average value falls.**

For the third assignment he receives 60 marks. This extra or additional mark now becomes his marginal mark. His total marks at this stage are 180 (ie 70 + 50 + 60). His average mark is 180 divided by 3, that is, 60. His average mark thus remains unchanged. **When the marginal value is equal to the previous average value, the average value remains unchanged.**

For the fourth assignment he is awarded 80 marks. His marginal mark is thus 80 and his total marks increase to 260 (ie 70 + 50 + 60 + 80). His average mark is 260 divided by 4,that is, 65. His average mark has increased. Why? Because his marginal mark is higher than his previous average mark. **When the marginal value is greater than the previous average value, the average value increases.** Sam's performance in the remaining six assignments and the corresponding total, marginal and average values are summarised in the following table. Work through the table and note how the three rules referred to above always hold.

Assignment number	Marks obtained	Total marks	Marginal mark	Average mark
1	70	70	70	70
2	50	120	50	60
3	60	180	60	60
4	80	260	80	65
5	40	300	40	60
6	60	360	60	60
7	67	427	67	61
8	93	520	93	65
9	20	540	20	60
10	80	620	80	62

Example 2: In the 2003 Cricket World Cup in South Africa, Jacques Kallis, the South African all-rounder of whom much was expected prior to the competition, played four innings, scoring 13 (against the West Indies), 33 (against New Zealand), 1 (against Canada) and 16 (against Sri Lanka). His total, marginal and average scores during the tournament are summarised below:

Innings	Score	Total score	Marginal score	Average score
1	13	13	13	13,0
2	33	46	33	23,0
3	1	47	1	15,7
4	16	63	16	15,8

Note, once again, how the total, marginal and average values are calculated and how they are related.

The relationships between total and marginal values and between marginal and average values can be summarised as follows:

Total and marginal values

- When a **total** magnitude is **rising**, the corresponding **marginal** magnitude is **positive**

  or

  When a marginal magnitude is positive, the corresponding total magnitude is rising
- When a **total** magnitude is **falling**, the corresponding **marginal** magnitude is **negative**

  or

  When a marginal magnitude is negative, the corresponding total magnitude is falling
- When a **total** magnitude reaches a **maximum** or a **minimum**, the corresponding **marginal** magnitude is **zero**

  or

  When a marginal magnitude is zero, the corresponding total magnitude remains unchanged

Marginal and average values

- When the **marginal** magnitude is **lower than the average** magnitude, the **average** magnitude **falls**

  or

  When the average magnitude is falling, the marginal magnitude must lie below it
- When the **marginal** magnitude is **higher than the average** magnitude, the **average** magnitude **increases**

  or

  When the average magnitude is rising, the marginal magnitude must lie above it
- When the **marginal** value is **equal** to the **average** value, the **average** value remains **unchanged**

  or

  When the average magnitude is neither rising nor falling (eg at a maximum or minimum) the marginal magnitude must be equal to it

A mathematical interpretation

Anyone with a mathematical background might have noticed that

- a marginal function is the first derivative of the corresponding total function
- a marginal function is given by the slope of the corresponding total function
- an average function is given by the slope of a line (ray) from the origin to the total function

al decisions if they have something like a scale of preferences at the back of their minds.

In Table 10-2 we show one such scale of preferences. We assume that a consumer, Katie Jantjies, consumes three goods – bread, meat and rice. Bread costs R1,00 per unit, meat costs R3,00 per unit and rice costs R2,00 per unit. The price of bread is labelled P_B, the price of meat P_M and the price of rice P_R. The table shows the marginal utilities (*MU*) and total utilities (*TU*) for one to ten units of bread, meat and rice that Katie could consume per week. In each case, the subscripts denote bread (B), meat (M) and rice (R). The table also shows the weighted marginal utilities. **Weighted marginal utility** is the marginal utility per unit divided by the price per unit (*MU/P*). The significance of the weighted marginal utility will become apparent as we proceed.

From the table we see, for example, that Katie's marginal utility derived from the consumption of the 5th unit of bread is 30 utils. We also see that her total utility from the consumption of 5 units of bread is 210 utils. Similarly, her marginal utility from the consumption of the 3rd unit of rice is 54 utils, and the total utility of 3 units of rice is 180 utils.

BOX 10-2 THE PARADOX OF VALUE

In his book, *The wealth of nations*, published in 1776, Adam Smith stated that there is no clear relation between the value in use (or utility) and the value in exchange (or price) of a product. To illustrate the point, he used the examples of water and diamonds. Water has a high value in use but a low value in exchange, whereas diamonds have a low value in use but a high value in exchange. Smith therefore concluded that exchange value is unrelated to value in use. He resolved this problem, which is usually called the paradox of value, by claiming that exchange values or relative prices are **supply determined** and depend on labour costs. This view is called the **labour theory of value**. It was extended by other classical writers such as David Ricardo, and was also used by Karl Marx.

The theory of marginal utility provided a possible solution to the paradox of value. According to this theory, the secret is to distinguish between total utility and marginal utility. The **total utility** of water is very high. The **marginal utility** of water, however, is very low. We consume so much water that the marginal utility of water, that is, the benefit or satisfaction we obtain by consuming an additional unit (say, a glass) of water, is very small. Diamonds, on the other hand, have a small total utility relative to water, but because diamonds are scarce and few diamonds are purchased, they have a high marginal utility. Marginal utility states that relative prices are **demand determined**, rather than supply determined, as was assumed by Smith, Ricardo, Marx and others.

Nowadays it is accepted that relative prices are determined by the interaction of supply **and** demand. This solution to the paradox of value was formulated towards the end of the 19th century by neoclassical economists such as Alfred Marshall. They emphasised both costs (or supply) and utility (or demand). In a market system, they argued, the value in exchange (or relative price) of a product is determined by **supply and demand**, as explained in Chapters 7 and 8 of this book.

If Katie consumes 10 units of bread, 10 units of meat and 10 units of rice per week, her total utility will be (270 + 495 + 390) = 1 155 utils. This is the maximum satisfaction that she can obtain, given the information in the table. The question, however, is whether she can **afford** to purchase 10 units of each good. Suppose she only has R12,00 available weekly to spend on bread, meat and rice. What should she do? To answer the question, we must determine the total utility of all the possible combinations of bread, meat and rice that she can purchase with R12,00. These combinations, along with the total utility of

TABLE 10-2 Katie's scale of preferences in respect of the weekly consumption of bread, meat and rice

	Goods								
	Bread (P_B = R1,00)			*Meat (P_M = R3,00)*			*Rice (P_R = R2,00)*		
Units	MU_B	TU_B	$\frac{MU_B}{P_B}$	MU_M	TU_M	$\frac{MU_M}{P_M}$	MU_R	TU_R	$\frac{MU_R}{P_R}$
1	54	54	54	90	90	**30**	66	66	33
2	48	102	48	81	171	27	60	126	**30**
3	42	144	42	72	243	24	54	180	27
4	36	180	36	63	306	21	48	228	24
5	30	210	**30**	54	360	18	42	270	21
6	24	234	24	45	405	15	36	306	18
7	18	252	18	36	441	12	30	336	15
8	12	264	12	27	468	9	24	360	12
9	6	270	6	18	486	6	18	378	9
10	0	270	0	9	495	3	12	390	6

TABLE 10-3 Possible combinations of bread, meat and rice that can be bought with R12,00 and the total utility of each combination

Combination	Units of Bread	Units of Meat	Units of Rice	Total utility (utils)
1	10	0	1	336
2	9	1	0	360
3	8	0	2	390
4	7	1	1	408
5	6	2	0	405
6	6	0	3	414
7	**5**	**1**	**2**	**426**
8	4	2	1	417
9	4	0	4	408
10	3	3	0	387
11	3	1	3	414
12	2	2	2	399
13	2	0	5	372
14	1	1	4	372
15	1	3	1	363
16	0	4	0	306
17	0	2	3	351
18	0	0	6	306

each combination, are summarised in Table 10-3. We see that there are 18 possible ways of spending the full R12,00 on up to ten units of each of the three goods concerned. For example, if she buys 3 units of bread, 1 unit of meat and 3 units of rice, it will cost her R12,00. This is depicted by combination 11. We also see that the highest total utility is obtained if Katie uses her R12,00 to purchase 5 units of bread, 1 unit of meat and 2 units of rice (ie combination 7), which yields a total utility of 426 utils.

Although this is one way of obtaining a solution, it is very cumbersome. Is there not **an easier way** of obtaining the solution, that is, of determining the consumer's equilibrium position?

A consumer like Katie will be in equilibrium if it is impossible to increase total utility (ie total satisfaction of wants) by purchasing more of one good and less of another. This position will be reached when the last monetary unit (rand in our example) spent on each good yields the same satisfaction or utility. This happens when the weighted marginal utility of each good is the same (provided that the specific combination is affordable). **To obtain the consumer's equilibrium position we must determine which combinations are affordable and at which of these combinations the weighted marginal utility (ie the marginal utility divided by the price of the product) is the same for all the goods in question.**

We now go back to Table 10-2 and see that this is indeed the case at an affordable combination of 5 units of bread, 1 unit of meat and 2 units of rice. At this combination the weighted marginal utility of each product (obtained by dividing the marginal utility by the price) is equal to 30.

This solution can also be reached as follows. Katie will start by selecting the product with the highest marginal utility per rand spent, that is, the one which gives the best value for money. She will thus select bread. In Table 10-2 we see that each of the first four units of bread yield a greater weighted marginal utility than the first unit of meat or rice. She will thus start by selecting four units of bread. She will then select one unit of rice, since it yields a greater weighted marginal utility (33) than the fifth unit of bread (30) or the first unit of meat (30). Next she will select a fifth unit of bread, the first unit of meat and a second unit of rice. They all yield a weighted marginal utility of 30. By this time she has selected 5 units of bread, one unit of meat and 2 units of rice. This combination costs (5 × R1,00) + (1 × R3,00) + (2 × R2,00) = R5 + R3 + R4 = R12, which means that she has allocated her available income. This is the best possible selection, since she cannot gain by switching her available income from one good to another. If she switches, the weighted marginal utility she sacrifices will be greater than the weighted marginal utility she gains. **When the weighted marginal utilities are equal and she has just spent her available income, she is in equilibrium. At equilibrium she derives the same utility from the last rand spent on each product.**

In symbols we can express the equilibrium condition as follows:

$$\frac{MU_B}{P_B} = \frac{MU_M}{P_M} = \frac{MU_R}{P_R}$$

where MU_B, MU_M and MU_R are the marginal utilities of bread, meat and rice respectively and P_B, P_M and P_R are the prices of bread, meat and rice respectively.

Note that it is not sufficient to compare the marginal utilities only. The marginal utilities (or consumer satisfaction) must first be related to the prices of the goods and services concerned. A motorcar, for example, will yield far greater consumer satisfaction than a kilogram of meat. The important aspect, however, is the value (or satisfaction) that the consumer obtains in relation to the amount of money he or she spends. This information is given by the weighted marginal utility. Although consumers do not actually think in terms of weighted marginal utility, this is what they are in effect doing when they decide which combination of goods and services to purchase, given their available income. The weighted marginal utility of a product is the utility derived from the last unit of money (eg rand) spent on the product. The equilibrium condition (that the weighted marginal utilities must be equal) thus means that equal utility is derived from the last rand spent on each product.

From Table 10-2 we see that there are also other combinations of bread, meat and rice where the weighted marginal utilities are equal. For example, 6 units of bread, 3 units of meat and 4 units of rice all have a weighted marginal utility of 24. But this combination costs R6 + R9 + R8 = R23 and is therefore not affordable in our example. The same applies to other similar combinations, for example, 7 units of bread, 5 units of meat and 6 units of rice; and 8 units of bread, 7 units of meat and 8 units of rice.

Two conditions have to be met for the consumer to be in equilibrium:

- The combination of goods purchased has to be affordable.
- The weighted marginal utilities of the different goods must be equal.

This is sometimes referred to as the **law of equalising the weighted marginal utilities** or Gossen's (improved) second law.

Equalising the weighted marginal utilities for any pair of goods implies that the **consumer's subjective valuation** of the relative importance of the two goods is the **same as** the **objective valuation of the market**, as reflected in the market prices of the goods concerned. Consider two goods, A and B. We know that there can only be consumer equilibrium if

$$\frac{MU_A}{P_A} = \frac{MU_B}{P_B} \qquad \text{(10-1)}$$

Multiplying both sides of the equation by $\frac{P_A}{MU_B}$ we obtain

$$\frac{MU_A}{MU_B} = \frac{P_A}{P_B} \qquad \text{(10-2)}$$

This means that the ratio of the marginal utilities (as assigned by the consumer) must be the same as the ratio between the market prices of the goods. In other words, the rate at which the consumer is subjectively willing to exchange the two goods must be the same as the rate at which the goods are exchanged in the market. You will encounter this result again in Section 10.9.

We have established the conditions for consumer equilibrium and can now proceed to derive a consumer's demand curve for a particular product.

10.4 Derivation of an individual demand curve for a product

A demand curve shows the quantities demanded of a good or service at different prices. We now use a simple example to illustrate how a consumer's equilibrium changes if the price of a product changes. Suppose that Henry Jones has R10,00 available per week to spend on chocolates and yoghurt, which cost R2,00 and R3,00 per unit respectively. His scale of preferences is illustrated in Table 10-4, which is constructed on the same basis as Katie's scale of preferences in Table 10-2. The subscript C denotes chocolates and the subscript Y denotes yoghurt. The best that Henry can do with his R10 is to purchase 2 units of chocolate and 2 units of yoghurt per week. The weighted marginal utility of chocolate (MU_C/P_C) is then equal to the weighted marginal utility of yoghurt (MU_Y/P_Y). His R10 yields a total utility of (50 + 69) = 119 utils. This is the maximum that he can achieve by spending his R10 on the two products.

Again note that the ratio between the marginal utilities at equilibrium is the same as the ratio between the prices of the two products:

$$\frac{MU_C}{MU_Y} = \frac{20}{30} = \frac{P_C}{P_Y} = \frac{2}{3}$$

Suppose the price of chocolates falls to R1,00 per unit, *ceteris paribus*. Henry's new position is illustrated in Table 10-5. The only things that have changed are the price of chocolates P_C and the weighted marginal util-

TABLE 10-4 Henry Jones's utility from chocolates and yoghurt (per week)

	Goods					
	Chocolates (P_C = R2,00)			*Yoghurt (P_Y = R3,00)*		
Units	MU_C	TU_C	$\frac{MU_C}{P_C}$	MU_Y	TU_Y	$\frac{MU_Y}{P_Y}$
1	30	30	15	39	39	13
2	20	50	10	30	69	10
3	14	64	7	24	93	8
4	10	74	5	18	111	6
5	6	80	3	15	126	5

ities of different quantities of chocolate. He now maximises his utility by consuming 4 units of chocolate and 2 units of yoghurt per week. The weighted marginal utility in each case is 10. His total utility increases from 119 utils to (74 + 69) = 143 utils.

Once again, the ratio between the marginal utilities of the two products at equilibrium is the same as the ratio between the prices of the products:

$$\frac{MU_C}{MU_Y} = \frac{10}{30} = \frac{P_C}{P_Y} = \frac{1}{3}$$

What does this mean? Simply that Henry will increase his utility by consuming a greater quantity of chocolates when the price of chocolates falls, *ceteris paribus*. This, of course, is what the demand curve (or the law of demand) is all about. A utility-maximising consumer will demand a greater quantity of a product when the price of the product falls, while all other things remain unchanged. The individual's demand curve thus slopes downward from left to right.

The two quantities of chocolates demanded by Henry are shown in Figure 10-1. At a price of R2,00 per unit of chocolate, Henry will plan to purchase 2 units. If the price falls to R1,00, he will plan to purchase 4 units. Other points can be obtained in a similar way. By joining these points, a downward-sloping demand curve *DD* is obtained, in accordance with the law of demand introduced in Chapter 7. In Figure 10-1 the demand curve is shown as a straight line. This is not necessarily always the case – it could have another shape. The important point is that the demand curve has a negative slope – as the price of the product falls, the quantity demanded will increase (and as the price rises, the quantity demanded will fall). The **market demand curve** is obtained by adding all the individual demand curves horizontally, as was shown in Figure 7-3. This curve will also have a negative slope.

We can use the same method to show how a consumer will react if the price of one of the products *increases* or if the *income* of the consumer changes. In both cases the results will confirm the conclusions in respect of the demand curve reached in Chapter 7. Some alleged exceptions to the law of demand are discussed in Box 10-3.

FIGURE 10-1 Henry Jones's demand curve for chocolates

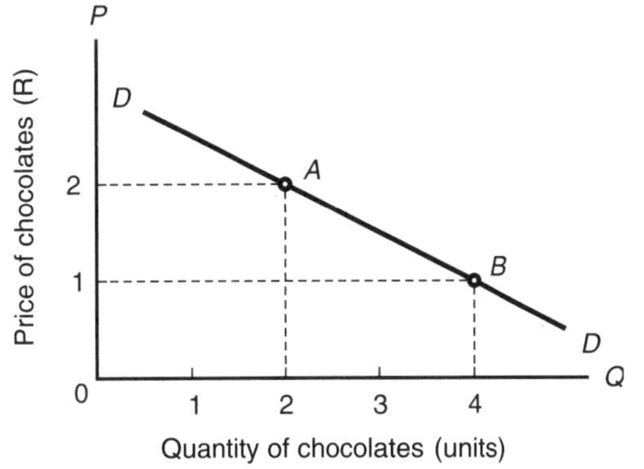

At a price of R2,00, two units are demanded (point A) and at a price of R1,00, four units are demanded (point B). By joining the two points, Henry's demand curve for chocolates is obtained. It slopes downwards from left to right.

10.5 Comments on the utility approach

We have now examined the decisions of an individual consumer by using the utility approach to consumer theory, which is based on the notion of cardinal utility. In the process we provided a theoretical justification for a downward sloping demand curve.

The key concept in the utility approach is **marginal utility**. Marginal concepts play an important role in economic analysis. It is important to understand what "marginal" means and how a marginal value relates to an average value and a total value.

TABLE 10-5 Henry Jones's utility from the weekly consumption of chocolates and yoghurt at a lower price of chocolates

	Goods					
	Chocolates (P_C = R1,00)			Yoghurt (P_Y = R3,00)		
Units	MU_C	TU_C	$\frac{MU_C}{P_C}$	MU_Y	TU_Y	$\frac{MU_Y}{P_Y}$
1	30	30	30	39	39	13
2	20	50	20	30	69	10
3	14	64	14	24	93	8
4	10	74	10	18	111	6
5	6	80	6	15	126	5

BOX 10-3 POSSIBLE EXCEPTIONS TO THE LAW OF DEMAND

The law of demand states that the higher the price of a product, the lower will be the quantity demanded, *ceteris paribus*, or that the lower the price of the product, the higher will be the quantity demanded, *ceteris paribus*. There are possible exceptions to this law. However, as we explain below, the alleged exceptions apply to individual demand rather than to market demand. At most, some of these "exceptions" will influence the price elasticity of market demand.

As explained in Box 7-2, and again later in this chapter, the impact of a price change can be split into a **substitution effect** and an **income effect**. When the price of a product increases, it means, first, that the product has become more expensive *relative* to other products, *ceteris paribus*. As a result, the quantity demanded will tend to decrease. Other products whose prices have remained unchanged will be subsituted for some of the product. Similarly, if the price of the product decreases, it will become *relatively* cheaper, *ceteris paribus*, and a greater quantity will tend to be demanded. This is the **substitution effect**. A possible exception is the case of a **snob** (or **Veblen**) **effect**, which occurs when consumers derive utility from owning or consuming expensive or exclusive goods (eg diamonds, gold Rolex watches, jewellery, mink coats, French champagne, designer clothing, expensive motorcars, oriental carpets). Thorstein Veblen (1857-1929) called this **conspicuous consumption**. Where certain high-priced goods have a "snob" value, an increase in price may lead to an increase in the quantity demanded and if such ostentatious goods become cheaper and less exclusive they might become less sought after in certain circles. The result may be an abnormal, positively-sloped demand curve. However, when the goods become cheaper other consumers will also be able to afford them and the quantity demanded by these consumers will tend to increase. There is no reason to assume that the total quantity demanded by all consumers will decline. The market demand will probably still reflect the law of demand, although it might become less price elastic as prices fall, due to the fact that certain consumers will no longer wish to purchase the product once it loses its snob appeal.

The impact of a price change is not confined to the substitution effect. When the price of a product changes, the **real income** of consumers also changes, *ceteris paribus*. When the price decreases, real income (or purchasing power) increases, *ceteris paribus*, and when the price increases, real income decreases. This is the **income effect**. Normally, an increase in income will lead to an increase in the quantity demanded, and a decrease in income to a decrease in the quantity demanded. However, as we have pointed out in Chapters 7 and 9, this need not always be the case. With some products, called **inferior goods**, the quantity demanded falls as income increases (or rises as income decreases). However, as long as the substitution effect is greater than the income effect, the law of demand will still apply.

The size of the income effect depends on the proportion of consumers' income that is spent on the product. The greater the proportion, the stronger the income effect will be. In the case of poor households who spend a large proportion of their income on a staple food (eg bread, rice or maize meal), the negative income effect caused by an increase in price of the staple food might exceed the substitution effect, thus violating the law of demand. This possibility is usually called the **Giffen case** (or Giffen paradox), after Sir Robert Giffen, who reputedly observed that an increase in the price of wheat led to an increase in the consumption of bread by 19th century English peasants and that an increase in the price of potatoes in the 1840s led to an increase in the consumption of potatoes by Irish peasants. Possible modern examples include the consumption of rice by poor households in Bangladesh and the consumption of maize meal by poor South African households. The argument is that a price increase will have such a strong income effect that the households will no longer be able to afford more expensive foodstuffs (eg meat) and will only be able to survive by purchasing more of the basic foodstuff. However, it is doubtful whether such Giffen goods really exist, and if they do exist they will be extremely rare (and confined to particular market segments).

The various possible substitution, income and price effects are summarised in the table below.

Effects of a price change

Type of good	Price change	Substitution effect	Income effect	Total price effect
Normal	*P* decreases	Q_d increases	Q_d increases	Q_d increases
	P increases	Q_d decreases	Q_d decreases	Q_d decreases
Inferior (but not Giffen)	*P* decreases	Q_d increases	Q_d decreases	Q_d increases
	P increases	Q_d decreases	Q_d increases	Q_d decreases
Giffen	*P* decreases	Q_d increases	Q_d decreases	Q_d decreases
	P increases	Q_d decreases	Q_d increases	Q_d increases

In our analysis of demand we have assumed that each consumer's demand is independent of other consumers' behaviour. This assumption, however, does not always hold. Exceptions include the snob effect, referred to earlier, as well as the **bandwagon effect**. The latter occurs when a consumer wants a good because other consumers have it – in other words, it is fashionable to possess the good. Examples include certain children's toys, items of clothing and swimming pools. Where a bandwagon effect exists, the demand curve will tend to become more price elastic, since a fall in price would lead to a greater increase in the quantity demanded than would otherwise have been the case.

The British social scientist, Jeremy Bentham (1748–1832), who was one of the earliest proponents of marginal utility, hoped that it would some day be possible to measure utility objectively, the way we measure length or temperature. He envisaged some kind of machine which could be connected to an individual to measure utility (ie the individual's degree of satisfaction or happiness). This, of course, was wishful thinking. Utility cannot be measured objectively – it can only be measured subjectively. Interpersonal comparisons of utility are therefore impossible. In fact, to many students (and economists) the idea that utility can be measured at all is quite ridiculous, with the result that they reject the whole utility approach.

Although such a reaction is quite understandable, it is not justified. Economic theory attempts to explain how people behave, and economists can use utility to analyse consumer choice although no economist has ever seen or measured a unit of utility. Even natural scientists use constructs which have never been observed (eg force) to analyse certain problems. The fact that utility cannot be measured objectively is not a sufficient reason to reject the utility approach to the analysis of consumer behaviour.

There is, however, an alternative approach to the analysis of consumer behaviour, which yields the same results but does not require the assumption of cardinally measurable utility. We now examine this approach, which is called the indifference approach.

10.6 Introduction to the indifference approach

The indifference approach was devised towards the end of the 19th century by a famous Italian economist, Vilfredo Pareto (1848-1923) and developed further by 20th century economists such as the Nobel Prize winner, Sir John Hicks. The indifference approach does not require the measurement of marginal utility. Nevertheless, it yields the same results as the utility approach.

But why bother with another approach if its results are the same as those of the one explained in the previous sections? First, many people are not impressed by the notion that consumer satisfaction can be measured and that changes in utility can be compared. Second, the indifference curve technique is an extremely useful tool which can be used to analyse a variety of other choices, over and above consumers' choices between different goods and services. Another advantage of the indifference approach is that it allows us to distinguish graphically between the income effect and the substitution effect of a price change.

In the remainder of this chapter we explain what **indifference curves** are, and indicate their important properties. We then introduce the **budget line** and combine it with indifference curves to explain **consumer equilibrium**. This is followed by an investigation of the effects of changes in income and prices.

The **income and substitution effects** of a price change are separated and a demand curve is derived.

As emphasised earlier, the indifference approach to consumer behaviour is based on ordinal utility. It is also confined to comparing different combinations or bundles of goods and services with each other, and therefore cannot be used to analyse the consumption of one good or service in isolation. Nevertheless, the indifference approach yields essentially the same results as the utility approach.

Three basic assumptions

The indifference approach is based on three basic assumptions: the assumption of completeness (or law of comparison), the assumption of consistency (or transitivity) and the assumption of non-satiation (or non-satiety). These assumptions may sound complicated, but they are actually quite simple. As you will see, they are also very reasonable and plausible assumptions.

- The assumption of **completeness** simply means that it is assumed that a consumer is able to rank **all** possible combinations (or bundles) of goods and services in order of preference. Consider two bundles of consumer goods: bundle *A* consists of three kilograms of meat and two dozen bottles of beer, while bundle *B* consists of two kilograms of meat and three dozen bottles of beer. A consumer must then be able to say whether he or she prefers *A* to *B*, prefers *B* to *A* or is indifferent to the differences between them (ie values them both equally). The consumer must be able to do the same for all other possible combinations of products.
- The assumption of **consistency** (or **transitivity**) simply means that consumers are assumed to act consistently. Consider three bundles, *X*, *Y* and *Z*. If the consumer prefers *X* to *Y* and prefers *Y* to *Z*, then he or she must (according to this assumption) also prefer *X* to *Z*. If not, then the consumer is acting inconsistently and his or her behaviour cannot be analysed.
- The assumption of **non-satiation** (or **non-satiety**) simply states that consumers are not yet fully satisfied and **prefer more to less**. Thus, if bundle *A* contains three kilograms of meat and two dozen bottles of beer and bundle *C* contains four kilograms of meat and three dozen bottles of beer, the consumer is assumed to prefer *C* to *A*.

The implications of the non-satiation assumption are illustrated in Figure 10-2. In the figure, meat (in kilograms) is shown on the vertical axis and beer (in dozens of bottles) on the horizontal axis. Point *A* shows the combination of three kilograms of meat and two dozen bottles of beer. By drawing a horizontal and a vertical line through point *A* we divide the area between the axes into four areas. Any point northeast of *A* (ie in the shaded area labelled I) is preferable to point *A* since the points in this area represent combinations of more meat and/or more beer than *A*. At worst the consumer will get more of at least one of the products while getting the same quantity of the other product.

FIGURE 10-2 A comparison of combinations of meat and beer

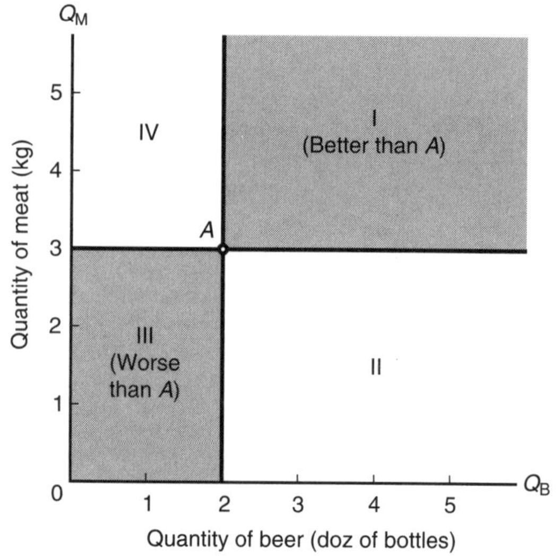

Point A represents a combination of 3 kilograms of meat and 2 dozen bottles of beer. By drawing horizontal and vertical lines through A we obtain four quadrants. Any point in quadrant I will be preferable to A, while A will be preferable to any point in quadrant III. In quadrants II and IV the position is uncertain. At some points in these quadrants the consumer will achieve the same satisfaction as at A.

Similarly, point *A* will be preferable to any point in area III (the shaded area to the southwest of *A*). But what about areas II and IV? Here we cannot make any deductions with certainty since these areas represent points where the consumer gets more of one good but fewer of the other. It is logical to expect that somewhere in these areas there will be points that will represent the same level of satisfaction as *A*. For the consumer these points are indifferent to point *A*. If we combine all these points between which the consumer is indifferent, we obtain an indifference curve.

10.7 Indifference curves

Given the three basic assumptions discussed in the previous section, a consumer's tastes and preferences can be indicated by means of an indifference curve.

An indifference curve is a curve which shows all the combinations of two products that will

provide the consumer with equal levels of satisfaction or utility. The combinations are equally desirable and the consumer is thus indifferent between them.

An example

To explain indifference curves, we consider an imaginary consumer, Koos van der Merwe, who consumes only two products, bread and meat. Koos decides that it does not matter to him whether he gets one portion of meat and six loaves of bread per week or two portions of meat and three loaves of bread. These two combinations provide him with the same amount of satisfaction, that is, he is indifferent between them. He also indicates some other combinations of meat and bread that will yield the same level of satisfaction or total utility as the previous two. The different combinations are shown in Table 10-6.

The information in Table 10-6 is shown graphically in Figure 10-3, with bread (loaves per week) on the vertical axis and meat (portions per week) on the horizontal axis. Each of the combinations in the table is represented by a single point in the figure. The points listed in Table 10-6 are not the only points between which Koos is indifferent – there are also other (intermediate) combinations (eg between *A* and *B*) which yield the same level of satisfaction. We draw a curve through points *A*, *B*, *C* and *D* which is called an **indifference curve**. The points on the curve (including those between *A*, *B*, *C* and *D*) represent different combinations of the two goods that are equally desirable or attractive to Koos – he will derive the same total satisfaction or utility from each of these combinations.

The indifference curve in Figure 10-3 bulges towards the origin – we say that the curve is **convex** when it is viewed from the origin. As we move downwards to the right along the indifference curve (ie as the loaves of bread decrease and the portions of meat increase), the curve becomes flatter (ie its slope decreases). This illustrates the **law of substitution**, which is similar to the law of diminishing marginal utility introduced in Section 10.2. The law of substitution states that **the scarcer a good becomes, the greater its substitution value will be**. In other

TABLE 10-6 Combinations of meat and bread that yield the same level of satisfaction to Koos van der Merwe

Combination	*Meat (portions per week)*	*Bread (loaves per week)*
A	1	6
B	2	3
C	3	2
D	4	1½

FIGURE 10-3 An indifference curve

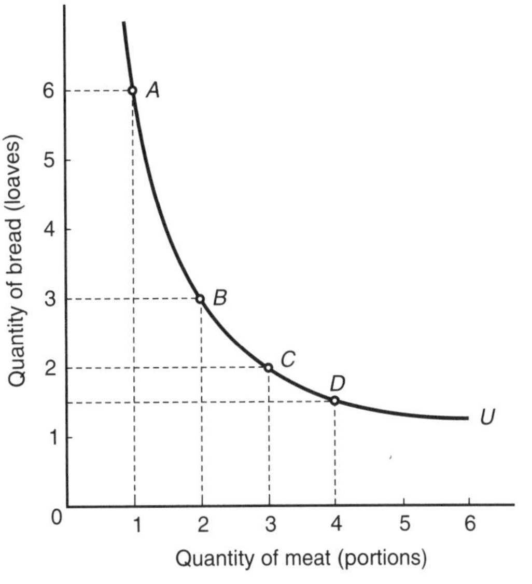

A, B, C and D are all combinations of bread and meat between which the consumer (Koos) is indifferent. By joining the points an indifference curve U is obtained. All points on the indifference curve represent combinations of the two products which yield the same level of consumer satisfaction.

words, the marginal utility of the good that becomes less plentiful rises in relation to the marginal utility of the good that becomes more plentiful. This can be explained by considering the various combinations listed in Table 10-6. The difference between combinations *A* and *B* indicates that Koos is willing to sacrifice three loaves of bread for a second portion of meat. However, between points *B* and *C* he is only prepared to sacrifice one loaf of bread for an extra (third) portion of meat. Moreover, he is prepared to sacrifice only half a loaf of bread to obtain a fourth portion of meat (points *C* and *D*). The fewer his loaves of bread (ie the less plentiful bread becomes) the less bread he is willing to swop for an additional portion of meat.

The rate at which Koos is prepared to substitute or exchange bread for meat between different points is given by the slope of a straight line between the points. For example, between *A* and *B* the slope of such a line is 3 (ignoring the negative sign); between points *B* and *C* it is 1, and so on. At any point on the indifference curve the exchange ratio or substitution ratio between the two goods is given by the slope of a tangent to the indifference curve (ie a line which just touches the curve at that particular point). The slope of the tangent (which is also the slope of the indifference curve at that point) indicates the rate at which the consumer is prepared to sacrifice a small quantity of one good (bread) for a little more of the other good (meat). This rate is called the **marginal rate of substitution** (*MRS*).

We can now restate our previous conclusion as follows: As we move downwards from left to right along an indifference curve, the marginal rate of substitution (which is equal to the slope of the curve) decreases. The law of substitution can therefore also be called the **law of the diminishing marginal rate of substitution**.

We shall return to the significance of the marginal rate of substitution later, but first we examine some properties of indifference curves and the consumer's equilibrium position.

Properties of indifference curves

The exact shape of an indifference curve will vary from one consumer to the next, but indifference curves usually slope downwards from left to right – for an exception to this rule, see Box 10-4.

An indifference curve shows various combinations of two goods or services which yield the same level of satisfaction or total utility to a particular consumer. For each level of satisfaction there will be a unique indifference curve, showing the various combinations which yield that particular level of satisfaction to the consumer. In principle it is therefore possible to draw an infinite number of indifference curves for any consumer's choice between two goods. Such a **collection of indifference curves** is called an **indifference map**. Table 10-7 contains two additional sets of combinations of bread and meat that yield equal satisfaction to Koos. These data can be used to plot two more indifference curves, U_1 and U_3, in Figure 10-4. The original indifference curve in Figure 10-3 is also shown and is labelled U_2.

BOX 10-4 TWO EXTREME CASES

The two limiting cases of indifference curves are perfect complements and perfect substitutes. If two goods are **perfect complements** it means that they can only be used together (ie in fixed proportions). A two-legged person can, for example, only use one left shoe with one right shoe. If he or she has only one left shoe, then more than one right shoe will yield no additional satisfaction. Similarly, if the consumer has only one right shoe, then the second, third or fourth left shoe will not increase his or her total utility. In the case of perfect complements the indifference curves will therefore be L-shaped, as in the figure below (on the left).

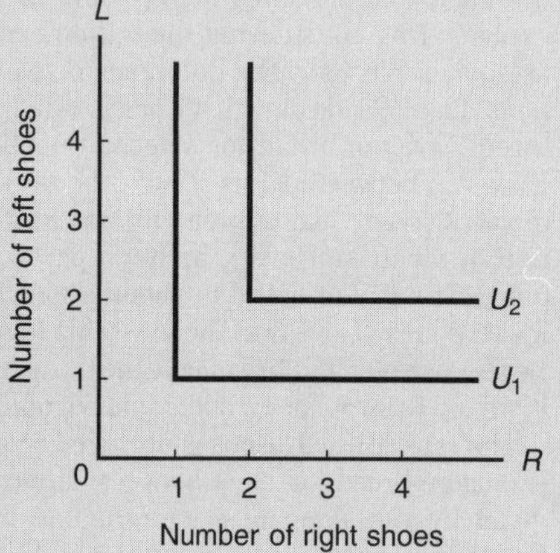

PERFECT COMPLEMENTS

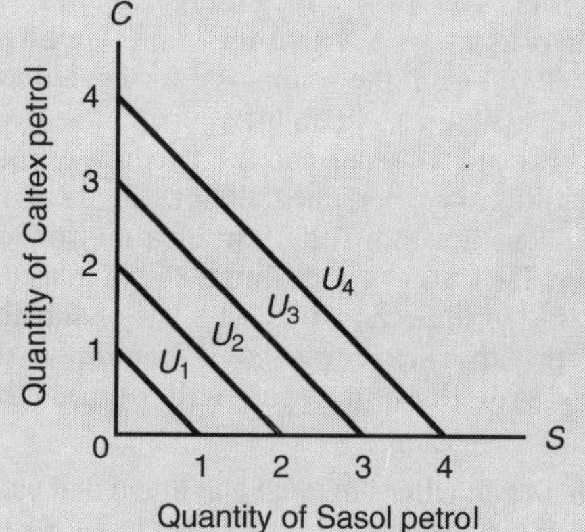

PERFECT SUBSTITUTES

The other extreme case occurs when the two goods are regarded as **perfect substitutes**. For example, if a consumer regards Sasol petrol as a perfect substitute for Caltex petrol, then one litre of Sasol petrol will always yield the same consumer satisfaction as one litre of Caltex petrol. In the case of perfect substitutes the indifference curve is a straight line which slopes downward from left to right as in the figure on the right. Note that "normal" indifference curves, such as the one illustrated in Figure 10-3, lie between the two extremes of perfect complements and perfect substitutes.

TABLE 10-7 Two further sets of combinations of bread and meat that yield equal satisfaction to Koos

U_1		U_3	
Bread (loaves per week)	Meat (portions per week)	Bread (loaves per week)	Meat (portions per week)
6	½	6	1½
4	1	4½	2
2	2	3	3
1	3	2¼	4½

Figure 10-4 is an example of an indifference map containing three indifference curves (U_1, U_2 and U_3). The further we move away from the origin, the larger the quantities of the two goods become and therefore the greater is the level of consumer satisfaction, as illustrated by the indifference curve. Given our assumption that the consumer is not satiated (ie not satisfied fully), it follows that he or she will derive greater utility from consuming more of both goods, as illustrated by a movement to a higher indifference curve (further away from the origin). Although we cannot quantify the amount of consumer satisfaction represented by each indifference curve, we can say that U_2 in Figure 10-4 represents a higher level of satisfaction than U_1, and that U_3 represents a greater level of satisfaction than either U_1 or U_2.

FIGURE 10-4 An indifference map

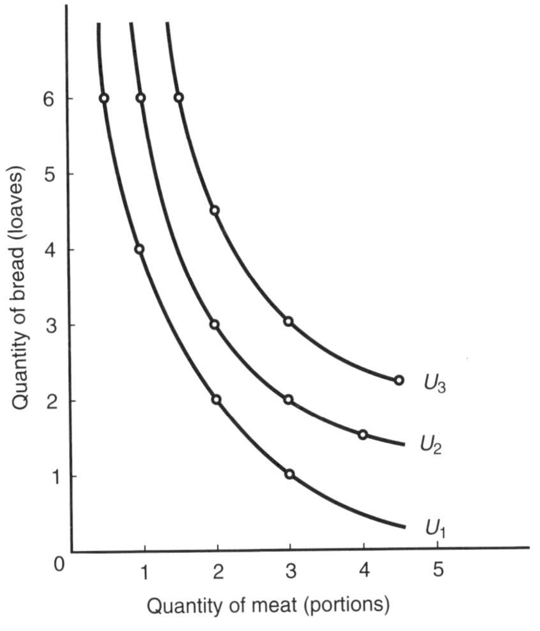

U_1, U_2 and U_3 are three indifference curves, each indicating different sets of combinations of bread and meat which yield the same level of satisfaction to the consumer. Each represents a certain level of satisfaction. As we move away from the origin, the level of satisfaction increases. Of the three curves U_3 represents the highest level of satisfaction and U_1 the lowest.

Another important property of indifference curves is that they never intersect or touch each other. This can be explained with the aid of Figure 10-5, which shows two "indifference curves" that intersect each other. It can easily be proved that such an intersection is impossible, given our assumptions. According to the definition of an indifference curve, all combinations of bread and meat on a particular curve will yield the same level of satisfaction or total utility to the consumer. This means that combinations *B* and *C* on curve *I* represent the same level of satisfaction. Similarly, *B* and *H* on curve *II* provide the consumer with the same level of satisfaction. If *B* and *C* (on curve *I*), and *B* and *H* (on curve *II*) yield the same level of satisfaction, then *C* and *H* should also yield equal satisfaction. But *H* represents a combination of more bread and meat than *C* (see also quadrant I in Figure 10-2), and we have assumed that consumers prefer more to less. It is therefore impossible for the consumer to be indifferent between *C* and *H* – he or she will always prefer *H* to *C*. This proves that indif-

FIGURE 10-5 Indifference curves cannot intersect

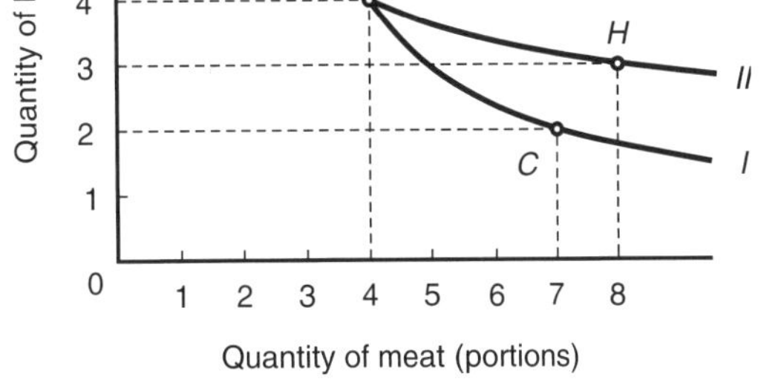

Consider the two intersecting curves, I and II. By comparing B, C and H it is easy to show that I and II cannot be indifference curves. If I and II were both indifference curves, then the consumer would have to be indifferent between C and H, which clearly cannot be the case.

ference curves cannot intersect each other (given our assumptions). You can use the same method to prove that indifference curves cannot ever touch each other.

10.8 The budget line

Now that we have considered the satisfaction the consumer obtains from various combinations of goods, we turn to the other element of the consumer's decision, namely the combinations that he or she **can afford**. As we have emphasised on a number of occasions, demand must not be confused with wants. Demand is a willingness to purchase which is backed by the means to purchase (ie by purchasing power). When analysing demand we must therefore restrict ourselves to the combinations that the consumer can afford.

We return to Koos van der Merwe's choice between bread and meat. We assume that he has a fixed amount of R24 per week to spend on bread and meat, and that bread costs R4 per loaf and meat R6 a portion. With his R24 Koos can afford a maximum of 6 loaves of bread (and no meat) or 4 portions of meat (and no bread). Table 10-8 indicates some of the ways in which Koos can spend his R24 on bread and meat, on the assumption that he always spends the full amount.

The combinations in Table 10-8 (as well as the intermediate combinations, such as five and a quarter loaves of bread and half a portion of meat) are illustrated graphically in Figure 10-6 by the straight line Q_BQ_M which runs through points *a* to *e*. At *a* Koos spends all his income on bread, while at *e* he spends everything on meat. This line is called the **budget line**, since it indicates all the combinations of the two products that the consumer (Koos) can afford to purchase with the amount of income at his disposal. The budget line is sometimes called the **consumption-possibilities curve**, **expenditure line** or **budget constraint**. All that is required to construct a budget line are the intercepts on the two axes (ie the maximum number of each good which the consumer can afford by spending the available amount of money on that good only). In the figure the intercepts are 6 loaves of bread and 4 portions of meat.

TABLE 10-8 Affordable combinations of bread and meat

Combination	Bread (loaves per week)	Meat (portions per week)
a	6	0
b	4½	1
c	3	2
d	1½	3
e	0	4

FIGURE 10-6 The budget line

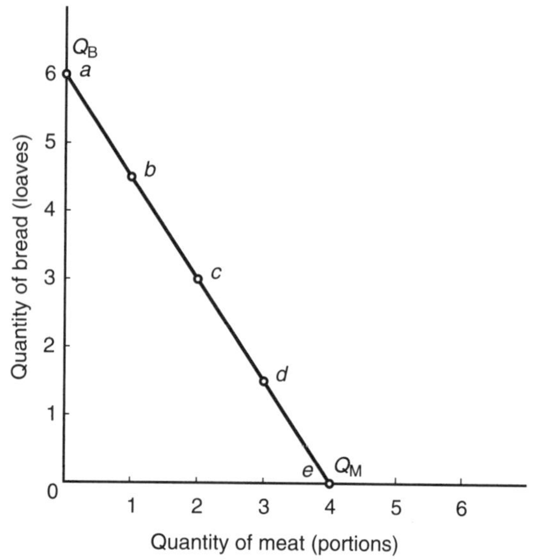

The line Q_BQ_M illustrates all the possible combinations of bread and meat that Koos can afford to purchase for R24, with the price of bread and meat being R4 per loaf and R6 per portion. Points a to e correspond to the combinations in Table 10-8.

The slope of the budget line Q_BQ_M is 6/4, which is the same as the ratio of the price of a portion of meat (R6) to the price of a loaf of bread (R4). It is easy to understand why this is the case. If Koos wants to purchase one more portion of meat, he must sacrifice 1½ (ie 6/4) loaves of bread. The exchange ratio between bread and meat is thus 6:4 or 3:2, which is the same as the ratio between the price of meat and the price of bread. This is, of course, also equal to the **opportunity cost** of meat in terms of bread.

We now combine indifference curves and the budget line to determine the consumer's equilibrium position.

10.9 Consumer equilibrium

Equilibrium in our example

The axes in Figure 10-6 are the same as those in Figure 10-4. In Figure 10-7 we superimpose the budget line from Figure 10-6 on the indifference map from Figure 10-4. In principle the indifference map contains an infinite number of indifference curves, but to explain equilibrium we show only three curves, as in Figure 10-4. Our consumer (Koos) can choose any point along the budget line (Q_BQ_M). Any position above and to the right of the budget line is unaffordable and any point below and to the left of the budget

FIGURE 10-7 Consumer equilibrium

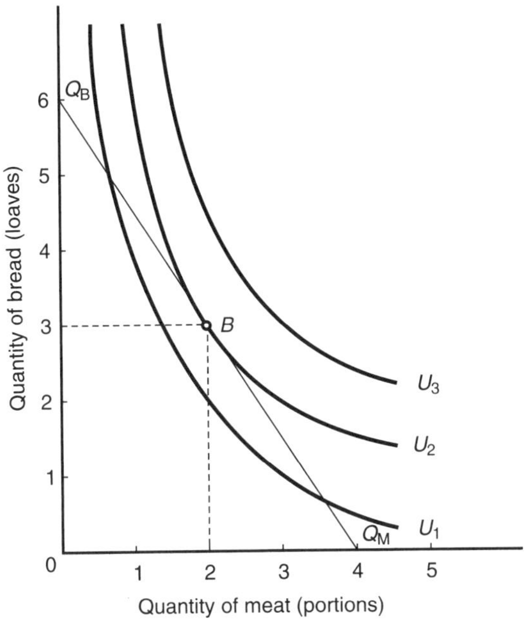

The consumer is in equilibrium (ie obtains the highest affordable level of satisfaction) where the highest indifference curve just touches the budget line. This point of tangency is indicated by B on indifference curve U_2. Points on U_1 are attainable (ie affordable) but yield less satisfaction than points on U_2. Points on U_3 yield greater satisfaction but are unattainable (ie not affordable).

line can be ignored, since we assume that Koos spends the full R24 that he has available.

The consumer (Koos) will be in equilibrium when he obtains the maximum amount of satisfaction for the amount he spends. This is indicated by point *B* in Figure 10-7, which is the same as point *B* in Figure 10-3. At *B* the budget line just touches the indifference curve U_2 without intersecting it. This is the highest indifference curve (ie the highest level of satisfaction or total utility) that Koos can reach, given the amount of money that he has available to spend. At equilibrium (point *B*) the slope of the indifference curve is equal to the slope of the budget line.

Any indifference curve which intersects the budget line, such as U_1 in Figure 10-7, represents a lower level of satisfaction than U_2. On the other hand, any indifference curve which does not touch or intersect the budget line, such as U_3 in Figure 10-7, is beyond the consumer's means.

A more general formulation

The consumer's equilibrium position, illustrated in Figure 10-7, can also be derived in more general terms. Consider the position of a consumer who spends his or her available income (I) during a certain period on two goods, good *x* and good *y*. Let Q_x be the quantity of *x* and let Q_y be the quantity of *y* that the consumer purchases in this period. The prices of *x* and *y* are P_x and P_y respectively.

We know that the budget line indicates the different combinations of the two goods the consumer can afford to purchase, given his or her income and the prices of the goods. To draw the budget line, we need only the intercepts on the horizontal axis and the vertical axis. If the consumer's total income (I) is spent on good *x*, the maximum quantity that can be purchased is I/P_x. This is the intercept on the horizontal axis. Likewise, if the consumer spends his or her total income on good *y*, a quantity of I/P_y can be purchased. This is the intercept on the vertical axis. The horizontal and vertical intercepts are shown in Figure 10-8(a).

Drawing the budget line is simply a matter of joining the two intercepts with a straight line. The slope of the budget line is

$$\frac{\text{vertical difference (rise)}}{\text{horizontal difference (run)}} = \left(\frac{I}{P_y}\right) \div \left(\frac{I}{P_x}\right)$$
$$= \frac{I}{P_y} \times \frac{P_x}{I} = \frac{P_x}{P_y}$$

The slope of the budget line is thus equal to the ratio of the price of good *x* (ie P_x) to the price of good *y* (ie P_y).

The same type of approach can be applied to indifference curves. All the points on an indifference curve indicate the same level of consumer satisfaction or total utility. Hence, total utility is unchanged as a consumer moves from one point on an indifference curve to another point, for example, from point *K* to point *L* in Figure 10-8(b). Total utility will remain unchanged only if the utility that the consumer sacrifices by consuming less of *y* is exactly compensated for by the additional utility derived from consuming more of *x*. This means that the following condition must be met:

$$\Delta Q_y \times MU_y = \Delta Q_x \times MU_x \quad \ldots\ldots\ldots\ (10\text{-}3)$$

where ΔQ_y = the change in the quantity of *y*
MU_y = the marginal utility of *y*
ΔQ_x = the change in the quantity of *x*
MU_x = the marginal utility of *x*

We can rearrange Equation 10-3 to obtain

$$\frac{\Delta Q_y}{\Delta Q_x} = \frac{MU_x}{MU_y} \quad \ldots\ldots\ldots\ (10\text{-}4)$$

where $\Delta Q_y/\Delta Q_x$ is the slope of the indifference curve and MU_x/MU_y is the ratio between the marginal util-

FIGURE 10-8 Further perspectives on the budget line and indifference curve

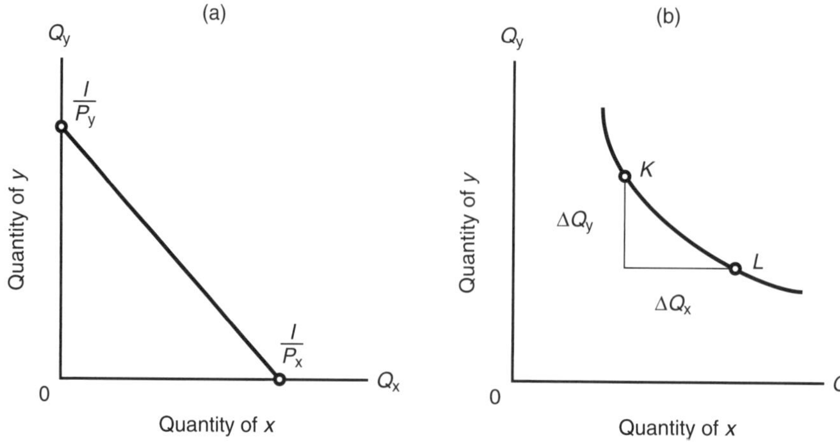

In (a) we indicate how the two intercepts are obtained. In (b) we show how the slope of an indifference curve can be measured between two points.

ities of the two goods. From Section 10.7 we also know that the slope of the indifference curve is equal to the marginal rate of substitution (*MRS*) between the two goods. It follows, therefore, that

$$\frac{\Delta Q_y}{\Delta Q_x} = \frac{MU_x}{MU_y} = MRS$$

We are now in a position to reconsider the equilibrium position illustrated in Figure 10-7. Maximum satisfaction (or consumer equilibrium) is attained at the point where the budget line is tangential to (ie just touches) the highest possible indifference curve, indicated by *B* in Figure 10-7. **At equilibrium the slope of the budget line is equal to the slope of the indifference curve.** The slope of the budget line is given by P_x/P_y while the slope of the indifference curve $(\Delta Q_y/\Delta Q_x)$ is equal to MU_x/MU_y and *MRS*. Equilibrium is thus attained where

$$MRS = \frac{\Delta Q_y}{\Delta Q_x} = \frac{MU_x}{MU_y} = \frac{P_x}{P_y} \quad \text{........... (10-5)}$$

At equilibrium the ratio of the marginal utilities of the two goods is thus equal to the ratio of their prices, that is,

$$\frac{MU_x}{MU_y} = \frac{P_x}{P_y} \quad \text{.......................... (10-6)}$$

which is the same as Equation 10-2 in Section 10.3. Multiplying both sides of Equation 10-6 by MU_y/P_x we obtain $MU_x/P_x = MU_y/P_y$. In other words, at equilibrium, the marginal utilities and prices of the consumer goods must be in proportion to one another. In Section 10.3 we called the latter result the law of equalising the weighted marginal utilities, which means that the consumer is only in equilibrium when he or she derives the same marginal utility from the last rand spent on good *x* as from the last rand spent on good *y*. This equation can be expanded to any number of goods, so that consumer equilibrium may be defined as

$$\frac{MU_x}{P_x} = \frac{MU_y}{P_y} = \frac{MU_z}{P_z} = \ldots = \frac{MU_n}{P_n} \quad \text{.. (10-7)}$$

As long as the ratios of marginal utility to price are not equal for all goods, the consumer can attain a higher level of total utility by adjusting his or her purchasing pattern. Should the marginal utility per rand spent, derived from the last unit of good *y* purchased, be greater than that derived from the last unit of good *x* purchased, then the consumer can increase his or her total utility by buying more of good *y* and less of good *x*. When the ratios are equal, however, total utility cannot increase further, and consumer equilibrium has been reached.

The consumer's valuation and the market valuation

At equilibrium the consumer's subjective valuation of the relative value of different consumer goods (indicated by the ratio of their marginal utilities) is the same as the objective valuation of the relative value of the goods in the market (indicated by the ratio of their market prices). This is essentially what the equilibrium position is all about. As long as there is a difference between the consumer's subjective valuation and the market's objective valuation of the relative importance of the goods, the consumer can improve his or her position by exchanging goods, but when the valuations coincide, no further improvement is possible and equilibrium is reached.

10.10 Changes in equilibrium

In this section we investigate how the equilibrium position changes if the consumer's income or the price of one of the goods changes.

A change in income

If the consumer's income changes, while prices remain constant, a new table of consumption possibilities, similar to Table 10-7, can be determined. For example, if the consumer's income increases from I_1 to I_2, then he or she can choose to purchase more of one or both goods. The budget line shifts to the right, as indicated in Figure 10-9. Since the price ratio P_x/P_y remains unchanged, the new budget line has the same slope as the original one (ie the two budget lines are parallel). The intercepts increase from I_1/P_x and I_1/P_y to I_2/P_x and I_2/P_y respectively. The new budget line will be at a tangent to a higher indifference curve than before. In Figure 10-9 the equilibrium shifts from

FIGURE 10-9 The effect of an increase in income

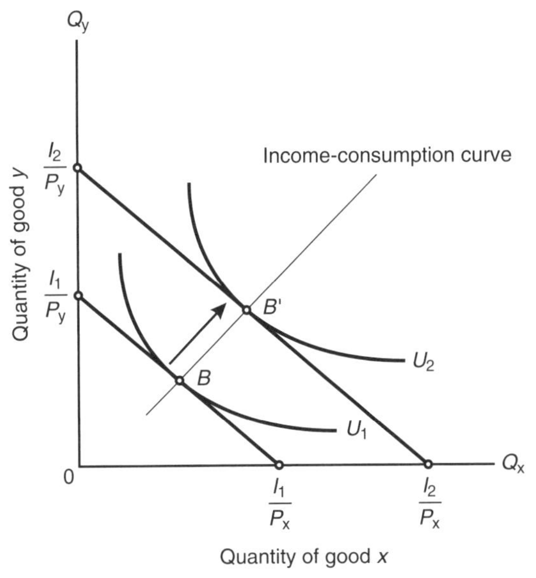

The original equilibrium is at B on indifference curve U_1. If income increases, the budget line shifts parallel to the right and a new equilibrium B' is obtained on a higher indifference curve U_2. By joining B and B' we obtain an income-consumption curve.

B to B'. If we join points such as B and B' we obtain an **income-consumption curve**, which indicates the effect of changing income on the consumer's consumption of the **two** goods.

If the consumer's income decreases, *ceteris paribus*, exactly the opposite will happen. The budget line will shift parallel to the left (ie closer to the origin). The previous indifference curve will no longer be attainable. The consumer's total utility will be reduced as a result of the decrease in income.

When the consumer's income changes, the equilibrium quantities of the goods concerned will not always change in the same direction. In Chapters 7 and 9 we distinguished between **normal goods** and **inferior goods**. In the case of a normal good an increase in income will result in an increase in the quantity of the good that is demanded. When an increase in income causes a decrease in the quantity demanded, the good is called an **inferior good**. See also Box 10-3.

We will return to the impact of changes in income when we analyse the effect of a price change.

A change in price

To explain the effect of a change in the price of a good, we return to Koos van der Merwe and his R24 per week that he can spend on bread and meat. Suppose that the price of meat rises from R6 to R12 per portion. What will be the effect on the budget line? As shown in Figure 10-10(a), the budget line changes from Q_BQ_M to $Q_BQ'_M$. Because the price of bread has not changed, Q_B remains at 6 loaves of bread. But because the price of meat has increased, Q_M (ie 4 portions of meat per week) is no longer attainable. Koos can now only afford a maximum of 2 (ie 24/12) portions of meat per week, indicated by Q'_M.

The budget line still starts at 6 loaves of bread but it rotates about this point to cut the horizontal axis closer to the origin, at 2 portions of meat. The new budget line has a slope of 3 (ignoring the minus sign). The new equilibrium is at point B', on a lower indifference curve (U_4) than before. The rise in the price of meat has caused a fall in the consumption of meat. By joining points such as B' (the new equilibrium) and B (the original equilibrium), a **price-consumption curve** is obtained. This curve shows the combinations of the **two** goods that are demanded if the price of one of the goods changes. The fact that the price-consumption curve in Figure 10-10(a) is horizontal is purely coincidental. The slope of this curve depends on what happens to the consumption of bread, which, in turn, depends on the consumer's indifference map. The curve could therefore also slope upwards or downwards to the right.

Should the price of meat fall, the budget line will swing towards the other side. For example, if B' was the original equilibrium (at a price of R12 per portion of meat), a fall in the price of meat to R6 per portion will swing the budget line to the right and *B* will be the new equilibrium point.

The demand curve

As in the case of the utility approach (based on cardinal utility), we can use the indifference approach (based on ordinal utility) to derive a demand curve.

In Figure 10-10(a) we derived two points of equilibrium for the consumer. At a price of R6 per portion the consumer will demand 2 portions of meat (point *B*) and at a price of R12 the consumer will demand one portion (point *B*'). This information can be used to draw a price-demand curve (a demand curve, for short) for this particular consumer. This is shown in Figure 10-10(b). Note that the demand curve falls from left to right, which is the normal shape of a demand curve. The demand curve shows the quantities of **one** specific good (meat in this instance) that will be demanded at various prices. The price of the good appears on the one axis and the quantity demanded on the other. Note that the demand curve differs from the price-consumption curve, which relates to the quantities of **both** goods, not just the one whose price changes. The price-consumption curve also does not explicitly show the price of the good.

Income and substitution effects of a price change

One of the major advantages of the indifference approach is that it allows us to graphically analyse the **income** and **substitution effects** of a price change, which were also discussed in Box 7-2 and Box 10-3.

To explain the income and substitution effects, we consider the case of a **decrease** in the price of a good. When the price of a good falls, while the prices of all other goods remain the same, consumers who buy that product experience an increase in their real incomes, even if their nominal incomes are unchanged. In terms of indifference curve analysis, an increase in real income means that the consumer is able to reach a higher level of satisfaction by moving to a higher indifference curve. The effect of a change in real income on the consumer's purchases of a certain good is called the **income effect**. This is similar to the effect of a change in real income as a result of a change in nominal income with prices unchanged, as explained earlier. We saw that a rise in real income leads to an increase in the consumption of a normal good, but causes a decrease in the consumption of an inferior good. In the case of a normal good, therefore, the income effect is positive, but in the case of an inferior good it is negative. Since inferior goods are the exception, we only analyse the case of a normal good.

FIGURE 10-10 The impact of a price change and the derivation of a demand curve

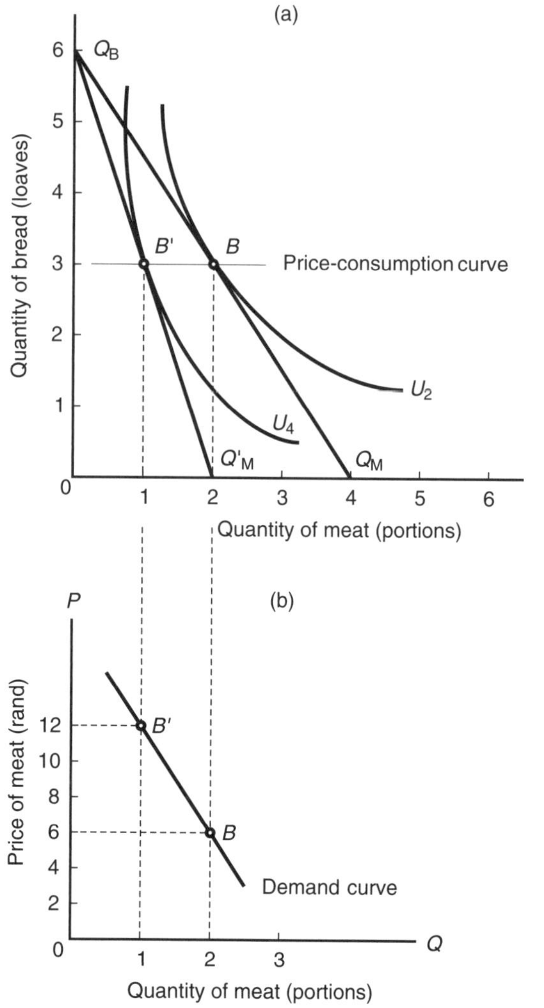

The impact of an increase in the price of meat is illustrated in (a). The original budget line is Q_BQ_M and the original equilibrium is B on indifference curve U_2. When the price of meat increases, the budget line swivels to $Q_BQ'_M$ and a new equilibrium B' is reached on a lower indifference curve U_4. By joining B' and B we obtain a price-consumption curve. The increase in the price of meat leads to a reduction in the quantity of meat demanded. This relationship is shown in (b), which is simply the familiar individual demand curve depicted in Chapter 7.

Quite apart from the income effect, a decrease in the price of a good also means that the good becomes cheaper relative to all other goods, if their prices have remained constant. Therefore it becomes an attractive option to purchase more of the good whose price has fallen. If our consumer buys only bread and meat, and the price of meat falls while the price of bread stays the same, then there will be a tendency for the consumer to buy more meat, **but less bread**. This is known as the **substitution effect**, because the consumer substitutes the good that has become relatively cheaper for the one that has become relatively more expensive.

The income and substitution effects in the case of a normal good can be analysed graphically as in Figure 10-11. If Q_BQ_M is the initial budget line, then the consumer is in equilibrium at point *A*. Here, the consumer purchases m_1 portions of meat. If the price of meat falls, while the price of bread and the consumer's money income remain constant, the position of the budget line will change to $Q_BQ'_M$. The new point of consumer equilibrium is at *B*, where m_2 units of meat are purchased. This increase in the consumption of meat, also depicted by the movement from *A* to *B*, represents the combined impact of the income and substitution effects.

We now analyse the separate contribution of each effect to this increase in consumption. We draw an auxiliary line, *ZZ*, parallel to the new budget line ($Q_BQ'_M$), which therefore has the same slope and indicates the same price ratio as $Q_BQ'_M$. Line *ZZ* is at a tangent to the original indifference curve U_1 at point *C*. The fact that a fall in the price of meat has increased the consumer's real income is reflected in the movement from indifference curve U_1 to U_2. The movement from *C* to *B* can be ascribed solely to the **income effect**. Any possibility that the movement could be due to the substitution effect is eliminated by the fact that lines $Q_BQ'_M$ and *ZZ* are parallel, and as such indicate the same price ratio.

FIGURE 10-11 The income and substitution effects of a price change

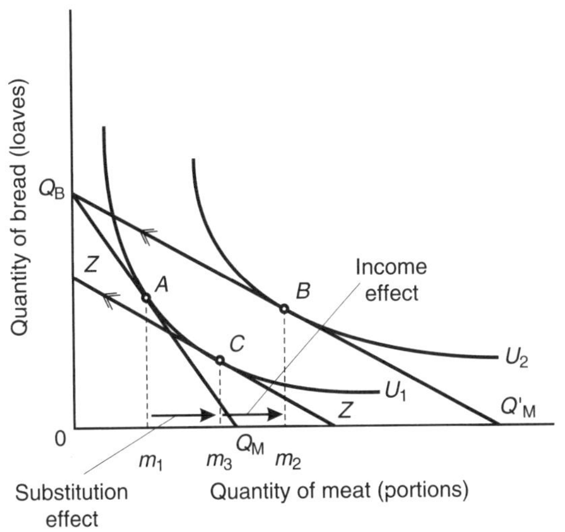

The original budget line is Q_BQ_M. When the price of meat falls, the budget line swivels to $Q_BQ'_M$. Equilibrium shifts from A (on indifference curve U_1) to B (on indifference curve U_2). The movement from A to B (or from m_1 portions of meat to m_2 portions of meat) is the price effect. This can be divided into a substitution effect A to C (or from m_1 to m_3) and an income effect C to B (or from m_3 to m_2). ZZ is an auxiliary line parallel to the new budget line ($Q_BQ'_M$) which enables us to isolate the substitution effect from the income effect.

What about the movement from *A* to *C*? At *A* the original price ratio applied, whereas at *C* the new price ratio applies. Because meat has become relatively cheaper, the consumer purchases more meat but less bread – that is to say the consumer substitutes meat for bread, which is shown in the movement from *A* to *C*. The movement from *A* to *C* can therefore be attributed to the **substitution effect**. Note that the movement from *A* to *C* takes place on the same indifference curve, which means that the consumer's real income is kept unchanged. Any possibility of income being even partly responsible for the movement from *A* to *C* is thereby eliminated. It is clear that the movement from *A* to *B*, termed the **price effect**, indeed comprises two separate effects, namely the **substitution effect** (*A* to *C*) and the **income effect** (*C* to *B*). In the case of a normal good both the income and substitution effects are in the same direction and reinforce one another. If we draw the demand curve for this normal good, it will have the standard shape of a demand curve, such as the one in Figure 10-10(b).

Further applications of the indifference curve technique

Indifference curves are versatile tools which can be used to analyse a variety of economic choices and policy issues, including:

- the choice between different factors of production in the production process – in this case the indifference curves are called isoquants (or equal output curves)
- an individual's choice between work and leisure (this is an important element of the analysis of the supply of labour) and his or her reaction to changes in wages or taxes
- the choice between consumption and saving (ie between present consumption and future consumption) and the impact of changes in interest rates on this choice
- international trade

You will encounter these and other applications of the indifference curve technique in intermediate courses in economics.

IMPORTANT CONCEPTS

Utility
Cardinal utility
Ordinal utility
Total utility
Marginal utility
Weighted marginal utility
Consumer equilibrium
Paradox of value
Indifference curve
Indifference map
Law of substitution
Marginal rate of substitution
Budget line
Income-consumption curve
Price-consumption curve
Income effect
Substitution effect

REVIEW QUESTIONS

1. Patrick Thahane's average utility from the consumption of 8 chocolates is 25 utils per slab. If the marginal utility of the 9th slab is 20 utils, will his average utility increase, decrease or stay constant if he consumes 9 slabs? Explain. What will happen to his total utility?
2. Explain in your own words what the law of equalising the weighted marginal utilities means.
3. Alfred Scott has R100 per week available to spend on beer and cigarettes. Beer costs R10 per bottle and cigarettes cost R15 per packet. Suppose Alfred buys 4 bottles of beer and 4 packets of cigarettes and that his marginal utility from beer is then 20 utils and that from cigarettes 25 utils. Is he in equilibrium? If not, should he buy more beer or more cigarettes? Explain.
4. You tell a friend that, as a consumer, she rearranges her purchases until the weighted marginal utility for all goods is equal. She replies: "That is ridiculous. I don't even know what marginal utility is. How can I be doing something I don't even know about?" How will you respond?
5. Suppose the marginal utility and total utility of Ntatho Moloi's weekly consumption of apples are both positive and that he subsequently consumes fewer apples per week. What will happen to his marginal and total utility of apples? Explain.
6. Use examples to explain the difference between cardinal utility and ordinal utility.
7. What variables are held constant along a budget line?
8. How will an increase in income affect the budget line?
9. Prove that the utility approach and the indifference curve approach yield the same consumer equilibrium.
10. Which of the following goods are more likely to be inferior goods: Mercedes Benz motorcars, imported beer, retreaded tyres, restaurant meals, polyester suits? Explain your answer.
11. Consider a consumer's choice between meat and fish. Use indifference curves to illustrate the income effect and substitution effect of an increase in the price of fish.

11 Background to supply: the theory of production and cost

Learning outcomes

Once you have studied this chapter you should be able to

- define the various revenue, cost and profit concepts
- distinguish between the total, average and marginal product of a variable input
- explain the relationship between the law of diminishing returns and the shapes of the total, average and marginal product curves in the short run
- distinguish between total, average and marginal cost
- explain the relationship between the product curves and the cost curves in the short run
- explain the nature of production and costs in the long run

Costs merely register competing attractions.

FRANK KNIGHT

Cost of production would have no effect on competitive price if it could have none on supply.

JOHN STUART MILL

In agriculture, the state of the art being given, doubling the labour does not double the produce.

JOHN STUART MILL

In this part of the book we have introduced demand and supply and the interaction between the two. We have also examined the theory behind the demand curve by looking at households' decisions about how much of a particular good or service they plan to purchase at each price. The time has now arrived to look at the theory behind the supply curve, and to examine firms' decisions about how many units of a good or a service to supply at each price. This theory is usually called the **theory of the firm**. One of the major tasks of microeconomic theory is to explain and predict how firms behave and respond to changes in market forces and economic policies.

Questions that must be answered include: Why do supply curves normally have positive slopes? How do the prices and productivity of the inputs or factors of production affect firms' decisions? What is the relationship between the returns on inputs and the cost of production? What is included in costs of production?

In this chapter and the next two chapters we examine the behaviour of firms. We assume that all firms aim to maximise profit. We start off by explaining what is meant by **revenue**, **cost** and **profit**. This is followed by a more detailed discussion of **production** and **cost**. We introduce **total**, **average** and **marginal product** and **total**, **average** and **marginal cost**, and we distinguish between the **short run** and the **long run**. Firms' decisions under different market conditions are examined in Chapters 12 and 13.

In Chapter 10, we introduced theories which explain demand. Supply also rests on a theoretical foundation, called **production and cost theory**, or simply **supply theory**. In many respects, supply theory is analogous to demand theory and a number of the techniques and concepts used to explain demand are also used to explain supply.

In microeconomics we examine the decisions of participants in the economy such as households or firms. When we examined the decisions of households as consumers, you could refer back to your own experience as a member of a household in order to understand how the typical household behaves. In this chapter we analyse the decisions of individual firms. However, since most people cannot rely on experience to understand how a firm behaves, we shall start with some introductory comments.

11.1 Introduction

Types of firm

In Chapter 3 we explained that firms can take various forms (see Box 3-2). The most common formal types of firm in South Africa are **individual proprietorships**, **partnerships**, **companies**, **close corporations**, **cooperatives**, **trusts** and **public corporations**. There are also numerous **informal businesses**, that is, businesses which are not formally registered. They include hawking, street vending, spaza shops, subsistence farming, smuggling, prostitution and shebeens.

Not all of these firms function in exactly the same way. Whereas an individual proprietorship or a one-person informal business often produces only one good or service, a large company or corporation usually produces a variety of products with inputs purchased in different markets. These products are then sold in a number of other markets. The South African formal private sector is dominated by a small number of large companies or "corporations". In South African jargon a "corporation" is a large group of companies under the control of the same group of people. It is sometimes also called a "pyramid" or a "conglomerate". A large company or corporation typically employs thousands of workers and has many managers who specialise in various fields. The decision-making processes of a corporation therefore tend to differ substantially from those of one-person businesses. To keep matters simple, however, we confine ourselves in this chapter to the functioning of a small, uncomplicated business.

The goal of the firm

The theory of the supply of goods (or supply theory) attempts to explain the behaviour of firms. That is why it is also called the **theory of the firm**. To understand how firms behave, we have to know what their goals are. In this book we assume that all **firms seek to maximise profits**.

Firms may, of course, also have other objectives. Some firms attempt to dominate the market by maximising their sales or market share, even though this might involve reducing their profit margins. Their ultimate aim is to dominate the market to such an extent that they feel stable and secure. The fact that most large firms are not owner managed also has implications for the objectives of these firms. Although the owners (the shareholders) may want the firm to make maximum profit, the managers may pursue their own objectives, such as expanding the size of the firm, since their status, power and remuneration tend to increase as the firm grows. This is an example of the **principal-agent problem** in economics – see Box 11-1.

A variety of managerial, behavioural and other theories have been developed to explain the behaviour of firms that pursue other, non-profit-maximising goals. For our purposes, however, it is sufficient to focus on profit maximisation.

Profit is an important objective of any privately-owned firm. If a firm is not profitable, it cannot continue to exist in the long run. That is why firms are sometimes defined as profit-seeking business enterprises.

Profit, revenue and cost: a brief introduction

What is profit? **Profit** is simply the surplus of **revenue** over **cost**. To understand the behaviour of a profit-maximising firm, we therefore have to examine its revenue structure as well as its cost structure, with a view to determining at which level of output the difference between total revenue and total cost (ie the firm's total profit) is at a maximum.

Total revenue (*TR*) was introduced in Chapter 9. A firm's total revenue is simply the total value of its sales and is equal to the price (*P*) of its product multiplied by the quantity sold (*Q*). **Average revenue** (*AR*) is equal to total revenue (*TR* or *PQ*) divided by the quantity sold (*Q*). If all units are sold at the same price, then average revenue is equal to the price of the product. **Marginal revenue** (*MR*) is the additional revenue earned by selling an additional unit of the product. More detail about the various revenue concepts is provided in Box 11-2.

As we explain in Chapters 12 and 13, the revenue structure of a firm is determined by the type of market in which it operates. Some firms are price takers. They have to accept the price determined in the market and cannot set their own prices. Other firms are price makers or price setters and can, within certain limits, decide at what prices to sell their products. The revenue structures of the two sets of firms will thus differ. All this will be explained when we examine the behaviour of firms in different types of market.

BOX 11-1 THE PRINCIPAL-AGENT PROBLEM

The separation of ownership and control of firms is an example of the **principal-agent problem**. In today's complex economy, people (principals) often employ others (agents) who have specialised skills or knowledge. Everyday examples include medical doctors, travel agents, estate agents, insurance brokers and stockbrokers. In the case of firms, the employees (particularly the managers) can be regarded as the "agents" of the owners. For example, senior managers are the agents of the directors, who themselves are the agents of the owners (shareholders) of the firm. The problem with this is that the agent knows more about the situation than the principal: there is **asymmetric information** between the agent(s) and the principal(s). As a result, the agent may well not act in the principal's interest and get away with it because of the principal's imperfect knowledge. Your insurance broker, for example, may sell you a policy on which he or she gets a large commission but which is not really suited to your particular needs. Likewise, your stockbroker or a fund manager with links to a stockbroking firm may repeatedly buy and sell shares on your behalf to maximise his or her commission or fees. In the case of firms, the owners (principals) must have some way of monitoring the performance of their agents (eg by using independent experts) and should also try to create incentives for agents to act in their (the principals') interests (eg by linking their remuneration more closely to the firm's profitability).

BOX 11-2 TOTAL, AVERAGE AND MARGINAL REVENUE

A firm's **total revenue *(TR)*** is the value of its sales, and is equal to the price *(P)* of its product multiplied by the quantity *(Q)* sold, that is

$$TR = P \times Q \text{ (or simply } PQ)$$

A firm's **average revenue (*AR*)** is equal to its total revenue (*TR* or *PQ*) divided by the quantity sold (*Q*), that is

$$AR = \frac{PQ}{Q}$$

If the firm sells all units of its product at the same price, then average revenue is equal to the price of the product.

A firm's **marginal revenue (*MR*)** is the additional revenue (ΔTR) earned by selling an additional unit of the product (ΔQ), that is

$$MR = \frac{\Delta TR}{\Delta Q}$$

The relationships between total, average and marginal revenue are the same as the relationships between other total, average and marginal magnitudes, which were explained in Box 10-1. For example, for an increase in quantity produced

- total revenue increases when marginal revenue is positive
- total revenue falls when marginal revenue is negative
- total revenue remains unchanged when marginal revenue is zero
- average revenue increases when marginal revenue is greater than average revenue
- average revenue decreases when marginal revenue is less than average revenue
- average revenue remains unchanged if marginal revenue is equal to average revenue

In contrast to their revenue structures, the cost structures of firms are more universal and are not specifically linked to the types of market in which they operate. In the rest of this chapter we focus mainly on the cost structure of firms. Firms use inputs (eg the various factors of production) to produce output. It follows that cost of production will depend on factors such as the technological link between inputs and outputs (ie the state of technology) and the prices and productivity of the various inputs. In other words, the theory of costs is based on the theory of production.

The short run and the long run in production and cost theory

An important distinction in production and cost theory is that between the short run and the long run. The **short run** is defined as the period during which **at least one of the inputs is fixed**. An example would be a firm which has a factory in which certain machinery has been installed and which can only vary its inputs of labour, raw materials etc. In the **long run all the inputs are variable**. For example, this would be a period that is long enough for the firm to decide whether or not to open another factory or install additional machines. The difference between the short run and the long run in production and cost theory depends on the variability of the inputs and not on calendar time. In some industries, for example the clothing industry, the actual period required for all inputs to be variable might be quite short, while in other industries, for example the steel industry, the actual period might be quite long.

Before analysing production and cost, in the short run as well as in the long run, we first have to explain the meaning of cost and profit in economic analysis.

11.2 Basic cost and profit concepts

Cost

In Chapters 1 and 2 we emphasised that cost has a specific meaning in economics. To the economist, the cost of using something in a particular way is the benefit forgone by not using it in the best alternative way. This is called **opportunity cost**, which we explained originally in Chapter 1. Whereas accountants, business people and others usually consider only the actual expenses incurred to produce a product, the economist measures the cost of production as the **best alternative sacrificed** (or forgone) by choosing to produce a particular product. The economist uses the opportunity cost principle to determine the value of **all the resources** used in production. See also Boxes 11-3 and 11-4.

The difference between accounting costs and economic costs can be explained by distinguishing between explicit costs and implicit costs. Accountants usually consider **explicit costs** only. Explicit costs are the monetary payments for the factors of production and other inputs bought or hired by the firm. These costs are, of course, also opportunity costs, since the payments for inputs reflect opportunities that are sacrificed. For example, if a firm pays R1 million for a certain machine, it means that it has decided not to do something else with the money (like purchasing a different machine, purchasing a building or depositing the money with a financial institution).

Economists, however, use a broader concept of opportunity cost and consider **implicit costs** as well as explicit costs. Implicit costs are those opportunity costs which are not reflected in monetary payments. They include the costs of self-owned or self-employed resources. The economist recognises that the use of resources owned by the firm is not free. For example, the owner of an individual proprietorship (ie a one-person business) must consider what he or she would have earned if he or she had not been running the firm (ie the opportunity cost of the owner's time must be included in the cost of production). Similar arguments apply in the case of all other self-owned resources, like land, plant and equipment. If these resources had not been used to produce the product in question, they could have been put to other uses that would have yielded an income to the owner. The **true economic cost** of using the resources in a particular way is the value of the best alternative uses (or opportunities) sacrificed. The importance of the difference between economic costs and accounting costs, and the difference between implicit costs and explicit costs, will become obvious when we examine the equilibrium of the firm in Chapters 12 and 13.

Consider the following hypothetical example. Jan van Tonder is a woodwork teacher who earns R100 000 a year (including his salary and other employment benefits, such as medical aid and pension benefits), and who has R50 000 in a savings account. Jan decides to resign from his teaching post and start his own business, making furniture on order. He uses the R50 000 in his savings account to purchase the machinery and equipment required to start the business. In addition to all the explicit money costs that he incurs, he has to consider the R100 000 a year which he sacrificed by resigning from his post, as well as the interest that he would have earned if he had kept the R50 000 in the savings account. These implicit opportunity costs are added to his explicit costs to arrive at his total economic (or opportunity) costs of producing furniture. We thus have:

economic costs of production
= opportunity costs
= explicit costs + implicit costs

The monetary payments that the firm's resources could have earned in their best alternative uses is

BOX 11-3 ACCOUNTING COSTS AND ECONOMIC COSTS

Accountants prepare income statements (or profit and loss accounts) which reflect the flows of revenue and cost during an accounting period. They want to determine the net income or accounting profit of the firm, which is equal to the difference between the firm's total revenue and its total expenses. The items in the income statement are measured at their historical costs (ie accountants use the actual monetary values of the transactions when they took place). Historical costs are objective and can usually be verified, but even historical costs are not necessarily measured accurately. Certain items such as depreciation allowances (to reflect the cost of capital goods during the accounting period) can be measured in different ways. There are different cost accounting systems, each employing different conventions for measuring costs, and two accountants can therefore arrive at different estimates of the historical costs incurred by a firm during an accounting period.

Economists, however, do not restrict themselves to actual monetary transactions when estimating the costs of production. They want to measure the true resource costs of an activity. In other words, they want to determine the value of all the resources used in production, including the use of the owner's time and financial resources (which form part of the firm's implicit costs). The estimation of implicit costs is not as straightforward as using or estimating actual expenses or historical costs. For example, values have to be assigned to the owner's time and money employed in the firm. These values are called **imputed costs** and their estimation inevitably involves a certain degree of subjectivity. Nevertheless, they have to be estimated in order to arrive at the true opportunity or resource costs of production.

Another difference between accounting costs and economic costs is that the economist does not necessarily include all historical costs as part of economic (or opportunity) costs. Some of the historical costs may be sunk costs. When a machine which has no alternative use but to produce a certain product is purchased and installed, its opportunity cost falls to zero, or almost to zero (depending on whether or not it has any scrap value). Instances where historical costs have been incurred but where opportunity costs are zero, are called **sunk costs**. The basic principle is that current decisions should be based on current costs – past costs should be regarded as bygones and should be ignored when deciding on the most profitable course of action.

In this chapter (and in the rest of the book) we always use the economic definition of costs (not the accounting definition).

called **normal profit**. Normal profit can be regarded as the minimum return required by the owner(s) of the firm to engage in a particular operation. If revenue is insufficient to cover the economic costs of production (including all implicit costs), the firm is not a viable concern. In our example, this means that Jan van Tonder should earn enough revenue to compensate for his loss of earnings as a woodwork teacher and the loss of interest on the amount he invested in his furniture-making business.[1] **Normal profit forms part of the firm's costs of production**. Thus, when an economist says that a firm is just covering its costs, it means that all explicit and implicit costs are being met and that the firm is earning a normal profit. Normal profit is explained in more detail in the next subsection.

As in the case of revenue, we distinguish between total, average and marginal cost. **Total cost** (*TC*) is simply the cost of producing a certain quantity of the firm's product. **Average cost** (*AC*) is the total cost (*TC*) divided by the number of units (or quantity) of the product produced (*Q*). **Marginal cost** (*MC*) is the addition to total cost (ΔTC) required to produce an additional (extra) unit of the product (ΔQ).

$$\text{Thus } AC = \frac{TC}{Q}$$

$$\text{and } MC = \frac{\Delta TC}{\Delta Q}, \left(\begin{array}{l}\text{thus if } \Delta Q = 1, \\ \text{then } MC = \Delta TC\end{array}\right)$$

The relationships between total, average and marginal cost are the same as the relationships between any other set of total, average and marginal magnitudes,

1. Owners of owner-run firms (like Jan) are, however, sometimes willing to pay a premium for self-employment (ie to be their own bosses) and may therefore be willing to continue with their business activities even if they do not make (or expect) a normal profit. Others may only be willing to go into business on their own if they expect to make more than a normal profit.

BOX 11-4 PRIVATE COSTS AND SOCIAL COSTS

Another important distinction is that between private and social costs. The costs considered in the text are all private costs. However, the full costs to society of the production of any good or service (ie the **social costs**) may be greater or smaller than the private costs faced by firms due to the existence of **external costs** or **benefits**, collectively called **externalities** in production.

External costs (also called **negative externalities**) are the costs borne by someone other than the firm(s) producing the good. For example, if a chemical firm dumps waste in a river or pollutes the air, society bears costs additional to those borne by the firm. Likewise, the heavy vehicles that travel on our national roads cause serious damage to the roads, atmospheric pollution, traffic congestion and noise. Residents of places like Secunda and Witbank and people staying near Johannesburg International Airport also regularly experience such costs. In all these cases social costs are greater than private costs. Where external costs are serious, society may impose charges or taxes on the firms that inflict the costs, thus forcing them to account for (and pay) at least part of the costs. In technical terms we say that such charges or taxes are an attempt to internalise the external costs. That is why, for example, heavy vehicles are subject to higher licence fees than motorcars and on toll roads, large trucks are subject to much higher toll fees than other vehicles.

External benefits (also called **positive externalities**) are the benefits enjoyed by someone other than the firm(s) producing the good. Beekeepers, for example, try to put their beehives in orchards on farms because the nectar from the fruit trees on the farms increases the production of honey. The farmers also benefit from the beehives because the bees stimulate pollination of the fruit. Another example is a firm that builds a swimming pool, sports fields or even a golf course that can also be enjoyed by non-employees of the firm. Where positive externalities occur, social costs are lower than private costs.

We return to the question of externalities in Chapter 16.

as explained in Box 10-1. For example, as the quantity produced increases

- total cost increases when marginal cost is positive
- average cost increases when marginal cost is greater than average cost
- average cost decreases when marginal cost is lower than average cost
- average cost remains unchanged when marginal cost is equal to average cost

These relationships are examined in greater detail in Section 11.4 .

Profit

The definition of profit is quite straightforward: **profit is the difference between revenue and cost**. In other words, a firm's profit is the difference between the revenue it earns by selling its product and the cost of producing it. The economist's definition of profit is, however, not the same as the accountant's definition of profit. Recall, from our discussion of cost, that accountants record events that have already occurred. Accounting profit is therefore an *ex post* concept based on recorded transactions. Economists, on the other hand, are interested in explaining and predicting behaviour and do not necessarily deal with things that have already occurred. Also recall that accountants usually only consider explicit costs, whereas economists consider **all costs**, including implicit costs. Implicit costs are those opportunity costs which are not reflected in actual payments.

As economists, we distinguish between total (or accounting) profit, normal profit and economic profit:

- **Total (or accounting) profit** is the difference between total revenue from the sale of the firm's product(s) and total explicit costs.
- **Normal profit** is equal to the best return that the firm's resources could earn elsewhere and forms part of the cost of production.
- **Economic profit** is the difference between total revenue from the sale of the firm's product(s) and total explicit and implicit costs (ie the total economic, or opportunity, costs of all resources, including normal profit).

We thus have:

Accounting profit = total revenue − total explicit costs

Economic profit = total revenue – total costs (explicit and implicit), including normal profit

These relationships are illustrated in Figure 11-1.

Economic profit is the additional return to the owners of the firm, over and above the opportunity cost of their own inputs (ie over and above normal profit). Economic profit is sometimes called **excess profit**, **abnormal profit**, **supernormal profit** or **pure profit**. It is equal to the amount by which revenue exceeds the opportunity cost of all the resources used in production.

If the firm's total sales revenue (or gross income) exceeds its total economic costs, the firm makes **economic profit**; if total revenue equals total economic costs, the firm makes **normal profit**; and if total economic costs exceed total revenue, the firm makes an **economic loss** (ie negative economic profit).

11.3 Production in the short run

To analyse the supply decisions of firms, we have to study their profit-maximising behaviour. Profit, we know, depends on revenue and cost, so to understand firms' behaviour we have to examine both revenue and cost. Cost, in turn, is determined by the prices and productivity of the various inputs used in the production process. Thus to examine cost we first have to examine the physical relationship between the quantity of inputs and the quantity of outputs produced using the inputs. In the next section we add the prices of inputs and examine the cost of production.

Production is the physical transformation of inputs into output. The world of production can be quite fascinating – see Box 11-5. Some goods and services (the inputs) are combined to produce other goods and services (the output). The **inputs** typically consist of factors of production and intermediate inputs. An **intermediate input** is any good or service other than the basic factors of production (natural resources, labour, capital and entrepreneurship) which is used to produce something else (eg screws, nails and hinges for making furniture, flour for producing bread, or parts assembled into an electric toaster or a computer). See also the explanation of the distinction between final and intermediate goods in Chapters 2 and 4. To keep matters simple, we use the term "product" for a good **or** a service throughout this chapter.

Remember that we have defined the short run as a period in which at least one of the inputs is fixed. A **fixed input** is thus an input whose quantity cannot be altered in the short run. By contrast, a **variable input** is one whose quantity can be changed in the short run (as well as the long run).

In analysing production in the short run we make the following simplifying assumptions:

- The firm produces only **one product**.
- All units of a given input are identical or **homogeneous**.
- The inputs can be used in **infinitely divisible amounts**.
- The technical relationship between inputs and output, called the **production function**, is **given** and therefore cannot be changed.

FIGURE 11-1 Economic profit and accounting profit

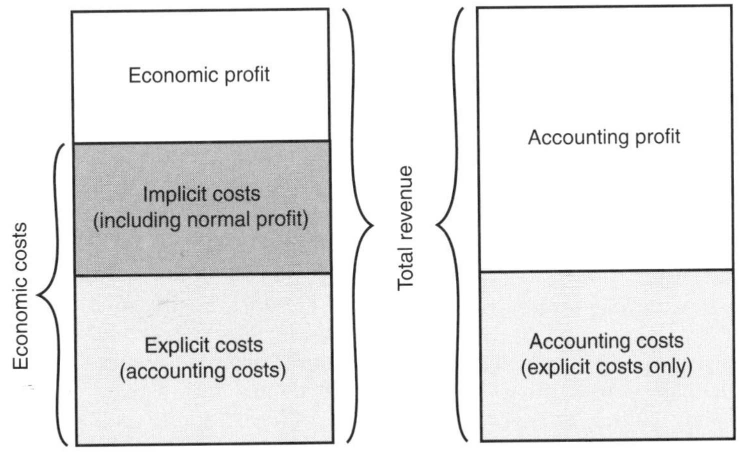

Economic profit is equal to total revenue minus economic costs (based on the opportunity cost principle). Economic (opportunity) costs are the sum of explicit and implicit costs and include a normal profit to the entrepreneur. Accounting profit is equal to total revenue less accounting (explicit) costs.

BOX 11-5 THE FASCINATING WORLD OF PRODUCTION: INTERMEDIATE GOODS, BY-PRODUCTS AND JOINT PRODUCTS

When one thinks of production, one usually thinks about the production of final goods, particularly consumer goods. Production processes, however, are complex and involve many intermediate goods, which also have to be produced, and which, in turn, yield a number of useful by-products. African Products, a subsidiary of Tongaat-Hulett, is one of the biggest direct maize buyers in South Africa, purchasing about 0,6 million tons annually. The maize is used to produce starch, which is then converted into products used in alcoholic beverages, adhesives, charcoal briquettes, mining, pharmaceuticals, intravenous drips, paper, sweets and animal feeds. About 30% of the unmodified starch ends up in paper, corrugated boxes and food products. The remaining starch is broken down into glucose. High converted glucose is used in brewing and energy drinks and is also the basis for sorbitol, the base ingredient of toothpaste. Medium converted glucose is used for sweets and chocolates and other food applications, such as ingredients of processed goods, while low converted glucose ends up in powdered milk and instant coffee. The total sales of the company amounted to about R1,6 billion in 2002. Who would have thought that there is so much more to maize than mealie pap and animal feeds? Incidentally, the company also produces guar gum, a by-product of the guar bean, which is used in the separation of precious metals (eg platinum) and base metals.

Also consider the following ways in which products from Sasol touch our everyday lives:

- The cardboard box containing your favourite breakfast cereal is sealed with hot-melt adhesives containing Sasol waxes and printed with the company's solvent-based inks.
- The wiring on the motor armature of your electric toothbrush is coated with a phenolic resin made by Sasol.
- The fragrance of perfumes, deodorants and aftershaves contains ethanol – Sasol produces that too.
- The polish with which you shine your shoes or polish your furniture is made from Sasol waxes.
- The paint, glass, plastic parts, carpets, brake fluids and other components in the bus, taxi, or car in which you travel to work are made from raw materials produced by Sasol.
- The drugs in your painkiller are derived, in part, from Sasol chemicals.
- Your favourite CD is sealed in a protective layer of polycarbonate produced from a Sasol product.
- And your DVD or VCR players need Sasol products for the coatings on their microchips and the base materials on their printed circuit boards.

Sources of basic information: *Financial Mail*, 6 December 2002, 17; *Sunday Times Business Times*, 16 February 2003, 16

- The **prices** of the product and of the inputs are **given**.
- The firm uses **fixed inputs** and **one variable input**.

These simplifying assumptions or abstractions allow us to construct simple models that can be applied to a wide range of production processes. The assumptions enable us to construct a general theory of supply. Once we have established the general theory, we can relax the assumptions in order to examine specific cases.

Let us assume that a typical firm is represented by a farmer with a fixed quantity of land on which he or she produces maize, using **labour** as the **variable input**. You will probably worry about the absence of other essential inputs, such as seed and implements (eg spades, shovels, ploughs and tractors). To keep matters simple, we assume that the land (the fixed input) comes with a fixed quantity of seed, picks, spades, shovels and so on.

Another of our simplifying assumptions is that all units of a given input are **homogeneous** (or identical). In this example, this means, for example, that all the labourers are equally intelligent, strong and diligent, and work equally hard.

We said that a fixed input is an input of which the quantity cannot be changed in the short run. But how long is the **short run**? Economists define it as the period which is so short that it is impossible to vary the quantity of at least one input! This definition might be regarded as a prime example of circular reasoning, but it is simply a way of saying that the exact time period is not important and that the length of the short run may differ from case to case. In our example of a maize farmer, land is a fixed factor of production, because it cannot be varied during the growth season. Once planting time has passed, it is impossible to increase the quantity of land on which maize is grown. (It is, of course possible to *reduce* the quantity of land devoted to maize by removing some of the plants, but we ignore this possibility, because doing this would normally be irrational.) In this example, the short run might be one growth season. But this is not necessarily the case. The institutional environment (ie the laws, rules, regulations, customs and rights governing land use) might be such that it will take the farmer more than one growth season to change the quantity of land he or she can use for maize production.

In the short run, a firm can expand output only by increasing the quantity of its variable inputs. However, the fixed inputs place an absolute limit on the quantity of output that the firm can produce (ie at some point output cannot be increased further by increasing the quantity of the variable inputs). The relationship between inputs and output is called a **production function**.

The short-run production function

As mentioned earlier, **production** occurs when inputs are combined to produce output. The inputs are not combined in a haphazard manner. For a given state of technology, there is a **relationship between** the **quantity of inputs** and the **maximum output** that can be obtained from these inputs. This relationship is called the **production function** and can be expressed in the form of a table (or schedule), an algebraic equation or a graph.

The production function depends on **the state of technology**. When technology changes, the production function also changes. To many people, technology is synonymous with equipment (eg computers). In the economist's language, however, technology refers to specific kinds of **knowledge** that can be used in production processes. A new technique can, for example, enable a firm to combine inputs differently and obtain a higher level of output with the same amount of inputs.

Our maize farmer's simple production function is presented as a schedule in Table 11-1. The first column shows how many units of land the farmer uses. Since we are examining the short run, the quantity of land (the fixed input), remains constant at 20 units. Various quantities of labour can be combined with this fixed quantity of land. Some possible quantities are

TABLE 11-1 Production schedule of a maize farmer with one variable input

Units of land	*Units of labour (N)*	*Total product (tons) TP*
20	0	0
20	1	16
20	2	44
20	3	78
20	4	113
20	5	145
20	6	171
20	7	190
20	8	200
20	9	200
20	10	187

indicated in the second column. Remember that, in addition to the assumptions we have already referred to, we are assuming that the inputs can be employed in infinitely divisible amounts. We could therefore have included something like 2,75 units of labour in the table. To keep matters simple, however, we only show integers. The third column shows the maximum quantities of output (in tons) that can be produced with the various combinations of the two inputs, given the current state of technology. In economics, we refer to these figures as **total product** (*TP*). Note that product is expressed in **physical units**, not in money terms.

The production function (or schedule) shows that if no labour is applied to the 20 units of land, no maize will be produced. The production function further shows that if one unit of labour is employed on 20 units of land, 16 tons of maize can be produced. The production function shows that with the current pool of knowledge, no more than 16 units of the product can be produced with this specific combination of inputs.

The rest of the table shows the total product (*TP*) that can be produced with other combinations of land and labour. For example, if two units of labour are applied to the land, *TP* will be 44 tons, and if seven units of labour are employed, *TP* will be 190 tons.

The production schedule can also be presented in the form of a graph. The total product of labour in Table 11-1 is presented graphically in Figure 11-2(a). The **quantity of labour** is measured on the **horizontal axis** and the **total product** on the **vertical axis**. The quantity of land is not shown, but we know it remains constant at 20 units. You will find Figure 11-2(a) a bit further on – for reasons that will become obvious, we place Figure 11-2(a) with Figure 11-2(b).

You can see clearly from the table as well as from the graph that as the quantity of labour is increased, total product (*TP*) increases from zero at an increasing rate, then starts increasing at a decreasing rate until a maximum point is reached, after which *TP* declines. Although this is a hypothetical production function, it has been found that total product *TP* follows this general trend in many practical situations. In fact, this S-shape of the total product curve reflects actual production functions so frequently that economists have formulated a "law" to express it. This is called **the law of diminishing returns**, or **the law of diminishing marginal returns**.

The law of diminishing returns

The law of diminishing returns (which was stated more than two centuries ago by the French writer Turgot) can be explained using our example of a maize farmer. One person with a pick, shovel, spade and tractor cannot cultivate 20 units of land very well in one season. In other words, if only one unit of labour (one person) is combined with the land, the land will not be utilised properly. If a second unit of labour is added to the first, the land will be cultivated more thoroughly and the total product will be higher.

Although this is not included in the law of diminishing returns, it has been found that in many production processes the second unit of a variable input will add more to the total product than the first. This is not because the second unit is superior to the first (remember, we have assumed that all units of a given input are identical or homogeneous). One reason may be that **specialisation** or **division of labour** becomes possible when more than one person is employed. One worker might, for example, prepare the soil, while the other does the sowing – recall Adam Smith's example of the production of pins, which we quoted in the explanation of specialisation and the division of labour in Box 2-1. Two labourers can prepare more than twice the land that one could prepare in the same time.

As the quantity of labour is increased, the initial benefits are gradually exhausted. All the possible savings from the division of labour have been gained and the addition of more labour brings no more savings of this kind. It is at this point that diminishing returns begin to set in. In our example, all the land will be properly utilised at some point, and adding more labour will not enable better cultivation. If still more units of labour are added, the workers may get into each other's way, slowing down instead of speeding up the work.

To formulate the law of diminishing returns more formally, we need first to explain **average product** and **marginal product**.

Average and marginal product

The **average product** (*AP*) of the variable input is simply the average number of units of output produced per unit of the variable input. It is obtained by dividing total product (*TP*) by the quantity of the variable input (*N*). *AP* is shown in column 5 of Table 11-2. The first three columns of Table 11-2 contain the same information as Table 11-1.

The **marginal product** (*MP*) of the variable input is the number of additional units of output produced by adding one additional unit (the marginal unit) of the variable input. As a marginal concept, *MP* is similar to all other marginal concepts. See also Box 10-1.

TABLE 11-2 Production schedule of a maize farmer with one variable input

1 Units of land	2 Units of labour (N)	3 Total product (tons) TP	4 Marginal product (tons) MP	5 Average product (tons) AP
20	0	0		0
			16	
20	1	16		16,00
			28	
20	2	44		22,00
			34	
20	3	78		26,00
			35	
20	4	113		28,25
			32	
20	5	145		**29,00**
			26	
20	6	171		28,50
			19	
20	7	190		27,14
			10	
20	8	200		25,00
			0	
20	9	200		22,22
			–13	
20	10	187		18,70

The marginal product of labour in our example is indicated in the fourth column of Table 11-2. The first unit of labour produces 16 tons of maize (ie the employment of the first unit of labour raises the total product from zero to 16 tons). The marginal product of the first unit of labour is thus 16 – 0 = 16 tons, as shown in column 4 between zero and the first unit of labour. The total product of the first two units of labour is 44 tons of the product. Employing a second unit of labour therefore adds 28 tons to total product, that is, the marginal product of the second unit of labour is 44 – 16 = 28 tons, as shown in column 4 between the first and the second unit of labour.

The highest marginal product shown in the table, namely 35 tons, occurs when the fourth unit of labour is employed. The marginal product of the fifth unit of labour is less than 35 tons. Once the maximum marginal product has been reached, it keeps on declining. The ninth unit of labour adds nothing to total product (ie the marginal product of nine units of labour is equal to zero). The marginal products of additional units of labour are negative, which means that their employment causes total product to decline! The state of technology places a limit on the total output that can be achieved by combining the variable input with the fixed input. Once that limit is exceeded, the workers get in each other's way, are given jobs too specialised to keep them occupied all day, or get on each other's nerves!

Column 5 indicates the average product of labour. The first unit of labour produces 16 tons of maize. Its average product is thus 16 ÷ 1 = 16 tons, as shown in column 5 opposite the first unit of labour. The average product of two units of labour is 44 ÷ 2 = 22 tons, and so on.

The highest average product (29 tons) is reached when 5 units of labour are employed. The figures in column 5 clearly show that *AP* increases until the fifth labourer is employed and then declines to only 18,7 tons when ten labourers are employed.

The information in columns 4 and 5 of Table 11-2 is depicted in Figure 11-2(b). The units of labour are shown on the horizontal axis and the average and marginal product of labour on the vertical axis. The curves show the average and marginal product of labour. The scale on the horizontal axis is the same as that used in Figure 11-2(a). Figure 11-2(b) is placed directly below Figure 11-2(a), so we can compare the trends of the total product, the average product and the marginal product of labour. Note, however, that the **scales on the vertical axes of the graphs are not the same**. The scale is more "stretched out" in the bottom graph, so we can see the movements in the average and marginal product more clearly.

We are now ready to formulate the law of diminishing returns more formally:

The **law of diminishing returns** states that **as more of a variable input is combined with one or more fixed inputs in a production process, points will eventually be reached where first the marginal product, then the average product and finally the total product start to decline.**

FIGURE 11-2 Total, average and marginal product of labour

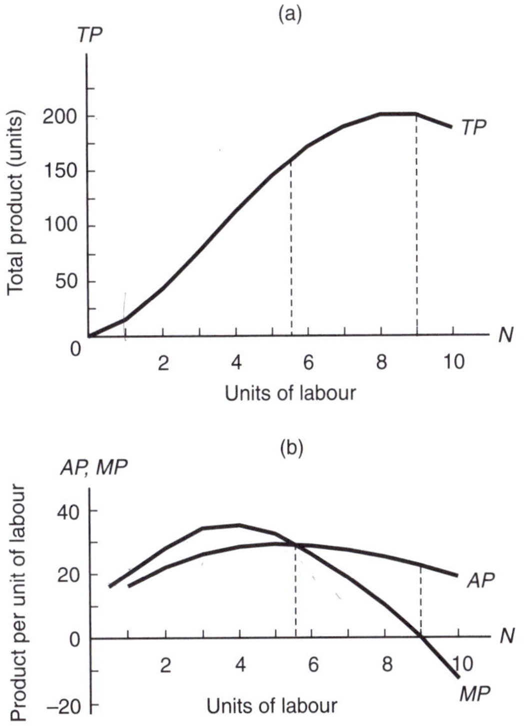

In (a) we show the total product of labour TP, while the average and marginal product of labour (AP and MP) are shown in (b). The same scales are used on the horizontal axes in (a) and (b) but the vertical scale in (b) is larger (more "stretched out") than in (a). TP increases as long as MP is positive, but falls once MP becomes negative. AP increases if MP is above it, reaches a maximum where it is equal to MP and then falls when MP is below it.

Comparison of total, average and marginal product

The effect of the law of diminishing returns is illustrated in Table 11-2 and Figure 11-2. Applied to our example, the law states that as more units of labour are combined with the fixed quantity of land, first the marginal product, then the average product and finally the total product will start to decline. The table and the graphs confirm that the marginal product (*MP*) starts to decline first (after the fourth unit of labour has been employed), followed by the average product

(*AP*) (after the fifth unit of labour) and then the total product (*TP*) (after the ninth unit of labour).

Because we only indicate full units of labour, the curves are not smooth or stepless, but consist of successive straight lines. Had we shown fractions of units of labour, the straight-line sections would be curved.

The total, average and marginal product of labour are all based on the same basic information and are therefore interrelated. If the total product curve is smooth, the average and marginal curves are also smooth, as shown in Figure 11-3. In this case the curves display the following mathematical characteristics (see also Box 11-6):

- *TP* is S-shaped. In other words, as the variable input is increased, *TP* increases from zero at an increasing rate, then at a decreasing rate, reaches a maximum point and then decreases.
- *AP* and *MP* are shaped like inverted "U"s, that is, as the variable input is increased, they rise at declining rates, reach maximum points and then decrease at increasing rates.
- *MP* reaches its maximum before *AP* reaches its maximum.
- Before *AP* reaches a maximum, *MP* lies above *AP*.

FIGURE 11-3 Marginal product and average product

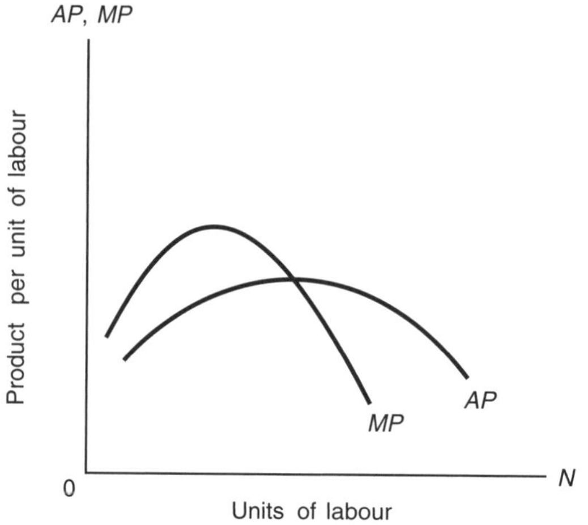

Marginal product MP increases, reaches a maximum and then decreases. When MP is greater than average product AP, AP also increases; when MP is lower than AP, AP falls. MP is equal to AP where AP is at a maximum.

BOX 11-6 TOTAL, AVERAGE AND MARGINAL PRODUCT: A MATHEMATICAL INTERPRETATION

The short-run production function can be written as:

$$TP = f(N)$$

where TP = total product

N = quantity of labour

This is simply another way of stating that total product is a function of labour input, *ceteris paribus*.

The average product of labour (*AP*) can be expressed as the ratio of total product (*TP*) to labour input (*N*):

$$AP = TP/N$$

which simply means that average product is equal to total product divided by the number of units of labour employed.

The marginal product (*MP*) of labour can be expressed as follows:

$$MP = d(TP)/dN$$

where $d(TP)$ = a small change in *TP*

dN = the corresponding small change in labour input

The changes denoted by the symbol d are so small that mathematicians say they tend towards zero. In mathematical terms the *MP* function is the **slope** or **first derivative** of the *TP* function. If the *TP* function is a continuous function, the *MP* function will also be a continuous function. In such a case *MP* differs slightly from the *MP* in Table 11-2, which was calculated by dividing relatively large changes in *TP* (ie ΔTP) by discrete changes in labour input (ΔN).

- *MP* equals *AP* at its maximum point.
- After the maximum point of *AP* is reached, *MP* lies below *AP*.
- *MP* equals zero where *TP* reaches its maximum.

From the table and graphs we can also see that as long as marginal product *MP* exceeds average product *AP*, average product increases. Similarly, when marginal product is less than average product, average product declines. These relationships are the same as those explained in Box 10-1.

11.4 Costs in the short run

Recall from Section 11.2 that economic costs are **opportunity costs**, which include both explicit costs and implicit costs. In the short run a firm's costs consist of fixed costs and variable costs.

Fixed and variable costs

As we explained earlier, the quantity of a **fixed input** cannot be altered in the short run. In our example of the maize farmer, the **quantity of land** remains constant at twenty units. We assume that the **rental** of a unit of land, that is, the price of using it for a specific period, is given and represents the opportunity cost of the land. The cost of the land to the farmer for a specific period, say one growth season, can therefore be calculated by multiplying the number of units of land by the rental per unit of land for that period. Because the number of units of land is fixed and the price of using a unit of land is given, the cost of using the land is fixed. It does not change when the quantity of labour is varied and the total product changes. **Fixed cost** is thus formally defined as cost that remains constant irrespective of the quantity of output produced. Fixed costs are sometimes also called overhead costs, indirect costs or unavoidable costs.

The quantity of a **variable input** can be varied in the short run. In the case of our hypothetical maize farmer, **labour** is the variable input. We assume that the price of a unit of labour is given and represents its opportunity cost. The cost of labour to the firm for the relevant period can therefore be calculated by multiplying the number of units of labour employed, by the price per unit of labour. Although the price of a unit of labour is given, the quantity of labour is variable and therefore the cost of labour is also variable. **Variable cost** is formally defined as cost that changes when total product changes – it represents the cost of the variable input(s). Variable costs are sometimes called direct costs, prime costs or avoidable costs.

Table 11-3 illustrates the relationship between the short-run production function and the short-run total cost function of the maize farmer. The first three columns simply repeat the information in Table 11-1. Assume that the cost of a unit of the fixed input (land) for the growth season is R450. Therefore, the cost of the twenty units is 20 × R450 = R9 000, irrespective of the quantity of maize produced during the growth season or the quantity of the variable input (labour) used. This represents the **total fixed cost** (*TFC*) of producing the various quantities of output indicated in column 3. *TFC* is shown in column 4 of Table 11-3. Columns 3 and 4 together are known as the **total fixed cost schedule**, because they indicate the relationship between total product (*TP*) and total fixed cost (*TFC*).

Suppose the price of a unit of labour for the full growth season is R2 400. To obtain the cost of labour, we have to multiply the units of labour by the price per unit of labour. Because there is only one variable

TABLE 11-3 Total, fixed and variable cost schedules of a maize farmer

1 *Units of land*	2 *Units of labour*	3 *Total product (units) TP*	4 *Total fixed cost (R) TFC*	5 *Total variable cost (R) TVC*	6 *Total cost (R) TC*
20	0	0	9 000	0	9 000
20	1	16	9 000	2 400	11 400
20	2	44	9 000	4 800	13 800
20	3	78	9 000	7 200	16 200
20	4	113	9 000	9 600	18 600
20	5	145	9 000	12 000	21 000
20	6	171	9 000	14 400	23 400
20	7	190	9 000	16 800	25 800
20	8	200	9 000	19 200	28 200
20	9	200	9 000	21 600	30 600
20	10	187	9 000	24 000	33 000

input in this example, the result represents the **total variable cost** (*TVC*) of producing the various quantities of output indicated in column 3. It is shown in column 5 of Table 11-3 and increases as the quantity of labour increases. Columns 3 and 5 together are known as the **total variable cost schedule**, because they indicate the relationship between total product (*TP*) and total variable cost (*TVC*).

The **total cost** (*TC*) is simply the sum of the total fixed cost *TFC* and the total variable cost *TVC* associated with each level of production. *TC* is shown in column 6 of Table 11-3 and increases as the quantity of labour employed increases. Columns 3 and 6 together are known as the **total cost schedule**, because they indicate the relationship between total product *TP* and total cost *TC*.

The three total cost schedules can be represented in graphical form as **cost functions** or **cost curves**. The curves are depicted in Figure 11-4. Note that **total product** (not units of labour, as in the previous graphs) is measured on the horizontal axis. Also note that cost (not product) is measured on the vertical axis. This is because we are measuring the costs of producing various levels of output.

The **total fixed cost** function or curve (*TFC*) is a horizontal line with an intercept of R9 000 on the vertical axis, indicating that total fixed cost remains constant at R9 000 irrespective of total product.

The **total variable cost** function or curve (*TVC*) has a reversed S-shape. It starts at the origin and then increases at a decreasing rate up to a point. Thereafter *TVC* increases at an increasing rate. It is only drawn up to 200 units of total product, the maximum number of units that can be produced with the specified inputs, given the state of technology (and considering only whole units of labour input).

FIGURE 11-4 Three total cost curves

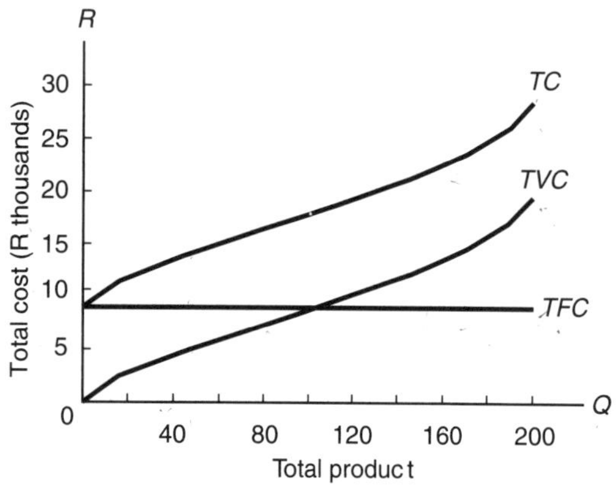

Total cost TC consists of total fixed cost TFC and total variable cost TVC. TFC is the same at all levels of output but TVC varies as output changes. Note that this means that the distance between TC and TVC is always equal to TFC.

The **total cost** function or curve (*TC*) has the same shape as the variable cost function, but does not start at the origin. It starts above the origin at the point on the vertical axis which represents the total fixed cost. **Total cost equals total fixed cost plus total variable cost**. Graphically, this means that at every point along the horizontal (*TP*) axis the vertical distance between the total cost curve and the total fixed cost curve is equal to the total variable cost. The total variable cost of zero units of output is zero and therefore the total cost of zero units of total product is equal to the total fixed cost. At all other points, total variable cost is positive and is added to total fixed cost to derive total cost. The vertical distance between total cost (*TC*) and total variable cost (*TVC*) is also always equal to total fixed cost (*TFC*).

Average and marginal cost

To analyse a firm's output decisions, we also have to examine **average cost** and **marginal cost**, which were introduced in Section 11.2.

Since there are three measures of total cost, there are also **three measures of average cost**:

- **average fixed cost** *AFC* (ie total fixed cost *TFC* divided by total product *TP*)
- **average variable cost** *AVC* (ie total variable cost *TVC* divided by total product *TP*)
- **average cost** *AC* (ie total cost *TC* divided by total product *TP*)

Note that average cost is obtained by dividing total cost by **total product** (not by units of labour, as in the case of average product). Average cost *AC* is sometimes called average total cost and abbreviated to *ATC*. However, to avoid this somewhat cumbersome term, we simply refer to average cost *AC*. Just remember that *AC* includes average fixed cost *and* average variable cost.

The various average cost figures for our hypothetical maize farmer are given in Table 11-4. Columns 1 to 5 are the same as columns 2 to 6 of Table 11-3. Note that average fixed cost *AFC* is the same (R45) whether eight or nine units of labour are used, because their total product is the same. However, when ten units of labour are used, *AFC* increases, because total product decreases. Average variable cost *AVC* is higher when nine units of labour are employed than when eight units are used, because total product is the same in both cases but it costs more to employ 9 units than 8 units of labour. This also applies to average cost *AC*.

Marginal cost *MC* is the increase in total cost when one additional unit of output is produced. Theoretically, we could distinguish between marginal

TABLE 11-4 Short-run total and unit cost schedule for a firm with one variable input

1 Units of labour	2 Total product (units) TP	3 Total fixed cost (R) TFC	4 Total variable cost (R) TVC	5 Total cost (R) TC	6 Average fixed cost (R) AFC	7 Average variable cost (R) AVC	8 Average cost (R) AC	9 Marginal cost (R) MC
0	0	9 000	0	9 000				
1	16	9 000	2 400	11 400	562,50	150,00	712,50	150,00
2	44	9 000	4 800	13 800	204,55	109,09	313,64	85,71
3	78	9 000	7 200	16 200	115,38	92,31	207,69	70,59
4	113	9 000	9 600	18 600	79,65	84,96	164,60	68,57
5	145	9 000	12 000	21 000	62,07	82,76	144,83	75,00
6	171	9 000	14 400	23 400	52,63	84,21	136,84	92,31
7	190	9 000	16 800	25 800	47,37	88,42	135,79	126,32
8	200	9 000	19 200	28 200	45,00	96,00	141,00	240,00
9	200	9 000	21 600	30 600	45,00	108,00	153,00	
10	187	9 000	24 000	33 000	48,13	128,34	176,47	

fixed cost, marginal variable cost and marginal (total) cost. However, total fixed cost remains unchanged when total product increases. Therefore, marginal fixed cost is always zero and **marginal cost is always equal to marginal variable cost**. By definition, marginal cost only consists of variable cost.

Whereas average cost could easily be calculated from the total cost figures in Table 11-4, it is not so straightforward to calculate marginal cost from such figures. The reason is that the total product figures in the table do not increase by one unit at a time, as required by the definition of marginal cost. The **marginal cost must be approximated by first calculating the increases in total cost and total product, and then dividing the increase in total cost by the increase in total product**, as shown in Table 11-5. Marginal cost is not defined for $\Delta TP = 0$, that is, in our example when nine units of labour are employed. Nor is it defined when total cost increases, but total product decreases. Therefore *MC* is not shown for these cases. For purposes of comparison, the marginal cost figures are included in colomn 9 of Table 11-4.

The average and marginal cost schedules are collectively referred to as **unit cost schedules**, to distinguish them from the total cost schedules. The unit cost schedules are depicted in Figure 11-5. As in Figure 11-4, total product is measured on the horizontal

TABLE 11-5 Calculation of marginal cost

Total product TP	Increase in total product ΔTP	Total cost (R) TC	Increase in total cost (R) ΔTC	Marginal cost (R) ΔTC/ΔTP
0		9 000		
16	16	11 400	2 400	150,00
44	28	13 800	2 400	85,71
78	34	16 200	2 400	70,59
113	35	18 600	2 400	68,57
145	32	21 000	2 400	75,00
171	26	23 400	2 400	92,31
190	19	25 800	2 400	126,32
200	10	28 200	2 400	240,00
200	0	30 600	2 400	
187	–13	33 000	2 400	

FIGURE 11-5 Marginal and average cost

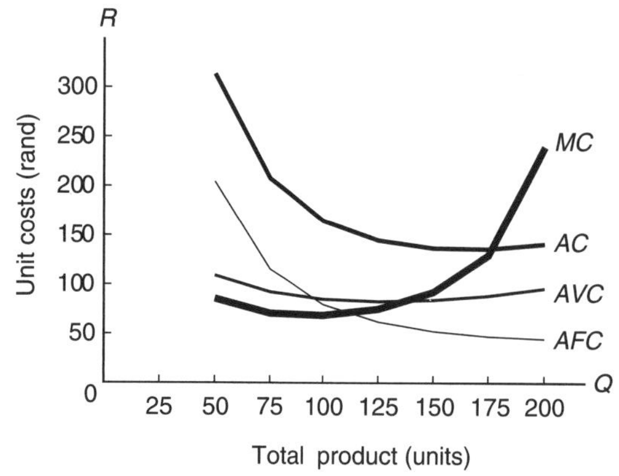

There is only one marginal cost curve MC, but there are three average cost curves: average fixed cost AFC (which falls as output increases), average variable cost AVC (which falls, reaches a minimum and then increases), and average total cost (or simply average cost) AC (which also falls, reaches a minimum and then increases). Both AVC and AC reach a minimum where they are intersected by MC.

FIGURE 11-6 Marginal and average cost

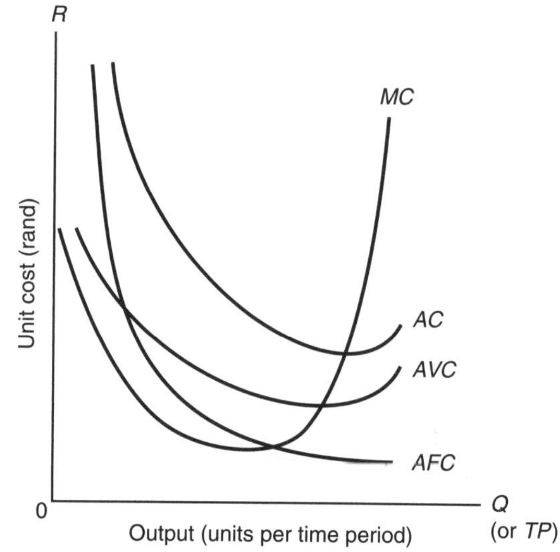

This set of smooth unit cost curves illustrates the conclusions reached in the text. Note, in particular, that MC intersects AC and AVC at their minimum points.

axis and cost on the vertical axis. However, the scale of the vertical axis is larger (more "stretched out"), because the unit costs are by definition much lower than the total costs. Note that the *AVC*, *AC* and *MC* curves are U-shaped. Recall that the average and marginal product curves, *AP* and *MP*, are shaped like inverted "U"s (see Figure 11-3).

As in the case of total, average and marginal product, from which the cost functions are derived, there are mathematical relationships between the cost functions. If the total cost curve is smooth, the average and marginal cost curves will also be smooth, as in Figure 11-6. In this case the curves will exhibit the following mathematical properties (see also Box 11-7):

- *TFC* is a horizontal line.
- *TVC* has a reversed S-shape. In other words, as *TP* increases from zero, *TVC* starts in the origin, increases at a decreasing rate up to a point and then at an increasing rate.
- *TC* is shaped like *TVC*, but starts at the same point on the vertical axis as *TFC*.
- *AFC* is L-shaped. In other words, as *TP* increases from zero, it starts at a very high value and then keeps on declining until the maximum *TP* is reached.
- *AVC*, *AC* and *MC* are U-shaped. In other words, as *TP* increases from zero, they start at high values, decline at decreasing rates, reach minimum points and then increase at increasing rates.
- *AC* lies above *AFC* and *AVC*, because it includes them both. The vertical distance between the *AC* and *AFC* curves is equal to *AVC*, and the vertical distance between the *AC* and *AVC* curves is equal to *AFC*. As *AFC* declines, the vertical distance between *AC* and *AVC* becomes smaller.
- *MC* reaches its minimum point before *AVC*.
- *AVC* reaches its minimum point before *AC*.
- *MC* equals *AVC* and *AC* at their respective minimum points. Before these points are reached, *MC* lies below *AVC* and *AC* respectively. Beyond these points, that is, when total product is increased further, *MC* lies above *AVC* and *AC* respectively.

Rather obvious implications of these relationships, which are also clear from the table and graphs, are that while *AVC* or *AC* is decreasing, it exceeds *MC*, and that while *AVC* or *AC* is increasing, it is exceeded by *MC*. All the properties of the unit cost curves are illustrated in Figure 11-6.

The relationship between production and cost in the short run

To conclude this section, we emphasise the relationship between the product (or productivity) of the input(s) and the cost of the output(s) in the short run, as illustrated in Figure 11-7.

One of the most important points to emerge from this chapter is that a firm's cost structure depends on the productivity of its inputs (given the prices of the inputs). In other words, the shape of the unit cost curves is determined by the shape of the unit product curves. In Figure 11-7(a) we show the average and marginal product of labour, which each represents a relationship between the quantity of labour (N) (on the horizontal axis) and output per unit of input (on the vertical axis). Marginal product (MP) reaches a maximum of MP_1 at N_1 units of labour. The average product of labour (AP) reaches a maximum of AP_1 where it intersects the marginal product (MP) at N_2 units of labour.

In Figure 11-7(b) we show the unit costs of the firm. Marginal cost (MC) and average variable cost (AVC) each represent a relationship between total output (Q) (on the horizontal axis) and unit cost (on the vertical axis). Marginal cost (MC) reaches a minimum of MC_1 at a total output level of Q_1. Average variable cost (AVC) reaches a minimum of AVC_1 where it intersects marginal cost (MC) at an output level of Q_2.

Although the axes in Figures 11-7(a) and (b) are different, the output of Q_1 in (b) is the **total** output produced by N_1 units of labour in (a). Likewise, total output Q_2 in (b) is the total output produced by N_2 units of labour in (a). The figure shows how the inversely U-shaped product curves give rise to the U-shaped cost curves. Both are grounded in the law of diminishing returns. When marginal product (MP) is increasing, the marginal cost (MC) of producing a good is falling, but when MP declines, MC increases.

FIGURE 11-7 The relationship between production (or productivity) and cost

(a)

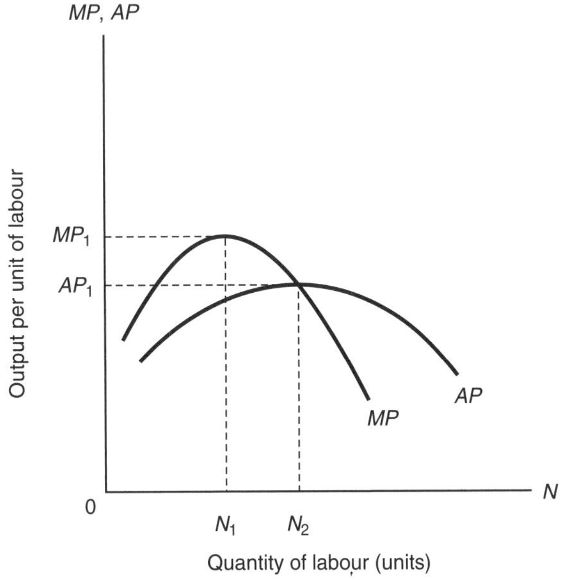

(b)

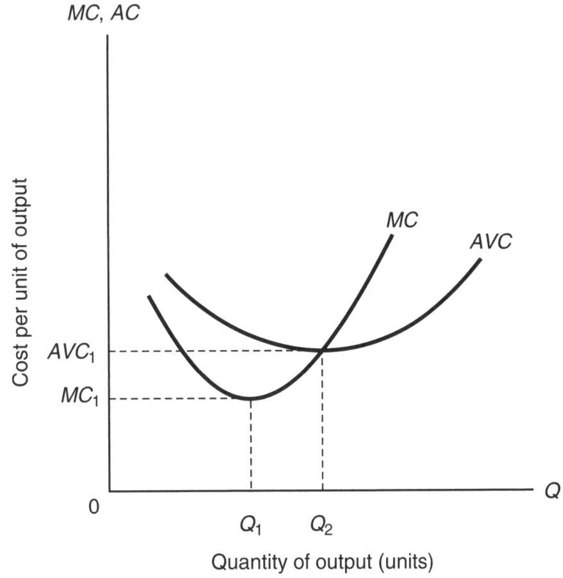

In (a) we show the average and marginal product of labour and in (b) we show the corresponding average variable cost and marginal cost of production. The maximum of MP (at N_1) corresponds to the minimum of MC (at Q_1). Similarly, the maximum of AP (at N_2) corresponds to the minimum of AVC (at Q_2).

11.5 Production and costs in the long run

What is meant by the long run?

In the long run there are **no fixed inputs** – all the inputs (including all the factors of production) are variable. In the long run there are thus no fixed costs – all the costs are variable. Moreover, the law of diminishing returns does not apply. (You will recall that this law refers to a situation where additional units of a variable input are added to the fixed inputs.[2]) There is therefore no compelling reason why long-run cost curves should exhibit the same features as short-run curves.

In production theory the long run is defined as a period that is long enough for the firm to change the quantities of all the inputs in the production process as well as the process itself. That would mean, for example, that there is enough time for the firm to build a new factory, to install new machines and to use new techniques of production. The actual time period required to vary all the inputs or to adopt new production techniques depends on the characteristics

2. Note also that marginal product has no meaning in long-run production theory since the marginal product of an input can only be derived if all the other inputs are held constant.

BOX 11-7 TOTAL, AVERAGE AND MARGINAL COST: A MATHEMATICAL INTERPRETATION

The total cost function TC can be written as:

$$TC = f(TP)$$

where TC = total cost
TP = total product

This simply states that total cost is a function of total output.

Since TP is expressed in units of output, we can also substitute it with Q (ie the quantity of output). Thus $TP = Q$.

Average cost (AC) can be expressed as the ratio of total cost (TC) to total product (TP) (or Q):

$$AC = TC/TP \text{ (or } TC/Q)$$

In the same way, average fixed cost (AFC) and average variable cost (AVC) can be expressed as functions of total fixed cost (TFC) and total variable cost (TVC) respectively:

$$AFC = TFC/TP \text{ (or } TFC/Q)$$
$$AVC = TVC/TP \text{ (or } TVC/Q)$$

Marginal cost (MC) can be expressed as follows:

$$MC = d(TC)/d(TP) \text{ (or } d(TC)/dQ)$$

where $d(TC)$ = a small change in TC
$d(TP)$ = the corresponding small change in TP (= dQ)

In mathematical terms the MC function is the **slope** or **first derivative** of the TC function. If the TC function is a continuous function, the MC function will also be a continuous function. In such a case MC differs slightly from the MC in Table 11-5, which was calculated by dividing large changes in TC (ie ΔTC) by relatively large changes in the quantity produced (ΔTP).

of the firm, the production processes and the institutional environment, and it may differ quite significantly from case to case. A street hawker, for example, might be able to vary all inputs (eg the stock for sale, the location and the hours worked) on a daily basis. A clothing manufacturer will take longer, while a cement producer or an aluminium producer might require several years to expand production by extending an existing factory or building an additional one.

In the long run, a firm has to take decisions about the scale of its operations, the location of its operations and the techniques of production it will use. All these decisions will affect the cost of production.

Returns to scale

The term "returns to scale" refers to the long-run relationship between inputs and output. Returns to scale are measured by varying **all** the inputs by a certain percentage and comparing the resulting percentage change in production with the percentage change in the inputs. Three possible situations can be distinguished:

Constant returns to scale. This is where a given percentage increase in inputs will give rise to the *same* percentage increase in output (eg a doubling of the inputs leads to a doubling in output).

Increasing returns to scale. This is where a given percentage increase in inputs will lead to a *larger* percentage increase in output (eg a doubling of the inputs leads to a trebling of output).

Decreasing returns to scale. This is where a given percentage increase in inputs will give rise to a smaller percentage increase in output (eg a 100% increase in the inputs leads to a 50% increase in output).

Returns to scale refer to a situation in which **all** inputs increase by the **same** proportion. Decreasing returns to scale (a long-run concept) should therefore not be confused with diminishing marginal returns (a short-run concept). Remember that in the case of diminishing marginal returns only the *variable* input increases.

The concept of increasing returns to scale is closely linked to that of **economies of scale**, a related but different concept.

Economies of scale

A firm experiences **economies of scale** if costs per unit of output fall as the scale of production increases. This may or may not be the result of increasing returns to scale. If a firm experiences increasing returns to scale from its inputs, it means that the firm will be using smaller and smaller amounts of inputs **per unit of output** as it expands. *Ceteris paribus*, this means that unit cost will decrease as output increases. In other words, economies of scale will be experienced.

As explained above, returns to scale refer to the relationship between **inputs** and output and specifically to a situation where **all** the inputs are increased by the same percentage. Economies of scale, on the other hand, refer to the relationship between **costs** and output and specifically to a decline in unit costs as output expands. Economies of scale are thus different from returns to scale. Moreover, economies of scale can be achieved by increasing the quantity or productivity of only one or a few of the inputs, and where all the inputs are increased they do not necessarily have to increase by the same percentage.

A firm might also experience **diseconomies of scale**. This occurs when unit costs rise as output increases.

Economies and diseconomies of scale can be classified into two broad groups: internal and external economies or diseconomies. **Internal** economies or diseconomies are those pertaining to the specific firm – they can be controlled by the firm. **External** economies or diseconomies, on the other hand, are outside the firm's control and relate to conditions and events in the industry and the broader environment within which the firm operates. Examples of the different types of economies and diseconomies of scale are provided in Box 11-8.

BOX 11-8 ECONOMIES AND DISECONOMIES OF SCALE

As mentioned in the text, there are both internal and external economies and diseconomies of scale. This box contains some examples of each type.

Internal economies of scale include the following:

- *Technical economies* refer to the techniques of production and are therefore related to increasing returns to scale. In some industries modern technology is such that efficient, low-cost production can be achieved only if producers are extremely large, both absolutely and in relation to the market. Examples include the production of aluminium, chemicals, stainless steel and other forms of steel (produced by Mittal SA). In some cases the economies of scale are so large that there is room for only one firm in the industry, and competition is either impossible or highly inefficient. Such **natural monopolies** are discussed in Chapter 13.
- *Indivisibilities* are a sub-category of technical economies and refer to the fact that some inputs (eg large machines) are of a minimum size (ie indivisible). In many cases it is only worthwhile installing the expensive machines if the scale of production warrants it.
- *Managerial, organisational or administrative economies*. As the size of the firm increases, economies may arise from the opportunities for division of labour and specialisation within management. A large firm, for example, can provide full-time activity for those with specialist managerial skills (eg accountants, buyers, lawyers, personnel, marketing, production and other managers). This is an example of the more general advantages of *specialisation and division of labour* (see Box 2-1).
- *Marketing economies* may arise both in the purchase of inputs (eg raw materials) and in the sale of the finished products. Large firms can usually negotiate bulk discounts and the larger the firm, the more efficient its marketing effort can be. For example, a product sold nationwide can be advertised efficiently on TV, but not a product that is sold in a limited geographic area.
- *Financial economies* occur when, for example, large firms are able to raise finance more easily and at more favourable terms than small firms. Moreover, financial institutions often levy certain fixed minimum charges with the result that average costs decline as the amounts involved increase.

- *Spreading overheads*. In general, the greater the firm's output, the more widely **overhead or fixed costs** (which include managerial, administrative, marketing and other costs as well) are spread, and the lower average costs become. This category therefore includes most of the others mentioned earlier. For example, the cost of producing this textbook is related to the number of books printed. The higher the number, the lower the average total costs and, therefore, the lower the selling price and/or the higher the profits of the publishing firm.

Internal diseconomies of scale include the following:

- *Managerial diseconomies*. As the firm becomes larger and more complex it may become more difficult to manage it efficiently. Lines of communication become longer and management may become less directly involved.
- *Worker alienation*. In Box 2-1 we explained that jobs might become so specialised, boring and repetitive that workers might feel alienated and become poorly motivated and unproductive.
- *Deteriorating industrial relations*. As the firm grows, the problems mentioned above and the increased complexity of the interrelationships between different categories of employees may result in a deterioration of industrial relations, giving rise to increased work stoppages and strikes.
- *Other problems of mass production*. The complex interrelationships between different production processes and the scale of production can give rise to great disruption and increased unit costs if, for example, a machine breaks down or workers in a particular section go on strike.

External economies of scale include the following:

- *Industry economies*. The firm may benefit from an expansion of the industry in which it operates. For example, as the industry grows in size, specialised markets may develop for buying raw materials or selling the finished product (eg in agriculture, mining); specialised labour skills may develop (eg in information technology); specialised component suppliers may develop (eg in the motor vehicle industry); or specialised financial services may develop (again, for example, in the motor vehicle industry). Such economies occur independently of any change in the size of a particular firm.
- *General economies*. A firm may also benefit from general infrastructural development of the area in which it is located, for example, the improved provision of roads, railways, housing, schools, hospitals and other services. Better services, in turn, also attract better workers and may lower the effective cost of labour. The available economic and social infrastructure is, of course, always an important determinant of a firm's decision to locate in a particular geographical area.

External diseconomies include the following:

- *Shortages*. As an industry grows, growing shortages of specific raw materials or skilled labour might ensue, pushing up their prices and hence the firm's costs.
- *Congestion*. Industrial areas might become overcrowded, pushing up the prices of land, labour and services. Traffic congestion and pollution of the environment may also occur.

These are just some of the possible types of economies and diseconomies of scale that firms may encounter and which will affect their unit or average costs of production. Strong economies of scale often result in firms with significant market power and sometimes pose major problems for public policy – see Chapter 13.

FIGURE 11-8 Alternative long-run average cost curves

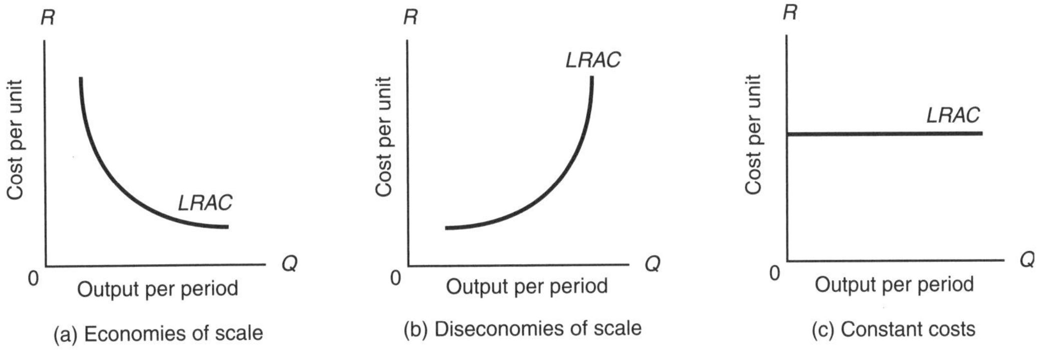

If cost per unit of output falls as output increases, economies of scale are experienced, as illustrated in (a). If cost per unit of output increases as output increases, diseconomies of scale are experienced, as illustrated in (b). The third possibility, illustrated in (c), is that cost per unit of output remains constant as output increases.

Economies of scope

Sometimes it is cheaper to produce two related goods in a single firm rather than in two separate firms. Motorcars and trucks, for example, use common inputs such as technical knowledge, engines and transmissions. The major motor vehicle manufacturers therefore usually produce both cars and trucks. The cost savings achieved by producing related goods in one firm rather than in two separate firms are called **economies of scope**. Another South African example is Sasol, which produces a wide range of related products, including those referred to in Box 11-5.

Long-run average costs

In the long run all inputs are variable and economies or diseconomies of scale may be experienced. Long-run average cost (*LRAC*) curves can therefore take various shapes. The three basic possibilities are illustrated in Figure 11-8. If economies of scale are experienced, the firm's *LRAC* curve will fall as output (ie the scale of production) increases. This is illustrated in Figure 11-8(a). On the other hand, if diseconomies of scale predominate, *LRAC* will rise as output increases. This is illustrated in Figure11-8(b). The third possibility is that neither economies nor diseconomies of scale are experienced. In this case, as illustrated in Figure 11-8(c), the *LRAC* curve is horizontal, indicating constant costs.

It is often assumed that, as a firm expands, it will initially experience economies of scale, illustrated by a downward-sloping *LRAC* curve. If it continues to expand, however, at some stage all economies of scale will have been achieved and the curve will flatten out, indicating constant long-run average cost. At some further stage the firm will get so large that diseconomies of scale set in, illustrated by a rising *LRAC* curve. At this stage, for example, technical and financial economies will begin to be offset by the managerial problems of running a giant undertaking. These three stages can be combined to yield a saucer-shaped *LRAC* curve, as in Figure 11-9. If the rising part of such an *LRAC* curve does not occur, or can be ignored, we speak of an L-shaped *LRAC* curve.

The *LRAC* curves in Figures 11-8 and 11-9 are based on three key assumptions, namely that:

- the prices of the factors of production are given
- the state of technology and the quality (or productivity) of the factors of production are given

FIGURE 11-9 A typical long-run average cost curve

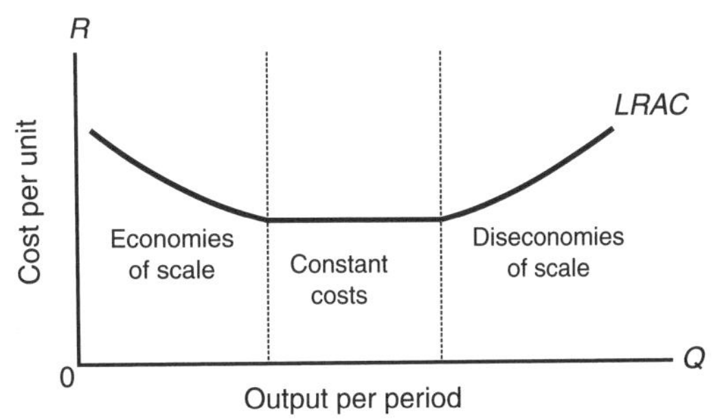

As long as economies of scale are experienced, average costs fall. This is followed by a range of output over which average costs remain constant. At some level of output diseconomies of scale may set in resulting in an increase in average costs.

- firms always choose the least-cost combination of the factors of production to produce each level of output

If, for example, there is a general increase in wages, costs will increase (*ceteris paribus*), illustrated by an upward shift of the *LRAC* curve. On the other hand, if new cost-saving techniques are introduced, costs will decrease (*ceteris paribus*), illustrated by a downward shift of the *LRAC* curve.

Long-run marginal cost

The relationship between long-run average cost (*LRAC*) and long-run marginal cost (*LRMC*) is similar to that between any other set of average and marginal variables. If there are economies of scale, the *LRMC* curve must lie below the *LRAC* curve. The only way in which *LRAC* can decline is if the cost of additional units of output (*LRMC*) is lower than the current average cost, thus pulling it down. This is illustrated in Figure 11-10(a). On the other hand, if there are diseconomies of scale, the *LRMC* curve must lie above the *LRAC* curve. The only way in which *LRAC* can increase is if the cost of additional units of output (*LRMC*) is higher than the current average cost, thus pulling it up. This is illustrated in Figure 11-10(b). If constant costs are experienced, the *LRAC* curve is horizontal. In this case the *LRMC* curve must coincide with the *LRAC* curve. The only way in which

FIGURE 11-10 The relationship between long-run average and marginal costs

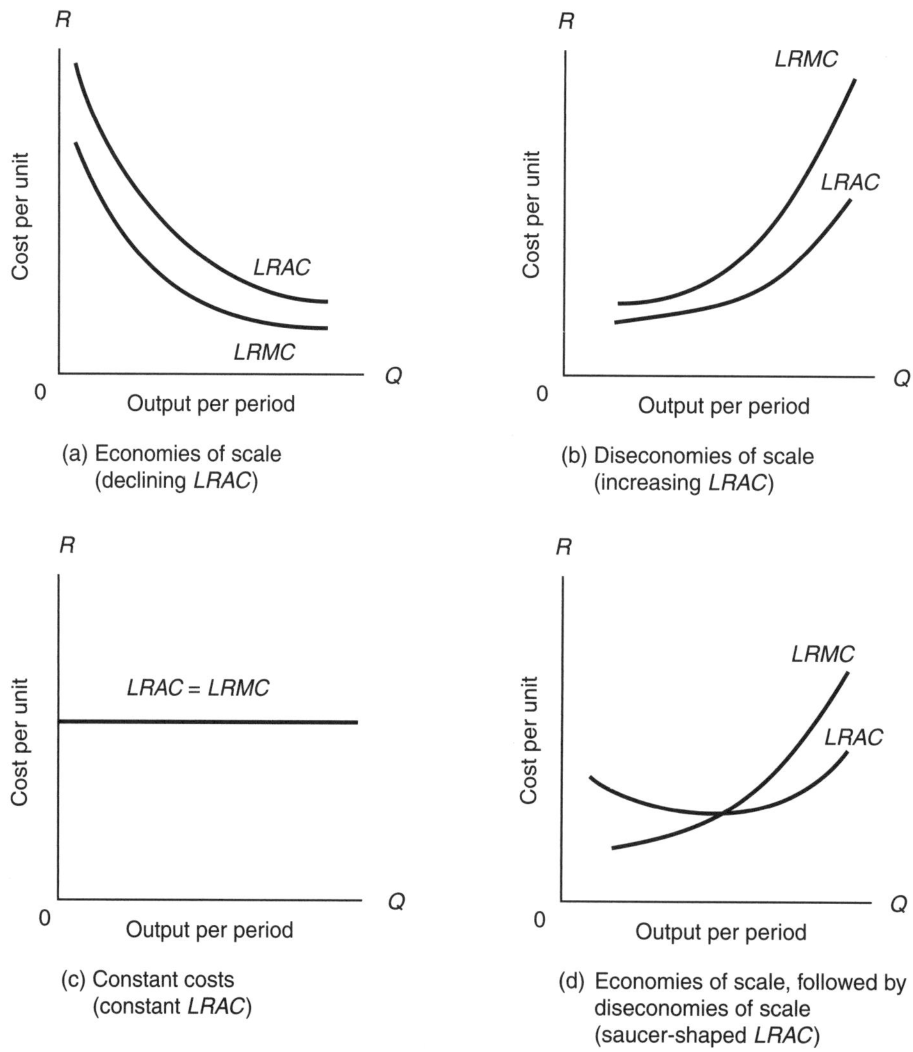

Parts (a) to (d) illustrate the four possible relationships between long-run average cost (LRAC) and long-run marginal cost (LRMC).

LRAC can remain unchanged is if the cost of any additional units of output (*LRMC*) is the same as the current average cost, thus keeping it constant. This is illustrated in Figure 11-10(c). If economies of scale are experienced only up to a certain level of output, followed by diseconomies of scale, the relationship between *LRMC* and *LRAC* will be the same as that explained in Section 11.4. As long as *LRMC* is below *LRAC*, *LRAC* will fall. When *LRMC* is above *LRAC*, *LRAC* will rise. It follows, therefore, that the *LRMC* curve will intersect the *LRAC* curve at the minimum of the *LRAC* curve. This is illustrated in Figure 11-10(d). If the *LRAC* curve has a horizontal section, as in Figure 11-9, then *LRMC* will coincide with *LRAC* along that section before rising above *LRAC*.

The relationship between long-run and short-run average cost curves

In the long run all inputs are variable. The firm can choose to use any quantity per period of, for example, land, buildings, machinery and management. In the long run there are thus no total or average **fixed** costs. In the short run at least one input is fixed and the firm is thus faced with total and average fixed costs.

The long run can be envisaged as a set of alternative short-run situations between which the firm can choose. In each short-run situation the firm faces a given set of short-run costs. In Figure 11-11 $SRAC_1$, $SRAC_2$ and $SRAC_3$ represent three different short-run average cost curves, each pertaining to a situation in which at least one input is fixed. For example, $SRAC_1$ may refer to a situation where the firm operates only one factory. If the firm builds another factory, the average cost curve (for the two factories) is $SRAC_2$ and if it builds a third factory, then average cost (for the three factories) is represented by $SRAC_3$. The long-run average cost (*LRAC*) curve is obtained by joining the lowest portions of the three short-run average cost curves, as indicated by the heavy line in the figure. The firm will never operate at the light portions of the *SRAC* curves in the long run because it will always be able to reduce costs by changing the size of the firm. The heavy line in Figure 11-11 thus represents the long-run average cost which illustrates the least-cost method of production for each level of output.

The *LRAC* curve is called an **envelope curve** since it envelops a series of *SRAC* curves. If we assume that the short-run fixed inputs can be varied by any amount in the long run, there will be an unlimited number of *SRAC* curves and the *LRAC* curve will become smooth, as in Figure 11-12.

FIGURE 11-11 A long-run average cost curve for three scales of production

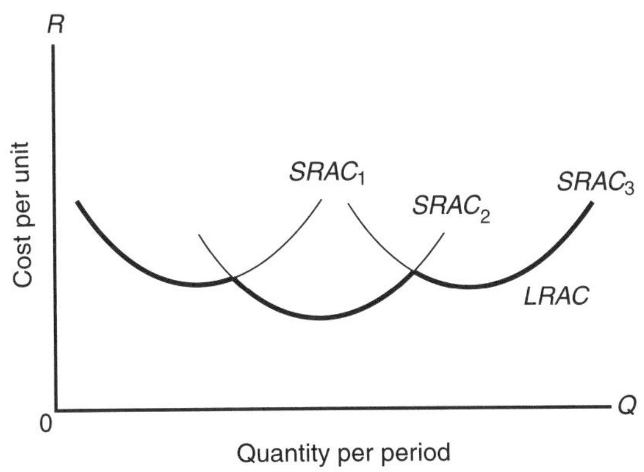

The short-run average cost curves for the three scales of production are $SRAC_1$, $SRAC_2$ and $SRAC_3$. The long-run average cost curve LRAC is obtained by combining the lowest parts of the three short-run curves.

FIGURE 11-12 The long-run average cost curve when short-run fixed inputs can be varied by any amount (in the long run)

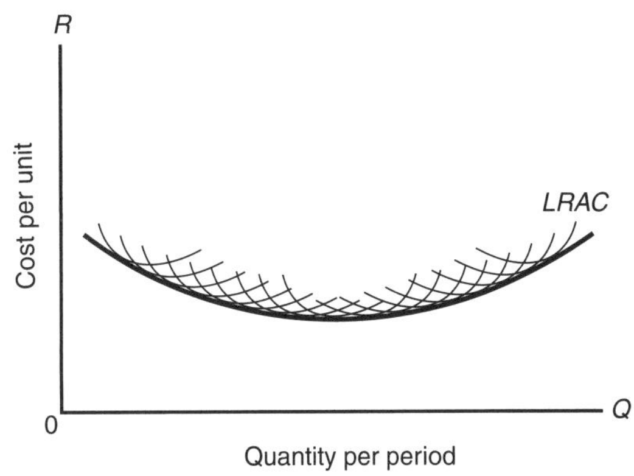

When there are many possible plant sizes, there are many short-run average cost curves, illustrated by the thin lines. By joining the lowest portions of these curves, a smooth long-run average cost curve LRAC is obtained.

Summary

In this chapter we examined production and cost in both the short run and the long run. The basic differences between the short run and the long run are summarised in Table 11-6.

In the following two chapters we use the concepts explained in this chapter to analyse the decisions of firms in different types of market, starting with a perfectly competitive market.

TABLE 11-6 The short run and long run in production and cost theory: a summary

Period	*Inputs used*	*Costs associated with inputs*	*Definition of costs*
Short run	Fixed	Fixed costs	Fixed costs do not change as output changes
	Variable	Variable costs	Variable costs change as output changes
Long run	All variable	Variable costs only	Variable costs change as output changes

IMPORTANT CONCEPTS

Principal-agent problem
Profit
Revenue
Cost
Production function
Total revenue *(TR)*
Average revenue *(AR)*
Marginal revenue *(MR)*
Long run
Short run
Fixed inputs
Variable inputs
Opportunity cost
Explicit costs
Implicit costs
Accounting costs
Economic costs
Private costs
Social costs
Externalities
Accounting profit
Normal profit
Economic profit
Total cost (*TC*)
Average cost (*AC*)
Marginal cost (*MC*)
Law of diminishing (marginal) returns
Total product (*TP*)
Average product (*AP*)
Marginal product (*MP*)
Fixed cost
Variable cost
Total fixed cost (*TFC*)
Total variable cost (*TVC*)
Average fixed cost (*AFC*)
Average variable cost (*AVC*)
Long-run costs
Returns to scale
Economies of scale
Diseconomies of scale
Internal economies
External economies
Economies of scope
Long-run average cost (*LRAC*)
Long-run marginal cost (*LRMC*)
Envelope curve

REVIEW QUESTIONS

1. Explain the difference between the short run and the long run in the theory of production.
2. Which of the following inputs would probably be classified as fixed and which as variable over a period of one month? Why?
   (a) cars to Budget Rent-a-car
   (b) labour to a Nando's franchise
   (c) apples to Liquifruit
   (d) ovens to Albany Bakeries
   (e) timber to Bakker & Steyger, a furniture manufacturer
3. Which of the following costs are fixed costs and which are variable costs if the period under consideration is a calendar year?
   (a) the salaries of permanent lecturers at the University of South Africa
   (b) the cost of cans to the bottlers of Coca-Cola
   (c) the cost of printing machines to the printers of this book
   (d) the cost of fuel to a transport company

4. Explain the difference between (a) accounting costs and economic costs and (b) accounting profit and economic profit.
5. Define normal profit and explain the relationship between total profit, normal profit and economic profit.
6. Many business people have never even heard of marginal cost. Why then do economists use this concept so often? Explain.
7. Explain the relationship between (a) the average product and marginal product of a variable factor of production employed by a firm and (b) the firm's short-run average cost and marginal cost.
8. Is there any connection between the law of diminishing returns and the shape of a firm's short-run average and marginal cost curves? Explain your answer.
9. Explain why average variable cost and average total cost get closer to each other as output increases. At what level of output is total cost equal to total fixed cost?

Nobel Laureates in economics, 1988–2006

1988	Maurice Allais (France)
1989	Trygve Haavelmo (Norway)
1990	Harry M Markowitz, Merton H Miller, William F Sharpe (United States)
1991	Ronald H Coase (Britain)
1992	Gary S Becker (United States)
1993	Robert W. Fogel, Douglass C North (United States)
1994	John C Harsanyi,* John F Nash Jr. (United States), Reinhard Selten* (Germany)
1995	Robert E Lucas Jr (United States)
1996	James A Mirrlees (Britain), William Vickrey* (United States)
1997	Robert C Merton, Myron S Scholes* (United States)
1998	Amartya Sen (India)
1999	Robert A Mundell* (United States)
2000	James J Heckman, Daniel L McFadden (United States)
2001	George A Akerlof, A Michael Spence, Joseph E Stiglitz (United States)
2002	Daniel Kahneman*, Vernon L Smith (United States)
2003	Robert F Engle (United States), Clive WJ Granger (Britain)
2004	Finn E Kydland*, Edward C Prescott (United States)
2005	Robert J Aumann* (Israel), Thomas C Schelling (United States)
2006	Edmund S Phelps (United States)

* Harsanyi was born in Hungary; Selten in Poland; Vickrey, Scholes and Mundell in Canada; Kahneman in Israel; Kydland in Norway; and Aumann in Germany.

Learning outcomes

Once you have studied this chapter you should be able to

- list the conditions which have to be met for perfect competition to exist
- explain the demand curve facing the firm under perfect competition
- explain the short-run equilibrium of the firm under perfect competition
- explain the long-run equilibrium of the firm and the industry under perfect competition
- explain allocative and productive efficiency

12 Perfect competition

By perfect competition I propose to mean a state of affairs in which the demand for the output of the individual seller is perfectly elastic.

JOAN ROBINSON

The system of free competition is a rather peculiar one. Its mechanism is one of fooling entrepreneurs. It requires the pursuit of maximum profit in order to function, but it destroys profits when they are actually pursued by a larger number of people.

OSKAR LANGE

In Chapter 11 we examined a firm's costs of production and distinguished between total, marginal and average cost. We also distinguished between the short run and the long run and showed how a firm's costs are determined by the prices and productivity of the factors of production that it uses.

In this chapter and the next one we derive the equilibrium positions of firms. We want to determine whether or not it is profitable for a firm to produce and, if so, what quantities of the product the firm should supply at different prices of the product. To do this, we have to consider demand conditions as well. In other words, we have to consider both supply and demand.

We assume that firms aim to maximise **profit** (the difference between **revenue** and **cost**). Cost was examined in detail in Chapter 11 but revenue has to be examined in more detail. Total revenue (*TR*) from the production and sale of a product is calculated by multiplying the quantity sold (*Q*) by the price (*P*) of the product. But the price of the product (and therefore also revenue) depends on the structure of the market. In this book we introduce you to the four standard forms of market structure: perfect competition, monopoly, monopolistic competition and oligopoly. In this chapter we focus on the position of a firm which operates under conditions of **perfect competition**. The other three types of market structure are examined in Chapter 13.

We start our analysis of the position of the firm under perfect competition by explaining what perfect competition means. We then introduce the concept of a demand curve for the product of the firm and explain the relationship between total, average and marginal revenue under conditions of perfect competition. In the next section the equilibrium conditions are explained and the equilibrium position of the firm is derived in two alternative ways. We also derive the firm's supply curve and the market supply curve. We then look at the long-run equilibrium of a perfectly competitive firm and industry.

12.1 Perfect competition

We commence our analysis of the behaviour of firms by assuming that there is perfect competition in the goods market. Recall from earlier chapters that a **market** consists of all the buyers (demanders) and sellers (suppliers) of the good or service concerned. Also recall that **competition** occurs on each side of the market. In the goods market the buyers compete to obtain the good and the sellers compete to sell the good to the buyers.

Perfect competition occurs when **none of the individual market participants (ie buyers or sellers) can influence the price of the product**. The price is determined by the interaction of demand and supply and all the participants have to accept that price. In perfectly competitive markets all the participants are therefore **price takers** – they have to accept the price as given and can only decide what quantities to supply or demand at that price.

Requirements

Perfect competition exists if the following conditions are met:

- There must be a **large number of buyers and sellers** of the product – the number must be so large that no individual buyer or seller can affect the market price. Each firm, for example, only supplies a fraction of the total market supply.
- There must be **no collusion** between sellers – each seller must act independently.
- All the goods sold in the market must be **identical** (ie the product must be **homogeneous** – see Section 2.1). There should therefore be no reason for buyers to prefer the product of one seller to the product of another seller.
- Buyers and sellers must be completely free to enter or leave the market – this condition is usually referred to as **complete freedom of entry and exit**. There must be no barriers to entry in the form of legal, financial, technological, physical or other restrictions which inhibit the free movement of buyers or sellers.
- All the buyers and sellers must have **perfect knowledge** of market conditions. For example, if one firm raises its price above the market price, it is assumed that all the buyers will know that the other firms are charging a lower price and will therefore not buy anything from the firm that is charging a higher price.
- There must be **no government intervention** influencing buyers or sellers.
- All the **factors of production must be perfectly mobile**. In other words, labour, capital and the other factors of production must be able to move freely from one market to another.

These conditions are clearly very restrictive and it is hardly surprising that no market meets all the requirements for perfect competition. Approximations to these conditions are found in agriculture, for example in the markets for maize, wheat, fruit and vegetables. An individual farmer is usually regarded as the best example of a perfect competitor. Other markets for fresh produce, like meat and fish markets, may also approximate perfect competition. However, producers often form cooperatives to control the supply of agricultural products, and government also tends to intervene in markets for agricultural products. The closest approximations to perfect competition are probably in the international commodity markets where there are thousands of sellers and ultimately millions of buyers; entry and exit are easy; the products are graded and those in a given grade are therefore identical; the participants are well informed about market conditions; and they can purchase or sell large quantities of the product at the ruling market price. In these markets no individual firm has any market power – all the firms are **price takers**.

Financial markets, like the JSE Securities Exchange, also approximate perfect competition. There are many buyers and sellers, the goods (eg shares in a company) are homogeneous and anyone is free to participate.

Relevance

But why study perfect competition if it is only approximated in a small percentage of markets?

- We can learn a lot about the functioning of those markets (particularly in agriculture) where the conditions for perfect competition come close to being satisfied.
- Perfect competition represents a clear and meaningful starting point for analysing the determination of price and output.
- Perfect competition represents a standard or norm against which the functioning of all other markets can be compared. This is common practice in all

branches of science – even in the natural sciences it is common to use a model based on a set of very restrictive conditions as a yardstick against which other situations can be compared.

- A good knowledge of the functioning of perfectly competitive markets, along with information about conditions in a particular market (including how it deviates from perfect competition), is often sufficient for a meaningful analysis of that market.

The model of perfect competition can therefore always be useful, provided it is used with sufficient care. Note, however, that the adjective "perfect" in perfect competition does not mean that it is necessarily the most desirable form of competition – it simply signifies the highest or most complete degree of competition.

12.2 The demand for the product of the firm

Under perfect competition the price of a product is determined by supply and demand. The individual firm is a price taker and can sell any quantity at the market price. No firm will charge a price higher than the prevailing market price because it will then lose all of its customers. Nor will a firm gain anything by charging a price that is lower than the existing market price, since it can sell as many units of its output as it wishes at the market price.

Under perfect competition the individual firm is faced by a demand curve which is horizontal (or perfectly elastic) at the existing market price. We call this curve the **demand curve for the product of the firm**. It is sometimes also called the **firm's sales curve**, the **firm's demand curve**, or the **demand curve facing the firm**. The position of the individual firm under perfect competition is illustrated in Figure 12-1. The graph on the left shows that the price of the product (P_1) is determined in the market by the forces of supply (*SS*) and demand (*DD*). The position of the individual firm is shown in the graph on the right. The firm can sell any quantity at the prevailing market price. At higher prices the quantity demanded will fall to zero (since consumers will be able to purchase the product at a price of P_1 from any other supplier). Nor will the firm charge a lower price than P_1 because it can sell all its output at a price of P_1. The horizontal curve at P_1 is the demand curve for the product of the firm.

Under perfect competition the firm receives the same price for any number of units of the product that it sells. Its **marginal revenue** (*MR*) and **average revenue** (*AR*) are thus both **equal to the market price**, that is, $MR = AR = P$. We know that a firm's total revenue (*TR*) is equal to the price of the product (*P*) multiplied by the quantity sold (*Q*), ie $TR = P \times Q$ ($= PQ$). Under perfect competition the price is given, thus for each additional unit that the firm sells, total revenue will increase by an amount equal to the price of the product. This is simply another way of stating that $MR = AR = P$. The firm's total revenue can be represented graphically by a straight line which starts at the origin and which has a slope equal to the price of the product, as shown in Figure 12-2.

FIGURE 12-1 The demand curve for the product of the firm under perfect competition

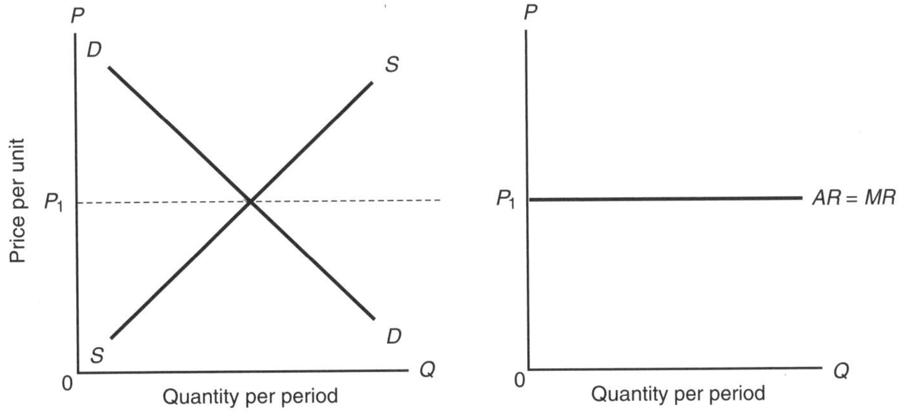

The graph on the left shows that the price of the product is determined in the market by demand and supply. The firm can sell its whole output at that price. This is indicated by the horizontal line on the right. This line is the demand curve for the product of the firm. It is also called the firm's sales curve, the firm's demand curve, or the demand curve facing the firm. The firm's average revenue (AR) and marginal revenue (MR) are equal to the price of the product.

FIGURE 12-2 Total revenue of the firm under perfect competition

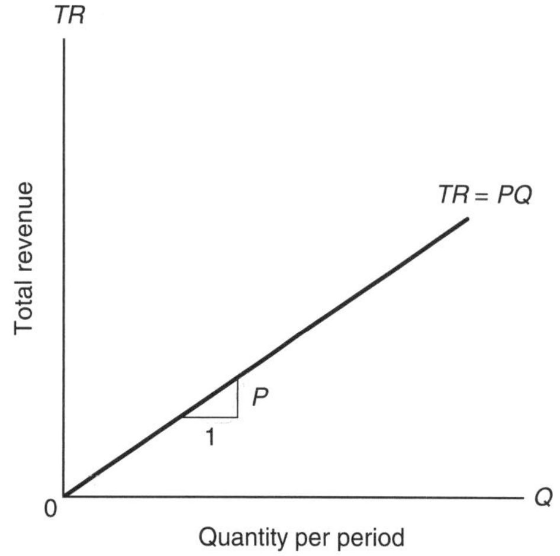

Since the firm is a price taker, the price of the product (P) is given and the firm's total revenue (TR) increases by a constant amount for each additional unit sold. TR is thus a straight line through the origin with a slope equal to the price (P). The equation for total revenue is TR = PQ.

In Box 12-1 the relationships between price, total revenue, marginal revenue and average revenue are explained with the aid of a numerical example.

12.3 The equilibrium of the firm under perfect competition

We now examine the equilibrium (or profit-maximising) position of the firm under conditions of perfect competition. We do so in two stages: first we examine the equilibrium conditions which apply to any firm, irrespective of the type of market in which it operates, and then we apply these conditions to the specific case of perfect competition.

The equilibrium conditions (for any firm)

Firms want to maximise profit. Economic profit is the difference between revenue and cost (which includes normal profit). To examine the behaviour of firms, we therefore have to examine and combine their revenue and cost structures. Once these are known, two decisions have to be taken:

- The firm must first decide whether or not it is worth producing at all. Under certain conditions it would not be in the firm's interest to produce (but rather to shut down its operations).

BOX 12-1 TOTAL, MARGINAL AND AVERAGE REVENUE UNDER PERFECT COMPETITION: A NUMERICAL EXAMPLE

Suppose a firm operates under conditions of perfect competition and that the market price of its product is R20 per unit. The firm is a price taker and its total, average and marginal revenue for the first five units sold will be as follows:

Quantity (units) Q	Price per unit (rand) P	Total revenue (rand) TR (= PQ)	Marginal revenue (rand) MR (= ΔTR/ΔQ = P)	Average revenue (rand) AR (= TR/Q =P)
0	20	0		0
			20	
1	20	20		20
			20	
2	20	40		20
			20	
3	20	60		20
			20	
4	20	80		20
			20	
5	20	100		20

The same relationships will apply at greater quantities. The demand curve facing the firm is a horizontal line at the level of the market price (R20), similar to the one illustrated in the right-hand part of Figure 12-1. The total revenue curve is a straight line through the origin with a positive slope equal to the price of the product (R20), similar to the curve in Figure 12-2.

- If it is worth producing, the firm must determine the level of production (ie the quantity) at which profit is maximised (or losses minimised).

These decisions have to be taken in *any* firm. Before examining the position of a firm under conditions of perfect competition, we take a look at the two rules for profit-maximisation which apply to all firms, irrespective of the market conditions under which they operate.

■ THE SHUT-DOWN RULE

The first rule is that a firm should produce only if **total revenue is equal to, or greater than, total variable cost** (which includes normal profit). This is often called the shut-down (or close-down) rule, but it can also be called the start-up rule because it does not just indicate when a firm should stop producing a product – it also indicates when a firm should start (or restart) production. The shut-down rule can also be stated in terms of unit costs – a firm should only produce if **average revenue (ie price) is equal to, or greater than, average variable cost**.

In the long run all costs are variable. Production should therefore only take place in the long run if total revenue is sufficient to cover *all* costs of production. This is quite straightforward. But what about the short run, when certain costs are fixed? Should production occur only if total revenue is sufficient to cover total costs (ie total fixed costs and total variable costs)? The answer is no.

Once a firm is established, it cannot escape its fixed costs. Fixed costs are incurred even if output is zero (ie if the firm does not produce at all). If the firm can earn a total revenue greater than its total variable cost (or an average revenue greater than its average variable cost), then the difference can help cover some of the unavoidable fixed costs of the firm. It would be advisable for the firm to maintain production in the short run, even though it is operating at an economic loss. If total revenue is just sufficient to cover total variable costs (ie if average revenue is equal to average variable costs) it is immaterial whether or not the firm continues production – its loss will be the same in both cases (ie equal to its fixed costs). In such conditions firms tend to continue production in order to retain their employees and clients.

If total revenue is not sufficient to cover total variable costs (ie if average revenue is lower than average variable cost), the firm will not produce, because to do so will result in a loss greater than its fixed costs. In other words, the firm's losses will be minimised by not producing at all.

■ THE PROFIT-MAXIMISING RULE

The second rule is that firms should produce that quantity of the product such that profits are maximised, or losses minimised. Since the same rule applies for profit maximisation and loss minimisation, we usually refer to profit maximisation only, and we do not always mention that the aim is also to minimise losses.

Profit maximisation can be explained in terms of total revenue (*TR*) and total cost (*TC*) or in terms of marginal revenue (*MR*) and marginal cost (*MC*). Since profit is the difference between revenue and cost it is obvious that **profits are maximised where the positive difference between total revenue and total cost is the greatest**. However, it is usually more useful to express the profit-maximisation condition in terms of revenue and cost **per unit** of production. The rule is that **profit is maximised where marginal revenue (*MR*) is equal to marginal cost (*MC*)**.

To explain why profits are maximised where *MR* = *MC*, it is useful to consider what happens if *MR* is not equal to *MC*. If marginal revenue *MR* (ie the addition to revenue as a result of the production of an extra unit of the product) is greater than marginal cost *MC* (ie the cost of producing that extra unit), the firm is still making a profit on the last (extra) unit produced. The firm can therefore add to its total profit by expanding its production until no extra profit is made on the last unit produced, that is, until the revenue earned from the last unit (*MR*) is equal to the cost of producing the last unit (*MC*). At that quantity the firm's profit is maximised.

If the firm continues producing beyond that point, the cost of producing each additional unit of output (*MC*) will be greater than the revenue gained from selling it (*MR*). In other words, the firm will make a loss on the production of each additional unit of output and its profit will therefore decrease. Profits are maximised when marginal revenue *MR* is just equal to marginal cost *MC*.

The different possibilities can be summarised as follows:

- When *MR* is greater than *MC* (ie $MR > MC$), output should be expanded.
- When *MR* is equal to *MC* (ie $MR = MC$), profits are maximised.
- When *MR* is lower than *MC* (ie $MR < MC$), output should be reduced.

As we mentioned earlier, this rule and the shut-down rule apply to any firm, irrespective of the type of market in which it operates – see Box 12-2. We now apply these rules to a firm operating in a perfectly competitive market.

The profit-maximising (or equilibrium) position of the firm under perfect competition

We now combine the cost curves derived in Chapter 11, the two profit-maximising rules which apply to all

BOX 12-2 SHORT-RUN DECISIONS OF A FIRM, THE IRRELEVANCE OF SUNK COSTS AND THE IMPORTANCE OF THE MARGINAL PRINCIPLE

In the long run, when all the inputs are variable, a firm will continue to produce only if total revenue is sufficient to cover total cost (including normal profit). In the short run, however, the situation is somewhat more complicated and can be summarised as follows:

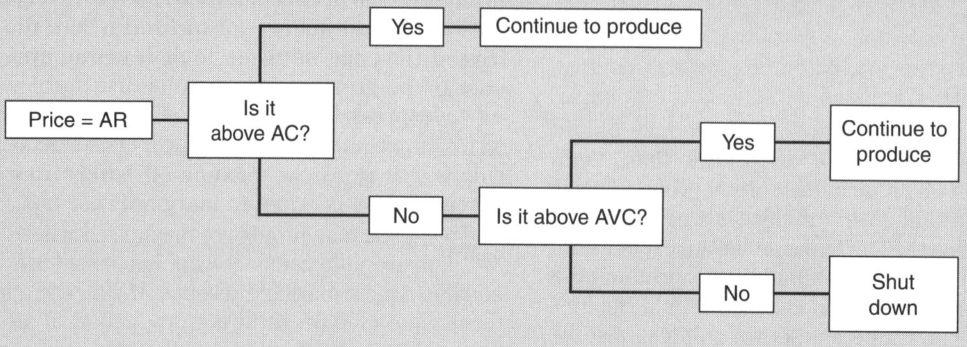

The basic difference between short-run and long-run costs is that while certain costs are fixed in the short run, all costs are variable in the long run. In Box 11-3 we also introduced the notion of **sunk costs**. A sunk cost is a cost incurred in the past that cannot be changed by current decisions and cannot be recovered. The firm's short-run fixed costs are an example of sunk costs. The firm cannot recover these costs by temporarily stopping production. The firm's fixed costs are sunk in the short run and the firm can ignore these costs when deciding whether or not to produce and how much to produce. Only the variable costs, over which the firm has control, should be taken into account. This explains why a number of large firms continue to produce despite reporting huge losses. Take a big airline, for example. If the airline has bought a number of aircraft and cannot resell them, this cost is a sunk cost in the short run. The opportunity cost of a flight includes only the variable costs of fuel, the wages of pilots and flight attendants, etc. As long as the total revenue from flying exceeds these variable costs, the airline should continue to operate. The same principle applies to any other firm. Sunk costs should not be taken into account in short-run decisions.

Sunk costs are also important in everyday life. The principle of "let bygones be bygones" or "do not cry over spilt milk" applies to many spheres of life. For example, if you buy an expensive pair of shoes and they turn out to be very uncomfortable you should not continue wearing them simply because you paid a lot of money for them. Likewise, if you purchase shares in a company at (say) R10 each and the price falls to R6, you should not take the R10 that you paid for them into account when deciding whether to keep or sell the shares. Your decision should be based only on the expected future price of the shares. If there is no prospect of an increase, you should sell them.

The examples in this box illustrate one of the most important lessons of economics: **always look at the marginal costs and marginal benefits of decisions and ignore past or sunk costs**. Do not complain about yesterday's losses. Calculate the extra costs you will incur by any decision, and weigh these against its advantages. Always base decisions on marginal costs and marginal benefits.

firms, and the demand curve for the product of the firm, to examine the equilibrium of the firm under perfect competition. We know that such a firm is a price taker (ie it has no control over the market price). The firm can only decide to sell or not to sell at the ruling price. This means that the firm does not have to make any pricing decisions – it can only choose the output (quantity) at which it will maximise its profits (or minimise its losses). That quantity, we have seen, is **where the positive difference between total revenue *TR* and total cost *TC* is at a maximum**, or (which amounts to the same thing) **where marginal revenue *MR* is equal to marginal cost *MC***, provided, of course, that average revenue *AR* (= *P*) is at least equal to short-run average variable cost *AVC* (the shut-down rule). We now examine the two different approaches to determine the profit-maximising position of the firm under perfect competition.

■ EQUILIBRIUM IN TERMS OF TOTAL REVENUE AND TOTAL COST

The cost structures of most firms follow the same pattern, irrespective of the type of market in which they function. The explanation of costs in Chapter 11 thus applies to most firms, including those which operate in perfectly competitive markets. The total cost curve is shaped like a reversed S, as illustrated in Figure 11-4. In the **short run** (to which we shall confine ourselves in the remainder of this section), the total cost curve does not start at the origin, since part of the firm's cost is fixed. This is illustrated in Figure 12-3.

Total revenue (*TR*) of the firm under perfect competition was illustrated in Figure 12-2 as a straight line with a positive slope which starts at the origin and has a slope equal to the price of the product. In Figure 12-4 we combine such a total revenue (*TR*) curve with the total cost (*TC*) curve illustrated in Figure 12-3. Economic profit is the difference between *TR* and *TC*. Graphically it is represented by the vertical distance between the *TR* curve and the *TC* curve. At levels of output below Q_1 in Figure 12-4, *TC* is greater than *TR* and the firm therefore incurs economic losses (indicated by the shaded area). At Q_1 the firm's total economic profit is zero (since $TR = TC$). Between Q_1 and Q_2 the firm makes an economic profit at each level of output (indicated by the shaded area), since $TR > TC$.

FIGURE 12-3 Total short-run costs of the firm

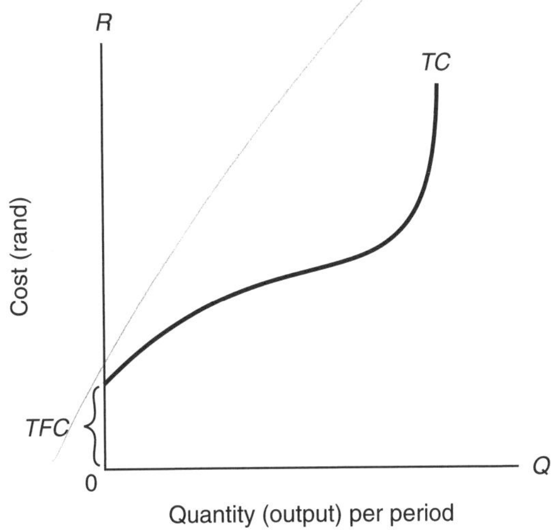

The total cost (TC) curve is shaped like a reversed S. It does not start at the origin, indicating that part of the firm's costs (TFC) is fixed.

At Q_2 total economic profit is zero once more and at higher levels of output the firm again incurs economic losses.

The firm's profit will be maximised where the positive vertical difference between *TR* and *TC* is the greatest (ie somewhere between Q_1 and Q_2). One can determine this with a ruler, by measuring the distance between *TR* and *TC* at each possible quantity. Alternatively, one can draw a tangent to the *TC* curve, parallel to the *TR* curve, such as the broken line in Figure 12-4. At the point of tangency the vertical difference (ie total profit) will be at a maximum. There is, however, a way of determining the level of output at which profit is maximised without using a graph or a ruler. This is by applying the $MR = MC$ rule which we explained earlier.

FIGURE 12-4 Total revenue, total cost and total economic profit

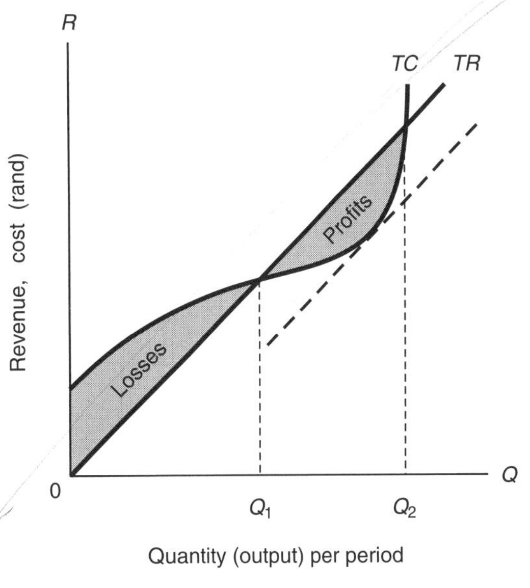

The firm's economic profits (or losses) are indicated by the vertical difference between total revenue TR and total cost TC. Between 0 and Q_1 the firm makes losses. At Q_1 the firm's economic profit (loss) is zero and between Q_1 and Q_2 the firm makes an economic profit. At Q_2 economic profit is again zero. The broken line is parallel to TR and tangent to TC. At the point of tangency profit is maximised.

■ EQUILIBRIUM IN TERMS OF MARGINAL REVENUE AND MARGINAL COST

Earlier in this section we explained that any firm maximises its profit (or minimises its losses) where marginal revenue *MR* is equal to marginal cost *MC*. The marginal revenue of a firm in a perfectly competitive market was derived in Section 12.2. In Figure 12-1 we showed that the firm's marginal revenue *MR* is equal to the market price *P* of the product (since each unit of output has to be sold at the market price, over which the individual firm has no control). The profit-maximising rule in the case of a perfectly competitive firm can therefore also be stated as *P* = *MC* (since *MR* = *P*).

Marginal cost was explained in Chapter 11. Recall that the marginal cost curve is U-shaped. However, as explained in Box 12-3, only the rising part of the *MC* curve is relevant to our analysis. We now use a numerical example to explain why profit is maximised when *MR* (or *P*, in this case) is equal to *MC*.

Suppose a firm produces a product which it sells in a perfectly competitive market where the price is R10 per unit. The firm's fixed cost amounts to R5. (The numbers have been kept small to keep the example as simple as possible.) The firm's daily output, revenue and cost are summarised in Table 12-1. The marginal revenue *MR* and marginal cost *MC* of the firm are also shown graphically in Figure 12-5.

BOX 12-3 MARGINAL COST AND PROFIT MAXIMISATION

In this box we explain why profits are only maximised along the rising part of the marginal cost curve *MC*. From Chapter 11 we know that *MC* usually falls before it starts rising. We also know that under perfect competition, marginal revenue *MR* is equal to the price *P* of the product. *MR* therefore stays constant at all levels of output. It follows that *MR* can be equal to *MC* at two different levels of output, as in the figure below, and the question arises as to what is signified at these two points (corresponding to quantities Q_1 and Q_2 in the figure). The answer is that losses are maximised at a quantity such as Q_1 (ie where *MR* = *MC* along the falling part of the *MC* curve), while profits are maximised at a quantity such as Q_2 (ie where *MR* = *MC* along the rising part of the *MC* curve).

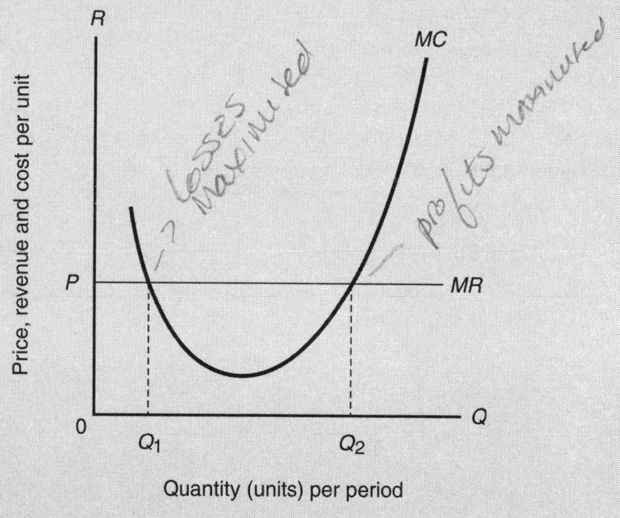

The latter case (ie the position at Q_2) is explained in detail in the text. All that remains is to show why losses are maximised at a point such as Q_1 and why we can therefore ignore the declining part of the marginal cost curve.

The answer is quite simple. At any point to the left of Q_1, *MC* lies above *MR*. In other words each additional unit of the product up to Q_1 costs more to produce than the price at which it can be sold. At this stage the firm's *AR* is also less than its *AC*. Up to Q_1 the firm therefore only makes losses. At quantities greater than Q_1 marginal revenue *MR* is greater than marginal cost *MC* and the firm starts earning a profit on each additional unit produced. The total loss of the firm thus starts to fall, and can turn into a total profit at some stage (ie where *AR* becomes greater than *AC*). At Q_2 the firm's profit is maximised (or its losses minimised). It should be clear therefore that the falling part of the *MC* curve can be disregarded when we analyse the equilibrium position of the firm.

TABLE 12-1 Revenue and cost of a hypothetical firm

Quantity of the product Q	Price per unit (R) P	Total revenue (R) TR	Marginal revenue (R) MR	Total cost (R) TC	Marginal cost (R) MC	Total profit (R) TR–TC
0	10	0		5		–5
			10		4	
1	10	10		9		1
			10		6	
2	10	20		15		5
			10		8	
3	10	30		23		7
			10		10	
4	10	40		33		7
			10		12	
5	10	50		45		5

The marginal cost *MC* of the first unit produced is R4, indicated by point *a* in Figure 12-5. This is lower than the marginal revenue of R10 (ie the price of the product). The production of the first unit thus adds R6 (ie R10 – R4) to the profit of the firm. Likewise, the *MC* of the second unit (R6) is also lower than the *MR* of the second unit (R10). The production of the second unit thus adds R4 (ie R10 – R6) to the profit of the firm. Point *c* in Figure 12-5 shows that the production of the third unit costs R8. It can be sold for R10 and

FIGURE 12-5 Marginal revenue and marginal cost of a firm operating in a perfectly competitive market

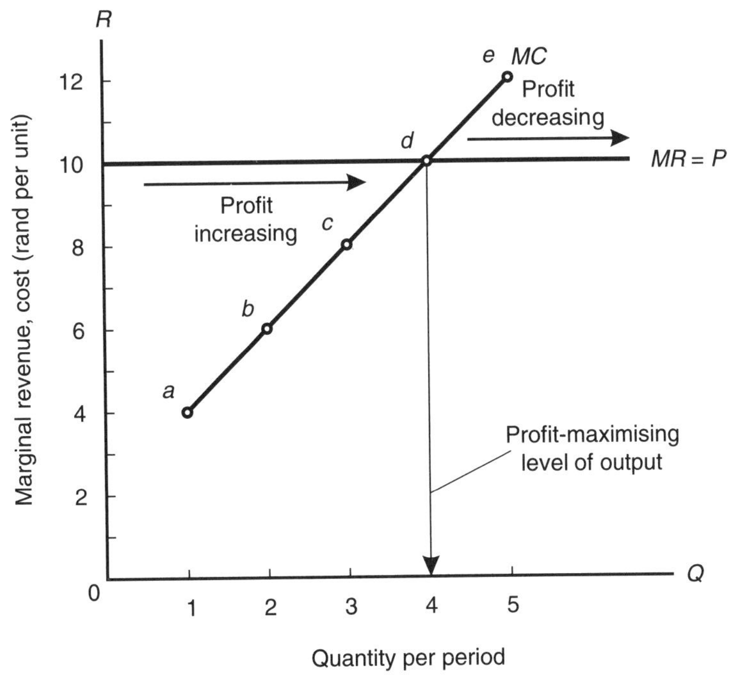

Marginal revenue MR is equal to the price P of the product. Marginal cost MC increases as more units of the product are produced. Profit is maximised where MR (or P) = MC, that is, at an output level of 4 units. At lower levels of production, profit can be increased by expanding production. If more than 4 units of the product are produced, profit starts falling.

the firm will therefore add to its profit by producing the third unit. The extra profit will be R2 (ie R10 – R8). For the fourth unit $MC = MR$ (= P) = R10 and the firm therefore makes no further profit. This serves as a signal that the point of maximum profit has been reached. If the firm produces 5 units of the product, MC (indicated by e in Figure 12-5) will be R12, which is greater than MR. The firm's profit will thus decline by R2 (ie R10 – R12) if a fifth unit of the product is produced.

This example confirms the conclusion reached earlier, namely that a firm should expand its production as long as $MR > MC$, up to the point where $MR = MC$ (at which point profit will be maximised). If it continues producing beyond that point, MR will be lower than MC and the firm's profit will fall.

The firm's profit position can be illustrated clearly by adding average cost AC to the diagram showing average revenue AR, marginal revenue MR and marginal cost MC. Recall, from Chapter 11, that average cost AC consists of average fixed cost AFC and average variable cost AVC. The firm's profit per unit of output (or average profit) is equal to the difference between average revenue AR and average cost AC. As long as AR is greater than AC the firm is earning an **economic profit**. When AR is equal to AC the firm only earns a **normal profit**. Recall, from Chapter 11, that normal profit is included in the firm's cost.

Figure 12-6 shows the average revenue AR, marginal revenue MR, average cost AC and marginal cost MC of a firm under perfect competition. AR and MR are both equal to the price P of the product and are represented by the same horizontal line at the level of the market price (as shown in Figure 12-1). The cost structure of the firm is the same as that explained in Chapter 11 (see, for example, Figure 11-6). In Figure 12-6 we show three different possibilities. The same set of unit cost curves is used throughout, but we show three different market prices, and therefore three different AR and MR curves.

In Figure 12-6(a) the market price is P_1. This is, of course, equal to the firm's AR and MR. Profit is maximised where MR (= P_1, in this case) is equal to MC. This occurs at a quantity of Q_1. At Q_1 the firm's average revenue AR (= P_1) is greater than its average total cost AC (which is indicated as C_1 on the vertical axis). The firm thus makes an **economic profit** (or supernormal profit) per unit of production of $P_1 - C_1$. The firm's total profit is given by the shaded area $C_1P_1E_1M$, which is equal to the profit per unit of output ($P_1 - C_1$) multiplied by the quantity produced (Q_1). Alternatively, the area representing total profit can be obtained by subtracting the firm's total cost from its total revenue. The firm's total revenue is equal to the price of the product P_1 multiplied by the quantity produced (and sold) Q_1. This is equal to the area $0P_1E_1Q_1$. Similarly, the firm's total cost is obtained by multiplying its average cost C_1 by the quantity produced Q_1. This is equal

FIGURE 12-6 Different possible short-run equilibrium positions of the firm under perfect competition

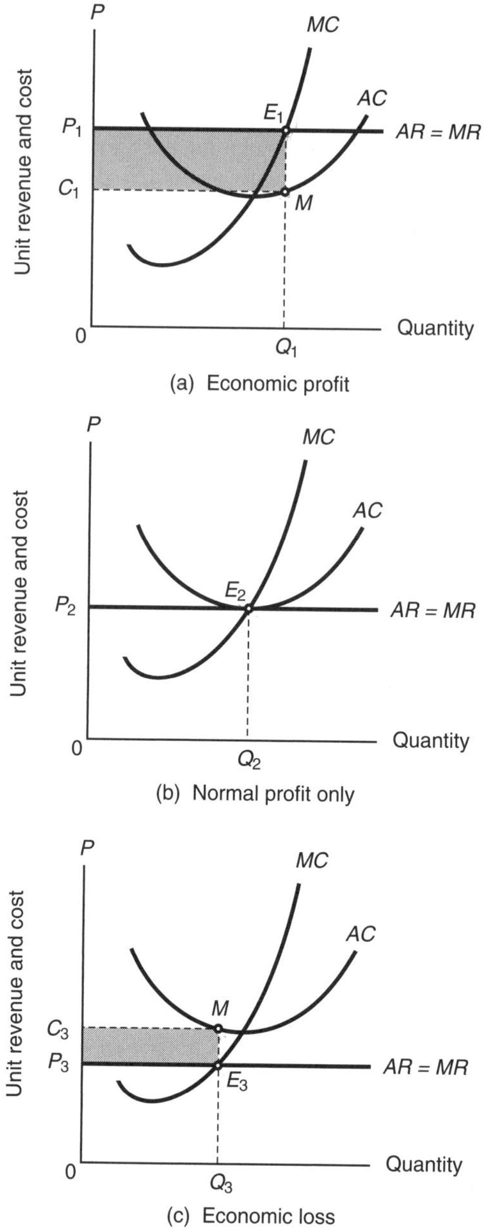

In the short run a firm's economic profit may be positive, zero or negative. In (a) we show a situation in which the firm makes an economic profit, equal to the shaded area. In (b) the firm just breaks even. It earns a normal profit but no economic profit. In (c) the firm incurs an economic loss, equal to the shaded area. If the price P (= AR) lies above the minimum AVC (not shown in the figure) the firm will continue production in the short run. If it lies below the minimum AVC, the firm will close down.

to the area $0C_1MQ_1$. The difference between these two areas is the shaded area $C_1P_1E_1M$, which represents the firm's total economic profit.

In Figure 12-6(b) the market price (and therefore also the firm's *AR* and *MR*) is P_2. It is equal to *MC* at the point where *MC* intersects *AC* (ie at the minimum point of *AC*). The corresponding level of output is Q_2. At that level of output *AR* is equal to *AC* (and *TR* = *TC*) and the firm therefore does not earn an economic profit. It does, however, earn a **normal profit**, since all its costs, which include normal profit, are fully covered.

In Figure 12-6(c) the market price (and therefore also the firm's *AR* and *MR*) is equal to P_3. *MR* or price is equal to *MC* at a quantity of Q_3. At Q_3 the firm's average revenue *AR* is lower than its average cost *AC*. It therefore makes an **economic loss** per unit of output, equal to the difference between C_3 and P_3. The total economic loss is indicated by the shaded area $P_3C_3ME_3$. Whether or not the firm should continue production will depend on the level of *AR* (ie P_3) relative to the firm's average variable cost *AVC*, which is not shown in the figure. If *AR* is greater than *AVC*, the firm will be able to recoup some of its fixed costs and should therefore continue producing in the short run. However, if *AR* is lower than *AVC*, the firm should close down in the short run, thereby restricting its losses to its fixed costs.

The situations illustrated in Figure 12-6 are also summarised in Figure 12-7 in the next section.

The equilibrium condition of the firm under perfect competition may be summarised as follows: **Profit is maximised (or loss minimised) when a firm produces an output where marginal revenue equals marginal cost, provided marginal cost is rising and lies above minimum average variable cost.**

12.4 The supply curve of the firm and the market supply curve

In the previous section we explained that a firm maximises its profits where marginal revenue (*MR*) is equal to marginal cost (*MC*), provided that average revenue *AR* (ie the price of the product) is sufficient to cover average variable cost (*AVC*). Under perfect competition, price *P* is equal to marginal revenue *MR* and average revenue *AR*. The firm will therefore produce the quantity where *P* is equal to *MC*, provided that this occurs where *P* is equal to, or greater than, *AVC*. The rising part of the firm's *MC* curve above the minimum of *AVC* can thus be regarded as the firm's supply curve. In Figure 12-7 this is illustrated by the part of the *MC* curve above point *b*. We show various quantities that will be supplied at different prices, and we also show the close-down point *b* and the break-even point *d*.

FIGURE 12-7 The supply curve of the firm

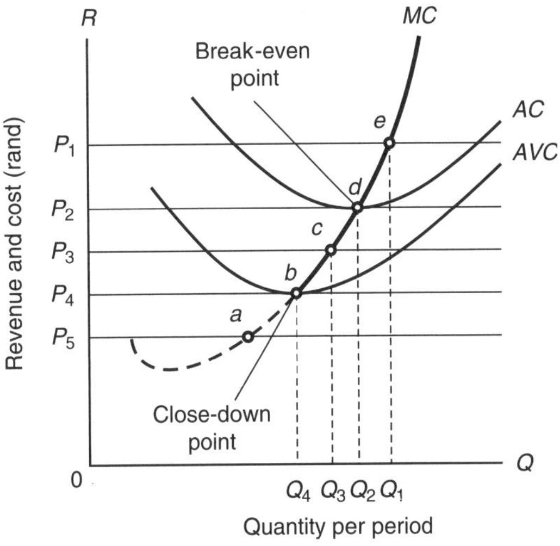

The rising portion of the firm's marginal cost curve above the minimum of its average variable cost curve at point b is the firm's supply curve. If the price is P_5, the firm will not produce at all. If the price is P_4, the firm will be at its close-down point (b) and it is immaterial if it shuts down or continues production. If the price is P_3, the firm will minimise its economic losses by producing a quantity Q_3, corresponding to point c. If the price is P_2, the firm will make normal profit (ie it will break even) at point d, which corresponds to a quantity Q_2. If the price is P_1, the firm will maximise economic profit at point e, that is, it will produce a quantity Q_1.

The market supply curve is obtained by adding the supply curves of the individual firms horizontally. This was explained in Chapter 7. There, however, we simply assumed that the firm's supply curve and the market supply curve slope upward from left to right. In the present chapter we have explained why this is the case. The supply curves slope upwards because the marginal cost curves slope upwards, that is, because marginal cost increases as output increases. (The marginal cost curves, in turn, slope upwards because the marginal product curves slope downwards – on account of the law of diminishing returns.)

We are now also in a better position to explain changes in supply, which are illustrated by shifts of the market supply curve. In Chapter 7 we mentioned, for example, that supply will change if the number of firms change or if the prices of the factors of production (eg labour) change. Since the market supply curve is the sum of the individual supply curves, an increase in the number of firms will shift the market supply curve to the right, and a reduction in the number of firms will move the market supply curve to the left, *ceteris paribus*. If the price of a variable input (such as labour) changes, both marginal cost MC and average variable cost AVC will change. For example, if the price of labour (ie the wage rate) increases, MC and AVC will move upwards and the market supply curve will also move upwards (ie to the left), indicating a fall in supply (of each individual firm and in the market).

12.5 Long-run equilibrium of the firm and the industry under perfect competition

So far we have examined only the position of an individual firm in the short run. We turn now to the long run and examine, in addition, the position of the industry (ie the collection of firms that supply a specific product in the market). In the long run, two things can change. First, new firms can enter the industry and existing firms can leave. Second, all factors of production become variable (recall the definition and analysis of the long run in the previous chapter) and existing firms earning economic profit in the short run may decide to expand their plant sizes to realise economies of scale. These two changes are now examined. Initially, we ignore changes in plant size and costs and focus only on the impact of entry and exit on the long-run equilibrium of the firm and the industry. After we have explained this, we use long-run cost curves to extend the analysis.

The impact of entry and exit on the equilibrium of the firm and the industry

In the previous two sections we saw that an individual firm can be in equilibrium in the short run where it makes an economic profit or an economic loss. These positions, however, are not sustainable in the long run under conditions of perfect competition. When firms are making economic profits, this will induce new firms to enter the industry and when this happens, the market (or industry) supply will increase, thus reducing the market price, *ceteris paribus*. Similarly, firms making economic losses will leave the industry in the long run, thus reducing the market (or industry) supply and raising the market price, *ceteris paribus*. **The industry will only be in equilibrium in the long run if all the firms are making normal profits.** Only then will there be no inducement for new firms to enter the industry, or for existing firms to leave the industry. With complete freedom of entry and exit, there will always be some movement (ie disequilibrium) in the industry when firms are making economic profits or losses. Disequilibrium, and the process whereby equilibrium is reached, can be explained with the aid of a series of diagrams.

We start, in Figure 12-8, by showing the long-run equilibrium of the firm and the industry. In Figure 12-8(a) we show that the individual firm is only making a normal profit. It is therefore covering all its costs (including normal profit). The firm is doing just as well as it could if its resources were employed elsewhere. There is thus no incentive for existing firms to leave the industry or for new firms to enter the industry. In Figure 12-8(b) we show the market demand and supply of the product, which determines the market price (and therefore the *AR* and *MR* of the individual firm). The vertical axes in (a) and (b) are exactly the same – both measure the price per unit of the product. The horizontal axes both measure quantities, but the horizontal scales are different since each firm supplies only a small, insignificant part of the whole market. In the figure this is indicated by using units on the horizontal axis in (a) and thousands of units on the horizontal axis in (b). (The reason why the price is labelled P_2 will become obvious as we proceed.)

In Figure 12-9 we show a situation in which the individual firm initially earns an economic profit. The initial demand and supply curves in (b) are D_1 and S_1 respectively, and the market price is P_1. The individual firm in (a) makes an economic profit at E_1 (ie at price P_1). However, because the existing firms are making economic profits, new firms enter the industry, and the market (or industry) supply curve shifts to the right. This process will continue until the new supply curve is S_2, and the market price is P_2 (corresponding to the equilibrium point E_2). At E_2 (ie at a price of P_2) the individual firm earns a normal profit only and there is no reason for more new firms to enter the industry. The industry and each individual firm is in equilibrium at a price of P_2. This corresponds to the equilibrium at price P_2 in Figure 12-8.

In Figure 12-10 we start off with a situation where the individual firm is making an economic loss. The initial demand and supply curves in (b) are D_1 and S_1 respectively, and the initial market price is P_1. At P_1 the individual firm makes an economic loss where MR_1 = MC at E_1. This loss, however, cannot be sustained in the long run and some firms leave the industry. As firms leave the industry, the market (or industry) supply curve shifts to the left. The process will continue until the new supply curve is S_2 and the market price is P_2 (corresponding to the equilibrium point E_2). At E_2 (ie at a price of P_2) the individual firm earns a normal profit only and there is no reason for more firms to leave the industry (or for new firms to enter the industry). The industry and each individual firm is in equilibrium at a price of P_2. This corresponds to the equilibrium at price P_2 in Figures 12-8 and 12-9.

To summarise: economic profits in a competitive industry are a signal for the entry of new firms; the industry will expand, pushing the price down until the economic profits fall to zero (ie only normal profits are earned). Economic losses in a competitive industry are a signal for the exit of loss-making firms; the industry will contract, driving the market price up

FIGURE 12-8 The firm and industry in long-run equilibrium

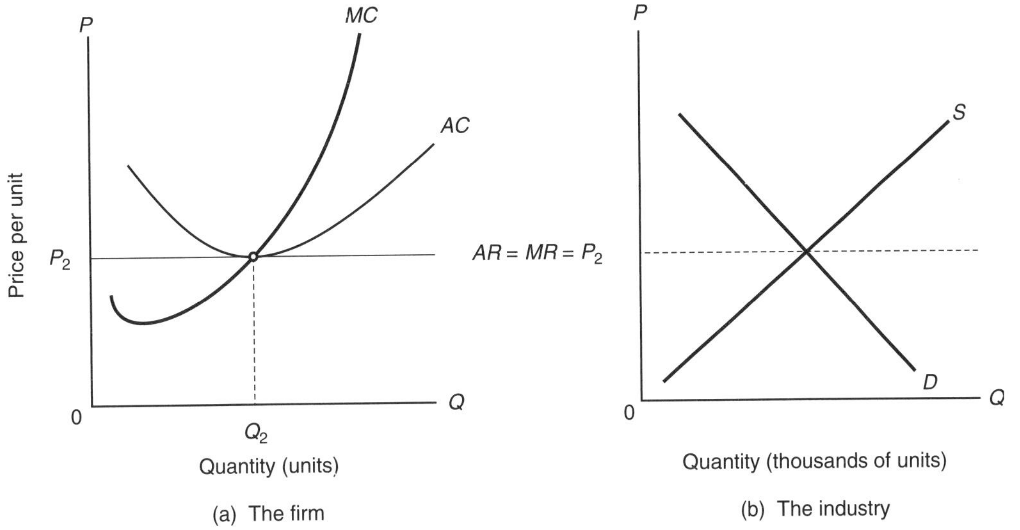

Equilibrium occurs when the price determined in the market (P_2 in (b)) is just sufficient for the individual firm to earn a normal profit. This is shown in (a) where MR = MC and AR = AC at the same quantity (Q_2).

FIGURE 12-9 The individual firm and the industry when the firm initially earns an economic profit

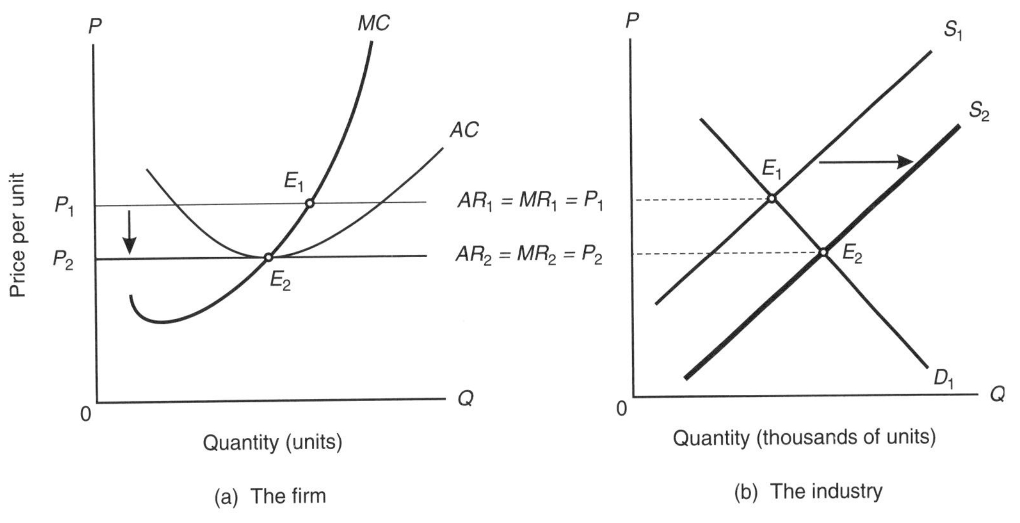

The original demand and supply curves in (b) are D_1 and S_1, yielding a price of P_1. At P_1 the individual firm earns an economic profit where MR_1 = MC, since AR > AC at that point (E_1). At E_1 the industry is in disequilibrium. The economic profits attract new firms to the industry, thus shifting the supply curve in (b) to S_2 in the long run. The price falls to P_2, where industry equilibrium is established, since the individual firm is only earning a normal profit and there is no incentive for firms to enter or leave the industry.

FIGURE 12-10 The individual firm and the industry when the firm initially makes an economic loss

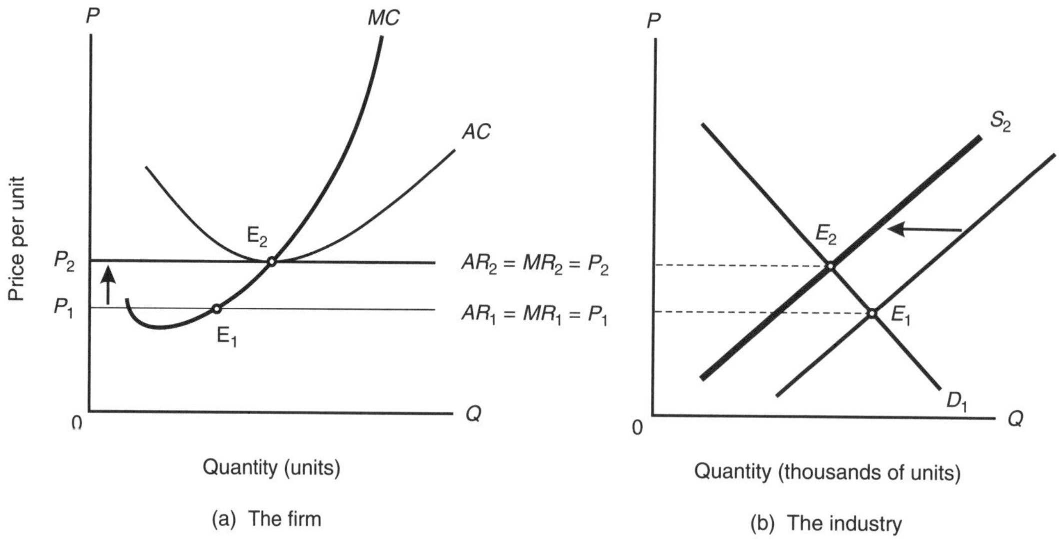

The original demand and supply curves in (b) are D_1 and S_1, yielding a price of P_1. At P_1 the individual firm cannot cover all its costs and makes an economic loss where $MR_1 = MC$ (since $AR < AC$ at E_1). At E_1 the industry is in disequilibrium. The economic losses force firms to leave the industry in the long run, thus shifting the supply curve in (b) to the left, to S_2. The price rises to P_2, where equilibrium is established for the industry. The individual firm earns a normal profit and there is no incentive for firms to leave or enter the industry.

until the remaining firms are covering their total costs (ie until normal profits are earned).

The impact of changes in the scale of production on the equilibrium of the firm and the industry

Until now we have assumed that the existing firms' scale of production remains unchanged. In the long run, however, all factors of production are variable and existing firms can therefore change their scale of production. If an existing firm is earning an economic profit and it can realise economies of scale (ie if average cost can be reduced), it will expand its scale of production. This is illustrated in Figure 12-11. Initially, the firm is producing at scale 1, with short-run marginal cost $SRMC_1$ and short-run average cost $SRAC_1$. The market price is P_1 and the firm maximises economic profit (indicated by the shaded area) by producing Q_1 units of the product. In the long run all the factors of production are variable and the firm can realise economies of scale (ie reduce average costs) by expanding to scale 2, indicated by the new short-run marginal and average costs, $SRMC_2$ and $SRAC_2$ respectively. The firm expands since it will increase profits at the original market price (P_1) if its average costs are reduced. However, the existence of positive economic profits in the industry attracts new entrants (as explained earlier) and also gives other existing firms an incentive to expand the scale of their operations. Both the entrance of new firms and the expansion of existing firms result in an increase in the supply of the product, which can be illustrated by a rightward shift of the supply curve. This increase in supply (not shown in the diagram) drives the price of the product down to P_2 and in the end all remaining firms in the industry (such as the one in Figure 12-11) again just earn a normal profit (ie zero economic profit).

In the long run, therefore, existing firms will continue to expand as long as there are economies of scale to be realised (ie as long as average costs can be reduced), and new firms will continue to enter the industry as long as positive economic profits are being earned. This process will continue until only normal profits are earned. In the long run, the firm is thus in equilibrium where $\boldsymbol{P = SRMC = SRAC = LRAC}$, as at price P_2 and quantity Q_2 in Figure 12-11. No other price can represent an equilibrium. At any higher price, economic profits will be earned and the existing firms will expand and/or new firms will enter. At any lower price, economic losses will be made and

FIGURE 12-11 Increasing the firm's scale of production to realise economies of scale

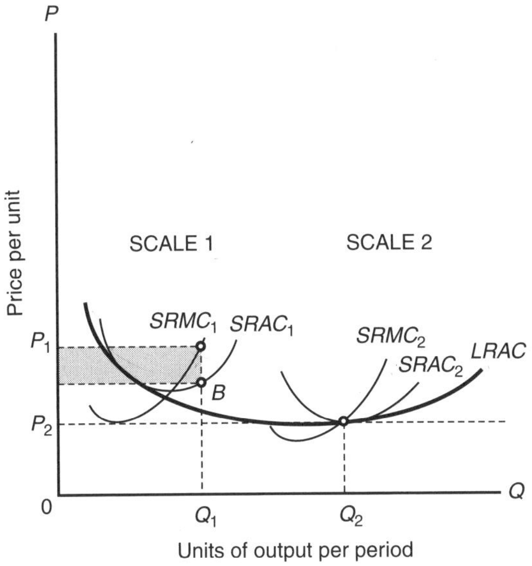

The firm initially produces at scale 1 when the market price is P_1. A quantity of Q_1 is produced and economic profit (indicated by the shaded area) is earned. In the long run, when all inputs are variable, the firm expands its plant size and produces at lower unit costs at scale 2. However, due to similar expansions at other existing firms and the entry of new firms, industry supply increases and the market price drops to P_2. In the long run, equilibrium is achieved at a quantity Q_2 where $P = SRMC_2 = SRAC_2 = LRAC$. The firm earns only normal profit in the long run.

the existing firms will contract and/or exit the industry. Only where $P = SRMC = SRAC = LRAC$ will economic profit be zero and will the industry be in equilibrium.

Throughout the analysis in this chapter we have assumed that the demand for the product remains unchanged. If the demand should change (illustrated by a shift of the demand curve), the price of the product will change and this, in turn, will set a whole chain of actions and reactions in motion. An analysis of these changes falls beyond the scope of this book, but you will encounter it in intermediate courses in microeconomics.

12.6 Perfect competition as a benchmark

In Section 12.1 we mentioned that one of the reasons why perfect competition is studied is that it represents a standard or norm against which the functioning of all other types of market can be compared. Two of the important criteria in this regard are allocative efficiency and productive efficiency.

Allocative efficiency

An allocation of resources is regarded as **efficient** when it is impossible to reallocate the resources to make at least one person better off without making someone else worse off. On the other hand, an allocation of resources is **inefficient** if it *is* possible to make at least one person better off without making someone else worse off. In such a case the welfare of society can be improved by reallocating the resources.

This notion of allocative efficiency is called Pareto efficiency or **Pareto optimality**, after the Italian economist, Vilfredo Pareto (1848-1923), who formulated it in 1906. Allocative efficiency is achieved when **the price of each product is equal to its marginal cost in the long run**. Marginal cost (MC) is the opportunity cost of **producing** an extra unit of output. Price (P), on the other hand, is the opportunity cost of **consuming** an extra unit of the product – it reflects the consumers' sacrifice required to obtain the extra unit. Society's welfare is maximised when the marginal cost of each product is equal to its price (ie when $MC = P$) and $AC \leq MC$ in the long run. If price is greater than marginal cost, society places a higher value on an additional unit of the product than the resources required to produce it, and society's welfare can be improved by producing more of the product (and less of other products). Conversely, if price is lower than marginal cost, society places a lower value on an additional unit of output than the cost of producing it. Society's welfare can then be improved by producing less of the product (and more of other products).

As we have seen, perfectly competitive firms produce where $MR = MC$, that is, where marginal cost (MC) is equal to price (P). Under perfect competition there is equilibrium when $MR = P = MC$ and the first condition for allocative efficiency is thus met. Moreover, perfectly competitive firms will only produce in the long run if AR ($= P = MR$) $\geq AC$. It therefore also follows that $AC \leq MC$ in the long run. The second condition for allocative efficiency is therefore also met.

Note that for a perfectly competitive firm, profit maximisation and allocative efficiency are not at odds. The perfectly competitive firm seeks to maximise profits by producing the quantity of output at which $MR = MC$, and because for the firm $P = MR$, it automatically achieves allocative efficiency ($P = MC$) when it maximises profit ($MR = MC$). However, as we shall see in the next chapter, profit maximisation and allocative efficiency might be at odds in other market structures.

Productive efficiency

Productive efficiency in an industry occurs when all the firms in the industry **produce where their long-run average or unit costs (*AC*) are at a minimum**. At any other level of output it is possible to reduce the average cost of production by producing more or less of the product. Productive efficiency is desirable for society since it means that firms are economising on society's scarce resources and therefore not wasting them. As we have seen in the previous section, perfectly competitive firms are only in equilibrium in the long run where average cost is at a minimum. Perfectly competitive firms thus satisfy the condition for productive efficiency. However, as we shall see in the next chapter, firms in other market structures are not necessarily productively efficient.

Concluding remarks

Perfect competition is intuitively attractive. It disciplines all the participants and satisfies the conditions for allocative and productive efficiency. In the impersonal world of perfect competition market forces call the tune and neither private firms nor public officials wield economic power. The market mechanism, acting like Adam Smith's invisible hand, determines the allocation of resources among competing uses. Perfectly competitive markets clearly have remarkable and desirable properties and are undoubtedly efficient.

But are such markets fair? Do they necessarily produce the greatest happiness for the greatest number of people? Unfortunately not. To participate in the market, one needs purchasing power – only money votes count – and people are not equally endowed with purchasing power. Some are very poor through no fault of their own and some are very rich through no virtue of their own. In a society in which the distribution of income and wealth is highly unequal, perfect competition will maintain and aggravate the inequalities. A perfectly competitive system might bc very efficient but it only benefits those who are in a position to compete. Societies do not live on efficiency alone. Equity is also important and societies often decide to take steps to improve the equity or fairness of the distribution of income and wealth. We return to this issue in Chapter 16, where we discuss the role of government in the economy.

IMPORTANT CONCEPTS

Perfect competition
Price taker
Homogeneous (identical) products
Entry and exit
Demand curve for the product of the firm
Total revenue (*TR*)
Marginal revenue (*MR*)
Average revenue (*AR*)
Shut-down rule
Profit-maximising rule
Total cost (*TC*)
Average cost (*AC*)
Average variable cost (*AVC*)
Marginal cost (*MC*)
Total profit
Normal profit
Economic profit
Break-even point
Supply curve of the firm
Industry (or market) supply
Industry equilibrium
Allocative efficiency
Productive efficiency

REVIEW QUESTIONS

1. Use diagrams to illustrate the fact that perfectly competitive firms are price takers. How are prices determined in perfectly competitive markets?
2. What is the point of studying perfect competition if it does not exist, or exists only very rarely, in the real world?
3. Explain how the profit-maximising level of output can be determined using (a) the total revenue and total cost approach and (b) the marginal revenue and marginal cost approach.
4. "A perfectly competitive firm maximises profit by producing at a level of output where marginal cost is lower than the market price of the good." Do you agree? Substantiate your answer.
5. Economists say that firms maximise profit by producing a level of output where marginal cost is equal to marginal revenue. The owner of a firm responds, "That's a lot of nonsense. I do not even know what marginal cost and marginal revenue mean. How can I be doing something I don't even know about?" How would you react to this response?
6. A perfectly competitive firm is producing at a level of output where marginal cost is equal to marginal revenue. Does this imply that the firm is earning a profit? Explain.
7. Why would a firm increase the quantity of its output even though marginal cost is increasing?
8. Explain the relationship, under conditions of perfect competition, between (a) total revenue and marginal revenue, (b) total revenue and average revenue and (c) average revenue and marginal revenue.

Points to ponder

The ideas of economists and political philosophers, both when they are right and when they are wrong, are more powerful than is commonly understood. Indeed the world is ruled by little else. Practical men, who believe themselves to be quite exempt from any intellectual influences, are usually the slaves of some defunct economist. Madmen in authority, who hear voices in the air, are distilling their frenzy from some academic scribbler of a few years back. I am sure that the power of vested interests is vastly exaggerated compared with the gradual encroachment of ideas. Not, indeed, immediately, but after a certain interval; for in the field of economic and political philosophy there are not many who are influenced by new theories after they are twenty-five or thirty years of age, so that the ideas which civil servants and politicians and even agitators apply to current events are not likely to be the newest. But, soon or late, it is ideas, not vested interests, which are dangerous for good or evil.

JOHN MAYNARD KEYNES
(*The general theory of employment, interest and money*: 383)

The basic problems of economics are simple; the hard part is to recognize simplicity when you see it. The next hardest part is to present simplicity as common sense rather than ivory tower insensitivity.

HARRY G JOHNSON

("The Study of Theory", *American Economic Review*, Papers and Proceedings, May 1974: 324)

Learning outcomes

Once you have studied this chapter you should be able to

- summarise the most important differences between perfect competition, monopolistic competition, oligopoly and monopoly
- explain the equilibrium position of a monopolist
- analyse the equilibrium position of a monopolistically competitive firm
- discuss the key features of oligopoly
- compare perfect competition with other market structures
- explain the purpose of competition policy

It is not enough to prove that a given industry is not competitive. The crucial question is: how far do conditions in the industry depart from competition? In many and perhaps most cases the answer is that the departures are not large.

GEORGE STIGLER

Like many businessmen of genius he learned that free competition was wasteful, monopoly efficient.

MARIO PUZO

I don't meet competition, I crush it.

CHARLES REVSON

13 Monopoly and imperfect competition

In Chapter 12 we examined the behaviour of a firm in a perfectly competitive market. Perfect competition is a theoretical construct which serves as a standard or norm against which we can compare other types of market. In the real world there are many different types of market. Nearly every market or industry is unique, and no simple classification system can accurately reflect this enormous variety. Nevertheless, economists usually distinguish between four broad sets of markets: perfect competition, monopoly, monopolistic competition and oligopoly.

In this chapter we examine the last three types. We start by explaining what **market structure** means, and distinguishing between the **four different types of market**. We then examine **monopoly**, **monopolistic competition** and **oligopoly**. The last two are usually collectively referred to as **imperfect competition**. This is followed by **comparisons** between perfect competition and the other three market structures. The chapter is concluded with a discussion of **government policy** with regard to monopoly and imperfect competition.

The theory of the behaviour of firms (ie the theory of the supply side of the goods market) is called the **theory of the firm**. The neoclassical version of this theory is based on the assumption that all firms seek to maximise their profits.

In this chapter we examine the behaviour of profit-maximising firms under conditions of monopoly and imperfect competition. Under **monopoly** there is only one supplier and entry to the industry is completely blocked (ie there is **no** competition), while **imperfect competition** refers to a situation in which at least one of the conditions for perfect competition listed in Section 12.1 is not satisfied. The two broad categories of imperfect competition are **oligopoly** and **monopolistic competition**.

In Chapter 12 we saw that the demand curve facing the perfectly competitive firm is horizontal (at the level of the market price). Under monopoly and imperfect competition, however, the demand curve for the product of an individual firm slopes downward, like a normal market demand curve. This is one of the distinguishing features of monopoly and imperfect competition. Another important feature of imperfect competition (but not of monopoly) is that an individual firm can be affected by the actions of competitors.

13.1 Market structure

The behaviour of a firm depends on the features of the market in which it sells its product(s) and on its production costs. The major organisational features of a market are called the structure of the market (or **market structure**). These features include the number and relative sizes of sellers and buyers, the degree of product differentiation, the availability of information and the barriers to entry and exit.

The different market structures: a preliminary overview

The key features of the four different types of market structure are summarised in Table 13-1. Eight features or criteria are listed in the first column and the remaining four columns show the position of each market type in respect of each criterion. Perfect competition is included in the table, since it serves as a benchmark against which the other market structures can be compared.

We now discuss each of the criteria briefly. Note that this is only a preliminary overview. We provide more detail about monopoly, monopolistic competition and oligopoly in the remaining sections of this chapter.

- The first criterion is the **number of firms**, which can vary between one and many. The actual number of firms as such is not particularly significant – the most important question is the *behaviour* of firms, in particular whether or not an individual firm can influence the price at which its product is sold. Perfectly competitive firms are all **price takers** (ie they cannot influence the price of their product), but monopolists and imperfectly competitive firms are **price makers** or **price setters** (ie they each have some influence on the price of their product).
- The second criterion is the **nature of the product**. The product can be homogeneous (identical, standardised) or it can be heterogeneous (differentiated, non-standardised). The distinction between homogeneous and heterogeneous products is not based on technical differences between them. As we emphasise later, consumers ultimately decide whether two products are identical or different. Two brands of the same product may be technically identical, but if they are different in the eyes of buyers, the product is classified as a heterogeneous or differentiated product.
- The third factor, **entry** (or mobility), refers to the ease or difficulty with which firms can enter and exit the market. Entry can vary from perfectly free (under perfect competition) to totally blocked (under monopoly). Various barriers to entry are discussed in Box 13-1.
- The fourth factor is the **information** (or degree of knowledge) about market conditions available to market participants. As we mentioned in Chapter 12, perfect competitors are assumed to possess full information (or perfect knowledge) of market conditions, which implies that there is no uncertainty under perfect competition. This assumption also applies in the case of monopoly. Under monopolistic competition and oligopoly, however, firms have incomplete information (ie they operate under conditions of uncertainty).
- Unlike the first four, the next four criteria in Table 13-1 are not basic assumptions, but logical consequences of the basic assumptions. The first of these (ie the fifth criterion in the table) is collusion. **Collusion** occurs when two or more sellers enter into an agreement, arrangement or understanding with each other to limit competition between or among themselves. Collusion, which is only common in oligopoly, is discussed in Section 13.4.
- We have already touched on the sixth criterion in the discussion on the number of firms. A perfectly competitive firm has no **control over the price** of its product (ie it is a price taker), whereas other firms have a varying degree of control (but never absolute control) over the prices of their products. They are price makers or price setters.
- The seventh criterion, the form or **shape of the demand curve for the product of the firm**, is

TABLE 13-1 Summary of market structures

Feature/criterion	*Perfect competition*	*Monopolistic competition*	*Oligopoly*	*Monopoly*
Number of firms	So many that no firm can influence the market price	So many that each firm thinks others will not detect its actions	So few that each firm must consider the others' actions and reactions	One
Nature of product	Homogeneous/ standardised	Heterogeneous/ differentiated	Homogeneous or heterogeneous	A unique product with no close substitutes
Entry	Completely free	Free	Varies from free to restricted	Completely blocked
Information	Complete	Incomplete	Incomplete	Complete
Collusion	Impossible	Impossible	Possible	Irrelevant
Firm's control over the price of the product	None	Some	Considerable, but less than in monopoly	Considerable, but limited by market demand and the goal of profit maximisation
Demand curve for the firm's product	Horizontal (perfectly elastic)	Downward-sloping	Downward-sloping, may be kinked	Equals market demand curve: downward-sloping
Long-run economic profit	Zero (normal profit only)	Zero (normal profit only)	Can be positive	Can be positive

related to the previous one. Under perfect competition the individual firm (as a price taker) is faced with a horizontal (or perfectly elastic) demand curve for its product (at the level of the market price). In contrast, other firms are all faced with downward-sloping demand curves for their products and therefore have some scope for "making" or "setting" their own prices. The price elasticities of the demand for their products can, however, vary quite significantly.

- The last criterion is the **possibility of earning an economic profit in the long run**. In Chapter 12 we explained that perfectly competitive firms do not earn any economic (or supernormal) profits in the long run (only normal profits). This also applies to the case of monopolistic competition. However, as we explain later, monopolistic and oligopolistic firms may earn economic profits in the long run.

Table 13-1 provides a concise summary of the most important features of the four basic market structures. You should refer back to the table while studying the rest of the chapter. The various elements of the table are explained in more detail as we proceed.

Market concentration

As we have mentioned, the number of sellers is one of the major determinants of the structure of a particular market or industry. The number and size distribution of firms in a market is called the degree of **concentration** in the market. Economists use measures to quantify the extent to which a market is dominated by a small number of large firms. One of these is the **four-firm concentration ratio** which is the fraction (or percentage) of the total value of assets, output or sales in an industry that is accounted for by the four largest firms in the industry. For example, a four-firm concentration ratio of 0,80 (or 80 per cent) means that the four largest firms account for 80 per cent of industry assets, output or sales.

In Table 13-2 we show the four-firm concentration ratios (in respect of sales) for a selection of South African manufacturing industries in 1996, the most recent available data at the time of writing. In each case we show the industry, the number of firms in the industry and the four-firm concentration ratio.

The figures in the table show a great variety of concentration in South African manufacturing. They also show that there is no definite correlation between the

TABLE 13-2 Seller concentration in selected South African manufacturing industries, 1996

Industry	*Number of firms*	*Four-firm concentration ratio*	*Herfindahl-Hirschman index*
Watches and clocks	4	1,00	0,46
Sugar, golden syrup and castor sugar	7	0,99	0,35
Tyres and tubes	10	0,98	0,26
Pulp, paper and paper board	22	0,98	0,30
Beer and other malt liquors and malt	23	0,97	0,70
Breakfast foods, starches and starch products	8	0,97	0,40
Cement, lime and plaster	10	0,93	0,25
Glass and glass products	72	0,88	0,29
Butter and cheese	17	0,86	0,21
Soft drinks and mineral waters	43	0,77	0,18
Soap and other cleaning compounds	163	0,76	0,27
Games and toys	55	0,68	0,17
Bakery products	522	0,51	0,08
Lifting and handling equipment	226	0,50	0,07
Footwear	256	0,37	0,06
Women's, girls' and infants' clothing	599	0,28	0,04
Men's and boys' clothing	650	0,21	0,02
Printing	1 415	0,21	0,02
Furniture	1 554	0,17	0,02
General mechanical engineering	1 200	0,11	0,01

Source: Statistics South Africa. 1999. *Census of manufacturing, 1996: statistics according to major groups and subgroups: South Africa.* Report No. 30-01-01 (1996). Pretoria: Government Printer

number of firms in an industry and the degree of economic concentration. In some cases practically the whole industry was accounted for by the four largest firms. In other cases there were a large number of firms, but the industry was still dominated by the four largest producers. Note, for example, that the baking industry consisted of more than twice as many firms than the footwear industry, but the degree of concentration in the baking industry was much larger. Also note the difference between soap and other cleaning products and games and toys, as well as the high degree of concentration in the glass industry. The last five entries in the table are examples of unconcentrated industries, each consisting of a relatively large number of firms.

Concentration ratios are not restricted to the four-firm ratio. In South Africa, for example, Statistics South Africa also publishes a ten-firm concentration ratio, while in other countries three-firm and five-firm concentration ratios are often used. Apart from these ratios there are also various indices that are used to measure market concentration, including the Herfindahl-Hirschman index, the Horvath index and the Rosenbluth index, all of which are calculated and published by Statistics South Africa. The Herfindahl-Hirschman index (HHI, sometimes simply called the Herfindahl index) has become increasingly popular among competition authorities in recent years, especially since the Justice Department in the United States started using it in June 1982. This index is calculated by adding the squares of the market shares of each firm in the industry (ie HHI = Σ(% market share)^2). For example, if there is only one firm in the industry, the value will be $(100)^2$ = 10 000. For an industry in which four firms each control 25 per cent of the market, the HHI = $25^2 + 25^2 + 25^2 + 25^2$ = 625 + 625 + 625 + 625 = 2 500. If, on the other hand, there are 100 firms with equal market shares of 1 per cent each, then the Herfindahl-Hirschman index will be equal to 100.

In the United States, an HHI of less than 1 000 is regarded as an indication that the industry is unconcentrated (ie competitive). A value of 1 000 to 1 800 indicates moderate concentration, while a value of higher than 1 800 is regarded as a sign of a concentrated industry. In South Africa the HHI, which is also included in Table 13-2, is calculated somewhat differently. The formula is basically the same but the market shares are expressed as fractions not percentages. As a result the index values are greater than zero but have a maximum value of 1, with the latter figure indicating that there is only one firm in the industry.

BOX 13-1 BARRIERS TO ENTRY

There are a number of potential barriers to entry that may give rise to monopoly or near-monopoly (or may protect existing monopolists from competition).

In some cases one firm can supply the entire market at a lower price than two or more firms can. When there is room for only one firm in an industry to produce a product efficiently (ie when one firm can supply the entire market at a lower price than two or more firms can), economists speak of a **natural monopoly**. This occurs when the average cost of production is still declining at levels of output that are greater than those likely to be demanded. The reason for the falling average cost is usually that production requires a large initial capital outlay (ie large fixed cost), as in the case of the supply of electricity, water and telephone services in a particular region. Recall from Chapter 11 that reductions in the average cost of production as the scale of operation increases are called **economies of scale**. We can therefore say that a natural monopoly occurs when the economies of scale are so large that there is room for only one firm in the industry. Examples include the railway system and the generation of electricity. Natural monopolies are usually owned or regulated by government and are discussed again later in this chapter.

Limited size of the market is another natural barrier to entry. This is particularly relevant in South Africa, since the economy is relatively small and isolated geographically from international markets. Many South (and southern) African markets can only support one or a few large firms, especially in industries that require large capital expenditure, while the distance from the international markets sometimes excludes export possibilities (because of the high transport costs).

A third possible reason for monopoly is the **exclusive ownership of raw materials**. The example most frequently cited in this regard is De Beers Consolidated Mines, which owns or controls a number of diamond mines and, through its Central Selling Organisation (CSO), largely controls the supply of diamonds on the world market.

A fourth barrier to entry is **patents**. A patent is the legal right granted to the inventor of a product, technique or process that allows him or her a temporary exclusive use of the product, technique or process patented (usually for 20 years). Patents play a very important role in the pharmaceutical industry. For example, SmithKline's patent on Tagamet, a product for treating ulcers, yielded large monopoly profits for that company. Other recent examples include Zantac, another product for treating ulcers (manufactured by Glaxo), Prozac, an antidepressant (manufactured by Eli Lilly) and Viagra, a male sexual stimulant (manufactured by Pfizer). A classic example is the exclusive right to photocopying that Rank-Xerox originally had in the United Kingdom.

A related type of barrier is **licensing**. Licences may be used to control entry into certain industries, occupations or professions. Governments may grant licences to one or a limited number of firms to supply a particular good or service. In South Africa, for example, Vodacom and MTN were the only companies that were licensed to provide a cellular phone service when this was introduced in South Africa in 1994. Subsequently Cell C was awarded the third licence, after a protracted struggle against other bidders. At the time of writing, Telkom still had the monopoly on fixed-line telephone services in South Africa, although a second licence had been awarded to Neotel. Other examples include liquor licences and broadcasting licences. In certain professions (eg law, accounting, medicine, dentistry, veterinary science, architecture and engineering), licensing requirements also have the effect of limiting competition. The Nobel laureate, George Stigler, who was also quoted at the beginning of this chapter, regularly emphasised the role of government in creating monopolistic conditions.

Sole rights to a particular product or service **can also be purchased by a private firm**. In June 1995, for example, the Australian tycoon, Rupert Murdoch, created a furore by purchasing the sole rights to telecast provincial and international rugby union matches in Australia, New Zealand and South Africa from 1996 to 2005, for an amount of US$550 million. In 2004 Murdoch's company, News Ltd, again bought the rights to broadcast the games from 2006 to 2010 for a further US $323 million.

Another barrier to entry is **import restrictions**. Even if there is only one producer of a particular good or service in a country, that producer is often subject to competition from foreign firms. To protect themselves from import competition, the domestic monopolies lobby (ie try to persuade) government to impose import restrictions (eg in the form of import quotas or tariffs – see Chapter 17). It is not surprising that the import tariff has been described as "the mother of monopoly".

Established firms can also create their own barriers to entry by applying strategies aimed at discouraging new firms from entering the market or forcing them out once they have entered. This can take many forms, including predatory pricing and maintaining excess capacity. **Predatory pricing** refers to the situation where existing firms lower their prices to below the new entrant's costs of production, in order to drive out the new entrant and discourage future entry. If experience shows that prices fall drastically in a particular market every time a new firm enters the market, potential new firms will be reluctant to enter. A well-known example occurred in the 1970s when a British businessman, Freddy Laker, started operating a passenger air service between London and New York at much lower prices than the established airlines. The existing companies responded by cutting their airfares on this route to the point where Laker Airways was driven into bankruptcy. Once Laker's company had been forced out, prices were raised to their former levels. Another possible strategy is for the existing firm(s) to build up **excess capacity** that can be used if new firms enter the market. If potential new firms realise that the existing firm(s) can increase production with little effort and little additional cost, they will probably refrain from entering the market.

These are some barriers to entry which may deter or prevent new firms from entering the industry and give rise to (or perpetuate) monopoly or oligopoly.

Note that there does not seem to be any correlation between the HHI and the four-firm concentration ratio in the highly concentrated industries, but as the level of concentration declines, a definite correlation emerges.

The main advantage of the HHI is that it provides information about the dispersion of firm size in an industry. However, as with all other concentration measures, there is an assumption that there are direct links from firm size to market power and the abuse of such power. Moreover, concentration ratios and indices are usually based on national data, while many goods and services are sold in local, regional or global markets, where these measures have little meaning. For example, the fact that there are hundreds or thousands of restaurants nationally does not mean that there is sufficient competition in every town or suburb. On the other hand, a domestic monopolist may be subject to intense competition from international firms, so a high concentration ratio or HHI does not necessarily signify the absence of actual competition. We return to the concentration issue in Section 13.6.

Market structure, conduct and performance

We have now established that there is no definite or necessary correlation between the number of firms in an industry and the degree of concentration. Moreover, even when concentration is high, it does not necessarily mean that there is little competition or that the market is inefficient. The **performance** of a market in attaining economic objectives such as efficiency, full employment, price stability and progressiveness depends on the conduct of the participants as well as on concentration. **Market conduct** refers to the efforts of suppliers to market their products, to gain a competitive advantage over rivals, or to limit competition among themselves.

The concern of governments and other interested parties over business concentration stems mainly from the neoclassical structure-conduct-performance (SCP) theory. According to this theory, market structure influences the conduct or behaviour of market participants, which, in turn, affects the performance of the market. In many countries the SCP theory has led to the adoption of measures aimed at limiting or regulating economic concentration (or power) and stimulating competition, such as the anti-trust laws in the United States and the competition legislation in South Africa. Competition policy in South Africa is discussed in Section 13.6.

13.2 Monopoly

The word **monopoly** is derived from the Greek words *monos*, meaning "single" and *polein*, meaning "sell". In its pure form, monopoly is a **market structure** in which there is only one seller of a good or service that has no close substitutes. A further requirement is that entry to the market should be completely blocked (see Table 13-1). The single seller or firm is called a **monopolist** or **monopolistic firm**.

Monopoly is at the opposite extreme to perfect competition in the spectrum of market structures. Whereas a perfectly competitive industry consists of a large number of small firms, the monopolistic industry consists of a single firm (ie the monopolistic firm is also the industry). This means that the demand for the product of the industry (or the market demand) is also the demand for the product of the single firm (or monopolist). The monopolistic firm faces a downward-sloping demand curve and can fix the price at which it sells its product. In other words, it can choose the point along the demand curve at which it wants to operate. However, once it decides on a price, the quantity sold depends on the market demand. A monopolist cannot set its sales *and* its price independently of each other. In other words, a monopolistic firm is always constrained by the demand for its product. This demand, however, might be highly price inelastic, thereby creating scope for the monopolist to exploit consumers by reducing the quantity supplied.

Contrary to what many people believe, pure monopoly is a relatively rare occurrence. Most "monopolies" are actually near-monopolies. Although there may be only one seller of a particular product in a market, that product may have substitutes. For example, there is only one railway system in South Africa, but that system has to compete with other modes of transport (air, road, sea). Similarly, there is only one postal system in the country, but in certain areas of its operations the Post Office has to compete with facsimiles, electronic mail, private courier services and even fixed-line and cellular phone services. SABMiller is usually regarded as a good example of a private monopoly, and it certainly dominates the beer market in South Africa. But it is not the only supplier of beer and has to compete with imported brands in certain segments of the market. Moreover, beer also has some potential substitutes (eg wine, spirits, soft drinks and even bottled water). The South African beer market definitely does not meet the requirements for pure monopoly and should therefore be classified as a near-monopoly rather than as a monopoly.

It should be borne in mind, however, that whether or not an industry or market can be classified as a monopoly depends, *inter alia*, on how narrowly the industry or market is defined. There are global, national, regional and local markets. A monopoly does not require that there be only one supplier of the good or service in the whole country. A monopoly may pertain to a specific market area, such as a suburb, town, city or province, with transport costs often being an important determinant of the geographical size of the market. Moreover, services and retail outlets usually have narrower markets, geographically speaking, than manufactured goods. As a result, a shop or trading store in an isolated rural area, the local hotel, the local bottle store, the local hairdresser and so on may all be virtual monopolists. On the other hand, the advent of the Internet and online trading has widened some markets. For example, the fact that one can purchase books electronically via *Kalahari.net* and *Amazon.com* has reduced the market power of local bookstores.

Even if there is only one firm in the market, this fact alone is not sufficient to label it a pure monopolist. A single firm can only be classified as a monopolist if entry into the market is blocked. Different barriers to entry are discussed in Box 13-1.

Why study the theory of pure monopoly if there are few, if any, actual examples of pure monopolies? The answer is basically the same as the one we gave in respect of perfect competition. The theory provides important insights into the behaviour of firms in markets which approximate conditions of monopoly. It also serves as a benchmark at the opposite extreme to perfect competition in the spectrum of market structures. As we shall see, many markets exhibit elements of competition and monopoly and we need theories of competition and monopoly to understand how these intermediate markets operate.

The equilibrium (or profit-maximising) position of a monopolist

We assume that the monopolistic firm aims to maximise profit. In principle the profit-maximising decision of a monopolist is exactly the same as that of any other firm. The monopolistic firm must consider its revenue and cost structures and follows the two basic rules explained in Section 12.3. Like any other firm, a monopolist should produce where marginal revenue *(MR)* is equal to marginal cost *(MC)* (the profit-maximising rule), provided that average revenue *(AR)* is greater than minimum average variable cost *(AVC)* in the short run or average total cost *AC* in the long run (the shut-down rule).

For the moment we also assume that a monopolist is subject to the same basic technology and cost constraints as any other firm and we assume that its cost structure is no different to that of any other firm. Its revenue structure, however, is different to that of a perfectly competitive firm and we have to examine this more closely before we can determine the profit-maximising position of a monopolist.

■ TOTAL, AVERAGE AND MARGINAL REVENUE UNDER MONOPOLY

Since a monopolist is the only supplier of the specific product, the demand curve for the product of a monopolistic firm is the market demand curve for the product of the industry. For example, if TP Cement is the sole supplier of cement in a particular market, the market demand for cement in that area is also the demand for TP Cement's product. Because the market demand curve slopes downward, the monopolist can only sell an additional quantity of output if it lowers the price of its product. But the lower price will usually apply to all units of output, which means that the marginal revenue from the sale of an extra unit of output is less than the price at which all units of the product are sold.

The relationship between a monopolist's average revenue (ie the price of the product) and its marginal revenue can be explained with the aid of a simple numerical example. **This relationship applies to imperfect competitors as well**. In Table 13-3 we show prices and quantities for a hypothetical monopoly. The first column shows the different quantities demanded at the different prices shown in the second column. For example, when the price of the product is R6 per unit, 3 units will be demanded and sold. Total revenue (*TR*) is equal to price (*P*) times quantity sold (*Q*) (ie $TR = P \times Q$, or *PQ*). Average revenue is equal to the price of the product (or to total revenue *TR* (= *PQ*) divided by the quantity *Q*). The firm's marginal revenue (*MR*) is the change in total revenue when one extra unit of output is sold. This is shown in the last column. Except for the first unit sold, the firm's marginal revenue (*MR*) is always lower than the price of the product.

The firm's total, average and marginal revenue are illustrated in Figure 13-1. In Figure 13-1(a) we show average revenue (*AR*) and marginal revenue (*MR*). Because *MR* is the change in total revenue resulting from the sale of an extra unit of output, it applies to the **movement** from one unit to the next, rather than to a specific unit. The value of *MR* is therefore plotted between the two units concerned, rather than against one of them. Figure 13-1(a) clearly shows that *MR* is lower than *AR* at all levels of output. This is an important result which always holds when *AR* is downward sloping, as in Figure 13-1(a). If *AR* is a straight line, *MR* lies exactly halfway between *AR* and the price axis (ie the vertical axis).

The firm's total revenue (*TR*) is shown in Figure 13-1(b). *TR* rises, reaches a maximum and then falls.

TABLE 13-3 Average, total and marginal revenue when the demand curve for the product of the firm slopes downward: a numerical example

Quantity Q	Average revenue (R) AR (or price P)	Total revenue (R) TR (= PQ)	Marginal revenue (R) MR
0	0	0	
			8
1	8	8	
			6
2	7	14	
			4
3	6	18	
			2
4	5	20	
			0
5	4	20	
			–2
6	3	18	

FIGURE 13-1 Marginal, average and total revenue under monopoly (and imperfect competition)

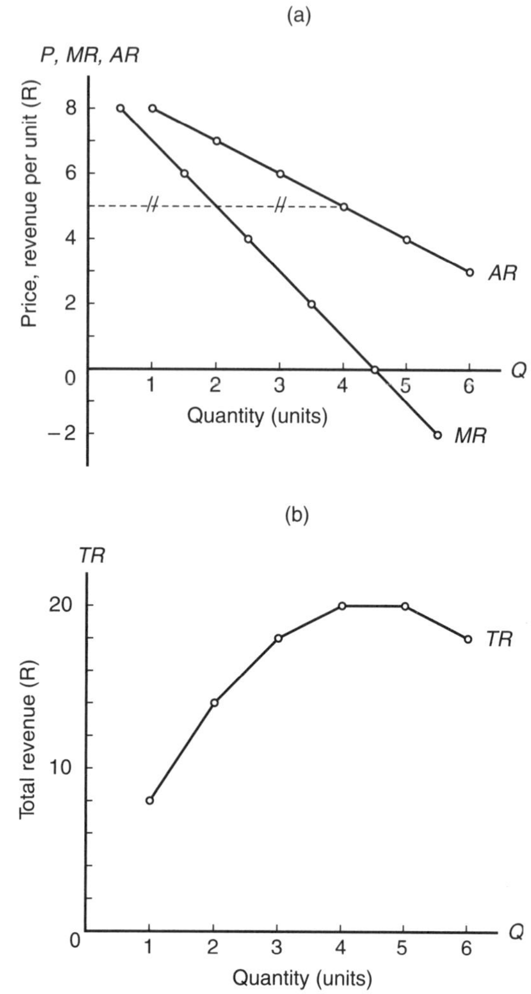

Under monopoly, a firm faces a downward-sloping demand curve, which is also its average revenue curve AR, as shown in (a). The marginal revenue curve MR is also downward sloping. If AR is a straight line, MR lies halfway between the AR curve and the price axis. The corresponding total revenue curve TR is shown in (b). When MR is positive, TR increases; when MR is zero, TR remains unchanged; and when MR is negative, TR falls. These relationships apply to imperfectly competitive firms as well.

As you can see if you compare (a) and (b) of Figure 13-1, as long as *MR* is positive, *TR* rises; where *MR* is zero, *TR* reaches a maximum; and when *MR* becomes negative, *TR* falls. This relationship between *MR* and *TR* is illustrated clearly in Figure 13-1. See also Box 13-2.[1]

The most important results illustrated in Figure 13-1 are that

- *MR* is always lower than *AR* when the firm's demand curve slopes downward
- if *AR* is a straight line, *MR* lies halfway between the price axis and the *AR* curve

These results apply to all cases where the firm's demand curve is downward sloping, including monopolistic competition and oligopoly, which are discussed in Sections 13.3 and 13.4.

THE SHORT-RUN EQUILIBRIUM OF THE MONOPOLISTIC FIRM

The short-run equilibrium position of a monopolistic firm is illustrated in Figure 13-2. The firm faces a downward-sloping demand curve (*D*) which is also its average revenue curve (*AR*). The firm's marginal revenue (*MR*) is lower than its average revenue, and the *MR* curve lies halfway between the *AR* curve and the price axis. The monopolist's marginal cost *MC* and average cost *AC* curves have the same shape as those of any other firm.

To maximise profit (or minimise loss), the monopolist has to produce where *MR* = *MC*.[2] In Figure 13-2 this is indicated by *E*, which points to an output of Q_1. At lower levels of output than Q_1, the firm's marginal revenue *MR* is greater than its marginal cost *MC*. The firm will therefore be able to add to its profit by expanding production. At Q_1 the additional revenue generated by the last unit of output is equal to the additional cost of producing that unit. At that quantity the firm's profit is maximised. If it increases its production beyond Q_1, the cost of each additional unit of output (*MC*) is greater than the additional revenue (*MR*) earned by selling it. Total profit will therefore decline if the firm continues producing beyond Q_1. Like any other firm, a monopolist maximises profit by producing that quantity where *MR* = *MC*.

FIGURE 13-2 The short-run equilibrium of the firm under monopoly.

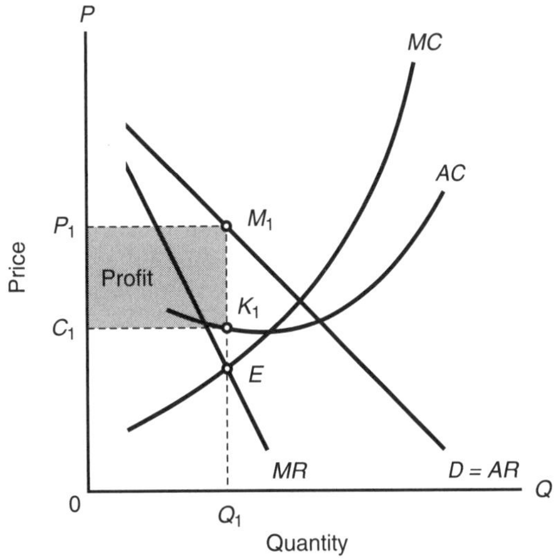

The figure shows the average revenue AR, marginal revenue MR, average cost AC and marginal cost MC of a monopolist. The monopolist's profit is maximised by producing a quantity Q_1 at a price P_1. The economic profit per unit of output is the difference between M_1 and K_1 (or between P_1 and C_1). The firm's total economic profit is the shaded area $C_1P_1M_1K_1$.

At what price should that output be sold? The answer is quite simple. The monopolist sells its output at the price which consumers are willing to pay for that particular quantity, as indicated by the demand curve. In Figure 13-2 point M_1 is the relevant point on the demand curve. It shows that consumers are willing to pay a price of P_1 for a quantity of Q_1. The equilibrium price is thus P_1 and the equilibrium quantity Q_1.

Does the monopolist make a profit in equilibrium? To determine whether a firm makes an economic profit or a loss, we have to compare total revenue with total cost, or average revenue with average cost. Contrary to what many people believe, a monopolist can also make a loss. The hypothetical monopolist in Figure 13-2 earns an economic profit, but it would also be possible to illustrate the position of a monopolistic firm that makes an economic loss, as well as one that earns normal profit only (ie when economic profit/loss is zero).

In Figure 13-2 the monopolist's average profit per unit of output is shown by the difference between average revenue (*AR*) and average cost (*AC*) at a quantity Q_1. In the figure these two points are labelled M_1 and K_1 respectively. The firm's total economic profit is indicated by the shaded rectangle $C_1P_1M_1K_1$.

1. Note that these relationships apply only if all output is sold at the same price. The exception is when the monopolist sells its product at different prices to different consumers (or groups of consumers). This practice, which is called price discrimination, is discussed later.
2. The profit-maximising position of a monopolist can also be illustrated using total revenue *TR* and total cost *TC* (instead of marginal revenue *MR* and marginal cost *MC*). The figure would in principle be the same as Figure 12-4, which illustrated *TR* and *TC* for a perfectly competitive firm. The only difference is that the monopolist's *TR* curve is not a straight line but is shaped like an inverted U (as in Figure 13-1(b)).

THE LONG-RUN EQUILIBRIUM OF THE MONOPOLISTIC FIRM

Under perfect competition any short-run economic profit is competed away in the long run by the entry of new firms or the expansion of existing firms. Under monopoly, however, entry into the industry is blocked (by definition) and short-run economic profits therefore cannot be reduced by new competing firms entering the industry. The monopolistic firm can thus continue to earn economic profits (also called monopoly profits) in the long run, as long as the demand for its product remains intact. If the monopolistic firm should expand its plant size (to achieve economies of scale), its average cost curve will become flatter but for the rest the long-run position of a monopolist will be essentially the same as that illustrated in Figure 13-2, the only difference being that the firm will produce where *MR* = **long-run** *MC*.

ABSENCE OF A SUPPLY CURVE UNDER MONOPOLY

A monopolist does not have a supply curve showing the quantities that will be supplied at different prices of the product. Under perfect competition, the short-

BOX 13-2 MARGINAL REVENUE AND PRICE ELASTICITY OF DEMAND

Figure 13-1 probably looks familiar. It should, since it is essentially the same as Figure 9-3. In Figure 9-3 we showed how total revenue (*TR*) depends on the price elasticity of demand for the product. As quantity increases, total revenue also increases when the price elasticity of demand (e_p) is greater than one. *TR* reaches a maximum where $e_p = 1$, and falls (as quantity increases) when e_p is lower than one. You should turn back to Figure 9-3 now to refresh your memory on this point.

From Figures 13-1 and 9-3 it follows that

- *MR* is positive when e_p is greater than one (ie when demand is elastic)
- *MR* is zero when e_p is equal to one (ie when demand is unit elastic)
- *MR* is negative when e_p is less than one (ie when demand is inelastic)

These results are illustrated in the following figure.

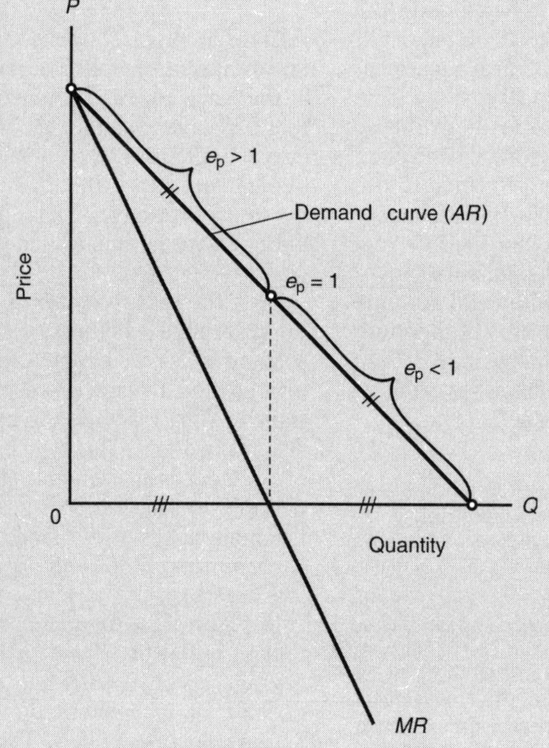

run supply curve of each individual firm is the rising (or upward-sloping) part of the marginal cost (*MC*) curve above the minimum average variable cost (*AVC*), and the market supply curve is obtained by adding all the individual supply curves horizontally. The monopolist, however, chooses the combination of price and output at which profit is maximised (or loss minimised), given the demand (or revenue) conditions and the cost conditions. Subject to the demand constraint, the monopolist is a price maker and does not move along a supply curve as the price of the product changes.

Price discrimination

Until now we have assumed that the monopolistic firm sells its product at a single price, irrespective of where or to whom it is sold. Sometimes, however, firms with market power find it profitable to sell the same product to different consumers or groups of consumers at different prices. This practice is called **price discrimination**. Price discrimination only occurs when price differences are based on different buyers' valuations of the same product. If price differences are based on cost differences they are not discriminatory.

It is said that in Ancient Egypt, during the reign of Rameses the Great, there was a toll road on an important route across a range of hills. Other routes were available, but they were much more difficult than this one. The person sent to administer the toll road found that he had some discretion over pricing. When he asked for guidelines on what he should charge, the reply was: "Charge what the traffic will bear." This is essentially what price discrimination is all about.

In Chapter 7 we explained that consumers as a group benefit when a good or service is sold at a fixed price. If the demand curve slopes downward, a single price implies that all the quantities except the last one is sold at a lower price than consumers are willing and able to pay. This benefit is called the **consumer surplus**. The purpose of price discrimination is to capture all or part of the consumer surplus, or to increase sales, thereby increasing profits. However, not all firms are in a position to practice price discrimination. Two basic conditions have to be met:

- The firm must be a price maker or price setter. Under perfect competition, where all firms are price takers, price discrimination is impossible.
- Consumers or markets must be independent. Consumers obtaining the product at a low price or in the low-priced market must not be able to resell the product at higher prices or in the high-priced market. The discriminating firm must thus be able to divide the market and keep the different parts separate. This is usually much easier for services than for goods. For example, one cannot resell the services of a hairdresser or a medical practitioner.

Three main varieties of price discrimination can be distinguished:

- **First-degree price discrimination** (sometimes also called discrimination among units) occurs when each consumer is charged the maximum price he or she is prepared to pay for each unit of the product. This is also what stall holders in a bazaar or fleamarket *attempt to do* when bargaining with their customers. In a bazaar, however, negotiation between sellers and buyers occurs at prices between that which the consumer is prepared to pay and that which the supplier is prepared to accept. The outcome will depend on the bargaining or negotiation skills of the two parties. In some instances, for example, the price at which the trade occurs might be the minimum price which the supplier is prepared to accept, rather than the maximum price the consumer is willing to pay. The price-discriminating firm, however, will only practise price discrimination if it can obtain a higher price than the equilibrium market price. If the firm succeeds in capturing the total consumer surplus by charging each consumer the full amount she is willing and able to pay, the consumer surplus is eliminated and the demand curve becomes the firm's marginal revenue curve. This is called **perfect price discrimination**.
- **Second-degree price discrimination** (sometimes also called discrimination among quantities) occurs when the firm charges its customers different prices according to how much they purchase. It may, for example, charge a high price for the first so many units, a lower price for the next so many units and a lower price again for the next. With different prices being charged for different quantities or blocks of the same product consumers may be encouraged to consume more of the product. For example, if you purchase a six-pack of Castle Lager you will pay less per can than if you buy fewer cans, and if you buy a case of 24 cans the unit price will be even lower. Likewise, if you subscribe to a magazine or newspaper for a certain period, you will pay less per copy than if you buy each one separately.
- **Third-degree price discrimination** (sometimes also called discrimination among buyers) occurs when consumers are grouped into two or more independent markets and a separate price is charged in each market. In this case the price elasticity of demand must differ between the different markets. The firm will charge the higher price in the market where demand is less price elastic, and thus less sensitive to an increase in price. By raising the price where demand is inelastic and reducing it where demand is elastic, revenue can be increased in both markets (or market segments).

Third-degree price discrimination is practised fairly widely. Eskom, for example, differentiates between domestic and industrial consumers, selling electricity to industrial users on more favourable terms than to domestic users. Electricity can also be sold at different prices during peak periods and off-peak periods. Since electricity cannot be stored for later use, such discrimination is possible.

South African Airways also practises price discrimination by charging different fares to different market segments and at different times of the day. Business travellers, whose fares are usually paid by their employers, tend to travel during peak times and are generally less sensitive to price than tourists, students or other casual travellers who have to pay out of their own pockets. More formally, business travellers' demand for air travel is relatively price inelastic and an increase in their fares will tend to result in higher revenue. Other travellers, however, tend to have a high price elasticity of demand and a reduction in the price of air travel (eg during off-peak periods or by booking well in advance or by staying over on weekends) will tend to attract additional passengers and raise revenue in this part of the market for air travel.

Another example is Telkom, which also provides a service that cannot be resold by its customers. Telkom charges higher tariffs during peak hours and lower tariffs during off-peak hours or Callmore time. Once again, the rationale is that calls during normal business hours will be made in any case (ie the demand is price inelastic) while lower off-peak tariffs will result in an increase in calls during this period (ie the demand is price elastic).

There are many other examples of price discrimination, particularly as far as services are concerned. Hairdressers, for example, offer special low rates for pensioners at slack times, as do many golf clubs. Bus and train services charge different rates per trip for daily, weekly and monthly tickets. Many cinemas charge lower prices for children than for adults during daytime, or to everyone on relatively "quiet" days (eg Tuesdays). Children or students are also often charged lower prices on public transport or at sporting events. Doctors in private practice tend to charge their non-medical aid patients according to what they can afford. Quite clearly, therefore, price discrimination is not practised only by monopolists (narrowly defined).

Natural monopoly

As mentioned in Box 13-1, natural monopoly is a situation that arises where it is most cost efficient for a single firm to produce all the output in an industry or market. This is illustrated in Figure 13-3. In the figure we see that average cost *AC* is still declining at the point where the quantity demanded reaches a maximum. Even if the price of the good or service is zero, market demand will still not be sufficient for the firm to achieve minimum *AC* (or maximum economies of scale). Thus, even where one firm supplies all the industry output, the firm will still not be operating at the minimum efficient scale. Clearly, if there were more than one firm sharing the output, the average cost of production of each firm would be higher. The situation illustrated in Figure 13-3 typically arises in the case of public utilities such as the supply of electricity and water.

Natural monopolies create a dilemma for government policy and regulation. Some form of government intervention is necessary, since a private firm would be able to produce at inefficient levels and earn large economic profits. Broadly speaking, there are two options. Either government can produce the good itself or production could be left to a private firm, which is then regulated by government in a variety of possible ways.

Government cannot force competition by legislating that there be a minimum number of firms in the industry, since the economy's resources would be wasted if there were more than one producer. Where production is left to a private firm, regulation can take the form of price control. But where should the price be set? In Chapter 12 we explained that there are two notions of efficiency. Allocative efficiency requires that the price P be such that $P = MC$, while productive efficiency is achieved where AC is at a minimum. In this case, the latter point cannot be reached and the logical conclusion is therefore that price should be equated with marginal cost to ensure allocative efficiency. This is called the marginal pricing rule. How-

FIGURE 13-3 Natural monopoly

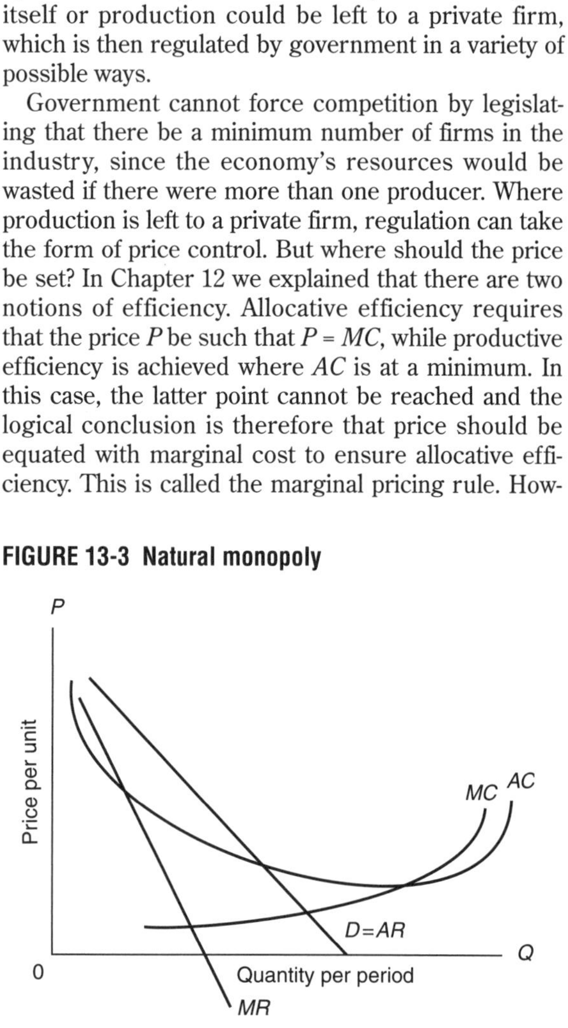

A natural monopoly exists if average cost AC is still declining when the quantity demanded reaches a maximum.

ever, imposing the marginal pricing rule will result in economic losses – see Figure 13-4. If price is equated to marginal cost, average revenue will be lower than average cost. What now? If the product is an essential one, like water or electricity, a solution needs to be found. At least four alternative strategies can be followed:

- Government can supply the good or service itself and use tax revenue to compensate for the losses. This is what has happened, for example, in the case of postal services in South Africa. A major problem with this strategy is that non-users have to help pay for the good or service.
- Government can leave production to a private firm and subsidise its losses.
- An alternative pricing strategy can be followed, for example, average cost pricing (ie setting $P = AC$). The firm (which could be government-owned or a private company) would then earn a normal profit and no subsidisation would be necessary. Output (Q_2 in Figure 13-4) will be lower than in the case of marginal cost pricing (Q_3) but higher than that of an unregulated monopolist (Q_1), which will produce where $MR = MC$ and at a price (P_1) corresponding to the demand (AR) curve. Theoretically, average cost pricing may seem a good option, but if firms are only allowed to earn normal profits they have no incentive to minimise costs. Higher costs (eg in the form of higher wages and salaries) will simply result in higher prices. This disadvantage is associated with the first two strategies as well.

FIGURE 13-4 Pricing options under natural monopoly

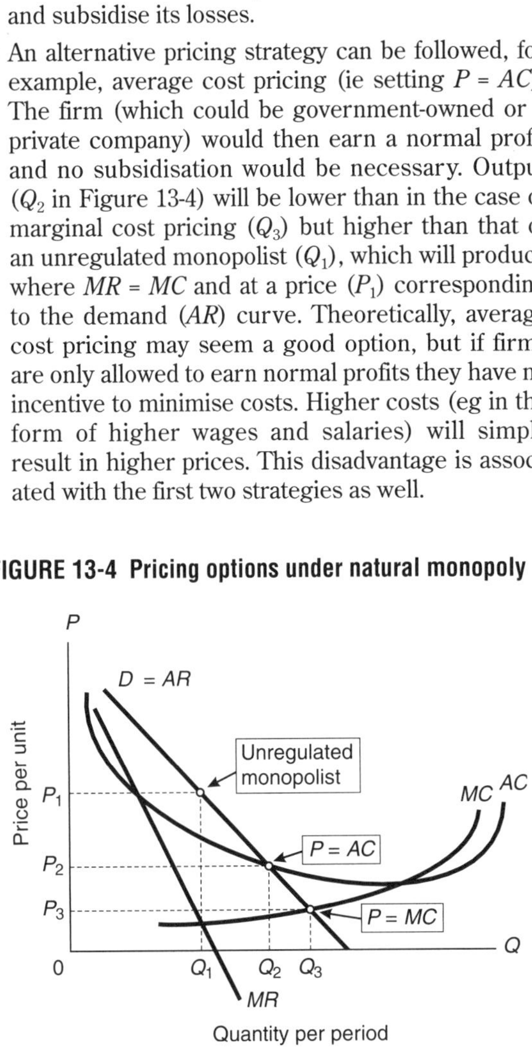

If the monopoly is unregulated, equilibrium will be at price P_1 and quantity Q_1. Marginal cost pricing will yield a price P_3 and quantity Q_3, but the monopolist will make a loss. Average cost pricing will yield a price P_2 and quantity Q_2.

- The fourth option is price discrimination. As explained earlier, public utilities like Eskom tend to charge different rates for different market segments. Price discrimination enables the supplier to capture some of the consumer surplus in certain market segments which can then be used to subsidise consumers in other market segments.

There are also other possible strategies, including the regulation of output, which we shall not discuss here. Regulation of natural monopolies is a complicated issue but our brief discussion should help you to understand some of the basic issues relating to privatisation and regulation of natural monopolies and to follow the debates on tariffs charged by public utilities, such as Eskom, Telkom, Rand Water and the Post Office, and on the role of the various regulating agencies to which these utilities have to report.

13.3 Monopolistic competition

Between the extremes of pure monopoly and perfect competition there is a range of actual market structures. Some industries (like the brick manufacturing industry) consist of a few very large firms and a large number of small ones. Other industries (like motor manufacturing) consist of a few large firms only. In some industries (like the clothing industry) there are many firms producing a variety of quite similar products. In other industries (like the cement industry) a few large firms produce virtually identical products.

One type of market in the spectrum between the extremes of perfect competition and monopoly is **monopolistic competition**. As the name indicates, monopolistic competition combines certain features of monopoly and perfect competition. The theories of perfect competition and monopoly were explained in detail by the famous British neoclassical economist, Alfred Marshall, in his *Principles of economics*, which was first published in 1890. For the next forty years or so most economists analysed the behaviour of the firm and the industry in terms of these two extreme market forms. In the early 1930s, however, two economists, working independently, developed similar theories of the firm which combined certain features of competition and monopoly. They were a British economist, Joan Robinson, and an American economist, Edward Chamberlin. Robinson and Chamberlin were concerned about the complete separation of the two existing models of firm and industry behaviour (perfect competition and monopoly), neither of which had many real-world applications. They pointed out that most goods and services are heterogeneous rather than homogeneous, and that many sellers are actually monopolists as far as their own goods and services are concerned. These "monopolists", however, compete against each other in markets for roughly similar goods. Many firms can thus be regarded as "competing monopolists", hence the name monopolistic competition. Under monopolistic competition each firm is small enough (relative to the total market) and the total number of firms large enough so that each firm can ignore the consequences of its actions on the other firms in the market.

In a monopolistically competitive market a large number of firms produce **similar but slightly different** products. Whereas both a monopolist and a perfectly competitive firm produce a homogeneous (standardised, identical) product, monopolistically competitive firms produce heterogeneous (differentiated) products. The act of making a product that is slightly different to the product of a competing firm is called product differentiation.

Product differentiation

The theory of perfect competition is based on the assumption that all the firms in the particular market produce absolutely identical (or homogeneous) products. When all the products are identical, the only form of competition in which firms can engage is price competition. A pure monopoly can also only exist if the product is unique. If there are close substitutes for the product of a firm, that firm cannot be a monopolist, since it then has to compete against the firms producing close substitutes for its product.

Most products, however, are not regarded as absolutely identical by all consumers. When there are different varieties of a product, the product is called a **differentiated** (or **heterogeneous**) **product**. In some cases different varieties of a product are technically different. The contents of two different painkillers may differ. However, the decision as to whether a product is homogeneous or heterogeneous ultimately rests with the consumers. For example, two different brands of painkillers may have identical contents, but certain consumers may prefer the one to the other. Like beauty, product differentiation is in the eye of the beholder. In some cases the contents of two different products may actually come from the same source. For example, the large supermarket chains (Pick 'n Pay, Shoprite Checkers, Spar) all have their own house-brands (or no-name brands) for washing powder, cooking oil, tea, coffee, canned foods, fruit juices, margarine, dog food and so on. In many instances these goods are exactly the same as well-known branded goods carrying the labels of their manufacturers. In some cases (eg canned fruit or vegetables) the no-name brand and the branded good may even contain identical products from the same farm and factory. The consumers decide whether or not the no-name goods are different to the other brands. Some consumers regard the products as identical and purchase the cheapest one. Others, however, prefer the well-known brands and are therefore willing to pay a higher price to obtain them.

Box 13-3 contains lists of the five most popular brands of selected goods and services in South Africa. Each brand has a large number of loyal customers who prefer that particular brand to any other, and who are willing to pay a premium for it, even though cheaper substitutes may be available.

Petrol is another example of a good which can be regarded as homogeneous or heterogeneous, depending on consumers' tastes or preferences. In South Africa, the price of petrol is fixed by government and there is thus no price competition. Some motorists believe that petrol is a homogeneous good and are therefore willing to fill up at any convenient service station. Others, however, prefer a certain brand (eg Sasol, Caltex, Shell), and always try to purchase that particular brand.

The example of petrol also illustrates certain elements of **non-price competition**. For the motorist who believes that all brands are identical, a convenient **location** is probably the most important determinant of his or her choice of filling station. Petrol companies therefore compete to obtain the best possible sites. But petrol companies also try to **differentiate** their product and to create consumer loyalty. They therefore spend large amounts on researching, developing and advertising additives that can enhance the performance of petrol-driven engines. Each company wants to create the impression that its product is technically superior to the similar products of other companies. They therefore spend massive amounts on **advertising** and other marketing strategies. Even in cases where the price of the product is fixed, competition can be fierce.

Deliberate product differentiation is a common phenomenon in the modern economy. Each firm wants to differentiate its product from similar products supplied by other firms. The greater the real or perceived differentiation a firm can establish, the less price elastic the demand for its product becomes. The techniques of product differentiation, such as advertising, packaging, and the provision of free gifts with purchases, are all elements of non-price competition. In the case of differentiated products, non-price competition is often much more important than price competition. Advertising is discussed in more detail in Section 13.4.

Salient features of monopolistic competition

The conditions for monopolistic competition can be summarised as follows (see also Table 13-1):

- Each firm produces a distinctive, differentiated product.
- Each firm therefore faces a downward-sloping demand curve for its particular product.
- There are a large number of firms in the industry.
- There are no barriers to entry or exit.

BOX 13-3 SOME OF THE MOST POPULAR BRANDS IN SOUTH AFRICA, 2006

Rank	Household cleaners and detergents	Clothing stores	Cars	Petrol
1	Omo	Jet	Toyota	BP
2	Sunlight	Edgars	BMW	Shell
3	Handy Andy	Pep Stores	Mercedes Benz	Engen
4	Jik	Woolworths	Volkswagen	Caltex
5	Surf	Ackermans	Mazda	Total

Rank	Over-the-counter medicine	Beer	Food (on shelf)	Fast-food outlets
1	Panado	Carling Black Label	Tastic	KFC
2	Disprin	Castle	Huletts	Nando's
3	Grand-Pa	Hansa	Koo	Chicken Licken
4	Compral	Amstel	Ace	Wimpy
5	Eno	Castle Milk Stout	White Star	Steers

Rank	Food (in fridge)	Soft drinks	Electrical goods	Banks
1	Rama	Coca-Cola	LG	Absa
2	Clover	Fanta	Defy	Standard
3	Parmalat	Sprite	Panasonic	FNB
4	I&J	Lemon Twist	Samsung	Nedbank
5	Enterprise	Schweppes	Philips	People's Bank

Source: *Markinor Sunday Times Top Brands Survey 2006*

Many markets in the economy can be classified as monopolistically competitive. Good examples are the markets for different types of clothing. As we showed in Table 13-2, men's and women's clothing manufacturing industries in South Africa are characterised by large numbers of firms and low levels of economic concentration. Other examples include printing, furniture manufacturing, restaurants in a city and service stations.

Each monopolistically competitive firm has a certain degree of monopoly power, as it is the only producer of the particular brand or variety of the product. Under monopolistic competition, each firm is thus in effect a mini-monopoly. But, in contrast to pure monopoly, monopolistically competitive firms compete with each other and new firms are free to enter the market for the differentiated product (eg shoes or shirts).

The essential difference between monopolistic competition and monopoly lies in the barriers to entry. Whereas entry is not restricted under monopolistic competition, it is completely blocked in the case of monopoly. On the other hand, the essential difference between monopolistic competition and perfect competition is found in the nature of the product. Whereas monopolistic competitors produce differentiated (heterogeneous) products, perfectly competitive firms produce identical (homogeneous) products.

Under monopolistic competition, each firm has its own identity. Each firm produces its own variety of a differentiated product and therefore faces a specific downward-sloping demand curve for its product. For example, the manufacturer of Pierre Cardin shirts faces a demand for Pierre Cardin shirts, rather than for shirts in general. If the price of Pierre Cardin shirts increases, consumers will, *ceteris paribus*, tend to switch to other brand names (eg Cambridge, Polo, Van Heusen), but the quantity of Pierre Cardin shirts demanded from the manufacturer will not fall to zero, as it would under perfect competition. Likewise, the manufacturers of Panado face a demand curve for Panado, rather than for painkillers in general, while

McDonald's faces a demand curve for McDonald's hamburgers, rather than for hamburgers in general.

The equilibrium of the firm under monopolistic competition

As we move away from the extremes of perfect competition and monopoly to the market structures which occur most frequently in the economy, it becomes increasingly difficult to formulate general theories of the behaviour of firms. It is impossible, for example, to construct a general theory or model of a monopolistically competitive **industry**. Although there is a market for, say, women's clothing (a differentiated product supplied by a large number of firms), there is no single product or single market price in that market. Instead, there is a range of similar products and a range of prices. Nevertheless, we can still analyse the equilibrium of a **representative firm** under monopolistic competition, in both the short run and the long run.

Analytically, the **short-run equilibrium** of a monopolistic competitor is the same as that of a monopolist, except that the demand curve for the product of the monopolistic competitor is significantly more price elastic than that of the monopolist. The reason is that the product of the monopolistically competitive firm has many close substitutes, whereas the product of the monopolist has no close substitutes. In the **long run**, however, there are important differences. The monopolist is protected by barriers to entry and can therefore make an economic profit in the long run, but monopolistic competition is characterised by freedom of entry. If monopolistically competitive firms earn economic profits in the short run, this will induce new firms to enter the market and they will eventually drive economic profits down to zero. In the long run, monopolistically competitive firms earn normal profits only, just like their perfectly competitive counterparts.

The short-run equilibrium of a monopolistically competitive firm is illustrated in Figure 13-5(a). Like a monopolist, the monopolistically competitive firm faces a downward-sloping demand curve (*D*) for its product, which is also its average revenue (*AR*) curve. The only difference with the monopolist is that the price elasticity of demand is larger, since there are many close substitutes for the product of the firm. The firm's marginal revenue curve (*MR*) is also downward-sloping and if *AR* is a straight line, it lies halfway between the price axis and the demand (or average revenue) curve. Profit is maximised at the quantity where marginal revenue (*MR*) is equal to marginal cost (*MC*). The short-run profit-maximising quantity is thus Q_1, for which the monopolistic competitor charges a price per unit of P_1. The economic profit per unit of production is the difference between average revenue (*AR*) and average cost (*AC*) at Q_1. The firm's total economic profit is indicated by the shaded rectangle in the figure.

This short-run equilibrium cannot be sustained in the long run. The economic profit attracts new entrants and as new firms enter the industry, two things happen. First, the demand for the product of the original firm falls. Graphically, this is illustrated by a leftward shift of the firm's demand curve (and a corresponding leftward shift of the firm's marginal revenue curve). Second, the demand curve for the product of the firm also becomes more price elastic, since there are now more close substitutes for the firm's product than before. This process will continue until all the economic profits have been eliminated and there is no further entry into the industry. The long-run equilibrium of the monopolistically competitive firm is illustrated in Figure 13-5(b). The only possible equilibrium in the long run is where the individual firm produces a quantity (Q_e) at which average revenue (*AR*) is equal to average cost (*AC*) (ie where economic profit is zero and only normal profit is earned). Graphically, this is indicated by a position where *MR* = *MC and AR* = *AC*. This implies that the *AR* curve must be at a tangent to the *AC* curve. In this respect the long-run profit position of the firm operating in a monopolistically competitive market is the same as that of a firm operating under conditions of perfect competition. However, for the reasons mentioned earlier, it is not possible to construct a diagram that illustrates the position of the **industry** under conditions of monopolistic competition, as can be done in the case of perfect competition.

In the movement towards the long-run equilibrium, the monopolistic competitor makes a series of adjustments and moves through a series of short-term equilibria based on perceived demand curves. The perceived demand curves differ from the actual demand curves shown in Figure 13-5 and are based on the incorrect assumption that the representative firm's competitors will not react to its own adjustments. This is the reason why we indicated in Table 13-1 that the monopolistic competitor has incomplete information.

13.4 Oligopoly

The word **oligopoly** comes from the Greek words *oligoi*, meaning "few", and *polein*, meaning "sell". Under oligopoly a few large firms dominate the market. When there are only two firms in the industry, it is called a duopoly. The product may be homogeneous (eg steel, cement), but it is mostly heterogeneous (eg motorcars, cigarettes, household appliances, electronic equipment, household detergents). When the product is homogeneous, the market is described as a pure or homogeneous oligopoly, and when the product is heterogeneous (or differentiated) the market is called a differentiated oligopoly. Oligopoly is the most common market form in modern economies.

FIGURE 13-5 The equilibrium of the firm under monopolistic competition

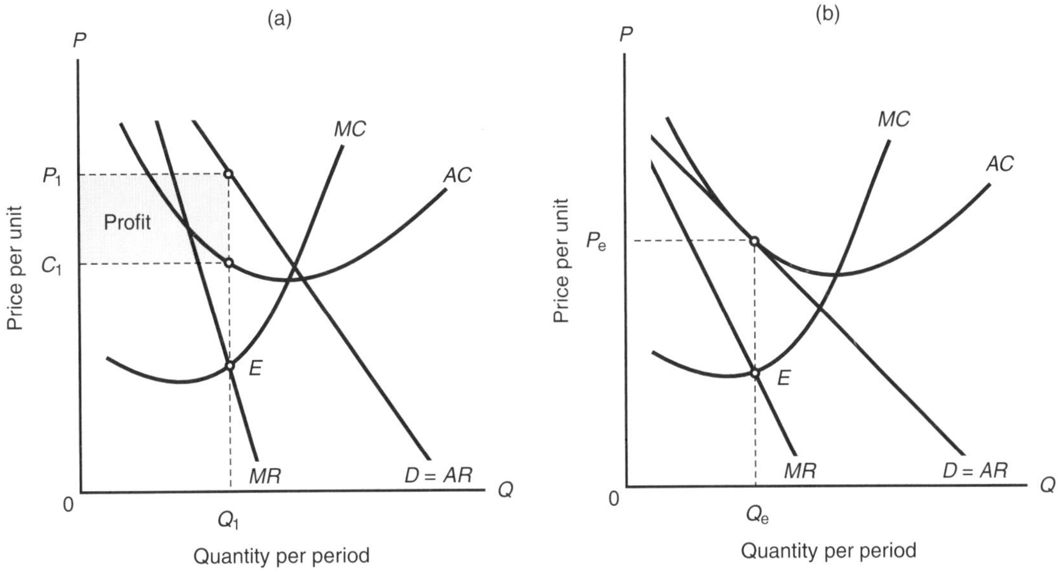

Short-run and long-run equilibrium positions of a monopolistically competitive firm are illustrated in (a) and (b) respectively. In both cases D is the demand curve for the product of the firm (or average revenue AR), MR is marginal revenue, MC is marginal cost and AC is average cost. The firm is in equilibrium where MR = MC. In the short-run conditions illustrated in (a), the firm is in equilibrium at output Q_1 and price P_1. The firm's total profit is illustrated by the shaded rectangle. In the long run, however, the firm only makes a normal profit at an output of Q_e and a price of P_e. At that price-output combination AR is tangent to AC, MR = MC and AR = AC.

When people talk about "big business" and "market power" they are usually referring to oligopolies (rather than to pure monopolies).

Examples of industries in which there are only a few firms, or in which a few firms dominate the market, were given in Table 13-2. Some further examples are sugar refining, insecticide production, domestic airlines, radio stations, television channels, golf equipment, computer hardware, retail supermarkets and other competing firms in a certain geographical area (eg television repair shops in a city). The list is almost endless. See also Box 13-4 and Table 13-4 at the end of the chapter.

As in many other countries, by far the largest proportion of the total value of manufacturing output in South Africa is produced by oligopolists.

The main feature of oligopoly is the high degree of **interdependence** between the firms. Interdependence refers to the degree to which the actions of one firm affect (or are determined by) the actions of other firms. Under oligopoly there are so few suppliers that each firm is affected by the actions of the other firms. Each oligopolist therefore always has to consider how its rivals will react to any action that it takes. Another important feature of oligopoly is **uncertainty**. This is related to the interdependence among the firms. Because the firms are interdependent and no firm can ever be certain of the policies of its competitors, the firms operate in an uncertain environment. A third key feature is **barriers to entry**, which may vary from industry to industry.

Strategy

In an oligopolistic industry or market each firm must act **strategically**, since its profit depends not only on its own actions but also on the other firms' actions. An oligopolistic firm must therefore always consider the possible impact of its decisions on the decisions and actions of its rivals. Under perfect competition and monopoly, strategic interactions are either unimportant (perfect competition) or absent (monopoly). Under oligopoly, however, each firm must constantly take strategic decisions. The most basic decision is whether to cooperate with the other firms in the industry or whether to compete with them. One of the techniques that can be used to analyse strategic oligopolistic behaviour is **game theory** which is studied in intermediate and advanced courses in microeconomics. In this book we only consider the broad principles of cooperation (or collusion) between oligopolists and competition between them.

BOX 13-4 CONCENTRATION IN THE SOUTH AFRICAN BANKING SECTOR

The South African banking sector is a good example of an oligopoly. At the end of 2001, Absa (21,1%), Standard Bank (18,6%), Nedcor (18,1%) and FirstRand (14,9%) had a combined market share of 72,7% of the market for bank deposits in South Africa. In 2002, Nedcor also took over BOE Bank, which had a 6,5% market share. The four big banks thus controlled about 80% of the market for bank deposits.

In 2000, the Competition Commission estimated that the Big Four controlled 96,5% of the market for cheque accounts, 88,7% of the market for transmission accounts, 93,3% of the overdrafts, 81,2% of the mortgages and 94,5% of the credit cards.

The oligopolistic nature of the banking sector helps to explain why the major banks invariably adjust their rates virtually simultaneously when the South African Reserve Bank adjusts its repurchase rate (ie the rate at which it lends to the banks) – see Chapter 15. As a result of this type of behaviour, the banking sector has often been accused of operating or acting like a cartel – see Box 13-5.

Source of basic information: *Competition News*, no. 10, December 2002

Oligopolists have two possible broad strategies:

- They can join forces and act as if they were a monopolist (the collusion option).
- They can compete with their rivals to gain a larger share of industry profits for themselves (the competition option). The competition, in turn, can be price competition or non-price competition.

■ COLLUSION

Oligopolists often collude by entering into an agreement, arrangement or understanding to limit competition in the industry and maintain high levels of profitability in the long run. Sellers can, for example, agree to charge the same prices for certain products, to grant uniform discounts, or to limit their marketing and distribution to certain regions. A specific arrangement among otherwise competitive firms to limit output, to set prices, or to share the market, is called a **cartel**. The purpose of the members is to operate in a particular market as a shared monopoly. Some examples of cartels are provided in Box 13-5.

Collusion is only successful if agreements can be enforced. When a large number of sellers are involved, successful collusion is highly unlikely (if not impossible). Some of the sellers will invariably break the agreement in the hope that the others will not notice or retaliate. With a small number of large producers, the distribution of profits among the members of a cartel is always a source of dispute. The conditions for successful collusion include the following:

- The number of firms must be small and they must be well known to each other.
- The firms should have similar production methods and average costs and therefore have an incentive to change prices at the same time by the same percentage.
- The product should be homogeneous rather than heterogeneous, making it easier to agree on price.
- There should be significant barriers to entry which reduce the possibility (and fear) of disruption by new firms.
- The market should be stable.
- There should be no government measures to curb or prohibit collusion.

In practice, however, governments often prohibit collusion between firms. Anti-cartel actions are therefore usually important elements of **competition policy**, which we discuss in Section 13.6.

Where open collusion is prohibited, firms nevertheless often try to get around the law. Construction firms, for example, often collude when tendering for contracts. They get together beforehand and allocate the various contracts among themselves. They then all submit high-priced estimates for a particular contract, but the chosen one puts in a slightly lower (but still high) estimate and is awarded the contract. Similar practices exist in other industries, for example where producers decide to share the clients between them and quote prices in such a way that a particular client is virtually forced to continue buying from the same producer. Although such practices are illegal, it may be very difficult to prove that firms are making informal agreements behind closed doors.

■ COMPETITION

When oligopolists compete, it is often in the form of non-price competition such as product development, advertising and other forms of marketing. Price competition tends to be avoided, since price competition will drive down the average industry profit. The more fiercely firms compete to obtain a larger share of industry profits, the smaller these industry profits will become. Even with non-price competition this will tend to occur because product development, advertising and other forms of marketing all raise industry costs.

BOX 13-5 CARTELS

A cartel is a formal collusive agreement whereby oligopolists agree on prices, market share, advertising expenditure, product development, etc. The classic example in South Africa was the cartel between the three major cement producers, Pretoria Portland Cement (PPC), Anglo-Alpha and Blue Circle, which together accounted for more than 90 per cent of the total cement sales in the country. These three firms long colluded on price setting and market share, and were even granted official permission to continue colluding after the practices concerned were prohibited in 1986. In October 1994, however, the government withdrew this permission and gave the cartel until the end of 1996 to wind up its affairs. Although the cartel was subsequently abandoned, cement users frequently allege that the cartel between the three companies, PPC, Holcim and Lafarge SA (as they are called nowadays) is still in place.

Early in 2007 it transpired that Pioneer Foods (trading as Sasko and Duens Bakeries), Tiger Food Brands (trading as Albany Bakeries) and Premier Foods (trading as Blue Ribbon Bakery) had operated a bread cartel in the Western Cape. The companies had (i) simultaneously increased the price of bread to independent distributors in the Western Cape by the same amount, (ii) simultaneously decreased and fixed the maximum discount given to independent distributors and (iii) agreed not to supply each other's independent distributors. The case was prosecuted by the Competition Commission (see Section 13-6), but Premier Foods was granted conditional leniency for co-operating with the Commission.

A well-known international example of collusion is the Organisation of Petroleum Exporting Countries (OPEC), the cartel that was set up in 1960 by the five major oil-producing countries at the time (Saudi Arabia, Iran, Iraq, Kuwait and Venezuela). In contrast to the cement example, which involved three price-making firms, the international oil market was supplied by a number of price-taking firms and the formation of OPEC was aimed at improving the position of its members. In 1973, OPEC countries, which now numbered 13 and which together accounted for 70 per cent of the world's supply of crude oil and 87 per cent of world oil exports, agreed to restrict their output by negotiating quotas. Even though the cartel was not a complete monopoly, it had substantial market power. Given the highly inelastic demand for oil (particularly in the short run), the output restrictions resulted in a quadrupling of the oil price within a year. Profits rose and many of the OPEC countries suddenly became very wealthy. By the end of the decade they were spending vast amounts on arms, infrastructure and economic development. Eager for yet more income they engineered a second output restriction that raised prices from \$10–\$12 per barrel to above \$30 per barrel. However, the world supply subsequently increased, spurred by the high oil prices, and by 1985 OPEC's share in world production had fallen to 30 per cent. The world demand for oil also became more price elastic in the long run as consumers and producers economised on the use of oil and new fuel-saving technologies were introduced.

As the world output grew, OPEC countries continually had to reduce their output to maintain world prices. With the more elastic demand, incomes in OPEC countries declined and the cartel came under increasing pressure. OPEC members started to violate their quotas and at the end of 1985 production quotas were eliminated. The OPEC example is typical of many cartel arrangements. Individual members of a cartel will always be tempted to cheat by cutting prices or (as in OPEC's case) by selling more than their allocated quota.

The OPEC example illustrates some basic problems associated with attempts to restrict output:

- Maintaining market power becomes more difficult over time.
- Producers with market power face a basic trade-off between short-run and long-run profits.
- Agreement over output restriction is difficult to maintain over time.

No general theory of oligopoly

Since oligopolistic firms are interdependent and rivalrous, and therefore act strategically, it is impossible to have a single, general theory of the pricing and output decisions of the firm under oligopoly. The general behaviour of oligopolists cannot be predicted with any certainty – under oligopoly almost anything can happen. The broad principle is that the closer we come to the real world, the more difficult it becomes to construct general theories. Instead of a general theory, there are many different oligopoly theories or models, each based on different assumptions about the reactions of rivals to the pricing and output decisions of the firm being studied. This prompted the American economist, Martin Shubik, to state:

> [W]ith action and reaction curves and marginal cost and revenue curves of a dozen varieties, diagram drawing has its finest hour when a new crop of seniors or fresh graduate students are given the one or two week special on oligopoly ...[3]

We do not discuss the different oligopoly models in this book, but to give you some idea of what oligopoly models are about, we outline one of the classic oligopoly theories (that of the kinked demand curve).

■ AN EXAMPLE OF A THEORY OF OLIGOPOLISTIC BEHAVIOUR: THE KINKED DEMAND CURVE

The theory of the kinked demand curve, devised in 1939 by the American economist, Paul Sweezy, is one of the many possible theories of oligopolistic behaviour. The kinked demand curve **does not explain how price and output are determined** under oligopoly, but it does illustrate the importance of **interdependence** and **uncertainty** in oligopolistic markets. It is also one of the possible explanations for the observed degree of relative **price stability** under oligopoly in the United States at the time Sweezy constructed the model.

Figure 13-6 illustrates the position of an oligopolistic firm. Instead of explaining the price of the product and the level of output, we start by assuming that the price of the product is P_1 and that the quantity supplied is Q_1. This is indicated by point *a* which is a point on the demand curve for the product of the firm. If the oligopolistic firm raises or reduces the price of its product, the outcome will depend on the reactions of its competitors. According to this particular theory, the oligopolist assumes that its competitors will not react to a price increase by also raising the prices of their products. A price increase will therefore lead to a relatively large fall in the quantity demanded of the firm's product (as consumers switch to the relatively cheaper products of the firm's competitors). This is indicated by the demand curve *Da*. The oligopolistic firm thus believes that it will lose market share if it increases the price of its product. However, the oligopolistic firm assumes that its competitors *will* react to a price *decrease* by lowering their prices as well. The oligopolistic firm will not therefore be able to increase its market share by lowering the price of its product. The quantity demanded of the firm's product will increase, but not to the same extent as it would decrease as a result of a comparable increase in the price of its product. This is indicated by the demand curve *ad*. This assumed **asymmetrical reaction** of competitors to a price increase and a price decrease gives rise to a kinked demand curve, with the kink at the level of the ruling price of the product. In effect the oligopolist is assuming that there are two demand curves for its product – one if competitors do not react to a price change (*DD*), and one if they do react (*dd*). The kinked demand curve *Dad* thus consists of portions of two different demand curves.

FIGURE 13-6 The kinked demand curve

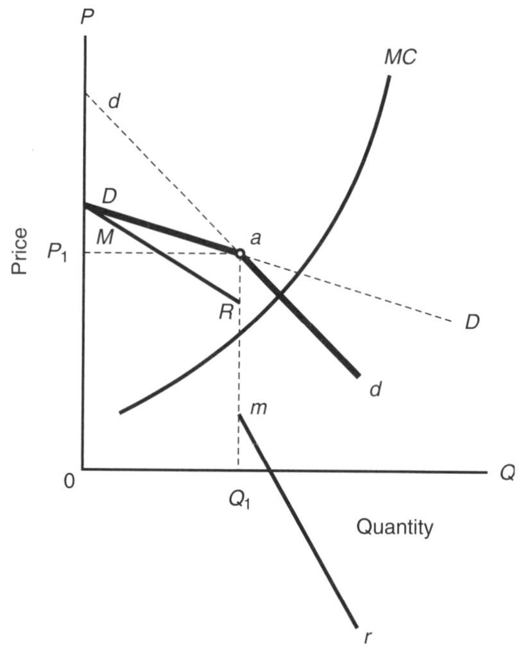

The initial price is P_1 and the quantity Q_1. Dad is the kinked demand curve facing the oligopolistic firm. It is based on asymmetric reaction by the firm's rivals to a price increase (Da) and a price decrease (ad). The corresponding marginal revenue is broken up into MR and mr, corresponding to Da and ad respectively. The gap between the two can accommodate a range of marginal cost curves such as MC. As a result the profit-maximising levels of price and quantity remain at P_1 and Q_1 respectively.

3. Shubik, M. 1970. A curmudgeon's guide to microeconomics. *Journal of Economic Literature*, 8(2): 416.

The demand curve for the product of the firm is also its average revenue (*AR*) curve, and its marginal revenue (*MR*) curve lies halfway between the *AR* curve and the price axis. In the figure we also show the marginal revenue curve corresponding to *Dad*. It consists of two separate portions, *MR* (corresponding to *Da*) and *mr* (corresponding to *ad*). We know that profit is maximised at the level of output where *MR* = *MC*. In the figure we also show a marginal cost (*MC*) curve which passes through the gap between the two marginal revenue curves. Profit is thus maximised at the existing quantity and price (Q_1 and P_1). The significance of the kinked demand curve lies in the fact that *MC* can increase or decrease significantly without affecting equilibrium output and price – any *MC* curve which passes through the gap between *MR* and *mr* will yield the same equilibrium quantity and price. In Sweezy's time oligopoly was characterised by stable prices and output levels. According to the theory of the kinked demand curve, this is the result of the high degree of interdependence among oligopolists, and the uncertainty about how competitors will react to price changes.

It should be emphasised, however, that the kinked demand curve is but one of a wide range of theories explaining oligopolistic behaviour. As we emphasised earlier, no general theory of oligopolistic behaviour is possible. Another possible pricing strategy under oligopoly, namely mark-up pricing, is discussed in Box 13-6.

Like a monopolist and a monopolistic competitor, an oligopolist faces a downward-sloping demand curve. However, the shape of the curve is uncertain, since this depends on how its competitors will react to price changes – they may decide to follow or not to follow any price change.

Under oligopoly the entry of new firms is more difficult than under perfect competition or monopolistic competition. However, in contrast to monopoly, entry is possible and the mere threat of possible entry by new firms may be as effective in disciplining oligopolists as actual competition would be – see the discus-

BOX 13-6 MARK-UP PRICING IN THE RETAIL SECTOR

A retailer offers a service that is differentiated by location, hours of service, product lines, quality of service and so on. Retailers purchase goods from manufacturers or wholesalers and usually add a percentage mark-up (the margin) to the prices they pay. Some products have high mark-ups while other have low mark-ups.

Food prices increased sharply in South Africa in 2002. In October 2002 food prices (measured by the food component of the CPI) were 19,3 per cent higher than a year earlier. Many consumers blamed the supermarkets and other food retailers for this state of affairs and in March 2002 the Minister of Trade and Industry called on the Competition Commission (see Section 13.6) to launch an investigation into the causes of rising food prices. In October 2002 the Commission's final report was published. In this report it is stated (in section 2.5) that Pick 'n Pay admitted to passing on all cost increases fully to maintain their margins. In other words, the supermarket chain applies mark-up pricing, that is, it adds a fixed percentage to the prices it pays for goods purchased from manufacturers and other suppliers.

Does this refute the theories we have explained thus far? What about marginal revenue, marginal cost and all the other concepts we have introduced? Do they have any application in real-world situations? The answer is that all the basic concepts and rules still apply, but in a different setting. A retailer provides a service – it does not produce goods – and there are significant differences between the cost structure of a retailer such as Pick 'n Pay and a firm which produces or manufactures goods. Once these differences are taken into account it becomes obvious that mark-up pricing in the retail sector is simply a special case of the more general theories we have explained.

Like any other firm, a supermarket like Pick 'n Pay maximises its profit where marginal revenue is equal to marginal cost. Since the firm purchases goods from producers or wholesalers at a fixed price per unit, the marginal cost of each product is fixed. The firm's marginal cost curve is thus horizontal at that price as in both figures in this box. In this case the typical U-shaped cost structure does not apply. As far as the firm's revenue structure is concerned, the price elasticity of the demand facing a particular supermarket will differ from product to product. For example, in the case of basic foodstuffs the price elasticity will tend to be high, as illustrated in diagram I, since each supermarket (eg Pick 'n Pay) has to compete with other supermarkets (eg Shoprite or Spar) in the town, suburb or city in which it is located. Note that we are dealing here with the demand for the products of a particular supermarket. The **market** demand for basic foodstuffs will probably be price **in**elastic, for the reasons outlined in Chapter 9, but for **a particular supermarket** the demand will be price elastic since a small rise in price might cause existing consumers to switch to rival supermarkets, while a small drop in price might increase the supermarket's market share, by persuading more households to purchase their weekly or monthly groceries at the store with the lower prices. With an elastic demand curve, the mark-up will be relatively low, as illustrated in diagram I. The firm operates at quantity Q_1, where $MR = MC$, and charges a price according to the demand curve (which is also the firm's AR curve). The price is A_1 and the mark-up over costs is A_1B_1*. What we have here is an illustration of the often-quoted phenomenon of "low margin, high turnover". This also explains why competing supermarkets advertise so extensively by offering various "specials" on basic consumer items. Each wants to create the impression that its products are the cheapest.

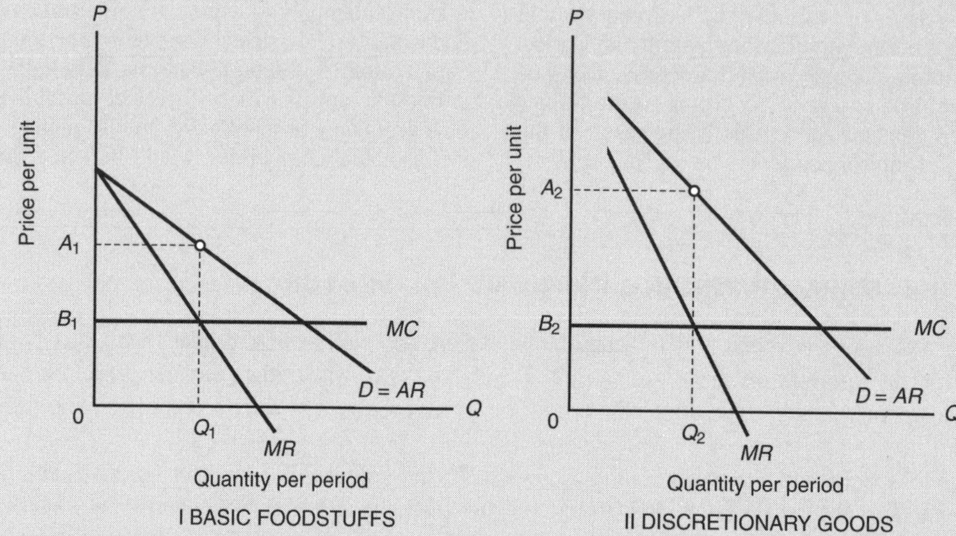

But supermarkets do not only sell basic foodstuffs and other basic consumer items. They also sell a variety of so-called discretionary items (eg stationery, beauty aids, health products, small appliances and small hardware items). The price elasticity of the demand for such items that the individual supermarket is faced with, tends to be much lower than for basic foodstuffs. Because discretionary products are purchased less frequently, shoppers tend to be less aware of their prices at competing stores. Even if they are aware of some price difference, it will probably not be worthwhile to go to another store to buy one or two relatively small items. Given the relatively inelastic demand facing the individual supermarket, the mark-up for discretionary goods or irregular purchases tends to be higher, as illustrated in diagram II. Profit is maximised where $MR = MC$ (ie at quantity Q_2). The price is A_2 and the mark-up is A_2B_2.

The differences in price elasticities provides a further incentive to supermarkets to advertise "specials" on basic items, sometimes even at or below cost. Once the consumer is enticed to visit the store, she will probably also buy other goods on which the mark-up is higher. In fact, sometimes the retailer will even temporarily raise the mark-up on other basic items to compensate for possible losses on the "specials". Also note that the massive purchasing of the major supermarket chains often enables them to negotiate special discounts on large purchases. When this happens, the firm's MC declines and lower prices can be charged.

The basic message of this box is that mark-up pricing in the retail sector does not refute the theory of costs and profit maximisation explained in this part of the book.

*Note that, as represented here, the firm's cost does not include normal profit.

sion of contestable markets in the next section. The fact that the market is dominated by a few large producers does not mean that there is little or no competition under oligopoly. On the contrary, competition is often intense, although it tends to be non-price competition, rather than price competition (which they tend to avoid). The more intensely oligopolists compete, the closer they are likely to come to perfectly competitive output and price.

Advertising and product diversification as barriers to entry

Oligopolistic firms often use advertising and product diversification to create barriers to entry. Some firms spend huge amounts on **advertising** to create product awareness and loyalty to well-known brands (eg Coca-Cola and Castle Lager), thereby making it very expensive for potential rivals to enter the market. Advertising is discussed further in Box 13-7.

Product diversification can also be used as a barrier to entry. In many industries the existing firms produce multiple brands of the same product aimed at different market segments, which compete actively against each other as well as against the products of other firms. In South Africa, for example, Unilever produces Omo, Surf, Skip and Sunlight (fabric cleaners), Lux, Dove, Vinolia, Breeze, Geisha and Sunlight (soaps), Shield, Impulse, Pears, Axe, Brut and Storm (deodorants), and Joko, Glen, Glenton, Pitco, Lipton Rooibos, Lipton Herbal, Lipton Ice and Lipton Laager (teas), to mention but a few, while Steinhoff produces

BOX 13-7 ADVERTISING

One of the main forms of non-price competition is advertising. Firms advertise to increase the demand for their particular product or to reduce the price elasticity of the demand for their particular brands of a differentiated product.

The following table lists the ten largest private advertisers in South Africa in 2006.

Rank	Advertiser	All media (Rm)	Print (Rm)	Radio (Rm)	TV (Rm)
1	MTN	398	180	56	162
2	Shoprite Checkers	393	260	49	84
3	Vodacom	364	139	75	150
4	Pick 'n Pay	332	233	16	83
5	Unilever HPC	266	18	37	211
6	Cell C	232	89	31	112
7	Nedbank	225	100	49	76
8	Standard Bank	225	115	57	53
9	FirstRand Bank	224	74	77	73
10	JD Group	223	60	14	149

Source: *Adfocus 2007*, Supplement to the *Financial Mail*, 25 May: 112

Not surprisingly, the companies listed in the table are near-monopolists or oligopolists. Oligopolists and monopolistic competitors have the largest incentive to advertise, but firms engaged in monopolistic competition are too small to feature in the list. Unilever, mentioned in the text, is a large producer of a variety of consumer products. Unilever Food also spent R131 million in 2006. Shoprite Checkers and Pick 'n Pay are two oligopolists that continuously try to maintain or increase their market share by advertising a range of "specials" to lure customers to their stores. The ultimate purpose is to convince shoppers that they offer the best value for money. Incidentally, Spar, the other main supermarket chain, was twentieth on the list. As mentioned earlier, MTN, Vodacom and Cell C, are the three oligopolists in the cellular phone market. As indicated in Box 13-4, the banking sector is also an oligopoly. Note the similarity in the amounts spent by Nedbank, Standard Bank and FirstRand Bank. Absa, the fourth member of the group, was in the eleventh position. JD Group is a large player in the furniture and appliances retail market.

As emphasised in the text, oligopolistic firms tend to refrain from price competition. Instead, they use advertising and other forms of non-price competition to maintain or increase their share of the market. Even monopolists or near-monopolists sometimes advertise extensively to increase the demand for their products. Only perfectly competitive firms have no incentive to advertise, since they can sell their output at the ruling market price. An organisation representing a perfectly competitive *industry*, however, might still advertise on behalf of the firms in the industry in an attempt to increase the demand for the product of the industry (eg milk, pork).

Many firms clearly have an incentive to advertise, but are the huge amounts spent on advertising justifiable from a broader economic perspective? Is society not simply wasting the scarce resources devoted to advertising? This is a controversial issue that often generates heated debate among economists and other observers. Critics argue that much advertising is psychological rather than informational, that firms attempt to manipulate people's tastes and to create desires that might otherwise not exist. They also argue that advertising reduces competition, for example by trying to convince consumers that products are more different than they actually are. Sasol, Engen, Shell, Caltex and BP are all among the top advertisers in South Africa, but do their products differ significantly? Also, to the extent that advertising succeeds in establishing brand loyalties, the price elasticity of demand for the products falls and the firms can increase their profits. Finally, critics point out that advertising costs are part of production costs and that it is ultimately the consumer that bears most, if not all, of the burden in the form of higher prices.

Against this, defenders of advertising argue that advertisements convey information (eg about prices, new products, the location of outlets) that enables customers to take more informed decisions, thereby promoting competition and improving the efficiency of resource allocation. They also argue that advertising allows new firms to enter more easily (which implies that they disagree with the view that advertising tends to raise barriers to entry).

Although the debate about the economic advantages and disadvantages of advertising is by no means settled, it is interesting to note that certain professions that were previously prohibited from advertising (eg medical doctors, dentists, lawyers) are nowadays allowed to advertise freely, presumably to increase competition. On the other hand, there has been a severe clampdown on the advertising of tobacco products, which are regarded as socially and physically undesirable, in South Africa and elsewhere.

Edblo, Softex, Slumberland, Sealy, Ther-a-pedic and Dreamland (mattresses) and a whole range of furniture brands. Why do oligopolistic firms act in this way? They want to gain a larger share of the market and make it harder for a new entrant to enter the market and to obtain a significant share of the market with a single product. By advertising all the different brands and creating brand loyalties they raise the barriers even further.

13.5 Comparison of monopoly and imperfect competition with perfect competition

In Section 12.6 we explained that perfect competition is both allocatively and productively efficient. You will recall that a market is allocatively efficient if $MC = P$ and productively efficient if production occurs where $LRAC$ is at a minimum. In this section we use allocative efficiency, productive efficiency and other criteria to compare monopoly and imperfect competition with perfect competition. We start with monopoly.

Monopoly versus perfect competition

Analytically, the only valid comparison is between the long-run equilibrium of a perfectly competitive industry (or market) and a monopoly. In other words, we compare a monopoly with the situation that would have prevailed if there had been a large number of firms producing the product under conditions of perfect competition. Moreover, the comparison must pertain to the long run, since all possible adjustments can only be made in the long run.

In Figure 13-7 MC represents the marginal cost of the industry, while the market demand curve is represented by the average revenue curve (AR). Under perfect competition the industry (or market) supply curve is obtained by adding all the individual supply curves (ie the rising parts of the marginal cost curves of all the firms in the industry). For a perfectly

FIGURE 13-7 Comparison between monopoly and a perfectly competitive industry

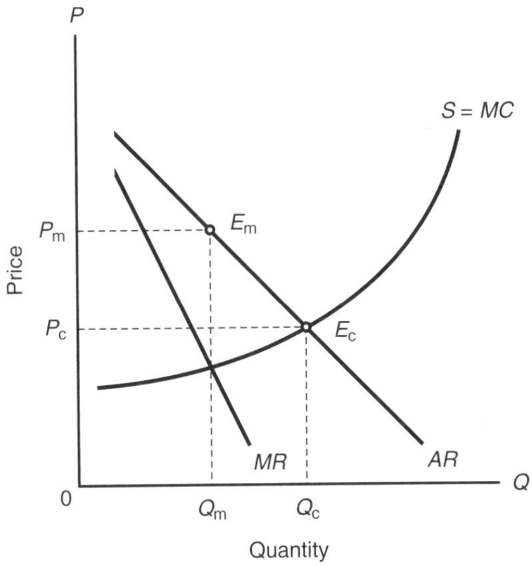

AR is the demand curve for the product of the industry and MR is the monopolist's marginal revenue curve. Marginal cost MC is also the supply curve S for the perfectly competitive industry. Under perfect competition, long-run equilibrium E_c is established by the interaction of demand AR and supply S at a price P_c and a quantity Q_c. Equilibrium for the monopolist E_m is at a price P_m and a quantity Q_m. Under monopoly the equilibrium price is higher, and the equilibrium quantity lower, than under perfect competition, ceteris paribus.

competitive industry, *MC* can thus be regarded as the industry (or market) supply curve (*S*). The equilibrium price and quantity are determined by the intersection of supply (*S*) and demand (*AR*). The equilibrium under perfect competition is at E_c, that is, at a price P_c and a quantity Q_c.

For the same cost and demand conditions, the equilibrium of a monopolist is at price P_m and quantity Q_m. **If the industry is a monopoly, the price *P* will thus be higher and the output *Q* lower than if perfect competition prevails.** An example would be if avocado farmers who initially operate under perfect competition set up a marketing agency through which they sell all their avocados. The agency then acts as a monopoly supplier to the market. Production cost would still be the same but prices will be higher and quantities lower than before.

Under perfect competition $MC = P$ and production occurs at the minimum of *AC* in the long run where all firms earn a normal profit only (see Figure 12-8). Perfect competition thus meets the criteria for allocative and productive efficiency. In contrast, monopoly does not meet either of these criteria. At equilibrium, *P* is greater than *MC* and the monopolist does not produce where *AC* is at a minimum. **Monopoly is thus an inefficient market structure.** The monopolist produces less, employs fewer resources, charges a higher price than society will prefer and does not produce at the lowest possible cost per unit of output.

This conclusion, however, is based on the assumption that the cost conditions are the same for a single, large producer as for a large number of small producers. If one large firm can produce a product (eg a motorcar) more cheaply than a large number of small producers, then monopoly is not necessarily inefficient (see the discussion of economies of scale and scope in Section 11.5 and Box 11-8).

In Figure 13-7 we assumed that the perfectly competitive industry and the monopolistic firm are subject to the same cost conditions. But what if the monopolist can achieve economies of scale that are not available to the numerous small producers in the perfectly competitive industry? The answer depends on the extent to which the monopolistic firm can reduce its costs. In Figure 13-8 we illustrate a situation in which the monopolistic firm produces at the same price and output as the perfectly competitive industry. The $S = MC$ curve indicates the supply curve of the competitive industry, which is equal to the sum of the rising parts of the *MC* curves of all the individual producers. As in Figure 13-7, P_c indicates the equilibrium price and Q_c the equilibrium quantity in the perfectly competitive market, since equilibrium occurs where demand *D* (= *AR*) intersects supply *S* (= *MC*). MC_m indicates the lower marginal cost of the monopolistic firm, which produces where $MC = MR$ (ie quantity Q_c) at price P_c (ie the same price and quantity as the perfectly competitive industry). This position serves as a reference point. If the monopolist's marginal cost lies between $S = MC$ and MC_m, the equilibrium price (for the monopolist) will still be higher and the equilibrium quantity still lower than under perfect competition. However, if the monopolist's *MC* curve lies below MC_m, then its equilibrium price will be lower and the equilibrium quantity higher than under perfect competition. In other words, if the economies of scale are large enough, then the classical case against monopoly need not hold. Note, however, that even in this case allocative efficiency will not be achieved, since *P* will still be greater than *MC*.

Social costs of monopoly power

We can use the notions of consumer surplus and producer surplus introduced in Chapter 7 to examine the social costs of monopoly power. For this purpose we assume again, as in Figure 13-7, that the monopolistic firm has the same cost structure as the perfectly competitive industry. This is illustrated in Figure 13-9 which is basically similar to Figure 13-7, with P_c and

FIGURE 13-8 Comparison between monopoly and perfect competition if monopolistic firm has a lower cost structure

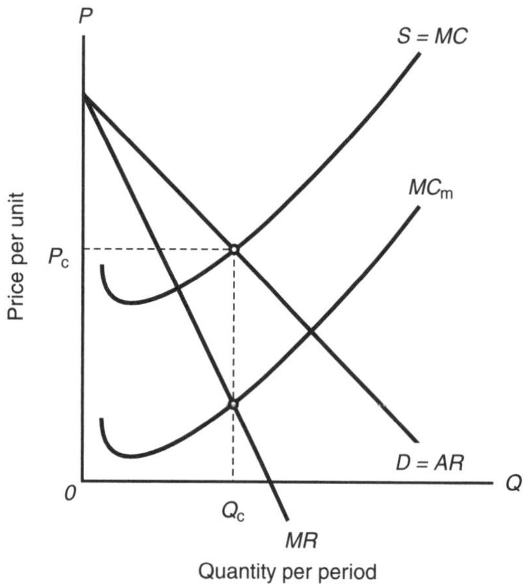

D is the demand curve and also the average revenue curve (AR) for the product of the industry, while MR is the monopolist's marginal revenue curve. Marginal cost (MC) is also the supply curve S for the perfectly competitive industry. Under perfect competition, long-run equilibrium is at price P_c and quantity Q_c. MC_m indicates the lower cost structure of the monopolistic firm. The firm will maximise profits where MR = MC at the same quantity Q_c and price P_c as under perfect competition. If the monopolist's MC lies above MC_m, the monopolist's price P will still be higher and quantity Q still lower than under perfect competition, but if MC lies below MC_m, then P will be lower and Q higher than under perfect competition.

Q_c indicating the equilibrium price and quantity under perfect competition and P_m and Q_m the corresponding values under monopoly.

As a result of the higher price P_m under monopoly, compared to price P_c under perfect competition, consumers lose areas *A* and *B*. Area *A* now becomes part of the producer surplus, but *B* is simply lost. This allocative loss is called a **deadweight loss** to society. Likewise, area *C*, which forms part of the producer surplus under perfect competition, is also lost. The total deadweight loss is thus *B* + *C*. What about the area under *MC* between Q_m and Q_c? The resources that would have been used to produce the difference between Q_c and Q_m are now released for use elsewhere in the economy. There is thus no deadweight loss in this case. With monopolisation, the monopolist thus gains at the expense of the consumers (area *A*) and society suffers a deadweight loss (areas *B* and *C*).

Similar techniques can be used to analyse situations where the cost structure of the monopolistic firm differs from that of a perfectly competitive industry.

Is monopoly a bad thing?

Most people will answer "yes" to this question. There are, however, a number of misconceptions about monopoly. In this subsection we first deal with some of the misconceptions, and then we discuss some of the arguments for and against monopoly. Many of these arguments apply to oligopoly as well.

■ SOME POPULAR MISCONCEPTIONS ABOUT MONOPOLY

It is often claimed that a monopolist can charge virtually any price it wants. This is not true. Like any other firm, a monopolist is constrained by the demand for its product. A monopolistic firm cannot sell whatever it wants at any price it decides to set.

FIGURE 13-9 The social costs of monopoly

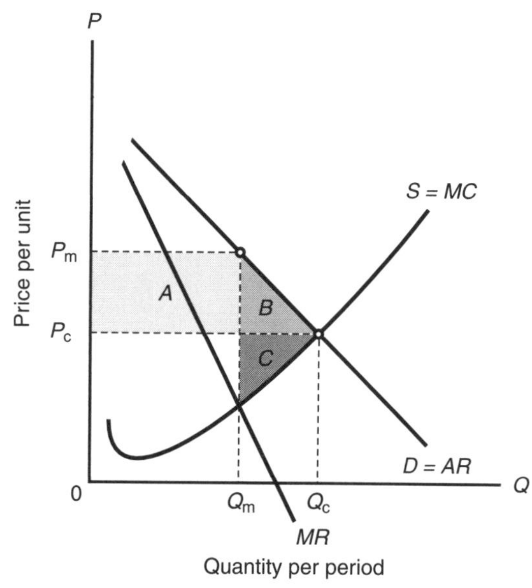

The curves are exactly the same as in Figure 13-7. When a perfectly competitive industry is monopolised, the equilibrium price rises from P_c to P_m and the equilibrium quantity falls from Q_c to Q_m. Area A illustrates the monopolist's gain at the expense of the consumers. Area B, which (like A) was part of the consumer surplus under perfect competition, simply disappears. This is a deadweight loss to society. Likewise, Area C, which formed part of the producer surplus under perfect competition, also disappears. The total deadweight loss is thus B + C.

A related claim is that a monopolist will charge the highest price it can get. This is not the case. The monopolist will set the price for its product at a level that will maximise total profit, not at the highest possible price it can charge.

Many people believe that monopoly guarantees economic profits (in the short run *and* in the long run). However, as we pointed out earlier, monopolists can also make losses. Whether a monopolist makes a profit or a loss depends on the demand for the product, the cost structure of the firm, and its pricing and output decisions. In fact, when the demand for its product falls drastically, a monopolist can be forced out of business. This happened, for example, when trams were replaced by buses, taxis and other forms of transport.

There is also a popular belief that once a profitable monopoly is established, its position is virtually unassailable and that it therefore has almost absolute economic power. This is not the case either. Even a monopolist must always consider potential competition from firms producing products which may become substitutes for its product if the price increases. For example, if the price of electricity is pushed up too high, consumers may switch to wood, paraffin, coal, petrol and other energy sources. Or if the relative price of beer is raised, consumers might switch to wine, spirits, soft drinks or even water.

The mere threat of competition may discipline a monopolist almost as much as actual competition would. Apart from potential domestic competition, a monopolist in a particular country is always subject to potential competition from similar firms in other countries. A monopolist must also be sensitive to the ruling political climate and the possibility of government regulation. If it is believed that a monopolist is abusing its economic or market power, government may decide to intervene and regulate or control its activities.

■ THE CASE AGAINST MONOPOLY (OR BIGNESS)

We now examine some of the arguments against monopoly and the counter-arguments of those who defend the existence of monopoly. You should note, however, that many of the arguments apply to all large, powerful firms, whether or not they are the sole suppliers of goods and services. The most powerful corporations in South Africa produce hundreds of different goods and services which are sold in a large number of markets in which they compete with other firms. Their financial strength, however, often gives them similar advantages to those they would have if they were the sole suppliers of the goods or services in the markets concerned.

As we have seen, **monopoly output is lower than perfectly competitive output and monopoly price is higher than perfectly competitive price**, for a given set of cost and demand conditions. Monopoly makes goods scarcer (and more expensive), *ceteris paribus*, than they would be if the industry were competitive, and this results in an inefficient allocation (or a misallocation) of resources. This conclusion is only valid, however, if the monopolist's cost structure is the same as that of a competitive industry. One of the reasons for the existence of monopoly is that it permits economies of scale. If one firm can produce a product at lower cost than a number of small, independent firms can (ie when there is a natural monopoly), monopoly is not necessarily an inefficient market structure. In a number of industries which require large capital outlays (eg the motorcar, cement, aluminium and heavy engineering industries), a small scale of production is inefficient and perfect competition is simply not feasible.

Critics of monopoly often argue that there is **little or no incentive for innovation or technological improvement** under monopoly. Since there is no competition, management may decide to take things easy, avoiding the risks associated with innovation. The British Nobel Laureate, John Hicks, once remarked that the "best of all monopoly profits is the quiet life." It may be argued, however, that only large firms have the resources required for significant innovation. It is also argued that although a patent gives the holder a monopoly (see Box 13-1), it also stimulates innovation. Why, for example, would a firm spend time and money on the development of a new product or idea if it can be copied by a rival firm?

Another argument against monopoly (or bigness) is that it leads to **managerial inefficiency**. Under perfect competition all firms are forced to produce as cheaply as possible to avoid bankruptcy, but monopolies are not forced to be efficient. If there is no competition, then inefficient, high-cost firms can survive. Economists call this X-inefficiency and it occurs, for example, if managers have other goals (eg firm growth, avoidance of risk, providing jobs for incompetent friends or relatives) which conflict with cost minimisation. X-inefficiency may also arise because the firm's workers are poorly motivated. The counter-argument is that monopolists are always subject to potential or indirect competition from firms in other industries, which try to develop substitute products, or from firms in other countries.

A related complaint is that monopolists **do not pay sufficient attention to the quality of their products or their service to customers**. The classic examples are state monopolists that leave consumers with little choice but to accept poor products and service. In a mixed economy, however, potential competition is always a disciplining factor. In South Africa, for example, Telkom (and previously the Post Office) traditionally had a monopoly on telecommunication, and customers invariably complained about the bad service. In recent years, however, Telkom has had to compete with cellular phones, electronic mail and other forms of communication, and has made a concerted effort to improve its service and its image (also with a view to privatisation and potential competition from a second fixed-line operator).

Critics also argue that monopoly **gives rise to an unfair or socially unacceptable distribution of income and wealth**. They argue that monopolists make substantial economic profits which accrue to the owners (or shareholders) at the expense of consumers, who have to pay high prices for the products. The counter-argument is that much of the profit is reinvested in the economy, and that the profits are required to finance continued economic growth. While there is no guarantee that this will indeed happen, it should be borne in mind that a monopolist is not an inherently evil institution which robs people or forces its products down consumers' throats. A monopolist simply exploits the fact that it is the sole seller of a good or service.

Monopolists and would-be monopolists, however, tend to engage in **rent-seeking** behaviour. This refers to activities designed to transfer income or wealth to a particular firm or resource supplier at someone else's or society's expense. Since a monopolist can earn economic profits in the long run, there is an incentive for monopolists and aspiring monopolists to do everything in their power to acquire or maintain monopoly privileges granted by government (eg in the form of an exclusive franchise or licence). They often spend large amounts on legal fees, lobbying and public relations advertising to persuade government to grant or sustain their privileged positions. Rent-seeking expenditures raise costs without adding anything to a firm's output and are thus socially wasteful. See also Section 16.5.

More generally, large monopolists (and all other large firms or corporations) have significant **economic power** and are often also **politically powerful**. There is thus a legitimate fear that they may be able to dictate the politics in the country and, in particular, the economic policy. On the other hand, one of the major arguments raised in favour of monopoly (or bigness) in South Africa is that the country needs large, powerful firms to be able to compete against foreign suppliers in the domestic and international markets.

What, then, is our conclusion? Is monopoly (or bigness) a good thing or a bad thing? On balance it is difficult to give an unqualified answer, but the burden of proof is on those who defend monopoly (or bigness). As we have seen, monopoly is subject to certain inherent inefficiencies and there is always the possibility that monopolists (or large firms) will abuse their economic power. Nor are there any guarantees that the potential advantages of monopoly will be realised, or passed on to consumers. It is not surprising, therefore, that most governments do not simply allow monopolists to do whatever they like. Policy with regard to monopoly and imperfect competition is discussed in Section 13.6.

Monopolistic competition versus perfect competition

The long-run equilibrium of a monopolistically competitive firm occurs when only normal profits are made. In this respect there is no difference between monopolistic competition and perfect competition. But in long-run equilibrium, the monopolistically competitive firm produces where price is higher than marginal cost and where average cost is not at a minimum – see Figure 13-5(b). Monopolistic competition is therefore neither allocatively nor productively efficient. Although monopolistically competitive firms do not make economic profits in the long run (as monopolists do), monopolistic competition is also characterised by an inefficient use of resources. Consumers pay a higher price and less output is produced than under perfect competition.

The long-run equilibrium of the firm under perfect and monopolistic competition can be compared formally as in Figure 13-10. We assume that both firms have the same long-run average cost curve *LRAC*. D_c indicates the horizontal demand curve facing the perfectly competitive firm while D_{mc} illustrates the downward-sloping, relatively price-elastic demand curve facing the monopolistic competitor. The perfectly competitive firm will produce quantity Q_c at price P_c while the monopolistically competitive firm will produce quantity Q_{mc} at price P_{mc}. Under monopolistic competition the price is higher and the quantity lower than under perfect competition. Moreover, in contrast

FIGURE 13-10 Long-run equilibrium of the firm under perfect and monopolistic competition

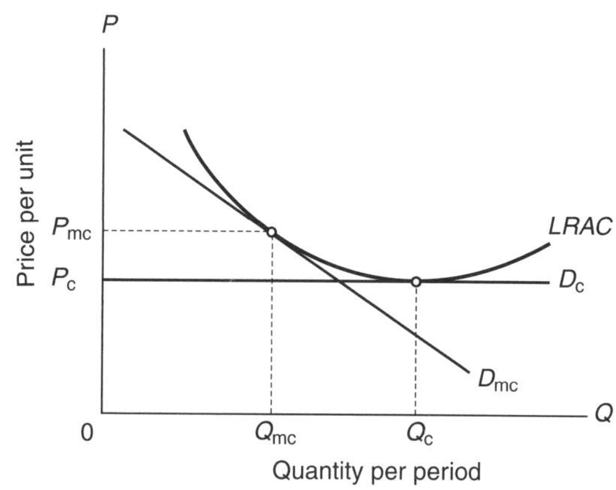

It is assumed that both firms have the same long-run average cost, illustrated by LRAC. D_c and D_{mc} represent the demand curves facing the perfect competitor and the monopolistic competitor, respectively. The perfectly competitive firm produces Q_c at price P_c, while the monopolistically competitive firm produces Q_{mc} at price P_{mc}.

to perfectly competitive firms, monopolistically competitive firms do not produce where *LRAC* is at a minimum. The latter therefore have **excess capacity**, indicated by the difference between Q_c and Q_{mc}.

Note that because we cannot illustrate the long-run equilibrium of a monopolistically competitive *industry* the only possible comparison is between a perfectly competitive and a monopolistically competitive *firm*.

The only way in which allocative and productive efficiency can be achieved is to standardise the product (ie to sacrifice the variety offered by the different firms) in which case monopolistic competition will no longer exist. Consumers are, however, normally willing to pay a slightly higher price in order to obtain a wider range of products (eg shirts, dresses) from which to choose. Another possible advantage of monopolistic competition is that it provides an incentive to firms to develop new varieties of the product in an attempt to achieve a competitive edge over their rivals. If consumers are willing to pay a premium for variety, then monopolistic competition does not necessarily reduce society's economic welfare.

Under perfect competition there is no incentive for the individual firm to advertise. As we explained in Section 13.4, the only possible advertising will be undertaken on behalf of the industry as a whole (to increase the market demand for the product). Monopolistic competitors, however, have a strong incentive to advertise and market their product in an attempt to differentiate it from the other varieties of the product and establish brand loyalty among consumers. The greater the degree of differentiation, the less elastic demand will be. Advertising and marketing costs, however, raise costs and prices. The *LRAC* curve of the monopolistic competitor is therefore likely to lie above that of the perfect competitor.

Oligopoly versus perfect competition

Although oligopoly is a form of imperfect competition, oligopolistic competition is much more active than perfect competition. Oligopolistic competition is an active, strategic process of moves and countermoves, in which one firm's gains are often at the expense of the other firms in the industry. But while oligopolistic competition can be intense and aggressive, perfect competition is entirely passive. Each firm is so insignificant that no one of them takes into account what the other individual firms do. Yet this passive competition is quite effective and prevents a perfectly competitive firm from "exploiting" consumers.

Since there is no general theory of oligopoly we cannot compare oligopoly with perfect competition in formal terms, as we could in the case of monopoly and monopolistic competition. However, if oligopolists collude and jointly maximise profits, they will in effect be acting together as a monopoly and all the disadvantages of monopoly will also be experienced under oligopoly. Graphically, the position of the industry will then be the same as that of a monopolist, as illustrated in Figure 13-2. Moreover, depending on the size of the individual oligopolists, there may be less scope for economies of scale than under monopoly. As emphasised earlier, oligopolists are also likely to engage in much more extensive advertising than monopolists.

On the positive side, oligopolists have a considerable incentive to engage in research and development (much more so than a monopolist). If an oligopolistic firm succeeds in producing a new or better product, it will gain an advantage over its rivals and it may be some time before the latter can respond by producing a similar product. Where patent rights are involved (eg in the pharmaceutical industry), the incentive will be even stronger. Research and development can also succeed in lowering costs and improving the competitive position of the oligopolistic firm. Another potential advantage, which we also mentioned in respect of monopolistic competition, is that non-price competition through product differentiation may result in a greater choice for the consumer. In many oligopolistic markets (eg in the case of cellular phones and motor vehicles) a huge range of products are supplied to meet the needs of different groups of consumers.

Sometimes the power of oligopolists in certain markets is offset to some extent if they sell their products to other oligopolists. Given the prevalence of oligopoly in the modern economy, this often happens. In the South African food industry, for example, there are some powerful producers of processed foods, but they sell most of their products to the equally powerful large supermarket chains, who can use their market power to keep prices down.[4] This phenomenon, where the power of a seller is offset by powerful buyers, who can prevent the price from being pushed up, is known as **countervailing power**. As early as the 1950s, John Kenneth Galbraith, an eminent American economist, emphasised the power and prevalence of oligopolists in the United States and noted that price competition between suppliers had declined but had been replaced (as a restraint on oligopolistic power) by countervailing power.

It should be clear that it is difficult to draw any general conclusions about the impact of oligopoly, particularly in relation to perfect competition. In some cases the disadvantages to society may outweigh the advantages but in other cases the outcome of the rivalrous behaviour of oligopolists may be little different from that under perfect competition. In recent decades the latter result has resulted in the identification of a different theory about markets, namely the theory of contestable markets.

4. For example, in 2002 Pick 'n Pay (40%), Shoprite Checkers (25%), Spar (23%) and Woolworths (6,5%) had a combined market share of 94,5% in the retail food sector. See Competition Commission. 2002. *Final report: Inquiry into food price rises,* 33.

CONTESTABLE MARKETS

In our discussion of monopoly we mentioned that potential competition can serve to discipline market behaviour in much the same way as actual competition. In the early 1980s, this idea was developed and formalised in the United States by William Baumol and others in the theory of **contestable markets**. According to this theory, there is no clear relationship between the *actual* number of competitors in a market and the extent to which price and quantity resemble or differ from what we would observe under perfect competition. The focus is on **potential** competition rather than actual competition and the argument is that the mere threat of potential competition may be sufficient to force existing firms to prevent prices and profits from rising too much, thereby attracting new entrants into the market. The idea of contestable markets thus broadened the application of competitive behaviour beyond the structure-conduct-performance (SCP) approach mentioned in Section 13.1.

For a market to be **perfectly contestable** the following conditions have to be met:

- There must be **easy entry** into the market as well as **costless exit** from the market. Apart from the absence of barriers to entry, there must be **no sunk costs**. You will recall that sunk costs are costs which cannot be recovered by selling the asset in question or by redeploying it in another market if the firm should exit the industry. Sunk costs increase the costs of exiting the industry and therefore make the existing firms more aggressive towards new entrants. Sunk costs also tend to deter potential new entrants. The original example used to illustrate contestability was the airline industry. If a firm that owns aircraft exits a particular route, it can sell its aircraft or switch them to other routes. Sunk costs are therefore low or zero.
- New firms entering the market should be able to produce the product at the same cost as existing firms. The potential entrant should be at no disadvantage (compared to existing firms) in respect of technology, perceived product quality and so on. In other words, it should be able to compete on equal terms with the existing firms.
- The new entrant must be able to engage in "hit and run" tactics, that is, enter a market, make a profit and exit before the existing firms can retaliate by adjusting their prices downwards.

If these conditions are met, the existing firms (irrespective of their actual number) will always be threatened with **potential** competition and will therefore tend to behave like competitive firms (ie efficiently), even in the absence of **actual** competition. In the case of perfect contestability the market outcome will be the same as under perfect competition, that is, the ideals of allocative and productive efficiency will be achieved. Firms will produce at the lowest possible long-run average costs and only normal profits will be earned.

How useful is this notion? A sceptical conclusion would be that perfect contestability is a figment of the imagination, an ideal that will rarely, if ever, be achieved. But does perfect competition ever occur in the real world? In Chapter 12 we said that perfect competition, although unrealistic (in the narrow sense), serves as a useful benchmark against which market behaviour and outcomes can be judged. The notion of perfect contestability must be viewed in the same light. It sets a context for behaviour in all types of market structure. Like perfect competition, it serves as a benchmark, but the focus is on contestability rather than on the actual number of firms, degree of competition and so on. From this different perspective, it is possible for even highly monopolistic and oligopolistic markets to experience a high degree of contestability and achieve a competitive-type market solution with prices close to long-run average costs and profits close to normal. The policy implications of this approach are that the emphasis should be on the removal of barriers to entry and the lowering of exit costs. Contestability thus provides a powerful argument in support of deregulation (see Footnote 5), which is aimed at opening up specific markets to potential new entrants as a means of securing efficiency gains.

It is increasingly argued that perfectly contestable markets provide a more useful ideal type than perfect competition. Whether or not perfect contestability will replace perfect competition as the standard yardstick for comparing markets remains to be seen. The theory is still comparatively young and not without its problems. For example, the airline industry, to which it was applied originally, turned out to be less contestable than was assumed. Nevertheless, the theory has succeeded in focusing the attention of many economists on barriers to entry and exit as important determinants of market behaviour, and policymakers increasingly apply this notion when applying policy, to which we now turn.

13.6 Policy with regard to monopoly and imperfect competition

Where monopolistic or oligopolistic conditions prevail, governments sometimes intervene in an attempt to reduce supernormal (or monopoly) profits, achieve a more efficient allocation of resources and prevent abuses of market power. Various types of intervention can be distinguished, including the following:

- Government can levy **taxes** on the firms concerned to reduce their profits. Powerful firms may, however, shift at least part of the tax to the consumers of the products. If this happens, prices will be raised and the quantities supplied will be reduced. The allocation of resources will then be even more inefficient after the introduction of the tax than it was before.

- A second alternative is **government ownership**. Certain products (eg water, electricity) are produced efficiently by monopolists. As indicated earlier, such natural monopolists are frequently owned by government. Government may also decide to purchase (or simply take over) private monopolists. This is called nationalisation (see Chapter 16). Nowadays, however, it is generally accepted that production should preferably be left to private firms and that government should regulate rather than nationalise these firms. In fact, the current trend is to privatise government-owned firms and to regulate them, rather than to maintain government ownership.
- A third alternative is **regulation**, which consists of laws, rules or regulations that are issued to control the pricing, production or other decisions of firms.[5] Such rules, laws or regulations prescribe the conditions under which the firms can do business. For example, to prevent powerful firms from raising prices, government may decide to fix maximum or ceiling prices for their products. However, as we explained in Chapter 8, such price controls are a blunt instrument which can cause a variety of distortions in the economy.
- A fourth alternative is **competition policy**. Most countries have a policy with respect to competition, economic concentration and possible abuses of economic power. In the United States it is called antitrust policy and in South Africa it is called competition policy. The objectives are to promote competition, curb the potential abuses of economic power and exploit the advantages of bigness to the benefit of society at large. Government can, for example, promote competition by opening up the economy to **imports**. Competition from imports is probably one of the most effective ways of preventing monopoly and the abuse of economic power. In South Africa, the lowering of import tariffs and the abolition of import quotas probably did more to promote competition in the domestic market than any other measures aimed at achieving this goal. Other barriers to entry can also be reduced or eliminated to encourage competition in the domestic market, for example by making it easier for small businesses to enter the market. We now take a closer look at competition policy.

5. The opposite of regulation is **deregulation**, that is, the elimination of laws, rules and regulations that govern particular industries and which limit competition or otherwise hamper the functioning of market forces. The case for deregulation is based partly on the conviction that regulation often reduces competition, rather than increase it. Industries that have been deregulated in South Africa and elsewhere include road transport and the airline industry.

Competition policy

Competition policy has three basic aims:

- to prevent existing monopolies and other powerful firms abusing their power (monopoly policy)
- to regulate the growth of market power through mergers and acquisitions (merger policy)
- to prevent the application of restrictive practices, particularly by oligopolistic firms (restrictive practice policy)

Some of the basic terms relating to merger policy are defined in Box 13-8. **Restrictive practices** include the fixing of selling prices (eg resale price maintenance), collusion with regard to tenders, price discrimination by a dominant firm, collusion in respect of market share (eg the division of markets by allocating customers, suppliers, territories or specific types of goods and services among the different firms in the industry), restrictions on output or technical development, making purchases of one item conditional upon purchases of another item and exclusive dealing agreements between manufacturers and retailers.

In the United States the first competition policy (called antitrust policy) was introduced in 1890 when Congress passed the Sherman Act. Monopoly and trade restraints were declared illegal but the solution was not sought in the form of regulation and government ownership. Instead, the focus was on competition and the market. Interestingly enough, one of the firms that regularly ran foul of the strict anti-trust laws in the United States was De Beers, the South African firm that supplies about 60 per cent of the world's diamonds and virtually controls the international diamond market.

In the United Kingdom competition policy dates back to 1946. At present there are two main bodies responsible for implementing the policy: the Office of Fair Trading and the Monopolies and Mergers Commission.

The European Union (EU) also has a strict competition policy. In 1996, for example, the European Commission, the body responsible for implementing the EU's competition policy, blocked a merger between the platinum operations of Lonrho (a British company) and Gencor (a South African company).

In South Africa, the first comprehensive legislation specifically aimed at dealing with these matters was the Regulation of Monopolistic Conditions Act 24 of 1955. In July 1979 a new Act, the Maintenance and Promotion of Competition Act 96 of 1979, was promulgated in response to a growing concern over economic concentration and obstacles to competition in South Africa. The thrust of the new Act was to promote com-

BOX 13-8 MERGER TERMINOLOGY

A major concern of competition policy is the potential impact of mergers between different firms on the degree of competition in the industry or market. The Competition Act defines a merger as "when one or more firms directly or indirectly acquire or establish direct or indirect control over the whole or part of the business of another firm." Mergers are usually aimed at eliminating competition or at achieving economies of scale, thereby reducing the cost of production per unit of output. Four basic types of merger can be distinguished:

- A **horizontal merger** occurs when two firms engaged in the same stage of production of the same good come together. For example, in 2002 SA Breweries (SAB) acquired Miller Brewing in the United States and formed a new company, SABMiller, which became the second largest brewer in the world. A few years earlier, two large mining companies, BHP and Billiton merged to form BHP-Billiton, one of the largest mining companies in the world. Other South African examples include the merger between Nampak and Malbak, two companies in the packaging industry, between JD Group and Profurn, two companies in the furniture industry and between Nedcor and BOE, two of the largest banking groups, as well as the purchase of Nestlé SA's sugar based confectionery business by Tiger Food Brands (owner of Beacon).

- A **vertical merger** occurs between two firms in the same industry but engaged in different stages of the production of the good. It can be *backward*, when a firm acquires another firm to safeguard or control its inputs, or it can be *forward*, for example, when a firm acquires outlets for its product. In 2003, for example, Coleus Packaging, a subsidiary of SABMiller, purchased Rheem Crown Plant, the largest producer of metal beer and soft-drink caps (known as crowns) in South Africa. Another example is the purchase (in 2005) of Midas Group, a dealer in motor vehicle parts and accessories, by General Motors SA.

- A **conglomerate** (or **diversifying) merger** occurs between firms that operate in different markets. The purpose is usually to diversify the activities of the acquiring company, by applying its managerial skills and expertise over a wider terrain or to safeguard the firm in anticipation of a decline in its principal market. A recent South African example was the acquisition (in 2002) of the large CNA stores by Edcon, the company that owns Edgars Stores. A few years earlier Woolworths had acquired CNA but this conglomerate merger proved unsuccessful.

  Conglomerate mergers are often frowned upon, especially if the acquiring firm is already a large conglomerate. Such mergers may lead to a centralisation of economic power, which refers to a situation in which a few large conglomerates control a large number of firms. At the end of 1987, for example, it was estimated that Anglo American effectively controlled 60 per cent of the total market capitalisation of the JSE Securities Exchange. Seven years later, the five largest conglomerates (Anglo American, Old Mutual, Liberty, Sanlam and Rembrandt) controlled an estimated 83,7 per cent of the market capitalisation of the JSE. However, by 2004 these conglomerates had sold or reduced their shareholding in many non-core assets and their combined control had fallen to an estimated 38,5 per cent, with Anglo American's share down to 18,7 per cent. Although such figures are often cited in the debate on competition and economic power, it should be emphasised that *centralisation* differs from market *concentration*, which refers to the pre-eminence of large firms supplying a particular market.

- A **lateral merger** involves two companies which produce related goods that do not compete directly with each other. The merger between Cadbury, a manufacturer of sweets and chocolates, and Schweppes, a manufacturer of beverages, serves as an example.

petition (instead of regulating monopolistic conditions) and a Competition Board was established to implement the policy. An interesting development during the 1980s was an increasing focus on government interference as a source of economic concentration or a lack of competition. During the early 1990s, the stated policy of the Competition Board was to promote what was labelled as "effective competition". The existence of large firms or the concentration of power in the hands of one or a few firms was not necessarily regarded as undesirable. The crucial factor was their behaviour. Restrictive practices such as resale price maintenance and various forms of collusion were regarded as undesirable. The Board was also empowered to investigate possible increases in economic power through mergers and acquisitions. Officials of the Board maintained that the fear of adverse publicity associated with formal investigations persuaded many firms to curtail or abolish restrictive practices or plans for mergers or acquisitions.

In 1994, competition policy received a further boost when the African National Congress, which had been propagating a vigorous anti-monopoly policy, came into power. Barriers to entry were perceived to be at variance with the aspirations of previously disadvantaged groups who needed to gain access to scarce resources and economic power if the country's economic transformation was to be market based. The economic power of the large conglomerates that were dominating the South African economy had to be curtailed in order to revitalise the economy and address the inequalities of income and wealth. In addition, South Africa's reintegration into the world economy demanded an improvement in the competitive ability of South African firms (although it is sometimes argued that large firms are required to compete effectively in international markets), while new trade agreements (eg with the European Union) also required that South African competition laws meet certain requirements.

All this led to vigorous analysis, controversy, debate and negotiations between government, business and labour, culminating in the promulgation of the Competition Act 89 of 1998. The Act provided for the establishment of a Competition Commission and a Competition Tribunal. In terms of the Act, the Competition Commission seeks to provide all South Africans with an equal opportunity to participate fairly in the national economy, in order to promote a more effective and efficient economy. More specifically, it is responsible for

- investigating complaints against firms engaging in restrictive business practices (restrictive practice policy)
- evaluating and subsequently approving or prohibiting mergers and acquisitions (merger policy)
- conducting research, providing policy inputs, educating and informing stakeholders, and conducting regulatory and legislative reviews

One of the features of the Act is that all mergers and acquisitions have to be notified to the Competition Commission. Moreover, intermediate and large mergers may only be implemented after the necessary approval has been obtained from the Commission. The Commission's recommendations are forwarded to the Competition Tribunal, which may accept or reject such recommendations, while subsequent disputes may be referred to the Competition Appeal Court.

In 2005/06 the Competition Commission was notified of 408 mergers and acquisitions, of which 97 were large, 300 intermediate and 11 small. During the same period, 394 cases were finalised. Only four (three large and one small) were prohibited. Eight cases were either withdrawn or fell outside the Commission's jurisdiction and 390 were approved. Similar patterns were observed during previous years. It should be noted, however, that some of the approvals (14 in 2005/06) were conditional approvals (ie certain, sometimes quite stringent, conditions had to be met) – see Box 13-9.

In evaluating mergers, the Commission has to consider competition concerns, possible efficiencies that could arise and public interest issues. The latter include the impact of the transaction on:

- a particular industrial sector or region
- employment
- the ability of small and medium-sized businesses and firms owned or controlled by historically disadvantaged individuals to become competitive
- the ability of South African firms to compete internationally

Concluding remarks

We started the chapter by outlining the different market structures. We now conclude it by summarising some key differences and providing examples of each type of market structure in Table 13-4.

BOX 13-9 EXAMPLES OF RULINGS BY THE COMPETITION COMMISSION

In the United States, the Department of Justice uses the following guidelines with regard to horizontal mergers. If the Herfindahl-Hirschman index (HHI), which was explained in Section 13.1, is less than 1 000 after the merger it will not be challenged. However, if the HHI lies between 1 000 and 1 800 and the merger raises it by more than 100 points, or if the HHI is above 1 800 and the merger raises it by more than 50 points, the merger is challenged. In South Africa, however, a more flexible approach is adopted and each case is examined on its merits.

Some insight into the application of competition policy in South Africa can be gained by considering a few examples of mergers approved unconditionally, approved conditionally and rejected by the Competition Commission.

One of the mergers approved in 2001/02 was the acquisition of Columbus, the sole producer of stainless steel in South Africa, by Acerinox SA, a Spanish stainless steel producer. Among the reasons given by the Competition Commission for the approval were that:

- the transaction was essentially the purchase of a domestic monopolist by a foreign company with a minimal presence in South Africa
- stainless steel imports are readily available
- the acquisition would result in foreign direct investment
- it would assist Columbus in becoming more competitive internationally

Another approved merger was the one between Iscor Ltd and Saldanha Steel (Pty) Ltd. Although the two firms overlapped in the production of hot rolled coil steel, Saldanha (which was to become a wholly owned subsidiary of Iscor (nowadays Mittal SA), a public company listed on the JSE Securities Exchange), focused solely on the export market and concentration in the domestic market would therefore not be affected by the merger.

The Commission recommended that the acquisition by Litotech Limited (part of the Bidvest Group) of Paragon Business Communications Limited (a horizontal merger) be prohibited since it would substantially prevent or lessen competition in the market for printed business forms (in which Litotech and Paragon are the two major players). The Competition Tribunal, however, subsequently approved the transaction.

The proposed merger between Astral Foods Limited (Astral) and National Chick Limited (Natchix) was prohibited by the Competition Commission on the grounds that it would substantially reduce competition in the animal feed market and supply of day-old broiler chicks. The Competition Tribunal subsequently conditionally approved the merger. The main conditions were that Astral may not discriminate in the supply of day-old chicks between entities in its own group and independent customers in relation to price, discounts or rebates offered for equivalent transactions, and that Nutrix, a subsidiary of Astral, had to be sold to either the minorities or an independent buyer.

Another conditionally approved merger was the one between Unifoods, a division of Unilever South Africa, and Robertsons Foods. The Commission was concerned about competition in a number of product markets (including packet soups, soya mince, salad dressings, recipe mixes, instant soups, dry marinades, dry pasta sauces, black spreads and pour-over sauces) where Royco and Oxo (Unilever) and Knorr, Bovril and Marmite (Robertsons) were the leading brands. It therefore recommended, *inter alia*, that Unifoods had to sell all the products, including the sub-brands, marketed under the Royco and Oxo brands, to an independent third party. The Competition Tribunal accepted the Commission's recommendation.

In 2006 the Competition Tribunal prohibited the proposed horizontal merger between Massmart (Makro, Game, Dion etc) and Moresport (Sportsmans Warehouse, Outdoor Warehouse and Sports Shoe World). The main reason for the decision was that the merger would have eliminated competition between the two largest, strongest, most committed and experienced players in the market for sports and outdoor goods.

The basic approach of the Competition Commission and the Competition Tribunal is thus not simply to ban mergers, but to consider the merits of each case (eg by examining possible rationalisation and economies of scale, as well as the effects on employment and economic development in a broader sense).

TABLE 13-4 The different market structures: a summary

Type of market	*Shape of demand curve facing the firm/firm's control over price/profit situation*	*Examples (often approximations)*
Perfect competition	Horizontal demand curve; the firm is a price taker; economic profits possible in short run, but only normal profits in the long run due to freedom of exit and entry	International commodity markets (gold, platinum, oil, maize, sugar), financial markets (JSE Securities Exchange, foreign exchange market – when exchange rates are free), local fresh produce markets (vegetables, fruit, meat, fish)
Monopolistic competition	Downward-sloping demand curve but relatively elastic; the firm has some control over price; economic profits possible in short run, but only normal profits in the long run due to freedom of exit and entry	Clothing, footwear, household furniture, fast-food outlets, restaurants, butcheries, plumbers, books, magazines, television repair, used cars, photographic development, filling stations – in some instances location might turn market into oligopoly or even monopoly, particularly as far as services are concerned (eg plumbers, electricians, television repair, supermarkets, hotels, filling stations)
Oligopoly	Downward-sloping demand curve, with elasticity depending on rival firms' reactions to price changes; the firm has some control over price; economic profits possible in short run and long run due to barriers to entry	Iron and steel, motorcars, tyres, breakfast cereals, banks, cellular phones, cigarettes, cement, petrol, chemical fertilisers, aluminium smelting, golf balls, golf clubs, photographic equipment, beer, soft drinks, car rental service
Monopoly	Downward-sloping demand curve (the market demand curve); the firm has considerable control over price; economic profits possible in short run and long run due to blocked entry	Electricity supply (Eskom), local water supply (Umgeni Water, Rand Water), satellite TV (DSTV), stainless steel (Columbus), local monopolies (hotels, bottle stores, universities)

IMPORTANT CONCEPTS

Monopoly
Imperfect competition
Monopolistic competition
Oligopoly
Market structure
Homogeneous (identical) products
Heterogeneous (differentiated) products
Price takers
Price makers (price setters)
Barriers to entry
Collusion
Demand for the product of the firm
Concentration
Concentration ratio
Herfindahl-Hirschman index
Market conduct
Natural monopoly
Economies of scale
Patents
Licensing
Predatory pricing
Total revenue *(TR)*
Average revenue *(AR)*
Marginal revenue *(MR)*
Short run
Long run
Total cost *(TC)*
Average cost *(AC)*
Marginal cost *(MC)*
Economic profit
Normal profit
Economic loss
Price discrimination
Consumer surplus
Product differentiation
Non-price competition
Interdependence
Uncertainty
Collusion
Cartel
Kinked demand curve
Mark-up pricing
Advertising
Allocative efficiency
Productive efficiency
Deadweight loss
X-inefficiency
Rent-seeking
Countervailing power
Contestable markets
Regulation
Competition policy
Mergers

REVIEW QUESTIONS

1. AM Bitious, the newly-appointed managing director of One and Only, a monopolistic firm, tells you that (as a monopolist) he can set any price he wishes and sell as many units of his product as he wants at that price. Do you agree? Explain.
2. What is the relationship between the market demand for the product of a (single-price) monopolistic firm and its average revenue? Explain.
3. Explain what is meant by a natural monopoly and give examples of natural monopoly in the South African economy.
4. The main heading in the *Business Times* section of the *Sunday Times* of 2 February 2003 read: "Telkom tightens its grips on monopoly." In the article it was stated that: "The delay in licensing a second national operator is a blow to consumers who have been awaiting the benefits of a competitive market."
   (a) Do you think Telkom had a monopoly in 2003 and, if so, in which market(s) did it act as a monopolist?
   (b) What are the benefits referred to in the article?
5. Why do we say that a monopolist is neither allocatively nor productively efficient?
6. Explain why some firms practise price discrimination.
7. How can the government react to the problem of monopoly power?
8. What is the focus point of the theory of contestable markets? Do you think that this theory has any particular merit? Why (not)?
9. What are the essential differences between: (a) perfect competition and monopoly; (b) perfect competition and monopolistic competition; (c) monopoly and monopolistic competition; (d) perfect competition and oligopoly; (e) monopoly and oligopoly; (f) monopolistic competition and oligopoly? What, if any, are the common features of each of these six pairs of market structure?

14 The labour market

Learning outcomes

Once you have studied this chapter you should be able to

- identify the main differences between the labour market and the goods market
- explain the main determinants of the supply of labour
- explain how the demand for labour is derived
- explain how a perfectly competitive labour market functions
- analyse various labour market imperfections
- discuss the desirability of minimum wages
- explain why wages differ
- explain what is meant by the informal sector

Labour ... is any painful exertion of mind or body undergone partly or wholly with a view to future good.

W STANLEY JEVONS

When a man says he wants to work, what he means is that he wants wages.

RICHARD WHATELY

One man's wage increase is another man's price increase.

HAROLD WILSON

Labour issues are often in the news. The creation of employment opportunities is an important macroeconomic objective and unemployment is generally regarded as the most important economic problem in South Africa. Increases in wages and salaries are often blamed for increases in costs and prices. Wage disputes and strikes are regularly in the headlines.

In the previous chapters we analysed different types of goods market. In this chapter we switch our attention to the market for factors of production (the factor markets) and we examine the labour market. The other factor markets (ie the markets for natural resources or land, capital and entrepreneurship) are dealt with briefly in the appendix to the chapter – the underlying principles tend to be the same in all cases. Most of this chapter is still concerned with microeconomic issues but we touch on some broader, macroeconomic issues in its last section.

We first explain how the **labour market differs from the goods market**. The next section focuses on the **perfectly competitive labour market**. We examine the **supply of labour**, the **demand for labour** and **wage determination** in the labour market. The third section deals with **imperfectly competitive labour markets**, more specifically with issues such as the impact of **trade unions**, **government intervention** (eg minimum wage fixing) and **monopolisation**. The next section deals with the interesting issue of **why wages are not uniform**. The chapter concludes with a discussion of certain **macroeconomic aspects** of the labour market, including the role of the **informal sector**.

Labour is an important factor of production. The cost of labour is the largest cost factor in the economy. In 2006 the compensation of labour represented 49,4 per cent of the cost of producing South Africa's GDP. Changes in the cost of labour therefore have a significant impact on cost and price trends in the economy. The cost of labour depends on the wages and salaries paid to workers and on the productivity of labour. If higher wages and salaries are not matched by increased productivity, the cost of labour, which is usually expressed as labour cost per unit of output, rises. But cost levels are unaffected if productivity rises to the same extent as wages and salaries. It is therefore obvious that the productivity (or quality) of labour is an important determinant of the cost of labour.

However, wages and salaries do not represent only costs. They are also an important demand factor in the economy. Wages and salaries are the main source of household income and therefore influence the demand for goods and services. In 2006 the compensation of labour represented 64,5 per cent of the income of South African households. If all employers pay low wages, they run the risk (in the short run at least) of dampening the total demand for goods and services in the economy. As we shall see in Part IV, this total (or aggregate) demand is an important determinant of total production, income and employment in the economy.

Most economists would agree that the creation of jobs is the most important objective of economic policy in any country. Unemployment is a costly phenomenon. It entails a variety of costs, both to the unemployed and to society at large. To keep unemployment as low as possible, jobs must be created at a sufficient rate. This, in turn, requires a well-disciplined, productive workforce and a steady expansion of aggregate demand.

Labour issues are often highly politicised. This is quite understandable, given that these issues involve human beings, their hopes, aspirations and fears. South Africa is no exception. At the height of apartheid, certain jobs were reserved for whites, while a number of further restrictions were placed on black workers. In the 1970s and 1980s trade unions representing mainly black workers played an important role in the political struggle against apartheid. In the 1990s affirmative action, black economic empowerment and employment equity became major issues and had a significant impact on the functioning of the labour market in South Africa.

In this chapter we introduce certain elements of the labour market. All the concepts and issues examined in this chapter are dealt with in greater detail in courses on labour economics.

14.1 The labour market versus the goods market

Like any other market, the labour market is a link between potential sellers (suppliers) and potential purchasers (demanders). Individuals (or households) supply their labour services to firms and the government, who hire these services at a price, called wages and salaries (or wages for short) – see Box 14-1. There are, however, a number of differences between the labour market and other markets (including the markets for other factors of production). Most of these differences relate to the fact that the labour market is concerned with human beings rather than with inanimate objects such as consumer goods, capital goods and natural resources.

The following are some of the most important differences:

- Workers usually have to be physically present when their services are used. As a result, **non-monetary factors**, such as location of employment and other working conditions, are more important in labour markets than in markets for other factors of production.
- Labour services are embodied in the persons concerned and are therefore **not transferable** to other people. Goods, in contrast, are fully transferable between purchasers and sellers.
- Labour markets differ from goods markets in that labour is always **rented rather than sold**. A person can rent a worker's services but nobody can buy him or her.
- Considerations other than material advantage enter the relationship between suppliers and demanders. This relationship does not involve only wages and productivity. It also involves considerations of equity and humanity, such as loyalty, fairness, appreciation and justice. It may also involve both actual and perceived discrimination on the basis of gender, race, age and marital status. The functioning of the labour market can therefore be affected by a wide range of **non-economic considerations**.
- Labour markets are typically characterised by **trade unions**, **employees' associations, collective bargaining** and **government intervention**. These features have to be taken into account when labour markets are analysed.
- Labour is usually employed by means of **long-term contracts**. In most cases labour is therefore not traded at the best price on a daily basis.
- Labour is intrinsically **heterogeneous** and unlike goods it cannot be classified or standardised.
- There are a **variety of labour markets**, each with its own features. For example, there are different markets for different occupations, different skills and different geographical locations. The labour market is therefore often described as a **segmented market**. Each segment has its own particular characteristics and workers cannot, in the short

BOX 14-1 SOME BASIC CONCEPTS RELATING TO THE REMUNERATION OF LABOUR

The remuneration of labour can take different forms, for example wages, salaries, bonuses, commissions, fees, allowances, royalties, overtime payments and fringe benefits (eg housing subsidies, car allowances, medical and pension fund contributions). Economists usually use the term **wage** to refer to the basic amount, excluding any benefits or allowances, that is paid in return for the use of labour in production. The price of labour is usually called the **wage rate**, that is, the amount of money to be paid to a worker for working for a specified period, or for performing a specified number of tasks. A wage rate may, for example, be expressed as R25 an hour, R200 a day, R1000 a week, R4 000 a month or R48 000 a year. Note that in economic analysis, we do not distinguish between wages (hourly, daily or weekly rates) and salaries (monthly or annual rates), but simply refer to wages or the wage rate. **Earnings** is a much broader concept which reflects the amounts actually earned by a worker during a specified period, including all bonuses, fringe benefits, and so on.

Another important distinction is made between money (or nominal) wages and real wages. The **nominal wage** is the amount of money actually received by a worker per hour, day, week, month or year. The **real wage** is the quantity of goods and services that can be purchased with the nominal or money wage. Real wages therefore refer to the purchasing power of money wages. They are determined by the nominal (money) wages and the prices of the goods and services purchased by the workers. For example, when money wages increase by 5 per cent while prices of consumer goods and services increase by 10 per cent, real wages decline by 5 per cent. Similarly, if the increase in nominal wages (say 15 per cent) exceeds the rate of increase in prices (say 10 per cent), then real wages increase (by 5 per cent). In this case the material standard of living of the workers increases (provided that employment and other conditions of service remain unchanged). See also the discussion of nominal values, real values and purchasing power in Boxes 4-1 and 4-5.

run, move freely between the different segments. There can therefore simultaneously be a shortage of labour in a certain segment of the market and an oversupply in another segment.

- The remuneration of labour does not consist only of its price (ie the wage). The remuneration package may include various **non-wage benefits** (such as housing, medical, pension, travel and holiday benefits).
- The **remuneration** of labour is **affected by** a number of **factors** which are **not directly related to labour market conditions**, for example, taxation and views as to what constitutes a living wage or a reasonable standard of living.

14.2 A perfectly competitive labour maket

Requirements for perfect competition

In the case of the goods market we used perfect competition as a benchmark against which the performance of other market structures could be compared. Likewise, we start our analysis of the labour market by examining a perfectly competitive labour market. The requirements for perfect competition in the labour market include the following:

- There must be a **large number of buyers** (employers) and a **large number of sellers** (employees) in the market. The number must be so large that no individual participant can influence the price of labour (ie the wage rate). In other words, all participants must be **price** (or, in this case, **wage**) **takers**.
- Labour must be **homogeneous**, that is, all workers must have identical skills. There must be no reason for employers to prefer one worker to another worker.
- Workers must be **completely mobile**, meaning that they must be able to move freely from one employer to another, from one market to another or from one region to another. Entry and exit must therefore be completely free.
- There must be **no government intervention** influencing employers or workers.
- All participants must have **perfect knowledge** of market conditions. Workers must have full information on jobs available and wage rates, while each

employer must have full information on wage rates paid by other employers.

- There must be **perfect competition in the goods market**. No employer must be able to pass increased labour costs on to consumers in the form of higher prices. In other words, all firms must be price takers in the goods market.

These requirements are very restrictive and it is doubtful whether any labour market actually meets these requirements. Nevertheless, as with perfect competition in the goods market, the notion of a perfectly competitive labour market provides a useful starting point for an analysis of the labour market.

Equilibrium in the labour market

In a perfectly competitive labour market (ie a market in which all the requirements for perfect competition are met) the equilibrium wage rate and the equilibrium quantity are determined by the interaction of supply and demand, as illustrated in Figure 14-1. *DD* represents the demand for labour, while the supply of labour is illustrated by *SS*. Equilibrium occurs when the quantity of labour demanded is equal to the quantity of labour supplied. This is illustrated by the intersection of the demand curve and the supply curve. In principle, this is the same as equilibrium in a perfectly competitive goods market, the only difference being that we are now dealing with the price of labour (the wage rate w) and the quantity of labour (N), instead of the price (P) and quantity (Q) of a good or service.

FIGURE 14-1 Equilibrium in a perfectly competitive labour market

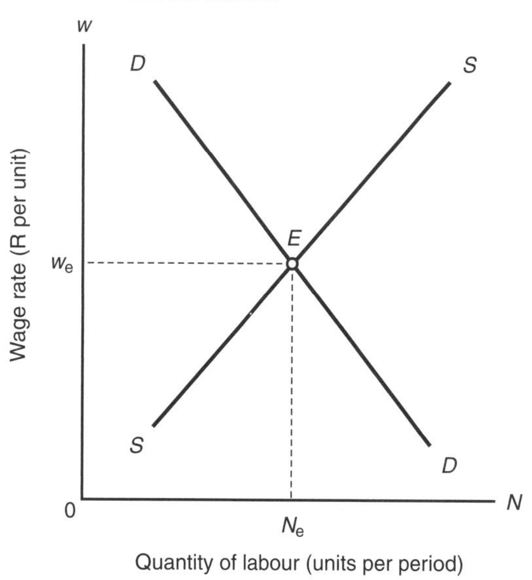

Equilibrium is determined by the interaction of the demand for labour DD and the supply of labour SS. The equilibrium wage rate (ie the price of labour) is w_e and the equilibrium quantity (ie the level of employment) is N_e.

In Figure 14-1 the equilibrium wage rate is w_e and the equilibrium quantity N_e. To analyse the labour market we have to examine the supply of labour and the demand for labour. We start with the individual supply of labour.

The individual supply of labour

Each individual has to decide how to divide his or her time between work and leisure. The quantity of labour supplied (ie the number of working hours offered by a worker) will tend to rise as the wage rate rises, but only up to a certain point. Consider the following example.

Eric Baloyi has to decide how to divide his time between work and leisure. His choice is illustrated in Figure 14-2. At an hourly wage rate of R10 or less he is not willing to work at all. This is shown by point *A* in the figure. Wage rates of R10 or less are not sufficient to cover his transport and other direct costs of taking a job, as well as his opportunity cost in terms of the leisure he has to sacrifice by working. However, he is willing to work at wage rates of more than R10 per hour and the higher the rate, the longer he is willing to work. At a wage rate of R50 per hour he is willing to work 45 hours per week. This is indicated by point *B* in the figure. If he is employed for 45 hours at R50 per hour, he will earn a weekly wage of R2 250 (= 45 × R50). This he regards as being sufficient to enjoy a reasonable standard of living, which includes having enough leisure time. At wage rates higher than R50 he can still earn at least R2 250 per week by working fewer hours and he will have more time for watching TV, going to soccer games or socialising with his friends. At a wage rate of R70 per hour, he is willing to work 40 hours, as indicated by point *C* in the figure. If he can find employment on such conditions (ie a wage rate of R70 per hour and a working week of 40 hours), he will earn R2 800 (= 40 × R70) per week. He will therefore earn an additional R550 per week *and* have an additional five hours of leisure time per week.

The individual labour supply curve illustrated in Figure 14-2 is called a **backward-bending supply curve**. This form of the supply curve can be ascribed to two forces, namely a **substitution effect** and an **income effect**:

- **Substitution effect**. As the wage rate increases, workers will tend to work more hours. In other words, they will be willing to sacrifice leisure to obtain a higher income. What this really means is that they will be willing to substitute a greater consumption of goods and services (which they will be

FIGURE 14-2 The individual supply of labour

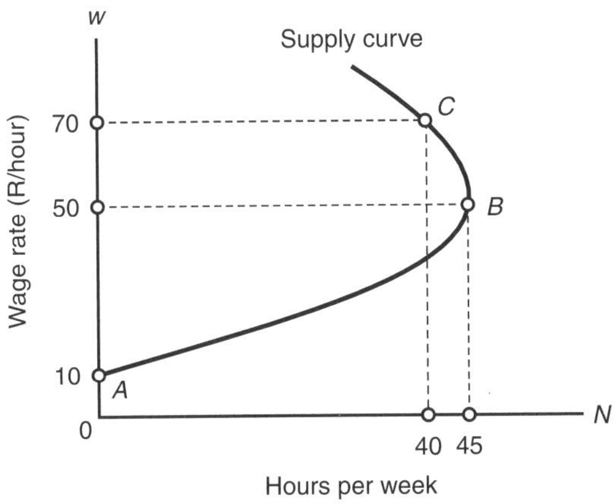

The quantity of labour supplied increases up to a certain point (B in the figure) and then declines as the wage rate increases further. This is called the backward-bending individual supply curve of labour.

able to afford with a higher income) for leisure. Increases in the wage rate raise the **opportunity cost** of leisure and will probably entice most workers to sacrifice leisure and to work longer, thus enabling them to purchase more goods and services. This is the **substitution effect** – increases in the price of labour persuade workers to substitute work for leisure.

- **Income effect**. As a worker's spending on goods and services increases, his or her marginal utility of consumption (see Chapter 10) decreases. Moreover, leisure is a normal good. Recall from earlier chapters that the demand for a normal good increases as income increases. As the worker's income increases (along with the wage rate), his or her demand for leisure will thus increase. This is the **income effect**.

The direction of the substitution effect always depends on the change in relative prices. As the price of labour increases, *relative* to the price of leisure, the quantity of labour supplied will increase and the quantity of leisure demanded will decrease. The income effect works in the opposite direction. As income increases, more leisure will be demanded and less labour will be supplied. From point *A* to point *B* in Figure 14-2 the substitution effect is stronger than the income effect and the quantity of labour supplied increases (while the quantity of leisure demanded decreases). At a given (but indeterminate) wage rate, however, the income effect becomes stronger than the substitution effect. In Figure 14-2 this occurs when the wage rate is R50 per hour. At higher wage rates there will be more to gain by working less than by working more. The quantity of leisure demanded increases and the quantity of labour supplied decreases. Note, however, that this supply curve, like all other supply curves, indicates the **plans** of the individual concerned. There is no guarantee that Eric will get a job or ever be offered a wage of R50 per hour or higher.

The market supply of labour

The theory of the backward-bending supply curve of labour is quite plausible as far as the behaviour of an individual worker is concerned. However, as in the case of many other aspects of economic life, what applies to the individual does not necessarily apply to the group or to the market. It is unlikely that all individual supply curves will bend backwards at the same wage rate. Moreover, an increase in the wage rate will induce more people to enter the labour market and supply their services. The market supply of labour will thus have a positive slope, like any normal supply curve, indicating that the quantity of labour supplied *(N)* will increase as the wage rate *(w)* increases. This is shown in Figure 14-3.

The market supply of a particular type of labour will **change** if any of the **non-wage** determinants of the supply of labour changes. This is illustrated by a **shift** of the market supply curve. The market supply will change if, for example:

- **new workers** enter the market (eg because the population has increased or on account of immigration)

FIGURE 14-3 The market supply of labour

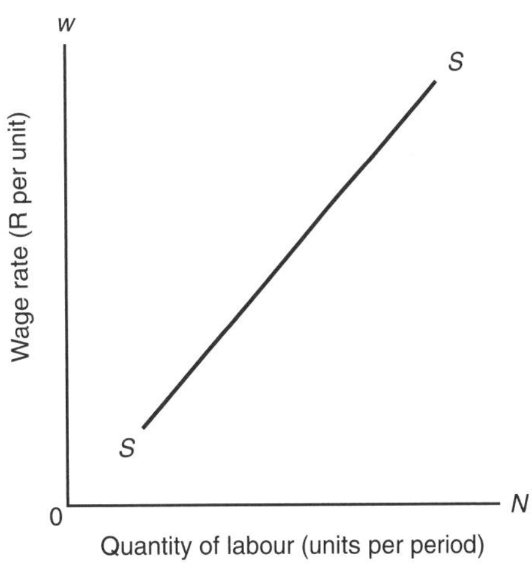

The quantity of labour supplied (N) increases as the wage rate (w) increases, ceteris paribus. *The market supply curve SS thus has a positive slope.*

- the **number of workers decreases** as a result of the impact of HIV/Aids
- the **wages** that can be earned **in other occupations** change, thereby making the particular occupation less or more attractive
- the **non-monetary aspects** of the occupation change (eg if the job becomes more pleasant or less dangerous as a result of the introduction of new safety measures, the market supply will tend to increase; likewise, if fringe benefits like holidays, the degree of job security, status or power change, the market supply will also change)

An individual firm's demand for labour

The most important aspect of the demand for labour is that it is a **derived demand**. Labour is not demanded for its own sake but rather for the value of the goods and services that can be produced when labour is combined with other factors of production. Firms will therefore demand and employ labour only if there is a demand for the goods and services produced by labour *and* if it is profitable for them to do so. In deciding whether or not to employ a worker (or an additional worker) a firm will compare the marginal benefit derived from employing the worker with the marginal cost of employing the worker. As long as the marginal benefit exceeds the marginal cost, the firm will continue to employ additional units of labour. This will continue until the marginal benefit is equal to the marginal cost.

To analyse the individual firm's demand for labour, we thus have to consider the determinants of the marginal cost of labour *(MCL)* and the marginal benefit of labour. In a perfectly competitive labour market, which is what we are dealing with here, the wage rate is determined in the labour market by the demand for and supply of labour, as illustrated in Figure 14-1. In such a market, no individual participant can influence the wage rate – all participants are **wage takers**. The position of an individual firm is illustrated in Figure 14-4. At any particular time the firm is faced with a horizontal (or perfectly elastic) supply curve. This indicates that the firm can employ any quantity of labour at the wage rate determined in the (perfectly competitive) labour market. Figure 14-4(a) illustrates how the wage rate is determined in the market and Figure 14-4(b) shows the position that confronts the individual firm. The equilibrium wage rate is indicated as w_e. The perfectly elastic supply of labour to the firm (S_f) at the wage rate is also the marginal cost of labour *(MCL),* as well as the average cost of labour *(ACL),* which is not shown in the figure.

How much labour will the firm employ at the given wage rate? To answer this question, we have to exam-

FIGURE 14-4 A perfectly competitive labour market

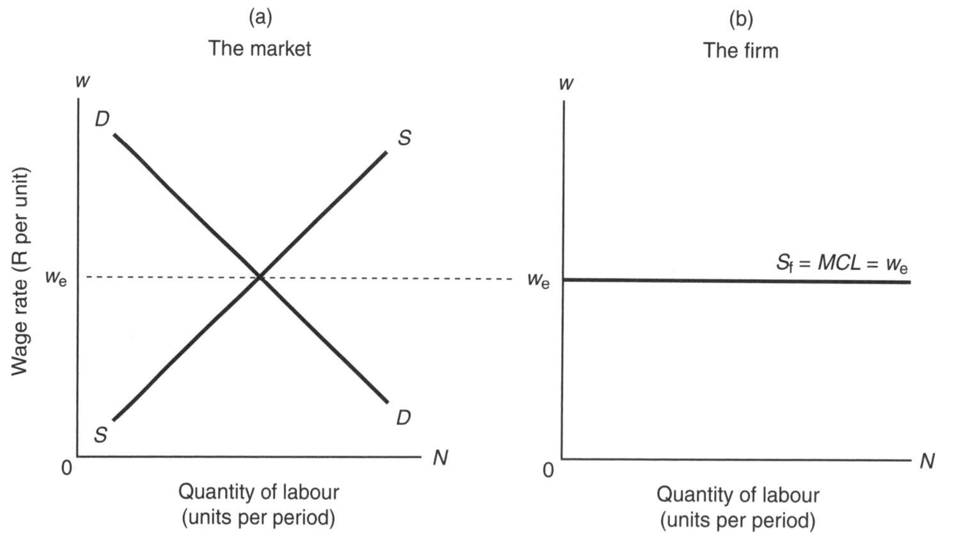

The perfectly competitive labour market is illustrated in (a). In this market the equilibrium wage rate (w_e) is determined by the interaction between the demand for labour DD and the supply for labour SS. The position of the individual firm is illustrated in (b). The firm can employ any quantity of labour at the equilibrium wage rate. The supply of labour to the firm (S_f) is thus represented by a horizontal line at the level of the equilibrium wage rate. This also represents the marginal cost of labour (MCL) to the firm.

ine the marginal benefit to the firm of employing additional units of labour. The two components of this benefit are the **physical productivity of labour** and the **marginal revenue** (in monetary terms) that accrues to the firm by selling an additional unit of its product. Since we are assuming that the firm sells its product in a perfectly competitive product market, the firm's marginal revenue is equal to the **price of the product** (as we explained in Chapter 12). The firm will continue to employ labour as long as the employment of each additional unit adds more to its total revenue than to its total cost (ie as long as marginal benefit exceeds marginal cost). We now consider the two components of the marginal benefit gained by employing labour.

Recall from Chapter 11 that the **law of diminishing returns** implies that the **marginal product of labour** has a declining tendency. As more units of the variable factor of production – labour – are added to the fixed quantities of the other factors (natural resources, capital and entrepreneurship), the additional output generated by the employment of each additional unit of labour decreases. The marginal product of labour may increase initially, but from a certain point diminishing returns start to set in and marginal product starts to decline. For the purposes of our discussion we ignore the rising part of the marginal product of labour and focus on the declining part only. Moreover, we refer to the marginal product of labour as the marginal **physical** product of labour (*MPP*), to distinguish it from the marginal **revenue** product, which is expressed in monetary terms.

The *MPP* indicates the physical value to the firm of employing an additional unit of labour. To determine the increase in total **revenue** of the firm (in monetary terms) as a result of the employment of an additional unit of labour, the physical value (*MPP*) has to be multiplied by the marginal revenue (*MR*) that accrues to the firm by selling an additional unit of the good or service that it produces. This is called the **marginal revenue product** (*MRP*). Thus

$$MRP = MPP \times MR \quad \text{(14-1)}$$

For a perfectly competitive firm, marginal revenue (*MR*) is equal to the price (*P*) of the product. For such a firm, marginal revenue product (*MRP*) is therefore equal to marginal physical product (*MPP*) multiplied by the price of the product (*P*). Thus

$$MRP = MPP \times P \quad \text{(14-2)}$$

See also Box 14-2.

To determine whether or not it will be profitable to employ an additional unit of labour, the marginal benefit to the firm (ie *MRP*) has to be compared to the marginal cost of labour (ie the wage rate). As long as *MRP* is greater than the wage rate (*w*), that is, as long as each additional worker's contribution to the firm's revenue is greater than the cost of hiring him or her, it will be profitable to expand employment. On the other hand, when *MRP* is less than the wage rate, marginal cost exceeds marginal benefit and it will therefore not be profitable to employ more workers – losses will be incurred as a result of the employment of each additional worker. Equilibrium (ie maximum profit) is achieved when *MRP* is equal to the wage rate (*w*), that is, when **marginal benefit** is equal to **marginal cost**. Thus, for equilibrium

$$MRP = w \quad \text{(14-3)}$$

We now use a numerical example to illustrate these points. Consider the information in Table 14-1. The first column gives the number of workers and the second column shows the total product (number of shirts) that can be produced by that number of workers, assuming that the quantities of all other factors of production remain constant. The third column shows the marginal physical product of labour, that is, the additional number of shirts that can be produced by hiring each additional worker. The next column gives the price of shirts (R50 per shirt). The fifth column shows the marginal revenue product (*MRP*) of labour. This is obtained by multiplying the marginal physical product (*MPP*) by the price of a shirt. (Alternatively, the total product – second column – can be multiplied by the price of a shirt to obtain total revenue. The

TABLE 14-1 Calculation of the marginal revenue product of labour: an example

Number of workers *N*	*Total physical product (number of shirts per week)*	*Marginal physical product (number of shirts per week) MPP*	*Price per shirt (R)* *P*	*Marginal revenue product (R per week) MRP*
0	0	0	50	0
1	10	10	50	500
2	18	8	50	400
3	24	6	50	300
4	28	4	50	200
5	30	2	50	100

MRP can then be derived by calculating the addition to total revenue as a result of employing each additional worker.)

Suppose the wage rate (*w*) is R200 per week. The firm will then maximise profits by employing a maximum of four workers. If the firm employs fewer workers, the *MRP* will be greater than the wage rate. This means that the firm can increase its profits by employing additional workers. Maximum profit is achieved when *MRP* = wage rate. If the firm employs five workers, the *MRP* of R100 will be less than the cost of the fifth worker (ie R200). It is therefore not profitable to employ five workers.

At different wage rates the quantity of labour demanded can be derived in a similar fashion. The firm in our example will employ a maximum of two workers if the wage rate is R400, three workers when the wage rate is R300, and so on. The derived demand curve for labour is then given by the marginal revenue product, as in Figure 14-5.

The equilibrium position of an individual firm operating in a perfectly competitive labour market is illustrated in Figure 14-6. The firm's demand for labour is given by the marginal revenue product of labour (*MRP*) which slopes downward as a result of diminishing returns to labour. The supply curve facing the firm is horizontal at the level of the wage rate (determined in the labour market). Equilibrium is reached where *MRP* (the marginal benefit of employing labour) is equal to *w* (the marginal cost of employing labour). This occurs at an employment level of N_e.

FIGURE 14-5 The individual firm's demand for labour

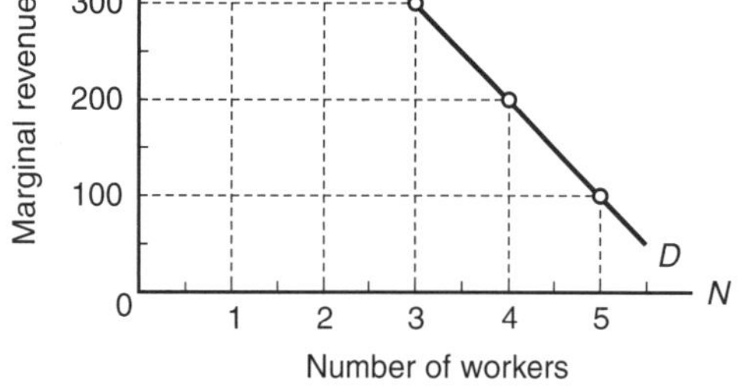

The demand curve for labour DD is given by the marginal revenue product of labour (MRP). It slopes downwards from left to right like a normal demand curve for a product.

FIGURE 14-6 The equilibrium position of a firm operating in a perfectly competitive labour market

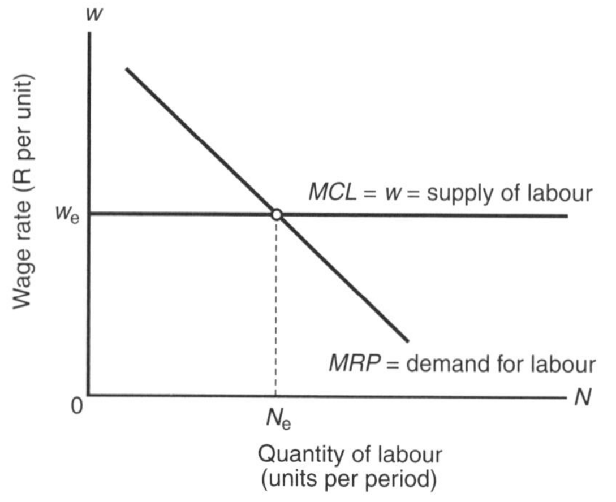

The firm is in equilibrium where MRP, which represents the firm's demand for labour, is equal to the wage rate w_e, which represents the supply of labour to the firm. This occurs at an employment level of N_e.

The market demand for labour

The market demand for a particular type of labour (which is assumed to be homogeneous) is obtained by adding all the individual firms' demand curves. It will therefore also have a negative slope. The market demand curve was illustrated as *DD* in Figure 14-1.

The market demand for a particular type of labour will change if any of the **non-wage** determinants of the quantity of labour demanded changes. This is illustrated by a **shift** of the market demand curve. The market demand will change, for example, if:

- the **number of firms** (employers) changes
- the **price of the product** changes – a change in the price of the product (eg as a result of a change in **demand**) will change the marginal revenue product *MRP* and therefore also the quantity of labour demanded at each wage rate (remember that *MRP* = *MPP* × *P*; thus if *P* changes, *MRP* will also change, *ceteris paribus*)
- the marginal physical product *MPP* (or **productivity**) of labour changes, since this will change *MRP*, *ceteris paribus*
- a **new substitute for labour** becomes available – for example, the introduction of automated teller machines (ATMs) resulted in a decrease in the demand for bank tellers, *ceteris paribus*
- the **price of a substitute factor of production** changes – for example, if the price of machinery

BOX 14-2 IMPERFECT COMPETITION IN THE PRODUCT MARKET AND THE DEMAND FOR LABOUR

Although the analysis of the demand for labour remains fundamentally unchanged if we relax the assumption of perfect competition in the goods market, one difference should be noted. With imperfect goods markets there are two reasons why marginal revenue product (*MRP*) declines as employment expands beyond a certain point. As in the case of perfect competition, diminishing returns will set in but, in addition, a firm faced with a downward-sloping demand curve for its product also has to reduce the price of all units in order to increase sales (ie in the absence of price discrimination). Thus, when a firm sells its product in an imperfect market, both elements of the *MRP* of labour (ie the marginal physical product *MPP* and the price of the product *P*) can vary. Because *P* falls as output increases, the *MRP* will *(ceteris paribus)* fall more rapidly for firms operating in imperfect goods markets than for those engaged in perfect competition.

To differentiate between the two cases, a distinction is sometimes made between the **marginal revenue product** (*MRP*) and the **value marginal product** (*VMP*, short for value of the marginal product) where the former is equal to the marginal physical product multiplied by the marginal revenue of the product in question (ie $MRP = MPP \times MR$), while the value marginal product is equal to the marginal physical product multiplied by the price of the product (ie $VMP = MPP \times P$).

In perfectly competitive goods markets marginal revenue (*MR*) is equal to price (*P*), therefore *MRP* = *VMP*. However, in the case of imperfect competition *MR* will be lower than *P* (since prices have to be lowered to increase sales volumes) and therefore *MRP* will be lower than *VMP*. Graphically, the *MRP* curve will be steeper than (or lie inside) the *VMP* curve. As a result, fewer workers will be employed *(ceteris paribus)* at any given wage by a firm operating in an imperfect goods market than by a firm that is subject to perfect competition in the goods market.

In the main text we ignore the difference between *MRP* and *VMP* and refer only to *MRP*, which is the broader concept.

(capital) decreases, the quantity of labour demanded will tend to decrease, as employers replace workers with machines

- the **price of a complementary factor of production** changes – for example, if the price of trucks decreases and the quantity of trucks increases, the number of truck drivers demanded will also increase

Each of these changes can be illustrated by a **shift** of the market demand curve.

A further look at labour market equilibrium and changes in equilibrium

In a perfectly competitive labour market all the participants are wage (or price) takers and the equilibrium wage rate and equilibrium level of employment are determined by the interaction of the demand for and supply of labour, as illustrated in Figure 14-1. In such a market there is a uniform wage rate, which implies that all employed workers except the last one actually receive a higher wage than the minimum wage at which they are prepared to offer their services. In technical terms they are earning an **economic rent** – see Box 14-3.

A change in any of the non-wage determinants of the demand for or supply of labour will give rise to a shift of the demand curve or the supply curve, as illustrated in Figure 14-7. Figure 14-7(a) depicts an increase in the demand for labour (eg as a result of an increase in the demand for the product in question, illustrated by a shift of the demand curve from D_0D_0 to D_1D_1). In a perfectly competitive labour market, the wage rate and the level of employment will adjust immediately, to w_1 and N_1 respectively. Figure 14-7(b) depicts a decrease in the demand for labour (eg as a result of the substitution of labour by capital, illustrated by a shift of the demand curve from D_0D_0 to D_2D_2). In a perfectly competitive labour market this will immediately result in a decrease in both the wage rate (to w_2) and the level of employment (to N_2). Likewise, Figures 14-7(c) and (d) illustrate an increase in the supply of labour (eg as a result of new entrants to the labour market) and a decrease in the supply of labour (eg as a result of a decline in the relative attractiveness of the particular type of job).

BOX 14-3 ECONOMIC RENT AND TRANSFER EARNINGS IN FACTOR MARKETS

In any factor market the price (ie remuneration) of the factor of production (ie labour, land, capital or entrepreneurship) consists of two components: economic rent and transfer earnings.

Transfer earnings are what the factor must earn to prevent it from moving to an alternative use. In the case of labour it is what workers must be paid to persuade them to stay in their present job, instead of transferring to another job (hence the name "transfer" earnings).

Economic rent is anything that the factor earns over and above transfer earnings. It is equivalent to the producer surplus introduced in Chapter 7.

Transfer earnings and economic rent can be explained with the aid of the following diagram:

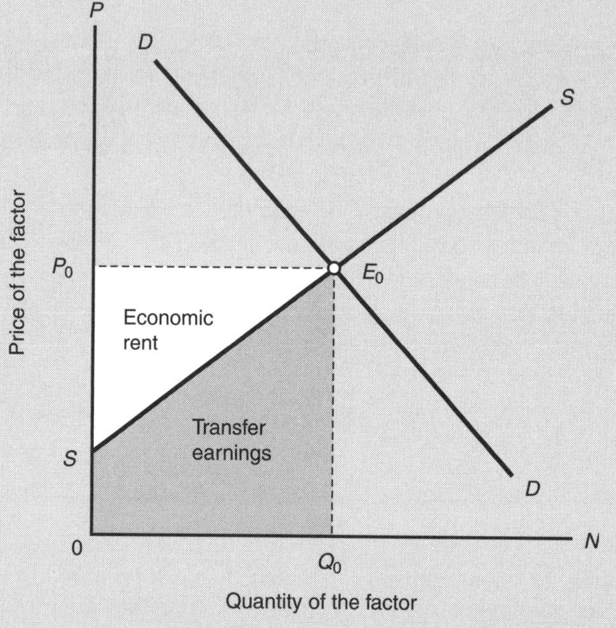

The demand for the factor is represented by *DD* and the supply by *SS*. The equilibrium price is P_0 and the equilibrium quantity Q_0. The total earnings of the factor is the rectangle $0P_0E_0Q_0$. The supply curve shows the prices at which the various quantities of the factor will be supplied. The area under the supply curve represents the **transfer earnings** of the factor. In this case it is equal to $0SE_0Q_0$. Apart from the last unit (ie at Q_0) all the previous units of the factor receive a price (P_0) which is higher than the owners of the factor would have been willing to accept (ie the earnings exceed the transfer earnings). The difference between the price received and the supply price (or transfer earnings) is the **economic rent**. The total economic rent in this case is equal to the triangle SP_0E_0. This is similar to the producer surplus in a goods market.

In the case of labour, for example, the economic rent is the difference between the actual wage rate and the wage rates at which the different quantities are supplied (ie the wage rates which the workers concerned would have accepted). In this case the economic rent is positive for all units except the last unit (Q_0) of labour.

The relative size of the transfer earnings and economic rent depends on the elasticity of supply of the factor. The more inelastic the supply is (ie the steeper the supply curve), the greater the economic rent becomes. In the extreme case of a perfectly inelastic supply, the economic rent is equal to the total earnings of the factor. See also Box 14-6.

In all these cases, the **magnitude** of the changes in the wage rate and the level of employment will depend on the **elasticities** of demand and supply. For example, if the demand for labour decreases, the impact will depend on the elasticity of the supply of labour. The more inelastic the supply of labour, the greater the impact on the wage rate and the smaller the impact on the level of employment will be. Likewise, the impact of a change in the supply of labour will depend on the elasticity of the demand for labour.

In Figure 14-7 it is assumed that the labour market adjusts fully and instantaneously to changes in demand or supply. In other words, the labour market is completely **flexible**. In practice, however, adjustment takes time and also need not be complete. In fact, most labour markets are imperfect markets characterised by various rigidities and deviations from the perfectly competitive model. In the next section we examine some of the imperfections and their implications.

FIGURE 14-7 Changes in labour market equilibrium

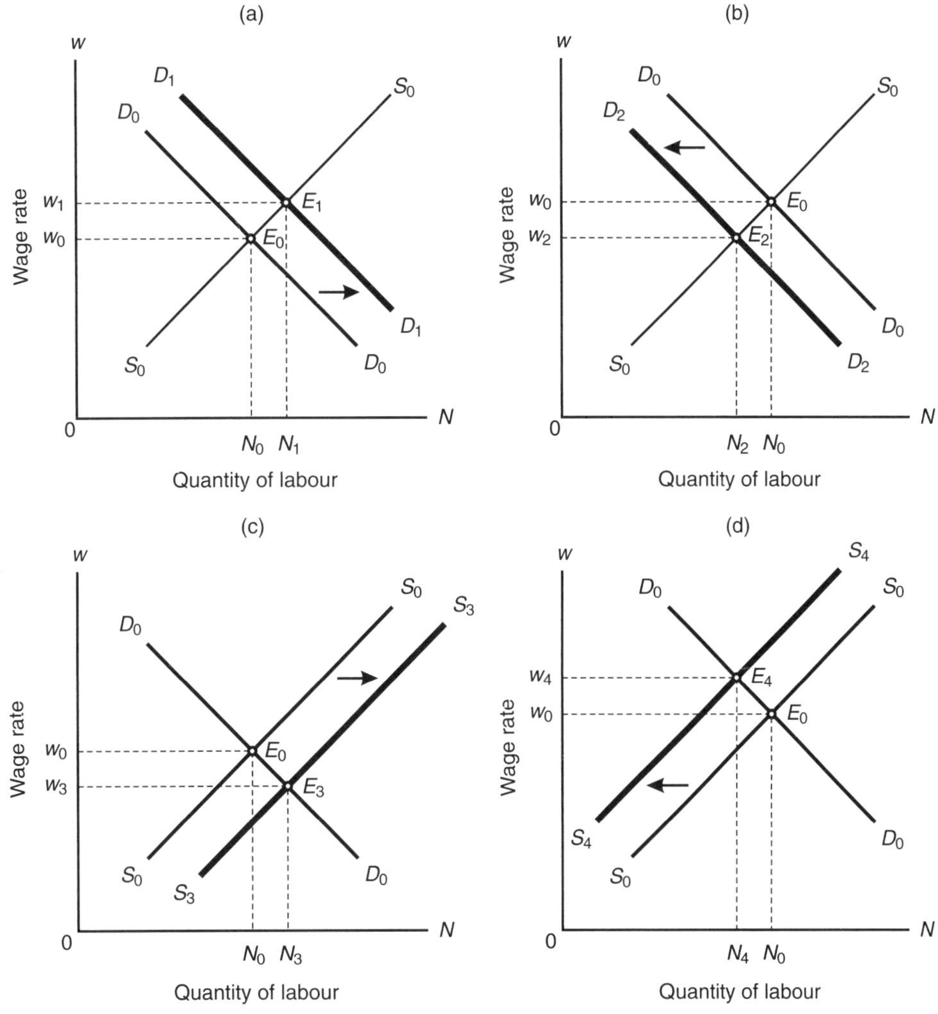

In all cases the initial equilibrium is illustrated by the intersection of the demand curve (D_0D_0) and the supply curve (S_0S_0). The equilibrium wage rate is w_0 and the equilibrium level of employment N_0. In (a) the demand for labour increases, illustrated by a rightward shift of the demand curve to D_1D_1. The wage rate increases to w_1 and the level of employment to N_1. In (b) the demand for labour decreases, illustrated by a leftward shift of the demand curve to D_2D_2. The equilibrium wage rate and employment level fall to w_2 and N_2 respectively. In (c) the supply of labour increases, illustrated by a rightward shift of the supply curve to S_3S_3. The wage rate falls to w_3 but the level of employment increases to N_3. In (d) the supply of labour decreases, illustrated by a leftward shift of the supply curve to S_4S_4. The wage rate increases to w_4 but the level of employment falls to N_4.

14.3 Imperfect labour markets

In Chapter 13 we saw that most goods markets are not characterised by perfect competition. Likewise, most labour markets are not characterised by perfect competition. We do not live in a world of perfect information, or in a world with perfectly competitive input and output markets. In this section we examine some of the reasons why labour markets tend to be imperfect, and we analyse some of these imperfections.

Some of the reasons that labour markets may be imperfect are the following:

- Workers in a particular market are organised in a **trade union** which then acts as a **monopolistic supplier** of labour.
- There is **only one buyer** of labour (ie only one major employer or employer organisation) in a particular market. This is called a **monopsony** (recall that when there is only one seller in a market it is called a **monopoly**).
- Labour is **heterogeneous**, not homogeneous, and each worker (or group of workers) has particular abilities, attributes, education, training or experience that differentiates him or her from other workers.
- Labour is **not completely mobile**, in the sense that workers cannot move freely from one occupation to another, from one employer to another or from one region to another. The labour market is a **segmented market** and workers often cannot move freely between the different segments.
- **Government intervenes** in the labour market by legislating conditions of employment, minimum wages and so on. Government is also the largest employer in the economy and its actions invariably affect the rest of the labour market.
- Employers and employees have **imperfect knowledge** (information) about market conditions (eg workers are often unaware of jobs that are available).

We now examine some of these market imperfections.

Trade unions

One of the requirements for perfect competition in the labour market is a large number of independent suppliers of labour. However, individual workers, particularly unskilled ones, are usually at a disadvantage when negotiating with employers. The employer decides whether or not to employ the worker and also determines the conditions of employment. Unless the worker has some special skills or other attributes, or unless labour is in short supply, he or she will have little or no individual bargaining power. Workers therefore often band together to form trade unions or other employees' organisations to pursue certain common aims and to serve as a **countervailing force** to the bargaining power of employers. Wages and other conditions of service are then negotiated on a collective basis between employees and employers. When matters cannot be settled through such **collective bargaining**, disputes are referred for mediation or arbitration by a third party, or the workers may go on strike in an attempt to enforce their demands.

The economic effects of trade unions are hotly debated. Do trade unions raise wages? Do they cause inflation? Do they increase or decrease economic efficiency? Do they make the distribution of income more equal or less equal? Do they cause unemployment? Economists and other observers differ on these issues. Some argue that trade unions raise wages at the cost of increased unemployment. It is often claimed, for example, that trade union pressure for higher wages has caused certain workers to be priced out of the market and replaced by machines. Some observers also argue that unions cause so much "hassle" that employers prefer to replace people with machines, which cannot go on strike or disrupt the production process in other ways.

Collective bargaining is not concerned only with wages. It covers a variety of issues, including matters such as hours of work, job security, overtime, fringe benefits, job evaluation and procedures for settling grievances. In this subsection, however, we restrict ourselves to an examination of the possible impact of trade unions on wages and employment. Some information about trade unions in South Africa is provided in Box 14-4.

There are two broad categories of trade union: craft unions and industrial unions. A **craft union** consists of workers with a common set of skills (eg plumbers, electricians, printers) who are joined together in a common association, irrespective of where, or for whom, they work. South African examples include the Airline Pilots' Association of South Africa (ALPA-SA), the Jewellers and Goldsmiths Union (J & GU), the South African Democratic Teachers' Union (Sadtu) and the South African Football Players' Union (Safpu). Professional bodies (eg in the medical, legal, engineering or accounting professions) operate along similar lines. Such unions can control the supply of skilled labour in particular trades or professions (eg by restricting membership, controlling the length of training or apprenticeship programmes or raising standards for entry). This is illustrated in Figure 14-8(a). The original demand and supply are represented by D_0D_0 and S_0S_0 respectively. The original equilibrium wage rate is w_0 and the level of employment N_0. If the union succeeds in reducing the supply of skills (illustrated by a leftward shift of the supply curve to S_1S_1), the wage rate increases to w_1 and the level of employment falls to N_1. The impact of the shift in supply will depend, *ceteris paribus*, on the elasticity

FIGURE 14-8 Ways in which a trade union can attempt to increase the wage rate

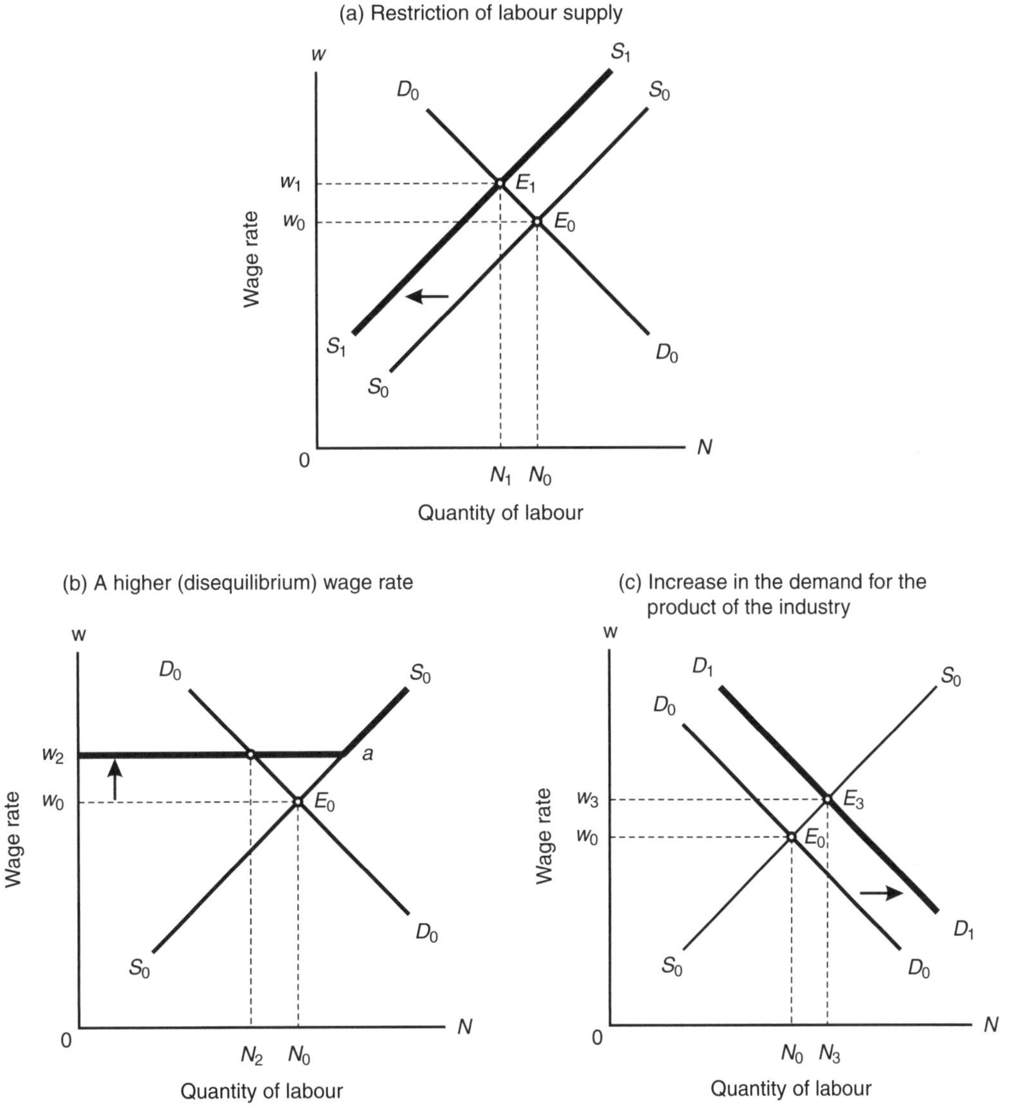

Trade unions can attempt to raise the wage rate by (a) restricting supply, (b) enforcing a higher disequilibrium wage or (c) assisting firms to raise the demand for the product of the industry. The restriction of supply is illustrated in part (a) by a leftward shift of the supply curve to S_1S_1. Part (b) illustrates a situation in which the union succeeds in raising the wage rate to w_2, which is higher than the equilibrium wage. As in (a), this is accompanied by a decline in employment. Part (c) illustrates a situation in which the union succeeds (in conjunction with the firms) in raising the demand for the product of the industry. This results in an increase in the derived demand for labour (to D_1D_1). The wage rate increases (to w_3) and the level of employment also increases.

of demand. The greater the elasticity of demand, the larger the drop in employment will be.

An **industrial union** tries to organise all workers (both skilled and unskilled) in a particular industry in a single bargaining unit. In contrast to a craft union, it does not restrict its membership to workers with particular skills or qualifications. South African examples include the National Union of Metalworkers of South Africa (Numsa), the Police and Prisons Civil Rights Union (Popcru), the Southern African Clothing and Textile Workers' Union (Sactwu), the South African Municipal Workers Union (Samwu) and the National Union of Mineworkers (NUM). The ultimate aim of an industrial union is to achieve complete control over

BOX 14-4 TRADE UNIONS IN SOUTH AFRICA

Trade union activity in South Africa was fairly subdued until the 1970s, mainly because black workers were not permitted to join or form trade unions, while the other trade unions shared in the fruits of economic growth. In the 1970s and 1980s things changed. Unofficial trade unions became a strong economic and political force and when these unions were eventually recognised, following the recommendations of the Wiehahn Commission, they formed one of the nuclei of the struggle against the political regime. Membership of registered trade unions increased from 782 000 in 1980 to about 3,5 million in 2000.

Most individual trade unions belong to larger trade union federations. The largest federations are:

- The **Congress of South African Trade Unions** (Cosatu) which claimed a paid-up membership of more than 1,8 million in 2007. Cosatu, which was formed in 1985, is one of the parties (along with the African National Congress and the South African Communist Party) in the tripartite alliance which effectively governs the country.
- The **Federation of Unions of South Africa** (Fedusa). Formed in 1997, it had a paid-up membership base of more than 550 000 in 2007. Fedusa is not aligned to any political party.
- The **National Council of Trade Unions** (Nactu), with a claimed membership of 397 000 in 2003. Although non-racial in principle, Nactu appears to be oriented towards the Pan African Congress (PAC) or the Azanian People's Organisation (Azapo).

The four largest trade unions in South Africa in 2007 were all affiliated to Cosatu. They are the:

- National Union of Mineworkers (NUM) with 262 042 members
- South African Democratic Teachers' Union (Sadtu), with 224 387 members
- National Union of Metalworkers of South Africa (Numsa), with 216 808 members
- National Education, Health and Allied Workers' Union (Nehawu), with 192 739 members

The oldest and largest independent trade union in South Africa is Solidariteit. Originally founded as the Mynwerkersunie (MWU) in 1913, it became Solidariteit in 2001, when four other unions joined the MWU. A further three unions joined in 2002, increasing the total membership to 128 000 (compared to 33 000 in 1994). It is a politically conservative union but is not aligned to a particular political party.

As in other countries, there is no consensus about the impact of trade unions on wages and employment in South Africa. The real wages of union members have increased but some researchers ascribe this to increased geographical and occupational labour mobility (eg as a result of better opportunities and improved qualifications) rather than to trade union pressure as such. Others, however, maintain that trade unions were co-responsible for the stagnation and decline of formal sector employment (and the consequent increase in unemployment) in South Africa after 1980.

These issues will continue to be debated. The only aspect about which everyone agrees is that trade unions are an important feature, not only of the labour market, but of the economy as a whole. In the 1990s, for example, the major trade union federations (particularly Cosatu) assumed an important role in the formulation of economic policy in South Africa, but their influence in the policy-making process tended to wane from 1996 onwards.

the labour supply in a particular industry, thereby forcing firms in the industry to bargain exclusively with it over wages and other conditions of employment. Although this aim is seldom, if ever, achieved in practice, powerful industrial unions have significant bargaining power and can severely disrupt firms or industries through strike action.

In contrast to craft unions, industrial unions use their bargaining power directly to increase wage rates. This is illustrated in Figure 14-8(b). Once again D_0D_0 and S_0S_0 represent the original demand and supply of labour. The equilibrium wage rate is w_0 and the equilibrium level of employment N_0. Suppose the union (which represents all the workers in the industry) succeeds (eg through strike action or the threat of such action) to raise the wage rate to w_2. The effective labour supply now becomes w_2aS_0 (illustrated by the thick line in the figure). The level of employment will fall to N_2 but the higher wage rate will persist as long as the union can prevent other (non-union) workers from accepting employment at lower wage rates. Once again the impact on employment will depend on the elasticity of the demand for labour. Other factors that affect the bargaining position of the union are discussed later in the subsection on bilateral monopoly.

Unions can also attempt to raise wages (and employment) by trying to increase the demand for labour in a particular industry. This is illustrated in Figure 14-8(c). The initial equilibrium is similar to the initial equilibria in Figures 14-8(a) and (b). If the demand for labour increases, illustrated by a rightward shift of the demand curve to D_1D_1, the wage rate rises to w_3 and the level of employment increases to N_3. This is clearly a win-win situation for both the workers and the firms in the industry. But how can this be achieved? A first possibility is an increase in labour productivity. As we saw earlier, the physical productivity of labour (represented by the marginal physical product *MPP*) is an essential element of the demand for labour. The higher the *MPP*, the greater the demand for labour, *ceteris paribus*. Trade unions often enter into **productivity agreements** with employers, whereby workers agree that they will increase productivity in exchange for higher wages. Unions also often join employers' organisations in lobbying government to impose or raise import tariffs or quotas to reduce competition from imports and raise the demand for domestically-produced goods (eg in the clothing and textile industries). If they succeed, the derived demand for labour will also increase.

The impact of trade unions on the labour market is a complex issue. We touch on it again in the subsection on bilateral monopoly. But first we have to examine monopsony.

Monopsony

A **monopsony** is a market structure in which one buyer purchases a good or service from many sellers. It can be regarded as the opposite of a monopoly, in which one supplier sells to many buyers. A labour market in which one employer, the **monopsonist**, confronts an unorganised (non-unionised) group of workers competing against each other for jobs, is called a monopsony. A monopsony also exists where such an unorganised group of workers is faced with an employers' organisation that represents all the employers in a particular industry. Examples include mining towns, where the mining company is the major employer, towns where a clothing or textile firm is the major employer or a rural area where a large farming business is the sole or major employer. Well-known South African examples were the Native Recruiting Corporation (NRC), established in 1898 to recruit labour for the gold mines from South Africa, Botswana, Lesotho and Swaziland, and the Witwatersrand Native Labour Association (WNLA), established at the same time to recruit workers from further afield. The NRC and WNLA controlled recruitment of labour for the gold mines for 80 years, until they were combined into one organisation, known as The Employment Bureau of Africa Limited (TEBA).

Unlike a perfectly competitive employer, a monopsonist employer of labour is not faced with a horizontal supply curve of labour at the ruling market price. Unless the monopsonist is faced with a perfectly elastic supply of labour (which was probably the case in the South African gold mining industry when the NRC and WNLA did the recruiting), a monopsonist has to raise the wage rate if it wishes to increase the level of employment. This means that the marginal cost of labour to the monopsonist is greater than the wage rate. Why? Because if the monopsonist wishes to employ an additional worker it has to pay that worker more than the ruling wage rate *and* also pay all the existing workers more. The marginal cost of labour *(MCL)* is thus no longer equal to the average cost of labour *(ACL)*, but greater than *ACL*.

Table 14-2 provides a numerical example of the cost of labour and the marginal revenue product of a monopsonist. The first column shows the quantity of labour (eg the number of workers). The second column shows the wage rate at which the quantities of labour in the first column will be supplied. The first two columns together thus represent the supply of labour, as well as the average cost of labour *(ACL)* to the monopsonist. The third column shows the total cost of labour *(TCL)* and the fourth the marginal cost of labour *(MCL)*. The *MCL* is, of course, the addition to *TCL* as a result of the employment of an additional unit of labour. The last column shows the marginal revenue product *(MRP)* which represents the monopsonist's demand for labour. It is equal to the marginal physical product *(MPP)* multiplied by the price of the product *(P)*. In order to focus on the key variables, neither *MPP* nor *P* is shown separately in the table. If this bothers you, you can assume that $P = 1$, and therefore that $MRP = MPP$ (bearing in mind that *MRP* is expressed in monetary terms and *MPP* in physical terms).

The data in Table 14-2 are illustrated in Figure 14-9.

A monopsonist will employ labour up to the level where the marginal cost of labour (*MCL*) is equal to the marginal benefit of labour, that is, the marginal revenue product of labour (*MRP*). In our example, this is at a level of 4 units of labour. What about the wage rate? The monopsonist will pay the wage rate at which the required quantity of labour will be supplied. In our example, 4 units of labour will be supplied at a

TABLE 14-2 The cost and marginal revenue product of labour in a monopsonistic labour market

1 Quantity of labour (units)	2 Wage rate or average cost of labour (R) ACL	3 Total cost of labour (R) TCL (= 1 × 2)	4 Marginal cost of labour (R) MCL	5 Marginal revenue product of labour (R) MRP
1	3	3	3	15
2	4	8	5	13
3	5	15	7	11
4	6	24	9	9
5	7	35	11	7
6	8	48	13	5

wage rate equal to R6 per unit. This, then, is the wage rate that the monopsonist will pay.

If, by contrast, the same market were a competitive labour market, the market demand for labour (*MRP*) would intersect the market supply of labour (*ACL*) at an employment level of 5 units and a wage rate of R7 per unit. In other words, a greater quantity of labour would be employed at a higher wage rate than in a monopsonistic labour market.

Bilateral monopoly

In many (if not most) labour markets, in South Africa and elsewhere, wages and other conditions of employment are determined through a process of **collective bargaining** between the representatives of the workers and the representatives of the employers. Where there is a single trade union representing the workers in an industry, and a single employers' organisation representing the employers in an industry, the result is a **bilateral monopoly**. In other words, a monopolist (the trade union) is pitted against a monopsonist (the employers' organisation). South African examples include the National Union of Mineworkers (NUM) and the Chamber of Mines of South Africa, and the National Union of Metalworkers of South Africa (Numsa) and the Steel and Engineering Industries Federation of South Africa (Seifsa).

The actual outcome of negotiations in a bilateral monopoly is uncertain. Trade unions desire relatively high wage rates, as illustrated in Figure 14-8(b). By contrast, monopsonistic employers desire relatively low wage rates, as illustrated in Figure 14-9. The actual outcome in a particular case will depend on the bargaining power of the union relative to that of the monopsonist. The greater the relative bargaining power of the union, the closer the actual wage rate will be to that desired by the union. Conversely, the greater the relative bargaining power of the monopsonist, the closer the actual wage rate will be to that desired by the employers' organisation. In practice, the relative bargaining power of the two parties may even be such that the same outcome is achieved as would be the case in a perfectly competitive labour market.

In collective bargaining about wages the typical points of reference in the negotiations are:

- what other workers are getting
- changes in the cost of living
- the employers' ability to pay
- productivity

The relative bargaining strength of the two parties is determined, *inter alia*, by:

- **The ratio of wage cost to total cost.** The smaller the ratio of wage cost to total cost, the more likely an employer or employers' organisation will be to concede a wage claim rather than risk a costly strike during which nothing is produced but significant overhead (fixed) costs still have to be met.
- **Changes in productivity.** For example, if it can be shown that workers' productivity has increased, or will increase, the union will be in a stronger bargaining position than if no such evidence is available.
- **The relationship between the wages paid in the industry and the wages paid elsewhere for similar work.** If it can be shown that workers are earning more for similar work elsewhere, the union's position will be strengthened. By the same token, an important successful wage claim elsewhere in the economy (eg in the public sector) will also strengthen the union's hand.
- **The nature of the product.** For example, if the workers supply an essential service or product, there might be pressure on employers to reach a quick settlement. In some cases, however, workers providing essential services are prohibited from

FIGURE 14-9 Wage and employment determination in a monopsonistic labour market

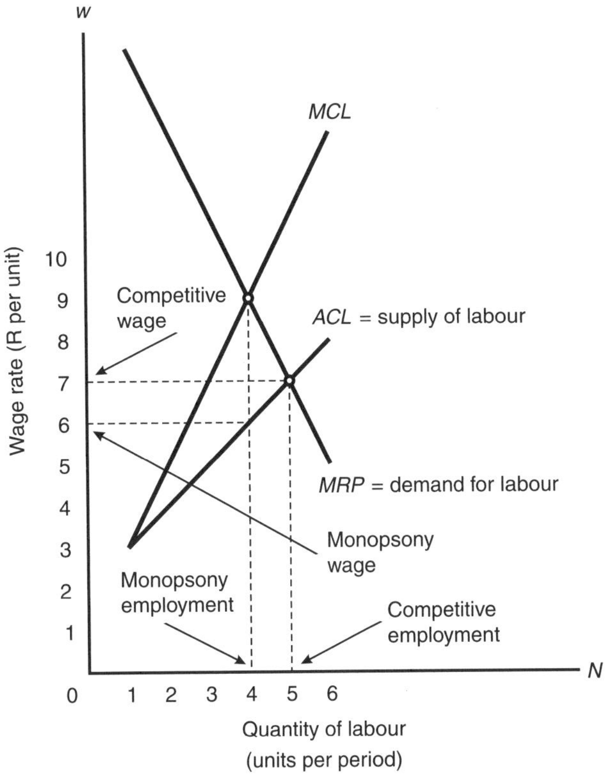

The monopsonistic firm faces the supply of labour in the market, which represents its average cost of labour (ACL). Its marginal cost of labour (MCL) is greater than its ACL because all existing workers also have to be paid more if an additional worker is hired. The firm will employ labour up to the point where its marginal cost of labour (MCL) equals its marginal revenue product (MRP) of labour. This is at an employment level of 4 units. The wage rate paid will be R6 per unit, since this is the wage rate at which 4 units of labour will be supplied. If the labour market were a competitive market, MRP would represent the demand for labour. MRP intersects the supply of labour at an employment level of 5 units and a wage rate of R7. Under monopsony, both the level of employment and the wage rate are thus lower than in a perfectly competitive labour market.

striking, which weakens the union's bargaining position.

- **The price elasticity of the demand for the product**. The more inelastic the demand for the product, the greater the scope for passing cost increases on to consumers and the stronger the union's bargaining position will be. The opposite applies when the demand for the product is price elastic.
- **The degree to which the union controls the supply of labour**. The greater the control of the union over the supply of labour, the stronger its position will be. On the other hand, if employers can easily obtain non-union labour, they will be in a stronger position.
- **The level of unemployment**. The greater the level of unemployment in the economy, region or industry, the weaker the union's position will be. On the other hand, the more buoyant the economy, the greater the union's bargaining power will be.
- **The extent to which machinery can readily replace labour**. The easier it is to substitute machinery for labour, the stronger the bargaining position of the employers will be.
- **Increases in the cost of living**. The cost of living is always an important factor in determining a wage claim. Although employers are not obliged to compensate workers for increases in the cost of living, the inflation rate (measured by the rate of increase in the consumer price index) is usually an impor-

tant yardstick in wage negotiations. In some contracts wage rates are even linked to the cost of living (see the discussion of indexation in Chapter 21), while in other cases increases in the cost of living beyond a certain threshold trigger additional payments to employees. When inflation is high and accelerating, unions are particularly preoccupied with securing cost-of-living increases and employers find it more difficult to resist wage increases than when inflation is low and stable.

- **The structure of the goods market**. If the employers are producing in competitive markets, firms are earning normal profit only (see Chapter 12) and any increase in costs will result in the bankruptcy of the marginal firms. In such circumstances, wages can only be increased at the expense of employment. If unemployment increases, there is also a danger that those who become unemployed will undercut the union wage. On the other hand, if the employers are powerful price makers, they may be able to pass on wage increases to their customers in the form of higher prices and may thus accede more readily to wage demands. However, if the employer is a monopolist who does not have to fear any loss of market share due to strike action, the firm may decide to vigorously resist any wage increase.

These are but some of the determinants of the relative bargaining strength of unions and employers in collective bargaining about wages. It should be obvious that the actual outcome of bilateral monopoly depends on the particular circumstances of each case. Negotiations are often intense and protracted but in most cases a compromise solution is found.

Government intervention in the labour market

One of the basic conditions for perfect competition is that there should be no government intervention in the labour market. In practice, however, governments intervene in various ways. Such intervention inhibits the functioning of the market mechanism and is often regarded as an important potential cause of unemployment and other labour market problems.

In the 1990s the South African government launched a comprehensive legislative programme aimed at reforming the labour market – see Box 14-5. Critics often cite the new labour laws as one of the most important causes of the high and increasing unemployment and sluggish economic growth subsequently experienced in South Africa. They propose a much less regulated (or more flexible) labour market in which it will be much easier for employers to adjust to changing circumstances, roughly similar to the perfectly competitive labour market explained in Section 14.2. Others, however, argue that **stability** is at least as important as **flexibility** and ascribe much of the instability and rigidity in the South African labour market to misguided policies of the past. Participants in the debate tend to present the choice as a simple one between an **employer-friendly, flexible labour market** (in which employers are able to adjust the size, remuneration and working conditions of their workforces speedily and at low cost) and a **worker-friendly, stable labour market** (in which employees are securely protected against arbitrary dismissal, reductions in earnings, discrimination and unhealthy or dangerous working conditions). In reality, however, the government opted for an intermediate position of **regulated flexibility**, in an attempt to strike a balance between labour market security or stability and the flexibility demanded by the globalised world economy. The debate continues. We do not analyse all the issues here. Instead, we focus on one form of intervention in labour markets, namely the fixing of minimum wages. In the analysis of minimum wages it will become clear that one should think carefully before expressing an opinion on matters related to the labour market.

Minimum wages

Wage determination is often an emotional process. When the pay of those at the bottom end of the wage structure is at issue, concepts such a basic needs, minimum living levels, living wages and calls for minimum wages tend to become emotionally loaded. We now examine the controversial issue of minimum wages.

Those who are in favour of minimum wages argue that individual workers, especially those who are unskilled or inexperienced, are often at a disadvantage when negotiating with employers. When job opportunities are scarce, employers may exploit workers and pay very low wages. In such circumstances market forces do not protect workers against possible exploitation. Minimum wages are therefore propagated as a means of avoiding exploitation and ensuring a certain minimum standard of living for all workers.

The proponents of minimum wages also justify them on other grounds. They argue, for example, that minimum wages will increase productivity. How? Firms using low-wage workers may be using labour inefficiently and the higher wages imposed by the minimum wage may shock them into using labour more efficiently. The higher wages may also improve the nutrition, health, vigour and motivation of workers, thus making them more productive.

Supporters of minimum wages also point out that wages are the most significant form of income and therefore constitute the largest source of the demand for goods and services. In South Africa, for example, it is argued that increases in wages as a result of the

BOX 14-5 SOUTH AFRICAN LABOUR LEGISLATION

During the second half of the 1990s the South African government adopted a legislative programme aimed at reforming the labour market, which stimulated a fair amount of controversy. This programme consisted of a series of new Acts, of which the following are the most important:

- **Labour Relations Act, 66 of 1995**. This Act, which came into force in 1996, establishes a common industrial relations framework for all civilian employees, including public servants (who were previously covered by a different Act) and farm workers and domestic workers (who were denied bargaining rights under the previous Labour Relations Act). The Act gives effect to the economic and social rights entrenched in the 1996 Constitution, including the right to strike, freedom of association, the right to picket the premises of an employer, to form industry-wide statutory councils and to democratise the workplace. It establishes the framework for collective bargaining and it also overhauls the procedures for dispute resolution by introducing new institutions such as the Commission for Conciliation, Mediation and Arbitration (CCMA) and endowing the Labour Court and the Labour Appeal Court with the same status as the Supreme Court.
- **Basic Conditions of Employment Act, 75 of 1997**. The purpose of this Act is to advance economic development and social justice by establishing and enforcing basic conditions of employment. It establishes a floor of basic rights for all workers (including those who were previously denied basic worker rights) and extends these rights by reducing the length of the working week, increasing annual and maternal leave periods and increasing overtime premiums.
- **Employment Equity Act, 55 of 1998**. This Act is aimed at achieving equity in the workplace by promoting equal opportunity and fair treatment in employment through the elimination of unfair discrimination, and by implementing affirmative action measures to redress the disparities in employment experienced by certain designated groups (ie women, black males and the disabled).
- **Skills Development Act, 97 of 1998**. This Act aims to develop the skills of the labour force by increasing the investment in education and training in the labour market. More specifically, the aim is to improve productivity and competitiveness, to improve the work prospects and occupational mobility of workers, to promote self-employment and to improve social services.

While the changes to South African labour legislation have created a labour market built on just and equitable labour practices, critics argue that the changes have given rise to an inflexible labour market that cannot respond adequately to market forces and therefore tends to stifle economic growth and raise unemployment. Many critics argue that a developing country like South Africa simply cannot afford a sophisticated set of labour laws similar to those in developed countries.

imposition of minimum wages will raise the demand for basic consumer goods and services. This, in turn, will stimulate production, income and employment in the domestic economy – see the discussion on inward industrialisation in Section 23.3.

No compassionate human being would deny anyone a job at a remuneration which is adequate to permit a decent or reasonable living standard, but unfortunately this is impossible to guarantee. While the arguments in favour of minimum wages all sound attractive, other economic forces also have to be taken into account. Wages are a significant cost item and the imposition of minimum wages will therefore tend to raise costs of production, unless productivity also increases. Increased costs of production will either be passed on to consumers (in the form of higher prices) or result in a drop in the demand for labour (ie unemployment).

We now examine the impact of minimum wages in perfectly competitive and monopsonistic labour markets.

■ A MINIMUM WAGE IN A PERFECTLY COMPETITIVE LABOUR MARKET

Figure 14-10 illustrates what will happen in a perfectly competitive labour market if a minimum wage **above** the equilibrium wage rate is imposed. *DD* is the

FIGURE 14-10 The impact of the imposition of a minimum wage in a perfectly competitive labour market

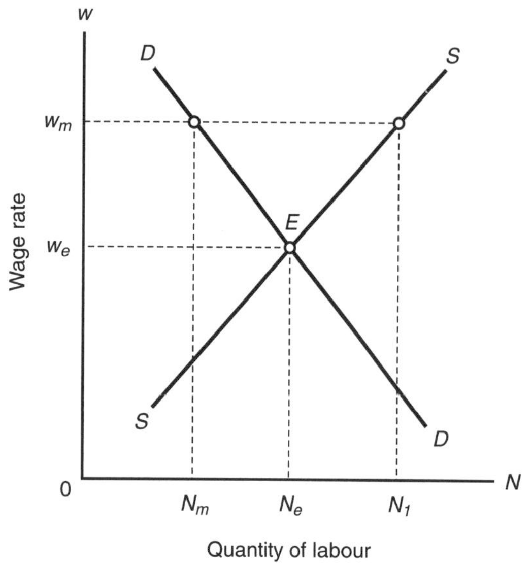

DD and SS are the demand and supply of labour respectively. The original equilibrium wage is w_e and the quantity of labour employed is N_e. The imposition of a minimum wage at w_m decreases the quantity of labour demanded to N_m and thus causes unemployment equal to the difference between N_e and N_m. At the minimum wage w_m there is an excess supply of labour equal to the difference between N_1

demand for labour, *SS* is the supply of labour, w_e the equilibrium wage rate and N_e the equilibrium quantity of labour employed. If the minimum wage rate is fixed at w_m, an excess supply of labour will develop. The quantity of labour demanded and employed will fall to N_m. At the minimum wage the quantity of labour supplied will increase to N_1. At that wage rate there will thus be unemployment (ie an excess supply of labour) equal to the difference between N_1 and N_m. However, if we compare the position after the introduction of the minimum wage to the position before its introduction, the fall in employment is given by the difference between N_e and N_m.

In South Africa, the markets for farm workers and domestic workers are relatively competitive markets, characterised by a large and relatively elastic supply of labour and low wages. When minimum wages for farm workers and domestic workers were introduced in recent years, many observers feared that the result would be increased unemployment, as illustrated in Figure 14-10. At the time of writing, no conclusive evidence was available yet, but anecdotal evidence seemed to suggest that some farm and domestic workers might have lost their jobs as a result of the imposition of minimum wages.

Minimum wages are also set in other industries, but in many instances the minimum wage rate appears to have been set at lower than the equilibrium wage rate. As we saw in the discussion of minimum price fixing in Chapter 8, a minimum price (in this case the wage rate) that is set below the equilibrium price has no impact on price or quantity. In other words, the imposition of a minimum wage rate **below** the equilibrium wage rate will have no effect on the wage rate or the level of employment.

As we have seen, labour markets tend to be imperfect, rather than perfectly competitive. The analysis of a perfectly competitive labour market therefore does not provide sufficient evidence to reject the case for minimum wages. In fact, in the case of a monopsonistic labour market the introduction of a minimum wage might even raise, rather than lower, the level of employment.

■ A MINIMUM WAGE IN A MONOPSONISTIC LABOUR MARKET

Figure 14-11 illustrates the impact of the imposition of a minimum wage if there is a single employer in a particular labour market (ie in the case of a monopsony). From our earlier discussion of monopsony we know that the marginal cost of labour *(MCL)* facing the monopsonist is greater than the average cost of labour *ACL* (which is also the market supply of labour). The equilibrium level of employment N_e is reached where the marginal cost of labour *(MCL)* is equal to the marginal revenue product of labour *(MRP)*. The equilibrium wage rate w_e is the wage rate at which the equilibrium level of employment will be supplied.

If the government now imposes a minimum wage w_m **above** the current equilibrium wage w_e, the supply of labour to the monopsonist (ie the monopsonist's *ACL*) becomes $w_m ab$ and its *MCL* becomes $w_m acd$. Between w_m and *a*, the supply curve to the employer is horizontal (as in the case of perfect competition) and *MCL* is thus equal to *ACL*. *MCL* returns to its original level beyond point *a*. The monopsonist will again employ labour up to the point where *MCL* = *MRP*. In Figure 14-11 this is at an employment level N_m, which is greater than N_e (ie the equilibrium level of employment in the absence of the minimum wage). In this example, therefore, the imposition of a minimum wage rate above the equilibrium wage rate actually increases the equilibrium level of employment. This result, however, will only be obtained as long as the minimum wage is set at a level lower than w_1. At any minimum wage greater than w_1 *MCL* will equal *MRP* at a level of employment lower than N_e. If the minimum wage rate is set at w_1, the level of employment will remain at N_e.

FIGURE 14-11 The impact of the imposition of a minimum wage in a monopsonistic labour market

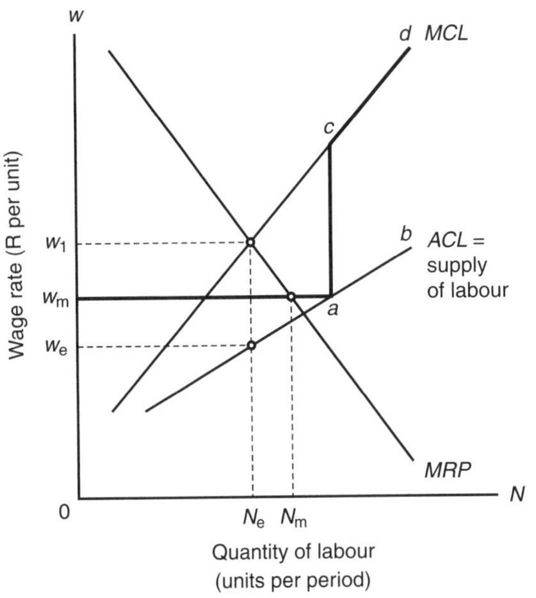

Before the imposition of the minimum wage, the equilibrium level of employment is N_e and the equilibrium wage rate is w_e. If a minimum wage rate of w_m is imposed, the supply of labour (or ACL) becomes $w_m$ab and the corresponding marginal cost of labour (MCL) becomes $w_m$acd. The monopsonist will employ labour up to the point where MCL = MRP. This will now be at a level of employment of N_m, which is greater than N_e. As long as the minimum wage rate is above the equilibrium rate but below w_1, the quantity of labour employed will increase after the imposition of the minimum wage.

If the minimum wage rate is imposed **below** the equilibrium wage rate, it will, of course, have no impact on the wage rate or the level of employment in the market.

■ CONCLUDING REMARKS ON MINIMUM WAGES

The analysis above shows that the minimum wage issue is not as clearcut as either the supporters or the opponents of minimum wages tend to argue. Empirical evidence on the impact of minimum wages is inconclusive.

South Africa does not have a national statutory minimum wage as in countries like France, Luxembourg, the Netherlands, Portugal, Spain and the United Kingdom, but minimum wages apply in certain industries and for certain categories of workers. In recent years the imposition of minimum wages for domestic workers and farm workers has been particularly controversial.

As in the case of all kinds of minimum prices (or price floors), the level at which minimum wages are imposed is crucial. If the minimum wage is below the average market wage, it should have no significant impact on the labour market. To the extent that such a minimum wage can be enforced, it will serve only to eliminate the exploitation of unskilled labour by unscrupulous employers. But if a minimum wage is imposed above the average market wage, it can potentially give rise to unemployment, although we have seen that this does not necessarily have to be the case. A minimum wage above the market wage rate clearly benefits those workers who receive higher wages, but if it results in unemployment some workers will lose their livelihood. Thus, setting a statutory minimum wage may raise the earnings of low-paid workers who remain employed, but may make those who become unemployed worse off. Minimum wages are therefore not necessarily an effective means of combating poverty, especially in a country like South Africa where the major cause of poverty is unemployment. The solution to poverty is to raise employment rather than to raise the wages of workers who already have a job. Moreover, there is always a danger that artificially raising the price of labour might lead to an increase in unemployment (and therefore to an increase in poverty).

Labour immobility and imperfect information

Among the other requirements for perfect competition in the labour market listed in Section 14.2 are perfect mobility and complete knowledge of market conditions. In practice, however, workers are often geographically and occupationally immobile and lack information about job opportunities, wage rates and so on.

Geographical immobility is the inability or unwillingness to move to a job in another part of the country or even in the same metropolitan area. This may be because of the financial costs of relocating, the inconvenience of moving, social or family ties, the availability and/or cost of housing or other facilities (eg schooling) in the new area, and so on.

Occupational immobility refers to the inability or unwillingness of people to move to different types of job, irrespective of location. This could, for example, be because they lack the qualifications or ability to do alternative jobs, or because of the less desirable working conditions or fringe benefits in the alternative jobs.

Geographical and occupational mobility are often also inhibited by a **lack of information** on the opportunities available in other areas or occupations. Moreover, information is not always available freely. Workers have to search for information, thereby incurring what economists call **search costs**.

If workers were perfectly mobile, unemployed and low-paid workers would move to areas and occupations where jobs were available or remuneration higher. In practice, however, some workers **choose** not to move while others are **unable** to move. For example, wages may be higher in Johannesburg than in Cape Town, but some people may prefer to live in Cape Town while others may not be able to afford to move to Johannesburg. Some workers may also not be allowed to move to particular labour markets because employers discriminate on the basis of race, gender or religion. Other workers may not have the necessary skills, qualifications or experience to qualify for certain occupations.

Having examined some labour market imperfections, we now turn our attention to some of the reasons for differences in wages.

14.4 Wage differentials

If labour were a homogeneous factor of production, and were sold in perfectly competitive markets, everyone would earn exactly the same when the labour market was in equilibrium. However, as we have emphasised, labour is not homogeneous and labour markets tend to be imperfect. As a result there are large differences between what different workers earn, even if all the various labour markets are in equilibrium. Wage differentials are permanent phenomena, not merely the result of temporary disequilibrium.

In this section we indicate some of the reasons why wages differ. One of the most important reasons for the inequality in the distribution of personal income and wealth is differences in the remuneration of labour. Some other possible causes of inequality are mentioned in Box 14-7.

To explain differences in wages, all the possible determinants of such differences have to be taken into account, since more than one usually applies to a particular occupation or group of workers. For example, a certain occupation might be unpleasant or dangerous and one may therefore expect the relevant wage to be relatively high. But the occupation might also require no particular skills and if the supply of labour is high, the actual wage might be relatively low. Likewise, a certain individual may possess certain scarce skills or abilities but the demand for those skills or abilities might be low, or the individual may be discriminated against on the basis of age, gender, race or religion, with the result that the actual wage might be relatively low. A single determinant therefore often provides an insufficient, possibly even inappropriate, explanation for actual wage differentials.

Job-related differences

A first reason why wages differ is that **jobs differ**. Some occupations are so dangerous, hazardous, uninviting, disagreeable, dirty, risky, monotonous or boring that many people prefer not to do them at all. Higher wages (called compensating wage differentials) must be paid to compensate for the undesirable characteristics of such occupations. A **compensating wage differential** is a wage difference that is required to compensate workers for entering a less desirable occupation or accepting a position in a dry, dusty, remote or otherwise unattractive location. This is the reason, for example, why people who work night shifts are usually paid more than those who work day shifts.

Against this, there are certain enjoyable and safe jobs which provide workers with a high degree of job security or job satisfaction. Such occupations will be less well paid than disagreeable or risky ones. University lecturers, for example, are often paid less than similarly qualified or experienced people employed elsewhere in the economy (particularly in the statutory professions and in the business world).

Other job-related differences include the educational, training or skill requirements of different occupations, the importance of experience and the degree of accountability or responsibility associated with the job.

Worker-related differences

A second reason why wages differ is that **people differ**. Workers are not homogeneous, as is assumed in the theory of perfect competition. Empirical studies across the world have found that wages tend to vary with education, age, gender and race. Some of these differences can perhaps be ascribed to discrimination (which is discussed later), but some are related to other determinants of wage differences, such as experience and mental and physical characteristics. Experience, for example, is one of the reasons why older workers tend to earn more than younger workers. Experience in a particular field, however, does not guarantee a higher wage rate. There must also be a demand for that particular type of experience. For example, people who were experienced in adding up long lists of figures mentally lost their relative advantage with the advent of calculators and computers.

Worker-related differences can be classified in two broad categories: innate characteristics that cannot be acquired and other characteristics that can be acquired.

Some people have certain special talents or abilities (eg intelligence or physical characteristics, such as beauty, strength and dexterity) which cannot be acquired. When such abilities are in great demand, the people concerned can earn above-average, sometimes astronomical, incomes. Examples include megastars in the cinema, television and music industries and in the sporting world – see Box 14-6. In a study conducted in the United States it was found, for

BOX 14-6 ECONOMIC RENT AND INEQUALITY

Some megastars in the world of sport and entertainment earn massive amounts of money. Take Tiger Woods as an example. As the world's best golfer (and possibly the best player ever) he can charge the organisers of golf tournaments huge amounts simply to play in their tournaments. Since he is unique, the supply of his services is totally inelastic, represented by a vertical supply curve, such as *SS* in the diagram below. There is only one Tiger Woods and his appearance fee is determined entirely by the demand for his presence (*DD* in the diagram). Moreover, his fee consists of **economic rent** only (see Box 14-3). The better he plays and the more popular he is, the greater the demand for his services becomes and the higher the appearance fee that he can command.

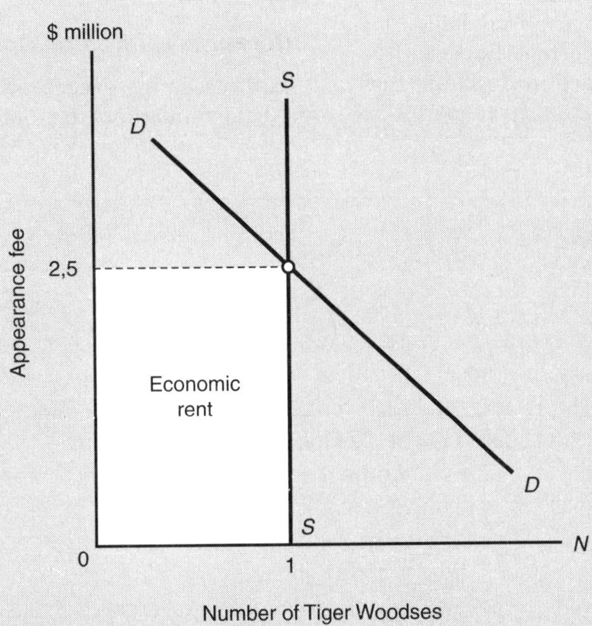

In the early 2000s, Tiger Woods's appearance fee was reputed to be US$2,5 million. This was apart from the prize money he could earn by participating in the tournament.

Other megastars (in the cinema, music and television industries and in other types of sport) earn similar economic rents as a result of their unique talents.

example, that attractive people tend to earn more, *ceteris paribus*, than people of average looks. People who are fortunate enough to genetically inherit special mental or physical features or talents thus appear to have an advantage over the less fortunate ones.

In most cases, however, people can acquire skills, education, expertise and experience that make them more productive and increase their earning capacity. Just as firms can invest in machinery and equipment to increase their productive and earning capacities, so human beings can invest in themselves to raise their future earning capacity. For example, individuals can invest in a university education or special training courses which improve their qualifications and skills. This is called **investment in human capital**. But, as with any other form of investment, costs are incurred. Someone who invests in a full-time university education has to pay tuition fees, purchase books, and so on. But the person also has to sacrifice current earnings in favour of expected future earnings. In other words, the **opportunity cost** of a full-time university education includes the wages that could have been earned if the person had taken a job instead of attending university. Because acquiring human capital is costly, the more highly skilled the job, the more it must pay if enough people are to be attracted to train for it. The demand for particular skills is, of course, also crucially important. For example, in recent years people with specialised (acquired) computer skills have commanded high rates of remuneration.

With regard to human capital, it is important to bear in mind that intellect is usually not sufficient. For many specialised occupations (eg in the various professions) investment in human capital is required before a person is qualified to engage in that occupation. Some talented people, however, may not be able to afford investment in human capital (eg in the form of higher education) because their parents are too poor or because the opportunity cost (in terms of income forgone) is simply too high. As in the case of innate talents, fortune or luck can therefore also be important as far as investment in human capital is concerned.

Apart from natural talents or acquired skills, the **attitude** of workers is also important. Some differences in earnings can be attributed to work effort or intensity. Some people work hard, are prepared to work long hours and are remunerated accordingly, while others are lazy and therefore earn less. Some people are also more willing to search for better jobs than others.

The **immobility** of labour is another important determinant of wage differentials. If all workers were occupationally or geographically mobile, wage differentials would be eliminated through occupational or geographical migration. However, as we emphasised earlier, workers are often unable or unwilling to move from one occupation to another or from one location to another.

Differences related to market structure

A third reason why wages differ is that **markets differ**. Labour markets are not perfectly competitive

BOX 14-7 OTHER SOURCES OF INEQUALITY

Labour is only one of the factors of production and labour income is thus only one of the possible sources of income. To explain income inequality, we also have to consider the income derived from the ownership of the other factors of production: natural resources (land), capital and entrepreneurship. Recall that the incomes of these factors are called **rent**, **interest** and **profit**. The different types of non-labour income are often collectively called **property income** or **asset income**.

Much of the inequality in the distribution of **income** is derived from the unequal distribution of **wealth** in the economy. Whereas income is a flow (the flow of earnings during a particular period), wealth is a stock (the stock of assets owned by an individual or household). Wealth can be kept in different forms, for example, cash, equities (shares), bonds, fixed property and works of art.

Most forms of wealth generate an income (eg in the form of rent, interest or profit) and wealthy people therefore tend to have larger incomes than people whose main source of income is in the form of wages and salaries.

Wealth can be inherited or acquired. A large proportion of very wealthy people have **inherited** most of their property (from which they derive large incomes). In the United States, for example, it has been estimated that two-thirds of the top one per cent of wealth holders inherited most of their property. The other major source of great wealth is **entrepreneurship**. In a market economy, successful entrepreneurs (ie those who put together new organisations and put new ideas into action) are richly rewarded. But to become a successful entrepreneur, one has to be willing to accept **risk**. Some of the individuals who are willing to take on risk succeed (sometimes after first failing a number of times) and become very rich. Most, however, do not make the grade and many fall to the bottom of the income distribution ladder. By contrast, those who prefer to play it safe and avoid risk, will never reach the top of the income distribution, but are also less likely to fall to the bottom.

Luck also plays a role. Some people are fortunate enough to be in the right place at the right time or to make the right choices, while others are less fortunate. Some inherit wealth, win the lottery, get ahead through personal contacts or invest in profitable ventures, while others suffer prolonged illness, become unemployed or are not afforded the opportunity of a good education.

Saving behaviour is another potential source of inequality of wealth and income. Some people spend all their income while others save, thereby increasing their stock of wealth and their future income.

We return to the question of inequality in Chapter 16, where we discuss the role of government in the economy.

markets and the imperfections in these markets can give rise to wage differences. The relative market power of employees and employers differs from market to market and can affect the outcome as far as wages are concerned. For example, wages tend to be higher in labour markets dominated by trade unions or professional bodies than in more competitive markets. On the other hand, wages tend to be lower in monopsonistic labour markets than in competitive markets.

Wages are not affected only by the structure of the labour market. The structure of the goods market is also important. Thus workers employed by firms operating in highly competitive goods markets (ie firms that cannot make a significant impact on the prices of their products) will tend to earn less, *ceteris paribus*, than workers employed by firms that have a significant degree of market power (ie those that operate in monopolistic or oligopolistic markets).

The structure of demand is also important. The less elastic the demand for the product, the higher the remuneration of labour will tend to be, *ceteris paribus*.

One of the possible types of market imperfection is government intervention (eg in the form of minimum wage fixing or occupational licensing, as in the case of the statutory professions – doctors, lawyers, accountants, etc). Such intervention can give rise to wage differences.

Differences as a result of discrimination

As mentioned earlier, men tend to earn more than women and whites tend to earn more than blacks. Employers often discriminate between workers on the basis of gender, race, age, religion, creed, nationality, ethnicity or social background. While discrimination is undoubtedly one of the determinants of wage differentials, in South Africa as well as elsewhere, one should be cautious about ascribing most or all differences in remuneration to discrimination. Differences in incomes between different groups (eg the genders, race groups, religious groups, age groups) do not provide evidence of discrimination. Only that part of wage differentials that cannot be explained by other factors can be ascribed to discrimination.

Labour market discrimination refers to the inferior treatment of certain workers with respect to employment policy or practices for reasons not related to the labour market. It can take several forms. For example, women may be restricted to "female" jobs such as nursing, teaching or secretarial work. The supply of labour in these occupations will be high and the remuneration relatively low. At the same time, men will be protected from competition in "male" jobs. This type of discrimination is sometimes called **occupational discrimination**. Another example is where certain workers (of, say, a particular race group) are afforded less opportunity for education and training than others. The resulting skill differences can be ascribed to discrimination, sometimes called **human-capital discrimination**. **Racial discrimination** has always been a feature of the South African labour market. During the apartheid era certain jobs were reserved for whites, while "non-whites" were often paid less than whites in similar jobs. Since the 1990s, new forms of discrimination have appeared in South Africa, such as affirmative action, employment equity and black economic empowerment. These measures or strategies are attempts to redress the inequities of the past and to compensate those groups who were previously subject to racial, gender or other forms of discrimination.

In conclusion it should be noted that **discrimination** (a pattern of behaviour) is not the same as **prejudice** (or attitude). Although discrimination may sometimes be rooted in prejudice, the latter does not necessarily result in discrimination. For example, an employer might be prejudiced against black workers, but could nevertheless hire them because they will work for lower wages than whites. By contrast, another employer who is not prejudiced against black workers at all might decide to employ white workers because they do not have to travel long distances to get to work.

Differences in productivity

The greater the value of workers' contributions to their employers' activities, the higher their wages will tend to be. In previous sections we defined these contributions in terms of their marginal revenue product (*MRP*). This, in turn, consists of the marginal physical product (*MPP*) and the price of the relevant product (*P*). Wages therefore tend to be related to physical labour productivity and the markets in which the products made by the workers are sold. Physical productivity, in turn, depends partly on labour quality, that is, the worker-related factors discussed earlier (eg skill, experience, education and work effort). But labour productivity also depends on factors beyond the workers' control, such as the availability and quality of other factors of production (eg capital and technology) and the quality of management. Moreover, the monetary value of workers' contributions will depend on the prices of the goods they produce. For example, the greater the demand for the particular goods, the higher the prices of the goods will be (*ceteris paribus*) and therefore the greater the *MRP* of the workers producing those goods. Because the demand for labour is a derived demand, anything that affects the demand for a particular product will, *ceteris paribus*, impact on the wages of the workers who produce the product. Likewise, changes in market supply can also affect the wages in the firm or industry in question.

14.5 Macroeconomic aspects of the labour market

In this section we briefly examine some macroeconomic aspects of the labour market, taking South Africa as our background. We discuss the total (or aggregate) supply of labour in the economy, the aggregate demand for labour, the level of employment, unemployment, the informal sector and the macroeconomic significance of the cost of labour. Most of these topics are analysed in more detail in Part IV.

The total supply of labour

The total supply of labour in a country is defined as all the people who are available to participate in the production of goods and services. It therefore comprises everyone who is willing and able to work. This is called the **labour force** or **economically active population**. The economically active population includes both employed and unemployed persons. It also includes the informal sector (which is explained later in this section) as well as the formal sector. The size and growth of the economically active population or labour force are determined by the size and growth of the **population** and the propensity to participate in the labour force, as reflected in the **labour force participation rate** according to age and gender. We now consider each of the main determinants of the labour force, with reference to the South African situation.

The total population: its size and growth

Population figures in South Africa are still compiled and presented separately for the four major population groups. The main reason is that the different population groups have different demographic characteristics (the adjective "demographic" is derived from the noun "demography" which means the study of populations).

Some estimates of the South African population are presented in Table 14-3. The first part of the table shows the estimated number of people per major population group and for the country as a whole. The second part shows the percentage distribution between the different populations groups. The first four years (1980, 1985, 1991 and 1996) were census years (in which the population was officially estimated by Statistics South Africa). The figures for 2005 are mid-year estimates. In the 2001 census the total population was estimated at 44,8 million.

Between 1980 and 2005 the South African population as a whole increased at an average annual rate of 1,9 per cent. The corresponding rates for the different population groups were: Asians 1,4 per cent; blacks 2,3 per cent; coloureds 1,8 per cent and whites –0,1 per cent.

From these growth rates, and from the data in Table 14-3, it is clear that the size and growth of the South African population, and therefore also of the labour force, are determined largely by the demographic features of the black group.

TABLE 14-3 Estimates of the South African population, selected years

Year	*Population (millions)*				
	Asians	*Blacks*	*Coloureds*	*Whites*	*Total*
1980	0,818	21,079	2,687	4,526	29,110
1985	0,898	24,462	2,958	4,853	33,171
1991	0,987	28,397	3,286	5,068	37,738
1996	1,046	31,503	3,600	4,435	40,584
2005	1,154	37,206	4,149	4,380	46,889

Year	*Population (percentage of total)*				
	Asians	*Blacks*	*Coloureds*	*Whites*	*Total*
1980	2,8	72,4	9,3	15,5	100,0
1985	2,7	73,7	8,9	14,7	100,0
1991	2,6	75,3	8,7	13,4	100,0
1996	2,6	77,6	8,9	10,9	100,0
2005	2,5	79,4	8,8	9,3	100,0

Source: Statistics South Africa

Demographers have identified a **demographic cycle**, consisting of four stages, through which any given population tends to move. **Stage I** is characterised by high birth rates and high death rates. Population growth is low during this stage (as is life expectancy). As modernisation occurs and health services improve, death rates fall. This is **Stage II**. With continued high birth rates, population growth increases quite rapidly during Stage II. Life expectancy also increases. During **Stage III** birth rates start to fall as a result of the forces and influences of modernisation. Although the death rate also falls further, the fall in the birth rate is much greater. The result is a fall in the rate of population growth (accompanied by a further increase in life expectancy). The final stage, **Stage IV**, is reached when birth rates fall so low that the size of the population starts to decline. Life expectancy, however, is very high. Most western European countries have undergone the full process of demographic transition. Population growth in these countries is approaching zero while life expectancy at birth is close to 80 years.

In South Africa, Asians and coloureds have been in Stage III of the cycle for some time, while blacks entered Stage III towards the end of the 1990s. Whites have already entered Stage IV.

It is important to note, however, that the demographic cycle pertains to **natural population growth** only. The overall growth of the population consists of natural growth plus net **migration**. If large numbers of foreigners enter the country, legally or illegally, in pursuit of employment and income, natural population growth can be overshadowed by the growth in the number of immigrants. If immigration reaches large proportions, as has been the case in South Africa since the 1990s, natural demographic trends may become relatively unimportant.

The greatest uncertainty regarding the future size and growth of the South African population is the impact of HIV/Aids. Southern Africa, including South Africa, has the highest incidence of HIV/Aids in the world and the rate of population growth is expected to decline significantly during the first decades of the 21st century.

Demographic changes have a variety of important consequences – see Box 14-8. Demographers argue that these changes underlie most of the important economic trends and issues, since the economy consists of people and their activities. A detailed discussion of these consequences is not possible here, and it is sufficient to note that:

- the size and growth of the population are among the most important determinants of the size and growth of the labour force
- the size and growth of the South African population (and therefore also of the labour force) are dominated by the demographic trends of the black population group, which constitutes the majority of the population

Labour force participation

The other major determinant of the size of labour force is the **labour force participation rate**

BOX 14-8 MALTHUS ON THE IMPORTANCE OF POPULATION GROWTH

In 1798 Thomas Malthus, a non-practising English clergyman, published his *Essay on the principle of population*. Malthus believed that there would be an imbalance between the rate of population growth and the rate of growth in food production in the long run and that workers would therefore usually find themselves on the verge of starvation. He argued that population tends to increase at a **geometric** rate (eg 1, 2, 4, 8, 16, 32, 64, ...), while food production tends to increase at an **arithmetic** rate (1, 2, 3, 4, 5, 6, 7, ...).

Malthus ascribed the rapid increase in population to mankind's strong sexual drive, which he called the "passion between the sexes". The slow increase in food production, on the other hand, was ascribed to the law of diminishing returns. Whenever wages rose above the subsistence level, Malthus argued, the rate of reproduction would tend to increase. This, in turn, would drive wages back to the subsistence level. In the absence of moral restraint, the only checks on population growth would be famine, epidemics, natural catastrophes and war.

Malthus was thus very pessimistic about the future of mankind. It was his pessimism which resulted in classical economics being described as the dismal science. Fortunately, history has proved Malthus wrong, at least as far as the industrial countries are concerned. He did not foresee the tremendous technological developments which have increased the production of food and other necessities. Nor did he foresee that improvements in the material standard of living of workers would lead to decreasing, rather than increasing, birth rates.

(LFPR). This is the fraction or percentage of the population which constitutes the labour force or economically active population. This can be expressed as follows:

$$\text{Labour force participation rate (LFPR)} = \frac{\text{Labour force (or economically active population)}}{\text{Population}}$$

The LFPR can also be expressed as a percentage by multiplying the ratio by 100. From the definition it follows that it is possible to have two countries with exactly the same population size but with different LFPRs (and therefore different labour force sizes). Factors which affect the LFPR include the following:

- **The age distribution of the population**. The greater the proportion of the population in the 15–64 age group, the greater the labour force. The age structure of the labour force, in turn, depends primarily on birth and death rates. For example, if birth rates and death rates are both high, the result is a young population and a relatively low LFPR.
- **Retirement rules and the availability of social security**. Compulsory retirement arrangements tend to reduce the LFPR, as does the availability of pensions and other forms of social security.
- **Social, cultural, religious or other conventions about the role of women in society**. In a society in which women are expected to stay at home to run the household and to bear and rear children, the labour force will be much smaller than in a society in which women are free (or even encouraged) to work outside the home.
- **The availability of household appliances** (like dishwashers), **child care centres** (such as pre-primary schools) and other institutions which enable women to take up paid employment outside the home.
- **The level of development and structure of the economy**. Countries where light industry (eg textiles, clothing, food processing) and services are relatively important will tend to have higher female LFPRs (and higher total LFPRs) than countries whose economies are dominated by mining and heavy industry.

The aggregate supply of labour is thus determined by demographic trends, economic conditions and a variety of social, cultural and moral values and psychological attitudes. The **effective** supply of labour in a country also depends on the **quality** of labour, which is determined, in turn, by education, training, ability, experience and so on.

The aggregate demand for labour and the level of employment

As emphasised earlier, the demand for labour is a **derived** demand. This is true at the macroeconomic as well as the microeconomic level. Labour is employed to produce goods and services and will only be demanded if there is a demand for the goods and services produced by labour. The quantity of labour demanded can thus be estimated by the level of employment in the economy. The determination of the aggregate level of employment is analysed in Part IV of this book. The aggregate level of employment depends on the aggregate level of production or income in the economy. All the factors that affect the total production or income in the economy therefore also affect the total demand for labour and the total level of employment.

However, while there is undoubtedly a link between the level of production and the level of employment, this link has tended to weaken in recent decades. One of the reasons for this is the increased **capital intensity of production** in South Africa (see Table 5-13), which means that labour has tended to be replaced by machines and other capital equipment in production processes. This is therefore also one of the reasons for the increase in the unemployment rate, which is examined in Chapter 22.

The link between employment and production can be expressed by the **employment coefficient** or **production elasticity of employment**, which measures the degree of responsiveness of employment to economic growth. This indicator is calculated by dividing the percentage change in formal employment over a period covering a full business cycle (see Chapter 23) by the growth in real GDP during the same period. This coefficient averaged about 0,50 in South Africa from the 1950s to the 1980s but actually became negative in the 1990s when formal employment tended to decline (see Table 5-4), despite positive (albeit low) economic growth. This phenomenon is often referred to as **jobless growth**. In the 2000s formal employment increased again.

Unemployment

When the quantity of labour supplied exceeds the quantity of labour demanded, the result is unemployment. As indicated in Chapter 4, the creation of employment opportunities (or the combating of unemployment) is one of the major macroeconomic objectives. Full employment (in the absolute sense) is unattainable. At any time there will always be people moving between jobs, particularly when the aggregate demand for labour is high (ie when the economy is booming). But high and increasing unemployment is a serious problem. The **unemployment rate** is obtained by expressing the number of unemployed persons as a percentage of the labour force. Most observers agree that the level of and growth in unemployment are the most serious social and economic problems in South Africa. Unemployment is examined in Chapter 22.

The informal sector

When economists talk about employment, they usually refer to **formal employment**, that is, to people who are employed in a full-time capacity in the modern or formal sector of the economy. But this does not mean that all those members of the labour force who are not formally employed have no income or other means of survival. Some are engaged in subsistence agriculture while others are engaged in the informal sector.

The **informal sector** (sometimes also called the shadow economy, unrecorded economy, underground economy or hidden economy) has often been in the news during the past three decades. As economic growth declined and formal employment stagnated in South Africa, increasing attention was paid to the informal sector as a source of employment and income. There are primarily three reasons why people engage in informal sector activity:

- They cannot find employment in the formal sector.
- They are engaged in illegal activities.
- They do not want to pay tax.

There is no precise definition of the informal sector, but Table 14-4 provides a good indication of the activities that are involved. Opinions differ as to the total size and the importance of the informal sector, but there is no doubt that it has grown significantly since the 1970s. That is why the Central Statistical Service (as Stats SA was formerly known) started estimating employment and income in the informal sector towards the end of the 1980s. Another significant step was taken in 1994 when estimates of informal sector activity were included in the official national accounts for the first time – see also Section 23.1.

Economists argue about the economic significance of the informal sector. Some regard it as a survival sector where people who cannot find formal employment can find legal or illegal means of survival. They therefore regard the growth of the informal sector as a symptom of a stagnating or declining economy. As far as economic policy is concerned, they believe this stagnation can be overcome by stimulating formal sector activity. Others regard the informal sector as an important source of income and employment creation. Free marketeers, for example, favour the stimulation of the informal sector by abolishing all laws, rules and regulations that could possibly suppress initiative and economic activity. The pragmatic view is that the informal sector essentially represents a means of survival but that it cannot be neglected by policymakers. It should be given all possible scope, especially in view of South Africa's pervasive poverty and the inability of the formal sector to create enough jobs for the growing labour force.

TABLE 14-4 Informal sector activities

Legal/socially acceptable	*Illegal/socially unacceptable*
Producers	**Producers**
Self-employed artisans, shoemakers, dressmakers and tailors, home brewers, craft and curio makers	Dagga producers, counterfeiters
Distributors	**Distributors**
Hawkers, flea-market traders, petty traders, carriers, runners, shebeeners	Pickpockets, burglars, robbers, embezzlers, confidence tricksters, gamblers, drug traffickers, black marketeers
Services	**Services**
Taxi operators, money lenders, musicians, launderers, repairers, shoeshiners, barbers, photographers, herbalists, traditional healers, backyard mechanics, pawnbrokers	Hustlers, pimps, prostitutes, smugglers, bribers, protection racketeers, loan sharks

Source: Vosloo, W.B. 1994. The small firm as a vehicle for entrepreneurship. *Entrepreneurship and economic growth*, Pretoria: HSRC, 171

The macroeconomic significance of the cost of labour

As emphasised at the beginning of this chapter, the cost of labour is the largest cost factor in the economy. The remuneration of labour represents about half the cost of producing the GDP. It therefore comes as no surprise that economists are keenly interested in movements in the cost of labour, particularly when it comes to explaining inflation. Inflation is examined in Chapter 21. In this subsection we focus on labour cost per unit of output, one of the key macroeconomic indicators.

Labour cost per unit of output is obtained by dividing the total wage bill (W) by the real value of output (Q), where the total wage bill is equal to the average wage rate (w) multiplied by the number of workers (N).[1] Thus, labour cost per unit of output is equal to $W/Q = wN/Q$.

1. Note that the average wage rate (or the general level of wages) is similar to the general level of prices – it is a composite concept that encompasses a wide range of specific wage rates.

The two key components of labour cost per unit of output are the average wage rate (w) and average labour productivity, where the latter is equal to the output per worker (ie Q/N). Labour cost per unit of output (wN/Q) can be rewritten as follows:

$wN/Q = w \times N/Q = w \div Q/N$, where Q/N is equal to average labour productivity.

Thus, the higher the wage rate, the higher the cost of labour per unit of output and the higher the average productivity of labour, the lower the cost of labour per unit of output, *ceteris paribus*. In a dynamic sense, the rate of change in unit labour cost is equal to the rate of change in the wage rate minus the rate of change in labour productivity. For example, if the rate of increase in wages is matched by an equal rate of increase in labour productivity, the cost of labour per unit of output remains unchanged. However, if the rate of increase in wages exceeds the rate of increase in labour productivity, the cost of labour per unit of output increases, thereby raising the cost of production and the prices of goods and services (*ceteris paribus*). That is why it is often stated that price stability can only be achieved if the rate of increase in nominal labour costs is matched by an equivalent rate of increase in labour productivity. The role of labour costs in the inflation process and the need to link wage increases to productivity increases are examined further in Chapters 21 and 22.

IMPORTANT CONCEPTS

Wage rate
Earnings
Nominal wage
Real wage
Supply of labour
Backward-bending supply curve
Demand for labour
Derived demand
Marginal physical product
Marginal revenue product
Marginal cost of labour
Economic rent
Transfer earnings
Trade union
Monopsony
Collective bargaining
Bilateral monopoly
Flexible labour market
Minimum wages
Mobility of labour
Wage differentials
Compensating wage differential
Investment in human capital
Discrimination
Productivity
Labour force
Labour force participation rate
Demographic cycle
Capital intensity of production
Unemployment
Informal sector
Unit labour cost

REVIEW QUESTIONS

1. Do you think that the market supply of labour can be represented by a backward-bending curve (as in the case of the individual supply of labour)? Explain your answer.
2. Explain the relationship between the market supply of labour in a perfectly competitive labour market and the supply curve facing an individual employer in such a market.
3. Explain why the demand for labour is a derived demand.
4. Explain why the curve representing the market demand for labour slopes downward from left to right.
5. Explain how labour productivity (represented by the marginal revenue product of labour) affects the wage rate in a perfectly competitive labour market.
6. Use diagrams to illustrate and explain the impact of each of the following on equilibrium in a perfectly competitive labour market:
   (a) More workers enter the labour market.
   (b) The physical productivity of labour increases.

(c) The price of the product produced by the workers increases.
(d) Wages in other, related occupations increase.
(e) The price of machinery (a substitute for labour) decreases.

7. "Minimum wages inevitably result in an increase in unemployment." Do you agree? Why (not)?
8. Explain how minimum wage legislation can affect a perfectly competitive labour market. Do you think that these effects can occur in the markets for domestic and farm workers in South Africa? Explain your answer.
9. Explain the different ways in which a trade union can try to increase the wage rates of its members.
10. "If the national average wage for men exceeds the national average wage for women, there is definitely sexual discrimination in the labour market." Do you agree? Substantiate your view.
11. Explain why a young chartered accountant without a masters degree or a doctorate earns more than an experienced professor of mathematics with a doctorate.
12. Why do people in pleasant jobs often earn higher wages than people doing unpleasant work?
13. Should the wage rates for all jobs be the same? Explain your answer.
14. In 2002 Brian Gilbertson, a South African, was chief executive officer of BHP Billiton, a major international mining company, and earned a basic annual remuneration package of R52 million (ie R1 million per week). Do you think a remuneration of this magnitude was justified, particularly compared to the earnings of mine workers working for the company? Substantiate your view.

APPENDIX 14-1
OTHER FACTOR MARKETS

In Chapter 14 we examined the labour market, the most important factor market in the economy. In this appendix we touch briefly on the markets for the other factors of production (ie natural resources or land, capital and entrepreneurship) and the remuneration (or prices) of these factors (ie rent, interest and profit).

Land (natural resources) and rent

Land and other natural resources (eg the ocean and minerals) are generally **fixed** in total **supply**. They are non-produced factors of production and can broadly be regarded as gifts of nature. As the American comedian, Will Rogers, once remarked: "Land is a good investment: they ain't making it no more." Like the demand for any other factor of production, the demand for land is a **derived demand**. It is demanded not for its own sake, but for what can be produced with it.

The **price** paid for the use of land and other natural resources is called **rent**. It is important to note that economists use the term rent in a specific fashion. Whereas people often speak of renting a car, house or flat, for economists rent is the payment made for the use of land. Since the supply of land is fixed, the price of land (ie rent) is essentially determined by the demand for land, as illustrated in the diagram.

In the diagram *SS* represents the fixed quantity of land. The original demand is represented by D_0D_0. The interaction of supply and demand yields an equilibrium rent of r_0. If the demand for land should increase, illustrated by a rightward (upward) shift of the demand curve to D_1D_1, the equilibrium rent will increase to r_1. Likewise, if the demand for land should decrease, depicted by a leftward (downward) shift of the demand curve to D_2D_2, the equilibrium rent will fall to r_2. Rent is thus completely demand determined.

In Boxes 14-3 and 14-6 we introduced the concept "economic rent". Recall that **economic rent** is the payment made to any factor of production over and above what is necessary to keep the factor in its pres-

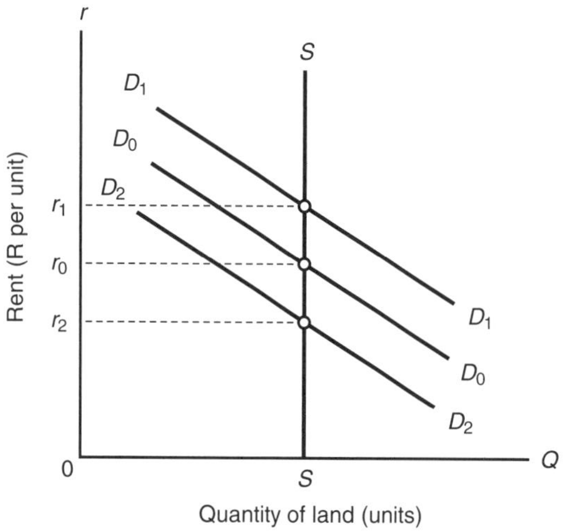

ent use and that it is similar to the producer surplus introduced in Chapter 7. Since the supply of land is fixed, irrespective of the price of land (ie rent), the total amount earned from land is therefore economic rent. This is where the term "economic rent" had its origin.

There are, of course, differences in the quality or productivity of land. Some land is fertile and is situated in areas with high rainfall and mild climates, while other land is less fertile and situated in areas with low rainfall and extreme climates (eg in the Kalahari or the Karoo). Some land contains valuable mineral resources while other land does not contain any such resources. Location is also important. For example, land in remote areas is much less sought after than land in metropolitan areas. These differences in productivity or location are reflected in the demand for land. The more productive the land or the more sought after the location, the greater the demand for land and the higher the rent will be.

It is sometimes argued that since land is a gift of nature it should be available to everyone. However, as we explain in Chapter 16, common property resources create a variety of problems, notably over-exploitation. This is often referred to as the tragedy of the commons. Private ownership and the payment of rent result in a more efficient and effective allocation of land and other scarce resources.

Capital and interest

In contrast to land, capital is a produced factor of production. Recall that capital as a factor of production refers to goods (eg plant, machinery, equipment, buildings, roads, bridges) that are used to produce other goods. Firms need capital (in the physical sense) to produce goods and services. As with any other factor of production, the demand for capital is a **derived demand**. Firms employ capital for the products which it creates. More specifically, firms will use capital goods up to the point where the marginal factor cost equals the marginal benefit (ie the marginal revenue product) of the factor.

The calculation of the benefit (or productivity) of capital is quite complicated. The return on investment in capital goods is spread out over the lifetime of the asset, which can be many years. Moreover, a benefit today is worth much more than the same benefit in ten years' time (even if there is no inflation). Future benefits therefore have to be discounted by using an appropriate interest rate. Alternatively, a percentage rate of return on capital can be calculated by determining the discount rate which will make the present value of the expected future benefits of the capital good equal to its cost. If this rate of return is greater than the rate of interest at which the firm can borrow funds, it will be worthwhile to make the investment. As explained further in Chapter 18, the rate of interest is thus an important factor in the investment decision (ie the decision to purchase capital goods).

Since resources are scarce, the production of capital goods entails a sacrifice or opportunity cost in terms of a reduced production of consumer goods. Put differently, society has to refrain from consumption (ie save) to expand its productive capacity. According to neo-classical theory, the crucial factor in this regard is the interest rate, which is determined by the interaction between the demand for borrowed funds (which is derived from the desire to invest in capital goods) and the supply of loanable funds (which is derived from the propensity to save). As illustrated in the diagram, the demand for borrowed funds (which can be regarded as the demand for capital) is inversely related to the interest rate, since more investment projects become profitable at lower interest rates. On the other hand, the supply of loanable funds (which is sometimes also called the supply of capital) is positively related to the rate of interest, since the higher the interest rate, the more attractive it becomes to save rather than to consume. According to this theory, which is called the **loanable funds theory**, the interest rate adjusts to equate the quantity of funds demanded with the quantity of funds supplied.

In the diagram, *DD* represents the demand for loanable funds (derived from the demand for capital goods, which in turn is derived from the productivity of capital), while *SS* represents the supply of loanable funds (which is determined by the propensity to save).

The equilibrium rate of interest (i_0) is determined by the interaction of demand and supply. Note, however, that the loanable funds theory is only one of a range of possible theories of the rate of interest and pertains only to long-term interest rates. Another approach to the determination of the interest rate, which applies to short-run interest rates, is explained in the next chapter.

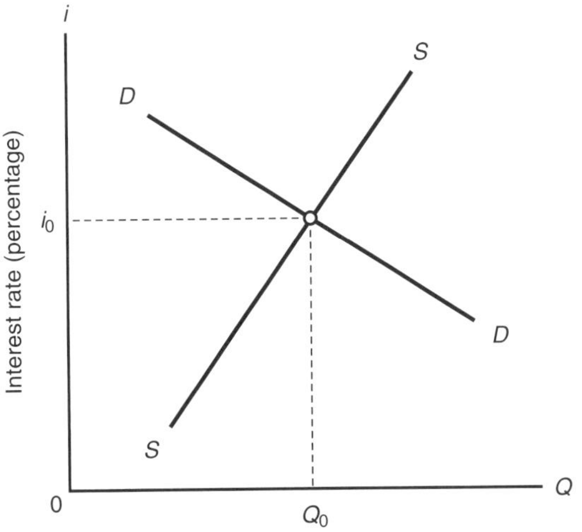

The loanable funds theory and other theories of the interest rate may create the impression that money or finance is a factor of production. As emphasised in Chapter 2, this is not the case. Money or finance cannot produce goods and services. The factors of production are land (natural resources), labour, capital and entrepreneurship. But firms have to finance the acquisition of capital goods, which contribute to production but only yield a return over long periods. In other words, firms have to obtain finance to buy the capital goods required to produce goods and services.

Although we often talk about "the interest rate" there is actually a **range of interest rates** on different types of financial instrument. These rates differ as a result of factors such as differences in risk, maturity, the liquidity or marketability of the instrument, the size of loans and market structure (including market imperfections).

Another important distinction is that between the **nominal interest rate** and the **real interest rate**. The real interest rate is the difference between the nominal interest rate and the inflation rate. For example, if the nominal interest rate is 15 per cent and the inflation rate is 10 per cent, the real interest rate is (15 – 10) = 5 per cent. Real interest rates can be positive or negative. For example, if the nominal interest rate is 8 per cent and the inflation rate is 10 per cent, the real interest rate is (8 – 10) = –2 per cent. The real interest rate is the important one as far as the allocation of factors of production is concerned. For example, if the real interest rate is negative and real wages are high, capital is relatively inexpensive and firms will tend to demand more capital and substitute capital for labour (compared to a situation where the relative price of capital is high).

Entrepreneurship and profit

The fourth factor of production is entrepreneurship. The entrepreneur is the person who takes the initiative to combine the other factors of production in producing a good or service; makes the basic, non-routine policy decisions for the firm; introduces innovations in the form of new products or production processes; and bears the economic risks associated with all these functions. Entrepreneurship is rewarded in the form of profit.

Profit acts as an incentive to produce, take risks and introduce new products and processes. It also acts as an indicator of efficiency or success. The meaning of profit was discussed in some detail in Chapter 11. The important point here is that profit is not something ominous, sinister or sinful. Profit is the remuneration of the entrepreneur, who is the driving force in a private enterprise economy. Moreover, only the successful entrepreneurs are rewarded. For each highly successful entrepreneur there are many would-be entrepreneurs who do not make the grade and therefore earn no profit, and even the successful ones often fail a number of times before achieving success.

The functional and personal distributions of income

In Chapter 2 we pointed out that the **functional distribution** of income refers to the distribution of income between the various factors of production (ie rent, wages, interest and profit), while the **personal distribution** of income refers to the distribution between the various individuals or households in the economy. No aggregate official data on the functional distribution of income are available in South Africa. The inequality of the personal distribution of income was emphasised in Chapter 5. It is important to bear in mind, however, that there are definite links between the functional and personal distributions of income. All factors of production are owned directly or indirectly by individuals or households and the remuneration of these factors (ie rent, wages, interest and profit) are the sources of personal income. To explain the inequality of the personal distribution of income, the various elements of the functional distribution therefore have to be taken into account.

PART III

From microeconomics to macroeconomics: three important sectors of the economy

In this part of the book we examine three important sectors of the economy: the monetary sector (Chapter 15), the public sector (Chapter 16) and the foreign sector (Chapter 17). Both microeconomic and macroeconomic issues are discussed. We use the concepts and analytical tools developed in Part II to analyse certain microeconomic aspects of the money market, the role of the public sector in the economy, taxes, exchange rates and international trade. We also discuss a number of macroeconomic concepts and issues and we introduce monetary and fiscal policy, thereby paving the way for the analysis of these issues in Part IV, in which we focus exclusively on macroeconomic theory and policy.

Once you have studied this part of the book, you should be able to

- define the various functions of money in the economy
- analyse the supply and demand of money
- describe what monetary policy is all about
- explain why and how the government intervenes in the economy
- define fiscal policy
- explain why countries trade
- discuss trade policy
- analyse the foreign exchange market
- explain the links between the foreign sector and the domestic economy

15 The monetary sector

Learning outcomes

Once you have studied this chapter you should be able to

- describe the functions of money
- define money
- describe the main functions of the South African Reserve Bank
- explain the demand for money
- explain how the supply of money is determined
- explain the basic instruments of monetary policy

Money is a good servant but a bad master.

ENGLISH PROVERB

Money speaks in a language all nations understand.

APHRA BEHN

Man is not nourished by money. He does not clothe himself with gold, he does not warm himself with silver.

FRÉDÉRIC BASTIAT

Money is like muck, not good except it be spread.

FRANCIS BACON

A bank is a place that will lend you money if you can prove that you don't need it.

BOB HOPE

Money is one of the most important institutions in the economy. Money, it is said, talks, makes the man (or woman), and makes the world go around. The Bible says that the love of money is the root of all evil. Everyone is fascinated by money. Writers write about it, singers sing about it and people dream about having enough money to satisfy all their wants. Through the centuries, money has taken different forms; cattle, seashells, cigarettes and gold have all served as money. In modern societies paper money is issued by central banks. The American comedian, Will Rogers, once said that there have been three great inventions since the beginning of time: fire, the wheel and central banking. Money is indeed a fascinating subject.

In this chapter we take a closer look at money and financial institutions. We start by examining the **functions of money**. This enables us to define money. We then look at different **forms of money** and how money is **measured** in South Africa. This is followed by brief discussions of **financial intermediaries** and the role of the **South African Reserve Bank**. The bulk of the chapter is concerned with an analysis of the money market. We examine the **supply of money**, the **demand for money** and **equilibrium in the money market**. We conclude the chapter with a discussion of **monetary policy in South Africa**.

Most people think that economics is largely concerned with money and with activities aimed at making money. Economists are therefore invariably approached for tips about how to become rich quickly. But you have now studied 14 chapters of this book without examining the properties, functions and role of money. It should thus be clear that much of economics is **not** concerned with money.

It is also a mistake to assume that economists are good business people or that they are skilled at making money. Of Adam Smith, the founder of modern economics, it was said: "He was the most unbusinesslike of mankind. He was an awkward Scotch professor ... choked with books and absorbed in abstractions. He was never engaged in any sort of trade, and would probably never have made sixpence by any if he had been."[1]

In earlier chapters we have pointed out that money is not a factor of production and that it should not be confused with income or wealth. We did show, however, that money was an important invention, since it eliminates the need for a double coincidence of wants which is a feature of the barter system.

The time has now come to take a closer look at money. Although everyone agrees that money is an important invention, there is still a lot of controversy about the role of money in the economy. After centuries of serious thought and analysis there is still no generally accepted theory about how money influences economic activity. It should be obvious that there can be no mechanical or technical connection between the quantity of money in the economy and the level of production and income. If this were the case, the world's poverty and development problems could have been solved long ago by printing more money.

Although there is no simple relation between money and real economic activity, economists nowadays accept that the influence of money on the economy is not entirely neutral. The supposed **neutrality of money** was for many years the cornerstone of classical economic theory. It was thought that the amount of money in circulation could influence only the absolute price level (eg a doubling of the money stock would lead to a doubling of the price level) without having any real effects on production or welfare.

Today, however, economists think differently about money. But before we can take a closer look at the way in which money affects economic activity (and the way in which economic activity affects money), we first have to examine a few of the basic characteristics of money and of the financial system. In this chapter we deal with the functions of money, its definition, and with the factors and institutions which determine the supply of and demand for money, and interest rates.

1. Walter Bagehot, as quoted in James, S. 1984. *A dictionary of economic quotations*, 2nd edition. London: Croom Helm, 162.

We also look at the role of the South African Reserve Bank and at monetary policy. The important question of how monetary variables are supposed to influence economic activity is examined in Chapter 20.

15.1 The functions of money

Money as a medium of exchange

Money is such an integral part of our daily lives that its significance is not always appreciated. To explain the importance of money, we again consider a **barter economy**, that is, an economy that functions without money. In a barter economy, you will recall, goods can only be exchanged for other goods. For example, a wheat farmer who needs clothing for his family first has to find a tailor who needs wheat. Then the exchange can take place. If no tailor who happens to want wheat can be found, the farmer will be obliged to exchange the wheat for something else that the tailor *does* require. In other words, before the exchange of two goods can take place, there has to be a **double coincidence of wants** between the parties concerned. A barter economy is therefore characterised by numerous unnecessary exchange transactions which are cumbersome and inefficient. For each of the farmer's (or anybody else's) many requirements, a particular person has to be found who has a specific need for the product he or she wishes to trade.

The inefficiency of the barter economy led, even in early primitive communities, to the use of some form of money. The advantages of a **monetary economy**, where exchange takes place through the medium of money, are just as obvious as the disadvantages of a barter economy. In a monetary economy a double coincidence of wants between parties is no longer required. The farmer no longer has to look for a tailor who needs wheat. As long as a buyer can be found for the wheat, the money received in exchange for the wheat can be used to buy clothes. Money therefore serves as a **lubricant** or **intermediary** to smooth the process of exchange and to make it more efficient. This is the first and most basic function of money. Money functions as a **medium of exchange**. When we discuss the other functions of money, you will see that this function is the only one that is unique to money. It can therefore be used to define money:

Money is anything that is generally accepted as payment for goods and services or that is accepted in settlement of debt.

If you look carefully at the wording of the definition, you will realise that it actually says that **money is what money does**. The meaning of money is so difficult to describe, that we are obliged to define it in terms of its main function. Money is a **generally acceptable means of payment**. Moreover, it is accepted as payment because people believe that it will be accepted as payment by other people.

Money as a unit of account

A **unit of account** is an agreed measure for stating the prices of goods and services. In a money economy the prices of all goods and services are expressed in monetary terms. Money thus functions as a unit of account. We need a common measure of the cost of various goods and services to be able to decide how best to spend our income. The fact that income and prices are all expressed in rands and cents enables us to calculate what we can afford. If we know that a beer costs R8 and a soft drink costs R5 then we can also immediately calculate the opportunity cost of a beer in terms of the number of soft drinks that we have to sacrifice for a beer. In addition, the use of money as a unit of account enables us to obtain measures of the total value of all goods and services produced in the economy, such as GDP. Money is not, however, the only possible unit of account. Any other commodity or product can serve as a unit of account. The item used as the medium of exchange (money) is simply the most convenient unit of account.

The function of money as a unit of account is closely related to its function as a medium of exchange. What serves as a medium of exchange usually also fulfils the function of an accounting unit. The accounting unit function is, however, secondary to the medium of exchange function. Money can also lose some of its usefulness as a unit of account during inflation. When prices increase, monetary or **nominal** values have to be adjusted for price increases to obtain **real** values, which are more meaningful.

Money as a store of value

Money is also a store of value. In any society there is a need to hold wealth (or surplus production) in some form or another. The most common form for holding wealth is money, since it can always be exchanged for other goods and services at a later date. Wealth can, however, also be held in other forms, such as fixed property, real assets, stocks and shares. The advantage of using money as a store of value lies in the fact that it is usually more convenient and can be used immediately in exchange for other assets. We therefore say that money is the most **liquid** form in which wealth can be kept.

But it is not always advantageous to use money as a store of value. In times of high inflation money loses its purchasing power and is not a good store of value. A person who keeps all her wealth in the form of money while there is inflation will soon realise that her wealth is not retaining its value. During inflation there is thus a tendency to use other objects as stores of value, for example, fixed property, shares, works of art and postage stamps. Therefore, unlike the medium of exchange function, the store of value function is not unique to money.

The function of money as a unit of account and the store of value function are both derived from the medium of exchange function. If money did not fulfil the function of a medium of exchange, it could not serve as an accounting unit or as a store of value.

The store of value function also implies that money serves as a **standard of deferred payment**. By this we mean that money is the measure of value for future payments. If you borrow money to buy a house, your future commitment will be agreed to in rands and cents. Money is also the means whereby credit is granted.

What money is not

We have now defined money and outlined its various functions. It is also important to know what money is not. As we show at various other places in this book, money is often confused with other things. Money should not, for example, be confused with **income** or **wealth**. Because income and wealth are usually measured or expressed in monetary terms (eg in rands), they are often confused with money.

Income is the reward earned in the production process. Natural resources, labour, capital and entrepreneurship are rewarded in the form of rent, wages and salaries, interest and profit. The fact that income is calculated and paid in monetary terms is coincidental. Income is something completely different to money. As we explain later, a certain amount of money (which is a **stock**) can finance a much larger **flow** of income during a particular period. This is because money can be used over and over – we say that money circulates through the economy.

Wealth consists of assets that have been accumulated over time. Wealth can take many forms, such as fixed property, shares, oriental carpets or paintings. It can, of course, also take the form of money. This is one of the possible reasons for the confusion between wealth and money. Another reason is that wealth, like income, is usually calculated in monetary terms. However, wealth and money are not synonymous. Money forms part of wealth, but wealth consists of other assets as well. In fact, many people who possess great wealth do not possess a great deal of money. They keep most of their wealth in other forms, particularly during inflation, when money loses much of its function as a store of value.

15.2 Different kinds of money

Through the ages various goods have served as money. For example, cocoa beans, beads, seashells, tea, cattle, silver and cigarettes (in modern prisoner of war camps and in jails) have all served as money at one time or another.

The earliest forms of money were **commodities**, where the intrinsic value of the commodity was equal to the exchange value assigned to it. Naturally, certain commodities were more suitable for use as money than others. Properties such as **uniformity, durability, divisibility** and the ability to be **carried** (which is determined by size and weight) were not to be found in all commodities. For example, cattle are not divisible into "change", nor can they be carried around easily.

In due course this type of commodity money made way for the more efficient **coins** made of various kinds of metal. Initially iron and copper coins were very popular forms of money but when they became too abundant they lost their value and were replaced by scarcer metals such as silver and gold.

In time, however, the exclusive use of coins as a medium of exchange also became inconvenient as the increasing specialisation of production led to greater dependence on trade. Particularly in large transactions, the coins became unwieldy and difficult to handle. This in turn led to the use of **paper money** which first appeared in England in the 16th century. The owners of gold (or silver) **deposited** it for safe-keeping with the goldsmiths of that time. In exchange for such **deposits** they received certificates of deposit, and these certificates could then be transferred to other persons to pay for goods and services. The certificate of deposit was the first form of paper money fully covered by the metal it was supposed to represent.

The next step in the evolutionary process was the replacement of paper money, fully backed by a commodity such as gold, by notes which were only partially covered by a commodity. The gold standard, which applied in most countries up to the 1930s, functioned under such a partial coverage of gold. This was called a fractional reserve system. The total value of the paper money in issue was thus greater than the value of the gold backing it. Such money is called **fiduciary** or **credit money**.

The modern banknote which is in use today bears no relationship to any commodity and its value is based solely on **confidence** in the government or monetary authorities to control the supply of notes in such a way that their purchasing power will not fall substantially. As long as we are assured that goods and services can be obtained in exchange for banknotes, the confidence in and acceptability of such paper money will be guaranteed. This confidence is further supported by the fact that the notes and coins issued by the central bank (in South Africa's case, the South African Reserve Bank) have been declared by law as **legal tender**. This means that such notes or coins cannot be refused if they are tendered as payment.

The next important development in the evolution of money was the use of **cheque accounts**. In any developed country this form of money constitutes the largest part of the money stock.

Continuous technological innovation in the monetary sector of the economy, such as the introduction of credit and debit cards and various forms of electronic payment, make it difficult to pinpoint exactly what money is, especially in countries with highly developed financial markets – see Box 15-1.

We now turn to the various definitions of money presently used in South Africa.

15.3 Money in South Africa

Although it is relatively easy to define money, it is quite difficult to measure it in practice. One reason is that there are several possible means of payment as well as a number of assets which can easily be converted to a medium of exchange of some kind. A second reason is that economists are also interested in the other functions of money, particularly the store of value function. The South African Reserve Bank, which is in charge of monetary matters in South Africa, uses three different measures of the quantity of money. These measures are labelled M1, M2 and M3 respectively.[2]

The conventional measure (M1)

M1 is defined solely on the basis of the function of money as a medium of exchange. According to this measure, the quantity of money includes all articles generally available as a medium of exchange (or means of payment).

M1 includes coins and notes (in circulation outside the monetary sector) as well as all demand deposits (including cheque and transmission deposits) of the domestic private sector with monetary institutions.

Note first, that only coins and notes **in circulation outside the monetary sector** constitute a part of the money supply. The reason is that only cash in the hands of the public can be used as a means of payment. The cash in the bank vaults obviously cannot be used directly to pay for goods and services. It must first be withdrawn by someone who intends to spend it. The **monetary sector** in South Africa includes the South African Reserve Bank, the Corporation for Public Deposits, the Land Bank, Postbank, private banking institutions and mutual building societies.

Secondly, **demand deposits** refer to deposits that can be withdrawn immediately by means of a cheque. It is simply a term that is used to describe the money against which cheques may be written out. The value of these deposits forms part of the quantity of money since the deposits are immediately available and are also generally accepted as payment in South Africa.

Everything that normally serves as a **means of payment** is included in the definition of M1.

This definition of money can be written in the form of an equality, as follows:

2. Actually there is also a fourth measure, called M1A. This is the narrowest possible measure of the quantity of money, but we do not deal with it separately.

BOX 15-1 CHEQUES, DEBIT CARDS AND CREDIT CARDS

Money (as a medium of exchange) consists of currency (ie notes and coins in circulation) and demand deposits. The latter can be accessed in a number of ways, for example by writing out a **cheque**. Cheques themselves, however, are not money. A demand deposit (eg a positive balance in a current account) is money; the cheque simply transfers that money from one person to another. **Debit cards** provide another way of making such transfers.

But what about **credit cards**? Are credit cards not a medium of exchange? Why are credit cards often called "plastic money"? Like cheques and debit cards (or, for that matter, electronic transfers from one account holder to another), credit cards are not a medium of exchange. Demand deposits are also not created when a person is issued with a credit card. The card is simply a convenient means of making purchases (by obtaining a short-term loan from the bank or other financial institution which has issued the card). The term "plastic money" is thus a misnomer.

For example, if Thabo Twala uses his Standard Bank Mastercard to purchase a DVD player from Game, Standard Bank will pay the money to Game. But at the end of the month Thabo will have to pay the amount to Standard Bank. The bank charges an annual fee for the services provided and if Thabo repays the bank in monthly instalments, he will pay a hefty interest charge. Credit cards are thus simply a means of **deferring** or **postponing** payment for a relatively short period.

Although credit cards are not a form of money, they have important implications for the monetary system. People who have credit cards "economise" on the holding of money and find it easier to synchronise their expenditure with their income. For example, a cardholder can use her card to do all her purchases during the month and then repay the bank at the end of the month when she receives her salary. Credit card holders thus probably hold less money on average than people who do not have credit cards.

$$M = C + D \quad \text{(15-1)}$$

where M = quantity of money
C = cash (coins and notes in circulation outside the monetary sector)
D = demand deposits

Contrary to what you might expect, D is by far the largest component of M1. In South Africa the composition of M1 on 31 December 2006 was as follows:

	R millions
Coins, Banknotes (C)	49 951
Demand deposits (D)	555 778
Quantity of money (M1)	605 729

On that date nearly 92 per cent of the total quantity of money consisted of demand deposits. This percentage remains fairly stable over time.

A broader definition of money (M2)

M2 is equal to M1 *plus* all other short-term and medium-term deposits of the domestic private sector with monetary institutions.

The short-term and medium-term deposits in question are not immediately available as a medium of exchange. They are deposits invested for a certain period (less than 30 days for short-term deposits and less than 6 months for medium-term deposits) and can only be withdrawn earlier at considerable cost. However, since the maturity of these deposits is not very long, they are quite similar to M1. They are therefore regarded as **quasi money** (or near money). M2 can thus be defined as money plus quasi money.

The most comprehensive measure of money (M3)

For many years M1 and M2 were the only measures used to quantify the money supply, but nowadays great significance is attached to the M3 measure.

M3 is equal to M2 *plus* all long-term deposits of the domestic private sector with monetary institutions.

The long-term deposits in question have a maturity of longer than six months. The monetary authorities regard M3 as the most reliable indicator of developments in the monetary (or financial) sector of the economy. This broad measure of the money supply was also used to evaluate the success of monetary policy when monetary growth targets, and later guidelines, were part of the monetary policy framework in South Africa. Note that M3 is a reflection of the **store**

of value function and not only the function of money as a medium of exchange. As we move from M1 to M2 and M3, the emphasis on the medium of exchange function decreases while the emphasis on the store of value function increases.

The narrow definition of money (M1) includes coins, banknotes and demand deposits only. The broader definition, M2, includes short-term and medium-term deposits (quasi money) and is more than one and a half times the value of M1. M3, which includes long-term deposits, is regarded as the best measure of developments in the monetary sector.

The relative values of the various measures in South Africa at certain dates are summarised in Table 15-1. Although all the measures point to a tendency for the quantity of money to increase, the rate of increase in the various totals can differ quite significantly.

15.4 Financial intermediaries

With the advent of money, a group of institutions emerged that specialised in purely financial transactions. These transactions can be distinguished from real transactions by the fact that no goods or non-financial services are involved. The goldsmiths of earlier times were probably the first institutions to earn their living by being involved in exclusively financial transactions. But even this could be disputed, since gold was actually exchanged (ie there was a product involved in each transaction). However, as a result of the development of credit money, there are many examples today of institutions which prosper without trading any goods (apart from bits of paper!).

The distinction between **real transactions** and **financial transactions** can be used to divide the economy into a real and a financial sector. In the financial sector there is a multitude of different kinds of institutions each specialising in a particular service or segment of the market. In spite of this specialisation, all these institutions have one main function, namely **to act as an intermediary between the surplus units and the deficit units in the monetary economy**. Recall the discussion about the place of the financial sector in the economy in Chapter 3. See also Box 15-2.

At any particular time there are units (eg households which have saved some of their income) that have a surplus of funds and other units (eg entrepreneurs wishing to start new business enterprises) who are in search of funds. They are called **surplus units** and **deficit units** respectively. Although the surplus units and deficit units can contact each other directly, the vast majority of financial transactions occur via financial intermediaries. These institutions specialise in the acceptance of deposits and the granting of credit.

Credit is granted when a person or institution lends funds to another person or institution. In exchange for the funds a piece of paper (known as a **security** or credit instrument) is normally issued. This document stipulates the **interest rate** at which the funds are loaned as well as when and how the loan is to be repaid. Examples of such credit instruments are bills of exchange, promissory notes and bankers' acceptances. When the government borrows money it uses Treasury bills and government stock or bonds as security.

We do not examine the activities of the financial sector in detail here. This is a specialised field of study which is dealt with in greater depth in courses in monetary economics or the financial sector of the economy. In the rest of this chapter we confine ourselves to those institutions and aspects which have a direct bearing on the quantity of money in the economy. We are primarily interested in the demand and supply of money and in the way in which they affect economic activity.

15.5 The South African Reserve Bank

The most important financial institution in any monetary economy is the central bank. South Africa's central bank is the South African Reserve Bank (**Reserve Bank**, the **Bank** or **SARB**), which was established in 1920 and started doing business in 1921. The Constitution of the Republic of South Africa clearly states that:

TABLE 15-1 Monetary aggregates in South Africa, 2002–2006 (R millions)

End of:	*Coins and banknotes*	*Demand deposits*	*M1*	*Quasi money*	*M2*	*Long-term deposits*	*M3*
2002	29 216	329 036	358 252	274 370	632 622	83 196	715 818
2003	33 715	354 073	387 788	345 665	733 453	74 594	808 047
2004	39 080	382 414	421 494	397 246	818 740	95 410	914 150
2005	43 419	459 634	503 053	457 924	960 977	135 264	1 096 241
2006	49 951	555 778	605 729	551 151	1 156 880	192 462	1 349 342

Source: South African Reserve Bank, *Quarterly Bulletin*, March 2007

BOX 15-2 MORE ABOUT FINANCIAL INTERMEDIARIES

The following diagram summarises the role of financial intermediaries as links between the **surplus units** (or savers) and the **deficit units** (or borrowers) in the economy.

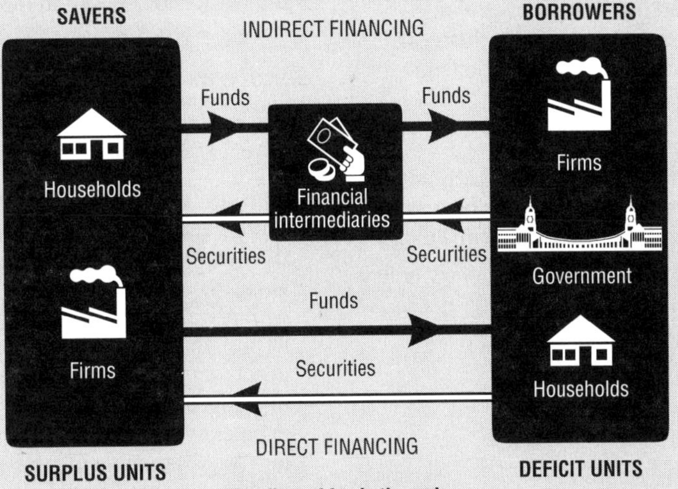

The flow of funds through the financial system

Certain households and firms with surplus funds save by depositing these funds with financial intermediaries, or by purchasing securities from them. Government can also save, but in most countries (including South Africa) the government is generally a net borrower of funds and is therefore not included among the surplus units in the diagram. The financial intermediaries lend the funds that they receive to other households and firms and to the government in exchange for securities. In the case of government, for example, they purchase government stock. In this way the financial intermediaries serve as links between surplus units and deficit units in the economy. This is called **indirect financing**. Surplus units and deficit units can also enter into direct transactions (called **direct financing**) but this is far less common than indirect financing.

There is a large variety of financial intermediaries in South Africa. The following are a few examples:

Monetary authority

South African Reserve Bank
Corporation for Public Deposits

Insurers

African Life Assurance Co Ltd
Old Mutual Life Assurance Co South Africa Ltd
Sanlam Life Assurance Ltd
South African Eagle Insurance Co Ltd

Pension and provident funds

Anglo American Group Pension Fund
Mineworkers Provident Fund

Other miscellaneous financial institutions

Land and Agricultural Bank of South Africa
Development Bank of Southern Africa
South African Housing Trust Ltd

Banks

ABSA Bank Ltd
First National Bank of Southern Africa Ltd
Investec Bank Ltd
Mercantile Bank Ltd
Nedcor Bank Ltd
The Standard Bank of South Africa Ltd

Unit trusts

Oasis General Equity Fund
Old Mutual Investors Fund
Standard Bank Mutual Fund

Finance companies

BMW Financial Services (Pty) Ltd
Genbel SA Ltd
Sasfin Holdings Ltd

(1) The primary object of the South African Reserve Bank is to protect the value of the currency in the interest of balanced and sustainable economic growth in the Republic.

(2) The South African Reserve Bank, in pursuit of its primary object must perform its functions independently and without fear, favour or prejudice, but there must be regular consultation between the Bank and the Cabinet member responsible for national financial matters.

See also Box 15-3.

The Reserve Bank is the **monetary authority** in South Africa and its current functions can be grouped into the following four major areas of responsibility:[3]

- formulation and implementation of monetary policy
- service to the government
- provision of economic and statistical services
- maintaining financial stability

Formulation and implementation of monetary policy

The SARB is responsible for formulating and implementing monetary policy. The way in which the Bank's other functions are fulfilled is determined mainly by the goals of monetary policy at that juncture. The Bank's accommodation policy (also referred to as the Bank's **refinancing system** or more commonly the **repo rate** tender system) is the main instrument through which monetary policy is conducted in South Africa. Through its refinancing system the Bank provides in the daily liquidity needs of private banks. In order to ensure that the refinancing system's influence on interest rates in general remains effective, the Bank has to compel the banks to borrow a substantial amount (the liquidity requirement) from the SARB. Other instruments like the imposition of a **cash reserve requirement** and **open market** transactions are used to drain excess liquidity from the money market in order to ensure a liquidity shortage at all times. South Africa's monetary policy framework is discussed in more detail in Section 15.9.

Service to the government

The services provided by the SARB to the central government are threefold:

- **Banker and advisor**: Until the early 1990s the Bank handled all financial receipts and payments of the central government. Nowadays the government also has accounts (called tax and loan accounts) with private banks. Nevertheless, the Reserve Bank is still the main banker for the government. It grants credit, deals with the weekly issues of Treasury bills on behalf of the Treasury, advises the government with regard to monetary and financial matters and is responsible for the administration of all exchange control regulations.
- **Custodian of gold and foreign exchange reserves**: With the exception of necessary balances held by banks and the Treasury, the Reserve Bank keeps all the country's gold and foreign exchange reserves. Gold coins and gold bullion are added to the reserves at a market-related price. The level of South Africa's gold and other foreign reserves is one of the main barometers of the state of the economy and of prospects for future economic growth. In this regard the Bank is also responsible for the formulation of **exchange rate policy**.

BOX 15-3 MISSION OF THE SOUTH AFRICAN RESERVE BANK

The following extract from the SARB's mission statement gives an indication of the primary aims of the Bank.

Mission

The South African Reserve Bank is the central bank of the Republic of South Africa. It regards its primary goal in the South African economic system as

the achievement and maintenance of financial stability

The Reserve Bank maintains that South Africa has a growing economy based on the principles of a market system, private and social initiative, effective competition and social fairness. It recognises, in the performance of its duties, the need to pursue balanced economic development and growth.

3. Based largely on Fact Sheet 1: *Introduction to the South African Reserve Bank*. Available at http://www. reservebank.co.za

- **Administration of exchange control:** The Reserve Bank is responsible for exchange control in South Africa. Exchange control restricts the movement of foreign exchange in order to protect an economy from disruptive fluctuations in capital movements and other international economic shocks. Exchange control in South Africa was introduced for the first time in 1939 and has never been totally abolished since then.

Provision of economic and statistical services

The Bank collects, processes, interprets and publishes economic statistics and other information. The data these publications contain are a major source of information for policymakers, analysts and researchers.

Maintaining financial stability

The SARB presently regards financial stability (particularly price stability) as its most important objective (see Box 15-3). In pursuit of this objective the Bank plays a pivotal role in the following areas:

- **Bank supervision:** The Reserve Bank is responsible for bank regulation and supervision in South Africa. The purpose is to achieve a sound, efficient banking system in the interest of depositors of banks and the economy as a whole. This function is performed by issuing banking licenses to banking institutions and monitoring their activities.
- **The National Payment System:** The Bank is responsible for overseeing the safety and soundness of the National Payment System (NPS). The main aim is to reduce interbank settlement risk with the objective of reducing the potential of a systemic risk crisis emanating from settlement default by one or more of the settlement banks.
- **Banker to other banks**: The Bank acts as custodian of the minimum cash reserves that banks are legally required to hold or prefer to hold voluntarily with the Bank. These reserves form part of the **monetary base** that the banks can use to create the demand deposits (D) which constitute the largest part of of the quantity of money. By exerting control over the level and composition of these reserves the Reserve Bank can, to a certain extent, control the quantity of money. The reserves are also used to clear the banks' mutual claims and obligations to one another. In this way the Reserve Bank acts as a **clearing bank**. Obviously the success of clearing bank activities is very closely related to the smooth operation of the National Payment System mentioned above. In terms of its **"lender-of-last-resort"** activities the Bank may in certain circumstances provide liquidity to banks experiencing liquidity problems. The way in which the Reserve Bank accommodates (or finances) the banking sector is known as the refinancing system, which has already been referred to.
- **Banknotes and coins:** The Reserve Bank has the sole right to make, issue and destroy banknotes and coins. The SA Mint Company, a subsidiary of the Bank, mints all coins on behalf of the Bank while the SA Bank Note Company, another subsidiary of the Bank, prints all banknotes on behalf of the Bank. In its issues of notes and coins the Bank is largely guided by the public's cash requirements. The cash comes into general circulation through the purchase of assets (usually financial assets) by the Bank.

15.6 The supply of money

In Section 15.3 we said that the SARB uses three definitions of money (M1, M2 and M3). These definitions are used to determine the **quantity of money**. The quantity of money is a **stock** concept which can only be measured at a particular time. To examine the quantity or supply of money we make the following simplifying assumptions:

- We use only one definition of money (M1) and therefore assume that money (*M*) consists of cash (*C*) and demand deposits (*D*). Therefore, as was stated in Equation 15-1, we have

  $M = C + D$
- We assume that only banks are authorised to hold demand deposits. This is quite plausible since most demand deposits are actually held by banks.
- We also assume that there is a central bank which exercises control over the activities of banks. This is quite true, of course, as has just been indicated in the previous section.

In Section 15.3 we showed that demand deposits (*D*) constitute the main share (more than 90%) of the quantity of money. In any analysis of the money supply it is therefore essential to establish what determines the size of these deposits.

The role of banks in the money creation process

By now it should be clear that money is created largely by banks and not by a mint or printing press. Banks accept deposits from the general public and lend these funds to borrowers (eg in the form of overdraft facilities). The difference between the lending rates and the deposit rates represents the income banks receive for their intermediation role. Because banking institutions, as defined in the Banks Act (No 94 of 1990), are the only institutions that may accept deposits from the general public, their activities are closely monitored by the Reserve Bank. The most notable feature of banks, however, is the fact that their clients can open cheque accounts and that they can therefore access their demand deposits by writing cheques.

Demand deposits are characterised by the fact that the bank is obliged to pay out the deposit in cash (banknotes) or to transfer it immediately on demand to another bank or account holder. The cheque account can therefore be treated like money (hence it forms part of M1). Since cheques are a form of money and also a very convenient form, banks pay little interest on cheque accounts. In fact, they even debit account holders with bank charges for the costs they incur in providing this service.

Demand deposits (*D*) can be created in the following ways:

- Provided a person has a reasonably good reputation and has a reasonable amount of money at his or her disposal, any bank will be prepared to create a demand deposit in favour of that person in exchange for cash deposited at that bank. For example, if a person deposits R1 000 in banknotes with a bank, the bank will issue that person with a cheque book which will give him or her the right to write out cheques to the value of R1 000.
- However, this is not the only way in which *D* can be created. Because the banks, like the goldsmiths in earlier times, noticed that the demand deposits held by them were not all withdrawn immediately or simultaneously, they got into the habit of lending some of these funds to deficit units in the form of **overdraft facilities**. Provided that the bank can be convinced of a person's creditworthiness, a demand deposit can be created in that person's favour without any cash deposit.

There is obviously a considerable difference between the two ways in which demand deposits are created. In the first case the bank's role is fairly **passive** since nothing has been done to change the money supply in the country. You will recall from the definition of M1 that only cash that is **in circulation outside the banking sector** can be regarded as part of the money supply. In this case, the creation of *D* has therefore been accompanied by a corresponding decline in *C*. The change in *M* can thus be expressed as follows:

$$\begin{aligned}\Delta M &= \Delta C + \Delta D\\ &= -R1\,000 + R1\,000\\ &= 0\end{aligned}$$

In the second case the conduct of the bank is more **active**. The bank has deliberately lent money and thus **created credit**. As a result, the money supply in the country has been increased. According to our equation, the change in *M* (when the person who has been granted an overdraft facility writes out cheques to the value of R1 000) can be expressed as follows:

$$\begin{aligned}\Delta M &= \Delta C + \Delta D\\ &= 0 + R1\,000\\ &= R1\,000\end{aligned}$$

The reserve asset position and the credit multiplier

Although banks can create credit, as illustrated above, there are definite limits to the amount that can be created.

In the first place, it must be remembered that *D* may be withdrawn at any time. Cash and demand deposits can be arbitrarily substituted for each other. Each bank must therefore ensure that it always has sufficient **cash reserves** available to provide for **cash withdrawals**.

In the second place, the bank, which forms part of a larger banking system, must provide for the claims of other banks, which may exceed its own claims. This happens when a bank's clients (including those who have obtained overdraft facilities) write cheques in favour of people who have accounts with other banks. Such transfers to other banks may be larger than the transfers received by the bank for similar cheques.

From experience banks know what percentage of the total deposits received by them should be set aside in the form of **cash reserves** for the above-mentioned eventualities. However, as we explain in the next paragraph, this judgement is no longer left to the discretion of individual banks.

In any business enterprise it is of the utmost importance that the **confidence** of creditors should be maintained. In the business of banking the creditors are a multitude of depositors – the holders of current accounts, savings accounts and time deposits – and it is vitally important to maintain their trust. The slightest crack in a bank's image of creditworthiness could give rise to a rush of withdrawals that could disrupt the entire financial system, as occurred with the collapse of Saambou in 2002. To maintain confidence in the banking system, the monetary authorities lay down legal requirements, stipulating the amount of cash reserves to be held against the total liabilities (demand deposits) of a bank.

At the time of writing the banks were obliged to hold 2½ per cent of their **total** liabilities to the public (demand deposits) in the form of cash reserves in a non-interest-bearing account with the Reserve Bank.

Any increase in a bank's demand deposits increases the amount that the bank has to hold in the form of cash reserves with the Reserve Bank.

The required increase in cash reserves (*R*) as a result of an increase in demand deposits (ΔD) can be calculated as follows:

$$\Delta R = b\,(\Delta D) \qquad (15\text{-}2)$$

where b = required cash reserve ratio (expressed as a fraction or a percentage). Any increase in demand deposits will raise the required minimum cash reserves. For example, if the cash reserve requirement is $2\frac{1}{2}$ per cent and the increase in demand deposits amounts to R2 000 it means that an additional R50 will be required as cash reserves:

$$\begin{aligned} \Delta R &= b\,(\Delta D) \\ &= 0{,}025\ (2000) \\ &= 50 \end{aligned}$$

Alternatively, the amount of demand deposits will have to be reduced to meet the cash reserve requirement. Equation 15-2 can be rewritten to express the change in demand deposits as a function of the change in required reserves. To do this, we switch the two sides of Equation 15-2 and divide both sides by b. Thus

$$\begin{aligned} b(\Delta D) &= \Delta R \\ \Delta D &= \tfrac{1}{b}\,(\Delta R) \qquad (15\text{-}3) \end{aligned}$$

where $\frac{1}{b}$ = **credit multiplier**

If b = 2,5 per cent (or 0,025), then $1/b = 1/0{,}025 = 40$. This means that if the banks receive an additional amount in cash, they can create an amount of demand deposits equal to 40 times the initial increase in cash reserves. Conversely, Equation 15-3 can be used to calculate the increase in demand deposits as a result of a R50 increase in cash reserves:

$$\begin{aligned} \Delta D &= \tfrac{1}{b}\,R \\ &= 40 \times 50 \\ &= \text{R2 000} \end{aligned}$$

See also the example in Box 15-4.

An increase in the cash reserve requirement of banks (ie an increase in b) will reduce the credit multiplier ($1/b$). To meet the new requirement the banks will (*ceteris paribus*) have to keep more cash reserves with the central bank or, alternatively, reduce the amount of demand deposits (eg by requiring some clients to repay the amounts they borrowed on overdraft). For example, if the cash reserve requirement (b) is doubled, from 2,5 per cent to 5 per cent, the credit multiplier ($1/b$) will be halved (from 40 to 20) and required cash reserves will double. To meet this requirement, the banks will either have to double their cash reserves or reduce the amount of demand deposits by a half. Put differently: with a required cash reserve ratio of 5 per cent and an increase in demand deposits of R2 000, the banks will have to keep an additional R100 in cash reserves with the central bank (compared to the additional R50 required when the ratio was 2,5 per cent).

Although variations in the cash reserve requirement may be used occasionally when structural changes in the financial sector occur, these variations are not an essential part of the present monetary control system in South Africa. Equation 15-3 shows the relation between demand deposits and required cash reserves, but it says little about the process whereby demand deposits are actually controlled.

The present system of monetary control in South Africa seeks to control the amount of demand deposits by influencing the **cost** of additional cash reserves, rather than by variations in the cash reserve ratio (b) or by seeking to control the actual amount of the banks' aggregate cash reserve holdings. The monetary authorities use various other supportive monetary policy measures to ensure that the banks experience a shortage of cash reserves on a more or less permanent basis. In this way the influence of the repo rate through the Bank's accommodation policy (which is discussed in Section 15.10) is made effective by forcing the banks to utilise the accommodation facilities of the Reserve Bank.

Any increase in demand deposits (ΔD) as a result of an increase in the provision or use of overdraft facilities forces the banks to acquire additional reserves (ΔR) which have to be borrowed from the SARB at the repo rate. The higher the repo rate, the more expensive credit becomes and the smaller the demand for credit (and demand deposits) will be. As the demand for credit falls, so too will the size of M1. This, in short, is the rationale behind South Africa's present monetary control system.

Under the present system, the creation of demand deposits is determined by the **demand** for credit at the interest rates quoted by the banks, rather than by the credit that the banks are able or willing to extend to their clients. The money supply process is thus essentially a function of the demand for money. The money supply is said to be **demand driven**. The fact that the money supply is demand driven weakens the monetary authorities' control over the size of the money supply.

Other factors that can influence the money supply

The money supply can also be influenced by **transactions with foreign countries** and by **government transactions**.

In Part I we emphasised that South Africa has an open economy. This means that South Africa has strong economic links with the rest of the world. These links have a considerable impact on economic activity. In addition, **foreign trade and international capital movements** can also exert a significant influence on the domestic money supply.

If a local exporter earns foreign currency (in payment for exports) and exchanges it at his or her bank for a demand deposit, the money supply will be directly increased. On the same principle, payment for

BOX 15-4 THE PROCESS WHEREBY DEMAND DEPOSITS ARE CREATED

We can use a simple example to illustrate how banks can create demand deposits. The example also illustrates how the cash reserve requirement imposed by the central bank determines the size of the credit multiplier. To keep matters simple, we assume a cash reserve requirement (*b*) of 20 per cent (or 0,2).

- Suppose Ms X receives R1 000 as a gift and deposits it with Bank A. Bank A's cash reserves increase by R1 000 and in exchange it creates a demand deposit to the amount of R1 000 in favour of Ms X. As indicated in the text, the money supply is unaffected at this stage.
- Since the cash reserve requirement is 20 per cent, Bank A has to keep R200 of the R1 000 deposited by Ms X as cash reserves.
- This leaves Bank A with R800 which it can lend to Mr Y in the form of an overdraft facility.
- Mr Y then uses this facility to write a cheque for R800 in favour of Ms Z, who deposits it with her own bank, Bank B.
- At this stage the total amount of demand deposits has increased from the original R1 000 to R1 800 (ie Ms X's deposit of R1 000 at Bank A and Ms Z's deposit of R800 at Bank B). The money creation process by the banks has thus begun.
- Ms Z's deposit of R800 raises Bank B's cash reserves. Again, 20 per cent of this increase in deposits (ie R160) has to be kept in the form of cash reserves. The other R640, however, can be lent to one of its customers, Mr W.
- This process will continue, as illustrated below, until it works itself out. For every rand received by a bank in the form of a cash deposit, 20 cents have to be kept as a cash reserve with the central bank, but the remaining 80 cents can go out on loan.

Bank	New deposits	Additional cash reserves required	New loans granted
A	R1 000,00	R200,00	R800,00
B	R800,00	R160,00	R640,00
C	R640,00	R128,00	R512,00
D	R512,00	R102,40	R409,60
.	.	.	.
.	.	.	.
.	.	.	.
Total	**R5 000,00**	**R1 000,00**	**R4 000,00**

- By working through the whole process it can be shown that the total increase in demand deposits will be equal to the original deposit (ie the original increase in cash reserves) multiplied by the credit multiplier. In this case, therefore, the total increase in demand deposits will be R1 000 x 5 = R5 000, since $b = 0{,}20$ and $1/b = 5$. In terms of Equation 15-3 in the text:

$$\Delta D = (1/b)\,\Delta R = (1/0{,}20) \times \text{R}1\,000 = 5 \times \text{R}1\,000 = \text{R}5\,000$$

The increase of R5 000 consists of the initial deposit of R1 000 plus new loans granted to the value of R4 000.

imports will have a negative effect on the quantity of money. Capital inflows have the same effect as exports while capital outflows decrease the money supply in the same way as imports do.

The effects of foreign transactions on the money supply can be summarised by stating that **a country's money supply generally increases when its gold and foreign exchange reserves increase and falls when the gold and foreign exchange reserves decrease**.

The **government** can also exert a significant influence on the money supply. When the government deposits funds (eg taxes that it collects) with the Reserve Bank, the money supply decreases since the money is withdrawn from circulation. On the other hand, when the government withdraws funds from its account with the South African Reserve Bank (eg by issuing a government cheque), the funds are put back into circulation and the money supply increases. The net impact of the government on the money supply thus depends on the size of its deposits with the SARB relative to the size of its withdrawals from the SARB.

Prior to the early 1990s the SARB acted as the only banker of the government. Nowadays, however, the government also keeps accounts (called tax and loan accounts) with the major private banks. This step was taken to reduce the disruptive impact on the monetary system of large government receipts (mainly in the form of tax revenue) and payments. If the government keeps some of the funds outside the SARB, the funds remain in circulation, just like the demand deposits of private clients of the banks concerned.

If the government cannot finance all its expenditure through tax revenue and borrowings from the private sector, it can borrow the remainder from the Reserve Bank (see the discussion on the financing of government expenditure in Chapter 16). Such a loan will increase the cash reserves of the banks and can therefore potentially increase the money supply. This type of financing is generally not desirable and is called **inflationary financing**.

15.7 The demand for money

Having examined the supply of money, we now turn our attention to the demand for money. At any moment all holders of wealth in the economy must decide in which form to hold their wealth. Wealth can be held in various forms. This includes **real assets**, such as fixed property (real estate) and valuable items such as oriental carpets, paintings, rare postage stamps and antiques, and **financial assets**. We distinguish between two types of financial asset, namely **money** and interest-bearing assets which we call **bonds** – see Box 15-5.

The demand for money is the amount that the various participants in the economy plan to hold in the form of money balances. Remember, however, that demand is not the same as wants. The demand for money does not relate to the amounts of money that people want. The demand for money is concerned with the choices of those participants who earn an income or possess wealth. They must decide in which form to hold their income and wealth. To explain the demand for money we therefore have to examine the choice between money and bonds.

Why do households and firms wish to hold money? The answer is not immediately obvious. There is, after all, a cost to holding money. Recall that money consists of cash (C) and demand deposits (D). Holders of cash earn no interest on it, while the interest on demand deposits is generally so low that it can, for all practical purposes, be ignored. Households and firms therefore earn little or no interest on their money holdings. The money could have been used to purchase bonds that earn higher interest than money does.

The opportunity cost of holding any money balance is the interest that could have been earned had the money been used to purchase bonds instead. Money will only be held if it provides a service that is valued at least as highly as the opportunity cost of holding it. The demand for money is therefore directly related to the functions that it performs. Recall from Section 15.1 that the two most important functions of money are the medium of exchange and the store of value functions. On the basis of these two functions we can distinguish two basic components of the demand for money:

- the **transactions demand** for money which arises from the medium of exchange function
- the **demand for money as an asset** which arises from the store of value function

The demand for money can be investigated in more detail by examining the three motives for holding money distinguished in the 1930s by John Maynard Keynes. Keynes identified two reasons for holding money as a medium of exchange and also explained why money is often held as a store of value. Because money is the most liquid of all assets, he referred to the demand for money as **liquidity preference**.

- The first reason for holding money is the **transactions motive**. In a money economy all participants have to hold money as a medium of exchange. Without money it is impossible to enter into transactions. The need to hold money arises because participants' payments and receipts of money do not coincide. For example, wages and salaries are normally paid weekly or monthly, while purchases of goods and services occur more regularly. Workers therefore have to hold money to buy food and other commodities between paydays. The amount of money required for transaction purposes will

BOX 15-5 BONDS, THE BOND MARKET AND THE CAPITAL MARKET

A **bond** is a financial instrument that promises that the issuer (the borrower) will regularly pay the holder interest and will repay the capital amount at a certain date. The government, for example, issues bonds to finance part of its expenditure.

A bond has a number of features:

- **The principal**: This is the amount (eg R1 million) that the issuer will repay to the bondholder when the bond expires.
- **The maturity date**: This is the date on which the bond will expire (ie the date at which the issuer will repay the principal to the bondholder).
- **The coupon rate**: This is the interest (expressed as an annual rate – eg 10%) that the issuer promises to pay the bondholder until the maturity date. The coupon rate is usually fixed and the coupon payment dates are also specified.

Holders of bonds do not have to keep them until they mature. Bonds are a form of marketable debt and can be traded in the secondary **bond market** (eg the Bond Exchange of South Africa, which is part of the JSE Securities Exchange). The bond market forms part of the capital market. The **capital market** is a market for **long-term** financial instruments. Four main categories of financial instruments are traded in the capital market: fixed-interest-bearing securities (or bonds), variable interest securities, shares and negotiable documents. Interest rates determined in the capital market (eg the rates on government bonds with different maturities) are long-term rates and are determined by market forces of supply and demand. Among the government bonds whose interest rates are regularly reported in the media are the R153, R157 and R186. As we explain in Box 15-9, there is an inverse relationship between bond prices and market interest rates.

For more information on bonds, the bond market and the capital market, see Van Zyl, C, Botha, Z and Skerritt, P (eds). 2006. *Understanding South African financial markets*. Second edition. Pretoria: Van Schaik Publishers.

depend mainly on the total value of the transactions concerned. This, in turn, will depend on the level of income. At the macro or aggregate level, the **transactions demand for money is therefore a function of national income**.

- The second motive for holding money is the **precautionary motive**. In principle this is the same as the transactions motive. The only difference is that the precautionary motive allows for unpredictable expenditures. Households and firms provide for unforeseen expenditures, over and above their normal transaction requirements. At the macro or aggregate level, the **precautionary demand is also a function of national income**. The distinction between the transactions demand and the precautionary demand is somewhat artificial and is often dropped when the demand for money is analysed further.
- The third motive for the demand for money distinguished by Keynes is both the most interesting and the most complicated. This is the **speculative motive**, which is related to the function of money as a store of value. The identification of the speculative demand for money was Keynes's most important contribution to monetary economics. To understand the speculative demand, we must consider the choice between holding money (which earns little or no interest) and holding bonds (which earn interest). The full explanation is quite complicated and we therefore use a short-cut method below to explain it. For those of you who are interested in this fascinating and important topic, we provide a more detailed explanation in the appendix to this chapter (Appendix 15-1). You should try to understand it, since you will encounter it time and again if you should continue your studies in monetary economics and macroeconomics.

  The short-cut explanation is that the choice between holding financial assets in the form of money or bonds will depend on the interest rate. As mentioned earlier, the **opportunity cost** of holding money is the interest that is forgone by not holding bonds. This is because interest is earned on bonds, while little or no interest is earned by holding money. It follows, therefore, that the quantity of money demanded for speculative purposes will be low when the interest rate is high (since the opportunity cost of money is then also high). Likewise, the quantity of money demanded for speculative purposes will be higher when the interest rate (and therefore the opportunity cost of money) is low.

Our conclusion is therefore that there is a negative (or inverse) relationship between the quantity of money demanded for speculative purposes and the level of the interest rate. This is illustrated by demand curve L_2 in Figure 15-1(b).

If interest rate expectations are also taken into account (as in Appendix 15-1), this inverse relationship between the quantity of money demanded for speculative purposes and the interest rate is reinforced.

There is yet another useful way of distinguishing between the various components of the demand for money (or liquidity preference). The transactions and precautionary demand are both related to the need to actively employ the money balances concerned. In these cases the purpose is to spend the money. We therefore add the transactions and precautionary demand for money together and call them the demand for **active balances**. By contrast, the speculative demand is not directly linked to transactions. In this case the purpose is to hold the money passively as a store of value. We therefore call the speculative demand for money the demand for **passive balances** (sometimes also called **idle balances**). This distinction is used in Figure 15-1 to derive the total demand for money (or the total liquidity preference). The different concepts that we have introduced in this section are summarised in Table 15-2.

The money demand curve can be represented as in Figure 15-1. In Figures 15-1(a) and 15-1(b) the demand for **active balances** (transaction and precautionary motives) and for **passive balances** (speculative motive) are shown separately. We use the symbol L to denote that we are dealing with **liquidity preference** and not with the demand for an ordinary commodity. The demand for active balances is denoted by a vertical line (L_1) which is not sensitive to interest rate variations, measured on the vertical axis. The position of L_1 is determined by the income level. The higher the income level, the further to the right L_1 will be. The demand for passive balances is represented by L_2. This curve demonstrates the negative relation between interest rates and the quantity of passive balances demanded. At a certain interest rate level (i_1) no funds will be demanded to be used for speculative purposes.

In Figure 15-1(c) the joint or **total money demand curve** or **total liquidity preference** (*LL*) is shown. This is merely the horizontal addition of the two individual demand curves in (a) and (b). The properties of the demand curve can be summarised as follows:

- The negative **slope** reflects the inverse relationship between the interest rate level and the quantity of money demanded for speculative purposes.
- The **position** of the demand curve is mainly determined by the demand for active balances, which is determined by the income level. Any increase in income shifts the total demand curve to the right, while a decrease in the income level will cause the *LL* curve to shift to the left.

TABLE 15-2 The demand for money (or liquidity preference): a summary

Function	*Motive*	*Active/passive*	*Main determinant*
Medium of exchange	Transactions, Precautionary	Active balances	Income
Store of value	Speculative	Passive balances	Interest rate

In general terms the demand for money (or liquidity preference) may be expressed in the following equation:

$L = f(Y, i)$, where
L = quantity of money demanded
Y = national income
i = interest rate

The equation states that the demand for money is a function of the **income level** and the **interest rate level**.

The interest rate

The interest rate level referred to above probably needs further clarification. Interest rates may generally be described as the prices of loanable funds. The suppliers of funds would like to earn an income on the funds invested or lent out, while the borrowers are usually willing to pay a price for the right to use these funds. Here as well as in the rest of the book, we often refer to "the interest rate" or "the interest rate level" as though there were only one such rate in the economy. This is certainly not the case, since there are numerous interest rates, each associated with the borrowing and lending of specific funds. For example, there is the repo rate (which plays a dominant role in

FIGURE 15-1 The demand for money

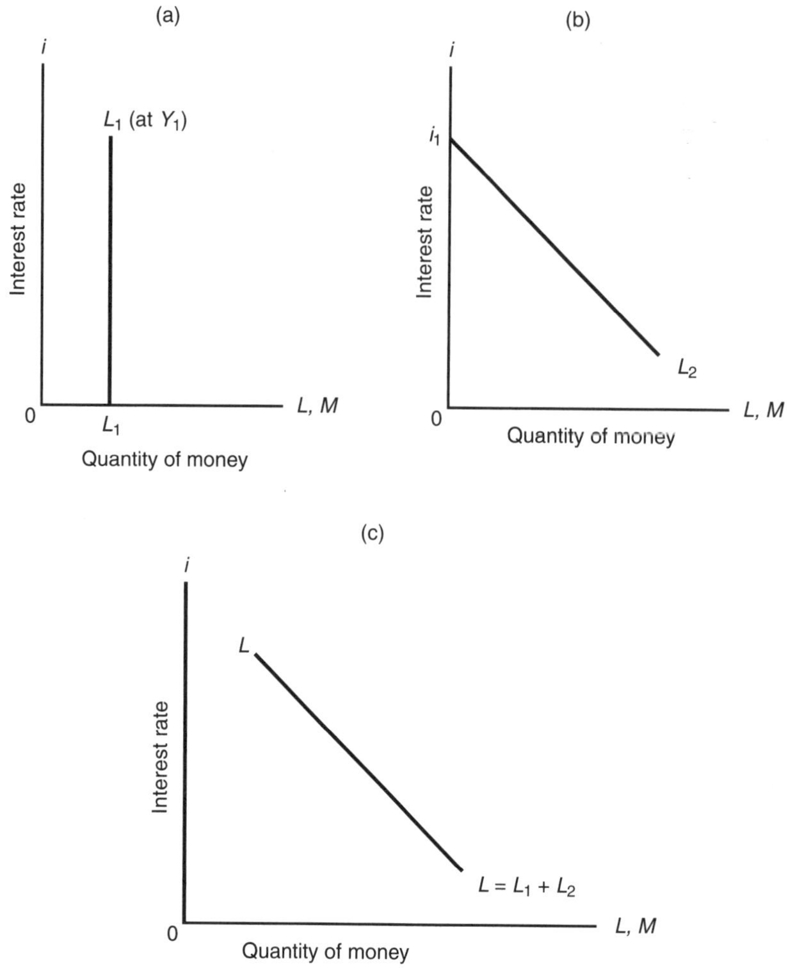

The demand for active balances (L_1), which is independent of the level of the interest rate, is shown in (a) for a given level of real income Y_1. The demand for passive balances (L_2), which is inversely related to the interest rate, is shown in (b). The total demand for money (LL) is obtained by adding the quantity of active balances (L_1) and the quantity of passive balances (L_2) at each interest rate. The total demand for money at the given level of income (Y_1) is shown in (c).

the money supply process), the interbank lending rate, the prime rate of banks, various rates on deposits, mortgage rates and the rate on government stock, to mention only a few.

Although all these rates differ and there are sound economic reasons for these differences, the rates nevertheless tend to move in harmony with each other. Therefore, when we refer to "the interest rate", it should be regarded as a representative rate for all the individual rates encountered in practice.

This simplification is not unique. Recall from Chapter 6 that theory always requires some simplification or abstraction from reality. We do it all the time. For example, we refer to total income in the economy without specifying whether we mean GDP, GNI or any other measure of total income. In macroeconomic theory, the differences between these magnitudes are not relevant. Likewise, we refer to the general price level without specifying which price index we are using.

15.8 Equilibrium in the money market

Is there an independent money supply curve?

In the previous section we established a money demand curve which indicated that the demand for money is a function of both income and the rate of interest. In order to determine how equilibrium in the money market is reached through the interaction of demand and supply we also have to derive an appropriate money supply curve. In Section 15.6 we indicated that the process of money creation and the supply of money are influenced and controlled by a variety of factors and transactions. The complex nature of the process of money creation makes it particularly difficult to derive a generally applicable supply curve of money. In fact, it can be argued that an independent money supply curve does not exist, in other words that the money supply is determined by the interaction of the demand for money and the interest rate level, where the latter is determined mainly by the monetary authorities. This interpretation is represented in Figure 15-2. The money demand curve *LL* is the same as the one explained in Section 15-7. The interest rate is determined or largely influenced by the monetary authorities through their accommodation policy (discussed in Section 15-10). The quantity of money is determined by the interaction of the interest rate and the demand for money. At an interest rate of i_0 the quantity of money will be M_0. A reduction in interest rates to i_1, initiated by a lowering of the repo rate, will raise the quantity of money to M_1, *ceteris paribus*.

FIGURE 15-2 The money market

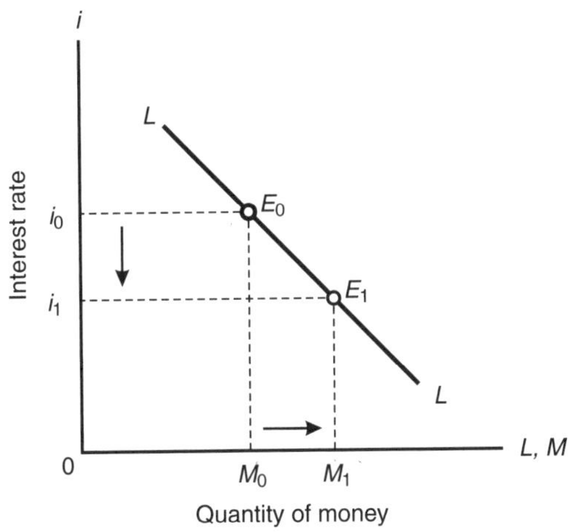

The quantity of money is determined by the interaction of the interest rate and the demand for money. At the initial interest rate i_0 the quantity of money is M_0. A reduction in the interest rate to i_1 will increase the quantity of money to M_1, ceteris paribus.

According to this interpretation there is no independent money supply curve. The money supply (or quantity of money) depends on the demand for money and the cost of credit (ie the interest rate). This is called a **demand-determined money supply**.

The approach adopted here differs from the traditional explanation of equilibrium in the money market, which is based on the assumption that the monetary authorities can control the money supply (ie on the notion that there is an independent money supply curve) – see Box 15-6.

Simultaneous control of the quantity of money and interest rates

It is important to note that the monetary authorities cannot simultaneously set both the interest rate and the quantity of money at given target levels. This is clearly illustrated in Figure 15-2. An interest rate of i_0 cannot be maintained if the money supply target is M_1. If the central bank wishes to peg the interest rate at a certain level, it loses control over the supply of money. The quantity of money demanded at that interest rate will determine the quantity that will be supplied.

Up to now we have assumed that the monetary authorities are in a position to change the rate of interest, but we have not explained how this is achieved in practice. In South Africa, changes in market interest rates through changes in the repo rate are a key element of monetary policy. To explain this, we have to examine the framework of monetary policy.

15.9 The monetary policy framework in South Africa

Monetary policy can be defined as the measures taken by the monetary authorities to influence the quantity of money or the rate of interest with a view to achieving stable prices, full employment and economic growth. Monetary policy in South Africa is formulated and implemented by the South African Reserve Bank. Decisions on the appropriate monetary policy stance are taken by the Monetary Policy Committee (MPC) of the SARB. The MPC consists of the governor of the SARB, the deputy governors and a few senior officials of the Bank. Regular Monetary Policy Forums are also held to provide a platform for discussion of monetary policy issues with a broad range of stakeholders.

The evolution of the monetary policy framework

In Section 15.5 it was clearly stated that the primary objective of the SARB is to protect the value of the

BOX 15-6 THE TRADITIONAL APPROACH TO THE SUPPLY OF MONEY AND EQUILIBRIUM IN THE MONEY MARKET

Most textbooks assume that the money supply is controlled by the central bank and that there is thus an independent money supply curve. Moreover, it is assumed that there is no relationship between the quantity of money supplied and the interest rate. The money supply curve is thus traditionally represented by a vertical straight line which is entirely inelastic with regard to the interest rate. In the figure below, M_1M_1 represents the (exogenous) supply of money. The supply of money and the demand for money (represented by *LL* in the figure) jointly determine the equilibrium rate of interest (i_1) in the money market. This is similar to any market situation where the equilibrium price is determined by supply and demand. The price of money (the interest rate) is determined by the supply of and demand for money. At interest rates above i_1 there will be an excess supply of money and at interest rates lower than i_1 there will be an excess demand for money.

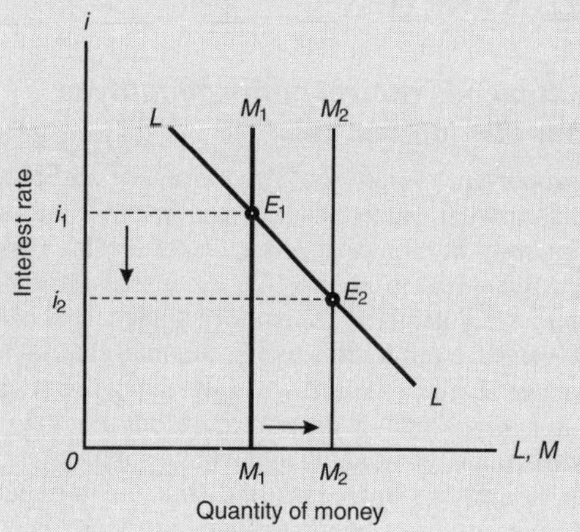

According to this view, the monetary authorities control the money supply and can change the interest rate by varying the money supply. For example, if the monetary authorities increase the money supply, illustrated by a rightward shift of the money supply curve (to M_2M_2), the equilibrium interest rate will fall (from i_1 to i_2). Exactly the opposite will happen if the money supply is reduced.

This view of the money supply and money market equilibrium is discussed further in Box 20-2.

rand in the interest of balanced and sustainable economic growth. The South African Reserve Bank Act of 1989 also states that "in order to achieve these objectives the Bank shall influence the total monetary demand in the economy through the exercise of control over the money supply and over the availability of credit."

Over the years, various policy regimes have been applied in an attempt to achieve the monetary stability required for balanced and sustainable economic growth. The policy regimes shifted from **direct intervention** in the 1960s and 1970s (when banks were simply instructed not to exceed certain quantitative restrictions on the extension of bank credit) to a more **market-oriented policy approach** where the authorities, through their own buying and selling conditions on financial markets, created incentives for financial institutions to react in the desired manner.

The monetary policy approaches (or framework) that have been used since the 1960s are outlined below and summarised in Table 15-3:[4]

4. This section draws on Casteleijn, AJH. 2001. South Africa's monetary policy framework. Paper presented at a conference on Monetary Policy Frameworks in Africa, Pretoria, 17 to 19 September.

- During the period from 1960 to 1981 a **liquid asset**-based system was used to control the extension of credit by banks. In this system, commercial banks were required to hold a certain minimum proportion of their total liabilities (eg demand deposits) in financial assets which were deemed to be "liquid". Monetary control was achieved by adjusting the ratio between these liquid assets and the demand deposits of banks. The level of interest rates (or the cost of credit) played a minor role in this system of control. In principle, this system worked in the way explained in Section 15.6, where the cash reserve ratio and the credit multiplier were discussed.
- Between 1981 and 1985 the policy framework underwent a transitionary period during which the liquid asset requirement was gradually replaced with a **cost of cash reserves**-based system. Instead of having to hold sufficient liquid assets against their liabilities, banks now had to hold a certain percentage of their liabilities in the form of **cash reserves** with the Reserve Bank. These cash reserves had to be held interest free in an account at the Reserve Bank and were obtained by discounting financial assets at the Bank's prevailing

discount rate. The element of an interest rate cost was thus firmly established in the South African monetary control system by the middle of 1985. Changes in the discount rates and other conditions on which cash reserves were made available to banks were referred to as the Reserve Bank's **discount policy**. Discount policy thus involves the regulation of the quantity of money through variations in the **cost of credit**. Changes in the discount rate led to adjustments in the interest rates charged by banks when extending credit to their clients. In other words, the cost of credit to the general public was linked to the Reserve Bank's discount rate.

- The system of variations in the cost of cash reserves was continued throughout the period from 1986 to 1998. The system of control was further enhanced when explicit **monetary growth targets** (later called **guidelines**) for M3 were announced annually from 1986 onwards. These pre-announced targets were pursued indirectly by changes in the Bank's official discount rate (also known as the **Bank rate**). If the Reserve Bank wanted to reduce the demand for credit, it increased the Bank rate and *vice versa*. Short-term interest rates effectively became the main instrument or operational variable of monetary policy. The monetary targets or guidelines were, however, invariably missed (usually exceeded) and were generally ineffective. This was ascribed, *inter alia*, to financial liberalisation and other structural changes in the economy.
- Although guidelines for the growth in M3 continued to be announced in 1998 and 1999, their importance in the formulation of policy diminished. It had become obvious that the policy of monetary targets or guidelines could not achieve the financial stability required for balanced economic growth. In March 1998 an **informal inflation target** of 1 to 5 per cent was set for the first time and a new system of monetary accommodation with daily tenders for cash reserves through **repurchase transactions** came into effect. This new monetary control system (discussed in more detail in the next section) replaced the old system whereby banks obtained cash reserves either through the discounting of eligible financial assets (discount policy) or later through the overnight lending facility at the Bank rate (refinancing policy). Through daily (since 2001 weekly) tenders banks were given the opportunity to tender for central Bank funds through repurchase transactions.
- The last phase in the evolution of South Africa's monetary policy framework was introduced on 23 February 2000 when the Minister of Finance announced a **formal inflation target** of between 3 and 6 per cent to be achieved by 2002. Some salient features of inflation targeting as a framework for monetary policy are summarised in Box 15-7.

TABLE 15-3 Evolution of South Africa's monetary policy framework

Period	*Monetary policy framework*
1960–1981	Liquid asset-based system with quantitative controls over interest rates and credit
1981–1985	Mixed system during transitionary period
1986–1998	Cost of cash reserves-based system with pre-announced monetary target (M3)
1998–1999	Daily tenders for cash reserves through repurchase transactions (repo system), plus pre-announced M3 target and informal targets for core inflation
2000–	Formal inflation targeting

Source: Casteleijn, *op cit*, 5

The main features of the South African **monetary policy framework** at the time of writing can be summarised as follows:

- The **ultimate objective** is balanced and sustainable economic growth.
- The **intermediate objective** is a pre-announced inflation target.
- The **operational variable** is short-term interest rates, which are governed by changes in the repo rate.
- The **monetary control system** is a classical cash reserve system.

The main elements of the **classical cash reserve system** are

- a minimum cash reserve requirement of 2,5 per cent of banks' total liabilities
- various policy instruments (mainly open market policy) aimed at creating a persistent liquidity shortage
- the provision of cash reserves through the repo system and the marginal lending facility (accommodation policy)
- the impact of the repo rate on short-term interest rates
- the impact of short-term interest rates on credit creation, the money supply and other variables and, ultimately, on the rate of inflation

We now take a closer look at the way in which the Reserve Bank provides cash reserves to the banks (ie its accommodation policy) and also provide a sum-

BOX 15-7 INFLATION TARGETING AS A FRAMEWORK FOR MONETARY POLICY

Formal inflation targeting as a framework for monetary policy was first introduced in New Zealand in March 1990. In February 2000 the South African Minister of Finance announced, in his annual budget speech, that South Africa would become the 15th country to formally adopt this framework. Many central banks have *informal* inflation targets, but *formal* inflation targeting is less widespread – by the middle of 2005 only about 20 countries were applying such a framework.

The cornerstone of an inflation-targeting framework is the public announcement of medium-term quantitative targets for inflation. In South Africa the target is set by the Minister of Finance in conjunction with the South African Reserve Bank. It is thus effectively the government that sets the target, which the Reserve Bank must then attempt to achieve. By doing so, the government indicates that price stability is the primary goal of monetary policy and that the Reserve Bank will be granted the freedom to use the instruments of monetary policy (see Section 15.10) to achieve the inflation target. In other words, the Reserve Bank is granted the necessary **operational independence** to pursue the inflation target. The main instrument used in this regard is the repo rate, that is, the interest rate at which the Reserve Bank accommodates the financing needs of the banks (see Section 15.10). The Monetary Policy Committee (MPC) of the Reserve Bank meets regularly (at the time of writing every quarter) to consider possible adjustments to the repo rate.

Inflation targeting is discussed in more detail in Chapter 21 (Section 21.5).

mary of other policy instruments that are used to create a persistent liquidity requirement.[5] "Liquidity" in this context refers to banks' balances at the SARB that are available to settle their transactions with other banks, over and above the minimum statutory level of reserves that they have to hold.

15.10 The instruments of monetary policy

As stated previously, a high priority is currently given to market-oriented policy instruments. The key instruments are:

- accommodation policy (or the refinancing of the liquidity requirement)
- open-market policy
- public debt management
- intervention in foreign exchange markets

Since the South African Reserve Bank relies extensively on its accommodation policy to influence interest rates, we provide a fairly detailed description of this instrument. Open-market policy is explained briefly, because it is the main supporting instrument of accommodation policy. Public debt management and intervention in foreign exchange markets are not discussed here.

Accommodation policy

A crucial element of the classical cash reserve system is the fact that banks are obliged to hold 2,5 per cent of their total liabilities to the public in the form of cash reserves with the Reserve Bank. When a bank experiences a shortage of cash reserves, it can either change other financial assets into cash or borrow funds on the interbank market to eliminate the shortage. Normally one would expect banks who are in need of funds to make use of the overnight interbank market where they borrow from other banks that have excess funds at their disposal. These funds are obtained at the interbank overnight rate. However, if all banks have the same liquidity problems, the Reserve Bank, as bankers' bank, acts as **lender of last resort** and the banks can then obtain funds by means of the repo system.

Through the **repurchase tender system** (repo system), which was introduced in March 1998 (see Box 15-8 for an explanation of a repurchase agreement), liquidity is provided to the banks by means of repurchase agreements (repos) between the Reserve Bank and its banking clients. Banks apply for refinancing by tendering for central bank funds at weekly auctions of repos with seven-day maturities. Eligible underlying assets for these repos are restricted to gov-

5. The liquidity requirement (or shortage) of **banks** is sometimes also referred to as the "money market shortage". This shortage should, however, not be confused with the excess demand for money by the **general public** referred to in Box 15-6.

BOX 15-8 REPURCHASE AGREEMENTS (REPOS)

A repo may be defined as the sale of an existing security (financial asset) at an agreed price, coupled with an agreement by the seller to purchase (buy back) the same security on a specified future date (normally seven days later) at the same price. The maturity value of the repo is determined in the initial agreement and consists of the price plus an agreed amount of interest. The interest represents the cost of obtaining the funds for a week.

In terms of the present accommodation policy of the Reserve Bank, repos are the main means whereby banks can obtain funds in order to comply with their cash reserve requirements. As a result of this refinancing system, repurchase agreements have become particularly important in South Africa. The underlying securities which may be used for this purpose are government bonds, Treasury bills, Land Bank bills and Reserve Bank debentures of all maturities.

The initial flow of cash in one direction and the underlying security in the opposite direction, is referred to as the "first leg" of the transaction. The offsetting flow of cash and the security in the opposite direction, after seven days, is known as the "second leg" of the transaction.

ernment bonds, Treasury bills, Land Bank bills and Reserve Bank debentures of all maturities.

The fixed rate determined by the Bank represented the interest rate that banks had to pay for their required reserves. If banks still experienced short or long liquidity positions after the main repo auction they would be accommodated by way of a supplementary square-off auction. If the Reserve Bank was of the opinion that the long or short positions were due to unacceptable activities on the interbank market, the banks would be accommodated at a penalty rate of 0,5 percentage points above the repo rate. In cases where the Reserve Bank unintentionally over- or under-estimated the market shortage, supplementary tenders would be conducted at the fixed repo rate.

The accommodation policy of the Reserve Bank thus mainly comprises changes in the repo rate and other conditions on which cash is made available to banks. It is therefore an instrument by which the SARB can regulate the quantity of money through variations in the **cost of credit**. Changes in the repo rate lead to adjustments in the interest rates at which credit is made available by the banks to their clients. The cost of credit in the economy is therefore directly linked to the repo rate. Other interest rates (eg deposit rates and mortgage rates) also tend to move in sympathy with the repo rate.

Open-market policy

Open-market transactions as an instrument of monetary policy consist of the sale or purchase of domestic financial assets (mainly Treasury bills and government bonds) by the central bank in order to exert a specific influence on interest rates and the quantity of money.

For example, when the SARB wishes to **increase** the money supply, it **buys** government bonds on the open market from a broker or an institution such as a bank. If bonds are purchased from a bank, the central bank will normally pay for them by increasing the cash reserves of the bank concerned by means of a book entry. The bank will now have excess reserves which it may use to create demand deposits. In this way the initial aim of the central bank is achieved.

Exactly the opposite procedure is followed when the intention is to **decrease** the quantity of money. Now the central bank **sells** government bonds on the open market and so reduces the cash reserves of banks (directly or indirectly), which in turn leads to a reduction of the money supply.

The important question, of course, is how the central bank persuades the various market participants (eg banks and other financial institutions) to buy or sell bonds (such as government stock, Land Bank bills and municipal stock) at any specific moment. In order to encourage institutions to **buy** securities, their **prices** have to be made attractive (ie **lowered**). Paying a lower price for a bond (or any similar security) implies that a higher yield will be realised on it.

The **inverse relationship between the price of a bond and the yield (interest rate) that can be earned on it** is explained in Box 15-9. This relationship plays a key role in financial markets.

When the central bank buys securities (ie increases the quantity of money), it will tend to pay higher prices to induce the bondholders to part with their bonds. The price of securities will therefore tend to rise and interest rates will drop. Open-market transactions consequently affect not only the quantity of money but also **interest rates**. These transactions

BOX 15-9 THE INVERSE RELATIONSHIP BETWEEN INTEREST RATES AND BOND PRICES

To explain the relationship between interest rates and bond prices, we consider a special type of bond called a **perpetuity**, which has an indefinite life with no maturity date printed on the face of the bond. In other words, the issuer of a perpetuity makes no promise to buy it back, but promises to pay the holder a fixed amount of money every year.

Let us take as an example a perpetuity that was originally sold for R1 000 with a percentage rate (the **coupon rate**) of 10 per cent printed on it. This means the face value of the perpetuity is R1 000 and the annual amount promised to the holder is R100 (ie 10 per cent of the face value of R1 000). Whoever holds this bond is therefore entitled to an annual interest payment of R100. The perpetuity can be traded in the secondary bond market. The price at which the bond is sold will fluctuate in accordance with changes in market interest rates. If market interest rates increase to, say, 12,5 per cent, no one will be prepared to buy this bond at the face value of R1 000, since it yields an annual interest of only R100. When the interest rate is 12,5 per cent, anyone can purchase a new interest-bearing security which yields 12,5 per cent. The market price for a new bond yielding interest of R100 will be R800. The price of our perpetuity will therefore probably drop to a level of R800. At a price of R800 the buyer will receive an effective return of 12,5 per cent (ie R100 on an investment of R800). The interest rate on the perpetuity is calculated by dividing the promised (fixed) annual payment by its current value and expressing the result as a percentage. The following table illustrates the mechanics of this relationship:

The relationship between the current value of a perpetuity and the interest rate

Current value (R)	Fixed interest payment (R)	Interest rate (%)
2 000	100	5,00
1 000	100	10,00
800	100	12,50
500	100	20,00

Comparing the first column with the last column reveals a distinct **inverse relationship** between the price of the bond and the interest rate. The higher the interest rate, the lower the price of the bond will be, and the lower the interest rate, the higher the price of the bond will be. When the market interest rate is 5 per cent, buyers will be prepared to pay R2 000 for the bond. At a market interest rate of 20 per cent they will only be prepared to pay R500.

We thus conclude that bond prices will be high when interest rates are low and that bond prices will be low when interest rates are high. Although we have used a simple, somewhat extreme example to illustrate the point, this general conclusion applies to all interest-bearing securities or bonds, irrespective of their type or maturity. The inverse relationship between interest rates and the prices of such securities is the most important relationship in the market for interest-bearing securities.

can therefore be used to support the accommodation policy of the central bank.

The main feature of open-market policy as it is applied in South Africa is that the sale of government stock may be undertaken in order to bring about a shortage of cash reserves in the banking system so that banks will be forced to make use of the financing facilities of the SARB through repurchase agreements, thus rendering the accommodation policy more effective.

Other instruments

In addition to the policy instruments mentioned above, a number of other measures may be used by the monetary authorities in pursuit of their goals. These include non-market-oriented measures such as **credit ceilings** and **deposit rate control**, (which were discontinued in South Africa some time ago), changes in the **terms of hire purchase agreements,** changes in **exchange control regulations**, Reserve Bank **intervention in foreign exchange markets** and **public debt management**.

A final instrument at the Reserve Bank's disposal is the informal measure of **moral suasion**. Although moral suasion is not a policy instrument in the strict sense of the word, the Reserve Bank can nevertheless, by means of consultation and persuasion, influence the banks in a certain direction when it does not wish to use other policy instruments.

15.11 Bank supervision

In addition to the cash reserve requirement of 2,5 per cent of banks' total liabilities which forms the basis of the Reserve Bank's accommodation policy, banking institutions must also adhere to various requirements in respect of their **capital** and **liquid asset** holdings. Although the latter could also exert a substantial influence on the credit creating abilities of banks, these requirements are more of a prudential (supervisory) nature and do not form part of the normal monetary policy arsenal of the Reserve Bank. The Banks Act (Act 94 of 1990) regulates these requirements and the supervisory role is performed by the Registrar of Banks.

Capital requirements

The present capital requirements are the higher of R250 million or a specified percentage of a bank's risk-weighted assets and off-balance sheet activities.

Liquid asset requirements

A bank has to hold at least 5 per cent of the value of total liabilities to the public in the form of approved liquid assets. The required cash reserves may not be counted as part of these liquid assets. Approved liquid assets include:

- cash reserve deposits with the SARB
- banknotes and coins in bank vaults and automated teller machines
- gold coin and bullion
- short-term Treasury bills
- short-term Land Bank bills
- securities of the Reserve Bank
- government bonds

As indicated above, the liquid asset requirement of 5 per cent was not meant to be varied for monetary policy purposes. It should rather be seen as a structural and prudential requirement to ensure the liquidity of all banking institutions in South Africa.

Concluding remarks

In this chapter we took a closer look at the monetary sector of the economy. We explained what money is, how it is created and why people hold money. We also described the functions of the South African Reserve Bank and the monetary policy instruments used by the Bank to affect important economic variables in South Africa. But we have not yet discussed a very important topic, namely the way in which developments in the monetary sector influence the rest of the economy. The link between the **monetary sector** and the **real sector** of the economy is called the **transmission mechanism**. The transmission mechanism describes how changes in the quantity of money and interest rates work their way through the economy, eventually to influence the price level, production, income and other important variables. This often controversial subject is introduced in Chapter 20.

IMPORTANT CONCEPTS

Medium of exchange	Financial intermediaries	Classical cash reserve system
Barter economy	Securities	Bonds
Unit of account	Monetary authority	Demand for money
Store of value	South African Reserve Bank	Liquidity preference
Commodity money	Supply of money	Liquidity requirement (shortage)
Credit money	Repurchase tender system	Transactions demand
Notes and coins in circulation	Repo rate	Precautionary demand
Demand deposits	Money-creation process	Speculative demand
Monetary aggregates	Credit multiplier	Active balances

Passive balances	Monetary policy framework	Open-market policy
Interest rate	Monetary growth targeting	Interest rates and bond prices
Demand-determined money supply	Inflation targeting	Bank supervision
Monetary policy	Cash reserve requirement	Liquid asset requirement
	Accommodation policy	

APPENDIX 15-1
KEYNES'S SPECULATIVE DEMAND FOR MONEY

Of the three motives put forward by Keynes for holding money, the speculative demand is the most interesting (and most complicated). It does not seem to make sense to hold money balances beyond those needed for transactions and precautionary purposes. Money balances do not earn any interest and they can easily be exchanged for interest-bearing securities (ie bonds) on which interest may be earned. It appears irrational to hold additional money balances and voluntarily forgo the interest that could otherwise be earned. Yet this is exactly what happened during the depression of the 1930s, when people accumulated large quantities of money in excess of the amounts required for transactions and precautionary purposes. This unexplained demand for money prompted Keynes to formulate his theory about the speculative demand for money.

According to Keynes, the speculative demand for money stems from uncertainty about the direction of changes in interest rates. If people feel the present level of interest rates is lower than it should be, they expect interest rates to rise in the near future. If interest rates do rise, as expected, it means that the price of bonds will fall (see Box 15-9). Anybody holding on to bonds under these circumstances may suffer a potential capital loss because of the decline in bond prices. When people expect interest rates to rise, there will be a demand for money balances. By holding money one can avoid the expected loss associated with holding bonds. Moreover, one will then be in a position to purchase bonds more cheaply, once their prices have fallen.

The following example illustrates the rationale of holding money instead of bonds. If the current interest on a bond paying R100 per year is 8 per cent, its price will be R1 250 (ie 100/1 250 × 100 = 8 per cent). An individual who expects interest rates to go up to 10 per cent will sell the bond and rather hold money because the capital loss if the bond price subsequently falls to R1 000 (100/1 000 × 100 = 10 per cent) is R250. This is more than the R100 interest that could be earned by holding on to the bond.

On the other hand, if people regard the current interest rate as being too high, relative to what might be considered "normal", they expect interest rates to fall. People who hold such expectations will speculate by holding greater amounts of their wealth in the form of bonds. In this way they can make a capital gain if interest rates do in fact fall and bond prices rise.

We can now summarise our conclusions: Anyone who expects interest rates to rise will hold money rather than bonds (to avoid possible capital losses and to be able to purchase bonds at cheaper prices). On the other hand, anyone who expects interest rates to fall, will hold bonds rather than money (to realise possible capital gains). The quantity of money demanded therefore also depends on **expectations about changes in interest rates**. This is what the speculative demand for money is all about.

In Section 15.7 we explained that the opportunity cost of holding money is the interest forgone by not holding interest-bearing securities. The higher the interest rate, the higher the opportunity cost of holding money and, therefore, the smaller the amount of money that people are likely to hold, *ceteris paribus*. This was illustrated graphically by the downward sloping liquidity preference schedule (L_2) in Figure 15-1. In this appendix we have shown that **interest rate expectations** confirm our conclusions regarding liquidity preference. When interest rates are generally high (at the top of the L_2 curve) most people expect rates to fall in the near future.

Prospects of capital gains are good if money balances are kept to a minimum and bonds are held instead. At the lower end of the L_2 curve more people expect interest rates to rise in the near future, with the threat of a possible capital loss if bonds are held. At lower interest rates more money will therefore be held. Interest rate expectations and the possibility of capital gains or losses add another dimension to the opportunity cost of holding money and liquidity preference.

REVIEW QUESTIONS

1. How would you explain to a family member what money is?
2. Describe the main functions of money and explain the role of each function in your personal life.
3. Describe the main motives for holding money.
4. What are the main functions of the South African Reserve Bank?
5. Business people and government officials often say that they can produce more goods or services if they have more money available. Does this mean that money is a factor of production (perhaps even the most important one)? Explain your answer.
6. What are the main determinants of the demand for money?
7. "The South African Reserve Bank is the sole issuer of notes and coins in South Africa and therefore has full control over the money supply." Do you agree with this statement? Substantiate your answer.
8. What do we mean when we say that the quantity (or supply) of money is demand determined and therefore not an exogenous variable?
9. What do we mean when we say that the South African Reserve Bank is independent?
10. What will happen to the money supply in each of the following cases, *ceteris paribus*? Explain each of your answers.
    (a) Depositors become concerned about the safety of their bank deposits and start withdrawing cash.
    (b) The SARB lowers the required cash reserve ratio.
    (c) The Monetary Policy Committee of the SARB raises the repo rate.
    (d) Economic activity is depressed and the banks find it difficult to find creditworthy borrowers, while many existing borrowers fail to meet their obligations to the banks.
11. Some economists argue that the central bank should implement a 100 per cent cash reserve requirement (ie $b = 1$). How would this affect the credit multiplier? How do you think banks would react to such a move? Explain your answer.
12. Suppose the South African Reserve Bank pursues an aggressive open-market policy by purchasing government bonds. What will happen to (a) the price of bonds and (b) the interest rate on bonds? Explain.
13. If you expect that interest rates are going to fall, will you hold cash or buy bonds? Explain your answer.

Some more points to ponder

Using official statistics to govern the country is like looking up today's trains in last year's timetable.

HAROLD MACMILLAN

Of all the quacks that ever quacked, political economists are the loudest. Instead of telling us what is meant by one's country, by what causes men are happy, moral, religious, or the contrary, they tell us how flannel jackets are exchanged for pork hams, and speak much of the land last taken into cultivation.

THOMAS CARLYLE

No real English gentleman, in his secret soul, was ever sorry for the death of a political economist.

WALTER BAGEHOT

Economists have not yet earned the right to be listened to attentively.

JOHN MAYNARD KEYNES

An economist: the only professional who sees something working in practice and then seriously wonders if it works in theory.

RONALD REAGAN

No one would remember the good Samaritan if he had only good intentions. He had money as well.

MARGARET THATCHER

The misery of being exploited by capitalists is nothing compared to the misery of not being exploited at all.

JOAN ROBINSON

The important thing for Government is not to do things that individuals are doing already, and to do them a little better or worse; but to do those things which at present are not done at all.

JOHN MAYNARD KEYNES

The age of chivalry is gone. That of … economists … has succeeded; and the glory of Europe is extinguished for ever.

EDMUND BURKE

16

The public sector

Learning outcomes

Once you have studied this chapter you should be able to

- explain why government participates in economic affairs
- describe how government intervenes in the economy
- explain why governments, like markets, can fail
- distinguish between nationalisation and privatisation
- explain what fiscal policy means
- discuss government spending and financing
- discuss the criteria for a good tax
- analyse who bears the burden of a specific excise tax

The market has a keen ear for private wants, but a deaf ear for public needs.

ROBERT HEILBRONER

The market needs a place but the market needs to be kept in its place.

ARTHUR OKUN

The point to remember is that what the government gives it must first take away.

JOHN S COLEMAN

The government that is big enough to give you all you want is big enough to take it all away.

BARRY GOLDWATER

Our lives are affected daily by the various laws, rules and regulations laid down by local, provincial and central government. Thus we drive on the left-hand side of the road and we stop at traffic lights. The government sector provides water, sewerage, electricity, education and health services. We and our property are protected by the police and the defence force. Some of these goods and services (eg electricity and water) are paid for directly, but others (such as defence) have to be financed in other ways. We therefore have to pay taxes. When we buy something we usually have to pay value-added tax (VAT) and some of us pay income tax. The annual budget speech of the Minister of Finance, which provides details of government spending and taxes, always attracts a lot of interest. Government has an important impact on our lives and it is not surprising that the role of government in the economy is invariably a contentious issue.

In this chapter we take a closer look at the government sector, which is also called the **public sector**. As we emphasised in our discussion of the mixed economy in Chapter 2, the government is a major participant in such an economy. In Chapter 3 we briefly described the government sector and showed how it interacts with the other major sectors in the economy. We also introduced aspects of the role of the government in other chapters. In this chapter we examine topics and issues such as the **reasons for government participation** in the economy, the difference between **public ownership and private ownership**, **fiscal policy**, **government spending** and **taxation**.

As indicated in Chapter 3, the government or public sector in South Africa consists of

- **central government**, which is mainly concerned with national issues such as defence and our relationship with the rest of the world (ie foreign affairs)
- **regional** (or **provincial**) **government**, which is mainly concerned with regional issues such as housing, health services and education
- **local government**, which deals with local issues such as the provision of sewerage, local roads, street lighting and traffic control
- **public corporations** and other government business enterprises such as Eskom, Transnet and Rand Water

The general departments (not business enterprises) of central, provincial and local government together form the **general government**. The general government plus the public corporations and other government enterprises form the **public sector**. (For a graphical illustration, see Box 3-3.)

These distinctions are important when various aspects of government activity are measured. When dealing with data about the role of government, you always have to check which definition of government the data refer to. In this book we usually refer simply to the government or to the public sector and we use these terms interchangeably.

In Figure 3-4 we showed how the government interacts with households and firms. The government provides them with goods and services (such as law and order, health services, education and housing). Apart from these goods and services, government also makes transfer payments to households (eg in the form of old-age pensions) and firms (eg in the form of export or other incentive payments or subsidies). To finance these goods and services, households and firms pay taxes to the government. In addition, the government also influences the economic activity of households and firms through regulation (ie through various laws, rules and regulations). This aspect of the role of the government is not captured in the circular flow models of Chapter 3.

Government uses its tax revenue to purchase the inputs required to provide public goods and services. These inputs include labour, which is purchased from households, and goods such as computer equipment, stationery, uniforms and building materials, which are purchased from firms. The payments by government constitute income for households and firms. There are thus continuous flows of goods, services and income between the public sector (government) and the private sector (households and firms).

16.1 The role of government in the economy: an overview

In Chapter 2 we suggested that all economies can nowadays be classified as mixed economies in which the government, the private sector and market forces all play an important role. The appropriate mix of markets and government intervention, however, remains a controversial issue. As indicated in Chapter 2, the market system (also called the free enterprise system or price system) is in many respects an amazing system which coordinates the activities of millions of people in an unplanned and decentralised way. In other chapters (eg Chapter 12) we also pointed out that the free market system is basically an **efficient** system, in the sense that, for a given distribution of income, it allocates the available resources in the best possible way. In Chapter 13, however, we showed that when markets do not function perfectly (ie when there is monopoly or imperfect competition), the market outcome might not be efficient. Moreover, we should always guard against confusing efficiency with **equity** (ie fairness). Even if market outcomes are efficient, they need not be fair. In a market system, only money votes count and those without income or wealth cannot register their wants in the market place.

What does this imply for the appropriate division (or mix) between government and the market? *First,* it should be recognised that private initiative and market forces are generally more efficient than any other possible solution to the basic economic problems of What? How? and For Whom? Government should not get involved in the production of goods and services that can be produced much more efficiently by the private sector. *Second,* it is generally accepted that free markets cannot function properly without government enforcement of the rules under which private households and firms make contracts. Market economies cannot function without well-defined property rights, the enforcement of contracts, and so on. Even Adam Smith, who is generally regarded as the intellectual father of the market economy, recognised that government always has a role to play (eg in providing national defence, upholding justice, maintaining law and order and recognising property rights).

Third, cognisance should be taken of the fact that markets do not always produce **efficient** outcomes. Markets sometimes fail and when they do, a case for government intervention arises. In other words, government intervention may be required in an attempt to correct **market failure**. *Fourth,* market systems produce relatively **efficient** outcomes but they often do not produce **equitable** outcomes. Thus, when society has other goals, such as an equitable distribution of income and wealth, which the market system cannot provide, a further justification for government intervention arises. This is the most controversial aspect of the government's role in the economy, since there is often a trade-off between equity and efficiency.

In the following two sections we examine efficiency considerations (ie market failure) and other considerations (eg equity considerations) as reasons for government intervention in the economy.

16.2 Market failure (as justification for government intervention)

In Section 12.6 we introduced the notion of **allocative efficiency**. Recall that an allocation of resources is efficient when it is impossible to reallocate the resources to make at least one person better off without making someone else worse off, and that society's welfare is maximised when the marginal cost of each product is equal to its price in the long run. **Market failure** occurs when the market system is unable to achieve an efficient allocation of resources. Note that market failure does not mean that nothing good has happened, but rather that the *best available outcome* has not been achieved. This is an important point. Some economists contend that market failure does not necessarily provide sufficient grounds for government intervention. They argue that even though the market may fail to achieve the best possible outcome (in terms of efficiency), government intervention will tend to worsen the situation, rather than improve it. In other words, they maintain that the problems created by government intervention are greater than the problems overcome by that intervention. We shall examine such **government failure** later. First we take a closer look at the main types of market failure and some of the ways in which government can try to correct these failures.

We examine five cases of market failure:

- monopoly and imperfect competition
- public goods
- externalities
- asymmetric information
- common property resources

Monopoly and imperfect competition

Monopoly and imperfect competition were dealt with extensively in Chapter 13, where we showed that (in contrast to perfect competition) monopoly, monopolistic competition and oligopoly are not allocatively efficient. We also noted possible responses to the existence of the market power of monopolists and oligopolists:

- A **first** option is to **do nothing** and to simply trust that large profits will attract competitors to the market concerned. Strong firms, however, can often protect their positions (eg by conducting a price war) whenever a competitor (even a potentially strong one) enters the market. In South Africa, for example, even financially strong and experienced entrepreneurs like Anton Rupert and Louis Luyt were unable to establish a foothold in the beer market.
- A **second** possibility is to **impose price control** in an attempt to prevent unduly high prices. This option is intuitively attractive and has often been applied in practice. However, as indicated in Chapter 8, price control is not without its problems. Apart from the problems mentioned in that chapter, it is also subject to various administrative problems (which we do not go into in this book).
- A **third** possibility is to **tax the full excess profits** of monopolists. This is, however, also subject to various problems. The monopolist can, for example, shift part of the tax to the consumer in the form of higher prices.
- A **fourth** option is to regulate monopoly through **competition policy**, which was discussed in Section 13.6.

In Chapter 13 we also discussed a specific type of monopoly which requires a different approach. This is a **natural monopoly**, which refers to a situation where the required capital expenditure or scale of production is so great that a single supplier can satisfy the demand in a particular region. Take a power station as an example. Once the power station has been built and is in operation, the marginal cost of providing power to additional customers declines rapidly to very low levels. As a result the average cost also declines significantly. In other words, the **economies of scale** are very large. In such cases, where the initial outlay is large and where average costs decline rapidly, the original supplier can easily force new entrants out of the market by lowering prices. The original supplier is therefore in a very powerful position.

In the case of a natural monopoly, government either regulates private production or undertakes the production itself. The latter includes the provision of railways and harbours by Transnet, the provision of electricity by Eskom and the provision of water by Umgeni Water (in KwaZulu-Natal) and Rand Water (in Gauteng). In recent years, however, the tendency has been to privatise government enterprises and to regulate the activities of the private enterprise or to promote competition in that particular industry.

Public goods (or non-private goods)

A second type of market failure arises from the failure of the market to provide sufficient quantities of certain goods and services. In Chapter 2 we introduced the distinction between private goods and public goods. We now examine this distinction more carefully and explain why public goods are not provided by the free market system.

In Table 16-1 we use two criteria, rivalry in consumption and excludability, to classify goods and services into four broad categories. A good is **rivalrous in consumption** if no two persons can consume the same unit of a good. For example, if you buy and eat a hotdog, no one else can buy and eat that same hotdog. Most consumer goods and services are rivalrous in consumption. On the other hand, a good is **non-rivalrous in consumption** if its consumption by one person does not reduce its consumption by others. National defence, for example, protects all the people in a particular geographical area, not just some, and the protection enjoyed by one person does not reduce the protection enjoyed by another person.

A good is **excludable** if it is possible, or not prohibitively costly, to exclude someone from receiving the benefits of the good after it has been produced. In other words, a good is excludable if people can be prevented from obtaining it. A good or service can only be excludable if its owner is able to exercise effective property rights over it in order to determine who uses it – usually only those who pay for the privilege. For example, if I do not pay for a packet of cigarettes I can be prevented from consuming it. Most consumer goods and services are excludable. On the other hand, a good or service is **non-excludable** if, once it has been produced, there is no way of stopping anyone from consuming it. National defence is again a good example. See also the other examples in Table 16-1.

Rivalry in consumption is usually determined by the nature of the good or service. An ice-cream is rivalrous in consumption; national defence is not. Excludability, however, depends on circumstances and the state of technology. In earlier years, for example, television programmes were broadcast openly to anyone who had a set. Nowadays, however, it is possible to provide programmes only to those who pay for the service. Likewise, the position-fixing service provided by lighthouses (which was traditionally regarded as an excellent example of a pure public good) can nowadays be replaced by electronic methods of position fixing that can be sold exclusively to those who are willing to pay for the service. In some cases it might be technically possible to make a good excludable, but it is too costly to do so. Such goods therefore remain non-excludable.

The four quadrants in Table 16-1 each represent a different type of good or service.

- The first quadrant contains goods and services that are both **rivalrous in consumption and excludable**. These are called **normal goods** or **pure private goods** and represent the type of goods and services that should preferably be produced by the market.
- The second quadrant contains goods that are **rivalrous in consumption but non-excludable**. They are called **common property resources**. As we shall explain later, they tend to be overused in the absence of government intervention.
- The third quadrant contains goods that are **excludable but non-rivalrous in consumption**. Such goods (called **mixed goods**) can be produced by the market but (as explained later) their efficient use requires a zero price.
- The fourth quadrant contains goods that are **non-rivalrous in consumption and non-excludable**.

TABLE 16-1 Four types of good

Consumption	*Exclusion*	
	Excludable	*Non-excludable*
Rivalrous	I *Pure private goods* Ice-cream cone Bananas Shirts DVD players Computers A seat in a cinema Medical services	II *Common property* Fisheries (fish in the ocean) Other marine resources Wildlife Air Rivers The environment Common grazing land
Non-rivalrous (up to capacity)	III *Mixed goods* Non-congested roads Museums Soccer stadiums Cinemas Satellite TV	IV *Public goods* Defence Street lights Public information Broadcast signals Basic research

These goods are called **public goods** and they are usually not produced at all by the free market. The non-production of public goods is thus an example of market failure and, therefore, a justification for government intervention. It is important to note that the term "public good" is a technical term which is not synonymous with a government-provided good. The government provides certain goods (eg education and postal services) that are also provided privately. In other words, not all goods provided by the public sector are public goods. Public goods and private goods are categorised according to their characteristics, not by which sector ends up providing them.

What are the broad implications of this classification for the role of government in the economy?

- First, the production of private (ie rivalrous and excludable) goods should be left to the market. Private firms can produce and sell these goods. If the firms are price takers, they will also fulfil the condition for allocative efficiency by operating where marginal cost is equal to price.
- Second, private firms will not provide public goods because they are non-excludable. The provision of public (ie non-rivalrous and non-excludable) goods is thus ultimately the responsibility of government. Note that we refer to the **provision** of public goods, not the **production** of public goods by the government. Once the government decides which goods or services it wants to provide, it often contracts the actual production to private firms. But who should pay for the provision of public goods, like national defence, weather forecasts and policy services? Such goods are usually paid for from tax revenue and provided free to all users. We return to this issue below.
- Third, mixed (ie excludable but non-rivalrous) goods can be provided by private firms. For example, a museum, fenced park or art gallery provides an excludable service, but as long as there is no overcrowding the consumption of the service is non-rivalrous (ie one person's use does not reduce the availability to another person). However, since the marginal cost of adding another user is zero (until capacity is reached), any admission fee that the owner charges will result in an inefficient allocation of resources (ie the non-optimal use of the facility). To avoid such inefficiency, the government often provides such mixed goods. However, even in such cases we usually find that a fee (called a **user charge**) is levied by government. Examples include toll roads and entrance fees to parks, museums and public swimming pools.
- Common property resources (quadrant II in Table 16-1) are dealt with separately below. Another category of excludable goods, namely merit goods, is also dealt with later.

Before discussing the next type of market failure it should be noted that non-excludability gives rise to a phenomenon called free riding. **Free riding** arises when some or all consumers believe that the product will be provided anyway, whether or not they pay for it. For example, everyone wants street lighting but no one wants to pay for it, knowing that they cannot be excluded from the benefits once the lights have been installed. This is why government usually levies taxes (ie compulsory charges) to finance such non-excludable goods.

Externalities

Externalities were introduced in Box 11-4. They are costs or benefits of a transaction or activity that are borne or enjoyed by parties not directly involved in the transaction or activity. They are also called third-party effects, spillover effects or neighbourhood effects. Where there are **external costs**, we refer to **negative externalities**. Where there are **external benefits**, the term **positive externalities** is used. Both consumption and production may be subject to externalities, but we confine our discussion to externalities in production.

When there are external costs or benefits to production, the full costs to society differ from the private costs faced by firms. Since markets register private costs only, the market mechanism fails to bring about a socially efficient allocation of resources in such cases. Consider the following examples:

■ EXTERNAL COSTS OF PRODUCTION

Suppose a perfectly competitive industry produces a chemical discharge that pollutes rivers. In other words, the producers impose costs on others that they themselves do not experience. In Figure 16-1, *DD* represents the market demand for the product and *SS* the market supply. Recall, from Chapter 12, that the market supply curve is obtained by adding the rising parts of the marginal cost curves of the different firms in the industry. *SS* thus also represents the marginal private cost of the industry (*MPC*). In the absence of any government intervention, the equilibrium is at E_1, the market price is P_1 and the quantity produced is Q_1. However, as a result of the pollution the marginal social cost (*MSC*) is greater than the marginal private cost *MPC*. The difference between the two represents the additional cost to society of the pollution caused by the industry. The socially efficient equilibrium (E_2) occurs at a price P_2 and quantity Q_2. This is where marginal social cost is equal to the price of the product. For each unit produced beyond Q_2, the cost imposed on society exceeds society's willingness to pay for that unit (as represented by the demand

FIGURE 16-1 Negative externalities in a perfectly competitive market

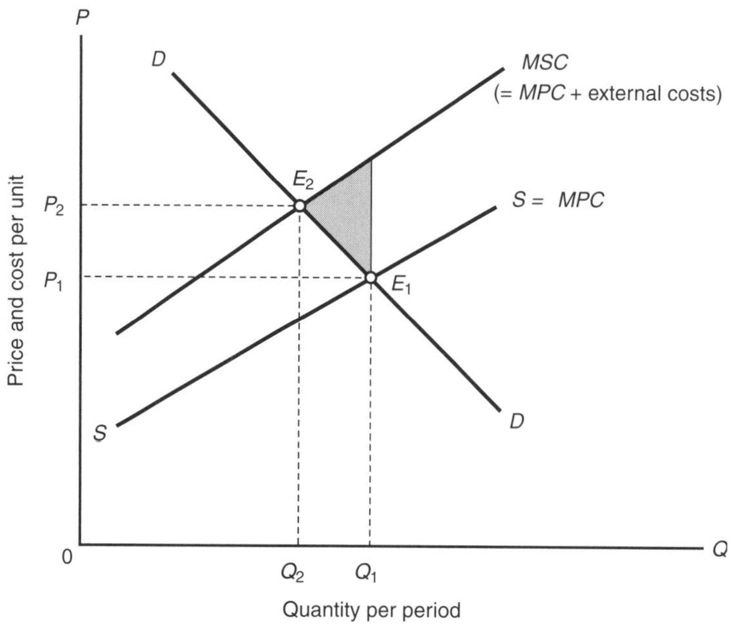

The demand for the product is represented by DD. The supply of the product, which is also the marginal private cost (MPC) of the industry, is represented by SS. As a result of the pollution, the marginal social cost (MSC) is greater than MPC. If the market is left to its own devices, a quantity Q_1 will be produced at price P_1. This is a socially inefficient solution. Social efficiency requires that MSC be equal to the price of the product. This occurs at price P_2 and quantity Q_2. The shaded triangle represents the welfare loss to society.

curve). The shaded triangle represents the welfare loss to society.

The same results will be obtained for other market structures as well. When external costs are experienced, markets tend to produce too much of the product concerned.

How can the socially efficient level of production be reached? Ronald Coase, who received the 1991 Nobel Prize in economics, has argued that if the two parties to an externality – the one causing it and the one suffering from it – can bargain with one another, they will reach an efficient allocation of resources. This result is now called the **Coase theorem**. This theorem, however, supposes that the parties can bargain effectively and that there are no transaction costs associated with the bargaining process. These assumptions are usually not satisfied and in most cases the government has to try to improve matters. One possibility is to levy a tax on those causing the external costs. If such a tax is equal to the difference between the marginal social cost (*MSC*) and the marginal private cost (*MPC*), the socially efficient level of production will be achieved. By levying such a tax, the government tries to **internalise the externality** by increasing the industry's private cost by the amount of the external cost. There are also further possibilities (eg direct control of the quantity produced or forcing the firms concerned to install anti-pollution equipment), which we do not examine here. The basic points are the following:

- External costs result in a socially inefficient allocation of resources.
- Governments should try to improve the situation.
- All potential solutions are subject to serious practical problems.

■ EXTERNAL BENEFITS OF PRODUCTION

Positive externalities arise when activities yield benefits for those not directly involved. Certain forms of medical care provide positive externalities. Thus the benefits of inoculation against a disease such as polio are not limited to those who are inoculated. Others benefit since they will not contract the disease from the inoculated person. Likewise, the opening up of a factory in a remote area might lead to the provision of facilities and services such as electricity, running water, telephones and shopping centres which would not have been provided otherwise. Other examples include housing and research and development, where the benefits also extend beyond the firms that finance the activity.

If external benefits are experienced, the marginal social cost (*MSC*) will be lower than the marginal private cost (*MPC*), again resulting in a socially inefficient allocation of resources. In this case, however, the problem is that too little is produced. Governments therefore often intervene by **subsidising** activities that are subject to external benefits. The aim is once again to **internalise the externality** but the problem and the solutions are the obverse of those pertaining to external costs.

Asymmetric information

Another possible cause of market failure is asymmetric information. In Chapter 12, we showed that perfect competition requires that all market participants have perfect knowledge of market conditions. To make informed choices, households and firms must have full information on the quality, availability and prices of goods, services and inputs. In the real world, however, there is often a great deal of ignorance and uncertainty which make it virtually impossible for consumers and firms to equate marginal benefit with marginal cost.

We can use the market for cigarettes to explain the effects of asymmetric information. Suppose the suppliers of cigarettes are aware of the health hazards of smoking but do not release this information to potential buyers of cigarettes. In Figure 16-2 the demand and supply of cigarettes are represented by *DD* and *SS* respectively. The equilibrium price is P_0 and the equilibrium quantity Q_0. Suppose the potential buyers then acquire the information about the health hazards associated with smoking. The demand thus decreases, illustrated by a leftward shift of the demand curve to D_1D_1. The new equilibrium price is P_1 and the quantity Q_1. In this example fewer units of the good are thus bought at a lower price with symmetric information (as assumed in the models of perfect competition) than in the case of asymmetric information. The new equilibrium is the socially efficient one. With asymmetric information there is an inefficient allocation of resources.

Asymmetric information can occur in any market. For example, there have been highly publicised court cases in which former workers at South African asbestos mines and other people living in the vicinity of the mines successfully claimed hundreds of millions of rands from mining companies as compensation for the asbestos-related diseases they contracted while working at or living near the mines. They argued that they had not been sufficiently informed of the health hazards associated with being employed at or residing near the mines. Similar court actions have been launched by smokers against the major tobacco companies in the United States and elsewhere. Asymmetric information probably exists in nearly all exchanges. The important question, however, is whether or not the asymmetric information results in an outcome that is significantly different from that which would have occurred with symmetric information. Only then does asymmetric information represent a market failure.

FIGURE 16-2 Asymmetric information in a goods market

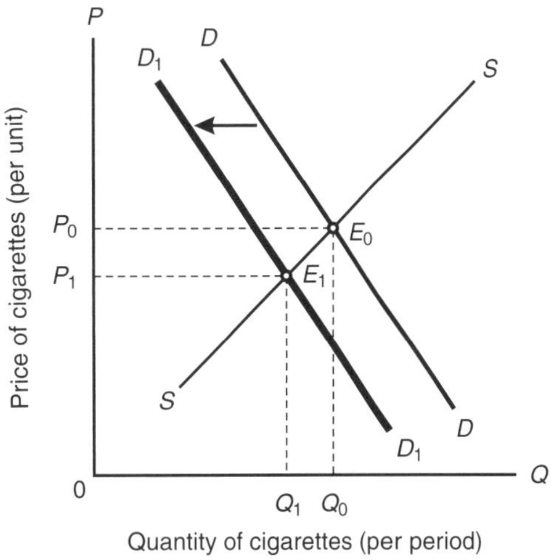

With asymmetric information, DD represents the demand for cigarettes and SS the supply. The equilibrium price is P_0 and the equilibrium quantity Q_0. If the consumers obtain all the available information, demand decreases, illustrated by a leftward shift of the demand curve to D_1D_1. The equilibrium price falls to P_1 and the equilibrium quantity to Q_1. This is the socially efficient equilibrium.

Asymmetric information is also the cause of the **principal-agent problem** which we introduced in Box 11-1. Management often has more information about a firm than the owners (shareholders), doctors have more information than their patients, lawyers have more information than their clients, and so on. In each case the party with the superior knowledge (the agent) can use it to his or her advantage. Doctors, for example, can influence the demand for their services by what they do or do not tell their patients, and the situation is exacerbated if payment occurs through a third party such as a medical aid or insurance scheme.

What can government do to remedy the situation? It can try to remove the differences in information by providing information about certain goods or services or requiring the disclosure of information to shareholders, customers and other interested parties (eg

BOX 16-1 MORAL HAZARD AND ADVERSE SELECTION

Moral hazard and adverse selection are two sources of market failure that arise as a result of asymmetric information.

Moral hazard occurs when one party to a transaction has both the incentive and the ability to shift the cost of its behaviour onto the other party. The classic example is insurance contracts which cause those who are insured against certain risks to take risks that they would have avoided if they had not been insured. In this way the cost of the insured person's behaviour is passed on to the insurance company. This raises social costs and causes an inefficient allocation of resources.

For example, if the contents of a person's house are insured, that person may be less careful about taking precautions against theft than a person who is not insured. Likewise, insured people tend to take risks that they would avoid if they did not have motorcar insurance, health insurance, life insurance, fire insurance, and so on. It has even been argued that the introduction of safety belts in the United States resulted in more accidents since drivers thought they could safely go faster if they wore safety belts. Another example is the person with medical insurance who unnecessarily visits the doctor or dentist because he or she does not have to pay in full for such consultations.

The problem of moral hazard is also related to the principal-agent problem. Suppose you ask an attorney whether you need legal assistance, a doctor whether you require medical treatment or a mechanic whether there is something wrong with your car's engine. In each case you, as the client, face moral hazard, since the service providers all have a financial interest in providing answers that will encourage you to buy their services. Moreover, it is difficult (and costly) for you to find out whether or not their advice is appropriate.

Insurance companies try to deal with moral hazard in various ways, for example by specifying certain precautions that an insured person must take. These include the installation of gear locks, tracking systems, burglar bars or fire extinguishers and the specification of excess payments that insured people have to make when they claim against their policies. Such requirements increase the private costs of the insured and provide them with an incentive to avoid unnecessary risks.

Adverse selection exists when the parties on one side of the market, who have information not known to others, self-select in a way that adversely affects the parties on the other side of the market. In the case of adverse selection, asymmetric information exists prior to an exchange. The classic example again relates to the insurance market, in which people who are most at risk tend to buy the most insurance. People who buy insurance almost always know more about themselves as individual insurance risks than their insurance companies do. Whenever a group of individuals are offered a common insurance rate, they alone tend to know how their own individual risks deviate from the average risk within the group. Those who are more at risk than the average person will tend to purchase insurance, while those who are less at risk than the average person will tend to remain uninsured. For example, elderly people, smokers and those with HIV/Aids or other health problems will be more likely to take out medical or life insurance than younger people, non-smokers and those who are not suffering from HIV/Aids or other health problems.

Insurance companies try to cope with adverse selection by defining a number of different groups according to the characteristics that affect their risk (eg smokers, people who are HIV positive, young drivers, people residing in crime-ridden suburbs or in houses with thatched roofs) and charging each group a different rate, or specifying different excess payments that have to be made when the insured groups claim against their policies.

Adverse selection occurs in other markets as well. A well-known example is the used car market, where adverse selection tends to cause an increase in the supply of bad cars and a decrease in the supply of good cars. The problem arises because the sellers know more about the conditions of the cars than the buyers. The average market price for a given "model-make-year" will be a good price for a bad car but a bad price for a good car. The owners of bad cars will regard the average market price as an excellent price and offer their cars for sale. However, the owners of good cars will regard the average price as being too low and will therefore tend to keep their cars. The socially inefficient outcome is that the supply of bad cars increases while the supply of good cars decreases. As a result, the average quality of used cars falls. To deal with this type of problem, the government can pass legislation to force car dealers to take back defective cars or to offer guarantees on second-hand cars. In the case of insurance markets, government may provide insurance or other services to high-risk groups who cannot obtain or afford insurance at market-related rates. Medical services are also provided free of charge or at low cost to those who cannot afford to join private insurance schemes.

about the hazards associated with smoking), or establishing codes of professional ethics, licensing or certification requirements. Government can also impose standards which consumer products have to meet, or safety standards in the workplace which employers have to adhere to; but it will never be able to eliminate the problem. See also Box 16-1.

Common property resources

Common property resources are those that are non-excludable but rivalrous in consumption – see quadrant II in Table 16-1. Common property resources belong to no one and are available free of charge to anyone who wants to use them. No one can be excluded from using them. But they are rivalrous in consumption. One person's use of the common resource reduces the availability to other persons. Examples of common property resources include the fish in the ocean, other wildlife, rivers and common land.

A common resource will be efficiently exploited if the marginal cost of exploitation is equal to the marginal benefit of exploitation. However, since no one owns the resource, no one can be excluded from using it, and the free market cannot produce an efficient result. Instead, common resources tend to be overexploited, even to the extent of destruction. This is often referred to as the **tragedy of the commons**.

Consider the example of fish in the ocean. No one owns the fish until they are caught, and in a free market no one can be excluded from catching them. But once a fish is caught by someone it is no longer available to others. Moreover, there are no incentives for any individual fisherman (or fishing company) to consider the impact of his (or its) activities on others (eg by limiting the catch or returning undersized fish). In the absence of regulation there will thus be a tendency to overexploit the resource.

A similar problem arises in the case of commonly-owned grazing land (eg in the rural areas of South Africa) or public roads. In each case, the use of the resource is rivalrous: if one cow eats the grass, another cannot; and if one car uses the space on the road another car cannot use the same space at the same time.

Because there are no incentives to limit the use of the common resource, overgrazing and peak-hour traffic jams tend to result. Even the failure of communism is sometimes regarded as the tragedy of the commons (on a grand scale).

The problem with common resources was recognised many years ago by the ancient Greek philosopher, Aristotle, when he stated that: "What is common to many is taken least care of, for all men have greater regard for what is their own than for what they possess in common with others."

Clearly the government has a role to play in protecting or avoiding the overexploitation of common property resources. One possibility is to regulate the use of the resource. For example, in the case of fishing it can issue and charge for fishing licences, declare limited fishing seasons for certain species, restrict numbers that may be caught (by issuing quotas or specifying maximum daily numbers) and specify the minimum size that may be kept. A major problem, however, is the enforcement of the restrictions. A common resource like the ocean is vast and although all the appropriate laws, rules and regulations may be in place, it may prove almost impossible to enforce them. A case in point is the overexploitation of South African marine resources such as abalone *(perlemoen)* and crayfish (rock lobsters).

Similar measures may be instituted to protect other marine resources and wildlife. In the case of congested roads, a toll (ie a user charge) may be levied. Enforcement (including collection costs) is, however, often subject to various practical problems.

Another potential solution to the problem of common property resources is to make them excludable by granting property rights to private owners. For example, common grazing land may be divided and allocated to individual owners. When a common property resource is "privatised" in such a way, it is usually used more efficiently, but those who are excluded in the process lose out. Moreover, many common property resources are so huge that single private ownership is impractical. In such cases public ownership or public regulation of private ownership is usually more realistic. The important point here, as in other cases of market failure, is that **markets cannot function effi-**

ciently if property rights are not well established. In such cases the government has a role to play, either by establishing property rights or by regulating the activities concerned through taxes, subsidies, user charges, laws, rules, regulations and so on.

We have now discussed different cases in which the free market system fails to generate an efficient allocation of resources, thereby providing a rationale for some form of government intervention. But market failure is not the only possible justification for government intervention in the economy. In the next section we discuss other possible reasons for the role of government in the economy.

16.3 Further reasons for government intervention in the economy

The great strength of the market system is its ability to generate reasonably efficient outcomes in a majority of cases through a system of decentralised decision-making in which each individual participant tries to maximise his or her benefit. Not surprisingly, however, markets do not perform well when broader social goals are at stake. Much of the justification for government's role in the economy can be traced to the inability of the market system to achieve such broader goals.

Income distribution

The free market tends to generate an unequal distribution of income. Proponents of free markets claim that the market produces the most efficient allocation of resources and that the problem of income distribution is not an economic one. Income distribution, they argue, is a "political" issue that lies outside the realm of economics. However, any particular market outcome depends on the initial distribution of income. For each income distribution there will be a different "efficient" allocation of resources. Clearly, therefore, there is nothing sacred about any particular allocation of resources. The distribution of income determines the structure of demand and economists cannot simply pretend that it is not an economic issue.

Consider the following example. If the government redistributes income from the wealthy to the poor, the demand for luxury goods (eg expensive cars, gold jewellery and fur coats) will fall and the demand for basic necessities (food, clothing, etc) will rise. The relative prices of these items will change and more necessities and fewer luxuries will be produced. The new market outcome will be as efficient as the initial outcome (prior to the redistribution), but will be the result of the redistribution of income. Clearly, the distribution of income has important economic effects.

Different causes of income inequality were discussed in Chapter 14. An absolutely equal distribution of income is, of course, unattainable in a market-based economic system. In fact, it is undesirable, since it is highly unlikely that everyone will make the same contribution to production (and therefore receive the same remuneration). In a well-functioning economic system there should always be some link between reward (or remuneration) and effort (or contribution to production). Nevertheless, a free market system rewards certain participants and penalises others. Because the workings of the market may be stern, even cruel, society often chooses to intervene in an attempt to produce more socially acceptable income distributions.

By definition, a socially undesirable income distribution is one with which society is unhappy. Government, as the representative of society, must therefore take steps to achieve a more acceptable (or more equitable) distribution. The measures that governments usually take in this regard include progressive income taxation (which means that the greater your income, the greater the percentage tax you pay), free or subsidised provision of certain goods and services (eg primary health care and primary education) to those who can least afford it, cash transfer payments to the needy (eg old-age pensioners and very poor families that have to raise children) and legislation and other forms of regulation (eg labour laws).

As we have mentioned in earlier chapters, the distribution issue can become very emotional. Government has to avoid a situation where certain individuals or groups simply claim a certain income or standard of living irrespective of their input or effort. Such **entitlement** can have disastrous economic implications. Nevertheless, government should recognise that a free market system tends to perpetuate and exacerbate income inequalities. Some form of redistribution is therefore always called for, bearing in mind that factor price differences (and therefore income differences) are an essential part of a dynamic market economy and that the goal of an equitable distribution of income may thus be in conflict with the goal of achieving a more efficient economy. Freemarketeers therefore argue that the best way to reduce inequality is to encourage greater factor mobility (eg through education and training and assisting people to help themselves) rather than to use taxes and transfer payments to simply redistribute income. The solution, they argue, is to create equal opportunities.

Macroeconomic growth and stability

Until now we have dealt mainly with microeconomic justifications for government intervention.

A number of economists argue that the free market system tends to fall short of achieving important macroeconomic objectives such as rapid economic growth, full employment and price stability and that governments have to intervene in an attempt to achieve these objectives. They emphasise that market systems tend to experience **business cycles**, that is, phases of rapid economic growth (called upswings or booms), followed by periods of stagnation or decline (called downswings or recessions).

Other economists disagree and maintain that unfettered market systems tend to produce the best possible results at the macroeconomic level (as well as at the microeconomic level). The debate on the appropriate role of government at the macroeconomic level is an ongoing (and often heated) one. We examine business cycles and the factors that determine economic growth, employment and inflation in Part IV of this book. At this point, however, you need only be aware that governments around the world try to achieve macroeconomic objectives such as economic growth, full employment and price stability by applying macroeconomic policy. **Macroeconomic policy** consists of monetary, fiscal and other policies. **Monetary policy** was introduced in Chapter 15. The major instrument of **fiscal policy** in South Africa is the **budget** presented annually by the Minister of Finance (usually in February). The meaning of fiscal policy and various elements of fiscal policy are explained later in this chapter.

Merit goods

Some goods are excludable but have social benefits (ie positive externalities), with the result that they are often provided by government in addition to, or in place of, private provision of such goods. **Merit goods** can be defined as goods that are regarded as so beneficial to society that everyone should be in a position, irrespective of their incomes, to receive or consume them. Examples include education, health, shelter, fire protection and sports facilities (particularly in poor neighbourhoods). Take education as an example. It is excludable, but society gains in various ways if its members are educated. However, if the provision of education were left to the private sector, many parents would not be able to afford to send their children to school. The higher the level of education, the smaller the social benefit becomes relative to the individual benefit, and therefore the weaker the merit goods argument tends to become. Note that the provision of merit goods to those who would otherwise not have access to such goods amounts to a redistribution of income in favour of the recipients. Also note that a decision to provide merit goods does not imply that government should actually produce the goods – the goods can, for example, be produced by the private sector and financed or subsidised by government.

Just as there are socially beneficial merit goods, there are also **merit bads** or **demerit goods** that are regarded as socially harmful. Examples include tobacco, other addictive drugs and gambling. In these cases governments often take steps to discourage consumption. Since merit goods and bads involve value judgements (by government, as the representative of society), the provision of such goods can be quite controversial. Some observers object, for example, to the paternalistic notion that government knows what is best for society and its members. Their objections are even stronger when government intervenes to protect people from others and, especially, from themselves by discouraging or prohibiting certain activities or products.

Summary

We have now examined various reasons **why** government intervenes in the economy. The role of government in the economy can be summarised by distinguishing between three broad functions of government:

- the **allocative function**, which refers to the role of government in correcting market failure and achieving a more efficient allocation of resources
- the **distributive function**, which refers to the steps taken by government to achieve a more equitable or socially acceptable distribution of income than that generated by market forces
- the **stabilisation function**, which refers to the measures taken by government to promote macroeconomic stability (eg full employment, price stability and balance of payments stability)

16.4 How does government intervene?

Having identified the rationale for government intervention, the next question is about **how** government intervenes. In other words, what instruments can government use to achieve its objectives?

A first option is **public provision** of goods and services (eg of public goods such as national defence, the justice system and infrastructure). This can be achieved by **public ownership** or by **public financing** of production undertaken by the private sector. At the time of writing, for example, the railway system and the largest supplier of electricity (Eskom) were still wholly owned by government. The issue of public versus private ownership is discussed further in Section 16.6, which deals with the often controversial issues of nationalisation and privatisation. In recent years there has also been an increasing tendency for government to finance the provision of public goods by the private sector. Examples include the construction and operation of prisons and hospitals by private firms on behalf of the government. Since 2000 the government has also entered into a number of public private partnerships (PPPs). A PPP is defined as a contractual arrangement whereby a private party performs part of a government function and assumes the associated risks. In return, the private party receives a fee according to predefined performance criteria.

Examples include hospitals, prisons, nature reserves, toll roads and the provision of accommodation to government departments.

A second way in which government can try to achieve its objectives is through its role as a **market participant**. For example, government is the largest employer of labour in the economy and through its wage policy and other employment practices it can try to achieve certain objectives (eg price stability, redistribution of income) and also set an example for other employers to follow. Likewise, government is an important purchaser of goods and services from the private sector and can use its purchasing policy to achieve certain objectives (eg to stimulate particular firms and promote employment).

Thirdly, **government spending** is a powerful tool. Both the level and the composition (or structure) of government spending have a powerful impact on the economy. Government spending is examined further in Section 16.8. Apart from deciding which and what quantity of goods and services to purchase, government also makes **transfer payments**, that is, payments for which it receives nothing in return. Examples include old-age pensions, child support grants, disability grants and various subsidies (eg agricultural subsidies, transport subsidies and export subsidies). Transfer payments are a powerful instrument that can be used to change the distribution of income. At the time of writing, various observers and interest groups were calling for the introduction of a basic income grant (BIG) to be paid to the poorest people in the economy to help alleviate their plight.

A fourth instrument at the disposal of government is **taxation**. Although the primary purpose of taxation is to finance government expenditure, the level and structure of taxation can be used to achieve various objectives. Taxation can be used to redistribute income, to promote certain desirable activities and to penalise other socially undesirable activities. For instance, tax incentives (possibly in the form of lower tax rates or tax holidays) are often provided to stimulate investment spending and small business development, while tobacco products and alcoholic beverages are subject to additional taxes. Taxation can also be used to internalise the social costs of negative externalities such as environmental pollution. Taxation is examined further in Sections 16.10 to 16.12.

A fifth important instrument that government can use to affect economic outcomes is **regulation**. Regulation refers to all laws, rules and regulations that affect private behaviour. Examples include the labour laws (which govern the labour market); competition policy (which governs the goods market); the anti-tobacco law (which regulates smoking in public places); the law prohibiting shops from providing free plastic bags to customers; and the fixing of maximum or minimum prices and minimum wages. Our lives are affected daily (and to an increasing extent) by various laws, rules and regulations. In many cases these regulations are enforced through a system of fines and criminal penalties.

16.5 Government failure

We have now established why government intervenes in the economy and we have identified the main types of government intervention. However, the fact that there are good reasons for government intervention and the fact that government has an array of instruments it can use to achieve its objectives do not imply that government intervention is necessarily successful. On the contrary, governments, like markets, can also fail. In this section we briefly examine some forms of **government failure**.

To understand government failure, one has to examine the nature of government's own objectives. Government is not merely an institution that automatically or mechanically serves the interests of society. Government consists of people (public officials) and while they undoubtedly do attempt to serve society to some extent, public officials are human beings with their own motives, ambitions, objectives and faults. An examination of the role of government thus requires an examination of the behaviour of decision makers in the public sector.

There are two broad groups of public officials: those who are elected (the **politicians**) and those who are appointed (the **bureaucrats** or civil servants). These officials are the agents of the public but, as elsewhere in the economy, the agents do not always serve the interests of the principals (in this case the public). This does not imply that politicians and bureaucrats are inherently less intelligent, less hardworking, less competent or more corrupt than other people. On the contrary, the problems arise because they have virtues, flaws and motives of their own, like all other participants in the economy.

Politicians, for example, may be viewed as vote-maximising agents whose main aim is to be re-elected. They therefore pursue vote-maximising strategies to secure or retain political office. Politicians want to be popular and try to please most of the people most of the time by proposing or supporting a variety of programmes which serve the interests of different groups in society. In other words, politicians tend to "buy" votes, without due consideration of the benefits, costs or consistency of their policies. Because they have to be re-elected every few years, they tend to have a short-term outlook and to favour programmes with immediate, clear-cut benefits and vague or deferred costs. Politicians also tend to support programmes or policies from which a relatively small, but identifiable and articulate, group will receive large gains at the expense of a larger number of people who suffer relatively small losses. In this way they succeed in securing the votes of the beneficiaries without necessarily losing the votes of the others. In addition, politicians tend to be slow to admit mistakes. It is often politically easier to proceed with failed projects than to abandon them. In fact, government often responds to the failure of a programme by allocating more funds and human resources to it. All these actions tend to result in an over-supply of goods and services by government.

Bureaucrats are not necessarily the lazy or incompetent people they are often made out to be. They are rational economic agents who respond to a particular set of incentives and try to maximise their salaries, status, power or prestige. In their attempt to achieve this, they try to maximise the size of their budget allocations and staff complements. The larger their budgets, the larger their departments become and therefore the larger their salaries, the greater the opportunities for promotion and the greater their power or status.

As agents for politicians and the public, bureaucrats are in a powerful position. They are the administrative or technical experts and usually know more about the functioning of government than politicians. Moreover, they have to formulate and implement spending plans. In other words, they are responsible for the supply of goods and services by the government and are often in a position to manipulate this supply to their own advantage. A typical example is the defence establishment, which tends to exaggerate the military threat of potential enemies in an attempt to obtain more funds and better equipment. The behaviour of bureaucrats thus tends to result in an excess supply of goods and services.

One of the basic causes of bureaucratic failure is the fact that governments are usually not subject to competition and are not constrained by a profit-and-loss account (the so-called "bottom line"). Bureaucracies do not face any market test and inefficiencies can persist, first, because it is often almost impossible to gauge the efficiency of a particular service and, second, because it is usually very difficult to dismiss inefficient bureaucrats. Whereas the market creates various incentives and pressures for internal efficiency, few such incentives and pressures exist in government. Bureaucrats tend to be less cost conscious than private sector employers. In fact, they can even try to increase their budget allocations by supplying goods and services more inefficiently (eg by using more inputs to produce a given level of output).[1] As a result of all this, the principal-agent problem is even more difficult to solve in the public sector than in the private sector. Various attempts are made to solve the problem, for example by linking the employment and remuneration of senior bureaucrats to performance criteria, but it is very difficult (sometimes even impossible) to measure the performance of bureaucrats or government institutions.

1. Recall, from Chapter 13, that this type of inefficiency is called X-inefficiency.

Another source of government failure is **rent-seeking**, which refers to attempts by private firms, households, organised business, organised labour and other interest groups to benefit at the expense of society at large. Because government can use the instruments at its disposal to affect the distribution of economic resources, various interest groups attempt to influence government behaviour to their own advantage. In technical terms we say that the interest groups use their political influence to seek economic rents from government, where **economic rent** is that part of the remuneration of the owners of factors of production over and above the payment that the resource would receive in the best possible alternative employment (ie over and above the supply price or opportunity cost of the factor) – see Box 14-3. Economic rent can be the result of favourable regulations, direct subsidies, special tax treatment, profitable contracts, import tariffs or quotas. Farmers lobby government for subsidies, some firms try to secure import tariffs or quotas to limit competition from imports, professions lobby for occupational licensing that will restrict entry to the professions, firms try to obtain special tax allowances, or try to bribe politicians or bureaucrats to secure profitable contracts or monopoly rights, and so on. Special interest groups spend large amounts of resources in their attempts to secure special benefits in these and other ways. Rent-seeking activity thus distorts the allocation of resources in various ways. Apart from giving rise to an unwarranted redistribution of resources in favour of the relevant special interests, the resources employed by the interest groups to influence government behaviour also amount to an inefficient or wasteful use of society's scarce resources.

Rent-seeking poses a difficult problem, since democratic governments tend to respond to special interest groups and are therefore vulnerable to this kind of manipulation. The only way in which it can be limited is by reducing the role of government in the economy and, in particular, the number of instruments (eg laws, rules and regulations) that can potentially be manipulated to serve the interests of particular individuals and groups.

We have now discussed the three primary sources of government failure: the behaviour of vote-maximising politicians, the behaviour of bureaucrats and the rent-seeking behaviour of interest groups. From this discussion it should be clear that the causes of government failure are inherent in government institutions, just as the causes of market failure are rooted in the nature of markets.

If both the market and government can fail, where does this leave us? The important point to recognise is that both are imperfect. When choosing between the market mechanism and government intervention, the choice is not between perfect markets and imperfect governments, or between flawed markets and omniscient, rational and benevolent governments: it is between inevitably imperfect institutions. The fact that both are imperfect often makes it very difficult to determine whether a particular activity can be performed better in the private or the public sector. In the next section we consider a further aspect of this problem, namely the choice between public ownership and private ownership.

16.6 Nationalisation and privatisation

One of the aspects of the role of the public sector that has been debated vigorously in South Africa is the desirability of nationalisation compared with privatisation (ie the desirability of public vs private ownership).

Nationalisation means that the government takes over the ownership or management of private enterprise (with or without compensation). Proponents of nationalisation in South Africa often argue that it was a significant element in the solution of the "poor white" problem, particularly during the 1920s and 1930s. They cite the establishment of a national transport system, a national posts and telecommunications system, Iscor and Sasol as examples of successful nationalisation by the South African government. This is, however, an incorrect interpretation. The establishment of state-owned industries is not the same as nationalisation (ie **the transfer of ownership from private enterprise to government**). During the early stages of a country's economic development, the private capital base is often too small to mobilise sufficient capital for industries that require a large initial capital outlay. Moreover, the time that has to elapse before the initial outlay can be recouped and positive returns earned is often too long for private companies to become interested. As a result, the state has to take the lead in establishing such industries. This is what happened in South Africa in the case of state-controlled firms like Iscor and Sasol. What South Africa experienced was the establishment of state-owned industry, not nationalisation. This type of government intervention was aimed primarily at improving the economic position of whites, rather than that of all South Africans.

For many years nationalisation was a key element of the economic policy of the African National Congress, but it was abandoned in the early 1990s, partly as a result of the dismal failure of eastern European socialism (which may be regarded as nationalisation on a grand scale). Nowadays most observers agree that nationalisation (in the correct sense of the term) is usually an economic failure. While nationalisation may be attractive to certain politicians and groups of voters or workers, who want to increase their power, any advantages that it may have in principle are usually not realised in practice. Instead, nationalisation often results in large bureaucracies, inefficiency and political interference. Where governments own and manage enterprises, the modern trend is towards the privatisation of these enterprises.

Privatisation is the opposite of nationalisation – it refers to **the transfer of ownership of assets from the public sector to the private sector** (ie the sale of state-owned assets to the private sector). The case for privatisation is usually based on three broad arguments. The *first* concerns the problem of financing increasing government expenditure in a situation where tax burdens are already very high. In South Africa, for example, privatisation is regarded as a possible way of obtaining funds that can be used to reduce the public debt and lower personal income tax. The *second* argument is based on the view that government ownership is always less efficient than private ownership. According to this argument the role of the government in the economy should be reduced and more scope should be created for private ownership and private initiative. The *third* is based on the view that the losses of inefficient state-owned enterprises are an important source of budget deficits and other fiscal problems.

Since the early 1980s, many governments around the world have privatised state-owned firms. In the United Kingdom, for example, the Thatcher and Major governments returned most of the previously nationalised industries to the private sector. In the 1990s many Latin American governments followed the same route, and after the collapse of communism and central planning, the formerly socialist eastern European countries (eg Poland, East Germany, Czechoslovakia and Russia) engaged in privatisation on a massive scale. The South African government also embarked on a privatisation drive in the 1980s, when Sasol and Iscor were privatised, but apart from these two large firms, state control of industry was never as pervasive in South Africa as in many other countries (including other African countries). Many of the arguments concerning the relative merits of public and private ownership were therefore not as important in South Africa as elsewhere. Nonetheless, some of the main arguments for and against privatisation (ie in addition to the broad arguments mentioned earlier) should be noted, particularly in view of the ongoing political controversy about privatisation or (as it is often euphemistically termed) the restructuring of state assets.

The arguments for privatisation include the following:

- State-owned enterprises are bureaucratic, inefficient, unresponsive to consumer wishes and often a burden on the taxpayer. They are also characterised by a lack of creativity and innovation by management, poor investment decisions, poor financial control, a lack of accountability to taxpayers and low levels of productivity. Privatisation, it is argued, will eliminate these shortcomings.

- Privatisation will attract foreign direct investment, thereby also augmenting the country's foreign exchange reserves.
- To the extent that public enterprises do not pay tax, privatisation will broaden the tax base (since the privatised enterprises have to pay tax).
- Privatised enterprises will have greater access to investment capital and will be able to adapt more easily to changing economic conditions.
- The proceeds from privatisation will make funds available for spending on housing, education, health, and so on.
- Privatisation will increase share ownership in the economy and serve as an instrument of black economic empowerment.

Arguments against privatisation include the following:

- Privatised firms will not necessarily be exposed to greater competition and be more efficient than state-owned firms. In the extreme case, privatisation may simply entail the replacement of a state monopoly with a private monopoly.
- Whereas state-owned firms are supposed to take account of any possible external costs or benefits, the same does not apply to privately owned firms.
- In contrast to state-owned firms, privately owned firms will not take a broader view of the public interest. For example, the provision of postal services, rail transport, telephone services and electricity to rural areas often entails losses which have to be recouped from (ie cross-subsidised by) the more profitable provision to metropolitan and urban areas. If these services are privatised, the services to the rural areas may be terminated or become more expensive.

In South Africa, the major trade union federations, particularly Cosatu, are vehemently opposed to privatisation. They want the government to stop the process of privatising basic services such as water, sewerage, waste disposal, electricity, transport and telecommunications. In addition, they insist that any other restructuring of state assets or state-run activities be considered only if it will lead to improved service delivery and no job losses, and that any possible action in this regard be negotiated with labour and the broader community.

The main reason why trade unions oppose privatisation is that it tends to lead to job losses. The problem is that state-owned enterprises that are indeed inefficient (as the proponents of privatisation believe) invariably tend to employ more labour than required. When such enterprises are privatised (or restructured in any other way – see below), the number of workers is typically reduced quite substantially.

Several state-owned enterprises have been partially or fully privatised (or restructured) in South Africa in recent years. They include Sasol and Iscor (in the 1980s) and Telkom, Sun Air, the Airports company, certain SABC radio stations, Denel and Aventura (since 1997). When privatisation occurs, it has to be decided how the proceeds from privatisation should be used. Governments may easily be tempted to use the proceeds to finance current government expenditure in the year in which the income is received. However, it would be folly to use a once-off revenue source to finance recurrent expenditure. This would amount to the proverbial selling of the family silver to buy groceries. The proceeds from privatisation should rather be used to reduce public debt or to finance capital expenditure (eg the creation of additional infrastructure). The latter would entail the substitution of one state asset (the privatised asset) by another asset (the infrastructure that is created).

Before leaving the topic of privatisation, it should be noted that the term is often interpreted much more widely than as simply referring to the sale of state assets to the private sector, to also include the following:

- the contracting out of services, such as cleaning services, information technology (IT) services and marketing services, to private firms
- build-operate-own-transfer (BOOT) schemes whereby the government contracts out the construction to a contractor who then operates the facility as its property for a predetermined number of years, after which the ownership reverts back to government (eg toll roads, prisons, schools, hospitals)
- public-private partnerships (PPPs) whereby a private party performs part of a government function and assumes the associated risks in return for a fee that is determined according to predetermined performance criteria
- deregulation
- opening up of state monopolies to greater competition
- reducing public subsidies and introducing or increasing user charges

Apart from privatisation (in the narrow sense) and the other forms of "privatisation" listed above, the restructuring of state assets does not necessarily require a transfer of ownership or private sector involvement. In recent years many state-owned enterprises in South Africa, whose budgets used to be subject to parliamentary approval, have been commercialised or corporatised. **Commercialisation** or **corporatisation** means the transformation of state-owned enterprises into commercial entities, subject to commercial legal requirements and governance structures, while retaining state ownership. In other words, the enterprise remains in the public sector but is run like a private company and is also liable for tax. This is what has happened in recent years at Transnet, Eskom and other state enterprises. In fact, for various reasons privatisation is usually preceded by corporatisation and many of the potential advantages and disadvantages of privatisation already become evident at this stage of restructuring.

Privatisation should not be regarded as a "quick-fix" programme. Instead, the question of whether or not to privatise (in all senses of the word) should be viewed as an ongoing process of choosing between public and private provision of goods and services, based on efficiency and equity considerations.

16.7 Fiscal policy and the budget

Every government purchases goods and services and raises taxes and borrows funds to finance its expenditure. Every government must therefore regularly decide how much to spend, what to spend it on and how to finance its expenditure. It must therefore have a **policy in respect of the level and composition of government spending, taxation and borrowing**. This is called **fiscal policy**. The word "fiscal" is derived from "fiscus", which was the name given to the public treasury of ancient Rome.

The main instrument of fiscal policy is the **budget** and the main policy variables are government spending and taxation. In South Africa the budget is presented to Parliament annually by the Minister of Finance, usually in February. In the budget the Minister outlines government's spending plans for the financial year, which runs from 1 April of the current calendar year to 31 March of the following calendar year, and indicates how government proposes to finance its expenditure. The budget speech is one of the most important events on the economic calendar and always attracts a lot of attention. Once the budget proposals are accepted, government is empowered to spend the funds and to collect taxes and borrow to finance the spending.

The budget is essentially a reflection of **political decisions** about how much to spend, what to spend it on and how to finance the spending. But the size and composition of government spending and the way in which it is financed can have significant effects on important macroeconomic variables such as aggregate production, income and employment and the price level, as well as on the distribution of income. These effects have to be taken into account when the budget is prepared. In fact, the government often uses the budget (or fiscal policy) to stimulate economic growth and employment, redistribute income, control inflation or address balance of payments problems. We examine the links between the fiscal variables (government spending (G) and taxation (T)) and important macroeconomic variables (eg total production or income (Y)) in Part IV of this book. Fiscal policy is often regarded as an effective means of influencing total spending (or the aggregate demand for goods and services) in the economy. It is therefore classified as an instrument of **demand management**, that is, as an instrument that can be used to manage or regulate the total demand for goods and services in the economy.

The other important instrument of demand management is **monetary policy**, which we introduced in Chapter 15. Whereas fiscal policy refers to the use of government spending, taxation and borrowing to affect economic activity, monetary policy entails the manipulation of interest rates. Fiscal policy is controlled directly by the government, while monetary policy is conducted by the central bank. But these policies have to be applied in harmony, otherwise the one may counteract or negate the effects of the other. There is, therefore, usually close liaison between the National Treasury, which is responsible for the execution of fiscal policy, and the South African Reserve Bank, which applies monetary policy in South Africa.

In Section 16.3 we noted that one of the functions of government in a mixed economy is to counteract economic instability (or to promote economic stability). When the economy is in a recession, the tendency is therefore to apply **expansionary** fiscal and monetary policies to stimulate economic activity. As far as fiscal policy is concerned, this usually means that government spending is raised and taxes reduced (or not increased). The difference between government spending and taxation, called the **budget deficit**, will therefore tend to increase. In contrast, when the economy is expanding too rapidly and inflation and balance of payments problems are being experienced, the appropriate response is to apply **restrictive** or **contractionary** fiscal and monetary policies. As far as fiscal policy is concerned, this means that government spending has to be reduced and/or taxes have to be increased. We analyse the impact of expansionary and contractionary (or restrictive) fiscal policies in Part IV, particularly in Chapters 19 and 20.

Whenever fiscal policy measures are considered, certain practical problems have to be taken into account. Some of these are associated with other types of policy as well. One of the basic difficulties associated with attempts to stabilise the economy is the existence of **delays**, or **lags** as they are called by economists. The lags associated with fiscal policy are discussed in Chapter 20.

Although the macroeconomic impact of fiscal policy always generates particular interest, it is important to note that fiscal policy has various sectoral and microeconomic impacts as well. For example, fiscal policy is often used to stimulate the development of a particular sector, region, city or town and it can also be used to achieve outcomes in particular markets (eg by taxing or subsidising certain products or activities).

In the rest of this chapter we take a closer look at some of the main elements of fiscal policy: government spending, the different ways in which government spending can be financed and the economics of taxation.

16.8 Government spending

In Part I of this book we indicated that government spending (*G*) is an important component of total spending in the economy. In this section we examine the trend of government spending in South Africa. We also show how the composition of government spending has changed in recent years. The way in which government spending affects the economy is examined in Part IV.

The government's involvement in economic activity is often measured by the share of government spending in total spending in the economy.[2] Government spending can be classified economically or functionally. Economically, we can distinguish between consumption spending and investment spending. Table 16-2 shows two measures of government spending in South Africa: final consumption expenditure by general government and total expenditure (ie consumption plus investment) by general government, both expressed as a percentage of gross domestic expenditure (GDE). From the table it is obvious that the share of government spending in total spending increased significantly in the 1970s and 1980s. Most observers were perturbed by this trend, particularly in view of the difficulties experienced in financing the growth in government expenditure and the implications for the growth of the private sector. Fortunately, the share of final consumption expenditure by general government in total spending stabilised in the 1990s and remained steady in the first years of the new millennium.

The growth in government spending during the postwar period is not unique to South Africa. Most other countries have had a similar experience. There are a number of possible explanations for this trend. Viewed in isolation, none of these explanations is sufficient, but together they provide a plausible account of what happened in South Africa.

- **Changing consumer preferences**. A first possible explanation is that income growth is accompanied by a proportionally greater growth in the demand for public goods and services. As their income rises, households tend to spend more of their additional income on services than on goods. In other words, the income elasticity of the demand for services is greater than one, and since some of these services are provided by government, government spending rises in proportion to total income and expenditure.

2. It is important to note, however, that the share of government spending in total spending is not necessarily a good indicator of the role of government in the economy. As we showed in Section 16.4, government intervenes in the economy in various ways and not all forms of intervention (eg regulation) are reflected in government spending.

TABLE 16-2 Government spending in South Africa as a percentage of gross domestic expenditure, 1960–2006

Year	*Final consumption expenditure by general government (% of GDE)*	*Total spending by general government (% of GDE)*
1960	9,8	12,7
1970	11,7	15,8
1980	14,5	17,6
1990	20,3	22,6
2000	19,3	21,6
2006	18,8	21,6

Source: South African Reserve Bank, *Quarterly Bulletin*, various issues

- **Political and other shocks**. Severe political or other shocks (eg wars) are important causes of increased government spending. For example, in the 1970s and 1980s, South Africa's involvement in wars in Namibia, Angola and Mozambique caused sharp increases in our defence expenditure. Similarly, the growing domestic unrest and attempts to appease the disenfranchised gave rise to increases in spending on law and order, education and other services. The imposition of sanctions against South Africa resulted in massive spending on the local manufacture of arms, synthetic fuel and natural gas by government or semi-government agencies such as Armscor, Sasol and Mossgas. In principle, government spending ought to fall once the shock or the threat to the country diminishes or disappears. In practice, however, the level and trend of government spending tend to be unaffected. At best there is a change in the composition of government spending, for example away from defence to social services such as education, health and housing.
- **Redistribution of income**. In a democratic society in which the majority of the population have relatively low incomes, income redistribution tends to be an important explanation of the growth of the public sector. In developing countries the low-income groups are numerous and often politically powerful, for they will determine who wins the next democratic election. They therefore use the political process to redistribute income from the high-income groups to themselves. In South Africa political democratisation shifted the balance of power towards the lower-income groups, and accordingly much more attention is being given nowadays to

redistribution measures than in the past. The primary focus is on social spending, aimed at improving the living conditions of the poor and the previously disenfranchised members of South African society. However, using government spending to redistribute income is not a new phenomenon in South Africa, nor is it unique to this country. In previous years, for example, the Nationalist government devoted much of its spending to the upliftment of Afrikaners, often at the expense of other South Africans.

- **Misconceptions and entitlement.** Society often has certain misconceptions about the financial and administrative capacity of the public sector. For example, many people do not realise the true cost of public services – some even think that they are free (in an absolute sense). Some people overestimate the government's capacity to deliver certain goods and services like housing, education, electricity and health services. This can result in excessive demands on government. People often feel entitled to a certain volume or standard of services, irrespective of whether these services are affordable or can be provided, given the lack of funds and the scarcity of factors of production. The fact that such demands are made is quite understandable. The crucial question is how government (ie the politicians and the bureaucrats) reacts to such entitlement. If government succumbs to popular demands, government spending will rapidly grow out of control.
- **Population growth and urbanisation.** Rapid population growth in South Africa has resulted in large increases in the demand for public goods and services like education and health services. This has been exacerbated by the rapid rate of urbanisation in recent years. As people have flocked to the cities, increased pressure has been put on government spending, particularly in areas such as infrastructure (roads, sewerage, electricity, etc), housing and the maintenance of law and order. The high incidence of HIV/Aids also contributes in various ways to rising government expenditure.

Apart from the overall growth in government spending, the **composition** of government spending has also changed significantly. Changes in the **functional** composition of government spending reflect changing economic and social conditions and changes in the priorities of the government. Table 16-3 indicates how the functional composition of government spending in South Africa changed between the 1990/91 and 2006/07 financial years.

Note, in particular, the decline in the share of defence spending and the increase in the share of spending on social services. Also note the high level of spending on interest on the public debt. In fact, the share of this item had been much higher (eg 19,1 per cent in 2000/01) but subsequently fell as a result of lower interest rates and a decline in the size of the public debt – see also Table 16-4.

TABLE 16-3 Functional composition of budget expenditure 1990/91 and 2006/7

Function	*Percentage of total expenditure*	
	1990/91	*2006/7*
General services	8,4	5,9
Protection services (total)	21,8	15,7
– Defence	13,7	5,4
– Police	5,6	6,9
Social services (total)	41,3	53,6
– Education	20,9	19,2
– Health	10,1	11,0
Economic services	13,7	14,2
Interest on public debt	14,8	10,6

Source: National Treasury, *Budget review*, 1995, 2007

16.9 Financing of government expenditure

Government spending has to be financed in one way or another. There are basically three ways of financing government spending: **income from property, taxes** and **borrowing.**

Government has certain property which yields income. **Income from property** includes the interest and dividend income that is derived from government's full or partial ownership of enterprises such as Eskom, Telkom and Transnet, profit earned from government production and the sale of agricultural, forestry and fishing products, rent (for example in the form of mining rights), and other license fees and user charges. But income from property is a relatively insignificant source of revenue. The main source of revenue is taxation, which we discuss in the next section.

But taxation is not sufficient to finance all government spending. **The difference between government spending and current revenue is called the budget deficit.** This deficit is financed by **borrowing.** The government can borrow money in the domestic and international capital markets or it can borrow from the central bank. Government borrows in the capital market by issuing government stock (ie bonds) on which it has to pay interest. The alternative is to borrow from the central bank by using, as it were, its overdraft facilities. This type of financing increases the money supply and is potentially inflationary. It is therefore called **inflationary financing** and is avoided as far as possible.

Government borrowing increases the **public debt**. In the early 1990s South African **budget deficits** were particularly high and large amounts had to be borrowed. As a result, the **public debt** grew significantly. This, in turn, led to substantial increases in the **interest on public debt**. Like any other borrower, government has to pay interest on all borrowed funds, and as its debt increases, its interest burden also increases.

The recent trends in these three interrelated variables (the budget deficit, the public debt and the interest on public debt) are shown in Table 16-4. In 1975 the interest on public debt represented a mere 8,3 per cent of current spending by general government. By 1995 this had reached 20,0 per cent. An increase in the interest burden means that a smaller proportion of government spending is available for social upliftment and other priorities. Viewed from another angle, a rising interest burden implies a higher tax burden than would otherwise have been necessary. Government borrowing places a burden on future generations who have to pay the interest and repay the debt. This explains the remark made by the American president, Herbert Hoover: "Blessed are the young, for they shall inherit the national debt." Fortunately, the share of interest payments in government spending declined significantly in the new millennium due to lower budget deficits, a lower government debt and lower interest rates.

In the 1980s and 1990s the budget deficit was always larger than the government's investment spending. This meant that the government was actually borrowing funds to finance part of its current expenditure (including the interest on public debt). Borrowing can still be justified if it is used to finance capital expenditure, which is expected to yield a return over a number of years. But borrowing to finance current expenditure cannot be justified on economic grounds, as it means that future generations will have to pay for the consumption enjoyed by the current generation. In 2006, the situation was reversed, when saving by general government became positive again, for the first time since 1983.

16.10 Taxation

Taxes are compulsory payments to government and are the largest source of government revenue. In 2006 taxes constituted 97,8 per cent of total budget revenue.

Taxation is one of the most emotional of all economic issues. People do not like paying taxes and every taxpayer feels that he or she is bearing the brunt of the overall tax burden. Sir Thomas White once said: "In such experience as I have had with taxation – and it has been considerable – there is only one tax that is popular, and that is the tax on the other fellow." When tax burdens are increasing, as was the case in South Africa in the 1980s and 1990s, taxation is a particularly sensitive social and political issue. In 1991, for example, Cosatu and other organisations launched a massive protest against the government for its decision to implement a broadly-based value-added tax (VAT).

Criteria for a good tax

Winston Churchill once said that there is no such thing as a good tax. J-B Say, the French economist who also formulated Say's law (see Chapters 2 and

TABLE 16-4 Budget deficits, public debt and interest on public debt in South Africa, 1997–2006

Year ended 31 March	*Budget deficit as percentage of GDP (%)*	*Public debt (at end of year) as percentage of GDP (%)*	*Interest on public debt as percentage of current expenditure of general government (%)*
1997	5,0	48,9	19,8
1998	3,7	48,1	20,7
1999	2,8	50,2	20,6
2000	2,2	47,7	19,8
2001	1,9	45,3	18,9
2002	1,4	38,9	17,1
2003	1,1	39,6	14,8
2004	2,3	37,1	13,4
2005	1,5	36,6	12,7
2006	0,4	33,3	11,7

Note: The figures in the last column relate to calendar years.
Source: South African Reserve Bank, *Quarterly Bulletin*, various issues

20), was somewhat less outspoken. In 1814 he wrote that "the best of all taxes is that which is least in amount." Few people would disagree with this statement.

Taxes do, however, have to be levied and paid and even if it is agreed that they should be as low as possible, choices still have to be made between various possible taxes and the respective contributions they are intended to make to government revenue.

Centuries ago, Adam Smith laid down four **canons** (or criteria) **of taxation**. A good tax, said Smith, should be equitable, economical, convenient and certain. These canons are still valid. Along the same lines we distinguish three slightly more modern criteria for a good tax: neutrality, equity and administrative simplicity.

■ NEUTRALITY

In a market-based economic system the economic problem is largely solved by the market mechanism. Market prices play a key role in determining what should be produced and how and for whom it should be produced. But taxes affect prices and therefore also the decisions of the various participants in the economy. They can therefore **distort** the allocation of resources and lower the welfare of society. Taxation can also act as a **disincentive** to the owners of the factors of production. For example, workers might decide to work less if they are taxed at high marginal rates of personal income tax.

These costs of taxation – economists refer to them as the excess burden or deadweight loss of taxation – have to be kept as low as possible. This is usually achieved through taxes which do not induce taxpayers to change their behaviour. Taxation should have the minimum possible effect on **relative prices**, which are the signals on which the various market participants base their decisions. They should therefore be as **neutral** as possible.

The case for neutral taxes is based on the assumption that the market mechanism is functioning effectively. However, as we saw earlier, in the case of market failure (eg because of externalities) there is a strong case for introducing taxes specifically aimed at compensating for the failure of the market to provide an efficient allocation of resources.

■ EQUITY

The tax burden should be spread as fairly as possible among the various taxpayers. If a tax system is generally perceived to be equitable, taxpayers might be quite willing to pay high taxes. But if it is perceived to be inequitable, the willingness to pay taxes might be undermined. But what is an equitable or fair tax system? Who should pay tax and who should pay the most tax?

Two principles can be used to answer these questions: the ability to pay principle and the benefit principle. As its name implies, the **ability to pay principle** means that people should pay according to their ability. For example, in the case of an income tax the ability to pay is determined by the level of income. There are two notions of equity in this regard: horizontal equity and vertical equity. **Horizontal equity** requires that people in the same position (ie two taxpayers who have the same income) should be taxed equally. **Vertical equity** requires that people in different positions should be taxed differently. Rich people should therefore pay more tax than poor people.

According to the **benefit principle,** the recipients of the benefits generated by a particular government expenditure should pay for the goods or services concerned. In this case taxation can therefore be viewed as a charge or levy that has to be paid for goods and services provided by government – the more you receive, the more you have to pay. As mentioned in the previous section, benefit taxes are usually called **user charges**. They can be levied where exclusion is possible (see Section 16.2). Examples include toll roads, parks, library services, hospital services, the provision of electricity and water and university education. In the case of public goods, however, exclusion is impossible and it is therefore also impossible to allocate the benefits of government services (eg defence, justice, law and order) among those who receive them. Even where the benefits can be estimated, services such as education or health services are often provided to the poor free of charge specifically because they cannot afford them (and the services have positive externalities).

Equity is always a contentious issue. This matter is complicated further by the fact that we often do not know who actually bears the burden of a tax. Part or all of the burden can sometimes be shifted to other participants in the economy – see Section 16.12.

■ ADMINISTRATIVE SIMPLICITY

Taxes are a cost to taxpayers. In addition to the tax payments that they have to make, taxpayers have to keep records and complete tax returns or pay accountants to do it for them. These costs are called **compliance costs**. Government also has to employ people to write tax laws, design tax forms, collect taxes and assess tax returns. These costs are called **administration costs**. A good tax (or tax system) is one that keeps the compliance and administration costs as low as possible. Taxes must therefore be simple. Complicated taxes entail high compliance and administration costs and also present taxpayers with a variety of tax loopholes. The practice of exploiting these loopholes is called **tax avoidance**. This is quite legal but it lowers the government's tax revenue. It can also create frustration among those taxpayers (like ordinary salaried workers) who are not in a position to avoid tax. Tax avoidance should be distinguished from **tax evasion**, which occurs when people do not pay the taxes that they are supposed to pay. For example, when someone makes shirts, sells them at a flea market and does not declare the profit as income, the person is evading tax. Tax evasion is illegal.

Different types of tax

■ DIRECT AND INDIRECT TAXES

Taxes are classified into two major categories: direct and indirect taxes. **Direct taxes** (also called taxes on income and wealth) are levied on *persons*, more specifically the income or wealth of individuals and organisations such as companies. They include personal income tax, company tax and estate duty. **Indirect taxes** (also called taxes on goods and services or taxes on products and production) are levied on *transactions* (eg the purchase of goods and services) and are usually paid by those who consume the goods and services in question. Examples include VAT, customs duties and excise duties.

■ GENERAL TAXES AND SELECTIVE TAXES

VAT is a **general tax** since it is levied on most goods and services. Excisc duties are **selective taxes** which are levied on specific goods only. In South Africa, excise duty is levied on tobacco and alcohol (these duties are commonly referred to as "sin taxes"), fuel and a few luxury goods.

■ PROGRESSIVE, PROPORTIONAL AND REGRESSIVE TAXES

The distinction between progressive, proportional and regressive taxes is based on the ratio of tax paid to taxable income (ie the average tax rate).

- A tax is **progressive** when the ratio of tax paid to taxable income increases as taxable income increases. In other words, a progressive tax means that people with high incomes pay a larger *percentage* of their income in tax than people with low incomes. As we explain later, personal income tax in South Africa is an example of a progressive tax.
- A tax is **proportional** if the ratio of tax paid to taxable income is the same at all levels of income. In other words, the average tax rate is the same for all taxpayers. The basic company tax in South Africa is an example of a proportional tax because it is levied as a fixed percentage of company profits.
- A tax is **regressive** if the ratio between tax paid and taxable income decreases as taxable income increases (or rises as taxable income falls). In other words, a regressive tax takes a larger percentage of the income of low-income individuals and groups than of those with higher incomes. Indirect taxes (eg VAT) are often regressive.

16.11 Taxation in South Africa

The contributions of the different types of tax

The major sources of tax revenue in South Africa in the 1980/81, 1990/91, 1998/99 and 2006/07 financial years are indicated in Table 16-5. Although 1980/81 was an abnormal year in which the gold price was very high and the South African economy grew rapidly, the trends shown in Table 16-5 are nevertheless significant.

Table 16-5 points to a number of important changes in the composition of South African tax revenue in recent decades. The share of personal income tax more than doubled between 1980/81 and 1998/99 but subsequently declined significantly as personal income tax rates were lowered in the new millennium. The share of GST/VAT also rose sharply in the 1980s. As a result, personal income tax and VAT together constituted more than 60 per cent of total tax revenue at the start of the new millennium. The contribution of company tax fell sharply in the 1980s and 1990s but a significant improvement in the efficiency and effectiveness of tax collection in the present century, along with sharp increases in profits, resulted in a strong increase in the relative contribution of this type of taxation, despite cuts in the nominal rates of taxation on companies. In earlier years, gold mines contributed significantly to tax revenue, although not nearly as much as in the exceptional 1980/81 financial year. By the 1990s, however, the contribution of gold mines had become almost negligible. Excise duties are still a significant source of tax revenue, although the fuel levies (which cannot all be classified as excise taxes) nowadays account for more than half of the figure shown in the table.

We now discuss the three main taxes: personal income tax, company tax and VAT.

Personal income tax

Personal income tax is the most important form of direct taxation in South Africa and also the most important single source of tax revenue, despite the decline in the relative contribution of this type of tax in the new millennium. These facts are clearly illustrated in Table 16-5. Small wonder that personal income tax is such a controversial issue.

Personal income tax is levied on individuals' **taxable income**. Taxable income is the legal **tax base** and is obtained by deducting personal and other allowances from an individual's total income. Tax tables are then used to determine how much tax should be paid. The tax tables consist of a number of tax brackets. For each bracket there is a minimum amount of tax and a tax rate that is applied to each rand by which taxable income exceeds the starting point of the bracket. This rate is called the **marginal tax rate**. The marginal tax rate is thus the rate at

TABLE 16-5 Percentage contribution of certain taxes to total tax revenue, selected financial years

Type of tax	Percentage contribution			
	1980/81	1990/91	1998/99	2006/07
Direct taxes				
Personal income tax	18,7	33,6	42,1	28,4
Company tax (excluding gold mines)	22,8	19,7	13,1	26,6[1]
Gold mines	23,6	0,9	0,1	n/a[2]
Indirect taxes				
GST/VAT[3]	14,1	25,4	23,8	27,5
Customs duties	6,2	3,5	3,2	4,8
Excise duties (including fuel levies)	10,7	10,4	12,0	8,0

Notes: 1. Includes tax on gold mines.
2. Not available.
3. VAT was introduced in the 1991/92 financial year. It replaced the earlier general sales tax (GST).

Source: National Treasury, *Budget review*, 1995, 2003, 2007

which each **additional** rand of income is taxed. The **average tax rate** is the ratio between the amount of tax paid and taxable income. The average tax rate is also called the **effective tax rate**.

Table 16-6 shows the tax table for individuals in the 2007/08 financial year. The first column shows the tax brackets, while the second column shows the basic amount payable in each bracket. The third column shows the marginal tax rate in each bracket, and the last column indicates the lowest average tax rate in each bracket. From this table, you can calculate, for example, that a taxpayer who earned a taxable income of R200 000 in the 2007/08 tax year had to pay income tax amounting to R37 125 plus 30 per cent of R20 000 (ie R200 000 – R180 000). The total amount payable is thus R37 125 + 0,3 (R20 000) = R37 125 + R6 000 = R43 125. This implies an average tax rate of (R43 125 ÷ R200 000) × 100 per cent = 21,6 per cent.

From Table 16-6 it is obvious that **personal income tax** in South Africa is a **progressive tax**. As taxable income increases, the proportion of taxable income that is paid in taxes increases. In other words, the average tax rate increases as income increases. Why does the average tax rate increase? It increases because the marginal tax rate increases. If each successive rand (or income interval) is taxed at a higher rate than the previous one, the average tax rate must increase.

One of the features of tax policy in South Africa in recent years was the reduction in the number of income brackets. In 1990/91, for example, there were still 15 income brackets. As shown in Table 16-6, this number had been reduced to six by 2007/08. Along with the reduction in the income brackets, the top marginal rate of taxation was also reduced from 44 per cent to 40 per cent. The combined effect of these measures was a sharp **reduction in the progressivity** of the personal income tax. One of the purposes of

TABLE 16-6 Personal income tax rates in South Africa, 2007/08

Taxable income bracket (R)	Basic amount (R)	Marginal rate (%)	Lowest average rate in each bracket (%)
0–112 500	0	18	–
112 501–180 000	20 250	25	18,0
180 001–250 000	37 125	30	20,6
250 001–350 000	58 125	35	23,2
350 001–450 000	93 125	38	26,6
450 001 and above	131 125	40	29,1

Notes: Marginal rates apply to amounts exceeding the starting point of the respective brackets. Figures do not include the primary rebate.

Source: National Treasury

the reduction in progressivity was to reduce the effect of inflation on a progressive income tax, also known as **bracket creep**. This phenomenon is discussed in Chapter 21. Along with the reduction in brackets and marginal tax rates, however, the personal income tax **base** was **broadened** significantly, for example, by taxing certain fringe benefits that were previously partially or wholly excluded from the definition of taxable income, and capital gains.

Capital gains tax (CGT), introduced in the 2001/2002 financial year, is not a separate tax. It only extends the definition of taxable income to capital gains, that is, gains resulting from the sale of assets such as shares and fixed property. To compensate for the fact that at least part of such gains may merely be **nominal** gains (as a result of inflation) and not **real** gains, only a portion (25 per cent in 2007/08) of capital gains above a certain limit (R15 000 in 2007/08) is taxable.

CGT was introduced primarily to protect the integrity of the personal income tax base and to ensure horizontal equity. If capital gains are not taxed (as was the case in South Africa prior to 2001), taxpayers have an incentive to convert income into capital gains in order to avoid taxation. Moreover, if two persons have the same net additions to wealth, but part of the first person's earnings is in the form of capital gains while the second person earns a salary only, they have the same ability to pay but are taxed differently in the absence of CGT. However, although CGT is a good tax in principle, it does not generate large amounts of tax revenue and is also difficult and costly to administer, for taxpayers and tax authorities alike.

Company tax

Companies are separate legal entities and are taxed independently from their shareholders and other individuals. In the case of companies the calculation of taxable income (ie the tax base) is quite complicated. This is because the calculation of company profits, on which company tax is levied, requires specialist knowledge of accounting techniques and tax law. Once the taxable income has been established, the calculation of the tax liability is quite simple, since all profits are taxed at a uniform rate. The company tax rate is thus an example of a **proportional** tax rate. In the 2007/08 financial year companies were subject to a basic tax rate of 29 per cent. Recall that in the case of a proportional tax the average tax rate is equal to the marginal tax rate (both equal to 29 per cent in this case). However, in addition to the basic rate, a secondary tax on companies (STC) was introduced in 1993. STC is levied on all profits distributed to shareholders in the form of dividends. From 1 October 2007 the rate was 10,0 per cent, but it was scheduled to be phased out completely in a few years and to be replaced by a tax on dividends.

As Table 16-5 shows, the contribution of company tax to total tax revenue declined significantly in the 1980s and 1990s. However, since then there has been a sharp increase. This can be ascribed to the broadening of the tax base (eg by eliminating various allowances that reduced taxable profit) and by a significant improvement in tax collection. The contribution of company tax also depends significantly, of course, on general economic conditions. The better the performance of the economy, the higher the company profits and therefore the greater the contribution of company tax.

Value-added tax (VAT)

On 30 September 1991 value-added tax (VAT) replaced the previous general sales tax (GST), which had been introduced on 1 July 1978. Like its predecessor, VAT is by far the most important source of indirect tax in South Africa (see Table 16-5). It is second only to personal income tax (a direct tax) as a source of tax revenue in South Africa. VAT is based on the concept of value added that we introduced originally in our discussion of the production method of calculating GDP (see Chapter 4). The working of VAT is explained in Box 16-2.

VAT is an important and effective source of revenue for government but it is a **regressive** tax. Politically it is therefore difficult for government to increase VAT, particularly in a country like South Africa, which has a vast number of poor households.

Most goods and services are taxed at the same standard rate (14 per cent in South Africa in 2007). However, since low-income consumers spend a greater proportion of their income on goods which carry VAT than high-income consumers (who save part of their income), the ratio between tax paid and income is greater for low-income households than for high-income households. In other words, the tax burden increases as income decreases (or falls as income rises). In South Africa the regressiveness of VAT has been reduced to a certain extent by taxing certain basic foodstuffs (eg brown bread, maize meal, fruit and vegetables) at a zero rate.

In 1994 a commission of inquiry into certain aspects of the tax structure (the Katz Commission) estimated that very poor households paid 8,8 per cent of their income as VAT, whereas high-income families paid only 6,6 per cent. The absolute amounts paid by high-income families are, however, far greater than the absolute amounts paid by poor households. Moreover, poor households do not pay personal income tax.

The rise in the overall tax burden

In Table 16-2 we showed how government spending in South Africa increased from 1960 onwards. This increase was accompanied by an increase in taxes. Table 16-7 indicates how the overall tax burden and

BOX 16-2 HOW VALUE-ADDED TAX WORKS

One of the main advantages of value-added tax is that it is based on a simple set of principles, according to which the tax is **collected** at different points in the production and distribution chains. Firms pay VAT on all their taxable inputs and then charge VAT on all their outputs. The amount paid over to the South African Revenue Service is simply the difference between the amount collected from the customers and the amount paid to the suppliers of inputs. The final consumer pays the tax.

Consider the following example: A shopkeeper purchases taxable inputs to the value of R100 000 (excluding VAT) and pays VAT at 14 per cent, that is, R14 000. This R14 000 is paid over to the Receiver of Revenue by the firms that supplied inputs to the shopkeeper. The shopkeeper's total outlay is thus R114 000. The shopkeeper adds 10 per cent to the cost of the inputs (excluding VAT) and sells the goods to consumers for R110 000 plus VAT, that is, R110 000 + (14 per cent of R110 000) = R110 000 + R15 400 = R125 400. The shopkeeper only pays R1 400 to the Receiver of Revenue, that is, the R15 400 received minus the R14 000 paid.

From Chapter 4 we know that the shopkeeper's value added is the difference between R110 000 and R100 000, that is, R10 000. The R1 400 paid over by the shopkeeper is exactly equal to 14 per cent of his value added. By paying over the difference between the VAT he paid and the VAT he receives, the shopkeeper is in effect paying on his value added. Note, however, that the shopkeeper does not actually pay VAT. He pays over only the difference between what he collected and what he paid. Finally, all VAT is paid by the purchasers of the final goods and services. From the consumer's point of view, a VAT of 14 per cent is thus exactly the same as a 14 per cent sales tax levied at the till.

the personal income tax burden increased in South Africa during the same period. Note that tax revenue as a percentage of GDP continued to increase after the growth in government spending had been arrested. This was due, *inter alia*, to improved tax collection, particularly in respect of company tax. The high and often rising share of tax revenue in GDP has frequently been a major cause for concern. Taxpayers are concerned about the fact that they are paying an ever-increasing share of their income to government in the form of taxes. Economists and business people are concerned about the large and often increasing share of government in the economy. They point out that government is **crowding out** the private sector, which is the ultimate source of sustainable growth and development.

TABLE 16-7 Taxation in South Africa, 1960–2006

Year	*Tax revenue as % of GDP*	*Personal income tax as % of current income of households*
1960	14,6	5,4
1965	16,1	6,7
1970	18,2	6,5
1975	19,2	8,2
1980	19,7	6,3
1985	24,2	11,3
1990	26,1	12,8
1995	24,1	13,0
2000	26,3	14,9
2006	29,1	11,9

Note: The first column indicates the tax revenue of general government.
Source: South African Reserve Bank, *Quarterly Bulletin*, various issues

Concern about taxes has given rise to many committees and commissions of inquiry to investigate the level and structure of taxation in South Africa. The only real solution, however, is to arrest the growth of government spending and to reduce it in real terms. Only then will the government be able to lower taxes across the board.

16.12 Tax incidence: who really pays the taxes?

Most people believe that the individuals, companies or other entities that pay the taxes over to the South African Revenue Service actually bear the burden of the taxes concerned. This is sometimes called the fly-paper theory of taxation – the burden of any tax sticks where the government puts it. Governments also act as if they determine the actual tax burden. Those who write the tax laws spend much time and effort in devising complex systems which, they believe, will determine precisely who pays the tax.

Governments can specify who has to hand over the money to them. In technical terms we say that government can determine the **statutory** or **legal incidence** of the different taxes. But governments cannot determine who will ultimately bear the burden of the taxes. This is because the economic system is an interdependent system and because taxes change decisions. No one wants to pay taxes. Everyone will therefore try to shift the tax forward or backward to someone else. But the individual households and firms cannot determine what will happen. When a tax is introduced or raised, it changes relative prices and affects the decisions of households and firms. Once all the direct and indirect effects of taxation on supply, demand, prices and quantities have been taken into account, the final tax burden can be very different from the apparent effects. In technical terms we say that the **effective incidence** can be quite different from the **statutory incidence**. **The effective incidence or burden of a tax cannot be established by determining who actually hands over the money to the government**.

A common mistake in reasoning about the burden of taxation is to assume that company tax is paid by companies. The distribution of the tax burden between individuals and companies is frequently the subject of heated debate. Politicians, voters and commentators often argue that companies must pay their fair share of taxes. This creates the impression that taxes on individuals can be lowered if companies pay more. Companies, however, are legal entities owned by individuals. **All taxes are paid by individuals**. Shifting the statutory tax burden from individuals to companies simply changes the group of individuals in the economy that bears the burden of the tax. The government cannot shift the tax from an individual to some other entity in the economy – such a shift is simply impossible. In the case of taxes on companies there are three groups who can potentially bear the burden of the tax – the owners or shareholders of the company, the workers employed by the company or the consumers. Companies will always try to shift the burden of the tax (away from their shareholders and employees) to their consumers by increasing the prices of the goods and services which they produce. The extent to which they can do this is, however, limited by the structure of the relevant market and the features of the demand and supply of the goods concerned.

We now analyse the effects of the imposition of a specific excise tax to illustrate the points we have raised.

The impact of a specific excise tax

There are two types of excise taxes: a **specific** excise tax is a fixed amount that is levied on each unit of the product and an **ad valorem** excise tax is a tax that is levied as a percentage of the value of the product. (VAT, for example, is also an **ad valorem** indirect tax.) To keep matters simple, we examine only a specific excise tax. The basic principles, however, apply to both types of excise tax.

Suppose cigarettes cost R12,00 a packet in the absence of any excise tax or duty on cigarettes and that the government then imposes a specific tax of R4,00 per packet. This tax has to be paid by the manufacturers on each packet of cigarettes that they produce. Who will bear the burden of the tax? Will cigarette smokers end up paying the tax or will it be borne by the manufacturers of cigarettes? The manufacturers will attempt to pass on the tax to the consumers. But the extent to which they are able to do so depends on the price elasticity of the demand and supply of cigarettes.

In Figure 16-3, the demand curve *(DD)* and the supply curve *(SS)* for cigarettes represent the position before the introduction of the tax. The equilibrium price is R12,00 and the quantity exchanged is 150 000 packets per week. When the tax is levied, the suppliers add R4,00 to the price at each level of production. For example, to receive R12,00 per packet, they plan to charge R16,00 since R4,00 has to be paid to government in the form of tax. This difference applies to each and every quantity. The supply curve will thus shift up by R4,00 at each level of production. The new supply curve, after the imposition of the tax, is S_TS_T. We now compare the original equilibrium at E with the new equilibrium at E_1. The new equilibrium price (R14,40) is higher than before but the equilibrium quantity (120 000) is lower. The amount per packet received by the suppliers is also lower than before. The price to the consumer (R14,40) is higher, but the suppliers have to pay R4,00 to the government, which means that they are left with only R10,40 per packet. This is indicated by point E_2 in the figure. The tax per packet is the difference between E_1 and E_2. The suppliers have not succeeded in passing the full tax on to the consumers. They also have to pay part of the tax (R12,00 – R10,40 = R1,60 per packet), not because they want to, but because the forces of demand and supply give them no alternative.

The burden of the excise tax is actually shared by three groups:

- the **consumers of cigarettes**, who have to pay more for each packet of cigarettes
- the suppliers, who receive less for each packet of cigarettes – this means that the profits of the **owners or shareholders of the cigarette companies** are lower than before
- the **employees of the cigarette companies** – since the production of cigarettes has fallen, there will be fewer jobs available in the cigarette industry (alternatively, the existing employees will have to accept wage cuts which will shift the supply curve to the right)

FIGURE 16-3 The incidence of an excise tax on cigarettes

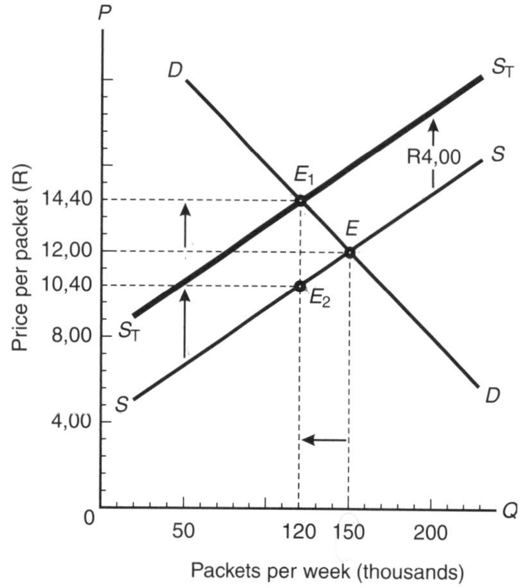

SS is the supply curve before the imposition of the tax of R4,00 per packet of cigarettes. DD is the demand curve. The original equilibrium price is R12,00 per packet and the equilibrium quantity is 150 000 packets per week. After the imposition of the tax, the supply curve shifts up by R4,00 to S_TS_T. The new equilibrium is indicated by E_1. The equilibrium price is R14,40 per packet and the equilibrium quantity is 120 000 packets per week. The suppliers receive the selling price less the tax, that is, R10,40 per packet. This is indicated by E_2 on the original supply curve. The difference between E_1 and E_2 is the tax. The consumers pay R2,40 extra per packet and the suppliers receive R1,60 less per packet than before.

This example illustrates that a tax cannot be passed on at will and that there are three groups who will potentially have to share the burden of the tax: the consumers, the owners of the firms and the employees of the firms. The distribution of the burden between these groups will depend on the relative price elasticities of the demand curve and the supply curve. We shall not analyse all the possible cases but we give you some of the results in Box 16-3. Tax incidence is examined more fully in courses on public economics or the economics of government.

The welfare implications of a specific excise tax

Figure 16-3 can also be used to illustrate the welfare cost of an excise tax. Figure 16-4 is a redrawn version of Figure 16-3 without the numbers. Before the introduction of the tax DE_0P_0 and SE_0P_0 represented the consumer surplus and producer surplus respectively. After the introduction of the tax, the government receives rectangles A and B in tax revenue. Rectangle A is transferred from the consumer surplus to government and rectangle B is transferred from the producer surplus to government. Because the imposition of the tax reduces the level of output, triangle X (which initially formed part of the consumer surplus) and triangle Y (which initially formed part of the producer surplus) both disappear. Triangle $E_1E_0E_2$ (ie $X + Y$) represents the total **deadweight loss** of the tax.

FIGURE 16-4 The deadweight loss of a specific excise tax

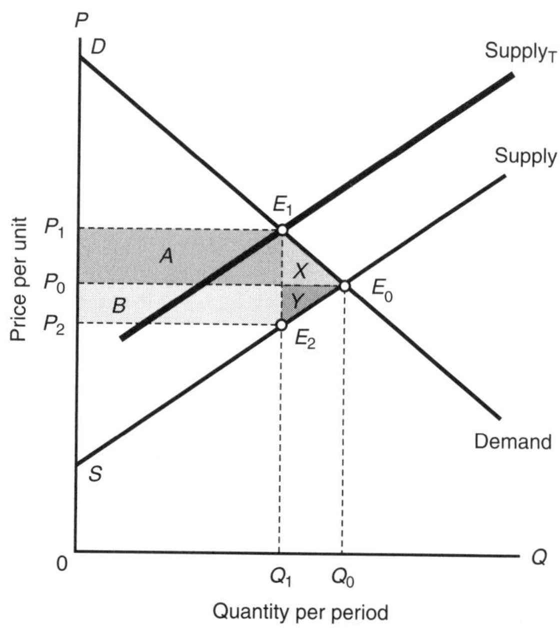

Before the imposition of the tax, the equilibrium price and quantity are P_0 and Q_0 respectively. After the imposition of the tax, the equilibrium price and quantity are P_1 and Q_1 respectively. The government gains rectangle A (at the expense of the consumers) and rectangle B (at the expense of the producers). Triangles X and Y disappear. X plus Y represents the deadweight loss of the tax.

BOX 16-3 TAX INCIDENCE AND THE PRICE ELASTICITY OF DEMAND AND SUPPLY

In Figure 16-3 we presented an example of how the tax burden is shared between consumers and suppliers. The results depend on the relative price elasticities of demand and supply. If different demand and supply curves are used, different results can be obtained, although the general principles still apply. We now summarise the possible results. You can check these results for yourself by replicating Figure 16-3 and drawing different demand and supply curves through point *E*. When you want to compare different cases, you always have to start at the same point and keep all the relevant information the same. For example, all the pre-tax supply curves that you use must pass through point *E* and all the after-tax supply curves must shift up by exactly R4,00 per packet, otherwise the comparison is not valid. Similarly, all the pre-tax demand curves must also pass through point *E*.

Price elasticity of demand

Extreme cases

- If the **demand is totally price inelastic**, that is, if the demand curve is vertical, the consumers will bear the full burden of the tax. The price will rise to R16,00 per packet and the equilibrium quantity will remain unchanged at 150 000 packets per week.
- If the **demand is totally price elastic**, that is, if the demand curve is horizontal, the suppliers (and their employees) will bear the full burden of the tax. The price will still be R12,00 per packet but the quantity will fall.

Intermediate cases

The two extreme cases are somewhat unrealistic but they do serve to indicate what will happen in the more normal, or intermediate, cases. Given the supply, the greater the price elasticity of demand, that is, the flatter the demand curve in Figure 16-3, the lower the price increase and the greater the fall in the equilibrium quantity. Similarly, given the supply, the smaller the price elasticity of demand, that is, the steeper the demand curve, the greater the price increase and the smaller the fall in production.

In other words, the greater the price elasticity of demand, the greater the relative burden on the suppliers, *ceteris paribus*. The smaller the price elasticity of demand, the greater the relative burden on the consumers, *ceteris paribus*.

Price elasticity of supply

Extreme cases

- If **supply is perfectly price inelastic**, that is, if the supply curve is vertical, the price will remain unchanged and the full burden of the tax will fall on the supplier, *ceteris paribus*.
- If **supply is perfectly elastic**, that is, if the supply curve is horizontal, the price will increase by the full amount of the tax, *ceteris paribus*. Consumers will therefore bear the full burden of the tax. The equilibrium quantity will, however, fall with the result that the employees of the firms supplying the good or service will also be affected.

Intermediate cases

Again, these two extreme cases serve to illustrate what happens in normal conditions where the supply is price elastic, that is, where the supply curve slopes upward from left to right. The greater the price elasticity of supply, the greater the proportion of the burden that falls on the consumers, *ceteris paribus*. The smaller the price elasticity of supply the greater the proportion of the burden that falls on the suppliers, *ceteris paribus*.

IMPORTANT CONCEPTS

General government
Public sector
Market failure
Public goods
Rivalry
Excludability
Mixed goods
User charge
Externalities
External costs
External benefits
Asymmetric information
Principal-agent problem
Moral hazard
Adverse selection
Common property resources
Tragedy of the commons
Business cycle
Macroeconomic policy
Fiscal policy
Merit goods
Government spending
Transfer payments
Taxation
Regulation
Government failure
Rent-seeking
Nationalisation
Privatisation
Commercialisation
Budget
Demand management
Expansionary policy
Contractionary policy
Lags
Budget deficit
Inflationary financing
Public debt
Interest on public debt
Tax neutrality
Horizontal equity
Vertical equity
Benefit principle
Tax avoidance
Tax evasion
Direct taxes
Indirect taxes
General tax
Selective tax
Progressive tax
Proportional tax
Regressive tax
Taxable income
Marginal tax rate
Average tax rate
Bracket creep
Capital gains tax
Value-added tax
Tax incidence
Statutory incidence
Effective incidence
Specific tax
Ad valorem tax
Deadweight loss

REVIEW QUESTIONS

1. Define market failure and list some of the main causes of market failure.
2. What is the difference between a public good and a private good? Give an example of each.
3. Can the free rider problem arise in the case of excludable goods? Explain.
4. Define externalities and give an example of a positive externality and a negative externality.
5. Are all goods and services provided by the South African government public goods? Discuss.
6. Give an example of each of the following:
   (a) a good that is rivalrous in consumption and excludable
   (b) a good that is non-rivalrous in consumption and excludable
   (c) a good that is rivalrous in consumption and non-excludable
   (d) a good that is non-rivalrous in consumption and non-excludable
7. Which is the most beneficial to society: privatisation or nationalisation? Substantiate your view.
8. List some of the advantages and disadvantages of the privatisation of Telkom.
9. Discuss the main economic arguments in favour of and against the privatisation of public corporations such as Eskom and Transnet.
10. Explain the difference between (a) a progressive tax and a regressive tax and (b) a direct tax and an indirect tax, and give examples of each.

11. Use the requirements of a good tax to evaluate the following South African taxes:
    (a) personal income tax
    (b) value-added tax (VAT)
    (c) fuel tax
    (d) capital gains tax
12. Define bracket creep.
13. Is the following statement true or false? "Under a proportional income tax a person earning a higher income will pay more in income tax than a person who earns a lower income." Explain your answer.

ECONOMIC GROWTH AND INFLATION IN SOUTH AFRICA, 1965–2006

Year	Economic growth		Inflation	
	Annual percentage change in:		Annual percentage increase in:	
	Real GDP	Real GNI	CPI	PPI
1965	6,1	3,7	3,9	3,0
1966	4,4	5,6	3,6	4,0
1967	7,2	8,9	3,4	2,4
1968	4,2	6,0	2,1	1,2
1969	4,7	4,9	3,2	2,3
1970	5,2	2,8	5,3	3,1
1971	4,3	6,7	6,1	4,6
1972	1,7	5,8	6,5	7,1
1973	4,6	13,0	9,4	15,0
1974	6,1	10,1	11,7	17,4
1975	1,7	–2,2	13,5	16,0
1976	2,2	–1,0	11,5	15,9
1977	–0,1	1,1	11,8	12,5
1978	3,0	4,0	10,5	10,0
1979	3,8	6,0	13,1	15,2
1980	6,6	10,6	13,7	16,7
1981	5,4	0,8	15,7	13,5
1982	–0,4	–3,6	14,4	13,9
1983	–1,8	–1,8	12,6	10,5
1984	5,1	6,8	11,2	8,4
1985	–1,2	–0,8	16,2	17,0
1986	0,0	0,8	18,8	19,5
1987	2,1	3,6	16,2	13,9
1988	4,2	4,1	12,9	13,1
1989	2,4	1,1	14,5	15,4
1990	–0,3	–1,2	14,3	11,9
1991	–1,0	–0,8	15,6	11,5
1992	–2,1	–2,1	13,7	8,2
1993	1,2	1,6	9,9	6,6
1994	3,2	5,1	8,8	8,3
1995	3,1	2,2	8,7	9,4
1996	4,3	4,6	7,3	7,0
1997	2,6	2,1	8,6	7,0
1998	0,5	–0,3	6,9	3,6
1999	2,4	1,2	5,2	5,8
2000	4,2	3,7	5,4	9,2
2001	2,7	2,5	5,7	8,4
2002	3,7	5,1	9,2	14,2
2003	3,1	3,5	5,8	1,7
2004	4,8	5,8	1,4	0,6
2005	5,1	5,3	3,4	3,1
2006	5,0	6,3	4,7	7,7

17 The foreign sector

Learning outcomes

Once you have studied this chapter you should be able to

- explain why international trade occurs
- analyse the impact of an import tariff
- evaluate the case for and against the use of trade barriers
- describe the major elements of the balance of payments
- explain how exchange rates are determined in the foreign exchange market
- define the terms of trade and explain their significance

The opening up of a foreign trade ... sometimes works a sort of industrial revolution in a country whose resources were previously underdeveloped.

JOHN STUART MILL

The notion dies hard that in some sort of way exports are patriotic but imports are immoral.

LORD HARLECH

No nation was ever ruined by trade.

BENJAMIN FRANKLIN

It is widely accepted nowadays that the most successful economies are those that have strong economic links with the rest of the world and are able to compete successfully in international markets. Economies that cannot compete tend to stagnate or decline. Exports, imports and international capital movements have all been important in the development of the South African economy. In recent decades, however, the South African balance of payments has not always been favourable. The precarious state of the balance of payments was frequently an important determinant of the relatively poor performance of the South African economy, particularly during the 1980s and early 1990s.

We introduced the foreign sector in Chapter 3. We defined the balance of payments in Chapter 4, and emphasised the importance of South Africa's economic links with the rest of the world in Chapter 5. In this chapter we examine some aspects of these links in more detail. In the first section we explain **why countries trade**. This is followed by a discussion of **trade policy**, including an analysis of the impact of **import tariffs**. In the third section we return to the balance of payments, which we discussed in Chapter 4 and which we now examine in more detail. We also discuss the links between the balance of payments, economic activity and economic policy. In the fourth section we examine the question of the determination and significance of **exchange rates**, following which we explain the **terms of trade**.

At the start of the new millennium the world's economies appear to be becoming more integrated: trade is expanding, capital markets have sprung up in developing and transition economies, tourism is increasing (and in some places migration as well) and new technologies have linked the farthest corners of the world. All these activities are evidence of a process that has come to be called **globalisation**. By opening new markets, sharing knowledge and increasing the efficiency of resources, globalisation can expand opportunities for people and reduce poverty. But there are also risks. Globalisation can increase vulnerability to external shocks, which have their origin in the foreign sector. Increased competition creates losers as well as winners. In addition, there is much disagreement among political and economic leaders as to whether increasing integration is a strategic choice or an inevitable consequence – for better or worse – of the economic and technological change that accompanies globalisation. The answers to these questions are important for shaping future development strategies.

The extent of a country's involvement in international trade and finance is referred to as the **openness** of its economy or its degree of **integration** into the international economy, and differs from country to country. In Table 5-15 we showed three measures of openness for a selection of countries: the ratio of exports to GDP, the ratio of imports to GDE and the average of these two ratios. In Table 17-1 we show similar measures for South Africa and some other countries not included in Table 5-15. The figures indicate clearly how the importance of international trade varies from country to country and how international trade has tended to increase in recent years. As indicated in Section 5.5, the South African economy can be described as an **open economy** – the degree of openness is not particularly high or low. However, it did not increase as much as those of most of the other countries included in the table.

The measures used in Table 17-1 pertain to international trade only and ought to be supplemented by other indicators, such as the ratio of gross private capital flows to GDP and the ratio of gross foreign direct investment to GDP, to obtain a more balanced indication of a country's degree of integration into the international economy. More information in this regard is provided in Box 17-1.

International trade has grown considerably since the end of World War II. Data on total world exports and world output (world GDP) show that real output and real exports rose at approximately the same rate from 1950 until 1955, and that exports then increased more rapidly. By the mid-1970s, world exports had increased fivefold over their 1950 level. By comparison global output had only doubled. At the beginning of 1990, world exports were more than 1 000 per cent higher than in 1950. During the same period world output grew by less than half this figure. The United States dominated international trade in the 1950s. Over the following two decades, its share of global trade declined, whereas the shares of Germany and Japan increased considerably. Since the 1980s, the newly industrialised countries (NICs), such as Korea, Taiwan and Malaysia, have expanded their contribution to trade at the expense of the established industrialised countries. More recently, the increase in China's share in world trade has been spectacular.

TABLE 17-1 Indicators of openness for selected countries, 1990 and 2005

Country	*1* *Exports as % of GDP*		*2* *Imports as % of GDE*		*3* *Average of **1** and **2***	
	1990	*2005*	*1990*	*2005*	*1990*	*2005*
Low-income countries						
India	7,1	19,0*	8,4	20,6*	7,8	19,8*
Tanzania	12,6	22,9	30,0	28,2	21,3	25,6
Middle-income countries						
Hungary	31,3	66,4	29,3	66,9	30,3	66,7
Turkey	13,3	27,4	16,8	31,9	15,1	29,7
South Africa	24,7	27,5	19,9	28,1	22,3	27,8
High-income countries						
South Korea	29,2	42,5	29,9	41,0	29,5	41,8
Sweden	29,9	48,7	29,7	44,5	29,8	46,6

Note: * Data pertain to 2004. Data for 2005 not available.
Source: International Monetary Fund, *International Financial Statistics*

BOX 17-1 MEASURING OPENNESS OR INTEGRATION

There are two broad approaches to measuring openness or economic integration: the first pertains to the **barriers to integration** and the second to the **outcomes of integration**. In a fully economically integrated world there would be no official barriers to negotiating and executing economic transactions. **Barriers to integration** begin at the border with tariffs and non-tariff barriers, but such barriers are only part of a wide range of domestic policies and practices which prevent full economic integration. Their outcomes can be seen in the volume of trade and capital flows.

Average tariffs, non-tariff barrier coverage ratios and indicators of capital controls are all useful indicators, and they are frequently cited as evidence of significant reductions in barriers to integration since World War II, especially in the past two decades. But the story they tell may be misleading. Posted tariffs are not always collected. Capital controls can be evaded. Behind-the-border barriers such as domestic regulation and private collusive behaviour – which are virtually impossible to measure – may be more restrictive. Obstacles to integration also extend beyond official actions to include market structures, technology, geography and access to information.

Given the difficulties associated with measuring the barriers to integration, one may instead measure the **outcomes of integration**. Studies in this regard focus on the impact of integration on trade or capital flows. Such studies suggest that global integration has increased in recent decades.

Ratios of exports to GDP and/or imports to GDE are used as measures of product market integration. However, before these ratios can be used for cross-country comparisons of integration, they ought to be adjusted for the influence of structural factors such as country size, factor endowment, geographic isolation and stage of development. For example:

- Large countries tend to trade less than small countries because they possess more diversified resources.
- Countries that are well endowed with natural resources, such as oil, gold or coal, tend to export and import more, *ceteris paribus*.
- Rich countries appear to be less integrated than they really are because they devote more of their output and consumption to services, which are harder to trade. They also tend to have higher prices for services, which again make them seem less integrated by their export to GDP or import to GDE ratios.

With outcome studies it is difficult to disentangle the separate influences of the many forces that affect market outcomes. As a result there is no single measure – or group of measures – that serves as an unambiguous indicator of the extent of openness or economic integration.

Data also show that the composition of trade has changed. At first, agricultural products, raw materials and a narrow range of simple manufactured goods were traded. After the industrial revolution, international trade came to be dominated by manufactured goods. In the past few decades trade in more advanced products (eg computers and other electronic goods) and in services has grown rapidly. To understand these trends we have to examine the reasons for trade.

17.1 Why countries trade

Why does international trade take place? Do countries gain from international trade or is it better for one country to produce everything that its citizens require? The notion of **self-sufficiency** (or **autarky**) used to be popular among politicians and citizens who wanted to be independent from other countries. But countries, like individuals, are economically interdependent. In Chapter 2 we explained that it is better for an individual to **specialise** in the activities that he or she does best, rather than to attempt to do everything (even if he or she can do everything better than anyone else). The same principle applies as far as countries are concerned. Countries (and the world at large) gain if every country specialises in the production of certain goods, exporting the surplus which is not consumed domestically and importing those goods which are not produced domestically.

Adam Smith began his famous book, *The wealth of nations* (see Chapter 2), by emphasising the benefits of specialisation and the division of labour. He then used the same kind of reasoning to argue for free international trade. On page 424 of *The wealth of nations* he wrote:

> It is the maxim of every prudent master of a family, never to attempt to make at home what it will cost him more to make than to buy ... What is prudence in the conduct of every private family, can scarce be folly in that of a great kingdom. If a foreign country can supply us with a commodity cheaper than we ourselves can make it, better buy it of them with some part of the produce of our own industry, employed in a way in which we have some advantage.

One of the basic reasons for international trade is the fact that factors of production (natural resources, labour, capital and entrepreneurship) are not evenly distributed among the nations of the world. In the case of natural resources the basic reason for trade is often quite simple – all countries do not possess every natural resource. South Africa, for example, has large reserves of platinum which most other countries do not have. On the other hand, it does not possess significant reserves of crude oil that can be profitably exploited. South Africa therefore exports platinum and imports crude oil.

The other factors of production are also important. For example, a country like Japan has limited natural resources, but it has large supplies of capital, entrepreneurship and skilled labour. Japan therefore produces and exports commodities such as electronic equipment that require capital and skilled labour.

If Australia produces wool but does not produce digital video cameras, while Japan produces digital video cameras but does not produce wool, both countries will obviously benefit by trading what they have for what they do not have. But what if both countries produce **both** wool and digital video cameras? Will trade still be desirable or possible under such conditions? We now examine different possibilities in this regard. To keep matters simple, we assume that there are only two countries, each of which produces two goods and that goods are exchanged directly for goods (ie we assume that each economy is a barter economy, which implies that money and exchange rates can be ignored).

Absolute advantage

Suppose that Australia and Japan can both produce wool and digital video cameras. One worker in Australia can produce 100 kg of wool *or* 5 digital video cameras per week. In contrast, one worker in Japan can produce 50 kg of wool *or* 10 digital video cameras per week. We say that Australia has an **absolute advantage** in the production of wool and Japan an **absolute advantage** in the production of digital video cameras. Both countries will obviously gain if each specialises in the production of the good in which it has an absolute advantage. Australia will then export some of its wool to Japan and Japan will export some of its digital video cameras to Australia. With complete specialisation, the Australian worker will produce 100 kg of wool per week and the Japanese worker 10 digital video cameras per week. Suppose the trading ratio is 10 kg wool for one digital video camera and that Australia exports 50 kg wool to Japan in exchange for 5 digital video cameras. With specialisation and trade, Australia and Japan will thus each be able to consume 50 kg of wool *and* 5 digital video cameras per week, which would have been impossible without trade – see Table 17-2. This simple example illustrates the advantages of trade if each country has an absolute advantage in the production of a particular good.

TABLE 17-2 Absolute advantage in international trade

	Production and consumption	
Country	*Before trade*	*After trade*
Australia	100 kg of wool *or* 5 digital video cameras	50 kg of wool *and* 5 digital video cameras
Japan	50 kg of wool *or* 10 digital video cameras	50 kg of wool *and* 5 digital video cameras

Comparative (or relative) advantage

Absolute advantage is not, however, a prerequisite for international trade. Trade can also be beneficial when one country is more efficient in the production of both goods. This possibility was explored in the early 19th century by the English economist David Ricardo (1772–1823), who formulated the **law of comparative (or relative) advantage**. According to Ricardo, both countries will benefit from trade if the **opportunity costs** of production (or **relative prices**) differ between the two countries. We now use another example to illustrate this law or principle.

Suppose there are only two countries, Germany and South Africa, and that a German worker can produce two cars or eight barrels of wine per day, while a South African worker can produce one car or six barrels of wine per day. According to this example (summarised below), it takes fewer resources in Germany to produce a car or a barrel of wine than in South Africa. Germany has an **absolute advantage** over South Africa in the production of both goods.

Maximum output per worker per day in Germany and South Africa:

Germany	2 cars *or* 8 barrels of wine
South Africa	1 car *or* 6 barrels of wine

Since Germany can produce both goods with fewer resources than South Africa, it would appear that Germany has nothing to gain from trading with South Africa. But is this the case? To answer this question we have to consider the cost of producing cars and wine in both countries, using the **opportunity cost** principle. In Germany the cost of producing 2 cars is 8 barrels of wine. By using its scarce labour resources to produce 2 cars, Germany forgoes the opportunity to produce 8 barrels of wine. Assuming constant opportunity costs, this means that the cost to Germany of producing 1 car is 4 barrels of wine. But in South Africa 6 barrels of wine have to be sacrificed to produce 1 car. Thus it costs **relatively** less to produce cars in Germany than it does in South Africa. Germany has to give up fewer barrels of wine to produce a car than South Africa.

On the other hand, the opportunity cost of producing wine is lower in South Africa than in Germany. To produce 6 barrels of wine, South Africa has to sacrifice 1 car. The opportunity cost of producing a barrel of wine in South Africa is thus $\frac{1}{6}$ of a car. In Germany the cost of producing 4 barrels of wine is 1 car. The opportunity cost of producing 1 barrel of wine in Germany is thus $\frac{1}{4}$ of a car. It thus costs **relatively** less to produce wine in South Africa than it does in Germany.

Thus, although Germany has an **absolute** advantage over South Africa in the production of both goods, it does not have a **relative** advantage in both. Put differently, Germany is **in absolute terms** twice as efficient in producing cars than South Africa, but it is only marginally more efficient in producing wine. This implies that Germany is relatively more efficient in the production of cars, whereas South Africa is relatively more efficient (or relatively less inefficient) in the production of wine. Germany has a relative or **comparative advantage** in the production of cars, while South Africa has a relative or **comparative advantage** in the production of wine.

According to the theory (or law) of comparative advantage, **each country will tend to specialise in and export those goods for which it has a comparative advantage**. In our example, both Germany and South Africa have an incentive to specialise and trade, provided that a mutually beneficial trading ratio is established. Each country will undertake the shift of resources required for specialisation only if there are clearly demonstrable gains to be had from trading. South Africa, for example, will only be willing to shift its resources into wine production if it can exchange fewer than 6 barrels of wine for a car from Germany. Likewise, Germany will only be willing to shift its resources into car production if it can obtain more than 4 barrels of wine for every car it sends to South Africa. In our example both countries will thus gain from trade only if 1 car is exchanged for more than 4 but fewer than 6 barrels of wine.

Suppose 1 car exchanges for 5 barrels of wine:

- Germany gains from trade. For each car Germany sends to South Africa, it receives 5 barrels of wine in exchange. It thus makes sense for Germany to shift labour resources from wine production to car production and trade the excess production of cars. Without international trade, Germany could only produce and consume 4 barrels of wine for each car sacrificed. After international trade, Germany can import and consume 5 barrels of wine for each car given up (ie exported).
- South Africa gains from trade. For each 5 barrels of wine South Africa sends to Germany, it receives 1 car in exchange. It thus makes sense for South Africa to shift labour resources from car production to wine production and trade the excess production of wine. Without international trade, South Africa could only produce and consume 1 car for each 6 barrels of wine sacrificed. After international trade, South Africa can import and consume 1 car for each 5 barrels of wine given up (ie exported).

Note, however, that:

- International trade will only occur if comparative advantages exist, that is, if the **opportunity costs** differ between countries. If the opportunity costs are the same in both countries (eg if a worker can produce 1 car or 6 barrels of wine in both countries) there is no basis for trade. In such a case **equal advantage** is said to exist. Even if one country has an absolute advantage in the production of both goods but the opportunity cost ratio (or relative price ratio) is the same in both countries, there is no basis for trade. For example, if a German worker can produce 2 cars or 8 barrels of wine and a South African worker can produce 1 car or 4 barrels of wine, the opportunity costs are the same in both countries and there are no gains from trade. Comparative advantage (reflected in differences in opportunity costs) is a necessary and sufficient condition for gains from trade.
- Both countries will gain only if the trading or exchange ratio lies somewhere between the opportunity cost ratios in the two countries. For example, if 1 car is exchanged for 4 barrels of wine in international trade, South Africa would gain but Germany would not. Germany would thus have no incentive to trade. By the same token, if 1 car is exchanged for 6 barrels of wine, Germany would gain but South Africa would not. South Africa would thus have no incentive to trade.

The gains from trade in our example are illustrated further in Box 17-2.

Our explanation for international trade has been very basic. We have, for example, ignored the possibility of increasing or decreasing costs as well as the impact of exchange rates and transport costs. These and other complications are dealt with in intermediate and advanced courses in international economics. In Box 17-3 we briefly touch upon intra-industry trade, an interesting phenomenon in international trade. The theory of comparative advantage nonetheless provides the basic explanation for international trade and we now briefly discuss some of the possible sources of comparative advantage.

Sources of comparative advantage

Although the discussion thus far has identified some of the likely consequences of comparative advantage, it does not help us understand why a country has a comparative advantage in one good as opposed to another. The sources of comparative advantage can be found in those factors that determine the relative demands for and the relative supplies of each of the goods produced.

■ TECHNOLOGY

If a country possesses a production process that is technologically superior to the processes used

BOX 17-2 A FURTHER ILLUSTRATION OF THE GAINS FROM TRADE

In this box we expand on the example in the text to illustrate the magnitude of the gains from trade. Suppose that Germany and South Africa both have 25 workers. Suppose further that **before trade** 15 workers in each country produce cars and 10 produce wine. This means that 30 cars and 80 barrels of wine are produced and consumed in Germany before trade, while 15 cars and 60 barrels of wine are produced and consumed in South Africa. This situation is summarised below:

Product	Production and consumption before trade and specialisation		
	Germany	South Africa	Total
Cars (units)	30	15	45
Wine (barrels)	80	60	140

Suppose Germany and South Africa decide to engage in trade at the ratio of 5 barrels of wine for each car. Germany will then devote all its resources to car production (ie specialise in the production of cars), while South Africa will specialise in the production of wine. Germany will thus produce 50 cars and South Africa will produce 150 barrels of wine. Both these levels of production are greater than the pre-trade levels of 45 cars and 140 barrels of wine respectively. Suppose Germany and South Africa agree to exchange 17 German cars for 85 barrels of South African wine. The outcome is summarised below:

Product	Production after specialisation			Consumption after trade		
	Germany	South Africa	Total	Germany	South Africa	Total
Cars (units)	50	0	50	33	17	50
Wine (barrels)	0	150	150	85	65	150

We thus see that, by specialising and engaging in trade at a mutually beneficial exchange ratio, both countries can increase their consumption of both products. Compared to the pre-trade position, Germans are able to consume 3 additional cars and 5 additional barrels of wine after trade. Likewise, South Africans gain 2 cars and 5 barrels of wine.

BOX 17-3 INTRA-INDUSTRY TRADE

Traditional trade theories explain only the phenomenon of **inter-industry trade**. This involves the exchange between nations of products of **different industries**. For example, South Africa exports minerals to Japan and imports electronic goods from Japan. In reality, much of inter-industry trade is between nations that have vastly different resource endowments (such as developing countries and industrial economies) and can be explained by either the principle of comparative advantage (the Heckscher-Ohlin model) or the product life cycle theory.

A growing proportion of international trade, however, involves **intra-industry** trade, the exchange of the products of **similar industries** between countries. For example, South Africa imports motorcars from Britain but also exports motorcars to Britain. Two-way trade in commodities like watches, computers, motorcars and wine cannot be explained by trade theories based on differences in factor requirements. Industrialised countries, which are largely responsible for this type of trade, are endowed with factors and technologies that have become increasingly similar over the years. It is for this reason that trade theories that take into account less traditional criteria such as demand-side factors, economies of scale and imperfect competition are better suited to explaining the phenomenon of intra-industry trade.

Intra-industry trade can take place in homogeneous goods as well as in differentiated products. In the case of homogeneous goods, the reasons for intra-industry trade are easy to grasp. A nation may export and import the same product because of transportation cost considerations or due to seasonal fluctuations (eg in the case of agricultural products). However, most intra-industry trade occurs in differentiated products. Two-way trade in these differentiated products can be explained by consumer tastes. For example, most Japanese consumers prefer Toyotas to Volkswagen vehicles; yet some Japanese consumers purchase vehicles from Volkswagen, while Toyotas are exported to Germany. Likewise, South Africa exports wine to Europe but also imports wine from Europe. Intra-industry trade increases the range of choices available to consumers in each country, as well as the degree of competition among manufacturers.

Intra-industry trade in differentiated products can be further explained by overlapping demand segments between trading nations. When South African manufacturers look overseas for markets in which to sell, they often find them in countries having market segments that are similar to those they sell in at home; for example, luxury motorcars sold to high-income consumers. Nations with similar income levels can be expected to have similar tastes, and thus sizeable overlapping market segments, and they would be expected to engage heavily in intra-industry trade.

Besides marketing factors, economies of scale associated with differentiated products may also help explain intra-industry trade. A nation may enjoy a cost advantage over its foreign competitor by specialising in a few varieties and styles of a product. Such specialisation permits longer production runs, economies of scale and decreasing unit costs. Since trade creates a larger market, a country can reduce the number of product varieties it produces, thereby lowering the production costs of each variety (economies of scale effects), and at the same time increase the number of product varieties available to consumers (via imports). In this way, intra-industry trade introduces an additional gain from international trade. The gains from trade include both lower product prices and a wider product choice.

abroad, this could be a source of that country's comparative advantage. Technological superiority here means more output per unit of input.

Many people mistakenly argued that South African industry should have been able to compete with foreign producers because wage costs were so much lower than in the industrial countries. But wage costs alone do not tell us what we need to know to determine unit costs (the costs for each unit of output). If wage costs are low and each worker produces a very small output (ie worker productivity is low), unit costs could be very high compared with a country whose wage costs are high but whose technique of production brings about a high level of output or productivity per worker. In other words, the technological superiority of some production processes may overcome the wage cost differences between countries.

It needs to be recognised, however, that the existence of a superior production process in one country does not mean that those technological differences will persist over time. Indeed, the transmission of technology from one country to another is an important factor that can change the comparative advantage position of countries in various goods. Initially, an advanced country like Germany may have a comparative advantage in the production of electrical appliances because of a technological superiority that overcomes its wage cost disadvantage. Germany therefore exports electrical appliances. In time, producers in less advanced countries like the Republic of Korea imitate the technology used in Germany. If wage and other input costs are lower in the Republic of Korea, Germany may lose its comparative advantage in electrical appliances and in time it may begin to import electrical appliances from the Republic of Korea. This idea forms the basis of what is known as the **product life cycle theory of international trade**.

In a dynamic world economy, any single country's comparative advantage could well be changing continuously. The international transmission of technology explains, in large measure, why developed countries like Germany and Japan have been losing out to newcomers like the newly industrialised economies in the production of such traditional goods as steel and textiles.

■ RESOURCE ENDOWMENTS

One of the most important explanations of each country's comparative advantage lies in the fact that different countries are endowed with different quantities of scarce resources. Furthermore, given the fact that the production of different goods requires the use of scarce resources in different proportions, differences in production costs for similar goods will emerge between countries.

Eli Heckscher and Bertil Ohlin developed the theory of comparative advantage based on differences in resource endowments among countries. The **Heckscher-Ohlin theory** can be stated as follows: *each country will tend to export those goods that most intensively use the country's relatively abundant resources.* The essentials of the theory can be explained in the following way. Assume a world of only two resources: capital and labour. Assume the United Kingdom has a relatively larger amount of capital than India, while India has a relatively larger amount of labour than the United Kingdom. As a consequence of these differences, the various goods produced in the two countries will reflect these factor endowment differences. In the United Kingdom it should cost relatively less to produce capital-intensive products whilst in India it should cost relatively less to produce labour-intensive products. According to Heckscher and Ohlin, these differences in relative costs form the basis of each country's comparative advantage.

In reality, however, there is a large variety of resources just as there are differences in the qualities of labour and capital. Trade between nations is thus more complicated than can be captured by any single trade theory.

■ DIFFERENCES IN TASTES OR DEMAND

The technology and resource endowments explanations of comparative advantage emphasise the conditions of supply in the various countries. However, relative prices cannot be determined on the basis of supply considerations alone. The forces of demand are also important in the determination of a country's comparative advantage.

For example, if consumers in Germany have a relative preference (or greater demand) for good X, whereas consumers in France have a relative preference (or greater demand) for good Y, pre-trade relative prices will differ between Germany and France even if they have similar resource endowments and production techniques. Tastes or demand differences are thus also important in explaining trade flows between countries. Religious, cultural, sociological and climatic differences among nations are some of the more critical factors that shape the consumption decisions of the countries of the world. Additionally, differences in the levels of economic development of nations help to explain differences in their consumption patterns. In poor countries, characterised by low per capita incomes, there is a sizeable market for necessities but only a small market for luxury goods. The market for luxury goods is much more extensive in developed countries. This partly explains why the major trading partners of the developed countries (like Germany and France) tend to be other developed countries, at least as far as trade in consumer goods is concerned.

17.2 Trade policy

By now it should be clear that the opening up of trade between countries leads to greater world production of traded goods and, by implication, to an increase in economic welfare. Nevertheless, every government takes steps to protect domestic firms against foreign competition and to control the volume of imports entering the country. The measures used include import tariffs, quotas, subsidies, other non-tariff barriers and exchange controls. We first discuss these measures before touching on some of the reasons for protection and barriers to trade.

Import tariffs

Import tariffs are duties or taxes imposed on products imported into a country. They are used to protect domestic firms against competition from imports (**protective tariffs**) or to raise government revenue

(revenue tariffs). There are two categories of tariffs: **specific tariffs** and **ad valorem** tariffs. A **specific tariff** is a fixed amount that is levied on each unit of the imported commodity. For example, a tariff of R5,00 levied on each imported bottle of wine is a specific tariff. An **ad valorem** tariff is a tariff that is levied as a percentage of the value of the imported item. For example, a tariff of 20 per cent on the price of an imported motor car is an **ad valorem** tariff.

Revenue tariffs are usually imposed on items that are not produced in the domestic economy. In South Africa this includes certain specialised computer and other electronic equipment. **Protective tariffs**, on the other hand, are imposed to protect a local industry or sector of the economy from foreign competition. Import tariffs can be quite high, placing foreign producers at a disadvantage (since the tariffs raise the prices of their products in the domestic market), but they are usually not sufficient to prevent imports altogether.

■ THE ECONOMIC IMPACT OF AN IMPORT TARIFF

We use an example of a **specific** tariff to explain the economic effects of a tariff by means of demand and supply analysis. In Figure 17-1, *DD* represents the domestic (South African) demand for textiles, a product in which the country has a competitive disadvantage. *SS* represents the domestic supply of textiles. In the absence of world trade the equilibrium price is P_d and the equilibrium quantity is Q_3, as indicated by point E_d. When the economy is opened up to international trade, countries with a relative or comparative advantage in the production of textiles, such as certain Asian countries, will export textiles to South Africa at a lower price, which we call the world price (P_w). The international supply of textiles in the domestic market will now be represented by the horizontal line P_wS_w. This indicates that any quantity of textiles can be imported and therefore supplied at the world price (P_w). The domestic price for textiles will thus fall to the world price. At the lower price the quantity of textiles demanded increases to Q_5. The new equilibrium point is indicated by E_w. The equilibrium price is P_w, and the equilibrium quantity is Q_5. Domestic production has fallen from Q_3 to Q_1. South African producers who cannot compete at a price of P_w are eliminated from the market. Imports are represented by the difference between Q_5 and Q_1.

In this example, international competition causes a decrease in domestic production and employment and a weakening of the balance of payments (since imports increase). Domestic consumers benefit, however, because they pay lower prices. Moreover, firms which use textiles as an intermediate product to produce clothing, linen and so on, also benefit. Their production and income may therefore expand. The net impact of the introduction of international competition is therefore uncertain.

FIGURE 17-1 The impact of a specific import tariff

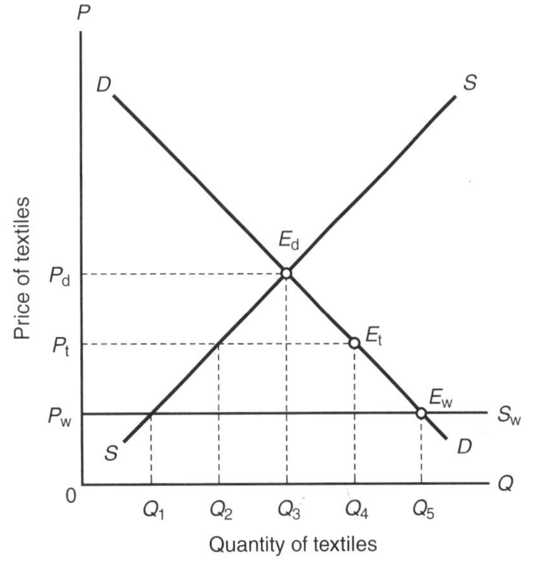

The original demand and supply of textiles before international trade are represented by DD and SS. As indicated by E_d, the domestic price is P_d and the quantity exchanged is Q_3. With the introduction of international competition the price falls to the world price P_w. The new equilibrium is E_w, indicating an equilibrium quantity of Q_5. The world supply of textiles is represented by P_wS_w. With the introduction of a specific tariff, the domestic price increases to P_t. The new equilibrium is E_t. The equilibrium quantity is Q_4 of which Q_2 is produced domestically. Domestic production increases and the volume of imports falls.

Suppose, however, that the government is perturbed about the loss of production and employment in the textile industry, as well as by the increase in imports, and therefore decides to impose a specific tariff on imported textiles. In Figure 17-1 the tariff is indicated by the difference between P_t and P_w, with P_t being the domestic price of textiles after the introduction of the tariff. The new equilibrium position is indicated by E_t. The higher price of textiles reduces the quantity demanded from Q_5 to Q_4. At the same time the higher price stimulates the domestic production of textiles and the quantity produced domestically increases to Q_2. The difference between Q_4 and Q_2 represents the quantity imported, which is now smaller than before the imposition of the tariff.

The imposition of the tariff raises domestic production (and employment) and reduces the quantity of imports. It also raises revenue for government. However, this is a mixed blessing. The domestic price of textiles is raised and if all the direct and indirect consequences are taken into account, the imposition of the tariff may prove to be an unwise move.

■ THE WELFARE EFFECTS OF AN IMPORT TARIFF

The welfare costs of a tariff can be explained with the aid of a modified version of Figure 17-1. In Figure 17-2 all the symbols have the same meaning as in Figure 17-1.

Prior to the imposition of the tariff, consumers could purchase quantity Q_5 at the world price (P_w). After the imposition of the tariff, they have to pay a price P_t (ie the world price plus the tariff) for the same quantity. The imposition of the tariff thus causes them to increase their spending by P_tABP_w, compared to what they were spending prior to the tariff, where $P_tABP_w = P_tAQ_40 - P_wBQ_40$. The question now is who receives the extra amount (represented by the rectangle P_tABP_w) that consumers pay. A part goes to government, whose revenue from the tariff is equal to the tariff per unit (ie P_t–P_w) multiplied by the quantity of units imported (ie Q_4–Q_2). The transfer from consumers to government is thus illustrated by the rectangle *FABG*.

Part of the increased consumer payments goes to firms as extra profits. After the imposition of the tariff, domestic producers receive more for their products, first, because they sell more, and second, because they are receiving a higher price. The firms' revenue increases from $0P_wEQ_1$ to $0P_tFQ_2$. Part of this increase, namely Q_1EFQ_2 (ie the area under the supply curve) is required to meet the costs of supplying a greater quantity (Q_2) than before (Q_1). The rest of the gain, however, represented by the area P_tFEP_w, consists of an increase in profits.

What about area *X*? This is part of the additional consumer payments but it is neither revenue for government nor extra profits for firms. Triangle *X* thus represents a net cost to society – it is the cost of supporting inefficient firms.

Area *Y* also represents a net loss to society. Prior to the imposition of the tariff, it was part of the consumer surplus (without affecting the domestic producers' surplus). After the imposition of the tariff, society loses this benefit (because the amount of textiles purchased by consumers has declined).

The imposition of a tariff thus results in **transfers** from one part of the economy to another (ie from consumers to government and firms), as well as **net costs** to society. The net costs are indicated by the two shaded triangles. They represent **pure waste** or

FIGURE 17-2 The welfare costs of a tariff

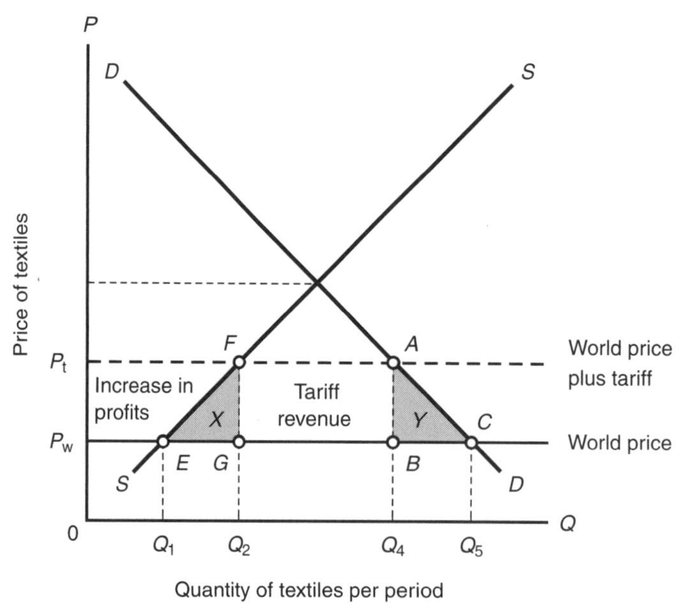

The imposition of a tariff results in transfers and net social losses. The tariff raises the domestic price from P_w to P_t and as a result consumers have to pay P_tABP_w more for quantity Q_4 than before the imposition of the tariff. FABG represents a transfer to government and P_tFEP_w a transfer to firms (in the form of extra profits). Triangles X and Y represent pure waste and net social losses, that is, the deadweight loss of the tariff.

the **deadweight loss** as a result of the tariff and therefore also represent the case for free trade.

Other measures

■ QUANTITATIVE RESTRICTIONS (IMPORT QUOTAS)

An **import quota** is a quantitative restriction on imports. Whereas tariffs are aimed at influencing the prices of imported goods, import quotas seek to control the physical level of imports. Import quotas are therefore a form of **direct intervention** in the market mechanism. The main difference between this kind of protection and tariffs is that, whereas with a tariff the government gains extra revenue, with quota restrictions the benefit of the higher price resulting from the limited supply goes to the seller of the goods, unless the government takes prior steps to prevent this. Government can, for example, auction import licenses to the highest bidders. Alternatively, licenses may simply be sold (or merely issued) to overseas suppliers on the basis of the pattern of supplies in earlier years.

The economic consequences of tariffs and quotas are much the same. For example, if an import quota of the difference between Q_4 and Q_2 in Figure 17-1 is imposed, it will also raise the domestic price to the tariff induced price of P_t. Most import quotas in South Africa have been abolished, as required by the World Trade Organisation (WTO) – see Box 17-4.

■ SUBSIDIES

Subsidies granted to home producers have the same impact as taxes on overseas goods. If, for example, maize produced in the United States costs R1 000 a ton delivered to South Africa and South African farmers need R1 100 to cover their costs and make a living, then they cannot compete. The government can assist South African agriculture either by imposing a tariff of R100 per ton of American maize imports or by granting the South African farmers a subsidy of R100 a ton, to enable them to sell at R1 000 a ton and compete with the imported grain. While the form of protection that is chosen will make little difference to the ultimate pattern of trade, the sources of the support for home agriculture are different. If tariffs are imposed on imports, consumers support home agriculture directly by paying a higher price than they would have paid in the absence of the tariff. However, if home producers receive a subsidy to enable them to compete, the support for agriculture comes indirectly from taxpayers. As most tax is paid by the relatively wealthy, support through taxpayers may be considered preferable to direct support from consumers, many of whom have very low incomes.

■ OTHER NON-TARIFF BARRIERS

Until recently the commercial barriers to trade tended to be assessed purely on the basis of tariffs and quantitative restrictions. With the complete removal of such barriers in terms of certain regional trade agreements, such as the North American Free Trade Agreement (NAFTA) and those incorporated in the European Union (EU), the significance of non-tariff barriers to trade has increased. These may take the form of discriminatory administrative practices, such as deliberately channelling government contracts to domestic firms even when their tenders are not competitive, insisting on certain technical standards or specifications that may be difficult for foreign firms to meet, special licensing requirements or simply unnecessary red tape. Non-tariff barriers will probably remain a hindrance to world trade for a long time to come.

■ EXCHANGE CONTROLS

An alternative to imposing limitations on internationally traded goods is to reduce the flow of these goods by restricting the amount of foreign exchange (currency) available for their purchase. For example, if the South African government wishes to reduce the flow of imports from the EU, it may set limits to the amount of euros that its citizens can acquire to buy European goods. The South African government also restricts the amount of currency available to people who want to take holidays overseas. The governments of developing countries frequently conserve foreign currency in this way.

■ EXCHANGE RATE POLICY

Many observers nowadays argue that trade policy, as discussed up to now, is not as relevant in the current era of flexible exchange rates as it was during the era of fixed exchange rates. Movements in exchange rates have significant effects on exports and imports and it is therefore argued that exchange rate policy can often be a much more effective instrument for influencing international trade than the traditional instruments of trade policy, such as tariffs, quotas and subsidies.

■ GENERAL COMMENTS

Whichever restraint is employed, the intention (except in the case of purely revenue-raising tariffs) is to increase the demand for home goods at the expense of foreign suppliers who can supply the goods more cheaply than domestic firms. By imposing tariffs or other controls, the government enables domestic firms to maintain or increase their sales, maintain employment in the industry, and perhaps increase profits. Those connected with the protected sector benefit at the expense of foreign producers as well as at the expense of domestic consumers, who are forced to pay a higher price than would be necessary under conditions of free trade. We now examine the case for and against tariffs and other obstacles to international trade.

Arguments for the use of trade barriers

■ INTRODUCTORY COMMENTS

Oskar Morgenstern, who was a prominent member of the Austrian school of economic thinking, once stated that economic policy is politics in the real sense. Nowhere is this more true than in the case of trade policy. Despite the benefits of free trade, all governments intervene to create barriers to free international trade. One of the reasons is that politicians tend to have a biased outlook and to be ignorant of the advantages of free trade. This is reflected in the following statement, reputed to have been made by Abraham Lincoln, the famous 19th century American president: "When I buy a coat from England, I have the coat and England has the money. But when I buy a coat in America, I have the coat and America has the money." Another reason is that trade barriers benefit some firms and workers a great deal, with the result that they exert a lot of pressure on government to adopt measures that will protect them against foreign competition. For example, if the economy of a town or region is dominated by a particular industry (eg the textile industry, steel industry or motor industry), the firms in question will pressurise their political representatives for import tariffs, import quotas or other protective measures.

A related problem is that the costs of protection (or the gains from trade) are spread over a large number of people, with the result that their political resistance to trade barriers is low. Put differently: free trade helps most people a little, but protection helps a few people a great deal. The latter group go to great lengths to achieve their goals, while the large numbers who each lose a little in the process tend to be unconcerned about their losses.

Supporters of free trade are highly critical of arguments for trade barriers. According to them all such arguments are biased and are aimed only at serving the interests of those who stand to gain from protection against international competition. It should be recognised, however, that firms and workers in industries that are subject to competition from abroad are hurt by a movement to free trade. Resources cannot be shifted instantly and costlessly between industries. Labour and capital are immobile and when an economy is opened up to international trade (as was the case in South Africa in the 1990s), unemployment and bankruptcy are inevitable.

Against this background we now examine some of the arguments that are advanced in defence of trade barriers.

■ THE BALANCE OF PAYMENTS

Tariffs and other controls may be imposed as a short-term method of correcting a deficit in the balance of payments. How successful measures which raise the prices of imports are, will depend on the price elasticity of demand for imports. The higher the price elasticity, the greater the saving of foreign currency will be. However, since the imposition of trade barriers is likely to invite retaliation from other countries, it is uncertain whether or not such a strategy will succeed in improving the country's balance of payments position in the long run.

■ DUMPING

Closely connected with the balance of payments motive is the imposition of trade barriers to counteract the practice of dumping. **Dumping** occurs when a firm sells its product in a foreign market at a lower price than in the domestic market or at a lower price than in other export markets. It may be that the firm in question is simply practising price discrimination (see Section 13.2), by selling at one price in its domestic market and at a lower price in an overseas market where the price elasticity of demand may be different. Or it may be that a firm charges high prices in the domestic market and lower prices elsewhere to expand its output and achieve economies of scale. Dumping may also mean that the price the firm charges in the protected home market is raised and part of the proceeds of the higher price is used to subsidise exports so that it can undercut competitors in the world market. This is known as **predatory dumping** and it is generally agreed that this type of dumping is unfair and that governments are entitled to impose protective tariffs, called **countervailing duties**, to counter it. Dumping is, however, difficult to prove. What might look like dumping may simply be comparative advantage. Foreign firms may be more efficient and allegations of dumping may simply be the political response of domestic firms that cannot compete with efficient foreign firms.

■ EXPORT SUBSIDIES

Free trade is desirable only if all countries play according to the same rules. When a country subsidises some or all of its exports or export industries, firms in other countries call for retaliatory measures (eg in the form of countervailing duties). The steel industry in the United States, for example, persistently called for special tariffs on products exported by Iscor, claiming that Iscor was subsidised in various ways by the South African government (a claim that Iscor consistently denied).

The export-subsidy issue once again illustrates the asymmetries inherent in such issues. For example, if country A subsidises its exports, consumers in country B benefit (at the expense of taxpayers in country A, who bear the burden of the subsidies), but producers in country B lose, and since they are the well-organised, vocal group their voices tend to be heard by the policymakers (rather than those of the consumers, who benefit from the subsidy).

■ INFANT INDUSTRIES

The "infant industry" argument is probably the best known and the oldest of the economic arguments for protection. According to this argument, many developing countries have a potential comparative advantage in manufacturing, but new manufacturing industries in such countries cannot initially compete with well-established industries in developed countries. It is argued that, to allow manufacturing to establish a foothold, governments should temporarily support new industries (with tariffs, import quotas, and subsidies) until they have grown strong enough to meet international competition. During the postwar period, the governments of developing countries found this argument very appealing, and the General Agreement on Tariffs and Trade (GATT) recognised the infant industry argument as a legitimate reason for protectionism. Nevertheless, many economists remain very critical of this argument. They maintain that protection from foreign competition serves no purpose unless the protection helps make the industry efficient. In case after case, protection seems to have done little more than foster the development of inefficient industries that have little hope of ever competing in the world market. Protection also tends to create monopolistic conditions in the domestic market (as was the case in South Africa), and the protected firms tend to become complacent and reluctant to adapt to changing circumstances. Another basic problem is that governments, influenced by political motives, are often poor judges of which industries ought to be protected. Even objective analysts find it difficult, if not impossible, to "pick winners", that is, to identify the industries that will be able to succeed in the long run.

■ EMPLOYMENT

Perhaps the most common political argument for the imposition of trade barriers is that they are necessary to protect jobs and industries from foreign competition. If tariffs are prohibitive they would exclude imports altogether and thus maintain a high level of employment in the domestic industry. Given that unemployment in South Africa is very high, this argument is favoured by trade unions, which regularly call upon government to intervene in international trade flows for the purpose of conserving jobs. A major disadvantage of such protection, however, is that it may delay the structural changes (including the restructuring of jobs) required to render the industry competitive again. Critics also argue that trade barriers are an inefficient way of stimulating employment or lowering unemployment. According to them there are better ways of doing this (eg through appropriate fiscal, monetary and exchange rate policies). It should also always be borne in mind that while one country can succeed with import restrictions, all countries cannot succeed simultaneously with such restrictions. What is true for one country is not true for all countries (recall the fallacy of composition explained in Chapter 1).

A variation of the employment argument is the argument that domestic industries should be protected against cheap foreign labour. In principle, this argument is not valid. Low wages are supposed to reflect low productivity and unit labour cost should not be affected by low wages. Even if unit labour costs are affected, exchange rates can always adjust in response to such differences. Moreover, the case for international trade is based on comparative advantage. If a country's comparative advantage lies in low wage cost, that advantage should be exploited. To deny this would be to argue that poor countries should not be allowed to trade with richer countries. Developed countries tend to respond by arguing that low wage costs in developing countries are often the result of the exploitation of labour and that this serves as a justification for trade barriers. However, to the extent that such exploitation can be proved to exist (and this might be very difficult), the problem should be addressed via the International Labour Organisation (ie through labour policy) rather than through trade policy.

■ GOVERNMENT REVENUE

In developing countries the import tariff is frequently not only a means of industrial protection but also a crucial source of government revenue. For developing countries, tariffs are often extremely efficient forms of revenue collection. Production, consumption, income and property cannot be effectively taxed or subsidised when they cannot be measured and monitored, and with import tariffs revenue can be raised more cheaply than through more elaborate kinds of taxes. Many low-income countries receive between one-quarter and three-fifths of their government revenue from customs duties, whereas in industrial countries the average figure is about two per cent.

■ NATIONAL SECURITY

For obvious reasons, governments prefer not to be entirely dependent upon foreign suppliers for essential resources. It is therefore often argued that industries that produce products that will be essential in times of war or international crisis should be protected. South African examples include the protection afforded to Armscor and Sasol during the country's international isolation under the Nationalist government. Virtually any industry can claim a direct or indirect contribution to national security, and firms or industries tend to exaggerate their strategic importance in an attempt to obtain protection from foreign competition. In the United States, for example, it has been alleged that no industry has ever asked for protection without invoking the national defence argument. In fact, even firms producing pens, pencils, pottery, peanuts, paper, candles and thumbtacks have used it!

National security is a political issue, not an economic one. Economists can only inform politicians and the public about the economic costs associated with attempts to achieve strategic self-sufficiency. As in all other policy matters, the final decisions rest with the politicians.

Arguments against trade barriers

Many of the arguments against obstacles to international trade have already been touched upon in examining the arguments for protection. Some of the most common arguments against trade barriers are the following:

■ RETALIATION BY TRADE PARTNERS

Trade restrictions tend to invite retaliation. For example, if South Africa imposes import controls on Japanese motorcars, then it is more than likely that Japan may do the same and impose import controls on South African products. Any gain to South African firms that compete in the domestic market with Japanese firms would then be offset by the losses made by South African firms that export to Japan. The overall result could well be a tit-for-tat trade war with no real winners.

■ WELFARE COST TO SOCIETY

Protectionist measures, particularly tariffs, impose a cost on society. With the aid of Figure 17-2 we have shown that the introduction of a tariff would be followed by an increase in the price paid by domestic consumers, a fall in the consumer surplus and a loss of welfare to society.

■ INEFFICIENCY

Since import controls protect particular industries from foreign competition, it means that these industries have less incentive to reduce their costs and increase their efficiency.

In general, the net gains and losses from trade barriers are largely unpredictable. Consumers in the protected economy lose since prices are higher than they would be otherwise; producers in the protected economy gain since demand for their products increases; and foreign producers lose since they are deprived of a market.

Trade policy in South Africa

As we explained in Chapter 5, the initial development of the South African economy was based on agriculture and mining. During the 1920s the government adopted a deliberate policy of industrialisation through import replacement. A key feature of the development of the manufacturing sector was the protection granted to South African firms. Import surcharges and quotas were also often used to reduce domestic demand, improve the country's balance of payments and generate government revenue.

By the 1970s, however, it had become increasingly clear that a significant change in trade policy was called for. The process of import substitution had nearly run its course and the country could not continue to rely on gold as the main earner of foreign exchange. Other export industries had to be developed and this required a more liberal approach to imports (eg to reduce the input costs of potential export industries). Export subsidies were instituted and on the import side quantitative restrictions (in the form of import quotas) were replaced by equivalent tariffs and other duties. During the 1980s further steps were taken to reduce the so-called "anti-export bias" and improve the position of exporters. These included exemptions from import duties or the drawback of such duties. However, by the end of the decade primary products, particularly minerals, still dominated the South African export basket and at the start of the 1990s the South African trade regime was still a complex, highly discretionary one with a significant anti-export bias.

In an attempt to improve matters, the government introduced a General Export Incentive Scheme (GEIS), comprising a significant set of export subsidies, in April 1990. GEIS was designed as an economy-wide package, based on value added and local content, and offered considerable incentive to export. Although GEIS was certainly more far-reaching than anything available during the 1980s, it still encouraged exports by addressing the anti-export bias on the output side of the equation, rather than on the input side through import liberalisation. When South Africa signed the GATT agreement, following the Uruguay Round of multilateral trade negotiations (see Box 17-4), at Marrakesh on 15 April 1994, it was agreed that GEIS would be phased out. A three-year phase-out period began in April 1995 and on 11 July 1997 all GEIS concessions were finally repealed (well ahead of schedule).

In signing the Marrakesh Agreement, South Africa agreed to liberalise international trade by lowering import tariffs and eliminating non-tariff barriers to trade. Thus began a more significant and sustained process of import liberalisation. The World Trade Organisation (WTO), which replaced the GATT on 1 January 1995 (see Box 17-4), played an important role in this regard. South Africa's offer to the WTO consisted of a five-year tariff reduction and rationalisation programme, which entailed reducing to six the number of tariff categories, which had previously numbered over 100. Since then, South Africa has demonstrated a clear commitment to opening up the economy to foreign competition.

Besides tariff liberalisation and the abolition of quantitative restrictions, South Africa has also made significant moves towards strengthening bilateral ties with its main trading partners. This has mainly taken the form of negotiating Free Trade Areas (FTAs), the most important of which are the EU-SA FTA, which came into force in January 2000, and the SADC Trade Protocol, which was concluded in August 1996. FTA negotiations were also held with both the United States and Singapore.

To conclude the discussion of trade policy, we reiterate that the international value of the currency also plays an important role in international trade. The exchange rates between the rand and the currencies of our major trading partners (eg the euro, the US dollar, the pound sterling and the yen) have a significant effect on exports and imports, and movements in exchange rates can sometimes be more effective than tariffs, quotas, subsidies and so on. Exchange rates are discussed in greater detail in Section 17.4.

BOX 17-4 THE GATT, THE URUGUAY ROUND, AND THE WORLD TRADE ORGANISATION

At the end of World War II, it was proposed that a global economic organisation, the International Trade Organisation (ITO), be established. Had it been implemented, the ITO's job would have been to establish rules relating to world trade, business practices and international investment. However, opposition from the United States killed the idea of the ITO, and in 1946 twenty-three countries (including South Africa) opened negotiations over tariff reductions. These negotiations led to some 45 000 tariff reductions, affecting one-fifth of world trade. In addition, a number of agreements were reached on rules for trade. This separate agreement, which came into effect on 1 January 1948, became known as the **General Agreement on Tariffs and Trade** (**GATT**). The GATT was quite successful in gradually bringing down trade barriers and increasing world trade. It is estimated that international trade grew at an average rate of more than 6 per cent per year during the second half of the twentieth century, which was much faster than before the war and faster than growth in the world's total output. The GATT functioned through a series of trade rounds during which countries negotiated sets of incremental tariff reductions. Gradually, through the Kennedy Round in the mid-1960s and the Tokyo Round of the 1970s, trade rules other than tariffs began to be addressed, including the problems of dumping, subsidies to industry, and non-tariff barriers to trade. As tariffs came down, these non-tariff issues became more prominent.

The GATT deliberately ignored the extremely contentious sectors of agriculture, textiles and clothing. In addition, trade in services was ignored because it was not important. The accumulation of unresolved issues in these sectors, however, along with the increased importance of non-tariff trade barriers, led to the demand for a new, more extensive set of negotiations. These demands culminated in the **Uruguay Round** of trade negotiations that began in 1986 and concluded in 1993. In 1994, 125 countries signed the new agreement, called the Marrakesh Agreement, and it was also decided to establish a **World Trade Organisation** (**WTO**) to replace the GATT. The WTO was established on 1 January 1995 and by January 2007 its membership had grown to 150 members, with another 20 or so in the process of negotiating to join.

Every two years, trade ministers from around the world meet to set the broad policy objectives of the WTO. Day-to-day work is done by the WTO's staff, under the leadership of its Director-General. The WTO's rules for trade consist of 29 separate legal texts, plus more than 25 declarations, memoranda of understanding and joint statements. The key concepts of all WTO agreements, carried over directly from the GATT, are **non-discrimination** and **national treatment**. These concepts are embodied in the general mission of the WTO, which includes insurance of market access, promotion of fair competition, and encouragement of economic development and economic reform.

The important concept of non-discrimination is embodied in the idea of **most favoured nation** status (MFN). MFN requires every member of the WTO to treat each of its trading partners as well as it treats its most favoured trading partner. In effect, it prohibits one country from discriminating against another. The main exception to MFN that is permitted is regional trade agreements such as the NAFTA (in North America) and Mercosur (in Latin America). **National treatment** requires that imports may not be treated differently than domestically produced goods. In other words, imports must have the same market access as similar domestic goods.

The Uruguay Round and the establishment of the WTO were genuine reforms to the rules of world trade. The WTO preserved the GATT while reaching into new areas, including agriculture, textiles and services; it replaced the GATT's dispute resolution procedure with a faster and more effective mechanism; and it monitors national trade practices more closely.

At the WTO's summit in November 2001 in Doha (in Qatar) a new round of trade negotiations, the **Doha Round**, was launched. The goal was to complete the talks and implement the resulting trade rules in 1 January 2005. Unfortunately, this goal was not met and by July 2006 the five-year Doha Development Round negotiations were suspended following the collapse of ministerial level negotiations of the WTO in Geneva. Calls to resume the negotiations as soon as possible emanated from various forums around the world but at the time of writing the future of the negotiations remained highly uncertain.

17.3 The balance of payments

International trade and other international transactions result in a flow of funds between countries. All transactions relating to the flow of goods, services and funds across national boundaries are recorded in the balance of payments of the countries concerned. We introduced the balance of payments in Chapter 4. In this section we revise the basic concepts and take a closer look at the major components of the balance of payments.

The balance of payments is a systematic statistical account of all the economic transactions between the residents of a country and the residents of other countries in a specific period. Recall, from Chapter 4, that the balance of payments consists of four basic accounts: the **current account**, the **capital transfer account**, the **financial account** (previously called the capital account) and the **unrecorded transactions**. The capital transfer account is relatively insignificant and we will not discuss it further. Payments and receipts relating to the flows of goods and services and other flows of income are recorded in the current account. International transactions in financial assets, including the borrowing and lending of funds, are recorded in the financial account. The balancing item in the balance of payments (in principle) is the **change in the country's gold and other foreign reserves**. In practice, however, the unrecorded transactions serve to balance the balance of payments, as will be explained later.

South Africa's balance of payments accounts for 2005 and 2006 are presented in Table 17-3.

We now take a closer look at some of the items in the balance of payments.

Current account

Merchandise exports and imports require no further explanation. These items simply reflect the rand value of the **goods** exported and imported during the period. Together with net gold exports they constitute what is often referred to as the **trade balance**.

A peculiar feature of South Africa's balance of payments is the fact that **net gold exports** are shown separately, instead of being included in merchandise exports. This is because gold is our most important export and because gold used to play an important role in the international monetary system (see Box 17-5).

The next important set of items is **service receipts** and **payments for services**. Trade in services includes the transportation of goods and passengers between countries, travel, construction services, financial and insurance services, various business, professional and technical services, as well as personal, cultural and recreational services and government services. Money spent by tourists on food and accommodation while travelling in foreign countries falls in this category. The third item in the current account of the balance of payments represents the total value of all service receipts during the period concerned (eg the money spent by foreign tourists in South Africa), while the sixth item represents the total value of payments for services (eg the money spent by South Africans when travelling abroad). In South Africa's case, the payments for services are larger than the service receipts.

Since June 1999, **income receipts** and **income payments** are identified separately in the South African balance of payments. Income receipts refer to income earned by South African residents in the rest of the world, while income payments refer to income earned by non-residents in South Africa. There are two categories of income flows: compensation of employees and investment income. Compensation of employees includes wages, salaries and other benefits earned by individuals from countries other than those in which they are resident (ie from the rest of the world). Investment income includes dividends, inter-

TABLE 17-3 South Africa's balance of payments, 2005 and 2006

	2005 (R millions)	*2006 (R millions)*
Current account		
Merchandise exports	325 103	398 532
Net gold exports	27 023	35 470
Service receipts	70 896	81 353
Income receipts	29 550	40 234
less Merchandise imports	–359 822	–476 545
less Payments for services	–77 384	–96 950
less Income payments	–60 975	–75 990
Current transfers (net receipts +)	–12 775	–17 186
Balance on current account	**–58 384**	**–111 082**
Capital transfer account (net receipts +)	**193**	**205**
Financial account		
Net direct investment	33 854	–47 350
Net portfolio investment	29 903	130 583
Net other investment	4 638	17 970
Balance on financial account	**68 395**	**101 203**
Unrecorded transactions	24 059	39 466
Change in net gold and other foreign reserves owing to balance of payments transactions	**34 263**	**29 792**
Change in liabilities related to reserves	2 577	–5 453
SDR allocations and valuation adjustments	10 777	23 513
Change in gross gold and other foreign reserves	**47 617**	**47 852**

Source: South African Reserve Bank, *Quarterly Bulletin*, March 2007

est, profits and other forms of income earned from the provision of financial capital. Income receipts in the balance of payments are equal to the "primary income from the rest of the world" identified in the national accounts. Likewise, income payments in the balance of payments are equal to the "primary income to the rest of the world" identified in the national accounts.

Recall, from Chapter 4, that gross national income (GNI) is equal to gross domestic product (GDP) plus primary income from the rest of the world minus primary income to the rest of the world. Note that income payments in the South African balance of payments are larger than income receipts. This accounts for the fact that the South African GNI is less than the South African GDP.

The last item in the current account is **current transfers**. This entry includes social security contributions and benefits, taxes imposed by government, and private transfers of income such as gifts, personal, immigrant and other remittances and charitable donations. By transfers we mean money, goods or services transferred without anything tangible being received in return (ie without any *quid pro quo*). In South Africa's case, the current transfer payments are usually significantly greater than the current transfer receipts.

One of the most significant features of Table 17-3 is the large and increasing deficit on the current account of the balance of payments. Note, however, that a current account surplus is not necessarily a good thing. By the same token, there is nothing inherently undesirable about a deficit on the current account, provided that it can be financed – see Box 17-6.

Financial account

The second main component of the balance of payments is the **financial account,** which records international transactions in assets and liabilities. (Before June 1999 it was called the capital account.) The financial account has three main components: direct investment, portfolio investment and other investment. **Direct investment** includes all transactions where the purpose of the investor is to gain control of or have a meaningful say in the management of the enterprise in which the investment is made (eg

BOX 17-5 GOLD IN THE INTERNATIONAL MONETARY SYSTEM

Gold played an important role in the international monetary system prior to 1971. In the late 19th and early 20th centuries most countries were on the **gold standard**. This was an international monetary system in which (i) currencies were defined in terms of gold, (ii) money supplies were linked to gold (in specified ratios) and (iii) balance of payments deficits were settled in gold. Each country adhering to the gold standard established as its monetary unit a gold coin containing a legally specified amount of gold. For example, the US dollar contained 23,22 grains of pure gold, while the British pound contained 113,0016 grains of pure gold. With currencies tied to gold there was a set of basic exchange rates expressing their relative gold content. For example, the exchange rate between the US dollar and the British pound was $4,86656 (ie 113,0016 divided by 23,22) to the pound. At the same time the domestic quantity of money was limited to a certain multiple of a country's gold holdings – in most countries the multiple was 4. Moreover, each central bank was obliged to buy or sell gold at the official price. All balance of payments imbalances between countries were also settled in gold. This system broke down in 1914 with the outbreak of World War I. Although it was restored in some countries between 1925 and 1931, the next few decades were generally characterised by the absence of an organised system for setting exchange rates. At the end of World War II a new exchange rate system was created. This was named the **gold exchange standard** or **Bretton Woods system**, after the place in the United States where a major conference was held in 1944 to establish a new international monetary system. Under this system each country again fixed the value of its currency in terms of gold, as under the gold standard, but the currencies were not backed by gold reserves. By fixing the various currencies in terms of a common denominator, exchange rates between the different currencies could be determined. These exchange rates could be changed by devaluing or revaluing currencies against gold and therefore against each other. The official price of gold was set at $35 an ounce (a price that had been constant since 1934) and countries could use gold to settle international payments at this price.

This international monetary system came under immense pressure during the late 1960s and eventually broke down in 1971, when the major industrialised countries switched to a system of floating currencies whereby exchange rates are determined by market demand and supply. At the same time the official price of gold was abandoned. Until that time South Africa had been guaranteed a price of at least $35 an ounce. In the 1970s, however, gold became an ordinary product, with a variable price (still quoted in US dollars) determined by demand and supply on the international gold markets. Nevertheless, gold exports are still shown separately in the South African balance of payments.

through the establishment of new businesses or the acquisition of shares in existing businesses). **Portfolio investment**, on the other hand, refers to purchases of assets such as shares or bonds where the investor is interested only in the expected financial return on the investment. **Other investment** is a residual category which includes all financial transactions not included under direct investment or portfolio investment. It includes loans, currency and deposits. An important category of other investment is short-term trade credit which is used to finance imports and exports. When a South African importer purchases foreign goods, the transaction is often financed through short-term trade credit obtained abroad. Likewise, South African exports to other countries may also be financed through credit granted to the foreign importer.

In Table 17-3 direct investment, portfolio investment and other investment are all shown on a **net** basis. In other words, the outflows (debits) have been deducted from the inflows (credits). The **balance on financial account** can be obtained by adding net direct investment, net portfolio investment and net other investment. As indicated in Table 17-3, a surplus was recorded on the South African financial account in 2005, followed by an even larger surplus in 2006. These surpluses were typical of the South African experience from 1994, with financial account surpluses generally being large enough to finance current account deficits.

The next item is **unrecorded transactions**. Since a double-entry accounting system is used to record balance of payments transactions, the net sum of all credit and debit entries should, in principle, equal the

BOX 17-6 IS A CURRENT ACCOUNT DEFICIT NECESSARILY A BAD THING?

A deficit on the current account of the balance of payments is not as bad as it may sound. Broadly speaking, a deficit means that a country is importing more than it is exporting. This means that the country is using or consuming more goods and services than it is producing. When imports *(Z)* are greater than exports *(X)*, domestic spending is greater than domestic production. Recall from Chapter 4 that gross domestic expenditure (GDE) consists of consumption spending *(C)*, investment spending *(I)* and government spending *(G)*, that is, $GDE = C + I + G$. Gross domestic product (GDP), on the other hand, consists of $C + I + G + (X - Z)$. When domestic spending (GDE) is greater than domestic production (GDP), imports are greater than exports, that is, $(X - Z)$ is negative. Similarly, when domestic production (GDP) is greater than domestic spending (GDE), exports are greater than imports, that is, $(X - Z)$ is positive.

A country, like an individual, always enjoys a higher standard of living when its residents are spending (or consuming) more than they are producing (or earning), compared to when they can only spend (or consume) what they produce (or earn). But the shortfall must be financed. If a country can obtain the necessary finance in the form of a sustained surplus on the financial account of the balance of payments, it can afford to keep running a deficit on the current account. This can be compared to an individual whose excess spending (over earnings) is financed by obtaining a loan from the bank. As long as the bank manager has sufficient confidence in the client's creditworthiness, the client can keep spending more than he or she is earning. Similarly, if the international community has confidence in the growth potential of an economy, financial account surpluses can be maintained. International confidence will depend, *inter alia*, on the type of import spending. Spending on capital goods enhances a country's long-term production potential and is therefore preferable to spending on consumer goods. Nevertheless, debts have to be settled eventually. When debts have to be repaid and there are no other foreign lenders or investors who are willing to supply the necessary finance, as was the case in South Africa from 1985 to 1993, domestic spending has to be kept lower than domestic production in order to generate the surplus on the current account that is required to finance the deficit on the financial account. When this happens, there is a corresponding drop in average living standards.

The important point is that there is nothing inherently undesirable about periodic deficits on the current account of the balance of payments. Similarly, there is nothing inherently desirable about sustained current account surpluses.

change in the country's net gold and other foreign reserves. In practice, however, this does not happen. All errors and omissions that occur in compiling the individual components of the balance of payments are entered as unrecorded transactions. In practice, therefore, unrecorded transactions serve to ensure that the balance of payments actually balances.

Gold and other foreign reserves

A country earns foreign currency by exporting goods and services and by receiving transfers as well as inflows on the financial account (generally known as capital inflows). On the other hand, it has to pay in foreign currency for imported goods and services and also loses currency through transfers and outflows on the financial account (generally known as capital outflows). If the receipts of foreign currency exceed the payments of foreign currency, the country's **foreign reserves** (ie its holdings of various foreign currencies) increase. If the receipts are smaller than the payments, the foreign reserves decrease.

The sum of the current account balance, the capital transfer balance, the financial account balance and the unrecorded transactions is therefore reflected in the change in foreign reserves. A portion of South Africa's gold production is held by the South African Reserve Bank as part of the country's foreign reserves. If necessary, the gold reserves can be sold to obtain foreign currency (eg US dollars). South Africa's foreign reserves thus consist of **gold and other foreign reserves**.

Gold and other foreign reserves are the most important total in the balance of payments for the following reasons:

- They reflect the overall balance of payments position.
- Since payments and receipts of foreign currency do not necessarily coincide – there may be large differ-

ences from week to week or month to month – foreign reserves are required to ensure a smooth flow of international trade and finance.

- Foreign reserves are required to prevent large fluctuations in exchange rates between the domestic currency and foreign currencies.
- Foreign reserves are an indicator of the authorities' scope to stimulate the economy without running into payment difficulties.

Table 17-3 also shows that there is a difference between changes in **net** and **gross** foreign reserves. The **change in net gold and other foreign reserves** reflects the combined balance on the current, capital transfer and financial accounts and the unrecorded transactions. This is why it is described as the change "owing to balance of payments transactions". The authorities can, however, supplement the reserves by borrowing specifically for this purpose, for instance from the International Monetary Fund – see Box 17-7. This increases the country's reserves, but the increase is only a "gross" change since the loans obtained have to be repaid as soon as the balance of payments improves. When the loans are repaid, the **gross reserves** decline accordingly.

As shown in Table 17-3, South Africa's net gold and other foreign reserves increased in 2005 and 2006, with the increases in the gross reserves being even larger.

The balance of payments and economic activity and policy in South Africa

International economic developments have important effects on economic activity and economic policy in the domestic economy. Modern economies are highly interdependent and those which can compete most effectively on international markets are generally the ones that succeed.

In South Africa, **exports** are a major source of demand for domestically produced goods and therefore also of production, income and employment in the domestic economy. Had it not been for South Africa's gold and other exports, the country would not have developed as it has. Exports are therefore of great significance. But how can exports be promoted? The following are some of the options:

- Take steps to keep domestic costs of production in check so that goods can be supplied on international markets at competitive prices.
- Assist potential exporters to find international markets, and subsidise some of their costs (this is usually called export promotion).
- Allow or engineer a depreciation of the rand against other currencies, thereby making exports more competitive, *ceteris paribus*.

Steps to boost exports are, however, easier to identify than to carry out. Moreover, they all entail significant costs or side-effects, such as the possibility of increased inflation (in the case of a depreciation of the international value of the currency). While some action usually has to be taken to boost exports, the major determinant of South African exports is, in fact, economic conditions in the rest of the world. When the world economy is booming, the value of South Africa's exports increases because more goods are demanded and prices are better. But when the country's major trading partners are suffering from a recession, the value of South Africa's exports tends to decline, because fewer goods are demanded and prices also tend to fall.

A large portion of domestic spending in South Africa is on **imported goods and services**, particularly on capital and intermediate goods required by domestic industry. As economic activity in South Africa increases, imports invariably increase as well (and usually at a much higher rate). This can create problems, since imports have to be paid for in foreign currency, which can only be obtained by exporting or from net inflows of foreign capital.

When the demand for imports increases, the demand for foreign exchange increases. If foreign exchange is lacking, or if there is no intervention, the rand will depreciate against other currencies. This will assist exporters in the short run, but will also lead to higher import prices which feed into the domestic inflation process. To promote international trade and economic growth and stability, the South African Reserve Bank (SARB) wants to avoid sharp fluctuations in the exchange rates between the rand and other currencies. If the SARB has the necessary foreign exchange reserves, it can intervene in the foreign exchange market, although it has been reluctant to do so in recent years. However, if it does not have sufficient reserves and cannot rely on a sustained surplus on the financial account (ie a sustained net inflow of foreign capital) then the demand for imports must be cut back. Tariffs and quotas can be used for this purpose, but both these measures have a variety of undesirable side-effects (including raising the costs of domestic production and possibly eliciting retaliatory measures by other countries against South Africa's exports) and are therefore generally not used for balance of payments purposes. The imposition of tariffs and quotas may also constitute a contravention of international trade agreements. One approach that has proved effective is to reduce domestic demand. Such a reduction will be accompanied by a fall in imports, but this means that domestic production, income and employment have to be sacrificed for balance of payments purposes. Unpalatable as it may seem, South Africa has often had to rely on this strategy to solve its balance of payments problems.

From 1985 to 1993 the need to cut back on domes-

BOX 17-7 THE INTERNATIONAL MONETARY FUND AND THE WORLD BANK

Apart from the WTO, two other global organisations are central to international economic relations: the **International Monetary Fund** (**IMF**) and the **World Bank**. During World War II, the United States, Great Britain and a few other allies held regular discussions about the shape of the post-war international economic order. They wanted to avoid the mistakes of the 1920s and 1930s, when the settlement of debts following World War I and a lack of international cooperation led to the complete collapse of economic relations. The culmination of these talks was the meetings held at Bretton Woods in the United States in July 1944, where the outlines of the International Monetary Fund (IMF) and the International Bank for Reconstruction and Development (World Bank) were agreed upon.

The IMF began operation on December 27, 1945 with a membership of 29 countries, including South Africa. By 2000, its membership had grown to 182 members. The IMF provides loans to its members under different short-, medium-, and long-term programmes. Each member is charged a fee, or quota, as the price of membership, the size of the quota varying with the size of the nation's economy and the importance of its currency in world trade and payments. Important decisions within the IMF are made by vote with the weight of each nation's vote proportional to its quota. This gives the high-income countries of the world a voting power that is disproportionate to their population. The size of the quota also determines a country's access to loans.

The most visible role for the IMF is to intercede, by invitation, whenever a nation experiences a crisis in its international payments. For example, if a country imports more than it exports, it may deplete its reserves of foreign exchange that are used to pay for foreign goods. If a country lacks reserves, it cannot pay for its imports, nor can it pay the interest and principal it owes on its international borrowings. This is one scenario that warrants a call to the IMF. The IMF makes loans to members that are experiencing problems, but it usually extracts a price above and beyond the interest it charges. The price is an agreement by the borrower to change its policies to avoid a recurrence of the problem. The IMF often requires a borrower to make fundamental changes to its economy (eg in the relationship between government and markets) in order to qualify for IMF funds. These requirements are known as **IMF conditionality**.

The IMF also performs several related functions. In the current world economy, it has been an important source of both technical expertise and capital for the transitional economies of central and eastern Europe. These economies lacked experience with open markets and large private sectors. They have had to create tax systems, social programmes and business codes from scratch, and the IMF has been a major source of information and financing. This role, however, and its role as the main provider of funds and advice to crisis-gripped economies in Latin America, Africa and East Asia, have frequently been criticised. Indeed, the advice given by the IMF and the conditions it imposes have often been extremely controversial.

The **World Bank** was founded at the same time as the IMF but started operating only in March 1947, with South Africa as a founder member. World economies that are members of the Bank buy shares in it and, similar to the quotas that determine voting rights in the IMF, shareholding determines the weight of each member in setting the Bank's policies and practices. Originally, the World Bank was known as the International Bank for Reconstruction and Development, or IBRD. The name reflected the fact that it was created primarily to assist with the reconstruction of countries that had been ravaged by the Second World War. By the 1950s, the field of development economics had begun to take off and several leading economists argued that the world's less economically developed regions could grow much faster if they could get around the constraints imposed by a lack of investment capital. The IBRD was therefore encouraged to lend to developing economies. Today, the IBRD is one of five separate subgroups that make up the World Bank. The role of the IBRD is to lend for specific development projects such as dams, highways and schools, and to support major adjustments in government policies that change the way a country manages its economy. Other sub-groups in the World Bank are focused on the very poor, private sector development, and loan guarantee programmes. Only developing countries can borrow from the World Bank.

tic demand to reduce imports was forced on South Africa by the position on the **financial account**. When there are large deficits on the financial account (eg because foreign debt has to be repaid or because people are taking their funds out of the country), these deficits have to be balanced by surpluses on the current account. The only exception is when the country can obtain the necessary loans to supplement its foreign exchange reserves. Between 1985 and 1993 South Africa did not have this option and the authorities therefore simply had to keep domestic demand in check to keep imports down and maintain a current account surplus.

With the emergence of democracy in 1994, South Africa's international economic relations improved substantially, but the interaction between the balance of payments, domestic economic activity and economic policy is still (and will always be) one of the most important aspects of South African economic life.

17.4 Exchange rates

Foreign trade involves payment in foreign currencies such as the euro (€), pound sterling (£), United States dollar ($) and Japanese yen (¥). South African **importers** have to pay in these currencies for the goods they buy and are therefore obliged to exchange South African rands for these currencies. There is thus a **demand** on the part of South African importers for euros, pounds, dollars, yen, etc. On the other hand, importers in other countries, such as Germany and the UK, have to pay in rands for South African exports and must therefore exchange euros, pounds, etc for rands. In this way South African **exports** lead to a **supply** of foreign currency. The rate at which currencies are exchanged is known as the **rate of exchange** or **exchange rate**. The rate of exchange therefore represents a **ratio**, that is, the **price** of one currency in terms of another currency. Like any other price, the exchange rate can be explained and analysed with the aid of supply and demand curves

In principle, the exchange rate is not a difficult concept to understand. It simply represents the price of one currency in terms of another currency. It is, however, important to be alert when dealing with exchange rates. One must, for example, be careful to establish from which point of view an exchange rate is approached in a particular situation. An increase in the value or price of one currency in terms of another currency (also known as **appreciation**) automatically implies a decrease (**depreciation**) in the value of the other currency. Note that an exchange rate, or the price of one currency in terms of a second currency, may just as well be quoted as the price of the second currency in terms of the first currency – see Box 17-8.

But how are exchange rates determined? Who decides what the exchange rates should be? In the next subsection we explain how the exchange rate between the United States dollar and the South African rand is determined in a freely functioning foreign exchange market. A **foreign exchange market** is the international market in which one currency can be exchanged for other currencies. The foreign exchange market does not have a specific location. The South African foreign exchange market consists of all the authorised currency dealers, among whom are included all the major banks. Since in South Africa the market for US dollars is the most important element of the foreign exchange market, we use the exchange rate between the rand and the dollar to

BOX 17-8 DIRECT AND INDIRECT QUOTATION OF EXCHANGE RATES

An exchange rate is simply the price of one currency in terms of another currency. It can always be quoted in two ways – a **direct** way and an **indirect** way. Most countries use the direct method. With this method the exchange rate shows how much of the local currency (rands in the case of South Africa) have to be exchanged for one unit of a foreign currency. For example, if you have to pay R10,00 to obtain one US dollar, the direct method is to state that $1 = R10,00. With the indirect method, on the other hand, the exchange rate is expressed as the amount of foreign currency that is required to purchase one unit of the domestic currency. In our example the indirect method involves stating that R1 = $0,10, that is, only 10 US cents are required to purchase one rand. The indirect method is thus simply the inverse of the direct method.

The indirect method of quotation can be useful to a South African tourist who can immediately determine how much of the foreign currency she can obtain for her rands. However, since foreign exchange is simply a commodity and the exchange rate is the price of that commodity, it is more logical to quote the price directly in terms of the domestic currency (eg rands). The SARB also uses the direct method to indicate exchange rates in its *Quarterly Bulletin*.

explain how a freely functioning foreign exchange market works. We later also explain how the Reserve Bank can intervene in the foreign exchange market in an attempt to manage the exchange rate.

The foreign exchange market

In Figure 17-3 we show the South African market for US dollars. The diagram is similar to the diagrams used in Part II to explain the prices of goods and services. The quantity of dollars is measured on the horizontal axis and the price of dollars (in South African rands) is measured on the vertical axis. The figure shows the demand and supply curves for US dollars. Financial institutions, firms, governments, investors, speculators, tourists and other individuals exchange rands for dollars and dollars for rands every day. In January 2007 the average *daily* turnover (in all currencies) on the South African foreign exchange market was more than $14,4 billion. We now take a closer look at the demand for and supply of dollars.

FIGURE 17-3 The foreign exchange market

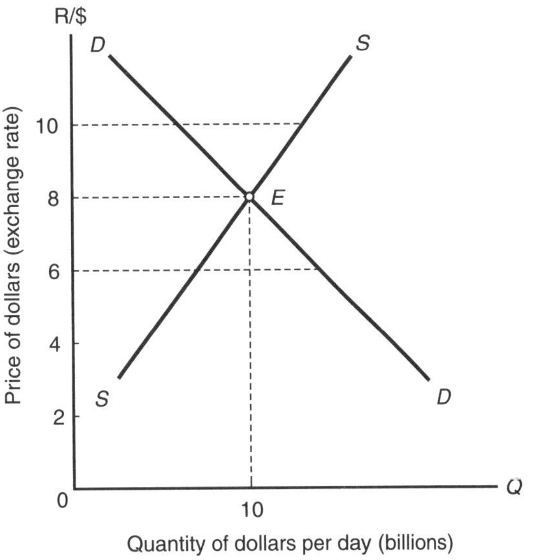

The figure shows the market for US dollars. The price of dollars (in rands) (ie the exchange rate) is indicated on the vertical axis. The quantity of dollars (billions per day) is indicated on the horizontal axis. DD represents the demand for US dollars and SS the supply of US dollars. The equilibrium exchange rate is $1 = R8. At lower prices there is an excess demand for dollars and at higher prices there is an excess supply of dollars. The equilibrium quantity is $10 billion per day.

■ THE DEMAND FOR DOLLARS

Those who demand dollars are holders of rands who are seeking to exchange them for dollars. The demand for dollars (which is the same as the supply of rands) comes from various sources. A first source is South African importers who import goods and services for which they pay in US dollars. A second source is South African residents who wish to purchase dollar denominated assets, such as shares of American companies. Another example is American investors who sell their South African assets (eg shares, bonds) and wish to convert the proceeds into US dollars. A fourth source is South African tourists who buy dollars or dollar denominated travellers' cheques. Another important source is speculators who anticipate a decline in the value of the rand relative to the dollar (ie a depreciation of the rand against the dollar, or an appreciation of the dollar against the rand) – see Box 17-9. The general rule is that the more expensive the dollars are (ie the higher the price of the dollar in terms of the rand), the smaller will be the quantity of dollars demanded, *ceteris paribus*.

In Figure 17-3 we show three exchange rates. When the exchange rate is $1 = R8 it means that a tractor which costs $100 000 in the United States will cost R800 000 in South Africa (if we ignore transport and other costs of importing the tractor). However, at an exchange rate of $1 = R6 the same tractor will cost only R600 000 in South Africa. The lower the price of dollars, the cheaper American goods will become and the greater the quantity of American goods and therefore also of dollars that will be demanded in South Africa. The demand curve therefore has a negative slope. Note that the demand for dollars is a **derived** demand – it is derived, for example, from the demand for imported goods and services and foreign assets, and foreigners' supply of domestic liabilities. The exchange rate determines the domestic price of the goods, services and assets and the foreign price of domestic liabilities, and therefore affects the quantity of foreign currency demanded.

■ THE SUPPLY OF DOLLARS

Those who supply dollars are holders of dollars seeking to exchange them for rands. The supply of dollars comes from various sources. A first source is South African exporters who export goods and services. The foreign buyers of South African exports whose prices are quoted in dollars supply dollars which are then exchanged for rands. A second source is foreign holders of dollars who purchase South African assets (eg shares on the JSE Securities Exchange or government stock). They also supply dollars. Another example is South African investors who sell foreign assets denominated in dollars and convert the proceeds back into rands. Further sources include foreign tourists in South Africa who exchange dollars or dollar denominated travellers' cheques for rands, and speculators who anticipate a rise in the value of the rand relative to the dollar (ie an appreciation of the rand against the dollar or a depreciation of the dollar against the rand) – see Box 17-9.

The supply of dollars is positively related to the rand/dollar exchange rate. For example, at an exchange rate of $1 = R7 a South African product which costs R420 000 will cost an American purchaser $60 000, but at an exchange rate of $1 = R6 the same product will cost $70 000 in the United States. As the rand price of the dollar falls, the quantity of South African exports demanded by Americans and therefore also the **derived** quantity of dollars **supplied** will fall. The supply curve therefore has a positive slope.

■ THE EQUILIBRIUM EXCHANGE RATE

The equilibrium exchange rate is the rate at which the quantity of dollars demanded equals the quantity of dollars supplied. In Figure 17-3 this is indicated by an exchange rate of $1 = R8. The quantity exchanged at this exchange rate is $10 billion. At a higher price of the dollar (eg $1 = R10) there will be an excess supply of dollars. At a lower price of the dollar (eg $1 = R6) there will be an excess demand for dollars.

This example shows how market forces determine an exchange rate. We chose the dollar because the rand/dollar exchange rate is the basic exchange rate in the South African foreign exchange market. The rates against all other currencies (eg pound sterling, euro or yen) are derived from those currencies' exchange rates with the dollar. For example, if $1 = R8,00 and $1 = € 0,80 then South African currency dealers will quote an exchange rate of € 1 = R(8,00 ÷ 0,80) = R10,00. Similar calculations are made in respect of other currencies. (The actual rates may, however, differ somewhat due to certain costs and margins that have to be taken into account.)

■ CHANGES IN SUPPLY AND DEMAND: CURRENCY DEPRECIATION AND APPRECIATION

Anything that causes a change in the supply or demand of foreign exchange will result in a change in the exchange rate, *ceteris paribus*. When dollars become more expensive, we say that the dollar has **appreciated** against the rand, or (what amounts to the same thing) that the rand has **depreciated** against the dollar. Similarly, a fall in the price of the dollar implies that the dollar has **depreciated** against the rand or that the rand has **appreciated** against the dollar. In terms of Figure 17-3 a **change in supply or demand** will be reflected by a **shift** of the relevant curve. We now use a **decrease in the supply of dollars** (ie a leftward shift of the supply curve in Figure 17-3) to illustrate how the exchange rate changes in response to a change in market forces.[1]

The supply of dollars decreases, for example, when households, firms or the government in the United States import fewer South African goods, or when the price of gold falls on the world market. In the case of a decrease in South African exports to the United States, fewer dollars will be earned. Since the gold price is quoted in dollars, a fall in the gold price also means that fewer dollars will be earned (ie **supplied** on the South African foreign exchange market) for a given volume of gold exports. In Figure 17-4 the original supply (*SS*), demand (*DD*), equilibrium exchange rate or price ($1 = R8) and equilibrium quantity ($10 billion) are all the same as in Figure 17-3. The subsequent decrease in supply is illustrated by a leftward shift of the supply curve to S_1S_1. The new equilibrium exchange rate is $1 = R9,00 and the equilibrium quantity falls to $8 billion.

What does this mean? What has happened to the exchange rate? In this case, the dollar has become more expensive in terms of rands, that is, the **dollar has appreciated** against the rand. This implies that the **rand has depreciated** against the dollar.

Diagrams similar to the one in Figure 17-4 can be used to obtain the rest of the results summarised in Table 17-4. When the dollar appreciates (ie when the

FIGURE 17-4 A decrease in the supply of dollars

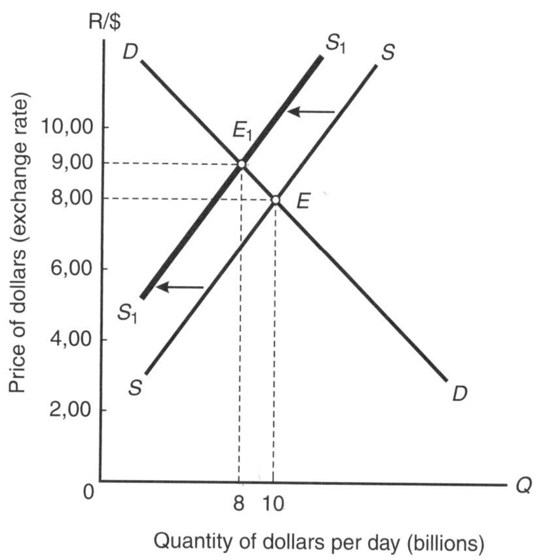

The original supply (SS), demand (DD), equilibrium price and quantity are the same as in Figure 17-3. The decrease in the supply of dollars shifts the supply curve to S_1S_1. The equilibrium price (or exchange rate) changes to $1 = R9,00 and the equilibrium quantity falls to $8 billion.

1. Note that, as in the case of all other demand and supply curves, a change in the exchange rate (ie in the price of a currency) causes a **movement along** the demand curve as well as a **movement along** the supply curve. The curves **shift** only if a non-price determinant (ie something other than the exchange rate) changes.

TABLE 17-4 Changes in supply and demand: a summary

Change	*Illustrated by*	*Impact on rand/dollar exchange rate (ceteris paribus)*	
		Rand	*Dollar*
Demand for dollars increases (eg because SA firms purchase more US capital goods at each exchange rate or because more SA tourists visit the United States)	A shift of the demand curve to the right	Depreciates	Appreciates
Supply of dollars increases (eg because the gold price increases or because US firms buy more South African minerals)	A shift of the supply curve to the right	Appreciates	Depreciates
Supply of dollars decreases (eg because gold price falls or because US citizens stop investing in South Africa)	A shift of the supply curve to the left	Depreciates	Appreciates
Demand for dollars falls (eg because a recession in South Africa causes a slump in the demand for US goods)	A shift of the demand curve to the left	Appreciates	Depreciates

rand depreciates), imports from the United States become more expensive (in rands) in South Africa and South African exports to the United States become cheaper (in dollars) in that country, *ceteris paribus*. This will tend to dampen imports and stimulate exports (ie to improve the balance on the current account). Similarly, when the dollar depreciates (ie when the rand appreciates), imports from the United States become cheaper in South Africa (in rands) but South African exports to the United States become more expensive (in dollars) in that country. This will tend to stimulate imports and dampen exports (ie to worsen the balance on the current account).

A change in the exchange rate is a double-edged sword. South African exporters, for example, generally prefer a depreciation of the rand since it makes their goods more competitive on international markets, *ceteris paribus*. But a depreciation raises the prices of imported goods and services. These price increases then feed into the inflation process and tend to raise inflation – see Chapter 21. When the authorities wish to combat inflation, they prefer an appreciation of the rand, but this tends to reduce the competitiveness of our exports (in the short run at least) and to stimulate imports. These effects are summarised in Table 17-5. See also Box 17-9. From this brief discussion it should be obvious that the question of the appropriate international value of the currency is quite complicated – see Box 17-10.

Intervention in the foreign exchange market

If the foreign exchange market is left to its own devices, exchange rates tend to fluctuate quite considerably, since the demand for and supply of foreign exchange are not synchronised on a day-to-day basis. As explained in Box 17-9, a freely floating exchange rate is also subject to speculation. Because of the potential volatility of exchange rates, and because the authorities often wish to use the exchange rate to pursue particular policy objectives, exchange rates are often managed or manipulated to some extent by central banks. This is called **managed floating** and was practised by the South African Reserve Bank from 24

TABLE 17-5 Impact of changes in rand/dollar exchange rate for South Africa

Change in R/$ exchange rate	*Impact on*			
	Export prices (in dollars)	*Import prices (in rands)*	*Current account*	*Domestic prices*
Rand depreciates against dollar	Decrease	Increase	Improves	Rise
Rand appreciates against dollar	Increase	Decrease	Worsens	Fall

BOX 17-9 THE SPECULATIVE NATURE OF THE FOREIGN EXCHANGE MARKET

The basic functioning of a speculative market was explained in Box 8-1. Foreign currency is a homogeneous, durable good and currency markets are subject to speculative activity. We now use the rand-dollar market to explain the basic elements and impact of speculation in a foreign exchange (or currency) market.

In the diagram below, *DD* represents the demand for dollars and *SS* the supply of dollars. The original equilibrium exchange rate is $1,00 = R7,50. Suppose that most market participants believe that the rand will depreciate against the dollar (ie that the price of dollars will increase). How will they react? Everyone who will have to purchase dollars in the near future (eg importers, South African tourists wishing to go abroad and South Africans planning to invest abroad) as well as speculators who wish to profit from movements in the exchange rate will immediately purchase as many dollars as they can (before the price of dollars increases).[1] This is illustrated by a rightward shift of the demand curve to D_1D_1.

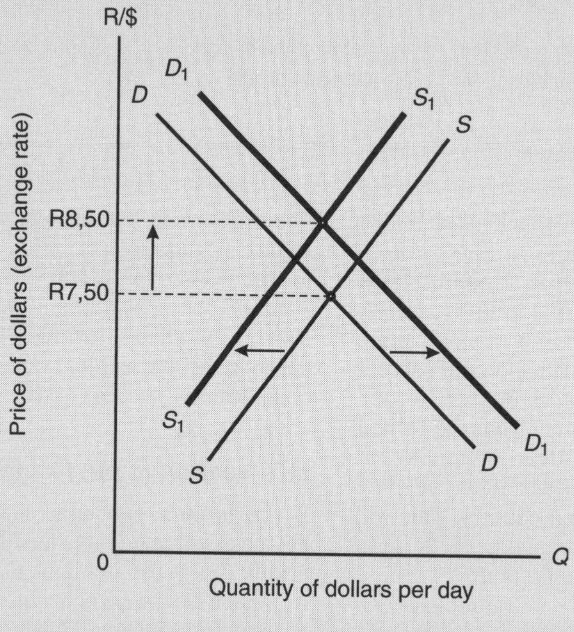

At the same time, the expected appreciation of the dollar reduces the supply of dollars. Everyone who will sell dollars in the near future (eg South African exporters, South Africans who wish to sell their foreign assets and foreigners who want to invest in South Africa) will postpone their dollar sales (or purchases of rand) for as long as possible (until the price of dollars has increased). This is illustrated by a leftward shift of the supply curve to S_1S_1.

As a result of the increase in demand and decrease in supply a new equilibrium is established at a higher price than before. In the diagram this is illustrated by the new exchange rate of $1,00 = R8,50.

If there is a general expectation that the dollar will appreciate and the majority of market participants incorporate this expectation into their behaviour, the dollar will appreciate **immediately** (purely as a result of **expected** price movements).

1. Speculators finance their purchases of dollars by borrowing rands. If the dollar subsequently appreciates, as they expect, they repay their loans with cheaper rands. The interest rate at which they can borrow rands is vitally important. The higher the interest rate, the greater the cost of currency speculation becomes. This is why the SARB has often raised interest rates during actual or perceived bouts of speculation against the rand. Higher interest rates curb speculative activity by reducing the potential profits from such speculation.

Likewise, if there is a general expectation that the dollar will depreciate (ie that the rand will appreciate) exactly the opposite will tend to occur, provided that market participants act on the basis of this expectation. On the other hand, if there are mixed expectations, or a general expectation that the exchange rate will remain fairly stable, a fairly stable exchange rate will tend to ensue.

From this brief discussion it should be obvious that **expectations** or **market sentiment** are often a crucial determinant of movements in exchange rates. The speculative nature of the foreign exchange market helps to explain, for example, why exchange rates tend to overshoot (in both directions), as happened in South Africa between September 2001 and the first half of 2003 – see Box 17-11.

January 1979 until the adoption of inflation targeting in February 2000.[2]

We now explain managed floating with the aid of Figure 17-5. The original demand and supply curves (*DD* and *SS* respectively) are the same as in Figure 17-3, as are the original equilibrium exchange rate ($1,00 = R8,00) and quantity traded ($10 billion). Suppose that the demand for dollars increases (eg because of an increase in South African imports from the United States), illustrated by a rightward shift of the demand curve to D_1D_1. At the original exchange rate ($1,00 = R8,00) there is now an excess demand for dollars of $1 billion, indicated by the difference between E_0 and E_2 (ie the difference between $11 billion and $10 billion).

In the absence of any intervention the excess demand for dollars will result in an increase in the price of dollars to $1,00 = R9,00, illustrated by the new equilibrium at E_1. In other words, the rand will depreciate against the dollar. Suppose that the SARB wishes to avoid such a depreciation of the rand (eg because it may result in inflationary pressure). What can it do?

If it has the necessary reserves, the SARB can supply $1 billion to the market. This can be illustrated by a rightward shift of the supply curve to S_1S_1. A new equilibrium is established at E_2 and the exchange rate remains at $1,00 = R8,00. What will actually happen in practice is that the SARB will be willing to supply additional dollars at the original exchange rate to avoid the development of an excess demand for dollars and a consequent appreciation of the dollar (ie depreciation of the rand).

2. Under a pure inflation targeting regime, the central bank does not intervene in the foreign exchange market. This was also the approach adopted by the South African Reserve Bank when inflation targeting was introduced. Even during the last quarter of 2001, when the rand depreciated sharply against the main currencies (see Box 17-11), the SARB steadfastly refrained from intervening in the foreign exchange market to support the rand. The State President did, however, appoint a commission of enquiry (the Myburgh Commission) to investigate the reasons for the depreciation of the rand, in response to allegations that exchange rates had been manipulated by certain financial institutions and large companies.

FIGURE 17-5 Managed floating

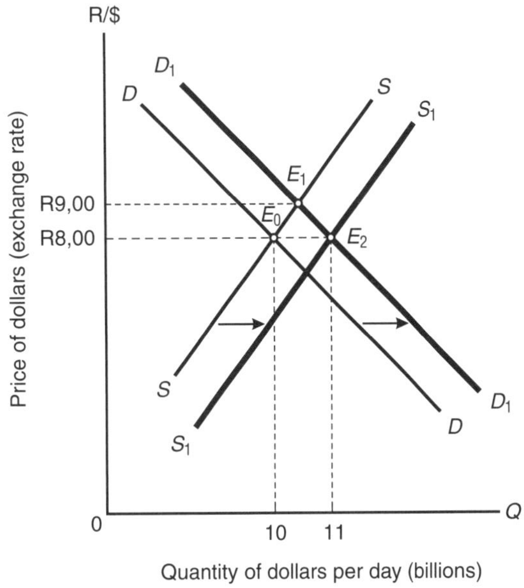

The original demand and supply curves (DD and SS), equilibrium (E_0), exchange rate ($1,00 = R8,00) and quantity traded ($10 billion) are the same as in Figure 17-4. The demand for dollars increases, illustrated by the shift of the demand curve to D_1D_1. In the absence of intervention, an excess demand of $1 billion (ie E_2-E_0) will develop at the original exchange rate and the equilibrium exchange rate will change to $1,00 = R9,00 (at E_1). The central bank can avoid this appreciation of the dollar by supplying an additional $1 billion to the market, illustrated by a shift of the supply curve to S_1S_1. The new equilibrium will be at E_2 (ie at an unchanged exchange rate).

This is how **managed floating** works. The central bank monitors developments in the foreign exchange market and decides whether or not to intervene. If it decides to intervene, it can also do so on a limited scale. For instance, in our example the SARB can supply fewer than a billion dollars. In such a case the

BOX 17-10 UNDERVALUED AND OVERVALUED CURRENCIES: PURCHASING POWER PARITY AND THE BIG MAC INDEX

Economists, policymakers and others frequently differ as to whether or not exchange rates are at appropriate levels. Put differently, there is often disagreement as to whether the domestic currency is correctly valued against other currencies. For example, at any particular time there are those who argue that the rand, for example, is undervalued while others contend that it is overvalued. But how does one determine whether a currency is undervalued, correctly valued or overvalued? One of the basic criteria is **purchasing power parity** (PPP). Purchasing power parity occurs when currencies have the same purchasing power in different countries. For example, the PPP exchange rate between the rand and the US dollar will be determined by the number of rands which will give the holder (in SA) the same command over goods and services as one US dollar (in the USA). Thus, if a basket of goods and services costs $10 in the US, and the same basket costs R100 in South Africa, the PPP exchange rate (or simply PPP) is $1,00 = R10,00.

International comparisons of the cost of similar baskets of goods and services are not conducted regularly, but since 1986 the well-known British financial weekly, *The Economist*, periodically publishes the Big Mac index, a light-hearted, simplistic version of PPP. Instead of using the cost of a basket of goods and services, a McDonald's Big Mac hamburger is used to determine PPP exchange rates. The Big Mac was selected because it is available, in similar shape and taste, in more than 115 countries.

The Big Mac PPP between the US and another country is the exchange rate that would mean hamburgers would cost the same in the US as in the other country. Comparing the actual exchange rate with the Big Mac PPP then gives an indication of whether a currency is overvalued, correctly valued or undervalued compared to the US dollar. The Big Mac standard can also be used to determine PPPs between other pairs of countries.

The following table contains some of the results of the survey conducted on 31 January 2007 (*The Economist*, 1 February 2007).

THE BIG MAC INDEX, 31 JANUARY 2007

Country	Big Mac prices		Implied PPP of the US dollar	Actual $ exchange rate	Local currency under (–)/over (+) valuation against $
	In local currency	In US dollars			
United States	$3,22	3,22	–	–	–
Australia	A$3,45	2,67	1,07	1,29	–17
Britain	£1,99	3,90	0,61	0,51	+20
China	Yuan 11,0	1,41	3,42	7,77	–56
Euro area	€2,94	3,82	0,91	0,77	+18
South Africa	R15,50	2,14	4,81	7,25	–34
South Korea	Won 2900	3,08	901	942	–4
Switzerland	SFr 6,30	5,04	1,96	1,25	+57

The first column shows the local currency prices of a Big Mac. In the second column these prices are converted into US dollars using the prevailing exchange rates. The third column shows the Big Mac PPPs. These are obtained by dividing the domestic price of a Big Mac by the price in US dollars ($3,22). This is what the exchange rate should be to make the dollar price of a Big Mac equal to the price in the domestic currency (eg rand). For example, dividing the South African price of R15,50 by the US price of $3,22 gives a PPP of R4,81 per dollar. The fourth column shows the actual exchange rates on 31 January 2007. By comparing the actual exchange rates with the PPP exchange rates, the degree of undervaluation or overvaluation can be determined. For example, on that date the rand was 34 per cent undervalued against the dollar, while the British pound (sterling) was overvalued by 20 per cent.

As mentioned earlier, the Big Mac standard can also be used to calculate PPPs between other sets of currencies. For example, a Big Mac cost A$3,45 in Australia and R15,50 in South Africa, implying a PPP exchange rate of R15,50 ÷ 3,45 = R4,49 to the Australian dollar. The actual exchange rate was R7,25 ÷ 1,29 = R5,62 to the Australian dollar, implying that the rand was 20 per cent undervalued against the Australian dollar in Big Mac PPP terms on 31 January 2007.

Although the Big Mac index is a crude measure, it often yields PPP estimates that are quite similar to those based on more sophisticated methods. The publication of the latest Big Mac index regularly receives extensive coverage in the media and the index is often used as a guide by tourists planning to visit foreign destinations.

Any standardised product that is sold in different countries can be used to estimate PPPs. For example, since *The Economist* itself is sold in different currencies, the different prices can be used to compile a set of *The Economist* PPP exchange rates. On 31 January 2007 the magazine cost €5,20 in the Euro area, R35,00 in South Africa and SFr10,00 in Switzerland. This implies PPP exchange rate of €1 = R6,73 and SFr1 = R3,50. The corresponding Big Mac PPP exchange rates were €1 = R5,27 and SFr1 = R2,46, and the actual exchange rates €1 = R9,42 and SFr1 = R5,80. All these data point to a significantly undervalued rand against those currencies on a PPP basis at that stage.

Note that, since exchange rates are determined by a variety of factors, PPP, especially not a simple estimate, is not necessarily always an appropriate indicator of whether a currency is undervalued or overvalued.

exchange rate will settle somewhere between R8,00 and R9,00 per dollar, depending on the amount of intervention.

On the other hand, if an excess supply of dollars develops at the original exchange rate (eg because of a decrease in the demand for dollars, ie a decrease in the supply of rands), and the SARB wishes to avoid a depreciation of the dollar (ie an appreciation of the rand), it will purchase the excess dollars at the original exchange rate and add them to the foreign exchange reserves.

While it is relatively easy for a central bank to purchase foreign exchange in an attempt to avoid an appreciation of the currency (because such an appreciation might, for example, stimulate imports and hurt exports), it is much more difficult to try to avoid a depreciation. **A central bank can only intervene to stabilise a depreciating currency if it has sufficient foreign exchange reserves to do so**. This further illustrates the importance of a country's gold and other foreign reserves, as discussed in Section 17.3. However, given the extremely large daily turnover on the foreign exchange market (which has exceeded $15 billion in South Africa) it is doubtful whether the SARB, or for that matter any other central bank, will ever have sufficient reserves to effectively manage the international value of the currency. In earlier years it was still possible (albeit not indefinitely), but the explosion of international financial transactions has almost eliminated this policy option.

Having explained how managed floating works, we now briefly discuss exchange rate policy in a somewhat broader context.

Exchange rate policy

Exchange rates are among the most important prices in the economy. Movements in exchange rates can have a significant impact on economic growth, employment, inflation and the balance of payments as well as on the well-being of individuals (eg people who have invested abroad or in rand hedge equities and people who wish to travel abroad). During the past few decades the rand depreciated significantly against the major currencies, and exchange rates were often quite volatile – see Box 17-11 – and both the depreciation of the rand and the volatility of exchange rates have frequently been major causes for concern.

How can policymakers react in such circumstances? This will depend on the exchange rate system that is in force. The most fundamental element of exchange rate policy is the choice of an exchange rate system or regime. The gold standard and the Bretton Woods system of fixed but adjustable exchange rates (see Box 17-5) were both variations of fixed rate systems. In the new millennium, however, such systems are no longer feasible, at least not on a global scale. At

BOX 17-11 THE RAND-DOLLAR EXCHANGE RATE, 1980–2007

The rand has depreciated significantly against the US dollar since 1980. In January 1980 the average rand-dollar exchange rate was $1,00 = R0,82. By October 1980 the rate was $1,00 = R0,75. Yes, it cost only 75 South African cents to purchase a dollar! At that stage South Africa had a dual exchange rate, in the form of a **commercial rand** (which applied to all import and export transactions as well as to all other international transactions by South African residents, who were still subject to stringent exchange controls at that stage) and a **financial rand**, a special investment currency (which applied to non-residents' purchases and sales of South African assets). The financial rand was, in effect, a form of exchange control on non-residents and protected the commercial rand from the impact of changes in investor sentiment.

The dual exchange rate system was discontinued when the financial rand was abolished on 7 February 1983. At that stage the exchange rate was approximately $1,00 = R1,10. Subsequently the rand strengthened somewhat, but then depreciated steadily against the dollar, *inter alia* as a result of the worsening domestic political situation and a decline in economic growth in South Africa. By the middle of 1985 the rate was about $1,00 = R1,97. In August 1985 South Africa experienced an international debt crisis, which has been referred to at various places in this book and which will be discussed further in Chapter 20. The rand depreciated sharply against the dollar and, despite the reinstatement of the financial rand on 2 September 1985, the exchange rate changed to about $1,00 = R2,70 at the end of the year. The rand subsequently recovered and by the end of 1987 a dollar cost R1,96. This was followed by a fairly steady depreciation, and at the end of 1989 the rate was $1,00 = R2,58. The declining trend, interrupted by sporadic moderate appreciations, continued until the dual exchange rate system was finally abolished on 13 March 1995, after the lifting of sanctions and the normalisation of South Africa's international economic relations. At that stage a dollar cost about R3,60.

Early in 1996, Mr Trevor Manuel took over as Minister of Finance and initially made some disparaging comments about international financial markets that caused some anxiety in these markets. At the same time rumours were spread about Mr Mandela's health. There was also a widely-held perception that the rand was overvalued against the dollar. These factors gave rise to a sharp depreciation of the rand. From January to April the average monthly rand-dollar exchange rate weakened from $1,00 = R3,64 to $1,00 = R4,24 (ie by 8,6 per cent). However, the rate stabilised fairly quickly and even strengthened somewhat after the announcement of the government's growth, employment and redistribution (Gear) strategy in June 1996.

In 1998 there was a major collapse of the rand, following currency collapses and systemic financial crises in a number of south-east Asian countries and in Russia. As an emerging market economy, the South African economy was affected by negative sentiment towards emerging market economies in general. Faced with acute pressures in the foreign exchange market in May 1998, the SARB tried to support the rand by substantial sales of dollars. This resulted in a dramatic fall in the country's net gold and foreign exchange reserves. At the same time, the SARB also increased interest rates aggressively in an attempt to curb currency speculation. The prime overdraft rate rose from 18,25 per cent at the beginning of June to 25,50 per cent at the end of August. The rand, which had depreciated on average by 19,5 per cent against the dollar between May and August, strengthened somewhat towards the end of 1998 and subsequently depreciated in a fairly orderly fashion until August 2001, despite the declared intention of Mr Tito Mboweni, who became the Governor of the SARB in August 1999, to adopt a freely floating exchange rate regime.

The SARB's non-interventionist policy stance was tested severely during the final months of 2001, when the rand depreciated more sharply than ever against the major international currencies. This collapse is illustrated even better in the following diagram, which shows the average Friday exchange rates between the rand and the US dollar from the last week of June 2001 to the last week of June 2003. **Note that the scale on the vertical axis is an inverted one.** A fall in the graph thus indicates a depreciation of the rand.

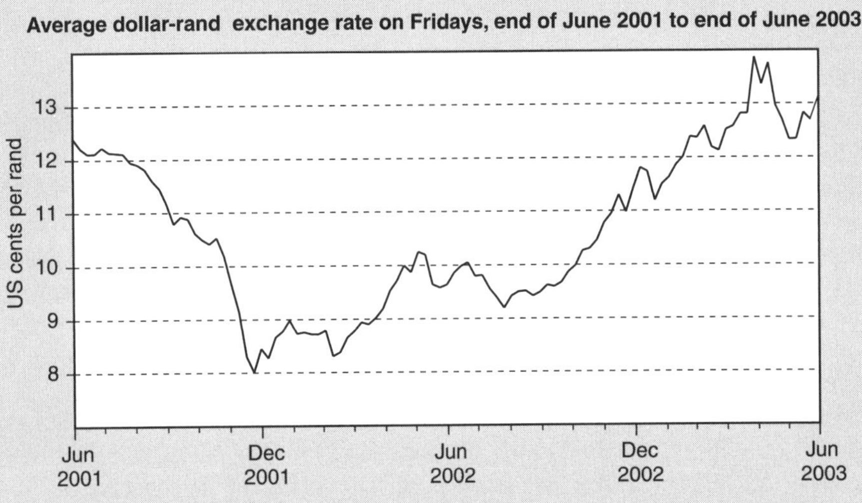

From August 2001 to December 2001 the rand depreciated, on average, by an unprecedented 28,1 per cent against the dollar. In fact, on 20 December 2001 the exchange rate reached $1,00 = R13,84, which was 40 per cent worse than the average rate during August. Among the reasons given for this massive depreciation were:

- the strength of the US dollar
- the reduction of the repo rate by half a percentage point in September (following the attack on the World Trade Centre)
- a sharp decline in non-gold exports, which resulted in a significant deterioration in the current account of the balance of payments
- capital outflows associated with the listing of a number of major South African companies (Anglo American, Billiton, Didata, Old Mutual and SA Breweries) on the London Stock Exchange
- the delay in the privatisation of Telkom (which meant that the expected associated inflow of foreign capital did not materialise)
- the low level of the country's foreign exchange reserves
- a decline in the volumes on the foreign exchange market (due to a tightening of the rules) – this increased volatility in the market and made the rand a more attractive target to speculators
- the impact of the crisis in Argentina on South Africa (as an emerging market country)
- the impact of the crisis in Zimbabwe on South Africa (as a neighbouring African country)
- the resignation (without any explanation) of the Senior Deputy Governor of the SARB (the next day the rand reached its worst level)

This incomplete list gives some indication of the complexity of the foreign exchange market and the potential determinants of exchange rate movements.

There were also allegations that certain financial institutions had collaborated with major South African companies to engineer the collapse of the rand. In response to these allegations and the general discontent about the depreciation of the rand, the State President appointed a commission of enquiry (the Myburgh Commission) on 8 January 2002 to investigate the reasons for the currency's rapid depreciation. By that time, however, the rand had started to recover and, as shown in the diagram, the upward trend continued almost unabated during the rest of the year. By February 2003 the currency had regained all its losses and continued to strengthen to levels last recorded in 2000. By the end of June 2003 the rand had appreciated by 84,5 per cent against the dollar from its weakest level on 20 December 2001.

Why did the rand appreciate so sharply and continuously? To some extent the appreciation can be ascribed to a reversal in some of the real or alleged causes of the depreciation listed above. For example, the dollar weakened significantly on the international currency markets, the current account of the balance of payments improved significantly (spurred by the positive impact of the depreciation on South African exports), and the SARB raised the repo rate by a total of four percentage points during 2002 (in an attempt to prevent or counter the possible inflationary impact of the increases in import prices as a result of the depreciation). The increases in the interest rate and the strengthening currency meant that South Africa became an attractive destination for foreign investors, and also curbed capital outflows. Interestingly, however, a number of the factors that had been mooted by certain observers (including the Myburgh Commission) as causes of the depreciation (eg the Zimbabwean crisis, the slow pace of privatisation and the weak global economy) were still present (and sometimes more strongly so) during the period of currency appreciation.

From 2004 onwards the exchange rate between the US dollar and the rand mostly stayed in a band between about $1,00 = R6,00 and $1,00 = R7,50, occasionally moving out of the band. However, it still tended to be quite volatile, complicating decision-making in all sectors of the economy.

From this discussion it should be obvious that exchange rates are difficult to explain and predict. However, there can be no doubt about the impact of exchange rate changes on the economy.

the time of writing, most of the larger countries, including South Africa, had independently floating currencies (ie if one includes the euro, the common currency of a number of European countries). Some countries (including India and Singapore) still practised managed floating, while others (eg China, Malaysia and Saudi Arabia) pegged their currencies to a single currency (eg the US dollar).

With a floating currency, there are basically only three policy options:

- **Do nothing**, that is, allow market forces, including the actions of currency speculators, to determine exchange rates.
- **Intervene in the foreign exchange market** by buying or selling foreign exchange, that is, practise **managed floating**. However, as explained above, such a course of action is subject to severe limitations, especially in view of the large turnover in the foreign exchange market.
- **Use interest rates** to influence exchange rates. For example, if the SARB wishes to avoid a depreciation of the rand against the major currencies, it can raise interest rates relative to the rates in the rest of the world. This will encourage an inflow of foreign capital and will also raise the costs of speculators who want to speculate against the rand. The result will be an increase in the demand for rands, relative to what it would have been otherwise, and therefore a stronger rand (than in the absence of intervention).

All three these approaches have been used in South Africa in recent years – see Box 17-11.

17.5 The terms of trade

The total value of a country's export earnings depends on the volume or quantity of exports *and* on the prices of the exports. Similarly, the total value of a country's payments for imports depends on the volume or quantity of imports *and* the prices of the imports. When export prices decline, a greater volume of exports have to be produced and sold merely to keep total export earnings constant. Export prices are therefore important. But even more important than the absolute level of export prices is the **ratio between export prices and import prices**. When the prices of a country's exports are falling **relative** to the prices of the goods and services it imports, the country actually becomes poorer. Why? Because the country has to sell more of its export products and use more of its scarce factors of production just so that it can afford the same volume of imports as before. Consider the following simple example: If the average price of exports falls from 3 foreign currency units to 2 currency units while the quantity remains at 100 units, then the value of the exports falls from 300 to 200. If, at the same time, the average price of imports remains unchanged at 3 while the volume is also 100, the value of imports remains at 300. Whereas the quantity of exports was initially sufficient to pay for the imports, the quantity of exports will now have to be increased to 150 to earn sufficient foreign exchange to afford a quantity of 100 units of imports.

Economists have a special name for the ratio between export prices (expressed as an index) and import prices (also expressed as an index). This relationship is called the **terms of trade**, which is normally expressed as an index. Thus

$$\text{terms of trade} = \frac{\text{export price index}}{\text{import price index}} \times 100$$

When a country's exports are dominated by an important product, like gold in South Africa, changes in the price of that product can have a significant impact on the country's terms of trade and therefore on the well-being of its residents. An increase or improvement in the terms of trade means that the welfare of the nation has increased, *ceteris paribus*. On the other hand, a fall or weakening of the terms of trade indicates a welfare loss, *ceteris paribus*.

South Africa's terms of trade have sometimes been subject to considerable fluctuation. The most dramatic decline was between 1980 and 1982 when they decreased by more than 23 per cent due to the sharp decline in the gold price. This meant that South Africa had to produce and sell at least 23 per cent more exports (in volume terms) in 1982 than in 1980 to afford the same volume of imports as in 1980. In recent years the country's terms of trade have been relatively stable. By 2006 they were 6 per cent higher than in 1994, but still 10 per cent lower than in 1980. A decline in the terms of trade is one of the possible causes of a deterioration in the overall performance of the economy. See also Box 23-1 and Section 23.4.

IMPORTANT CONCEPTS

Open economy	Revenue tariffs	Portfolio investment
Globalisation	Protective tariffs	Gold and other foreign reserves
Absolute advantage	Deadweight loss	Gross reserves
Comparative (or relative) advantage	Import quotas	Net reserves
Equal advantage	Dumping	Exchange rate
Inter-industry trade	Export subsidies	Appreciation
Intra-industry trade	Infant industries	Depreciation
Trade policy	Balance of payments	Foreign exchange market
Import tariffs	Current account	Floating exchange rates
Specific tariffs	Trade balance	Managed floating
Ad valorem tariffs	Financial account	Exchange rate policy
	Direct investment	Terms of trade

REVIEW QUESTIONS

1. Suppose you are hired by a group of South African clothing manufacturers to prepare a case for the introduction of new barriers to international trade in the clothing industry. List the arguments that you would use.
2. Suppose you are hired by the South African government to argue against the case for the introduction of new trade barriers in the clothing industry. What counter-arguments would you use?
3. What does the infant industry argument mean?
4. Explain two sources of comparative advantage.
5. Explain the difference between an import tariff and an import quota.
6. How can high tariffs on imports affect domestic producers that export goods to the rest of the world?
7. Explain who would benefit and who would lose if the South African government doubled the tariff on imported frozen chickens.

8. Why would the South African Clothing and Textile Workers Union tend to support an application by the South African Clothing Manufacturers Organisation for the imposition of a quota on imported clothing?

9. Explain the difference between absolute advantage and comparative (or relative) advantage in international trade.

10. The balance of payments must always balance (like any other set of accounts). Does this mean that policymakers need not be concerned about the balance of payments? Explain your answer.

11. List four possible reasons for a depreciation of the rand against the US dollar.

12. Explain how exchange rate changes can affect exports and imports.

13. In 2002 the Myburgh Commission concluded that the following factors contributed towards the sharp depreciation of the rand against the US dollar towards the end of 2001. Use graphs to explain how each factor might have given rise to a depreciation of the rand:
    (a) the crisis in Zimbabwe
    (b) the delay in the privatisation of Telkom
    (c) the weakening of the world economy

14. Define the terms of trade and explain their significance.

15. South Africa's terms of trade (including gold) improved by 13,6 per cent between 2000 and 2006. What does this statement mean and what were the implications for the South African economy?

PART IV

Macroeconomics

In the first three parts of the book we introduced you to a variety of economic issues. Some of the issues were only mentioned or defined while others were studied in detail, particularly in Part II. But we have not yet examined more closely the big economic issues of the day, like economic growth, inflation and unemployment. In this final part of the book, we focus on macroeconomics. In other words, we look at the "Big Picture" and we examine the economic issues which regularly make the news headlines. What causes economic growth? What is a recession? What can the authorities do to stimulate the economy? What is inflation? Why is it a problem? What can we do about it? Why is unemployment so high? Can it be reduced? Are there any links between inflation and unemployment? These are some of the questions that we investigate in this part of the book. But before we can focus on them, we first have to find out how the whole economy fits together. In other words, we first have to construct theories or models about the functioning of the economy as a whole. As is the case with all other theories or models we have to abstract from (or remove) the details which are not of immediate concern. In this part of the book we take a macro view and we focus on flows such as total production, total income and total spending in the economy.

In Chapters 18 and 19 we develop a simple Keynesian model of the economy. In Chapter 20 we also introduce you to some other, non-Keynesian approaches to macroeconomics. We conclude the book by taking a closer look at inflation (Chapter 21), unemployment (Chapter 22) and economic growth and development (Chapter 23).

When you have studied this part of the book you should be able to

- explain how the equilibrium level of income is determined in a simple Keynesian model
- use a simple Keynesian model to predict the effects of a change in government spending, exports or imports
- describe the monetary transmission mechanism
- use aggregate demand and supply curves to analyse the effects of monetary and fiscal policies and supply shocks
- describe the important features of inflation and unemployment
- explain the major causes of economic growth
- distinguish between economic growth and economic development

18 Income determination in a simple Keynesian macroeconomic model

Learning outcomes

Once you have studied this chapter you should be able to

- explain the equilibrium level of total income in the economy
- describe the major features of the consumption function
- indicate what the determinants of investment are
- determine the equilibrium level of income in an economy which consists of households and firms only
- describe what the multiplier is and explain how it works

The right dichotomy is, I suggest, between the Theory of the Individual Industry or Firm and … the Theory of Output and Employment ***as a whole.***

JOHN MAYNARD KEYNES

If men ceased to consume, they would cease to produce.

DAVID RICARDO

Unexpected new investment … can simply mean that stocks at the end of the period are different from what the entrepreneur expected.

BERTIL OHLIN

In this chapter we develop a simple macroeconomic model of an economy which consists of households and firms only. In other words, we ignore both the foreign sector and the government sector. To understand the working of the model, you have to go back to the concepts we developed in Chapter 3. These include the three central macroeconomic flows: **total production** (or output), **total income** and **total spending** (or expenditure). We examine the relationships between these flows. We then focus on the two components of total spending in an economy that has no government or foreign sector. These two components are **consumption spending** by households and **investment spending** by firms. Together they determine the **equilibrium level of output and income** in our model. We show how this equilibrium is achieved and we then investigate how a change in spending (eg a change in investment spending) affects the equilibrium level of output and income. In the process we introduce the important concept of the **multiplier**.

We are now entering the world of macroeconomic theory which is aimed at **explaining** the functioning of the economy, **predicting** what might happen and analysing economic **policy**.

In macroeconomic theory we do not deal directly with real world variables such as gross domestic product (GDP) and gross national income (GNI) which we introduced in Chapter 4. We abstract from (or ignore) the differences between GDP and GNI and simply talk about total, aggregate or national product, output or income without referring to specific national accounting concepts. Nevertheless, you might find it useful to regard GDP as the focus of our study.

The model developed in this chapter is called a simple Keynesian model. By now you should be well aware that all models are simplifications of reality. This model is most elementary, since we leave out all details that might confuse the issue at this stage. It is therefore explicitly called a simple model. The "Keynesian" in the name of the model refers to the famous British economist, John Maynard Keynes, who developed the idea that total output and income are essentially determined by total spending (or total demand) in the economy.

18.1 Production, income and spending

In Chapter 3 we introduced you to the three central flows in the economy at large: total production (or output), total income and total spending (or expenditure). We also indicated the interrelationships between these flows. When you are studying macroeconomics you must try to visualise these flows and their interrelationships. One way of doing this is to use the flow diagrams presented in Chapter 3.

In Chapter 4 we also showed that total production, income and spending are identically equal in the national accounts. The national accounting system is essentially a bookkeeping system which is used to measure economic activity **after it has occurred**. Economists often use the Latin term *ex post* to denote that measurement occurs after the event (or after the fact).

The *ex post* equality of total production, income and spending in the national accounts is guaranteed by the way in which these concepts are defined. Recall that total production or output is always equal to total income because economists are only interested in income that is earned in the process of production. The only way in which total income in the economy can be increased is by expanding total production. Total production (or output) and total income are therefore two sides of the same coin. This is always true, in macroeconomic theory as well as in the national accounts.

In the **national accounts**, total spending (or expenditure) during any particular period is also always equal to total production and income during that period. This is the result of the way in which total spending is defined in the national accounts – changes in inventories are added to total investment spending (ie capital formation), one of the components of total spending. In **macroeconomic theory**, however, there is no guarantee that total spending will be equal to total production or income. To clarify this statement, we have to take another look at the relationships between total production, income and spending in the economy.

Although production, income and spending all occur simultaneously, it is useful to consider these three flows in sequence, starting with production. Production creates income which is then used to purchase the products that were produced in the first place. By definition, income is always equal to production but there is no guarantee that all income will be spent. Spending may be equal to, greater than or less than income. When all income is spent, total production will be sold and we would expect this process to continue at the current level of production. In other words, if spending is just sufficient to purchase the total product there will be no incentive for producers to expand production. In this case production is at its equilibrium level. **Recall that equilibrium is a situation in which there is no tendency for change. Equilibrium occurs when none of the participants have any incentive to change their behaviour. Things will therefore remain the same (as long as the underlying forces do not change).**

But what happens if total spending is not equal to total income in the economy? If spending exceeds income, then the demand for goods and services is greater than the available production or supply. In this case there will be a decrease in producers' stocks or inventories which serves as an incentive for them to expand their production. Production is therefore not at its equilibrium level. But how is it possible for total spending to exceed total income? To understand this, you must remember that production, income and spending are all **flows** which are measured during a particular period, say one year. There are two reasons why spending in any particular period can be greater than the income earned during that period: households and firms can use savings from a previous period to finance their spending or they can purchase goods and services on credit.

Total spending can also be less than total income. In this case the total demand for goods and services will be less than total production. Producers find that they cannot sell all their goods and services – in other words, their stocks or inventories increase. They therefore have an incentive to cut back on their production. When is total spending in the economy less than total income? This happens when part of the income is saved and those savings do not find their way back into the circular flow of production, income and spending. Remember, from Chapter 3, that saving is a leakage or withdrawal from the circular flow.

We therefore have three possibilities:

- **Spending may be equal to production and income**. In this case production and income are at their equilibrium levels – there is no tendency to change.
- **Spending may be greater than production and income**. In this case production and income will tend to increase. They are therefore not at their equilibrium levels.
- **Spending may be less than production and income**. In this case production and income will tend to fall. They are therefore not at their equilibrium levels.

In macroeconomics we use the symbol Y to denote total production, output or income in the economy, which we often simply call national product or national income. Y is the theoretical equivalent of variables such as GDP or GNI. We use the symbol A to denote total or aggregate spending (or aggregate demand) in the economy. See Box 18-1.

The three possible relationships between production, income and spending can therefore be summarised as follows:

- $A = Y$, which denotes the equilibrium level of production and income.
- $A > Y$, which denotes a disequilibrium in which the level of production and income will tend to increase (because total spending is greater than total production or income).
- $A < Y$, which denotes a disequilibrium in which the level of production and income will tend to fall (because total spending is lower than total production or income).

There were some economists who believed that total spending (A) will **always** be equal to total production or income (Y), and that this will always occur at the **full-employment level of production or income** (ie the level of production or income where all the factors of production are fully employed). We use the symbol Y_f to denote the full-employment level of income. According to these economists there was therefore only one equilibrium level of production and income, namely Y_f. This belief was based on the notion that **supply creates its own demand**, which is called **Say's law**, after the Frenchman Jean-Baptiste Say who is said to have formulated the idea at the beginning of the 19th century – see Box 2-7. According to Say's law, all leakages will automatically find their way back into the circular flow of income and spending. If this happens, total spending will always be equal to total income. According to Say's law there can never be an insufficient demand for goods and services in the economy.

In due course it became clear, however, that total spending or aggregate demand is not always sufficient to purchase all the goods and services produced in the economy. The most noted example is the Great Depression (1929–1933) during which production, income and employment fell in all major economies (as well as South Africa). The Great Depression clearly indicated that there are no automatic mechanisms which keep the economy at the full-employment level of income, or that restore full employment if something happens to create unemployment. It was in response to these events that John Maynard Keynes wrote his famous book, *The general theory of employment, interest and money* – see Section 2.5. The central theme of *The general theory* was that the level of income (Y) is determined by the level of aggregate spending or demand (A) and that there are various

BOX 18-1 SOME SYNONYMS IN MACROECONOMICS

The two central variables that are used in the models of Chapters 18 and 19 are Y and A. Y represents total production or income in the economy, while A represents total spending. There are, however, a number of other terms which have the same meaning as total production, total income and total spending in macroeconomic theory. Some of these terms are also used in this part of the book. To avoid any possible confusion, we provide a number of synonyms for total production, total income and total spending.

We have shown on a number of occasions that total production in the economy is always equal to total income. In macroeconomic theory total production means the same thing as total output, aggregate output, national output, aggregate production, aggregate income, national product and national income. All these terms are represented by the symbol Y. In the models developed in Chapters 18 and 19, Y also represents total supply or aggregate supply in the economy.

Total spending, on the other hand, has the same meaning as aggregate spending, total expenditure and aggregate expenditure. All these terms are represented by the symbol A. In the models in Chapters 18 and 19, A also represents total demand or aggregate demand in the economy.

reasons why spending can be insufficient to achieve full employment.

Whereas Say believed that aggregate production or supply (Y) creates its own demand (A), Keynes claimed that aggregate demand (A) is the force which determines total production or income (Y). The direction of causality in the two theories can be summarised as follows:

Say's law $Y \rightarrow A$
Keynes $A \rightarrow Y$

The macroeconomic model developed in this chapter and the next is based on Keynes's idea that the level of economic activity (Y) is determined by aggregate spending or demand (A). That is why it is called a Keynesian model. In this model the equilibrium condition is still that aggregate demand (A) must equal total income (Y). The major differences with Say's law are that the direction of causality is from A to Y and that equilibrium can occur at **any** level of income, not necessarily at the full-employment level (Y_f). If the economy is operating at a level of income below the full-employment level, there will be no automatic tendency towards full employment – measures have to be taken to stimulate aggregate spending. On the other hand, if the economy is operating at a level of income beyond the full-employment level (eg because workers and other factors of production are working overtime), measures may have to be taken to reduce aggregate spending. In our Keynesian model there is therefore often a **need for government to intervene** in the economy to stimulate or dampen aggregate spending. By contrast, Say's law does not require government to take any steps to influence aggregate demand. We shall return to Say's law in Chapter 20, but first we study the Keynesian model in more detail.

18.2 The basic assumptions of the model

The aim of the Keynesian macroeconomic model is to explain how national income is determined. We start with the simplest possible model which excludes the government and the foreign sector. In this model the economy therefore consists of only households and firms. We also assume that prices, wages and interest rates are given. These variables are not explained in the model.

These simplifying assumptions mean that the money market (or the financial markets in general) cannot be analysed with this model. The fact that government is excluded, also means that we cannot use the model to analyse or explain macroeconomic policy.

The assumptions of the model, which are summarised in Box 18-2, may appear to be unduly restrictive. It is important, however, to start with the most elementary model of the economy. This enables us to focus on some of the important relationships in the economy without being distracted by unnecessary details. Once these important relationships have been established, the assumptions can then be relaxed.

When you are working with a particular model of the economy, the assumptions on which it is based must always be kept in mind. These assumptions determine what can or cannot be done with the model. Box 18-2 therefore includes a list of the things we *cannot* do with the model.

In an economy which consists of households and firms only, there are only two types of spending on goods and services. The first is spending by households on consumer goods and services. In Chapter 3 we called this **consumption spending** (or simply consumption) and denoted it with the symbol C. The equivalent term in the national accounts is final consumption expenditure by households. The other type is spending by firms on capital goods. In Chapter 3 we called this **investment spending** and denoted it with the symbol I. In the national accounts it is called capital formation.

From Section 18.1 we know that the economy is in equilibrium when aggregate spending A is equal to aggregate income Y. If aggregate spending A consists of consumption spending C and investment spending I, then it follows that the economy is in equilibrium when consumption spending C plus investment spending I is equal to aggregate income Y. In other words, there is equilibrium when $C + I = Y$.

Before we can analyse how national income Y is determined, we therefore first have to analyse consumption C and investment I. This is done in the next two sections. Once that has been done, we can put the various elements of the model together and investigate some of its important features and implications.

A very important point

In our analysis of the decisions of individual households and firms and of market demand and supply, we emphasised that demand and supply are concerned with the **plans** or **decisions** of households and firms. Demand and supply are analytical concepts which are used to explain and predict certain phenomena and to analyse policy decisions. Similarly, when we refer to consumption spending C and investment spending I in macroeconomic theory, we are referring to the **decisions** or **plans** of households and firms.

This is a very important point. Our macroeconomic variables and models do not describe something that has happened. They are devices that are used to **explain** how the various sectors of the economy operate, to **predict** how they will react under certain circumstances and to analyse the possible effects of **policy**. As we explained in Chapter 6, a theory or model

BOX 18-2 THE ASSUMPTIONS OF OUR SIMPLE KEYNESIAN MODEL AND THEIR IMPLICATIONS

Assumption	Implication
The economy consists of households and firms only	Total spending consists of consumption spending and investment spending
There is no government	The model cannot be used to analyse government spending or taxes
There is no foreign sector	The model cannot be used to analyse exports, imports, exchange rates, trade policy and exchange rate policy
Prices are given	The model cannot be used to study inflation
Wages are given	The model cannot be used to study the workings of the labour market
The money supply and interest rates are given	The model cannot be used to study the financial markets or monetary policy
Spending (demand) is the driving force that determines the level of economic activity	Production (supply) adjusts passively to changes in spending (demand)

When we say that prices, wages, the money supply and interest rates are given, we mean that their values are determined outside the model. These variables are used to determine other variables but they are not explained by the model. In the context of economic models they are usually referred to as exogenous variables.

is a simplification of reality or an abstract device which helps us to understand how the economy functions. In macroeconomic theory it is important to understand how the major groups of participants in the economy operate. This means that we have to analyse the **plans** or **intentions** of households and firms, and later of the government and the foreign sector as well.

Macroeconomic theory is aimed at understanding what happens. It deals with **plans** and **intentions**, not with events that occurred in the past. In contrast, the **national accounts**, introduced in Chapter 4, are a set of accounts which record what actually happened in the economy during a particular period. The whole national accounting system is based on a set of accounting identities that ensure that the accounts balance. The national accounts can only describe what has already happened. Things that happened in the past can be used as a guide in the search for fundamental relationships in the economy. It is important, however, to remember that theory does not involve a description of particular events that have already taken place. Economists often use the Latin term *ex ante* to denote that theory occurs before the event (or before the fact). Measurement, you will recall, always occurs *ex post* (ie after the event).

18.3 Consumption spending

Consumption spending by households was introduced in Chapters 2 and 3. In Chapter 2 we indicated, for example, that there are four major types of consumer goods and services: durable goods, semi-durable goods, non-durable goods and services. Spending on non-durable goods, such as food, beverages, tobacco, petrol and pharmaceutical products, is a large component of total consumption spending. This is also the most stable component of consumption spending. Purchases of semi-durable goods (eg clothing, footwear and motorcar parts) and, in particular, durable goods (eg furniture, household appliances and transport equipment) are much more erratic. Purchases of these goods are influenced by factors such as changes in consumers' income and the availability and cost of credit. However, despite the fluctuations in its durable component, aggregate consumption expenditure by households constitutes a relatively stable (and high) proportion of total income in any economy. When the data are plotted on a diagram, a strong positive correlation between consumption spending and total income is clearly visible. This relationship is an important element of our theory or model of the economy.

The consumption function

The relationship between consumption expenditure by households and total income is called the **consumption function**. The consumption function has three important characteristics:

- Consumption increases as income increases (ie there is a positive relationship between consumption spending and income).
- Consumption is positive even if income is zero – this reflects the influence of the non-income determinants of consumption spending.
- When income increases, consumption increases but the increase in consumption is less than the increase in income – part of the additional income is saved.

The consumption function is illustrated graphically in Figure 18-1. Consumption (*C*) is measured along the vertical axis and total production or income (*Y*) is measured along the horizontal axis. The consumption function shows the level of consumption spending at each level of income.

Figure 18-1 confirms the three features mentioned earlier. First it is obvious that consumption spending increases as income increases. The second feature is that consumption does not fall to zero even if income falls to zero. When *Y* is zero, consumption is still at some positive level, indicated by C_1 in the figure. The fact that C_1 is positive means that income *Y* is not the only determinant of consumption. The distance from the origin (0) to C_1 is called autonomous consumption. **Autonomous consumption** is that part of consumption which is independent of the level of income. This can also be regarded as a minimum level of consumption that is financed from sources other than income, for example, from past savings or credit.

Total consumption spending can therefore be split up into two components: an **autonomous** component which is independent of income, and an **induced** component which is determined by the level of income. The area under the consumption function thus consists of two parts, as indicated in Figure 18-2. The autonomous component is not affected by the level of income, while the induced component increases as income increases. Autonomous consumption is shown by the **position** or **intercept** of the consumption function. Induced consumption is indicated by the **slope** of the consumption function.

As income increases, consumption increases, but the increase in consumption is smaller than the increase in income. As income increases from Y_1 to Y_2, in Figure 18-1, consumption increases from C_2 to C_3. However, the change in *C* (ie ΔC) is smaller than the change in *Y* (ie ΔY). This is the third important feature of the consumption function. The ratio

FIGURE 18-1 The consumption function

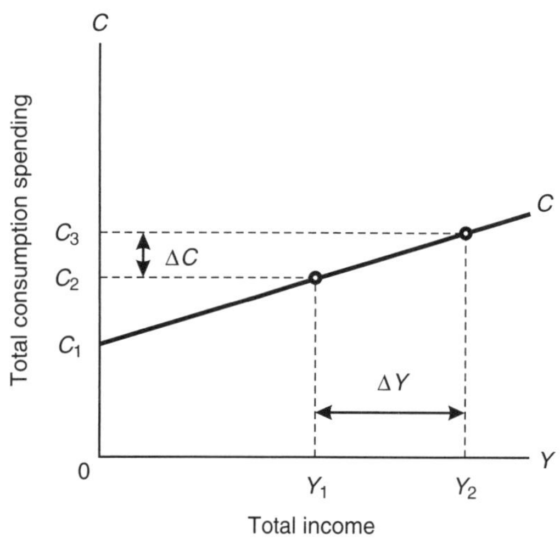

Both axes in the figure are drawn to the same scale. The line C is called the consumption function. It has three important features. It shows that households spend more as their total income increases; that consumption does not fall to zero when income falls to zero; and that the increase in consumption when income increases is smaller than the increase in income.

FIGURE 18-2 Autonomous and induced consumption

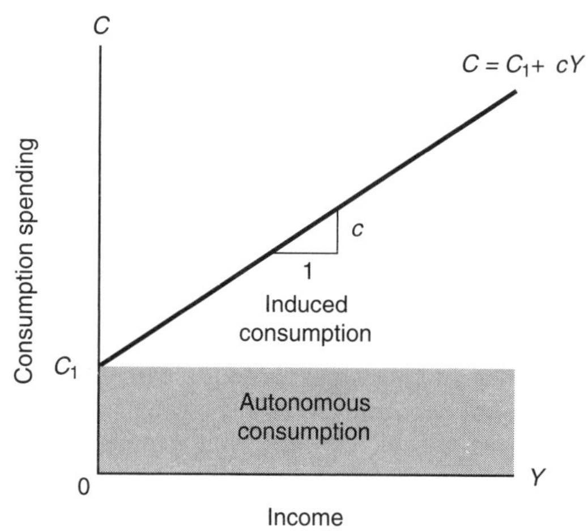

The shaded area represents autonomous consumption while the remainder of the area under the consumption function represents induced consumption. Autonomous consumption is independent of the level of income, while induced consumption increases as income increases. Autonomous consumption changes as a result of a change in one of the non-income determinants of consumption – see Box 18-3.

between the change in consumption (ΔC) and the change in income (ΔY) is one of the most important ratios in macroeconomics. It is called the **marginal propensity to consume** and it is usually indicated by the symbol c. Note that it is **equal to the slope of the consumption function**.

In symbols the marginal propensity to consume may be expressed as

$$c = \frac{\Delta C}{\Delta Y}$$

The marginal propensity (or tendency) to consume indicates the proportion of an **increase** in income that will be used for consumption. It can never be greater than one, since the additional amount used for consumption out of additional income can never exceed the additional income. The marginal propensity to consume therefore lies somewhere between zero and one. In symbols we can therefore write $0 < c < 1$.

The position of the consumption function

As indicated above, the position of the consumption function is determined by the level of autonomous consumption. When the consumption function shifts, the **intercept** of the line, indicated by C_1 in Figures 18-1 and 18-2, changes. The position of the consumption function is determined by all non-income factors that affect consumption spending, (ie the factors that determine autonomous consumption). These include the distribution of income, the age distribution of the population, consumers' holdings of financial assets and the availability and cost of consumer credit – see Box 18-3.

The equation for the consumption function

The consumption function illustrated in Figures 18-1 and 18-2 can also be expressed as an equation. We use the symbol $\bar{C}$ for **autonomous consumption**, where the bar above the symbol indicates that it is autonomous (ie independent of the level of income Y). Recall that the value of autonomous consumption ($\bar{C}$) is given by the vertical **intercept** of the consumption function. It therefore relates to the **position** of the consumption function.

The value of **induced consumption** depends on two things:

- the marginal propensity to consume (c) (which gives the **slope** of the consumption function)
- the level of income (Y)

Induced consumption can therefore be expressed as the product of c and Y, that is, cY. For example, if the marginal propensity to consume (c) is ¾ (or 0,75) and the level of income (Y) is R1 000, then induced consumption (cY) = ¾ × R1 000 (or 0,75 × R1 000) = R750. This means that R750 of the R1 000 earned will be spent on consumption.

Total consumption (C) is the sum of autonomous consumption ($\bar{C}$) and induced consumption (cY). Thus

$$C = \bar{C} + cY \qquad (18\text{-}1)$$

Equation 18-1 is the equation for the consumption function. As indicated earlier, $\bar{C}$ is always greater than zero while c has a value between 0 and 1.

The consumption function also implies a **saving function** – see Box 18-4.

BOX 18-3 NON-INCOME DETERMINANTS OF CONSUMPTION

Income (Y) is the most important determinant of consumption spending (C). But it is not the only determinant. There are a variety of other factors which influence consumption spending. Graphically this is indicated by the positive **intercept** of the consumption function ($\bar{C}$). The position of this intercept, and therefore the position of the whole consumption function, is determined by all the non-income factors that affect aggregate consumption spending. A change in any of these factors affect **autonomous consumption** and will therefore cause a **shift** of the consumption function.

There are similarities between the slope and intercept of the macroeconomic consumption function and the slope and intercept of the microeconomic demand curve introduced in Chapter 7. In the case of the demand for a particular product, the emphasis is on the relationship between the quantity demanded and the price of the product. This relationship is indicated by the **slope** of the demand curve. But there are also other factors which affect the quantity demanded (eg income, the prices of other products and consumers' taste). These factors determine the position of the demand curve. A change in any of these other factors leads to a change in demand. Graphically this is shown by a shift of the demand curve.

In the case of consumption spending (C) (ie the total spending on consumer goods and services in the economy) we focus on the relationship between consumption (C) and its most important determinant (Y). This relationship is indicated by the **slope** of the consumption function (ie the marginal propensity to consume). But there are also other determinants of aggregate consumption spending. These determinants determine the position or **intercept** of the consumption function. They are therefore determinants of autonomous consumption. Any change in these other determinants will lead to a **shift** of the whole consumption function.

But what are these other determinants? Because the consumption function is concerned with total spending in the economy, we can expect that many other factors may affect consumption. The following are among the most important:

- **Interest rates**. Interest rates can affect consumption spending in two ways. First, most consumers purchase durable goods such as motorcars, washing machines, refrigerators and video recorders on credit. The cost of such consumer credit is the interest that consumers have to pay on the amount that they borrow. The higher the interest rate, the more expensive credit becomes and the smaller the consumption spending will be, *ceteris paribus*. Second, interest rates also represent the return on saving. The higher the interest rate on saving deposits and other financial instruments, the greater the return on saving and the more attractive it is to save. If households save a greater portion of their incomes, it follows that they will spend less. Put differently: an increase in the interest rate raises the opportunity cost of consumption and therefore tends to reduce consumption spending, *ceteris paribus*. Both arguments in this paragraph point to the same result: a higher interest rate will tend to reduce consumption, *ceteris paribus*.
- **Expectations**. The level of consumption spending will also depend on households' expectations. For example, if shortages are expected or if people are convinced that inflation will accelerate, households may increase their consumption spending. The effect of expectations is, however, difficult to predict. For example, in the 1970s many households in the industrial countries reacted to the increase in inflation by saving more. They were uncertain about what was going to happen and tried to protect themselves against possible future developments by saving more. This surprising result was contrary to the predictions of conventional economic theory. But although the effects of changes in expectations are difficult to predict, there is no doubt that they can have a significant impact on consumption behaviour.
- **Wealth**. Consumption spending is also affected by consumers' wealth and by changes in their wealth. Wealth consists of the net money value of assets people own, such as money, shares and fixed property. As the value of these assets rises (eg when share prices on the JSE Securities Exchange rise), the holders of the assets feel richer and are therefore likely to spend more, *ceteris paribus*. The money value of such assets may, however, also fall, in which case consumption may be reduced. Moreover, the **real** value of consumers' assets is affected by the price level. A rise in the price level reduces the real value of assets, *ceteris paribus*. People will feel poorer and will therefore spend less.
- **Income distribution**. Low-income households spend a larger portion of their income than high-income families. The level of consumption spending will therefore depend on the distribution of total income (Y). Moreover, changes in the income distribution will tend to change total consumption spending. For example, if income is redistributed from rich to poor families, the level of consumption spending will tend to increase, *ceteris paribus*. Similarly, a redistribution of income in favour of high-income households will tend to raise saving and lower consumption spending.
- **Other factors**. Other non-income factors which may affect the level of consumption spending include the age distribution of the population and the level of taxation.

Concluding note: Our present model excludes the government, and certain influences on consumption spending such as taxation are therefore also excluded. Note, however, that the model does not exclude the possibility of changes in prices, wages and interest rates. Although the model cannot explain changes in prices, wages and interest rates (which are assumed to be given in any particular situation), the possibility of changes in these variables is not ruled out, and such changes can affect the **position** of the consumption function.

BOX 18-4 SAVING

In the highly simplified economy we are examining, households can only do two things with their income: they can spend it or they can save it. All income is either spent (on consumer goods and services) or saved. Using the symbol *S* for saving, we can thus write $Y \equiv C + S$. This identity indicates that income must, by definition, either be spent or saved. Saving can thus also be defined as **not spending**.

Moreover, the marginal propensity to save (*s*), that is, the proportion of an **increase** in income that is saved, plus the marginal propensity to consume (*c*), must be equal to one. This is because any **increase** in income can only be spent or saved. If three-quarters of each rand (ie 75 cents) is spent, then it follows that the other quarter (ie 25 cents) is saved (ie not spent). Therefore, if $c = ¾$ (or 0,75), then it follows that $s = ¼$ (or 0,25).

Since the decision to save is a decision not to spend, and *vice versa*, it follows that the factors that determine aggregate saving in the economy are the same factors that affect aggregate consumption. Anything that increases the marginal propensity to consume (*c*) will reduce the marginal propensity to save (*s*), and anything that decreases *c* will increase *s*. Similarly, anything that changes $\bar{C}$ will also change $-\bar{C}$ (ie the intercept of the saving function). This intercept can also be denoted by $\bar{S}$.

To derive the equation for the saving function we simply subtract consumption *C* from income *Y*. The difference, by definition, is saving. Thus:

$$S = Y - C$$
$$= Y - (\bar{C} + cY) \text{ since } C = \bar{C} + cY$$
$$= Y - \bar{C} - cY$$
$$= -\bar{C} + Y - cY$$
$$= -\bar{C} + (1 - c)Y$$
$$\text{or } S = \bar{S} + (1 - c)Y, \text{ where } \bar{S} = -\bar{C}$$

For example, if $\bar{C} = 50$ and $c = ¾$, then

$$S = -50 + (1 - \tfrac{3}{4})Y$$
$$= -50 + \tfrac{1}{4}Y$$

This can also be shown graphically as follows:

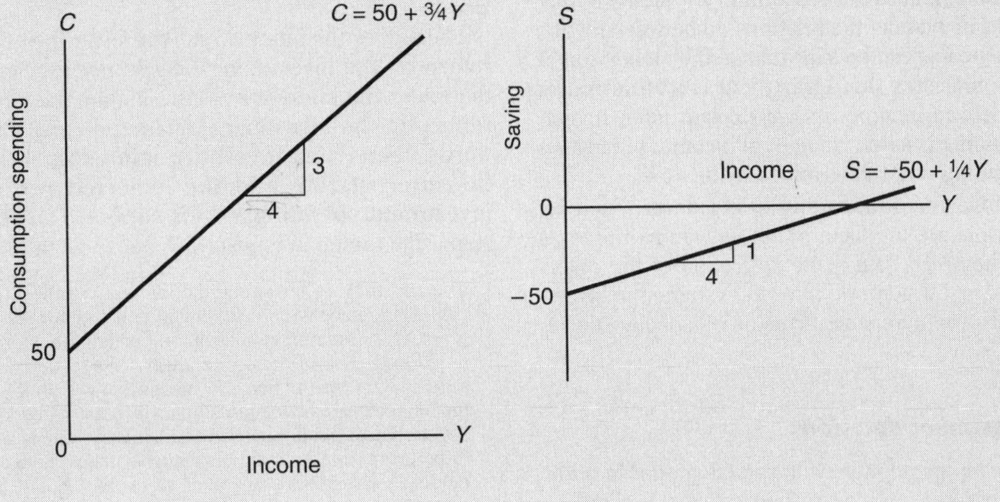

The diagram on the left shows the consumption function. The intercept $\bar{C}$ is 50. This means that *C* will equal 50 if *Y* = 0. If $\bar{C}$ = 50, then $-\bar{C}$ (or $\bar{S}$), the intercept of the saving function, must be –50. This means that households will dissave (ie reduce their stock of past savings) by 50 if income *Y* is zero. The slope of the consumption function (*c*) is shown as ¾. If the marginal propensity to consume *c* is ¾ then the marginal propensity to save (*s*) must be ¼ (ie 1 – ¾).

18.4 Investment spending

Aggregate spending in our hypothetical economy consists of consumption spending by households (*C*) and investment spending by firms (*I*). Now that we have examined consumption spending, we turn to investment spending. Whereas consumption spending is the largest component of total spending, investment spending is more variable and less predictable than consumption spending. In fact, investment spending, called capital formation in the national accounts, is the **most volatile** of all the components of aggregate spending, including those that are not studied in this chapter.

Because it is so volatile, investment spending is often the main cause of fluctuations in economic activity. In earlier chapters we explained that investment spending (*I*) refers to the production and purchase of capital goods, that is, man-made means of production such as buildings, plant, machinery and equipment. Investment thus relates to **capital** as a factor of production.

In contrast to consumption spending, investment spending is not primarily a function of income. The level of investment is usually regarded as independent of the level of income. An examination of South African data substantiates this view. It clearly shows that there is no systematic positive or inverse relationship between total investment and total income in the economy.

If investment does not respond in a systematic way to changes in income, the relationship between investment and income can be approximated by a horizontal line. This indicates that investment is **autonomous** with respect to income. As we explain later, investment spending is a determinant of income, but investment spending is not determined by income.

But if investment spending is not determined by income, what are the factors that determine the level of investment? To gain some indication of the determinants of investment, we have to examine the investment decisions of existing firms or prospective entrepreneurs.

The investment decision

Why do firms spend money on capital goods? In other words, why do they invest? The answer is simple – firms invest because they hope to earn profits. They estimate the cost of the capital goods concerned (eg buildings, machinery, equipment) and compare these costs to the amounts they expect to earn from the investment. The greater the expected profit, the greater investment will be. If no profit is expected, there will be no investment.

The profit that a firm expects to make from a specific investment depends on the **cost** of obtaining the capital goods and the **revenue** that these goods are **expected** to yield in future. For example, if a firm plans to buy a new machine, it must consider the cost of the machine and the income that the machine is expected to generate in future. But it must also consider the cost of borrowing the funds required to buy the machine. A large portion of investment spending by firms is financed by borrowing. When they borrow, firms have to pay interest on the borrowed funds. The **interest rate** is therefore an important element of the investment decision. Even if a firm plans to use its own funds (ie retained earnings) to buy the machine, the interest rate is still relevant. The firm must then consider the interest income that it can earn by depositing the funds in a bank or other financial institution. In other words it has to consider the **opportunity cost** of using the funds to purchase the machine.[1]

The investment decision thus involves three important variables: the **cost of the capital goods**, the **interest rate** and the **expected revenue** to be earned from the capital goods. See the example in Box 18-5.

The higher the interest rate, the lower the expected return on the investment, *ceteris paribus*. Similarly, the lower the interest rate, the higher the expected return on the investment, *ceteris paribus*. In other words, there is an **inverse relationship between the interest rate and the expected return on investment spending,** *ceteris paribus*. This relationship is illustrated in Figure 18-3.

1. The fact that we introduce the interest rate here may be confusing, since we are assuming that the interest rate is given. Our assumption does not imply that the interest rate is ignored. The interest rate always has to be taken into account. Our assumption only means that we cannot use the model to explain how interest rates increase and decline. At any particular point, the level of the interest rate is assumed to be given, that is, it is independent of any change in our model. Interest rates are used to explain *Y*, but interest rates are not explained by the model.

FIGURE 18-3 The investment function

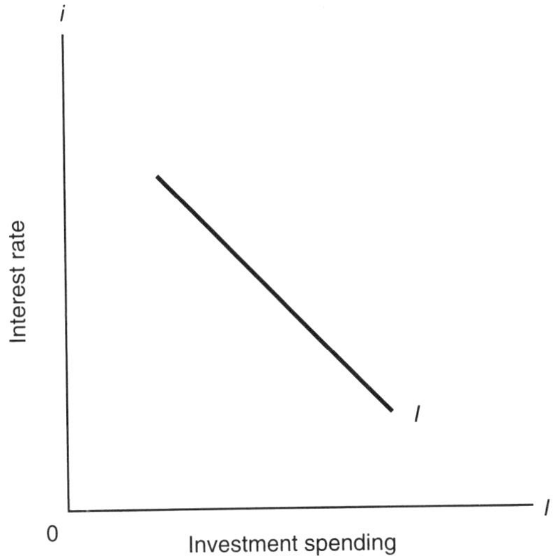

The level of investment I is inversely related to the interest rate i, ceteris paribus.

Although the interest rate is an important determinant of investment spending, it is not the only determinant. A particularly important feature of the investment decision is the fact that the expected profits are uncertain. When a firm purchases a machine, it has no guarantee that the expected revenue will be earned. For example, there may be an insufficient demand for the goods produced by the machine, and the price of the goods may fall. The machine may also wear out sooner than expected or it may become obsolete as a result of technological innovation.

Investment spending is an inherently risky affair. The level of investment spending thus depends on the willingness of firms or entrepreneurs to take chances. Their willingness, in turn, depends on their expectations about future economic and business conditions. When there is a great deal of economic and political uncertainty, as was the case in South Africa during the second half of the 1980s and early 1990s, investment spending is low.

In terms of Figure 18-3 an improvement in profit expectations or business sentiment will be illustrated by a rightward **shift** of the investment function. Likewise, a deterioration in business confidence will be

BOX 18-5 THE INVESTMENT DECISION: AN EXAMPLE

Consider the following hypothetical example. Gariep Investments can purchase a machine for R1 000. We assume that the machine will have to be replaced after a year. The company expects that the machine will increase the value of its sales by R1 210 during the year. Whether or not the owners will be willing to undertake this investment will depend on whether or not the firm expects to earn a sufficient rate of return on the investment. The rate of return is the profit from the investment, expressed as a percentage of its cost.

If Gariep Investments has to borrow R1 000 from the bank for one year to pay for the machine, it will have to pay interest to the bank. Suppose the interest rate is 10 per cent per year. The firm will then have to pay R100 interest (ie 10 per cent of R1 000) and repay the loan at the end of the year. This raises the cost of the investment from R1 000 to R1 100, that is, the cost of the machine (R1 000) plus the R100 interest. In this example the rate of return on the investment is 10,0 per cent. This is calculated as follows: the net benefit of the investment = extra sales, less cost of investment = R1 210 – R1 100 = R110. The **rate** of return on the investment is obtained by expressing the net benefit (R110) as a percentage of the cost of the investment (R1 100), that is,

$$\text{rate of return on investment} = \frac{R110}{R1100} \times \frac{100}{1}$$
$$= 10 \text{ per cent}$$

If the interest rate is 21 per cent per year, the cost of the investment will be R1 000 (cost of machine) plus R210 (interest) = R1 210. This will be equal to the expected income. The return of the investment will be zero and there will thus be no incentive for Gariep Investments to purchase the machine. On the other hand, if the interest rate is 5 per cent per year (instead of 10 per cent) the rate of return on the investment will be greater than 10 per cent (15,2 per cent to be precise). The incentive to invest will be greater than it will be at an interest rate of 10 per cent.

reflected by a leftward **shift** of the investment curve. These shifts often overshadow the effects of movements along the curve as a result of changes in interest rates.[2]

Investment spending (*I*) is therefore related to expectations and interest rates and not to the level of national income (*Y*). The absence of a systematic relationship between *I* and *Y* is illustrated in Figure 18-4.

FIGURE 18-4 Investment and the level of income

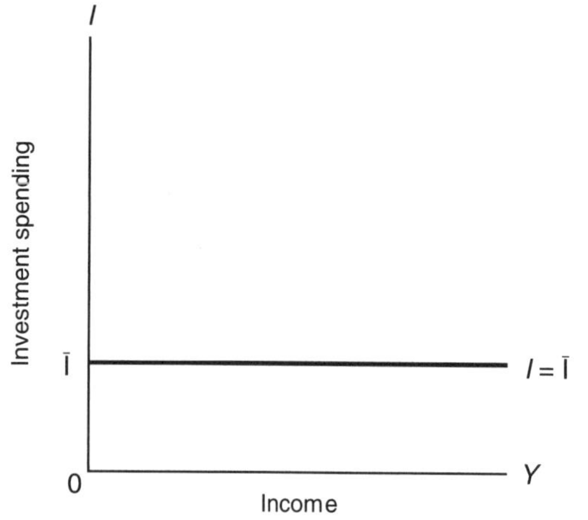

Investment spending I is independent of the level of income Y. Investment is thus autonomous with regard to the level of total income in the economy.

The equation for the investment function

As we have indicated, investment (*I*) is independent of the level of income (*Y*). It is therefore **autonomous** with respect to income. As in the case of the autonomous component of consumption spending ($\bar{C}$), we indicate the fact that investment (*I*) is autonomous by putting a bar above the symbol. Thus

$$I = \bar{I} \qquad (18\text{-}2)$$

Equation 18-2 represents the investment function.

18.5 The simple Keynesian model of a closed economy without a government

Now that we have examined the determinants of the two components of aggregate spending, we are in a position to construct a simple macroeconomic model of income determination.

2. Note again that we do not ignore interest rates in this model. We do not explain interest rates but they are important. At any given level of the interest rate there will be a certain level of investment, *ceteris paribus*.

Total spending (or aggregate demand)

We have established that consumption (*C*) is primarily a function of income (*Y*). We have also established that investment (*I*) is *not* a function of income (*Y*). These two relationships are illustrated in Figure 18-5(a) and (b). To obtain aggregate spending, we have to add *C* and *I* at each level of *Y*. This yields the total or aggregate spending function in Figure 18-5(c). We also know that there is equilibrium when aggregate spending (*A*) is equal to total income (*Y*). We therefore have to establish at which point along the *A* curve aggregate spending is equal to total income (*Y*). This is done by using a 45-degree line, like the one in Figure 6-5 of Chapter 6.

The 45-degree line

In Figure 18-6(a) we have total spending (*A*) on the vertical axis and total income (*Y*) on the horizontal axis. If **both axes are drawn to the same scale**, a 45-degree line running through the origin represents all the points at which total spending (*A*) is equal to total income (*Y*). This line therefore shows **all the possible equilibrium points**. (See also the explanation in Section 6.5.)

If income (*Y*) is equal to 100, then there will be equilibrium only if total spending (*A*) is also equal to 100. This equilibrium is indicated by point 1. At any point above the line, total spending (*A*) is greater than total income (*Y*). Point 2 is an example of such a point. If *A* is 150 while *Y* is only 100, total spending on goods and services (or the total demand for goods and services) is greater than total income (or the total production of goods and services). In other words, there is an **excess demand** for goods and services.

Similarly, there is an **excess supply** of goods and services at any point below the 45-degree line, for example at point 3. At point 3 the total level of production and income is 100 but aggregate spending is only 50. Firms will therefore not be able to sell their full production. Their stocks (or inventories) of unsold goods will therefore increase.

We now have the aggregate spending function *A* (= *C* + *I*) and a 45-degree line which shows all the possible equilibrium points (where $A = Y$). All points above the line indicate excess demand ($A > Y$) and all the points below the line indicate excess supply ($Y > A$), as in Figure 18-6(b). All that remains is to combine the aggregate spending function and the 45-degree line to obtain a specific equilibrium point. This is illustrated in Figure 18-7. The equilibrium level of income, which we denote by Y_0, is the level of income at which aggregate spending (*A*) is equal to income (*Y*). In the figure it is shown as the income level at which the aggregate spending function (*A*) intersects the 45-degree line ($0A_0 = 0Y_0$). At any other level of income there is either excess demand or excess supply along the *A* function, and therefore an unplanned

FIGURE 18-5 The aggregate spending function

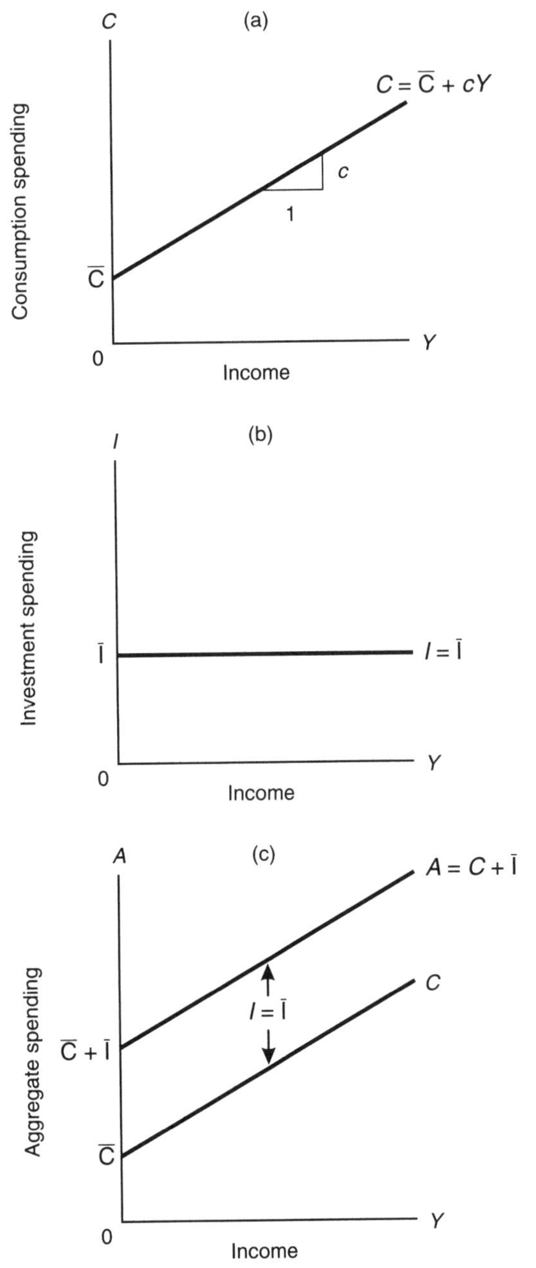

The consumption function of Figure 18-1 is shown in (a). Consumption spending C is positively related to the level of income Y. The investment function of Figure 18-4 is shown in (b). Investment spending I is not related to the level of income Y. The aggregate spending function A is shown in (c). This is obtained by adding consumption C and investment I at each level of income. The A function is parallel to the C function. The vertical difference between the two is the autonomous level of investment $\bar{I}$.

FIGURE 18-6 The 45-degree line

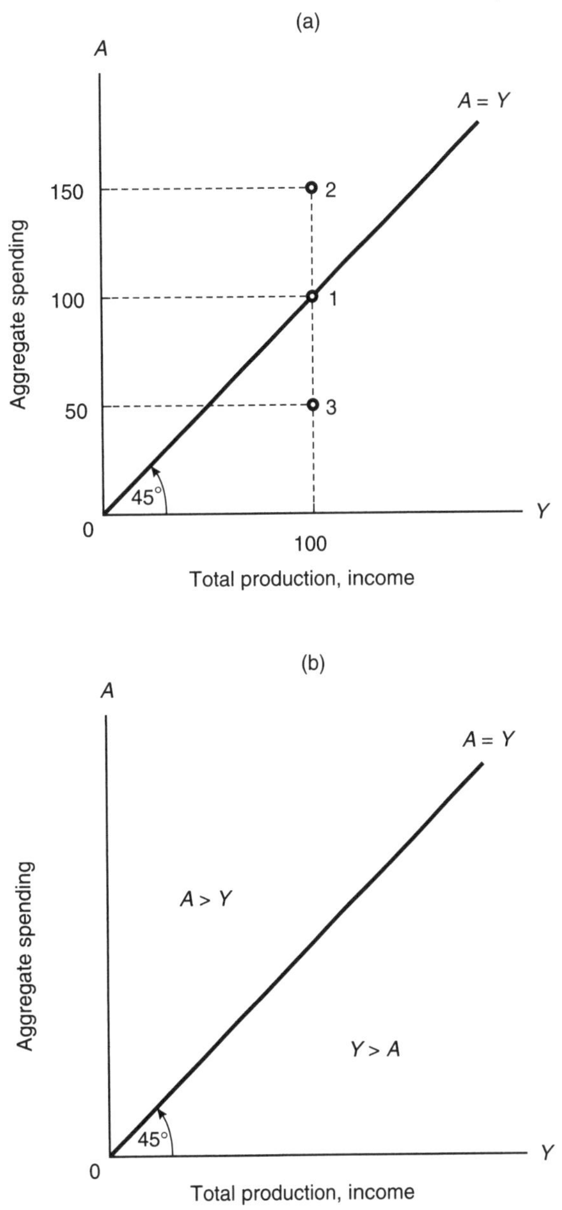

In (a) we have aggregate spending A on the vertical axis and aggregate income Y on the horizontal axis. Both axes are drawn to the same scale. A 45-degree line running from the origin indicates all the points at which A = Y. For example, at point 1 both A and Y are equal to 100. At any point above the line (eg point 2) A is greater than Y. Similarly, at any point below the line (eg point 3) Y is greater than A. These positions are summarised in (b). The 45-degree line indicates all the possible equilibrium points. Above the line there is excess demand (ie A > Y). Below the line there is excess supply (ie Y > A).

FIGURE 18-7 The equilibrium level of income

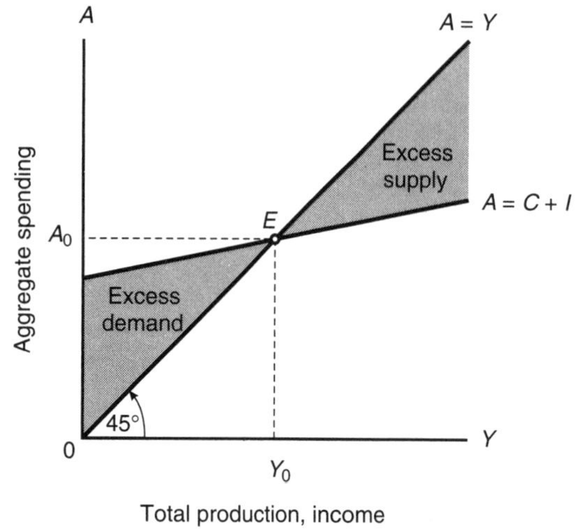

The equilibrium level of income Y_0 is the level of income at which the aggregate spending function A intersects the 45-degree line. At any level of income lower than Y_0 there is excess demand and at any level of income higher than Y_0 there is excess supply along the aggregate spending function.

change in inventories. At any level of income lower than Y_0 aggregate spending is greater than income. Here the aggregate spending curve lies above the 45-degree line, indicating excess demand for goods and services. Similarly, at any income level greater than Y_0 the aggregate spending curve lies below the 45-degree line, indicating excess supply. The only possible equilibrium is where $A = Y$, that is, where the aggregate spending curve intersects the 45-degree line at E. We now examine how to determine the equilibrium level of income in more detail.

The equilibrium level of income

In Part II we showed that economic theory can be expressed in words, numbers, graphs or symbols. In this section we use a simple example to show how the equilibrium level of income (Y) can be expressed, or determined, in various ways.

■ USING WORDS

Income (Y) is at its equilibrium level when it is equal to the level of aggregate spending (A). When aggregate spending (A) is **greater** than total production or income (Y), firms experience an **unplanned decrease in their inventories**. The reason is that current production is insufficient to meet the demand for goods and services. Firms therefore have to draw on their stocks or inventories to meet the demand. The unplanned decrease in inventories acts as an incentive to firms to increase their production of goods and services in the next period. When aggregate spending (A) is **less** than total production or income (Y), then firms experience an **unplanned increase in their inventories**. Firms find that they cannot sell all the goods and services produced during the period and therefore lower their production during the following period. Equilibrium only occurs when aggregate spending (A) is equal to total production or income (Y).

■ USING SYMBOLS (AND EQUATIONS)

Suppose the consumption and investment functions are as follows:

$$C = 50 + \tfrac{4}{5}Y \quad (\text{or } C = 50 + 0{,}8Y)$$
$$I = 150$$

To obtain aggregate spending (A), we have to add C and I. Thus

$$\begin{aligned} A &= C + I \\ &= \left(50 + \tfrac{4}{5}Y\right) + 150 \\ &= 200 + \tfrac{4}{5}Y \end{aligned}$$

or

$$\begin{aligned} A &= C + I \\ &= \left(50 + 0{,}8Y\right) + 150 \\ &= 200 + 0{,}8Y \end{aligned}$$

We know that there is equilibrium when $Y = A$. By substituting A in this equilibrium condition with $200 + \tfrac{4}{5}Y$ or $200 + 0{,}8Y$ (as above), we obtain

$$\begin{aligned} Y &= 200 + \tfrac{4}{5}Y \\ \therefore Y - \tfrac{4}{5}Y &= 200 \\ \therefore \tfrac{1}{5}Y &= 200 \\ \therefore Y &= \frac{200}{\tfrac{1}{5}} \\ &= 200 \times 5 \\ Y_0 &= 1\,000 \end{aligned}$$

or

$$\begin{aligned} Y &= 200 + 0{,}8Y \\ \therefore Y - 0{,}8Y &= 200 \\ \therefore 0{,}2Y &= 200 \\ \therefore Y &= \frac{200}{0{,}2} \\ &= \frac{2\,000}{2} \\ Y_0 &= 1\,000 \end{aligned}$$

The general algebraic derivation of the equilibrium level of income is explained more fully in the next section.

▪ USING NUMBERS

The concept of macroeconomic equilibrium can also be illustrated by means of a numerical example. Table 18-1 shows different combinations of aggregate spending (A) and total production or income (Y) that correspond to the equations in the previous subsection. As we have shown, aggregate spending is represented by the equation $A = 200 + 0{,}8\,Y$. When $Y = 500$, then $A = 200 + 0{,}8(500) = 200 + 400 = 600$. This is indicated by combination 1 in Table 18-1. When $Y = 750$, then $A = 200 + 0{,}8(750) = 200 + 600 = 800$. This is shown by combination 2 in the table. The other entries in Table 18-1 can be calculated in the same way.

Equilibrium occurs when aggregate spending (A) equals aggregate production (Y) (or, more precisely, when **planned** spending is equal to **planned** production). The only possible combination where aggregate spending and aggregate production are equal, is combination 3 where both are equal to 1 000. At every other combination there is disequilibrium in the form of excess demand or excess supply. Excess demand and excess supply cause changes in the level of production and income. Equilibrium only occurs when there is no excess demand or excess supply.

▪ USING GRAPHS

The information in the example can be illustrated graphically as in Figure 18-8.

Equilibrium occurs where the aggregate spending curve (A) intersects the 45-degree line, that is, at an income level (Y) of 1 000. The intersection is indicated by E. At any point to the left of E the aggregate spending curve (A) lies above the 45-degree line. This means that aggregate spending (A) is greater than total production (Y). There will be excess demand and an unplanned reduction in inventories. Firms will react by expanding their production. At any point to the right of E the aggregate spending curve (A) lies below the 45-degree line. This means that aggregate spending (A) is less than total production (Y). There will be excess supply and an unintended increase in inventories. Firms will react by reducing their production. Equilibrium only occurs at a production or income level of 1 000.

An alternative approach to determining the equilibrium level of income in this simple Keynesian model is given in Box 18-6.

18.6 The algebraic version of the simple Keynesian model

We have already used an example to indicate that the equilibrium level of income can be determined with the use of symbols. In this section we give a formal summary of the algebraic version of the model.

The model has three elements: a consumption function, an investment function and an equilibrium condition. As explained earlier, the **consumption function** is given by

$$C = \bar{C} + cY \quad \text{(18-1)}$$

where C = total consumption spending
$\bar{C}$ = automomous consumption
c = marginal propensity to consume
Y = income
cY = induced consumption

Recall that **investment spending** is fully autonomous with respect to income. Thus

$$I = \bar{I} \quad \text{(18-2)}$$

The **equilibrium condition** is given by

$$Y = A \quad \text{(18-3)}$$

Equation 18-3 states that there is equilibrium when total income (Y) is equal to total spending (A).

We also know that **total spending** (A) consists of consumption spending (C) and investment spending (I). Thus

$$A = C + I \quad \text{(18-4)}$$

TABLE 18-1 Macroeconomic equilibrium: a numerical example

Combination	*Aggregate spending A*	*Aggregate production Y*	*Result*
1	600	500	Unplanned decrease in inventories (excess demand) of 100
2	800	750	Unplanned decrease in inventories (excess demand) of 50
3	1 000	1 000	Equilibrium
4	1 200	1 250	Unplanned increase in inventories (excess supply) of 50
5	1 400	1 500	Unplanned increase in inventories (excess supply) of 100

FIGURE 18-8 The equilibrium level of income

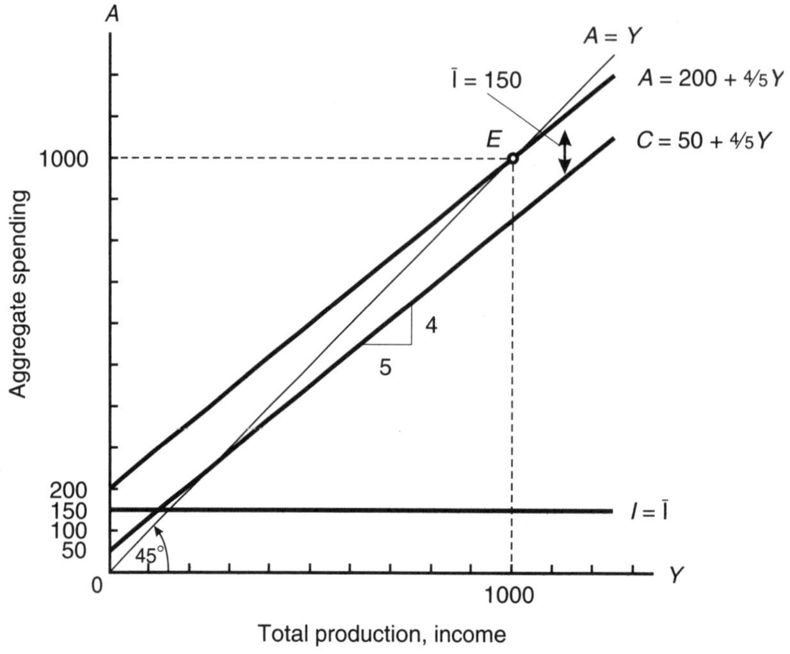

The figure shows the consumption function, C = 50 + 4⁄5Y, the investment function Ī = 150, the aggregate spending function, A = 200 + 4⁄5Y and the equilibrium condition Y = A. The equilibrium level of income is determined by the intersection of the A curve and the 45-degree line at point E. The equilibrium level of income in this case is therefore 1 000. At levels of Y lower than 1 000 there is excess demand and at levels of Y higher than 1 000 there is excess supply.

We now have to put all these ingredients together. We always start with the **equilibrium condition** (in this case Equation 18-3), that is,

$Y = A$

Next we substitute A with its components as indicated in Equation 18-4.

$Y = A$ therefore becomes
$Y = C + I$

Next we substitute C and I with their values as indicated in Equations 18-1 and 18-2.

$Y = C + I$ therefore becomes
$$Y = \bar{C} + cY + \bar{I} \quad \text{.........................} \quad (18\text{-}5)$$

All that remains is to solve Equation 18-5 to determine the equilibrium level of Y. This is done as follows:

$$Y = \bar{C} + cY + \bar{I}$$
$$\therefore \quad Y - cY = \bar{C} + \bar{I}$$
$$\therefore \quad (1 - c)Y = (\bar{C} + \bar{I})$$
$$\therefore \quad Y_0 = \frac{1}{(1 - c)}(\bar{C} + \bar{I}) \quad \text{...........} \quad (18\text{-}6)$$

or

$$Y_0 = \frac{1}{1 - c}(\bar{A}) \quad \text{..............} \quad (18\text{-}6a)$$

where $\bar{A} = \bar{C} + \bar{I}$

This is the general statement of the equilibrium level of income (Y_0) in our model. Note that the formula for the equilibrium level of income contains two elements, $1/(1 - c)$ and $(\bar{C} + \bar{I})$ or $(\bar{A})$ The significance of these elements will be explained shortly.

At this stage you must first work through the numerical example in Box 18-7 to ensure that you can handle this model.

18.7 The impact of a change in investment spending: the multiplier

Having explained the equilibrium level of income (Y_0), we now turn to changes in Y. In other words, we want to establish what will happen if the equilibrium is disturbed. This will enable us to **predict** what may happen in the economy if aggregate spending (or aggregate demand) changes.

Suppose that SABMiller decides to spend R100 million to build a new factory in Gauteng. When SAB-

BOX 18-6 EQUILIBRIUM IN TERMS OF SAVING AND INVESTMENT

In an economy that consists only of households and firms there is an alternative way of obtaining the equilibrium level of income. At equilibrium, planned saving (S) will be equal to planned investment spending (I). Saving is a leakage or withdrawal from the circular flow of spending and income while investment is an injection or addition. Income and spending can only be in equilibrium if the withdrawals or leakages (saving) equal the injections (investment).

Take the example used in the text where $C = 50 + \frac{4}{5}Y$ and $\bar{I} = 150$. As explained in Box 18-4, consumption (C) plus saving (S) must equal income (Y). Income that is not spent is saved.

This means that saving $(S) = -50 + \frac{1}{5}Y$.

Setting saving (S) equal to investment (I), we have

$$\begin{aligned} S &= I \\ \therefore -50 + \tfrac{1}{5}Y &= 150 \\ \therefore \tfrac{1}{5}Y &= 150 + 50 = 200 \\ \therefore Y &= \frac{200}{\frac{1}{5}} \\ &= 200 \times 5 \\ Y_0 &= 1\,000, \text{ as before.} \end{aligned}$$

Graphically this can be illustrated as follows:

In the diagram we show the investment function, $\bar{I} = 150$, and the saving function, $S = -50 + \frac{1}{5}Y$. The equilibrium level of income (Y_0) is the level of income where saving (withdrawals) equals investment (injections). As before, this is where $Y = 1\,000$.

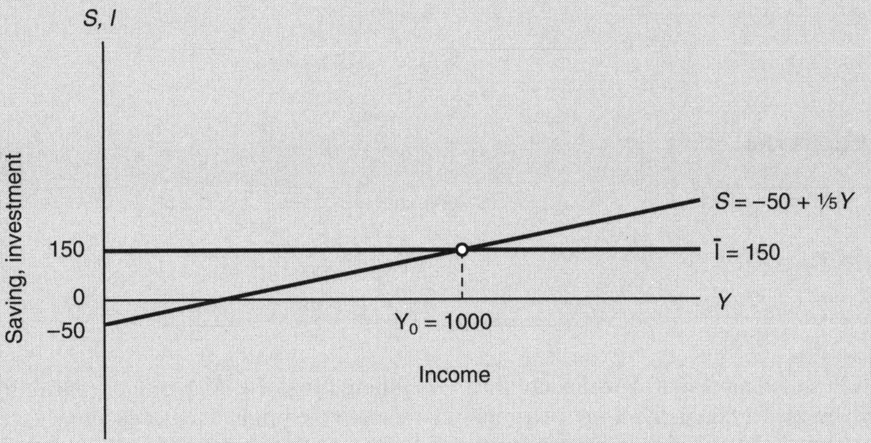

Note that saving is equal to investment at the equilibrium level of income only. At any other level of income S will not be equal to I. The Keynesian equilibrium condition ($S = I$) must not be confused with the idea (based on Say's law) that S is **always** equal to I. Also note that the injections-withdrawals approach can be applied to more complex models, as will be explained in Chapter 19.

Miller spends the R100 million, the money goes to the workers and owners of construction companies, and to the companies that supply materials and equipment to the construction industry. They receive the income in the form of wages, salaries and profits. The investment spending of R100 million thus raises the incomes of households in the economy by a similar amount.

But the process does not stop there. The owners and workers of the firms involved in the construction of the factory will not simply keep the R100 million in

BOX 18-7 CALCULATING THE EQUILIBRIUM LEVEL OF INCOME: A NUMERICAL EXAMPLE

If $\overline{C}$ = R10 million, c = ¾ (or 0,75) and $\overline{I}$ = R5 million, what will the equilibrium level of income (Y_0) be?

The answer can be obtained in various ways. We use a long method and a short method.

If $\overline{C}$ = R10 million and c = ¾, it follows that C = R10 million + ¾Y. If $\overline{I}$ = R5 million, then $I = \overline{I}$ = R5 million. By adding C and I we obtain A. Thus

$$A = C + I = \text{R10 million} + \tfrac{3}{4}Y + \text{R5 million}$$
$$= \text{R15 million} + \tfrac{3}{4}Y$$

Equilibrium is where $Y = A$, thus where

$$Y = \text{R15 million} + \tfrac{3}{4}Y$$
$$\text{or} \quad Y - \tfrac{3}{4}Y = \text{R15 million}$$
$$\therefore \tfrac{1}{4}Y = \text{R15 million}$$
$$\therefore Y = \frac{\text{R15 m}}{\tfrac{1}{4}}$$
$$= \text{R15 million} \times 4$$
$$Y_0 = \text{R60 million}$$

Alternatively we could simply have substituted the values of $\overline{C}$, c and $\overline{I}$ in the equations for the equilibrium level of income (Y_0) (ie Equation 18-6 or 18-6a):

$$Y_0 = \frac{1}{1-c}(\overline{C} + \overline{I}) \quad \textit{or} \quad Y_0 = \frac{1}{1-c}(\overline{A})$$
$$= \frac{1}{1-\tfrac{3}{4}}(\text{R10 million} + \text{R5 million}) \qquad = \frac{1}{1-\tfrac{3}{4}}(\text{R15 million})$$
$$= \frac{1}{\tfrac{1}{4}}(\text{R15 million}) \qquad = \frac{1}{\tfrac{1}{4}}(\text{R15 million})$$
$$= 4 \times \text{R15 million} \qquad = 4 \times \text{R15 million}$$
$$= \text{R60 million} \qquad = \text{R60 million}$$

the bank. They will spend most of it. The amount that they spend will be determined by their marginal propensity to consume. If the marginal propensity to consume (c) is ⅘ (or 0,8) they will spend 80 cents out of each rand and they will save the rest. Total spending in the economy will therefore increase by R80 million (ie ⅘ × R100 million). **This R80 million is an addition to the demand for goods and services in the economy in the same way as SABMiller's original investment of R100 million was.** The households concerned buy goods and services to the value of R80 million and this then raises the income of the workers and owners of the shops and other firms that sell the goods and services to them. At this stage the total spending and income in the economy have already increased by R180 million (ie the original R100 million **plus** the R80 million spent by those who received the original R100 million).

This is still not the end of the story. The shopkeepers and others who receive the R80 million also spend most of it. With a marginal propensity to consume of ⅘, they will spend R64 million (ie ⅘ × R80 million). And so the process continues. In each round there is additional spending and income. Every additional rand that is spent lands in someone's pocket and part of that rand is spent again. The additional amounts become progressively smaller but by the time the process ends, the total increase in income will be much greater than the initial injection of R100 million in the form of investment spending by SABMiller. **The ratio between the eventual change in income and the initial investment is called the multipli-**

er. The size of the multiplier depends on the fraction of the additional income generated in each round that is spent in the next round, that is, on the marginal propensity to consume (*c*).

Having described how the multiplier process works, we now examine it in more detail, using a simple numerical example. Suppose we have an economy in which C = R2 million + ⅗ (or 0,6) Y and $\bar{I}$ = R2 million. By this time you should be able to calculate the equilibrium level of income (Y_0). In this case it is R10 million. Suppose that there is then a spectacular improvement in business confidence and that investment spending increases by R12 million (to R14 million). We now examine the impact of this increase on the equilibrium level of income graphically and numerically.

The original aggregate spending function (A_1) and the new one after the increase in investment spending (A_2) are both shown in Figure 18-9. Note that the intercept ($\bar{A} = \bar{C} + \bar{I}$) increases from R4 million to R16 million (because $\bar{I}$ increased by R12 million) while the slope of both curves is ⅗ (or 0,6). The slope remains constant, since the marginal propensity to consume (*c*) has not changed. The intersection between the 45-degree line and the *A* curve (ie the equilibrium point) changes from E_1 to E_2. In Figure 18-9 we see that this implies that the equilibrium level of income increases from R10 million to R40 million. We now trace the process whereby the initial increase in investment of R12 million raises the equilibrium level of income by R30 million (from R10 million to R40 million).

- The increased investment expenditure immediately causes a shift from E_1 to point *z*. At this point total expenditure is equal to R22 million while production still remains temporarily at a level of R10 million. There is thus an excess demand for goods.
- Over the next period (approximately as long as it takes to produce the goods) production will also expand to the level of R22 million in order to meet the increased demand. We are therefore moving towards point *y* in the figure.
- At point *y* income has also increased by R12 million (ie from *z* to *y*), which means that consumption expenditure will, as a result of the marginal propensity to consume, increase by R7,2 million ($c\Delta Y = 0{,}6 \times 12 = 7{,}2$) and we move to point *x*.

FIGURE 18-9 The multiplier process

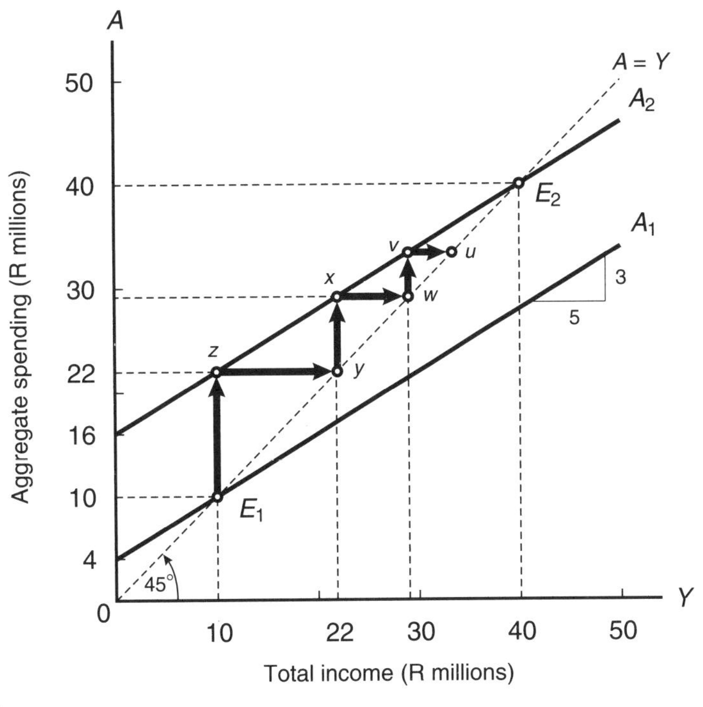

The original aggregate spending function is indicated by A_1 and the original equilibrium by E_1. Investment spending then increases, raising the aggregate spending curve to A_2. The new equilibrium is indicated by E_2. To explain the multiplier, the movement from E_1 to E_2 is broken up into different periods or rounds. The step-by-step process is indicated by the movements to z, y, x, w, v, u, and so on.

- The increased demand (from y to x) encourages manufacturers once more to increase production by the same amount (R7,2 million) to point w.
- The process repeats itself with diminishing increments of expenditure and income until the new equilibrium point E_2 is reached. At point E_2 the gap between expenditure and the level of income (ie the excess demand) is completely eliminated and there is no reason to increase or reduce production.

The different rounds in the multiplier process can also be traced by using numbers. The chain of spending and income in our example is summarised in Table 18-2.

The immediate effect of the additional investment spending of R12 million is to raise spending and income by R12 million. In the next round households spend three-fifths of the additional income (since $c = \frac{3}{5}$ or 0,6). This means that spending increases by R7,2 million. This spending raises the income of those who produced and sold the goods and services concerned. The cumulative impact at this stage is R19,2 million (ie R12 million plus R7,2 million). In the third round spending and income increase by R4,32 million (ie 0,6 × R7,2 million), raising the cumulative impact to R23,52 million. During the next round households again spend three-fifths of the additional income. By the seventh round the cumulative impact is already more than R29 million. The additional spending in each round gets smaller and smaller as the cumulative total approaches R30 million. It can be shown mathematically (see Box 18-8 and Appendix 18-1) that the total increase in income (ΔY) can be expressed as:

$$\Delta Y = \frac{1}{1-c}(\Delta I)$$

where c = marginal propensity to consume

ΔI = initial change in investment spending

In our example ΔY can thus be calculated as follows:

$$\begin{aligned}\Delta Y &= \left(\frac{1}{1-\frac{3}{5}}\right) \times (\text{R12 million})\\ &= \left(\frac{1}{\frac{2}{5}}\right) \times (\text{R12 million})\\ &= \tfrac{5}{2} \times \text{R12 million}\\ &= \text{R30 million}\end{aligned}$$

The equilibrium level of income thus increases by R30 million from R10 million to R40 million, as in Figure 18-9.

To obtain the change in income (ΔY) we therefore have to multiply the change in investment spending (ΔI) by $1/(1-c)$, where c is the marginal propensity to consume and $1/(1-c)$ is called **the multiplier**.

This is an important result, which can be generalised as follows: Any change in autonomous spending ($\bar{A}$) will set a multiplier process in motion and change the equilibrium level of income (Y) by a multiple of the initial change. **The ratio between the change in income and the change in autonomous spending ($\Delta Y/\Delta A$) is called the multiplier.**

In an economy which consists of households and firms only, the size of the multiplier is determined by the marginal propensity to consume (c). The greater the marginal propensity to consume, the greater the multiplier will be. Since the multiplier is such an important concept, we denote it with a separate symbol, α. In this case

$$\alpha = \frac{1}{1-c}$$

We can also write $\Delta Y = \alpha(\Delta\bar{A})$ which is simply another way of stating that the change in income will be equal to the multiplier times the change in autonomous spending.

TABLE 18-2 The multiplier chain of spending and income

Round number	*Additional spending and income in this round (R millions)*	*Cumulative total (R millions)*
1	12,0	12,0
2	7,2	19,2
3	4,32	23,52
4	2,592	26,112
5	1,5552	27,6672
6	0,93312	28,60032
7	0,559872	29,160192
8	0,3359232	29,4961152
9	0,2015539	29,6976691
...	...	...
...	...	...
n	...	30,0

BOX 18-8 THE MULTIPLIER AS THE SUM OF A GEOMETRIC SERIES

The cumulative increase in income as a result of an increase in investment spending can also be expressed by using a geometric series. In the example in Table 18-2 the change in income (ΔY) can be written as:

$$\begin{aligned}\Delta Y &= 12 + (0{,}6 \times 12) + 0{,}6 \times (0{,}6 \times 12) + 0{,}6 \times (0{,}6 \times 0{,}6 \times 12) + \ldots \\ &= 12 + (0{,}6 \times 12) + (0{,}6^2 \times 12) + (0{,}6^3 \times 12) + \ldots \\ &= 12(1 + 0{,}6 + 0{,}6^2 + 0{,}6^3 + \ldots)\end{aligned}$$

The expression in brackets is a geometric series. Each term is obtained by multiplying the previous term by 0,6. In each round the additional amount thus becomes smaller until it eventually approaches zero.

The series can also be expressed more generally in symbols. The fraction by which each successive term is multiplied is the marginal propensity to consume (c). Thus

$$\begin{aligned}\Delta Y &= \Delta I + c(\Delta I) + c^2(\Delta I) + c^3(\Delta I) \ldots + c^n(\Delta I) \\ &= \Delta I(1 + c + c^2 + c^3 + \ldots + c^n)\end{aligned}$$

Fortunately we do not have to keep adding new terms indefinitely. Mathematicians have shown that there is a general formula for the sum of the geometric series $(1 + c + c^2 + c^3 + \ldots + c^n)$. The sum is equal to $1/(1 - c)$.

We thus have $$\Delta Y = \frac{1}{1-c}(\Delta I)$$

or $$\frac{\Delta Y}{\Delta I} = \frac{1}{1-c}$$

The last equation represents the multiplier. **The multiplier is the ratio between the change in income (ΔY) and the initial change in spending (ΔI).** In this model the size of the multiplier is $1/(1 - c)$. With $c = 3/5$ (or 0,6), as in our example, the multiplier is thus

$$\frac{1}{1-c} = \frac{1}{1-\frac{3}{5}} = \frac{1}{\frac{2}{5}} = \frac{5}{2} = 2{,}5$$

The size of the multiplier depends on the marginal propensity to consume (c): the greater the value of c, the greater the value of the multiplier.

The multiplier can also be used to determine the equilibrium level of income. In Equation 18-6 we expressed the equilibrium level of income Y_0 as follows:

$$Y_0 = \frac{1}{1-c}\left(\bar{C} + \bar{I}\right)$$

The expression on the right-hand side consists of two components, $1/(1 - c)$ and $(\bar{C} + \bar{I})$. The former is the multiplier while the latter represents total autonomous spending in our model. **The equilibrium level of income can therefore always be obtained by multiplying the total of all the autonomous components of aggregate spending by the multiplier. In symbols we can therefore write**

$$Y_0 = \alpha \bar{A} \qquad (18\text{-}7)$$

This is an important general result which applies to all variants of the simple Keynesian model, including the ones to be discussed in Chapter 19.

The multiplier can also be derived algebraically by using the various equations of our model. This is shown in Appendix 18-1.

18.8 The simple Keynesian model: a brief summary

In this chapter we developed a simple model to determine total production and income in an economy that consists of households and firms only. We explained how the equilibrium level of income is determined by aggregate spending in the economy. In the model used in this chapter, aggregate spending (A) consists of consumption spending (C) and investment spending (I). Having explained how the equilibrium level of income is obtained, we examined the impact of a change in autonomous spending. We used the example of an increase in investment spending to explain the important concept called the multiplier.

The multiplier (α) is the ratio between a change in income (ΔY) and the change in autonomous spending ($\Delta\bar{A}$) which causes the change in income. The multiplier can never be less than one. In our present model its size depends on the marginal propensity to consume (c), that is, the slope of the aggregate spending function. The greater the value of c, the greater the multiplier will be. The equation for the multiplier (α) of this chapter is $\alpha = \Delta Y/\Delta A = 1/(1-c)$.

Figure 18-10 provides a graphical summary of the multiplier. When autonomous spending increases from $\bar{A}_1$ to $\bar{A}_2$, total income increases from Y_1 to Y_2. The multiplier is the ratio between the change in income (ΔY) and the change in autonomous spending ($\Delta\bar{A}$). In Chapter 19 you will encounter a slightly more complicated multiplier but the basic principles will be exactly the same as in Figure 18-10. The only thing that will change is the slope of the A function.

In some of the boxes in this chapter we presented an alternative explanation of equilibrium in terms of saving and investment. In the model developed in this chapter, production and income are determined by spending. The higher the level of spending, the higher the equilibrium level of income will be. If all households suddenly start saving a greater proportion of their income, aggregate spending and income will fall. This strange result is called the **paradox of thrift** and is explained in Box 18-9.

When you use a macroeconomic model (or any other theory), you must always remember the assumptions on which the model (or theory) is based. In the next chapter we drop some of the assumptions listed in Box 18-2 and we incorporate the government and the foreign sector into our Keynesian model. The model therefore becomes somewhat more complex. However, the basic principles developed in this chapter still apply. If you understand the determination of the equilibrium level of income and the principle of the multiplier you should have little difficulty in dealing with the models we work with in Chapter 19.

FIGURE 18-10 The multiplier: a summary

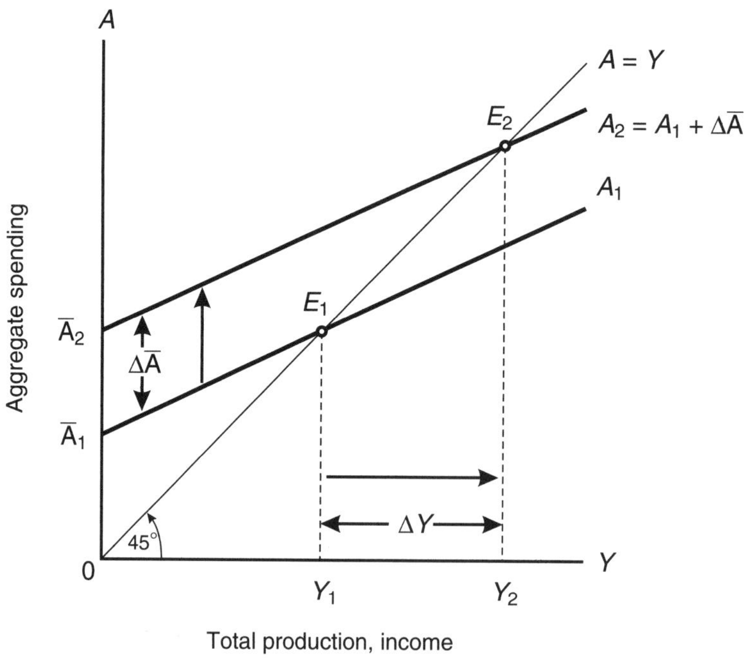

If autonomous spending increases from $\bar{A}_1$ to $\bar{A}_2$, the equilibrium level of income will increase from Y_1 to Y_2. The increase in income (ΔY) is greater than the increase in autonomous spending ($\Delta\bar{A}$). The ratio between these two increases is the multiplier.

BOX 18-9 THE PARADOX OF THRIFT

In Section 1.3 we explained the **fallacy of composition**. This is the logical fallacy of assuming that what is true for the part is also true for the whole. One of the examples we mentioned was the **paradox of thrift**. This paradox refers to the fact that while an individual or single household can increase its income by saving more, the same result does not hold for society as a whole. We are now in a position to explain this paradox.

If a household saves a larger portion of its income, it increases its stock of assets, and it will earn additional income from the additional assets. For example, if a household starts saving R1 000 per year instead of spending it and the interest rate is 10 per cent, it will receive an additional income of R100 per year which it would not have received otherwise. But if **all** households save a larger portion of their income, aggregate consumption spending (C) will fall, *ceteris paribus*. Aggregate spending (A) and total income (Y) will thus also fall and in the end households (as a group) will have a lower total income than before. The simple Keynesian model thus predicts that an increase in saving (at each level of income) will reduce the equilibrium level of income in the economy. If everyone saves more, aggregate spending on goods and services will fall. Firms will reduce their production of goods and services and total income will fall.

Graphically, this can be shown by a downward shift of the consumption function (C) and therefore also of the aggregate spending function (A). Alternatively, the equilibrium condition in Box 18-6, (ie $S = I$), can also be used. In terms of the diagram in Box 18-6, an increase in saving will be illustrated by an upward shift of the saving function and a consequent fall in the equilibrium level of income. You can prove for yourself that an upward shift of the saving function or a downward shift of the consumption function will result in a fall in the equilibrium level of income.

IMPORTANT CONCEPTS

- Macroeconomics
- Consumption spending
- Investment spending
- Aggregate spending (demand)
- Total production or income
- Keynesian model
- Equilibrium
- Inventories (stocks)
- Say's law
- Consumption function
- Autonomous consumption
- Induced consumption
- Marginal propensity to consume
- Saving
- Investment function
- Excess demand
- Excess supply
- 45-degree line
- Equilibrium level of income
- Multiplier
- Paradox of thrift

APPENDIX 18-1
AN ALGEBRAIC DERIVATION OF THE MULTIPLIER

With $C = \bar{C} + cY$ and $I = \bar{I}$, the original equilibrium level of income Y_0 is calculated as follows:

$$\begin{aligned} Y &= A \\ &= C + I \\ &= \bar{C} + cY + \bar{I} \\ &= \bar{C} + \bar{I} + cY \\ \therefore\ Y - cY &= \bar{C} + \bar{I} \\ (1 - c)Y &= \bar{C} + \bar{I} \\ \therefore\ Y_0 &= \frac{1}{1-c}(\bar{C} + \bar{I}) \quad \ldots\ldots\ldots\ldots\ (1) \end{aligned}$$

This is the same as Equation 18-6 (see Section 18.6).

If I increases by ΔI from $\bar{I}$ to $(\bar{I} + \Delta I)$ then the new equilibrium level of income will be $(Y_0 + \Delta Y)$. By substituting Y_0 with $(Y_0 + \Delta Y)$ and $\bar{I}$ with $(\bar{I} + \Delta I)$ we obtain

$$\begin{aligned} Y_0 + \Delta Y &= \frac{1}{1-c}(\bar{C} + \bar{I} + \Delta I) \\ &= \frac{1}{1-c}(\bar{C} + \bar{I}) + \frac{1}{1-c}(\Delta I) \quad \ldots\ (2) \end{aligned}$$

To obtain ΔY we have to subtract Equation (1) from Equation (2). This yields the following result:

$$\begin{aligned} \Delta Y &= \frac{1}{1-c}(\bar{C} + \bar{I}) + \frac{1}{1-c}(\Delta I) \\ &\quad - \frac{1}{1-c}(\bar{C} + \bar{I}) \\ \therefore\ \Delta Y &= \frac{1}{1-c}(\Delta I) \quad \text{or} \quad \frac{\Delta Y}{\Delta I} = \frac{1}{1-c} \end{aligned}$$

Once again we have shown that the multiplier α is equal to

$$\left(\frac{1}{1-c}\right)$$

In more general terms we can write

$$\begin{aligned} \Delta Y &= \alpha(\Delta\bar{A}) \\ \text{where } \alpha &= \text{multiplier} \\ \Delta\bar{A} &= \text{change in autonomous spending} \end{aligned}$$

REVIEW QUESTIONS

1. Can the model discussed in this chapter be used to explain (a) inflation, (b) the balance of payments and (c) developments in the monetary sector of the economy? Why (not)?
2. Explain the meaning of the marginal propensity to consume and the relationship between the marginal propensity to consume and the marginal propensity to save.
3. What do we mean when we say that investment is regarded as an *exogenous* variable in the Keynesian model of the determination of total production or income in the economy?
4. Why is the model developed in this chapter called a Keynesian model?
5. What is meant by autonomous consumption?
6. What happens in the economy when total production (*Y*) is greater than aggregate spending (*A*)?
7. Explain the meaning or purpose of the 45-degree line in the model used in this chapter.
8. How would you explain the multiplier to a friend or family member?
9. Explain why there is equilibrium in the economy when total spending (*A*) is equal to total production or income (*Y*).

10. Suppose the marginal propensity to consume is 0,75 and investment spending increases by R100 million. By how much will total production or income in the economy change?

11. Why does a marginal propensity to invest not feature in the model introduced in this chapter?

12. What determines the size of the multiplier in an economy without a government or foreign sector?

13. Use (a) an *AY* diagram (ie one with an aggregate spending curve and a 45-degree line) and (b) a saving-investment diagram to explain the paradox of thrift.

Some notable technological landmarks

1764	Spinning jenny (Hargreaves)
1769	Spinning frame (Arkwright)
1776	Steam engine (Boulton-Watt)
1779	Spinning mule (Crompton)
1785	Power loom (Cartwright)
1793	Cotton gin (Whitney)
1804	Steam-powered locomotive (Trevithick)
1816	Photography (Niepce)
1823	Digital calculator (Babbage)
1831	Electric transformer (Faraday)
1833	Telegraph (Gauss)
1848	Colour photography (Becquerel)
1852	Elevator/lift (Otis)
1862	Machine gun (Gatling)
1865	Cylinder lock (Yale)
1866	Dynamite (Nobel) Aluminium (Hall)
1877	Telephone (Bell)
1885	Motorcycle (Daimler) Automobile with internal combustion engine Commercial adding machine (Burroughs)
1888	Hand-held camera (Eastman)
1890	Steam turbine (Parsons)
1893	Motion pictures (Edison)
1895	Radio (Marconi) X-rays (Roëntgen)
1899	Bayer aspirin Electric home refrigerator Tape recorder
1900	Tractor (Holt)
1901	Mercedes car
1903	Airplane flight (Wright brothers)
1911	Air conditioning (Carrier)
1926	Motion pictures with sound
1928	Mechanically-operated computer (Bush) Penicillin (Fleming) Electric shaver (Schick)
1930	Jet-propulsion aircraft (Whittle)
1932	Polaroid (Land)
1935	Nylon
1938	Ball-point pen
1941	Aerosol spray
1946	Electronic computer (Eckert)
1948	Transistor Long-playing record
1951	Colour television in the United States
1953	Polio vaccine (Salk)
1958	Boeing 707
1961	First astronaut in space
1966	Boeing 747
1967	Microwave oven
1969	First walk on the moon Concorde supersonic jet
1972	World Trade Centre completed

19

Keynesian models including the government and the foreign sector

Learning outcomes

Once you have studied this chapter you should be able to

- explain how government spending affects the level of production and income
- describe how the introduction of a proportional income tax affects the multiplier
- use the simple Keynesian model to analyse the effects of fiscal policy
- explain how exports and imports affect the level of income in the domestic economy
- analyse the effects of changes in government spending in the open economy

Government is the great fiction, through which everybody endeavours to live at the expense of everyone else.

FRÉDÉRIC BASTIAT

You can no more define equilibrium in international trade than you can define a pretty girl, but you can recognise one if you meet one.

PER JACOBSSON

If the propensity to consume and the rate of new investment result in a deficient effective demand, the actual level of employment will fall short of the supply of labour potentially available.

JOHN MAYNARD KEYNES

In Chapter 18 you encountered your first macroeconomic model. This simple model was used to introduce a number of important concepts and relationships such as aggregate spending (A), total income (Y), macroeconomic equilibrium ($A = Y$), the marginal propensity to consume (c) and the multiplier (α). The time has now arrived to drop some of the simplifying assumptions made in Chapter 18. In this chapter we introduce the **government** and the **foreign sector** into the simple macroeconomic model. This means that we also consider **government spending** (G), **taxes** (T), **exports** (X) and **imports** (Z). As you will see, the basic principles developed in Chapter 18 still apply. The only real difference is that aggregate spending includes more elements than before and that there are now more leakages from the circular flow of income and spending. As the leakages increase, the **multiplier** becomes smaller.

In this chapter we introduce the government and the foreign sector into the simple Keynesian model. This means that we include four additional **flows** into our analysis: **government spending** (G), **taxes** (T), **exports** (X) and **imports** (Z). By this time you should be thoroughly acquainted with these flows. We originally introduced them in Chapter 3 and they have been dealt with at various other places in the book. For example, we discussed government spending and taxation at some length in Chapter 16, which focused on the government sector. Similarly, Chapter 17 (which focused on the foreign sector) dealt with exports and imports.

The time has now arrived to include these flows into our model and to see what effects they have on total production and income in the economy. In particular wc want to see how each of these flows influences aggregate spending A, the multiplier α and the equilibrium level of income Y. Once the government sector is included, we can also start to analyse macroeconomic policy. Remember that economic theory essentially has three purposes:

- to **explain** what is happening in the economy
- to **predict** what will happen if something changes
- to help us to analyse economic **policy**

In this chapter we focus on explanation, prediction and the analysis of policy decisions. In the process you will learn more about the interaction between the major flows in the economy. But this is by no means the end of the macroeconomic story. Although two of the simplifying assumptions made in Chapter 18 are relaxed, all the other assumptions (see Box 18-2) still apply. In other words, we still assume that prices, wages and interest rates are given (ie exogenous). We cannot, therefore, analyse inflation, changes in wages or developments in the financial markets by means of the models we introduce in this chapter. The remaining assumptions in Box 18-2 will only be dropped in later chapters and in more advanced courses in macroeconomics.

In this chapter we first introduce the government sector and, once we have done this, we add the foreign sector. This means that the model of Chapter 18 becomes somewhat more complicated. You will notice, however, that **all the underlying principles remain exactly the same**. The only real differences are that we add new components to aggregate spending A, and we introduce new leakages from the flow of income and spending, which reduce the size of the multiplier. If you followed the argument in Chapter 18, you should have no difficulty in understanding this chapter. The main requirement is to keep **thinking** about the basic principles involved.

19.1 Introducing the government into our model

The introduction of the government means that we have to consider the impact of government spending G and taxes T on:

- the level of aggregate spending A
- the multiplier α
- equilibrium income Y

In addition we must also determine how government spending and taxes can be used as policy instruments to affect the level of income Y. Recall, from Chapter 16, that government spending and taxes are the essential ingredients of the **budget** and that they are the main instruments of **fiscal policy**. By introducing the government we are therefore incorporating thc budget and fiscal policy into our analysis.

We start by examining the **determinants** of government spending G and taxes T, that is, by **explaining** G and T. In particular we want to know whether there are any systematic links between G or T and the level of income Y.

Government spending (G)

What determines government spending? In earlier chapters we indicated that government spending in South Africa has increased quite rapidly in recent decades. In Chapter 16 we also gave a number of reasons for this increase. In the 1980s and 1990s, for example, there was pressure on government to spend more on education, housing, health and safety and security, while defence spending increased rapidly during the 1970s and early 1980s. The important point is that **government spending is essentially a political issue**. In other words, government spending is related to political objectives rather than to the level of income Y. In fact, government spending G has often been increased after income Y has fallen. There is thus **no systematic relationship between G and Y**. In **symbols** we express this as

$$G = \overline{G}$$

where the bar above the G indicates that G is **autonomous** with respect to Y.

Graphically the relationship between government spending G and Y is illustrated by a horizontal line as in Figure 19-1.

How does the introduction of G affect the level of aggregate spending A? The answer is quite simple. Government spending on goods and services G has to be added to the other components of aggregate spending, that is, consumption spending C and investment spending I. When we add the government, aggregate spending A thus becomes equal to $C + I + G$.

In **symbols** we have

$$A = C + I + G$$

Graphically we have to add G to $C + I$ at each level of Y. This is illustrated by a parallel upward shift of the A curve as indicated in Figure 19-2. Since G is autonomous (ie $G = \overline{G}$), it affects the **position** of the A curve, but the **slope** of the curve remains unchanged. As in Chapter 18, the aggregate spending curve A is still parallel to the consumption function C. Remember that the multiplier α is related to the marginal propensity to consume c, that is, to the slope of the A curve. The introduction of government spending therefore does not affect the size of the multiplier α.

The 45-degree line is also shown in Figure 19-2. Note that the introduction of government spending moves the intersection between aggregate spending and the 45-degree line from E_1 to E_2. The equilibrium level of income increases from Y_1 to Y_2 – the introduction of government spending increases the equilibrium level of income, *ceteris paribus*. By **how much** will it increase the equilibrium level of income? As we explained in the previous chapter, the change in income will be equal to **the change in autonomous spending** (in this case the introduction of G) **multiplied by the multiplier**. In Figure 19-2 the increase from Y_1 to Y_2 will therefore be greater than G.

Algebraically the model can be represented as follows:

$$Y = A \quad \text{.......... (19-1)}$$
$$A = C + \overline{I} + \overline{G} \quad \text{.......... (19-2)}$$
$$C = \overline{C} + cY \quad \text{.......... (19-3)}$$

FIGURE 19-1 Government spending

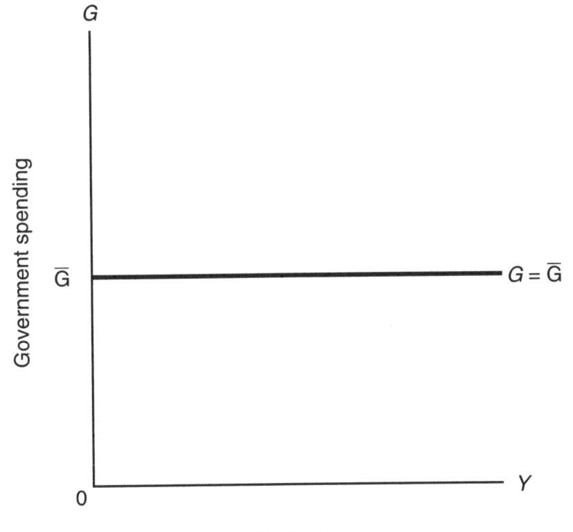

The horizontal line $\overline{G}$ indicates that government spending G is autonomous with respect to income Y. In other words, the level of G is independent of the level of Y. It is determined by other factors.

Equation 19-1 is the same as Equation 18-3. It represents the equilibrium condition – total income Y is only in equilibrium when it is equal to aggregate spending A. Equation 19-3 is also the same as Equation 18-1. It represents the consumption function. The only difference between this model and the model of the previous chapter is that aggregate spending A now has an additional component $\overline{G}$, as indicated in Equation 19-2.

To calculate the equilibrium level of income Y, we start with the equilibrium condition (Equation 19-1):

$$Y = A$$

The next step is to substitute A with the right-hand side of Equation 19-2:

$$\therefore\ Y = C + \overline{I} + \overline{G}$$

Then substitute C with the right-hand side of Equation 19-3:

$$\therefore\ Y = (\overline{C} + cY) + \overline{I} + \overline{G}$$

All that remains is to solve the equation:

$$Y - cY = \overline{C} + \overline{I} + \overline{G}$$

$$\therefore\ Y(1 - c) = \overline{C} + \overline{I} + \overline{G}$$

$$\therefore\ Y_0 = \frac{1}{1-c}(\overline{C} + \overline{I} + \overline{G}) \quad \text{.......... (19-4)}$$

The only difference between Equation 19-4 and Equation 18-6 is the addition of government spending $\overline{G}$ to autonomous spending. As in Equation 18-7, the general formula is still

$$Y_0 = \alpha(\overline{A}) \quad \text{.......... (19-5)}$$

where Y_0 = equilibrium level of income
α = multiplier
$\overline{A}$ = total autonomous spending

To prove for yourself that this is the case, work through the numerical example in Box 19-1.

The impact of government spending G can be summarised by considering the three aspects mentioned at the beginning of this section. The introduction of government spending G

- increases the level of aggregate spending A
- leaves the multiplier α unchanged
- raises the equilibrium level of income Y_0, *ceteris paribus*

It follows that **increases in government spending can be used to raise the level of production and income** Y. Any increase in government spending will raise production and income by a multiple of the ori-

FIGURE 19-2 Aggregate spending in an economy with a government sector

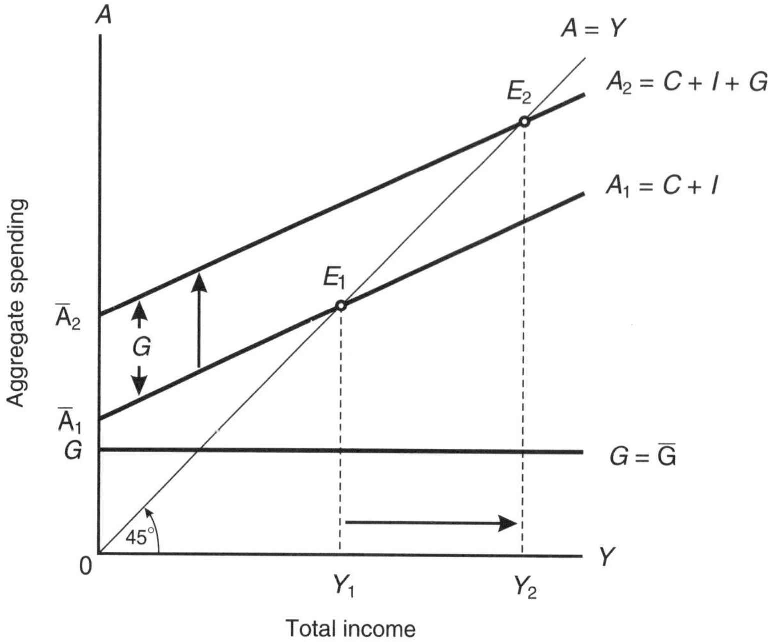

To obtain the level of aggregate spending A, we simply add G, which is independent of Y, to C + I at each level of Y. The intercept $\overline{A}_1$ increases by G to $\overline{A}_2$ and the whole curve shifts upwards by the same distance. The new aggregate spending curve is C + I + G.

ginal increase. This seems to indicate that government spending is a powerful instrument that can be used to increase production and income, and lower unemployment. The problem, however, is that this result only applies in a world in which there is no foreign sector and in which prices, wages and interest rates are fixed – recall the simplifying assumptions in Box 18-2. Once these assumptions are dropped, government spending becomes a less powerful and more complicated instrument of economic policy. Moreover, government spending has to be financed. As we explained in Chapter 16, government spending is financed largely by taxes, to which we now turn.

Taxes (T)

If government wishes to spend, it should levy taxes. In the circular flow models introduced in Chapter 3, we emphasised that **government spending** *G* is an **injection** into the circular flow of income and spending in the economy. We also indicated that **taxes** *T* constitute a **leakage** or **withdrawal** from the circular flow. We would therefore expect that the impact of taxes *T* would be the opposite of the impact of government spending *G*. As a general principle this is indeed the case. But there is a subtle difference between the impact of *T* and the impact of *G*. Whereas *G* affects the level of spending and income in a **direct** way, by adding to the demand for goods and services, taxes *T* operate in a more **indirect** fashion. Taxes reduce the income that households have available to spend on goods and services. We say that **taxes reduce the disposable (or after-tax) income** of households, with the result that households can afford to purchase fewer goods and services than before. By reducing disposable income, taxes indirectly reduce consumption spending *C* by households.

As in the case of government spending *G*, we wish to know how the introduction of taxes *T* will affect

- the level of aggregate spending *A*
- the size of the multiplier α
- the equilibrium level of income *Y*

We also want to know how the government can use taxes to affect the level of income. In other words, we want to know how taxation can be used as an instrument of fiscal policy.

To answer these questions, we must first find out **what determines the level of taxes**. In particular, we want to know whether there is a systematic relationship between the level of taxes *T* and the level of national income *Y*.

BOX 19-1 THE IMPACT OF THE INTRODUCTION OF GOVERNMENT SPENDING: A NUMERICAL EXAMPLE

Suppose a small economy, Economia, originally consists only of households and firms. There is no government and there are no trade links with the rest of the world. The currency unit is the econ. Autonomous consumption is 10 million econs per year and households consume 60 per cent (or ⅗) of each addition to their income. Firms spend 30 million econs on capital goods each year, that is, investment spending is 30 million econs per year.

This means that C = 10 million econs + $\frac{3}{5}Y$ and $\bar{I}$ = 30 million econs. The multiplier α is

$$\frac{1}{1-c} = \frac{1}{1-\frac{3}{5}} = \frac{1}{\frac{2}{5}} = \frac{5}{2} = 2\tfrac{1}{2} \text{ (or 2,5).}$$

The equilibrium level of income Y_0 is equal to $\alpha\bar{A}$, that is, $2\frac{1}{2} \times 40$ million econs = 100 million econs.

Suppose that a government is then formed and that it spends 20 million econs per year, that is, G = 20 million econs. (At this stage we are not concerned with the way in which this spending is financed.) The introduction of government spending raises autonomous spending from 40 million econs to 60 million econs:

$$\bar{A} = \bar{C} + \bar{I} + \bar{G} = 10 \text{ million} + 30 \text{ million} + 20 \text{ million} = 60 \text{ million econs}$$

The equilibrium level of income is obtained by multiplying autonomous spending ($\bar{A}$) by the multiplier α. Thus

$$\begin{aligned} Y_0 &= \alpha\bar{A} \\ &= 2\tfrac{1}{2} \times 60 \text{ million econs} \\ &= 150 \text{ million econs} \end{aligned}$$

This answer could also have been obtained by multiplying government spending $\bar{G}$ (20 million econs) by the multiplier ($2\frac{1}{2}$) and adding the result (50 million econs) to the original equilibrium level of income of 100 million econs.

The different types of tax in South Africa were introduced in Chapter 16. Recall, for example, that we distinguished between **direct** taxes (ie taxes on income and wealth) and **indirect** taxes (ie taxes on goods and services). Also remember that personal income tax and value-added tax (VAT) are two of the most important sources of government revenue in South Africa. Personal income tax is a direct tax, while VAT is an indirect tax.

As their incomes increase, people have to pay more income tax. Similarly, as people spend more, they pay more VAT. Company tax is levied on profits and is therefore also related to the level of production and income. There are thus clearly definite links between income and spending in the economy and the total amount of tax that is paid. We therefore cannot realistically assume that taxes T are unrelated to income Y. T is clearly **not autonomous** (as is the case with G). To be realistic, we have to assume a link between taxes T and income Y. We assume that taxes T are a certain proportion (t) of income Y. This proportion is called the **tax rate**. Thus

$$T = tY \quad \text{(19-6)}$$

For example, if the tax rate $t = 0{,}2$ we have $T = 0{,}2Y$, which means that 20 per cent of the total income in the economy, or 20 cents out of each rand, has to be paid to government in the form of taxes.

Graphically this relationship can be illustrated as in Figure 19-3. The assumption of a fixed income tax rate t may seem a bit unrealistic. In Chapter 16 we saw that personal income tax in South Africa is progressive – as taxpayers' income increases, their tax **rate** also increases. However, for the economy as a whole (which is what we are dealing with here) a fixed tax rate (or a **proportional tax**, as it is usually called) is quite realistic. During any particular year taxes T for the economy as a whole are a certain proportion of income Y. In other words, T/Y = t or $T = tY$, as indicated in Equation 19-6.

FIGURE 19-3 Taxation as a function of income

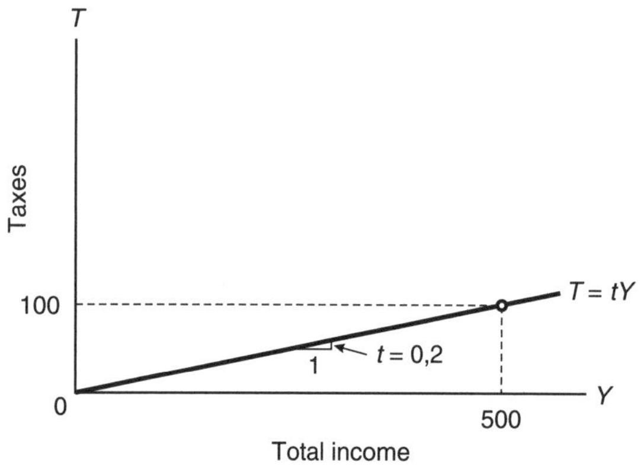

Taxes T are a certain proportion t of income Y. This proportion is called the tax rate. In the figure t = 0,2. When Y = 0, then T is also equal to zero. When Y = 500, then T = 0,2Y = 0,2(500) = 100. The slope of the curve is given by t. In this case the slope is therefore 0,2.

Now that we have introduced taxation, we must establish how taxes affect spending and income in the economy. As mentioned earlier, the immediate effect is to reduce disposable (or after-tax) income, that is, the income that is available for spending. We must therefore distinguish between **total income (Y)** and **disposable income (Y_d)**. Disposable income Y_d is simply the income that households have available after they have paid taxes. Thus

$$Y_d = Y - T \quad \text{.............................} \quad (19\text{-}7)$$

Since $T = tY$ we can also write

$$Y_d = Y - tY$$

or, by collecting terms on the right-hand side,

$$Y_d = (1 - t)Y \quad \text{.............................} \quad (19\text{-}8)$$

Equation 19-8 states that disposable income Y_d is equal to a fraction $(1 - t)$ of total income Y. For example, if $t = 0{,}20$, as before (ie if 20 per cent of income is paid to the government in the form of taxes) then $(1 - t) = 0{,}80$. In this case, Equation 19-8 simply states that disposable income is 80 per cent of total income. What happens to the other 20 per cent? It is paid to government in the form of taxes.

When we introduce taxes we have to distinguish between total income and disposable income. This also means that we have to modify the consumption function to indicate that households cannot spend their total income. They can only spend their disposable (or after-tax) income. We therefore have to substitute total income Y in the consumption function with disposable income Y_d. Thus

$$C = \bar{C} + cY_d \quad \text{.............................} \quad (19\text{-}9)$$

This might seem complicated, but it is actually quite straightforward. Equation 19-9 simply states that households can only spend a proportion (c) (the marginal propensity to consume) of their disposable (or after-tax) income Y_d.

How does this consumption function compare with the one in Chapter 18? The answer is that the introduction of taxes reduces consumption spending at each positive level of income Y. If we now plot consumption spending against total income Y (as we usually do), we find that the consumption function has a smaller slope (ie it is flatter) than before.

This result can also be shown **algebraically**. We start with Equation 19-9:

$$C = \bar{C} + cY_d$$

We then substitute Y_d with $Y - tY$ (since $Y_d = Y - T = Y - tY$):

$$\therefore C = \bar{C} + c(Y - tY)$$

By collecting terms this transforms to

$$C = \bar{C} + c(1 - t)Y \quad \text{.......................} \quad (19\text{-}10)$$

The slope of this curve is given by $c(1 - t)$ which is smaller than c.

Since a proportional income tax is a **leakage** or **withdrawal** from the circular flow, the introduction of such a tax means that a smaller proportion of any addition to aggregate spending A will be passed on in each round of the multiplier process. The introduction of a proportional income tax thus reduces the size of the multiplier:

$$\text{Multiplier without taxes} = \frac{1}{1 - c}$$

$$\text{Multiplier with taxes} = \frac{1}{1 - c(1 - t)}$$

This result is confirmed in the next subsection. It can also be tested by using a numerical example. Suppose $c = \frac{3}{4}$ and $t = \frac{1}{5}$, then

$$\text{Multiplier without taxes} = \frac{1}{1 - \frac{3}{4}} = \frac{1}{\frac{1}{4}} = 4$$

$$\text{Multiplier with taxes} = \frac{1}{1 - \frac{3}{4}\left(1 - \frac{1}{5}\right)} = \frac{1}{1 - \frac{3}{4}\left(\frac{4}{5}\right)} = \frac{1}{1 - \frac{3}{5}} = \frac{1}{\frac{2}{5}} = \frac{5}{2} \ \left(\text{or } 2\tfrac{1}{2}\right)$$

Important note: When calculating the multiplier with taxes, the calculation in brackets $(1 - t)$ must be made first. The result of this calculation is then multiplied by the marginal propensity to consume c, and only then is the subsequent result subtracted from 1 and inverted (ie divided into 1) to obtain the multiplier. The economic logic of this calculation is as follows: Instead of simply using the marginal propensity to consume, the first step is to subtract the proportion of each additional rand that has to be paid as tax. This yields the fraction of each rand $(1 - t)$ that is available for consumption. This fraction is then multiplied by the marginal propensity to consume. We thus have $(1 - t) \times c = c(1 - t)$. The rest of the argument is the same as for the multiplier without taxes, as explained in Chapter 18.

Graphically, the introduction of taxes swivels the consumption function downwards, as illustrated in Figure 19-4. In other words, the consumption function becomes flatter. The difference between the original consumption function (without taxes) and the new consumption function (after taxes) at each level of income is the difference between what households would have planned to spend in the absence of taxes and what they plan to spend after the introduction of taxes.

The slope of the new consumption function (and of the new aggregate spending function, since I and G are both autonomous) is given by $c(1 - t)$. This is quite easy to explain. Without taxes, households plan to spend a certain fraction (c) (say 0,75, or 75 per cent – as in the previous example) of their available income on consumer goods and services. When taxes are introduced, they first have to pay a fraction (t) of their income (say 0,20, or 20 per cent) in taxes. Out of each rand they therefore have only R0,80 or 80 cents (ie 80 per cent) left. If they still spend the same fraction c (75 per cent in our example), they ultimately spend a smaller fraction of their total income. In our example they will spend 75 per cent of each 80 cents rather than 75 per cent of R1,00. They thus spend 60 cents instead of 75 cents out of every rand. The remainder goes to taxes (20 cents) and saving (20 cents).

Now work through the numerical example in Box 19-2 to ensure that you understand how the introduction of taxes affects the consumption function and the multiplier. Since an income tax is a leakage, it reduces the equilibrium level of income, ***ceteris paribus***. In terms of our model, this reduction is caused by the fact that the tax rate reduces the size of the multiplier. The introduction of a proportional tax thus

- leaves autonomous spending $\bar{A}$ unchanged
- reduces the multiplier α
- reduces the equilibrium level of income Y_0, ***ceteris paribus***

FIGURE 19-4 The impact of the introduction of taxes on the consumption function

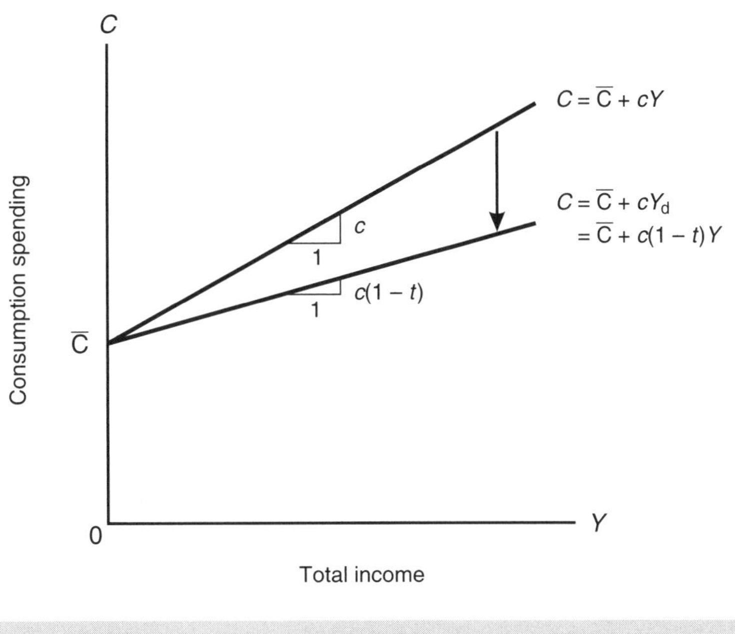

The original consumption function is given by $C = \bar{C} + cY$. With the introduction of a proportional income tax, households cannot spend all their income. They first have to pay tax. The difference between income earned and tax paid is disposable income Y_d. The new consumption function is lower than the previous one, except at an income of zero, where tax is also zero. The consumption function therefore becomes flatter, as indicated by $C = \bar{C} + c(1 - t)Y$.

The equilibrium level of income in an economy with a government sector

We are now in a position to determine the equilibrium level of income in an economy with a government sector. Government spending *G* is an injection into the circular flow of spending and income. It raises the level of aggregate spending *A* at each level of income. Taxes represent a leakage from the circular flow. A proportional income tax reduces disposable income, thus reducing consumption spending *C* at each positive level of income *Y*. As we have explained, a proportional income tax thus reduces the size of the multiplier.

Graphically the effect of the introduction of government can be illustrated as in Figure 19-5. The original aggregate spending curve, prior to the introduction of the government, is given by $A_1 = \overline{A}_1 + cY$. The intercept is $\overline{A}_1$ (where $\overline{A}_1 = \overline{C} + \overline{I}$) and the slope is *c*, that is, the marginal propensity to consume. The initial equilibrium is indicated by E_1 and the equilibrium level of income is Y_1. When government spending *G* is introduced, aggregate spending at each level of income *Y* increases by the amount of government spending *G*. This is illustrated by a parallel upward shift of aggregate spending to A_2. The intercept is now higher at $\overline{A}_2$ (= $\overline{C} + \overline{I} + \overline{G}$) but the slope *c* is still the same. In the absence of taxes, the equilibrium will change to E_2 and the equilibrium level of income will increase to Y_2. However, when a proportional income tax is introduced to finance part of the government spending, households have to pay a certain portion *t* of their income in the form of taxes. This reduces their disposable income and therefore also their consumption spending at each level of income. The aggregate spending curve becomes flatter, as indicated by A_3, since a smaller portion of any increase in income is spent on consumer goods and services. The slope of the aggregate spending curve falls to $c(1 - t)$ where t = tax rate. In the figure we show the eventual equilibrium as E_3, corresponding to an equilibrium level of income of Y_3, which is higher than Y_1. Total income will, however, not necessarily increase when the government is introduced into the model. The eventual impact of the introduction of government on the equilibrium level of income will depend on the relative sizes of the level of government spending and the tax rate.

FIGURE 19-5 The impact of government spending and a proportional income tax on the equilibrium level of income

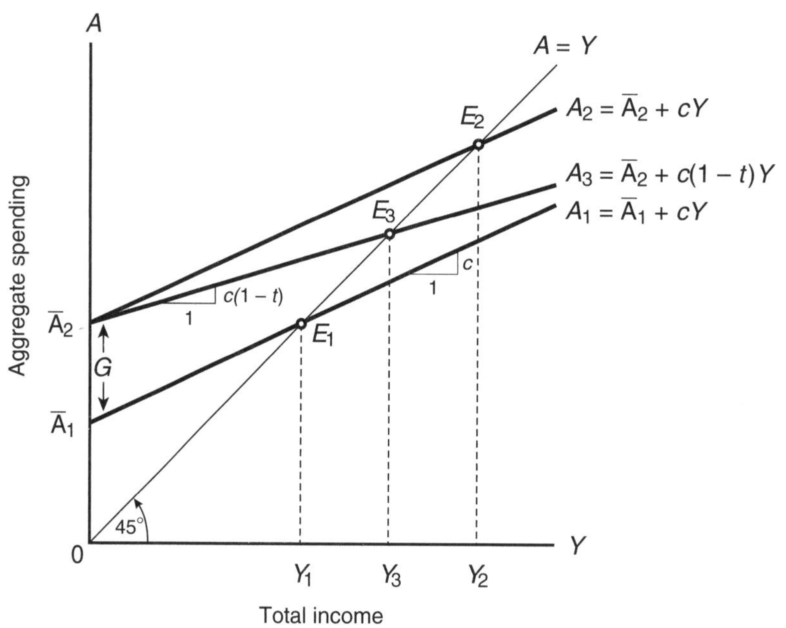

The original aggregate spending curve prior to the introduction of government is indicated by A_1. The equilibrium level of income is Y_1. With the introduction of government spending the aggregate spending curve shifts parallel to A_2. With the introduction of a proportional income tax, the aggregate spending curve becomes flatter, as indicated by A_3. The eventual equilibrium level of income is indicated by Y_3.

BOX 19-2 IMPACT OF THE INTRODUCTION OF A PROPORTIONAL INCOME TAX ON THE CONSUMPTION FUNCTION AND THE MULTIPLIER: A NUMERICAL EXAMPLE

Suppose that autonomous consumption $\overline{C}$ is R100 million and that the marginal propensity to consume c is ⅔. This yields the following consumption function:

$$C = \text{R100 million} + \tfrac{2}{3}Y$$

The government then introduces a proportional income tax at a rate of 25 per cent (or ¼) of income. Households now first have to pay taxes before they can spend. With a tax rate of 25 per cent, this means that only 75 per cent (or ¾) of their income is available for consumption and saving. Disposable income Y_d is equal to income Y minus taxes T, where $T = tY$. With a tax rate of 25 per cent, it follows that $Y_d = Y - \tfrac{1}{4}Y = \tfrac{3}{4}Y$.

If the marginal propensity to consume c is ⅔, it means that households spend ⅔ of any addition to their income. But now they first have to pay ¼ of any additional income to the government in the form of taxes. This means that only ⅔ of ¾ of every additional rand of income is consumed. When a proportional income tax is levied, the increase in consumption spending due to an increase in income is thus lower than in the absence of taxes. This means that the slope of the aggregate spending curve decreases (ie the curve becomes flatter), as illustrated in Figure 19-4. In our numerical example the slope falls from ⅔ to ½ (= ⅔ × ¾). Only half of every increase in income is thus consumed by households and the multiplier falls from 3 to 2:

$$\text{Multiplier without taxes} = \frac{1}{1-c} = \frac{1}{1-\frac{2}{3}} = \frac{1}{\frac{1}{3}} = 3$$

$$\text{Multiplier with taxes} = \frac{1}{1-c(1-t)} = \frac{1}{1-\frac{2}{3}\left(1-\frac{1}{4}\right)} = \frac{1}{1-\frac{2}{3}\left(\frac{3}{4}\right)}$$

$$= \frac{1}{1-\frac{2}{4}} = \frac{1}{\frac{2}{4}} = 2$$

The introduction of a proportional income tax reduces the slope of the consumption function and the multiplier. It therefore also reduces the equilibrium level of production and income, *ceteris paribus*.

Algebraically we now have the following model

$Y = A$ (equilibrium condition) .... (19-11)

$A = C + \overline{I} + \overline{G}$ (aggregate spending) .... (19-12)

$C = \overline{C} + c(1 - t)Y$ (consumption function) .... (19-13)

Substituting Equations 19-12 and 19-13 into Equation 19-11 yields the following:

$$\begin{aligned} Y &= A \\ &= C + \overline{I} + \overline{G} \\ &= \left(\overline{C} + c(1-t)Y\right) + \overline{I} + \overline{G} \\ Y - c(1-t)Y &= \overline{C} + \overline{I} + \overline{G} \\ Y\left(1 - c(1-t)\right) &= \overline{C} + \overline{I} + \overline{G} \end{aligned}$$

$$\therefore Y_0 = \frac{1}{1-c(1-t)}\left(\overline{C} + \overline{I} + \overline{G}\right) \quad \text{...... (19-14)}$$

where Y_0 = equilibrium level of income

$\frac{1}{1-c(1-t)}$ = multiplier (α)

$(\overline{C} + \overline{I} + \overline{G})$ = autonomous spending ($\overline{A}$)

Once again we therefore have the same general result as in Equations 18-7 and 19-5:

$$Y_0 = \alpha\overline{A}$$

The equilibrium level of income can always be obtained by multiplying autonomous spending $\overline{A}$ by the multiplier α. All that changes when the government is introduced is that

- autonomous spending $\bar{A}$ has an additional component $\bar{G}$
- the multiplier α becomes smaller, thus reducing induced consumption

Now work through the numerical example in Box 19-3 to ensure that you understand these results. See also the alternative approach to equilibruim outlined in Box 19-4.

Fiscal policy

Fiscal policy was introduced in Section 16.6. Recall that fiscal policy refers to the use of government spending (*G*) and taxes (*T*) to affect important macroeconomic variables such as aggregate production or income (*Y*). Various aspects of fiscal policy, including certain practical problems associated with its formulation and implementation, were discussed in Section 16.6. In this subsection we use the Keynesian model to analyse the use of fiscal policy. Having **explained** government spending and taxes and **predicted** the impact of changes in these variables, we now focus on the **policy implications** of our analysis.

We know that a change in government spending *G* will change total production or income by a multiple of the change in *G*. We also know that the tax rate *t* affects the size of the multiplier α. The impact of changes in our two fiscal variables, government spending *G* and the tax rate *t*, can be summarised as follows:

- If the government wishes to **increase** the equilibrium level of income, it can **increase** *G* and/or **decrease** *t*. The increase in *G* will initially have a **direct** impact on aggregate spending *A*, which will

BOX 19-3 THE EQUILIBRIUM LEVEL OF INCOME WITH GOVERNMENT SPENDING AND A PROPORTIONAL TAX: A NUMERICAL EXAMPLE

To illustrate the impact of government spending and taxes on the equilibrium level of income, we now return to the example of Economia which we used in Box 19-1. In Box 19-1 we showed how, with $c = 3/5$, $\bar{C}$ = 10 million econs and $\bar{I}$ = 30 million econs, the introduction of government spending *G* of 20 million econs (ie $\bar{G}$ = 20 million) raised the equilibrium level of income from 100 million econs to 150 million econs. But government spending has to be financed. Suppose Economia's Minister of Finance decides to levy a proportional tax rate of one-sixth of income, that is, $T = 1/6Y$. What will be the impact on the equilibrium level of income in Economia?

After the introduction of the tax, the multiplier (which was previously 2,5) will now be given by the following expression:

$$\text{Multiplier } (\alpha) = \frac{1}{1 - c(1 - t)}$$

With $c = 3/5$ (as before) and $t = 1/6$ this yields

$$\alpha = \frac{1}{1 - 3/5\,(1 - 1/6)} = \frac{1}{1 - 3/5\,(5/6)} = \frac{1}{1 - 1/2} = \frac{1}{1/2} = 2$$

The introduction of the proportional income tax thus reduces the multiplier from 2,5 to 2. To obtain the equilibrium level of income, autonomous spending $\bar{A}$ must be multiplied by the multiplier. In this case autonomous spending is:

$$\begin{aligned}\bar{A} &= \bar{C} + \bar{I} + \bar{G} \\ &= (10 \text{ million} + 30 \text{ million} + 20 \text{ million}) \text{ econs} \\ &= 60 \text{ million econs (as before)}\end{aligned}$$

The equilibrium level of income Y_0 in Economia is obtained by multiplying autonomous spending by the multiplier:

$$\begin{aligned}Y_0 &= \alpha\bar{A} \\ &= 2 \times 60 \text{ million econs} \\ &= 120 \text{ million econs}\end{aligned}$$

BOX 19-4 EQUILIBRIUM IN TERMS OF INJECTIONS AND WITHDRAWALS

In Box 18-6 we presented an alternative approach to equilibrium in the simple Keynesian model (excluding the government). This approach involved the equality between investment (an injection into the basic circular flow of income and spending) and saving (a withdrawal or leakage from the circular flow). The injections-withdrawals approach can be extended to include government spending (an injection) and taxes (a withdrawal).

Once the government is included, the equilibrium level of income can be defined as the level where injections (J) equal withdrawals (W), where $J = I + G$ and $W = S + T$. By substituting the expressions for I, G, S and T, that is, $I = \bar{I}$, $G = \bar{G}$, $S = -\bar{C} + (1 - c)(1 - t)Y$ and $T = tY$, it can be shown that the equilibrium condition is the same as in Equation 19-14.

Graphically, the equilibrium level of income can be illustrated as follows:

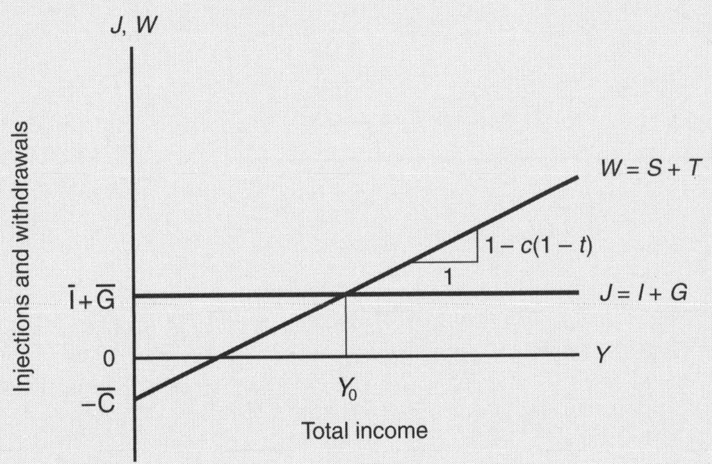

The injections-withdrawals approach can also be used to analyse changes in the equilibrium level of income as a result of changes in I, G, S or T.

then be multiplied as a result of an increase in induced consumption spending. The decrease in t will increase the multiplier. A decrease in t will raise the equilibrium level of income in an **indirect** way by increasing disposable income and consumption at each level of income, that is, it raises induced consumption spending.

- If the government wishes to **reduce** the equilibrium level of income, it can **decrease** G and/or **increase** t. The effects will be in exactly the opposite direction to those described above.

To keep things as simple as possible, we only examine a change in government spending G. For those who are interested, we present a numerical example of a change in the tax rate in Box 19-6.

Suppose the equilibrium level of income Y_0 is below the full-employment level of income (Y_f) and that the government wishes to close this income gap by raising its spending. Since any change in government spending will set a multiplier process in motion, the increase in G must be less than the required increase in Y. If we denote the income gap by ΔY and the change in G by ΔG, then

$$\Delta Y = \alpha \Delta G$$

$$\therefore \quad \Delta G = \frac{\Delta Y}{\alpha}$$

In other words, the increase in government spending must be equal to the income gap that has to be closed, divided by the multiplier. This is illustrated graphically in Figure 19-6.

In Figure 19-6 the original level of aggregate spending is A_0 and government spending is G_0. This yields an equilibrium level of income of Y_0, which is lower than the full-employment level of income Y_f. The government wishes to close the gap (ΔY) between Y_0 and Y_f by raising government spending. This can be

FIGURE 19-6 Fiscal policy in the simple Keynesian model

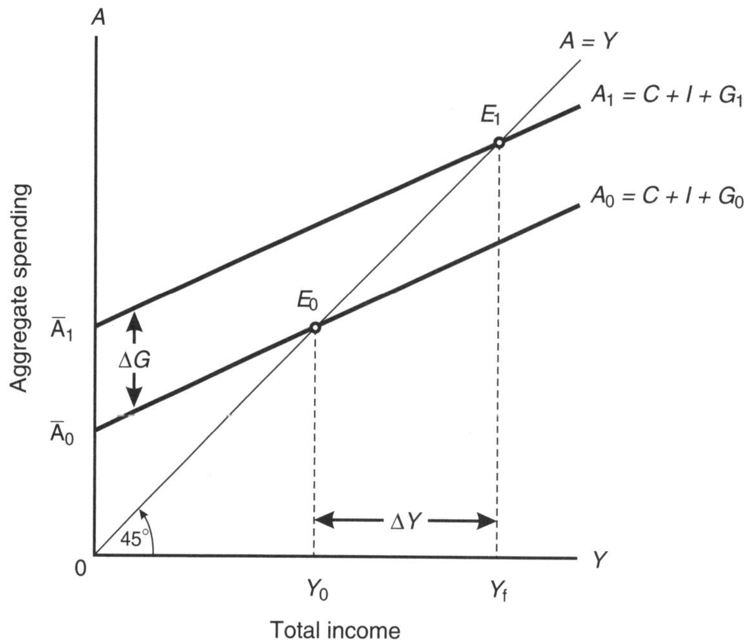

The original equilibrium level of income (with aggregate spending at A_0) is Y_0, which is lower than the full-employment level of income Y_f. Government can close the gap between Y_0 and Y_f (ie ΔY) by raising government spending by ΔG (from G_0 to G_1). The increase in income is greater than the increase in government spending, because of the effect of the multiplier.

achieved by raising government spending by ΔG from (G_0 to G_1). The new aggregate spending function (A_1) yields an equilibrium of E_1, which corresponds to an income level of Y_f. Note that the increase in income (ΔY) is larger than the increase in government spending (ΔG). The ratio between ΔY and ΔG is the multiplier. Now work through the numerical example in Box 19-5 to ensure that you understand how this works.

19.2 Introducing the foreign sector into the model: the open economy

We have now introduced the government sector into the model. The next step is to introduce the foreign sector. This means that we have to incorporate **exports** (X) and **imports** (Z). As we have emphasised in several parts of this book, a country's links with the rest of the world are often of crucial importance to the growth and stability of the domestic economy.

Domestic expenditure ($C + I + G$) does not represent all expenditure on the domestic product. Part of the domestic product is exported and the spending on these exports comes from the rest of the world. As we emphasised in Chapter 3, spending on **exports** constitutes an **injection** into the circular flow of income and spending in the domestic economy.

On the other hand, part of the domestic expenditure is spent on imported goods and services. Such spending on **imports** constitutes a **leakage** or **withdrawal** from the circular flow of income and spending in the country. In this section we investigate how exports and imports affect

- the level of aggregate spending A
- the multiplier α
- the equilibrium level of income Y

We also examine how the introduction of the foreign sector affects our previous conclusions about fiscal policy. The emphasis is therefore again on **explanation**, **prediction** and **policy**.

Because exports X are an injection, we expect them to have the same type of effect as any other injection such as government spending G. Similarly, we expect that imports Z will have the same type of effect as other leakages or withdrawals such as saving S or taxes T. This is indeed the case. But there are a few differences that have to be taken into account.

BOX 19-5 FISCAL POLICY IN THE KEYNESIAN MODEL: A NUMERICAL EXAMPLE

To illustrate the impact of fiscal policy, we return to our example of Economia which we introduced in Box 19-1 and developed further in Box 19-3.

In Box 19-3 we showed that with $c = 3/5$, $t = 1/6$, $\bar{C} = 10$ million econs, $\bar{I} = 30$ million econs and $\bar{G} = 20$ million econs, the equilibrium level of income in Economia is 120 million econs and the multiplier is equal to 2. Suppose that the economic adviser to the President of Economia determines that the potential or full-employment level of income is 150 million econs. The government then decides to close the gap between the equilibrium level of income (120 million econs) and the full-employment level of income (150 million econs) by increasing government spending while keeping the tax rate unchanged. By how much must government spending be increased? By 30 million econs? No. Why not? Because any increase in government spending will have a multiplier effect on the economy. With a multiplier of 2, government spending only needs to be raised by 15 million econs (to 35 million econs) to reach the full-employment level of income in Economia.

We now work through the complete model to prove that an increase in $\bar{G}$ from 20 million econs to 35 million econs will be sufficient to raise the equilibrium level of income from 120 million econs to 150 million econs ($\Delta Y = \alpha \Delta G$ or $\Delta G = \Delta Y/\alpha = 30/2 = 15$).

The full model is:

$$Y = A \quad \text{............} \quad (1)$$

$$A = C + \bar{I} + \bar{G} \quad \text{............} \quad (2)$$

$$C = \bar{C} + cY_d, \text{ where } Y_d = Y - T \text{ and } T = tY \quad \text{............} \quad (3)$$

As before, we use the equilibrium condition (Equation 1) and substitute the values of A and C with Equations 2 and 3 above. Thus

$$\begin{aligned}
Y &= A \\
&= C + \bar{I} + \bar{G} \\
&= \left(\bar{C} + c(Y - tY)\right) + \bar{I} + \bar{G} \\
&= \bar{C} + c(1 - t)Y + \bar{I} + \bar{G} \\
&= 10 \text{ million} + \tfrac{3}{5}\left(Y - \tfrac{1}{6}Y\right) + 30 \text{ million} + 35 \text{ million} \\
&= 75 \text{ million} + \tfrac{3}{5}\left(\tfrac{5}{6}Y\right) \\
&= 75 \text{ million} + \tfrac{1}{2}Y \\
\therefore Y - \tfrac{1}{2}Y &= 75 \text{ million econs} \\
\therefore \tfrac{1}{2}Y &= 75 \text{ million econs} \\
\therefore Y &= 150 \text{ million econs}
\end{aligned}$$

Alternatively we could simply have used the formula for the equilibrium level of income:

$$\begin{aligned}
Y_0 &= \alpha \bar{A} \\
&= \frac{1}{1 - c(1 - t)}(\bar{C} + \bar{I} + \bar{G}) \\
&= \frac{1}{1 - \frac{3}{5}\left(1 - \frac{1}{6}\right)}(10 \text{ million} + 30 \text{ million} + 35 \text{ million}) \\
&= 2 \times 75 \text{ million econs} \\
&= 150 \text{ million econs}
\end{aligned}$$

BOX 19-6 CHANGING THE TAX RATE TO ACHIEVE A CHANGE IN INCOME

We now move to a different "country", which we shall call Capitalia. Suppose the government of Capitalia wishes to increase the equilibrium level of production and income to achieve full employment. However, as a strong supporter of a free-market approach, it wishes to use a tax cut rather than an increase in government spending to achieve this goal. The particulars of the economy are as follows: $c = \frac{3}{4}$; $t = \frac{1}{5}$; $\bar{A} = 120$. This yields a multiplier α of $2\frac{1}{2}$ and an equilibrium income Y_0 of 300. The full employment level of income Y_f is 320.

What must the new tax rate be to achieve full employment?

We know that $Y = \alpha\bar{A}$. To achieve a level of income of 320 with $\bar{A} = 120$, the multiplier must be $\frac{320}{120} = \frac{8}{3}$. All that remains is to find the value of t (ie the tax rate) which will yield a multiplier of $\frac{8}{3}$ when $c = \frac{3}{4}$. This amounts to solving the following equation to obtain t:

$$\frac{1}{1 - \frac{3}{4}(1 - t)} = \frac{8}{3}$$

$$\therefore \frac{1}{1 - \frac{3}{4} + \frac{3}{4}t} = \frac{8}{3}$$

$$\therefore 8(1 - \tfrac{3}{4} + \tfrac{3}{4}t) = 3 \quad \text{(by cross-multiplication)}$$

$$\therefore 8 - 6 + 6t = 3$$

$$\therefore 2 + 6t = 3$$

$$6t = 1$$

$$t = \frac{1}{6}$$

By lowering the tax rate from $\frac{1}{5}$ to $\frac{1}{6}$ the government will raise the multiplier from $2\frac{1}{2}$ to $2\frac{2}{3}$ and will increase the equilibrium level of income from 300 to 320. We leave it to you to verify this result using the full model.

Exports (X)

What determines exports? Are there systematic links between the level of exports *X* and the level of total income in the domestic economy *Y*? In other words, does the level of exports depend on the level of income? In Chapter 17 we discussed certain aspects of international trade. In the process we introduced concepts such as relative advantage and the exchange rate. In Chapter 5 we also examined the composition of South Africa's exports, and we noted that they consist mainly of mineral products (eg gold). From these discussions it should be clear that the demand for South Africa's exports depends largely on **economic conditions in the rest of the world**, our **international competitiveness**, and **exchange rates**. There are no systematic relationships between the level of exports *X* and the level of income in the domestic economy *Y*. We can therefore realistically assume that **exports** *X*, like investment spending *I* and government spending *G*, are **autonomous** with respect to total income *Y*. In **symbols** this can be expressed as

$$X = \bar{X} \quad \text{.................................... (19-15)}$$

where the bar above the *X* indicates that it is autonomous with respect to *Y*.

Graphically the relationship between exports *X* and income *Y* is illustrated by a horizontal line as in Figure 19-7.

How does the introduction of exports *X* affect the level of aggregate spending *A*? Foreign spending on the goods and services exported from the country has to be added to the other components of aggregate spending, namely *C*, *I* and *G*. The introduction of exports *X* thus increases aggregate spending *A* on domestic production, *ceteris paribus*. Like any other injection into the domestic flow of income and spending it is **subject to a multiplier effect. But exports do not affect the size of the multiplier**, that is, they leave the slope of the *A* curve unchanged.

The impact of exports is thus quite straightforward. Any increase in exports *X* will increase aggregate spending *A*. The multiplier process will be set in motion and the eventual result will be an increase in the equilibrium level of income *Y* that is greater than the original increase in exports *X*.

We shall return to the impact of exports later in this

FIGURE 19-7 Exports

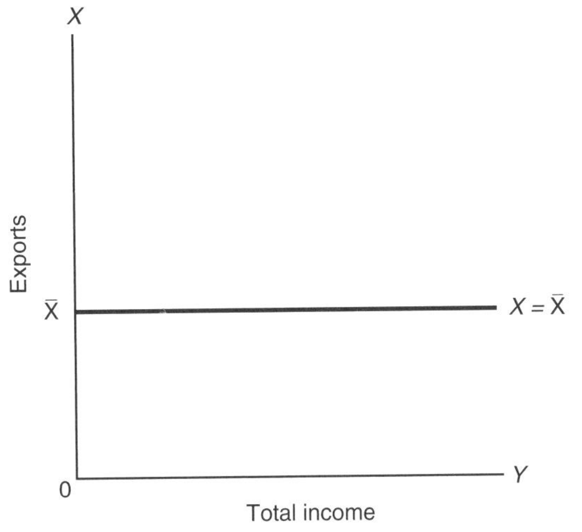

The horizontal line $X = \bar{X}$ indicates that exports X are autonomous with respect to income Y. In other words, the level of X is determined by other factors and is independent of the level of Y.

chapter, and shall provide numerical, graphical and algebraic examples, once we have introduced imports.

Imports (Z)

What determines imports? Are there systematic links between the level of imports *Z* and the level of income *Y* in the domestic economy? In other words, does the level of imports depend on the level of income? In Part I and in Chapter 17 we indicated that South Africa is an open, developing economy and that it is highly dependent on imported capital and intermediate goods. About 80 per cent of South Africa's imports consist of capital and intermediate goods. When spending and income in the domestic economy increase, this almost automatically results in an increase in imports. **The positive relationship between domestic economic activity and imports is one of the strongest macroeconomic relationships in the South African economy**. It would therefore be unrealistic to assume that imports *Z* are autonomous with respect to total income *Y*.

This creates a problem, which illustrates the trade-off between realism and complexity in economic theory. If we make the unrealistic assumption that imports *Z* are autonomous with respect to income *Y*, the impact of imports is straightforward. But if we make the more realistic assumption of a positive link between *Z* and *Y*, the analysis becomes somewhat more complex. If we make the unrealistic assumption, you will learn something about the foreign sector, but if we want to teach you more, we have to make the more realistic assumption. Since imports are the final addition to the model, we present both cases. We first consider what happens when imports *Z* are autonomous, and we then proceed to investigate what happens when imports *Z* are a function of income *Y*.

■ AUTONOMOUS IMPORTS

The most important fact about **imports** is that they represent a **leakage** or **withdrawal** from the circular flow of income and spending. In other words, when households, firms and the government spend on imported goods and services, they reduce aggregate spending on domestically produced goods and services, *ceteris paribus*. Whereas exports *X* have to be added to the other components of aggregate spending *A*, imports *Z* have to be subtracted. Taking both exports *X* and imports *Z* into account, aggregate spending *A* can therefore be written as

$$A = C + I + G + X - Z \quad \text{.............. (19-16)}$$

Because the last two terms in Equation 19-16 both relate to the country's links with the rest of the world, they are often joined together in brackets, as in Equation 19-17.

$$A = C + I + G + (X - Z) \quad \text{............. (19-17)}$$

The term in brackets $(X - Z)$ is the difference between exports and imports and is usually referred to as **net exports**. See also Box 19-7.

Exports *X* are autonomous with respect to income *Y*. If we assume that imports *Z* are also autonomous, then we can write

$$Z = \bar{Z} \quad \text{.................................. (19-18)}$$

Net exports $(\bar{X} - \bar{Z})$ are then also autonomous and the aggregate spending function becomes

$$A = C + \bar{I} + \bar{G} + (\bar{X} - \bar{Z}) \quad \text{.............. (19-19)}$$

If exports $(\bar{X})$ are greater than imports $(\bar{Z})$, net exports will be positive and aggregate spending (*A*) will be greater at each level of income (*Y*) than before the introduction of the foreign sector. If $\bar{Z}$ is greater than $\bar{X}$, then $(\bar{X} - \bar{Z})$ is negative and *A* will be lower at each level of *Y* than before. This is illustrated graphically in Figure 19-8.

In Figure 19-8(a) we show both a positive and a negative level of autonomous net exports, indicated by $(\bar{X} - \bar{Z})_2$ and $(\bar{X} - \bar{Z})_1$ respectively. In Figure 19-8(b) the aggregate spending curve prior to the introduction of the foreign section is given by A_0. The corresponding equilibrium level of income is Y_0. When negative net exports $(\bar{X} - \bar{Z})_1$ are added to aggregate spending A_0 (ie $C + I + G$), the curve shifts parallel downwards to A_1. The equilibrium level of income

BOX 19-7 NET EXPORTS, THE BALANCE OF PAYMENTS, DOMESTIC SPENDING AND DOMESTIC PRODUCTION

Recall from Chapters 4 and 17 that exports and imports of goods and services are recorded in the current account of the balance of payments. Net exports can be regarded as the theoretical equivalent of the **current account of the balance of payments**.

The first three terms in Equation 19-17, namely $C + I + G$, represent domestic spending, which is the theoretical equivalent of **gross domestic expenditure (GDE)**. Total income Y, in turn, is the theoretical equivalent of gross domestic product (GDP). We know that there is equilibrium when $Y = A$, that is, when

$$Y = C + I + G + (X - Z)$$

When net exports $(X - Z)$ are zero, that is, when $X = Z$, aggregate domestic spending $(C + I + G)$ is equal to total production or income Y. When aggregate domestic spending $(C + I + G)$ is greater than Y, net exports $(X - Z)$ are negative, that is, imports Z are greater than exports X. Thus, if households, firms and the government are (in aggregate) spending more than they are producing or earning, the result is negative net exports, or a deficit on the current account of the balance of payments. Similarly, if a country wants to achieve a surplus on the current account of the balance of payments (ie positive net exports), then domestic spending $(C + I + G)$ must be kept lower than domestic production and income Y. As we emphasised earlier, the relationship between domestic spending, domestic production and the balance of payments is one of the most important macroeconomic relationships in South Africa. For example, when South Africa was forced to repay foreign debt, the authorities had to keep domestic spending lower than domestic production and income. This was necessary to achieve a surplus on the current account of the balance of payments (ie positive net exports), which in turn was needed to finance the deficit on the financial account as a result of the repayment of foreign debt.

falls to Y_1. When positive net exports $(\bar{X} - \bar{Z})_2$ are added to the original aggregate spending curve A_0 (ie $C + I + G$), this yields a new aggregate spending curve A_2, which is above A_0 and parallel to it. The equilibrium level of income increases to Y_2. In both cases the change in income will be equal to net exports $(\bar{X} - \bar{Z})$ multiplied by the multiplier α.

Algebraically, the model is as follows:

$$Y = A \text{ (equilibrium condition)} \quad \text{(19-20)}$$

$$A = \bar{C} + \bar{I} + \bar{G} + (\bar{X} - \bar{Z}) \text{ (aggregate spending)} \quad \text{(19-21)}$$

$$C = \bar{C} + c(1 - t)Y \text{ (consumption function)} \quad \text{(19-22)}$$

The equilibrium level of income Y_0 is given by the following equation

$$Y_0 = \frac{1}{1 - c(1 - t)} (\bar{C} + \bar{I} + \bar{G} + \bar{X} - \bar{Z}) \quad \text{(19-23)}$$

where $\frac{1}{1 - c(1 - t)}$ = the multiplier (α)

$(\bar{C} + \bar{I} + \bar{G} + \bar{X} - \bar{Z})$ = autonomous spending $(\bar{A})$

The only difference between Equation 19-23 and Equation 19-14 is that net exports $(\bar{X} - \bar{Z})$ have been added to autonomous spending. The general form of the equation is $Y_0 = \alpha\bar{A}$, as before.

■ INDUCED IMPORTS: IMPORTS AS A FUNCTION OF INCOME

Imports reduce aggregate spending A, and therefore also total income Y, *ceteris paribus*. These conclusions always apply, irrespective of the assumptions we make. However, if we assume (realistically) that the level of imports depends, in part at least, on the level of income Y, then matters become slightly more complicated, since the multiplier will also be affected. Let us explain.

If income Y is the main determinant of imports Z, then the import function resembles the consumption function. Imports then have an **autonomous component** $(\bar{Z})$ as well as an **induced component** (mY), where m is the **marginal propensity to import**. This import function can be written as

$$Z = \bar{Z} + mY \quad \text{(19-24)}$$

where the bar above the Z indicates autonomous imports (as before) and m indicates the fraction of

FIGURE 19-8 The impact of autonomous net exports

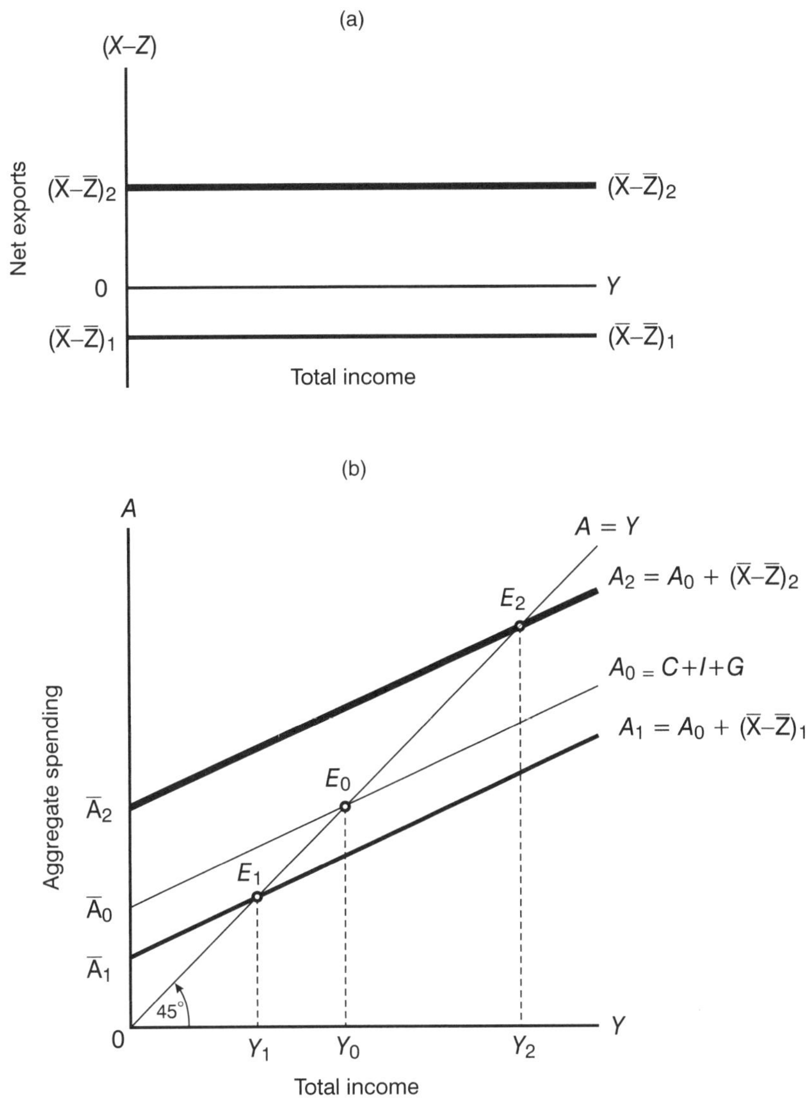

In (a) we show that autonomous net exports can be positive or negative. This is indicated by $(\bar{X}-\bar{Z})_2$ and $(\bar{X}-\bar{Z})_1$ respectively. Prior to the introduction of the foreign sector, aggregate spending is A_0 and equilibrium is at E_0, corresponding to an equilibrium level of income of Y_0. This is shown in (b). If autonomous net exports are negative, as indicated by $(\bar{X}-\bar{Z})_1$, the aggregate spending function shifts parallel downwards from A_0 to A_1 and the equilibrium level of income falls to Y_1. If autonomous net exports are positive, as indicated by $(\bar{X}-\bar{Z})_2$, the aggregate spending function shifts parallel upwards from A_0 to A_2 and the equilibrium level of income increases to Y_2.

any increase in domestic income that is spent on imports.

For example, if 20 per cent of any increase in domestic income is spent on imports, then m = 0,20. Note that if m = 0 then $Z = \bar{Z}$ as assumed earlier. However, when m is positive, a portion of any increase in income Y is spent on imports. The leakages from the circular flow of income and spending increase as income increases. A smaller portion of any increase in income is therefore passed on in each round of the multiplier process, that is, the multiplier becomes smaller. This can be illustrated algebraically as well as graphically.

Algebraically the model now looks as follows:

$$Y = A \quad (19\text{-}25)$$
$$A = C + \bar{I} + \bar{G} + \bar{X} - Z \quad (19\text{-}26)$$
$$C = \bar{C} + c(1 - t)Y \quad (19\text{-}27)$$
$$Z = \bar{Z} + mY \quad (19\text{-}28)$$

To obtain the equilibrium level of income Y, we first substitute A in Equation 19-25 (the equilibrium condition) with the right-hand side of Equation 19-26. This yields

$$Y = C + \bar{I} + \bar{G} + \bar{X} - Z \quad (19\text{-}29)$$

Next we substitute C and Z in Equation 19-29 with the right-hand sides of Equations 19-27 and 19-28 respectively. Therefore

$$Y = (\bar{C} + c(1-t)Y) + \bar{I} + \bar{G} + \bar{X} - (\bar{Z} + mY)$$
$$\therefore Y = \bar{C} + c(1 - t)Y + \bar{I} + \bar{G} + \bar{X} - \bar{Z} - mY$$

All that remains, is to collect terms and solve for Y:

$$Y - c(1 - t)Y + mY = \bar{C} + \bar{I} + \bar{G} + \bar{X} - \bar{Z}$$
$$Y(1 - c(1 - t) + m) = \bar{C} + \bar{I} + \bar{G} + \bar{X} - \bar{Z}$$

$$Y = \frac{1}{1 - c(1 - t) + m}(\bar{C} + \bar{I} + \bar{G} + \bar{X} - \bar{Z})$$
$$= \alpha(\bar{A}) \quad (19\text{-}30)$$

where

$$\frac{1}{1 - c(1 - t) + m} = \text{the multiplier } (\alpha)$$
$$\bar{C} + \bar{I} + \bar{G} + \bar{X} - \bar{Z} = \text{autonomous aggregate spending } (\bar{A})$$

This may seem complicated, but actually it is quite simple. As emphasised earlier, **the equilibrium level of income is always equal to the multiplier multiplied by the autonomous components of aggregate spending, that is, $Y_0 = \alpha\bar{A}$.**

The multiplier α includes a new term m, the marginal propensity to import. Since it is below the line, it follows that the greater m is, the smaller the multiplier becomes. This is quite understandable. The greater the proportion of income that leaks from the flow of spending and income to the rest of the world in each round, the smaller the multiplier becomes. Autonomous spending $\bar{A}$ consists of the same components as before. Work through the example in Box 19-8 to ensure that you understand this model.

The import function, $Z = \bar{Z} + mY$, is shown **graphically** in Figure 19-9(a), along with autonomous exports $\bar{X}$. The vertical intercept of the import function (ie $\bar{Z}$) represents autonomous imports, while the slope of the function (ie m) represents the marginal propensity to import. Note that there is only one level of income where exports are equal to imports, that is, where net exports are zero. This represents the level of income at which the balance on the current account of the balance of payments is zero, and we denote it by Y_B.

Net exports (X – Z) are shown in Figure 19-9(b). At Y_B net exports are zero. At levels of income lower than Y_B net exports are positive and at levels of income higher than Y_B net exports are negative. Because imports increase as income increases, net exports fall as income rises.

In Figure 19-9(c) net exports are added to the other components of aggregate spending (C, I and G). The aggregate spending function before the introduction of the foreign sector is represented by A. When net exports are added, the intercept and the slope of the aggregate spending function change. In the figure net exports (X – Z) are positive when Y = 0. The vertical intercept of the aggregate spending function therefore increases when net exports are added. The slope of the aggregate spending function becomes smaller than before (ie the A function becomes flatter), since the leakages (imports) increase as income increases. The new aggregate spending function intersects the previous aggregate spending function at Y_B, that is, where (X – Z) = 0 (or X = Z).

In Figure 19-9(c) the original equilibrium is at Y_0. In this particular example, the introduction of the foreign sector reduces the equilibrium level of income to Y_1. This is not, however, necessarily the case – the actual impact will depend on the position and slope of the net export function illustrated in Figure 19-9(b). The only result that will always hold is that the introduction of induced imports into the model reduces the size of the multiplier, as we have indicated earlier. See Box 19-9 for an alternative approach to equilibrium in a model which includes the government and the foreign sector.

Fiscal policy in the open economy

Before the introduction of the foreign sector into the model, fiscal policy (particularly changes in government spending) appeared to be a very powerful instrument of economic policy. If we make the unrealistic assumption that both exports and imports are autonomous, this conclusion still applies (since the multiplier does not change). However, once we accept that imports are positively related to total income in the economy, the multiplier becomes smaller, *ceteris paribus*, and the impact of fiscal variables such as changes in government spending becomes less powerful. If we also take the balance of payments into account, the situation becomes even more complicated, since an expansionary fiscal policy will raise income and imports and reduce net exports. In other words the current account of the balance of payments will also be adversely affected. The relationship between economic policy and the balance of payments is analysed further in the next chapter.

FIGURE 19-9 Net exports, aggregate spending and equilibrium income in the open economy

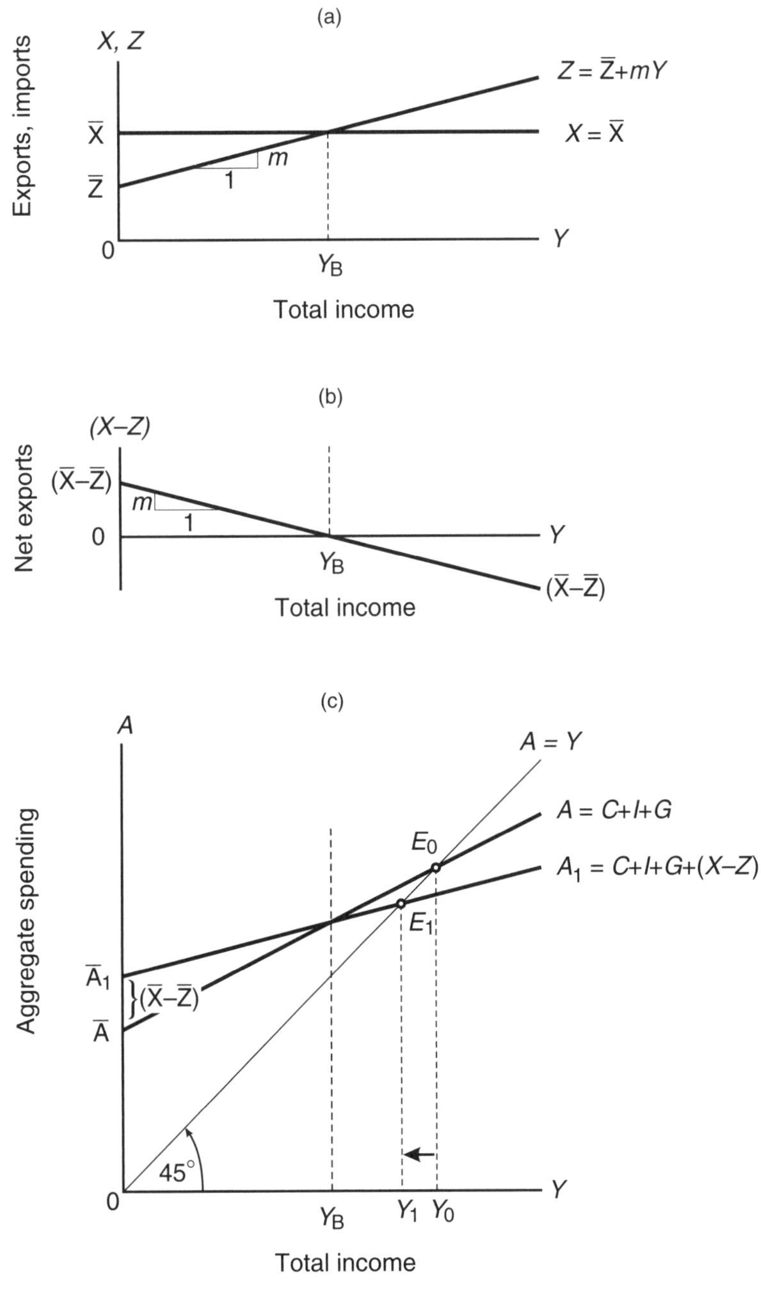

In panel (a) exports are represented by a horizontal line $X = \overline{X}$. The import function slopes upwards, with an intercept of $\overline{Z}$ and a slope of m. Exports are equal to imports at Y_B. Panel (b) shows net exports (X – Z) and is derived from (a). At Y_B net exports are zero. At lower levels of income (X – Z) is positive and at higher levels of income (X – Z) is negative. In panel (c) the net exports in panel (b) are added to the other components of aggregate spending A. A_1 is the new aggregate spending function. It is flatter than A, indicating that the multiplier has decreased. In this particular case the equilibrium level of income Y_1 is lower than Y_0, the level of income before the introduction of the foreign sector.

BOX 19-8 THE IMPACT OF THE FOREIGN SECTOR: A NUMERICAL EXAMPLE

To illustrate the impact of the foreign sector, we return to the example of Economia used in previous boxes. We first give an example of what happens when imports are autonomous and then we consider the impact of induced imports.

When we last visited Economia (in Box 19-4) the government had just increased its spending to 35 million econs (ie $\bar{G}$ = 35 million econs). $\bar{C}$ and $\bar{I}$ were 10 million econs and 30 million econs respectively. The marginal propensity to consume c was ⅗ and the tax rate t was ⅙. This yielded a multiplier of 2 and an equilibrium level of income of 150 million econs. What will happen if the economy is opened up to international trade and this results in autonomous exports ($\bar{X}$) of 10 million econs and autonomous imports ($\bar{Z}$) of 15 million econs? The answer is simple. The autonomous net exports ($\bar{X} - \bar{Z}$) of minus 5 million econs will have a multiplier effect on income in Economia. With a multiplier of 2, the total impact will be a fall in the equilibrium income of (2 × 5) million econs, from 150 million econs to 140 million econs. (If exports had been greater than imports, the equilibrium income would have risen by an amount equal to the multiplier times the positive net exports.)

But what will happen if imports are a positive function of income? We return to the original equilibrium level of income of 150 million econs and suppose that exports are again 10 million econs but that autonomous imports are only 5 million econs. However, as income increases, imports also increase. Suppose the marginal propensity to import m is ⅛. What will the new equilibrium income be? Autonomous spending ($\bar{A}$) is equal to $\bar{C} + \bar{I} + \bar{G} + \bar{X} - \bar{Z}$ = (10 + 30 + 35 + 10 – 5) million econs = 80 million econs. The multiplier is given by the expression

$$\alpha = \frac{1}{1 - c(1 - t) + m} = \frac{1}{1 - \frac{3}{5}(1 - \frac{1}{6}) + \frac{1}{8}} = \frac{1}{1 - \frac{3}{5}(\frac{5}{6}) + \frac{1}{8}}$$

$$= \frac{1}{1 - \frac{1}{2} + \frac{1}{8}} = \frac{1}{\frac{5}{8}} = \frac{8}{5}$$

The equilibrium level of income (Y_0) is given by the expression

$$Y_0 = \alpha\bar{A} = \frac{8}{5} \times 80 \text{ million econs} = 128 \text{ million econs}$$

19.3 The impact of the government and the foreign sector: a brief summary

The main conclusions of this chapter can be summarised as follows:

- The introduction of government spending increases autonomous aggregate spending and raises the equilibrium level of income, *ceteris paribus*. The increase in income is a multiple of the change in autonomous spending, that is, government spending has a multiplier effect on income. Government spending, however, does not affect the size of the multiplier.
- The introduction of a proportional income tax reduces the size of the multiplier and therefore reduces the equilibrium level of income, *ceteris paribus*. Such a tax affects spending and income indirectly, via its influence on disposable income.
- Exports constitute an autonomous injection into the flow of income and spending, and they have the same impact on the equilibrium level of income as any other component of aggregate autonomous spending (such as investment spending or government spending).
- Imports are a leakage or withdrawal from the domestic flow of income and spending. If imports are wholly autonomous, the multiplier remains unchanged; but if imports are positively related to income, the multiplier decreases, since income will "leak" to the rest of the world in each round of the multiplier process.
- As our model becomes more involved, the impact of fiscal policy is reduced.

It is important to remember that these conclusions are all based on the assumptions underlying the models we have introduced in this chapter and in the pre-

BOX 19-9 EQUILIBRIUM IN TERMS OF INJECTIONS AND WITHDRAWALS

Once again we can use the equality between injections and withdrawals as an alternative approach to determining the equilibrium level of income and analysing changes in equilibrium. Once we add the foreign sector, the injections (J) consist of investment spending (I), government spending (G) and exports (X), while withdrawals (W) consist of saving (S), taxes (T) and imports (Z). By substituting the expressions for the different variables in the equilibrium condition $J = W$ it can be shown that the equilibrium condition is the same as in Equation 19-30.

Graphically, the equilibrium level of income can be illustrated as follows:

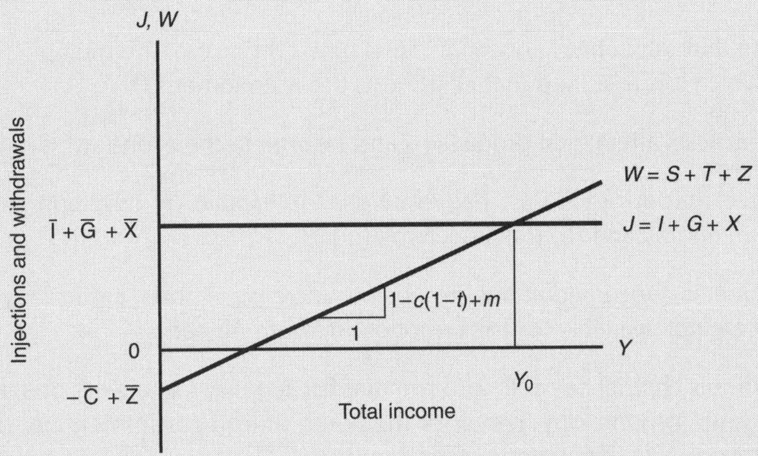

The injections-withdrawals approach can also be used to analyse changes in the equilibrium level of income as a result of a change in I, G, X, S, T or Z.

vious one. Once the remaining assumptions are relaxed, the model becomes more complicated and the conclusions listed above have to be modified accordingly. In the next chapter we consider some of these adjustments, along with some other approaches to macroeconomic theory.

IMPORTANT CONCEPTS

Aggregate spending	Proportional income tax	Exports
Autonomous spending	Tax rate	Imports
Equilibrium level of income	Disposable income	Net exports
Multiplier	Injections	Autonomous imports
Government spending	Withdrawals	Induced imports
Taxes	Fiscal policy	Marginal propensity to import

REVIEW QUESTIONS

1. What do we mean when we say that exports are exogenous in the Keynesian model of income determination that includes the foreign sector?
2. What determines the size of the multiplier in a Keynesian model that includes both the government and the foreign sector?
3. How does the introduction of a proportional tax rate (t) affect the size of the multiplier (compared to the situation before the introduction of such a tax)?
4. How does the introduction of induced imports affect the size of the multiplier (compared to a situation in which it is assumed that all imports are autonomous)?
5. Explain how exports affect total production and income in the economy.
6. Can the models introduced in this chapter be used to explain (a) developments in the monetary sector of the economy and (b) inflation? Why (not)?
7. Why is everyone so concerned about the need to increase exports, particularly since goods that are exported are not available for consumption in South Africa?
8. The models in this chapter seem to indicate that fiscal policy can always be used to establish or maintain full employment. Why then does the South African government not use the instruments of fiscal policy to eliminate unemployment?

20 More on macroeconomic theory and policy

Learning outcomes

Once you have studied this chapter, you should be able to

- use aggregate demand and supply curves to analyse changes in aggregate demand and supply, including the impact of monetary and fiscal policy
- describe how changes in interest rates can affect important macroeconomic variables such as total production and the price level
- use the *AD-AS* model to illustrate the policy dilemma in the open economy
- describe the major features of monetarism and supply-side economics

Economics has been defined as the logic of choice ... Economists have said that their subject is about reason ... But almost none of them have said that their subject is concerned with imagination.

GEORGE SHACKLE

Let us beware of this dangerous theory of equilibrium which is supposed to be automatically established. A certain kind of equilibrium, it is true, is re-established in the long run, but it is only after a frightful amount of suffering.

SIMONDE DE SISMONDI

What used to be called the quantity theory of money ... is now called monetarism.

MILTON FRIEDMAN

In Chapter 18 we considered an economy that consists of households and firms only and assumed that prices, wages and interest rates are fixed and that output is determined by aggregate demand. In Chapter 19 we expanded on this model by including the government and the foreign sector. The time has now arrived to discard the remaining assumptions and to allow for variable prices, wages and interest rates as well as for other factors that could affect aggregate supply. We start by introducing **aggregate demand *(AD)*** and **aggregate supply *(AS)***. This is followed by an examination of the **monetary transmission mechanism**, which examines how changes in interest rates affect important macroeconomic variables such as total output and the price level. The next section discusses **monetary and fiscal policy** in the *AD-AS* framework. Policy lags are explained, as well as the policy dilemma in the open economy. In the final section we briefly examine some **other approaches to macroeconomics**, particularly the monetarist approach, usually associated with Milton Friedman, and the supply-side approach, which was very popular when Ronald Reagan was President of the United States and Margaret Thatcher was Prime Minister of Britain.

20.1 The aggregate demand-aggregate supply model

As mentioned on the previous page, the time has now arrived to incorporate variable prices, wages and interest rates into our explanation of how the economy functions. This implies that we have to incorporate the monetary sector, introduced in Chapter 15, and also allow for the impact of independent changes in aggregate supply. Until now we have not allowed for monetary influences and we have also assumed that aggregate supply adjusts passively to changes in aggregate demand. See Box 20-1.

The most popular macroeconomic model used nowadays is the **aggregate demand–aggregate supply model** (abbreviated as the *AD-AS* **model**), which allows for all these changes and which can be adapted to incorporate the views of different schools of thought about macroeconomics. The *AD-AS* model also serves as a guide to policy-making.

The formal derivation of the *AD-AS* model can be quite complicated and falls beyond the scope of this book. However, since you are well acquainted with microeconomic demand and supply models you should be able to follow the basics of the *AD-AS* model and use it to illustrate various macroeconomic issues and possible ways of dealing with them.

The *AD* and *AS* curves have much in common with the demand and supply curves that you are familiar with. It is important to emphasise, however, that we are now dealing with **the economy as a whole** and not with a particular commodity or service. The *AD-AS* model deals with the **general level of prices** in the economy (represented, for example, by the consumer price index), instead of the price of a particular good or service. Likewise, the model deals with the **total production of goods and services** in the economy (represented, for example, by the gross domestic product), instead of the quantity of a particular good or service. Moreover, the *AD* and *AS* curves are not simply sum-

BOX 20-1 THE ASSUMPTIONS OF THE SIMPLE KEYNESIAN AND *AD-AS* MODELS

In Box 18-2 we listed the key assumptions on which the simple Keynesian model is based, along with the implications of these assumptions. We discarded the first few assumptions in Chapter 19, where we introduced the government and the foreign sector into the model. The remaining assumptions are discarded in the current chapter. In the columns below we list the original assumptions (in Chapter 18) that are relaxed in this chapter. In the last column we also indicate the implications of these relaxations for the *AD-AS* model.

Assumptions in Keynesian models	Assumptions in *AD-AS* model	Implications for *AD-AS* model
Prices are given	Prices are variable	The model can be used to study inflation
Wages are given	Wages are variable	Aggregate supply can change independently from aggregate demand; the impact of changes in the general level of wages on production, income, employment (and unemployment) and inflation can be analysed
The money supply and interest rates are given	Interest rates are variable and the money supply can change	The model can be used to study the impact of changes in the monetary sector, including monetary policy
Spending (demand) is the driving force that determines the level of economic activity; supply adjusts passively to demand	The level of economic activity is determined by the interaction of aggregate supply and aggregate demand	Changes can originate on both the supply and the demand side of the economy and the interaction between the two always has to be taken into account

mations of market demand and supply curves for the different goods and services produced in the economy. As emphasised earlier, the macroeconomy is not simply the sum of its microeconomic parts.

In Figure 20-1 we show an aggregate demand (*AD*) curve as sloping down from the left to right just like any normal demand curve. The **general price level** (*P*) and **total production or income** (*Y*)[1] are drawn on the vertical and horizontal axes respectively. The *AD* curve indicates the levels of total expenditure (or aggregate demand) at various price levels. Similarly, the *AS* curve slopes upward to the right and indicates the various levels of output which will be supplied at different price levels. The equilibrium price level (P_0) and the equilibrium level of real production or income (Y_0) are determined by the interaction between aggregate demand and aggregate supply.

The *AD-AS* model differs in two important respects from the Keynesian model discussed in Chapters 18 and 19. In the first place it explicitly allows for supply conditions – in the Keynesian model we simply assumed that aggregate supply would adjust passively to aggregate spending. Secondly, it also incorporates a variable price level *P*. In the Keynesian model prices were assumed to be constant.

As mentioned earlier, we shall not go into the details of the derivation of the *AD* and *AS* curves. We accept that a decrease in the price level will be accompanied by an increase in total real expenditure (or the total quantity demanded) and that an increase in the price level will give rise to a decrease in total real expenditure (or the aggregate quantity demanded), ***ceteris paribus***. Likewise, we accept that an increase in the price level will give rise to an increase in real production (or the aggregate quantity supplied) and that a decrease in the price level will lead to a fall in real production (or the total quantity supplied). However, to be able to use these curves to analyse particular situations you have to know what lies behind them, that is, what determines their **position. Changes** in any of these non-price determinants of aggregate demand and aggregate supply will give rise to **shifts** of the curves.

FIGURE 20-1 Aggregate demand and aggregate supply

On the vertical axis we have the general level of prices P in the economy (represented by a price index). On the horizontal axis we have the real value of total production or income Y in the economy. AD is the aggregate demand curve which shows the relationship between the total real expenditure on goods and services and the price level. AS is the aggregate supply curve which shows the relationship between real production or output and the price level. The equilibrium is indicated by E_0. The equilibrium price level is P_0 and the equilibrium output level is Y_0.

The aggregate demand curve

The aggregate demand curve is determined by everything that influences total expenditure (*A*) in the economy. All the determinants of aggregate spending (*A*) introduced in Chapters 18 and 19 thus also influence aggregate demand (*AD*). These include consumption expenditure by households (*C*), investment spending by firms (*I*), government spending (*G*), taxes (*T*), exports (*X*) and imports (*Z*), as well as all the factors which influence *C, I, G, T, X* and *Z*. The most important of these factors is the interest rate *i*, which influences consumption and investment spending in the economy. Along with government spending and taxes (the two basic instruments of **fiscal policy**) the interest rate (the basic instrument of **monetary policy**) is an important policy variable which influences aggregate demand in the economy. An **expansionary fiscal policy** (ie an increase in government spending *G* and/or a decrease in taxes *T*) will increase aggregate demand in the economy at each price level and this can be illustrated by a rightward shift of the *AD* curve. By the same token, a **contractionary fiscal policy** (ie a decrease in *G* and/or an

1. It is important to note that *Y* represents total **real** production or income in the economy. In Chapters 18 and 19 it was assumed that the price level does not change. In those chapters, therefore, there was no significant difference between **real** and **nominal** production or income. Since the price level could not change, a change in nominal production was synonymous with a change in real production. In this chapter and in the rest of the book, however, it is extremely important to distinguish between real and nominal values and changes. With a variable price level (*P*) we use *Y* to indicate **real** production or income, while *PY* represents the **nominal** value of production or income.

increase in T) can be illustrated by a leftward shift of the *AD* curve. As far as monetary policy is concerned, an increase in the repo rate (ie a **contractionary monetary policy**) can be illustrated by a leftward shift of the *AD* curve and a decrease in the repo rate (ie an **expansionary monetary policy**) by a rightward shift of the *AD* curve. The main causes of shifts of the *AD* curve are summarised in Table 20-1.

TABLE 20-1 Impact of key changes on the aggregate demand curve

Change	*Impact on AD curve*
Price level *P* increases	Upward movement **along** the curve
Price level *P* decreases	Downward movement **along** the curve
Autonomous consumption $\bar{C}$ increases	Shifts to the right
Investment spending *I* increases	Shifts to the right
Government spending *G* increases	Shifts to the right
Taxes *T* decrease	Shifts to the right
Net exports (*X-Z*) increase	Shifts to the right
Interest rate (*i*) decreases	Shifts to the right
Autonomous consumption $\bar{C}$ decreases	Shifts to the left
Investment spending *I* decreases	Shifts to the left
Government spending *G* decreases	Shifts to the left
Taxes *T* increase	Shifts to the left
Net exports (*X-Z*) decrease	Shifts to the left
Interest rate (*i*) increases	Shifts to the left

The aggregate supply curve

Like the microeconomic supply curve, the aggregate supply (*AS*) curve is primarily governed by the costs of production. The main difference is that the *AS* curve is concerned with the cost of producing the **total** output of goods and services (eg GDP), whereas a microeconomic supply curve deals only with a specific good or service.

The costs of production are governed by the prices and productivity of the various factors of production. For a given set of factor prices (rent, wages and salaries, interest and profit) and prices of imported capital and intermediate goods, and for a given level of productivity, we have an aggregate supply curve which normally slopes upwards from left to right. Any factor that changes the prices at which firms produce a given level of output will shift the aggregate supply curve. For example, an increase in factor prices or import prices and/or a decrease in productivity will shift the aggregate supply curve upward (to the left). Similarly, a decrease in factor and import prices and/or an increase in productivity will shift the aggregate supply curve downward (to the right).

These effects are summarised in Table 20-2. In contrast to the *AD* curve, the *AS* curve is usually not affected directly by expansionary or contractionary monetary and fiscal policies.[2]

The slope of the aggregate supply curve

Although we usually depict the *AS* curve as an upward-sloping straight line, the curve can sometimes be quite flat or steep, as illustrated in Figure 20-2. In the figure Y_f represents the full-employment level of real output and income. When economic conditions are very depressed and there is substantial excess production capacity (ie when the economy is operating way below the full-employment level of out-

TABLE 20-2 Impact of key changes on the aggregate supply curve

Change	*Impact on AS curve*
Price level *P* increases	Upward movement **along** the curve
Price level *P* decreases	Downward movement **along** the curve
Prices of factors of production (eg wages) increase	Curve shifts upward (to the left)
Prices of imported capital and intermediate goods (eg oil) increase	Curve shifts upward (to the left)
Productivity decreases	Curve shifts upward (to the left)
Weather conditions deteriorate	Curve shifts upward (to the left)
Prices of factors of production (eg wages) decrease	Curve shifts downward (to the right)
Prices of imported capital and intermediate goods (eg oil) decrease	Curve shifts downward (to the right)
Productivity increases	Curve shifts downward (to the right)
Weather conditions improve	Curve shifts downward (to the right)

2. The main exception is in the case of interest rates, which impact on both aggregate demand and aggregate supply, the latter because interest costs can be an important element of the cost of production. In this book, however, we focus almost exclusively on the impact of interest rates on *AD* rather than on *AS*.

FIGURE 20-2 The slope of the *AS* curve

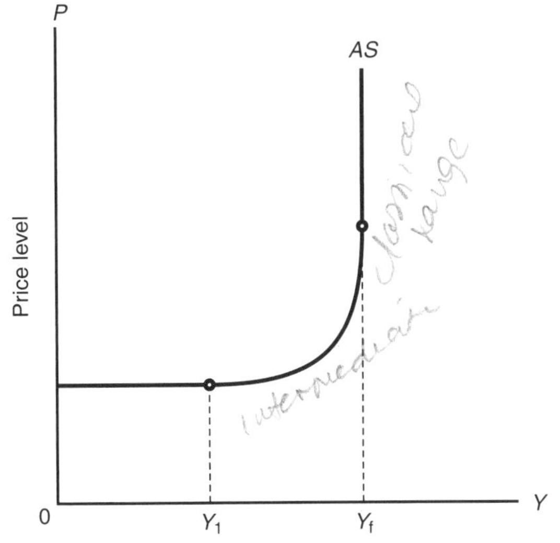

The AS curve can have a flat part, a rising part and a vertical part. Along the flat part, sometimes called the Keynesian range, an increase in aggregate demand will result in increases in real output (up to Y_1), without an increase in the price level. Along the vertical part (sometimes called the classical range), an increase in aggregate demand will result only in an increase in the price level. Between these two parts (ie in the so-called intermediate range), both the price level and real output will increase if aggregate demand increases.

put), production can be expanded without putting significant pressure on the price level. This is illustrated by the area between the origin and Y_1 on the horizontal axis. This describes the situation that prevailed, for example, during the Great Depression when Keynes was formulating his *General theory*. This also explains why Keynes was not unduly concerned about inflation at that stage. The major problem that he was concerned with was how to get an economy out of a depression or serious recession. In terms of the diagram, the purpose was to move Y in the direction of Y_f.

On the other hand, if there is little or no excess capacity in the economy, that is, when most factors of production are almost fully employed, the *AS* curve is quite steep. When full employment is reached (at Y_f), the curve actually becomes vertical, since production cannot be expanded beyond the full-employment level in the short run.

Between the two extremes (ie between Y_1 and Y_f in the figure), the *AS* curve has a positive slope. We shall return to these three parts of the *AS* curve when we discuss inflation in the next chapter.

Changes in aggregate demand

When the *AS* curve is very flat, an increase in aggregate demand (illustrated by a rightward shift of the *AD* curve), leads to an increase in real output or income (Y) with little or no increase in the price level (P). This corresponds to the analysis in Chapters 18 and 19 where it was assumed that the price level P is constant.

Similarly, when the *AS* curve is very steep (or even vertical), an increase in aggregate demand will result in an increase in the price level with little or no increase in production.

In the remainder of this section we deal only with the more general case of an upward-sloping *AS* curve, that is, a situation in which the economy is neither in a depression nor at full employment. This is the situation indicated in Figure 20-1 at the beginning of this section.

We examine a situation in which **aggregate demand increases**. This can be the result of any of the factors identified in Table 20-1 as possible causes of rightward shifts of the *AD* curve. Suppose the authorities decide to stimulate the economy by implementing an expansionary monetary or fiscal policy. In Figure 20-3 the increase in aggregate demand is illustrated by a rightward shift of the *AD* curve, from AD_0 to AD_1. The original equilibrium was E_0. The new equilibrium is indicated by E_1. The result is an increase in the equilibrium level of real output or income from Y_0 to Y_1 *and* an increase in the equilibrium price level from P_0 to P_1. The authorities can therefore still use expansionary monetary and fiscal policies to stimulate production and income, as well as employment (since employment increases along with real production and income), but this is achieved at the cost of an increase in the price level. When supply conditions and the price level are introduced explicitly, policy choices thus become more complicated. The monetary and fiscal authorities now have to consider the **trade-off** between increased production and employment (on the one hand) and increased prices (on the other). In this model, **demand management** (ie monetary and fiscal policy) can only be used to achieve one objective (eg increased production and employment) at the cost of the other (eg increased prices). If the Reserve Bank and the Department of Finance are more worried about unemployment than about inflation, they will apply expansionary policies. If they are more worried about inflation, they will apply contractionary policies. When contractionary monetary and fiscal policies are applied, aggregate demand will decrease. This is illustrated by a leftward shift of the *AD* curve (ie exactly the opposite situation to that shown in Figure 20-3). In this case the price level P declines but real production Y also declines and since employment is positively related to real production, employment will also decrease (ie unemployment will increase).

FIGURE 20-3 Expansionary monetary and fiscal policy in the *AD-AS* framework.

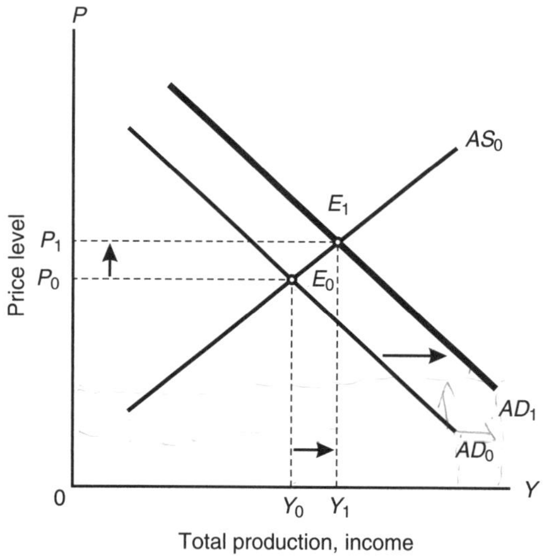

The original aggregate demand and supply curves are indicated by AD_0 and AS_0. The original equilibrium is at E_0 with the price level at P_0 and output at Y_0. The authorities then apply expansionary monetary and fiscal policies to stimulate aggregate expenditure, production and income. This is illustrated by a rightward shift of the AD curve to AD_1. The new equilibrium is indicated by E_1. Production increases to Y_1 but the price level also increases, to P_1.

Changes in aggregate supply

What happens if aggregate supply changes? In Table 20-2 we identified a number of possible causes of changes in aggregate supply, illustrated by shifts of the *AS* curve. To illustrate the impact of a change in aggregate supply, we use the example of an increase in the price of imported oil. Such an increase raises the domestic cost of production at each level of real output *Y*. This is illustrated by an upward shift of the aggregate supply curve, as illustrated in Figure 20-4.

AS_0 is the original aggregate supply curve. Given the aggregate demand curve (AD_0), the equilibrium levels of production and the price level are Y_0 and P_0 respectively, as indicated by the original equilibrium point (E_0). As a result of the increase in the oil price, the costs of production increase. This is illustrated by a shift of the *AS* curve to AS_1. The equilibrium point shifts to E_1. The equilibrium price level increases to P_1 while the equilibrium level of production falls to Y_1. This is clearly a very undesirable situation. An increase in the cost of producing the total product (eg GDP) results in higher prices, lower production, income and employment and higher unemployment. What we have here is a situation of **stagflation**, which describes a situation of **stag**nation plus in**flation**.

Such a situation can also be caused by any other factor which causes a general increase in production costs in the economy. This includes increases in wages and salaries without corresponding increases in productivity, decreases in productivity, increased profit margins and increases in the prices of other important inputs.

Upward shifts of the *AS* curve are often referred to as **supply shocks**. They present policymakers with a difficult situation. Expansionary fiscal or monetary policies will increase aggregate demand and therefore production, income and employment, but at the same time the price level will be increased even further. In other words, demand management policies can be used to counteract the effects of a supply shock on production, income and employment but only at the cost of even higher inflation. This describes quite accurately what happened in most countries after the first oil crisis of 1973/74. The authorities tried to combat the production and employment effects of the increased oil prices but in the process they pushed inflation up to its highest level since the Korean conflict in the early 1950s.

FIGURE 20-4 An increase in the price of imported oil in the *AD-AS* framework

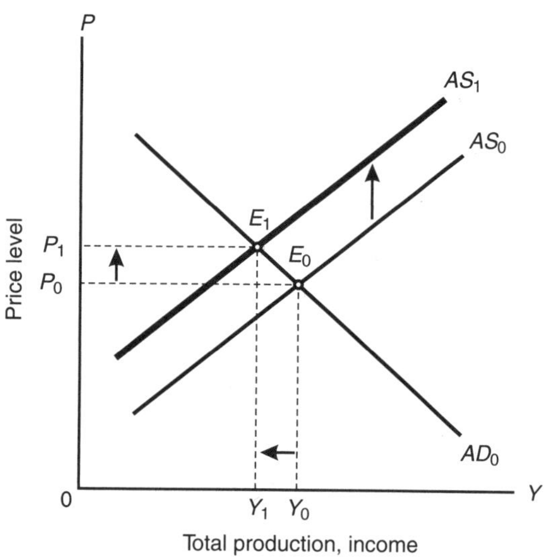

The original aggregate demand and supply curves are indicated by AD_0 and AS_0. The original equilibrium is at E_0 with the price level at P_0 and output at Y_0. An increase in the price of imported oil raises the costs of production. This is illustrated by an upward shift of the AS curve to AS_1. The new equilibrium is indicated by E_1. Production falls to Y_1, while the price level increases to P_1.

When the next oil crisis occurred in 1979/80, the industrial countries tried exactly the opposite strategy. They implemented restrictive monetary and fiscal policies to counteract the inflationary impact of the oil price increases. In terms of Figure 20-4, they applied policies which shifted the *AD* curve to the left. This induced the deepest and most prolonged recession since World War II. Production, income and employment fell in many countries, for the first time since the war.

There is, of course, a solution to a supply shock that avoids the worst of both of these experiences. The solution is to take steps to lower costs of production. In terms of our graphs the aim would therefore be to shift the *AS* curve downwards (to the right). Lower costs of production require a reduction in factor prices (ie lower wages, salaries, profits, etc) and/or increased productivity without a corresponding increase in remuneration. Technically, what is required is an anti-inflationary **incomes policy**. The aim of such a policy is to establish a balance between the growth in incomes and the growth in productivity. The problem is that while the solution is simple in principle, it is very difficult (sometimes virtually impossible) to achieve in practice. The reason for this will become clear when we discuss incomes policies in Chapter 22.

To round off this section, we illustrate the benefits of an increase in productivity without any concomitant increase in the remuneration of the factors of production (eg capital and labour). By now we know that such a decrease in the costs of production can be illustrated by a downward (rightward) shift of the *AS* curve, as in Figure 20-5. Total real output, income and employment increase *and* the price level falls. Clearly this is the most desirable of all the possible changes in aggregate supply or aggregate demand.

FIGURE 20-5 An increase in productivity without any increase in remuneration

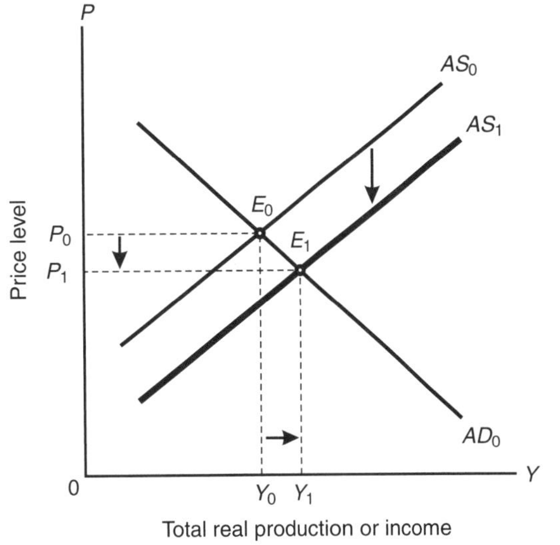

The original aggregate demand and supply curves are indicated by AD_0 and AS_0. The original equilibrium is at E_0 with the price level at P_0 and real output at Y_0. An increase in productivity without any increase in remuneration lowers the costs of production. This is illustrated by a downward shift of the AS curve to AS_1. The new equilibrium is indicated by E_1. Real output increases to Y_1, while the price level falls to P_1.

20.2 The monetary transmission mechanism

In the macroeconomic model developed in Chapters 18 and 19 it was assumed that the money supply and the interest rate are fixed. By assuming a fixed money supply and a fixed interest rate we actually eliminated the impact of money and monetary policy. In the *AD-AS* model developed in the previous section we dropped these assumptions and allowed for the impact of a variable interest rate on aggregate demand. We said that a fall in the interest rate will increase aggregate demand (illustrated by a rightward shift of the *AD* curve) and that an increase in the interest rate will reduce aggregate demand (illustrated by a leftward shift of the *AD* curve). We now need to examine these links more closely, that is, to examine *how* changes in interest rates affect total spending, production, income and prices in the economy. The way in which changes in the monetary sector are transmitted to the rest of the economy is called the **monetary transmission mechanism**.

Most textbooks explain the monetary transmission mechanism by starting with an increase in the money supply, which is assumed to be **exogenous** (ie under the control of the monetary authorities). However, as we explained in Chapter 15, this is not a realistic starting point, since the money supply is not exogenous but **endogenous** (in the sense of being determined by the interaction between the interest rate and the demand for money). This does not mean that the money supply is ignored. It is still an important variable in the economy. The important point, however, is that changes in the monetary sector are triggered by changes in the interest rate (which is for all practical purposes determined by the central bank) and not by (exogenous) changes in the money supply. In other words, the monetary transmission mechanism starts with a change in interest rates, not a change in the money supply (as assumed in most textbooks).

The traditional treatment of the transmission mechanism is outlined in Box 20-2. This treatment is no longer useful in the South African context, but it will still be appropriate in countries where the money sup-

BOX 20-2 THE TRADITIONAL EXPLANATION OF THE TRANSMISSION MECHANISM

As explained in Box 15-6 it is assumed in most textbooks that the money supply is controlled by the monetary authorities. In other words, it is assumed that the money supply is **exogenous**, illustrated by a vertical money supply curve. According to this view, the interest rate is determined by the interaction between the demand for and supply of money (ie the interest rate is **endogenous**). Monetary policy is implemented by changing the money supply, which then affects the interest rate and other important variables in the economy (via the interest rate).

The initial phase of this approach to the monetary transmission mechanism can be explained with the aid of the diagram.

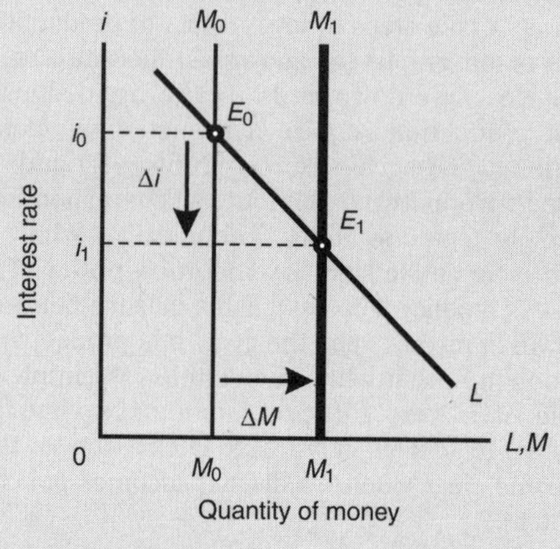

The demand for money is represented by L and the initial money supply M_0. The initial equilibrium interest rate is thus i_0. Suppose the monetary authorities then increase the money supply, illustrated by a rightward shift of the money supply curve to M_1. The increase in the money supply results in a decrease in the equilibrium interest rate to i_1. At the lower interest rate, investment spending will be higher than before, *ceteris paribus*, and other variables in the economy will also be affected. In other words, the diagram in this box can be linked to Figure 20-6.

The only real difference between this view of the transmission mechanism and the one explained in the text, is that this one starts with an **exogenous** change in the **money supply**, which then affects the interest rate, while the more realistic version in the text commences with an **exogenous** change in the **interest rate**. The remainder of the process may be similar in both cases.

ply is largely under the control of the monetary authorities (eg because the financial system is still undeveloped). Note that it is only the initial part of the mechanism that is affected. Once the interest rate changes, the rest of the process is basically the same in both our treatment and the traditional treatment.

The links between interest rates, investment spending and the rest of the economy

When the Monetary Policy Committee (MPC) of the South African Reserve Bank (SARB) adjusts the repo rate, all other short-term interest rates (eg the prime overdraft rates of the banks) change in the same direction. In our models we use a single interest rate to represent all these rates. The question now is how a change in the interest rate will affect other important variables in the economy such as aggregate demand, aggregate supply, production, income and the price level. This is what the transmission mechanism is all about.

A key element of the transmission mechanism is the relationship between the interest rate (i) and investment spending (I), which is an important component of aggregate spending (A) and aggregate demand (AD). The inverse relationship between the interest rate and investment spending was illustrated in Figure 18-3 in Chapter 18. This diagram is reproduced in Figure 20-6(a).

At any particular interest rate, such as i_0 in Figure 20-6(a), there will be a certain level of investment spending (I) in the economy, *ceteris paribus*. Suppose the interest rate is now reduced to i_1. At this lower interest rate more investment projects will be profitable than before. Investment spending (I) will thus increase from I_0 to I_1. The difference between I_1 and I_0 is indicated as ΔI. But the process will not stop there. We use two diagrams to illustrate the rest of the process. In Figure 20-6(b) we show what will happen in terms of the models derived in Chapters 18 and 19, where it was assumed that prices and wages are fixed. Since investment spending is an important component of aggregate spending (A), it follows that total spending in the economy will increase, illustrated by

FIGURE 20-6 The monetary transmission mechanism

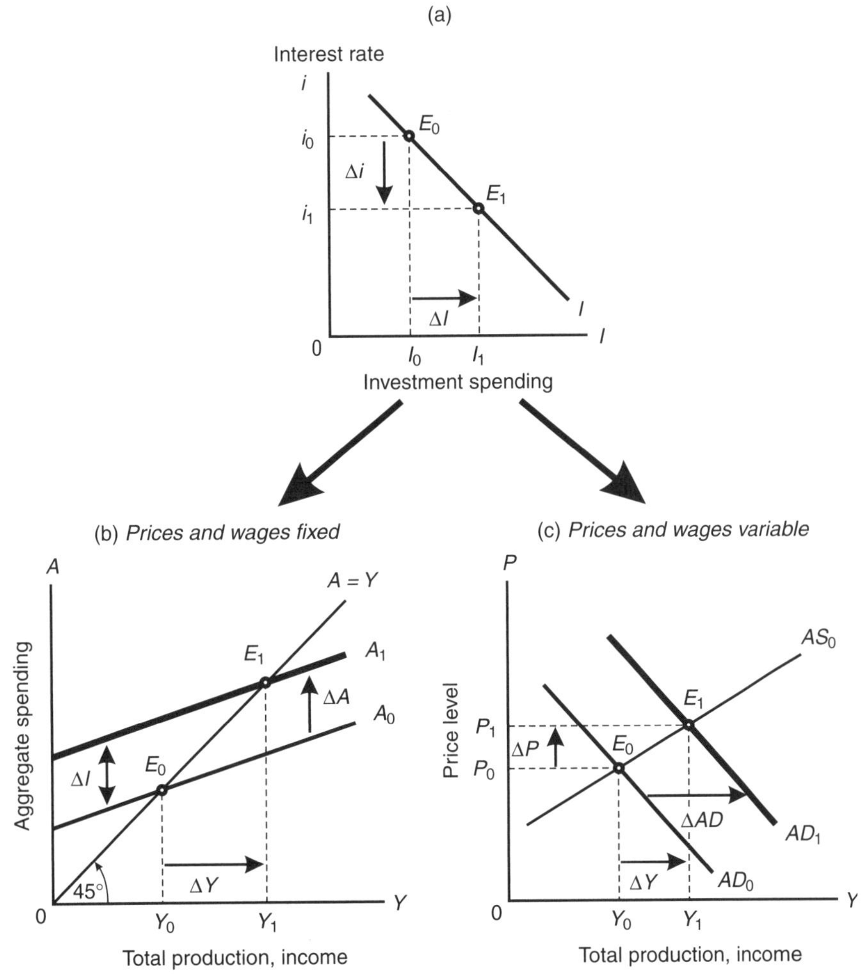

Graph (a) shows the investment function, graph (b) shows the simple Keynesian model and graph (c) shows the AD-AS model. The original equilibrium position in each part is indicated by E_0. Graph (a) shows that a fall in the interest rate to i_1 will lead to an increase in investment spending to I_1. If prices and wages are fixed, total production or income will increase to Y_1, as in graph (b), with the multiplier having its full effect. However, if prices and wages are variable, as in graph (c), production and output will increase by a smaller amount, while the price level also increases, from P_0 to P_1.

an upward shift of aggregate spending (A) curve from A_0 to A_1. The amount of the shift (ΔA) is equal to the change in investment spending (ΔI). Because total spending increases, total production and income (Y) will also increase. In Figure 20-6(b) this is illustrated by the increase from Y_0 to Y_1 (ie ΔY). Moreover, the increase in Y will be a multiple of the increase in I. For a given *increase* in investment (ΔI) the extent of the *increase* in total production and income (Y) will depend on the size of the multiplier (α). In symbols: $\Delta Y = \alpha\Delta I$ (as in Chapter 18). This chain of events (or transmission mechanism) can be summarised as follows:

In symbols: $\Delta i \Rightarrow \Delta I \Rightarrow \Delta A \Rightarrow \Delta Y$

In words: A change in the interest rate leads to a change in investment spending, a change in aggregate spending and a change in total production or income.

The transmission mechanism which we have just explained is based on the assumption that prices and wages are fixed. Once we drop this assumption, the models of Chapters 18 and 19 no longer tell the full story. The appropriate model is now the *AD-AS* model, which was explained in the previous section and is illustrated in Figure 20-6(c). With the *AD-AS* model (ie with variable prices and wages) the first part of the transmission mechanism is exactly the same as in the previous model. The only difference is that, since prices are no longer fixed, an increase in aggregate spending (*A*), which causes an increase in aggregate demand (*AD*), now results in increases in the price level (*P*) as well as in total (real) production and income (*Y*). In Figure 20-6(c) the impact of an increase in investment spending is illustrated by a rightward shift of the *AD* curve, from AD_0 to AD_1. This results in an increase in the price level, from P_0 to P_1, as well as an increase in total production and income, from Y_0 to Y_1. Note, however, that since the full impact of the increase in investment spending does not fall on production and income (because prices can increase), the increase in *Y* in Figure 20-6(c) is smaller than in Figure 20-6(b). In other words, the introduction of variable prices and wages reduces the size of the multiplier.

The monetary transmission mechanism with variable prices and wages (ie in terms of the *AD-AS* model) can be summarised as follows:

In symbols: $\Delta i \Rightarrow \Delta I \Rightarrow \Delta A \Rightarrow \Delta AD \rightarrow \Delta Y$ and ΔP

In words: A change in the interest rate leads to a change in investment spending, a change in aggregate spending and a change in aggregate demand. The change in aggregate demand results in a change in total production or income *and* a change in the price level. The split between ΔY and ΔP depends on aggregate supply conditions in the economy (represented by the slope of the *AS* curve).

There are some crucial links in the monetary transmission mechanism. The first is the link between the **interest rate** and **investment spending**. If changes in the interest rate do not affect investment spending, the chain breaks down. In other words, if investment demand is completely interest inelastic (illustrated by a vertical investment demand curve) a change in the interest rate will not have any impact on investment spending.[3]

The second important link is between **aggregate demand** (on the one hand) and the **price level** and **total production or income** (on the other). When aggregate demand (*AD*) changes, the relative impact on the price level (*P*) and the level of total production or income (*Y*) will depend on aggregate supply conditions. For example, if the aggregate supply (*AS*) curve is relatively flat, an increase in *AD* will result in a relatively large increase in *Y* and a relatively small increase in *P*. On the other hand, if the *AS* curve is relatively steep, an increase in *AD* will cause a relatively large increase in *P* and a relatively small increase in *Y*. The opposite will occur in both cases when *AD* decreases.

To summarise: The smaller the interest elasticity of investment demand, and also the steeper the *AS* curve, the less effective an expansionary monetary policy will be as a means of stimulating the economy. However, the steeper the *AS* curve, the more effective a contractionary monetary policy will be as a means of combating inflation.

Other links between interest rates and the rest of the economy

We have now discussed one of the channels through which changes in the interest rate can affect the price level (*P*) and real output (*Y*) in the economy. It is widely accepted nowadays that there are also other channels through which the interest rate (and therefore monetary policy) can influence the price level and real output. We now outline the most important channels of monetary influence, which are also considered by the SARB when decisions on the appropriate level of the repo rate have to be made. The SARB's view of the monetary transmission mechanism is summarised in Figure 20-7. Note that this broad framework includes the links discussed previously.

When the SARB changes the repo rate, a number of variables are affected, including:

- domestic market interest rates
- the amount of money and bank credit
- expectations
- asset prices
- exchange rates

When these variables change, those changes (in turn) affect the various components of aggregate demand in the economy (ie *C, I, G, X* and *Z*). The change in aggregate demand (*AD*) then impacts on domestic output and inflation, depending on the prevailing conditions of aggregate supply (as illustrated by the *AS* curve). The various channels through which a change in the repo rate can affect real output and inflation can

3. The chain will also break down if the change in the interest rate is neutralised by a **shift** of the investment demand function. The investment demand curve in Figure 20-6(a) can shift as a result of changes in sentiment or expectations. For example, if firms become pessimistic about future prospects, the investment demand curve will shift downward (to the left). Thus, when the central bank lowers the repo rate to stimulate the economy the stimulatory impact of such a decrease in the interest rate may be offset by an inward (downward) shift of the investment demand curve. The opposite can occur when the central bank increases the repo rate to curb spending but firms become more optimistic, with the result that they invest more at each level of the interest rate than before (illustrated by a rightward shift of the investment demand curve).

FIGURE 20-7 The South African Reserve Bank's view of the monetary transmission mechanism

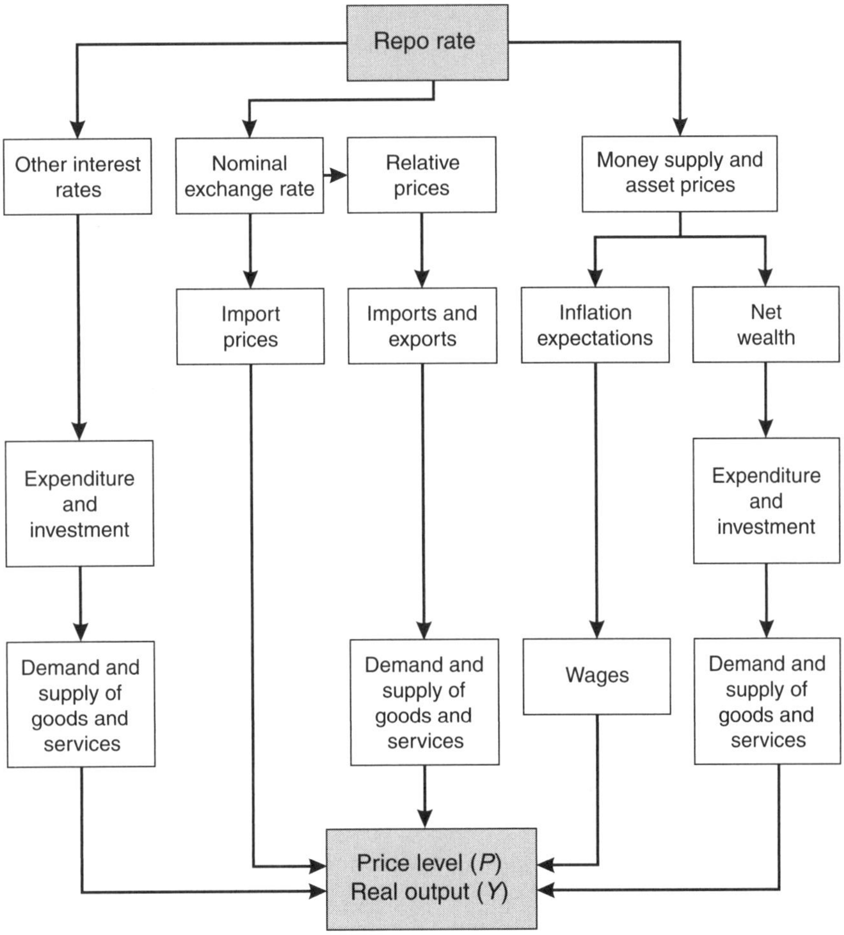

Source: Adapted from Smal, MM & de Jager, S. 2001. The monetary transmission mechanism in South Africa. Occasional paper no 16. Pretoria: South African Reserve Bank (September), 5

be summarised as follows (using an *increase* in the repo rate as an example – in each case a decrease will have the opposite effect):

■ THE INTEREST RATE CHANNEL

The SARB raises the repo rate:

⇒ Market interest rates (*i*) increase.

⇒ Investment spending (*I*) and consumption spending (*C*) decrease.

⇒ Aggregate demand (*AD*) decreases.

⇒ The relative impact on the price level (*P*) and real output (*Y*) depends on aggregate supply (*AS*) conditions.

■ THE EXCHANGE RATE CHANNEL

The SARB raises the repo rate:

⇒ Market interest rates (*i*) increase.

⇒ If foreign interest rates remain unchanged, there will be an increase in net capital inflows (stimulated by the increase in domestic interest rates).

⇒ The rand appreciates against other currencies (because of the greater demand for rands).

⇒ Exports decline and imports increase.

⇒ Aggregate demand (*AD*) decreases.

⇒ The relative impact on *P* and *Y* depends on *AS* conditions.

■ THE ASSET PRICE CHANNEL

The SARB raises the repo rate:

⇒ Market interest rates (*i*) increase.

⇒ Equity (share) prices and property prices fall.

⇒ Firms and consumers become (or feel) poorer and spend less – in other words, there is a decline in investment spending and consumer spending via the wealth effect.

⇒ Aggregate demand (AD) decreases.

⇒ The relative impact on P and Y depends on AS conditions.

■ THE CREDIT CHANNEL

The SARB raises the repo rate:

⇒ Market interest rates (i) increase.

⇒ Bank deposits increase and bank loans decrease.

⇒ Investment spending (I) and consumption spending (C) decrease.

⇒ Aggregate demand (AD) decreases.

⇒ The relative impact on P and Y depends on AS conditions.

In all these channels **expectations** can have a significant (albeit often uncertain) effect.

Four aspects of this modern view of the monetary transmission mechanism have to be emphasised:

- The link between the interest rate and investment spending, discussed in the previous subsection, is still a crucial part of the mechanism.
- It is a complex transmission mechanism which works through various channels (in contrast to the relatively simple transmission mechanism explained earlier).
- The outcome of the process is uncertain (more so than in the case of the simpler transmission mechanism).
- The time lag between the policy action (a change in the repo rate) and its eventual impact on the price level (P) and real output (Y) is also variable and uncertain. (The lags associated with monetary and fiscal policy are discussed in the next section.)

20.3 Monetary and fiscal policy in the *AD-AS* framework

Monetary and fiscal policy have already been discussed at various places. In this section we summarise some of the earlier discussion and add a few further topics with regard to monetary and fiscal policy.

Expansionary and contractionary monetary and fiscal policies

Monetary and fiscal policy (sometimes collectively called **demand management**) can be expansionary or contractionary. An **expansionary monetary policy** is implemented when the central bank (eg the SARB) reduces the interest rate (eg the repo rate) at which it provides credit to the banks. In terms of the *AD-AS* model this is illustrated by a rightward (upward) shift of the AD curve. Monetary policy is **contractionary** when the central bank raises the interest, illustrated by a leftward (downward) shift of the AD curve.

An **expansionary fiscal policy** is applied when the government (in the person of the Minister of Finance) increases government spending (G) and/or reduces taxes (T). This is illustrated by a rightward (upward) shift of the AD curve. Fiscal policy is **contractionary** when government spending is reduced and/or taxes are increased, illustrated by a leftward (downward) shift of the AD curve.

Monetary and fiscal policy can also be **neutral**, in the sense of not being aimed at increasing or decreasing aggregate demand in the economy. However, since we are primarily interested in what would happen if things change, we do not pay specific attention to a neutral policy stance.

While it is in principle always possible for the monetary and fiscal authorities to influence aggregate demand in the economy, the actual outcome of monetary and fiscal policy depends on aggregate supply. As we have seen, a change in AD will sometimes have a relatively greater impact on the price level, and at other times a relatively greater impact on total real production and income in the economy. In practice, it also takes time to formulate and implement monetary and fiscal policies, while a considerable period may also elapse before these policies take effect. We now discuss some of the practical problems associated with monetary and fiscal policies.

Monetary and fiscal policy lags

Whenever monetary and fiscal policy measures are considered, certain **practical problems** have to be taken into account. One of the basic difficulties associated with attempts to stabilise the economy by using monetary and/or fiscal policy is the existence of **delays** or **lags**. Four types of lag can be distinguished: the recognition lag, the decision lag, the implementation lag and the impact lag.

■ THE RECOGNITION LAG

This is the lag between changes in economic activity and the recognition or realisation that the changes have occurred. Economic data do not become available immediately – it takes time, for example, to compile the national accounts. Even the consumer price index takes some time to compile. It thus takes time for policymakers to establish or confirm that the economy has moved into a recession or a boom – see also the discussion of the business cycle in Section 23.2. The recognition lag is the same for monetary and fiscal policy.

■ THE DECISION LAG

Once it has been established what is happening, the authorities have to decide how to react. In the case of

fiscal policy this means that ministers and officials from different departments, and eventually the Cabinet, have to meet to discuss matters and to consider various policy options. This also takes time. In fact, the most important fiscal policy measures are announced only once a year, in the budget speech of the Minister of Finance (usually in February). With **monetary policy** the lag is generally much shorter. At the time of writing, the MPC of the SARB met six times a year to consider possible changes in the repo rate. However, nothing prevents the Governor of the SARB from convening a meeting of the MPC at any time, and decisions can be taken within a day or two.

■ THE IMPLEMENTATION LAG

Once the decisions have been taken, it takes time to implement them. In the case of **fiscal policy**, government spending and taxes cannot be changed overnight. Plans have to be drawn up and Parliamentary approval usually has to be obtained before the plan can be put into action. Certain changes can only be implemented via the budget and may therefore have to wait up to a year before they can be applied. Income tax rates, for example, are only adjusted annually. In contrast, the implementation lag associated with **monetary policy** is very short. In fact, when a change in the repo rate is announced, it comes into effect immediately. Thus, as in the case of the decision lag, the implementation lag is much shorter for monetary policy than for fiscal policy.

■ THE IMPACT LAG

When the policy measures are introduced, a further period elapses before they actually affect economic behaviour. In the case of **fiscal policy**, an increase in taxes will, for example, not have its full impact on the economy immediately. The same applies in the case of a change in government spending, although you will recall that government spending has a more direct impact on spending, production and income than taxes, which have an indirect impact (eg via disposable income and consumption). The impact lag is often referred to as the **outside lag**, to distinguish it from the first three types of lag, which together constitute the **inside lag** (ie the delay from the time a need for action arises until the appropriate policies are implemented). In the case of **monetary policy** the impact lag is very long. Most economists estimate that it takes between 12 and 18 months (and even up to 24 months) for a change in the repo rate to have its full impact on prices, production, income and employment. It is generally accepted that the impact lag is significantly longer for monetary policy than for fiscal policy. The different lags are summarised in Table 20-3.

It should be clear, therefore, that the formulation and implementation of economic policy is no easy task. In fact, by the time the policy measures become effective, circumstances may have changed to such an extent that the measures may even have perverse effects. For example, by the time an expansionary policy comes into effect, the prevailing conditions may call for a contractionary policy. **Timing** is thus of the utmost importance. If the authorities' timing is wrong, monetary and fiscal policy may prove to have a destabilising, instead of a stabilising, effect on the economy. The practical difficulties we have referred to have led certain economists to recommend that the government should not attempt to achieve too much through monetary and fiscal policy. Their recommendation, therefore, is that monetary and fiscal policy should be as **neutral** as possible. As far as fiscal policy is concerned, they tend to call for balanced budgets. A **balanced budget** refers to a situation in which all government spending is financed by taxes, that is, where the budget deficit is zero. With regard to monetary policy, some economists call for stable interest rates, while others call on the monetary authorities to try to achieve low and stable rates of growth in the money supply – see the discussion of monetarism in the next section.

TABLE 20-3 Lags associated with monetary and fiscal policy

Type of lag	*Relative length*
Recognition lag	Same for monetary and fiscal policy
Decision lag	Long for fiscal policy, short for monetary policy
Implementation lag	Long for fiscal policy, extremely short for monetary policy
Impact lag	Longer for monetary policy than for fiscal policy

The relative effectiveness of monetary and fiscal policy

You may have gained the impression that the authorities use either monetary or fiscal policy to guide the economy in a certain direction. What actually happens, or should happen, however, is that the two types of policies should be used in conjunction with each other to pursue the objectives of macroeconomic policy. Nowadays most economists agree that fiscal and monetary policy are both important instruments for stabilising aggregate demand.

There are, however, certain circumstances in which the one type of policy may be more successful than the other. **Fiscal policy** has generally been more successful in **stimulating** a depressed economy, while **monetary policy** can be employed with greater assurance to **dampen** an overheated economy in which inflationary pressures are severe.

Apart from the policy lags discussed in the previous subsection, the **institutional features** of the two sets of policy instruments also have to be taken into account. Fiscal policy is subject to parliamentary approval and the decisions in this respect are normally taken by politicians. Monetary policy, on the other hand, is formulated by the central bank (the Reserve Bank in South Africa), which enjoys a greater degree of autonomy. The pressure on politicians to act in the interest of voters has resulted in fiscal policy being generally aimed at stimulating aggregate demand, while the Reserve Bank and other central banks traditionally take a more conservative and restrictive attitude towards economic policy.

To achieve macroeconomic objectives such as economic growth and price stability, a suitable combination of the different types of policy instrument has to be applied. Continual consultation between the Reserve Bank, the Treasury and other government departments is thus of the utmost importance to ensure that different types of economic policy are sufficiently **coordinated**. This is particularly important when there are trade-offs between different policy objectives.

The policy dilemma in an open economy

As indicated earlier, policymakers are often confronted with a dilemma, since steps taken to increase production, income and employment may raise the general price level, while steps taken to lower the price level may result in lower production and income and increased unemployment. In this section we introduce a further dimension by adding the balance of payments. Once exports and imports are taken into account, macroeconomic policy becomes even more complicated, particularly in developing countries where economic growth requires the importation of capital goods. This additional complication is often referred to as a **balance of payments constraint**.

In Chapter 19 we incorporated the foreign sector into the simple Keynesian model. We explained that exports (X) are autonomous with respect to income (Y) and that there is a positive relationship between imports (Z) and income (Y). This means that there is a unique level of income at which exports are equal to imports, that is, where net exports ($X - Z$) are zero. This is shown in Figure 20-8.

Figure 20-8(a) shows that exports (X) are autonomous (ie independent of the level of income (Y)). It also shows that there is a positive relationship between imports (Z) and income (Y) – as Y increases Z also increases. The unique level of income at which net exports ($X - Z$) are zero is labelled Y_B and is indicated by a vertical line in Figure 20-8(b). At any level of income lower than Y_B, exports are greater than imports. This can be seen clearly in (a). In (b) we call this the **surplus area**, since it corresponds to a surplus on the current account of the balance of payments. At any level of income greater than Y_B imports are greater than exports. This can be seen clearly in (a). In (b) we call this the **deficit area**, since it corresponds to a deficit on the current account of the balance of payments. As the level of income increases from zero, the surplus falls until it disappears at Y_B.

FIGURE 20-8 Net exports at different levels of income

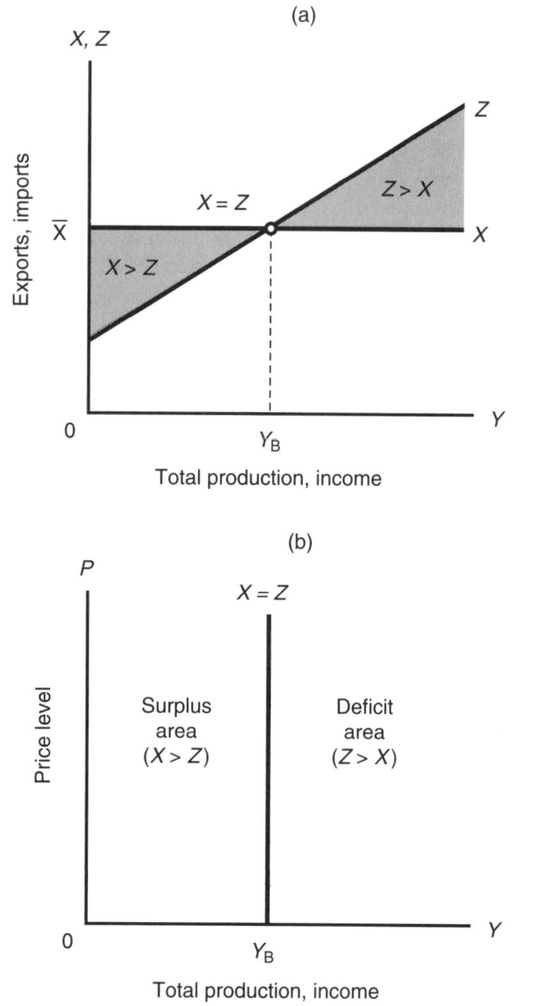

In (a) we show that the level of exports X is independent of the level of income Y, while the level of imports Z increases as Y increases. Exports are equal to imports at Y_B. Y_B is also shown in (b). When Y is less than Y_B there is a surplus of exports over imports. When Y is greater than Y_B imports are greater than exports. Any point to the left of Y_B thus indicates a surplus on the current account of the balance of payments, while any point to the right of Y_B indicates a deficit. As income moves away from Y_B, the surplus or deficit increases.

Increases in income above Y_B will be accompanied by increases in the deficit.

The level of income (Y_B), at which net exports are zero, thus serves as a dividing line between the surplus and deficit areas. We now incorporate Y_B into the *AD-AS* model to explain how balance of payments considerations can further complicate economic policy-making.

In Figure 20-9 we show aggregate demand (*AD*), aggregate supply (*AS*) and the level of income (Y_B) at which net exports are zero. We also show the level of income corresponding to full employment. This is indicated by Y_f. In the figure the equilibrium level of income (Y_0) (determined by *AD* and *AS*) is greater than Y_B. From Figure 20-8 we know that this means that there is a deficit on the current account of the balance of payments at Y_0. The equilibrium level of income (Y_0) is also lower than the full-employment level of income (Y_f). This means that there is unemployment at Y_0.

In this particular case, policymakers are confronted with a dilemma. Any measures that they take to raise the level of production and income (to reduce unemployment) will increase the deficit on the current account of the balance of payments. Similarly, any measures taken to reduce the level of income (to reduce the current account deficit) will increase unemployment. When the balance of payments is introduced into the analysis, matters are therefore even more complicated than before. The dilemma can, of course, be resolved if current account deficits are financed by net inflows of foreign capital, that is, by surpluses on the financial account of the balance of payments. However, countries like South Africa cannot always rely on such inflows and therefore have to maintain some balance between exports and imports.

FIGURE 20-9 A policy dilemma

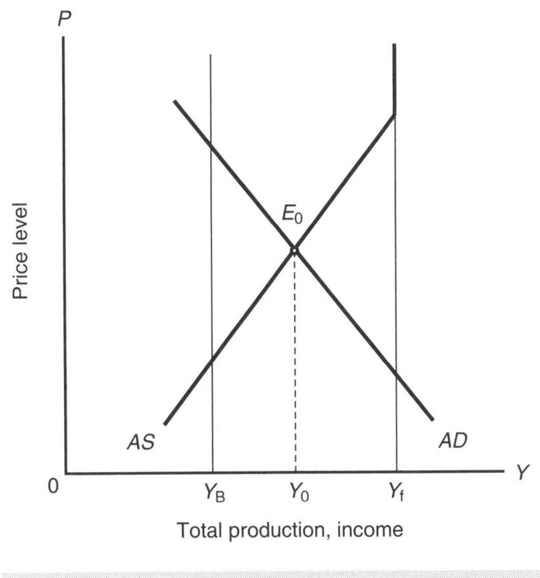

The equilibrium level of income Y_0 is determined by aggregate demand AD and aggregate supply AS. Y_B indicates the level of income at which exports X equal imports Z. Y_f indicates the full-employment level of income. At Y_0 there is unemployment ***and*** *a deficit on the current account of the balance of payments. Measures to reduce the deficit will increase unemployment, while measures to reduce unemployment will increase the deficit.*

The authorities always want to stimulate production and income to reduce unemployment, but balance of payments considerations can prevent such a strategy. This was particularly true in South Africa between 1985 and 1993 when the country experienced large outflows of foreign capital. After the foreign debt standstill of 1985 the country was forced to repay a substantial portion of its foreign debt. The problem was exacerbated by political and economic uncertainty which gave rise to further outflows of capital and large deficits on the financial account of the balance of payments. To finance these deficits, considerable current account surpluses had to be maintained. This meant that income *Y* had to be kept low in order to keep imports *Z* down. In these circumstances, the authorities could not even afford to let the level of income rise to Y_B. The economy had to be kept in the surplus area by maintaining restrictive policies. Balance of payments considerations thus prevented the authorities from applying the policies which they probably would have preferred to apply (to reduce unemployment). This dilemma is a practical example of a **balance of payments constraint** on economic policy. When faced with such a dilemma or constraint, conventional monetary and fiscal policies have to be supplemented by other policies in an attempt to find a solution. If you pursue your study of economics further, you will analyse this dilemma more closely in more advanced courses in macroeconomics and international economics. At this stage it is only important to realise that balance of payments considerations can complicate policy-making in an open economy, particularly if there is a persistent deficit on the financial account of the balance of payments.

20.4 Other approaches to macroeconomics

Before discussing some other approaches to macroeconomic theory and policy, we first provide a brief overview of the development of macroeconomic thought.

The development of macroeconomic thought

Prior to the Great Depression of the early 1930s, nobody used the term macroeconomics. Economic analysis was mainly concerned with microeconomics and fluctuations in aggregate economic activity, which were generally regarded as short-term deviations from the full-employment level of production and income. At the aggregate level, most economists tended to believe in Say's law, which states that "supply creates its own demand." The basic idea underlying Say's law (which you have already encountered in Chapter 18) is that production creates income, and therefore also the necessary means to purchase the goods and services that are produced. An important element of this line of reasoning is that saving (a withdrawal from the flow of income and spending) will automatically be invested (and thus be injected back into the flow of income and spending).

All output will thus always be sold, that is, there will never be insufficient demand at the macroeconomic level. Moreover, since the willingness to work is motivated by the desire to consume, there is no reason for unemployment. Output should expand to the point where the labour force is fully employed in the long run. Unemployment was regarded as a short-run, temporary phenomenon which would be eliminated in due course by the working of the market mechanism (ie by natural economic forces). This pre-Keynesian view of how the economy functions is usually called "classical economics," a term that was originally coined by Karl Marx and which was also used by Keynes to describe the conventional (ie non-Marxist) economic theory in the early 1930s when he wrote his *General theory.*

The Great Depression of the early 1930s forced economists to reconsider the basic principles of Classical economics. As we have seen, John Maynard Keynes turned Say's law around completely by stating that aggregate supply will adjust passively to aggregate demand. Thus, instead of supply creating its own demand, Keynes emphasised the importance of aggregate demand, thus creating the possibility that demand could be insufficient to ensure full employment. Keynes's emphasis on aggregate spending (or aggregate demand) as the driving force that determines aggregate economic activity and his view that the Great Depression was caused by a lack of aggregate demand became very popular among academics and policymakers. Many Western governments followed this line of thought and applied expansionary fiscal policies to stimulate economic activity. A number of other factors also served to stimulate aggregate spending. These included World War II (which many observers believe was the factor which finally freed the world from the Great Depression) and the spending boom following the war. The latter was the result of the pent-up demand for civilian goods (which could not be satisfied during wartime) and the spending that was required to reconstruct the war-ravaged countries. The end result was a strong expansion in aggregate spending in most countries, especially the industrialised countries. Production, income and employment grew fairly rapidly and policymakers tended to believe that they had found the solution to recessions, depressions and unemployment. Keynesian economics provided all the answers.

During this period, however, a new problem emerged, namely **inflation**. Inflationary episodes had been experienced before but they tended to be linked to specific events, like wars, and usually disappeared once the event had ceased. Moreover, the inflationary episodes tended to be confined to particular countries. During the post-war period, however, *all* countries experienced inflation and kept experiencing it. Initially the rates were fairly low, except for the temporary increase as a result of the Korean conflict in the early 1950s. But by the 1960s the rates had started to creep up. This presented Keynesian policymakers with a serious problem since they had no theory with which to understand the phenomenon, and no remedy for it except to apply restrictive policies which would inevitably increase unemployment. A more detailed discussion of this problem is provided in the discussion of the Phillips curve in Chapter 22.

It was during this period that the **monetarists**, a group of economists led by Milton Friedman of the University of Chicago (winner of the Nobel Prize for Economics in 1976), came to the fore and provided a theory of inflation, the quantity theory, which we discuss in the next chapter. According to the monetarists, the problem was the excessive rate of increase in the money supply. To combat inflation, the authorities had to bring the money supply under control.

In the 1970s, however, a new problem emerged, namely the simultaneous occurrence of high inflation, low economic growth and increased unemployment. The term **stagflation** was coined for this combination of economic **stag**nation and high in**flation**. This phenomenon and its solution posed a serious challenge to all the various schools of thought. It also brought to the fore new schools of thought which professed to have solutions to the problem. Among these were the **supply-side economists**. By the time Ronald Reagan was elected as President of the United States in 1980, supply-side economics was all the rage in the United States. In fact, his whole political campaign was based on this approach, and when he took office, supply-side economics (or Reaganomics, as it was soon named) became the official economic policy of the United States. The supply-siders claimed a lot of the credit for the strong performance of the United States economy during Reagan's second term of office.

Supply-side economics was also popular in other countries. In Britain, for example, Margaret Thatcher, who had become Prime Minister in 1979, also adopted the kind of policies that supply-side economists were calling for. Her approach to economic policy was also given a label, namely Thatcherism. In South Africa many elements of supply-side economics were incorporated into the *Normative economic model* (NEM) published by the South African government in 1993. However, the NEM was overtaken by political developments and was never officially adopted as government policy in South Africa. Certain elements of the NEM, such as the need to curtail the growth in government spending, maintain monetary discipline and liberalise international trade and payments, were, however, accepted by the 1994 Government of National Unity. Most of these elements were also incorporated into *Growth, employment and redistribution: a macro-economic strategy* (generally known as the Gear strategy) which was adopted by the South African government in June 1996.

In the 1970s Keynesian economics was also attacked from a somewhat different angle by a group of economists led by Robert Lucas, who was awarded the Nobel Prize for Economics in 1995. The school of thought that developed around the ideas of Lucas and his followers became known as the **new classical school** and was very influential during the last quarter of the 20th century.

In response to the attacks from the monetarists, supply-siders and new classicists, two groups of economists defended Keynesian economics and the economics of Keynes. The first is the **Post Keynesians,** who argue that many of Keynes's important insights were neglected or ignored by the so-called Keynesians. They argue that mainstream Keynesians are simply neoclassical economists who adapted their theories to include some Keynesian insights. This group owes its origins to the work of economists such as Joan Robinson, George Shackle and Nicolas Kaldor in the United Kingdom and Sidney Weintraub, Paul Davidson and Hyman Minsky in the United States. The Post Keynesians are a rather diverse group of economists and each has placed a unique emphasis on what he or she considers to be the fundamental theoretical contribution made by Keynes.

A second group of economists, the **new Keynesians**, responded to the attack by the new classical school by combining certain aspects of new classical economics with more traditional mainstream Keynesian notions.

The macroeconomics in this book is largely a mixture of Keynesian and Post Keynesian economics. In the rest of this subsection we briefly discuss the ideas of the monetarists, the supply-side economists, new classical economists and the new Keynesians.

Monetarism

Monetarism has its origins in classical macroeconomics. One of the basic elements of classical macroeconomics was Say's law, which we have already outlined. Another distinguishing feature was a belief that there were no strong links between the monetary sector of the economy and the real sector of the economy. This separation of the monetary sector and the real sector is known as the **classical dichotomy**. The classical economists believed that a change in the money supply (ΔM) would lead to a proportional change in the price level (ΔP). For example, a 10 per cent increase in the quantity of money would lead to a 10 per cent increase in prices. Money, according to the classical economists, was simply a lubricant which facilitated exchange but which had no impact on real variables such as real production, income and spending.

Classical economics was largely overtaken by Keynesian economics in the 1940s and 1950s but its main ideas were brought to the fore again in the 1960s by the monetarists, under the leadership of Milton Friedman. Whereas Keynesian economics emphasised fiscal policy and tended to neglect money and monetary policy, the monetarists re-emphasised the role of money in the economy and raised doubts about the effectiveness of fiscal policy. This resulted in an often fierce debate between the monetarists and the Keynesians. The key elements of this debate can be summarised as follows:

- Like the classical economists, the monetarists generally believe that a free-market economy is intrinsically stable and effective in achieving macroeconomic objectives. In contrast, Keynesians believe that the free-market economy is inherently unstable.
- Monetarists therefore believe that government intervention should be restricted to the minimum. In particular, the government should not use discretionary fiscal and monetary policies to try to stabilise the economy. Keynesians, on the other hand, favour government intervention and believe that appropriate fiscal policy should be implemented to stabilise the economy.
- Monetarists believe that inflation is caused by excessive increases in the money supply (see the discussion of the monetarist approach to explaining the causes of inflation in Section 21.4). They therefore believe that the growth in the money supply should be regulated in such a way that it merely keeps abreast of the growth in real production. Such action will avoid inflation and have the least disturbing effect on the free-market economy. Keynesians, on the other hand, believe that inflation is a more complex phenomenon and that the monetary transmission mechanism works via changes in interest rates, as explained earlier.

Further perspective on monetarism can be gained by considering the essential elements of monetarism, which follow a logical pattern. The monetarists believe that:

- The money supply is an important determinant of nominal production or income (PY).

- Movements in the quantity of money are the best indicator of the stance of monetary policy.
- The velocity of circulation of money (*V*) (and therefore also the demand for money) is stable.
- Changes in the money supply can affect real production or output (*Y*) only in the short run.
- Changes in the money supply affect only the price level (*P*) in the long run.
- The private sector is inherently stable.
- Changes in the money supply can disturb the stability of the private sector.
- The timing of the effects of monetary policy are unpredictable.
- The unpredictable effects of monetary policy can be spread out over a number of years.
- Attempts to stimulate or dampen economic activity through discretionary monetary and fiscal policies (ie through decisions taken from time to time by the monetary and fiscal authorities) are a major cause of poor economic performance (eg low growth, high inflation).
- The monetary authorities should therefore only try to keep the growth in the money supply steady (at a low rate) to avoid disturbing the inherent stability of the economy (and thus causing inflation).

The monetarist approach to inflation is explained in more detail in Section 21.4.

Supply-side economics

What is supply-side economics, Reagonomics or Thatcherism all about? Unlike the Keynesians and the monetarists, the supply-siders do not have a single theory or model which represents their basic ideas and which can be explained in a graph or equation. One of the reasons is that supply-siders place greater emphasis on the microeconomic aspects of economic policy and particularly on the incentive effects of taxation.

As the name indicates, the distinguishing feature of supply-side economics is an emphasis on aggregate supply, which had been largely neglected during the previous decades. The focus is therefore on policies aimed at increasing the aggregate supply of goods and services in the economy.

The major problems identified by the supply-siders relate to the role of government in the economy. *First*, they believe that government spending in general is too high; *second*, they argue that there are too many rules and regulations which inhibit private initiative; and, *third*, they believe that tax rates are too high (partly because government spending is too high). They therefore recommend cuts in government spending, deregulation and lower tax rates. Let us look briefly at each of these points.

Supply-siders argue that cuts in **government spending** on goods and services will release some resources which can then be used by the private sector. Supply-siders believe that the private sector uses resources more productively than the public sector. They therefore believe that such a transfer of resources from the public sector to the private sector will raise total production in the economy. For the same reason they also believe in the **privatisation** of state assets.

The second element of the supply-side programme is **deregulation**. This means that all rules and regulations which restrict the exercise of entrepreneurship should be reviewed and preferably scrapped. This will free producers from the red tape of government bureaucracy and simulate innovation and investment.

The third, and most important, element of supply-side economics concerns **tax rates**. Supply-siders believe that tax rates are too high. These high rates, they argue, have disincentive effects on saving, investment and work effort. The higher the marginal tax rate, the greater the incentive to avoid paying taxes – by avoidance (legal), evasion (illegal) or simply by working, saving or investing less. Reducing the company tax rate will give businesses a greater incentive to invest. Likewise, lower marginal rates of personal income tax will make it more worthwhile for individuals to work and save. Some supply-siders even call for exempting saving completely from income tax by allowing firms and individuals to deduct their total saving from their taxable income. In the tradition of Say's law they believe that higher saving will lead to higher investment (and therefore to higher production, income and employment).

The idea that tax cuts can be used to stimulate economic activity is not new. Economists of different persuasions agree that tax cuts are stimulatory. They warn, however, that such cuts may increase the budget deficit. The novel element of the supply-side argument is the idea that tax cuts will stimulate the economy **and reduce the budget deficit**. Supply-siders argue that the additional economic activity and the income generated by the tax cuts will raise additional tax revenue. This view is based on the **Laffer curve** which was developed by Arthur Laffer, one of Reagan's advisers. Laffer argued that government revenue is maximised at a certain tax rate. After that it becomes counterproductive to raise tax rates further since people will evade tax or avoid it by not working, saving or investing. If the economy is beyond that point, as he believed the United States economy to be, a reduction in tax rates will actually raise tax revenue. The Laffer curve and certain other aspects of supply-side economics are still hotly debated among economists and policymakers. However, irrespective of the merits of the various elements of their approach, the supply-siders succeeded in drawing attention once again to the importance of aggregate supply in determining production, income and employment.

From a macroeconomic point of view, supply-side economics is concerned with attempts to raise the aggregate supply of goods and services in the economy to combat stagflation. In terms of the *AD-AS* model, the essence of supply-side economics can thus be illustrated as attempts to shift the *AS* curve to the right, thereby increasing production, income and employment, while simultaneously reducing the price level.

New classical economics

For the new classical economists, macroeconomics must have solid microeconomic foundations. In fact, to them macroeconomics is simply the sum of the microeconomic parts. Their key assumptions are that all economic agents have **rational expectations** and that all **markets always clear**. Their theory of rational expectations extends the neo-classical assumption of rationality to the formation of expectations. More formally, rational expectations can be defined as extending the application of the principle of rational behaviour to the acquisition and processing of information and the formation of expectations. The theory is that people form their views of the future by taking account of all available information, including their understanding of how the economy works. They do not know the future but they use the imperfect information at their disposal in the best possible way. Although they can and will make mistakes, they will not repeat them.

The other important hypothesis is that markets continuously clear in a framework of competitive markets. Rational expectations and market clearing have serious implications for the effectiveness of monetary and fiscal policies. If (i) an expansionary policy is correctly anticipated, (ii) individuals form their expectations rationally and (iii) wages and prices are flexible, expansionary monetary and fiscal policies will not succeed in increasing real GDP and reducing unemployment. One of the main implications of this theory is that policymakers should be **credible**, and to achieve this they have to apply **policy rules** rather than discretionary policies (which will destabilise the economy).

New Keynesian economics

The new Keynesians responded to the new classical challenge by combining certain aspects of new classical economics with more traditional Keynesian ideas. Like the new classical economists, they argue that macroeconomics requires solid microeconomic foundations and most (but not all) accept the idea of rational expectations. However, new Keynesians strongly reject the notion of continuous market clearing in a perfectly competitive environment. Instead, they believe that a typical market economy is characterised by numerous **imperfections**. They spend a lot of time and effort on explaining *why* wages and prices tend to be inflexible and on investigating the implications of wage and price stickiness.

In contrast to the new classical economists, the new Keynesians favour policy intervention (like all other Keynesians). There is, however, no consensus among them about how desirable or feasible discretionary policy is or whether monetary or fiscal policy should be favoured. In summary: new Keynesians argue for policy measures to improve the performance of the economy, but differ among themselves about which policies are desirable.

IMPORTANT CONCEPTS

Aggregate demand
Aggregate supply
Fiscal policy
Monetary policy
Contractionary policy
Expansionary policy
Trade-off
Demand management
Stagflation
Supply shock
Incomes policy
Monetary transmission mechanism
Recognition lag
Decision lag
Implementation lag
Impact lag
Policy dilemma
Balance of payments constraint
Monetarism
Supply-side economics
Classical dichotomy

REVIEW QUESTIONS

1. Use the *AD-AS* model to explain how government can stimulate the economy by applying expansionary monetary and fiscal policies. What would the side-effects of such policy be? What role does the price elasticity (or slope) of the *AS* curve play in this regard?
2. Use the *AD-AS* model to explain the impact of an increase in productivity (*ceteris paribus*) on the price level and the level of real output and income in the economy.
3. What does stagflation mean? Use the *AD-AS* model to illustrate this phenomenon.
4. Explain the difference between Say's law and Keynes's views about the relationship between aggregate demand and aggregate supply in the economy.
5. Explain what the monetary transmission mechanism means.
6. Briefly describe the various channels through which a change in the repo rate can affect the price level and real output in the economy.
7. Describe the various lags associated with monetary and fiscal policy and explain why the timing of policy decisions and actions is so important.
8. Use the *AD-AS* model to illustrate and explain the policy dilemma in an open economy.
9. Under what conditions can the balance of payments impose a binding constraint on economic activity and economic policy in an open economy such as the South African economy?
10. What are the central ideas of (a) the monetarists, (b) the supply-side economists, (c) the new classical economists, and (d) the new Keynesians?

21 Inflation

Learning outcomes

Once you have studied this chapter, you should be able to

- define inflation
- describe how inflation is measured
- distinguish between different measures of inflation
- explain why inflation is regarded as a problem
- distinguish between four approaches to explaining what causes inflation
- explain demand-pull and cost-push inflation
- mention the different policies that can be used to combat inflation

Inflation is like sin; every government denounces it and every government practises it.

SIR FREDERICK KEITH-ROSS

If all prices and incomes rose equally, no harm would be done to any one. But the rise is not equal. Many lose and some gain.

IRVING FISHER

South Africans are getting stronger. Thirty years ago it took five people to carry fifty rands' worth of groceries. Today a child can do it.

ANONYMOUS

In this chapter we focus on inflation, which has often been described as "Public Enemy Number One". The first section deals with the **definition** of inflation. In the second section we explain various ways of **measuring inflation**. This is followed by a discussion of the effects or **costs of inflation**. In contrast to a problem such as unemployment, which is undoubtedly a serious one, the costs of inflation are less obvious. The fourth section deals with the **causes of inflation**. We explain four different approaches: the **monetarist approach**, the **demand-pull versus cost-push approach**, the **structuralist approach** and the **conflict approach**. We also indicate the broad policy implications of the different approaches. The final section deals with some of the **policy measures** that can be used to combat inflation. The question of anti-inflation policy is dealt with further in the next chapter, where the relationship between inflation and unemployment is examined.

Since World War II, and particularly since the early 1970s, the prices of most goods and services in South Africa have increased quite significantly every year. Price increases have become a feature of South African life. When consumers inquire about the cause of the increases, they are usually informed that "inflation" is to blame – see Box 21-1. But what exactly is inflation? How is it measured? Why is it a problem? What causes inflation and how can it be combated? We investigate these questions in this chapter.

21.1 Definition of inflation

Inflation is one of those economic concepts that can easily cause great confusion if it is incorrectly defined. Someone once defined inflation as a phenomenon which means that you can buy less with your money now than you could when you had no money at all! There is some truth in this definition. On a more serious note, however, inflation is defined as a **continuous and considerable rise in prices in general**.

Four aspects of this definition have to be emphasised:

- It is a **neutral definition** which does not attempt to define inflation in terms of specific causes. Inflation is often defined in the media as "too much money chasing too few goods" or as "excessive increases in the money supply". Such definitions highlight a particular cause of inflation and therefore exclude all other possible causes. These are called **causal definitions**. One of the drawbacks of causal definitions is that they can result in the formulation of inappropriate policies for fighting inflation. A neutral definition, on the other hand, allows for all possible causes of inflation to be taken into account. It also provides a sounder basis for anti-inflation policy.
- Another important element of the definition is that it describes inflation as a **process**. Inflation does not refer to a once-and-for-all increase in prices. What is at issue here is a **continuous** increase in prices. Inflation refers to a process in which the prices of most goods and services are increasing from year to year (or even from month to month).
- Inflation is concerned with a **considerable** increase in prices. If prices are, on average, increasing by only 1 or 2 per cent per year, it is questionable whether this should be described as inflation. Such price rises could, for example, have resulted from increases in the quality of the goods and services concerned, in which case it would be wrong to describe them as inflation.
- Inflation refers to an increase in prices **in general**. An increase in the price of a particular good (eg meat or petrol) is not inflation. Even when the overall level of prices remains constant some prices will increase while others will decrease in response to changes in supply and demand. There is inflation only when the prices of most goods and services in the economy are increasing. Economists therefore often refer to inflation as increases in the general (or average) price level.

BOX 21-1 WHY DO PRICES INCREASE?

Many people have a simple explanation for price increases: they blame them, quite simply, on inflation. For example, when the price of cigarettes was raised in December 1994, a spokesman for United Tobacco said that the increase "was due to inflation" (*Pretoria News*, 9 December 1994: 1). This reminds one of the explanation of the origin of the word "inflation" once offered by the American humorist, Art Buchwald. He told the following story:

> In 1887 there was a bar and grill owner in San Francisco named George Inflation. One day he failed to receive a shipment of booze from the East. Since the demand for booze was great, George Inflation decided to charge 15 cents for a shot of whiskey, instead of the standard 10 cents. He also made the shot glass smaller. This did not stop his customers from buying booze, so he raised the price to 20 cents, then 25 cents. The other bars in San Francisco raised their prices accordingly and when their customers complained the other bar and grill owners would say, "Blame it on Inflation."
>
> Thus inflation soon became part of the English language.

(Art Buchwald, quoted in MacEwan, A & Weisskopf, TE (Eds). 1973. *Perspectives on the economic problem*, 2nd edition. Englewood Cliffs, NJ: Prentice-Hall, 101)

21.2 The measurement of inflation

The consumer price index

Since inflation is a continuous and considerable increase in the general price level, it follows that the measurement of inflation requires some yardstick for the general price level. The most commonly used indicator of the general price level is the **consumer price index (CPI)** which we explained in Chapter 4. Recall that the CPI is an index which reflects the cost of a representative basket of consumer goods and services. The unadjusted CPI is nowadays often referred to as the **headline CPI**.

Once we have a set of CPI figures we can calculate the inflation rate. This is done by calculating the **percentage change in the CPI** from one period to the next. Inflation is always expressed as an annual rate. In other words, when we say that the inflation rate is 10 per cent, this means that prices are increasing at a rate of 10 per cent **per year**. For various reasons it does not make much sense to calculate an inflation rate over a period of less than one year.

But how do we measure the inflation rate for a particular year? The CPI is estimated and published on a monthly basis. For any particular year we therefore have twelve figures – one for each month, as in Table 21-1, which gives the figures for 2005 and 2006. When the figure for December 2006 was published, two methods could be used to calculate an inflation rate for 2006.

TABLE 21-1 The consumer price index and inflation in South Africa (metropolitan areas), 2005–2006

Month	*Consumer price index (2000 = 100)* 2005	2006	*Inflation rate (%)*
January	125,4	130,4	4,0
February	125,6	130,5	3,9
March	126,9	131,2	3,4
April	127,6	131,8	3,3
May	127,6	132,6	3,9
June	127,4	133,6	4,9
July	128,5	134,9	5,0
August	129,0	136,0	5,4
September	129,5	136,3	5,3
October	129,6	136,6	5,4
November	129,5	136,5	5,4
December	129,5	137,0	5,8
Average for year	**128,0**	**134,0**	**4,7**

Source of basic data: Statistics South Africa

■ MONTH ON THE SAME MONTH DURING THE PREVIOUS YEAR

The most common practice in South Africa is to compare the index for a particular month with the index of the corresponding month in the previous year. The result is then expressed as a percentage increase. For example, if we compare the index value for the metropolitan areas for December 2006 (ie 137,0) with that of December 2005 (129,5) an inflation rate of 5,8 per cent is obtained. The calculation is as follows:

$$\frac{137{,}0 - 129{,}5}{129{,}5} \times 100 = 5{,}8\%$$

The rates for the other months in the last column of Table 21-1 were obtained in the same manner.

This method is very popular. This is how the inflation rate reported in the media each month is calculated. The method covers a period of 12 months and therefore indicates what happened to prices during the most recent "year". Inflation rates calculated according to this method are, however, subject to considerable fluctuations. For example, a change in the petrol price, interest rates or value-added tax may suddenly raise or lower the inflation rate in a particular month. The following example illustrates the point: On 15 June 2001 the Reserve Bank reduced the repo rate by one percentage point (or 100 basis points). This reduction was reflected in the decline in the **level** of the CPI in July 2001 from 106,2 to 106,1. The **rate of increase** in the CPI fell from 6,3 per cent in June to 5,3 per cent in July. In September 2001 the Reserve Bank again reduced the repo rate and again both the CPI and the inflation rate declined in October (when the reduction was reflected in the figures). In 2002 the opposite happened. The Reserve Bank raised the repo rate by a full percentage point (100 basis points) on four occasions (on 16 January, 15 March, 14 June and 13 September), resulting in sharp increases in both the CPI and the rate of increase in the CPI in February, April, July and October. The impact of changes in interest rates on the headline CPI is the main reason why the CPIX (see below), rather than the unadjusted CPI, is used as the basis for calculating the Reserve Bank's inflation target.

Another problem with this method is that not all prices are measured every month. Some prices (like the prices of motorcars) are only collected every three months while other prices (like the cost of education) are only collected annually.

■ ANNUAL AVERAGE ON ANNUAL AVERAGE

When the inflation rate has to be calculated for a calendar year, the usual procedure is to compare the average of all the monthly indices in a particular year with the corresponding average for the previous year. The annual averages for 2005 and 2006 are given in the last row of Table 21-1. The percentage change in the last column of the last row is obtained as follows:

$$\frac{134{,}0 - 128{,}0}{128{,}0} \times 100 = 4{,}7\%$$

Note that this figure differs from the result obtained by simply comparing the figures for December 2005 and December 2006. The reason is that the figure of 4,7 per cent is based on all 24 monthly figures in Table 21-1. In this way, short-term fluctuations in the index figures for particular months are eliminated. This measure therefore gives a better indication of the inflation **process** over a longer period. Note that this method is not restricted to calendar years. Any 12-month average (eg from June to May) may be compared with the previous 12-month average (also from June to May) in order to calculate an inflation rate.

There are other methods of calculating an annual inflation rate. One such method is to calculate the difference in the CPI between two successive months or quarters and to express the result as an annual rate. These methods fall beyond the scope of this book.

As indicated above, various inflation rates can be calculated from a particular set of CPI figures. Each of these methods has certain advantages and drawbacks. In practice, therefore, economists apply more than one method when analysing the inflation process. They also examine other price indices which can be used to calculate inflation rates and to analyse inflation.

Core inflation

During the second half of the 1990s Statistics South Africa started publishing a **core inflation rate** in addition to the unadjusted or **headline inflation rate**. The main objective of estimating core inflation is to capture the underlying inflationary pressures in the economy. Core inflation is estimated by excluding items from the CPI basket on the basis that their prices are highly volatile, subject to temporary influences or affected by government intervention and policy. In this way some of the problems associated with the unadjusted inflation rate are eliminated. The following items are excluded from the CPI basket to obtain the basket which is used to calculate the core inflation rate (with the reasons for their exclusion in brackets):

- Fresh and frozen meat and fish (prices may be highly volatile)
- Fresh and frozen vegetables and fresh fruit and nuts (prices may be highly volatile)
- Interest rates on mortgage bonds and overdrafts/personal loans (excluded to eliminate the effects of changes in monetary policy)
- Value-added tax (VAT) (to eliminate the distorting effects of changes in VAT)
- Assessment rates (since they are determined by local government)

Table 21-2 shows movements in both the unadjusted or headline inflation rate and the core inflation rate (for metropolitan areas) during 2006. The monthly rates were obtained by comparing each monthly CPI figure with that of the corresponding month of the previous year. Note how stable the movements in the core inflation rate were.

The CPIX

When the authorities decided to adopt **inflation targeting** in South Africa in 2000, one of the main decisions that they had to take was to choose which inflation rate they would target: headline inflation, core inflation or something in between? After much research and debate it was decided to use the rate calculated on the basis of the CPI for metropolitan and other urban areas but to exclude mortgage interest rates from the basket. The decision to exclude mortgage interest rates arises from the significant impact of changes in interest rates (the main instrument of monetary policy) on the CPI. If these rates are not excluded, changes in interest rates will tend to have a perverse impact. For example, if the Reserve Bank raises the repo rate to dampen the inflation **process**, the immediate impact would be to raise the measured rate of inflation. In view of the large impact of changes in interest rates on headline inflation in South Africa,

TABLE 21-2 Headline, core and CPIX inflation, 2006

	Annual rate of increase in		
Month	*Headline CPI (%)*	*Core CPI (%)*	*CPIX (%)*
January	4,0	4,1	4,3
February	3,9	4,1	4,5
March	3,4	2,9	3,8
April	3,3	2,8	3,7
May	3,9	3,0	4,1
June	4,9	3,7	4,8
July	5,0	3,8	4,9
August	5,4	3,9	5,0
September	5,3	3,8	5,1
October	5,4	3,3	5,0
November	5,4	3,4	5,0
December	5,8	3,8	5,0
Annual average	**4,7**	**3,5**	**4,6**

Note: The first two columns pertain to metropolitan areas only, while the last pertains to the metropolitan and other urban areas.
Source: Statistics South Africa

it was clearly necessary to exclude the most important interest rates that impact on the cost of living (ie mortgage interest rates) from the index used to calculate the inflation target. The adjusted index is called the **CPIX**, where the X indicates that interest rates have been excluded. The movements in the CPIX inflation rate during 2006 are also shown in Table 21-2. Note that CPIX inflation did not accelerate quite as fast as headline CPI inflation during 2006. This was because CPIX inflation did not reflect the increases in the repo rate (and therefore also in mortgage interest rates) during the course of the year.

The production price index

Another important price index is the **production price index (PPI)**. Whereas the CPI measures the cost of a representative basket of goods and services to the consumer, the PPI measures prices at the level of the first significant commercial transaction. For example, the prices of imported goods are measured at the point where they enter the country and not where they are sold to consumers. Likewise, manufactured goods are priced when they leave the factory, not when they are sold to consumers.

Another important feature of the PPI is that it includes capital and intermediate goods, but excludes services (which account for 45 per cent of the CPI basket). The PPI is therefore based on a completely different basket of items than the CPI. Where certain items overlap, their weights also differ significantly between the PPI and the CPI. For example, foodstuffs have a much larger weight in the CPI than in the PPI. The main differences between the CPI and the PPI are summarised in Table 21-3.

The PPI, which is also estimated and published on a monthly basis by Statistics South Africa, measures the **cost of production** rather than the **cost of living**. It can therefore not be related directly to consumers' living standards. Nevertheless, it is very useful in the analysis of inflation. Because the PPI measures the cost of production, a significant change in its rate of increase is usually regarded as an indication that the rate of increase in the CPI is also going to change some months later. Another useful feature of the PPI is the distinction that is drawn between goods produced in South Africa and imported goods. It is thus possible to determine to what extent the cost pressures are emanating from the domestic economy or from the country's economic links with the rest of the world. For example, when the rand depreciates against the major currencies, as during 2006, the prices of imported capital and intermediate goods usually tend to increase. These increases are reflected immediately in the PPI and, after a time lag of some months, also in the CPI.

The methods used for calculating the rate of increase in the PPI are the same as the methods explained above with reference to the CPI. Table 21-4 compares the results obtained for 2006 in respect of the PPI with the comparable rates in respect of headline CPI.

TABLE 21-3 Main differences between the CPI and PPI

Consumer price index	*Production price index*
Pertains to cost of living	Pertains to cost of production
Basket consists of consumer goods and services	Basket consists of goods only (no services)
Capital and intermediate goods excluded	Capital and intermediate goods included
Prices include VAT	Prices exclude VAT
Interest rates taken into account	Interest rates excluded
Prices of imported goods not shown explicitly	Prices of imported goods shown explicitly

TABLE 21-4 Annual rates of increase in CPI and PPI, 2006

Month	*Annual rate of increase in*	
	PPI (%)	*Headline CPI (%)*
January	5,5	4,0
February	5,5	3,9
March	5,4	3,4
April	5,5	3,3
May	5,9	3,9
June	7,5	4,9
July	8,1	5,0
August	9,2	5,4
September	9,0	5.3
October	10,0	5,4
November	10,0	5,4
December	9,3	5,8
Annual average	**7,7**	**4,7**

Note: The rates for the various months and the annual averages were calculated as explained in the subsection on the CPI. The figures in the last column are therefore the same as the figures in the last column of Table 21-1 and the first column of Table 21-2.

Source: Statistics South Africa

The implicit GDP deflator

Each of the two indices discussed thus far measures the prices of a particular basket. In the case of the

PPI, the basket consists of various consumer, capital and intermediate goods. The CPI basket contains consumer goods and services. Economists are often interested in what happened to the prices of **all** final goods and services produced in the economy in a particular year. In other words, they want to know what happened, on average, to the prices of all goods and services included in GDP.

In the case of the CPI and the PPI, Statistics South Africa regularly determines the prices of all the elements of the respective baskets. It is impossible, however, to measure all prices in the economy on a regular basis. Fortunately there is a solution to this problem. As explained in Chapter 4, GDP is first measured at current prices. By using a variety of complicated techniques the national accountants at Statistics South Africa and the South African Reserve Bank then transform GDP at current prices (or nominal GDP) to GDP at constant prices (or real GDP). This is done to eliminate the effects of inflation. Real GDP measures GDP in terms of the prices ruling in a certain base year (ie at constant prices). This provides the basis for calculating economic growth. Although the major purpose of the transformation of GDP at current prices to GDP at constant prices is to measure economic growth, it also yields a measure of inflation. This is because the difference between nominal GDP and real GDP indicates what happened to prices. There is therefore another index that can be used to calculate an inflation rate. We call this the **implicit GDP deflator**. It is an **implicit** index since it is a side-effect of the calculation of economic growth. The CPI and PPI, on the other hand, are explicit indices that are specifically designed to measure price increases.

To understand the derivation of the GDP deflator, it is important to realise that GDP at constant prices (real GDP) is not simply obtained by deflating GDP at current prices (nominal GDP) by a specific index. What actually happens is that the various components of GDP at current prices are each converted separately to constant prices. Moreover, all three methods for calculating GDP that were explained in Chapter 4 are used during this conversion process. The transformation of GDP at current prices to GDP at constant prices is a complicated process. Fortunately, all we need to know is that the difference between nominal GDP and real GDP yields an index which we can use to calculate an inflation rate for the economy as a whole.

This can be explained with the aid of Table 21-5. The first two columns of the table show GDP at current prices and GDP at constant (2000) prices for each year from 1997 to 2006. The third column shows the ratio between the first two columns expressed as a percentage. For example, the figure for 1998 is obtained by dividing 742 424 by 864 968 and multiplying the result by 100. This ratio between nominal and real GDP is called the GDP deflator. Note that the GDP deflator for 2000 is 100. This is no accident, since during the base year GDP at current prices must be the same as GDP at constant prices.

The GDP deflator can now be used to calculate an inflation rate for each year. The inflation rates calculated on the basis of the GDP deflator are shown in the last column. The figures are obtained by simply calculating the percentage difference between the values of the GDP deflator for successive years. For example, the rate of change in the GDP deflator for 2002, or the inflation rate, is obtained as follows:

TABLE 21-5 The GDP deflator and corresponding inflation rates, 1997–2006

Year	*GDP at current prices (R millions)*	*GDP at constant 2000 prices (R millions)*	*GDP deflator (2000 = 100)*	*Inflation rate (%)*
1997	685 730	860 516	79,7	–
1998	742 424	864 968	85,8	7,7
1999	813 683	885 365	91,9	7,1
2000	922 148	922 148	100,0	8,8
2001	1 020 007	947 373	107,7	7,7
2002	1 168 699	982 121	119,0	10,5
2003	1 260 693	1 012 763	124,5	4,6
2004	1 398 157	1 061 768	131,7	5,8
2005	1 539 253	1 115 875	137,9	4,7
2006	1 726 688	1 171 508	147,4	6,9

Note: An inflation rate for 1997 cannot be calculated from the data in the table.
Source of GDP data: South African Reserve Bank, *Quarterly Bulletin*, March 2005, 2006, 2007

GDP deflator for 2002 = 119,0

GDP deflator for 2001 = 107,7

$$\text{Inflation rate for 2002} = \frac{119{,}0 - 107{,}7}{107{,}7} \times 100\%$$

$$= \frac{11{,}3}{107{,}7} \times 100\%$$

$$= 0{,}105 \times 100\%$$

$$= 10{,}5\%$$

The implicit GDP deflator is a much broader-based index than the CPI or the PPI. Although it does not reflect consumers' cost of living, it seems to be an extremely useful indicator of inflation. Unfortunately, it has one potential drawback. Since GDP includes exports and excludes imports, it follows that the GDP deflator reflects changes in export prices, while excluding changes in import prices. From an inflation point of view, however, import prices (such as the price of imported oil) are important, while export prices (such as the price of gold) are of little significance. Thus, when the price of gold falls, it pushes down the rate of increase in the GDP deflator. The GDP deflator may thus indicate that the inflation rate has fallen while the rate of increase in prices in the domestic economy may actually have been constant or even increasing. When export prices and import prices are increasing at the same rate (ie when the **terms of trade** are constant) this does not present a serious problem. But when export prices and import prices are increasing at significantly different rates, the inflation rate calculated on the basis of the GDP deflator can become misleading. This is one of the reasons for the occasional divergence between the annual rates of change in the GDP deflator and in the CPI and PPI. (See also Box 23-1.) In such circumstances it is better to use the GDE or GNI deflators, which are obtained in a similar way.

Comparison between different measures of inflation

Table 21-6 shows the annual inflation rates for the period 1994 to 2006 calculated on the basis of the headline CPI, the PPI and the GDP deflator. While these figures do not show the same results, the differences are usually not very significant and tend to become smaller over time. This is illustrated by the last row which shows the compounded annual average increases in the three indices over the period as a whole.

Economists consider all these indices, as well as other implicit deflators not discussed here, when analysing the inflation process. However, for consumers (and therefore also for politicians) the CPI and the CPIX are by far the most important bases for calculating inflation since these indices relate to their cost of living (or the purchasing power of their incomes) and to the interest rate policy of the Reserve Bank (which further affects consumers' cost of living).[1]

TABLE 21-6 Annual inflation in South Africa according to the CPI, PPI and GDP deflator, 1994–2006

	Inflation according to the rate of increase in		
Year	*CPI (%)*	*PPI (%)*	*GDP deflator (%)*
1994	8,8	8,3	9,5
1995	8,7	9,4	10,3
1996	7,3	7,0	8,1
1997	8,6	7,0	8,1
1998	6,9	3,6	7,7
1999	5,2	5,8	7,1
2000	5,4	9,2	8,8
2001	5,7	8,4	7,7
2002	9,2	14,2	10,5
2003	5,8	1,7	4,6
2004	1,4	0,6	5,8
2005	3,4	3,1	4,7
2006	4,7	7,7	6,9
Average 1994–2006 (compound rate)	**6,2**	**6,6**	**7,6**

Sources: CPI and PPI: Statistics South Africa
GDP figures: South African Reserve Bank

21.3 The effects of inflation

The costs of unemployment require little or no explanation. Everyone can understand why unemployment is bad, for the unemployed as well as for society at large. But the costs of inflation are not immediately obvious. Certainly, everyone is perturbed by inflation, but does it hurt everyone? In this section we consider three sets of effects of inflation: distribution effects, economic effects and social and political effects.

Distribution effects

Inflation affects the distribution of income and wealth among the various participants in the economy. The first significant distribution effect is the redistribution between creditors and debtors. The basic rule is that **inflation benefits debtors (borrowers) at the expense of creditors (lenders)**. To understand this you have to remember that the real value (or purchas-

1. Note that CPIX inflation could not be included in the table since data on CPIX inflation are only available from 1998.

ing power) of money falls when prices increase (see Box 4-1 and Box 4-5).

The redistribution between creditors and debtors can be explained by using a simple example. Suppose Peter borrowed R10 000 from Paul on 1 January 2005 on the understanding that the principal amount of R10 000 was to be repaid on 31 December 2006. In addition Peter would pay Paul interest at 10 per cent per annum, that is, Peter would pay Paul interest of R1 000 per year. Table 21-1 shows that the CPI rose from 125,4 in January 2005 to 137,0 in December 2006. The real value or the purchasing power of the R10 000 (in January 2005) therefore fell to R10 000 × 125,4/137,5 = R9 153 in December 2006. In real (or purchasing power) terms Paul thus did not receive the full amount he loaned to Peter in January 2005 when the loan was repaid in December 2006. This clearly indicates a redistribution of wealth from the lender (Paul) to the borrower (Peter).

Peter can also gain in another way. If the interest rate that he has to pay Paul is lower than the inflation rate, Paul will also receive less real interest (ie in terms of purchasing power) than the R1 000 per year they had agreed to. The difference between the nominal interest rate (10 per cent in this case) and the inflation rate is called the **real interest rate**. If the nominal interest rate is lower than the inflation rate, then the real interest rate is negative. In such a case the lender is prejudiced in two ways by inflation: the real value of his wealth (the R10 000) declines *and* the interest income he receives is also not sufficient to compensate him for inflation. However, if the real interest rate is significantly positive, the redistribution of **income** (interest) falls away and only **wealth** is redistributed.

This redistribution of wealth naturally applies to all assets whose nominal value is fixed, such as money, government securities, bonds, certain insurance policies and certain pensions. Who then are the people that lose and who are the people that gain? This is not an easy question to answer, since most people are creditors (lenders) as well as debtors (borrowers). Anyone who holds money in a bank account or who has a savings or fixed deposit is a creditor and therefore loses. On the other hand, many people live in homes financed by bonds (called mortgage bonds), the nominal value of which is fixed. People with mortgage bonds are debtors who benefit from inflation because the real value of their loans decreases as prices increase. Similarly, people who borrow money to purchase expensive consumer goods such as motorcars also benefit from inflation, because it reduces the real value of their debt. It should be clear, therefore, that many people lose and gain during inflation. As a result it is difficult to pinpoint exactly who the losers and who the winners are. However, since younger people are more likely to be net borrowers while old people tend to have relatively fixed nominal incomes (eg pensions or interest income), inflation tends to **redistribute income and wealth from the elderly to the young**.

Apart from the redistribution between private lenders and private borrowers there is also a significant **redistribution from the private sector to the government**. In this case there is no doubt as to who benefits from inflation – it is always the government. The government is always a debtor – in South Africa the total debt of the government was more than R575 billion on 31 December 2006. During inflation the government therefore gains at the expense of the holders of the public debt (eg the holders of government stock).

The government can also gain via the tax system. As explained in Chapter 16, South Africa has a progressive personal income tax, which means that marginal and average tax rates increase with the income level (see Table 16-6). The higher an individual's income is, the greater the percentage income tax that he or she has to pay. When there is inflation, taxpayers' **nominal** incomes (eg wages and salaries) rise even when their **real** incomes remain unchanged. Taxes, however, are levied on nominal income and not on real income. Therefore, if the income tax schedule remains unchanged, inflation raises the average rates of personal income tax. In other words, individuals will have to pay higher taxes even if they are actually no better off than before. This phenomenon, which is known as **bracket creep**, results in a redistribution of income from taxpayers to the government. Bracket creep results from a combination of inflation and a progressive income tax. It has the same effect as an increase in the tax rate. Increased government revenue from taxation through inflation is also called the **fiscal dividend**.

Although the distribution effects of inflation are unintended and undoubtedly hurt those who lose in the process, they do not necessarily affect the overall performance of the economy. Moreover, the distribution effects can be counteracted (at least in principle) by linking nominal values (eg debt, pensions, taxes) to a price index such as the CPI – see the discussion of indexation in Section 21.5. From a macroeconomic point of view, the main question is how inflation affects variables such as economic growth, employment and the balance of payments.

Economic effects

Inflation has various economic effects which may result in lower economic growth and higher unemployment than would otherwise have occurred. For example, decision makers in the private sector tend to become more concerned with **anticipating inflation** than with seeking out profitable new production opportunities. The efforts of entrepreneurs are diverted, from innovation and risk-taking, to anticipating inflation. Inflation also stimulates **speculative**

practices that do not add to the country's productive capacity. People try to outwit others by speculating in shares, property (real estate), foreign currencies, precious metals, works of art, antiques, postage stamps and other existing assets which may have a good chance of at least maintaining their real value during inflation. Such speculative activity often occurs in place of productive investment in new factories, machines and other equipment.

By reducing the value of existing savings, inflation may also **discourage saving** in traditional forms such as fixed deposits and pension fund contributions.

One of the most serious economic effects of inflation is that it can produce **balance of payments problems**. Inflation increases the costs of export industries and import-competing industries. If inflation in South Africa is higher than in the economies of our major trading partners and international competitors, the result will be a loss of international competitiveness. This can be compensated for in the short run by a depreciation of the rand against foreign currencies but such a depreciation will again feed into the inflation process by raising the cost of imported goods. Since most of South Africa's imports consist of capital and intermediate goods, the depreciation will raise production costs and prices even further. This process will continue as long as South Africa's inflation rate remains out of step with the inflation rates of the most important trading countries in the world.

Social and political effects

Apart from its distribution and economic effects, inflation also has **social and political consequences**, which can further undermine the performance of the economy. Price increases make people unhappy and different groups in society start blaming one another for increases in the cost of living. When rents, service charges, bus fares or taxi fares go up, the frustration often gives rise to social and political unrest. Inflation creates a climate of conflict and tension which is not conducive to economic progress. It is therefore not surprising that Lenin is reputed to have said that inflation is the easiest way to destroy capitalism – see Box 21-2.

When the general price level is increasing at a rate of 10 per cent per year, this does not mean that all prices are rising at the same rate or that price hikes are the same in all shops or supermarkets. Since ordinary consumers purchase many different articles on a regular basis, it becomes more and more difficult for them to keep up with the relative prices of the art-

BOX 21-2 THE DESTRUCTIVE POWER OF INFLATION

John Maynard Keynes claimed that the Communist leader, Lenin, stated that inflation is the best way to destroy capitalism:

> Lenin is said to have declared that the best way to destroy the capitalist system is to debauch its currency. By a continuing process of inflation, governments can confiscate, secretly and unobserved, an important part of the wealth of their citizens. By this method they not only confiscate, but they confiscate **arbitrarily**; and, while the process impoverishes many, it actually enriches some. The sight of this arbitrary rearrangement of riches strikes not only at security, but at confidence in the equity of the existing distribution of wealth. Those to whom the system brings windfalls, beyond their deserts and even beyond their expectations or desires, become "profiteers", who are the object of the hatred of the bourgeoisie, whom the inflationism has impoverished, no less than of the proletariat. As the inflation proceeds and the real value of the currency fluctuates wildly from month to month, all permanent relations between debtors and creditors which form the ultimate foundation of capitalism, become so utterly disordered as to be almost meaningless; and the process of wealthgetting degenerates into a gamble and a lottery.

Keynes then added:

> Lenin was certainly right. There is no subtler, no surer means of overturning the existing basis of society than to debauch the currency. The process engages all the hidden forces of economic law on the side of destruction, and does it in a manner which not one man in a million is able to recognise.

(Keynes, JM. 1919. *The economic consequences of the peace*. London: Macmillan, 220–221; emphasis in the original) icles. The household budgeting process therefore becomes all the more complicated. The constant struggle against the assault of increasingly expensive consumer goods therefore often leads to a feeling of uncertainty and even despair. It should therefore come as no surprise that inflation is often regarded as Public Enemy Number One. There are, however, even worse possibilities – see Box 21-3.

The greatest cost of inflation

An American economist, Gardner Ackley, once claimed that the greatest cost of inflation is the inflation it causes. This may seem a strange statement but there is a lot of truth in it. There is a great deal of evidence to support the view that an increase in the rate of inflation often leads people to expect that it will increase further. They therefore try to be compensated for the expected higher inflation. If they succeed, this results in raising the actual rate of inflation. For example, unions may base their wage claims on the expected higher inflation. If these claims are granted, production costs and prices will rise more rapidly than during the previous period. Similarly, firms may raise the prices of their products in anticipation of expected cost increases. They may also increase prices because of the need to raise sufficient funds to purchase materials which they expect to be more expensive in future. When the rate of inflation is expected to increase, consumers may also rush to buy things now instead of later. This will put further upward pressure on prices. If unchecked, such a process may eventually result in very high inflation or **hyperinflation** – see Box 21-4.

21.4 The causes of inflation

Causes of inflation are not difficult to find. Ask any group of people what causes inflation and a host of culprits will be identified. Some will blame the government, while others will say that the problem is that the central bank prints too much money. Consumers will blame the farmers for increases in food prices, while the farmers will blame the shopkeepers and large retail chains for taking excess profits on the produce they supply to them. Business people will blame the trade unions for pushing up wages and salaries without increasing productivity. The trade unions will claim that they are only trying to be compensated for the erosion of their purchasing power by past inflation.

The fact of the matter is that inflation is a complex, dynamic process which cannot be ascribed to a single cause. We can explain some elements of this process by examining four approaches to diagnosing (or explaining) inflation. These approaches also provide useful frameworks for discussing policies that can be used to combat inflation. The approaches are:

- the monetarist approach (the quantity theory of money)
- the demand-pull and cost-push approach
- the structuralist approach
- the conflict approach

The monetarist approach to inflation: the quantity theory of money

The monetarists, whom we introduced in Chapter 20, regard inflation as a purely monetary phenomenon.

BOX 21-3 FALLING PRICES: A CONSUMER'S HEAVEN?

Consumers who are battered by continuous price increases often long for the day when prices will start falling. But are falling prices a good thing? When a group of people are asked whether they would prefer continuously increasing prices or continuously decreasing prices the majority always choose the latter. But are continuously falling prices (or **deflation**, as it is called) a good thing? On the contrary, deflation is arguably even worse than inflation. When prices are falling continuously, firms find it almost impossible to survive. They produce goods and services, but by the time they sell them the prices are too low to recover their costs of production. They therefore have to lay off workers or cut their wages and salaries. Deflation thus tends to be accompanied by increasing unemployment and falling incomes, as was the case during the Great Depression of the 1930s. Farmers are hit particularly hard. They have to incur costs to plant their crops, feed their animals, etc, but by the time they sell their products the prices have fallen and they therefore incur losses. Borrowers are also adversely affected by deflation – in contrast to inflation, deflation continuously increases the real value of debts such as mortgage bonds. Everyone who wins during inflation, loses during deflation while total production, income and employment tend to fall. When faced with a choice between inflation and deflation, inflation is therefore usually still the lesser of the two evils, unless it deteriorates into hyperinflation (see Box 21-4).

BOX 21-4 HYPERINFLATION

South Africa experienced double-digit inflation between 1974 and 1992. In every year from 1974 to 1992 the rate of increase in the CPI was above 10 per cent. The highest annual rate during this period was 18,6 per cent (1986) and the lowest annual rate was 10,9 per cent (1978). The cumulative price increase between 1974 and 1992 was 933,9 per cent, in other words a basket of goods which cost R100 in 1974 cost R1 033,90 in 1992. South Africans who experienced these price increases regard this period as one of high inflation. Viewed in an historical perspective this is quite true. South Africa had never previously experienced such a sustained period of double-digit inflation. But the rates of inflation experienced during this period come nowhere near the rates that have been experienced in some other countries.

When the inflation rate becomes very high, it is usually called **hyperinflation**. The highest recorded annual inflation rate was experienced in Hungary between August 1945 and July 1946. During this period the price level increased by an almost unimaginable 100 000 000 000 000 000 000 000 000 times! The most serious hyperinflations have all been associated with wars. Germany, for example, experienced massive hyperinflation after World War I. It has been said that a newspaper which cost 0,30 marks in Germany in January 1921 cost 70 million marks in November 1923. Other countries that experienced such war-related hyperinflation include Austria (1921–22), Russia (1921–24), Poland (1923–24), Greece (1943–44) and China (1945–49).

In recent years the highest annual inflation rates have been recorded in developing countries that have experienced social and political conflict or civil war. The following are a few examples:

Country	Year	Annual inflation rate (%)
Angola	1996	4 145,1
Argentina	1989	3 079,8
Armenia	1994	4 962,2
Azerbaijan	1994	1 664,5
Belarus	1994	2 221,0
Bolivia	1985	11 749,6
Brazil	1990	2 937,8
Bulgaria	1997	1 058,4
Congo (Dem. Rep. of)	1994	23 773,0
Kazakhstan	1994	1 877,4
Nicaragua	1988	10 205,0
Peru	1990	7 481,7
Ukraine	1993	4 734,9
Yugoslavia	1989	1 239,9

Source: International Monetary Fund, *International Financial Statistics*, various issues

According to them, sustained high rates of monetary growth *cause* high inflation, while low rates of money growth will eventually produce low inflation. In other words, they argue that high rates of inflation cannot be sustained without persistently high rates of growth in the money supply. This view is based on the **quantity theory of money** which, in turn, is based on the **equation (or equality) of exchange**.

The equation of exchange is actually an **identity** and may be stated as follows:

$$MV \equiv PY$$

where M = the quantity of money
V = the velocity of circulation of money
P = the average (or general) price level
Y = the real value of goods and services produced

The identity states that the real value (or quantity) of goods and services (Y) produced during a period, multiplied by their average prices (P) is equal to the quantity of money (M), multiplied by the velocity of circulation of money (V). We now examine the meaning of the equality and, in particular, the concept of **velocity of circulation**

The monetary or nominal value of GDP (PY) is greater than the value of the quantity of money (M) in circulation. This is because money is used more than once during the year to accommodate the final transactions represented by GDP. The velocity of circulation (V) is an indication of the number of times the average rand changes hands (or circulates) during a particular period. The value of V can be derived from the equation of exchange:

$$MV \equiv PY$$

$$\therefore V \equiv \frac{PY}{M}$$

For example, in 2006 the South African GDP at current prices amounted to R1 727 billion, while the average value of the narrowly-defined quantity of money M1 was R562 billion. This yielded a value of V of 3,07, which is calculated as follows:

$$V = \frac{PY}{\text{M1}} = \frac{\text{R1 727 billion}}{\text{R562 billion}} = 3{,}07$$

The average rand therefore had to pass from hand to hand more than 3 times during 2006 to accommodate the monetary value of the final goods and services produced in South Africa. See also Box 21-5.

As mentioned earlier, the equation of exchange formulated above is no more than an **identity**. By definition this equality is always true (hence the ≡ sign instead of =). The value of PY must necessarily be equal to MV since we define V in terms of the other three variables. If P, Y or M changes, V changes so as to ensure that $MV = PY$. The question that must be asked is how the monetarists convert this identity into a theory of inflation.

They do so by making three key assumptions, namely:

- The velocity of circulation of money (V) is stable – this assumption is based on the empirical finding that V tends to be relatively stable in practice.
- The quantity of money (M) is exogenously determined by the monetary authorities and is not influenced by changes in output (Y) or prices (P).
- Real output (Y) is determined by the quantity and quality of the various factors of production and is not influenced by changes in the quantity of money – in terms of the equation, Y is thus assumed to be fixed (given the quantity and quality of the factors of production) and will only change as a result of changes in real factors.

Together these assumptions imply that the price level (P) is determined by the quantity of money (M). In symbols we can write that $M\bar{V} \Rightarrow P\bar{Y}$ where the bars indicate variables whose values are fixed and the arrow indicates the direction of causation.

This equation represents a theory of the **price level**. To transform it into a theory of **inflation** (ie the rate of increase in prices) we have to consider the

BOX 21-5 THE VELOCITY OF CIRCULATION OF MONEY

The following story illustrates the concept of the velocity of circulation of money. It is an adaptation of a story by DH Robertson, who in turn adapted it from an original story told by Edgeworth in an article published in the *Economic Journal* in 1919.

On the day of the final of the SAA Super Eight, two men, Thabo and Sipho, set off from Diepkloof to the FNB Stadium with a barrel of home-brewed beer. They intended to sell it to soccer fans outside the gates at R2 a mug and to share the proceeds between them. On the way Thabo, who just had one R1 coin left on him, began to feel thirsty and drank a mug of the beer, paying Sipho R1 as his share of the market price. A little later Sipho yielded to the same desire. He also drank a mug of beer, returning the R1 to Thabo. The day was hot, and before long Thabo was thirsty again, and so, a little later, was Sipho. When they arrived at the FNB Stadium, the R1 was back in Thabo's pocket. Each had paid his debts to the other in full but the beer was all gone. One R1 coin had performed a volume of transactions that would have required many rand coins had the beer been sold to soccer fans as Thabo and Sipho originally intended.

Adapted from Robertson, DH. 1922. *Money*. Cambridge: Cambridge University Press, 27.

rates of change in the components of the equation. Since V is assumed to be fixed and Y is determined by real factors, we are left with a theory that states that the rate of growth in the quantity of money is the *cause* of inflation. For example, if real output Y grows by 3 per cent per year and the nominal quantity of money increases by 15 per cent per year, the inflation rate will be approximately 12 (ie 15 – 3) per cent. Conversely, if the real growth rate is 3 per cent, price stability will be achieved only if the nominal money stock also increases by 3 per cent per year.

Although this brief outline is a simplification of the monetarist approach, it nevertheless captures the essence of the theory on which monetarists base their case for a low and constant rate of increase in the money supply. This theory is still quite popular, even among certain policymakers. It is, however, a flawed theory. Many economists question the assumption that changes in the quantity of money do not affect real variables such as output and employment. Moreover, the assumption that the monetary authorities are able to control the money supply is also controversial. As explained in Chapters 15 and 20, the money supply in South Africa is endogenous, rather than exogenous (as the monetarists assume).

Nowadays most economists agree that a broader approach to inflation is required. One such approach is the demand-pull and cost-push approach, based on the *AD-AS* model, which we introduced in Chapter 20.

Demand-pull and cost-push inflation

■ DEMAND-PULL INFLATION

Demand-pull inflation occurs when the aggregate demand for goods and services increases while aggregate supply remains unchanged. This type of inflation is often described as a case of "too much money chasing too few goods". The excess demand **pulls up** the prices of goods and services.

Demand-pull inflation can be caused by any (or a combination) of the various components of aggregate demand:

- increased **consumption spending** by households (C), for example as a result of a greater availability of consumer credit or the availability of cheaper credit as a result of a drop in interest rates
- increased **investment spending** by firms (I), for example as a result of lower interest rates or an improvement in business sentiment and profit expectations
- increased **government spending** (G), for example to combat unemployment or to provide more or better services to the population at large
- increased **export earnings** (X), for example as a result of improved economic conditions in the rest of the world or because of increases in the prices of important export products (such as minerals, in the case of South Africa)

All these causes of demand-pull inflation are accompanied by **increases in the money supply**. Increases in the money supply do not simply happen – they are usually related to increases in one or more of the components of aggregate demand in the economy.

Demand-pull inflation can be illustrated with the aid of the aggregate demand-aggregate supply model (*AD-AS* model) introduced in Chapter 20. Demand-pull is illustrated by a rightward shift of the *AD* curve, as in Figure 21-1. An increase in aggregate demand leads to an increase in the price level (P) ***and*** an increase in production and income (Y).

Demand-pull inflation thus has a positive impact on production, income and employment, provided that there are still some unemployed resources and scope for increases in Y. When the economy is at full employment, further increases in aggregate demand simply lead to price increases. This is indicated in Figure 21-1 by the shift of the *AD* curve from AD_3 to AD_4 along the vertical part of the *AS* curve.

To combat demand-pull inflation, the authorities have to keep the aggregate demand for goods and services in check. This can be done by applying

FIGURE 21-1 Demand-pull inflation

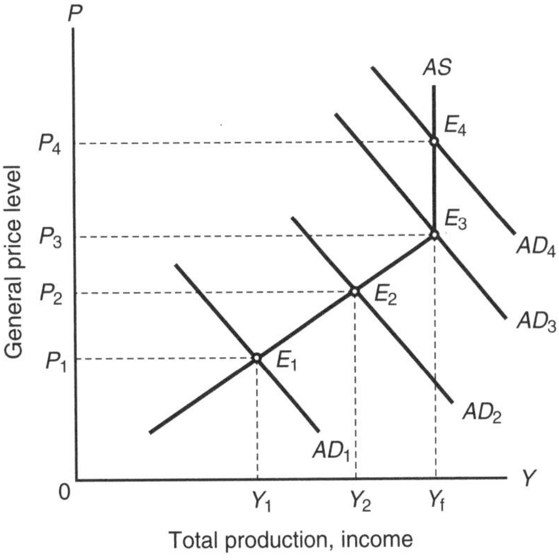

Demand-pull inflation occurs when the aggregate demand for goods and services increases. This is illustrated by the rightward shifts of the AD curve from AD_1 to AD_2, AD_3 and AD_4. As long as there is still excess capacity in the economy, the increases in the price level will be accompanied by increases in production and income. However, when full employment is reached, further shifts in the AD curve (from AD_3 to AD_4) lead to price increases only.

restrictive monetary and fiscal policies. Restrictive monetary policy entails raising interest rates and limiting the increase in the money supply. This raises the cost of credit and also reduces the availability of credit to the various sectors of the economy. Restrictive fiscal policy entails a reduction in government spending and/or increased taxation. These policies will tend to reduce aggregate demand. In terms of Figure 21-1 they will cause a leftward shift of the *AD* curve. This will result in a fall in prices, but it may have costly side-effects since production, income and employment will also tend to fall. We shall return to this dilemma in Chapter 22.

■ COST-PUSH INFLATION

As the term indicates, cost-push inflation is triggered by increases in the cost of production. Increases in production costs **push up** the price level. There are five main sources of cost-push inflation.

- The first source is **increases in wages and salaries**. Wages and salaries are the largest single cost item in any economy – in South Africa the remuneration of labour constitutes about 50 per cent of the cost of producing the gross domestic product. Increases in wages and salaries are therefore an important source of cost-push inflation.
- A second important cost item in the South African economy is the **cost of imported capital and intermediate goods**. These goods are essential to the functioning of the domestic economy, particularly the manufacturing sector. When the prices of imported goods such as oil, machinery and equipment increase, the domestic costs of production are raised. These increases could be the result of price increases in the rest of the world or of a depreciation of the domestic currency against the currencies of the exporting countries.
- A third source is **increases in profit margins**. Like wages, interest and rent, profit is also included in the cost of production. When firms push up their profit margins they are therefore raising the cost of production (and the prices that consumers have to pay).
- A fourth source is **decreased productivity**. If the various factors of production become less productive while still receiving the same remuneration, the costs of producing each unit of output increases.
- A fifth source is **natural disasters**, such as droughts or floods, which occur periodically. They raise the costs of production and the prices of agricultural and other related products.

Cost-push inflation can also be illustrated with the aid of the *AD-AS* model. Cost-push is reflected in an upward (or leftward) shift of the *AS* curve, as in Figure 21-2. Note that this is the same type of figure as the one used to explain the oil shock (ie Figure 20-4 in Chapter 20). An increase in the cost of production results in an increase in the price level *(P) and* a decrease in production and income (*Y*). Cost-push inflation thus has a negative impact on production, income and employment. In Chapter 20 we called this phenomenon **stagflation**, since price increases (inflation) are accompanied by increased unemployment (stagnation).

Cost-push inflation is caused by factors which push up the costs of production. To avoid cost-push inflation, measures have to be taken to avoid increases in the costs of production. Increases in wages and salaries and profits therefore have to be kept under control. Increases in productivity can also help to avoid or combat cost-push inflation. One of the possible measures is to apply an **incomes policy**. This type of policy is discussed in Chapter 22. The main point to note at this stage is that cost-push inflation cannot be combated by applying restrictive monetary and fiscal policies. Such policies may succeed in reducing the price level but this would be achieved at

FIGURE 21-2 Cost-push inflation

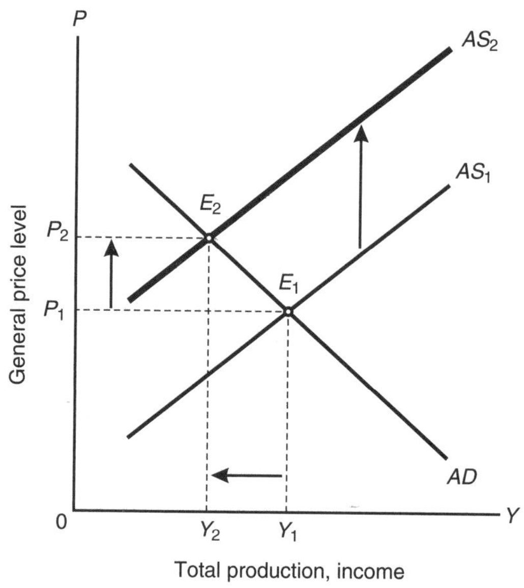

Cost-push inflation occurs when the cost of producing each level of total production Y increases. This is illustrated by an upward (leftward) shift of the AS curve from AS_1 to AS_2. Increases in the price level are accompanied by reductions in aggregate production or income Y (and therefore also by increases in unemployment). In the diagram the price level increases from P_1 to P_2 and the level of income falls from Y_1 to Y_2.

the expense of even greater unemployment. The dilemma of a possible trade-off between unemployment and inflation is investigated in Chapter 22.

Although it is easy (and important) to distinguish between demand-pull and cost-push inflation with the aid of diagrams, it is difficult to distinguish between the two in practice. The major problem is that demand-pull and cost-push become intertwined in the inflation process.

The distinction between demand-pull and cost-push inflation is a useful first step in analysing inflation. It helps to identify certain possible causes of inflation and also serves as a framework for the analysis of anti-inflation policy. But it also has a number of drawbacks, mainly that:

- It ignores possible linkages between aggregate demand and aggregate supply in the economy.
- It can only explain changes in the price **level** and does not deal with the dynamic **process** of inflation.

The demand-pull and cost-push factors listed in this section can all act as triggers which can set an inflation process in motion. However, once the process gets under way the distinction between aggregate demand and aggregate supply becomes blurred and other factors also come into play. To fully understand the process of inflation one therefore has to investigate the mechanisms which transmit price increases through the economy and over time, and which in so doing generate **a continuous and considerable rise in prices in general**, which is how we defined inflation at the beginning of this chapter.

The structuralist approach to inflation

The fact that the demand-pull versus cost-push approach to diagnosing inflation does not provide a satisfactory explanation of the inflation process, has given rise to an alternative approach to the diagnosis of inflation, which we call the **structuralist approach**. This approach retains the distinction between demand-pull and cost-push but places it in a much broader context. According to the structuralist approach the inflation process is the result of the interaction between three interrelated sets of factors:

- the **underlying factors**, which provide the background against which the inflation process occurs
- the **initiating factors**, which trigger or intensify a particular inflation process
- the **propagating factors**, which transmit the initiating impulse(s) through the economy and over time, and in so doing generate or sustain the process of rising prices

To explain inflation, all three sets of factors have to be taken into account. Moreover, a sustained process of inflation can occur only if all three are present. For example, even if the economy is particularly vulnerable to inflation (as a result of the underlying factors), specific initiating factors are still required to set the inflation process in motion or to raise the inflation rate. Once this has occurred, the propagating factors are required to generate or sustain a **process** of rising prices.

Some of the most important underlying, initiating and propagating factors are summarised in Table 21-7. We now briefly discuss each of these three sets of factors to give you some idea of the structuralist view on how the inflation process works.

■ UNDERLYING FACTORS

The **underlying factors**, also called the **structural factors** (hence the term "structuralist approach"), lie at the root of the inflation process. They provide the background against which the process occurs. An examination of the underlying factors gives an indication of how vulnerable an economy is to inflation. For

TABLE 21-7 Underlying, initiating and propagating factors in the inflation process

Underlying factors
Traditions, values and norms of society
Degree of conflict (or cohesion) between different groups in society
Political strength and bargaining power of trade unions
Degree of competition in the goods market
Degree of protection from international competition
Extent of administered pricing
Extent of formal and informal indexation
Size of the public sector
Degree of fiscal discipline
Degree of independence of the monetary authorities
Openness of the economy
Exchange rate regime
Initiating factors
Demand-pull factors (eg exogenous increases in *C*, *I*, *G* or *X*)
Cost-push factors (eg exogenous increases in wages, profits or import prices)
Other price increases (eg as a result of natural disasters or increases in indirect taxes)
Propagating factors
The various wage-price, price-price, price-wage and wage-wage interrelationships in the economy
Inflationary expectations
Interaction between domestic prices, the balance of payments and the exchange rate
Endogenous increases in the money supply

example, the greater the degree of class or race conflict in society, the greater the chances that high inflation will occur. Not surprisingly, therefore, the highest inflation rates tend to occur during wars or civil wars (see Box 21-4). On the other hand, the greater the degree of social and political cohesion, the greater the chances will be that disputes about the distribution of income and wealth can be settled without generating a process of inflation.

To understand inflation, the processes whereby the prices of goods and services and of the factors of production are determined also have to be examined. This means that, amongst others, the **structures** of the goods market and the labour market have to be examined. For example, if the goods markets are characterised by a high degree of concentration and the absence of competition, the chances of high inflation are greater than in a situation in which there is a high degree of price competition in the goods markets. Actual and potential competition from imports also have to be considered. One of the main reasons why inflation in South Africa fell significantly in the 1990s was the liberalisation of imports and the resulting exposure of South African firms to competition from abroad. Likewise, the structure of the labour market also has to be considered. Factors to be taken into account include the political strength and bargaining power of trade unions, the existence (or absence) of wage indexation (ie the practice whereby wages are automatically linked to price indices such as the CPI) and the existence of measures that protect certain workers from competition from other workers in the labour market. Again, a significant cause of the lower inflation in South Africa in the 1990s was greater discipline in the labour market where the bargaining power of the trade unions was curtailed by the scarcity of jobs and the increase in unemployment, as well as by the inability of firms to pass on wage increases (ie cost increases) to consumers and other firms in the form of higher prices (due to the greater degree of competition in the goods market).

Other important underlying factors include the fiscal discipline exercised by government and whether or not the central bank is in a position to pursue an independent monetary policy (ie free from political interference). In South Africa, for example, the curtailment of the growth in public spending towards the end of the 1990s and the independence granted to the South African Reserve Bank were important underlying or structural causes of the lower inflation rates recorded since the mid-1990s.

This discussion of the underlying factors is by no means complete, but it should give you some indication of what these factors are all about. In essence they determine the vulnerability of the economy to inflation and also lie at the root of the initiating and propagating factors.

■ INITIATING FACTORS

Although the underlying factors are important, they cannot explain why the inflation rate is what it is, why it sometimes falls and why it sometimes accelerates. Against the background of the underlying factors, specific cost and/or price increases are required to initiate or aggravate a particular inflationary episode. The immediate causes of such increases are called the **initiating factors**. These factors can be classified into three broad categories: **demand-pull factors**, **cost-push factors** and **"other" price or cost increases**. The demand-pull factors and cost-push factors are the same as those already discussed in the section on demand-pull and cost-push inflation. The distinction between demand pull and cost push is thus retained, but in a much narrower context. The demand-pull and cost-push factors set the process in motion but do not in themselves explain the whole process. Towards the end of 2001, for example, the rand depreciated sharply against the major international currencies. As a result, the prices of imported capital, intermediate and consumer goods increased sharply. Such increases, however, are in themselves insufficient to explain a *process* of inflation – see Box 21-6. They have to be transmitted through the economy and over time by the propagating factors.

The residual category of "other" price increases includes all those price increases that cannot easily be classified as demand-pull or cost-push factors but which can nevertheless act as initiating factors in the inflation process. For example, if the rate of value-added tax (VAT) were to be increased, the increase would be reflected in an increase in the CPI (which includes VAT), thereby possibly triggering further price and cost increases in the economy.

An interesting case in this regard is that of interest rates. The Reserve Bank uses the repo rate as its main policy instrument. The Bank will thus raise interest rates in its attempt to lower inflation (by reducing the level of, or growth in, aggregate demand). But interest rates are also a cost factor to net borrowers in the economy. Thus, while attempting to reduce inflation by reducing the rate of spending, the Reserve Bank also raises the costs of some economic agents. The important question, of course, is whether those who experience cost increases can pass such increases on to other agents in the form of increased prices or whether they are forced to adjust to the price increases (eg by cutting back on their consumption). This brings us to the third, arguably the most crucial, set of factors, namely the propagating factors.

■ PROPAGATING FACTORS

Once prices and/or costs have risen somewhere in the economy, these increases have to be transmitted to the rest of the economy and over time to generate or sustain an inflation **process**. This is where the **propag-**

BOX 21-6 THE INFLATION PROCESS: A CASE STUDY

During the first oil crisis in 1973/74, the price of oil increased more than fourfold. Japan does not produce oil and imports all its oil requirements. The oil crisis thus had a significant immediate impact on costs and prices in the Japanese economy. This can be illustrated by an upward shift of the aggregate supply curve (as in Figure 21-2). The price level in Japan rocketed and in 1974 consumer prices were on average 23,2 per cent higher in Japan than in 1973. Put differently, the Japanese inflation rate increased from 11,6 per cent in 1973 to 23,2 per cent in 1974. The various interest groups in Japan (eg government, business and labour) realised, however, that the increase in the price of oil meant that the country had become poorer, since Japan now had to produce and export more goods and services than before to be able to afford the same volume of oil and other imports as before (ie the country's terms of trade had deteriorated). They therefore decided to absorb the increases in the oil price and to refrain from using the higher rate of increase in the CPI as a basis for claiming higher prices and wages. In other words, it was decided not to pass on the cost increases due to the higher oil prices. By 1975, the Japanese inflation rate (based on the CPI) was back to 11,8 per cent and it declined further in subsequent years. The 23,2 per cent rate of increase in prices in 1974 thus cannot be regarded as a true reflection of inflation in Japan. It was rather the unavoidable consequence of the oil price shock and it did not result in a **process** of high inflation. Deciding to absorb the price increases by accepting lower living standards, rather than attempting to pass the increases on down the line, meant that Japanese society avoided the transformation of the price shock into a higher **process** of inflation.

But what typically happens in other countries, including South Africa? When import prices rise faster than export prices (ie when the terms of trade deteriorate - see Section 17.5) individuals and groups in society generally refuse to accept that they have, in effect, become poorer. Everyone tries to pass the increased costs on to someone else (eg in the form of higher prices or wages) and as a result the initial price increases are transformed into an inflation process.

This example illustrates that it is not the initiating factors (whatever they may be) that cause the inflation **process**. The process depends on how the individuals and groups in society react to the initial impulse. When import prices increase, as in the Japanese case, it is often said that the country is "importing" inflation. This is not true. Import prices can increase (as a result of price increases elsewhere and/or because of a depreciation of the domestic currency against the major currencies), but the **process** of inflation cannot be imported. Inflation in South Africa, for example, is made in South Africa, by South Africans for South Africans. Proudly South African!

ating factors come in. Broadly speaking, three sets of propagating factors can be distinguished. The first is the *various interrelationships that exist between prices, wages and profits* in the economy. In this regard, economists often refer to price-wage, price-price, wage-price and wage-wage spirals. These spirals have their origin in the underlying factors, for example the structure or degree of competition in the goods markets and the labour market, and are explained by the statement (attributed to Harold Wilson) that one man's price (or income) increase is another man's price (or cost) increase. For example, if a trade union in a key industry succeeds with a claim for a wage increase well above the current inflation rate (and unrelated to any productivity increase), the costs of the firms in that industry increase. If prices in that industry are set on a cost-plus basis, it means that prices in that industry will also increase. The firms or consumers who purchase the industry's goods will experience cost increases and will try to pass those increases on to their customers or employers. Workers, for example, will demand higher wages, first, because prices have increased and, second, because the workers in the other industry have received high wage increases. Firms purchasing from the first industry will experience cost increases which will be exacerbated if their workers succeed with wage increases similar to those in the first industry, and so on. This simple and incomplete example gives some indication of how price or wage increases originating in a particular sector or industry can generate a **process** of inflation in the economy. Such a process will, of course, be facilitated by a practice of linking wages or prices to the CPI or any other price index (ie indexation – see Section 21.5) as well as by **expectations** of further inflation (once the process has taken root).

A second set of propagating factors (or elements of the inflationary transmission mechanism) is to be found in the *interaction between domestic prices, the balance of payments and the exchange rate*. Consider the following sequence of events: One of the domestic initiating factors (eg a sharp increase in wages) causes price increases in the domestic economy. This leads, through a process of substitution, to an increased demand for imports and/or a decreased demand for exports at the current exchange rate. Under a floating exchange rate regime, this could result in a vicious circle of exchange rate depreciation and domestic inflation. The initial trigger could also have been the depreciation of the currency (as happened in South Africa towards the end of 2001), which then results in higher import prices. If these higher prices are passed on to domestic consumers and they, in turn, claim higher wages to compensate for the higher prices (and succeed with such claims) the same type of vicious circle may ensue.

This brings us to the third, and often crucial, propagating factor, namely the *increase in the money supply*. Inflation is indeed "always and everywhere a monetary phenomenon," as Friedman claimed. But this is not really a meaningful statement. By definition, inflation can occur only in a money economy. It is impossible to have inflation in a moneyless (ie barter) economy. If there is no generally accepted medium of exchange, as in a barter economy, an increase in the price of one good implies that the price of another good has fallen. In such an economy a general increase in the price level is thus impossible. But this does not mean that we can ignore money. Inflation can be sustained only if the supply of money increases. The supply of money over a period has two components: the quantity of money (M) and the velocity of circulation of money (V). An increase in M and/or V is thus required to sustain the process of inflation. The monetarists assume that the quantity of money is exogenously determined by the monetary authorities (the central bank). They therefore believe that inflation can be halted by fixing the money supply. However, as we explained in Chapters 15 and 20, the money supply is determined by the interaction between the interest rate and the demand for money. In other words, the money supply is endogenous rather than exogenous. In terms of the structuralist approach to inflation, this means that expansions in the money supply tend to be part of the inflation process (ie endogenous) rather than directly under the control of the monetary authorities (ie exogenous).

The general policy implication of the structuralist approach is that inflation can be effectively combated only through a broad, coordinated anti-inflation strategy that is aimed at all three sets of factors in the inflation process. The contents of such a strategy will vary from country to country and even from time to time within a particular country. An important determinant of the strategy will be the nature of the underlying factors, in particular the degree of conflict or cohesion between the different interest groups and the degree of competition in the goods and factor markets. In some countries the structure of society and the economy is such that the vulnerability to inflation is quite low, while in other cases the vulnerability may be high. In South Africa, for example, the decline in inflation in the recent decade would have been impossible without the significant structural economic reforms that were implemented during this period (eg the liberalisation of international trade, the structural changes in government spending and taxation, the granting of independence to the South African Reserve Bank and other measures which increased the efficiency, the degree of competition and the competitiveness of the South African economy).

Most economists agree that the structuralist approach provides a useful **description** of the inflation **process**. Some argue, however, that it is too broad (or eclectic) and therefore does not provide an adequate **explanation** of inflation or an adequate basis for forecasting what might happen to inflation. This leads us to a fourth approach to inflation, which abstracts from the details of the inflation process, but focuses on what are regarded to be the fundamental **causes** of inflation. This is called the conflict approach to inflation.

The conflict approach to inflation

According to the **conflict approach**, inflation is a symptom of a fundamental disharmony in society which results in a continuous imbalance between the rate of growth in the real national income and the rate of growth of the total effective claims on this income. There is no consensus on the appropriate division or distribution of the national income. Neither the market mechanism nor the political process works with sufficient authority to balance the contributions and the claims of the various groups in the economy and society. The different economic and social groups together claim more income than is produced. Moreover, each group has the economic or political bargaining power to raise its money income. The rival interest groups each strive to gain larger shares of the "pie" by claiming higher money incomes, and this results in inflation.

Although inflation is essentially a dynamic process, it is easier to explain the salient features of the conflict approach with the aid of a simple, comparative-static model.

Each of the different interest groups in society (eg trade unions, other employee organisations, large firms, business organisations, professional associations, bureaucrats and politicians) has a certain degree of economic and/or political power which governs its **effective** claims on the national income.[2] Suppose that there is no economic and/or political mechanism which guarantees a balance between the claims on the national income and the contributions to the national income. Put differently, there is no mechanism which guarantees *ex ante* equilibrium between the total effective claims and contributions at the existing price level.[3] This is illustrated in Figure 21-3(a).

Since there is no reason why contributions should increase in response to such an *ex ante* imbalance, there are only two possible equilibrating forces (*ex post*): an increase in net imports (to supplement the domestic contributions) and/or an increase in prices (ie inflation). Any increase in imports will have to be financed through an equivalent net inflow of foreign capital, decrease in net foreign reserves or a combination of the two. If we disregard this (non-sustainable) option, the only remaining equilibrating mechanism at the aggregate level is an increase in the price level (ie inflation). This can be viewed either as an increase in the **nominal** value of the national product (to equate the nominal income with the claims on that income) or as a decrease in the **real** value of the effective income claims (to equate the real claims with the real value of the product). In other words, in the first case the value of the product is inflated by price increases and in the second case the value of the claims is deflated by price increases. In the latter case, the interest groups still receive the nominal amounts they claimed, but the real value of those amounts is eroded by inflation. The two equilibrating possibilities, which amount to exactly the same thing, are illustrated in Figure 21-3(b) and (c) respectively.

To summarise: According to the conflict approach, inflation is the symptom of a lack of effective economic and/or political mechanisms to achieve a prior (*ex ante*) reconciliation of the conflicting claims on the national income.

The broad policy implication of this approach is that the only real remedy for inflation lies in the creation of an effective mechanism to achieve an *ex ante* reconciliation of the competing claims on the national income. This points to the need for some form of anti-inflationary incomes policy. Incomes policies are discussed towards the end of the next chapter.

FIGURE 21-3 A simplified view of the conflict approach

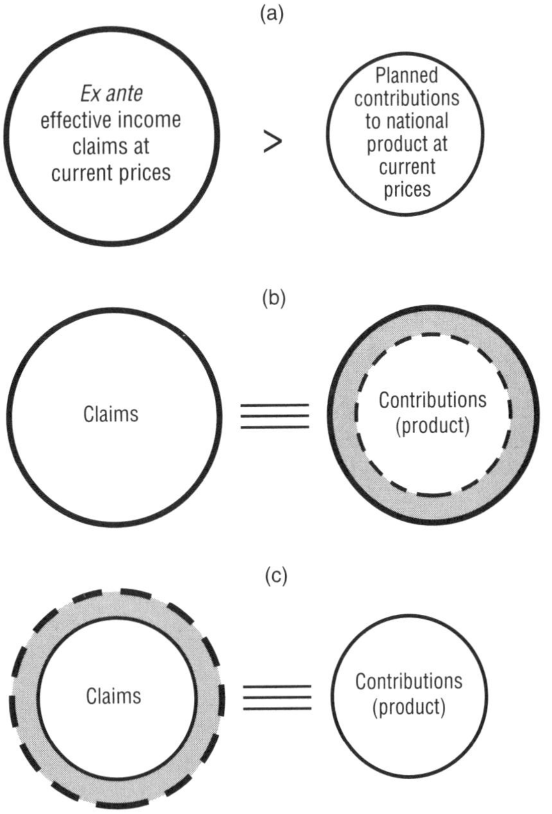

An ex ante *imbalance between effective claims and contributions (at current prices) is shown in (a). The* ex post *position is shown in (b) and (c). Equality is restored* ex post *through price increases (inflation). This can be viewed either as a nominal increase in the value of the product (contributions) or as a real decrease in the value of the effective claims. In (b) the shaded area represents the nominal increase in the value of the product due to price increases (inflation). In (c) the shaded area represents the real decrease in the value of the effective claims due to price increases (inflation).*

21.5 Anti-inflation policy

The broad policy implications of the various approaches to inflation have already been indicated. **Monetarists** want the central bank to control inflation by controlling the rate of increase in the money supply. They believe that inflation can be avoided by restricting the rate of increase in the money supply to a rate approximately equal to the growth in real output. The first problem with such a policy prescription, however, is that the money supply is not exogenously determined or controlled by the central bank (at least not in South Africa). Moreover, even if it were technically possible to control the rate of increase in the quantity of money, it does not necessarily follow that a restrictive monetary policy will affect only nominal variables such as inflation. Output, employment and

2. Note that the claims have to be effective, that is, they have to be backed up by some kind of power. We all want everything, but in order to get something we must have the means to do so.
3. Recall, from footnote 1 in Chapter 7, that *ex ante* (before the fact) refers to plans and *ex post* (after the fact) to events that have already occurred.

other real variables might also be affected. A related problem is that the velocity of circulation of money is probably not as stable as the monetarists would have us believe.

In terms of the **demand-pull versus cost-push approach**, the appropriate anti-inflation policy will depend on the type of inflation being experienced. In the case of **demand-pull inflation**, the appropriate response would be to apply contractionary (or restrictive) monetary and fiscal policies, raising the interest rate and tax rates and reducing the rate of increase in government spending. Such an approach would succeed in reducing inflation (or even the price level), but this would be achieved at the cost of lower production and income, and therefore higher unemployment. If **cost-push inflation** is being experienced, the situation is even more complex. Pure cost-push inflation by definition is already accompanied by a decline in production and income (and therefore an increase in unemployment). If contractionary monetary and fiscal policies are applied to combat such a type of inflation, the initial negative impact on production, income and employment will be reinforced, pushing the economy even deeper into recession. In principle, the appropriate response would be to increase aggregate supply, illustrated by a rightward (or downward) shift of the *AS* curve. One of the options is to apply an **incomes policy**, while another option is to apply the policy recommendations of the supply-side economists – see Section 22.3.

The **structuralist approach** and the **conflict approach** also point to the need for an incomes policy to combat inflation. Incomes policies, however, are subject to various practical problems, which we discuss towards the end of Chapter 22.

In the remainder of this section we first indicate the importance of taking account of the possible **costs of anti-inflation policy**. This is followed by a brief discussion of **indexation** as a means of coping with inflation. Finally, we outline the policy of **inflation targeting**, the current monetary policy framework in South Africa and also the cornerstone of the government's anti-inflation strategy.

The costs of anti-inflation policy

In Section 21.3 we outlined some of the negative effects (or costs) of inflation. Inflation is undoubtedly a problem and everyone would prefer a low inflation rate (preferably zero). But this does not necessarily mean that the elimination of inflation should be the most important (or the only) objective of macroeconomic policy. Other macroeconomic policy objectives such as economic growth, full employment and balance of payments stability are also important, and the possible impact of anti-inflation policy on these objectives therefore also has to be taken into account. Before deciding on the appropriate steps to combat inflation, policymakers should therefore consider the following:

- the nature of the inflation being experienced
- the possible interrelationships between inflation and other objectives or problems such as economic growth and unemployment
- the possible costs of failing to achieve other objectives such as economic growth and full employment
- the benefits of a reduction in the inflation rate (bearing in mind that a marginal reduction is often the only realistic possibility)
- the possible costs or side-effects of the policy measures that are to be implemented in the attempt to reduce the inflation rate to the desired level

When these things are considered, it becomes less obvious that everything possible should be done to combat inflation. The priority accorded to the fight against inflation will depend, among other things, on the nature of the particular inflation process and on the scope for implementing appropriate anti-inflation policy. In certain circumstances it might even be better to err on the permissive side, rather than to place too much emphasis on the fight against inflation. There is always the danger that inappropriate anti-inflation policies may be applied that could cause greater damage to the economy and society than the inflation which they were supposed to combat.

Indexation

In some countries the fight against inflation proved particularly difficult and various institutional measures designed to counteract the negative effects of inflation as far as possible were implemented. If it is not possible to stop inflation, it was argued, one can at least attempt to reduce its consequences. The most important compensatory measure introduced was indexation. **Indexation** means that prices, wages, pensions and so on are linked to price indices (for example, the CPI) to eliminate the distribution effects of inflation.

Formal indexation has been applied in countries like Brazil and Israel. When the inflation rate rises to very high levels (say 100 per cent or more), governments often have no alternative but to introduce indexation in all spheres of the economy in an attempt to counteract the distribution effects of inflation. Formal indexation can help communities to cope with high inflation or hyper-inflation in the short run. Unfortunately, it simultaneously impedes the fight against inflation since indexation means that today's price increases serve as the basis for tomorrow's price increases. It also reduces the pressure on government to take effective steps against inflation. Indexation should therefore only be resorted to in emergency conditions.

Inflation targeting

In Chapter 15 we pointed out that inflation targeting is a possible framework for monetary policy and that South Africa adopted this framework in 2000. In this section we provide more information on inflation targeting and we examine how it has been applied in the South African context.

In his budget speech in February 2000, the Minister of Finance announced that South Africa was to become the 15th country to adopt **formal** inflation targeting as its monetary policy framework.

■ WHAT IS INFLATION TARGETING?

Inflation targeting has five essential features. The *first* is the public announcement of quantitative inflation targets. Before the target can be announced, a number of decisions have to be taken, for example: Who should determine the target? What index should be used to calculate the target? Should the target be a specific inflation rate (ie a point target) or should the aim be to achieve an inflation rate within a certain range of possible rates (ie a target range)? Over what period should the target be achieved?

The *second* feature of an inflation-targeting framework is the acceptance by government that the primary goal of monetary policy (and therefore of the central bank) is to achieve price stability (ie to combat inflation). Coupled with this, the central bank should be operationally independent, that is, it should have the freedom to use the instruments of monetary policy as it deems fit in its attempt to achieve the inflation target.

The *third* feature is the use of a wide range of variables, and not just monetary aggregates or the exchange rate, to decide on the appropriate setting of the policy instruments (eg the repo rate).

The *fourth* feature is increased transparency, which implies that the central bank should regularly inform the public and the markets about its plans, objectives and decisions.

The *fifth* feature is that the central bank should be held accountable (eg to Parliament and the public at large) for attaining its inflation objectives.

The key features are thus:

- the announcement of quantitative targets
- the primacy of price stability as the objective of monetary policy
- a broad-based, pragmatic approach to the analysis of inflation
- transparency
- accountability

■ THE CASE FOR INFLATION TARGETING

The case for inflation targeting is essentially based on the view that the complex transmission mechanism of monetary policy (see Figure 20-7), the varying lags and strengths of effects through different channels, unpredictable shocks and inherent uncertainty combine to prevent the use of monetary policy for fine-tuning. Under an inflation-targeting framework there are limits to the discretionary powers of the central bank. Discretion is still regarded as essential, but it is constrained by the framework. Inflation targeting is thus often described as "constrained discretion". Many of the benefits of inflation targeting arise from the forward-looking nature of the framework and the constraints it places on central bank behaviour.

More specifically, the following **advantages** have been ascribed to inflation targeting:

- It is easily understandable, with the policy objective formulated in the form of an explicit quantitative target – this makes the framework extremely transparent.
- It makes it very clear that monetary policy is aimed at achieving price stability – this reduces uncertainty and enhances sound planning in both the private and public sectors.
- By providing an explicit yardstick, it serves to discipline monetary policy and improve the accountability of the central bank.
- It eliminates the need to identify and rely on a stable relationship between changes in the money supply and inflation.
- It enhances the coordination of economic policy since both the government and the central bank are publicly committed to the same inflation target.
- It serves as an anchor or coordination device for inflation expectations, particularly with regard to price and wage determination, thereby avoiding or reducing the problems arising from widely differing inflation expectations.
- By affecting inflationary expectations it can also help to reduce inflation.
- It reduces the danger of serious policy errors, particularly a tendency to overreact to short-term economic developments (eg exchange rate crises).
- It limits the discretion of the governor of the central bank in so far as important decisions have to be taken after consultation with a committee of experts – in other words, it provides a guide for the operational conduct of monetary policy.
- It commits policymakers to sound fundamentals.

Some potential **disadvantages** should also be noted:

- It is a complicated approach which relies heavily on forecasts in an uncertain economic environment.
- If forecasts turn out to be wrong, the central bank's credibility could be impaired.
- A major problem is how to react to external economic shocks – if the central bank tries to counter-

act the possible effects of such shocks on inflation it may apply too-stringent policy measures, thereby reducing economic growth and employment; on the other hand if the bank uses an escape clause to avoid doing this, it may lose credibility if inflation exceeds the pre-announced target.

- Many elements of the inflation process are beyond the control of the central bank. For example, it will be difficult for the SARB to control inflation if government raises administered prices sharply, if government spending is out of control or if trade unions succeed with demands for high wage increases. In such circumstances the inflation-targeting framework might lose its credibility. On the other hand, if the SARB is faced with such problems but nevertheless tries to achieve the target at all costs, the implications for economic growth and unemployment could be severe. In the final analysis, inflation can only be combated effectively if all stakeholders cooperate.

INFLATION TARGETING IN SOUTH AFRICA

As mentioned earlier, the Minister of Finance announced the adoption of an inflation-targeting framework for monetary policy in South Africa in 2000. The initial target, set by the Minister in consultation with the SARB, was to achieve an average inflation rate of between six and three per cent in 2002. South Africa thus opted for a target *range* rather than a *point* target. The time horizon chosen was approximately two years, with the target being revised every year on a rolling basis. This was in line with international thinking that the long and variable lags associated with monetary policy require a horizon of at least 18 months. As explained earlier, the target variable chosen was the rate of increase in the CPIX, that is, the consumer price index (CPI) for metropolitan and other urban areas, excluding mortgage interest rates. The SARB uses the repo rate as its policy instrument and this rate is set by the Governor of the SARB in consultation with the Bank's Monetary Policy Committee (MPC). The MPC consists of the governor, deputy governors and a few senior bank officials who meet on a regular basis. At its meetings the MPC considers a wide range of economic information, including the latest forecasts prepared by SARB staff. Once a decision is taken, it is announced immediately in a press statement that also sets out the reasons for the decision. In addition, a *Monetary Policy Review* is published every six months (in May and November), providing a more detailed analysis of monetary policy and inflation. Regular meetings are also held with various interested parties, including organised business, organised labour and private sector and academic economists. The Governor of the SARB reports regularly to the Parliamentary Portfolio Committee on Finance and also frequently explains the SARB's policy stance in the media and in public addresses.

When inflation targeting was introduced in South Africa, the annual rate of increase in the CPIX was about 7 per cent (ie above the target range). The rate accelerated somewhat during the second half of 2000 and on 17 October the SARB raised the repo rate by 25 basis points, from 11,75 per cent to 12 per cent. When the CPIX inflation rate subsequently declined in 2001, the repo rate was reduced on three occasions, to 11 per cent on 15 June, to 10 per cent on 5 September and to 9,5 per cent on 21 September (in the wake of the terrorist attack on the World Trade Centre). At that stage the annual rate of increase in the CPIX was slightly below 6 per cent, but it soon accelerated following the massive depreciation of thc rand against the major currencies towards the end of 2001. By December CPIX inflation had increased to 6,6 per cent and on 16 January 2002 the SARB raised the repo rate by 100 basis points (to 10,5 per cent). Inflation continued to accelerate, however, and the SARB again raised the repo rate by 100 basis points on a further three occasions in 2002 (to 11,5 per cent on 15 March, to 12,5 per cent on 14 June and to 13,5 per cent on 13 September). The rate of increase in the CPIX reached a peak of 12,7 per cent in November 2002 and subsequently started to decline. In September 2003 the annual rate of increase in the CPIX moved into the target range, but for the year as a whole the target was still not achieved. In November 2003 it was decided to move from an annual average target range to a continuous target of 3 to 6 per cent for the period beyond 2006. The main reason for moving away from a calendar-year average target was that it complicated communication. By changing to a continuous target, South Africa also came into line with ruling international practice. It is important to note, however, that a continuous target does not mean that the SARB must react if the inflation rate moves outside the target range. It is not the current inflation rate that is important in making policy decisions in an inflation-targeting framework, but the expected future trend of inflation.

The repo rate was reduced on five occasions in 2003 by a total of 5,5 percentage points (or 550 basis points), and by a further 50 basis points in each of 2004 and 2005. In 2006, however, the rate was increased on four occasions (by a total of 200 basis points). The favourable inflation performance was maintained through 2004, 2005 and 2006 and in March 2007 the rate of increase in the CPIX was still in the target range.

Although there had initially been some serious misgivings about the decision to adopt an inflation-targeting framework, most observers later tended to agree that the decision had been appropriate.

IMPORTANT CONCEPTS

Inflation
Consumer price index
Headline inflation
Core inflation
CPIX inflation
Production price index
GDP deflator
Distribution effects
Real interest rate
Bracket creep
Fiscal dividend
Economic effects
Social and political effects
Hyperinflation
Deflation
Quantity theory
Equation of exchange
Velocity of circulation
Demand-pull inflation
Cost-push inflation
Stagflation
Incomes policy
Underlying factors
Initiating factors
Propagating factors
Conflict approach
Effective claims
Indexation
Inflation targeting

REVIEW QUESTIONS

1. Explain the difference between the headline CPI, core CPI and CPIX.
2. What are the main similarities and differences between the CPI, the production price index (PPI) and the GDP deflator?
3. Discuss the following statement: "Maize is becoming more expensive; therefore we are experiencing inflation."
4. Can the inflation rate (a) decrease when prices in the economy are increasing and (b) increase when some prices in the economy are falling? Explain.
5. Is there any difference between the consumer price index (CPI) and the inflation rate? Explain.
6. What are the main costs (or consequences) of inflation? Should the South African Reserve Bank do everything in its power to combat inflation?
7. If all wages are indexed to inflation (ie if all wage increases are equal to the rate of increase in prices), would inflation still be a problem?
8. Which will be the most costly: a steady inflation rate of 5 per cent per year or an inflation rate that is sometimes high and sometimes low but averages 5 per cent per year over a 10-year period? Substantiate your viewpoint.
9. Why does the combination of inflation and a progressive tax system tend to redistribute income from taxpayers to the government? What is this phenomenon called?
10. What assumptions have to be made to transform the equation (or equality) of exchange into the quantity theory of money?
11. Explain how monetarists explain inflation.
12. Use an example to explain the velocity of circulation of money.
13. Use diagrams to explain the difference between demand-pull inflation and cost-push inflation.
14. Explain the difference between the underlying, initiating and propagating factors in the inflation process.

15. Explain the essence of the conflict approach to inflation.
16. Why is it difficult to distinguish between demand-pull inflation and cost-push inflation in practice?
17. Explain how the South African Reserve Bank tries to control or reduce inflation in South Africa.
18. What are the most important advantages of inflation targeting as a monetary policy framework?

22

Unemployment and the Phillips curve

Learning outcomes

Once you have studied this chapter, you should be able to

- Describe the costs of unemployment
- Distinguish between different types of unemployment
- Discuss the policies that can be used to reduce unemployment
- Explain what the Phillips curve means and how it is related to the aggregate supply curve
- Explain how an incomes policy can be used to combat stagflation

A man willing to work, and unable to find work, is perhaps the saddest sight that Fortune's inequality exhibits under this sun.

THOMAS CARLYLE

The rate of unemployment is 100 per cent if it is you that is unemployed.

ANONYMOUS

I believe that what looks like involuntary unemployment is involuntary unemployment.

ROBERT SOLOW

In this chapter we take a closer look at unemployment and the possible trade-off between unemployment and inflation. Unemployment is undoubtedly the most important economic problem in South Africa. We have already introduced and discussed it at various places in this book. In this chapter we expand on our previous discussions and we also consider the relationship between unemployment and inflation, which are often referred to as the twin evils of macroeconomics.

The first section of the chapter deals with unemployment. We discuss the **costs of unemployment** and distinguish between four different **types of unemployment**. This is followed by brief discussions of **unemployment in the context of our macroeconomic models** and **policies to reduce unemployment**. The second section focuses on whether or not there is any **relationship between unemployment and inflation**. We introduce the **Phillips curve**, which points to an inverse relationship between unemployment and inflation, and show how it is related to the aggregate supply curve. Shifts of the Phillips curve are explained and finally some **policies** to deal with the unemployment-inflation trade-off are discussed.

22.1 Unemployment

Unemployment is one of those things which everybody understands but which turns out to be quite difficult to define and to measure. Everyone knows that unemployment is a bad thing – for society as well as for the unemployed. We also know that a person who is searching for a job but cannot find one is unemployed. But what about a person who is not actively seeking work? What about someone who only has a part-time job or who is employed only for certain weeks or months of the year? And what about someone who makes a living either legally or illegally in the informal sector? If you pause to think about these problems, you will understand why researchers find it difficult to define and to measure unemployment. You will also understand why estimates of unemployment sometimes differ quite significantly.

The unemployment pool

The level or rate of unemployment is a **stock** concept, that is, it is measured at a particular date. The rate of unemployment is obtained by expressing the number of unemployed persons as a percentage of the labour force (ie the number of people who are willing and able to work, also called the economically active population, or EAP). There are, however, continuous **flows** in and out of unemployment as people enter and leave the **unemployment pool**.

A person may enter the unemployment pool for one of four reasons. First, the person may be a new entrant into the labour force, looking for work for the first time, or a re-entrant – someone returning to the labour force after not having looked for work for some time. Second, a person may leave a job in order to look for other employment and will be counted as unemployed while searching. Third, the person may be laid off. A lay-off means that the worker is not fired but might return to the old job if the demand for the firm's product recovers. Finally, a worker may lose a job to which there is no chance of returning, either on account of being retrenched (or fired) or because the firm closes down.

These sources of inflow into the pool of unemployment have a counterpart in the outflow from the unemployment pool. Apart from dying, there are essentially three ways of moving out of the pool. First, a person may be hired. Second, someone laid off may be recalled. Third, an unemployed person may become discouraged and stop looking for a job and thus, by definition, leave the labour force.

Measuring unemployment

In principle, data on unemployment can be obtained in various ways. A first option is to use official census data, but censuses are only conducted every five years and there is a significant lag before the detailed data are published. A second option is to use data on registered unemployment. In South Africa, however, such data are not very significant, since only a small portion of the unemployed register as such (mainly only those who qualify for unemployment benefits). Moreover, since September 1998 the Department of Labour no longer publishes data on registered unemployment in South Africa. A third option is to subtract the number of persons who are (a) formally employed, (b) engaged in the informal sector and (c) engaged in subsistence agriculture from the EAP. This yields the estimated number of unemployed people and this number can then be expressed as a percentage of the EAP to arrive at an unemployment rate. The final and most popular option is to use the official estimates of the unemployment rate published by Stats SA. Even in this instance, however, there is still some controversy about whether the strict or expanded definition of unemployment should be used. According to the **strict definition**, unemployed persons are those persons who, being 15 years and older, (a) are not in paid employment or self-employment, (b) were available for paid employment or self-employment during the seven days preceding the interview and (c) took specific steps during the four weeks preceding the interview to find paid employment or self-employment. The **expanded definition**, on the other hand, omits requirement (c). In other words, the expanded definition requires only a *desire* to find employment. Prior to 1994, the strict definition was used by Stats SA to estimate unemployment in South Africa, with the result that the official estimates were generally regarded as being too low. Stats SA subsequently switched to the expanded definition, but some observers (including the International Labour Office) regarded the new official estimates as being too high. In June 1998 Stats SA reverted to using the strict definition as the official definition, although estimates based on the expanded definition are also published. Table 22-1 indicates the estimated unemployment rates in South Africa from 1994 to 2006.

We shall not deal with the definition and measurement of unemployment any further in this chapter. Irrespective of how it is defined or measured, there is no doubt that South Africa is suffering from high unemployment. It is the most serious social and economic problem facing the country. In this section we deal with some of the costs of unemployment, different types of unemployment and some of the policies that can be applied in an attempt to reduce unemployment. We also explain how unemployment is treated in our macroeconomic models.

The costs of unemployment

Unemployment entails significant costs – to the individuals who are unemployed as well as to society at large.

TABLE 22-1 Unemployment in South Africa (expressed as a percentage of the labour force), 1994–2006

Month and year	*Strict definition*	*Expanded definition*
October 1994	20,3	32,6
October 1995	16,5	29,3
October 1996	20,3	34,4
October 1997	22,0	37,4
October 1998	25,2	37,5
October 1999	23,3	36,2
September 2000	25,8	35,9
September 2001	29,4	41,5
September 2002	30,4	41,8
September 2003	28,0	42,0
September 2004	26,2	41,0
September 2005	26,7	38,8
September 2006	25,5	37,3

Sources: 1994–1999: Statistics South Africa, *October Household Survey*
2000–2006: Statistics South Africa, *Labour Force Survey*

The **individual** who becomes unemployed suffers a loss of income, shock and frustration. In certain circumstances unemployment can result in hunger, cold, ill health and even death. In the industrial countries the private or individual costs of unemployment have been considerably reduced by the availability of unemployment benefits and other social welfare programmes. In South Africa, however, the social security system is not nearly as extensive and well developed as in the major industrial countries. Unemployment benefits are moderate and are generally available only to workers who have contributed to unemployment insurance schemes. Many people do not have access to unemployment benefits, and those who do receive benefits for a limited period only.

But even the best system of unemployment benefits cannot entirely eliminate the costs of unemployment. The unemployed also suffer psychological costs: enforced joblessness is demoralising and results in a loss of confidence and self-esteem. Increased unemployment tends to result in an increase in psychological disorders, divorces, suicides and criminal activity.

Unemployment also means a loss of experience and human development. Workers become unaccustomed to using their skills and may even lose them. When they apply for a position, workers who have lost their jobs may find it difficult to compete with others who are simply changing jobs or who are entering the labour market for the first time. Moreover, unemployment does not refer only to people who have lost their jobs. It also includes people who have never been able to find employment. This is arguably the most serious aspect of unemployment in South Africa. If new entrants to the labour market cannot find a job, they often have to resort to crime to survive. After surviving for a number of years without a job they may eventually become unemployable.

Unemployment is always a **loss to society**. Unlike other factors of production, labour cannot be saved and used later. If labour is not used when it is available it is lost forever. Unemployment is also damaging to the social and political structure. It tends to give rise to crime as well as to demonstrations, riots and other violent forms of unrest. In South Africa there appears to be a definite correlation between criminal, social and political violence and the level of unemployment. Unemployment can also lead to the overthrow of democratic institutions and processes. Some observers argue, for example, that Hitler would not have risen to power in Germany if the country had not been experiencing massive unemployment at the time.

Unemployment benefits and other social welfare programmes to assist the unemployed also entail significant financial costs as well as opportunity costs (since other spending possibilities have to be sacrificed). When unemployment is high, large amounts of money are required to support the unemployed, and spending on public goods and services has to be sacrificed.

Types of unemployment

There are various types of unemployment. The most basic distinction is between **voluntary** and **involuntary** unemployment, but this classification can be questioned. In Chapter 14 we pointed out that people who do not want to work are not regarded as part of the labour force. Accordingly, they cannot be classified as unemployed. The unemployment rate is expressed as the percentage of the labour force (ie people who are willing and able to work) who cannot find a job. Strictly speaking, all unemployment should therefore be classified as involuntary unemployment.

Economists usually distinguish between frictional unemployment, seasonal unemployment, structural unemployment and cyclical (or demand-deficiency) unemployment.

Frictional unemployment (sometimes also called search unemployment) arises because it takes time to find a job or to move from one job to another. At any particular time there will always be workers who are moving from one job to another. Individuals who leave one job, or who are looking for a first job, often do not find employment immediately, although there are vacancies in the economy. This kind of unemployment is unavoidable and is not considered a serious problem. In societies in which people are free to move from job to job, there will always be some frictional unemployment. Moreover, unemployment for any particular individual is temporary. As some individuals find jobs, others quit to look for new jobs and still others enter the labour force. The composition of frictional unemployment changes the whole time.

Seasonal unemployment arises because certain occupations require workers only for part of each year. This includes activities such as picking and processing fruit and vegetables which have particular growing seasons. Some tourist regions or resorts also have more jobs available during peak seasons – the summer season in the Western Cape is a good example. Certain jobs are also linked to increased sales activity during the Christmas and Easter periods. Father Christmases, for example, are employed only during the Christmas season. People who depend on seasonal occupations are often unemployed for part of the year. They are then classified as seasonally unemployed.

Cyclical (or **demand-deficiency) unemployment** occurs when a slump or recession in the economy (as a result of a temporary lack of demand) gives rise to unemployment. Aggregate demand in the economy does not increase smoothly. Periods of rapid increase in aggregate demand (called booms) are followed by periods of slower increase or decline (called recessions). This phenomenon is called the **business cycle** – see the discussion of the business cycle in Section 23.2. When the economy experiences a recession there is a general downturn in economic activity. Sales drop and some workers lose their jobs because there is **insufficient demand** for the goods and services they produce. However, when aggregate demand increases again the reverse happens and unemployment falls.

Structural unemployment is somewhat more complex. Whereas cyclical unemployment is related to fluctuations in the general state of the economy (ie to the business cycle), structural unemployment is usually confined to certain industries, sectors or categories of workers. Structural unemployment occurs when there is a mismatch between worker qualifications and job requirements or when jobs disappear because of structural changes in the economy. Consider the following examples:

- Certain workers **lack** the necessary **education, training** or **skills** required to obtain a job, even when the economy is booming.
- Changes in **production methods** or **techniques** can cause a drop in the demand for people with particular qualifications or skills. Nowadays machines can perform many tasks which previously required qualified or skilled people. For example, the introduction of automatic teller machines reduced the number of job opportunities for bank tellers. Automation has also resulted in the loss of many jobs in the manufacturing sector. People who are replaced by labour-saving machines are sometimes classified as **technologically unemployed**.
- Changes in the types of goods and services being produced (eg as a result of **changing consumer preferences**) can also cause unemployment. For example, a fall in the demand for cigarettes because of the health risk associated with smoking can lead to unemployment in the tobacco industry.
- **Foreign competition** can also result in a loss of jobs. For example, the growth of the highly competitive textile and clothing industries in Asia has destroyed many jobs in the textile and clothing industries in the industrial countries (as well as in South Africa). Generally speaking, the increased foreign competition as a result of trade liberalisation and globalisation resulted in many South Africans becoming unemployed.
- Jobs can also be lost as a result of a **structural decline in certain industries**. In South Africa, for example, the closure of gold mines and the general decline in gold production has destroyed many job opportunities.
- **Discrimination** can also cause unemployment. In South Africa many jobs were reserved for whites during the apartheid era. Qualified people from other population groups did not have access to these jobs. By contrast, since the mid-1990s affirmative action (or employment equity) has caused unemployment among qualified, skilled and experienced people who happened to belong to a particular race group.

Structural unemployment is a serious problem for which there are no easy solutions. Workers who are structurally unemployed often have to be trained or retrained, or they have to be moved to locations where their experience, qualifications or skills are in demand.

Some examples of the different types of unemployment are provided in Box 22-1.

Policies to reduce unemployment

When there are not enough jobs available for everyone who is willing and able to work, there is unemployment. When the growth in the labour force is greater than the growth in the number of job opportunities, unemployment increases. In South Africa the rapid increase in the unemployment rate in the past two decades originated from the **supply side** of the labour market as well as from the **demand side**. A large number of workers (approximately 350 000) entered the labour market each year, but few new job opportunities were created in a stagnating and declining economy. South Africa's unemployment problem therefore stems from both a rapid increase in the supply of labour and a constant, slowly growing or declining demand for labour. To combat unemploy-

BOX 22-1 THE DIFFERENT TYPES OF UNEMPLOYMENT: SOME EXAMPLES

The following examples may assist you in understanding the different types of unemployment:

- Jack Skwambane resigns from his occupation as a clerk with the Germiston City Council to look for a better job. Until he finds a new job, Jack is **frictionally unemployed**.
- Lucy Tomlinson works as a tourist guide on the Cape Wine Route during the summer months. For the rest of the year she is **seasonally unemployed**.
- Joseph Goodman is a nuclear scientist who was employed by the Atomic Energy Corporation (AEC) in its uranium enrichment division. When the AEC decided to close its uranium enrichment plant (after sanctions had been lifted) Joseph became **structurally unemployed**.
- Paula van der Merwe is a factory worker who was employed by Defy Industries. During the recession of the late 1990s Defy reduced its work force because of the fall in sales of household appliances. Paula was among those who were retrenched. She became **cyclically unemployed**. She expected to be employed again when economic activity and appliance sales picked up.

ment, steps need to be taken to limit the supply of labour and to stimulate the demand for labour.

On the **supply side**, rapid population growth can be a significant cause of unemployment. Steps taken to limit **population growth** can thus be regarded as part of the strategy to reduce unemployment. However, this is at best a long-term strategy. At any particular time, the next generation of entrants to the labour market have already been born. Nevertheless, any decrease in the birth rate will eventually result in a decrease in the rate of growth of the labour force. In South Africa the rate of population growth has declined significantly in recent years as a result of the HIV/Aids pandemic and this impact is projected to escalate during the current decade. Some cynics may regard this as a "natural" solution to the unemployment problem. However, apart from the strong moral objections to such an attitude, account has to be taken of the fact that many of the victims are experienced and skilled people whose loss reduces the productive capacity of the economy. Moreover, any decline in the growth (or even the level) of the domestic population can be negated by a net increase in **immigration**. This is a particularly serious problem in South Africa, since many unemployed workers from other sub-Saharan countries and others seeking their fortunes in South Africa enter the country legally or illegally in pursuit of employment and income. Stricter immigration control can therefore also be regarded as an element of a policy strategy to reduce unemployment.

Other relevant features of the supply of labour in South Africa are the **shortage of skills** and the **oversupply of unskilled and semi-skilled labour**. There is too much of the wrong type of labour. Even when the aggregate demand for goods and services (and therefore also for labour) is low, there are always vacancies for people with certain technical or professional skills or qualifications. On the other hand, people with no training or skills have difficulty finding employment, even when there is an excess demand for skilled workers. Any strategy to reduce unemployment in South Africa must therefore include policies to improve the quality of labour, for example through education and training.

On the **demand side**, additional employment opportunities can be created by raising the aggregate demand for goods and services and increasing the labour intensity of production. If more goods and services have to be produced, more job opportunities will be created and the greater the labour intensity of production, the more favourable the ratio between the growth in output and the growth in labour demand will be.

Government can, of course, always raise the aggregate demand for goods and services by spending more. But increased **government spending** has to be financed. If it is financed by raising taxes, private consumption and investment spending may fall, thus negating the positive impact of the increase in government spending. If it is financed through borrowing, interest rates will tend to rise and this will tend to dampen consumption and investment spending. If it is financed by increasing the money supply, the result will probably be inflation.

Another possible option is to stimulate **consumption** and **investment** spending by lowering taxes or interest rates. However, any excessive stimulation of domestic demand will result in inflation or balance of payments problems. There are thus definite limits to the extent to which domestic demand can be stimulated to reduce unemployment.

A more promising strategy would be to raise the demand for domestically produced goods and services by increasing the demand for **exports**. This is, however, easier said than done, since the demand for exports originates in the rest of the world. But steps have to be taken to increase the country's international competitiveness, for example by maintaining a realistic exchange rate and keeping domestic costs of production in check.

Apart from stimulating aggregate demand in the economy, steps can also be taken to increase the **labour intensity of production**. The idea here is to promote types of economic activity which are relatively labour intensive. It is often argued, for example, that government spending on housing will create more jobs than most other forms of government spending, both directly and through the linkages between the construction sector and the rest of the economy. The government can also embark on **special employment programmes** that are aimed at employing as many people as possible to build and maintain roads, build dams, clean the environment, develop new agricultural land and so on. Such programmes can, however, only be regarded as emergency measures. They are expensive and do not constitute a lasting solution to unemployment.

Another possible avenue is to promote **small businesses** and the **informal sector**. It is often claimed that small businesses are much more labour intensive than larger enterprises and that the promotion of such businesses will thus raise employment (and reduce unemployment). Yet another possibility is **tax incentives or subsidies** to stimulate employment. The idea is that employers will receive tax benefits or subsidies if they employ more people. However, such incentives have a number of drawbacks and are often abused. In South Africa, for example, firms hired people at very low wages simply to claim the subsidies.

Attempts to stimulate labour intensity will have sustained benefits only if the **relative price of labour** is kept within certain limits. One of the reasons for the increased capital intensity of production in South Africa (illustrated in Table 5-13) was an increase in the cost of labour (wages) relative to the cost of capital (interest). When interest rates are low and wages are increasing rapidly, as was the case in South Africa at some stages during the 1970s, there is an incentive for employers to do whatever they can to replace workers with machines. This trend is strengthened when there is a high incidence of strike activity among workers. Unless wage rates remain realistic and strike activity is kept within reasonable limits, other attempts at creating employment in the private sector are bound to fail.

Towards the end of the 20th century many observers argued that the **labour legislation** introduced in South Africa during the latter half of the 1990s had raised unemployment by making it more expensive and cumbersome for firms and other employers to continue to employ all their workers, or to employ more workers. They therefore recommended that the legislation be revised or relaxed to make it easier or cheaper for employers to maintain or expand employment and to dismiss or retrench workers, if necessary. This remains a highly controversial issue.

This brief discussion should give you some idea of the policies that can be applied to reduce unemployment, as well as of the possible pitfalls associated with some of the measures that are often proposed by politicians and other non-economists.

Unemployment in the Keynesian and AD-AS models

The Keynesian models of Chapters 18 and 19 and the *AD-AS* model of Chapter 20 did not explicitly include the level of employment or the level of unemployment. In these macroeconomic models we studied the forces that determine total real production or income (Y) in the economy and assumed that the **level** of employment is positively related to the **level** of production (or, in a dynamic sense, that the **growth** in employment is positively related to the **growth** in production). The relationship between the level of employment (N) and the level of real production (Y) can be illustrated by an aggregate **production function** as in Figure 22-1. The level of employment (N) is shown on the horizontal axis and the level of real production (Y) on the vertical axis. Since all other inputs (eg capital) are assumed to be fixed, this production function reflects the law of diminishing returns, that is, as employment (N) increases, real output (Y) also increases, but at a declining rate. The slope of this production function (which is equal to the marginal product of labour) thus declines as employment increases.

In Figure 22-1 full employment in the labour market is indicated by N_f and the corresponding full-employment level of production or income by Y_f. However, full employment will never be achieved in an absolute sense. As explained earlier, there will always be some frictional unemployment, while most types of structural unemployment will also not be eliminated by raising the level of production in the economy. For example, workers without the required skills or experience will tend to remain unemployed when the economy expands. Moreover, when production processes become more capital intensive (which can be illustrated by a leftward (or upward) shift of the production function in Figure 22-1), a higher level of output can be achieved without any increase in employment.

In a **dynamic** sense, an increase in production and employment also does not necessarily imply that the unemployment **rate** will decline, since the increase in employment may not be sufficient to accommodate all the **new entrants** into the labour market. Nevertheless, in the absence of any growth in real output there will probably not be any growth in employment, and therefore certainly an increase in unemployment.

FIGURE 22-1 An aggregate production function

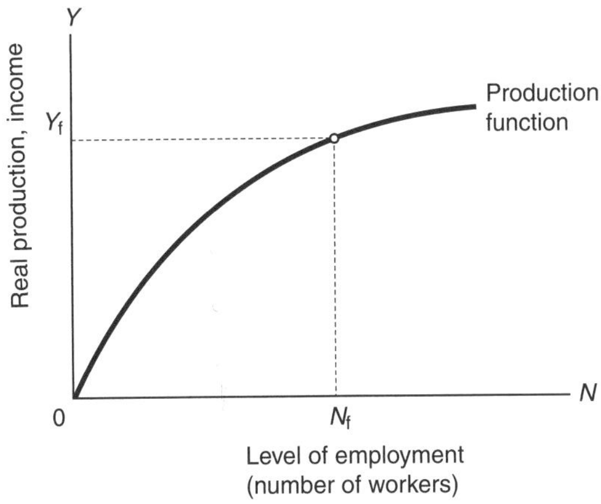

The production function shows the link between the level of real production Y and the level of employment N. Full employment in the labour market is indicated by N_f and the corresponding full-employment level of production or income by Y_f.

The upshot of all this is that **an increase in real production (ie economic growth) is a necessary but not sufficient condition for reducing unemployment**. This means that if real production (*Y*) increases, employment will not necessarily increase (and unemployment will not necessarily decrease), but if real production (*Y*) does *not* increase, employment will not increase (and unemployment will not decrease). However, since our comparative-static macroeconomic models cannot accommodate dynamic changes, it is still sensible to assume that an increase in real production (*Y*) will result in an increase in employment and that an increase in employment implies a decrease in unemployment.

22.2 Unemployment and inflation: the Phillips curve

In the *AD-AS* model, introduced in Section 20.1, an increase in aggregate demand (illustrated by a rightward shift of the *AD* curve) usually leads to an increase in production and income (*Y*) *and* a simultaneous increase in the price level (*P*). Similarly, a decrease in aggregate demand (illustrated by a lcftward shift of the *AD* curve) results in a decrease in production and income (*Y*) *and* a simultaneous decrease in the price level (*P*). Since the level of employment is related to the level of production, we expect employment to increase (and unemployment to fall) when production increases. Likewise, we expect employment to fall (and unemployment to increase) when the level of production falls. This suggests that there may be a relationship between changes in prices (ie inflation) and changes in unemployment. The links between aggregate demand, production, prices and employment in the *AD-AS* model are summarised in Table 22-2.

TABLE 22-2 Aggregate demand, production, prices and unemployment

Change in aggregate demand AD	Impact on Production Y	Price level P	Unemployment U
Increase	Increase	Increase	Decrease
Decrease	Decrease	Decrease	Increase

From Table 22-2 we see that the *AD-AS* model predicts that an increase in the price level (*P*) will be accompanied by a decrease in unemployment. Similarly, it predicts that a fall in the price level (*P*) will be accompanied by an increase in unemployment. This type of reasoning led economists to suspect that there may be an inverse relationship between inflation and unemployment. When inflation increases, unemployment falls, and *vice versa*.

In 1958 a New Zealand engineer turned economist, AW Phillips, published the results of a detailed study of the United Kingdom's experience with inflation and unemployment between 1861 and 1957. His results indicated an inverse relationship between inflation and unemployment, such as the relationship indicated in Figure 22-2.

In the figure the percentage of workers who are unemployed is measured on the horizontal axis and the inflation rate is indicated on the vertical axis. Phillips found that the statistical relation between inflation and unemployment could be illustrated by a curve running downwards from left to right. According to the Phillips curve, lower unemployment levels are associated with higher rates of increase in the general price level, and *vice versa*. For example, in Figure 22-2 we show that inflation will be 4 per cent at an unemployment rate of 2 per cent. According to the figure, the inflation rate can be reduced to nil only if the unemployment rate (*u*) is allowed to increase to 5 per cent.

The trade-off principle

The Phillips curve was originally regarded as a clear indication that **unemployment** and **inflation** could be **traded off** against each other. In other words, a lower inflation rate could be achieved by trading it off against, or exchanging it, for greater unemployment.

The original Phillips curve was essentially a statistical device with little theoretical background. After its publication, various theories were developed to pro-

FIGURE 22-2 The Phillips curve

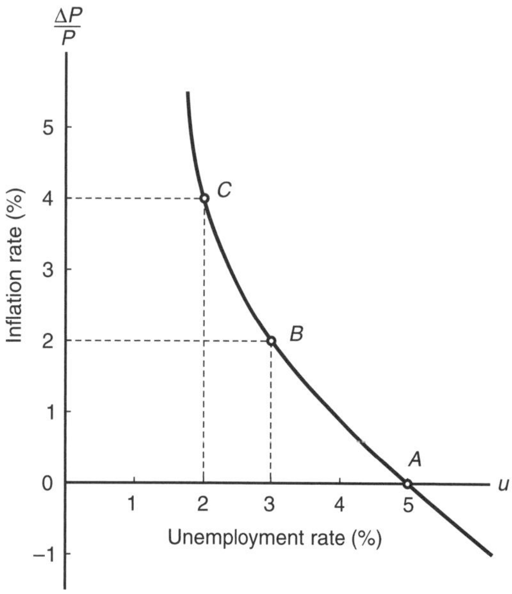

The Phillips curve relates the unemployment rate (u) to the inflation rate. Lower inflation is related to higher unemployment and vice versa.

FIGURE 22-3 A simultaneous increase in inflation and unemployment

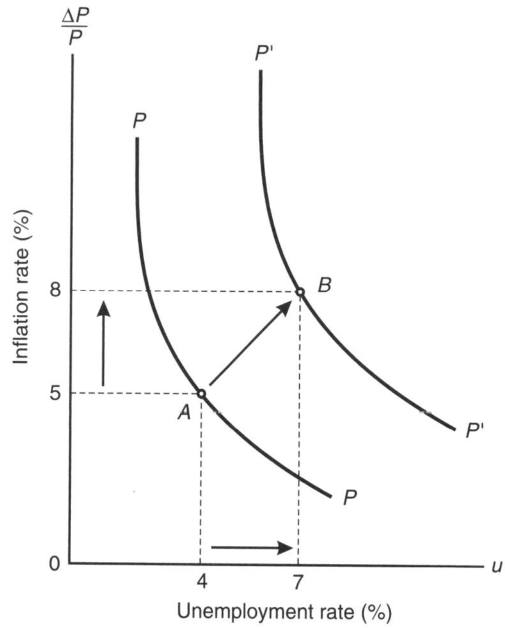

If the Phillips curve shifts to the right, an increase in inflation can be accompanied by an increase in unemployment. This is called stagflation and is indicated by a movement from point A to point B in the figure. The rightward shift of the Phillips curve is caused by the same factors which give rise to a leftward shift of the AS curve. See Table 20-2.

vide a theoretical justification for it. This popularised the idea that there is a trade-off between inflation and unemployment. According to Figure 22-2 a decrease in unemployment from 3 per cent to 2 per cent can be "bought" by stimulating aggregate demand and allowing the inflation rate to increase from 2 per cent to 4 per cent. This idea remained popular during the 1960s when both inflation and unemployment were generally low and increases in inflation were often accompanied by decreases in unemployment.

In the 1970s, however, inflation and unemployment increased at the same time. Recall that this phenomenon is called **stagflation**. Also recall that this is associated with a supply shock, which is illustrated by a leftward movement of the aggregate supply curve (Figure 20-4) or cost-push inflation (Figure 21-2). In terms of the Phillips curve, stagflation is illustrated by a rightward shift of the curve, as illustrated in Figure 22-3. The same factors which cause a leftward shift of the *AS* curve give rise to a rightward shift of the Phillips curve.

In Figure 22-3 the original Phillips curve is indicated by *PP*. Suppose the economy starts off at point *A* with an inflation rate of 5 per cent and an unemployment rate of 4 per cent. Factors such as a higher rate of increase in import prices, higher rates of increase in wages as a result of trade union pressure or higher profit margins then shift the Phillips curve to *P'P'*. As a result the economy moves to point *B* with a higher inflation rate (8 per cent) and a higher unemployment rate (7 per cent) than before. On the new Phillips curve *P'P'* there is again a trade-off between inflation and unemployment, but all the possible combinations are worse than before. For an alternative explanation, see Box 22-2.

As we have seen previously, such a situation of stagflation or cost-push inflation cannot be remedied by policies that affect aggregate demand in the economy. If expansionary monetary and fiscal policies are used to stimulate aggregate demand, unemployment can be lowered but inflation will increase further. Similarly, if contractionary monetary and fiscal policies are used to dampen aggregate demand and reduce inflation, unemployment will increase further. The appropriate solution is to apply policies which will lower both inflation *and* unemployment. This is a difficult task.

In principle it is possible to devise policies which can reduce inflation and unemployment but these policies are difficult to apply in practice. We now take a closer look at one such policy which can be used to solve the dilemma of stagflation or cost-push inflation.

BOX 22-2 A VERTICAL PHILLIPS CURVE?

Many economists, including the monetarists, argue that there is no trade-off between inflation and unemployment in the long run. According to them the long-run Phillips curve, and therefore also the long-run *AS* curve, is vertical at a level of unemployment which is called the natural rate of unemployment. Any change in aggregate demand will thus only affect the price level or the inflation rate in the long run, leaving the unemployment rate unchanged at the natural level. The natural rate of unemployment may change, however, due to structural changes in the economy. An increase in the natural rate of unemployment (illustrated as a rightward shift of the long-run Phillips curve and the *AS* curve) might be accompanied by an increase in the inflation rate, for example, due to a lax monetary policy. This represents another possible explanation for a simultaneous increase in unemployment and inflation.

The distinction between the short-run and long-run Phillips curves and *AS* curves is analysed in more detail in intermediate courses in macroeconomics.

Incomes policy

Cost-push inflation or stagflation creates a policy dilemma which cannot be solved by demand management (ie monetary and fiscal policies that are aimed at influencing aggregate demand in the economy). If the problem has its origin on the supply side, then the solution must also be sought on the supply side. This means that steps have to be taken to reduce production costs. In terms of our figures, measures have to be found to shift the *AS* curve downwards (to the right) or, what amounts to the same thing, to shift the Phillips curve to the left. If an absolute reduction in production costs is not feasible, then costs should be contained. In terms of our figures this means that the policies should prevent the *AS* and Phillips curves from shifting any further.

As we have indicated previously, many countries were faced with stagflation in the 1970s. As a result a number of countries experimented with **incomes policies** in an attempt to contain or reduce both inflation and unemployment. We have already referred to incomes policy in the discussions of supply shocks and cost-push inflation. We now take a closer look at this type of policy.

An incomes policy implies some form of government intervention in the determination of wages and prices. The action taken by the authorities may vary from the formulation of **guidelines** for the determination of wages and prices to **compulsory control measures**. For any incomes policy to be successful, it has to appear equitable to all parties involved. It also requires a tripartite agreement (between the government, employers and trade unions) on how national income is to be distributed. Incomes policy usually entails a call to workers to limit their demands for nominal wage adjustments to the average productivity increase in the economy, and to firms to limit their profit margins. If prices can then be kept constant, such an agreement ensures that the relative shares of wages and profits in the economy also remain constant. This principle can be illustrated by means of a numerical example.

In Table 22-3 we show data for a hypothetical economy for two consecutive years. Assume that labour productivity increased by 10 per cent from Year 1 to Year 2. The incomes policy being applied stipulates that wages may be increased only in accordance with increases in productivity. If we accept that the number of workers remains constant, this means that the real national income also increases by only 10 per cent. We assume that the national income is divided between wages and profits in the ratio of 80 to 20 per cent. Since wages may increase by only 10 per cent, the relative shares of labour and profit remain con-

TABLE 22-3 The operation of an incomes policy: a numerical example

	Year 1	*Year 2*	*Percentage change*
Labour productivity (index)	1,00	1,10	10
Employment (number)	100	100	0
Real national income (rand)	100	110	10
Remuneration of employees (rand)	80	88	10
Profit (rand)	20	22	10
Nominal wage (rand)	0,80	0,88	10
Unit cost of labour (rand)	0,80	0,80	0
Price level (index)	1,00	1,00	0
Real wage (rand)	0,80	0,88	10

stant over the two years, provided profit margins remain the same and prices do not rise. **Increases in the wage rate equal to the increases in productivity mean that the relative shares of workers (remuneration of labour) and employers (profit) remain the same if profit margins and prices do not change**. The unit cost of labour is calculated by dividing money wages by labour productivity. These variables both increase by 10 per cent, which means that the unit cost of labour does not change.

If everything works out as presented in the table (that is, the shares of the different market participants remain constant), there is no reason for price hikes and the fight against inflation is won without sacrificing any jobs.

In practice, however, it is extremely difficult to implement such an incomes policy successfully. One of the basic problems is that no single party has a guarantee that every other party will act in the spirit of the agreement – see Box 22-3. Another problem is that the average increase in productivity does not apply to individual industries – in some industries productivity will be falling while other industries will experience a rapid increase in productivity. It would be unrealistic to expect all industries to grant uniform increases in wages and salaries. And how will a rapidly growing industry be able to attract additional labour if it cannot offer higher than average wage increases? It is also unrealistic to expect no price increases if unit costs are not kept down in all industries. For a market system to function effectively, **relative prices** have to change. One of the major problems of an incomes policy is that it inhibits the working of the market mechanism at the microeconomic level.

Largely as a result of these problems, comprehensive incomes policies, such as those applied in the United States (1971–1974), the United Kingdom (1972–1974) and Canada (1975–1978), generally do not last very long. Except for short periods, comprehensive incomes policies have never been very successful in market-oriented economies.

Comprehensive, enforceable wage and price controls have never been introduced in peacetime in South Africa. The possible negative effects on economic efficiency and labour relations have caused policymakers to shy away from such policies. In 1975 a tentative effort was made to introduce an incomes policy in South Africa when representatives of the authorities and various private sector bodies signed the **Anti-Inflation Manifesto**. It was a voluntary agreement in terms of which the different parties undertook to absorb 30 per cent of all increases in the CPI. This meant that only 70 per cent of any increase in the CPI would be taken into account when fixing wages and prices. The experiment continued until

BOX 22-3 THE PROBLEMS OF APPLYING AN INCOMES POLICY: AN ANALOGY

The following analogy gives an indication of the problems associated with the implementation of an incomes policy.

A crowd is seated in a soccer stadium. Everyone is sitting down and everyone can see all the action. Suddenly a player breaks away and starts dribbling the ball along the touchline. A spectator gets excited and jumps up to get an even better view. This forces other spectators to follow suit. Eventually everybody is standing. But nobody can see any better than they would have if everybody had remained seated in the first place. In fact, the short spectators will probably be worse off when everyone is standing than when everyone is sitting down.

This example can be used to illustrate two aspects of the problems associated with applying an incomes policy. First, an incomes policy can be viewed as an attempt to prevent the first spectator from jumping up and setting the whole process in motion. An appeal can be made to spectators but this will usually not be sufficient. Spectators can, of course, be strapped to their seats but this will impinge on their personal freedom (as well as making them quite uncomfortable).

Once everyone is standing, the problem is how to get them to sit down again. An individual spectator will only sit down if he or she is certain that everyone else will sit down at the same time. But how do the organisers convince everyone to sit down simultaneously and to remain seated? This action is clearly in the interest of the spectators as a group, but how do you convince each individual to behave accordingly?

This is essentially what the problem of applying an incomes policy is all about. In some societies there may be enough social consensus and cohesion to achieve the goal but in other societies it may prove to be impossible.

Recall that we used a similar example to illustrate the fallacy of composition in Section 1.3.

March 1977, but its success remains doubtful.

These difficulties do not mean that the authorities should give up completely on a wage and price policy. It is a fact that the governments of the world, including the South African government, have a very important role to play in fixing wages and prices in modern society. The South African government, for example, is the single largest employer in the country and determines almost a third of all wages and salaries in the non-agricultural sectors. Moreover, the wages and salaries established in the public sector influence wages and salaries in the private sector.

In South Africa some important prices are also fixed directly or indirectly by the government, including the price of petrol, post and railway tariffs and the price of electricity. Seen from this angle, the government has to adhere to the same principles, albeit on a smaller scale, as those stipulated by an incomes policy. Put somewhat differently: the government always has to have an incomes policy – the only questions therefore are those surrounding the principles on which this policy must be based and whether or not the policy should be extended to cover the private sector.

Other supply-side policy actions

Recall from Section 20.4 that the supply-side economists also propose a solution for the twin evils of inflation and unemployment. A discussion of policies to deal with the unemployment-inflation trade-off would therefore not be complete without recalling the supply-side solution. Supply-siders call for a decrease in tax rates aimed at encouraging people to save more, invest more and work harder. Increased saving would keep interest rates low which, in turn, would stimulate further investment and growth. In this way the aggregate supply of goods and services would increase. At the same time they also call for a tight monetary policy to keep inflation under control.

In the United States in the 1980s this policy initially appeared to be successful. Unfortunately both measures began to put pressure on interest rates. On the one hand the restrictive monetary policy caused interest rates to rise. On the other, private saving increased at the expense of an increased **budget deficit**, which also resulted in higher interest rates. The higher interest rates had negative effects on investment and expectations of economic growth were not fully realised. Inflation was brought under control, but unemployment did not fall as had been anticipated.

Is there a trade-off between inflation and unemployment?

The existence of a trade-off between inflation and unemployment is still a hotly debated issue among economists and policymakers alike. Most participants in this debate agree that a Phillips curve, in the sense of a stable, long-run inverse relationship between inflation and unemployment, does not exist. Many argue that there is no trade-off in the long run (ie the long-run Phillips curve is vertical), but that there is probably still a short-run trade-off. The important question, however, remains whether such a short-run trade-off is stable enough to serve as a basis for policy decisions.

IMPORTANT CONCEPTS

Unemployment
Frictional unemployment
Seasonal unemployment
Cyclical unemployment
Structural unemployment
Phillips curve
Stagflation
Incomes policy

REVIEW QUESTIONS

1. What type of unemployment does each of the following examples represent? Explain your answers.
   (a) Workers at the Toyota plant in Durban are laid off as a result of the depressed state of the South African economy.
   (b) Workers at a factory making cassette tapes lose their jobs when the firm goes bankrupt due to competition from compact discs.
   (c) Migrant farm workers' employment is terminated when the harvest is finished.
   (d) Workers at a clothing factory in Dimbaza lose their jobs when the firm relocates to Malawi.
2. Give four possible reasons for the increase in unemployment in South Africa in recent decades.

3. Is an increase in real GDP always accompanied by an increase in formal employment? Explain your answer.
4. A friend or family member hears about the Phillips curve and asks you what it means. Answer him or her.
5. Does a conventional, stable Phillips curve provide a good illustration of stagflation? Discuss.
6. Explain what is meant by an incomes policy.

23 Economic growth and development

Learning outcomes

Once you have studied this chapter you should be able to

- define economic growth and economic development
- explain how economic growth and economic development are measured
- explain what is meant by the business cycle
- identify the major sources of economic growth
- enumerate the major problems experienced by developing countries

The rate of growth at a given time is a phenomenon rooted in past economic, social and technological developments.

MICHAL KALECKI

Economic advance is not the same thing as human progress.

SIR JOHN CLAPHAM

Growth for the sake of growth is the ideology of the cancer cell.

EDWARD ABBEY

In Chapter 5 we indicated that South Africa is a middle-income developing country with relatively poor social indicators. We also showed that economic growth in South Africa has been low since the early 1970s, both in relation to earlier growth in this country and relative to the growth in most other countries. This is also a cause of concern. Economic development and economic growth are both particularly important issues in South Africa today.

In this chapter we take a closer look at these two processes. For many years most economists did not distinguish between **economic growth** and **economic development**. Nowadays, however, it is generally accepted that economic development is a much broader concept than economic growth. In fact, development economics is often regarded as a separate subdiscipline of economics.

The **difference between economic growth and economic development** is explained in Section 23.5. The earlier parts of the chapter deal with the narrower concept, namely economic growth. Topics discussed include the **definition**, **measurement** and **sources** of **economic growth**. We also emphasise the uneven nature of economic growth as reflected in the **business cycle**. The discussion of economic growth is concluded by indicating some of the **reasons for South Africa's variable growth performance since the 1950s**. In the last section we look at the **definition and measurement of economic development, some typical problems of developing countries, theories of economic development** and aspects of **development policy**.

23.1 The definition and measurement of economic growth

Economic growth is traditionally defined as the annual rate of increase in total production or income in the economy. This definition has to be qualified in two important respects. First, the production or income should be measured in **real terms**, that is, the effects of inflation should be eliminated. Second, the figures should also be adjusted for population growth. In other words, they should be expressed on a **per capita** basis. Positive economic growth actually occurs only when total real production or income is growing at a faster rate than the population. In practice, however, economic growth is usually simply measured by determining the annual growth in real production or income.

Total real production is commonly represented by real gross domestic product (real GDP) or real gross national income (real GNI). Recall from Chapter 4 that **real** GDP or **real** GNI means that the measurement is at **constant prices**. Also remember that the difference between GDP and GNI is the net primary income payments to the rest of the world. However, as explained in Box 23-1, there is another difference between real GDP and real GNI which we have not mentioned up to now. But first we look at a few problems associated with GDP (and GNI) as measures of total production or income in the country.

Some problems associated with GDP

GDP and the other national accounting totals explained in Chapter 4 are all subject to certain shortcomings. As a result, GDP is sometimes jokingly referred to as the "grossly deceptive product" or the "grossly distorted picture". The problems associated with GDP include the following:

- **Non-market production**. It is difficult to measure or estimate the value of activities that are not sold in a market. This problem applies, for example, to the production of goods and services by the government. Since most of these goods and services are not sold in a market, they have to be valued at cost. It is assumed, for example, that the value of the output of a civil servant is equal to his or her salary. Another example of non-market production is farmers' consumption of their own produce.
- **Unrecorded activity**. A more serious problem is that many transactions or activities in the economy are never recorded. Such transactions or activities are described by terms such as the unrecorded economy, the underground economy, the shadow economy and the informal sector. The informal sector was discussed in Chapter 14. There it was pointed out that unrecorded activities range from smuggling, drug-trafficking and prostitution to cash transactions aimed at evading taxation. The existence of such unrecorded activities can result in a serious underestimation of the value of GDP. As a result, GDP figures are nowadays adjusted by including estimates of the total value of unrecorded activity. In South Africa, estimates of informal sector activity were first included in GDP in 1994. The reliability of these estimates is, however, open to question.
- **Data revisions**. Another problem associated with GDP and the other national accounting aggregates is that the original estimates are frequently adjusted as new and better data become available. This can be quite frustrating to analysts, since they are never sure whether or by how much the figures are going to be revised.
- **Economic welfare**. Many economists argue that GDP and the other national accounting totals are not good measures of economic welfare. They point out, for example, that **unwanted by-products** (or negative externalities – see Chapter 16) such as pollution, congestion and noise are not taken into account. They argue that the value of these "bads" should be subtracted from the value of "goods" included in GDP. They also argue that it is inappropriate to regard R1 billion spent on military equipment in the same light as R1 billion spent on health and education. Moreover, it is difficult to account for changes in the **quality** of goods and services. Allowance should also be made for the exhaustion of scarce mineral resources. In addition, GDP does not take account of the **distribution** of production and income. For example, some oil-rich countries, like Kuwait, have a high GDP per capita but the income is distributed unevenly. Growth in real GDP may also be accompanied by an increase in the inequality of the distribution of income. In certain industrial countries the published GDP figures have been adjusted for some of these influences in an attempt to arrive at a better measure of economic welfare (this is referred to as the Measure of Economic Welfare or MEW). No attempt has yet been made to estimate South Africa's MEW and, even in countries where the MEW has been estimated, these estimates are not updated and published regularly.

Despite all these criticisms, GDP and the other national accounting aggregates are still the best indicators of the total level of economic activity in a country. They therefore usually serve as the basis for calculating economic growth. One remaining shortcoming of GDP should, however, be noted – see Box 23-1.

Calculating economic growth

Economic growth is usually calculated on an annual basis. For example, to obtain a figure for economic

BOX 23-1 REAL GDP, REAL GNI AND THE TERMS OF TRADE

GDP includes exports but excludes imports. When real GDP is estimated, changes in export prices are therefore taken into account but changes in import prices are ignored (since imports do not form part of GDP). For example, when the price of gold increases, it affects the GDP deflator and real GDP but when the price of imported oil increases, both the GDP deflator and real GDP are unaffected. Recall, from Chapter 17, that the ratio between export prices and import prices is called the **terms of trade**. When the terms of trade improve, it means that the country can import a greater volume of goods and services in exchange for a given volume of exports. Similarly, when the terms of trade deteriorate, the country can import fewer goods and services in exchange for a given volume of exports. Changes in the terms of trade can have significant effects in open economies, particularly in those economies (like South Africa's) that rely heavily on the export of one or two major commodities. The fact that changes in the terms of trade are not taken into account when estimating real GDP can be a serious drawback if the terms of trade are subject to large swings. For example, if the gold price increases sharply, while gold production does not change significantly, real GDP is not really affected (*ceteris paribus*), while the GDP deflator (a basis for measuring inflation) increases sharply. Economic growth is thus understated, while inflation is overstated. Because imports are excluded from GDP, changes in oil prices are also not reflected in real GDP or the GDP deflator.

Changes in the terms of trade are, however, taken into account when calculating real GNI. The fact that the adjustment is only made when real GNI is estimated is an accounting convention. GNI figures are adjusted for changes in the terms of trade in an attempt to obtain better estimates of the changes in the income or welfare of the nation – remember that the N in GNI refers to "national".

This might seem somewhat complicated, but you should not feel anxious if you cannot follow the argument fully at this early stage of your studies in economics. It is important to note, however, that the difference between real GDP and real GNI is not only net primary income payments to the rest of the world (at constant prices). In estimating real GNI, the national accounts also make an adjustment for changes in the terms of trade. When the terms of trade are fluctuating significantly, real GNI is therefore a better basis for calculating changes in **national income** (or economic welfare) than real GDP. Real GDP is, however, still the best basis for calculating changes in **domestic production**, and it is also the national accounting total which bears the closest positive relationship to employment (or negative relationship to unemployment).

growth in 2008, real GDP (ie GDP at constant prices) for 2008 is compared with real GDP for 2007 and the difference is expressed as a percentage of the 2007 figure. In Table 23-1 we show four possible measures of economic growth in South Africa for the period 1990 to 2006. All the figures refer to annual rates of change. The four bases that are used are **real GDP**, **real GNI**, **real GDP per capita** (ie adjusted for population growth) and **real GNI per capita**. Note that some of the figures in the table (particularly the per capita figures) are indicated by a minus sign. This indicates that economic activity actually declined from one year to the next. This is often referred to as negative economic growth.

Another feature of the figures in Table 23-1 is that economic growth is not a smooth process – it can vary significantly from year to year. This feature of economic growth is related to a phenomenon called the business cycle.

23.2 The business cycle

The business cycle is the pattern of upswing (expansion) and downswing (contraction) that can be discerned in economic activity over a number of years. One complete cycle has four elements: a **trough**, an **upswing** or expansion (often called a boom), a **peak**, and a **downswing** or contraction (often called a recession). The different elements of the business cycle are illustrated in Figure 23-1.

Causes of business cycles

Economists have always been interested in fluctuations in the level and growth of economic activity and a great deal has been written about the subject. The **classical economists** of the 19th century believed that market economies are inherently stable. They therefore spent considerable time and effort to explain why economic activity does not grow smooth-

TABLE 23-1 Economic growth in South Africa, 1990–2006

Year	Annual percentage change in Real GDP (%)	Real GNI (%)	Real GDP per capita (%)	Real GNI per capita (%)
1990	–0,3	–1,2	–2,4	–3,3
1991	–1,0	–0,8	–3,1	–2,8
1992	–2,1	–2,1	–4,2	–4,1
1993	1,2	1,6	–0,9	–0,5
1994	3,2	5,1	1,1	2,9
1995	3,1	2,2	1,0	0,0
1996	4,3	4,6	2,1	2,4
1997	2,6	2,1	0,5	0,0
1998	0,5	–0,3	–1,6	–2,3
1999	2,4	1,2	0,2	–0,9
2000	4,2	3,7	2,1	1,6
2001	2,7	2,5	0,8	0,5
2002	3,7	5,1	1,9	3,3
2003	3,1	3,5	1,5	1,9
2004	4,8	5,8	3,4	4,4
2005	5,1	5,3	3,7	3,8
2006	5,0	6,3	3,6	5,0

Source: South African Reserve Bank, *Quarterly Bulletin*, March 2007

FIGURE 23-1 The business cycle

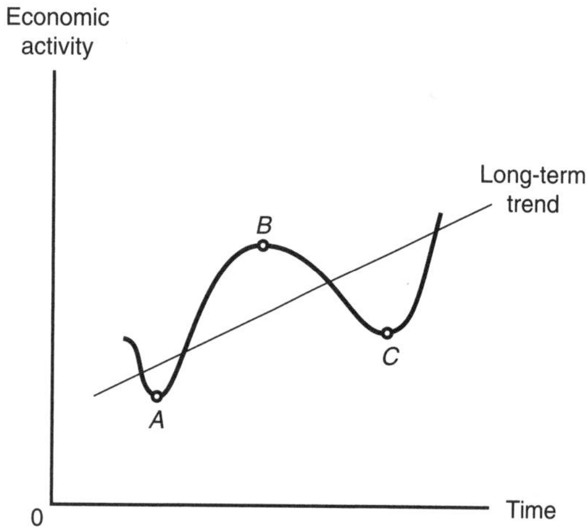

The figure shows a complete business cycle from one trough (point A) to the next trough (point C). The cycle describes a pattern of fluctuation around the long-term trend. After the trough there is an upswing, indicated by AB in the figure. The peak is reached at point B, followed by a downswing from B to C.

ly. They regarded fluctuations in the growth of economic activity as temporary phenomena that could be ascribed to **exogenous** factors (ie factors which originate outside the market system). An extreme version of this theory was formulated by the 19th century British economist, William Stanley Jevons, who formulated the "sunspot" theory of the business cycle. According to Jevons, periodic changes in solar radiation (popularly called sunspots) cause changes in weather conditions. The changes in weather conditions affect agricultural production and therefore also the total level of economic activity. This might seem quite far-fetched and even ridiculous. However, in the 19th century agricultural production still accounted for a large portion of total economic activity. Changes in agricultural conditions therefore had a significant impact on the overall performance of the economy. In fact, although the relative importance of agriculture has declined substantially, changes in agricultural production still have strong effects on economic growth in countries like South Africa. For example, in the 1980s and early 1990s the changes in weather conditions associated with the El Niño phenomenon had a significant impact on the changes in South African GDP at constant prices. Following Jevons, some South African economists may yet formulate an El Niño theory of the South African business cycle!

Many other classical economists formulated theories of the business cycle. The common element in all of these theories is that the causes of the business cycle are sought outside the market system, that is, in **exogenous** factors. Modern followers of the classical tradition, such as the monetarists, also trace the major causes of economic fluctuations to such "outside" influences. The monetarists, for example, ascribe the fluctuations to faulty or inappropriate government policy which results in fluctuations in the rate of increase in the money supply. These fluctuations then cause changes in the rate of increase in prices, production and employment.

Those economists who ascribe the business cycle to exogenous or "outside" forces believe that government should leave the market system to its own devices. They believe that market forces will, if given the opportunity, sort out all the important economic problems of the day. The government should not intervene, since such intervention will simply cause further problems rather than solve the existing ones.

Keynesian economists, on the other hand, do not believe that the business cycle is caused by exogenous factors. In contrast to the classical economists, they believe, further, that governments have a duty to intervene in the economy by applying appropriate monetary and fiscal policies. Keynesians believe that business cycles are part and parcel of the way in which market economies operate. In other words, they believe that the business cycle is an **endogen-**

ous phenomenon. For example, if business conditions improve, such an improvement is reinforced by mechanisms such as the multiplier. A strong upswing therefore results. However, the upswing carries the seeds of its own destruction. As the economy grows, interest rates increase, imports increase, foreign exchange reserves fall, and so on, until a peak is reached. The whole process is then reversed and an economic decline sets in. As the economy declines, interest rates fall, imports decrease, foreign exchange reserves increase, and so on. This continues until the economy reaches a trough. The process is then reversed yet again. In other words, Keynesians regard the business cycle as an inherent feature of modern market economies. As far as economic policy is concerned, they recommend government intervention to smooth the peaks and troughs as far as possible. When the economy is in a cyclical downswing, expansionary monetary and fiscal policies are recommended. When the economy is booming, restrictive measures are proposed.

A description of the various stages of the "typical" South African business cycle is presented in Box 23-2. This description is based on the Keynesian notion that the business cycle is an integral part of the way in which a modern market economy functions.

There is also a third possible explanation for fluctuations in economic activity. According to this explanation, which may be called the **structuralist or institutionalist** explanation, economic fluctuations are caused by various structural or institutional changes. Adherents to this view do not believe that the market system is inherently stable or systematically unstable. Instead, they focus on structural changes and unpredictable events. For example, in South Africa's case they emphasise events like the oil shocks of the 1970s, the imposition of trade and financial sanctions, the political unrest and uncertainty of the 1980s, the political transition of the 1990s and changes in technology and production techniques. Adherents to this view do not have set ideas on economic policy. According to them, the appropriate policy approach will vary from time to time as circumstances change.

The three broad approaches to the business cycle are illustrated in Figure 23-2. These three fundamental viewpoints should, however, be regarded as extremes, rather than watertight categories. Few (if any) economists subscribe fully to any one of these approaches. Most economists hold an *eclectic* view incorporating elements of the three extreme views, although one of the three approaches will usually still be found to dominate.

BOX 23-2 THE DYNAMICS OF THE SOUTH AFRICAN BUSINESS CYCLE

Stage of business cycle	Salient features of the economy
Latter stages of downswing	Business sentiment depressed Low demand for credit Interest rates low Surplus on current account of balance of payments Property market depressed Share prices start increasing Eventually a trough is reached
Trigger	Exports increase (eg because of increased overseas demand or increase in gold price)
Early stages of upswing	Exports grow Manufacturing production increases Inventories decrease Interest rates fall further Rand appreciates Inflation decreases Current account still in surplus
Latter stages of upswing	High utilisation of production capacity Higher demand and prices for capital goods Inflation increases Deficit on current account of balance of payments Share prices lose momentum High demand for credit Property prices rise Interest rates increase Eventually a peak is reached
Early stages of downswing	Rand depreciates Inflation increases Interest rates increase Property prices still high Unplanned increase in inventories Manufacturing production falls rapidly Surplus on current account of balance of payments Demand for credit starts falling

FIGURE 23-2 Different views on business cycles

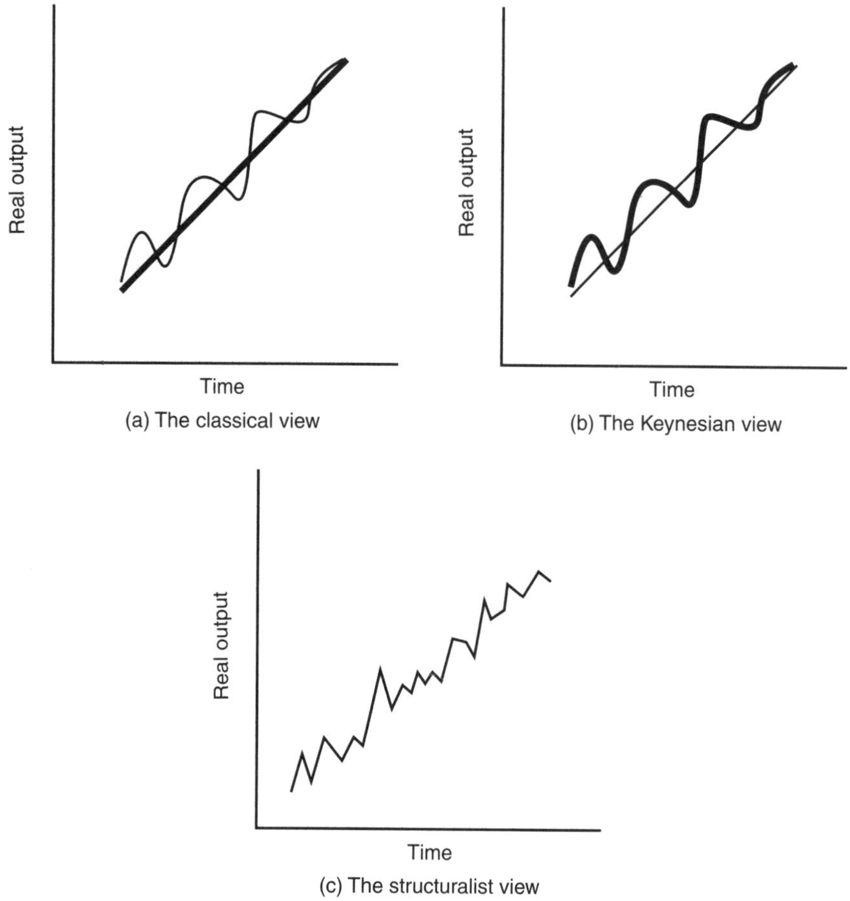

According to the Classical view, illustrated in (a), the economy is inherently stable (indicated by the thick line) and business cycles are caused by exogenous disturbances. According to the Keynesian view, illustrated in (b), the economy is inherently cyclically unstable (indicated by the thick wavy line), in other words, business cycles are endogenous to private market economies. The structuralist view, illustrated in (c), denies the notion of natural economic tendencies in market economies and views business cycles as random occurrences.

Measuring business cycles

From the brief discussion above it should be clear that the business cycle is an important phenomenon. Quite understandably, there is a lively interest in the business cycle, not only among economists, but also among business people and ordinary citizens. Economists are regularly confronted by people who want to know whether economic conditions are improving or worsening. What people are really asking is where the economy is on the business cycle. A major portion of the time and effort of private sector economists is devoted to answering this type of question. An important problem, however, is that information about the performance of the economy as a whole only becomes available weeks, even months, after the events have occurred.

To overcome this problem, economists try to identify certain critical variables or indicators that possibly reflect or predict movements in overall economic activity. These variables are called **business cycle indicators**. The most important indicators are the so-called **leading indicators**, which tend to peak before the peak in aggregate economic activity and reach a trough before the trough in aggregate economic activity. They thus give advance warning of changes in aggregate economic activity. To establish which indicators are leading indicators, economists examine the movements of different variables in relation to the overall changes of economic activity. Leading indicators used in South Africa include the number of new motorcars sold, the number of new companies registered and merchandise exports. Data on these variables become available relatively quickly (compared to the national accounting data). The official peaks and troughs of the South African business cycle are dated by economists at the South African Reserve Bank. The upswings and downswings of the post-war South African business cycle are indicated in Box 23-3.

23.3 Sources of economic growth

As mentioned in the previous section, business cycles are the deviations from the underlying trend in economic activity. While it is an established fact that economic growth does not occur in a smooth fashion, the theories of the business cycle do not explain the underlying growth trend of the economy. We now examine some of the fundamental causes or sources of this long-run economic growth. These sources can be grouped into two broad categories: **supply factors** and **demand factors**. Economic growth requires an expansion of the production capacity of the economy, as well as an expansion of the demand for the goods and services produced in the economy. Both the supply factors and the demand factors are therefore necessary for sustained economic growth.

Supply factors

The supply factors are those which cause an expansion in production capacity, also called the **potential output** of the economy. As you have probably guessed, they relate to the factors of production: natural resources, labour, capital and entrepreneurship. An expansion of the country's production capacity requires an increase in the quantity and/or quality of the factors of production.

■ NATURAL RESOURCES

In a narrow sense, a country's natural resources are fixed. A country is endowed with minerals, arable land, a favourable climate, and so on – these natural resources are either present or absent. The matter is, however, not quite as simple as that. Minerals have to be discovered, either by accident or through exploration; arable land has to be cultivated, and so on. In addition, new techniques or price increases may, for example, make it profitable to exploit certain mineral deposits which were previously impossible or unprofitable to exploit. It is therefore always possible to increase the exploitation of the available natural resources. On the other hand, minerals are non-renewable or exhaustible assets and the deposits may therefore become exhausted or too expensive to exploit. In South Africa, for example, the production of gold has fallen sharply since 1970.

BOX 23-3 THE SOUTH AFRICAN BUSINESS CYCLE SINCE WORLD WAR II

Upswings	Downswings
Post-war – July 1946	August 1946 – April 1947
May 1947 – November 1948	December 1948 – February 1950
March 1950 – December 1951	January 1952 – March 1953
April 1953 – April 1955	May 1955 – September 1956
October 1956 – January 1958	February 1958 – March 1959
April 1959 – April 1960	May 1960 – August 1961
September 1961 – April 1965	May 1965 – December 1965
January 1966 – May 1967	June 1967 – December 1967
January 1968 – December 1970	January 1971 – August 1972
September 1972 – August 1974	September 1974 – December 1977
January 1978 – August 1981	September 1981 – March 1983
April 1983 – June 1984	July 1984 – March 1986
April 1986 – February 1989	March 1989 – May 1993
June 1993 – November 1996	December 1996 – August 1999
September 1999 –	

Source: South African Reserve Bank, *Quarterly Bulletin*, March 2007

■ LABOUR

A second supply factor is the size and quality of the labour force. As explained in Chapter 14, the **size** of the labour force depends on factors such as the size and the age and gender distribution of the population. The **growth** of the labour force depends on the natural increase in the population and migration between countries. The supply of labour can also be increased by increasing the number of working hours (eg by working overtime). Even more important, however, is the **quality** of the labour force. The quality of the labour force depends on factors such as education, training, health, nutrition and attitude to work. As indicated in Chapter 5, South Africa has an abundance of labour but the quality of the labour force still leaves a great deal to be desired. It is therefore not surprising that improved education, training, nutrition, health and hygiene are among the most important priorities of the South African government.

The size and quality of the South African labour force in the next decade will be affected significantly by the prevalence of **HIV/Aids**. Most observers agree that the size, composition and productivity of the labour force will be affected through absenteeism, illness and a loss of skills and experience as a result of the pandemic.

Another important determinant of the size and quality of the South African labour force is the **net migration rate**. On the one hand, South Africa is losing many young professionals to countries such as Australia, Canada, the United Kingdom, the United States and countries on the European continent. On the other hand, there are many legal and illegal immigrants from sub-Saharan African countries who look to South Africa for job opportunities. Unless the economic performance of the other countries in the region improves markedly, this inflow of largely lesser skilled workers can be expected to continue and even increase in the years to come, bringing increasing pressure to bear on the job-creating capacity of the South African economy.

■ CAPITAL

The third supply factor is the quantity and quality of the country's capital (ie the manufactured means of production such as buildings, machinery, equipment and roads). Economic growth requires more and better capital equipment. An increase in the capital stock may take the form of either capital widening or capital deepening.

- **Capital widening** occurs when the capital stock is increased to accommodate an increasing labour force. For example, if the stock of capital is expanded by 10 per cent in response to a 10 per cent increase in the number of workers, there is capital widening. In this case, the average amount of capital per worker remains unchanged.
- **Capital deepening** occurs when the amount of capital per worker is increased, that is, when the growth in the stock of capital is greater than the growth in the number of workers. In Chapter 5 we referred to such a situation as an increase in the capital intensity of production.

As with the other factors of production, the **quality** of capital is also very important. The quality of capital is increased by applying **new technology** to capital equipment. Technology is such an important factor in the process of economic growth that it is often regarded as a separate factor of production. However, as mentioned in Chapter 2, new technology has to be embodied in capital equipment to become effective. We therefore do not regard it as a separate factor of production. Nevertheless, technological progress has always been crucial to world economic growth. For example, the steam engine, the internal combustion engine and the computer all had a major impact on economic growth. One of the consequences of modern, highly developed technology is that it requires a sophisticated, well-trained labour force to install, operate and maintain the specialised equipment. Capital, technology and skilled labour have become highly interdependent in the process of economic growth.

Another important aspect of additions to the capital stock is that such additions have to be **financed** in one way or another. Both the physical availability of capital goods and the availability of finance therefore have to be considered when economic policy is formulated. When many of the capital goods have to be imported, as in the case of South Africa, the availability and cost of foreign exchange also become important.

■ ENTREPRENEURSHIP

The fourth supply factor is **entrepreneurship**. As indicated in Chapter 2, a country needs people who can identify opportunities and exploit them by combining the other factors of production. The entrepreneur is the driving force behind economic growth. Entrepreneurial talent should therefore be fostered. At the very least there should be no obstacles (such as unnecessary laws, rules and regulations) that could act as a deterrent to the development of entrepreneurship. If the necessary entrepreneurship is lacking, the government may also have to act as an entrepreneur, particularly in the earlier stages of economic development.

Demand factors

The supply factors listed above all contribute to the country's production capacity, or the potential output of the economy. Whether or not this potential will be realised will depend upon whether there is a sufficient demand for the goods and services that can be produced. In other words, an increase in the quantity and quality of the factors of production is not sufficient to ensure economic growth. There also has to be an adequate and growing **demand** for goods and services produced in the country.

As we have seen in Chapters 4 and 19, the total demand for goods and services consists of consumption demand (*C*), investment demand (*I*), government demand (*G*) and net exports ($X - Z$). The various components of aggregate spending or demand can be used to distinguish between three sets of demand factors:

- **domestic demand**, which consists of consumption (*C*), investment (*I*) and government spending (*G*)
- **export demand** (*X*)
- **import substitution**, which involves attempts to reduce imports (*Z*)

Economic growth can thus be stimulated by a rise in domestic demand ($C + I + G$), a rise in exports (*X*) or a reduction in imports (*Z*).

■ DOMESTIC DEMAND

The determinants of domestic demand were discussed in Chapters 18 and 19. Consumption (*C*) is primarily a function of income (*Y*), investment spending (*I*) is a function of the expected profitability of investment projects (and therefore also of the interest rate), and government spending (*G*) is determined by government policy. In principle it is always possible to increase domestic demand by increasing government spending. Any expansion in domestic demand should, however, be matched by an increase in supply, otherwise it will result in inflation and balance of payments problems. This is the major weakness of the strategy of inward industrialisation that has often been propagated in South Africa.

Inward industrialisation is essentially a growth strategy that is based on meeting the wants of the rapidly growing poor population in the urban areas of South Africa. These wants, which include the need for basic consumer goods (food, clothing, etc), low-cost housing, sanitation, roads and electricity, constitute a large potential source of demand. To transform these wants or needs into an effective demand, the proponents of inward industrialisation propose a redistribution of income in favour of poorer households (to provide them with the necessary purchasing power) and large-scale government investment in housing and infrastructure such as electricity. Such investment, they argue, will have strong multiplier or linkage effects on the rest of the economy.

In principle these ideas are very attractive, but in practice supply constraints, inflation and balance of payments effects also have to be taken into account. Inward industrialisation is therefore at best a mixed blessing which should never be pursued in isolation from other growth policies.

■ EXPORTS

International trade is an important factor in economic growth and much of South Africa's economic growth has been based on the export of minerals and mineral products. An increase in exports raises the growth rate and also relieves the balance of payments constraint discussed in Chapters 5 and 17. It is therefore generally accepted nowadays that the promotion of exports is a more sensible growth strategy than stimulating domestic demand.

From a policy point of view, the main problem is that the demand for exports is largely determined by economic conditions in other countries. Nevertheless, the South African government can take certain steps to stimulate exports. These steps include the establishment or maintenance of a realistic exchange rate of the rand against other currencies (or perhaps even a slightly undervalued domestic currency) and the provision of finance, marketing and other assistance to South African exporters.

■ IMPORT SUBSTITUTION

Another growth strategy linked to the balance of payments is to reduce imports by manufacturing previously imported goods domestically. This is called import substitution and it played a significant role in the initial growth of the South African manufacturing sector. Nowadays many of the consumer products that were previously imported are manufactured in South Africa.

Import substitution has not, however, reduced the country's dependence on imports. To manufacture the goods locally, capital and intermediate goods have to be imported. As indicated in Chapter 5, South Africa's imports consist largely of capital and intermediate goods. What has happened, therefore, is that the **composition** of imports has changed – the **level** of imports has not been reduced. In fact, since the manufacturing sector cannot function without imported goods, South Africa is probably even more dependent on imports today than during the first half of the 20th century.

Import substitution has a number of other drawbacks. To make domestic production viable, local firms usually have to be protected against foreign competition during the initial stages. This protection (eg by means of import quotas or high import tariffs) should be withdrawn once local manufacturing has been established. In practice, however, the protection tends to continue, with the result that local manufacturing often becomes an inefficient and high-cost exercise (recall the infant industry argument discussed in Chapter 17). Moreover, since import substitution is directed at the domestic market, local manufacturers do not focus on the international market. Firms established to manufacture previously imported goods locally tend to neglect export opportunities and, being used to protection, seldom develop into enterprises that can compete effectively in the international market.

23.4 Economic growth in South Africa since World War II

Further perspective on the sources of economic growth in South Africa can be obtained by examining some broad trends in the country's economic growth during the postwar period. South Africa's growth experience during this period can be classified into three distinct phases: a phase of rapid economic growth from 1946 to 1974; a phase of lower growth, stagnation and decline from 1975 to 1993; and a period of sustained growth from 1994 onwards. During the first period real GDP grew at an average annual rate of almost 5 per cent, which implies a significant increase in real GDP per capita. From 1975 to 1993, however, real GDP grew at an average annual rate of only 1,6 per cent. In fact, from 1990 to 1993 real GDP *declined* at an average annual rate of 0,6 per cent. As a result, real GDP per capita was more than 11 per cent lower in 1993 than in 1974. From 1994 to 2006 real GDP increased at an average annual rate of 3,3 per cent and real GDP per capita was 22,1 per cent higher in 2006 than in 1993 (but only 4,8 per cent higher than in 1980).

Why did the long-term growth rate differ between these three periods? Some observers ascribe the broad economic developments to political developments such as the apartheid system (or its gradual demise), the imposition of trade and financial sanctions against the apartheid regime and their subsequent abolition after the democratic elections in 1994. Although the impact of political developments cannot be discounted altogether, there were a number of economic developments that contributed to the broad trends in South African economic growth and which have to be taken into account in any analysis of postwar economic growth in South Africa. They include

- variations in economic growth in the industrial countries
- variations in the growth of world trade
- technological changes
- developments related to gold
- the process of import substitution
- developments in the financial account of the balance of payments
- wage increases

Each of these factors is now discussed briefly.

Economic growth in the industrial countries

The first twenty to thirty years after World War II are often described as the Golden Age of capitalism – during the 1950s and 1960s most non-communist economies grew faster than they had ever grown before. Between 1950 and 1973 the average annual growth in the industrial countries was about 4,5 per cent. This changed dramatically after the first oil crisis in 1973. Between 1974 and 1993 average annual growth in the industrial countries fell to about 2,7 per cent. The decline in South Africa's economic growth after 1974 was therefore not unique. To some extent, the postwar growth of the South African economy was simply a reflection of international trends. For example, in Table 5-3 it was shown that economic growth in Japan declined from an average annual rate of 10 per cent in the 1960s to about 2 per cent in the 1990s. Similar, though less pronounced, trends were recorded in other industrial countries. Since these countries are South Africa's main trading partners, it stands to reason that our export performance was affected by the slowdown in growth in their economies.

From 1994 to 2005, annual real economic growth in the industrial countries averaged 2,6 per cent (about the same as the average rate recorded from 1974 to 1993).

World trade

The trends in world trade have been even more pronounced than the trends in world economic growth. Between 1950 and 1973 the volume of imports by the industrial countries rose on average by about 8,3 per cent per year, compared to a rate of 4,0 per cent between 1974 and 1993. The prolonged upswing in the industrial countries during the 1980s resulted in a renewed boom in international trade during the second half of the decade, but the growth rates attained during the 1950s and 1960s were not equalled. From 1994 to 2004 the volume of imports by the industrial countries grew at an average rate of 7,8 per cent per year. The fluctuations in the growth of world trade had significant implications for the exports of developing countries such as South Africa and therefore also for the rates of economic growth achieved in these countries.

Technology

Another change, probably even more important than the changes in the growth of production and international trade, was the shift from the natural-resource-intensive, smoke-stack manufacturing industries (eg iron, steel and heavy engineering) to knowledge-intensive and skill-intensive production of goods and services.

The replacement of natural-resource-intensive mechanical and chemical technologies has had profound implications for the structure of production, both domestically and internationally. Microelectronics, the computer revolution, robotics, computer-assisted design and biotechnology have generally favoured East Asian and other countries that are poor in natural resources but rich in human resources. Mineral-rich countries like South Africa have found it difficult to adjust to these changes.

Technological change has been identified as the most important structural economic change since the early 1970s. All industrial countries have experienced significant shifts in real output towards services and high-technology manufacturing. The rapid expansion of technologically sophisticated industries such as information technology and communications has also had significant impacts on the structure of world trade. In the industrial countries, imports of high-technology manufactures grew two or three times as fast as total imports. This helps to explain why South Africa did not share fully in the revival of international trade from the second half of the 1980s.

In the new millennium, however, an extraordiary economic boom in China and rapid growth in other countries (eg India) initiated a prolonged commodity boom, which again benefited mineral-exporting countries like South Africa.

The international environment: a summary

Until 1973 the South African economy was functioning in a rapidly growing world economy in which there was a substantial and growing demand for its mineral exports. From 1974 onwards all this changed. There were significant declines in the growth of the world economy and world trade, as well as major changes in the composition of production and industrial countries' imports. Whereas South Africa had benefited from international economic trends prior to 1974, these changes contributed to the country's impoverishment in subsequent years. The volume of South African exports grew at a slower pace than before and the country's terms of trade (excluding gold) declined by 66 per cent between 1974 and 1992. The volume of exports grew significantly again from 1993 onwards and the terms of trade were more stable, contributing to a slightly better growth performance during the second half of the 1990s. From 1994 to 2006 the volume of South African exports increased at an average annual rate of 4,7 per cent, boosted by significant growth in the country's non-traditional manufacturing exports. The volume of non-gold exports increased at an average annual rate of 6,3 per cent during this period, while the country's terms of trade (excluding gold) increased by 9,1 per cent between 1994 and 2006.

Gold

Gold dominated South African exports throughout the postwar period. The contribution of gold to South African export earnings was an important growth factor during most of this period. Even more important, however, was the volume of gold mining activity and its backward linkages to the South African economy. During the 1950s, for example, the opening up of the Free State goldfields provided a major stimulus to economic activity in South Africa. The annual volume of gold production increased from 380 tons in 1945 to 1 002 tons in 1970. Subsequently it declined to 713 tons in 1975, 619 tons in 1993 and 275 tons in 2006.

Prior to the early 1970s, South African gold exports were also a key stabilising force in the performance of the economy. During this period, South African export earnings were much more stable than those of most industrialised countries. From 1973 onwards, however, gold became a major source of instability in the South African economy, mainly because of fluctuations in the gold price. For example, the average London gold price was \$193 in 1978, \$613 in 1980, \$317 in 1985, \$360 in 1993, \$271 in 2001 and \$604 in 2006.

The decline in gold production and the instability of the gold price were important causes of the weaker performance of the South African economy from the early 1970s. Towards the end of the 20th century, however, platinum took up some of the slack and eventually overtook gold as the country's main mineral export.

Import substitution

During the period 1947 to 1974 manufacturing output grew at an average annual rate of 7,4 per cent. This manufacturing growth was largely based on the local production of previously imported consumer goods, often undertaken by, or under license from, multinational firms that had previously exported to South Africa. These firms also supplied much of the capital and know-how required to establish a domestic manufacturing industry. Import substitution provided a major stimulus to the growth of manufacturing in South Africa in the 1950s and 1960s, but this process reached its zenith in the early 1970s. The subsequent decline in import substitution contributed to a decline in the average annual real growth in manufacturing, from 7,4 per cent in the period 1947 to 1974, to 1,6 per cent during the period 1975 to 1993. Much of the import substitution that occurred during this period was undertaken for strategic reasons. Projects such as Atlantis Diesel Engines and Mossgas were costly ventures that would not have been undertaken in normal circumstances. These uneconomic projects further dampened economic growth. From 1994 to 2006 manufacturing growth increased to an average annual growth rate of 2,9 per cent, mainly as a result of the growth in manufacturing exports.

Foreign capital

A large portion of the finance required to establish and expand the manufacturing industry was obtained from abroad. During the period 1946 to 1974, South Africa experienced an average annual net inflow of capital equal to about 2,5 per cent of GDP. Between 1975 and 1984 this inflow disappeared and between 1985 and 1993 there was an average annual net outflow of capital of more than 4 per cent of GDP.

Between 1946 and 1974 South Africa could afford to run large deficits on the current account of its balance of payments because these deficits were financed by net inflows of foreign capital. Moreover, a significant portion of these inflows was in the form of foreign direct investment, which is arguably the best type of capital inflow. Between 1975 and 1984 the financial account was roughly in balance. South Africa periodically had to curtail its domestic spending and imports of capital goods to avoid serious balance of payments problems. During this period, the bulk of the capital inflows also switched from direct investment in the private sector to short-term loans by the public and banking sectors, culminating in the debt crisis of 1985. Subsequently, significant net outflows of foreign capital occurred, in the form of capital flight and repayments of foreign debt. The authorities were forced to apply restrictive economic policies aimed at generating the required surplus on the current account of the balance of payments to finance these outflows. The worsening position of the balance of payments during the postwar period was mirrored in the decline in gold and foreign exchange reserves, perhaps the most important single indicator of the economic health of the country.

From 1994 onwards the situation improved again. Between 1994 and 2006 South Africa experienced a net inflow of foreign capital of more than 2 per cent of GDP. Most of this inflow, however, was in the form of confidence-sensitive portfolio investment which could quite easily be reversed. Nevertheless, the capital inflows provided scope for renewed economic growth and were important determinants of the higher growth experienced between 1994 and 2006 (compared to the previous eight years).

Wages

Another change that occurred during the early 1970s was the surge in wages, especially those of unskilled workers. Whereas South Africa had low and stable wages during the 1950s and 1960s, a variety of factors resulted in sharp wage increases from the 1970s onwards. These increases were awarded in a stagnating and declining economy and exerted strong upward pressure on labour costs per unit of output produced, thus undermining the international competitiveness of South African industry. From 1995 onwards, however, the growth in labour costs per unit of output stabilised markedly.

The factors listed above do not provide a full explanation of the decline in South Africa's economic growth between 1974 and 1993, and the improvement since 1994, but they do provide a significant part of the explanation. They also serve to emphasise yet again the importance of the country's economic links with the rest of the world. As a developing country, South Africa's economic fortunes are closely linked to economic developments in the major industrial countries.

Having discussed economic growth, wc now turn to the related issue of economic development.

23.5 Economic development

In earlier chapters we indicated that the countries of the world can be classified into different groups. The World Bank, for example, distinguishes four groups of countries: low-income countries, lower-middle-income countries, upper-middle-income countries and high-income countries (see Table 5-9). A number of other classifications are also possible. The most general classification is the distinction between less developed countries (LDCs), often also called developing countries, and the developed countries (DCs). The LDCs include the countries of Africa, South and Central America, most Asian countries and certain southern and eastern European countries. The DCs, on the other hand, include the United States, Canada, Japan, Australia, New Zealand and most Western European countries.

Economic development refers to the improvement of living conditions in the LDCs. It entails an improvement in the quality of life of the majority of the population as a result of economic growth, the reduction of inequality and the eradication of absolute poverty. In this final section of the book we give an overview of some aspects of economic development.

Economic development versus economic growth

The distinction between economic development and economic growth is relatively new. The study of economic development, which is called **development economics**, only really came into its own after World War II. There had long been large differences in average living standards between the DCs and LDCs but these differences did not attract particular attention until the second half of the twentieth century. One of the reasons for this was that many LDCs were, or had been, colonies of the DCs and their development needs were therefore regarded as secondary to the needs of the colonial powers.

After World War II a number of things happened which stimulated interest in the LDCs and in economic development (or development economics) as a separate subdiscipline of economics. These included:

- the **rapid growth of the DCs** after the war and a concomitant improvement in the living conditions of the majority of inhabitants of these countries – this increased the gap in average living standards between the DCs and LDCs and gave rise to the notion that the success achieved in the DCs could be duplicated in the LDCs
- the **communications revolution**, which made people in the DCs more aware of the poverty in the LDCs and which also made people in the LDCs more aware of the affluence of the inhabitants of the DCs and of the gaps in living standards
- the **Cold War**, which led to competition between the United States and the Soviet Union to find favour among the LDCs
- the growing international awareness of the consequences of the **population explosion** in LDCs
- **decolonisation** and the consequent **political independence** of the former colonies, which resulted in an upsurge in nationalism and the establishment of a new power bloc in international politics (eg via the presence of many former colonies in the United Nations)

Initially economic development was simply a term for economic growth in LDCs. The aim of development was to emulate the high rates of growth and the structural changes in production that had occurred in DCs. The latter essentially involved attempts to increase the share of manufacturing in income and employment at the expense of agriculture. The emphasis on growth was reflected in the objectives of the Development Decades declared by the United Nations. The aim of the First Development Decade was to achieve a target annual growth rate of 5 per cent in the real GNI of LDCs during the 1960s. This was largely achieved and the target rate for the Second Development Decade was raised to 6 per cent, which was not achieved.

Partly as a result of this failure it was realised that economic development encompasses more than economic growth along developed country lines. In LDCs that had achieved high growth rates in the 1950s and 1960s, the growth had not been accompanied by reductions in poverty, inequality or unemployment. Many inhabitants therefore did not share in the fruits of economic growth. This led to a redefinition of economic development in terms of the **reduction or elimination of poverty, inequality and unemployment in a growing economy**. Economic growth came to be regarded as only one of the components of economic development. Development, it was argued, also requires changes in structures, institutions and attitudes, including a specific focus on the conditions and needs of the deprived majority. In due course an even greater emphasis was placed on the **human aspects of development**, such as the satisfaction of basic human needs and the importance of self-esteem and the freedom to choose. It was emphasised that people are the subjects or beneficiaries of development, not merely the agents or instruments of the development process. Nowadays, economic development is regarded as an improvement in living conditions in the broadest possible sense. Indicators of development (or underdevelopment) include the level and growth of real GDP (or GNI) per capita, infant mortality rates, life expectancy, literacy, nutrition, unemployment and inequality.

In 1990 the United Nations Development Programme published its first *Human Development Report* in which member countries were ranked according to a human development index (HDI). This index is based on three main criteria: real per capita income in US dollars (adjusted for changes in purchasing power and other influences), life expectancy at birth, and education. Table 23-2 lists some of these development indicators for a number of countries for 2004.

In the 2006 report, 177 countries were ranked from 1 (highest human development) to 177 (lowest human development). The countries were classified into three groups: those with high human development (1 to 63), those with medium human development (64 to 146) and those with low human development (147 to 177). Table 23-2 shows figures for five countries in each category. The first three columns show the information used to calculate the index in the fourth column and the last column shows the country's rank. Note the large differences in human development between the DCs and LDCs. Also note that South Africa is placed in the bottom half of the spectrum. This is due mainly to the low average life expectancy as a result of HIV/Aids. In terms of real GDP per capita South Africa was ranked 55th in 2004.

Features and problems of developing countries

Most countries of the world are classified as LDCs. Some LDCs (like Lesotho and Swaziland) are small while others (like China, India and Brazil) are among the largest nations in the world. Moreover, every country is unique, with its own history, factor endowment, and social, political and economic institutions. The differences among the LDCs are therefore large, in fact much larger than the differences among the DCs. Nevertheless, there are certain broad differences between LDCs and DCs which explain why the LDCs, as a group, are poorer than the DCs.

TABLE 23-2 Human development, selected countries, 2004

Country	*Life expectancy index*	*Education index*	*GDP index*	*Human development index*	*HDI rank*
Norway	0,91	0,99	0,99	0,965	1
Iceland	0,93	0,98	0,97	0,960	2
Australia	0,92	0,99	0,95	0,957	3
Ireland	0,88	0,99	1,00	0,956	4
Sweden	0,92	0,98	0,95	0,951	5
Japan	0,95	0,94	0,95	0,949	7
United States	0,88	0,97	1,00	0,948	8
Italy	0,92	0,96	0,94	0,940	17
United Kingdom	0,89	0,97	0,96	0,940	18
Germany	0,90	0,96	0,94	0,932	21
Russian Federation	0,67	0,95	0,77	0,797	65
Brazil	0,76	0,88	0,74	0,792	69
South Africa	**0,37**	**0,80**	**0,79**	**0,653**	**121**
Namibia	0,37	0,79	0,72	0,626	125
Botswana	0,16	0,78	0,77	0,570	131
Zambia	0,21	0,63	0,37	0,407	165
Malawi	0,25	0,64	0,31	0,400	166
Mozambique	0,28	0,47	0,42	0,390	168
Sierra Leone	0,27	0,45	0,29	0,335	176
Niger	0,33	0,26	0,34	0,311	177

Source: United Nations Development Programme, *Human Development Report 2006*

■ POPULATION GROWTH

LDCs generally have a much higher population growth than DCs. During the past few decades the populations of Asia, Africa and South America increased at an average annual rate of more than 2 per cent compared with an average annual growth of less than 1 per cent in the DCs. Rapid population growth can create a number of problems. Many new jobs have to be created to accommodate the increase in the labour force. If this cannot be achieved, unemployment increases. A rapidly growing population also puts pressure on housing, education and health services. If these services are lacking in quantity and quality, the quality of the labour force will also tend to be low.

Towards the end of the 20th century population growth in some LDCs, particularly in sub-Saharan Africa, started to decline significantly as a result of the impact of HIV/Aids. Although this might, in some perverse sense, be deemed a positive development, the loss of skills and experience and the costs of treating Aids sufferers and caring for their dependants will negate any possible positive impact of the lower population growth.

■ NATURAL RESOURCES

Many LDCs have been poorly endowed with natural resources such as mineral deposits, energy sources and agricultural land. For example, many are situated in the tropics where the climate is not conducive to farming, and crop and livestock diseases are common. There are, of course, exceptions. Some LDCs, like Brazil, South Africa and Chile, have an abundance of natural resources. But having natural resources such as minerals is not enough – scarce capital resources are required to extract mineral deposits.

Natural resources are, of course, not a prerequisite for economic development and growth. Countries such as Japan and Switzerland have attained high standards of living without significant natural resources. But their human and manufactured resources rank among the best in the world.

■ AGRICULTURAL PRACTICES

In many LDCs agricultural productivity is very low. This can often be attributed to traditional farming methods and land ownership (or tenure) systems. In some societies a few wealthy absentee landowners own the land and the rest of the population work as tenants. In other societies or areas the land is owned communally, so no individual owns any land. In these instances there is no incentive for the absentee landlord or the individual farmer to protect or improve the soil since others will benefit from the investment without having to bear any of the costs. Agricultural development is therefore impeded.

■ CAPITAL

LDCs generally suffer from a critical shortage of capital goods and access to finance to promote economic development. They do not have their own capital goods industries and therefore have to import capital goods. But these goods have to be paid for in foreign currency which is in short supply. As far as domestic saving and investment are concerned, the strong pressure on government spending means that governments of LDCs are unable to reduce consumption spending to generate saving and investment. Wealthy individuals and companies in LDCs, who have the capacity to save and invest, often channel their savings into unproductive activities (eg land speculation), or physical assets (eg jewellery and precious metals) and foreign bank accounts.

In many cases LDCs therefore rely on foreign aid, foreign loans and foreign direct investment to purchase capital goods. But even foreign direct investment is a mixed blessing. Although it has certain advantages, foreign companies are sometimes unwilling to train local workers and are reluctant to reinvest their profits in the LDCs.

■ INFRASTRUCTURE

A related problem of LDCs is that their infrastructure is generally poorly developed. Roads, power generation facilities, communication systems, education, health and housing facilities are often lacking. As a result, access to markets is usually a major problem. Companies investing in LDCs frequently have to invest in infrastructure before they can start their operations. In many countries the problem of limited access to markets is compounded by the limited size of domestic markets. Firms in LDCs usually cannot exploit economies of scale to the same extent as their counterparts in DCs are able to.

Theories of economic development

Economic development is a complex phenomenon that involves a variety of social and economic processes. It is therefore not surprising that there is no single theory of economic development. Various authors and schools of thought have developed theories about the process of economic development and about the causes of development or underdevelopment. In this subsection we outline some approaches to economic development to give the reader an idea of what development theory is all about.

■ ROSTOW'S STAGES OF ECONOMIC GROWTH

In 1960 the American economist, WW Rostow, published a theory of the stages of economic growth which immediately became popular in courses on economic development. He proposed that each country passes through certain stages during the course of development. His theory was based on the empirical observation that a rise in per capita income in different countries was accompanied by a fall in the proportion of the labour force employed in agriculture and a corresponding rise in the proportion of the labour force employed in secondary and tertiary activities – see also Box 2-2. This indicated that countries become more industrialised and service oriented as development proceeds.

Rostow distinguished five stages of economic development and maintained that every country can be classified according to these stages.

- **Traditional society**. This is the first stage during which farming and handicrafts are the main forms of economic activity. This stage is characterised by a low per capita income.
- **The preconditions for take-off**. This is the second stage in which many LDCs find themselves today. There is some accumulation of capital in the form of infrastructure, as well as a movement from traditional economic activity to industry.
- **The take-off**. This third stage lasts about one generation. Modern methods of production are spread from the leading industries to the rest of the economy and there is a sharp increase in saving and investment, including foreign investment.
- **The drive to maturity**. During this fourth stage the benefits of the investments made during the take-off stage are realised. Industrial activity becomes firmly established.
- **High mass consumption**. This final stage has been reached by DCs such as the United States and Germany. Material standards of living are high and social welfare systems are also well developed.

Like many mainstream development economists of the 1950s and 1960s, Rostow regarded saving, investment and foreign aid as critical elements of economic development. This group of theories did not differ significantly from the standard theories of economic growth in industrial countries. They all focused on the lack of saving, investment and foreign exchange in LDCs and called for the DCs to supply the necessary means to LDCs to overcome these bottlenecks. This type of approach, which is sometimes called "capital fundamentalism", formed (and in many respects still forms) the basis of the approach adopted by the IMF and the World Bank to problems of economic development.

■ DEPENDENCY THEORIES

Economists in the LDCs, particularly those in Latin America, were not impressed with conventional growth theories. They argued that these theories were not applicable to their countries and therefore developed their own theories to explain why many LDCs found it difficult to develop economically. One of these theories is the dependency theory which was originally proposed by the well-known Marxist economist, Paul Baran, and popularised by people such as André Gunder Frank.

The dependency theorists believe that the underdevelopment of the LDCs is functionally related to the economic development of the advanced capitalist countries. They see the development of the industrial countries, which they refer to as the **core**, as being dependent on the poverty and underdevelopment of the LDCs, which they refer to as the **periphery**. Similarly, they regard the development of the urban areas in LDCs (the core) as being dependent on poverty and underdevelopment in the rural areas (the periphery). According to the dependency theorists, development in certain countries (or regions within a country) occurs at the expense of other countries (or regions). For example, the depressed countries or regions provide a reservoir of cheap industrial labour for the growing countries or regions.

This relationship between core and periphery has also been used to explain different patterns and levels of economic development in South Africa. It is argued that the apartheid system with its Bantustans, influx control and migrant labour, provided an army of cheap labour for the industrial core. It is claimed, for example, that the migrant labour system lowered the cost of employment to employers, since they only had to support single workers, instead of families who were expected to fend for themselves in the rural areas.

■ THE BASIC NEEDS APPROACH

In the 1970s there was a widespread realisation that rising income is only one of the means of reducing poverty. In other words, it was realised that economic growth is *not* a *sufficient* condition for economic development. The focus then shifted to **basic needs**, which include

- certain minimum requirements for private consumption (eg food, shelter and clothing)
- essential services, such as clean drinking water, sanitation, public transport, health and education

The focus on basic needs was propagated as a modification to existing development strategies, rather than as an alternative strategy. It was accepted, for example, that basic needs could only be met in an environment of economic growth and increased employment. The major feature or advantage of the basic needs approach is its focus on concrete, measurable aspects of the quality of life, instead of on vague goals such as the reduction of poverty.

■ A BROADER CONCEPT OF ECONOMIC DEVELOPMENT

Nowadays the focus is on a much broader concept of economic development than the growth in total or per capita real GDP. Most development economists argue that there is no development if concrete indicators of poverty, inequality and unemployment do not improve, even if real GDP is growing. As pointed out earlier (see Table 23-2), this approach has also been adopted by the United Nations Development Programme, which bases its measurement of human development on indicators such as life expectancy, education and material living standards. Currently there is a widely held view among development economists that people should have access to food, clothing, protection, water and sanitation for development to occur. It is also accepted that they should be able to participate in decision making and be free from servitude, to increase their self-esteem and sense of self-worth. The question is, however, where the resources required to achieve these goals will come from.

■ FUNDAMENTAL CAUSES OF UNDER-DEVELOPMENT (AND LOW GROWTH)

In recent years economists have increasingly focused on trying to identify the fundamental causes of underdevelopment and low economic growth. Among those that have been identified are institutions, geography and culture and vigorous debates have ensued between proponents of each of these different causes.

Institutions are humanly devised constraints that shape human interaction and provide the incentives which people react to. They relate to the political, legal and regulatory framework and include property rights, laws, constitutions, traditions and markets. A classic example usually quoted by the proponents of the importance of institutions is the case of North and South Korea, two similar countries with different institutions. From a development perspective the important questions are *why* some countries have worse institutions than others and *what can be done* to remedy the situation.

Geography refers to the physical and geographical environment and includes climate and ecology. The region in which a country is situated can be important, since economic success, or the lack thereof, in one country may spill over to its neighbours. In East Asia, for example, it has been a positive factor, while it has tended to be negative in sub-Saharan Africa. More directly, climate may affect productivity and health, and thereby impact on economic development.

Those who emphasise **culture** argue that different societies have different cultures because of different shared experiences or different religions. According to them, culture is an important determinant of values, preferences and beliefs which ultimately help to shape economic performance. Examples in this regard include the emphasis on the link between Calvinism and capitalism and the virtues of Confucianism.

Development policy

As we have emphasised, economic development is not simply an increase in real GDP or real GDP per capita. It is a **process** whereby countries or societies are transformed. This process involves the interaction of economic, social and political change.

Economic development policy comprises a wide range of policy measures. In South Africa, for example, much of the *Reconstruction and Development Programme* could be regarded as development policy. Development policy includes measures aimed at achieving industrial development, agricultural development and human development.

■ INDUSTRIAL DEVELOPMENT

In the 1950s and 1960s **industrial development** was generally regarded as the panacea for the problems of LDCs. Industrial development was seen as the means of supplying goods and services to the domestic market and providing jobs for the large number of unemployed workers in the rural areas. The initial focus was on large-scale industrial activity financed by foreign loans and foreign aid, and involving foreign companies and incentives to foreign investors. In due course it was realised, however, that development comprises much more than industrial development. Moreover, large-scale industrial activity modelled on experience in industrial countries is often inappropriate in LDCs where capital and skilled labour are in short supply. The emphasis has therefore shifted to other forms of development. As far as industrial development is concerned, the focus has shifted to small, medium and micro-enterprises (SMMEs), which are often more suited to local conditions.

■ AGRICULTURAL DEVELOPMENT

In many LDCs the agricultural sector is characterised by traditional farming methods, low productivity and land tenure systems that inhibit agricultural development. Part of the underdevelopment of agriculture in many LDCs can also be attributed to policymakers' emphasis on the development of the industrial and service sectors. These sectors were often promoted at the expense of agricultural development. Nowadays, however, agriculture and the development of rural areas are much higher on the development agenda. Much more attention is being given to investment in drainage, irrigation and soil conservation, the development of seeds, fertilisers and farming methods, and improvement in the marketing and distribution of agricultural produce. The provision of infrastructure and other facilities in rural areas is also receiving attention as part of the attempt to stem the migration to the urban areas.

■ HUMAN DEVELOPMENT

The development of a country's human potential is unquestionably the single most important determinant of the pace of economic development. Human development issues include population growth, health, nutrition and education. Rapid population growth is often described as the primary villain in LDCs. Improvements in water supplies, sanitation, medical care and nutrition have reduced the death rate in many LDCs. However, the reduction in the death rate has not always been accompanied by a similar reduction in the birth rate. This has often resulted in a high natural rate of increase in the population. To address this issue, governments in LDCs have implemented various programmes to reduce the birth rate. Attempts have been made, for example, to introduce contraceptive measures and to convince people of the advantages of smaller families. In some Asian countries the rate of population growth has slowed dramatically. In other countries, however, particularly in Africa, the rate of population growth remained high. Towards the end of the 20th century a new determinant of population growth emerged, particularly in sub-Saharan Africa. This is the prevalence of HIV/Aids which has assumed epidemic proportions in a number of LDCs. While HIV/Aids slows population growth, it imposes great cost on the economy and society through a loss of productivity, skills and experience and the high cost of treating those suffering from Aids and caring for their dependants.

While it is generally accepted that economic development in poor countries requires a decrease in birth rates, the causation between population growth and development is a complex one. As economic development proceeds, living standards improve, the rate of urbanisation increases, education improves and more women become employed outside the home. These factors all increase the opportunity cost of having children and the birth rate therefore tends to decline. There is thus a two-way causation between development and population growth. A lower population growth makes development easier but, at the same time, development is the best way to lower the rate of increase in the population. For example, with improved standards of living, chances of survival are greater and this reduces the incentive to have large families as a form of insurance for old age. If the quality of human resources can be improved through improved education, health, nutrition, housing, etc, then the population problem will be much easier to deal with.

In many LDCs a large proportion of government spending is devoted to education, but much can still be done to improve education facilities and systems, particularly in Africa, where only about half the children of school-going age have access to primary schooling and the adult illiteracy rate is approximately 50 per cent. In countries where pupil enrolments have increased rapidly in recent years, this has often been accompanied by inadequate physical facilities, teacher shortages, poor quality teachers and increasing class sizes. Education systems in LDCs are not always appropriate, being based on elitist European models, and insufficient attention is given to primary education and technical training which probably yield the highest return in these countries.

Another important area of development policy is the improvement of health and nutrition. Health standards are not only determined by access to doctors and medical facilities. They also depend on basic nutrition and access to clean water and sanitation. In poorer LDCs only a small proportion of the population has access to safe water and medical services. Although there have been significant improvements in recent years, diseases such as tuberculosis, malaria and cholera are still major causes of death in LDCs. More recently, HIV/Aids has also reduced the life expectancy in LDCs. Health services in LDCs still leave much to be desired, particularly in the rural areas. The consensus nowadays is that the focus should be on community health, preventive measures and the training of health workers.

Concluding note

In this chapter we introduced you to two important but vast issues in economics: economic growth and economic development. As with many other topics introduced in this book, we have only been able to give you a broad outline of the most important aspects of each topic. We trust, however, that it will increase your understanding of economic life in South Africa and that you will decide to continue your studies in economics.

IMPORTANT CONCEPTS

Economic growth	Boom (upswing)	Import substitution
Real GDP	Recession (downswing)	Economic development
Real per capita GDP	Leading indicators	Human development
Real GNI	Capital widening	Stages of economic growth
Unrecorded activity	Capital deepening	Dependency theory
Business cycle	Technology	Basic needs

REVIEW QUESTIONS

1. Is GDP an appropriate measure of a country's economic development?
2. Discuss some of the problems associated with GDP as a measure of welfare.
3. What does economic growth mean and how can it be measured?
4. In 2004 South Africa's per capita GDP (in US dollars) was more than 13 times larger than the per capita GDP in Mozambique. Does this mean that everyone in South Africa was at least 13 times better off than everyone in Mozambique in 2004? Explain your answer.
5. At what stage of the business cycle is the South African economy at present? Substantiate your view.
6. What do Keynesians mean when they say that the economy is inherently unstable?

7. Distinguish between the classical, Keynesian and structuralist approaches to the explanation of the business cycle.
8. Will an increase in the potential output of the economy necessarily increase the level of production and income in the economy? Explain.
9. Will an increase in the output of the South African economy necessarily raise the standard of living of (a) all South Africans and (b) the average South African resident? Discuss.
10. Explain why population growth can be regarded as a mixed blessing as far as economic growth is concerned.
11. The State President requests people to submit suggestions about how the potential output of the South African economy can be increased. Make three suggestions in this regard and explain how they might serve to increase potential output.
12. South Africa is extremely well endowed with minerals and other natural resources. Are natural resources a necessary or sufficient condition for economic growth? Discuss.
13. Discuss the role of entrepreneurship in economic growth.
14. Is it possible to stimulate economic growth from the supply side only? Discuss.
15. Consider the following statement: "An average annual economic growth rate of 7 per cent is required to reduce unemployment in South Africa." Do you think such a growth rate is attainable? Use your knowledge about the determinants of South African economic growth to substantiate your view.
16. Distinguish between economic development and economic growth.
17. Discuss some of the main features and problems of developing countries.

INDEX

